Learning Disabilities

The Interaction of Learner, Task, and Setting

FOURTH EDITION

Corinne Roth Smith
Syracuse University

Allyn and Bacon
Boston • London • Toronto • Sydney • Tokyo • Singapore

Vice President and Publisher, Education: Nancy Forsyth
Senior Editor: Raymond Short
Editorial Assistant: Karin Huang
Marketing Manager: Kathy Hunter
Editorial Production Service: Omegatype Typography, Inc.
Manufacturing Buyer: David Suspanic
Cover Administrator: Linda Knowles

Library of Congress Cataloging-in-Publication Data
Smith, Corinne Roth.
     Learning disabilities : the interaction of learner, task, and
setting / Corinne Roth Smith. — 4th ed.
        p.   cm.
     Includes bibliographical references (p.   ) and indexes.
     ISBN 0-205-27203-7 (alk. paper)
     1. Learning disabilities.   2. Learning disabled children—
Education.   I. Title.
LC4704.S618   1998
371.92′6—dc21   97-4407
                                                 CIP

Printed in the Unites States of America

10   9   8   7   6   5   4   3   2   1   02   01   00   99   98   97

Photo Credits: Rachael Eliza Smith for photos appearing on pages 1, 141, 281, and 430 and Robin
M. Smith for the photo appearing on page 52.

To my husband Lynn
With gratitude for your
Unlimited faith in me,
Endless patience,
And cherished partnership

Contents

Part Three   The Learner

Preface

This book is written primarily for students enrolled in undergraduate and graduate introductory learning disabilities courses. Due to the overlapping characteristics and intervention needs of pupils with learning disabilities, low achievers, and others with mild disabilities, however, students may find that this text has wider applicability. In its broad overview of the field of learning disabilities, this text attempts to meet the informational needs of many who work with these students: special and general education teachers, administrators, psychologists, counselors, speech-language pathologists, and parents.

It is interesting to consider that a book on learning disabilities is necessary only because of the times in which we live. It is society's priorities that determine who is to be considered disabled, and in every age there will be people who have difficulty meeting the demands that society has placed on them, whether it be the value on physical prowess in Greek and Roman times, musical talent in the Elizabethan era, or social reparté in Edwardian days. In the case of learning disabilities, it is the academic expectations that our society has for its citizens which render those who are unable to meet these demands disabled. In the past, many had focused on learning disabilities in the most narrow sense, as reading disabilities. However, given the growing recognition that numeracy, written expression, poor strategy use, and accompanying social skills weaknesses also contribute in important ways to academic, vocational, and personal adjustment, these too of late have received the attention they deserve.

An unfortunate consequence of society's focus on a disability is that we often tend to overlook both these individuals' strengths and the ways in which home and school environments influence the extent of the disability and its impact on life adjustment. If we stop to think about it, we must admit that it is in large measure our expectations and attitudes that will determine whether student's learning is optimized, or whether difficulties become lifelong handicaps. Therefore, it is by no means sufficient to try to meet the educational, vocational, and personal-social needs of individuals with learning disabilities by merely trying to understand their personal characteristics and teaching needs. We are compelled at the same time to turn our looking glasses inward to ourselves, and outward to society as well, in order to consider how our families and schools may be contributing to the individual's difficulties, or how they could help to overcome these difficulties. Success needs to be as much our concern as are weaknesses. People with learning disabilities have strengths and talents. These too are our responsibility to nurture.

The empirical orientation of this book contrasts the learning and behavior of children, teenagers, and adults with learning disabilities with normal patterns of development. This book tries to achieve a broad view of learning disabilities by bringing together the most relevant theory and research from child development, psychology, the medical sciences, and special and general education. This is necessary because a major problem in the field of learning disabilities is that we have become very insular, reading primarily our own literature and not enriching our focus with the implications of other bodies of knowledge. Therefore, in an attempt to expand our scope, at times the research presented in this text will not yet have been tested with individuals who are learning disabled. Nevertheless, the relevance of these works is noteworthy. Because the instructional needs of students with learning disabilities do overlap in many ways with those of other students with mild disabilities, it makes sense to draw on a broad body of best practices when planning interventions.

This book reviews the most recent work in the field in the context of various learner, task, and setting factors that play a role in learning disabilities. Such an eclectic approach not only offers a comprehensive survey of current theory and practice but also reflects the fact that no one viewpoint adequately addresses the characteristics and needs of all children and adults with learning disabilities. Much can be learned from different perspectives. Each offers a valuable vantage point from which to evaluate the relative roles of learner, task, and setting factors in learning disabilities. While the text presents the controversies and lack of consensus in learning disabilities, it also acknowledges the healthy nature of our differences in opinion. It is these very differences that have promoted the proliferation of research on learning difficulties in recent years, the greater appreciation of individual differences within the classroom, the intensification of efforts to individualize teaching, and a fresh look at our curricular, vocational, and life adjustment expectations.

An effort has been made to give voice to parents, teachers, and individuals with learning disabilities. Throughout the text they tell their stories in a way that teaches best, through sharing of very personal fears, frustrations, joys, and triumphs. Illustrations of student work offer helpful examples, and simulations may help the reader develop some notion of what it is like to have a learning disability, if only for a moment.

An important focus of this book is multicultural issues in learning disabilities. At times children who differ in national origin, language background, or socioeconomic status, or those who come from different areas of the country, have been made to feel like strangers in our classrooms. Rather than celebrating the richness offered by this diversity, school personnel at times have conveyed the message that there is only one way of being and thinking; difference is misunderstood as deviance. This text examines the role of multicultural diversity in learning disabilities and offers suggestions on how to build schools in which family traditions, culture, and language are integral to the educational process, and in which teachers and students learn to value one another, to learn with and from each other.

This book is divided into five parts. The first part introduces students to the historical, definitional, identification, and prevalence issues in learning disabilities. Part Two reviews the many learner, task, and setting factors that may contribute to learning disabilities. Part Three explores the development of academic skills, learning strategies, information-processing abilities, and social–emotional adjustment of preschoolers, children, and teenagers with learning disabilities. Because learning problems tend to persist in different forms over time, transition planning for the vocational, independent living, and social–emotional needs of the adult with learn-

ing disabilities is explored as well. Part Four focuses on the academic tasks that we expect students to accomplish by examining multidimensional assessment approaches and programming strategies. Because learning problems can be accentuated by mismatches between learner and task characteristics, we also look at the facilitative effects of matching teaching content and methods to the student's abilities and learning styles. Part Five is devoted to the notion that one's learning and behavior must be understood within the context of his or her social networks. Emphasis is placed on the role of the parent as model, advocate, and teacher. Human, physical, and organizational attributes of the school environment that may impact the student, such as grouping patterns or teacher attitudes and practices, also are highlighted. Because each individual with learning disabilities is unique, only by understanding how the student's characteristics interact with the nature of the tasks he or she is expected to accomplish and the expectations and personalities within his or her social settings can we comprehend the student's learning and adjustment needs, and how best to intervene.

Writing a major textbook involves the assistance of many people. I am especially indebted to Ray Short, Senior Editor, for guiding this revision. It is also with gratitude that I acknowledge several reviewers whose feedback offered direction for this revision: Professor Beverly Barkon, Jersey City State College; Professor Charmaine Lepley, University of Rio Grande; Professor Judith Winn, University of Wisconsin-Milwaukee; and Professor Ralph Zalma, Hofstra University. My students deserve very special acknowledgment. Their questions, valued feedback, and insights over the past twenty-seven years have taught me far more than any books. In more ways than they will ever know, they have influenced this text's philosophical approach and the selection and organization of its content. Finally, I would know little were it not for the children, teenagers, parents, and teachers who, over the years, trusted those of us at Syracuse University's Psychoeducational Teaching Laboratory to take a keen look at their situations and join them in problem solving. To these people especially, I give thanks for teaching me and enriching me through the pleasure of sharing a small piece of their lives.

**Part One
The Concept of
Learning Disabilities**

Chapter One

History, Definition, and Prevalence

Learning disabilities is the newest, the fastest growing, and perhaps the most controversial and confusing area within special education. Some of the finest mathematics students at Harvard University have learning disabilities. Yet many students who find it hard simply to meet high school graduation requirements or to hold onto the most menial job also have learning disabilities. How can this be? What do these two types of individuals have in common? The answer is *unexpected underachievement.*

Our Harvard mathematician excels at his architectural design, engineering, and physics courses. Yet when he has to read his sociology textbook, it takes him three times longer than it takes his classmates, and he doesn't remember much of what he has read. When classes require thousands of pages of reading, he finds it much easier to absorb the material if he listens to a taped version of the book and takes notes. He is vice president of his fraternity and an intramural soccer star, and his friends find him to be an asset in their study group.

Our high school student, on the other hand, reads and comprehends at an average level but cannot add even such simple numbers as 38 + 15. His handwriting is illegible, he is uncoordinated, he doesn't know how to begin to socialize, and he is lonely and friendless. He cannot meet the high school math and science graduation requirements and has been fired repeatedly from part-time jobs because he is awkward with the patrons and easily sidetracked from his responsibilities.

Although these students are different, both are learning disabled. Both have exceptionally uneven ability to learn and, as a result, achievement in some areas is unexpectedly lower than in others. Each person's brain processes certain types of information very inefficiently, despite adequate intelligence, schooling, and eagerness to learn.

Perhaps now it is clearer why learning disabilities is the most confusing area in special education. Although all people with learning disabilities have uneven development of skills, the precise cause of their brains' inefficiency, the way it affects learning and adjustment, and the effect of families and schools on the problem can be very different from one person to another. It is for this reason that our current federal definition of learning disabilities lays out a general concept but avoids specificity:

"Specific learning disability" means a disorder in one or more of the basic psychological processes involved in understanding or in using language, spoken or written, which may manifest itself in an imperfect ability to listen, think, speak, read, write, spell, or to do mathematical calculations. The term includes such conditions as perceptual handicaps, brain injury, minimal brain dysfunction, dyslexia, and developmental aphasia. The term does not include children who have learning problems which are primarily the result of visual, hearing, or motor handicaps, of mental retardation, of emotional disturbance, or of environmental, cultural, or economic disadvantage. (Federal Register, Dec. 29, 1977, p. 65083)

In order to be identified as learning disabled, an individual must demonstrate a severe discrepancy between intellectual potential and achievement in reading, math, written expression, or language skills. In other words, the individual is achieving far less than would be expected for his or her age and intellectual ability.

Although biology does contribute significantly to learning disabilities, the person's learning patterns and behavior are also influenced greatly by the person's personality, and his or her educational and life experiences. A wide range of factors can contribute to learning disabilities beyond physical causes within the learner, including characteristics of the curriculum, school, and home environment. These learner, task, and setting contributors are illustrated in Figure 1–1. Each can adversely affect the development or application of an individual's information-processing capabilities. As a result, the person who is learning disabled experiences difficulty taking in, organizing, storing, recalling, or reproducing information. The extent of these difficulties and the degree to which they can be overcome depend on a complicated set of interactions among personal characteristics, curriculum variables, and family and school influences. Different combinations of these influences can lead to mild, moderate, or severe degrees of learning disabilities. Because these factors impact so many aspects of a person's life, professionals from many different disciplines have become involved in prevention, research, and intervention efforts.

Maintaining a broad perspective on learning disabilities is essential because no one theory is sufficient to explain the various causes, characteristics, and intervention needs of the learning disabled. Each theory offers unique strengths that, when taken together, help us to understand the needs of the individual with learning disabilities as an interaction of learner, task, and setting factors.

We begin by tracing the educational philosophies, advocacy efforts, and research that led to the birth of learning disabilities (LD) as a new field in special education. We also shall explore how the term *learning disabilities* evolved, its definition, common identification practices, and the numbers of students being identified.

We will see how the LD field emerged from a long line of theory and research dating to the 1800s. In the 1950s to 1960s this work helped to stimulate public awareness regarding the special educational needs of children who achieved less than expected academically, yet fit no existing category of disability. By the late 1960s the learning disabilities concept had a large following and, in 1975, special services for students with learning disabilities finally were mandated by federal law.

While the major identifying characteristic of an individual with learning disabilities is a major discrepancy between his or her potential for

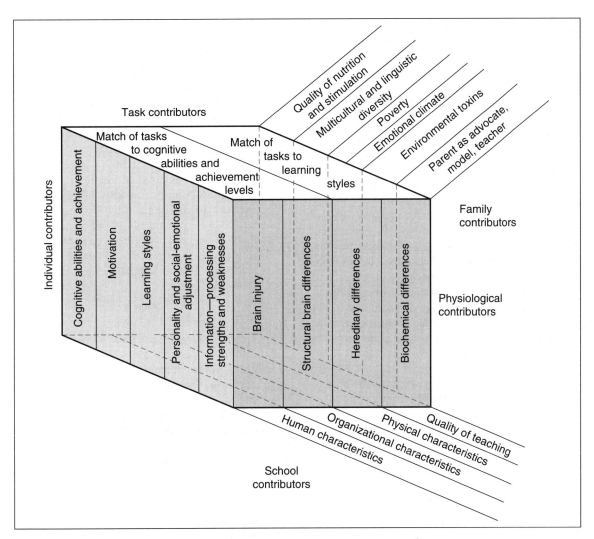

Figure 1–1 Learner, task, and setting contributors to learning success and failure.

achievement and actual achievement levels, we have not settled on one best way to measure these discrepancies or describe the characteristics of individuals with learning disabilities because these students differ markedly from one another in their strength and weakness patterns. Whether an individual ultimately is identified as learning disabled depends on a clinical judgment that considers such multiple dimensions as intelligence, achievement, quality of schooling, opportunities to learn at home, learning rate, motivation, and age. Although one in twenty school children currently are identified as learning disabled, research suggests that even greater numbers may qualify for LD services. Males far outnumber females in these estimates.

Educational Philosophy and Practices

The birth of the field of learning disabilities was influenced by parents and professionals seeking an instructional philosophy that would address each child's unique strengths, weaknesses, and learning style. It was important to them that teachers focus not only on what children could not do but also on what they could do, and how they might learn best. They urged that the academic tasks required of children, and the settings in which children studied, be altered to accelerate progress. By living and working with these children, they understood that whether a child's particular strengths became assets or whether weaknesses became liabilities depended on how specific child, task, and setting characteristics influenced one another. This multidimensional, individualized focus departed in three important ways from special education identification, grouping, and instructional practices in the 1950s and 1960s:

1. *Focus on individual learning needs rather than planning instruction based on the category of disability.* It was customary in the 1950s and 1960s to group children having the same disability together in special classes because they were assumed to have similar educational needs. More often than not, however, teachers found that each child had unique needs, even if they all had the same disability. Moreover, despite the assumption that a child with one disability would have little in common with a child having a different disability, their learning and behavior proved again and again that children with mild to moderate disabilities often had similar abilities and educational needs, despite being identified as having different disabling conditions. In fact, researchers showed that some children with mental retardation could learn certain types of information just as well as their brighter peers and the social skills of some of these children even surpassed those of typical youngsters (Jensen, 1963; Klausmeier,

Feldhusen, & Check, 1959; Spicker & Bartel, 1968; Lapp, 1957). Given the differing needs of children within a particular disability group—yet the similarities between children having different disabilities—parents and professionals argued that children should be grouped for instruction based on their individual instructional needs rather than on the basis of their disability category. Against this background, the learning disabilities concept was appealing because it focused on children's individual strengths, weaknesses, and learning styles so that instruction could be geared to each child's unique needs, rather than to the disability category. This individualized focus opened the door for attention to be directed to a new group of children who did not clearly fit existing special education classifications.

2. *Focus on intensive teaching.* The learning disabilities concept also arose because parents were demanding intensified teaching; they challenged the prevailing special class philosophy that children would learn automatically "when they're ripe and ready." Children with disabilities had been placed in segregated classes so that special instruction, in smaller groups, and with specially trained teachers, would help them progress. Yet progress was not overwhelming, and it was unclear whether there was anything very special about the methods used (Dunn, 1968; Morse, Cutler, & Fink, 1964). Johnson (1962) proposed that children profited no more from special classes than from regular classes because the special class therapeutic environment was geared toward children's inadequacies, thereby lowering teachers' expectations and children's motivation. Parents and professionals were beginning to question whether their children's failures were due in part to nonindividualized teaching approaches that neglected to match teaching goals and strategies to what children were ready to learn or to how they learned best. They urged school personnel

to stop emphasizing children's weaknesses by trying to eliminate their disabilities, and instead to concentrate on their strengths by teaching new talents and skills. Teachers were challenged to develop more positive expectations, and researchers were challenged to provide a solid scientific foundation for intensive teaching practices, tailored toward individual learning needs.

3. *Focus on overcoming behavioral and intellectual limitations.* Noting the marked intellectual gains of economically disadvantaged children who attended preschool programs (Klaus and Gray, 1968; Kohlberg, 1968), parents and professionals began to question whether some children's unique learning problems were causing them to be misunderstood as emotionally disturbed or mentally retarded. For example, Kirk (1976) reported that after intensive language and reading remediation, some institutionalized children with mental retardation had improved significantly not only in these skills but also in intelligence scores. These children were deinstitutionalized and eventually became self-supporting citizens. Similarly, Kirk (1958) found that intelligence quotients (IQ) of institutionalized preschoolers with mental retardation increased over time after enrollment in a school program, whereas IQs of children not enrolled decreased. Six of the fifteen enrolled children later left the institution, and one became a college graduate. None of the nonenrolled children ever left the institution (Kirk, 1976). Kirk felt that many of these children had been misidentified as retarded. Rather, they had specific learning disabilities in some areas but were normal in many other respects. The individualized focus of the learning disabilities concept proved attractive because it advocated sorting out and remediating specific disabilities that mistakenly could masquerade as retardation or emotional disturbance. Certainly, the term *learning disabled* appealed to parents

because it might avoid the devaluation, segregation, and compromise of potential often faced by children identified as retarded or disturbed. A more acceptable alternative, the term LD implied that these children's difficulties were correctable and that the responsibility for correction rested with the schools.

Interestingly, the mental retardation field actually spurred on the LD movement in 1973, when the American Association on Mental Deficiency (AAMD) dropped 13 percent of those identified as mentally retarded because it eliminated the borderline category (IQ 68–70 to 84–85). The AAMD's decision had been influenced by the consciousness-raising of the civil rights movement, which brought to light the overrepresentation of racial and ethnic minorities and children from lower socioeconomic backgrounds in classes for the retarded (Sleeter, 1986). Because the newly declassified children still needed intensive, individualized teaching, their parents worked to secure appropriate educational programming under the new learning disabilities category (Kirk, 1976).

Advocacy

A mix of advocacy efforts contributed to the emergence of learning disabilities as a new category of disability. These included federal bodies that assumed a role in special education, as well as professional and parent organizations.

Growing Federal Role in Special Education

The growth of the learning disabilities field was encouraged by federal court decisions that guaranteed the right of all children to equal educational opportunities. In 1975, Congress responded by enacting Public Law 94-142, which mandated special services for all children with disabilities. It was the first law to include the learning disabled among those identified as disabled.

Court Guarantee of Equal Education Opportunities. The Soviet launching of Sputnik I in October 1957 shocked America into upgrading its educational system. Schools were criticized for failing to produce the scientists and technicians necessary for the United States to retain its international lead. Schools were pressed to accelerate reading instruction, set standards for promotion and graduation, use national exams to test for mastery, group students for instruction by ability, and assign the most intellectually capable teachers to the highest achieving students (Sleeter, 1986). In 1969, when humans walked on the moon, the American Commissioner of Education launched the "right to read" program for all citizens (Allen, 1969). In addition, the Federal War on Poverty funded preschool programs in response to reports that children of low socioeconomic status often were ill-prepared for school entry.

With this greater press for literacy came increasing numbers of children who were unable to keep up. Yet federal funding for special educational programs was slow in coming. Of the seven million children identified with disabilities in 1971, one million received no educational services because of exclusion, suspension, or denial or postponement of school entry by school officials (Weintraub & Abeson, 1974).

Equal educational opportunities for the disabled eventually were won on two arguments: (1) that unequal educational practices violated the equal protection clause of the 14th Amendment to the U.S. Constitution and (2) that the Civil Rights Act of 1964 guaranteed an equal educational opportunity to every citizen.

Access to a free public education for the retarded was first recognized by the federal judicial system in *Pennsylvania ARC v. Pennsylvania*, 1971. A year later, the same rights were extended to all children regardless of disability (*Mills v. Board of Education*, 1972). But learning disabilities still were not listed among the disabling conditions for which special educational programs could receive federal funding: mental retardation, hard of hearing, deaf, speech impaired, visually handicapped, seriously emotionally disturbed, and crippled. In order to receive federal aid for children with learning disabilities, school systems had to apply under one of these categories or "other health impaired."

Legislative Recognition of Learning Disabilities. Formal federal recognition of learning disabilities began when the Elementary and Secondary Education Amendments of 1966 (PL 89-750) added a new Title VI, Education of Handicapped Children, to the 1965 act (PL 89-10). This authorized formation of a National Adisory Committee on Handicapped Children, which in turn urged Congress to deal with learning disabilities. In 1969, the Second Task Force of the Minimal Brain Damage National Project on Learning Disabilities urged Congress to legislate LD as a disability category.

Pressure from these committees and from parent organizations resulted in the Children with Specific Learning Disabilities Act of 1969 (Title VI of the Elementary and Secondary Education Act of April 13, 1970; PL 91-230). This act authorized one million dollars for teacher training, research, and demonstration projects in learning disabilities, but appropriated no money for educational services (United States Office of Education, 1970a). Shortly thereafter, the U.S. Office of Education disbursed funds to forty-four states to establish LD Child Service Demonstration Centers (Kirk & Elkins, 1975a).

By 1975, forty-five states had created their own LD categories to facilitate funding of special education services. The remaining five states served the learning disabled within other disability categories (Gillespie, Miller, & Fielder, 1975). It was not until November 29, 1975, with the passage of the Education for All Handicapped Children Act (PL 94-142), that special education services to students with learning disabilities were federally mandated and reimbursable. Full implementation of the law was required by the 1978–1979 school year.

Services to School-Age Students. Public Law 94-142, reenacted in 1990 as the Individuals with Disabilities Education Act (IDEA; PL 101-476) and amended in 1997 (PL 105-17), has had a dramatic impact on special services, financial aid, assessment practices, educational planning, due process rights, and personnel preparation. Those states accepting federal funds for education are mandated by IDEA to provide a free, appropriate education to all children aged six through seventeen with disabilities. PL 94-142 added learning disabilities and IDEA added autism and traumatic brain injury to the categories of disabilities eligible for federal funding. Students with attention deficit disorders may qualify for special education services by meeting the eligibility criteria of other categories of disability, such as "other health impaired," "seriously emotionally disturbed," or "specific learning disability." Federal funding to states is based on state census data and numbers of children living in poverty.

With implementation of these laws, the learning disabled quickly grew to be the largest group of students with disabilities served. When in 1979 approximately 8 percent of school-aged children were being identified as disabled (*The Condition of Education*, 1980), individual states' LD percentages varied from approximately one half of 1 percent to over 4 percent of the school-age population. By the 1995–1996 school year, however, 10.6 percent of six- to seventeen-year-old students (about 4.82 million) were being identified as disabled. Of these, 51 percent, nearly 2.5 million, were being educated under the LD classification. State LD percentages varied from 2.9 percent (Georgia) to 9 percent (Massachusetts) of school-aged children (U.S. Office of Education, 1997). Because of this rapid growth in the LD population, the number of teachers specializing in learning disabilities also has increased dramatically, as has the number of university training programs in learning disabilities.

IDEA mandates that students with disabilities be educated in as close to normal a setting as possible, the "least restrictive environment." They should participate for as much of the school day as appropriate with typical peers in academic instruction and special subject activities (homeroom, lunch, art, gym, music, or vocational education).

IDEA also mandates that a variety of assessment procedures as well as observation within the classroom be used when identifying children as disabled. The testing materials cannot be racially or culturally discriminatory, and test administra-

tion must be in the student's native language. The curriculum is detailed yearly in an *Individualized Education Program* (IEP), which is prepared and signed by appropriate school personnel and the parents or guardian. Beginning at age fourteen, and annually thereafter, the IEP must include a statement of the coursework that will meet the child's transition needs. By age sixteen, a comprehensive transition service plan must be detailed in the IEP in order to prepare the student for vocational training, employment, postsecondary education, and independent and community living. The transition plan must link the student to appropriate services in the adult system. IDEA's regulations give parents very specific rights to involvement in the educational planning process.

If a student's disability does not meet the level of severity required under IDEA to qualify for special education services, accommodations and specialized instruction may be accessed through the protections of Section 504 of the Rehabilitation Act of 1973. Section 504 requires public schools that receive federal funds to serve the needs of persons with disabilities as adequately as they serve the needs of the nondisabled. Section 504's definition of *handicapped person* is broad: any person who has a physical or mental impairment that substantially limits a major life activity (including learning).

Services to Preschoolers and Young Adults. PL 94-142 mandated that a free appropriate education be extended to all three to five and eighteen to twenty-one year olds with disabilities only if consistent with state law and practice. Therefore, services for the disabled at these ages were slower to develop. Federal incentive grants did fund some preschool services and child identification projects, but it was not until 1986 that Congress called for an intensive preschool education initiative. PL 99-457, an amendment to the Education for All Handicapped Children Act, mandated that all states accepting federal education reimbursements must provide services for three- to five-year-old children with disabilities by the school year 1990–1991. PL 99-457 also established programs to assist states in developing services for infants and toddlers with disabilities from birth through two years. Parents have the right to choose whether to enroll their child in all these preschool programs. Through an *Individualized Family Service Plan* (IFSP), the child's strengths and needs are outlined, along with the supports necessary to enhance the family's capacity to meet the developmental needs of their child.

As of the 1995–1996 school year, over 722,000 infants and preschoolers, and 252,000 eighteen- to twenty-one-year-old students with disabilities were receiving educational services (U.S. Office of Education, 1997). All states permitted adolescents with disabilities to stay in school to age twenty-one.

Growth of Professional and Parent Organizations

Parent and professional advocacy groups played a powerful role in bringing about the litigation and legislation just described. As parent advocacy grew in response to society's increasing understanding of and tolerance for the disabled (Cruickshank, 1967), parents began demanding instructional practices that addressed their children's unique strengths and weaknesses. Parents were tired of hearing their children described as "dumb," "mixed up," and "lazy." They knew that their children were smart in some ways, were not crazy, often tried very hard, and "would learn if only they could." Cruickshank (1972, p. 381) aptly described the situation: "Parents of tens of thousands of children in the United States knew that [their children] had [learning disabilities], even if professional educators and psychologists and pediatricians did not." Therefore, parents demanded a category distinct from all other recognized disability conditions.

Advocacy groups for children with these more subtle learning problems began at the local level (for example, the Fund for Perceptually Handicapped Children in Evanston, Illinois; the New York (City) Association for Brain-Injured Children). On April 6, 1963, these local parent organizations banned together at a national conference in Chicago, at which the term *learning*

disabilities was used in an address by Samuel Kirk. He had never intended this term to become another label for children, and he cautioned parents against establishing another category of exceptionality (Kirk, 1976). Nevertheless, the title Association for Children with Learning Disabilities was adopted, and this parent advocacy group, now renamed Learning Disabilities Association of America (LDA), was formalized in 1964. Spurred on by this strong parent advocacy, in 1968 educators formed what is now called the Division for Learning Disabilities (DLD) within the Council for Exceptional Children. In order to secure special education funding for children who did not fit existing disability classifications, both groups worked to establish LD as a legislated category of disability.

The conferences and newsletters sponsored by LDA, DLD, and another impressive group, the Orton Dyslexia Society, have been valuable means for disseminating information and catalyzing research, program development, and advocacy through the judicial and legislative systems. The lobbying of these strong national groups strengthened state and local affiliates, thereby influencing legislation and practice at the state and local levels as well.

Research and Program Development

The LD field emerged from a long line of theory and research on visual-perceptual development, language development, and program development dating to the 1800s. These research strands took place simultaneously, and findings in each influenced the other. Each area had its pioneers who challenged existing assumptions and practices and whose insights laid the foundation for today's theories, research, and intervention strategies.

The pioneers were all wise people with tremendous observational powers and the ability to integrate diverse information. None harbored fanatically narrow views regarding the cause of learning difficulties. The visual-perceptual theorists acknowledged the importance to learning of language. The language theorists acknowledged the role of visual and motor difficulties. Most developed sensible teaching approaches. They understood that an eclectic approach was important because many different abilities come together to contribute to learning and behavior. Although the pioneers certainly focused on what was wrong within the learner, the effectiveness of their curricular and environmental modifications highlighted the critical role that the curriculum, family, and school can play in overcoming learning disabilities.

Visual Perceptual Research

The examination of individual differences that may result in learning disorders can be traced to the study of the brain-injured adult. The scientific excitement that must have been engendered by studying behavioral deviations after brain injury is exemplified in Oliver Sacks's account of one of his patients, a brilliantly talented choir director (pages 11–12). It was not long before researchers noted that some children displayed characteristics similar to those of the adult with brain injury. These pioneers believed that the visual-motor difficulties of these individuals adversely affected their behavioral styles and achievement. Because development of visual and motor skills was believed to precede higher-level cognitive skills, some developed visual-perceptual and motor assessment measures and remediation programs. Although these practices were later challenged, they did lead to important research regarding the relationship between visual-motor processes and learning. The work of these pioneers established very important building blocks for current LD practices.

An important contributor to this research, *Kurt Goldstein,* found that the brain abnormalities of World War I soldiers who had sustained head injuries could alter their behavior. He attributed certain of their unusual behavior patterns to defective processing of visual information and to their reaction to these misperceptions (Goldstein, 1936, 1942):

1. *Forced responsiveness to stimuli:* They were easily distracted by objects and people around them; any fleeting movement, noise, or thought might compel attention.

2. *Figure-ground confusion:* Because they reacted indiscriminately to everything, the soldiers were unable to sort out the essential (a speaker) from the trivial (dining room noise).

3. *Perseveration:* Because their attention was caught and recaught by the same stimuli, the soldiers kept repeating behaviors in which they had just engaged.

4. *Hyperactivity:* The constant attention shifts created extreme, purposeless motor activity.

5. *Catastrophic reaction:* The soldiers suffered emotional breakdowns when they were unable to alleviate their bizarre perceptions and chaotic behavior. Goal-oriented, energetic, or creative activities were difficult to initiate.

6. *Meticulousness:* As a defense against excessive stimulus input, which produced a confusing world of misperceptions, soldiers became overly rigid in arranging their personal time schedules and possessions.

Goldstein's patients had much the same difficulty you are probably experiencing in distinguishing the object in Figure 1–2. But their problem extended even to such everyday necessities as finding a matching sock in the laundry basket or focusing on what one person was saying, to the exclusion of other random chatter. Perseveration, hyperactivity, emotional breakdowns, and a strong need for sameness were understandable consequences of this processing confusion. Attention to these characteristics remains important in the assessment of children with learning difficulties even today.

At the Wayne County Training School for retarded children near Detroit, a number of psychologists, neuropsychiatrists, and educators adapted additional observations regarding visual-perceptual deficits to new ways of facilitating

Figure 1–2   In this picture of a cow, the white space, which is customarily background, has become the figure. The dark space has become the background. The cow's head is to the left and its upper body extends to the right. *Source:* Van Witsen, B. (1967). *Perceptual Training Activities.* NYC: Teacher's College Press. Reprinted with permission from the Optometric Extension Program Foundation, Santa Ana, CA.

children's overall development. From his work, for example, *Heinz Werner* hypothesized that it was best to teach following the normal developmental sequence from earlier to later developing skills: for example, learn the concept "2" first by using manipulative materials such as blocks, then more visually complex but less manipulative materials such as counting dashes or drawings of objects, and finally learning to read the abstract numeral itself. Point-

ing out that children often answered correctly on tests merely by chance, or they answered incorrectly even though their reasoning had been appropriate (Werner, 1937, 1944), Werner, like those who came after him, urged that careful observation of how children perform tasks is far more useful than test scores in planning remedial programming (Werner & Strauss, 1939). He observed that some children were well organized,

Dr. P.: The Man Who Mistook His Wife for a Hat

Dr. P. was a musician of distinction, well-known for many years as a singer, and then, at the local School of Music, as a teacher. It was here, in relation to his students, that certain strange problems were first observed. Sometimes a student would present himself, and Dr. P. would not recognize him; or, specifically, would not recognize his face. The moment the student spoke, he would be recognized by his voice. Such incidents multiplied, causing embarrassment, perplexity, fear and, sometimes, comedy. For not only did Dr. P. increasingly fail to see faces, but he saw faces when there were no faces to see: genially, Magoo-like, when in the street, he might pat the heads of water-hydrants and parking-meters, taking these to be the heads of children; he would amiably address carved knobs on furniture, and be astounded when they did not reply. At first these old mistakes were laughed off as jokes, not least by Dr. P. himself. Had he not always had a quirky sense of humor, and been given to Zen-like paradoxes and jests? His musical powers were as dazzling as ever; he did not feel ill—he had never felt better; and the mistakes were so ludicrous—and so ingenious—that they could hardly be serious or betoken anything serious. The notion of there being "something the matter" did not emerge until some three years later. . . .

He was a man of great cultivation and charm, who talked well and fluently, with imagination and humor. I couldn't think why he had been referred to our clinic.

And yet there *was* something a bit odd. He faced me as he spoke, was oriented towards me, and yet there was something the matter—it was difficult to formulate. He faced me with his *ears*, I came to think, but not with his eyes. These, instead of looking, gazing, at me, "taking me in," in the normal way, made sudden strange fixations—on my nose, on my right ear, down to my chin, up to my right eye—as if noting (even studying) these individual features, but not seeing my whole face, its changing expressions, "me," as a whole. . . .

It was while examining his reflexes—a trifle abnormal on the left side—that the first bizarre experience occurred. I had taken off his left shoe and scratched the sole of his foot with a key—a frivolous-seeming but essential test of a reflex—and then, excusing myself to screw my ophthalmoscope together, left him to put on the shoe himself. To my surprise, a minute later, he had not done this. . . .

He continued to look downwards, though not at the shoe, with an intense but misplaced concentration. Finally his gaze settled on his foot: "That is my shoe, yes?" . . .

"No, it is not. That is your foot. *There* is your shoe."

"Ah! I thought that was my foot."

Was he joking? Was he mad? Was he blind? If this was one of his "strange mistakes," it was the strangest mistake I had ever come across. . . .

I resumed my examination. His visual acuity was good: he had no difficulty seeing a pin on the floor, though sometimes he missed it if it was placed to his left. He saw all right, but what did he see? I opened out a copy of the *National Geographic Magazine*, and asked him to describe some pictures in it.

His responses here were very curious. His eyes would dart from one thing to another, picking up tiny features, individual features, as they had done with my face. A striking brightness, a colour, a shape would arrest his attention and elicit comment—but in no case did he

(Continues on following page)

Dr. P. *(Continued from preceding page)*

get the scene-as-a-whole. He failed to see the whole, seeing only details, which he spotted like blips on a radar screen. . . .

He had no sense whatever of a landscape or scene. I showed him the cover, an unbroken expanse of Sahara dunes.

"What do you see here?" I asked.

"I see a river," he said. "And a little guest-house with its terrace on the water. People are dining out on the terrace. I see coloured parasols here and there." He was looking, if it was "looking," right off the cover, into mid-air and confabulating nonexistent features, as if the absence of features in the actual picture had driven him to imagine the river and the terrace and the coloured parasols.

I must have looked aghast, but he seemed to think he had done rather well. There was a hint of a smile on his face. He also appeared to have decided that the examination was over, and started to look round for his hat. He reached out his hand, and took hold of his wife's head, tried to lift it off, to put it on. He had apparently mistaken his wife for a hat! His wife looked as if she was used to such things. . . .

[At a later house visit] I decided I would show him a volume of cartoons which I had in my briefcase. Here, again, for the most part, he did well. Churchill's cigar, Schnozzle's nose: as soon as he had picked out a key feature he could identify the face. . . .

I turned on the television, keeping the sound off, and found an early Bette Davis film. A love scene was in progress. . . .

What was . . . striking was that he failed to identify the expressions on her face or her partner's, though in the course of a single torrid scene these passed from sultry yearning through passion, surprise, disgust and fury to a melting reconciliation. Dr. P. could make nothing of any of this. He was very unclear as to what was going on, or who was who or even what sex they were. His comments on the scene were positively Martian. . . .

On the walls of the apartment there were photographs of his family, his colleagues, his pupils, himself. I gathered a pile of these together and, with some misgivings, presented them to him. . . .

What had been funny, or farcical, in relation to the movie, was tragic in relation to real life. By and large, he recognised nobody: neither his family, nor his colleagues, nor his pupils, nor himself. He recognised a portrait of Einstein, because he picked up the characteristic hair and moustache. . . .

. . . he approached these faces—even of those near and dear—as if they were abstract puzzles or tests. . . .

He saw nothing as familiar. Visually, he was lost in a world of lifeless abstractions.

whereas others were disorganized. Some had *global* mental processing styles, for example, attending to outlines of shapes; others had *analytical* styles, attending to parts. Each style called for different programming strategies (see Research Box 1–1).

RESEARCH BOX 1–1

Performance Differences between Werner and Strauss's Exogenous and Endogenous Children

Werner and Strauss's investigations compared the performances of what they called *exogenously retarded* children, who had presumably suffered brain injury, with *endogenously retarded* children who had not. They found that exogenous children behaved very similarly to Goldstein's adult brain-injured: forced responsiveness to stimuli (impulsive and distractible), repetitiveness (inappropriate fixation on a task or thought), visual-motor disorganization (hyperactivity), figure-ground confusion, use of nonessential elements when categorizing, and inability to integrate parts into a whole.

One example of differences between the two groups occurred when they looked through a tachistoscope at common objects (a hat, a bird). Endogenous children reported seeing the object, but exogenous children instead were attracted to the nonessential background (Werner & Strauss, 1941). On a visual-motor task requiring copying a marble design on a marble board and then drawing the pattern, the exogenous children had no sense of form or organizational pattern. Their approach was erratic and incoherent. The endogenous children produced continuous, symmetrical patterns in a planned manner, as did nonretarded children of a similar mental age (Werner & Bowers, 1941). Similarly, exogenous, but not endogenous, children performed very poorly on a task in which children were to reproduce vocally simple melodic patterns played on a piano. The endogenous children improved with age, resembling the performance of normal children. The exogenous children did not improve. The errors of the latter children were "of a kind not known in normal development" (p. 98).

Because of the exogenous children's difficulties in all modalities, Werner concluded that the responsible factors are general and not specific to any one sense. The difference found between children in strategies for problem solving (organized vs. disorganized, global vs. analytical) continues to be a major area of research for cognitive psychologists. Strauss's (Strauss & Kephart, 1955; Strauss & Lehtinen, 1947) emphasis on matching academic materials and classroom environments to these children's different learning styles remains a key element in learning disabilities practice today.

When Werner and his partner, *Alfred Strauss,* noted similarities between some of their children's behaviors and Goldstein's brain-injured adults, they assumed that these children's unique behaviors also could be explained by brain injury (Strauss & Werner, 1942; Werner & Strauss, 1940, 1941). Although this tendency to infer neurological problems from behavior rather than from medical evidence was later severely criticized, their observation that children with the same disability can differ greatly from one another nevertheless was influential. Werner and Strauss focused on individuality, on how children solve problems, and on ordering the teaching process to parallel typical development. These remain key concepts within learning disabilities today. Werner's work also encouraged others to research the causes of brain injury, its effect on learning and behavior, and the implications of different information-processing styles. Werner's observations that some children's learning and behavior are unlike anything known in normal development and that other children learn and behave very much like younger, typical children, continue to be important distinctions in LD assessment today. For the former child, very special teaching approaches are necessary, whereas the latter child could benefit from the same approaches used with younger, typical learners.

Noting a slight decline over time in the IQs of institutionalized children who were believed to be retarded due to brain injury, Strauss blamed the IQ drop on their distractibility and overreaction in the overstimulating educational program to which they were exposed. Therefore, Strauss decided to reduce irrelevant environmental stimuli and increase the saliency of materials essential to learning, so that the children's attention could be captured appropriately before irrelevant stimuli did so (Strauss, 1943; Werner & Strauss, 1940). Strauss believed that as these methods decreased the children's hyperactivity and distractibility, their perceptual, conceptual, mental organizational, and behavioral skills would increase (Strauss & Lehtinen, 1947).

One way Strauss diminished hyperactivity and distractibility and engaged attention was by incorporating movement into learning tasks. For example, he had children place pegs into a pegboard while counting, in order to slow them down and coordinate their touching and counting, thereby deterring several objects from being counted as one. Similarly, when pictures were removed from reading materials or only a few words were exposed at a time, he found that children became more focused. Additional environmental modifications to reduce distractions included instructing children in small groups, seating children apart from one another, having teachers wear plain clothing with no accessories, using minimal room decorations, screening the lower quarter of windows and study areas, and facing desks toward the wall.

Though Strauss and his colleagues emphasized building a firm visual-perceptual foundation for further learning, academic instruction was not delayed until the perceptual weaknesses were resolved. Instead, special teaching methods were used to compensate for the perceptual problems: for example, heavy black crayon was used to outline a figure to be colored, so confusion with the background was avoided; letters that could be confused (b, d) were color-coded; only one math problem was presented on a page at a time. Active teacher guidance was essential to accommodate the child's learning style. For example, a teacher might work with a child at a rapid pace so that several steps were completed before the child became distracted.

When using methods tailored to individual children's learning styles, Strauss (1943) reported remarkable academic gains in short periods. As is the case with Strauss's client J, described on page 15, many of these children eventually moved on to normal school programs (Strauss & Lehtinen, 1947). Fifty years ago J may have been called emotionally disturbed or brain injured. Today the same child would be identified as learning disabled due to an attention deficit.

It was not long before Werner and Strauss's observations were expanded by their student, *William Cruickshank,* to children who were brain injured with cerebral palsy, yet of near-average (IQ above 75) to above-average intelligence. Finding these children's perceptual attributes to be similar to those of children thought to be retarded due to brain injury, Cruickshank reasoned that perceptual disabilities were due to brain dysfunction rather than to mental retardation (Cruickshank, 1976; Cruickshank, Bice, & Wallen, 1957). Cruickshank then expanded his work to children who were extremely hyperactive, behaviorally disordered, and had perceptual difficulties, yet had no record of brain injury (Cruickshank et al., 1961). He taught these children perceptual and academic skills in the same way as had Werner and Strauss. These children's successes suggested that Werner and Strauss's way of understanding and meeting individual needs was applicable to children at all intelligence levels. Cruickshank's practice of grouping children into classes based on their instructional needs, rather than on their diagnostic category, was an important forerunner of today's noncategorical grouping practices.

Another of Werner and Strauss's colleagues, *Newell Kephart,* also worked with brain-injured children of normal intelligence. Reflecting Werner and Strauss's assumption that perceptual and

J

J . . . Father a prominent attorney, mother educated according to the standards of the upper social class. Parents 31 and 17 years old respectively at the time of marriage. An only child. Pregnancy and delivery were both normal but the child was blue [oxygen deprived] at birth. . . . He walked and talked somewhat later than usual and had no serious childhood diseases. He was an extremely disobedient and "obstinate" child with destructive tendencies, very easily excited. He seemed to be fearless. Not accepted by other children because of his constant teasing and tormenting. . . . When six years old, he was entered in a private school but could not be admitted to a class with other children. Two teachers were employed for him alone since one teacher refused to stand it without relief for the entire day.

At eight years and six months of age he was admitted to our clinic. He had a second grade school achievement; psychometric testing was impossible because of extreme restlessness and distractibility. He was always "on the move," exploring everything in the house, particularly technical equipment, electric switches, door bells, elevators, etc. Asked questions incessantly, like a machine gun. Very affectionate with all the persons in the house. When taken to bed, he did not sleep until midnight but asked another question every five minutes. On the days following his admission he was still very restless and disinhibited [did whatever he wished; continually active and impulsive] but meticulous and pedantic in the arrangement of his belongings and everything handled by him at the table or in the classroom. Play in the garden consisted in trying to destroy flowers or bushes but without illhumor or anger. Always smiling and good-humored. At dinner time he ate enormous quantities of food and drank a glass of water or milk in one gulp. In church he was very distractible, wishing to give money to all the collection boxes. After two weeks in the clinic, he was more adjusted but still very distractible. He was discharged after one and one half years with an intelligence quotient within the normal range and admitted to a private school. Then attended class with children of his age and in an examination proved to be ninth in placement among forty children.

Source: Strauss, A. A., & Lehtinen, L. E. (1947). *Psychopathology and education of the brain-injured child.* New York: Grune & Stratton (p. 2). Reprinted by permission.

motor development form the basis for behavior, language, and conceptual learning, Kephart (1960) believed that all school information that was seen or heard had to be linked with a spoken or movement response (*perceptual-motor match*) in order to lay the foundation for learning (for instance, learning to differentiate left from right body parts first would help to clarify left from right when later learning confusable letters . . . b-d, p-q).

Kephart (1960) devised a perceptual-motor remediation program (balance, coordination, eye movements, eye-hand coordination, visual percep-

tion) for his students, whom he referred to as *slow learners.* Kephart's perceptual-motor training assumptions subsequently came under a great deal of criticism because learning of school information did not automatically improve with such training. Nevertheless, Kephart's assumptions did stimulate needed research into the relationship between motor, perceptual, and academic development.

Also noting that many children with neurological impairments have deficits in particular areas of visual perception, *Marianne Frostig* developed an assessment measure and a related gross-motor and workbook program to remediate these perceptual dysfunctions (Frostig & Horne, 1964; Frostig, LeFever, & Whittlesey, 1964; Frostig et al., 1961). Popular acceptance of Frostig's belief that most learning is acquired visually led to wide use of her program through the early 1970s. As with Kephart's work, however, studies soon surfaced challenging the validity of Frostig's assessment measure and showing unimpressive reading gains after perceptual training (Larsen & Hammill, 1975). Unfortunately, practitioners had hoped that Frostig's workbooks alone would resolve their students' reading problems. They did not heed Frostig's cautions that the exercises would only facilitate efficient use of visual skills during reading; reading improvement could not occur unless reading instruction also accompanied the visual-perceptual training (Frostig et al., 1961). Frostig emphasized that appropriate programming also must take into account the effects of such factors as past education, social environment, interests, attitudes, temperament, abilities, and disabilities (Frostig, 1967). This philosophy is followed today when we try to understand and deal with the various task and setting factors that contribute to a student's learning disabilities. Frostig's (1976) emphasis on the development of moral, socially appropriate, and cooperative behaviors in her students was unusual at the time, but has since become an important focus in LD research and practice.

Language Development Research

Since reading and writing are translations of our language into a new symbol system, it makes sense that a child who cannot understand what is said is likely to have difficulty understanding and remembering what he or she reads. Similarly, a child who is poor at communicating thoughts orally is likely to have trouble with written expression. Clearly, the development of language competency is an important prerequisite for academic progress.

Theories about how the brain processes language and the relationship between language development and literacy date to the early 1800s. Both have significantly influenced assessment strategies and individualized instruction in the

classroom. As language became appreciated for its significant role in higher-level learning, early remediation of language disabilities became an important means of trying to prevent learning disabilities.

Cassandra's story (page 17) illustrates one type of individual with whom the pioneers in language disabilities worked. Today, people like Cassandra, whose reading difficulties relate to delays in language and auditory processing, are called learning disabled.

The investigation of spoken language disorders can be traced to *Franz Gall,* a Viennese physician who practiced phrenology, the analysis of skull size, shape, and bumps (Wiederholt, 1974). In the early 1800s Gall hypothesized that loss of speech and memory for words resulted from injury to the brain's frontal lobes (Head, 1920a). After Gall's death, *John Baptiste Bouillaud,* a French physician and ardent follower of Gall, continued to try to locate speech in these lobes by offering "a sum of money to anyone who would produce the brain of an individual who had lost his speech in which the anterior lobes presented no lesion" (Head, 1920a, p. 393).

Continuing Gall's and Bouillaud's study of brain-behavior relationships in the 1860s, *Pierre Paul Broca,* a French physician, hypothesized that language was located in the left hemisphere of the brain. The right hemisphere was presumed to have a different function. When Broca autopsied the brains of two men who had lost their ability to talk, he found that a portion of each brain's left frontal lobe was atrophied (Osgood & Miron, 1963). Thus, he anatomically demonstrated a relationship between the left hemisphere and the ability to speak. This area of the brain was later labeled *Broca's area,* and the loss of ability to speak became referred to as *expressive aphasia.*

Broca observed that some children in whom these areas had been destroyed nevertheless developed normal speech. He attributed this to speech having been transferred to the corresponding areas of their right hemispheres (Smith, 1984). Both hemispheric specialization for language and the readiness of certain brain areas to take over for malfunctioning areas remain much researched topics today.

Cassandra

I can remember, to this very day, my mother making me wear a letter of the alphabet around my neck to school. I believe it was the letter *J*. I knew the letter before I left the house and tried so hard not to forget it all day. Picture a child, five years of age, walking out of her house knowing that when she comes back through that very same door she better know the letter.

I walked all the way to school saying that letter *J* over and over again. But do you know over the course of the day I had forgotten that letter? After school was out I tried so hard, I mean I looked at that letter so hard praying that a voice or something would give me the answer before I got home. I love my mother and I know she loves me, and all she wanted was for me to know my alphabet. But I feared her so and hated the fact that I couldn't remember or couldn't begin to remember what she tried so hard to teach me. I remember crying so hard and being mad at myself, because I just couldn't get it. I wanted so much to yell at her, "I'm trying, damn it, I'm trying. Can't you see I'm trying! Just help me please!"

As I got older, reading and spelling got harder and harder for me. Teachers, my family, and friends all seemed to be picking on me all the time. Teachers blamed me for cutting up in class everytime. So since everyone wanted to laugh or blame me for things, I stopped trying to read either to myself or out loud and became a clown in school and stayed to myself at home. By the time I reached eleventh grade I realized the damage that was done.

Going to college never entered my mind or what I wanted out of life or what kind of job I was going to get, since I wasn't going to college. Then I found myself feeling disappointed, not because the people that I cared about or the teachers that were supposed to teach had put me down, but because I had put my ownself down. I finally came to realize that I was always going to run into people who thought I was stupid, but I knew and really believed that I wasn't. I was going to graduate from high school without anyone's help, so I knew I wasn't stupid.

Therefore, why is it to this very day, now 28, I still fear reading and speaking to people I meet? I find myself only speaking to those I know won't pick on me, even at my job, or only speaking to someone if it's just me and them. I'll tell you why. It's because my mother, as well as other family members, and teachers have stopped me from trying. They have made me think that everyone I talk to is going to pick and pick on me until they can't pick any more. In other words every human being on this earth is smarter than me. And that is wrong.

No child should ever feel like that. I have asked myself how in the hell can someone do that to a child who is trying? Each and every child deserves the right to learn and should feel that they can speak their mind without someone stopping them by making them feel belittled.

Source: Reprinted by permission of Cassandra Branch.

Broca's work was an important beginning for subsequent theorists who studied how auditory information was received, understood, memorized, and then repeated. In fact, shortly after Broca's discoveries, a fellow Frenchman, Déjèrine (1891), reported postmortem findings on a person who could comprehend well, yet who had lost the ability to read and write. Like Broca, Déjèrine found a lesion in the left hemisphere but farther back in the brain where the temporal, parietal, and occipital lobes come together (Geschwind, 1986). This area subsequently has been identified as critical to the ability to read.

Carl Wernicke, a German physician, continued Broca's work in the 1870s but focused primarily on the inability to understand speech (Wernicke, 1874, in Eggert, 1977). While working with adult stroke victims, Wernicke noted instances in which they had lost their ability to comprehend language. These patients were unable to think of words when speaking, but the overall meaning of their garbled sentences was always reasonable. Even though they could not name simple objects such as a hat or pencil, the patients did know how to use them correctly. Along with their inability to understand, think of, or use words appropriately, they lost their ability to read and write words. As the patients recovered their ability to understand words, speech and reading also improved. However, the ability to call a word to mind quickly or to express oneself in writing remained very poor (Wernicke, 1906, in Eggert, 1977).

Prior to Wernicke's work, similar severe comprehension problems were attributed to low intelligence, hearing deficits, craziness, or brain deterioration due to aging. In contrast, Wernicke suggested that this loss was the result of damage to certain portions of the temporal lobe (*Wernicke's area*) that had neural connections to the frontal areas described by Broca. Wernicke (1906, in Eggert, 1977) hypothesized that when these connections were damaged, speech that had been understood could not be translated into spoken language. This explained why some stroke victims could understand what others said but could respond only with unrelated emotional, jargonlike expressions.

After Wernicke's death, his theories were validated anatomically (Geschwind, 1968). The comprehension difficulty became known as a *receptive* or *sensory aphasia*. The disorder in the neural connections between Wernicke's and Broca's areas became known as a *conduction aphasia*. The difficulty searching one's memory to come up with the right word is now called a *word-finding problem*. These word-finding difficulties have been identified as a common characteristic of learning disorders. Assessment and remediation methods in use in schools today commonly analyze behavior along Wernicke's receptive, expressive, and connectionist dimensions and link language-processing skills with achievement in reading and writing.

Hughlings Jackson, a contemporary of Broca's, agreed that the left hemisphere was used for speaking and that damage to it usually caused aphasia (Head, 1915). However, he was among the first to suggest that, in some people (for example, left-handers), language could be located in the right hemisphere. Although some of his patients had suffered left hemisphere damage, it was remarkable that they still had command of all or certain types of speech. Jackson therefore hypothesized that the right hemisphere processes and controls certain types of messages, such as emotional and habitual responses ("Oh my God," "Come on," "yes," "no," "very well").

Because behavioral disturbances often accompanied speech disorders, Jackson argued that speech was controlled by complex interconnections within the whole brain (Jackson, 1931). Consequently, damage to any single portion of the brain would reduce a person's overall abilities. This reasoning led Jackson to propose that language is thought and is therefore linked to intelligence. Aphasia, according to Jackson, diminishes intelligence by interfering with one's ability to understand or express thoughts.

Jackson's ideas about the right hemisphere's role in language have been confirmed and have helped us to understand ability differences among individuals. In addition, research suggests that a diminution in one ability due to brain damage may in fact impact several other skills that depend on that ability. Jackson's linking of language proficiency to intelligence is an important concept because what our society defines as intelligent achievement and problem solving depends a great deal on verbal skills.

Sir Henry Head, editor of the British journal *Brain* from 1905 to 1922, monopolized its pages by lauding Jackson's work and cruelly chastising Broca's and Wernicke's simple assignment of specific behaviors to specific brain regions (Head, 1926). Because he saw the brain as a complex neural network crossing different brain regions, Head (1920a) did not believe that a brain injury would produce a receptive or expressive disorder alone. Rather, it also would affect functions not associated with language, yet leave some speech functions intact. Because of the brain's complex connections, he urged that professionals plan interventions based on observation of patients' behaviors rather than by trying to pinpoint sites of brain lesions. He also stressed the meaninglessness of terms like *aphasia* because they do not describe the specific behaviors affected by the lesions.

Studying the language losses of World War I victims of gunshot wounds to the head, Head followed Jackson's lead in pointing out that abstract conceptual ability is the most serious process affected by aphasia (Head, 1920b). Insofar as conceptual processes depend on the perfect exercise of all mental aptitudes, language disabilities dull a person's reasoning skills (Head, 1923). These individuals' intellectual capacities may function well in some ways (for example, speaking) but be dull in other ways (for example, reading). Head noted that once a person appears less competent to others, he or she unfortunately becomes isolated from communication and information that might sharpen his or her intelligence.

Many of Head's ideas are reflected in key premises within current learning disability theories: children may have intellectual potential that shows up only through specific sensory modalities and on certain types of tasks; describing behaviors is more important than diagnosing sites of brain lesions; if language and intelligence are synonymous in our society, then early language intervention is critical.

Jon Eisenson (1954), another language theorist, cautioned about generalizing from adult brain injury to children's brains. Eisenson hypothesized that, while children could experience *developmental aphasias* (poor language development) as a result of brain damage before, during, or after birth, their language delays also could result from a lag in their brains' rate of maturation. Like adult aphasics, Eisenson found that these children's irregular brain waves often indicated problems in the left cerebral hemisphere (Eisenson, 1968). However, these children differed from the adults

in that, instead of losing the ability to speak, they were slow to develop speech.

Like his predecessors' work with adults, Eisenson found that language deficits such as small vocabulary, poor grammar, short sentence length, and poor comprehension were not the only difficulties experienced by these children. They frequently did not realize that people were speaking to them; had inconsistent responses to sound; experienced disorders in other sensory modalities; had intellectual, attention, and memory inefficiencies; perseverated; showed emotional ups and downs; and responded inconsistently from day to day (Eisenson, 1968). He believed that the majority of these children could not speak correctly because they lacked the capacity to derive meaning from the speech they heard (Eisenson, 1954). Eisenson's (1968) speculations stimulated research into auditory information-processing inefficiencies that he thought might underlie children's learning difficulties: a defective storage system for speech signals, difficulty processing auditory signals at a normal rate, and impaired ability to tell sounds apart and sequence sounds, words, or events.

Whereas Eisenson dealt with theories of disordered language in children, *Charles Osgood* (1957) proposed a normal language development model as a way of understanding learning disorders. Osgood suggested that there were two stages to all behaviors: *decoding,* interpreting the significance of signals received from the environment, and *encoding,* expressing intentions through overt acts. Each stage has three levels of organization: (1) a projection level, where sensory and motor action signals are wired to appropriate brain areas; (2) an integration level, where incoming and outgoing neural events are organized; and (3) a representation level, where meaning and thinking take place. The integration and representation of information were thought to depend on the number and strength of stimulus-response pairings at the projection level.

Osgood's normal language development model, like those of his colleagues *Joseph Wepman* (Wepman et al., 1960; Wepman & Jones, 1961), *Helmer Myklebust* (1965), and *Samuel Kirk* (Kirk, McCarthy, & Kirk, 1968), influenced the development of tests and remedial programs for children with learning problems. By proposing that reading is the second highest, and writing the highest, level of language development, Myklebust firmly linked language disorders to learning disabilities.

Beyond receptive, expressive, and mixed forms of aphasia in children, Myklebust (1952, 1954) also suggested a category of *central aphasia,* in which thinking and reasoning through inner speech (verbal or nonverbal silent reasoning) are disturbed. *Amnesic aphasia* occurred when language functioning was well established but patients could not remember words, even though they knew what they intended to say and could recognize the correct words when spoken or written. Today we refer to amnesic aphasia as *word-finding difficulties.*

Myklebust (1965) suggested that reading depends on proficiency in lower-level inner language, comprehension, and speaking skills. In turn, written expression competence depends on each of these plus reading. He noted that written language disorders also could be due to difficulty with the motor movements required in writing (*dysgraphia*) and with remembering (*revisualizing*) what letters or words look like.

Much of our reading and writing theory, assessment tools, and intervention strategies today are based on the important work of connecting language, reading, and composition skills. The work of these language theorists focused attention on the critical need for individually tailored, intensive, early remediation efforts that can raise not only children's language ability but also their intellectual, academic, and social skills.

Program Development

By the 1960s, the theoretical work in visual-perceptual and language development and a proliferation of new educational materials, methods, and equipment made individualized instruction more sophisticated and manageable. Emphasizing multisensory methods, programming concern shifted beyond reading to written expression, arithmetic, comprehension, and content area learning as well.

These advances in program development were stimulated by the work of several pioneers, some of whom viewed learning difficulties primarily from a visual-perceptual perspective, while others took a language approach. These pioneers developed creative remedial strategies for a broad range of youngsters displaying mild to severe problems in one or more areas of development and learning.

The story of Percy F., a young man who appeared normal in all respects yet who had great difficulty learning to read, is presented below. One of the earliest reports on reading disorders, this report illustrates how such puzzling children could excite the pioneers' clinical interests.

Percy F.

Percy F.—a well-grown lad, aged 14—is the eldest son of intelligent parents, the second child of a family of seven. He has always been a bright and intelligent boy, quick at games, and in no way inferior to others of his age.

His great difficulty has been—and is now—his inability to learn to read. This inability is so remarkable, and so pronounced, that I have no doubt it is due to some congenital defect.

(Continues on following page)

Percy F. *(Continued from preceding page)*

He has been at school or under tutors since he was 7 years old, and the greatest efforts have been made to teach him to read, but, in spite of this laborious and persistent training, he can only with difficulty spell out words of one syllable.

The following is the result of an examination I made a short time since. He knows all his letters and can write them and read them. In writing from dictation he comes to grief over any but the simplest words. For instance, I dictated the following sentence: "Now, you watch me while I spin it." He wrote: "Now you word me wale I spin it"; and, again, "Carefully winding the string round the peg" was written: "calfuly winder the sturng rond the pag."

In writing his own name he made a mistake, putting "Precy" for "Percy," and he did not notice the mistake until his attention was called to it more than once. I asked him to write the following words:

Song	he wrote	scone
Subject	"	Scojock
Without	"	wichout
English	"	Englis
Shilling	"	sening
Seashore	"	seasoiv

He was quite unable to spell the name of his father's house though he must have seen it and spelt it scores of times. In asking him to read the sentences he had just written a short time previously, he could not do so, but made mistakes over every word except the very simplest. Words such as "and" and "the" he always recognizes.

I then asked him to read me a sentence out of an easy child's book without spelling the words. The result was curious. He did not read a single word correctly, with the exception of "and," "the," "of," "that," etc.; the other words seemed to be quite unknown to him, and he could not even make an attempt to pronounce them.

I next tried his ability to read figures, and found he could do so easily. He read off quickly the following: 785, 852017, 20, 969, and worked out correctly: $(a + x)(a - x) = a - x$. He could not do the simple calculation $4 \times \frac{1}{2}$, but he multiplied 749 by 867 quickly and correctly. He says he is fond of arithmetic, and finds no difficulty with it, but that printed or written words "have no meaning to him," and my examination of him quite convinces me that he is correct in that opinion. Words written or printed seem to convey no impression to his mind, and it is only after laboriously spelling them that he is able, by the sounds of the letters, to discover their import. His memory for written or printed words is so defective that he can only recognize such simple ones as "and," "the," "of," etc. Other words he never seems to remember no matter how frequently he may have met them. . . .

I may add that the boy is bright and of average intelligence in conversation . . . his eyesight is good. The schoolmaster who has taught him for some years says that he would be the smartest lad in the school if the instruction were entirely oral. It will be interesting to see what effect further training will have on his condition.

Source: Morgan, W. P. (1896). A case of congenital word blindness. *British Medical Journal, 2,* 1378. Reprinted by pemission of *British Medical Journal* Publishing Group.

One such pioneer in the late 1800s, a Glasgow ophthalmologist named *James Hinshelwood,* published observations about the effects of brain damage on adult reading skills. Hinshelwood's case studies, summarized in Research Box 1–2, led him to hypothesize that the brain had separate contiguous centers for the storage of visual memories of everyday objects and places, letters, numerals, and words. He supported his thesis by noting that each of these functions returned separately, not simultaneously, as brain-injured adults recovered (Hinshelwood, 1899). Hinshelwood believed that a proficient reader remembered words merely by recalling a visual picture.

Hinshelwood applied the term *congenital word blindness* to children of normal vision and intelligence whose reading disabilities were similar to those acquired by his adult patients. He hypothesized that they had a defect in the portions of the left hemisphere where visual word and letter memories were stored (Hinshelwood, 1917). This brain defect was attributed to brain injury at birth, faulty brain development, or disease. Hinshelwood recommended a three-stage process for overcoming word blindness: (1) teach individual letters to be stored in the visual-memory center of the brain; (2) teach word recognition by spelling the printed words out loud, capitalizing on the person's good memory for letter sounds; and (3) use oral and written practice to enhance storage of the reading words. Hinshelwood's belief that analyzing each word into its individual sounds would help children recognize words as complete pictures had a strong impact on later intervention approaches designed to utilize presumed brain strengths to overcome children's weaknesses.

Like Hinshelwood, *Samuel Orton* (1937), a neuropathologist, also noted similarities between children's reading, writing, spelling, and speaking

RESEARCH BOX 1–2
Hinshelwood's Case Studies

Hinshelwood's clients suffered from brain insults caused by strokes and chronic alcoholism and had acquired strange forms of "word blindness" or "dyslexia" (inability to read). One individual had lost the ability to read print or write more than the first few words of a line, after which the words lost meaning for him. He was a tailor and could not remember how to fit pieces together, where he had just placed objects, and where his home was located (Hinshelwood, 1896). Another client could not read words but could read letters and numbers, write from dictation, and copy words. If allowed to spell each word aloud, letter by letter, he could read the words laboriously (Hinshelwood, 1898).

Hinshelwood found that word blindness was often accompanied by letter blindness. One patient could not recognize letters but, if allowed to trace them with his finger, could eventually name them (Hinshelwood, 1898). Another client, Tom, exhibited letter blindness without word blindness. He could not read, write, or point to individual letters (with the exception of *T*, which he called "Tom"). However, Tom could read familiar and unfamiliar words rapidly and also wrote well (Hinshelwood, 1899). It was not long before Hinshelwood and others generalized the theoretical notions about the injured brain processes in these adults to children who also experienced significant difficulties acquiring reading and writing skills.

delays and the disorders of brain-injured adults. Orton (1925, 1928) proposed that when one cerebral hemisphere fails to establish dominance over the other, it cannot suppress the intruding mirror-images of words presumably stored in the nondominant hemisphere. Although the resulting reversals were thought to cause reading difficulties, these were not believed to be nearly as serious as those caused by difficulties in "the process of synthesizing the word as a spoken unit from its component sounds" (Orton, 1937, p. 162).

To remediate reading disorders in children who also had writing, speech, and coordination problems, and who had no hand preference, Orton (1937) suggested training body movements on one side of the body in order to strengthen cerebral dominance and reduce interference from the opposing hemisphere. Once one hemisphere had become superior and a hand preference had been established, progress in language, reading, and reasoning was expected to follow.

Because most children had already developed handedness, they did not meet Orton's qualifications for dominance training. For these children, he urged reading remediation methods that built associations between auditory, visual, and kinesthetic (feedback from body movements) information. For example, he suggested "having the child trace [the letter] over a pattern drawn by the teacher, at the same time giving its sound or phonetic equivalent" (Orton, 1937, p. 159). Maintaining consistent left-to-right tracing was essential to aid recall of "word pictures" and to overcome confusion caused by reversed letter and word images supposedly stored in the nondominant hemisphere. Orton recommended repetitive oral and written drills on letter-sound associations (Orton, 1925). Because spelling presented even greater obstacles than reading, Orton (1937) urged that spelling be trained through analysis of the sequence of sounds in words.

Orton (1928) believed that the "look-say" approach in America's schools was responsible for a great deal of reading failure because the nondominant hemisphere's reversed letter and word images confused recall. Therefore, Orton influenced educators to use phonetic analysis and kinesthetic activities in their teaching. The value of phonetic over sight approaches to reading has since been affirmed, as have several other of Orton's influences: gearing materials to the student's ability and interest levels; no one remediation package being suitable for all children; individualizing instruction by analyzing the content and processes involved in learning; recognizing and dealing with negative personality characteristics (apathy, emotional blocking, inferiority, antagonism) that can arise from academic struggle and failure; researching the degree to which one hemisphere of the brain can interfere with the efficient operation of the other hemisphere. Most important, Orton's emphasis on the relationship between phonetic analysis and reading created a shift away from the visual-perceptual perspective on learning problems. By the 1970s, the language, rather than perceptual, viewpoint had become predominant.

Orton's methods were developed further by many individuals interested in reading remediation (for example, Marion Monroe, Anna Gillingham, Bessie Stillman, Romalda Spalding, Grace Fernald). Of these, *Grace Fernald* had the most widespread influence. Fernald (1943) blamed much of reading disability on the fact that the schools' visual teaching methods were incongruent with the needs of children who had difficulty remembering (revisualizing) what they had seen. Instead, she suggested a multisensory approach to reading and spelling that combined kinesthetic methods, such as tracing, with phonetic associations, such as saying word sounds, while looking at the whole word. Kinesthetic instructional methods never before had been advocated with as much energy and focus.

Fernald's *Remedial Techniques in Basic School Subjects* (1943) was a landmark work. She described specific reading and arithmetic remediation methods, and explained how to apply these in the course of teaching typical classroom subject matter.

Fernald's creative remedial approaches were developed further by *Doris Johnson* and *Helmer Myklebust* (1967) who proposed that information could be received, processed, and expressed via one sensory system (e.g., visual inputs–motor outputs, as in copying designs) and be relatively independent from another system (e.g., auditory inputs–vocal outputs, as in repeating oral directions). In contrast to such *intraneurosensory integration* tasks, they proposed that academic tasks like reading required the *interneurosensory integration* of information being transferred from one system to another (visual-vocal as in reading, or auditory-motor as in spelling). In reading, for example, a visual stimulus (letter) must be looked at, matched to its auditory correlate (sound), and then expressed vocally (read).

Johnson and Myklebust conceptualized several categories of *dyslexia*, or reading failure: *auditory dyslexia* (inability to process sounds), *visual dyslexia* (difficulty processing information that has been seen), *comprehension disorders*, and *written production* problems. They believed that *dyscalculia*, difficulty learning arithmetic, could be related to language or reading problems, disturbances in quantitative thinking, difficulty revisualizing or writing numbers, and difficulty recalling instructions. They also described the spatial, conceptual, memory, and social difficulties of children with learning difficulties and offered detailed instructional ideas.

As had their predecessors, Myklebust and Johnson developed excellent educational strategies that are used by today's teachers to adapt curricula to individual children's needs. Their emphasis on *clinical teaching* (ongoing assessment while teaching) greatly influenced the subsequent development of assessment strategies, teaching materials, and methods.

The 1960s to 1990s

Stimulated by the work of the pioneers, the 1960s to 1990s were years of significant growth in learning disabilities theory, research, and application. The 1960s were marked by particular controversy because of misapplication of the pioneers' beliefs about designing instruction around students' information-processing characteristics; often classroom practices would aim at remediating the inferred visual-motor, language, or motor causes of learning problems, sometimes to the neglect of solid academic teaching.

The 1960s were also characterized by accusations and counteraccusations between camps of individuals who had adopted one or another of the pioneers' beliefs. Unfortunately, many of these individuals had pursued a single theoretical position, despite the pioneers' more eclectic intentions and the limited research support for one theory over another. For example, Orton's followers jumped onto a cerebral dominance training bandwagon. Yet, in his entire book, Orton (1937) devoted less than one page to this type of training. Similarly, Marianne Frostig developed a visual-perceptual test and program but never intended, as her followers assumed, that remediation of these abilities alone, without concurrent reading instruction, automatically would increase a child's reading skills. In reaction to these narrow approaches, many individuals led severe, unwarranted attacks on the pioneering works.

As reaction to questionable practices grew, many researchers shifted their focus toward observable behaviors that had a more certain relationship to academic progress. The application of sophisticated behavior modification techniques moved from the laboratory to the classroom and grew in popularity (Haring & Lovitt, 1967; Whalen, 1966). Behavior modification's systematic reinforcement of appropriate behavior and learning responses offered a promising approach for modifying learning and behavior disorders in the classroom. Much of this behavioral technology was developed by Werner, Strauss, and Cruickshank's students, who modeled their mentors' environmental structuring techniques. These methods grew in favor because they focused only on behaviors that could be observed, rather than making presumptions about the underlying causes of learning difficulties. Methods were developed for analyzing curricular tasks so that teachers would know exactly which step to teach next and exactly how to teach it. Very rigidly sequenced reading and math programs were developed, even going so far as to specify the words, actions, and reinforcers teachers were to use. This behavioral technology made implementation of individualized instruction all the more possible (Bijou, 1970; Mann, 1971).

Toward the late 1960s, attention to visual and motor disabilities declined as educators discovered that language delays often led to far more serious learning problems. When educators looked back into the histories of children with reading delays, they found that many had been language-delayed as preschoolers. Moreover, these children continued to display subtle communicative disorders at older ages. Therefore, language remediation, early identification, and prevention of handicapping conditions became important priorities.

The heated debates of the 1960s spurred on scientific inquiry that modified theory and practice in learning disabilities yet also confirmed many of the pioneering notions; if we look closely enough, we recognize them: when we teach a child "through all his senses," that's Fernald; when we build a study carrel to help a child attend, that's Strauss; when we caution not to teach too much, too soon, too fast, that's Werner. The behavioral emphasis on observation, task analysis, and systematic reinforcement also would continue to flourish, as would research on basic information processing within medical and neurological circles. Language-processing weaknesses and attention deficits gradually replaced the visual-motor emphasis as focal points for understanding learning disabilities. By the mid-1970s, sophisticated neuropsychological studies had begun to connect specific information-processing patterns to different kinds of academic delays, and the effectiveness of various drugs, diets, and teaching strategies to learning and behavioral outcomes.

Despite this progress, it was disheartening that, as we watched children with learning disabilities grow up, we noted that their difficulties did not disappear. Rather, new hurdles would appear as the demands of the academic, social, and adult work worlds became more complex. Consequently, secondary and postsecondary educational and vocational preparation began receiving heightened attention in the 1970s, as did planning transitional living services. Accompanying these changes was a growing interest in the emotional and social aspects of learning difficulties. In addition, it became apparent that, besides brain differences, adverse circumstances such as poor parenting, schooling, and teacher attitudes required attention, because they too contributed to poor achievement (Quay, 1973).

The broadening focus of learning disabilities was accompanied by confusion and conflict. During the 1970s, the schism widened between the behaviorists (who concentrated on building basic academic competencies) and those who remediated underlying perceptual or language readiness skills because they viewed learning disabilities as a brain-related information-processing disorder (Smead, 1977; Ysseldyke & Salvia, 1974). Behaviorists were especially critical of the information-processing theorists because, when researchers tried to improve children's skills in the weaker visual perceptual, language, or motor areas, academic gains did not follow (Hammill & Larsen, 1974b, 1978). Besides, with the growing sensitivity to equal rights and the impact of nurture over nature, behaviorists looked askance at the notion that some students had inherent deficits that forecast poorer potential for learning.

In the 1980s, the battles softened. Eclecticism became an acceptable approach to learning disabilities because the research evidence was too powerful to refute either the information-processing or the behavioral approaches. With advances in neuropsychological research instrumentation, we witnessed an explosion in knowledge regarding the neurological underpinnings of learning and behavior. The intricate interplay between both biological and environmental influences on human development could no longer be ignored.

Some behaviorists actually began using physiological measures in their research because the new instrumentation had made brain functions observable. Educators biased toward remediating information-processing weaknesses, on the other hand, acknowledged that their neuropsychological data were too new and contradictory to definitely predict whether instruction geared to a particular brain strength or weakness would increase academic progress. While information about uneven brain development helped one understand the nature of a child's difficulties, these educators, like behaviorists, geared instruction toward actual academic and life skills. Both groups placed increasing emphasis on experimenting with curricular and environmental modifications that could help focus the attention of students with attention deficits.

Interestingly, it was behaviorists who introduced a whole new notion of information processing that would greatly influence intervention strategies—*metacognition*. Metacognitive strategies teach children how to plan their learning, in effect self-instructing their brains about how to pay attention, organize information, and remember. Because students often do not generalize what they learn in one setting to another, educators saw in these cognitive strategies the potential to impact how students learn, so that knowledge and skills acquired in one situation would be accessible in a wide range of circumstances.

The learning disabled participated fully in the computer revolution of the 1980s. Some children who were undermotivated and inattentive, who resisted workbooks, and who were sidetracked by the slightest distraction amazingly persisted when difficult tasks were presented via computer. Some children who resisted writing found success on the word processor. Software development mushroomed, and computers became commonplace in the classroom.

It had taken a long time, but by the 1980s we finally reconciled ourselves to the fact that learning disabilities are not a unitary disorder. The causes and characteristics of LD differ from person to person; consequently, each person's intervention needs also would vary. We also came to terms with the fact that attention to the social, emotional, vocational, and independent living side of learning disabilities was just as important as the academic achievement side of the picture.

Several concerns have been high priorities in the 1990s. Embarrassingly large numbers of students are being identified as learning disabled because the LD concept's popularity and the group's heterogeneity have led people to misinterpret normal variability as abnormal. There is a need for refined definitions of LD subtypes and identification criteria, so that we can stop misidentification, interpret our research accurately, and determine which instructional approaches are the most promising for different types of individuals. The sooner we come to grips with these issues,

the sooner we will begin to bridge the backlash created by critics of policies and practices in the LD field—the most extreme of whom question whether there even is such a thing as learning disabilities.

There are concerns on other fronts as well: fine-tuning the use of informal and curriculum-based assessment approaches as adjuncts to standardized testing; exploring ways to help adolescents make the transition to the adult world; identifying the best preventative strategies; countering the inflexibility and lack of personalization of the regular classroom curriculum; identifying strategies to help the student with learning disabilities fully access the curriculum and social life within the typical classroom. These concerns necessitate intensified preparation of regular educators to deal with the needs of the learning disabled, and better familiarity of the special educator with normal academic development and the regular education curriculum. There also is growing recognition that our reductionist approach to intervening with these students must be tempered. Rather than have teachers dictate every bit of information students are to learn, students must be approached from a more holistic perspective, one that gives them more autonomy in their learning and greater trust in the integrity of their minds. The learning experience must become more personally constructed and meaningful, guided more by each student's creativity, subjective feelings, interests, and cultural and linguistic background.

As we face these challenges, we find ourselves holding philosophies surprisingly similar to those of many of the pioneers in learning disabilities. They were the ones who originally conceptualized learning disabilities as an interaction of learner, task, and setting factors, and today's research builds on the many constructs that originated with their work.

Definition

Before the term *learning disabilities* became accepted, many terms were used interchangeably to describe children with unexpected underachievement, and whose learning and behavior patterns did not fit existing disability categories. These labels had little meaning because one term could refer to different behaviors, or different terms could be used to refer to the same behaviors.

In 1964, Clements's (1966) national task force on minimal brain dysfunction tried to come to grips with the terminology issue. It found that thirty-eight terms were being applied to this group of children. Some terms referenced the brain as causing the learning problem (for example, *organic brain damage, cerebral dysfunction*), whereas others described specific behaviors associated with the disorder (for example, *hyperkinetic behavior syndrome, character impulse disorder, hyperexcitability syndrome, primary reading retardation, clumsy child syndrome, learning disabilities*). Common terms not on Clements's list included *slow learner, neurological handicap, brain injury, Strauss syndrome, developmental imbalance,* and *educational handicap*. Strauss (1943) had even tried out the term *cripple-brained*.

The first of these terms to gain general acceptance was *brain injury*. This term was short-lived, however, because many people found it offensive:

1. It implied that the child's situation was hopeless; injured brain cells cannot be repaired.

2. It was too global a term to be meaningful. There are many types of brain-injured people, and they differ greatly. The term neither described a child's characteristics nor suggested appropriate teaching methods (Stevens & Birch, 1957; Wortis, 1956).

3. Knowing the nature and extent of brain injury cannot help a teacher decide on a remedial approach because the damage is not directly related to the nature and extent of functional problems. For example, Cohn's (1964) autopsy studies showed that it was possible for massive neurological destruction to result in only a few learning and behavioral abnormalities. Conversely, numerous learning and behavioral

deficiencies could result from very limited neurological damage.

4. The term *brain injured* was used most often when the label could not be validated (Gallagher, 1966). When brain injury could be proved, the label was more specific: for example, cerebral palsy, hydrocephaly. Making inferences about brain injury could not be justified given the practical uselessness of the term.

5. Even if children had verified brain injury, it was their actual abilities, not the underlying cause, that needed to be dealt with (Gallagher, 1966). These ability patterns could guide programming; the "brain injury" label could not.

An alternative term, *minimal brain dysfunction* (MBD), was met with similar objections. The term was used widely during the 1960s to refer to children of near average or higher intelligence who had sustained no known brain damage, yet had learning and behavior difficulties similar to the brain injured. Prior to this time, their underachievement often had been blamed on parental pressure, birth order, sibling rivalry, anxiety, poor motivation, or an inadequate home environment for studying.

Many youngsters identified as MBD tried very hard academically but still could not succeed. Others achieved adequately but had to put forth extraordinary effort just to keep up. Their behavioral characteristics were similar to, although less striking than, those of children known to be brain injured. For example, instead of having a dysfunctional limb due to a stroke, a child might have very poor handwriting or be physically uncoordinated; although able to speak, a youngster might have difficulty remembering a simple word like *house* in a conversation. It was believed that MBD could result from an immaturely developing central nervous system as well as from brain injury.

Clements's (1966) task force compiled ninety-nine symptoms of MBD. The ten most frequently agreed-on characteristics, in descending order of frequency, included hyperactivity, perceptual-motor impairments, emotional lability, general coordination deficits, disorders of attention, impulsivity, disorders of memory and thinking, specific learning disabilities (reading, arithmetic, writing, spelling), disorders of speech and hearing, and equivocal neurological signs and electroencephalographic irregularities. Because of the great variation in behaviors exhibited by students with learning disorders, seldom were any two students expected to share identical characteristics and instructional needs.

By the late 1960s, the term MBD fell into disfavor. It had lost any practical meaning because it was used as a catch-all label for all underachievers (McIntosh & Dunn 1973). Besides, it was argued that a cerebral abnormality is a major event; there is nothing minimal about it (Benton, 1973). Although the term *MBD* can still be heard in some medical circles, the term *learning disability* has become the accepted alternative.

Specific learning disabilities was one of the ten most frequent MBD characteristics listed by Clements's task force. In 1963, Kirk popularized the term when he used it in his keynote address at a conference on children with perceptual handicaps. The term *learning disabilities* was met with favor by most leaders in the field because its definition shifted away from the medical focus, to an educational focus (Cruickshank, 1976).

The definition of learning disabilities that we currently follow (see page 2), as put forth in The Individuals with Disabilities Act (IDEA) (PL 101-476), originated with a proposed definition at a 1964 U.S. Office of Education–sponsored conference at the University of Kansas Medical Center (Bateman, 1965). Much dissatisfaction exists with this definition because it is so broad, imprecise, and says more about what a learning disability is not than what it is.

Many definitions for LD have been put forth by one or another researcher or task force over the years. The definition that has drawn the broadest support was endorsed in 1988 by the National Joint Committee for Learning Disabilities (NJCLD), a group of nine national organizations that deal with the learning disabled:

Learning disabilities is a general term that refers to a heterogeneous group of disorders manifested by sig-

nificant difficulties in the acquisition and use of listening, speaking, reading, writing, reasoning, or mathematical abilities. These disorders are intrinsic to the individual, presumed to be due to central nervous system dysfunction, and may occur across the life span. Problems in self-regulatory behaviors, social perception, and social interaction may exist with learning disabilities but do not by themselves constitute a learning disability. Although disabilities may occur concomitantly with other handicapping conditions (for example, sensory impairment, mental retardation, serious emotional disturbance) or with extrinsic influences (such as cultural differences, insufficient or inappropriate instruction), they are not the result of those conditions or influences. (Hammill, 1990, p. 77)

This definition intended to show that learning disabilities apply across the entire life span, to adults as well as to children. It cleared up the ambiguity of the phrase *basic psychological processes* in IDEA by clearly stating that the underachievement is due to a neurological dysfunction within the individual. Here spelling is subsumed under writing, and poor social skills are recognized as accompanying, but not by themselves constituting, a learning disability. The NJCLD did not confuse the definition by including such terms as *dyslexia* and *developmental aphasia,* and the committee tried to clarify that LD is not caused by, but may coexist with, other handicapping conditions and adverse environmental circumstances.

When IDEA's predecessor, PL 94-142, recognized LD as a fundable handicapping condition, the law's regulations set the following identification criteria:

(a) A team may determine that a child has a specific learning disability if:
   (1) The child does not achieve commensurate with his or her age and ability levels in one or more of the areas listed in paragraph (a) (2) of this section, when provided with learning experiences appropriate for the child's age and ability levels; and
   (2) The team finds that a child has a severe discrepancy between achievement and intellectual ability in one or more of the following areas:
      (i) Oral expression;
      (ii) Listening comprehension;
      (iii) Written expression;

(iv) Basic reading skill;
(v) Reading comprehension;
(vi) Mathematics calculation; or
(vii) Mathematics reasoning.
(b) The team may not identify a child as having a specific learning disability if the severe discrepancy between ability and achievement is primarily the result of:
(1) A visual, hearing, or motor handicap;
(2) Mental retardation;
(3) Emotional disturbance; or
(4) Environmental, cultural or economic disadvantage.
(Federal Register, Dec. 29, 1977, p. 65083)

The federal regulations state that before a student can be identified as learning disabled, it must be documented that learning outcome has been poor in spite of good educational opportunities. In addition, the student with learning disabilities must require special educational strategies beyond those generally used at his or her age or ability level (Federal Register, Dec. 29, 1977). The story that Randal tells about himself (page 30), highlights the constant effort it takes for people with learning disabilities to keep up, an effort that is exhausting both physically and psychologically.

Approximately 70 percent of states use the federal definition of learning disabilities or one very similar (Mercer et al., 1996). Because the federal definition overrides state definitions, state definitions cannot be more restrictive than the federal intent. Several key implications of and concerns about our current LD definition and regulations deserve mention.

Severe Discrepancy between Achievement and Potential

People with learning disabilities, by definition, are achieving below what would be expected for their intellectual ability. This underachievement can occur in oral language, listening comprehension, reading comprehension, reading, writing, spelling, arithmetic reasoning, or calculation. Although the student has areas of intellectual strength, development is uneven. Part, but not all, of their cognitive functioning has been affected. For example, a student may be especially talented artistically and

mathematically, but she may be weak in comprehension, verbal communication, and reading.

Ninety-eight percent of states include the discrepancy notion in their LD definition or identification procedures, and two-thirds of states provide guidelines on how to quantify a severe discrepancy (Mercer et al., 1996). Each state determines how large the discrepancy between ability and achievement must be before it is considered severe. When the discrepancy is set high, only the most severely learning disabled are identified and served.

Educational Orientation

Federal regulations deal less with medical causes of learning disabilities than with educational performance. Underachievement is what determines LD identification. Proving central nervous system dysfunction is unnecessary.

The educational orientation of the LD regulations, however, does not mean that the brain is considered irrelevant to learning. IDEA's LD definition clearly states that underachievement is caused by an intrinsic disorder in one's "basic psychological processes," and brain-related terms are referenced: *perceptual handicaps, brain injury, minimal brain dysfunction, dyslexia,* and *developmental aphasia.* The basic psychological processes mentioned in the law refer to information-processing abilities that are critical to taking in information (listening, looking, touching), processing this information (attention, discrimination, memory, integration, concept formation, problem solving), or responding (speech, body movements).

Although research is offering plenty of clues about how brain functions may be linked with underachievement, there are good reasons for IDEA's educational, rather than basic psychological process, orientation: (1) we are still researching the psychological processes underlying different types of learning disabilities and which academic approaches might work best with whom; (2) because we do not know whether academic progress would be any more rapid even if we encouraged the exercise of specific brain regions, it is pragmatic to emphasize the academic objectives and interventions.

Randal

Life for this 48-year-old college professor with an earned doctorate began on a very shaky foundation. At birth, there was identified brain damage on the right side of the brain. The first week of life was spent in an incubator, with only a fair chance to live. Early childhood was complete with eye surgery at three, a heart problem at nine, frailness, overweight, and awkwardness. Not exactly the most popular child in school. Teachers felt that as long as the behavior was OK, "just let him sit in the class."

High school was four years of struggle—mostly alone. Ignored by teachers and peers—"he's different," we don't "want him in our crowd." When graduation came finally, class rank was lower half. High enough to get into a state college. The independence of being away from home resulted in failing out in the sophomore year. Laying out five years, only made the desire for a degree stronger—"I'll show everybody."

During this return to college, my interest was peaked with the new field of learning disabilities. After many hours in the library "stacks," I came to the realization that I was not mildly retarded. That was the high water point of my life. I could learn, but I needed to find out how. As a special education major, I only needed to change my major emphasis to the new field. I will learn how I can learn while I learn how to teach others. Not a bad plan. To enhance the process, marriage came into the picture. She is a gifted learner who also majored in special education. Together, we finished the first degree, and marched together to receive our master's degrees. At last my life both professionally and personally was on the right track.

With much support and even some pushing from my wife, I completed an Ed.D. in curriculum for special education, but I was too sick from a stroke to march in graduation— but, I did make it!!

In the workforce, my inability to handle large amounts of reading, and the comprehension of it, led to my loss of three special education jobs. Getting lost, no sense of direction, the inability to remember names, loss of details in planning meetings, and what appeared to be disinterest, caused me to job hunt on many occasions. It is frustrating, maddening, and yes, very depressing. Here is an individual who knows how it feels to be a misunderstood LD, but I can't help myself, only everyone else.

When I get lost driving between schools, panic attacks take over for a time, and I am not able to function for ten to fifteen minutes. This is always seen as a poor attempt at getting out of work or making an excuse for not completing a task. The age of computers has been a godsend for all of us. Spell check is the most wonderful invention since sliced bread.

My goal for the rest of my professional life is to make a difference for others like me. I promise relentless work to assure that every needy child will receive the services deserved. Repeating my life will not be fun for anyone: avoid it; fight against it; realize that it will be a lifelong fight to have others understand that there are many of us out there in the work force who try harder than most people to function as normally as we can. It makes you crazy, angry, frustrated, and very tired.

Source: Reprinted by permission of Randal L. Becker.

Exclusion Clauses

The federal "exclusion clause" that excludes mental retardation, emotional disturbance, visual (blind), hearing (deaf), and motor (for example, polio, muscular dystrophy) disabilities from being the "primary" cause of learning disabilities has been subject to much misinterpretation. Learning disabilities **can** coexist with these conditions. Even if children are mentally retarded, emotionally disturbed, or physically disabled, their development can be uneven due to a coexisting learning disability, which causes these children to achieve less than expected given their intellectual potential. For example, a blind teenager who reads braille also may have a learning disability in language processing because she can't comprehend what she has read. An emotionally disturbed child, whose mind is everywhere but on classwork, also may lag significantly behind his age and intelligence in the perceptual skills necessary for beginning reading. A learning disability seems apparent because, even when his attention is engaged and he tries hard, he makes no progress in reading. Unfortunately the law is easily misinterpreted to mean "if you're mentally retarded, emotionally disturbed, or physically disabled you can't also be learning disabled."

In reality, it is often difficult to determine whether underachievement is due to one's mental retardation, emotional disturbance, or physical disability, or whether there also is a coexisting learning disability. For example, a psychologist might argue that a child is emotionally disturbed as a result of poor family relationships and also learning disabled because of oxygen deprivation at birth. However, a physician may argue that the birth history had no significant effect on developmental milestones, so the emotional disturbance must be causing the academic underachievement. On the other hand, the special education teacher might argue that the academic and social frustrations of the learning disability actually promoted the child's disobedience and acting out, which then led to poor family relationships and emotional disturbance. To untangle who is right is very difficult.

Let us consider another example, this time of a teenager who is mildly retarded, and lagging in reading comprehension so far behind her achievement in reading decoding and arithmetic that there appears to be a coexisting learning disability. It may be, however, that it is the mental retardation that has put an upper limit on how far comprehension skills can develop, no matter how intensive the remedial efforts. Or perhaps this teenager's lags in language comprehension decreased her performance on the intelligence test's verbal reasoning items, so that her potential is underestimated; she is really learning disabled, and not retarded. Whether one or two disabilities exist and which caused what are hard to determine.

Currently, 98 percent of states include an exclusion clause in their LD regulations. Seven states limit learning disabilities identification to children who have intelligence quotients (IQs) in the average ranges or above, and six states set a minimum IQ above the mental retardation level (Mercer et al., 1996).

IDEA also excludes environmental, cultural, and economic disadvantages as primary reasons for LD identification. Clearly poor teaching, inability to speak English, poor home encouragement to study, and cultural diversity are environmental circumstances that can lead to underachievement. But they are not justifications for assuming an information-processing problem and identifying a student as learning disabled. Nevertheless, IDEA's exclusion clause does raise particular concerns for the poor achievers from low-income families because their poor health care and social conditions often compromise information-processing ability and increase the probability of academic failure. Children raised in low-income families tend to have more characteristics of learning disabilities than do children raised in middle-income homes (e.g., impulsivity, hyperactivity, immature language development, difficulty distinguishing sounds in words) (Smith, 1994). Despite neurodevelopmental disabilities similar to those of middle-income children whom we identify as learning disabled (Gottesman, Croen, & Rotkin, 1982), lower-income children risk not being identified for special services if IDEA's exclusion clause is interpreted too literally. It is hard to differentiate whether the low-income child was born with a learning disability, or whether the disadvantaged circumstances are what altered the child's information-processing abilities. In either case, intervention is essential. Yet, because we do not presume the environment of a middle-income child with the same uneven learning patterns to be at fault, professionals often are less hesitant to identify this child as learning disabled.

Overidentification

The vague LD definition has resulted in over-labeling. Many students who get misidentified as learning disabled perform poorly because of insufficient motivation, poor teaching, little home support for school achievement, general immaturity, general low ability, or English being their second language—not because of a learning disability (Ames, 1977; Gottlieb et al., 1994; Kirk & Elkins, 1975a; Valus, 1986). In a study of identification practices in Colorado, 57 percent of the learning disabled could be described more accurately as achieving poorly because they were slow learners, from second language backgrounds, emotionally disturbed, mentally retarded, or average learners who were out of place in above-average schools (Shepard & Smith, 1983). Several investigators report that one-third to one-half or more of children identified as learning disabled do not display a significant discrepancy between achievement and potential (Gottlieb et al., 1994; Kavale & Reese, 1992; McLeskey, 1992; McLeskey & Waldron, 1991; Norman & Zigmond, 1980; Sinclair & Alexson, 1986).

In their zeal to serve students and receive some reimbursement for their expenses, school personnel have been identifying a large number of underachievers as learning disabled, regardless of the factors responsible for their poor academic progress. They argue that the LD classification provides services to students who have no alternative funding sources, is the most flexible, least stigmatizing, and least restrictive label, and forces an individualized approach to instruction. Besides, the LD classification is easier for parents to accept than is mental retardation or emotional dis-

turbance (Kavale, 1987a; Mann et al., 1983). In addition, school districts are likely to stretch criteria for LD identification because they have no alternative programs, or because funds have been cut to bilingual or remedial programs (Gottlieb et al., 1994; McLeskey & Waldron, 1991; Shepard & Smith, 1983; Tugend, 1985).

Unfortunately, these liberal identification practices have prevented a consistent focus to LD programs, and remedial efforts are diluted by including pupils who don't require this intensity of service. Consequently, students with the most severe learning disabilities often are cheated of the intensive help that legislators had intended for them. In addition, overlabeling unwittingly relieves regular educators of the responsibility for teaching students who function at the bottom of their class (Shepard, 1987).

Because researchers often trust selection of their research subjects to schools, this LD overidentification has produced a confusing body of research regarding LD characteristics and the interventions that are likely to work best with different children. Our research findings, rather than reflecting the effects of a learning disability, often instead reflect the effects of low intelligence, emotional, or other factors. Research Box 1–3 explores this problem and offers recommendations for change.

Further Concerns

A number of additional concerns about the vagueness of the federal LD definition and regulations highlight the need to establish more specific definitions, identification criteria, and service guidelines.

1. The learning disabled population's characteristics are heterogeneous. More than one area of learning and performance can be affected, each in different ways. Describing all these individuals with one common term, LD, erroneously implies that they have the same causes of learning disorders, the same characteristics, and that they all profit from the same teaching methodology.

RESEARCH BOX 1–3

Dealing with the Inconsistency and Confusion in Learning Disabilities Research

In the first four years after implementation of PL 94-142, over 4,500 articles on LD were published in the professional literature (Keogh & Babbitt, 1986). This bustling of research effort has continued unabated. Unfortunately, with this great activity comes enormous inconsistency in research findings and confusion. The problem is due to two factors: (1) the heterogeneity of the LD group, and (2) incomplete descriptions of the characteristics of research subjects.

With the exception of some broad generalizations (for example, many students with learning disabilities are slow information processors, have motor and language weaknesses, don't feel themselves capable of succeeding), very few more specific observations hold true for the majority of students with learning disabilities. Because we are dealing with such a diverse group of individuals, in order to gain more meaning from our research we must start to study subgroups of children who are alike on a subset of variables that can impact learning.

Because of the diversity among students with learning disabilities, the vagueness of our LD definition, and the variety of perspectives on learning disabilities, researchers tend to study heterogeneous groups of subjects, rather than subjects who fit one circumscribed profile of learning disabilities. To complicate the matter, most of our subjects are identified for researchers by nonresearchers' standards and for nonresearch purposes (e.g., by clinics or school districts) (Keogh & Babbitt, 1986). Since LD is in the end a clinical judgment, who is called learning disabled will differ markedly from one institution to another. Some clinics, for example, will identify only children with neurological impairments as LD, whereas others identify only children with language impairments. Some school districts with tight budgets identify only children with severe delays, whereas wealthier districts and those with few intervention alternatives may decide to include children who are only slightly underachieving.

Because subject populations will continue to be heterogeneous, researchers must begin to carefully choose subgroups of students who share specific characteristics in common. If these attributes are described in detail, then we will be in a better position to sort out our research findings. That is, we may begin to understand why an information-processing weakness causes particular difficulties for one type of child but not for another, or why one teaching technique works for the first type of child but not for the second. With better descriptions of our samples, we will know which subjects to choose for replication studies; and if replication confirms the original findings, then we will know precisely to whom we can generalize our conclusions. Currently too little of our experimental work has been replicated. This, of course, limits generalizability.

Barbara Keogh and her colleagues (1982) suggested a group of important marker variables to specify when describing subject groups. As each of these variables can account for similarities and differences in the outcomes of studies, knowledge of these markers helps us to compare results obtained by different research groups:

(Continues on following page)

RESEARCH BOX 1–3 *(Continued from preceding page)*

Descriptive Markers	Topical Markers	Substantive Markers
Number of subjects by sex	Activity level	Intellectual ability
Chronological age	Attention	Reading achievement
Grade level	Auditory perception	Arithmetic achievement
Race/ethnicity	Fine motor coordination	Behavioral and emotional
Source of subjects	Gross motor coordination	adjustment
Socioeconomic status	Memory	**Background Markers**
Language background	Oral language	
Educational history	Visual perception	Month/year of study
Educational placement		Geographic location
Physical and health status		Locale
		Exclusionary criteria
		Control/comparison group

Keogh and Babbitt (1986) point out that it is equally important to specify the precise nature of the tasks subjects engage in and the measurement techniques. Rosenberg et al. (1993) add the importance of specifying the LD identification criteria used as well as narrative information such as student motivation, medical considerations, and history of teaching approaches. Morris et al. (1994) add specification of the qualifications of the examiners, the subjects' time in special education services, and the type of placement, while Bos and Fletcher (1997) also urge delineation of the child's primary and secondary language proficiency, cultural background, and detailed characteristics of the school and classroom context. All of these can influence the study's results, so that the findings are due to something other than the learning disability.

Because any of the variables listed above could influence a study's findings, it is critical that control subjects who are not learning disabled match the students who are learning disabled on all variables except the one being studied. If the groups are not matched, then any differences found between the subjects could be attributable to extraneous variables rather than to the learning disability.

An age-matched control group is very important because it matches subjects for years of experience. An achievement-matched control group also is important; this is a younger control group that equals the LD group's achievement (Fisher & Athey, 1986). For example, when the ability to sequence sounds in words is found to be poorer in an LD group than for same-age peers, it may be that sound sequencing is not the cause of the reading delay. The results may simply be due to the reduced reading experience of the LD group, which offers fewer opportunities to sharpen their sound sequencing skills. But if the students with learning disabilities do differ in sequencing of sounds from even younger subjects who read and spell at comparable levels, then it is likely that a sound-sequencing deficit is contributing to their reading delays. Qualitatively, they are very different learners. If, on the other hand, the student with a learning disability is like the younger child in all ways, then the learning delay could be explained in terms of slow maturation; the student is maturing at a level expected for a younger child. The immature student who is merely behind for his or her age may be expected to progress at a steadier pace than the student whose learning characteristics are atypical at even younger developmental levels.

(Continues on following page)

RESEARCH BOX 1–3   *(Continued from preceding page)*

Torgesen (1987) describes the value of two additional control groups: (1) a longitudinal comparison of the developmental course of different types of children who have used different intervention approaches and (2) children who have experienced similar failure but who do not have the cognitive disability being investigated. In his reading investigations, Stanovich (1988) refers to the latter group as "garden variety" poor readers; they are of the same age and reading level as the learning disabled, but they have not been identified as disabled. If the reading subskills and cognitive characteristics of the two groups differ, then we've identified different ways in which particular children master the same reading objectives. Stanovich stresses the importance of controlling separately for decoding and reading comprehension levels in these studies because they are two separate things.

By using these types of controls, the critical variables contributing to LD will begin to stand out. Simply comparing same-age students with and without learning disabilities tells us only what differences exist between the two without shedding light on the responsible factors.

Admonishing researchers who contribute to the confused state of research in learning disabilities, Senf (1987) reflects:

LD is that flexible sponge that lives in the region between alleged normalcy and alleged handicap, expanding and contracting with a myriad of external events (philosophy of education, parental aspirations for their children, professional status, values) only a fraction of which concern the state of the individual so labeled. . . . In a "publish or perish" atmosphere and being embedded in the broader discipline of education, not known for its demanding standards, self-examination, or intellect, researchers might easily accept for research whatever is rung from the sponge. . . . A research sample squeezed from a public school (university clinic, hospital, or private practice) LD sponge would be a heterogeneous mess, containing subjects conforming to few knowledgeable persons' concept of LD. . . . Sample selection proceeds atheoretically, based principally on convenience, that is, the nearest "sponge" (p. 92). . . .
Squeeze the sample from the LD sponge: If a reasonably pure color appears, conduct the experiment. If the water is cloudy, so likely will be your results (p. 96). . . .

Keogh (1987b) adds:

The heterogeneity within LD mirrors that of the sponge in its natural surround. . . . Many sponges harbour commensal worms, brittle stars, barnacles, shrimp, crabs, copepods, and amphipods. . . . Over 13,000 animals representing 19 species were found in a single Caribbean sponge (p. 56). . . . Some might argue that shrimp, barnacles, crabs, and brittle stars more accurately describe the researchers than the subjects of research (p. 97).

Clearly, better delineation of research samples, tasks, measurement tools, and control groups can help us understand the characteristics and needs of different subgroups of students with learning disabilities, even if drawn from the public school sponge. If learner, task, and setting variables are specified in our studies, we may begin to overcome the "unfortunate outcome of these methodological problems. . . . Many researchers draw inappropriate interpretations from the data or attach undue importance to the many epiphenomena that sometimes exhibit themselves in these research efforts" (Fisher & Athey, 1986, pp. 23–24).

2. The LD definition implies that the deficit is solely within the student, and that this disability needs to be cured. It ignores the possibility that our curricular expectations and learning environments also may aggravate the disability (Smith, 1985, 1986). When the child is blamed for every nonconforming behavior, schools and society are relieved from responsibility for modifying their ways (Bateman, 1974; Divoky, 1974).

3. The LD definition ignores nonacademic manifestations of learning disorders such as social skills, planning ability, organization, and problem-solving strategies.

4. The LD definition does not specifically recognize the adult whose persistent learning disabilities require unique vocational, emotional, social, independent living, and academic interventions.

5. A surprising extent of uneven development is normal. Yet, because of the LD regulations' appreciation of disparities in development, every variation from the norm is in danger of being misinterpreted as a disability. This leads to misidentification of normal people as disabled (Blatt, 1979; Divoky, 1974; Silberman, 1976). Alexander's story is one such example (pages 36–37). Only an unevenness in ability that is extremely uncommon and requires intense, out-of-the-ordinary teaching interventions should be considered a learning disability.

6. The LD definition may lead one to believe that the very complicated service needs of the learning disabled are simple (Senf, 1978). Due to the proliferation of poorly identified research groups, we have yet to pinpoint which intervention strategies will work best for different types of students.

7. The LD definition reflects society's valuing of academic achievement. Only in the regulations on transition planning are the postschool vocational and social adjustment needs of the learning disabled addressed.

Alexander

Alexander's parents and school psychologist referred him to a university clinic for evaluation. Because his written language difficulties have persisted, they wondered whether it would be appropriate to identify Alexander as "learning disabled."

Alexander's background reveals a great deal of turmoil. He has moved seventeen times and has been enrolled in four schools. His parents divorced when he was three years old. His mother recently remarried, and Alexander is having trouble accepting the new authority figure in the house. To complicate matters, Alexander's biological father sees so much of himself in Alexander that he generally dislikes Alexander, instead showering Alexander's younger sister with affection.

Alexander is an incredibly gifted ten-year-old. His vocabulary and reasoning ability are matches for any adult. Alexander scores at high school levels in all areas of achievement, with the exception of written expression, where he performs at average levels for his age and

(Continues on following page)

Alexander *(Continued from preceding page)*

grade. When writing, Alexander's spelling is perfect, as is his use of complex sentence structure and punctuation. However, he cuts his writing short, takes unduly long to put anything down on paper, and develops themes in such a detail-oriented way that the reader has no clue about the main idea he is trying to convey. In conversations also, Alexander spouts unnecessary detail after unnecessary detail but doesn't let the listener in on what the basic point is. This, in addition to his clumsiness and emotional difficulties, has left him friendless.

The evaluation revealed a captivating young man struggling with many personal issues. In addition, he abhors writing. The writing difficulties were found to be due to very poor motor planning. Alexander could not write a word without actually having to think about telling his hand how to move. His body movements and spatial judgments were equally nonautomatic; for example, it was a struggle for Alexander to touch his thumb to each successive finger, to figure out how to skip, to walk through a doorway without bumping the frame, or even to stand upright without falling over when he closed his eyes. No wonder he hated his worksheets and essays and took so long to do them. Interestingly, when given sufficient time to plan and think, Alexander eventually could figure out how to perform all motor activities and visual-perceptual exercises (puzzles, mazes, finding missing objects in pictures) perfectly.

Complicating Alexander's written and oral communication was his overanalytic style. Alexander focused on all the "trees" but seldom gave equal attention to the "forest" unless specifically asked to think about the main idea. It was found that simply telling Alexander to start each paragraph with a main idea, instructing him in the use of a prewriting, brainstorming strategy, and allowing him to tape his compositions resulted in products that were superior for his age and grade.

In order to accommodate his written language needs, Alexander's school psychologist and parents wanted him identified as learning disabled. Without this classification, there would be no way to convince Alexander's rigid classroom teachers to give him extra time on written work, to reduce unnecessary written assignments, to let him use the computer, or to let him tape and then transcribe his compositions. Alexander couldn't understand all this. He simply asked "Why not?"

Alexander was right. The evaluation team recommended the accommodations that had been successful at the clinic, as well as counseling services. The team felt that despite Alexander's significant weaknesses, these did not require an unusual intensity or quality of instruction. Simple adaptations within the classroom could promote success. Besides, Alexander said that he would feel dumb having to leave the class for a special education teacher's help. The team worried that the stigma of an LD label may be more detrimental to Alexander's social adjustment than the frustration he experienced from written work. The team recommended that Alexander's school initiate a gifted program and that Alexander be its first enrollee. The team explained Alexander's weaknesses to him and described how he could work around these difficulties. The team pointed out that his pattern of strengths and weaknesses was not unlike that of countless professors at the university!

Identification Practices

In this section we discuss issues surrounding LD identification of the preschooler, the young elementary school child, and the older student. Parts Four and Five of the text are devoted to more detailed descriptions of assessment procedures and programming options.

The Preschooler

It is important to identify and work with developmental weaknesses in preschoolers as early as possible in order to prevent these weaknesses from deterring later learning. Yet, LD identification of the preschooler is not possible because the child is not yet underachieving on the academic criteria by which federal regulations suggest we measure learning disabilities. Since LD prediction remains a calculated guess until a child is old enough to be tested for underachievement on the school's academic criteria, and because of the danger of stigmatizing preschoolers as LD and lowering expectations for their achievement, PL 99-457 simply identifies a preschooler as a child with a "developmental delay" if his or her delays in physical, cognitive, communication, social, emotional, or adaptive development necessitate special education services. In this way the dangers of inaccurate forecasts are overcome; professionals can devote their energies to teaching rather than to trying to assess a child's exact disability.

There is no one test battery that can predict for certain whether the developmental delays of a preschooler will develop into a learning disability once he or she enters school—that is, whether academic progress will be unexpectedly slow. This is because the preschooler's rapid developmental spurts, followed by plateaus, make preschool tests, especially IQ tests (McCall, Hogarty, & Hurlburt, 1972), highly unreliable. A child's scores may vary greatly in the span of several months depending on whether we have tested at a high or low point within these cycles. Nevertheless, these measures can identify preschoolers who show such unusually uneven developmental patterns that they are at high risk for learning disabilities, and immediate intervention is warranted.

The level of confidence in a learning disabilities prediction increases as:

1. the severity of a preschooler's delays in language, attention, visual-perceptual, and motor abilities increase.

2. the child nears the age of kindergarten entry and the assessment criteria become more similar to what children are expected to learn in school. It makes sense that observing a five-year-old's, rather than a four-year-old's, learning style, relationships with others, and performance on school-type tasks (impulsivity, attention span, sharing, patience, independent work habits, alphabet and number knowledge) will more accurately predict whether the child is likely to encounter difficulty in school.

3. environmental circumstances that can cause, aggravate, or help overcome developmental delays are taken into consideration. Although scales for evaluating setting variables tend to have uncertain validity for predicting learning problems (Bradley & Caldwell, 1978; Walberg & Marjoribanks, 1976), when used in combination with cognitive measures, these scales do enhance the accuracy of predictions regarding cognitive and language development.

The Young Elementary School Student

LD identification of a five or six year old is still not an easy matter. Identification depends on whether the child can handle the school curriculum as well as might be expected for his or her age, intelligence, and past learning opportunities. Because the origin of a child's developmental delay (whether due to a learning disability, emotional disturbance, or mental retardation) becomes clearer after age nine, and the child's gap between achievement and potential may not become large enough for LD identification until this age, the 1997 IDEA reauthorization allows states the discretion to identify a child with a developmental delay as a "child with a disability"; a specific disability does not have to be designated until after age nine. Early identification of developmental delays, not testing for LD per se, is critical so that developmental gaps do not widen, appropriate curriculum modifications can be made, and special services implemented as soon as possible. In order to identify lags, three techniques are used: tests administered to children, teacher checklists, and parent checklists. In kindergarten, poor performance (relative to what might be expected for a child's age, intelligence, and background) on the visual, language, motor, or attentional components of preacademic tasks frequently forecasts later learning disabilities. The best of these preacademic predictors are:

- reciting the order of the alphabet

- naming letters of the alphabet speedily and accurately

- identifying rhyming words

- identifying which words begin with a given sound, begin with the same sound, or do not share a common sound

- segmenting dictated words into individual syllables and sounds; blending syllables and sounds into words

- discriminating the position of sounds in words

- naming common colors and objects

- comprehending age-appropriate vocabulary

- writing one's name

- copying designs

- succeeding on readiness tests that, in addition to the above skills, sample vocabulary use, number concepts, numeral recognition, sentence memory and comprehension, visual discrimination, following directions, categorization, substituting initial and final sounds in words, and general knowledge

(Adams, 1990; Badian, 1988; Blachman, 1991; Bradley & Bryant, 1983, 1985; Colligan, 1977a, b; Glazzard, 1977; Jansky & de Hirsch, 1973; Jorm et al., 1986; Liberman & Shankweiler, 1985;

Lowell, 1971; Lundberg, Olofsson, & Wall, 1980; Mann, 1993; Roth, McCaul, & Barnes, 1993; Satz et al., 1978; Torgesen, Wagner, & Rashotte, 1994).

Teacher ratings of a child's readiness skills and learning strategies are sometimes even better predictors of learning problems than screening tests (Coleman & Dover, 1993; Glazzard, 1981; Gresham, MacMillan, and Bocian, 1997; Jorgenson et al., 1993; Stevenson, Parker, & Wilkenson, 1976). Teacher observations are particularly valuable because teachers' ratings reflect what tests cannot—how a child actually fares in a particular classroom's curriculum and setting: for example, readiness for what is taught in that classroom, rate of learning, ability to focus and sustain attention within that classroom's structure, ability to avoid distractions, creativity, social relationships, ability to work independently and in groups, motivation to learn, and verbal participation. In an analysis of fifty-eight studies that correlated kindergarten measures with reading achievement several years later, teacher ratings of attention, distractibility, and internalizing behaviors (for example, anxiety, depression) proved to be among the best predictors (Horn & Packard, 1985).

Parent observations are another valuable academic predictor, as are environmental indicators such as the amount of schooling the family desires for the child and learning activities encouraged by the parents (Bee et al., 1982; Colligan, 1981; Haywood & Switzky, 1986). The longer one waits before testing for LD identification purposes, the more the test items will resemble academic criteria so that a marked discrepancy between achievement and potential will be discernible.

The Older Elementary and Secondary School Student

The 1997 reauthorization of IDEA requires that a specific handicapping condition be designated after age nine. Professionals agree that students who have had sufficient opportunities to profit from instruction should be considered for LD identification if they show severe discrepancies between expected and actual achievement. Numerous formulas have been used to measure these discrepancies. Despite their inherent inaccuracies, these formulas have several advantages:

1. Formulas add some objective balance to the subjective judgments used in LD identification.
2. They provide a means of choosing research samples that have the same percentage of discrepancy; therefore, findings from different studies can be compared and interpreted more accurately.
3. They place no limits on intelligence level, so the degree of underachievement of all children, even the mentally retarded, can be evaluated.

To make wise use of these formulas, we must understand what constitutes a severe discrepancy, common means of calculating discrepancies, and the statistical weaknesses of discrepancy formulas. The final judgment about whether a learning disability exists is a clinical one, made after careful evaluation of multiple learner, curricular, family, teacher, and school variables that go far beyond the use of discrepancy formulas.

Severe Discrepancy. As a rule of thumb, in order to be judged severe, a discrepancy between one's expected and actual achievement needs to be unusually large when compared to normal variability in individuals of similar age, intelligence, and backgrounds. As information processing weaknesses are likely to lead to underachievement in more than one academic area, it is the exception to find a severe discrepancy in only one area of a student's learning.

How large must the discrepancy between expected and actual achievement be in order to be considered severe? Because federal and most state LD regulations do not dictate this decision, school districts usually can decide for themselves whether they will serve the mild to moderate underachiever or only the student with severe difficulties. Cutoffs generally are determined by setting a percentage by which a child's achievement must lag behind age or grade expectations given his or her intellectual potential (for example, an average-intelligence fourth grader would be 50 percent behind her

grade level expectations if achieving like a second grader). If the percentage discrepancy is set too high, then students with milder discrepancies will not be identified for help. High cutoffs also exacerbate school failure among young children in states that identify LD in the early school years, because the children will have to wait for years until their discrepancies grow large enough to meet the percentage of discrepancy needed for identification and special services.

A problem with establishing rigid discrepancy cutoffs is that the meaning of a set percentage of discrepancy is more serious at lower than higher grade levels. Because the most rapid escalation of basic skills occurs in the primary grades, followed by slower increments, it takes a deficiency of more grade levels at older ages to equal the seriousness of a few grade levels behind at younger ages. For example, although both show a 50 percent discrepancy between ability and achievement, an average third grader who still hasn't mastered the letter sounds expected of a first grader is more seriously delayed than the average eighth grader who can read at the fourth grade level. The eighth grader already has mastered a sight vocabulary, letter sounds, and blending, although at a slower than expected rate. The only way to equalize the significance of discrepancy cutoffs as grade levels increase is to gradually increase the percentage of discrepancy necessary for LD identification (Hammill, 1976).

A frequently made mistake is identifying learning disabilities on the basis of a grade-level deviation criterion. That is, if children's achievement is a certain number of years below their current grade levels, then they would be identified as learning disabled (for example, a criterion of one year behind for grades one through three, two years behind for the next few grades, and so forth). Currently three states recommend that LD eligibility be determined on this basis (Mercer et al., 1996).

There are several problems with this grade-level deviation method:

1. The student's potential for achievement, as required by IDEA, is ignored. Therefore, the question of whether a student should be expected to learn the curriculum in the

first place is overlooked. For example, under IDEA a very bright sixth grader who is one grade level behind in reading could be identified as learning disabled. A much slower classmate who is achieving two grade levels behind in reading, but is working to capacity, would not be identified as learning disabled. Yet the grade-level cutoff method could lead to the opposite results.

2. Grade equivalent scores are of questionable validity. Because achievement tests sample only a few items at each difficulty level, error in measurement and interpretation can be high. The grade level score merely indicates that a student got as many test items correct as the average student in a particular grade, but the actual items and skills composing this score may be far from typical. Furthermore, it is possible to achieve as well as one's peers simply because the test items were too easy for everyone (for example, if the hardest passage on a reading test given to tenth graders is at a sixth-grade equivalency, then a student with a learning disability could score like a tenth grader, and the student's underachievement would not be detected).

3. Because different academic subjects are acquired at different rates, and because society does not value all subjects equally, the same degree of underachievement may have different implications, depending on the subject area. For example, at age fifteen a four-year lag in spelling may not be considered as ominous as a four-year lag in reading. Therefore, judgments about whether to request remediation in different subject areas will influence whether parents and educators decide to identify a student as learning disabled.

Calculating Discrepancies. Reading clinicians were the first to use formulas to assess the reading level that different students should be expected to attain. These formulas were then applied to the many achievement areas in which one could experience learning disabilities.

Most formulas first estimate a student's expectancy for achievement from intelligence test scores. The IQ reflects mental ability relative to one's age group, with a score of 100 being average. The achievement test scores are then compared with this expectancy. In some formulas math achievement levels are added to the numerator in the IQ formula (Monroe, 1932), the number of years of schooling are added (Bond & Tinker, 1973), or age and grade are factored in (Myklebust, 1968). When achievement is below expectation, school personnel must determine whether the underachievement is severe enough to warrant LD identification.

Harris's (1962) formula is the most frequently used and simplest method of quantifying a severe discrepancy (Cone & Wilson, 1981):

$$RE = MA - 5$$

RE = reading expectancy grade level

MA = mental age (mental age = chronological age × IQ/100)

5 = 5 years old at school entry

Using this formula, Harris charted expected reading grade levels for children of different IQs and ages. For example, Nancy, who is eight years old and has an IQ of 100, would be expected to be spelling at the third grade level.

$$RE = (8 \times 100/100) - 5$$
$$= 3$$

If her actual achievement is below the third grade level, she is performing below her potential. It is up to the school to determine how much of a discrepancy qualifies as a learning disability.

Alice Horn (1941) based her formula on actual data indicating that, as one gets older, intelligence is more important to achievement than is age. She weighted mental age (MA) and chronological age (CA) equally up to age 8½ ($RE = \frac{MA + CA}{2} - 5$); three MA and two CA from age 8½ to 10; two MA and one CA from age 10 to 12; three MA and one CA above age 12 (in Bruininks, Glaman, & Clark, 1973).

Statistical Weaknesses of Discrepancy Formulas. The estimate of a student's expected achievement will depend on the particular discrepancy formula used. Whereas one formula might indicate that Nancy is a severe underachiever and in need of LD services, another formula might suggest that she is achieving as well as can be expected. Even among students who achieve at average levels, anywhere from 4 to 25 percent could be identified as learning disabled by applying one or another discrepancy formula (Ysseldyke, Algozzine, & Epps, 1983). The usefulness of any one formula will vary across different grade levels, genders, ethnic groups, and tests (Macy, Baker, & Kosinski, 1979). The clever clinician often can find just the right IQ and achievement measures that will result in a severe discrepancy. In fact, probability dictates that if twenty tests are administered, one test is likely to yield a significant discrepancy just by chance (Willson, 1987). To try to deal with the weaknesses of discrepancy formulas, conversion of students' test scores to standard scores and the use of regression equations have been suggested.

Standard Scores.   One way of circumventing the weaknesses in the age and grade discrepancies described above is to compare standard scores on IQ and achievement tests. This method answers the following question: Is the child's percentile rank on the achievement test roughly the same as his or her percentile rank on the IQ test? The same standard score is assigned to a 50th percentile performance, 16th percentile performance, and so forth, on every test. Most often a standard score of 100 is set as the mean (50th percentile), and every 15 standard score points above or below the mean represents a significant deviation from this mean. The school district can then decide how discrepant the standard scores earned on the IQ and achievement tests must be in order to qualify for LD identification. This standard score difference typically is set at 15 to 30 points (Mercer et al., 1996). Using standard scores, the variability of IQ and achievement in the child's age group is taken into account (for example, the greater range and variability of achievement scores in the upper grades), as are the errors of measurement due to a test's unreliability (Cone & Wilson, 1981). Standard score comparisons, however, tend to overidentify children with IQs over 100 and underidentify children with IQs below 100 (Fletcher et al., 1989; Kavale, 1987b).

Twenty-one states recommend using standard score comparisons for LD identification (Mercer et al., 1996). Although standard score comparisons are an improvement over the age and grade discrepancy formulas, they nevertheless make the faulty assumption that IQ correlates perfectly with achievement.

Regression Equations.   A major problem with all discrepancy formulas, including standard scores, is the assumption that as IQ goes up, achievement should go up an equal amount. But this isn't true. In fact, correlations show that, at best, we can predict reading level from intelligence only about 50 percent of the time. Put another way, only 50 percent of the attributes measured on intelligence tests are the same attributes required for performance on reading tests. Achievement predictions become more and more inaccurate the higher and lower the IQ because reading achievement will tend to "regress toward the mean." That is, whenever two skills are tested and one score is above or below average, the other is likely to be closer to average. Because standard score discrepancies do not take this regression phenomenon into account, very bright children with average reading levels may be misidentified as learning disabled, and less intelligent children who don't test as poorly as expected in reading may be underidentified.

To take into account this imperfect relationship between IQ and achievement, and the fact that every test score reflects some error, the regression equation has been developed. It factors in the actual correlation between the IQ and achievement measure and the likely degree of measurement error on each test. These equations have been able to bring uniformity and credibility to states' identification procedures, so that most of the students identified as learning disabled do indeed display significant discrepancies (T. E. Cone et al., 1985). With the regression method, African American students gain the same probability of being identified learning disabled as do white students (Kamphaus, Frick, & Lahey, 1991).

Using a regression equation, the underachievement of a student of average intelligence might not be identified as a learning disability if, among students in that school district, reading achievement is so highly variable that IQ measures are not very predictive of reading achievement. In other words, the student's level of underachievement is not unexpected given the student body.

The use of regression equations is standard practice in sixteen states (Mercer et al., 1996). They are complicated to develop because they require testing a sample of children who match the pupil being tested in age, sex, socioeconomic status, and number of years of schooling, and then calculating the correlation between their IQ and achievement tests and the measurement error on each test (Pennington, 1986). Given the complexity of the regression equation, a federally sponsored national task force concluded that standard scores were the method of choice, provided that highly reliable standardized tests were used, that the norm sample was comparable to the school population, and that the phenomenon of regression was considered (Chalfant, 1985).

Clinical Judgments. No matter which discrepancy technique is chosen, clinical judgment must be used to interpret the meaning of any discrepancies between expected and actual achievement. Discrepancy methods represent only one piece of data about whether a student may have a learning disability. These formulas can never be the sole criteria for LD identification because they do not address the many learner, task, and setting factors that also can influence learning failure: for example, the youngster's motivation; teacher expectations, materials, class settings; home support for study; information-processing delays; whether a slower instructional pace is all that's needed, rather than special teaching.

In LD identification, there is no substitute for the good clinical judgment that comes with experience. Often there is a high similarity in the degree of discrepancy shown by students with learning disabilities and underachieving students who are not identified as learning disabled (Furlong & Yanagida, 1985; McLeskey, 1989; Ysseldyke et al., 1983). Yet, the same degree of discrepancy in children of equal age, intelligence, and grade levels may have entirely different meanings. One child, for example, may be underachieving because of an impulsive learning style and a

language delay. Another may have moved so often that the child received little consistent instruction and lost the motivation to try. The former student is learning disabled, whereas the latter is not. If both students put forth equal effort, the former student would not profit as much from the typical curriculum.

Clearly, "the educational significance of any score needs to be considered independently of the discrepancy model" (Sinclair & Alexson, 1986, p. 116). For example, the information-processing patterns of a child who does not quite meet a discrepancy criterion nevertheless may still be diagnostically significant, thereby suggesting the appropriateness of LD identification. As Kavale (1987b) points out, discrepancy merely means underachievement; because much more than underachievement constitutes learning disabilities, "Discrepancy may be a necessary condition for LD but it is hardly sufficient. Discrepancy alone . . . does not capture the complexity of the LD phenomenon" (p. 19).

In practice, it seems that professionals seldom exclude students from LD services if they show large discrepancies. Yet they also often identify substantial numbers of students who do not in fact meet discrepancy cutoffs. In several studies, for example, 20 percent of students identified as learning disabled did not meet discrepancy cutoffs (Dangel & Ensminger, 1988; McLeskey, 1989).

Not surprisingly, team members show a good deal of inconsistency in interpreting student profiles because they differ from one another in their conception of learning disabilities, the degree to which they are willing to overlabel, and their understanding of the statistics needed for valid test interpretation (Shepard & Smith, 1983). Too often, teams interpret low scores as "meaningful," and indicative of LD, when in fact they were due to nothing more than the student's erratic test-taking strategies or to invalid tests.

One of the most important identification considerations that team members all too often forget to keep in mind is whether the student does, in fact, need a quality and intensity of instruction that could not possibly be met within the regular education system without input from special educators. To answer this question, consideration of multiple data, including the student's intellectual abilities, achievement levels, past educational experiences, and age is imperative, as is openness to alternative identification approaches.

Intellectual Abilities. In general, intelligence tests are the best predictors of school achievement. McClelland (1973) humorously explains that, "The games people are required to play on aptitude tests are similar to the games teachers require in the classroom" (p. 1). Doing well on IQ tests and in school programs depends on several common features: amount of past knowledge acquired from the school or environment, cognitive processes (for example, abstract reasoning ability, speed of information processing), and motivational and personality factors (Zigler & Trickett, 1978). Because of these commonalities, IQ tests do help to predict children's academic successes. While IQ tests are equally good predictors of academic achievement levels attained by African American, Hispanic American, and white children, in some cases they may underestimate students' actual potential for achievement (Sattler, 1992). For these and other reasons, we must be mindful of several cautions in using IQ tests for LD identification, and be sure to substitute alternative measures when necessary.

1. Although they do predict achievement, intelligence tests nevertheless underestimate the intellectual potential of lower-income Americans and some culturally underrepresented groups. Having learned different things than the information required by IQ test questions, these students often score lower than they should. Clearly, the scores of students who do not share the language abilities, reading skills, problem-solving approaches, concepts, and background knowledge of the test's majority white, middle-income norm group will suffer (Sattler, 1992).

    When youngsters from culturally diverse and low-income families show low IQs, the likelihood of LD identification is reduced because the discrepancy with

achievement becomes less apparent. This results in educational inequities and in a high disproportion of minorities to whites in special classes for the mildly mentally retarded (Chinn & Hughes, 1987; Messick, Heller, & Finn, 1982). Likewise, setting IQ cutoffs for LD identification discriminates against the identification of African Americans (McLeskey, Waldron, & Wornhoff, 1990).

Alternate approaches must be explored when IQ tests do not fairly assess the cognitive potential of lower income students and those from culturally underrepresented groups. For students with limited English proficiency, IDEA and the Office for Civil Rights require that a bilingual psychologist conduct the assessment in the student's native language. Adaptive behavior measures, which assess a student's independence in everyday life activities and correlate well with IQ, provide another alternative. Chapter 8 will review further the issue of intelligence test bias and explore possible alternatives.

2. When intelligence test items draw too much on students' weaker skills, their IQs will be underestimated, thereby reducing their opportunities for LD identification. Because standard intelligence tests tap verbal skills, children with severe language difficulties or those for whom English is not their native language are hampered in demonstrating their knowledge and reasoning abilities. Similarly, the student with severe reading disabilities cannot succeed on portions of IQ tests that demand reading or knowledge gained from reading. IQ tests also underestimate intelligence when performance taps weaknesses in short-term memory, rapid problem solving, visual perception, fine-motor coordination, attention, or organization.

    Because different IQ tests include different types of items, it is often possible to select one that bypasses some of a student's weaker abilities and taps more of his or her strengths. Alternatives include tests that do not award bonus points for rapid responses, tests that avoid verbal responses by requiring manipulation of objects or pointing to pictures, or tests that capitalize on language strengths and minimize items requiring visual perceptual judgments and motor manipulation.

3. Although IQ becomes more stable above ages five or six, the score still may vary by as much as fifteen points from one test to another (Bayley, 1949; Honzik, Macfarlane, & Allen, 1948; Sattler, 1992). This is due to differences between tests, differences in effort put forth by the student with different test administrators, and inconsistency across examiners in test administration or scoring. Therefore, when calculating discrepancies, it is always better to consider IQ as a range of probable functioning rather than as a fixed value.

4. IQ may become a poorer index of potential as students grow older because these scores tend to decline quite a bit as the students' learning problems diminish their knowledge acquisition, vocabulary growth, reasoning, and motivation (Stanovich, 1993).

5. Since IQ frequently predicts as little as 25 to 30 percent of variance in achievement, perhaps more weight in identification decisions should be placed on additional factors that are known to impact one's potential for achievement, such as interest and persistence in learning, family and teacher encouragement of achievement, and willingness to try hard.

6. IQ tests are not equally good predictors of potential for achievement in all school subjects. For example, IQ is a much more powerful contributor to reading comprehension than it is to handwriting. Years of instruction in writing might be a more relevant index for evaluating a child's expectations for handwriting quality.

Achievement Levels. Several considerations are important in choosing the best achievement test to use in the LD identification process. First and foremost, because we are trying to determine how much of what the student should have learned was actually learned, achievement test content must match classroom content as closely as possible. When these contents do not overlap, we are not assessing achievement fairly. For example, reading tests require students to read words that commonly appear in standard reading programs. If a student has been taught through a literature-based, whole language approach, rather than from a standard reading series, the overlap may be poor. The youngster's low score may represent nothing more than a difference in content. Yet such an erroneous discrepancy could lead to an LD classification.

Second, achievement tests must evaluate achievement in the same way that the student is expected to demonstrate this knowledge in the classroom. For example, if the teacher's concern is slow work speed, then timed tests should be contrasted with performance in untimed conditions. If spelling is an issue, the test should have the child write words rather than simply point to the one of four choices spelled correctly; if the pointing test is used, the student's score may be inflated, thereby reducing the chances of identification for special education help.

A special problem arises when new Americans and students for whom English is not their native language are tested. Achievement can be greatly underestimated because they are unfamiliar with the content of our schools and the language on our achievement tests. In these cases, testing of achievement in one's native language and curriculum is recommended. If this results in a marked discrepancy from expected achievement based on intelligence estimates, it may be that the student has a learning disability.

Finally, it is important to interpret grade-equivalent scores as reflecting ranges of achievement rather than absolute values. Often these tests overestimate achievement by one year or more because scores are derived by adding up successes on a variety of item types, and test items are not hard enough to distinguish older from younger students' abilities. In addition, the heightened motivation and attention in an individual testing situation raises performance beyond what a child could do independently in the classroom. This overestimation of achievement results in lower discrepancy figures and denial of LD services to students who could benefit from them.

Educational Experience. The number of years a pupil has spent in school, the quality of the instruction, and home learning experiences are all important to consider. A student who continues to have severe, persistent learning difficulties despite adequate educational opportunities and ability has a learning disability. When opportunities have been poor, however, we tend to overestimate expected achievement levels and therefore misidentify children as learning disabled.

Age. Age is important to consider in LD identification. Some children are mistaken as learning disabled simply because they are young for their grade and too much is being expected. Age is an important factor in skill areas such as reading comprehension, which continues to develop with additional years. However, age declines in relevance in areas such as grammar and handwriting, which reach maturity at fairly young ages.

Alternatives to Discrepancy Formulas. Several alternatives, used independently or together with discrepancy formulas, can help us broaden the array of factors we consider in the LD identification process.

Many individuals have suggested that a much slower learning rate than expected, despite the use of a variety of teaching approaches, is the critical factor for LD identification. This identification approach involves measurement of success on class assignments, and systematic evaluation of the teacher's behaviors and the quality of instruction. The model for learning and behavior laid down by the parents is equally important to assess.

Others have suggested that listening comprehension be used as an estimate of a student's expected reading achievement, since listening comprehension tends to be even more highly related than IQ to reading achievement (Harris &

Sipay, 1979; Stanovich, 1991a). In skilled readers, reading and listening comprehension levels tend to be comparable (Perfetti, 1985; Sticht & James, 1984; Vellutino et al., 1991). Therefore, a student may have a reading disability if he or she can comprehend dictated information at a level that is much higher than the student's oral reading ability.

Because learning disabilities are characterized by uneven maturation in information-processing abilities, some have suggested that these be measured for identification purposes (Kirk, McCarthy, & Kirk, 1968; Shaw et al., 1995). This method contrasts with IDEA's regulations in that it emphasizes the information-processing causes of learning disabilities (for example, language, visual perception, fine-motor coordination, attention, memory). The overall score on a comprehensive battery of information-processing tests is presumed to reflect potential. Any major deviation of a subtest score would be considered a significant discrepancy. The problem with this method is that it presumes that children should develop all their information-processing subskills at the same rate. But not all children do. Because strengths and weaknesses are common, these tests may inaccurately identify typical learners as disabled (Kaufman, 1976; Larsen, Rogers, & Sowell, 1976). A further problem posed by process-oriented tests is that most do not have adequate subtest reliabilities or validities to support these types of profile interpretations (Sattler, 1992). Besides, we are not certain whether specific subskill weaknesses are definitely predictive of poor achievement in specific academic areas (Colarusso, Martin, & Hartung, 1975; Hammill & Larsen, 1974a; Larsen & Hammill, 1975); clinicians are continually amazed by students whose information-processing weaknesses would have predicted a learning disability—nevertheless they are good achievers.

Some individuals calculate discrepancies by presuming that a high achievement score in one academic area represents potential. Relatively poor performance in another academic area would suggest a specific learning disorder (Kirk & Elkins, 1975b; Shaw et al., 1995). The problem with this method is that at times the higher score does not represent hope for greater functioning in weaker areas. The high score may merely be a special talent (for example, sight vocabulary or number fact knowledge) that has no implications for what should be expected of a student in other areas of achievement. Likewise, particularly when one's weakest achievement is still in average ranges for one's age, it may be that this particular weakness is so common that it should not be considered a disability (for example, the average spelling of a gifted high school student who demonstrates no other noteworthy learning difficulties).

Finally, Algozzine and Ysseldyke (1986) recommend that we do away with our screening and diagnostic efforts altogether because of their inherent flaws and their high cost in terms of money, time, and personnel. Instead, they suggest monitoring performance daily within the classroom curriculum and then offering special/remedial education to all students making inadequate progress, regardless of handicapping condition. Others too advocate dropping IQ/achievement discrepancy assessments, given the considerable overlap in the academic characteristics of students with learning disabilities and those who are simply catching on to academics at a slower pace (Fletcher et al., 1993; Siegel, 1989). Reynolds and Heistad (1997) suggest simply offering special services to every student who ranks in the lowest 20th percentile in his or her grade on a standard achievement criterion; since most students with disabilities will fall in this lowest 20th percentile, additional testing often is not warranted. These suggestions have the advantage of reducing the inordinate amounts of time spent testing for identification purposes, instead increasing the time available for developing, implementing, and monitoring effective interventions.

Prevalence of Learning Disabilities

How many students with learning disabilities are there? While over 5 percent of our school population is identified as learning disabled, estimates from research studies have varied from 2 percent to over 20 percent (Silver, 1988). The larger estimates reflect the LD definition's broadness and

the liberal way in which school teams and researchers have interpreted the federal identification guidelines. The smaller estimates come from school districts that serve only the severely learning disabled and from those that find the bureaucratic process too cumbersome and professional salaries too expensive to warrant full identification of the learning disabled (Luick & Senf, 1979).

Accurate prevalence estimates are essential to preparing adequate numbers of teachers, programs, and financial allocations to meet the service needs of the learning disabled. Definitive estimates will be possible only when uniform assessment measures and discrepancy criteria are used across states and studies. Three types of prevalence figures are currently available: national policy estimates, state counts of identified students, and findings from experimental studies.

National Policy Estimates

Over the years, national bodies have set guidelines that assumed 1 to 5 percent of school children to be learning disabled: U.S. Office of Education (1971–1972), 1 percent; National Advisory Committee on Handicapped Children (1970) and the U.S. Office of Education (1970a, b), 1 to 3 percent; U.S. Department of Health, Education, and Welfare (1977), 5 percent. The current recommendation to Congress stands at 5 to 10 percent (Interagency Committee on Learning Disabilities Report, 1987).

State Counts

The first count of students with learning disabilities was done in 1970. Approximately 2,000 public elementary and secondary school principals were surveyed by the National Center for Educational Statistics of the U.S. Office of Education (Farnham-Diggory, 1978). The percentage of students considered to be learning disabled averaged 2.6, but only 1.3 percent were receiving special services. The lower the socioeconomic status of the school district, the greater was the incidence of learning disabilities. By the 1978–79 school year, approximately 2.3 percent of the nation's six- to seventeen-year-old students were being served within the LD category (*The Condition of Education*, 1980). By 1995–96, the LD six- to seventeen-year-old group had grown to nearly 2.5 million, 5.4 percent of all six- to seventeen-year-old school-age youngsters. The learning disabled constituted 51 percent of the disabled enrolled in school programs (U.S. Office of Education, 1997). Large discrepancies exist from state to state in percentages of students being identified as learning disabled (for example, Georgia, 2.9 percent; Massachusetts, 9 percent). Those states that identify fewer students as LD also tend to identify fewer children overall as disabled. For the nation as a whole, in 1995–96, 10.6 percent of all six- to seventeen-year-old students, over 4.8 million, were identified as disabled.

Although we know how many students are being identified as learning disabled, we still do not know the nature and extent of their strengths and weaknesses, how many are falsely identified as learning disabled, or how many remain unidentified. This is due to variability across school districts and states in the degree of discrepancy between potential and achievement required for identification, measures used for identification, philosophies regarding learning disabilities, and alternate service possibilities.

Experimental Studies

Empirical studies would seem to be the way to determine how many students actually could qualify for LD identification. Studies that administered individual tests to 2,000–29,000 school children, and applied the same discrepancy formula, report a 4 to 7 percent incidence of learning disabilities when the criterion is one or two areas of underachievement (Smith, 1991). When group tests are used, 13 percent of students with at least average intelligence display significant discrepancies; this figure rises to 16 percent if children of borderline intelligence also are counted. Certainly, this does not mean that all these pupils are learning disabled. The lower numbers of students actually identified as learning disabled can be explained by several factors:

1. Many students are underachieving for reasons other than learning disabilities (for example, excessive school absence, little home encouragement to study, poor motivation, emotional difficulties, or poor teaching).

2. Politics, appropriations, and tax issues dictate how many students are identified.

3. Large LD teenage drop-out rates (nearly 40 percent) decrease the number of students eligible for identification.

4. The development by some students of compensatory techniques masks the existence of underlying problems, thereby delaying identification.

5. Enrollment in high school programs such as work study or vocational courses, by the very nature of their less rigorous academic requirements, camouflages the existence of certain learning problems.

Although studies find males and females to be equally intelligent (Aiken, 1987), learning difficulties are identified far more frequently among males than females. Some recent research suggests that the male to female ratio in LD may in fact be equal (Alexander, Gray, & Lyon, 1993; Shaywitz et al., 1990), despite other large-scale screening evidence showing male to female ratios of 1.5:1, 2:1, 3:1, 4:1, or 6:1 (Smith, 1994) Researchers have offered various medical, maturational, sociological, and brain organization explanations for the greater numbers of males than females being identified as learning disabled. These hypotheses are summarized in Table 1–1. Whether or not research ultimately determines if sex differences in learning disabilities actually exist, the fact is that boys are at greater risk of being identified as learning disabled than are girls.

Summary

In the mid-1960s several forces came together to catalyze the birth of learning disabilities as a new field in special education. Parents whose children showed unexpected underachievement and uneven patterns of development found that existing educational classification and placement practices did not

Table 1–1   Hypotheses regarding greater male than female incidence of learning disabilities

Hypothesis	*Investigator*
Medical Factors	
• The male may be more biologically vulnerable to brain damage prenatally and postnatally than the female. Although more males than females are conceived, more males die in utero or in infancy, females outlive males, and males face a higher risk of disease that may lead to learning disorders (for example, meningitis).	• Bentzen (1963), Critchley (1970), McMillen (1979), Novitski (1977)
• Boys tend to have greater birth weights and larger heads and are more often firstborns. These conditions are associated with increased risk of brain injury and learning disorders.	• Silver (1971), Strauss & Lehtinen (1947)
• More males than females experience difficulties during the birth process, resulting in more males than females with birth defects. Even in normal deliveries, births of males take an average of an hour longer than the births of females.	• Jacklin & Maccoby (1982)
• Boys experience one-and-one-half to three times greater numbers of head injuries than girls.	• Goethe & Levin (1984), Segalowitz & Lawson (1995)
• The left hemisphere, which is critical to language and reading achievement, develops more slowly prenatally than the right hemisphere. Therefore, it is vulnerable over a longer period of time to events that may alter development. The male's left hemisphere is particularly vulnerable because abnormalities in the development of the immune system are associated with excess testosterone, a male hormone. During fetal life, immune system malfunction can retard or disrupt migration of cells to the cortex. In addition, testosterone acts as a growth stimulus for the right hemisphere by decreasing the amount of normal cell death (which is intended to facilitate growth of more appropriate tissue). Not only can an overfunctioning right hemisphere block and distort left hemisphere processing, but if high levels of testosterone actually cause a shift in left-hemisphere handedness and language functions to the right hemisphere, developmental disorders may ensue.	• Galaburda (1986), Geshwind & Behan (1982)
• The inheritance of learning disabilities appears to be influenced by the offspring's sex, with a male to female inheritance ratio of 1.5:1.0.	• Pennington (1995)
Maturational Factors	
• Males lag behind females from the start. At birth males are one month less mature than females; they complete maturation at age 18, 2 years later than girls. Growth rate is 80% that of the female through adolescence. Slow physical maturation often is correlated with slow behavioral maturation.	• Bayley (1943), Bayley & Jones (1955), Farnham-Diggory (1978)

(Continues on following page)

Table 1–1   *(Continued from preceding page)*

- The male brain's protective sheath has been found to grow slower than the female's. Therefore, the male has more prenatal and postnatal opportunities for damage to later developing cortical functions.
- The neural maturation of boys' cortical regions is known to differ from that of females; these differences may increase the probability of learning failure. Males have been found to lag behind females in development of brain regions responsible for attention and such reading-related left hemisphere skills as verbal expression, articulation, and perception of the order of sounds in words; stuttering is more common in males than in females; the male delays may be related in part to girls experiencing a greater spurt in brain growth at 10 to 12 years of age

- Males' greater variability in development may make them more susceptible to learning and behavior disorders.

Sociological Factors

- Because males mature at a slower rate, research indicates that they often are unready for school entrance or the work of their grade.
- It has been suggested that our society expects more achievement from boys than from girls and therefore is more apt to be aware of their learning difficulties or put pressures on them that they are too immature to meet; their more aggressive general behavior and reaction to failure seems to increase chances for LD referral.
- Males and females show equal frequencies of low reading achievement relative to their intelligence, but because males are perceived by teachers as more active, inattentive, disruptive, and delayed in language, motor, and academic skills, this bias initiates a greater referral rate of males for assessment and identification.
- Failing boys have been more apt to develop secondary behavioral difficulties; their socially sanctioned alternatives for success, being leaders and athletes, have been harder to accomplish than girls' alternatives of being nice and quiet.
- Males show more inappropriate physical activity than do females. This activity is particularly disturbing to female teachers, who are more apt than male teachers to refer such students for special education evaluation—and more teachers are females.

Brain Organization Factors

- Impulsivity and certain types of information-processing disorders have been found to be male-linked genetically.

- Goldman, Crawford, Stokes, Galkin, & Rosvold (1974)

- Bakker (1970, 1972), Denckla & Heilman (1979), Denckla & Rudel, in Denckla (1979), Epstein (1980), Goldman et al. (1974), Hier (1979), Hines (1990), Kinsbourne & Warrington (1963), Townes, Trupin, Martin, & Goldstein (1980)
- Kinsbourne & Caplan (1979)

- Ames (1968)

- Bentzen (1963), Caplan (1977), Caplan & Kinsbourne (1974), Lambert & Sandoval (1980), Vernon (1957), in Critchley (1970)
- Shaywitz, Shaywitz, Fletcher, & Escobar (1990)

- McIntyre (1988)

- Kinsbourne & Caplan (1979)

(Continues on following page)

Table 1–1 *(Continued from preceding page)*

- The male's cerebral hemispheres are known to be more strongly specialized than the female's (presumably due to increased levels of prenatal testosterone); therefore, in the event of left hemisphere damage, their right hemispheres are less flexible in assuming language functions important to academic achievement. In the event of right hemisphere damage, data indicate that boys' left hemispheres may become overloaded with inappropriate right hemisphere strategies (global, holistic), thereby compromising the left hemisphere analytic, sequential reasoning skills that are so important to reading.

- Davidoff, Cone, & Scully (1978), Hier (1979), Hier, LeMay, Rosenberger, & Perlo (1978), Witelson (1976a, 1977)

meet their children's needs. They sought a way to focus greater attention on their children's unique strengths and weaknesses, what they needed to learn, and how they could best be taught.

Parents and professionals advocated for intensified instruction, and modification of teaching methods and settings to accommodate each child's unique abilities and learning styles. The possibility for such individualized instruction was enhanced by research relating visual-perceptual and language difficulties to learning disorders, development of individualized programming materials and methods, and classroom application of behavior modification techniques. That a specific information processing disorder could be responsible for learning difficulties had special appeal to parents because it avoided their children's identification as mentally retarded or disturbed, and encouraged intensive teaching efforts. With the urging of parent–professional advocacy groups and the backing of judicial decisions, the federal government took a greater role in education and, in 1975, mandated special education services to children with learning disabilities.

Our current definition defines learning disabilities as an information-processing disorder that causes achievement to be far below a student's intellectual potential. According to the federal definition, the retarded, emotionally disturbed, physically handicapped, and economically disadvantaged also can be considered learning disabled if these conditions are not directly responsible for their severe discrepancy from expected achievement.

Unfortunately, the conceptual vagueness of our LD definition has led to overidentification of students as learning disabled. When these students then become part of our research samples, and researchers do not establish uniform criteria to decide which students really belong, we end up with confusing findings that do not help us determine which programs work best for whom.

The judgment of whether a learning disability exists is difficult. It involves consideration of intelligence, achievement, past educational experiences, age, rate of learning with various instructional approaches, quality of present teaching, motivation, and many other personal, task-related, and setting-related factors. Currently, 51 percent of all students with disabilities, over 5 percent of all students, are identified as learning disabled. However, experimental studies and national estimates suggest that even more pupils may be identifiable. The fact that boys are identified with learning disabilities in far greater numbers than girls has been linked to possible medical, maturational, sociological, and brain organization factors

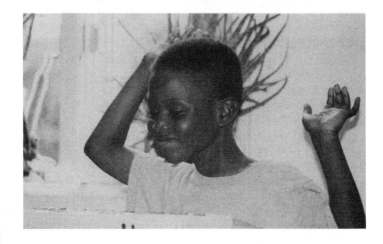

Chapter Two

Physiological Differences

While experts agree that the information-processing inefficiencies that underlie learning disabilities are of physiological
origin, they warn that task and setting contributors should not
be overlooked. Characteristics of the curriculum, school, and
home environment, such as school tasks that make demands on
the maturity levels or learning styles of students that they are
unprepared to meet, inadequate nutrition, or poor home climate, also can adversely impact the development or use of
one's information-processing capabilities. An understanding of
these learner, task, and setting influences will help us to better
assess the variety of factors that can contribute to different students' learning disabilities and plan appropriate interventions.

Our definitions of learning disabilities stress the intrinsic
nature of this disorder. Researchers who have focused on these
physiological differences have been able to identify a number of
brain functioning patterns that relate to the unique learning
and behavior patterns of individuals with learning disabilities.
This chapter will consider four physiological factors that may
lead to learning disabilities: brain injury, structural brain differences, heredity, and biochemical irregularities.

Brain Injury

Injury to brain tissue can cause a wide gamut of delays in the
development of a child and lead to difficulties in school learning. Yet brain injury and learning disabilities are not the same
thing. Brain injury does not always deter learning, and there
are other causes for learning disabilities. Strauss and Lehtinen's

classic case study of J.S. (below) illustrates the types of learning difficulties that may follow an insult to the brain.

J.S.'s accident is only one of many possible causes of brain injury. Although brain injury is often associated with learning difficulties, the brain injury diagnosis by itself tells us little about how to teach a student. Our growing understanding of the unique information-processing patterns of various subtypes of poor learners is far more useful in guiding our instructional programming. We will explore the causes, effects, and diagnosis of brain injury and the neuropsychological patterns that make these individuals' learning styles unique.

Causes of Brain Injury

Those areas of the brain that are the latest to mature carry the responsibility for high-level cognitive and academic reasoning abilities (Calanchini & Trout, 1971). Many events make these areas susceptible to damage: carbon monoxide (for example, during suffocation or unconscious states), nutrient and oxygen deprivation (for example, inadequate blood flow due to blood vessel constriction or blockage), free-flowing blood (for example, hemorrhages after strokes or concussions that block nutrients from cells), and pressure (for example, tumor, pus infection). These events may occur in prenatal, perinatal, or postnatal life and are more common among students with learning and behavior difficulties than among average learners.

Prenatal Factors. Prior to birth, brain injury can be associated with RH factor incompatibility, maternal diabetes and hypothyroidism, X rays, too young or old maternal age, many previous pregnancies, maternal measles or drug and alcohol abuse, cigarette smoking, medication that leads to oxygen deprivation, placental insufficiency, maternal kidney malfunction or bleeding, and fetal infections such as rubella, cytomegalovirus, or the herpes simplex virus (Pasamanick & Knobloch, 1973; Touwen & Huisjes, 1984). The nervous

J.S.

J.S., youngest son of American parents of average intelligence and economic level. Two older children were progressing normally in school. Birth normal, psychophysical development uneventful until eighth year of age, when he fell 35 feet from a viaduct, landing on the fender of a passing car. He was unconscious for 24 hours, with bleeding from the nose and left ear and a severe black eye. Hospital diagnosed a fractured skull. In personality he had always been attractive and alert; this had not changed but his mother observed that he was more stubborn and impulsive at home following the accident. On returning to school, he no longer recognized the letters of the alphabet which he knew before, had "forgotten" how to read everything but a few words. Teachers soon saw that the earlier skills showed no evidence of returning. He could not read or write without scribbling, could not memorize or remember things from one day to the next. When admitted to the institution at 10 years of age his intelligence quotient was 82, performance quotient . . . 106. Still showed slight neurological signs of brain-injury. After 18 months of special training, he reached the end of the third or beginning of the fourth grade in reading and arithmetic. He returned to his family to enter school with a slow group of normal children.

Source: Strauss, A. A., & Lehtinen, L. E. (1947). *Psychopathology and education of the brain-injured child.* New York: Grune & Stratton (p. 3). Reprinted by permission.

systems of premature children (birth weight under 5½ pounds) are far more vulnerable to injury than those of full-term infants (Touwen & Huisjes, 1984), and a significantly higher incidence of prematurity exists among children who subsequently develop academic and behavioral difficulties (Als, 1985; Rossetti, 1986).

Minor physical anomalies that have their origins prior to birth often are associated with later learning difficulties. These include facial asymmetry, atypical placement of ears or tear ducts, skin at the inside corner of the eye covering the tear ducts, unusually long index finger and short or curved fifth finger, tongue furrows, malformations of teeth, high arch in the mouth, and large gaps between toes or unusual length of toes (Steg & Rapoport, 1975; von Hilsheimer & Kurko, 1979). These physical anomalies do not disappear with age, are inversely related to intelligence, and are predictive of first grade school failure (Bell & Waldrop, 1989; Rosenberg & Weller, 1973).

Perinatal Factors.   At the time of labor and delivery, brain injury may occur because of shortage of oxygen, prolonged or precipitous labor, premature separation of the placenta, or difficult delivery. Studies have found that 9 to 12 percent of all surviving newborns have evidence of intracranial hemorrhages at birth (Colletti, 1979). This figure rises to 40 percent or more among infants who are born premature (Raz et al., 1995). Colletti reports that, as a group, those children who underachieved in school were atypical at birth in a number of ways: greater numbers of mild to severe problems at birth, short first and longer second stages of labor, poorer general health, birth more often induced by the physician, longer hospitalization, more labor complications, and more forceps deliveries.

Postnatal Factors.   After birth, events that may cause brain injury include serious head injuries, accidents, strokes, high fevers, dehydration, brain tumors, and diseases such as encephalitis and meningitis. Colletti (1979) suggests that by age six as many as 20 percent of all children may have suffered a significant insult to the brain. High school students report that about one in three

have incurred mild head injuries, with 15 percent of the incidents involving unconsciousness; 12 percent of students report multiple head-injury experiences (Segalowitz & Lawson, 1995). Given that brain injury is only one cause of disabilities, why then is the national count of children with disabilities only slightly more than 10 percent? Clearly, there is no one-to-one relationship between extent of brain damage and subsequent learning and adjustment difficulties. The next section describes why this is so.

Effects of Brain Injury

Knowing that a child is brain injured does not help a teacher understand which learning functions are impaired and to what degree. Individuals who have cerebral palsy or seizure disorders are all brain injured, as are many individuals who are learning disabled, blind, or deaf. Yet all have different abilities, behaviors, and instructional needs. Some have severe learning difficulties, whereas others have very few. Why is there such variability?

The effect of brain injury on learning and behavior varies because it depends on several factors: the reason for the damage, its location, the extent of the damage, the individual's developmental maturity at the time of damage, how much time the damage has been progressing, the time passed since the insult, the individual's state of development at the time of testing, and the nature and extent of retraining attempts (Reitan, 1974). Fortunately, our brains are "plastic." That is, although a brain cell won't regenerate or repair itself once destroyed, new neural connections often are formed between nondamaged cells so that learning continues. Therefore, brain areas that are malfunctioning, but not totally destroyed, may be able to recover function if stimulated appropriately. Moreover, some cells may give up their original functions in order to take over the lost function. In other cases, cells that were inhibited when the damaged tissue was active now adopt the function. Finally, existing cell systems can reorganize to handle the old function in a new way. Consequently, precise predictions of the functional outcome of a brain injury are very difficult to make (Hartlage & Telzrow, 1986).

Although the brain's "plasticity" declines with age, brain insults in infancy nevertheless may create greater damage and long-term functional losses than equivalent injury in later childhood or adulthood (Goethe & Levin, 1984). Because the brain is so modifiable, professionals hesitate to give up hope if students are older, yet critical skills such as speaking and reading have not yet emerged. Research Box 2–1 further explores research on the brain's modifiability.

Because of the brain's plasticity, a diagnosis of brain injury does not predict for certain

RESEARCH BOX 2–1
Brain Plasticity

Damage to a specific brain site reduces the ability of the individual to perform the function usually assumed by that area. However, this functional loss may not be permanent. The human brain has approximately 100 billion neurons, with each connected to approximately 15,000 other neurons (Kolb, 1989). Therefore, neurons from adjacent or distant areas often are capable of taking over functions of other damaged regions. This occurs provided that the primary, densely enervated, receptive (visual, auditory, tactile) and expressive (motor, speech) areas are not totally destroyed and provided that the dysfunction is in the more sparsely enervated secondary areas that analyze and integrate this information or in the tertiary areas where interaction and integration of neurons from various primary sites occur (Alajouanine & Lhermitte, 1965; Lenneberg, 1967). For example, before age two a child's right hemisphere will take over many of the left hemisphere's language functions when the latter is damaged; between ages two to five, language zones will shift within the left hemisphere. The trade-off is that the functions slated for these other brain areas may decline severely, as may overall language and cognitive capacities (Fletcher, Levin, & Landry, 1984; Kolb, 1989; Searleman, 1977). Most research finds that verbal abilities are better spared after left hemisphere damage than are visual-spatial abilities after right hemisphere damage, but that this sparing is uneven (Rourke et al., 1983; Taylor, 1984).

Animal research indicates that neuronal recovery after brain injury occurs in several ways (Finger & Almli, 1984; Kolb, 1989; Rodier, 1984):

1. Inactive, intact axons (nerves that send messages) take over for the inability of cut axons to repair themselves.

2. New connections sprout from the axons of undamaged neurons to repair damaged circuits; at times this sprouting may result in aberrant connections. In essence, one abnormality may be traded for another.

3. Synapses (areas where nerve endings meet) that had been vacated by other axon terminals are a growth stimulus for new neuronal sprouting; the sprouting pattern is not similar to the original normal connections.

4. Groups of dendrite branchings (nerves that receive messages) may form new circuits if stimulated appropriately; at times dendrites elaborate in response to a loss of input.

(*Continues on following page*)

RESEARCH BOX 2–1   *(Continued from preceding page)*

5. Glial (connecting) cells regenerate and make contact with neurons so that transmission can occur.

6. Enriched environments may result in positive changes in brain structure (for example, glial/neuronal ratio, enzyme activity, nucleic acid concentration, cortical weight).

7. The outer membrane of neurons near the site of injury may become more responsive to neurotransmitters, thereby improving recovery.

8. Better conduction may occur because of changes in synapse density after stimulation or a gain in numbers of synapses.

9. If injury occurs prior to birth, the brain may respond shortly after injury by producing new cells of the correct type; however, permanent reductions in the total numbers of neurons is still likely.

10. The fetus overproduces neurons by close to a factor of two, and after birth undergoes a period of natural cell death; if too few neurons are produced initially, the brain may respond by reducing the subsequent rate of cell death.

These findings are promising for people, but for obvious reasons cannot be tested out. We do know that the human's central nervous system recovery ability varies with the nature and location of the damage, the size of damage, the age at which the injury occurred, as well as the intensity, length, and type of retraining efforts (Reitan, 1974). Often the brain-injured child's brain reorganizes so that old problems can be solved in new ways (Rourke et al., 1983). No data on brain plasticity are more astounding than the remarkable relearning that takes place after an entire cerebral hemisphere or lobe has been surgically removed because of epilepsy, tumor, or trauma; however, overall functioning is nevertheless compromised, with some new learning occurring with ease while other more naturally developing sensitivities remain underdeveloped (Bigler, 1992; Fletcher et al., 1984; Dennis & Whitaker, 1976; Kolb, 1989).

Despite the brain's plasticity, complete recovery is the exception rather than the rule. That is, even if a brain insult has produced no obvious diminution in function, when problem solving demands require greater neurological maturity, the deficit may very well become apparent.

It has been a general belief that the adult recovers less function after equivalent brain injury than the child because (1) neuron regeneration is less efficient the older one gets, and (2) there is less room for one area of the brain to take over the activities of another because the former has already specialized for a specific function. More recently, however, evidence has accumulated indicating that young children may demonstrate as much or even more cognitive impairment when suffering from the same severity of brain injury as older children and adults (Hartlage & Telzrow, 1986; Kolb, 1989; Lord-Maes & Obrzut, 1996). Hynd and Willis (1988) explain that at birth the primary cortical zones appear mature, in contrast to the secondary and tertiary zones, which require months and years to mature

(Continues on following page)

RESEARCH BOX 2–1 *(Continued from preceding page)*

(Luria, 1980). Therefore, lesions in early childhood to primary regions may deleteriously affect higher-order cognitive processes because the necessary foundations for this learning have been disturbed. Similar lesions during adulthood would have a more limited effect because the functional system for higher-order cognitive processing already has been formed. An alternative explanation for more devastating effects from early brain injury considers the fact that injury to brain tissue also produces secondary cell loss or reorganization in areas with which the tissue anatomically or functionally interrelates, even if remote from the area of damage (Rosenzweig, Bennett, & Alberti, 1984). Therefore, early brain damage in one area may alter the neuroanatomy, function, neurochemistry, and growth patterns of remaining brain systems (Isaacson & Spear, 1984). Even if the effects of the damage are not evident on simple sensory, perceptual, or motor tasks, their adverse effects may be quite apparent in higher cognitive functions (O'Leary & Boll, 1984).

Once damage and recovery have occurred, the reserve power of the brain is limited in the event of further damage (Lehrer, 1974). Nevertheless, the reserve is usually large enough to help develop some compensatory skills. The fact that the brain is plastic is critical to the success of special education interventions.

whether the child will have learning difficulties, and the extent of these difficulties. Nor does it suggest the best instructional approaches.

Diagnosing Brain Injury

Diagnosing brain injury involves examination of prenatal, perinatal, and postnatal indicators of brain injury, electroencephalograms, and hard and soft neurological signs. When these measures indicate positive findings for children with learning difficulties, brain injury has been presumed to be the cause of their learning problems. However, research has questioned this conclusion for several reasons: (1) many factors besides brain injury can cause learning problems (for example, school absence, inappropriate teaching style), (2) brain injury indicators are extremely common among normal learners as well (their brains have compensated for the adverse cognitive consequences of injury), and (3) brain injury indicators tap lower-level brain integrity rather than skills necessary for high-level academic reasoning. Consequently, even if a child does test positive on brain injury indicators, it still cannot be concluded that this brain abnormality definitely has caused or will cause a learning problem.

Research shows that although prenatal, perinatal, and postnatal factors associated with brain injury are more prevalent among children with learning difficulties, they also are very prevalent among typical learners. For example, Coleman and Sandhu (1967) determined the following percentages of brain injury indicators among middle-income, seven- to fifteen-year-old children with different levels of reading achievement:

2 or more years behind in reading	1–2 years behind in reading	Less than 1 year behind in reading	Over 1 year ahead in reading
Birth difficulties			
30%	23%	17%	19%
Serious injuries			
26%	23%	11%	15%

Even though events related to brain injury were more prevalent among the poorer learners, they nevertheless were present in substantial percentages among the students who were one year ahead as well. In another study, there was no correlation between data on pregnancy history, maternal medical factors, labor, delivery, or birth trauma and whether students became identified as disabled by adolescence (Kochanek, Kabacoff, & Lipsitt, 1990). Therefore, positive findings on these prenatal, perinatal, and postnatal brain injury indicators cannot be used to definitely predict a future learning disorder in any one individual or to explain that an existing disorder is due to this brain insult.

The same is true for electroencephalograms (EEGs), which use electrodes to measure electrical activity at many points near the outer surface of the brain. The following percentages show that visual inspection of the graphed EEG signals reveals no differences in the numbers of typical and disabled learners who show abnormal EEGs:

Typical learners	Poor learners	
10%	10%	Meier (1971)
30%	41%	Myklebust & Boshes (1969)
22%	14%	Owen, Adams, Forrest, Stolz, & Fisher (1971)
32%	23%	Harris (1983)

This is because our brains can compensate for brain abnormalities so that learning remains unimpaired. Due to this compensation, even children known to have suffered brain injury often have normal EEGs (Black, 1973; Freeman, 1971). Even if EEG abnormalities persist in these children, the complicated patterns are difficult to discern on visual inspection of EEG recordings (Duffy & McAnulty, 1985). Because the EEG could readily distinguish tumors, malformations, convulsive disorders, sleep states, and coma, researchers assumed that these signals also might shed light on the brain functioning of the learning disabled. Unfortunately, these hopes were not fulfilled. Visually inspected EEGs could not even discriminate people of different intelligence and achievement levels, let alone detect different learning patterns (Hartlage & Green, 1971, 1972; McCauley & Ciesielski, 1982). Because both typical and poor learners have abnormal EEGs, an abnormal EEG is of uncertain value in determining whether a brain injury is causing or is likely to cause learning difficulties.

Hard and soft neurological signs have fared no better than prenatal, perinatal, and postnatal indicators or EEGs as predictors of learning disabilities. *Hard neurological signs* are behavioral signs that always reflect brain injury: for example, seizures, cerebral palsy, cranial nerve abnormalities leading to blindness and deafness, and microcephaly. Investigators also note lags in children's gross- and fine-motor development, such as persistent primitive reflexes, poor balance, and coordination difficulties. These lags are called *soft neurological signs* because, although normal at younger ages, they are abnormal relative to the child's current age.

Studies find that underachievers who have no obvious brain injuries, such as cerebral palsy, generally have no more hard or soft signs than do typical learners, and often their neurological examinations are entirely normal (Bortner, Hertzig, & Birch, 1972; Dykman et al., 1971; Myklebust & Boshes, 1969; Owen et al., 1971; Rutter, 1982; Shaffer et al., 1983). In one study, in fact, children with the most neurological signs actually had the fewest learning disorders (Ingram, Mason, & Blackburn, 1970). In another study, the children who were learning disabled did have more hard (95 percent) and soft (90 percent) signs than did typical learners; nevertheless hard (55 percent) and soft (75 percent) signs were highly prevalent in the control group as well (Meier, 1971). In the largest study of this type, the National Collaborative Perinatal Project, the relationship between neurological signs and learning disabilities in seven-year-old children could account for only 1 percent of the learning problem (Nichols & Chen, 1981). Because hard and soft signs are so prevalent among normal learners, their presence can-not prove that a brain defect has caused or will cause learning problems. This is because, like the prenatal, perinatal, and postnatal indicators and visually inspected EEGs, hard and soft signs do not measure brain processes necessary for high-level academic achievement and because our brains can compensate for these impairments. Besides, many factors other than brain injury can cause positive hard and soft signs: inherited traits (Owen et al., 1971; Matoušek & Petersén, 1973), maturational patterns that will be outgrown over time (Dykman et al., 1971; Routh & Roberts, 1972), or environmental influences that have affected brain development, such as inadequate health care or nutrition (Bortner et al., 1972; John et al., 1977).

Because these tests for brain injury have not been accurate predictors or explainers of learning disorders, they are not useful to instructional planning. Therefore, researchers no longer concern themselves with diagnosing brain injury among students with learning difficulties. Instead they are trying to better understand how certain patterns of brain functioning relate to specific strengths and weaknesses in these students' learning abilities and styles. Let us look at some of these patterns.

Neuropsychological Patterns

By comparing differences in the patterns of brain functioning of typical and poor learners, we have begun to shed light on the relationship between the brain, learning, and behavior. These patterns have become apparent through the newer neuropsychological assessment methods described in Research Box 2–2.

RESEARCH BOX 2–2
Neuropsychological Research Methods

Researchers in the 1950s and 1960s studied brain-behavior relationships by noting behavior changes due to brain lesions or stimulation of specific brain sites during surgery (Penfield & Roberts, 1959). Advances in instrumentation and computer technology in the 1970s and 1980s brought rapid gains in knowledge concerning patterns of typical and atypical brain functioning. The brain's asymmetry, each hemisphere's preference for certain types of tasks, was found to be very important to normal maturation and learning. The poor learner often showed atypical asymmetries. Several methods for studying brain-behavior relationships are described below.

Split-Brain Studies
Neuropsychologists isolated the function of one brain hemisphere from another by studying individuals whose severe seizures were terminated when the *corpus callosum*, a band of nerve fibers connecting the two cerebral hemispheres, was severed. Once this was severed, it was possible to present information to either hemisphere alone, thereby isolating the function of each cerebral hemisphere and observing which activities necessitate interhemispheric communication.

Sperry's (1968) studies used the apparatus pictured on the next page. Visual information is presented only to the left or right halves (visual field) of each eye. A picture presented to the left visual field is represented in the right cerebral hemisphere; Sperry's patients could not report in speech or writing what had been seen because these language

(Continues on following page)

RESEARCH BOX 2–2   *(Continued from preceding page)*

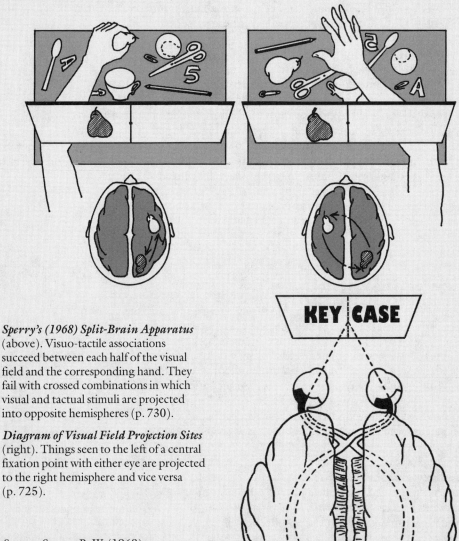

Sperry's (1968) Split-Brain Apparatus (above). Visuo-tactile associations succeed between each half of the visual field and the corresponding hand. They fail with crossed combinations in which visual and tactual stimuli are projected into opposite hemispheres (p. 730).

Diagram of Visual Field Projection Sites (right). Things seen to the left of a central fixation point with either eye are projected to the right hemisphere and vice versa (p. 725).

Source: Sperry, R. W. (1968). Hemisphere deconnection and unity in conscious awareness. *American Psychologist, 23,* pp. 723–733. Copyright 1968 by the American Psychological Association. Reprinted by permission of the publisher and the author.

(Continues on following page)

RESEARCH BOX 2–2 *(Continued from preceding page)*

functions are controlled by the left hemisphere. Some subjects even reported seeing nothing or just a flash of light. However, these same subjects' left hands were able to find the objects through touch because both the left side of the body and vision in the left visual fields are controlled by the right cerebral hemisphere. Only input to the right visual field (which projects to the left hemisphere) could be described in speech or writing. Likewise, only objects placed in the right hand could be named because all these functions are controlled by the left hemisphere. Even though they could perform the high-level task of naming when the object remained in their right hands, subjects could not match the object or name a picture of the object if the latter were projected to their right cerebral hemisphere (through the left visual field).

Visual-Half Field, Dichotic Listening, and Dichhaptic Stimulation Techniques

Simultaneous presentation of two different stimuli to both visual fields or ears is one means of examining the relative efficiency of each hemisphere in processing certain types of information. Each visual field is represented in the opposite hemisphere. In contrast, the left and right ears project only approximately 60 percent of auditory information to the opposite hemisphere. By determining which hemisphere is more accurate on a task, investigators presume its greater specialization for that particular function.

These techniques have been adapted to a tactile *dichhaptic stimulation task* (Witelson, 1974). This method asks the subject to use touch to perceive or name letters and meaningless shapes. Objects in the left hand are perceived primarily by the right cerebral hemisphere and vice versa. In naming letters, the right hemisphere is useful because it analyzes the spatial information, while the left hemisphere provides the name. With nonlinguistic stimuli, however, the left hand's perceptions prove to be superior because their interpretation relies on the right hemisphere's spatial skills. Using these measures, researchers are discovering the degree of specialization of each hemisphere for different functions, as well as the inefficiencies of the poor learner.

Event-Related Potentials

Event-related potentials, the computer summing of EEG recordings of electrical potentials, also reveal differences between good and poor learners. Recordings may be taken from as many as twenty brain sites while the subject has eyes open/closed, reads letters/words, looks at meaningful/nonmeaningful shapes and objects, looks at light flashes, or listens to sounds or words. Usually 50 to 100 stimuli are presented at one-second intervals. The computer sums the amplitude (microvolts) of peaks and measures the milliseconds from the onset of stimulation to peaks and the return to normal. This procedure allows the brain's responses to the stimuli to stand out against its background electrical activity. In the noncomputerized EEG, this background activity, as well as unreliable judgments, may obscure significant, abnormal wave patterns.

(Continues on following page)

RESEARCH BOX 2–2   *(Continued from preceding page)*

Brain Electrical Activity Mapping
The average evoked potential technique is used to create a moving visual display of brain
wave activity. The computer divides the head into 4,096 picture elements (pixels), each of
which takes on a color of the rainbow representing the electrode's reading. Electrodes measure the response to a stimulus (for example, listening to spoken words) every four msec for
a total of 512 msec. The 128 frames are viewed as a continuous movie of the spread of electrical activity in the brain. Using this technique, Duffy and McAnulty (1985) were able to
demonstrate electroneurological differences among boys whose reading disabilities
stemmed from three different types of language difficulties.

Computer-Assisted Tomographic Scanning (CAT Scan)
The CAT scan is an X ray that scans the skull and detects the absorption differences
between spinal fluid, bone, white and gray matter, and blood. Although brain lesion detection is enhanced by an intravenous injection of an X ray dense dye, the subtle differences of
the learning disabled are hard to detect (Denckla, LeMay, & Chapman, 1985).

Regional Cerebral Blood Flow
In order for brain tissue to be activated, glucose and oxygen are required. These nutrients
are supplied by means of the blood vessels. Consequently, measurement of blood flow in
the cerebral hemispheres can indicate which hemisphere has been activated by a particular
cognitive process.

  An extension of the CAT scan method, regional cerebral blood flow, (also called
positron-emission tomography, or PET), involves inhaling trace amounts of xenon or inject-
ing radioactive isotopes into the carotid artery, which feeds most cerebral areas. When the
subject is asked to do something, blood flow concentrations change because the more active
areas take up more oxygen and metabolize more glucose (80 percent of the brain's energy
comes from glucose). Blood flow concentrations are apparent in photographs of the cortical
areas being activated by these activities. Thus, we can discover the degree of activation
required of different areas when performing certain tasks.

  A simpler blood temperature measure also has been found useful. Blood temperature
measures taken at the eardrum reflect which hemisphere has been activated because, when
blood flow is increased, the brain tissue cools (Meiners & Dabbs, 1977).

Magnetic Resonance Imaging (MRI)
MRI images the brain's structure by means of low-energy radio waves generated within a
magnetic field. The brain's hydrogen protons resonate in response to these pulses. The
MRI measures the time it takes for the pulsing of the hydrogen protons to decay; the rate of
decay varies according to the density of the hydrogen. The MRI is sensitive to alterations in
the white matter, water content, bone marrow, and lower brain areas (brainstem, cerebel-
lum, upper spinal cord) that other techniques have difficulty scanning. The sensitivity to

(Continues on following page)

RESEARCH BOX 2–2 *(Continued from preceding page)*

white matter lesions is particularly helpful in that the white matter is the "superhighway" connecting different brain regions, yet is not well imaged on CAT scans (Hynd & Willis, 1988). MRI white matter lesions correlate well with neuropsychological findings (Levin, Handel, Goldman, Eisenberg, & Guinto, 1985). Because of this technology, subcortical white matter deficiency in the connections between different brain regions is becoming an important area of study. New imaging techniques, *functional MRI* and *Magnetic Source Imaging,* give the structural resolution of MRI but also highlight areas of activity, as do PET and event-related potentials.

Ultrasonography
In ultrasonography, high-frequency sound waves are generated by a transducer and directed into the body. The resulting echoes vary according to the tissue scanned. These sound waves are then converted into an image. Ultrasound is particularly valuable for viewing the brain's ventricles (four cavities that help to circulate the cerebrospinal fluid cushioning the brain and spinal nerves) and the corpus callosum (band of fibers connecting the two cerebral hemispheres).

Drugs
Drugs may be used to anesthetize a hemisphere temporarily so that we can observe which functions become impaired. Osgood and Miron (1963) used this technique to demonstrate that a numbing of the left hemisphere could induce language impairment in an adult. Their subject had been able to name common objects displayed to him: cigarette, spring, paper clip, colors, fingers. Injection of Nembutal into the right carotid artery (which feeds the right cerebral hemisphere) had no effect on this naming ability. But an injection into the left carotid artery produced jargon-like misnaming of the same articles. In addition, movement difficulties on the right side of the body became apparent. The Nembutal effect lasted four minutes, after which the subject again could identify the objects correctly. Obviously his speech functions were located in his left hemisphere. This method has been named *Wada's technique,* after its discoverer. It often is used prior to brain surgery to detect whether the patient's language centers are in danger of being disturbed.

Patterns of Typical Learners. We know that *primary brain regions* are critical to performance of very specific basic functions such as vision, hearing, or movement. It is the areas that connect these primary regions that form functional systems to carry out higher-level functions (Luria, 1980). As the child matures, one or the other cerebral hemisphere becomes specialized to contribute more actively to specific functions. Adequate hemispheric specialization and attention processes are essential to normal learning.

Structure-Function Relationships. Figure 2–1 shows the functions of various areas of the cerebral cortex. Figure 2–2 depicts the arrangement of brain cells responsible for body movements and sensations.

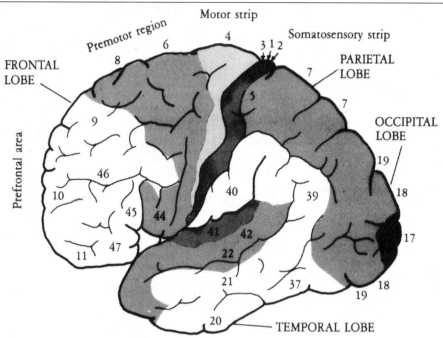

The cerebral cortex controls all conscious activity. The two halves of the cerebral cortex are almost identical in construction and metabolism but differ in function. All brain activity is controlled by the biological structure and chemical transmissions of the nervous system.

Left Hemisphere: In most individuals, the *left hemisphere* responds to language stimuli such as inner thought, words, symbols that have verbal meaning, and memory for verbal material (Luria, 1976). It usually contains Broca's area, the region for speech. Over 95 percent of right-handed individuals and about 60 percent of left-handers (Segalowitz & Bryden 1983) have speech located in the left hemisphere. The left hemisphere receives information from the right visual field of each eye and the right side of the body. It specializes in information processing that involves analytical thinking, evaluating details, and sequencing. Because of the left hemisphere's use of words to reason, it plays an important role in skilled reading, math analysis, and computation.

Right Hemisphere: The *right hemisphere* processes information as wholes (rather than details)

and deals primarily with nonverbal stimuli such as body awareness (orientation in space), time sense, directional orientation (up-down), pictorial perception, mental imagery, spatial perception (Ketchum, 1967), memory for visual stimuli (Luria, 1976), complex forms, color, and environmental sounds. Because of its visual-perceptual skills the right hemisphere plays an important role in appreciation of and talent in music, art, dance, sculpture, and geometrical/ perspective drawing (Tarnopol & Tarnopol, 1977). The right hemisphere's role in appreciation of the overall configuration of elements, its ability to see the big picture, is important to organizational skills and social perception. If not dominant for language, the right hemisphere is still able to understand simple language and perform simple arithmetic (adding two digits). It receives information from the left visual field of each eye and the left side of the body.

Temporal Lobe: The *temporal lobe* is responsible for language reception and comprehension. Sixty percent of nerve fibers that transmit sound come from the opposite body side's ear, and 40

Figure 2–1   Brain structure-function relationship. *Source:* Tarnopol, L., & Tarnopol, M. (1977). *Brain function and reading disabilities.* Baltimore: University Park Press, p. 9. Reprinted by permission of the authors. *General sources:* Hécaen & Albert (1978), Heilman & Valenstein (1979), Hynd & Willis (1988), Luria (1977, 1980), Tarnopol & Tarnopol (1977), Walsh (1978).

percent come from the same side's ear. Because language is important in learning, the hemisphere that contains these skills is called "dominant," even when one's writing hand is controlled by the opposite cerebral hemisphere. The temporal lobe also plays an important role in emotions and behavior because of its proximity to the limbic system.

Area 41: primary auditory reception field.

Area 42: also receives auditory input; together with area 41, it contains Heschl's gyrus, which analyzes sound frequencies, lower frequencies being more centrally located.

Areas 21, 22: auditory association area capable of higher-order auditory analysis because of connections with other regions; works with area 42.

Areas 21, 37: controls auditory memory and sequencing, word meaning, searching for words.

Frontal Lobe: The *frontal lobe* is active in focusing attention, integrating awareness of the whole with the component elements, and organizing output. It is active in judgment, controlling impulsivity, assessment of risks and consequences of behaviors, and appropriateness of emotional reactions. The *primary motor strip* (area 4) in the right hemisphere controls voluntary muscular movements of the left side of the body. The left hemisphere's motor area controls right side voluntary muscular movements. Each hemisphere contains some nerve fibers that control minor movements of the same side hand and arm.

Areas 6, 8, 44: These are the secondary or "premotor" regions that coordinate, organize, stop, or change movement that has already begun. They formulate complex motor activities through interconnections with the sensory association regions, primary motor strip, and somatosensory strip. Area 44 is called *Broca's area* and is usually located in the left hemisphere. It controls speech movements and, if damaged, results in articulation difficulties.

Area 4 + premotor + sensory connections: Permit visual-motor, auditory-motor, and tactile, kinesthetic-motor associations.

Prefrontal Areas (9, 10, 45, 46, 47): Control judgment, reasoning, abstract thinking, motives, planning, perseveration, following plans, vigilance, and restraint of emotional impulses and impulsivity; appropriateness of emotional reactions; organization of goal-directed, selective behavior; regulation of states of attention or activity; activation of motor, speech, and intellectual acts as well as consciousness and affective states; organization of information into temporal-based, sequential schemas.

Parietal Lobe: In contrast to the frontal lobe, which prefers a sequential strategy for surveying information, the parietal and occipital lobes take a more simultaneous approach, surveying stimuli in a unitary, holistic fashion. The *somatosensory strip* (areas 1, 2, 3) in the right hemisphere receives feelings of touch, texture, pain, movement, weight, and temperature from the left side of the body. The left hemisphere's strip receives sensations from the right side. Lesions on the strip result in a loss of sensation for specific body parts (see Figure 2–2).

Areas 5, 7: These are the secondary association areas, which, through their connections with other regions, can analyze and synthesize more complex tactile-kinesthetic information. Lesions in these areas result in partial loss of sensitivity.

Angular Gyrus: The *angular gyrus* (area 39) is located in the dominant cerebral hemisphere and works together with area 40. Visual, auditory, and kinesthetic areas of the brain are connected here. If it is damaged, the individual will have deficits in reading, writing, spelling, understanding language, and body image.

Occipital Lobe: The *occipital lobe* processes visual stimuli. The right occipital lobe processes information from the left visual field of each eye. The left occipital lobe processes information from each eye's right visual field.

Area 17: Responds to simple visual stimuli (lines and edges).

Areas 18 and 19: Secondary visual areas with connections to other areas that permit higher-order visual functions: analyzing angles, rectangles, movements, figure- ground discriminations; recognizing and describing one or more objects; synthesizing parts of objects into wholes; controlling eye tracking; visual-auditory, visual-motor, and visual-sensory associations.

Figure 2–1 *(Continued from preceding page)*

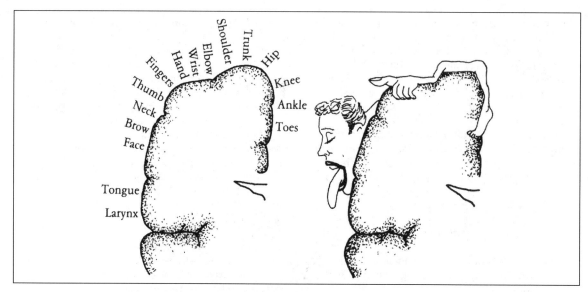

Figure 2–2 The homunculus. The human body is represented in each hemisphere's motor strip (area 4 of the frontal lobe) and somatosensory strip (areas 1, 2, 3 of the parietal lobe) as an inverted fetus, a "homunculus." A relatively large brain area is devoted to the face, tongue, thumb, and fingers. These body parts, in turn, are able to move in more specialized fashions and to sense more acutely than are other body parts. *Source:* Tarnopol, L., & Tarnopol, M. (1977). *Brain function and reading disabilities.* Baltimore: University Park Press, p. 222. Reprinted by permission of the authors.

Dynamic Interrelationship of Brain Areas. Brain regions rarely work in isolation. The areas are intimately interconnected, and any type of information processing generally activates several regions, each to a different degree. Therefore, complex learning and behavior is dependent on the activation of an organized, functional system of different brain regions. Because of this, an impairment in one brain region may decrease performance in seemingly unrelated areas as well.

Have you ever considered what your brain activity looks like when you are reading? Figure 2–3, a photograph of the actual activation of brain areas, shows that reading aloud activates seven cortical centers in each hemisphere. Even during silent reading, the areas responsible for listening and speech are stimulated slightly. This may be why, after reading all day for exams, your mouth feels stiff and dry and you have a scratchy

throat. Similar photographs have shown that even when you are resting with your eyes closed, listening to nothing and doing nothing, your frontal lobes are still likely to be extremely active, even though merely thinking.

Computerized brain wave recordings from different brain regions produce patterns that are able to distinguish females from males and left- from right-handers (Dimond & Beaumont, 1974). Furthermore, the latency, variance, and complexity of certain waves can reflect increases in mental maturity level, verbal and performance IQ, and age (Eysenck, 1984b; Kok & Rooijakkers, 1985; Licht et al., 1988; Matoušek & Petersén, 1973; Matarazzo, 1992; Myklebust & Boshes, 1969; Robinson et al., 1984).

Maturation of Brain Functions. As a child grows up, one cerebral hemisphere becomes more spe-

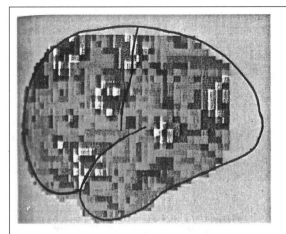
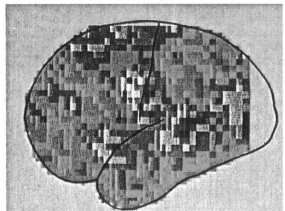

Normal brain cell activity during reading was revealed by measuring regional blood flow, which is closely related to metabolic rate and hence to functional activity. The images were generated by a computer and the data obtained by detecting the passage of the radioactive isotope xenon 133 through the cortex. Each pixel, or picture element, represents a square centimeter of cortex. On the color scale for these figures, flow rates up to 20 percent below the mean are in gray, and flow rates 20 percent above the mean or more are the black areas surrounded by white.

These images show that reading silently and reading aloud involve different patterns of activity in the cortex. Reading silently (left) activates four areas: the visual association area, the frontal eye field, the supplementary motor area, and Broca's speech center in the lower part of the frontal lobe. Reading aloud (right) activates two more centers: the mouth area and the auditory cortex. The left hemisphere is shown in both cases, but similar results have been obtained from the right hemisphere. Adding the primary visual cortex, which is not reached by the radioactive isotope, the act of reading aloud calls for simultaneous activity in seven discrete cortical centers in each hemisphere.

Figure 2–3 Emission tomographic recordings of brain structure-function relationships. *Source:* Lassen, N. A., Ingvar, D. H., & Skinhøj, E. (1978). Brain function and blood flow. *Scientific American, 239,* 62–71. Used by permission of N. A. Lassen, M.D.

cialized than the other for certain functions, such as talking or artistic talent. This specialization process continues in predictable ways through adolescence (Lenneberg, 1967; Satz et al., 1975). The more specialized an area becomes, the less capable it will be of taking over for another area that becomes damaged.

We refer to the specialization differences between the two hemispheres as *brain asymmetry.* Although the same regions in both hemispheres will be activated during information processing, the left hemisphere appears to be more active approximately 65 percent of the time, and the right hemi-sphere is more active about 12 percent of the time (Hartlage & Telzrow, 1986). Brain asymmetry is an important area of study in learning disabilities because one's efficiency and style of learning are influenced by the extent to which one cerebral hemisphere has become superior to the other for given functions (for example, visual-perceptual versus language processing). Conversely, the style one prefers to use also is an important area of study because this influences which part of the brain will be the more active during a certain activity. For example, despite music appreciation being primarily a right hemisphere skill, the hemisphere that actually is used depends on how one decides to listen. The untrained person seems to listen to music holistically, thereby using more right hemisphere processing, which prefers holistic styles. But because skilled musicians analyze the detailed sequence of musical attributes, they activate more left hemisphere processing, which prefers analytic-sequential reasoning (Bever & Chiarello, 1974).

In addition to a normal degree of brain asymmetry, adequate attention processes are critical to learning efficiency. As children pay greater attention, their brain wave amplitudes increase, and the time needed for the brain to respond decreases (Klorman, 1991). Interestingly, it takes more neural energy to be alerted to something and then inhibit reaction than to actually respond. In fact, Soviet research has found that the function of some brain cells is to inhibit response—they tell us to do nothing (Ekel, 1974). Because the brain finds stopping oneself from attending to be harder than attending, this explains teachers' observations that many children with learning disabilities just can't help becoming sidetracked by distractions, even when they are trying so hard to attend only to their work. As we learn more about the typical student's brain development, we also gain a better understanding of the atypical patterns of individuals with learning disabilities.

Patterns of Poor Learners.   Neuropsychological measurement techniques show clear patterns of differences between good and poor learners. Some patterns are shared by the majority of children with learning disabilities, whereas other patterns differentiate one LD subgroup from another.

Features Common to Poor Learners.   Teachers often comment that students with learning disabilities are immature in far more than their academic achievement. They tend to be more distractible and impulsive than their peers, must try much harder to pay attention, and take a longer time to finish tasks. Neuropsychological measures are now offering clues as to why this is so. We find that the brain wave patterns of immature and less intelligent children approximate those of younger, normally developing children

(Buchsbaum & Wender, 1973; Matoušek & Petersén, 1973). Whereas the resting brain waves of normal learners are extremely symmetrical in shape and amplitude, there is a high incidence of brain wave asymmetry in the underachiever (John et al., 1985).

Among poor learners, the natural preference for one hemisphere to be just a bit more active than the other hemisphere during a certain activity is often poorly developed (Obrzut, 1991). Whereas good learners share a great deal of activity between the same locations in the two hemispheres, poor readers seem to overuse one hemisphere instead of adequately activating the weaker one. The weaker hemisphere is not as strongly specialized as it should be.

Brain waves that represent attention and active mental processing often are lower in amplitude in students who are learning disabled than in typical achievers (Ackerman et al., 1994; Klorman, 1991). Therefore, in order to process information, many children with learning disabilities must put far greater than normal effort into paying attention.

The nervous systems of individuals with learning disabilities also respond more slowly than is typical; therefore, they require a longer time to process information and perform even simple tasks such as starting and stopping the sweep of an oscilloscope (Chiarenza, 1990; Klorman, 1991; Richards et al., 1990). Fisher and Athey (1986), for example, found that although their children with reading disabilities could read alphabet letters and sentences, they were slower than their agemates, and even slower than younger children with similar reading skills. Manis's (1985) disabled readers were about 300 msec slower than nondisabled readers in initiating the pronunciation of words that they knew how to read. This slow information processing persists into adulthood, even if good progress has been made academically (Bruck, 1993a, b; Miles, 1986).

Many youngsters with learning disabilities also suffer some amount of motor incoordination because smooth, well-planned motor movements depend on the brain's ability to integrate all incoming and stored information with motor output. When there are deficiencies in any of these functions, motor actions become impaired (Calanchini & Trout, 1971).

Patterns Differentiating LD Subgroups. Sensitive to atypical brain asymmetries, computerized measures of brain wave patterns have been able to discriminate children with higher verbal IQs from those with higher performance IQs; higher- from lower-scoring children on visual-perceptual, reading, and spelling tests; children with and without attention problems; arithmetic from verbal underachievers; and the most from the least learning-impaired children (Dool, Stelmack, & Rourke, 1993; John et al., 1977; Prichep et al., 1983). Depending on the subjects studied, measurement methods, and experimental tasks, we are finding patterns of brain functioning unique to specific subgroups of poor achievers. Three major patterns seem to repeat themselves across studies: overuse of right hemisphere/inefficient left hemisphere strategies, overuse of left hemisphere/inefficient right hemisphere strategies, and more frontally located inefficiencies that interfere with the organization, planning, and modulation of attention, motor, and other behaviors.

Children who overuse right hemisphere strategies and apply left hemisphere strategies inefficiently are at risk for difficulty with many tasks that require language and analytic proficiency: reading, spelling, paying attention to and memorizing facts, mathematical calculations, writing essays, sequencing details and thoughts, and engaging in social conversation (Holmes, 1987). The highly specialized left hemisphere language proficiency of good learners is important to achievement in these areas. When mature readers read words projected to one or the other cerebral hemisphere, their left hemispheres generally read far more accurately than do their right hemispheres (MacKavey, Curcio, & Rosen, 1975; Marcel, Katz, & Smith, 1974; Miller & Turner, 1973). In contrast, poor readers often are less accurate than good readers in their left hemisphere language processing and ability to recognize letters or words (Bakker, Smink, & Reitsma, 1973; Leong, 1976; Marcel & Rajan, 1975; Mc-

Keever & Van Deventer, 1975; Witelson, 1976b). In some cases, poor readers seem to shift unusual amounts of language processing to their right hemispheres, so that their right hemispheres actually process language and read more efficiently than do their left hemispheres (Bakker, 1984; Bakker & Vinke, 1985; Obrzut, Hynd, & Boliek, 1986; Witelson & Rabinovitch, 1972; Zurif & Carson, 1970). Such a right hemisphere superiority seldom is found even among those good readers who process unusual amounts of language with their right hemispheres.

Unfortunately, the right hemisphere's style of attending to wholes (for example, word shapes) is incompatible with the phonetic analysis of words and the linguistic sequencing of sentence and story meaning that is required for reading progress. This analysis and sequencing is a left hemisphere function. Some investigators believe that, rather than actual underdevelopment of left hemisphere abilities, these types of left hemisphere inefficiencies may be due to a situation-specific maladaptive allocation of attentional resources in the left hemisphere (Kerschner & Stringer, 1991; Obrzut et al., 1986).

A second subgroup of poor readers overuses left hemisphere learning strategies and is inefficient in right hemisphere information processing (Flynn et al., 1992; Witelson, 1976b). To illustrate, Bakker and Licht (1986) describe how EEGs were recorded while children read words flashed to one and then the other hemisphere. It was found that good readers processed these words more actively with their right hemispheres at young ages but by the end of second grade switched to their left hemispheres. In contrast, some poor readers overused their right hemispheres at all ages; others consistently overused left hemisphere processing strategies. Unlike the former group, the left hemisphere overusers could not recognize words rapidly by sight because they concentrated too much on analyzing word parts. These types of students are at risk for difficulty with many tasks that require visual-perceptual skills and the ability to get the big picture: recognizing sight words, spelling irregular words that can't be sounded out, nonverbal problem solving and inferential reasoning, planning essays, being socially perceptive and aware of emotional cues, mathematical reasoning, fine- and gross-motor coordination, and employing well-organized note-taking and outlining skills (Harnadek & Rourke, 1994; Holmes, 1987).

A third major pattern that poor learners show is inefficiency in functions controlled by the more frontal brain regions: planning, organizing, articulating, demonstrating well-planned fine- and gross-motor coordination, focusing attention, coordinating the whole picture with its component elements, and modulating behavior. These functions can be inefficient even when higher-level learning processes appear intact (Mattis, French, & Rapin, 1975).

As our knowledge grows regarding the ways in which the brains of individuals with disabilities may be electroneurologically unique, so does our potential to use this information to direct the teaching strategies we use with students. Some preliminary evidence has emerged, for example, regarding the potential for altering abilities by direct stimulation of various brain regions. Zihl (1981) trained brain-damaged adults with visual-field defects to move their eyes toward lights flashed into the defective field. This practice restored not only a portion of the visual field but also related visual functions. On a more educational note, Bakker et al. (1981) found that children's reading ability improved much faster if they practiced reading through the visual half-field that projected to their weaker hemisphere. EEG changes after brief periods of practice were striking. These findings have been replicated for the most part, with the additional finding that teaching materials designed to stimulate left or right hemisphere processing also positively affected reading accuracy, speed, and EEG changes (Bakker, 1984; Bakker, Bouma, & Gardien, 1990; Bakker & Vinke, 1985). In other words, the nervous system can change its wiring in response to changes in the individual's behavioral patterns or in the sensory environment; neurons will wire together if we encourage them to fire together (Sporns, 1994). Evidence suggests that the more a brain region is stimulated through practice, the more responsive it becomes to future input (Elbert et al., 1995).

In line with this research, some have expressed the view that teaching could be more effective if it would go beyond remediation of the end product, the academic disability (for example, reading, math computation), and instead remediate the common cause of these academic disabilities. Frostig and Maslow (1979) explain it this way:

Any disturbed brain function that finds its expression in behavior change will probably cause other behavior changes as well. Treatment directed solely to isolated behaviors or disabilities will probably not carry over to other situations. On the other hand, sometimes seemingly unrelated behaviors have a common origin in the same brain function. For example, difficulties in verbal logical behavior, mathematical skills, and spatial orientation may be overcome if the perception of spatial relationship is improved.

A teaching rule is suggested by neuropsychological research: *do not neglect to train basic psychological functions*—that is, functions that are necessary for a wide variety of behaviors. (p. 543)

We have long known that stimulation facilitates brain development (Greenough, 1976). The question that neuropsychologists must now deal with is exactly what type of stimulation is best for whom. Because researchers are just now learning which factors to investigate and how to study them, many studies are still methodologically weak, and results contradictory. Therefore, a comprehensive picture of different information-processing patterns in students with learning disabilities is a long way off. Likewise, research on how to match intervention techniques with specific brain patterns is still in its infancy. Therefore, our school programs continue to be broad in scope, using students' stronger information-processing skills to facilitate new learning, while also trying to remediate the weaknesses that interfere with progress.

Structural Brain Differences

It seems that some children are born with atypical brains because of maldevelopment of the brain's tissue, neuronal circuitry, or brain organization in fetal life. This has been linked to small fetal strokes, drugs, hormones, diet, toxins, infections, maternal stress, genetic predisposition, and more.

Evidence suggests that some individuals with learning disabilities are born with abnormalities in the size of their left and right hemispheres. In 65 percent of normal infants and adults, the upper portion of the left temporal lobe, which is important to reading, is larger than the corresponding area in the right hemisphere. Eleven percent show larger right lobes, and 24 percent are equal in size. The left posterior brain regions also typically are larger on the left than on the right (Geschwind, 1985). These anatomical findings actually correlate with the cerebral hemisphere these individuals use to control speech and hand preference (Ratcliff et al., 1980). Given this knowledge, it is striking that, on CAT scan or magnetic resonance images of brain areas involved in reading (see Research Box 2–2), a greater than expected number of people with reading disabilities show either larger right than left brain regions or equality of both regions (Flowers, 1993; Galaburda et al., 1985; Hynd, Marshall, & Gonzalez, 1991).

Autopsies of eight brains of individuals with learning disabilities suggest that their brain deviations occurred in the fifth to seventh months of pregnancy (Galaburda et al., 1985; Humphreys, Kaufman, & Galaburda, 1990; Hynd et al., 1991). This is the time when cells migrate upward from the base of the skull and interconnect to form the gray matter. This migration seemed incomplete, in that islands of nerve cells were misplaced, never having reached the cortex. The anomalies were most apparent in the left hemisphere, especially its language areas (smaller than normal, abnormal arrangement of neurons and cell connections), though anomalies also appeared in the right hemisphere. The frontal and subcortical regions also were affected, and some scarring seems to have continued into the early postnatal period. Investigations using magnetic resonance imaging also find abnormal electrophysiological activation patterns in nonlanguage areas of the brain (Bigler, 1992; Semrud-Clikeman et al., 1991).

Unfortunately, there is evidence that lack of development or damage to parts of the cortex in intrauterine life may lead to lifelong diminution in the talent usually performed by that brain region (Geschwind, 1985). Brain plasticity in intrauterine life is not the same as when injury occurs to the intact brain after birth. In the latter case, undamaged areas give up some space allocated to their own functions in order to take over the lost ability. In the fetus, however, the corresponding healthy region in the opposite hemisphere develops a more extensive pattern of connections than is normal. This region also sends connections to regions to which the damaged area would normally have projected. In other words, rather than taking over functions of the underdeveloped or damaged area, the healthy brain region seems to overdevelop its own talents. Therefore, children born with structurally different brains may have less reserve ability to compensate for their deficits than children who are born with brains that are appropriately wired and only subsequently incur damage.

Current findings suggest that at least some individuals with learning disabilities have distorted left hemisphere development and overdeveloped right hemispheres. Basically, the left hemisphere isn't wired to do its job efficiently, and its efficiency is further distorted when rivaled by an overactive right hemisphere. While these findings are intriguing, we must remember that this type of research is in its infancy; contradictory findings remain the rule due to variations in subject selection and methodology (Filipek, 1995). Brains, like behavior, are heterogeneous, and we are likely to find myriad brain anomalies that can significantly influence learning.

Hereditary Factors

The evidence for genetic influences on learning disabilities is substantial. It seems that different brain structures, patterns of brain maturation, biochemical irregularities, or susceptibility to diseases that impair brain functioning may be genetically transmitted. This should come as no surprise, given that hereditary factors have been linked to so many other disorders that affect learning: for example, phenylketonuria, schizophrenia, major depression, neuroticism, panic disorder, antisocial personality, hyperactivity, and alcoholism (Hynd et al., 1991; Kinney, Woods, & Yorgelun-Todd, 1986; Pennington, 1986, 1995; Plomin, 1989; Plomin et al., 1997).

Many early investigators documented cases in which reading disorders seemed to be passed down from one generation to the next or were shared by siblings (Eustis, 1947; Fisher, 1905; Hinshelwood, 1907, 1911; Marshall & Ferguson, 1939; Stephenson, 1907; Thomas, 1905). Jimmy's story below describes one youngster whose reading disorder seems related to many other disabilities among his relatives.

Large-scale research projects support the observation that learning disorders often run in families, with an overall risk factor to offspring of approximately 30 to 50 percent when one parent has learning difficulties. In these studies, approximately 40 percent of siblings shared learning disorders in common (Pennington & Gilger, 1996; Smith, 1994). In Oliver, Cole, and Hollingsworth's (1991) study, for example, 60 percent of children with learning disabilities had a parent or sibling with learning problems; 21 to 25 percent had a grandparent, aunt, uncle, half-sibling, or cousin with learning problems. In Vogler, DeFries,

Jimmy

When Jimmy's mother called the clinic to refer her son for an evaluation, the first hint that Jimmy's learning difficulties may be hereditary in nature came over the phone. Jimmy's mother expressed her deep "flustration" in obtaining adequate services for her son's "dilekia." For a woman with a Ph.D., who was director of a counseling center, such mispronunciations were unexpected. Jimmy's mother's worst fears were that he had inherited "dilekia" from both sides of the family.

Jimmy's mother had two siblings, neither of whom had learned to read until adolescence. One now writes books, but remains a terrible speller. One child of the other sibling has been identified as learning disabled, and her younger child, a preschooler, is receiving speech and language therapy.

Jimmy's father has a master's degree in social work, a Ph.D. in philosophy, and now spends all his time back in law school. He is never satisfied with his accomplishments and keeps trying to prove his competence in new ways. Jimmy's father was very late in learning to read and still reads, in his words, "a word an hour." What he reads he remembers, however, and he is an excellent student. His professors have always allowed him to use a spellchecker on exams.

Jimmy's father comes from a family of five children, of which every one has a reading disability. All but one sibling, who suffers from severe depression, have become vocationally successful. One of his brothers stutters, and a sister gets stuck on very simple words when speaking. Her conversations are punctuated by referring to objects as "thing" and elaborating when recounting an event by adding "or some such thing." Another brother is described as extremely disorganized; he gets lost in supermarkets and shopping malls and panics at the idea of traveling through a strange city.

Jimmy's mother had reason to believe that her son may not have been lucky enough to escape his genetic history. Take a look at his spelling on page 153 and judge for yourself the outcome of his assessment.

and Decker's (1985) study, the risk to sons of a parent with reading disabilities was 34 to 39 percent, a five- to sevenfold increase over that found in sons of parents without reading disabilities; the risk to daughters was 17 to 18 percent, a ten- to twelvefold increase over that found in daughters of parents without reading disabilities.

A major objection to studies on the heritability of learning disorders is that concordance of learning disorders could be due to some unique environment that the individuals have shared. Just think how many times you have been told that you look, behave, or achieve just like your parents, sister, or brother. Are these characteristics genetically endowed? How many could be due to your family's influence on you to dress, act, or value achievement just as they do? If you have an inherited disability, are you doomed to failure, or can you learn to overcome it?

One way to explore this heredity-environment question is to control for genetic and environmental influences by contrasting twins with siblings and parents. These studies have examined the heritability of learning disorders, intelligence, and handedness.

Heritability of Learning Disabilities

Studies of genetic versus environmental contributors to learning disorders compare identical twins with fraternal twins, siblings, and parents. Identical twins come from the same ovum and share the same genetic material. Fraternal twins share no more genetic material than do sibling pairs, but they are more likely to share environmental influences. These studies have found a genetic link to psychological and physiological characteristics that can influence learning, such as hyperactivity, autonomic responses underlying emotionality, and personality type (Goldsmith & Gottesman, 1981; Jost & Sontag, 1944; Morrison & Stewart, 1973; Nichols & Chen, 1981; Wilson & Matheny, 1986). They also have revealed a powerful genetic role in learning disabilities. Studies of normal readers reveal remarkable consistency, with fraternal twins' reading levels being very similar 20 to 50 percent of the time and the reading

achievement of one identical twin predicting that of another about 75 to 85 percent of the time (Harris, 1986). In the largest study of this type conducted with children with learning disorders, the Colorado Reading Project, the likelihood of identical twins both having learning disorders was found to be much greater (71 percent) than that for fraternal twins (49 percent) (DeFries & Gillis, 1991). Overall, it appears as though roughly 45 percent of the traits contributing to reading are inherited, with spelling (60 percent) and phonemic word analysis skills (75 percent) having higher heritabilities than do reading disabilities that are related to poor visual recall of letter sequences in words (about 30 percent) (Pennington & Gilger, 1996; Rack & Olson, 1993). In other words, the phonological skills necessary for reading are inherited to a far greater extent than are the skills necessary for recognizing word and letter patterns by sight (Rack & Olson, 1993).

Some of the most fascinating data on the heredity-environment question come from comparing the brain wave patterns of twins and siblings. Several studies of identical twin pairs report that the EEGs of one twin resemble those of the other as closely as the records of the same person on successive tests (Davis & Davis, 1936, p. 1222; Lennox, Gibbs, & Gibbs, 1945; Lykken et al., 1992; Matoušek & Petersén, 1973). The EEG records of fraternal twins bear far less relation to one another. Conners (1970) reported the same abnormal flattening of EEG waves in a father and his four children. All had reading problems. The mother had no learning problems and no EEG abnormality.

Not surprisingly, studies of precise types of reading disabilities show some consistency among siblings (Decker & DeFries, 1981). Even spelling patterns, such as whether misspellings are phonetic or nonphonetic (sound or don't sound like the target word), are remarkably similar among family members (Finucci, 1978; Omenn & Weber, 1978).

A new research focus in learning disabilities, *linkage analysis,* has attempted to locate a gene for learning disabilities by determining if a learning problem coexists with some other trait whose genetic origin is already known. Because genes that lie close together on the same chromosome tend to be inherited as a unit (rather than splitting), individuals with learning disabilities who share a known genetic marker (for example, blood or enzyme type) may have the gene for their learning disability lying on the same chromosome as that marker. With this type of analysis, the learning problems of some families have been linked to variations on chromosomes 6 and 15 (Pennington & Gilger, 1996). Given the many types of learning disorders, studies are concluding that there are probably many genetic modes of LD inheritance (Childs & Finucci, 1983; Pennington et al., 1991).

Despite evidence for a genetic influence on learning and behavior, we must not forget that what has been laid down by the genes can be strongly modified by the environment. This is evident in the simple fact that, among genetically identical twins, it sometimes happens that one twin has a learning disability, but the other twin is a good student. LaBuda and DeFries (1988a) point out that, despite the strong genetic contribution to reading deficits, approximately 60 percent of twins' reading achievement nevertheless is attributable to shared environmental influences, environmental factors unique to the individual, or to unknown factors. Olson and his colleagues (1989) report similar findings. In other words, the environment is a more powerful influence than the genes. No body of literature attests more strongly to the power of environmental influences than does the investigation of genetic versus environmental contributions to intelligence.

Heritability of Intelligence

Intelligence plays a significant role in academic achievement and LD identification. It is natural to expect children to function at intellectual levels commensurate with that of their parents and the stimulation afforded by their upbringing. Studies find that children's learning potential is genetically predetermined but that the achievement level attained is extremely modifiable through positive environmental events (Haywood & Switzky, 1986; Plomin et al., 1997).

Investigations find that IQ correlations increase in direct proportion to the increase in genetic relationship and the sharing of environmental influences. Therefore, fraternal twins' IQs are more highly correlated than siblings' IQs, even though both share the same genetic endowment. Likewise, identical twins who are reared together have higher IQ correlations than those reared apart, which still are similar 68 to 78 percent of the time (McGue et al., 1993).

Despite the high correlation between genetic endowment and IQ, the actual level to which intelligence can be developed is dependent on the environment. Marjorie Honzik's (1957) work found that, whether children were reared by their biological parents or by adoptive parents, their IQs correlated significantly with their biological mothers' IQs and the educational levels of their biological mothers and fathers. No IQ relationship existed between the adopted children and their foster parents. Yet, the adopted children's average IQ was 106, whereas their biological mothers' average IQ was only 86. Similarly, Scarr, Weinberg, and Waldman (1993) found that for nearly 100 black and interracial children adopted as infants by white, advantaged families, IQs at average ages of seven and seventeen had risen to average ranges, despite continuing to correlate significantly with the IQ level expected for their biological families. Their IQ scores did not reach those of their adoptive siblings. Likewise, in a sample of French adopted children, the average IQ increase was 14 points above that of the adopted children's biological siblings, who continued to live with their natural parents (Schiff et al., 1982).

Another classic example of the impact of environment on intelligence is Skeels and Skodak's (1966) follow-up of orphans who were retarded and who, before they were two and a half years old, had been placed in the care of adult women institutionalized due to mental retardation. These children were returned to the orphanage six months to four years later. Their average IQ on return was 92. The IQ of the group that had remained in the orphanage had decreased steadily to 51. Twenty-one years later, the average experimental child had graduated from high school, and one third had gone on to college. In contrast, half of the control group was unemployed; of the remainder, most worked as unskilled laborers.

Clearly, even if genetic endowment does significantly correlate with intellectual abilities, these abilities can be greatly altered through parenting and teaching. Heredity seems to establish an upper limit to intelligence, and by implication learning, but whether one reaches this limit is up to the environment.

Inherited Handedness

Handedness is often an inherited trait. Eight to 12 percent of the population is left-handed, with somewhat higher rates among males (Annett, 1985).

Although hand preference already is established at birth, it only becomes obvious later in the preschool years (Fennell, Satz, & Morris, 1983; Gesell, 1939). Whereas right-handers use their right hands for most activities, left-handers usually show some degree of ambidexterity and smaller discrepancies between right- and left-hand abilities. This is presumably because society has encouraged left-handers to practice right-handed skills. This same encouragement only makes right-handers even stronger in right-versus-left dexterity (Del Dotto & Rourke, 1985).

Left-handers have been deprecated throughout the centuries, with *left* being a synonym for bad or odd qualities (*sinister* in Latin, *gauche* in French). These deprecations are not deserved. Left-handedness causes neither learning difficulties nor odd behavior. These difficulties occur only when a brain dysfunction has caused both the poor performance and the left-handedness. Left-handers are interesting to study because the way their brains distribute functions, especially language, can be unique.

Handedness and Brain Dysfunction. Studies of individuals whose left-handedness is definitely *familial* (genetic) in origin find that they have no greater incidence of learning disorders than do right-handers (Hardyck & Petrinovich, 1977). Studies also find no differences in intelligence,

academic achievement, or perceptual skills between familial left-handers and right-handers (Newcombe & Ratcliffe, 1973; Nichols & Chen, 1981; Richardson & Firlej, 1979). These data seemingly contradict studies reporting two to ten times greater prevalence of learning disorders among left-handers than right-handers (Geschwind, 1986; Harris, 1957; Wall, 1945, 1946, in Critchley, 1970).

It is hypothesized that in those studies reporting a higher incidence of learning disorders among left-handers, many of the left-handed individuals with disabilities may not have been genetically slated to be left-handed. Rather, an injury, structural defect, or severe delay in maturation of their left hemispheres forced them to prefer their right hemispheres to direct fine-motor activities. This resulted in left-handedness. This is a common finding among children with cerebral palsy, seizure disorders, and mental retardation (Kinsbourne & Caplan, 1979). Geschwind and Behan (1982) suggest that, in males, prenatal suppression of the immune system by testosterone may retard or disrupt left hemisphere development so that the person develops learning disabilities and, due to the stronger right hemisphere, becomes left-handed. Most of these individuals would have been right-handed had it not been for the underlying condition that caused both the switch in handedness and the learning disability (Satz, Yanowitz, & Willmore, 1983). Therefore, it is believed that left-handedness does not cause learning problems (Hicks & Kinsbourne, 1978a). When left-handedness and learning disorders do coexist, oftentimes both may be symptoms of a common underlying brain dysfunction.

Handedness and Language Dominance. In the past, the preferred hand mistakenly was thought to indicate which hemisphere was dominant (more specialized) for language. Because language abilities are highly related to reading and higher-level reasoning, some clinicians had hoped to increase language and learning efficiency by training right- or left-sided body movements (Delacato, 1966). The flaw in this reasoning, however, is that language and hand dominance do not always lie in the same hemisphere. Neuropsychological assessment techniques reveal that, whereas over 95 percent of right-handers have speech located in their left hemispheres, the location of speech in the left-hander is far less predictable: about 60 percent have speech located in the left hemisphere, 20 percent in the right hemisphere, and another 20 percent in both hemispheres (Segalowitz & Bryden, 1983).

The advantages or disadvantages facing the familial left-hander who has language skills located in either or both hemispheres have been debated. Many familial left-handers who have language represented in both hemispheres recover function following brain injury much more rapidly than do individuals who have language in only one hemisphere (Luria, 1970). Hardyck and Petrinovich (1977) conclude, therefore, that the familial left-hander's two heads might in fact be better than the right-hander's one! Kinsbourne (1987), however, suggests that because of their differently distributed skills, many left-handers probably activate their cerebral hemispheres less asymmetrically than do right-handers. Therefore, one or another mental ability may not be sufficiently activated for information processing to be accurate and efficient. Others suggest that the left-handers' unique, at times imbalanced and crowded, cerebral organization actually may increase the risk of learning disorders (Denckla, 1979; Witelson, 1976a, b).

Biochemical Irregularities, Attention Deficit Disorder, and Hyperactivity

Several biochemical irregularities may lead to learning disorders in youngsters who otherwise may have had good potential to learn. Some of these imbalances can cause severe brain injury. Others create a hyperactive or hypoactive state that makes it difficult for the student to focus and sustain attention on learning tasks. Although the activity level itself is not an important issue, the inattention it represents is critical. If a child can't attend to pertinent information, the ability to process that information obviously will be hampered. This, of course, may result in learning disabilities.

Most investigators agree that the incidence of hyperactivity among children is approximately 3 to 5 percent (Hynd et al., 1991). Although 5 to 10 times as many boys as girls have been reported to be hyperactive, recent evidence suggests equal frequency among girls. Girls, however, are less likely to be noticed because their behavior is far less active and aggressive. Among hyperactive youngsters, about 20 to 40 percent have been estimated to be learning disabled (Barkley, DuPaul, & McMurray, 1990; Lambert & Sandoval, 1980). Among only students with learning disabilities, approximately 15 to 20 percent are hyperactive (Bruck & Hébert, 1982; Nichols & Chen, 1981; Porter & Rourke, 1985; Silver, 1987).

Generally, hyperactive children are more active than their peers in situations that require them to sustain attention and sit still, such as the classroom. Their activity levels may be very normal, however, in settings that do not require sustained attention, such as the lunchroom, recess, or physical education class (Porrino et al., 1983). Even when their activity level does not gain notice, these children nevertheless tend to be distinguishable from their nonhyperactive peers in other ways, such as overtalkativeness or attention shifts (Zentall, 1985). For example, when activity level is measured in the classroom over an entire week, many hyperactive children will get up and down no more often than other children, but they will do so at the wrong times, as their attention waxes and wanes (McNew, 1984). These students' inappropriate activity, restlessness, impulsivity, distractibility, and poor concentration do not go unnoticed by parents and teachers. Teachers often comment that the only consistent thing about these children is their inconsistency. Because attention deficits appear to be at the root of their difficulties, these children have been said to suffer from *attention deficit hyperactivity disorder* (ADHD) (American Psychiatric Association, 1994).

At least eleven different physiological hypotheses have been put forth to account for hyperactivity (Zametkin & Rapoport, 1986). The one addressed in this section is biochemical irregularity: extremely short attention span, distractibility, and poor impulse control, which become evident early in life and persist from year to year.

These in turn can lead to hyperactive behavior: restless, overactive, inappropriate body movements. Causes of hyperactivity besides biochemical irregularity include genetic predisposition, brain injury, maternal smoking during pregnancy, lead poisoning, chromosomal anomalies, anxiety, emotional disturbance, stress, distractibility when bored, and temperament (Denckla & Heilman, 1979; Hynd et al. 1991; Plomin et al., 1997; Pribram & McGuinness, 1987).

Parents report that their hyperactive children can't sit still, are disobedient and moody, can't complete what they begin, jump from one activity to another, and can't play cooperatively for long periods of time. They are "unleashed tornadoes" (O'Malley & Eisenberg, 1973, p. 95) because they run much of the time, seem not to tire, and injure themselves and objects around them. In class these children may disturb others, not stay on a task for any length of time, not respond to directions, become easily frustrated, get distracted when working in a group, impulsively raise their hands, or rush into activities without thinking. Immaturity, poor self-esteem, and conduct problems such as not following class rules, impulsive hitting, disrupting others, and having temper tantrums when frustrated are common (Gadow, 1986).

Darrell's story (page 78) vividly describes how hyperactivity can interfere with school success. It also highlights how there is often more than inattention behind the extreme impulsivity, social difficulties, and poor learning of some children with learning disabilities (Denckla & Heilman, 1979). When the teacher demands work on a structured task, Darrell cannot modulate his attention; it wanders to other things. He impulsively responds to these attention getters, and he is consequently more active and restless than his classmates. Clearly, opportunities for learning the assigned material are lost. It is important to recognize that Darrell's mind does not go blank and stop thinking when his attention drifts. Rather, he is learning many other things, most of which are irrelevant to the teacher's intentions (Kinsbourne & Caplan, 1979).

Whereas the attention of hyperactive children is underfocused, *hypoactive children's* attention is overfocused. They ponder too long, are overly attentive to details, and cannot arrive at decisions rapidly. They are lethargic, sluggish, and need more sleep. Often these youngsters are unmotivated and ask few questions; they command very little attention and are easy to overlook in the classroom because they are not disruptive. Over time, however, the slow completion of assignments and difficulty answering rapidly does get noticed. In the National Collaborative Perinatal Project's study of nearly 30,000 seven-year-old children, 12 percent of the children with learning disabilities were diagnosed as hypoactive (Nichols & Chen, 1981). We shall discuss two types of biochemical irregularities that have been linked to learning disorders and hyperactive/hypoactive behavior: abnormal neurochemical transmissions and endocrine disorders. There has been no research supporting a link between a third type of biochemical irregularity, vitamin deficiencies, and learning disabilities.

Abnormal Neurochemical Transmissions

Biochemical imbalances in the brain cannot be measured directly. Therefore, a neurochemical transmission problem has been inferred from reduced numbers of neurotransmitter metabolites in the urine and blood, from differences in cerebrospinal fluid, or from observation of how drugs known to alter brain chemistry improve attention, learning, and behavior (Barkley, 1991).

Many hyperactive youngsters focus attention better and refrain from mentally, physically, or verbally responding to diversions when given stimulant medication. These stimulants seem to energize their brains' inhibitory mechanisms so that distractions are screened out. The stimulants also heighten the sensitivity of specific brain systems to incoming stimuli. Although stimulants facilitate these students' attention span, motor performance, behavior management, productivity, accuracy, and speed on classroom work, drugs at times have negative side effects and do not improve long-term social adjustment or academic achievement.

In contrast to hyperactive youngsters, many hypoactive individuals seem to suffer from overactive inhibitory mechanisms. Sedatives quiet these mechanisms and allow more stimuli to come to their attention.

Darrell

At the time of evaluation, Darrell was 8 years and 7 months of age. He started school in the fall of 1966 at the age of 6 years and 2 months. His parents saw him as a bright, likeable little boy—not perfect, of course, for he seemed on the immature side. He could not dress himself and his speech was somewhat unclear. His father worried a bit about his lack of coordination; his mother was anxious that the other children might not let him play with them.

In his second year of school, his teacher referred him to the school's Special Services Department for psychological testing "to determine why he was not achieving at the level of average intelligence indicated by a group test." After the evaluation the parents were told Darrell's intellectual functioning was above average, but that he was below average on certain tasks requiring visual perception and visual-motor integration. Testing also revealed he was hyperactive and could not concentrate well. . . .

A year later, in February, 1969, his parents had become quite concerned about him. His rate of academic progress was slower than in the previous two years. They had had many conferences at school, always hearing that Darrell was "immature, fidgety, distractible, and unable to concentrate." The teacher said he required constant personal attention and help. They had tried seating him at the back of the room, at the front, and immediately beside the teacher, but nothing seemed to help. The parents were confused and discouraged. . . .

The following is a direct quote from the father, a nice-looking, personable, 30-year-old college graduate: "I'm concerned mainly about two things: his lack of coordination and his inability to concentrate on anything for over sixty seconds. He wants to compete and to excel in sports—he wants to so badly!—but he can't. He gets his feet mixed up and can't even kick a football. He is uncoordinated. . . .

The mother has a warm, ready smile. She is 29 years old and has a high school education. She expresses in a healthy way her mixed feelings about her son. There was the hint of tears as she said, "It upsets me when he comes home and says the kids don't want to play with him because he's not as good as they are." Later, her irritation came through as she fumed, "He can never find anything to occupy him for longer than a few minutes. He nags me for something else to do, somewhere to go, someone to see. My patience wears out. Sometimes I feel like knocking him down."

She told us about a visit to his classroom this year. It was depressing for her. Darrell was up and down, distracting other children from their work and constantly wiggling. He got very little work done; he couldn't copy things from the board. She felt like shaking him and wondered how the teacher could abide him.

Source: Clements, S. D., Davis, J. S., Edgington, R., Goolsby, C. M., & Peters, J. E. (1971). Two cases of learning disabilities. In L. Tarnopol (Ed.) *Learning disorders in children: Diagnosis, medication, education.* Boston: Little, Brown. © 1971 by Little, Brown and Company. Reprinted by permission.

Underactive Inhibitory Mechanisms and Attention Deficit Hyperactivity Disorder. Most researchers concur that the hyperactive individual's problem is one of underarousal rather than overarousal. The hyperactive individual does not appear to show the normal increase in blood flow or glucose utilization in specific brain regions that should be activated through speech, reading, and other activities (Lou, Henriksen, & Bruhn, 1984; Zametkin et al., 1990). Similar under-arousal appears to exist in the diminished supply of chemicals needed to inhibit neural transmissions: the neurons containing these chemicals may have been destroyed, or the synapses (where nerve endings come together) may not be sensitive enough to these chemical inhibitors (Kinsbourne & Caplan, 1979; Wender, 1976). Consequently, these students cannot inhibit attending. They respond to everything.

Stimulants such as dextroamphetamine (Dexadrine), methylphenidate (Ritalin), pemoline (Cylert), and Benedryl activate the chemicals that inhibit neurotransmissions. Ninety percent of children receiving medication for hyperactivity take Ritalin (DuPaul, Barkley, & McMurray, 1991). When taking stimulants, both normal and hyperactive people become more able to screen out distracting and irrelevant stimuli (Rapoport et al., 1980; Shetty, 1971). The ability to concentrate is generally enhanced, and motor restlessness is reduced. With greater ability to attend to relevant information, the ability to memorize is enhanced for both normal and hyperactive individuals (Weingartner et al., 1980).

Many excellently controlled, double-blind, cross-over studies (see Research Box 2–3) support this underarousal theory. Soviet laboratories have shown that the cerebral process involved in inhibiting action is much more complex, delicate, vulnerable, and difficult than the process involved in paying attention (Ekel, 1974). Stimulants seem to increase the activity of these inhibitory mechanisms. They also make specific brain systems more sensitive, thereby augmenting the impact of incoming stimuli on sensory and attending systems (Barkley, 1977).

Stimulant Medication and Attention Deficit Hyperactivity Disorder. Numerous surveys have shown that 1 to 2 percent of all elementary-age school children receive stimulant medication for hyperactivity (Gadow, 1986). Anywhere from 70 to 80 percent of these children improve to varying degrees (DuPaul et al., 1991). On rating scales, parents and teachers indicate large reductions in restlessness, crying, temper outbursts, dis-

tractibility, excitability, frustration, pouting, and other hyperactive symptoms when the children are taking medication. Ratings by parents and teachers often disagree, however, because these scales are subject to the bias of adult perceptions. In addition, the ratings do not always agree with objective psychological and physical measures of attention (Barkley, 1977). These objective measures of drug effects on attention span, activity level, motor performance, and productivity/accuracy in daily classwork have been positive. However, drugs often are accompanied by negative side effects, and optimum dosage is difficult to determine. Despite short-term improvements, the impact of drugs on standardized achievement measures and long-term adjustment has been modest at best. Clearly, learning disabilities are multifaceted, and biochemical irregularities represent only one piece of the puzzle.

Attention Span. Many physiological (brain wave amplitude/frequency and blood flow measures that reflect increased attention, inhibition, and strategy shifts) and behavioral (increased reaction time and hit rate on vigilance tasks, reduced impulsivity and greater reflectivity on tasks) measures show that the drug responder's attention does increase when taking stimulant medication (Barkley, 1977; Lou, Henriksen, & Bruhn, 1984; Keith & Engineer, 1991; Klorman, 1991; Rapport et al., 1994). Douglas (1972) described these children's enhanced impulse control, concentration, and planning as due to gains in ability to "stop, look, and listen." Intelligence test scores also tend to increase by about 15 percentile points because better attention enables these students to use their problem-solving capabilities and past knowledge to their best advantage (Barkley, 1977; Kavale, 1982a). These children's reaction to medication is not unusual; even children and adults who are not hyperactive improve attention and concentration when taking stimulants (McNew, 1984; Rapoport et al., 1980).

Activity Level. In structured classroom or laboratory situations that demand sitting still and paying attention, children's in-seat wiggling and arm/foot movements do decrease when taking

RESEARCH BOX 2–3
Stimulant Medication Research Methods

Studies measuring the effects of stimulant medication on behavior are quite complex to design because they must control for the *placebo effect*, changes in behavior merely because people think they are on medication. In addition, these studies must not let the group data mask the children's individual responses to medication. Therefore, the *double-blind, cross-over design* has been developed.

To control for placebo effects, in *double-blind* methods neither the experimenter nor the subjects know who is on drugs and who is on placebos. The *placebo* is a fake pill given to control subjects who believe they are receiving stimulants. In eight studies that used placebos, there was a 39 percent improvement rate (range = 8–67%) in hyperactivity within the placebo groups, presumably due to positive expectations fostered by taking medication (Barkley, 1977). Therefore, on average, 39 percent of the improvement in the drug groups can be attributed to positive expectancies alone. Placebo effects also can be negative. For example, Conners (1975) found that the mothers of children receiving placebos reported just as many side effects of the "drug" as did mothers of children taking Ritalin. Unfortunately, even double-blind studies aren't perfect, however; from the side effects alone, individuals may be able to guess who is on drugs (Sprague & Sleator, 1973).

Because of the individual variability in drug responses, the best studies use each child as his or her own control. This method is called a *cross-over* design because children receive the drug treatment followed by placebo, or vice versa. Because drug effects may show up if both instruction and posttesting occur when the child is receiving drugs (Swanson & Kinsbourne, 1976), some studies make sure children take (or don't take) drugs at both pre- and posttesting times. In addition, data on drug responders are separated from data on nonresponders to clarify differential drug effects for different people. These complex research designs help to determine exactly for whom, in which situations, and on which criteria stimulants may be helpful.

medication (Barkley, 1977; Kavale, 1982a). In free-play situations, however, these children's activity level is only sometimes reduced, depending on the situation and measure used (Barkley, 1977). It seems that activity level consistently decreases only when attention is engaged on a task. During these times, medication helps to channel the child's attention and activity so that there is less flitting from one thing to another (Gadow, 1986). This occurs most often in highly structured classroom situations.

Motor Performance. Children receiving stimulant medication show remarkable improvement on a number of fine- and gross-motor coordination tasks. Figure 2–4 illustrates the dramatic handwriting gains sometimes seen in form, spacing, size, and consistency of letter formation. Reaction time also has been enhanced, as has speed of copying a code and motor performance on tasks such as moving a stylus through a maze without touching the sides, or balancing on a tilted, rotating board (Dykman & Ackerman, 1991; Gadow, 1986; Klor-

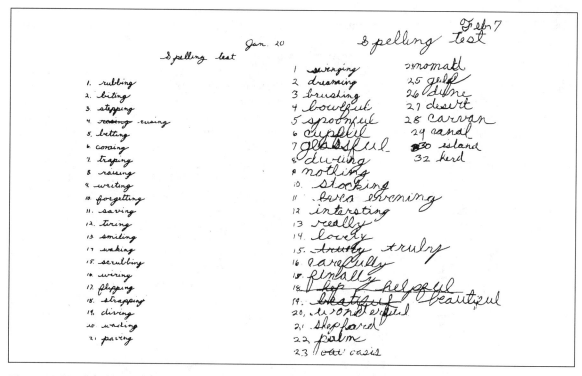

Figure 2–4 Effects of Ritalin on handwriting. When taking the spelling test dated January 20, this fourth-grade girl was receiving Ritalin. While she was receiving placebo on February 7, her writing skills rapidly deteriorated after the third word. *Source:* Gadow, K. D. (1986). *Children on medication: Vol. 1.: Hyperactivity, learning disabilities, and mental retardation.* San Diego: College-Hill Press, p. 118. Reprinted by permission of PRO-ED, Inc.

man, 1991). It appears that Ritalin has a direct effect on the metabolic and neural mechanisms that speed and control motor responses after the brain has evaluated information, searched one's memory, and decided on a course of action (Hynd et al., 1991; Klorman, 1991).

Academic Achievement. Studies that have looked at the effect of stimulants on academic achievement are difficult to interpret because they have been conducted with diverse types of subjects (some, for example, had no learning difficulties), intervention typically lasted only brief periods of time, and many outcome measures were not designed to be sensitive to short-term academic gains. Therefore, when looking at any one study, gains in academic achievement after a period of drug intervention tend not to be dramatic (Barkley, 1977; Carlson & Bunner, 1993; Gadow, 1983a, b). Nevertheless, when data from large numbers of studies are pooled, it appears that students taking stimulants do show about a 15 percentile point gain on standardized reading and spelling tests, though not in mathematics (Kavale, 1982a).

Several laboratory studies have shown that short-term enhancement of thinking and memory does occur when either typical students or those with learning difficulties take stimulants. These studies report improved persistence on frustrating tasks and better short-term memory for word pairs, spelling of nonsense-words, and tasks such as memorizing which animal lives in a particular zoo (Milich, 1994; Rapport et al., 1985; Stephens, Pelham, & Skinner, 1984; Swanson et al., 1978; Weingartner et al., 1980; Whalen & Henker, 1976).

In the classroom, investigations report as much as 25 to 40 percent improvements in accuracy, quantity, and speed of completing daily reading, spelling, and math assignments (Douglas et al., 1986; Pelham et al., 1985; Rapport et al., 1985, 1986, 1994). Significant improvements in quiz and test grades also have been reported (Carlson & Bunner, 1993). These academic gains presumably are due to enhanced attention, motivation, cooperation, and self-regulatory processes (Henker & Whalen, 1989). Nevertheless, long-term academic gains are not remarkable (Carlson & Bunner, 1993). Gadow (1986) concludes that "it is plausible that a dramatic improvement in productivity and proficiency may even be more clinically meaningful than a modest increase in standardized achievement test performance" (p. 130).

Behavior and Long-Term Adjustment. Fortunately, hyperactive children do become more compliant and manageable with age (Barkley et al., 1984; Hechtman, 1985). Adolescents no longer run away from their mothers in a supermarket, tear everything off the shelves, or break grandma's best china. Nevertheless, they remain fidgety, restless, impulsive, and often speak out or do something reckless without thinking. Studying may continue to be difficult for more than a few minutes at a time (Gadow, 1986). In general, it seems that now their minds, rather than their bodies, are doing the wandering (Kinsbourne, 1973a). Denckla and Heilman (1979) quote one adolescent as complaining, "My mind is like a television set on which someone is always switching the channels" (p. 576).

A number of studies report that stimulants can suppress demanding, antisocial, aggressive, disruptive, and noncompliant behaviors, so that the home and classroom environments become more manageable, less negative, and less control-

ling (constantly supervising and directing the child) (Dykman & Ackerman, 1991; Gadow, 1986; Rapport et al., 1994). Teacher behavior toward hyperactive children receiving stimulants has been shown to be less negative than when these children receive placebos: less guidance is necessary; fewer admonitions or commands are given; there is less calling out of the child's name; and the teacher has a quieter, less emotionally intense, and slower-paced demeanor (Whalen, Henker, & Dotemoto, 1980). Peer acceptance also is improved (DuPaul et al., 1991). Despite this, when compared with their peers, children who have been taking stimulants for over two years usually still are judged to be more active, inattentive, impulsive, rebellious, failing in school, distractible, aggressive, and difficult to discipline (Barkley, 1977). They have few friends, engage in more antisocial behavior, lack ambition, have poor self-concepts, are sad, and often find themselves in trouble with the law (Hechtman, 1985; Henker & Whalen, 1989; Pelham & Bender, 1982).

No studies have shown peer relations or emotional adjustment to be any better for youngsters who have been on medication several years than for those who had never been on stimulants. When these children's medication is discontinued, seldom are any treatment gains maintained (Douglas, 1975; Gadow, 1986). It seems that stimulant medication may set the stage for more positive social relations because aversive behaviors have diminished, yet more than medication is needed to generate longlasting change in socially appropriate behavior and friendships.

Henker and Whalen (1989) point out that it is hard to catch up for all the lost learning time or to erase the debilitating effects of past experience on motivation and self-concept. It is also hard to turn around the negative expectancies held by others, especially peers. It is no wonder that these youngsters continue to have difficulty negotiating their social worlds, especially when it comes to friendship and intimacy.

Many studies have found that behavior problems may be ameliorated and school productivity, accuracy, and learning enhanced more readily if hyperactive children are given medication than if behavior modification alone is implemented. In some cases, behavior management techniques have been more effective or just as effective as stimulant drug therapy. In a number of studies a combination of stimulant therapy and behavioral intervention have proved superior to either alone. Unfortunately, the behavioral and academic achievement/productivity patterns of hyperactive children are particularly difficult to modify, and for behavior gains to last intensive behavior modification, cognitive self-control, strategy training, social skill training, and attributional training, together with effective instruction, are essential. Behavior management and academic interventions (e.g., peer tutoring) appear to be more effective than the problem-solving strategy approaches with respect to improving attention and behavior; no one method, however, has proved clearly superior when it comes to enhancing academic achievement (DuPaul & Eckert, 1997; Gadow, 1986; Henker & Whalen, 1989; Pelham, 1993; Pelham et al., 1993; Reid & Borkowski, 1987). In other words, stimulants may create greater readiness to adapt socially, but the environment needs to be appropriately structured to allow this change to occur, and these children need to be systematically taught alternatives for coping with problematic situations.

Side Effects and Dosage. Not all hyperactive children respond positively to medication. Twenty to 30 percent may exhibit no response or even get worse (DuPaul et al., 1991). Therefore, careful teacher and parent observation, pretreatment versus treatment comparisons of different dosage levels, and controlled tests of learning and behavioral progress are essential to determine the drug's efficacy.

The most frequently noted side effects of stimulant medication are insomnia and decreased appetite. The next most frequent are weight loss, irritability, lethargy, and abdominal pains. Also observed are abnormal inactivity, headaches, drowsiness, sadness, dizziness, nausea, weepiness, euphoria, nightmares, tremor, dry mouth, pallor, apathy, serious facial expression, dark hollows under the eyes, fearfulness, constipation, depression, dazed appearance, nervous tics, hallucinations, increased talkativeness, and anxiety (Barkley,

1977; Gadow, 1986). It has been noted that individuals prone to tic disorders such as Tourette's syndrome are at risk for having the illness induced by stimulants (DuPaul et al., 1991).

With moderate doses of Ritalin, some growth suppression occurs during the first year of treatment, but rebound in growth does occur (DuPaul et al., 1991). Likewise, in children taking Dexadrine or high doses of Ritalin, height and weight may be suppressed very slightly; with time, maturation, and termination of drug treatment, however, height and weight expectations seem to be attained. To deal with the temporary growth delays, some experts advocate "drug holidays" during school vacations, in order to allow for growth rebound. Others, however, argue that growth will catch up anyhow, and it is far more important for the child to be thinking and behaving more intelligently, even on vacations. After all, learning does not occur in the classroom alone.

Children generally develop tolerance for many side effects of stimulants within a few weeks. At times tolerance also develops toward the medication, so that slight dosage increases are required to maintain therapeutic responses (Gadow, 1986).

The drug dosage at which optimal thinking will occur is different for different children. Many children's accuracy and productivity on school tasks, and ability to memorize, appear to be enhanced best at drug levels that are lower than the dosage needed to maximally reduce hyperactivity, dosages that may remain the same despite increases in height and weight (Gadow, 1986; McNew, 1984; Rapport et al., 1994; Swanson et al., 1991). When the child's behavior is completely calmed by medication, the child may become so overfocused that learning and productivity in fact deteriorate to a level equal to or below that before taking stimulants. This is particularly apparent on more complex tasks. Therefore, it is essential to begin with a small dose and gradually increase dosage until optimal learning, rather than optimal behavior, is achieved.

Dosage is a major concern because attention, thinking, and behavior see-saw as short-acting drugs reach their peak effect within one or two hours after ingestion, and wear off about two or three hours later; the effects of sustained release forms last up to 8 hours, but their effectiveness is not as powerful (DuPaul et al., 1991). At times these children experience a rebound effect as the drug wears off, becoming even more active and irritable than prior to taking the medication. If rebound occurs around bedtime, the child may require another dose of stimulants to calm down enough to permit sleep. Longer-acting agents help avoid this four-hour up-down cycle.

Because of the positive reports regarding stimulant effects with elementary school children, physicians have begun to prescribe these drugs to preschoolers, adolescents, and adults as well (DuPaul et al., 1991; Wender et al., 1985). The effects for adolescents have been favorable (Klorman et al., 1990). The effectiveness in preschoolers, however, appears to be more variable and unpredictable, and young children seem to be particularly sensitive to the effects of overmedication (Gadow, 1986). Despite concerns expressed by parents, no link between taking stimulants and later substance abuse has been documented (DuPaul et al., 1991).

Although coffee, as a substitute for stimulant medication, has been the object of experimentation, there is no clear evidence that it increases attention or suppresses behavior problems to any meaningful degree (DuPaul et al., 1991; Rapoport et al., 1984). When individuals do not respond favorably to stimulants, alternate drugs such as antidepressants, clonidine, or monoamine oxidase inhibitors have been found effective for some (DuPaul et al., 1991).

Stimulant Medication and Attention Deficit Disorder without Hyperactivity. Many students with learning disabilities have been identified as having an attention deficit disorder (ADD) that is not accompanied by hyperactivity. Although not as troubling to parents and teachers because of their more appropriate behavior, youngsters with ADD nevertheless show deficits in attention very similar to those who react to their attention deficit with hyperactivity.

Because stimulant medication aids attention and short-term memory in typical as well as hyperactive students, some researchers have investigated whether stimulants would be helpful to students who are not hyperactive yet who underachieve because of unknown reasons or an attention deficit disorder without hyperactivity (Aman & Werry, 1982; Dykman, Ackerman, & McCray, 1980; Gittelman, Klein, & Feingold, 1983; Lahey & Carlson, 1991). This line of research makes sense in that students with attention deficits, but no hyperactivity, show the same deficits in reaction time, speed of cognitive processing, and cognitive/perceptual skills on neuropsychological batteries as do those with hyperactivity; and when given medication, they respond similarly (Dykman et al., 1980; Hynd & Willis, 1988). As in studies of hyperactive children, children with attention deficits have made modest gains when taking medication. While short-term gains in some skills (for example, phonics, arithmetic calculations) have been seen, these generally have not persisted as the students continued taking medication or after termination of medication.

Overactive-Inhibitory Mechanisms and Hypoactivity. The biochemical problem of the hypoactive child appears to be opposite that of the hyperactive child in that the central nervous system inhibitory mechanisms appear to be overactive rather than underactive. This child's sluggishness may be helped by sedatives, which tone down the overactive inhibitory mechanisms and allow more stimuli to come to the child's attention (Silver, 1977).

Endocrine Disorders and Vitamin Deficiencies

The biochemical imbalances induced by glandular disorders, hypoglycemia, and vitamin deficiencies also have received attention for their role in learning and behavior disorders. Thyroid deficiencies and hypothroidism in the infant and toddler can cause permanent damage to the brain, as can elevated calcium levels. While excess thyroid hormone does lead to hyperactive behavior, studies suggest that for only a small number of children does sugar ingestion stimulate hyperactivity. Finally, there is no evidence that megavitamin treatments positively impact learning and behavior.

Thyroid Imbalances.   While excess thyroid hormone leads to restlessness and distractibility, thyroid deficiencies create a listless individual who may not be motivated or activated to learn. Severe intellectual deficits occur if thyroid deficiencies are not detected and treated as soon as possible after birth. While most children do respond favorably to continuous treatment, subtle diminution in intellectual and learning ability may nevertheless be apparent (Sandberg & Barrick, 1995).

Calcium Imbalances.   Abnormal elevation of calcium due to a calcium metabolism disorder can cause personality alterations bordering on psychosis and permanent intellectual deficits (Fraser et al., 1966; Karpati & Frame, 1964). Fortunately, early diagnosis can prevent these outcomes. Abnormally low calcium levels in the body have not been associated with learning disorders.

Hyper- and Hypoglycemia.   In diabetic children the body does not produce enough insulin for glucose to move from the bloodstream into the cells, where it is broken down for energy. Despite getting insulin therapy for this hyperglycemia, some diminution in intellectual and learning ability is common, especially when disease onset is before age five (Rovet et al., 1993). Hyperglycemic episodes often are accompanied by tiredness, thirst, headaches, frequent urination, and nausea (Hanson, 1990), all of which can disrupt attention to one's studies.

Hypoglycemia, low blood sugar, can severely compromise brain development during its most rapid growth period, the first two years of life (Green & Perlman, 1971; Griffiths & Laurence, 1974; Koivisto, Blanco-Sequeiros, & Krause, 1972). Early treatment can limit central nervous system damage, but if the condition goes untreated the brain's nerve and glial (support) cells begin to deteriorate (Anderson, Milner, & Strich, 1967). Convulsions and permanent brain damage may set in by the second day of life (Koivisto et al., 1972). The most common result is mental retardation, delayed motor development, and reduced brain size (Brandt, 1981; Green & Perlman, 1971). Severe hypoglycemia is present in more than 10 percent of newborns

(Lubchenco & Bard, 1971), especially among twins, newborns of low birthweight, infants whose mothers had kidney dysfunction or were diabetic during pregnancy, and those with inadequate intrauterine nutrition (Koivisto et al., 1972). The more severe the hypoglycemic episodes of a pregnant diabetic mother, the lower the intellectual abilities of her offspring (Turkington, 1992).

Central nervous system abnormalities are evident among as many as 75 percent of children who had experienced hypoglycemia as infants (Griffiths & Laurence, 1974; Koivisto et al., 1972). At older ages, single hypoglycemic episodes usually do not result in brain damage, although they do temporarily create abnormal EEGs (Green & Perlman, 1971). Temporary weakness, dizziness, fatigue, sweating, headaches, shakiness, and irritability accompany these episodes (Hanson, 1990). While episodic low blood sugar has been blamed for some children's hyperactivity, research has not substantiated this claim (Satterfield, Schell, & Barb, 1980).

Many parents limit their children's intake of foods such as sugar, cake, candy, soda, potato chips, white rice, and white flour because they believe that excess refined carbohydrates make their children "hyper." The depression, irritability, hyperactivity, and impaired mental functioning that some people report after sugar ingestion have been related to the influence of glucose metabolism on hormone secretions and on the production of brain neurotransmitters. However, well-controlled studies have shown little to no support for these clinical reports (Fishbein & Meduski, 1987; Wolraich, Wilson, & White, 1995). While a handful of studies have found a correlation between sugar intake and disruptive, aggressive, restless behavior, the remaining studies have found no deterioration, or clinically insignificant deterioration, in behavior after hyperactive children, children in a psychiatric ward, preschoolers, or children nominated by their parents as particularly sensitive to sugar ingested sugar drinks versus placebo (Milich, Lindgren, & Wolraich, 1986; Rosen et al., 1988; Wolraich et al., 1995). In fact, in many of these studies, activity level actually decreased and academic performance increased after ingestion of sugar. Milich and colleagues conclude that if some children respond adversely to sugar, just as they do to many different foods, these numbers appear to be small.

Vitamin Deficiencies. Allen Cott's (1985) orthomolecular approach prescribes megavitamin treatments, often over 1,000 times the usual daily requirement, to reduce hyperactivity and improve attention, concentration, and learning in psychotic children and in vitamin-deficient children with learning disabilities. Although case reports suggest improvement with megavitamin treatments (Brenner, 1982; Sieben, 1977), there have been no well-controlled studies using the methods detailed in Research Box 2–3. Supporters of the orthomolecular approach claim that it is impossible to get control groups similar in behavior to the treated children and that the need to frequently adjust dosage precludes double-blind research designs (Adler, 1979). In Haslam, Dalby, and Rademaker's (1984) study, no differences were found in most behavior scores when children reported to respond favorably to megavitamins alternated vitamin and placebo trials. In fact, when treated with vitamins, these children exhibited 25 percent more disruptive behavior. Because of the lack of evidence from controlled studies, the American Academy of Pediatrics' Committee on Nutrition (1976) declared that megavitamin therapy was unjustified as a treatment for psychoses and learning disorders, although it was appropriate in the case of some physical diseases.

Summary

Research on physiological differences between good and poor learners has found that learning disabilities may be caused by brain injury, prenatal maldevelopment of the brain, heredity, or biochemical irregularities. Any of these, to varying degrees, may affect a student's abilities in different areas of development.

Because of the brain's plasticity, the nature and extent of impairment in learning caused by brain injury is hard to predict. Therefore, nearly as many positive indicators of brain damage are found among typical learners as among poor learners. Because these indicators are so common to good learners and do not tap the higher cognitive processes involved in academic achievement, they often cannot explain or predict any one student's learning problems. A more fruitful way to explore brain-behavior relationships is to identify neuropsychological patterns that differentiate individuals with various learning strengths and weaknesses. This knowledge is just beginning to be linked with instructional approaches.

Structural brain differences also can result in learning disabilities. Atypical development of the cerebral cortex has been traced to disruptions during the second trimester of pregnancy. Autopsy evidence thus far has found atypical clusters of cells in the left hemisphere, as well as overly developed right hemispheres.

Because learning disabilities have a hereditary component, family history information may help us to understand a student's developmental patterns and teaching approaches that have succeeded with relatives. Left-handedness too runs in families, and many left-handers differ from right-handers in their cerebral organization patterns. Nevertheless, left-handedness appears to be associated with learning disorders only when both have stemmed from a common, underlying brain dysfunction.

Biochemical irregularities appear to be responsible for the attention difficulties, and consequent hyperactive and hypoactive behavior, of some students with learning disabilities. Judging from the effects of stimulant medication, which activate neural attention and inhibitory mechanisms, it seems that many hyperactive youngsters need their inhibitory, attention, and sensory systems aroused so that they will be able to block out irrelevant information and attend in a more focused manner. Seventy to 80 percent of hyperactive children respond to stimulants with some degree of improved attentiveness, motor performance, productivity, and speed and accuracy, as well as reduced activity in structured situations. Academic gains on standardized tests are modest, and long-term learning and behavior gains have not yet been demonstrated.

In infancy, untreated low blood sugar, low thyroid levels, and elevated body calcium can be devastating to learning potential. If these imbalances appear after the first few years of life, learning efficiency, energy, and motivation may be adversely affected as well. These biochemical imbalances can be rectified through diet and standard medical practices. Finally, megavitamin proponents have yet to support their claims with well-controlled research and, although a popular belief, it has not been consistently documented that excess sugar ingestion leads to hyperactive behavior.

Although physiological differences in students do account for some portion of their learning disabilities, it is important to remember that the environment can play a major role in helping students reach the limits of their potential. Good parenting and teaching may enhance brain functioning, learning, and ultimate life adjustment far beyond what might have been expected from the child's physiological makeup alone.

Chapter Three

Task and Setting Contributors

Although our LD definition presumes that physiological differences underlie students' learning disabilities, we cannot overlook the fact that the tasks we require students to accomplish and the settings in which they live and learn can do much to aggravate these disabilities or help overcome them. In fact, given appropriate parenting and teaching, the learning disability may emerge as only a minor deterrent to academic and social progress. On the other hand, with inappropriate parenting and teaching, a mild disability may be exacerbated to such a degree that very intensive, extraordinary intervention efforts become necessary. In some circumstances environmental factors cause academic achievement in otherwise typical learners to become so delayed that they eventually are identified as learning disabled. Clearly, attention must be given to task and setting factors that contribute to learning and development so that we can optimize development, intercede in situations that place the child at risk, and prevent exacerbation of learning and adjustment difficulties.

Several task-based factors contribute to learning disabilities. Consider that students with learning disabilities have such uneven development that they experience significant lags in some abilities but relative strengths in others. They also often have unique learning styles. It makes sense then that these youngsters' weaknesses may be aggravated by curriculum materials and methods that make demands on them that they are unable to meet. An appropriate match of task characteristics to these students' uneven ability patterns and unique learning styles can do much to facilitate their development.

Several setting-based contributors to learning disabilities also may be operating in a student's family or school climate. Like task-based factors, setting factors are influences beyond children's control, such as inadequate accommodation by school personnel to a student's cultural or linguistic diversity, that aggravate learning problems. In extreme cases, such as nutritional deprivation or exposure to environmental toxins, these setting factors in fact can cause physiological differences that result in developmental delays and learning disabilities.

In assessing the contributors to a particular student's learning difficulties, we must give equal weight to learner, task, and setting considerations. The better we understand both the strengths and weaknesses of different students and their curricula, schools, and families, the better we can intervene on each student's behalf.

Task-Based Contributors

All too often, school work is mismatched with the uneven ability patterns and unique learning styles of students with learning disabilities. When what and how the teacher teaches do not match what a student already knows, what the student is ready to learn, and how the student learns best, then learning disorders can be aggravated. School tasks that facilitate development are those that build on students' strengths, remediate their weaker abilities, and minimize the interference of these weaknesses with learning progress.

Maturational lag theorists stress the importance of modifying curricular content to better match what students are ready to learn. Cognitive style theorists stress modification of teaching approaches to better match these students' unique learning styles. These perspectives focus attention on modifying what and how students are asked to learn, so that academic achievement is facilitated.

Maturational Lags

Learning disabilities reflect slow maturation of visual-perceptual, motor, language, or attention processes that underlie higher cognitive development. Because each child with learning disabilities has different immaturities, each passes through the various stages of development with his or her own rate and style. The maturational lag perspective assumes that these stages of child development follow a patterned, predictable, and orderly sequence.

Uneven patterns of development are common to youngsters with learning disabilities. It is said that "these children's mental maturation proceeds by fits and starts" (Kinsbourne & Caplan, 1979). Adam, for example, is a bright third grader with superb drawing and mathematics skills. But his oral reading and ability to follow the teacher's instructions are more like that of a first grader. Tracy, Adam's classmate, is an excellent reader, listener, and storyteller. But when asked to translate her thoughts into a written composition she barely manages to scribble three short sentences, and the words are nearly illegible. Adam and Tracy each have some skills developing at normal rates while others have been slower to mature.

Delays such as Adam's and Tracy's are attributed to a time lag in the neurodevelopmental maturation of specific portions of their brains, which may be caused by such factors as genetic predisposition, brain injury, neurochemical imbalances, structural brain differences, or environmental stimulation. Adam's and Tracy's slower developing skills are understood to be very much like those of younger typical children. Though Adam's difficulty following directions and reading, and Tracy's difficulty with writing, are quantitatively behind the skill level of their classmates, these weaker abilities nevertheless qualitatively match the normal achievement levels of entering first graders. The cause of these delays is not much of a concern to maturational lag theorists because the treatment will always be the same, appropriate teaching geared toward the child's level of readiness.

Maturational lag theorists generally view the development of children with learning disabilities as following the normal continuum of child development, although they are at the low end of the continuum in their weaker areas (Shaywitz, Fletcher, & Shaywitz, 1995). Others, however, point out that some children do learn and behave differently from what is considered normal at any stage of development (Kinsbourne & Caplan, 1979). For example, six-year-old Jonah's level of inattention and hyperactivity in the classroom may be atypical for even a one-and-a-half-year-old child, who will walk around chairs rather than try to walk through them. The one-and-a-half-year-old child will delight in dumping a pile of paper on the floor, sit down, and joyfully crumple the papers piece by piece. But Jonah is unaware that he knocked the papers over, and he glances down without concern as he steps on them on his way to the hamster's cage. Similarly, Richard's (see his story on page 276) total arrest in reading development, being unable to recognize his name in print despite

being a college graduate, is unknown in normal child development.

Because the school curriculum is geared above the readiness levels of children like Adam, Tracy, and Jonah who have various developmental immaturities, these children are at risk for school failure. Pamela's and Larry's stories (below) illustrate the maturational lag theorist's tendency to favor retention rather than push a child who is unready to profit from a given curriculum into faulty learning. When a child is "pushed into error by a hasty environment," delays are aggravated, errors become well practiced, and more serious learning disorders are likely to develop (Ames, 1968, p. 39). Bombarded by excess amounts of

Pamela and Larry

Pamela

A girl of seven years and six months, in June Pamela was a first grade failure. The public school first grade teacher indicated that Pamela would have only a social promotion to second grade as she has not completed the work satisfactorily. . . .

. . . It is unfortunate that at the beginning of first grade when her maturity, perceptual and learning problems were evident almost at once to the teacher, she wasn't replaced in reading readiness class, to enter first grade only a year later, when she was seven.

At present, with her immaturity and fuzziness of behavior, her piecemeal way of thinking, her need of help in pulling things together and in thinking in an organized fashion, she is not ready for second grade work . . .

Repeating first grade should help to synchronize her learning ability and the demands of the learning situation. . . .

A slower course in school should improve her academic performance (Ames, 1968, pp. 52–53).

Larry

Larry was examined in June 1981, at the age of five years eight months shortly after the close of his kindergarten year, which had not been successful. Larry was a mid-October boy, which meant that he had started kindergarten just before his fifth birthday. Because school had been a disaster, he was referred to us to find out just what his academic and personal potentials actually were.

(Continues on following page)

information, these students absorb only fragments. This fragmented knowledge results in spotty, inaccurate understanding of concepts, which provides an unstable base for further learning and makes it hard for pupils to apply those skills they have mastered.

In contrast to those favoring retention, other educators believe that children with maturational lags should remain with their grade but that the curriculum should be modified to present only objectives that the children are absolutely ready to handle. With appropriate programming, minor lags may be able to resolve themselves over time. As can be seen from the examples of Adam, Tracy, and Jonah, different maturational lag patterns will necessitate very different educational interventions.

Maturational Lag Patterns. Children with learning disabilities often have more than one area of developmental immaturity. The resulting disability may become noticeable in different ways at different ages, as both the cognitive demands of tasks and the child's strengths and weaknesses change (Denckla & Heilman, 1979; Kinbourne, 1973b; Maxwell & Wallach, 1984). For example, Adam was slow to talk but by school entrance spoke well. He was the kindergarten teacher's dream pupil because he excelled at eye-hand coordination activities. But when reading was introduced, it again taxed Adam's weakness with language symbols. Adam finally did learn to read, but his language difficulties surfaced once again in ninth grade when he found it impossible to handle

---

Pamela and Larry   *(Continued from preceding page)*

He was a delightful child to examine. Though small and immature-looking for his age, he was attractive, friendly, and cooperative. Findings on the Gesell Developmental Examination showed that he ranged in behavior from 3½ years to around 5½ . . . .

Printing any letters or numbers was cumbersome and difficult for this boy, and his copies of square and triangle were not up to his age. His intelligence quotient was in the bright normal range, and there were no outstanding visual difficulties.

Larry showed himself, in our opinion, to be [a] good candidate for kindergarten in the coming fall when he would be five years eleven months old. That a whole year of overplacement had not caused him to fall apart or to lose his enthusiasm for school was remarkable.

Larry's parents had come to us in a state of considerable anxiety. They had been told by the school psychologist that their son was a trifle "backward" and that his failure to succeed in kindergarten was due to a clear-cut learning disability. The school's recommendation was that he proceed to first grade but be given special help in the coming year, and that in all likelihood throughout the rest of his school career he would need to be classified as learning disabled and would require special help.

It was fortunate for Larry that his parents questioned what the school had told them. It is sad to think of the all too many children in this country whose parents do not seek a second opinion and regretfully accept the diagnosis of learning disability without at least pursuing the possibility that their child's poor school adjustment may be due simply to immaturity and unreadiness for the work of the grade in which the school has placed him or her (Ames, 1983, pp. 19–20).

French classes. Brian, on the other hand, showed perceptual problems with puzzles and drawing as a preschooler. Once he got to school, however, his poor awareness of sound sequences when reading words was even more worrisome. With remediation, Brian did learn these phonological skills and became an accurate reader. He graduated law school, but as an adult still shows vestiges of perceptual difficulties in his slow reading speed, poor handwriting, and difficulty spelling irregular words.

Certain lags will cause problems at well-recognized "stress points" in the academic curriculum: kindergarten's set to learn, first grade's reading, fourth grade's reading comprehension, junior high's demands on organized approaches to learning, and high school's expectations for independent learning (Holmes, 1987). Kinsbourne (1973b) emphasizes that since "there is no known way of hurrying the brain maturation on its way" (p. 273), the school curriculum and methods will need to be adjusted to help a youngster both circumvent and remediate his or her weaknesses.

Some lags in neural maturation catch up over time, but others do not. Catch-up occurs on those skills in which all children reach high levels of sophistication at relatively young ages. Denckla (1979) comments that these early maturing skills need to reach only a "good-enough floor" in order to no longer interfere with academic progress (p. 560). One example of a such a skill is left-right letter reversals. By age nine the reversal tendency has disappeared in most children and no longer complicates reading and writing. Copying is another skill that reaches "good-enough" levels rather early—by age twelve to thirteen (Denckla, 1979; Rudel, 1985). When the child's deficits are only in these types of early emerging skills, the prognosis for later, high-level learning is excellent. The student may stumble through the first few years of school, but once the developmental interferences resolve themselves, the child can "lag and then leap" (Denckla, 1979, p. 561).

Unfortunately, catch-up does not occur on more complex, late-emerging skills that have higher "good enough" thresholds (La Buda & DeFries, 1988b; Rourke, 1976). This is because the educational and social demands on these abilities continue to grow as one gets older. For example, even if reading skill does over time begin to approach the level of one's peers, spelling is such a high-threshold skill that the gap tends to remain wide (Bruck, 1993a, b; Rourke & Orr, 1977). Similarly, we have found that verbal deficits are not likely to improve as rapidly as visual-spatial weaknesses (Fletcher & Satz, 1985). One example of such a high-threshold verbal skill is the ability to retrieve names rapidly from memory (Rudel, 1985). Rapid "naming" is important to success in high-level learning because most people memorize information by naming and then silently rehearsing this material. When students can't rapidly name what they see (for example, words or images seen momentarily on an overhead projector), their ability to rehearse, organize, store, and retrieve this information becomes depressed. Naming is one of those slow-maturing skills in which lags get greater through the elementary years, persist into adolescence, and are troublesome even in adulthood (Blalock, 1982; Brainerd, Kingma, & Howe, 1986; Korhonen, 1995; Wolf, 1991). These individuals have trouble retrieving facts that they know, words remain "on the tip of their tongue," and they can't recall names that are important to them, such as celebrities and restaurants. While searching for a number in the telephone book they suddenly may forget the name of the person they are looking up. This difficulty is what we all experience occasionally when we "block" on our best friends' names. But for some individuals with learning disabilities it happens all the time, with all types of information, even simple names of objects.

When they experience persistent information-processing lags, children's academic achievement often does not catch up with that of their peers (Fletcher & Satz, 1980; Francis et al., 1994; Juel, 1988; Korhonen, 1995; Lyon, 1995). In fact, the gap between the academic achievement of students with learning disabilities and their peers often gets larger from year to year (Horn, O'Donnell, & Vitulano, 1983; McKinney, Osborne, & Schulte, 1993; O'Shea & Valcante, 1986; Rutter, 1978; Shinn, 1986; Stanovich, 1988). Studies find that students who have learning disabilities make less academic progress than do less intelligent students who, though lagging behind their classmates, are achieving as well as can be expected for their intelligence (Rutter et al., 1976). Even when they score the same as non–learning disabled, low-achieving peers on standardized achievement tests, children who are learning disabled may appear qualitatively different: for example, significantly slower reading rate and word retrieval, fewer correct sequences of letter pairs when spelling, and slower reading progress (Badian, 1993; Shinn et al., 1986; Wolf & Obregón, 1992). It is not uncommon to find that the learning disabled take longer to learn novel tasks than do equally bright peers, or younger children who read at similar levels (Mauer & Kamhi, 1996). Even bone growth and weight gain frequently lag relative to what would be expected for one's age or family background (Dolan & Matheny, 1978; Gold, 1978; Oettinger et al., 1974).

Developmental immaturities are far more prevalent among boys than girls. It is not uncommon for the development of normal boys to be approximately six months behind that of girls at the time of school entry (Ilg & Ames, 1964). Boys' language and reading skills tend to reach maturity at the end of elementary school, whereas these skills in girls mature two years earlier (Bakker, Teunissen, & Bosch, 1976; Bryden, 1970). Boys' social behavior also matures later than that of girls (Rubin & Balow, 1971). These observations are by no means new. Even the Bible proclaimed a girl to be a mature woman at twelve years and one day, but a boy did not make it to manhood until age thirteen.

Matching Tasks to Readiness Levels. Maturational lag theorists urge that we gear academic tasks to what students are ready to master and not to what the curriculum expects them to accomplish for their age or grade. When the rate of instruction is slowed, so that children are taught precisely what they are ready to learn, the need for special teaching techniques often is reduced (Kinsbourne & Caplan, 1979). Whether grade retention is an appropriate way to slow the rate of instruction, however, is the subject of much debate.

Slowing the Rate of Instruction. Maturational lag theorists caution against teaching too much too soon because transitory immaturities may then become permanent deficits. If Allison is forced to read before she is ready, she will make errors, learn bad habits, hate reading, avoid practicing, and take up much of the teacher's time later on undoing the faulty learning. Therefore, delaying reading instruction is advised until she is absolutely ready to absorb instruction at a high success rate.

Despite this readiness emphasis, maturational lag theorists by no means sit back and wait for development to take its course. They urge immediate intervention to develop the necessary learning readiness. At times this demands very unique, intense teaching that differs from the typical strategies used even with younger children. They take issue with the wait-and-see attitude of those pediatricians who, when questioned by worried parents about their child's delayed walking, talking, restlessness, or hatred of school, too often reply "don't worry, your child will outgrow it." Quite the opposite is true. Each child has a lot to grow into: "Our society is a pressure cooker and doesn't allow a child to outgrow it" (Richardson, 1979).

Katrina de Hirsch (1963) offers one of the best statements of the maturational lag perspective on instruction:

We know from animal experiments that the nonuse of a function leads to atrophy. Thus, the emphasis on maturation should not be understood to mean that one should sit back and let development do the rest. The clinician's and educator's task is to study carefully the maturational level of the different modalities in each child who has difficulties. Thus, in the framework of a warm and supportive relationship, the teacher can help the child perform at the highest level of his potential. (p. 69)

In other words, find out precisely what the child is ready to learn in stronger and weaker areas—and teach it.

Grade Placement. Ames (1977, 1983) asserts that the tendency of school officials to fix a definite curriculum and to promote children automatically from year to year aggravates learning disorders. She cites findings that children who had entered kindergarten ready for the school's curriculum remained among the top students from grade to grade. Children who had been questionably ready for kindergarten were only average learners six years later. Those who had been unready were, years later, at the bottom of the class or had been dropped to a lower grade (Ames, 1968; Ilg & Ames, 1964). These findings have been replicated by other investigators as well (Book, 1980; Derienzo, 1981; Glazzard, 1982; Roth, McCaul & Barnes, 1993). Juel (1988), for example, reports that eight of ten students who entered first grade with poor awareness of the position of sounds in spoken words ranked in the bottom quartile of the class on decoding and comprehension four years later. Ames believes that if the unready and questionably ready children had not been promoted for one year, the school curriculum would have better matched their readiness levels, and their achievement would have been enhanced.

Ames (1968) claims that over 50 percent of children entering kindergarten are unready for the curriculum. She suggested that children begin school when their behavioral and learning maturity, rather than chronological ages, indicate that they are ready. In general, girls should have reached age six, but boys six and a half by September of first grade (Ilg, Ames, & Apell, 1965). This recommendation concurs with findings from several studies, including one of nearly 30,000 children, that children who are young for their grade are far more likely to lag academically in the early school years or develop learning difficulties than those who are older (DiPasquale, Moule, & Flewelling, 1980; Donofrio, 1977; Maddux, Green, & Horner, 1986; Nichols & Chen, 1981; Shepard and Smith, 1986). Ames believes that once school failure sets in, retention may become necessary because the school curriculum does not give children time to catch up.

Kinsbourne and Caplan (1979) warn that multiple problems can result from teaching above the level of a youngster with developmental lags. The student's daily failure may lead to a lowered self-image, suspended effort, depression, withdrawal, or acting out, all of which are complicated

by the reactions of disappointed parents and frustrated teachers.

The influence of the maturational lag view has resulted in many more children being advised to remain another year in preschool before entering kindergarten. In addition, some states and communities have advanced their school entry cut-off ages (for example, age six by September of first grade) (Ames, 1986; Lieberman, 1986a). Retention rates have increased due to both the maturational lag perspective and the public's outcry over high illiteracy rates, which forced stricter standards for promotion. Estimates report retention of as many as 15 to 25 percent of students, and these numbers continue to rise (McLeskey & Grizzle, 1992; Smith & Shepard, 1987).

Research suggests that retention can be helpful academically and socially up to second grade if children are of average intelligence, show normal emotional and social adjustment, have no serious academic deficits, do not oppose retention, and their parents are supportive educationally and favor retention (Medway, 1985). These children subsequently fit in well with the curriculum; they just needed more time, which the retention provided. When students who do not fit these characteristics are retained, their gains do not match those of similar children who were promoted. Moreover, within a few years, the retained children's declining rate of progress results in a second retention or special education placement (Medway & Rose, 1986; Rafoth, Dawson, & Carey, 1988; Safer, 1986). Very seldom does a second retention lead to positive academic or behavioral changes.

Research suggests that retention has particularly little benefit after sixth grade, and that it hurts self-image (Medway & Rose, 1986). Junior high school retentions tend to be marked by continued failure, deportment problems, and excessive absences (Safer, 1986). The fact that about 20 percent of retained students subsequently drop out of school, compared with about 9 percent of those never retained (*Condition of Education,* 1994), has been linked by some to the stigma associated with retention (Grissom & Shephard, 1989; Hammack, 1986; Rafoth et al., 1988).

Retention's generally negative outcome has been linked to the fact that often retention alone has been expected to solve the achievement problem (McLeskey & Grizzle, 1992). Few special services are offered. In contrast, the outcome seems far more positive when retention is accompanied by remedial education (Medway, 1985; Peterson, DeGracie, & Ayabe, 1987).

Clearly, many children need more time to absorb a curriculum before they are advanced to the next level, and they need to be offered special education immediately rather than being expected to outgrow their lags. Retention rates of students with learning disabilities are reported to be 2½ to 4 times that of children without disabilities (McKinney et al., 1993; McLeskey & Grizzle, 1992); yet these are the children who are least likely to benefit from retention. Therefore, school personnel have developed a number of options that maintain strict standards yet permit students to remain with their peers and learn at their own pace. These options include individualized instruction by adapting the grade-level curriculum, flexibly advancing levels of instruction as competency criteria are met, tutoring, summer programs, learning laboratories, multi-age grouping, cooperative learning strategies, remedial reading/math, and special education services. When flexibility and special services are not built into the school's organizational framework, the rigid school curriculum may exacerbate the learning problems of students with maturational lags.

Cognitive Styles

Cognitive style theorists stress that school tasks can contribute to learning disabilities when they require students to use problem-solving strategies that they find unnatural. Every individual has a preferred way, a preferred *cognitive style,* for looking at and interacting with the world. At times this way of perceiving, remembering, and problem solving helps, and at other times it hinders success, depending on the demands of the tasks. Cognitive styles have been found to be relatively stable temperaments (Keogh, 1973; Smith, 1997; Witkin, Goodenough, & Karp, 1967) caused by factors such as personality disposition, brain injury, and heredity (Kagan & Kogan, 1970; Kinsbourne &

Caplan, 1979; Morrison & Stewart, 1974; Smith, 1997).

Recall Jonah, our hyperactive first grader. His teacher asks him to choose an educational game to play quietly while she works with a small reading group. He flits from game to game, discarding each in favor of the next one that catches his attention. In the end, Jonah's activity level becomes a disturbance to others, and he learns little from any one game. Julie, his classmate, is much more reflective. Given the same directions, she chooses a game and plays it over and over again, intrigued with all its details and trying to improve her performance. Time is up before she even thinks about trying another game. When the teacher asks Jonah and Julie to tell the reading group what games are available, Jonah has the answer because he has tried them all. But if the teacher had asked that a game be demonstrated, only Julie would be able to do so.

Which child is the better learner, Jonah or Julie? In general, our society prefers Julie's style. Julie is more task oriented, takes more time to arrive at solutions, and likes to analyze and memorize details. School tasks are more compatible with Julie's disposition than with Jonah's (Ramirez & Castaneda, 1974; Zelniker & Jeffrey, 1976). Yet, cognitive style theorists remind us that Jonah's style too has some important virtues. For example, if the teacher asks both children to run into the classroom to find her pen, Jonah probably would find it first because his attention is all over the place at once. When looking at the theater listings in the newspaper, Jonah is likely to spot the movie he's looking for quite rapidly. In contrast, Julie is more likely to search one section of the room or newspaper systematically, and then another, until she finds what she's looking for. Julie's style takes too long. Whether each child performs well depends on how well the tasks are matched to their individual styles.

Cognitive style theorists presume that in many cases the basic learning ability of students with learning disabilities is intact. However, their styles are inappropriate to classroom demands, thereby interfering with achievement. When the student's cognitive style reduces the amount of information learned, this in turn may create a cumulative information deficit and a potential learning disability (Keogh, 1973).

On the other hand, when task demands are well-suited to these students' preferred styles, when they are taught better learning strategies, or when more appropriate strategies mature, these students can learn well (Torgesen, 1980). The most commonly discussed styles among students with learning disabilities are impulsivity-reflectivity, low-high conceptual levels, simultaneous-successive processing preferences, and efficient-inefficient learner strategies.

Impulsive and Reflective Learners. In the stories about Jennifer and Sandy (below), Jennifer has an impulsive cognitive style while Sandy is reflective. Jennifer makes others more aware of her learning problems because she creates the greater disturbance and fails more frequently.

Impulsive characteristics like Jennifer's quite often differentiate the learning disabled, from typical learners (Walker, 1985).

Jennifer's and Sandy's cognitive styles vary along a continuum of underfocused attention/premature decision maker to overfocused attention/postmature decision maker (Kinsbourne & Caplan, 1979). Jerome Kagan and his colleagues (1964) led the theorizing about these impulsive and reflective styles with their use of the Matching Familiar Figures Test (MFFT). Some of the MFFT items are reproduced in Figure 3–1. On the MFFT, children were required to find which one of the lower six figures matched the standard. Children who were fast and inaccurate were considered to be impulsive. Those who were slow and accurate were considered to be reflective.

Kagan and Kogan (1970) believed that the difference between the time impulsive and reflec-

Jennifer and Sandy

Jennifer's teachers complain that she is overly impulsive. When she must concentrate on a social studies paragraph, her attention is extremely underfocused. Her efforts to pay attention and the length of time that she concentrates are like that of a much younger child. She doesn't maintain attention long enough to get through the passage and therefore there's no hope of learning the material. She appears restless as her attention is continually drawn to other events. Jennifer is very capable of learning, if only she wouldn't leave tasks before she grasps the concepts. Her answers are often wrong because she makes decisions too soon, before considering enough information and comparing this with what she already knows about the topic. Jennifer frequently stops listening to the teacher before all directions are given, answers before hearing or reading all the questions, is hard to discipline because she considers neither what the adults expect from her nor alternative behaviors, and has social difficulties because she doesn't ponder how her actions may be perceived by her peers.

Sandy is also having learning difficulties, but for quite different reasons. She is overly compulsive, concentrating so long on one bit of information that she never learns enough about the overall subject. Sandy's attention is overfocused. She is extremely slow in shifting her attention from one thing to another. In contrast to Jennifer's style on a multiple-choice test, Sandy will go over and over a problem. She eventually does poorly on the test because she does not complete all the items and keeps switching answers. When disciplined, she is oversensitive to what is said and done, and she withdraws. Sandy's teachers say that she is overly reflective.

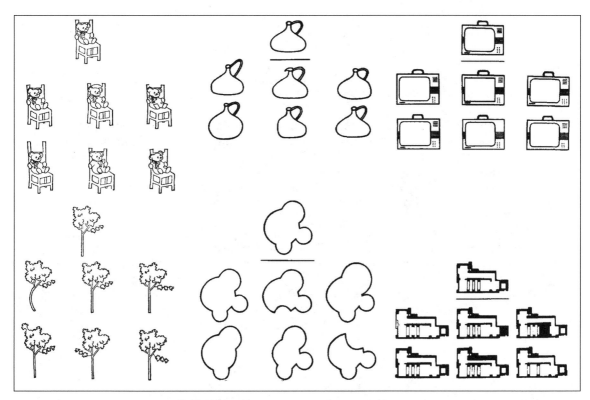

Figure 3–1 Kagen's Matching Familiar Figures Test items. *Source:* Kagan, J. (1965). Reflection-impulsivity and reading ability in primary grade children. *Child Development, 36,* p. 613. © 1965 The Society for Research in Child Development, and Zelniker, T., & Jeffrey, W. E. (1976). Reflective and impulsive children: Strategies of information processing underlying differences in problem solving. *Monographs of the Society for Research in Child Development, 41* (5), Serial No. 168. © 1976 The Society for Research in Child Development. Reprinted by permission.

tive children took to problem solve was caused by the latter's greater anxiety over being correct. They hypothesized that impulsive children would leave tasks early because they were not concerned enough about their performance to take the time to avoid errors (Yap & Peters, 1985). Zelniker and Jeffrey (1976), however, presented an alternate proposal, that children were fast or slow because they differed in their basic information-processing approaches. Their research had found that reflective children preferred to pay attention to fine details; therefore, they took the time to search stimuli exhaustively, and their responses very

often were accurate. Impulsive children, on the other hand, preferred to focus on the stimulus as a whole, which necessitates a shorter response time; when detail analysis was required, their style resulted in errors. Reflective children were superior to impulsive children only when analyzing details. On items requiring more global analysis, such as dealing with outlines and themes, impulsive children were equal, if not superior, to reflective children, and faster. Zelniker and Jeffrey's studies are summarized in Research Box 3–1.

Subsequent research has supported Zelnicker and Jeffrey's findings that the primary dif-

RESEARCH BOX 3–1

Zelniker and Jeffrey's Study of Impulsive and Reflective Search Strategies

Zelniker and Jeffrey (1976) conducted four studies to test their hypothesis that impulsive children and reflective children differ in the way in which they search information.

In the first study they analyzed MFFT items by whether the correct answers required attention to global (the contour, overview) or detail features. Findings indicated that reflective children were consistently superior to impulsive children on items requiring attention to detail. Although both groups performed equally well on global items, the impulsive children arrived at the solution faster.

In the second study, Zelniker and Jeffrey found that impulsive children gave more non-analytic (looking at wholes) than analytic (looking at details) responses on the Conceptual Style Test. Reflective children showed the opposite pattern. This test requires the child to describe similarities between line drawings. The children are specifically told to be analytic and nonanalytic in responding. Impulsive children made more errors when told to be analytic than nonanalytic. Reflective children made more errors when told to be nonanalytic.

Children in the third study listened to sentences or looked at pictures. Impulsive children recalled themes rather than details. Reflective children recalled details rather than themes.

The fourth study used Bruner's Concept-Attainment Task, which required descriptions of stimulus similarities by shape, color, and size. The impulsive children named more dimensions than did the reflective children, who preferred to scan parts.

Zelniker and Jeffrey's findings suggest that impulsive and reflective children differ in information-processing strategies. These strategies may influence their response speeds and accuracy, rather than speed itself being responsible for their level of performance.

ference between impulsive and reflective children's rapid and slow response times rests in search strategies (Kemler Nelson & Smith, 1989). For example, in Zentall and Gohs's (1984) very clever study of hyperactive four- to six-year-old low achievers, and equal intelligence typical learners, the children were given blocks with drawings of abstract designs. The children were to decide which block to place on a stand after listening to a global cue (for example, it looks like a ray gun; it looks like a man's shirt) or a detail cue (for example, it has two things on the side that curve up, with a hole in the middle). When the children had trouble making a decision and needed an addi-

tional cue, they would sound a buzzer. If a global cue had been given first, the buzzer would elicit a detail cue, and vice versa. Hyperactive children more often sounded the buzzer after hearing a detail cue than after hearing a global cue. The typical children had the opposite pattern; they needed more information when given a global cue than when given a detail cue. In other words, global information seems to be more meaningful to the hyperactive, poor learner than detailed information. The typical student, however, finds details more informative.

Researchers have found that the problem-solving errors of impulsive children can be reduced by teaching them to focus on details when scanning material, to use alternate strategies, and to understand why and when these strategies are appropriate. Merely telling them to take more time is not helpful because they need to be shown how to spend this time more profitably (Egeland, 1974; Heider, 1971; Kurtz & Borkowski, 1987; Meichenbaum & Goodman, 1971; Orbach, 1977; Ridberg, Parke, & Hetherington, 1971).

Both impulsive and reflective styles have advantages and disadvantages, depending on the type of information the student is being asked to learn. School tasks most often are geared toward the reflective student's style because they demand attention to details, and directions urge students to take their time. Impulsive youngsters are at a clear disadvantage. On the other hand, impulsive students are at an advantage when it comes to overviewing situations quickly, being sensitive to social cues, and solving problems that don't contain the answers (Keogh, 1973). They are more open to incidental learning, processing rapidly exposed simple patterns, and a broad array of information (Fitzgibbons, Goldberger, & Eagle, 1965; Kaswan, Haralson, & Cline, 1965; Messick & Damarin, 1964). Unfortunately, many students with learning disabilities are impulsive, and the demands of school tasks for the most part are not well suited to their global learning styles.

Low and High Conceptual Level Learners. David Hunt (1974) described a student's conceptual level (CL) as his or her ability to handle different complexities of information processing under low to high task structure. Students who are low CL learners are viewed as categorical thinkers, dependent on rules, and less capable of generating their own concepts or considering a number of alternatives. Therefore, they have difficulty directing their own learning. Students who are high CL learners, on the other hand, can generate their own concepts, provide their own rules, and consider different viewpoints; they have more alternatives available for problem solving. Consequently they are more inquiring, self-assertive, and capable of independently handling complex conceptual material. The majority of students with learning disabilities fit Hunt's low conceptual level category.

Hunt and his colleagues identified students who were low and high CL learners based on open-ended questions that assessed the amount of input they needed from others in various circumstances. They found that students who were low CL learners learned better from a lecture than a discovery method, and when a rule was presented before, rather than after, an example (McLachlan & Hunt, 1973; Tomlinson & Hunt, 1971). These students needed to be explicitly told all the information that required attention and the precise point being illustrated by examples. Students who were high CL learners learned equally well under all conditions, but they preferred rules after an example and discovery methods that gave them more autonomy in learning (Hunt et al., 1974).

Maier (1980), too, found that good learners preferred to be asked questions after they had heard a folk tale because they liked to organize the information in their own way. Poor learners, however, could retell the tale only if the questions were asked right before they heard the information, so that they knew what to listen for.

Teachers commonly encourage pupils to discover relationships for themselves. Children often are asked "How do you think we could solve this problem?" "What are the likely consequences?" and "Why did that happen?" Less often are they directly told the key concepts or given precise choices to ponder. There is evidence that direct teaching of the pertinent facts and concepts, and teacher guidance through explicit rules, may be just what the problem learner needs to promote greater integration and generalization of information and an ordered approach to learning (Hunt et al., 1974; Scott & Sigel, 1965, in Coop & Sigel, 1971). Such directed instruction will decrease the student's confusion and actually increase his or her conceptual flexibility. Because many students with learning disabilities are low conceptual level learners, our teaching approaches must become more structured and explicit in order to match their preferred instructional styles.

Simultaneous and Successive Learners. Imagine arriving at an airport and needing to use the "hotel hotline" telephone to alert the hotel's van to pick you up. The telephone number is buried within fifty hotel pictures and logos on the wall. While you're trying to figure out how to handle this confusion, your ten-year-old nephew says "There it is." How he sorted through that morass seems incomprehensible to you; after all, it takes time to systematically scan the wall column by column, hotel after hotel. For this child, however, the picture and logo he had in mind just jumped out at him as in a three-dimensional movie. This child took a *simultaneous* approach (global, holistic) to the task, whereas you preferred a *successive* (analytical, sequential) strategy. You too would have found the hotel number in time, but it would have taken you much longer.

Das, Kirby, and Jarman's (1979) simultaneous-successive information-processing theory, adapted from Luria's (1980) work, suggests that people choose to process information and make decisions in simultaneous or successive fashions based on genetic propensity, task demands, past experiences, and sociocultural influences (Das & Varnhagen, 1986). Youngsters who prefer simultaneous processing strategies do better on spatial-conceptual tasks: for example, conservation tasks that require one to reason whether two different sized beakers contain the same amount of liquid or whether two lines are still the same length when the distance between them has been increased (Mwamwenda, Dash, & Das, 1984). Simultaneous processors also have an advantage in comprehending spatial language constructs, such as "taller than," "below," or "inside" (Das & Varnhagen, 1986). In contrast, successive analysis and integration skills appear critical to the grammatical sequencing of language, so as to comprehend and produce it accurately. Studies have found successive processing to be important to beginning reading because letter sounds must be linked in sequence. As a child gets older and must conceptually organize compositions, simultaneous processing gains in importance.

As in the hotel example, research suggests that students may experience academic difficulties because they bring inappropriate simultaneous or successive styles to a task (Cherkes-Julkowski, Gertner, & Norlander, 1986; Das & Varnhagen, 1986). Whereas children typically adopt simultaneous approaches to visual and motor tasks, but

successive approaches to auditory-verbal tasks (Hynd & Willis, 1988), children with learning disabilities may approach these tasks with the least-suited strategy. Even though this strategy may solve the problem, it may take longer and be more effortful, leaving little room for higher-level reasoning or enjoyment of what has been accomplished. If the child looks at the world in an overly global way, attention to details will be sacrificed. In contrast, the child who is overly detailed may get the fine points but miss the overall idea. Social insensitivity and imperceptiveness are not uncommon among children with overly successive information-processing patterns (Voeller, 1986; Weintraub & Mesulam, 1983).

The stories of Gina and JJ (page 101) illustrate how overly rigid styles, whether successive or simultaneous, can interfere with learning. In order to be successful in school, both Gina and JJ require help to become more flexible in shifting strategies. They also benefit when teachers adapt their methods to suit each child's preferred strategy. For example, Gina's social interactions became far more positive when her boring, overly successive style was addressed by teaching her to first tell classmates what her conclusion was and then why ("I don't want our group project to be on recycling because . . . "). Shifting board work to the beginning of class gave Gina more time to compensate for her slow copying, so that she could finish without stress. To organize her writing, a brainstorming and outlining method proved useful. For JJ, who adopts an overly simultaneous strategy, drawing sticks next to numerals helped him to add, and forecasting what he thought would happen in a story based on his past experiences helped him to focus on subsequent details and time sequences. Task modifications like these adapt to children's conceptual styles and are exactly what students with learning disabilities who maintain overly rigid simultaneous or successive styles require to meet with greater success.

Efficient-Inefficient Learner Strategies.   Many students with learning disabilities are inefficient, inactive, and disorganized learners. They are not aware of how to go about learning, nor do they analyze what the task is demanding of them

(Flavell, 1971; Torgesen, 1977a, 1980). Because they often have little awareness that they are to put energy into learning, their efforts are not sustained or organized, and they seem unaware that memory is possible and desirable (Hagen, 1971; Norman, 1969).

Stone and Michals (1986) summarize research describing the typical problem-solving approaches of students who have learning disabilities: failure to use a systematic plan to approach a problem (for example, in the game "Twenty Questions," asking questions that focus on isolated possibilities rather than on categories), failure to identify the critical from irrelevant attributes in a problem situation, failure to make use of feedback concerning accuracy to alter task approaches (for example, abandoning a previously correct choice or returning to wrong choices), failure to generate new inferences or make use of data to revise actions, and failure to draw specific conclusions (for example, remaining highly general).

Left to their own styles, students with learning disabilities often are more dependent in their intellectual activities, less hard-working, more impulsive, and less capable of understanding directions than are typical learners (Stevenson,

Gina and JJ

Gina, a twelve year old who preferred a successive style, illustrates what can happen when a youngster is overly bound to one style. Instead of switching between strategies or letting them complement one another, Gina stuck to a successive strategy on all tasks. When looking at the teacher's concept map of continents, for example, Gina focussed on the countries within the various bubbles but did not notice that each bubble represented a different continent. Copying from the board was a very slow process for Gina. She proceeded letter by letter despite her ability to read these as sight words; therefore, she continually lagged behind the rest of the class. When Gina was telling about an incident, the listener had no idea what point she was trying to make because she rambled off sequences of events and ideas without connecting them to any major point. Although reading and spelling at high school levels, Gina's written compositions were a series of disconnected statements. Even when scanning a picture for the most important missing part, Gina would list many parts but have difficulty distinguishing the one whose absence was most critical. Despite high grades in school, Gina was very unhappy with taking longer than everyone else, and often missing the main point. The disconnectedness of her conversations caused problems in making friends. Squabbles and misperceptions about what others had said to her were daily occurrences.

In contrast to Gina, JJ took a simultaneous approach to most tasks. When shown a worksheet in first grade with a picture of two pigs connected by a plus sign, and the teacher asked "If there are three pigs and five more pigs come along, how many will there be all together?," JJ responded "two." He became visually bound by the pictures and could no longer attend to the teacher's words. When told to work the problem 3 + 5, JJ would randomly record a sum that "looked right" instead of counting up the answer. In stories, JJ would recognize the main ideas but could recall few of the details and seldom in the correct sequence. As a friend, however, he was empathic and great. Catching on to the rules of games was not a strength, but his friends somehow knew to show him how to play rather than to tell him the rules.

Friedricks, & Simpson, 1970). Often they do not know what kinds of strategies might help them learn. When studying, poor readers tend to ask themselves fewer questions to aid their comprehension, take fewer notes, look for fewer main ideas, and be less exhaustive in considering various ideas. They often ignore the fact that they don't understand words and phrases, and they fail to use a dictionary to look these up. They also do not take time to study difficult material more thoroughly than easy material (Worden, 1986). Even when they do rehearse information for memory as much as typical students, the precision with which students who are learning disabled elaborate their sentences is qualitatively different and potentially less effective in aiding recall (Wong & Sawatsky, 1984).

In many cases students with learning disabilities do not have deficits in their actual ability to learn. Rather, their learning strategies prevent them from using their basic abilities to their best advantage. They seem to have *performance deficits* rather than *ability deficits* (Brown, 1975; Gibson & Levin, 1975). When these students are taught appropriate strategies or when teaching methods circumvent their inefficiencies, their learning may equal that of their peers. For example, Torgesen (1977b) asked good and poor readers to push one button at a time to reveal each of seven pictures. The goal was to remember the pictures in order. Not only did the poor readers demonstrate worse recall than the good readers, but they also had little insight into a strategy to use for learning. Some didn't rehearse at all, others pushed the buttons in reverse order, and others rehearsed in random order. The good readers, on the other hand, systematically named the pictures and rehearsed in sequence from left to right. But, when Torgesen decided to push the buttons in sequence for the poor readers, their recall became equal to that of good readers.

Torgesen next required that twenty-four cards belonging in four categories be memorized. Good readers were initially superior to poor readers. They more often named the cards and grouped them into categories, spent more time moving the cards around, and had less off-task behavior than did the poor readers. But when the poor readers were trained to look for categories and use mnemonic devices (verbal memory tricks), their off-task behavior dropped and their memory no longer differed from that of the good readers. Poor readers also learned well when they were instructed to name the cards and actively sort them into categories (Torgesen et al., 1991).

As many youngsters with learning disabilities may underachieve because their learning strategies are inappropriate, inactive, and inefficient, *metacognitive* methods have been developed to teach them more appropriate learning strategies (Abikoff, 1979; Deshler et al., 1983; Digangi, Maag, & Rutherford, 1991; Hallahan, Kneedler, & Lloyd, 1983; Kamann & Wong, 1993; Meichenbaum, 1977; Salend et al., 1991; Wong, 1987). These methods teach children to stop and think before responding, to verbalize and rehearse what they have seen, to monitor their attention and what they are to do, to visually image what they must remember, to preplan task approaches, to use memory tricks, to reinforce their own appropriate behavior, and to organize their time. When students are encouraged to take an approach to a task that systematizes their learning, what seemed to be basic ability deficits often disappear. These task modifications can be significant aids in attenuating learning disabilities.

Setting-Based Contributors

Many environmental factors can create learning disorders in perfectly normal, healthy children, or aggravate weaknesses that already exist. One of the clearest ways in which society creates disabilities is through its value system, which puts forth one way of thinking and behaving as the right way, and rejects anything else as deviant (Blatt, 1970; Szasz, 1967). Homosexuality, for example, used to be listed by the American Psychological Association (APA) as a disease requiring treatment. Yet societal attitudes changed, and, in the 1970s, the APA dropped homosexuality from its list of psychological disorders.

The learning disabled are our most recent educationally handicapped because they fail to meet society's standards for academic success. Many individuals with learning disabilities could acquire knowledge well, were it not for the fact that reading is usually the required vehicle for this learning. Often other strengths and talents in the individual remain overlooked and undeveloped as we endlessly pursue progress in reading. Society places such importance on reading as a tool for acquiring knowledge that this value structure forces otherwise knowledgeable and well-adjusted individuals to be considered disabled. This is highlighted in the sad story of The Unlettered reprinted below.

The Unlettered

"Although sharp at all other things," the boy could not read. He was thirteen years old: at thirteen years a boy's reading lessons should be over and done. Yet he could not read: or, if he might read at all, it was only such words as "cat" and "rat."

Therefore he died, which seems heavy punishment for being dull at his reading. The tramway which runs on Southend Pier is an electric tramway. It is fenced about with railings. What are railings that they should keep a boy from climbing over them? But, besides the railings, there were placards warning all who should approach of the dangers of the live rail.

If the boy could have read the placards he would not have climbed the railing. But the placards told him nothing, he being able to spell out only the simplest of words. So he climbed and took his death from the current.

The world is like that, a perilous world for those who cannot learn to read. It must be so. We cannot fence every peril so that the unlettered may take no harm from it. There is free and compulsory education: at least everybody has his chance of learning his lessons in school. The world's business is ordered on the understanding that everybody can at least spell out words.

We walk in obedience to the written word. All about us are boards and placards, telling us to do this thing or to keep from doing that other thing. Keep to the Right, we are bidden, or else we are to Keep to the Left. By this stairway we are to descend to enter the train that goes Westward; by that we go to the Eastward train. Way Out and Way In; Private; Trespassers will be Prosecuted; Pit Entrance; the street's name and the name of the railway station—all of these things are cried out to us by that wonderful device of letters, a babble of voices which make no sound.

It is hard for us to understand the case of those to whom these many signs and warnings say nothing. They must move as though bewildered, as though they were blind and deaf. No warning touches them, not even that of the board which, like the board of the Southend tramway, cries Danger and Beware.

For such as he is, the days of school-time must be long days and weary days. I will not say that all the time is mis-spent: life nowadays is safer for the boy who can read the warning board, although painfully. But the case of the boy who could read only "cat" and "rat," although he was "sharp at other things," should have its lesson for those who are taken by the strong delusion that we may see a world of book-learned men and women if we will spend the money handsomely. For it is not so: there will always be those who cannot get beyond "cat" and "rat," even some who cannot get so far.

Source: Critchley, M. (1970). *The dyslexic child.* Springfield, IL: Charles C. Thomas (pp. xiii–xv). Reprinted by permission.

Certainly, in our culture academic competence is equated with self-worth. Those who can't meet these standards of competency are devalued and at risk for being identified disabled. There are many ways in which environments can reduce learning opportunities, motivation, and a person's ability to learn to his or her full potential: insufficient nutrition and stimulation, mismatches between an individual's cultural and linguistic background and the expectations of the school, poverty, adverse emotional climate, environmental toxins, and poor teaching.

Insufficient Nutrition and Stimulation

School breakfast and hot lunch programs demonstrate the concern of educators over nutrition's effect on learning. Certainly, a hungry child, or one who is in poor physical health, is not likely to be very motivated to put effort into school work.

Nutritional deficiencies negatively affect the maturation of the brain and central nervous system. Malnutrition interferes with brain cell production, reduces brain weight, and is particularly damaging during the first six months of life when the brain's nerve cells grow larger and the majority of synapses are formed (Brandt, 1981; Chase, 1973; Cravioto & DeLicardie, 1975; Rodier, 1984).

Cravioto's (1972) research demonstrated the long-lasting impact of malnutrition by testing Mexican children who had been admitted to a hospital for malnutrition prior to age two and a half and the sibling closest in age to them. IQ and performance on learning tasks were significantly lower for the previously malnourished children than for their siblings. Other studies, too, find long-lasting effects of early malnutrition, including soft neurological signs, reduced drive and initiative, and poorer social adaptation (Cravioto & Arrieta, 1983; Galler, Ramsey, & Solimano, 1985; Palmer & Barba, 1981; Stoch et al., 1982). Fortunately, some reversal is possible after several years of adequate nourishment and enriched caregiving (Haywood & Switzky, 1986; Pollitt et al., 1993; Winick, Meyer, & Harris, 1975; Zeskind & Ramey, 1981).

Early sensory deprivation also adversely affects brain maturation and learning (Dennis, 1960; Spitz, 1945). Research Box 3–2 reviews how reduced learning opportunities affect animal brain tissue and impair subsequent learning. It is assumed that the same is true in humans as well. Even milder losses in stimulation, such as delaying school entry, intermittent school attendance, or dropping out negatively impact intelligence (Ceci, 1991). Clearly, insufficient nutrition and stimulation can contribute to learning difficulties. Intervention is critical in order to avoid the unnecessary compromise of children's learning potentials.

Multicultural and Linguistic Diversity

We live in a society that is enriched by the traditions and values of people from different national origins, different language backgrounds, different areas of the country, different genders, sexual orientations, and so forth. Yet with this diversity comes the dilemma of having been steeped in customs, knowledge, languages, modes of thought, and styles of behavior that may not be well matched to the expectations of our schools. Our school curricula are built on middle income white expectations for the appropriate language to use, the best knowledge to learn, and the behaviors that are most acceptable. Rather than celebrating the differences among different people, our curricula all too often give the message that the white middle class way of behaving and thinking is more important than any other. How disappointing and defeating to be an African American student and study only about slavery, seldom reading the works of black authors or learning the music of the black composer. How humiliating for the Native American student to read about how the "indians" were conquered, without any mention of the rich culture that was beaten down. How frustrating for an immigrant Russian, Italian, or Castilian Spanish child, in whose language nearly each letter represents a single sound, to now learn that in English the same sounds can be represented by different letters. How difficult for a student, who doesn't know the American ways or

RESEARCH BOX 3–2
The Environment's Impact on the Brain

The environment has a powerful role in modifying the brain's structure and function. In a fascinating series of studies, Mark Rosenzweig and David Krech were able to prove Sömmering's (1791) suggestion that thinking induces growth of the brain and Spurzheim's (1815) hypothesis that brain "organs increase by exercise" (in Rosenzweig, 1966). Their subjects were rats who, at twenty-five days of age, were placed in either environmentally rich or impoverished living circumstances. The enriched condition consisted of ten to twelve animals housed in a large cage, a bright room with much other research activity going on, different toys each day (ladders, wheels, boxes, platforms), half-hour group (five or six rats) exploration of a 3-by-3-foot field whose pattern of barriers was changed daily, and formal maze training after thirty days in this stimulating environment. The impoverished situation consisted of one rat per cage with no way of seeing or touching another rat, and a quiet, dimly lit room. The animals were from the same litters and were fed similarly. Experimenters who later analyzed the rats' brains were unaware of which brain belonged to which condition.

Data from twelve of these experiments conducted over a five-year period showed that the cortex of 80 percent of the enriched rats weighed 4 percent more than that of the restricted rats (Rosenzweig, 1966). This was due to the development of thicker gray matter in enriched rats' visual centers. Their brains also contained greater numbers of glial cells (which provide structural and nutritional support for the brain's neurons) and more of the chemicals used in neural transmission. Even metabolic activity seemed higher, as suggested by increased RNA/DNA ratios (Rosenzweig, Bennett, & Diamond, 1972). Control groups indicated that these results could not be accounted for by the differences in locomotion, handling, and isolation alone. Animals reared in complex but dark environments demonstrated shrinkage of the visual centers but growth in touch and body movement areas. Those reared in isolation had decreased brain tissue growth (Krech, Rosenzweig, & Bennett, 1966).

Rosenzweig found that brain weight could be increased even in old rats. Their learning ability also increased. He jokingly commented that, "If these cerebral changes reflect learning and storage of memory, these results may be encouraging to those of us who are gray around the edges" (Krech et al., 1966, p. 327).

Many other investigations have supported Rosenzweig's and Krech's findings (Coleman & Riesen, 1968; Kratz, Sherman, & Kalil, 1979; Pysh & Weiss, 1979; Valverde, 1967). For example, Bell's research group (1971) found that mice reared in crowded living conditions had reduced concentrations of brain protein and nucleic acids, reduced brain weight, and decreased DNA synthesis. Conversely, Greenough and Juraska (1979) reported that rats reared in enriched environments, relative to littermates reared in isolation, showed more extensive dendritic fields for electric conduction in several brain regions. Similar findings were reported in monkeys. Rats handled in the first twenty-one days of life have appeared to develop different brain asymmetries than unhandled rats (Marx, 1983). Rosenzweig (1979) found that rats who had to learn their way through a complex maze to get

(Continues on following page)

RESEARCH BOX 3–2 *(Continued from preceding page)*

food and water had heavier brains with different amounts of RNA than less challenged rats. Even jewel fish raised in a community tank had far greater dendritic branching and spine formation than fish raised in isolation (Coss & Globus, 1978).

Enriched environments clearly have been beneficial to animals with surgically induced brain injury. When these animals are exposed to stimulation either prior to, after, or in between brain operations, they generally recover better than animals deprived of these enriching experiences (Finger, 1978; Rosenzweig, Bennett, & Alberti, 1984). The same is true when mental retardation is induced with hypothyroidism (Davenport, 1976).

Only recently has the influence of learning on the human brain's neural transmissions been demonstrated (Bakker, 1984; Bakker & Vinke, 1985; Elbert et al., 1995; John et al., 1977; Karni et al., 1995; Tzavaras, Kaprinis, & Gatzoyas, 1981). In his 1983 Presidential Address to the International Neuropsychological Society Meetings in Lisbon, Bakker (1984) introduced this exciting new research era in the following way:

> "As the heart pumps blood, the brain pumps behavior" has been asserted by Filskov, Grimm, and Lewis (1981, p. 39). I would like to call attention to the reverse, i.e. to behavior that "pumps the brain" (p. 1).
>
> Life does not prosper without food, water, and air. Life does not prosper without a stimulating environment either. Bad food and bad air are not good for the brain, and poor psychological stimulation does not help either. It is the environment which provides stimuli and it is man who, on the basis of whatever philosophy or social demand, decides what good and poor environments are. That is to say, we all, to some significant extent, determine not only what behaviors are called for, but also what brains, as the carriers of these behaviors, ultimately will look like (p. 13).

Research is just beginning to help us understand how teaching programs can actually modify children's information processing on a physiological level.

whose native language is not English, to feel valued and motivated to do well in this strange environment. No wonder some students feel alienated, unappreciated, unwelcome, unmotivated, and confused. It is easy to see how the clash between their backgrounds and the culture of the school can contribute to learning disabilities.

Many children who are multiculturally and linguistically diverse enter school with sociolinguistic conventions that are mismatched with the content and structure of the school curriculum, thereby causing confusion and misunderstanding. For example, it is reported that some Native American and Asian children may hesitate to initiate interaction with the teacher or respond to questions because, in their cultures, it is impolite and unnatural to set oneself apart from the group. Blending in, even if it means denying their knowledge of subject matter, is the course of action they have been acculturated to view as correct (Nazarro, 1981). Many Native Americans have been taught that it is disrespectful to make eye contact or give a firm handshake, that direct questions are rude, that personal information is to be shared only if others share as well, that following in the ways of the elders (maintaining the status quo) is good, that anonymity and submissiveness are preferable to asserting individuality, and that time moves with the flow of events rather than with the hands of the clock (Sattler, 1992).

Clearly such teachings, which having enriched the lives of those who share this heritage, are at odds with much of the individualism, competitiveness, and punctuality stressed in our classrooms.

Just as the Native American student may be acculturated not to answer direct questions, the Hawaiian student may feel picked on when questioned by teachers because in many Hawaiian homes there is little direct questioning by adults. Many African American students may simply not answer when questioned because they don't understand why a teacher would ask something they already know; they are not accustomed to this type of questioning from their parents (Ambert, 1991). The school's stress on competition, staying in one's seat, and working on one's own further conflicts with a common African American cultural emphasis on harmony, movement, and communalism (Boykin, 1994).

Hispanic students may look away from the teacher out of respect; to be polite, they will avoid disagreement with a directive, and simply won't follow through. If they do follow through, it may be mañana, because their culture is less time bound than the American culture (Langdon, 1992). These customs are misunderstood by teachers, as is the Mexican American child's tendency to copy classwork from another student; for this they have been wrongfully labeled dishonest, lazy, poorly motivated, and bad students. Yet sharing of knowledge and responsibilities is the way they have learned to function within their families. Seldom are things done alone; even carrying out the garbage is a family affair. If these children conform to individualism and competition, they are being untrue to the lessons learned from their roots; this presents quite a dilemma for them (Delgado-Gaitan & Trueba, 1985).

Language differences constitute another major mismatch with our school expectations. By the year 2000, approximately 15 percent of school children will be immigrants whose first language is something other than English, and one-third will be from sociocultural minority groups (American Council on Education, 1988; Langdon, 1992). Because the language of different ethnic groups and lower socioeconomic status children represents a significant mismatch with the language of the school, the teacher's verbally based content and methods may play an important role in handicapping their learning (Baratz & Shuy, 1969; Bernstein, 1960; Hallahan & Cruickshank, 1973).

Consider the difficulty of phonics instruction, for example, with immigrants from China; they will be handicapped because many English consonant sounds do not exist in Chinese (Chan, 1986). How confusing phonics instruction must be for the Korean child who cannot formulate our f, r, th, v, and z sounds (Smith & Luckasson, 1992). Even when a child finally does gain conversational facility in English, it will take many more years until the child has mastered the language of the books and classroom (Collier & Hoover, 1987). Research Box 3–3 explores why teachers cannot assume that their students will look at the world in the same way they do. Because language and culture are so closely intertwined, a concept that exists in the American culture may be totally meaningless to a child speaking another native tongue.

Clearly, it is essential for us to be sensitive to the multicultural and linguistic diversity among our students, so that these students' perspectives, backgrounds, and knowledge are valued. Curricula, attitudes, and teaching approaches must be modified to foster these students' self-respect and intrinsic motivation, by welcoming use of their native language in the school and giving them opportunities to contribute to the culture of the classroom. Such inclusiveness can mitigate chances of these students beginning to view themselves as failures, sapped of the will and effort to succeed. These children will make more rapid academic and social gains if their language and culture are utilized as rich sources of learning (Ambert, 1991; Langdon, 1992).

Poverty

Poverty is clearly associated with learning disabilities. Even among the learning disabled, progress tends to be more limited for those who live in poverty (Schonhaut & Satz, 1983). Today, one in five American children lives in poverty, as do over 40 percent of African American and Hispanic

RESEARCH BOX 3–3

The Influence of Language on What We See and Think

The idea that language has a fundamental influence on thought itself was advanced by Benjamin Whorf (1956). For example, Eskimos have hundreds of terms to differentiate one type of snow from another. Non-Eskimos have very few names for types of snow and can't imagine or even recognize all the varieties that the Eskimos say exist. On the other hand, Eskimos have only one name for what we label as blue, purple, and violet; therefore, they do not interpret these hues with the same complexity that we do. Likewise, Eskimos and Navajos label red, orange, and yellow as only two colors (Collier & Hoover, 1987). Eskimos also have no word for bread, and consequently have no idea what it is. To the average American, a camel is a camel, but to the average Arab, the conception of camels is far richer, with over fifty words to describe these animals. For the American, rhyming games are important precursors to reading. But in most Asian languages rhymes do not exist, so the Asian American will have difficulty appreciating important preschool rhyming activities, and nursery rhymes will hold little appeal (Welton, 1990). Clearly, language and culture are so tied to one another that teachers cannot assume that pupils from socioculturally and linguistically diverse backgrounds will see the world as they do. These children quite literally do not. Their differences must not only be understood, but also used to enrich the cultural and conceptual fabric of the classroom

families with young children and Native Americans living on reservations (Children's Defense Fund, 1996; Quality Education for Minorities Project, 1990; in Smith & Luckasson, 1992). One in every four homeless individuals is a child (U.S. Conference of Mayors, 1994).

Approximately 25 percent of Caucasian, 64 percent of African American, and 36 percent of Hispanic families are headed by only one parent, usually a mother (U.S. Bureau of the Census, 1995). Thirty percent of single mothers have not completed high school, 50 percent are unemployed, and 62 percent live on incomes below $10,000 (Hickman, 1989). Nearly half of all female school dropouts are pregnant, and half of these teens (and teen fathers) never graudate (Hodgkinson, 1986).

Unfortunately, the school and home education that many of these young people receive is insufficient to promote academic and vocational success. Today's eighth graders who are African American, Hispanic, Native American, or from low socioeconomic backgrounds are deficient in basic reading and mathematics skills when compared with other students (*Characteristics of At-Risk Students in NELS: 88*, 1992; *Condition of Education*, 1996). The high school dropout rate in low-income families is 25 percent, compared to a national dropout rate of 11 percent (*Condition of Education*, 1994). The earnings of dropouts are one-third less than the earnings of those who graduate high school (*Condition of Education*, 1997).

In 1995, 87 percent of African American and 57 percent of Hispanic youth had graduated from high school. This is in contrast to 92 percent of whites. Of white young adults, 31 percent go on to complete college: this contrasts with only around 18 percent of African American and 16 percent of Hispanic young adults (*Condition of Education*, 1996). The earnings of college graduates are over twice that of high school dropouts (*Condition of Education,* 1997).

The poor achievement of some low-income individuals is due in part to insufficiencies in nutrition and medical care, both of which compromise brain development. Almost all complications of prenatal life, pregnancy, labor, and delivery, as well as postnatal diseases and accidents that potentially can harm the infant's brain development, occur at a disproportionately higher rate among low-income groups (Kavale, 1980a; Teberg, Walther, & Pena, 1988). As a result, neurodevelopmental abnormalities are more likely (American Council on Education, 1988; Coll, 1990; Kirchner & Peterson, 1988; Pasamanick & Knobloch, 1961; Task Force on Pediatric AIDS, 1989). The adverse health effects of lower rates of physical activity among those living in poverty, and higher rates of tobacco and alcohol consumption, depression, hostile attitudes, and psychological stress don't help matters (Adler et al., 1994).

Other poverty-related correlates of poor learning include low immunization rates, lead poisoning, encephalitis, malnutrition (American Council on Education, 1988); immature language development (Broman, Bien, & Shaughnessy, 1985); delayed language specialization in the brain (Geffner & Hochberg, 1971; Kimura, 1967); poor ability to recognize and transpose sounds in words (Wallach et al., 1977); impulsivity (Schwebel, 1966); hyperactivity (Nichols & Chen, 1981); low fund of information and problem-solving abilities important to success in standard curricula (Mumbauer & Miller, 1970; Sattler, 1992; Skeels & Skodak, 1966); lack of variety in sensory stimuli (Uzgiris, 1970); minimal home encouragement of scholastic success (Larsen, 1978); less time spent on task in the classroom and in homework (Lerner, 1981); and low parental educational level; loss of one or more parents; families with many children; late birth order in a large family; migrancy; inadequate home climate (toys; books; playing rhyming, sound analysis, and alphabet games; enriching experiences; parental example and encouragement; emotional atmosphere) (Aiken, 1987; Broman et al., 1985; Ehri, 1989; Kochanek, Kabacoff, & Lipsitt, 1990;

Patterson, Kupersmidt, & Vaden, 1990; Smith & Luckasson, 1992).

The need for low-income women to work, thereby delaying childbirth, also is of concern. With over half of American women in the workforce, women are postponing first pregnancies beyond the optimal childbearing period (ages twenty to thirty). As a result, concern has heightened about increased risk to the offspring of older mothers (Kopp & Kaler, 1989).

Because what has been learned from one's home, school, and general environment is neurochemically represented in the brain and alters the brain's general capacities (Elbert et al., 1995; Rourke et al., 1983; Starck et al., 1977), this learning is likely to affect future achievement. Therefore, it is essential that we offer parent education programs pertaining to health and child-rearing concerns, as well as job training and continuing education, to help fight the adverse effects of poverty on learning potential. Unfortunately, illiteracy and fewer years of education are predictive of unemployment, underemployment, and poverty. High school graduation and home environments that foster the type of learning expected in our schools are critical to breaking the cycle of poverty.

Adverse Emotional Climate

Beyond their poverty, cultural, and language differences, it is understandable that children who have fled war, torture, or famine, only to face a new culture without one of their parents, or orphaned, can be so emotionally disrupted that school achievement is virtually impossible. Osofsky (1995) documents the large percentage of children living in "urban war zones" who have witnessed murders and serious assaults. How could these children possibly be motivated to concentrate in school given their increased anxiety, depression, sleep disturbances, aggression, and withdrawal? In 1994 alone, 3.1 million reports of child abuse and neglect were made to juvenile authorities in the United States (Children's Defense Fund, 1996). Unfortunately, far less than such extreme trauma also can disrupt learning:

family disorganization; divorce and emotional instability; maternal stress during pregnancy; harsh, critical, and neglectful maternal infant care-giving; paternal job/income loss; difficult parental temperaments; and reinforcement of behaviors incompatible with school success (McLoyd, 1989; Meier, 1971; Nichols & Chen, 1981; Owen et al., 1971; Ross & Ross, 1976; Stott, 1973).

Emotional stress can develop in response to the frustrations of school failure as well. Finding that children with learning disabilities tend to be more depressed than children with no learning disabilities, Goldstein and Dundon (1987) suggest that their negative mood reduces the amount of energy these children have available to put into effortful mental activities, such as academics. Irrelevant thoughts will sidetrack their attention, and sadness, poor self-esteem, and anxiety can subtly influence and direct children's cognitive activities. There is some evidence that, when teachers induce more positive moods, these students may for the moment improve the amount, accuracy, and rate of their learning (Yasutake & Bryan, 1995).

Emotional states can alter neuroendocrine and immune responses in such a way as to increase risk of illness (for example, gastrointestinal disorders, heart disease, stroke, infections, growth retardation), which in turn can affect learning (Adler et al., 1994; Sandberg & Barrick, 1995). Emotional states also can cause neurological diseases (such as tension headaches), intensify a disease process (for example, bring on seizures), or simulate a neurological disorder (for example, hysterical paralysis of a limb) (Valenstein & Heilman, 1979). Because any type of stress, pain, or effort activates the brain through increased blood flow (Lassen, Ingvar, & Skinhøj, 1978), emotional states actually are represented as changes in the brain, just as learning strengths and weaknesses are.

If environmental stress can trigger emotional states that then become unique brain states, then these brain states in turn can contribute to learning disabilities. The more we can alleviate such stresses, the more we prevent their contributing to learning disabilities.

Environmental Toxins

Environmental toxins can predispose us before or after birth to severe learning and health problems. Most of the over 53,000 chemicals in our pesticides, drugs, cosmetics, food additives, and commercial substances have not been pretested for their neurobehavioral effects (Fisher, 1985). To date, occupational standards have been set for only about 600 chemicals. Of these, nearly one third have deleterious effects on the central nervous system. It is important for us to be aware of these potential hazards in our environments so that we can help students and their families avoid agents that may deter learning. We will discuss prenatal and postnatal effects of toxins, food allergies, and nonfood allergies. Although allergies do interfere with the ability to maintain attention to instruction, allergies are not considered causal in learning disabilities, except in a very few young children who react to food additives with hyperactivity.

Prenatal Toxic Effects. Prenatal exposure to toxins can affect the brain development of the fetus and lead to later learning disorders. The brain in utero is generating neurons at the rate of 250,000 per minute. Yet, the fetus has neither a placental barrier against toxic substances nor the capacity to detoxify them (Kolb, 1989; Moya & Smith, 1965; Spyker, 1974). Consequently, prenatal exposure to toxins such as mercury and cadmium can adversely affect later health and cognitive status (Lewis et al., 1992; Rodier, 1984). Mercury arrests the division of neurons, and cadmium damages the circulatory system, resulting in brain hemorrhages. Inhalant anesthetics, too, are known to interfere with cell proliferation. Lead, a long-known offender, causes problems with the brain's blood vessels and reduces the number of neurons and dendrite connections. Low-dose prenatal lead exposure can result in preterm delivery, and higher doses can lead to spontaneous abortion (McMichael et al., 1986). A high lead concentration in umbilical cord blood at delivery has been related to a five-point decrease in overall intellectual and motor development in preschoolers (Bellinger et al., 1987). Marijuana smoking during pregnancy increases the risk for premature delivery and subsequent learning problems (Clayman, 1988). In addition, illicit drugs such as cocaine can cause structural malformation of the brain due to the oxygen deprivation caused by constricted blood supply to the placenta (Adler, 1992). Delayed langauge and fine-motor development, marked hyperactivity, irritability, distractibility, and depressed interactive behavior after birth are typical in these children (Phelps & Cox, 1993); in this country, 1,000 cocaine-involved children are born every day (National Task Force for Children's Constitutional Rights, 1991).

Maternal cigarette smoking is associated with hyperactivity and mild intellectual and academic decrements in the offspring (Denson, Nanson, & McWatters, 1975; Dunn et al., 1977; Nichols & Chen, 1981). Excessive maternal alcohol consumption may lead to neurological and physical abnormalities, significant cognitive delays, hyperactivity, attention and memory problems, fine- and gross-motor delays, language deficits, difficulty with organization and problem solving, and emotional lability in the child (Phelps, 1995; Streissguth, Sampson, & Barr, 1989). As little as one drink a day during pregnancy can be harmful.

Although the harmful effects of mercury, cadmium, lead, illicit drugs, tobacco, and alcohol are evident in both the mother and fetus, some toxins do not have toxic effects on the pregnant mother but do affect the developing fetus: for example, the sleeping pill thalidomide, which led to missing limbs (Taussig, 1962) or the acne medicine Acutane, which results in severe heart or craniofacial deformities (microcephaly, absent ears, small eyes) (Hansen, 1985). The effects of other prenatal toxins are not immediately apparent at birth. For example, a high incidence of vaginal cancer and a 69 percent greater chance of miscarriage or giving premature birth have been found among adult daughters whose mothers took diethylstilbestrol (DES) to prevent miscarriage (Barnes et al., 1980); when babies are born prematurely, there is a greater risk of subsequent learning disabilities. Based on animal studies, there is growing concern that our relief at the disappearance of some children's neurotoxic symptoms early in life may be premature, in that symptoms may reappear again at an older age (Azar, 1995). Clearly, many prenatal toxic agents can increase the risk of later learning disorders.

Postnatal Toxic Effects. The neurological, psychological, intellectual, learning, and behavioral effects of contact with environmental toxins after birth have been well documented, including lead, arsenic, aluminum, cadmium, carbon monoxide, mercury, radiation, chemotherapy, and illicit drugs (Smith, 1991). Often parents carry toxic particles or dust home on their clothing, shoes, or bodies from work (e.g., auto repair, battery manufacturing) or from their hobbies (e.g., pottery, stained glass, furniture refinishing). Family members are contaminated further by pesticides, air pollution, drugs, and possible toxins in cosmetics (Rosenstock et al., 1991; Science Agenda, 1990; Wood, Weiss, & Weiss, 1973). There is some evidence that exposure to neurotoxic substances actually may trigger such neurological disorders as Parkinson's, Alzheimer's, and Lou Gehrig's disease.

Although the dangers of high lead exposure have been recognized for centuries, low-level lead exposure, as from lead-based gasoline emissions, paint chips, soil, or water pipes, only recently has come under scrutiny. Low-level lead exposure does diminish cognitive functioning, often by four to five IQ points. Although this may seem to be a trifling reduction, toxicologists are quick to point out that if everyone in the United States suffered this reduction, we would nearly cut by 50 percent (by over 2½ million) the numbers of people testing at superior levels of intelligence.

The long-term learning and behavior changes that students bring on themselves with abuse of licit and illicit drugs are very serious concerns. It is heartbreaking to see a friend's son return home after one semester at Harvard devoid of any affect, frightening people as he stares suspiciously into their eyes, without common sense as to whether to shower or change clothes from day to day, and no longer able to manage more than the cash register at his parents' store—all because he took LSD laced with PCP. The brain damage was permanent, with little improvement even fifteen years later. As educators, we have the responsibility to be aware of how toxins may impair students' neurological and behavioral development, and to work preventively with students, parents, and politicians to reduce dangers from drug abuse, industrial hazards, and environmental pollution.

Food Allergies. Another toxin that has attracted interest in recent years is individual sensitivity to certain foods. Mayron (1979) estimated that 60 to 80 percent of individuals are allergic to at least one food. Toxic reactions include hives, headaches, and stomach problems. There have been many clinical observations of hyperactive behavior following ingestion of artificial food colors and flavors (Feingold, 1976; Green, 1974; Lockey, 1977), salicylates (aspirin-like compounds occurring in natural fruits and vegetables), aspirin (Settipane & Pudupakkam, 1975), and preservatives (Lockey, 1972; Michaelsson & Juhlin, 1973). Feingold (1975) attributed these responses to a toxic effect on the central nervous system. It has been reported that Americans typically ingest 5 pounds of these food additives per year (Sabo, 1976).

Research at the National Institute of Neurological and Communicative Disorders and Stroke has supported Feingold's contention that some children are sensitive to artificial food colors. This research group found that some dyes readily enter brain cells and interfere with chemical communication by inhibiting the nerve cells' uptake of neurotransmitters. Because the particular enzyme that the dye affects is controlled by a child's genetic makeup, it was hypothesized that some children may respond negatively to food dyes, whereas others may not (*ACLD Newsbriefs,* 1982).

Feingold's diet, which eliminates artificial flavorings, colorings, and salicylates, has been used in an attempt to reduce hyperactivity in children. In several well-controlled studies children alternated two experimental diets: Feingold's diet and one disguised as Feingold's diet but containing additives. Neither children, parents, teachers, nor experimenters knew when a child was on or off Feingold's diet. These studies conclude that

only a very small subgroup of young, hyperactive children appear to respond to food additives with an increase in hyperactivity.

Despite clinical reports of improvement on Feingold's diet, there is little consistency within each experimental study. In general, behavior has improved only slightly better than what might be expected by chance. In addition, essentially no gains have been shown in attention and learning ability, although in two studies deterioration in learning and visual-motor tracking was evident after ingestion of dyes and additives (Goyette et al., 1978; Kavale & Forness, 1983; Swanson & Kinsbourne, 1980). At times teachers note significant improvement whereas parents do not (Conners et al., 1976). At other times parents note positive changes, whereas teachers note fewer changes, and neuropsychological tests, objective observers, and laboratory observations indicate none (Harley, Matthews, & Eichman, 1978). When children who responded favorably to Feingold's diet continued on the diet but ingested cookies, candy bars, or sodas containing additives, they demonstrated very little of the expected deterioration in behavior. Behavioral deterioration occurred in only one child of nine (Harley et al., 1978), one child of twenty-two (Weiss et al., 1980), and three children of fifteen (Goyette et al., 1978). Those who responded to the additives with hyperactivity were generally the youngest in the study.

Because of these inconsistent findings, some experts suggest that most favorable results on Feingold's diet actually are a result of other things: heightened expectations when families guess their child is on the diet, increased attention to the child, altered family dynamics, or changes in general nutritional status (Stare, Whelan, & Sheridan, 1980). Others argue that positive results would be more striking if children were removed from all possible contact with additives (Mayron, 1979), if ratings of behavior were frequent enough to reflect small changes in behavior, and if quantities of additives tested were not so far below the typical amount ingested in any one day (Conners, 1980).

Certainly the deleterious effects of additives do not seem to be as widespread as Feingold and his supporters have claimed. If artificial flavors, colors, and preservatives do produce toxic behavioral responses, then this seems to occur in only an extremely small subgroup of young, hyperactive children.

Nonfood Allergies. A growing area of interest is the relationship between learning disabilities and allergies to far more than foods. Case studies have linked allergies to learning difficulties and to school absenteeism, which further deters achievement (McLoughlin, Nall, & Petrosko, 1985). However, well-designed studies have not found that more youngsters with learning disabilities than those without learning disabilities suffer from allergies (McLoughlin et al., 1983, 1985). Nor has the achievement of allergic students with disabilities been any lower than that of nonallergic students with disabilities.

Most experts believe that allergies aggravate rather than cause learning disabilities. When students must live with the discomfort of wheezing, itchy eyes, and runny noses, it is no wonder that they will be diverted from paying attention and studying. Moreover, allergy-related ear infections do cause intermittent hearing and comprehension losses in the classroom. Ironically, the side effects of allergy medications may themselves complicate learning by causing attention difficulties, hyperactivity, visual disturbances, restlessness, dizziness, irritability, lethargy, insomnia, and reduced problem-solving energy (McLoughlin et al., 1985).

Often parents will seek allergy treatments for their children, in hopes of alleviating learning disorders. Evidence thus far supports such treatments as a way to help students become sufficiently comfortable to attend to instruction, but not as a means to attenuate the learning disability itself.

Poor Teaching

Poor teaching has received much attention as a contributor to learning disorders. Poor teaching involves far more than an inappropriate match of tasks to learner characteristics. It also involves the kinds of expectations teachers communicate to students, the teacher's ability to deal with special needs in the classroom, his or her knowledge of normal child development, sensitivity to the different learning strategies/behavioral styles youngsters bring to the school environment, and understanding that when English is a second language students may seem conversationally fluent yet still lack the necessary academic language proficiency. Poor teaching also implicates inappropriate teaching environments, narrow bands of behavioral expectations, nonmotivating materials and methods, inflexible and stigmatizing school grouping practices, the radical adoption of unvalidated instructional methods, and narrow curricula (for example, that about 80% of middle school math textbooks consist of reviews of the same material; Englemann, Carnine, & Steely, 1991). When teachers do not personalize instruction to accommodate individual differences, the numbers of children with learning problems increase (Adelman, 1971).

Certainly, poor teaching can aggravate preexisting learning problems. Yet other students may be erroneously identified as learning disabled because they have fallen behind as a result of inappropriate learning opportunities (Larsen, 1978). Their discrepancy between potential and achievement is a pseudodiscrepancy that would not have occurred had teaching been personalized. They were never learning disabled in the first place.

Lieberman (1980a) points out that "in some school systems 30 to 40 percent of the children are functioning below grade level. This is not an epidemiological survey of handicapping conditions but an indictment of educational practices" (p. 67). Given such staggering underachievement, Bateman (1974) recommended that the term *learning disabilities* be replaced by the term *teaching disabilities,* which focuses on the inadequacies of teachers' skills and the teaching environment. Clearly, the problem is not in the child alone. If students are to change, it is only because teachers and parents have made changes in tasks and settings that will facilitate their learning and development. Because responsibility for child development must rest with the system, not just with the child, it is imperative that we examine the adequacy of the regular class environment before judging a student disabled. We must direct at least as many diagnostic and remedial procedures toward school systems as we do toward school children.

Implications for Assessment and Intervention

We have learned that students with learning disabilities differ from one another in their personal characteristics as well as the life experiences that have moderated or exacerbated their learning difficulties. Consequently, careful assessment of the student and his or her learning environments is essential before deciding on the most appropriate classroom modifications or family interventions.

The learner, task, and setting factors that can contribute to learning disabilities do place particular students at higher risk for learning and adjustment difficulties. However, the influence of these factors is not a sure thing. For example, in spite of coming from the most impoverished or dysfunctional homes, many children do very well in school and excel in all aspects of life (Werner, 1989). Despite emotional turmoil, many students are resilient and may even be strengthened by these conflicts. Despite maturational lags, some children do catch up (Fletcher & Satz, 1980; Lyon, 1995). Although generally less efficient than typical learners in their strategy use, many students with learning disabilities nevertheless do employ appropriate strategies on some tasks (Shepherd & Gelzheiser, 1987; Swanson, 1983; Torgesen, Murphy, & Ivey, 1979; Warner et al., 1989).

When a learning disability does become apparent, the youngster's situation requires very careful examination before intervention plans are formulated. Learning strategy training, counseling, parent education, nutritional adjustments, allergy treatments, and so forth can never be proposed dogmatically for every student with a learning disability. Each student is an individual, whose learning and adjustment is the result of a unique interaction between personal characteristics and the tasks and settings to which he or she has been exposed. The nature of this interaction must guide the programming efforts.

Summary

Students with learning disabilities enter the classroom with unique patterns of strengths and weaknesses. Some abilities that are important for academic achievement are well developed, whereas others are immature. These youngsters often have fairly stable styles in approaching learning tasks. Whether any of these students' uneven ability patterns and unique learning styles become liabilities depends on the nature of the school tasks they are expected to accomplish and the settings in which they study, live, and play.

Learning success is facilitated when school tasks are well matched to what a student is ready to learn and to his or her learning styles. Maturational lag theorists believe that the selective immaturities of students with learning disabilities make them unready for the work of their grade. Because their delays for the most part are qualitatively like that of younger normally developing children, similar teaching strategies often can be employed for both groups. However, if we teach beyond these students' capability levels, then distortions in the normal learning process may occur, leading to more permanent and severe deficits. Cognitive style theorists note that students' stable predispositions toward perceiving and interacting with information are advantageous to learning in some circumstances but detrimental in others. Detail-oriented teaching objectives and discovery-oriented teaching methods are particularly mismatched with the cognitive styles and learning strategies that many students bring to school tasks, thereby contributing to learning disorders.

Besides appropriately matching the curriculum to students' learning needs, intervention is necessary to avoid learning delays associated with inadequate nutrition and stimulation, poverty, adverse emotional climate, environmental toxins, and poor teaching. In addition, it is very important for teachers to be sensitive to the multicultural and linguistic diversity in their classrooms, and to modify the curriculum to welcome these students and meet their academic needs.

Much responsibility for learning success falls on the modifications educators and parents make in tasks and settings. Consequently, when we explore what might be contributing to a student's learning problems, we must consider how specific task and setting factors are interacting with the youngster's unique physiological, learning, and personality characteristics. When the positive attributes of each are combined, the effects of the learning disability can be moderated, and the chances for academic and behavioral progress are enhanced.

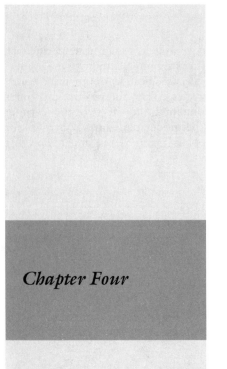

Chapter Four

Information-Processing Patterns in Learning Disabilities

When a learner, task, or setting factor contributes to a learning disability, what exactly has happened? We have learned that any of these factors can contribute to diminished knowledge, so that a student might be unprepared to deal with the school's curriculum. We also have learned that when the curriculum is not adapted to a student's unique learning styles school achievement can be adversely affected. In this chapter we focus on the underlying reason why learning becomes such a challenge for students with learning disabilities: the development of their information-processing abilities is inadequate to support the school's learning expectations.

By definition, students with learning disabilities are not remembering the information to which they are exposed. This chapter explores the way in which information-processing immaturities can contribute to these memory difficulties. Our information-processing abilities must work in concert with our cognitive abilities, learning styles, current knowledge, social skills, and motivation to determine exactly what we will learn and how well we will remember.

Studies have focused on four information-processing abilities that can be affected by learner, task, or setting contributors to learning disabilities: visual-perceptual skills, language and phonological-processing skills, attention, and motor skills. We have found that peripheral visual defects do not seem to cause learning disabilities, although they can aggravate existing disorders. Motor difficulties make expression of knowledge difficult, thereby interfering with success. Visual-perceptual processes appear to be important to reading and math achievement at young ages and, in very subtle ways, relate to some later spelling, writing, mathematical, and conceptual difficulties. They do not seem to be a major contributor to the skills needed for progress in many higher-level academic areas. Instead, researchers find that language, phonological-processing, and attention deficits play the greatest role in the most severe, long-lasting learning problems.

Visual-Perceptual Skills

As Cara's and Mimi's stories (below) illustrate, for most people poor vision and uncoordinated eye movements do not seem to be at the root of their reading disorders. The efficiency with which children with visual impairments scan visual material is equivalent to that of children with no visual impairments (Knowlton, 1997). Even farsightedness aggravates rather than causes reading disorders, and we find that people with poor eye movements usually read well (Gruber, 1962; Stein, Riddell, & Fowler, 1986). Interestingly, at times good readers have been reported to have more fusion and muscle imbalance problems than poor readers (Witty & Kopel, 1936).

Despite the popular belief fifty years ago that the eye itself is to blame for reading disorders (Betts, 1936; Dearborn, 1933; Eames, 1934),

studies find no differences between the peripheral visual functions of good and poor readers (Benton, 1969; Brown et al., 1983; Helveston et al., 1985; Letourneau, Lapierre, & Lamont, 1979). The only exception is for individuals whose documented prematurity, brain lesions, or seizure disorders led to brain dysfunctions that caused both the irregular eye movements and the reading delays (Eames, 1955; Elterman et al., 1980; Pavlidis, 1986; Rayner, 1986). These individuals have been reported to prefer moving their eyes to the left whether reading or following jumping lights, and some even report reading better when the reading material is held upside down. It is these people's brain dysfunction that has caused both the reading delays and the strange eye movements, although the latter certainly don't make the reading task any easier.

Because reading involves the mental translation of visual symbols into language, reading depends primarily on the ability to process information at a perceptual and cognitive level, well beyond the peripheral level of the eye. That is why we find that children with reading disorders also are deficient in learning symbol systems that avoid vision, such as Morse Code and Braille (Rudel, Denckla, & Spalten, 1976).

When reading, the typical reader's eyes proceed through a succession of pauses (fixations), each followed by a smooth, fast jump (saccades). The eyes are in a state of fixation for about 87 to

Cara and Mimi

Cara was born with a congenital defect of the iris. She is legally blind and must hold paper 4 inches from her face in order to be able to see print. Mimi was born with a muscle imbalance in her eyes. Because the muscles of her eyes don't coordinate with one another, she can use only one eye at a time. When Mimi is reading with her left eye, it all of a sudden may wander off and the right eye then takes over the reading. In spite of their visual difficulties, both girls read extremely well. They are well liked by their classmates and are actively involved in all class activities and discussions. Only in art class is their work never chosen for display, nor are they chosen first for any team in physical education classes.

95 percent of total reading time (Pavlidis, 1981). When the text becomes harder to sound out or comprehend, both good and poor readers' eye movements will regress to reread a word or phrase, or their eyes will move forward slowly to gain time for analysis (Fletcher, 1991; Rayner, 1986). Because the task of decoding and comprehending is so much more difficult for students with reading disabilities, these youngsters generally need more fixations, longer fixations, and more regressions (instead of a large leftward sweep once a line is finished, they use multiple, small fixations or diagonal movements to retrace part of the line toward the left) (Pavlidis, 1986; Zangwill & Blakemore, 1972). That the complexities of the reading task itself may be prompting these irregular eye movements, rather than an eye movement problem causing the reading disability, is consistent with data showing that the eye movements of many people with reading disabilities are not irregular when tasks do not involve reading, such as while scanning pictures or following patterns of light, or when the reading material is easy to decode and comprehend (Brown et al., 1983; Fletcher, 1991; Olson, Kliegl, & Davidson, 1983; Stanley, Smith, & Howell, 1983).

In order to alleviate any peripheral visual difficulties that could aggravate reading disorders by causing discomfort, fatigue, inefficiency, confusion, or avoidance when reading, optometrists often engage in visual training to improve the coordination and efficiency of the visual system. They nevertheless urge that reading remediation accompany the visual training (Getman, 1977).

In a special report of the American Optometric Association, 238 citations were used to support visual training's usefulness in facilitating the functioning of the eyes (lazy eye, eyes turning out or in, poor focusing, poor eye aiming, involuntary oscillation of the eyeball) (Cohen, 1988). Only one of these citations, however, studied the effect of visual training on the reading performance of children with learning disabilities, and the effects were weak (Punnett & Steinhauer, 1984). Consequently, the American Academies of Ophthalmology (1981) and Pediatrics, Ophthalmology and Otolaryngology, with the American Association of Pediatric Ophthalmology and Stra-

bismus issued an advisory for medical specialists to correct peripheral visual problems, but then leave the remediation of reading difficulties to the educator: "Medical specialists may assist in bringing the child's potential to the best level, but the actual remedial educational procedures remain the responsibility of educators" (Flax, 1973, pp. 332–333). Concern was raised that visual training could create a false sense of security that might delay proper instructional programming (Flax, Mozlin, & Solan, 1984).

With growing evidence that peripheral visual functions at best aggravate rather than cause learning problems, the thrust of visual research shifted to visual perception, the brain's ability to process visual information. The term *visual perception* is applied to the process of taking in visual information, interpreting what is seen, organizing this information, and storing and transmitting it.

Joseph's story (page 119) illustrates several ways in which severe visual-perceptual lags may interfere with performance even into adulthood. Researchers have found that visual-perceptual difficulties have the greatest relationship to academic progress in the early school years. For some individuals, however, visual-perceptual interferences persist at mild to moderate levels throughout life. For some, their inefficient visual processing appears related to slower pick-up of information from the visual images they see. Therefore, less information, or more confusing information, is available to the individual for storage. Others, despite having learned to sound out words, never seem to have mastered the visual-perceptual initial phases of reading. Just as you may have difficulty seeing the correct image jump out at you in Figure 4–1 (page 120), these adults continue to have trouble recognizing words at a glance, remembering common English spelling patterns, or remembering the spellings of irregular words that cannot be sounded out. Related math and social reasoning difficulties are not uncommon.

Table 4–1 (page 121) lists some visual-perceptual areas in which researchers find that students like Joseph perform poorly. Because many of these abilities involve language, motor, attention, and memory skills, in addition to the visual input, many weaknesses that appear related to

Joseph

Despite his subtle visual-perceptual difficulties, Joseph graduated from college and earned a master's degree in political science. Now, at age twenty-three, he is applying to law school.

Joseph's accomplishments did not come easily. They required determination and hard work. He had to drop some advanced math and business statistics courses because he could not envision how two-dimensional circles became three-dimensional, how planes intersected, and how graphs were constructed. He could not perceive where certain numbers fell along a continuum, as in estimating the height of an average woman or the temperature at which water would feel hot. Because Joseph cannot conjure up mental images, his spelling of phonetically irregular words has remained poor. Although a slow reader, Joseph learned to read at a satisfactory level because he could analyze the words' sounds, and he could use his good language comprehension to guess at words from a passage's context.

Joseph generally overanalyzes and must force himself to attend to the overall concepts being conveyed. Typically, he will memorize all the details in an assignment, understand the ideas to which they relate, yet be unable to list the main ideas in an organized fashion. For example, if Joseph is shown two circles (one red, one blue) that transformed into two squares (one black, one green) and asked how the two sets differ, he will say the red circle turned into a black square and the blue circle turned into a green square. When asked for the overall principle that transformed one set into another, Joseph will repeat his analysis of the details. However, when then given a choice of categorical concepts (color, size, number, or shape), he will immediately recognize "shape" as the correct concept. It is typical for Joseph to know the answer all along, yet the generalities are not automatically prominent in his awareness.

Because he has excellent language abilities, Joseph did make it through law school, but he had to work hard to overcome his detail-bound style. He needed the help of an advanced student in each course to guide him in looking at the big picture. "Canned briefs" were very helpful in alerting him to what is important and what is irrelevant. Joseph also dictated his examinations to compensate for his spelling difficulties, and he requested extra time to fulfill required reading assignments.

visual perception actually may be due to weaknesses in these other skills. Therefore, our research cautions against hastily blaming students' visual-perceptual systems for their learning difficulties. Let us explore what we have learned about the relationship of visual perception to reading and mathematics achievement.

Visual Perception and Reading

Studies using psychometric tests, pattern-contrast sensitivity measures, and the tachistoscope (an apparatus that briefly exposes visual stimuli) find that visual perception correlates highly with reading achievement in kindergarten and first grade. By second or third grade, however, the correlation begins to decline so that only a small amount of the skills used in visual perception appear to overlap with those necessary for reading (Lovegrove et al., 1986; Solan & Mozlin, 1986). Early in the elementary school years, language and phonological-processing abilities become more highly related to reading success than are visual-perceptual skills. Nevertheless,

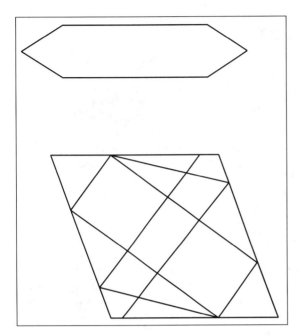

Figure 4–1   Instructions: Find the design on the top within the drawing below. *Source: unknown.*

correlations of visual-perceptual competencies with reading success continue, albeit at low levels, into the high school years and beyond (Bakker & Licht, 1986; Kershner, 1977; Kirby & Robinson, 1987; Licht et al., 1988; Shafrir & Siegel, 1994; Silverberg et al., 1979, 1980).

Because a critical component of beginning reading is the ability to attach sounds to letters and blend these together, and because higher-level reading relies more on the comprehension of a language system than on the visual analysis of the symbols themselves, it is understandable that visual-perceptual weaknesses are not major contributors to the most persistent, severe reading disabilities. Nevertheless, a few very subtle visual-processing differences do distinguish some poor readers from good readers. These weaknesses present continuing, mild to moderate obstacles to learning and adjustment.

Research suggests that weaknesses in right hemisphere visual-perceptual strategies may result in poor recognition of words at a glance, poor

memory for typical English spelling patterns, difficulty remembering phonetically irregular spellings, and poor comprehension of main ideas. Slow visual information processing also may create difficulty in remembering what is seen. Let us examine this work.

Right Hemisphere Strategy Weaknesses.   Visual processing appears to be an important element in beginning reading, whereas language functions play a greater role later on. What we are learning about the neuropsychology of the reading process is fascinating. The right hemisphere of the brain appears to specialize in functions involving perception of visual forms and the overall arrangement of these forms in their allotted space (visuospatial functions). The left hemisphere usually specializes in language skills and the analysis and sequencing of details. An easy way to remember this difference is to think of the person with right hemisphere strengths as an artist and the individual with stronger left hemisphere abilities as an English professor. It has been suggested that reading acquisition first relies more on the artist's strengths and later switches to using more of the talents of the English professor.

The right hemisphere appears best equipped to process novel information (Goldberg & Costa, 1981). This, together with its visuospatial strengths, makes the right hemisphere better at processing complex and novel typefaces. Certainly the young child would perceive letters and words to be novel and visually complex. With experience, however, print loses its novelty, and people begin to recall it better with their left hemispheres (Bryden & Allard, 1976). Using this information, Bakker (1983) proposed that young children need to use their right hemispheres' visuospatial abilities to help them in beginning reading. With practice, however, these words no longer appear visually complex, thereby making fewer demands on the right hemisphere. Numerous studies support Bakker's theory in that children aged six to seven can distinguish letters better when the letters are flashed to their right hemispheres; but older children recognize letters better when the letters are flashed to their left hemispheres (Rourke et al., 1983). As familiarity with letter

Table 4–1   Visual-perceptual weaknesses associated with reading disabilities

Visual-perceptual weaknesses

- Discriminating visual forms
- Figure-ground perception
- Finding embedded figures
- Ability to reverse figure and ground
- Spatial judgment
- Spatial orientation
- Directional sense
- Visual memory for sequence, form, and directionality
- Visual imagery: given unassembled pieces, recognize completed geometric design; given an incomplete drawing, choose the part that completes the figure
- Ability to perceive and integrate wholes
- Time perception
- Sensitivity to body language

Motor-related visual-perceptual functions

- Clumsy gait and movements
- Labored handwriting (slow, poor execution)
- Confusion in direction of letters during writing
- Fine-motor control (drawing a human figure; copying designs)

- Visual-motor organization (planning space; construction)
- Poor manual skills and sloppy work
- Reversals and rotations of figures when drawing from memory
- Balance and reaction time
- Awkward body movements
- Subtle fine-motor anomalies (finger movements)
- Performance IQ lower than Verbal IQ

Language-related visual-perceptual weaknesses

- Reversal of letter sequence in reading and spelling
- Confusion of letter name when letter recognition depends on directional cues (*p, q, d, b*)
- Auditory-visual integration
- Visual-auditory integration
- Visual sequential memory for letters and numbers
- Recall of flashed letters, words, and nonwords
- Differentiation of right from left

shapes increases, it seems that the need for perceptual analysis declines. In order to analyze words phonetically and comprehend sentence meanings, the left hemisphere's language abilities begin to take on a greater role in reading.

As children's reading skills develop, they gradually seem to shift from attending to how words look as whole shapes to how word parts sound, how they are strung together, and what the words mean. The initial visual reliance on global shapes may explain why Andrea can recognize her name at age three, long before she can name any of the letters. It also explains why she can recognize the words *McDonald's* and *Coca-Cola*. Andrea's reading relies on the shapes of

these names and the contexts in which they appear, rather than on how their parts sound. Even though research suggests that one hemisphere may be somewhat more active than the other at different ages, it is important to remember that both hemispheres continue to have a dynamic interaction during the reading process.

Unfortunately some children never develop a strong visual-perceptual strategy in beginning reading (Bakker, 1983; Boder, 1973; Ingram, Mason, & Blackburn, 1970; Myklebust, 1965). Basically, they underuse right hemisphere strategies, instead preferring to approach reading in an overanalytic, linguistic manner. They have trouble looking at words and quickly sensing, from their configurations alone, what they are. Instead, they sound out words or guess after gaining clues from the sentence's meaning.

Most children who are weak in their visual-perceptual approach to reading do learn the sounds of letters. They can sound out and spell words that sound exactly as they look (for example, *park*). Their language skills also help them to manage high-level comprehension demands. However, their ability to recognize words quickly when read or flashed (as in television commercials) remains deficient. They especially continue to have trouble remembering typical spelling patterns (for example, which words end in "le" versus "el") (Frith, 1983) and spelling words that cannot be sounded out; the latter words can be remembered only by mentally imaging how they look (for example, *precious, knight*) (Boder, 1971). Also reported is difficulty inferring main ideas when reading, because of these students' conceptual difficulty grasping the big picture.

Slow Visual Information Processing. It seems that some individuals with learning disabilities have difficulty quickly recognizing sight words or calling visual images to mind (for example, words with irregular spellings) because they pick up information from visual images at a slower than typical rate (Blackwell, McIntyre, & Murray, 1983; Bryant et al., 1983; Richards et al., 1990). They need a longer time period without any interference from a new stimulus (often as much as 100 milliseconds) to interpret what they have seen. Several studies have shown that these children's afterimages seem to persist too long so that the first image is still being processed when a subsequent image overlaps with it and confuses its perception (DiLollo, Hanson, & McIntyre, 1983; Lovegrove, Billing, & Slaghuis, 1978; O'Neill & Stanley, 1976; Stanley & Hall, 1973). Recent evidence from EEG and autopsy studies supports irregularities in the brain's ability to rapidly process visual information (Galaburda & Livingstone, 1993; Lehmkuhle et al., 1993).

Imagine the beginning reader whose zealous teacher points to the first letter in a word, the second letter, the third letter, and so forth. If the teacher proceeds too rapidly and the child's visual images persist too long, the second image may even overlap a prior image (for example, when a *c* is followed by *l*, they may appear to be a *d*; a *d* following an *o* may occlude the *o* altogether) (DiLollo et al., 1983; Stanley & Hall, 1973).

All of this visual information processing occurs extremely rapidly. Apparently visual information can persist as an image in our minds for at best only one-third to one-half of a second (Bauer, 1987; Stanley & Hall, 1973). During this period, we code what we have seen and transfer it to short-term storage. This short-term storage can last only a few seconds longer. If we don't figure out some way to remember what we have seen (for example, naming the letter or word, conjuring up its image again, thinking of a rhyming word or association), then we won't remember it. Clearly, the person who processes visual information slowly is at a disadvantage. Because important information can be held in memory for only a short period of time, the faster this information is processed the more capacity will be left over to devote to comprehension and storage (Lesgold & Perfetti, 1978). This is why, the faster one can read the more information is likely to be remembered (Baddeley, 1981; Nicolson, 1981). This is also why children who process visual information slowly have trouble learning common letter sequences in reading and spelling; if it takes too long to study the identity of a letter, the first letter will have dissipated in memory, making it difficult to learn the two as a team (e.g., *ch, br, an*) (Adams, 1990).

Visual Perception and Mathematics

Students with learning disabilities often are delayed in mathematics skills. As with reading, visual-perceptual abilities do play a role in mathematics achievement, but good language skills also are critical to handling the verbal reasoning involved in mathematical problem solving. Youngsters whose math deficits persist into adolescence and adulthood, despite adequate language, reading, or spelling skills, often exhibit right hemisphere weaknesses. These weaknesses are accompanied by such nonverbal learning difficulties as perceptual and coordination weaknesses, social imperceptiveness, and difficulty reasoning about the big picture (Shafrir & Siegel, 1994; Strang & Rourke, 1985a; Van der Vlugt & Satz, 1985).

Arithmetic success at young ages is facilitated by such abilities as visual discrimination (noting differences between figures), visuospatial organization, visual-motor coordination, and memory for visual sequences (Larsen & Hammill, 1975; Rosner, 1973). For example, when a kindergartner counts ten blocks, the ability to space the blocks in an orderly fashion certainly will come in handy; if the blocks are scattered all over the table, the child is likely to overlook some and double count others (Johnson & Myklebust, 1967). The child also must coordinate his or her visual-motor movements so that only one block is touched and counted at a time (Kaliski, 1962). With age, children must guide their hands to align columns properly, know in which direction to add or borrow, and attend to visual details such as decimals and + or − signs. The ability to imagine and mentally manipulate spatial relationships also is important. When dealing with the number five, for example, a third grader can mentally manipulate three and two dots, or four and one oranges. The child recognizes "fiveness" in all of its visual combinations and easily can count up four more oranges to combine with the five already visualized. This type of reasoning lies behind children's ability to judge whether the size of an answer to a problem appears reasonable.

In a review of 600 studies, Larsen and Hammill (1975) found that only 10 percent of the skills assessed on visual-perceptual tasks appear related to arithmetic achievement. As in reading, strong verbal abilities are essential to mathematics success. Try solving the third math problem in Figure 4–2. Does it now make sense why mathematics involves far more than visual perception? When dealing with money, time, and measurement problems as well, language facility is essential to analyze the problem, sequence one's thoughts, and reason (McLeod & Crump, 1978). In spite of good language skills, however, if a child's perceptual abilities remain markedly deficient, arithmetic disabilities are predictable due to difficulty with the nonverbal reasoning important

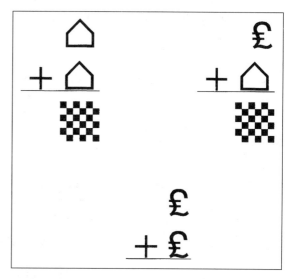

Figure 4–2 Simulation of a math problem.

in mathematical thinking (Harnadek & Rourke, 1994; Shafrir & Siegel, 1994).

Given the strong role of language in most learning, experts agree that the student with visual-perceptual deficits but strong language abilities generally has a good chance of making up for his or her perceptual weaknesses. Nevertheless, when the perceptual deficits are severe, mathematical and other more subtle weaknesses (problems with irregular spellings, handwriting, social imperceptiveness, catching the gist of conversations and authors' arguments) may linger.

Language and Phonological-Processing Skills

A majority of individuals with reading disorders display weaknesses in processing, storing, retrieving, or expressing language or phonological information. Many had been delayed in language acquisition at younger ages, and their reading delays became evident just as their language delays began to resolve themselves. When such children finally become proficient in the ability to read words, language weaknesses still may interfere with reading comprehension and written expression. It makes sense that foreign languages and poetry also would present predictable stumbling blocks. It follows that those reading-disabled children who have the higher verbal skills will tend to improve the fastest in reading ability (Kuder, 1991; Trites & Fiedorowicz, 1976). Conversely, the poorer one's language skills, the more severe the learning disability is likely to be (Smith et al., 1988).

As with many students with learning disabilities, Peter's story (below) reflects a multitude of language weaknesses. Many of the language weaknesses that researchers have associated with reading disabilities are listed in Table 4–2. In contrast to the diminishing relationship between visual-perceptual skills and reading as children get older, language and phonological-processing delays continue to differentiate good from poor readers. The language and phonological-processing weaknesses that seem to contribute most directly to reading disorders include left hemisphere strategy weaknesses, immature phonological awareness, poor phonological and verbal coding in working memory, difficulty with retrieval of phonological and verbal codes, and linguistic weaknesses. Studies using psychometric and brain electrical mapping technology have been able to differentiate among children with many of these difficulties (Bowers & Swanson, 1991; Duffy & McAnulty, 1985).

Left Hemisphere Strategy Weaknesses

It is believed that some students experience learning disabilities because they are weak in those left hemisphere language and analytic strategies that are essential to reading progress. In the normal

Peter

Peter is now in second grade and has had a terrible time learning to read. He is a cute fellow and is well liked by his peers. On the playground, or in physical education and art classes, he's as much a member of the in-group as anyone else. But in music class, reading group, and class discussion he is on the periphery. Peter has a terrible time in music class because he can't say the words in a song fast enough to keep up with the beat. It is not uncommon for the group to pause at the completion of a phrase of music and for all heads to suddenly turn. Giggles are heard as Peter trails the rest with the final phrase.

In his reading group, Peter takes so long to think of which sound goes with which letter in a word that he's forgotten the beginning sounds by the time he gets to the end of the word. Often the word he comes up with is utter nonsense. He can't even guess at words well because he doesn't understand the grammatical structure of the sentences and word meanings well enough to guess correctly. In class discussions Peter raises his hand eagerly because he knows the answers. But when he is called on, the light fades from his eyes as he struggles to pull the right words out of his head. He finally gives up as his classmates echo "call on me, I know."

Peter has severe deficits in several aspects of language: awareness of the phonological segments that make up words, learning phonetic rules, learning meanings of words, and being able to quickly retrieve sounds and words from memory. Because all these abilities are involved in reading, he has significant reading difficulties.

Table 4–2   Language weaknesses associated with reading disabilities

- Rate of early language development
- Auditory memory (recalling digits, words, or sentences)
- Memory for idea units in a dictated story
- Auditory closure (reconstituting fragmented words)
- Verbal-coding ability (translating nonverbal events into a verbal code to aid recall)
- Auditory discrimination
- Identifying words masked by noise
- Story retelling: includes fewer words and idea units, fewer events, fewer syntactically complex sentences, pronouns for which referents have not been specified, fewer descriptions of internal (seeing, feeling) responses, fewer gerunds and participles, less use of pronouns and conjunctions to make the story cohesive; less mature plot elements (major character, motivating conflict, appropriate sequence)
- Less mature verbal associations (e.g., responding red goes with *bird* vs. red goes with *blue*)
- Understanding ambiguous sentences and proverbs
- Ability to differentiate statements of information from questions
- Comprehension of complex semantics and sentence structures
- Speaking vocabulary, fluency, complex sentence types, and linguistic patterns
- Knowledge of grammatical rules
- Ability to define words, provide verbal opposites, formulate sentences and converse

- (conveying directions, elaborate with appropriate syntax), give logical reasons for common events
- Sequencing of verbal information
- Understanding verbal categories of space and time
- Learning puns, synonyms, homonyms
- Lower verbal intelligence scores than performance scores
- Forming sentences; cluttered and disorganized speech
- Inefficient use of prosodic cues (stress, pitch, pauses) to aid comprehension
- Minor articulation difficulties
- Comprehension of rapid, lengthy, complex, spoken language
- Speech production and repetition of multisyllabic words (e.g., *aluminum, specific*) and phonologically complex phrases (e.g., *the brown and blue plaid pants*)
- Rapid naming of pictured objects, colored shapes, letters, or numerals
- Inappropriate labels given for common objects
- Insensitivity to rhymes and alliterations
- Pig Latin games
- Rhyming (identifying which of three to four words does not begin, end, or contain in the middle, a common sound; identifying which two words begin or end with a specific sound)
- Segmenting words into syllables and sounds
- Deleting and substituting sounds in words
- Blending sounds in words
- Listening comprehension

process of development, the left hemisphere in most individuals becomes more specialized for language processing than does the parallel area in the right hemisphere. Even as young as four and five years of age, American children comprehend more accurately when words are heard through the right ear (which processes sound primarily in

the left hemisphere) than through the left ear (which processes sound primarily in the right hemisphere) (Berlin et al., 1973; Geffner & Hochberg, 1971). Some children with learning disabilities follow this same pattern (Witelson & Rabinovitch, 1972), but many others do not. Instead, they may have no language dominance differences between hemispheres, have right hemisphere preferences, or process one type of material (for example, digits) with one hemisphere and another type (for example, words) with the other hemisphere (Pettit & Helms, 1979; Sommers & Taylor, 1972; Sparrow & Satz, 1970; Zurif & Carson, 1970).

These language specialization differences have led to very interesting speculation regarding the role of language in reading disorders. Recall the hypothesis that the typical reading process involves a developmental shift from right to left hemisphere processing preferences. This shift seems to occur around second or third grade and corresponds with a change to a more mature reading style (Bakker & Licht, 1986; Kershner, 1977). Instead of concentrating primarily on the visual configurations of words, words now are also phonetically analyzed and guessed from the passage's meaning. We learned that some children with reading disabilities seem not to have mastered the right hemisphere phase. But it appears that the opposite also can happen; some children overuse right hemisphere strategies in reading and do not switch preferences to the left hemisphere's more analytic, language-processing mode (Bakker, Moerland, & Goekoop-Hoefkens, 1981). Unfortunately, the right hemisphere's holistic information-processing style is not well suited to the high-level, analytic language functions involved in reading and comprehension (Bakker, 1983; Hier et al., 1978; LeMay, 1977).

Students who underuse left hemisphere information-processing styles and overuse right hemisphere styles seem to be more severely reading disabled than those who show the opposite pattern. They read by fixating on the visual configuration of words rather than on their sounds. Phonetic analysis is a slow, laborious process, and reading proceeds syllable by syllable (Boder, 1973; Denckla, 1977; Ingram et al., 1970; Myklebust, 1965). When these students spell, it is hard to make out which words were intended because the wrong sounds are inserted, some are omitted, and letter order is confused. Furthermore, their comprehension and written expression tend to focus on main ideas rather than on analyzing and organizing these into a logical sequence of ideas.

Phonological Awareness

Data from over 100 studies show that auditory-perceptual abilities are second only to intelligence in contributing to reading success (Kavale, 1981a). The ability to analyze, sequence, and remember auditory stimuli is critical to reading progress (Felton & Wood, 1989; Liberman & Shankweiler, 1985). The more proficient a young child is at segmenting words into their individual sounds, the better he or she is likely to read and the faster the reading progress (Blachman, 1991; Catts, 1991; Fox & Routh, 1983; Griffith & Olson, 1992; Juel, 1988; Perfetti et al., 1987; Torgesen, Wagner, & Rashotte, 1994). Many disabled readers are far less aware of the sound structure of spoken language, even at the word and sentence level, than are average readers.

Most children with learning disabilities are able to auditorily discriminate sounds of letters from one another (for example, *b* from *f*) (Keir, 1977). If they couldn't discriminate sounds they would have significant articulation difficulties when speaking. When these children are required to make discriminations that involve finer cognitive and perceptual organization, however, such as breaking apart the order of individual sounds in words, they run into trouble (for example, what sound do you hear at the beginning of *mail?*).

Children with learning disabilities often experience difficulty in breaking down sentences into words, words into syllables, and syllables into their sequences of individual sounds. Snowling (1981), for example, showed that children with reading disabilities, compared to younger children reading at the same level, were impaired in their ability to repeat back words that, because of their unfamiliarity, required a good deal of phonemic processing (for example, *karpinular,* a modification of *particular; bagmivishent,* a modification of *magnificent*). Similarly, Bradley and Bryant (1978) found that poor readers had greater difficulty indicating which of four spoken words did not belong (for example, *weed, peel, need, deed*) than did normally developing children who were four years younger and read at an equivalent level. Cermak's (1983) eight- to ten-year-old students with learning disabilities were just as proficient as normal readers in detecting whether a word had been repeated in a list. However, they were significantly worse at indicating whether a word rhymed with a previous word. Similarly, Cermak found that boys who were learning disabled could push a button to indicate whether two letters, numbers, or geometric figures looked alike (for example, A, A) just as rapidly as boys without learning disabilities. But those with learning disabilities were much slower when required to indicate whether the names of these forms were alike (for example, A, a).

The ability of older preschoolers and kindergartners to group words based on rhyme or shared initial sounds is highly related to subsequent reading and spelling achievement (Bradley & Bryant, 1985). The young school child's understanding of how to break spoken words down into even smaller units is a powerful predictor of reading and spelling acquisition; sometimes this phonemic awareness is an even more powerful predictor than IQ, and difficulties can be detected into the high school and college years (Adams, 1990; Bradley, 1988; Bradley & Bryant, 1983; Hurford et al., 1994; Jorm & Share, 1983; MacDonald & Cornwall, 1995; Stanovich, Cunningham, & Cramer, 1984; Tornéus, 1984; Tummer & Nesdale, 1985).

The mechanism underlying phonological processing weaknesses is debated. One possibility is underactivation of relevant regions of the left hemisphere. For example, Rumsey et al. (1992) found lower than normal activation of left hemisphere blood flow in adults with severe reading disabilities even on a task that they found easy: pushing a button to indicate that two dictated words rhymed. This research implicates slow and inefficient auditory information processing as a mechanism underlying learning disabilities.

Research suggests that, just as with visual processing, some youngsters with learning disabilities seem to need a significantly longer time between auditory stimuli in order to process them (McCroskey & Kidder, 1980; Tallal & Piercy, 1978; Tallal ct al., 1980). When two syllables or sounds are presented too close in succession (less than 150 msec apart), some children can't tell which came first; they can't even tell whether the

two sounds are the same in pitch (Tallal, 1980). In contrast, typical learners do these tasks quite well, even when stimuli are separated by only eight milliseconds. When the interval between the two sounds is made longer or the stimuli themselves last longer (one-quarter of a second or more), then students with reading impairments can perform on these tasks as well as typical children. Interestingly, the more difficulty Tallal's students had with rapid acoustic analysis, the more errors they made when reading nonsense words.

Children who process auditory information slowly have the most trouble with brief stop consonant sounds (for example, *p, t, b*) because these sounds can't be sustained to allow time for auditory processing to occur (Godfrey et al., 1981). Vowel sounds, on the other hand, present less of a problem because they can be sustained. Because it is the brief consonant sounds rather than vowels that carry the meaning in our language, Tallal and Piercy (1978) suggest that some children may be unable to comprehend much of what is said because consonant sounds pass by before they can be processed. When these children are reading, this slow auditory-processing time may interfere with analysis, sequencing, and recall of sounds, as well as comprehension.

Henderson (1980) suggests yet another explanation for difficulty analyzing words into their component sounds: children not knowing where to focus their attention. Other experts suggest that the auditory-analysis weakness reflects short-term auditory memory or encoding limitations (Bauer, 1979a; Kamhi, Catts, & Mauer, 1990). These children can't remember a sound or word from one moment to the next. It makes sense that being able to simultaneously hold onto and compare groups of words or word segments in short-term memory should contribute to phonological awareness. We examine the research implicating short-term memory weaknesses in the next section.

Phonological and Verbal Coding in Working Memory

When we hear or see information, our *working memory* (short-term memory) allows us only 250 milliseconds to 25 seconds to think of a way to remember this information, or it will be forgotten (Siegler, 1983). It is common for people to use verbal labeling during working memory in order to increase the chance of remembering. For example, many people prefer to store visual images of letters, words, and objects in memory as sounds rather than as images (Baddeley, 1986; Kintsch & Buschke, 1969); the picture of the animal *bat,* for instance, might be recalled a month later as a *baseball bat* because the sounds, not the images, were stored. Similarly, when words are sounded out, it is the sounds, not images, that are held in memory. This is why reading errors that on the surface appear to be due to visual misperceptions (*din/bin, cob/cod, sung/snug*) often are due to difficulty analyzing and holding onto the sequence of sounds in working memory.

Clearly, our memory abilities are strongly tied to the use of language to label what we have seen. These labels help us to organize, rehearse, store, and recall the visual information. This labeling process is called *phonological coding* when referring to the analysis of sound sequences in words during reading, or *verbal mediation* when referring to the analysis of meaningful word units. Studies show that students who label what they see remember material better than those who don't. Interestingly, children who label lose their advantage over those who don't label when memorizing meaningless designs, because these figures cannot be named (Groenendaal & Bakker, 1971; Torgesen, 1988).

It appears that some children with learning disabilities have difficulty decoding words and remembering what they have just read because they don't use their working memory time to phonologically or verbally code the information. Even when given the verbal label to aid memorization (for example, "remember this shape—it looks like a house"), some children with learning disabilities will not use this verbal information to aid their recall as efficiently as do children without learning disabilities (Swanson, 1986). In Swanson's study, even the memory of students who were deaf was facilitated by verbal labels, but that of students with learning disabilities was not. In fact, verbal labeling actually disrupted the recall of the students with learning disabilities.

As indicated in Table 4–1, it is common for poor readers to have difficulty remembering what they have seen. While some may not remember well because of weak perceptual strategies and slow visual information processing, more often poor readers seem not to remember because of phonological awareness difficulties or not using verbal labeling to aid memory. The latter students tend to remember the perceptual image of what they have seen most recently. But they have difficulty remembering information they saw earlier because the more distant in time the information, the more language needs to be used to hold it in memory (for example, repeating it or thinking up a mnemonic trick) (Spring & Capps, 1974).

Because reading is a meaningful language task, researchers find that underachievement more often is due to failure to use language to mediate what has been seen, rather than to misperceptions of letters and words or other visual-processing inefficiencies (Denckla, Rudel, & Broman, 1981). For example, Vellutino's research group (1973) found that both poor and good readers had equal difficulty remembering images of Hebrew words. Both groups showed such classic visual-perceptual errors as omissions and distortions of what they had seen. Yet children who had studied Hebrew were better at remembering the letters because they could call on their language knowledge as a memory aid (Vellutino et al., 1975a, b). Likewise, Liberman's and Torgesen's research finds that poor readers do not differ from good readers in recalling which designs, doodles, unfamiliar faces, or block sequences they had seen, provided that these items are hard to describe in words. However, when three-letter nonwords, numbers, strings of words, or sentences are used, the poor readers' memory is significantly worse than that of good readers (Katz, Shankweiler, & Liberman, 1981; Liberman, 1985; Torgesen et al., 1991). Similarly, while children with reading disabilities might be able to write from memory short words that they have just seen, longer words become problematic because language must be used to help remember them (Vellutino, Steger, & Kandel, 1972).

Professionals frequently use the term *auditory-sequential memory difficulties* to describe the working memory weaknesses of children who cannot remember items in sequence, such as letters, numbers, words, and sounds (Fisher & Athey, 1986; Pennington, 1986). If children can't retain sounds in sequence, then they will have trouble reading from the beginning to the end of a word. They also will have trouble recognizing that a word reminds them of a word they already know, and then figuring out the new word by omitting one letter's sound and substituting a new sound (for example, *pat* for *sat, cub* for *cut*). Analyzing, omitting, substituting, and retaining sounds in sequence are important to beginning reading, where a sound must be applied to a letter, then remembered while the next sound is recalled, then the two are blended, and so on.

For any of us to remember more than five, six, or seven letters that we have just seen, these need to be recoded into more manageable chunks (Miller, 1956). Good readers use their verbal reading and spelling knowledge to do this chunking. But poor readers who can't read or spell the words have difficulty committing to memory the longer words they had seen because the words remind them of no known pattern and therefore must be remembered letter by letter.

Because good readers seem to verbally label meaningful material more automatically, frequently, and efficiently than do poor readers, they remember it better. Research finds that when a child's auditory working memory span is extremely limited, reading progress is far poorer than in children who have longer working memory spans (Torgesen et al., 1990).

Certainly, the ability to phonologically or verbally code information in working memory is critical to learning progress. Another reason hypothesized to underlie this working memory weakness is difficulty with retrieval, which we discuss in the next section.

Retrieval of Phonological and Verbal Codes

We commonly find that students with reading disabilities, despite knowing the names of common objects, colors, digits, letters, and letter sounds, are much slower and less accurate at naming them than are average readers (Fawcett & Nicolson, 1994; Torgesen, Wagner & Rashotte, 1994; Wolf,

1991). This slowness carries over into their speed of word recognition when reading.

When speaking, it is not unusual for poor readers to have unusually long silent periods between words, choose the wrong words, describe the word they're groping for, name another object in the same category, mispronounce, missequence syllables, use fillers (uh, you know, whatchamacallit), or talk around a topic. This is because they can't quickly retrieve the words they are searching for. This auditory retrieval difficulty is called a *naming* or *word-finding* problem. Try the exercise in Figure 4–3 to get some sense of the helpless feeling when you know that you know something, yet you have no cues available to help spark retrieval of this information.

Children with word-finding difficulties make these errors despite having full knowledge of object names or letter sounds. It is understandable that for these children sounding out words is arduous and often unsuccessful. They forget the sounds of previous letters by the time they struggle to recall the sound of the next letter in a word. It is not unusual to find that although they fail to read a word, they can find it quite readily on a page of print when dictated. These children are much slower in pronouncing even those words they do know how to read (Torgesen, 1988). Unfortunately, as poor readers belabor the decoding of each word, their capacity to remember and integrate information from previous sentences is reduced, and comprehension becomes impaired (Perfetti & Lesgold, 1977).

Children typically become faster namers with age, as the words they store become elaborated with knowledge that helps cue their retrieval (synonyms, words in the same category, related ideas) (Denckla & Rudel, 1974; Milianti & Cullinan, 1974). Spring and Capps (1974) found that when children do not reach a naming rate of one object per second, they don't even attempt to use verbal mediation as a memory aid. Consequently, their memory is poor. Spring and Capps's children were shown eight cards, which were then laid face down in a row. Their task was to match a ninth card with one already on the table. Poor readers never even tried to name the cards to help them remember, whereas good readers did. Studies show that as overt (speaking aloud) or covert

---

INSTRUCTIONS: Complete the missing word that begins with each initial.

EXAMPLE: 16 O. in a P.   16 ounces in a pound _____

1. 26 L. in the A.   _____

2. 7 W. of the A. W.   _____

3. 54 C. in a D. (WITH THE J.) _____

4. 88 P. K.   _____

5. 32 D. F. at which W. F.   _____

6. 200 D. for P. G. in M.   _____

7. 3 B. M. (S.H.T.R.)   _____

8. 11 P. on a F. T.   _____

Figure 4–3   Simulation of word-finding difficulties. *Source:* unknown.

(speaking to oneself) speech increases, so does one's success on memory tasks (Sheingold & Shapiro, 1976).

Unfortunately, a word finding problem can be a lifelong source of reading, learning, and expressive difficulties. Time may not help the naming speeds of poor readers catch up to even that of the younger child who reads at the same level (Fisher & Athey, 1986; Wolf & Obregón, 1992). There is evidence that the naming ability of the reading disabled may plateau as early as eight to ten years of age (Wolf, 1980). In contrast, in typical readers, as well as in children who read poorly for reasons other than learning disabilities, naming speed may continue to mature at least into the junior high school years (Stanovich, 1988). Jason's story (page 131) illustrates how significantly naming difficulties can affect many aspects of one's life that go far beyond reading.

It is not uncommon for a child with a word finding difficulty to read a word with effort on the first line of a passage but no longer be able to sound it out twenty lines later, no matter how much effort is expended. Some poor readers require increasingly longer times to scan their auditory memories as scanning continues, for example, when retrieving letter sounds while reading a series of words. If too much auditory retrieval is called for at once, the child may be unable to recall what he or she had remembered a little while earlier. Good readers do not have this problem (Farnham-Diggory & Gregg, 1975). The visual-memory scanning of poor readers often is more efficient than their auditory-memory scanning. Farnham-Diggory and Gregg suggest that these children's reading confusions might be due in part to their eyes moving on to a second letter before they have been able to retrieve the first letter's sound.

Children who cannot name efficiently not only have trouble decoding but also have difficulty using language as a comprehension and memory aid. When reading, normal readers generally pause about every two seconds to translate what has been read, or else it will be lost (Bauer, 1987). Spear and Sternberg (1987) explain that because their inefficient access to stored sounds and words slows reading speed, the material read by children with reading disabilities gets broken up into too many small chunks; this makes the content even more difficult to follow. Consequently, comprehension suffers, and so does memory.

Jason

Jason, an engineering college graduate who owns his own heating repair business, explains how his naming difficulties have affected his life. Jason always did well at remembering concepts but could never remember names, places, dates, baseball batting averages, and so forth. Consequently, he believed that he could contribute little to conversations because he wouldn't know what to say next. He says that he enters conversations "from the perimeter," waiting for people to get beyond the exchange of facts to the idea level.

A 6-foot, brawny, handsome fellow, Jason's social reticence began in elementary school when classmates in the lunchroom would outargue him with more accurate facts, no matter what the topic of conversation. He soon learned not to trust any information he offered and retreated socially. Still an exceptional tennis player, Jason never calls the score. When Jason returned to his tenth-year high school reunion, no one remembered him.

Jason's reading and spelling difficulties have continued into adulthood. He has read one novel in his entire life and never reads the newspaper. TV is his source of information. When writing, Jason can only catch his misspellings after he finishes each word and inspects whether it "looks right." Number reversals occur continually on his order sheets, but he catches these when the sums don't make sense and the order numbers don't match those in the catalogue. Jason has learned to check and double check any written work.

Jason is a sympathetic, pleasant fellow for whom finding business partners is easy. He has always sought partners who could be the upfront salespeople, good at making small talk. Jason, on the other hand, is the mechanical genius on whose skills everyone relies, and without whom there could be no business. He describes himself as an accommodating, honest, dependable person who is always on time and always helping others out. "Since I can't teach people anything new besides engineering, I've become the nice guy. When I was sixteen, I was the first person to get my license, and so I drove everyone around. What else can I do? I want to be liked."

It is not surprising that the speed of naming objects, letters, colors, and the like is an excellent predictor of reading success (Blachman, 1984; Wolf, 1991). It also has been found that the faster one can name, the faster one can calculate simple math facts. Students with learning disabilities are slower on both tasks (Garnett & Fleischner, 1983). Poor naming causes trouble at every interface of spoken and written language because sounds can't be retrieved to read words, and words can't be retrieved to express ideas (Shankweiler & Liberman, 1976). Research Box 4–1 reviews several hypotheses regarding the origin of these word-finding difficulties.

Linguistic Weaknesses

Receptive and expressive language abilities are significant factors in decoding, reading comprehension, writing, and even social interaction. Consider what might happen if Peter, described in the story on page 124, cannot understand common directions such as, "set the oven to 350° and, after you stir in the ingredients one at a time, be sure to bake the brownies for 30 minutes in a greased pan." Some children with learning disabilities are unable to comprehend such basic grammatical relations. As a result, their ability to understand and infer, whether from oral language

RESEARCH BOX 4–1

Hypotheses Regarding the Origin of Word-Finding Difficulties

Several investigators have concluded that word-finding difficulties represent a structural brain deficit that keeps students from accessing the verbal/phonological information or cues that could help them remember (Swanson, 1982; Torgesen & Houck, 1980). Others suggest that a slow articulation rate slows both oral and inner language so that decoding and rehearsal of information to be memorized are hampered (Baddeley, 1986; Ackerman, Dykman, & Gardner, 1990a). Kail and Leonard (1986), however, suggest that the problem is more at the word-knowledge end; children do not have a rich enough base of information about a word's meaning to facilitate rapid retrieval of the word for use in a variety of grammatical forms or contexts. Kail and Leonard demonstrated that children with word-finding problems did have the words they were trying to retrieve present in memory. However, their retrieval was slower and less accurate because they had associated less elaborate knowledge with these words: fewer synonyms, related ideas, other words belonging to the same category, and fewer multiple meanings of the same word. Therefore, even though the words were known, they were less distinct in the children's memories. Kail and Leonard also found some of the problem to be due to these children's inefficient and inappropriate retrieval strategies (for example, not using category or initial sound cues to help them recall), but this contributed less to poor retrieval than did the weak original elaboration of word knowledge. When words are stored more elaborately and multiple cues can be used for retrieval, access to words is facilitated and children are less likely to experience word-finding difficulties.

or reading material, suffers. Certainly, their ability to use context to help them decode difficult words also will be affected. For example, when reading a passage about a camping trip that occurred last week, a child with good language skills does not even have to look at the "ed" in *hiked*. He or she will just glance at the "hik" and know that the rest must be "ed" if the passage is to make sense. This lack of awareness of grammatical speech sequences (for example, prefixes and suffixes) makes it all the harder for the beginning reader to understand how alphabet sounds are segmented and ordered (Shankweiler & Liberman, 1976). Delays in vocabulary acquisition and understanding of idioms and metaphors only further complicate reading, comprehension, and composition ability.

Many experts believe that children with these types of language and reading disabilities have a common problem using any symbol system, including oral and written words, to represent thought (Bloom, 1978; Denckla, 1979). Other children may have a good understanding of language concepts, yet fail because of difficulty with the expressive language needed to explain the concepts, either orally or in writing.

Fisher and Athey (1986) poignantly demonstrated the weak linguistic abilities of children with reading disabilities in a study using pictographs (designs that stand for words). They found that these children could learn to read individual pictographs just as quickly as non-reading-disabled children. However, when the pictographs were put into sentences, the children with reading difficulties read at a slower rate. Fisher and Athey posited that these children read slower because their language systems were inefficient in allowing them to forecast meaning. When these children were asked to compose sentences using the pictographs, their sentences were brief, had many grammatical errors, and often contained pictographs that did not convey the intended meaning.

In order to read, comprehend, and compose accurately and rapidly, the written symbol must be translated into sound, grammar, and meaning. These multiple routes need to operate in parallel. If a student's access to any one of these is not automatic, then reading and written language progress will be hampered (Coltheart et al., 1983; Rudel, 1985). Try the exercise in Figure 4–4. No doubt this will give you some sense of the frustration and loss of self-confidence experienced by people who have the basic knowledge but are shut out of conversations and textbooks when the language is geared to a level that is beyond their comprehension.

Attention

Have you ever watched a five-year-old child eat a messy chocolate ice cream cone and, when she is thoroughly covered with brown drips, you ask her to go into the bathroom to wash her hands and face? She walks down the hallway and two minutes later returns, still a mess. She innocently looks up and asks, "What did you tell me to do?" You smile, hug her, repeat the directions, pat her on the head, and send her on her way again. Think about what your response might have been had she been ten years old? Presumably it would be quite negative. You might wonder whether the child can't hear, understand, pay attention, or remember, or if she is just plain insolent.

When these questions arise with students who are learning disabled, the answer in many cases is that there is insufficient focusing and sustaining of attention, so that the information isn't learned in the first place (Swanson, 1988). Attention seems to be a problem at the initial storage end because, when students attend to and practice information long enough to learn it, forgetting usually occurs no faster for students with learning disabilities than for typical learners (Bauer, 1979b; Brainerd, 1985; Brainerd, Kingma, & Howe, 1986; Gregory & Bunch, 1959; Kail & Leonard, 1986; Schoer, 1962; Shuell & Keppel, 1970; Underwood, 1964). In other words, even if it takes students with learning disabilities longer to

---

INSTRUCTIONS: Translate the following common sayings.

EXAMPLE: Scintillate, scintillate, asteroid minific. (Twinkle, twinkle, little star.)

1. Members of an avian species of identical plumage congregate.
2. Pulchritude possesses solely cutaneous profundity.
3. It is fruitless to become lachrymose over precipitately departed lactic fluid.
4. Freedom from the incrustation of grime is contiguous to rectitude.
5. The stylus is more potent than the claymore.
6. It is fruitless to try to indoctrinate a superannuated canine with innovate maneuvers.
7. The temperature of the aqueous content of an unremittingly ogled vessel does not attain 671.4 degrees Kelvin.
8. All articles that coruscate with resplendence, are not truly aurific.

Figure 4–4   Simulation of linguistic weaknesses *Source:* unknown.

learn something, once they have learned it their retention can be just as good as that of typical students. Many learning disabled may have adequate memory capabilities yet fail to remember because they take, or are given, insufficient time and practice to store information in the first place. Their recall difficulties appear to get worse as they get older because their peers begin to use sophisticated strategies to increase their memory capacities, but the learning disabled usually do not.

Another problem for students with learning disabilities seems to be thinking of ways to facilitate retrieval of information once they've learned it. Although the ability to store new information does increase with age for both students with learning disabilities and typical students, retrieval abilities do not seem to mature from year to year in students with learning disabilities, as they do for the non–learning disabled (Brainerd et al., 1986).

Whether the disabilities are at the storage or retrieval end of memory, researchers have long recognized that a fundamental contributor, and perhaps the most common characteristic of students with learning disabilities, is immature attending ability (Dykman et al., 1983; Keogh, 1973; Tarver & Hallahan, 1974). This includes the ability to be alert to a stimulus, decide on a goal, get ready to respond, focus on the appropriate stimuli, sustain attention for adequate time periods, delay responding while considering alternatives, and then decide on an answer or action. Whether essential information is attended to and how the learner then organizes it for storage are critical if the material is to be remembered.

Studies show that the attention of many students who have learning disabilities is easily caught. Once caught, however, they may have a problem focusing on relevant stimuli and sustaining this attention. An easy way to conceptualize the difference between caught and focused attention is to imagine that you are tired from a long day of studying, and it is your five-year-old niece's bedtime. You have just read a ten-page story aloud to her. Apparently you read the correct words because she understood the content and is now asking all the usual "but why did" questions. Yet, you can't answer. You obviously had allowed your attention to be caught by the words and

therefore read them correctly. But you failed to deliberately focus your attention to derive meaning from them. To answer the questions you'll have to reread the material and this time focus your attention. Similarly, a number of studies suggest that, among the learning disabled, it is their ability to focus and sustain attention that is deficient rather than their ability to have their attention caught (Porges et al., 1975; Richards et al., 1990). They remember content less well than the typical learner because they have difficulty focusing attention on the critical, distinctive features that need to be learned (Keogh & Margolis, 1976; Samuels, 1973). Goldstein and Dundon (1987) suggest that students with learning disabilities have difficulty arousing and maintaining the intense degree of selective attention required for conscious effort. Several reasons for this weakness have been proposed: physiological difficulties, cognitive styles incompatible with selective attention, and poor use of verbal mediation to aid attention and memory.

Physiological Difficulties

Poor attending processes are a physiological fact among many students with learning disabilities, particularly those who are hyperactive. On laboratory tasks that demand attention, these youngsters have trouble maintaining constant attention levels, take longer to react to stimuli, and do not have the typical physiological indices associated with attention: lower EEG arousal levels and amplitudes, slower EEG response to stimuli, EEG's remaining at peak for less time, less selective left hemisphere activation, lower metabolic activity in the white matter of the frontal lobes, lower cerebral glucose metabolism, and lower changes in heart rate (Mann et al., 1992; Smith, 1991; Zametkin et al., 1990). These inefficient attention processes may interfere with learning to such a degree that the development of visual- and auditory-processing abilities also is diminished, and these too become deficits (Denckla, 1979; Samuels & Anderson, 1973). Donahue (1986), for example, explains that when a child's attentional deficits cause failure in reading or listening efficiency (for example, to stories) this child is deprived of the opportunity to learn the sophisti-cated vocabulary and grammatical structures that comprise written language. This cumulative loss of exposure may cause language deficits when there were none to begin with.

Remember that we used to joke about one of our past presidents not being able to chew gum and walk down the street at the same time? Well, this seems to be true of many youngsters with learning disabilities. It is believed that while their left or right hemispheres are engaged in one activ-ity, they have difficulty also allocating energy to another activity that is mediated by that same hemisphere (for example, talking and at the same time rapidly tapping the right hand's fingers or writing down dictated numbers (Kershner & Stringer, 1991; Obrzut, Hynd, & Boliek, 1986). When this interference occurs with typical chil-dren, verbal processing tends to be maintained, but the motor functions diminish (Hiscock, 1982). The opposite, however, seems to be true for some children who are language disabled (Hughes & Sussman, 1983). Clearly, if language efficiency is sacrificed when the student is required to do too many competing things at once, the achievement of these students will suffer even further.

Because it is difficult for some students to allocate cognitive energy to two tasks at once, these students miss things that others simply "absorb" without even trying. Using a unique experimental design, Ceci and Baker (1989) and Baker, Ceci, and Herrmann (1987) had children play a computer game in which they were to land a spaceship on as many planets as possible and avoid being blown up by anti-aircraft rocket launchers. But, of course, the spaceships were pro-grammed to blow up at specified times. As the spaceship disintegrated amidst a loud crashing sound, the child (who had been told to ignore lists of words being read through earphones) heard the word *black*. Within nine to fifteen trials chil-dren's skin conductance indicated that they had become physiologically conditioned to the word *black* (because of the excitement accompanying the blow ups), even if no blow up was occurring. Then children stopped playing the game. Next, the children repeated words that were presented so rapidly to one ear that they were unaware that

competing words were being presented simulta-neously to the other ear. Incredibly, the skin con-ductance of children without learning disabilities showed the conditioned response to *black*, even though they were totally unaware that the word had been presented to the unattended ear. But the children with learning disabilities had far less of a response. The non-LD children even reacted to a rhyming word (*back*) and synonyms (*dark, brown*); the children who were learning disabled showed less of a reaction. Both groups' skin con-ductance was alike, however, when they were asked to repeat a list of words that included *black*.

This research suggests that the attention of some students with learning disabilities may be impaired at an automatic level that requires no purposeful awareness or attention. Certainly, teachers comment all the time that for some stu-dents "sound goes in one ear and out the other"; in other cases a teacher will wave a hand in front of the student's face asking "Are you there?" after the student's attention has wandered off. When these students' attention finally is regained, they have no idea what they did to cause their teacher's reaction.

Parents too are disturbed when their chil-dren don't automatically pick up on what else is going on (for example, hearing the call to dinner) if engrossed in some activity. Given the many physiological indices reflecting poor attention, it is likely that some children experience attention deficits at the automatic level, some at the level that takes conscious effort, and yet others at both levels. In all cases, these students need to put inor-dinate effort into actively processing information, because of inefficiencies in attentional processes that are activated involuntarily in the typical learner (Sternberg & Wagner, 1982).

Cognitive Style and Attention

Unique cognitive styles also can predispose a per-son to poor attention. These cognitive styles may deter attention to the important features of tasks and also encourage inappropriate task strategies. For example, distractible children whose style is to look at all stimuli around them are unable to organize the perceptual input in order to attend only to a task's most important features (Keogh, 1973). For this reason pictures on a page actually may hinder rather than help a distractible child when reading (Lamman & Bakker, in Bakker & de Wit, 1977; Samuels, 1967).

Impulsive response styles also are highly related to poor sustained attention (Douglas, 1976). The impulsive child is described as an underfocuser who relinquishes concentration too quickly, thereby making premature decisions and responding too rapidly. This impulsivity impacts performance in areas that depend on sustained attention, such as short-term memory and oral reading accuracy (Kagan, 1965; Messer, 1976). As these children learn to focus, sustain, and organize their attention better, their tendency to respond rapidly and make errors decreases (Ross, 1976; Yap & Peters, 1985). Their memory improves.

As with the impulsive student, when we help the student with a simultaneous processing style focus on critical details, learning improves. Similarly, when we draw the attention of a student with a successive style to main ideas, learning also improves. Clearly, a major priority in teaching students with learning disabilities is to draw their attention to important task features and to help them learn strategies to work around their less efficient cognitive styles.

Verbal Mediation and Attention

Immature verbal mediation also may underlie many students' poor attention. When a person does not use verbal labeling to focus attention on the relevant stimuli, the information that caught attention is not likely to be organized for storage; recall is typically hampered.

Ceci (1983) found that his ten-year-old students with reading disabilities, unlike typical readers, did not try to use verbal cues to help on a task, even when these were offered to them. These children merely had to name slides of familiar objects (for example, *horse*). In one condition 80 percent of the slides were preceded by a relevant cue (for example, when looking at a slide of a horse, the examiner would say "here's an animal"); in the second condition 80 percent of the cues were irrelevant (for example, "here's a fruit"). Whereas typical readers used the relevant cues to help them

name the slides faster, the students with reading disabilities did not. They were just as unaffected by this cue as were four-year-old control subjects. In other words, even when given helpful verbal information, the children with reading disabilities did not recognize how this could be useful to them. Ceci (1984) drew similar conclusions in another study where children had to recall words, four of which were semantically related.

Torgesen and Goldman's (1977) study was among the first to explore how much children could improve performance if specifically instructed to use verbal mediation. Good and poor readers were shown a picture containing seven drawings of common objects. The experimenter pointed to two, three, four, or five pictures. The child then covered his or her eyes with goggles for fifteen seconds. After taking off the goggles, the children looked at the same pictures presented in a different order on a new page and pointed to the sequence they had previously seen. Good readers verbalized significantly more during the fifteen-second delay and remembered better than did the poor readers. Those poor readers who did use verbal rehearsal applied this strategy less consistently than did the good readers. Torgesen and Goldman then repeated the task but instructed the children to point to and name the pictures on presentation and also during the delay. Interestingly, the good and poor readers no longer differed in the amount of verbal rehearsal, and they now remembered the material equally well.

The above results suggest that some students who do not spontaneously use verbal mediation to help them remember may seem to have memory deficiencies when in fact they do not. Because speech helps people to abstract, remember, and generalize information, many students with learning disabilities have been taught to increase their problem-solving and memory skills by literally talking to themselves (Leon & Pepe, 1983; Meichenbaum, 1977).

Motor Skills

Students with learning disabilities very often have difficulty with their gross-motor, hand, and oral movements. Sensorimotor disturbances in gaining information through touch and movement also are common. Slow motor speed is typical, paralleling the children's poor automatization in reading and number fact recall, articulation, pick-up of visual cues, word finding, and so forth. Joseph, our law school student, also has severe motor difficulties. The effect of these throughout his life is presented below.

As many as 75 to 90 percent of all poor readers seem to have motor disturbances (Clements et al., 1971; Critchley, 1970; Tarnopol & Tarnopol, 1977). In nearly three-quarters of these individuals, their motor weaknesses do not appear related to underlying visual-perceptual deficits. Benton and Pearl's (1978) study of all reading underachievers in Palo Alto, California, illustrates this point. The underachievers were poorer at copying designs than were their normal-achieving siblings and peers. Yet, when asked to score another child's drawings, the poor readers were better than the others at detecting the errors. In other words, their visual-perceptual systems were functioning well, and perceptual distortions could not have caused their poor copying. Similarly, the articulation difficulties of children with learning disabilities only infrequently are due to an inability to hear sounds accurately; more often they represent a problem specific to oral movements.

Despite the prevalence of motor incoordination among the learning disabled, motor difficulties do not relate highly to learning problems. Instead, they make it difficult for students to show what they have learned. For example, a child may misarticulate information that had been heard accurately (Matthews & Seymour, 1981), or a student may curtail the amount of information in an essay because the mere act of writing is so onerous. Merely keeping up is a problem due to slowness.

Motor incoordination is among the least powerful variables that have an impact on learning progress. Although studies find that copying ability is one of the most consistent correlates of early math and reading success (Kavale, 1982b; Keogh & Smith, 1967; Larsen & Hammill, 1975), these correlations are of such low magnitude that a motor difficulty cannot predict whether any single individual actually will fail academically.

It seems that coordination difficulties frequently accompany learning disorders because a very large area of the sensorimotor and motor

Joseph

As a youngster, Joseph always had a difficult time with recess, physical education class, youth-group dances, and summer camp sports activities. His coordination has not improved with time. At the age of twenty-three, Joseph cannot walk a straight line, or touch his nose when his eyes are closed. He skips and jumps with difficulty.

When Joseph is unsure of what he wants to say, his speech becomes slurred. Because he has difficulty visualizing symbols in his mind, he still reverses letters and numbers when he writes. He cannot correct these errors through proofreading because he has no mental picture against which to check his spelling. Joseph's handwriting is illegible.

Fortunately, these weaknesses need not deter Joseph's career as a lawyer. He can dictate his work and delegate proofreading to someone else. Furthermore, his coordination difficulties need not affect his social life. Given the enthusiasm of Americans for spectator sports, Joseph fits in nicely. He did, however, encounter a problem at his wedding, where he knocked over a candelabra on the way down the aisle, and, despite months of practicing, appeared very awkward and unnatural when the band leader invited Joseph and his bride to dance the first dance.

cortex subserves hand, finger, body, and oral sensations and movements; when there is a dysfunction in adjacent brain regions that are essential to higher-level cognitive and academic performance, there is a good deal of opportunity for things to go wrong in the sensorimotor and motor cortex as well. Since these areas receive messages about how to feel and move from all other brain areas, any inability to attend to, organize, store, or retrieve visual, auditory, tactile, or kinesthetic (sensations from body movements) information will be reflected in motor or verbal inefficiencies. This is why a child who hasn't watched the ball bats poorly. This is also why children stutter when they're not sure of what they want to say.

Coordination difficulties result in such problems as sloppy and illegible handwriting, reluctance to complete lengthy written assignments, math computation errors due to illegibility and poor alignment of numerals, articulation difficulties, slowness, incompetence in sports, social difficulties on the playground, and sloppiness in dressing. As in Joseph's case, such problems do not help youngsters to win friends. They're often frustrated by understanding much more than they can express orally or in writing. Their grades suffer. Their anger and frustration at not being able to "do it right" is evident in Nathan's coloring and his mother's commentary (Figure 4–5). Nathan is now in third grade and is very proud of how well he reads. Because of continuing handwriting difficulties he dictates compositions, uses a computer, tape records homework assignments, and works with a peer to record math computations. If a student's difficulties are only at the motor end, and he or she can bear the deprecation and poor grades that unfortunately may accompany written work, then the outlook for eventual success is good.

Implications for Assessment and Intervention

Although we have discussed the information-processing patterns in learning disabilities one at a time, in many cases several of these contribute simultaneously to a student's learning disability (Badian, 1996). Matějček and Sturma (1986)

explain the complexity of information-processing weaknesses in learning disabilities in this way:

> . . . every complex mental activity is a functional system that requires the concerted action of three principal units. One regulates the tone and alerts the brain; a second collects, processes, and stores information; and a third unit programs, regulates, and verifies mental activity. All three of them are interrelated. . . .We seem to be concerned with a certain functional inefficiency of this three phase system. The moment one of the component units is pressured, the other two malfunction under a type of law of limited effort. The logical conclusion is that to explain dyslexic difficulties, we must look for causes in the imperfect cooperation of the cerebral functional complexes . . . relatively wide-ranging, general, and complex dysfunctions of multiple and interacting origins. (p. 212)

Therefore, in assessing a student's learning strengths and weaknesses, we must look at the role of information-processing weaknesses as part of a larger, interconnected, functional system. We must then decide how we can help remediate or compensate for these weaknesses.

Learning disabilities are far from simple to understand because no one type of weakness can explain all the academic disorders we see in students (Fletcher & Satz, 1979a, b). Any of the learner, task, or setting contributors that the text has explored thus far may be operative to varying degrees in different individuals. Therefore, youngsters with learning disabilities are of a "mixed" variety. This makes it especially difficult to understand them, to predict the exact nature and course of any one student's learning progress, and to know how best to intervene.

As Keogh (1987a) put it, " . . . LD is not a single condition, but rather represents a class of related and partially overlapping conditions. . . . Rather than a single LD, we have a number of learning disabilities" (pp. 6–7). Given this heterogeneity, it is understandable why, in the learning disabilities field, inconsistencies with any general theory are the rule rather than the exception. For example, at times children are good readers although they do not use verbal mediation (Groenendaal & Bakker, 1971), or they are poor readers despite good phonemic awareness (Lenchner, Gerber, & Routh, 1990). They may be good decoders, despite word finding problems, or poor

When Nathan Colors

When Nathan colors, his crayon
becomes a weapon against the white paper.
It is his mission to color in every bit of
available background.
His coloring brain comes from his toes
and grips his entire body driving its power
down into his he-man fingers.
He sucks in drool as his concentration grows.

When Nathan colors, his crayons
make a popping sound as weapon after weapon
is broken by the paper enemy.
On December 26th, Nathan's coloring can
is filled with new, smooth shiny soldiers.
By January, his army is broken into small
midget fighters.
His mother watches as he pushes ¼" nubs
into the paper with his he-man thumb ends.

When Nathan colors, his world is
lost in the mission of wiping out white.
This is no calming, passive playtime
like it might be for other children.
Coloring is exhausting and sometimes,
it must be followed by a snack break
or, on rainy days,
a doze on the couch.

Figure 4–5 Nathan's coloring. *Source:* Reprinted by permission of Debra L. Morse-Little (1989).

decoders despite no word finding problems (Tallal, 1980; Wolf & Obregón 1992). Such evidence teaches us that, as with task and setting contributors to learning disabilities, no one information-processing weakness can definitely predict a learning disability. It is merely a risk factor that must be watched and dealt with when warranted.

Summary

Several information-processing weaknesses may underlie learning disabilities. Peripheral visual factors, such as poor acuity and inefficient eye movements, do not cause learning disabilities. Nevertheless, they can make the use of the eyes when reading uncomfortable, possibly aggravating an existing learning difficulty. Visual-perceptual factors influence learning at young ages and continue to do so in subtle ways at older ages. The most frequent and powerful contributors to academic achievement are language and phonological-processing skills as well as attention abilities. All are complexly interrelated and greatly influence how information is organized for storage, rehearsed, and recalled. Although motor disabilities often accompany the visual-perceptual, language, and attention weaknesses of students with learning disabilities, they do not contribute to the learning difficulty. Rather, they make it difficult for these youngsters to express what they know.

All the possible combinations of learner, task, and setting contributers to learning disabilities make it difficult to define exactly what a learning disability is, to assess the disability, and to decide how to intervene. It makes most sense to try to understand any one person's learning disability by specifying the precise ways in which task and setting contributors seem to be interacting with a student's information-processing abilities, background knowledge, cognitive style, and personal characteristics to influence learning outcome. Intervention is then geared toward capitalizing on any learner, task, and setting strengths in order to eliminate, minimize, remediate, or work around the factors that contribute to the student's learning and adjustment difficulties.

**Part Three
The Learner**

Chapter Five

Academic Development

In order to understand research related to the academic development of students with learning disabilities, how to sequence curriculum objectives, and how to choose the most appropriate teaching strategies, we must first familiarize ourselves with the way in which typical learners mature academically. Therefore, we will explore how academic skills normally are acquired and how the development of students with learning disabilities differs. We will discuss acquisition of reading, handwriting, spelling, and mathematics skills at the primary grade levels; the more complex aspects of reading comprehension, content area learning, written expression, and mathematics achievement will be addressed within the context of the intermediate grade curriculum requirements.

Unfortunately, the learning problems of many students with learning disabilities tend not to disappear with time, despite extensive elementary school intervention. Although these students do make progress, they generally continue to achieve significantly behind their age and grade expectations (Baker, Decker, & DeFries, 1984; Bruck, 1993a; Korhonen, 1995; McKinney, Osborne, & Schulte, 1993). One of the most disheartening realizations has been that some of the disabilities that were thought to have been outgrown or remediated tend to reappear in somewhat different forms in the secondary years, when youngsters are faced with new cognitive and environmental demands. Still other students whose problems had not been sufficiently acute to draw attention in the early grades, and who had managed to compensate for their weaknesses, find themselves ill-equipped to cope when faced with the more complex challenges of secondary education.

In addition to their areas of academic weakness, many secondary school students also demonstrate significant areas of strength and talent. To maximize these students' eventual adult adjustment, their needs in multiple areas must be addressed, including remedial help, tutoring, learning strategy training, intensified vocational preparation programs, and transition planning. Because in many cases weaknesses persist into adulthood despite remedial gains, an important focus in the secondary years is finding ways to work around and compensate for these weaknesses, so that the students' strengths can be fully developed and they will be more apt to avail themselves of postsecondary educational opportunities.

The Primary Grades

The incredible number of life's lessons that are part of a child's first experiences in elementary school is exemplified in the excerpt on page 143. Kindergarten is a year in which the teacher tries to reinforce those cognitive and information-processing skills that are of direct relevance to academic goals. In addition, children learn how to organize their approach to tasks, regulate their attention and physical activity, work independently and in a group, and get along with teachers and peers. Long-lasting attitudes toward oneself as a learner and toward school begin to take shape.

Researchers have identified some important prerequisite skills that will help increase kindergarteners' readiness to progress academically. These include alphabet and number knowledge, ability to rhyme, segmenting words by syllable and phoneme, naming common colors, objects, and designs, copying designs, writing one's name, vocabulary comprehension, and following directions (Badian, 1988; Blachman, 1991; Griffith & Olson, 1992; Jorm et al., 1986; Mann, 1993; Torgesen et al., 1994). As the teacher helps develop these subskills, the child gains a richer, more efficient knowledge and strategy base on which higher-level learning can be built.

For the majority of children, academic development will proceed in an orderly, predictable fashion. In fact, many children enter school already knowing a good deal about interpreting print, spelling, and numerical reasoning. Whereas the typical student then proceeds to elaborate on this knowledge, the child with learning disabilities has yet to begin laying the foundation for this learning. The information-processing inefficiencies of students with learning disabilities and their unique cognitive styles often interfere with the normal process of acquiring academic skills. For them, learning is a struggle to keep up. They are confused, overwhelmed, and eventually may question their own worth as individuals.

The ultimate success of any of these children in the school curriculum will depend on such learner, task, and setting factors as the child's cognitive and information-processing abilities, the child's motivation and perseverance, the attitude toward education and the fund of background knowledge he or she brings from home, teachers' skills and attitudes, class size, classroom organization, and peer characteristics. Let us begin by exploring the typical reading acquisition process and the way in which this process can differ for the child with a learning disability.

Reading

Reading acquisition involves a progression from attending to the whole visual configurations of words, to analyzing and sequencing the individual sounds in words, to reading for meaning with little conscious attention to decoding. Some children who are learning disabled follow the same developmental course as typical readers but at a slower rate. For these students, a well-chosen curriculum geared toward their readiness levels may be sufficient to ensure reading progress. In contrast, other students' reading patterns differ qualitatively from the typical process. They overuse either the visual/attending to wholes strategy or the phonological/analyzing details strategy and underuse the alternate approach. The most severely learning disabled tend to be inefficient with both processes and require very specialized teaching approaches.

All I Really Need to Know I Learned in Kindergarten

ALL I REALLY NEED TO KNOW about how to live and what to do and how to be I learned in kindergarten. Wisdom was not at the top of the graduate-school mountain, but there in the sandpile at Sunday School. These are the things I learned:

> Share everything.
> Play fair.
> Don't hit people.
> Put things back where you found them.
> Clean up your own mess.
> Don't take things that aren't yours.
> Say you're sorry when you hurt somebody.
> Wash your hands before you eat.
> Flush.
> Warm cookies and cold milk are good for you.

Live a balanced life—learn some and think some and draw and paint and sing and dance and play and work every day some.

> Take a nap every afternoon.
> When you go out into the world, watch out for traffic, hold hands, and stick together.
> Be aware of wonder. Remember the little seed in the Styrofoam cup: The roots go down and the plant goes up and nobody really knows how or why, but we are all like that.
> Goldfish and hamsters and white mice and even the little seed in the Styrofoam cup— they all die. So do we.
> And then remember the Dick-and-Jane books and the first word you learned—the biggest word of all—LOOK.

Everything you need to know is in there somewhere. The Golden Rule and love and basic sanitation. Ecology and politics and equality and sane living.

Take any one of those items and extrapolate it into sophisticated adult terms and apply it to your family life or your work or your government or your world and it holds true and clear and firm. Think what a better world it would be if we all—the whole world—had cookies and milk about three o'clock every afternoon and then lay down with our blankies for a nap. Or if all governments had a basic policy to always put things back where they found them and to clean up their own mess.

And it is still true, no matter how old you are—when you go out into the world, it is best to hold hands and stick together.

Source: Fulghum, R. (1988). *All I really need to know I learned in kindergarten: Uncommon thoughts on common things.* New York: Villard Books, pp. 6–8. Copyright © 1986, 1988 by Robert Fulghum. Reprinted by permission of Villard Books, a division of Random House, Inc.

Reading Acquisition.   Reading acquisition involves a gradual shift from reading being primarily a global, visual-processing task to one that also analyzes and sequences sounds and attributes meaning to written language (Berninger, 1990; Frith, 1985; Perfetti, 1985; Spear-Swerling & Sternberg, 1994). It is likely that the teaching methods we use influence this progression to some degree. There is general agreement on the series of broad, overlapping stages that characterize reading development:

Stage 1.   *Attention to Wholes.* In this stage, children rely on clues from the visual configuration of words. Preschoolers are in this stage when they recognize "Dunkin Donuts" from the orange and pink logo, or when they read Burger King signs as in the figure below. Preschoolers tend to see and remember these images more as patterns of shapes than as groupings of individual letters or words.

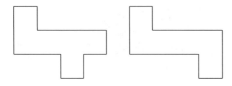

Stage 2.   *Attention to Parts.*
    a. *Initial phase.* The child now begins to attend to the separate words that make up a phrase. Word shape and length are important clues to meaning (Haber & Haber, 1981). To recognize the word *King* in *Burger King,* the child now attends to the "up then down" shape.

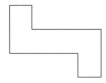

    b. *Secondary phase.* The child begins to attend to the details within each word. The child is able to discriminate the word *king* from *wing,* although still unaware of the letter sounds. Eventually the child learns the sounds associated with each of the letters. Finally, the child is able to sequence the sounds in order to sound out unfamiliar words. The child's visual attentiveness to the sequence of letters within words at this stage promotes recognition of common spelling patterns in the English language (Frith, 1983).

Stage 3.   *Reading for comprehension.* As facility is gained with analyzing and sequencing the sounds in words, and the common letter sequences of the English language gain familiarity, the child becomes able to read while attending to fewer and fewer letter cues. The visual, *orthographic* (common spelling patterns), and phonetic aspects of words are processed with such little effort that a focus on comprehension of the material becomes possible.

These three stages of reading acquisition are supported by a good deal of neuropsychological research suggesting that the child begins to shift from right to left hemisphere processing preferences during stage 2 (Bakker & Licht, 1986; Carmon, Nachshon, & Starinsky, 1976; Kershner, 1977; Licht et al., 1988; Silverberg et al., 1979, 1980). At this stage the left hemisphere's style of analyzing the visual details of words (individual letters and common letter sequences) is introduced, followed by application of its phonological analysis and sequencing abilities. By stage 3, the left hemisphere's phonological/analytic strategies (to a greater extent) and the right hemisphere's visual/holistic processing strategies (to a lesser extent) cooperate in such an automatic fashion that it becomes easy to allocate attention to the passage's meaning. The eye merely glances at the visual features of words to get a clue as to what they are. The phonetic associations with these letters are effortless. Orthographic awareness becomes mature at this stage: the child is familiar with the conventional combinations of letters in our alphabetic system, those that are unlikely to follow one another (for example, *hg* or *fz* are not English), and those that sound different in combination than in isolation (for example, *ight* or *kn*). The interplay of visual and phonological processes in reading and the anticipation of grammar and meaning have received considerable research attention.

Visual and Phonological Processes. Normal readers appear to recognize familiar words instantly because they use their efficient visual channels, which focus on whole words and familiar letter sequences (Adams, 1990; Boder, 1973; Frith, 1983; Myklebust, 1965). Decoding of unfamiliar words, however, must be helped by the phonological channel, which analyzes and sequences sound patterns according to what has been learned about letter order in the English language. This process also is rapid because good readers have become efficient at dealing with word parts that can have inconsistent pronunciations; for example, whereas *ail* and *ore* always are pronounced the same, *aid* and *ove* are inconsistent (*maid-said, stove-love*), and many pronunciations are contingent on rules (for example, vowel sounds are "short" in a consonant-vowel-consonant formation but "long" if a silent *e* is added) (Morrison, 1987).

Frith (1983) points out that the orthographic route (recognizing conventional spelling patterns) is a faster way to get to meaning than the phonological (sounding out), which goes from print to sound and only then to meaning. Research suggests that during instant visual recognition of sight words, it is orthographic cues rather than word shape that help us decode, because we continue to recognize these words even when they are written in unfamiliar typefaces (Adams, 1990; Frith, 1983). In other words, what we are recognizing by "sight" are the identity and position of letter patterns within words. This orthographic recognition develops after repeated successful encounters with print through the phonological route.

In normal reading, there is an automatic interplay between the visual and phonological process just described. No one process is entirely responsible because fluent reading requires that many cognitive abilities come together "simultaneously and successively" (Das, Kirby, & Jarman, 1975). While one is learning to read, it appears that each stage benefits from the simultaneous assistance of the cognitive systems that are active during the other stages as well (Chase & Tallal, 1991). For example, while good phonological awareness certainly aids word recognition, learning to sound out and recognize words further improves phonological awareness (Adams, 1990; Perfetti et al., 1987; Torgesen, Wagner, & Rashotte, 1994).

Anticipation of Grammar and Meaning. Goodman (1976) described an important component of the stage 3 process as a "linguistic guessing game." That is, the reader merely samples words from the text, making hypotheses about what the words will be based on semantic (meaning), syntactic (grammar), and graphic (form) cues. A fluent reader will miscall words that fit according to the meaning and grammar of the sentence. This poses no problem, since the meaning of the sentence is preserved. This is why, when the third grader reads "Mother told father to go to the grocery store to buy meat" as "Mom told dad to stop by the market and get meat," the teacher need not be concerned. The child is using good linguistic skills to anticipate what the passage is saying. The child is accomplishing the purpose of reading, which is to gain meaning, rather than just meaninglessly pronouncing words.

To get a feel for how the good reader can allow the grammar and meaning of the passage to guide reading, look quickly at the sign in Figure 5–1. What does it say? Now look at it again. Did you read the word *to* twice? In all likelihood you didn't even notice that the word *to* appeared twice. Bakker and Licht (1986) explain that because you are a good reader, your semantic bias actually induced you to neglect the perceptual features of the words. Similarly, your good linguistic skills allow you to correctly read the sentences in Figure 5–2, despite two of the words having common print. These same skills allow you to read the

Figure 5–1   Passage syntax and semantics can help guide decoding. *Source:* Bakker, D. J., & Licht, R. (1986). Learning to read: Changing horses in mid-stream. In G. Th. Pavlidis & D. F. Fisher (Eds.), *Dyslexia: Its neuropsychology and treatment.* New York: John Wiley & Sons, p. 88. © 1986 by John Wiley & Sons. Reprinted by permission.

There is evidence that the efficient reader switches between semantic, syntactic, orthographic, and phonological cues, using only a few at a time. Research suggests that good readers may have little need to use context to aid decoding. They recognize words so rapidly using their visual and phonological competencies that comprehension cues have little time to be processed and influence decoding (Spear & Sternberg, 1987; Vellutino, 1991). It is the poor reader, far more than the good reader, who relies on context to supplement slow, nonsystematic decoding abilities (Adams, 1990; Perfetti, 1982; Spear & Sternberg, 1987; Stanovich, 1986). In fact, the context's facilitation of word identification actually decreases with age for the typical reader (Stanovich, 1991b). It is only when especially difficult or novel words are encountered that context becomes a significant aid to word recognition (Adams, 1990).

The typical reading process is not really as clearcut as this presentation suggests. Experts continue to debate whether context aids decoding, whether we sample orthographic patterns or attend to all visual aspects of words at once when reading, whether beginning readers associate sounds with orthographic units as well as single letters, and whether instruction in phonetic analysis is as great a priority as early exposure to the rich language and ideas of good literature.

following sentence correctly on the first try, despite several words that are spelled alike but have different pronunciations and meanings: "Did you notice Judy's content when she discovered the content of her birthday package?"

Typical Reading Patterns.   Instruction in word recognition (reading words at a glance), word analysis (sounding out), and comprehension typically follows a sequence like that presented in Figure 5–3. By second grade the child is well into

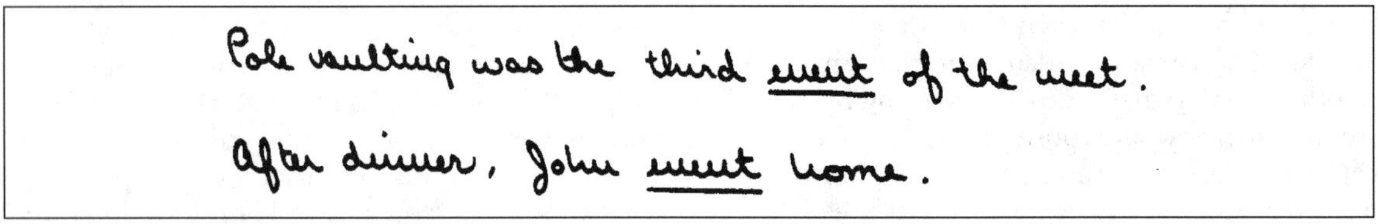

> *Pole vaulting was the third event of the meet.*
> *After dinner, John went home.*

Figure 5–2   Linguistic skills help guide decoding when the orthographic information is vague. *Source:* Nash-Webber, B. (1975). The role of semantics in automatic speech understanding. In D. G. Bobrow & A. Collins (Eds.), *Representation and understanding.* New York: Academic Press. Reprinted by permission of Daniel G. Bobrow.

Middle School

Understands paradoxes; appreciates elements of style (e.g., imagery/ foreshadowing/flashback/symbolism/irony/mood); recognizes biased writings and propaganda; uses appendices, *Readers Guide to Periodicals,* atlas, almanac, appropriate reference sources; recognizes figures of speech such as personification (e.g., *the computer yawned and spit out the disk*), hyperbole (intentional exaggeration, e.g., *waiting for an eternity*), onomatopoeia (word that imitates sounds, e.g., *cuckoo*); can read many adult level books

Fifth Grade

Makes generalizations; recognizes theme; uses copyright page, preface, cross-references; familiar with more literary forms (e.g., autobiography, fable, legend); reasons using syllogisms (e.g., if a=b and b=c, then a=c); can read many popular magazines

Fourth Grade

Begins to develop different reading styles/rates for different purposes (e.g., skimming); locates and uses references; increases silent reading rate; expands vocabulary; recognizes plot and implied main idea; understands idioms/multiple meanings; paraphrases or summarizes a story or article; selects/evaluates/organizes study materials; discriminates different forms of writing (e.g., folk tale, science fiction, biography); appreciates author's point of view; considerable independent reading expected; can read newspaper, restaurant menu

Third Grade

Reading focus shifts from decoding to comprehension; rapid expansion of sight vocabulary and word-analysis skills (e.g., igh, eight); interprets homophones (e.g., way, weigh) and homographs (e.g., grizzly *bear*, to *bear* arms); reversals of letters and words generally disappear; reads selectively to locate information; reading speed increases with development of silent reading skills; distinguishes fiction/nonfiction, fact/opinion, synonym/antonym; recalls prior knowledge and relates to new text; recognizes author's purpose; uses index, captions, subheadings, margin notes; uses encyclopedia, telephone directory; interprets diagrams; reads for both knowledge and recreation

Second Grade

Mastery of harder phonetic skills (e.g., kn, wr, gh, ck, lk, ir, ur, oi, au, oa); sounds out unfamiliar words based on individual letter sounds, familiar spelling patterns, root words, endings; identifies words from contextual clues; less confusion with reversible letters; varies in pitch, stress, volume when reading aloud; aware of syllabication rules, prefixes/suffixes, changing y to i or f/fe to v before adding ending; compares/evaluates information; recognizes character, setting, motive, resolution of a story; uses library for simple research purposes; interprets graphs; uses dictionary

First Grade

Identifies consonants in all positions in a word; reads long and short vowels, some vowel teams (e.g., ee, ae) and consonant diagraphs (e.g., ch, sh, th); growing ability to break dictated words into individual sounds; reads word families (e.g., cat, hat, rat); growing sight vocabulary; aware of root words, endings, compound words, contractions; recognizes main idea and cause/effect in story; draws conclusions; follows simple written directions; aware of author, title, table of contents, alphabetical order; recognizes a play; interprets maps and globes

Kindergarten

Points to/names upper and lowercase alphabet letters; recognizes some commonly seen words (e.g., STOP, McDonald's, Sesame Street); begins to associate letters with their sounds; matches simple words to corresponding pictures; rhymes; growing awareness of whether words begin or end with the same sound; developing ability to break spoken words into syllables; blends dictated sounds to make a word; recognizes that reading proceeds from left to right and from top to bottom on a page; interprets picture stories; recognizes/compares/contrasts facts in a story; aware of time sequence in a story and predicts outcome; recognizes poetry; distinguishes reality from fantasy

Figure 5–3 Sequence of reading development.

stage 2 of reading acquisition. By third grade the typical student is making a transition to stage 3. Traditional curricula have been arranged so that by fourth grade children typically stop "learning to read" and instead emphasize "reading to learn" (Chall, 1983a). More recent curricula, however, stress reading to learn from the start. By the middle school years students are expected to be independent readers, who enjoy reading for pleasure.

Most children enter school already knowing a great deal about the alphabet, its sounds, and the order of sounds in words (Adams, 1990; Goodman & Goodman, 1979; Read, 1975; Reid & Hresko, 1980). In fact, three year olds already are aware that sentences are comprised of discrete words, and a three or four year old's ability to detect rhymes is predictive of beginning word reading (Blachman, 1991; Sawyer et al., 1990).

Upon entering kindergarten, children's ability to match letters visually is nearly perfect (Calfee, Chapman, & Venezky, 1972), and they generally can discriminate among at least three stimuli at once (for example, recognizing why *rat* is different from *tar,* or listening to three rhyming words and identifying the common sound) (Eimas, 1969; Epstein, 1985). The ability to follow a line of print from left to right and to compare words visually is well established (Elkind & Weiss, 1967).

When they begin kindergarten, children typically are correct about half the time when asked to identify/provide rhymes or blend a phoneme with a stem (for example, *d-og*) (Majsterek & Ellenwood, 1995). Seventy-five percent of kindergarten children can represent short strings of individual letter sounds with different-colored blocks; they can also represent with blocks that two different sounds have been blended (for example, *ip*) (Calfee, Lindamood, & Lindamood, 1973). About half the time kindergarteners can tell whether two words begin or end with the same sound. Breaking a dictated word into its individual sounds and telling how many sounds they hear in a word are more difficult (Stanovich, Cunningham, & Cramer, 1984; Yopp, 1988). The findings of Liberman and colleagues (1974) support others, indicating that about half of kindergartners can segment words into syllables,

but less than 20 percent are able to segment the syllables into their individual phonemes.

By age six, approximately 90 percent of children are capable of segmenting words into syllables, and 70 percent can segment by phoneme (Liberman et al., 1974). By the end of first grade most children can count the phonemes they hear in words and delete initial phonemes (Blachman, 1991). Substituting phonemes to form new words develops next, with 75 percent of children being accurate by second grade, and nearly 95 percent by fifth grade (Calfee et al., 1973).

By age seven the child's letter identification is less confused by the orientation of reversible letters (Belmont & Birch, 1963), and by age eight reading reversals generally disappear (Boder, 1973). For the typical student, horizontal transformations (*b-d*) appear no more difficult to deal with than vertical transformations (*p-b*); more reading errors are made with *b* than with *d* or *p*; and very few errors are made with the letter *g* (Liberman et al., 1971). The average student requires two visual fixations per word in first grade but less than one per word by the intermediate grades (Taylor, 1966). Fixations generally last 200–250 msec, after which the eye jumps roughly eight letter spaces to the right. By adulthood, the individual scans about fifteen characters per fixation. The first eight characters are used to identify words and letters, and the remaining characters provide cues about word length to help guide the eyes' movements. About 10 to 15 percent of the time our eyes move back in the text to try to comprehend material we've already seen (Rayner, 1986, 1996). It is normal for about half of five to six year olds to be weak in their fixation ability, so that letters may tend to "move around." By ages seven to eight, 70 percent of children have achieved fixation stability, and 90 percent by age ten (Stein, Riddell, & Fowler, 1986).

By third grade, children generally are adept at analyzing words based on their sounds, configurations (length, shape), structure (roots, prefixes), orthography, and clues gained from context. The faster and more accurately children decode, the more their attention is freed to comprehend what has been read (Stanovich, 1982; Vellutino, 1991). Therefore, we find that those children who are the most automatic decoders also tend to be the ones who comprehend the best (Perfetti, 1984; Shinn et al., 1992).

Deno's (1985) research has found that in the fall of first grade, beginning readers can read about five words correctly in one minute. Within a year, their accuracy and speed increase dramatically, with the average child accurately reading about forty-five words per minute. This rate doubles again between second and third grades (about 95 words/minute), after which the rate of gain begins to taper. By sixth grade, the average student can read approximately 140 words per minute. Skillful readers eventually read faster than five words per second, over 300 words per minute (Rayner & Pollatsek, 1987).

Beginning readers generally read up to ten words incorrectly in one minute, and this number gradually decreases to one to two words incorrect by sixth grade. Reading errors typically made by elementary school children include:

- omitting letters or syllables in a word
- omitting words in a sentence
- omitting or inserting word endings
- inserting extra sounds in words or extra words in sentences
- substituting words that look, sound, or have meanings similar to the printed word
- mispronouncing initial letters, final letters, medial vowels, and so on
- reversing whole words and the order of letters or syllables in a word (these usually are due to phonological sequencing or attention factors rather than to visual confusion)
- transposing the order of words in a sentence
- repeating words
- using the wrong inflection, ignoring punctuation, having dialect differences

Sound substitution errors are far more frequent in the beginning reader than errors caused by misperception of the letter's shape. Vowels pose far greater difficulties than consonants (Adams, 1990; Liberman, 1985).

By third grade the teacher seldom listens to students read aloud anymore. Although they are reading silently, many children subvocalize (Edfeldt, 1959).

Reading Patterns of Students with Learning Disabilities. Students with reading disabilities obviously lag behind their classmates in how much they have learned about reading. Whereas some of these students may be progressing through reading stages in the expected way, albeit at a slower rate, others show patterns that are qualitatively different from those of even younger typical learners. Many children never get beyond stage 2 reading because they get stuck overusing either their visual/holistic or phonological/analytical information-processing abilities and underusing the alternate strategy, or they underuse both strategies. The normal interplay between visual and phonological processes never gets established. Yet other children's reading difficulties relate primarily to problems focusing and sustaining attention. Because reading merely translates language into another symbol system, the better a child's language skills, the more rapid reading progress is likely to be (Reid & Hresko, 1980; Vellutino et al., 1991).

Electroencephalogram and visual half-field studies have supported the visual and phonological weakness subtypes of individuals with reading disabilities (Dalby & Gibson, 1981; Dool, Stelmack, & Rourke, 1993; Fletcher, 1985; Riccio & Hynd, 1995; Rosenthal, 1982). Children whose reading difficulties relate to visual-processing weaknesses show their primary deficit in the ability to recognize and remember how letter and whole-word configurations look. They seem to attend only to partial cues in words, overlooking a systematic analysis of English orthography (Frith, 1983; Henderson & Chard, 1980). Children whose reading delays are associated with phonological-processing weaknesses often are unaware that spoken language is segmented (Williams, 1987). They have difficulty remembering letter sounds, analyzing the individual sounds in words, and sequencing/blending these into words. The most severely reading-disabled students are weak in both visual- and phonological-processing abilities (Badian, 1996; Bateman, 1968; Boder, 1973).

Tables 5–1 and 5–2 list the reading and spelling patterns of children with visual- and phonological-processing weaknesses. The spelling samples in Figure 5–4 illustrate the persistence of these students' processing preferences into the upper grades, despite improvement in reading ability. Other common behaviors among children with reading disabilities include holding the book closer than fifteen to eighteen inches (because of the effort being expended), fidgeting, refusing to read, reading slowly and word by word, using an unnatural voice quality, and ignoring words they can't read (Jones, 1980). Students with learning disabilities, when compared to typical readers, often read less than one half to two-thirds as many words accurately (Deno, Mirkin, & Chiang, 1982). After such a struggle, it is unlikely that the child will comprehend or remember much of the passage's message.

Because children with learning disabilities more often have difficulty with the sounds than with the visual forms of words, teachers are advised to concentrate on teaching phonological awareness and phonics skills rather than on elimination of reversals. It may surprise you to learn that, as a proportion of total errors, reading reversals are no greater for poor readers than for good readers (Stanovich, 1982). Reversals only seem to occur more often for poor readers because these students' overall error rates are greater. Even when writing (see Figure 5–5), only 15 percent of the errors of children with reading disabilities tend to be reversals of letter orientation, a visual error (Liberman, 1985). In contrast, Liberman found that consonant sounds accounted for 32 percent of errors, vowel sounds for 43 percent, and transpositions of the order of sounds in words 10 percent. When their reading reversals are ana-

Table 5–1   Reading and spelling patterns of children with visual-processing weaknesses

- Confusion with letters that differ in orientation (*b-d, p-q*)
- Confusion with words whose parts can be reversed (*was-saw; bread-beard*)
- Very limited sight vocabulary; few words are instantly recognized from their configuration—they need to be sounded out laboriously, as though being seen for the first time
- Losing the place because one doesn't instantly recognize what had already been read, as when switching one's gaze from the end of one line to the beginning of the next
- Omitting letters and words because they weren't noticed
- Masking the image of one letter, by moving the eye too rapidly to the next letter, may result in omission of the first letter when reading
- Difficulty learning irregular words that can't be sounded out (for example, *sight*)
- Difficulty with rapid retrieval of words when spelling due to revisualization weaknesses
- Visual stimuli when reading prove so confusing that it is easier for the child to learn to read by first spelling the words orally and then putting them in print
- Insertions, omissions, and substitutions, when the meaning of the passage is guiding reading
- Strengths in left hemisphere language-processing, analytic and sequential abilities, and detail analysis; can sound out phonetically regular words even up to grade level
- Difficulty recalling the shape of a letter when writing
- Spells phonetically but not bizarrely (*laf-laugh; bisnis-business*)
- Can spell difficult phonetic words but not simple irregular words

Table 5–2   Reading and spelling patterns of children with phonological-processing weaknesses

- Difficulty discriminating between individual sounds (occurs very seldom)
- Difficulty processing rapid auditory inputs: if the teacher models a word but the child does not perceive consonant sounds that cannot be sustained (e.g., *p-b*), these may then be omitted in reading and spelling
- Poor ability to analyze the sequence of sounds and syllables in words; leads to reversals in reading; analysis and sequencing errors when speaking are common (e.g., "lead a snot into temptation" and "Harold be thy name" in the Lord's Prayer, or "elmenopee" being one lumped cluster in the alphabet song
- Poor ability to remember individual sounds or combinations of sounds
- Difficulty blending individual sounds into words
- Difficulty listening to words and omitting one sound and substituting another (say *cat*; now take off the /*c*/ and put on a /*f*/); such abilities are essential to word analysis, during which children decode by matching the new word to known words, and making the appropriate substitutions; skill with initial consonants develops first, then final consonants, and then medial vowels and consonants
- Difficulty remembering the sounds of letters and letter combinations
- Difficulty with rapid retrieval of letter sounds, so that the beginning of a word is forgotten by the time the last letter sound is recalled (word finding problem)
- Difficulty analyzing new words because of poor knowledge of phonetic rules
- Vowel sounds are particularly troublesome
- Word substitutions may be conceptually (*person, human*) or visually (*horse, house*) related
- Limited sight vocabulary because phonetic cues can't aid memory
- Guessing at unfamiliar words rather than employing word-analysis skills
- Spelling is extremely poor because it is attempted by sight rather than by ear
- Correct spellings occur primarily on words that the child has encountered repeatedly and can revisualize
- Bizarre spellings that seldom can be identified, even by the child, because they do not follow phonetic patterns
- Extraneous letters and omitted syllables in spelling

lyzed, poor readers seem to have more difficulty with horizontal than with vertical transformations (Fischer, Liberman, & Shankweiler, 1978).

Of Boder's (1973) students with learning disabilities, 60 percent revealed a phonetic weakness. Less than 10 percent showed visual processing weaknesses. Approximately 20 percent showed both patterns at once; sometimes this appeared to be due to one area of weakness acting to impair the capabilities of the other area as well. A number of investigators concur with this distribution of different types of reading disabilities (Manis et al., 1988; Sweeney & Rourke, 1985; Telzrow et al., 1983). Children with either a phonological or

visual-processing weakness have a more favorable prognosis than do those with both weaknesses.

Language and phonological-processing weaknesses contribute more severely to reading disorders than do visual-processing deficits (Byrne, Freebody, & Gates, 1992; Stanovich, 1988). Children with phonological-processing strengths at least can sound out unfamiliar words, though their reading is likely to be labored because they cannot quickly recognize words from their configurations or orthographic patterns. The child with phonological-processing disabilities, on the other hand, has trouble sounding out unfamiliar words and is hampered by most people's limited capacity to

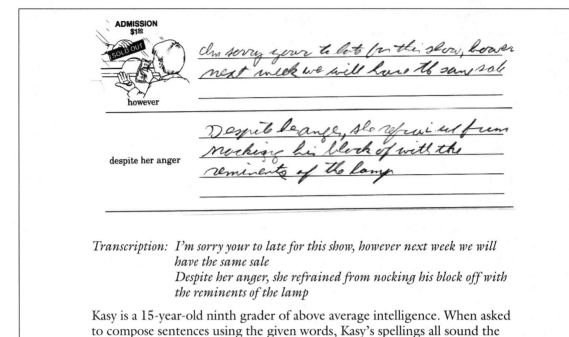

Transcription: *I'm sorry your to late for this show, however next week we will have the same sale*
Despite her anger, she refrained from nocking his block off with the reminents of the lamp

Kasy is a 15-year-old ninth grader of above average intelligence. When asked to compose sentences using the given words, Kasy's spellings all sound the way they should. Because of her perceptual disability, however, she does not recognize how these words should look. Likewise, she overlooks periods.

(Continues on following page)

Figure 5–4   Spelling patterns of a student with visual-processing weaknesses.

remember the visual forms of words without the aid of phonetic analysis. If the syntax and semantics of language also are problematic, then the child will be limited even further by difficulty using predictions of grammar or meaning to aid decoding (Goodman & Goodman, 1977).

Very often, the visual- and phonological-processing difficulties of poor readers are complicated by poor attending abilities. At other times, inattention may give the impression that a child has a visual- or phonological-processing disorder when the child in fact has none. This type of child guesses wildly at words from their first and last letters, does not take the time to sound out, and does not attend to the order of letters in words or the order of words in a sentence. This child tends not to pay attention to the orientation of reversible letters and does not organize what has been read for comprehension and recall. Errors often increase as the reading continues because the child's attention gets caught by irrelevant stimuli (Ross, 1976). Once the teacher helps this child attend systematically to the important features of words and passages, the teacher often finds that the child has some good abilities to bring to the reading task.

Goodman and Burke (1972) explain that children's reading errors usually are not random mistakes. Rather, they are miscues generated by the children's information-processing styles or past learning, which induce them to respond to one cue over a more relevant cue. Miscues have a graphic, sound, or grammatical similarity to the written word. Miscues that change the meaning of a passage (*pet-pit*) are considered more serious than word substitutions that do not interfere with comprehension (*mom-mother*). Because omissions and insertions seldom change the meaning of a

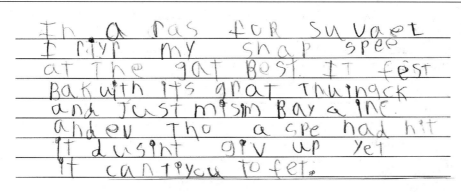

Known Words		Unknown Words	
friendship	friendship	*bage*	badge
remember	remember	*demoracte*	democrat
important	important	*gation*	quotation
comb	comb	*sowres*	source
unless	unless	*jusus*	justice
flower	flower	*onlibel*	honorable
whole	whole	*haytion*	hasten

A gifted seventh grader, Ethan earned over 500 on both the verbal and quantitative Scholastic Achievement Tests administered orally in seventh grade. He can spell "known" words within his sight vocabulary by remembering how they look but, unlike typical students, has difficulty phonetically approximating the spellings of "unknown" words that he has not yet learned to read.

Transcription: In a race for survival I raised my sharp spear at the great beast. It fought back with its great trunk and just missed him by an inch and even though a spear had hit it doesn't give up yet it can tire you to fight.

Jimmy is a 10 year old of high average intelligence whose parents and seven aunts and uncles have severe reading disabilities. His older sister is an honor student. Jimmy does not spell with good phonetic equivalents, and he can spell very few words in his limited sight vocabulary.

Figure 5–4 *Continued.*
(top) Spelling patterns of a student with phonological-processing weaknesses.
(bottom) Spelling patterns of a student with visual- and phonological-processing weaknesses.

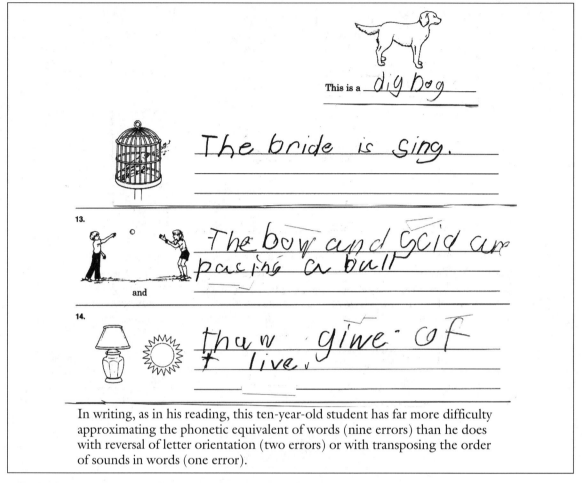

In writing, as in his reading, this ten-year-old student has far more difficulty approximating the phonetic equivalent of words (nine errors) than he does with reversal of letter orientation (two errors) or with transposing the order of sounds in words (one error).

Figure 5–5   Low frequency of letter reversals compared to other errors in the writing of students with learning disabilities.

sentence, teachers have been advised to attend primarily to word-substitution errors that alter meaning (D'Angelo & Mahlios, 1983). By analyzing the error patterns of children with learning disabilities, teachers can determine which strengths to capitalize on and which weaknesses to remediate, to speed reading progress.

Handwriting

A great deal of time is spent on handwriting instruction in the primary grades. Despite the availability of word processors, young children still handwrite the majority of their homework assignments, in-class assignments, and tests.

One study in which elementary classrooms were observed all day suggests that 30 to 60 percent of the school day is spent in paper-pencil and other fine-motor activities (cutting, pasting, computer) (McHale & Cermak, 1992). This poses quite an obstacle for the 75 to 90 percent of students with learning disabilities who have fine-motor difficulties (Clements et al., 1971; Critchley, 1970; Tarnopol & Tarnopol, 1977). Unfortunately, these children's handwriting problems often mask their underlying knowledge. Patterns of typical and atypical handwriting acquisition are important to understand because they can help direct the remediation process.

Typical Handwriting Acquisition. By the time children enter first grade, they usually can hold a pencil in a comfortable three-finger grasp, print letters from memory, and copy three- to four-letter words. They know that printing proceeds from left to right, and they can stay reasonably close to the line. Their letters may vary in size, spacing, alignment, proportion, pencil pressure (heavy, light), slant, and form (Freeman, 1965). Reversals of the orientation and sequence of letters in words are common among young elementary school students, though far less common than form errors (add, delete, or misalign letter parts) (Critchley, 1970; Simner, 1982). Writing reversals usually decline by age eight to eight and one-half (Boder, 1973; Kinsbourne & Caplan, 1979).

Figure 5–6 presents handwriting samples of children who are weak, average, and strong writers. The quality of these samples contrasts sharply with the handwriting of students with learning disabilities in Figure 5–6 and elsewhere throughout this chapter. As you can see, by the end of third grade children typically have made the transition from manuscript (printing) to cursive writing. Cursive writing continues to be refined in fourth and fifth grades. By sixth grade, children (especially girls) have experimented with many styles of penmanship (size, shape, slant, spacing) and usually have adopted one that will continue to distinguish their script from that of others. The left-hander seldom has more trouble writing than does the right-hander. By slanting the paper in the opposite direction from that of the right-hander, the left-hander's characteristic hook can be prevented (Otto, McMenemy, & Smith, 1973).

Handwriting Patterns of Students with Learning Disabilities. Children with handwriting difficulties generally write slowly and in a labored fashion (Clements et al., 1971; Deuel, 1995). Their writing often is sloppy and illegible, and

they seldom develop an individual style of handwriting. Written tests pose difficulties because these students' painstaking writing impedes their thought processes. So much effort needs to go into directing their pencils to form the letters that little energy is left to develop ideas. Sustaining energy long enough to put what they know down on paper is extremely difficult. As can be imagined from looking at Kasy's writing in Figure 5–4, these students' writing creates a real problem with teacher evaluation.

Many of these students have pencil grips that are awkward and too tight. Often their writing postures are uncomfortable, and they exert too much pressure on the paper. As illustrated in Figure 5–7, their letters seldom meet the line. These children have difficulty with letter size, slant, and formation, as well as spacing between letters and words (Poteet, 1980). Formation of letters containing vertical and horizontal strokes (*T, L, F*) seems to present less of a problem than those containing diagonals (*K*) and curves that meet lines (*R*). Interspersing capital letters with lowercase letters is common.

The cursive writing and mathematics calculations in Figure 5–7 illustrate the common finding that writing reversals continue longer than customary among children with learning disabilities. This is especially true for boys (Critchley, 1970). These reversals seem to occur because the children do not allocate sufficient attention to the distinctive features that discriminate one letter or numeral from another. Reversals are not due to actually seeing reversed images. If this were the case, children would pick up mugs from the wrong side, pierce their forks into the other side of the plate instead of their food, and so forth. Resolution of reversals comes as the children learn to use their visual, language, and cognitive competencies to discriminate ups from downs (*p-b; u-n; m-w*), lefts from rights (*b-d; E-3*), and rotations (*b-q; 6-9*). Reversals of numbers tend to be resolved before reversals of letters, perhaps because there are fewer of them to confuse.

Handwriting problems of students with learning disabilities have been related to underlying visual-perceptual difficulties, motor incoordination, or attention weaknesses.

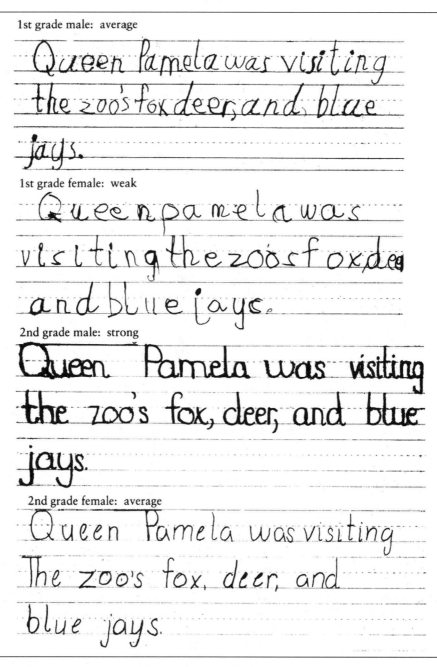

Figure 5–6 Handwriting samples of average, weak, and strong writers as well as students with learning disabilities. The typical samples were collected by having each student in a suburban elementary school copy the same sentence. The samples were sorted by sex into weak, average, and strong piles at each grade level. The middle most sample in each pile is what has been reproduced here.

3rd grade female: strong

Queen Pamela was visiting the zoo's fox, deer and bluejays.

3rd grade female: weak

Queen Pamela was visiting the zoo fox, deer and blue jays.

4th grade female: strong

Queen Pamela was visiting the zoo's fox, deer, and blue jays.

4th grade female: average

Queen Pamela was visiting the zoo's fox, deer, and blue jays.

4th grade female: weak

Queen Pamela was visiting the zoo's fox, deer and blue jays.

3rd grade male: weak

Queen Pamela was visiting the zoo's fox deer and blue jays.

3rd grade male: average

Queen Pamela was visiting the zoo's fox deer and blue jays.

4th grade male: average

Queen Pamela was visiting the zoo's fox, deer, and blue jays.

4th grade male: weak

Queen Pamela was visiting the zoo's fox, deer and blue jays.

4th grade male: strong

Queen Pamela was visiting the zoo's fox, deer, and blue jays.

Figure 5–6 *Continued.*

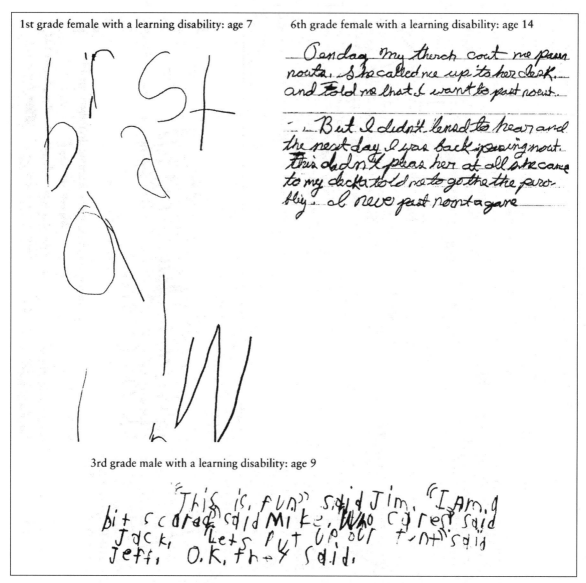

1st grade female with a learning disability: age 7

6th grade female with a learning disability: age 14

3rd grade male with a learning disability: age 9

Figure 5–6 *Continued.*

Visual-Perceptual Difficulties. Perceptual weaknesses, the inefficient storage and recall of visual images, seem to underlie the handwriting difficulties of only about 25 percent of children with learning disabilities (Tarnopol & Tarnopol, 1977). These children occasionally may pause while writing because they can't mentally picture how a letter is supposed to look, or they have trouble holding in mind the letter images they are copying. Their poor spatial judgment also compromises handwriting quality (Deuel, 1995).

Uncoordinated Motor Movements. The uncoordinated application of motor movements to the

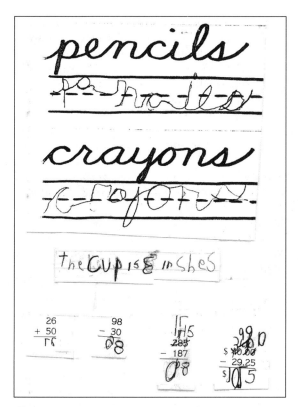

Figure 5–7 Cursive copying and mathematical calculation of an eight-year-old boy with average intelligence who has learning disabilities.

sive writing because manuscript requires less complex movements, and the letters are more similar to the print in books (Johnson & Myklebust, 1967). They believe that it is better for the child to learn one system well than to be confused about two. Others advocate cursive writing because spacing judgments are easier when letters connect, reversals are less likely, and the writing process is more rapid, continuous, and rhythmic (Orton, 1937; Strauss & Lehtinen, 1947). These considerations, together with evaluation of which form of writing comes closest to the quality of one's classmates' writing, can guide the teacher's decision on this matter (Poteet, 1980).

Inattention. Inattention can have an impact at the input as well as output ends of writing. Details of letters and words are not observed or recalled, relationships among letters and words are not evaluated, and space or motor movements are not preplanned. Because maintaining attention is difficult, the child's ideas and productivity suffer. This type of child hands in a paper that looks like it has gone through a war. When the child notices errors, he or she may just write over them impulsively in bolder print. Erasing, when done, is seldom complete, and the paper looks like a black smudge. Homework, by the time it gets back to school (if at all), is folded haphazardly, and the edges are torn. The inattentive child can do far better when attention is appropriately focused and sustained.

Spelling

Children's spelling reflects both their ability to hear positions of sounds in spoken words and what they have been able to store and recall about the words they read. For most individuals, spelling is a much more difficult task than reading, and difficulties persist long after reading problems have been resolved. We will contrast the typical process of spelling acquisition with the patterns shown by youngsters with learning disabilities.

Typical Spelling Acquisition. Spelling instruction generally does not get under way seriously until the middle of second grade because children need to become familiar with the visual and phonic

writing space is the most common cause of handwriting problems (Gerard & Junkala, 1980). These children's hands do not seem to move automatically. Their minds need to consciously direct attention to the appropriate cues (for example, spacing) or to explicitly revisualize the letters so their hand has an image to follow while copying (Fernald, 1943). Contrary to what happens with mature writers, these children cannot daydream while writing, then look down and say, "Did I write that?" Instead, they must actively plan and guide their motor movements. When so much energy goes into the mechanics, it is no wonder that ideas become muddled, abbreviated, disorganized, or lost altogether.

Some educators believe that the child with learning disabilities should not transition to cur-

(letter sound) elements of reading words before they can be expected to recall their spellings. In the meantime, use of "invented" spellings is encouraged, that is spelling words the way they sound (for example, *blt—built*). Children become able to point to correct spellings of words long before they are able to write their spellings. As adults, too, though we recognize correct spellings of words such as *conscientious,* we often have difficulty with their spelling.

There is evidence that the spelling acquisition process is the reverse of stages 1 and 2 in reading acquisition (Bryant & Bradley, 1983; Griffith, 1991). Children seem to attack spelling first with phonological strategies and then add visual strategies gained from familiarity with print conventions. Young elementary school children invent spellings that approximate phonetic portions of the spoken word (for example, *pickle = PL; quick = KWK*) (Ehri, 1989). Perhaps this phonic preference is why children tend to subvocalize when first learning to spell in the early grades (Luria, 1980; Tarnopol & Tarnopol, 1977). When they are not allowed to subvocalize, spelling errors increase.

Young elementary school children are most accurate in spelling the first sound in a word, second best at the last sound, and poorest with the sounds in the medial position. Vowels prove particularly troublesome, especially because they so often appear in the medial position between other sounds (Stage & Wagner, 1992). By third grade, vowel knowledge has improved and awareness of common English letter patterns is evident as children begin to approximate conventional spellings and rules (Ehri, 1989; Henderson & Beers, 1980). It seems that students typically continue to spell by this *lexical* route (conventional English letter patterns); when it fails, they fall back on the phonological route (Ehri, 1989; Frith, 1983). Basically, the mature speller imagines the possible combinations of spelling patterns in our language and resorts to phonetic analysis when the letter sequences do not look right.

English is particularly difficult because only approximately 50 percent of spellings follow regular phonetic rules (Hanna, Hodges, & Hanna, 1971). The only way to remember the remaining

irregular words is to revisualize them or to deduce their spellings from derivations (roots, prefixes, suffixes), from syntactic cues (for example, a past tense signals an "ed" rather than "t" spelling as in *passed* versus *past*), or from words that might follow similar orthographic patterns. The latter ability (for example, recognizing that *ite* goes with *bite* but *ight* goes with *sight*) develops later than phonetic word spellings. In the English language one orthographic form can have multiple pronunciations (for example, *cough, through, dough*) and different patterns can have the same pronunciation (for example, *weigh, way; threw, through*). Theodore Roosevelt was correct in commenting, "It's a damn fool who can't see more than one way to spell a word!" How very confusing for the child with learning disabilities.

Figure 5–8 illustrates the spelling of a typical second grader who can analyze and sequence sounds in words and who is beginning to take note of irregular spellings. Primary grade children's invented spellings are often good phonetic approximations. Although these are incorrect, the intent is clear. By the intermediate grades children usually are able to spell over 80 percent of words they recognize by sight, even if the words are phonetically irregular (Boder, 1973). Spelling instruction in the primary grades is integrated with other aspects of the language arts curriculum such as reading, vocabulary development, grammar, and composition skills.

Spelling Patterns of Students with Learning Disabilities. Children with learning disabilities typically can spell less than half of their sight vocabularies. Their spelling errors are typified by insertion of unnecessary letters (*umberella* for *umbrella*), omission of letters (*famly* for *family*), substitution of letters (*kast* for *cast*), phonetic spelling of irregular words (*sed* for *said*), directional confusion (*was* for *saw*), vowel-consonant order changes (*tabel* for *table*), vowel substitutions (*doller* for *dollar*), letter orientation confusion (*d, b; p, q; n, u; m, w*), and reversed letter sequences (*aminals* for *animals*) (Poteet, 1980).

As illustrated in Figure 5–4, children with learning disabilities may have difficulty with the phonetic or revisualization/orthographic awareness

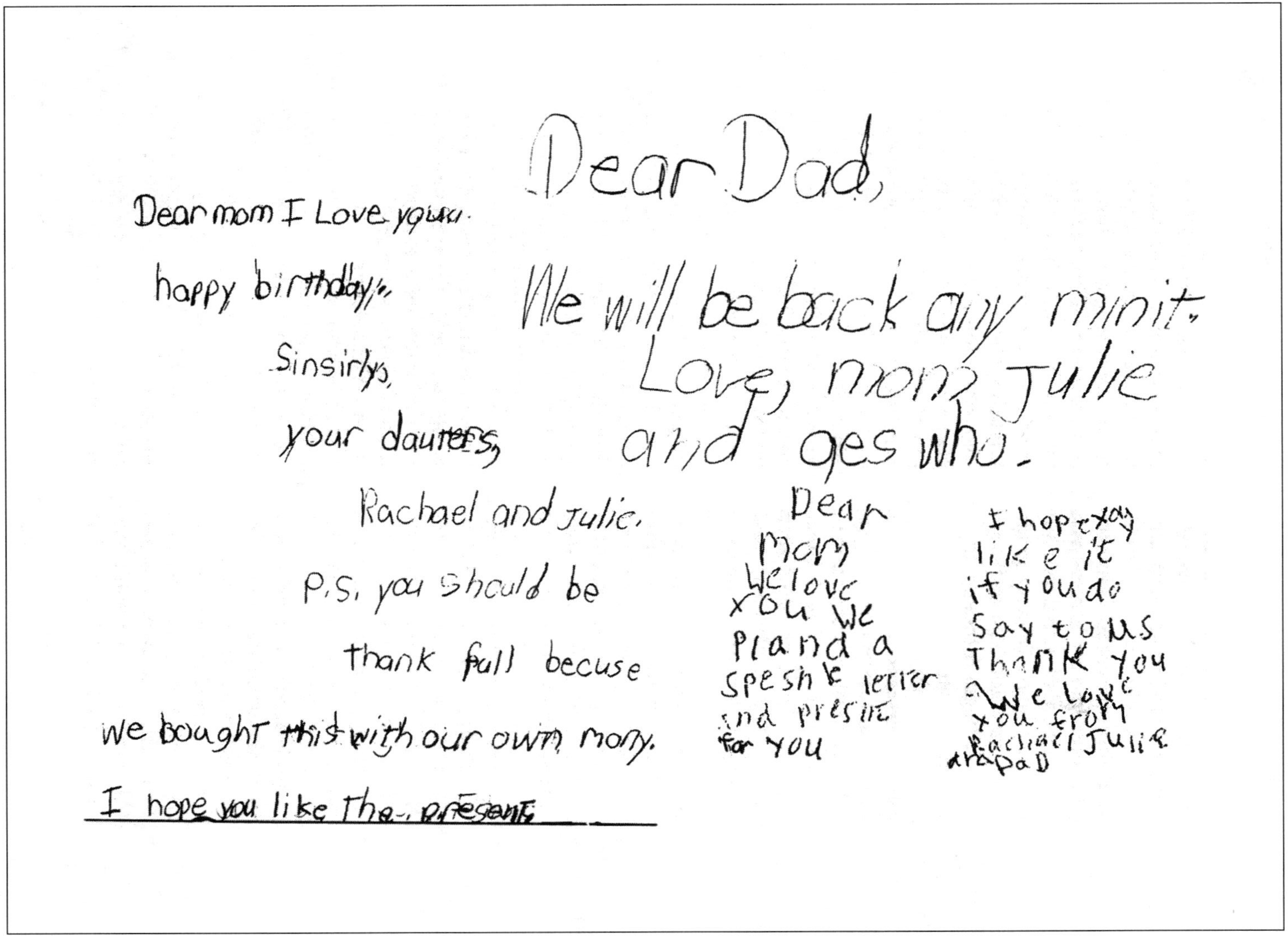

Dear mom I Love youu.

happy birthday's

Sinsirlys

your dauters,

Rachael and Julie.

P.S. you Should be

thank full becuse

We bought this with our own mony.

I hope you like the PRESENT

Dear Dad,

We will be back any minit.

Love, mom, Julie

and yes who.

Dear
mom
we love
you we
plan a
speshe letter
and presint
for you

I hopexxx
like it
if you do
Say to us
Thank You
we love
you from
Rachael Julie
and Dad

Figure 5-8 Phonetic spelling of an average second grader.

elements of the spelling process or with both. They typically show the same types of errors in their spelling as in their reading. The child with phonological-processing weaknesses has trouble analyzing the sound sequences in words. The child may be able to spell irregular words that have familiar derivations or whose orthographic sequences have been visually recalled, yet be unable to spell easier phonetically regular words. This child cannot spell words that he or she is unfamiliar with. In contrast, the child with visual-processing or orthographic awareness weaknesses may be able to spell phonetic words that he or she has never read, yet have trouble revisualizing the letter patterns that make up familiar words. This child is inattentive to which letter sequences are conventional in English spelling (Boder, 1973; Frith, 1983).

As in reading, the child with phonological-processing difficulties will be the more impaired in spelling. There is a limit to how many spelling words can be stored through revisualization alone; when this lexical route fails, the child will have difficulty falling back on phonetic analysis. Moreover, any linguistic deficiencies will deter the use of language cues to help figure out spellings (for example, knowing that a past tense is being used may cue the typical learner to spell *spilled* instead of *spilt*).

Because language and phonological-processing skills are so important in reading development, it makes sense that good readers who have spelling disorders tend to make far fewer phonetic spelling errors than do children with both reading and spelling difficulties (Frith, 1983). The good reader's greatest problem tends to be with the revisualization/orthographic alertness process, so that the wrong letters are substituted for similar-sounding letter combinations (*ow* for *ou*; *uf* for *ough*); the spellings are plausible, but the letter sequences are unconventional in English (Frith, 1983; Nelson & Warrington, 1976).

Finally, attention deficits also may result in poor spelling productions despite a good capacity to learn to spell. When the inattentive child is prompted to think about whether the word has been seen before, which other words sound similar, different ways in which the word might be spelled, and parts of the words that are particularly troublesome, spelling often improves (Gerber, 1984).

Figure 5–9 illustrates the spelling of ten-year-old Joe, who is trying to use orthographic and visualization strategies to recall spellings; his phonic skills are progressing, but one can still detect the underlying language and phonological difficulties in his syntactic errors and phoneme omissions and substitutions.

Mathematics

The computer revolution has helped us recognize that, just as with reading, failure in mathematics can seriously interfere with adaptive functioning. Even the supermarket checkout clerk has become an account analyst of sorts, memorizing hundreds of codes for products, calculating which coupons cannot be doubled because the sum is greater than the item's cost, estimating whether the computer's price calculation for oranges makes sense given their weight, and so forth. In other words, even lower-paying jobs are requiring a good deal more mathematical reasoning ability than in the past.

Like reading and spelling, mathematics involves the integration of important cognitive and information-processing abilities. Visual-spatial abilities, for example, enable one to imagine and rearrange objects in one's mind, thereby facilitating mental addition and subtraction. Fine-motor coordination helps a child to keep track of each object counted, to write the numerals, and to align numerals properly while calculating. Focused attention is always an important prerequisite to instruction; in word problems it helps a student spot the extraneous information to ignore and the words that cue how to go about solving the problem. Language skills also are highly related to math success because mathematics symbols are just another way of recording numerical language concepts. Word problems need to be read and understood, and mathematics reasoning depends on a good deal of language flexibility, for example, searching one's mind for a number fact while holding another fact in abeyance (as in borrowing). The greater the linguistic complexity of a

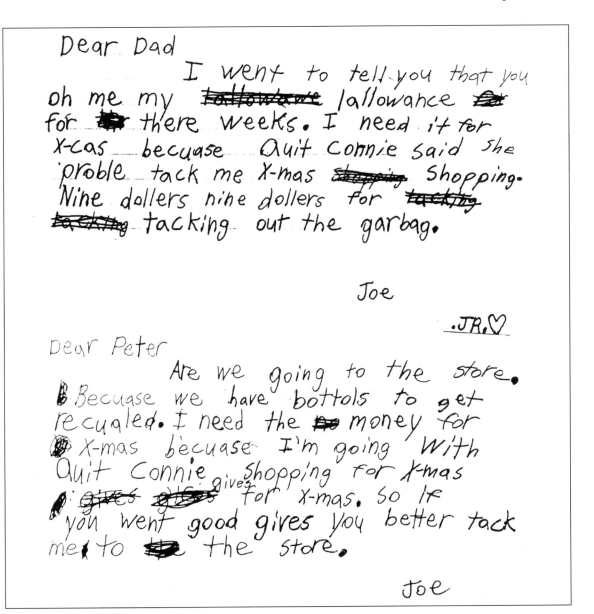

Figure 5–9 Correspondence of Joe, a ten-year-old boy with learning disabilities.

problem (vocabulary, syntax, sentence length), the more difficult mathematics solutions become for students with learning disabilities (Zentall & Ferkis, 1993).

Although the male superiority gap in math abilities is moderate and closing, girls do tend to be more proficient than boys in the computation and number-fact aspects of math; boys tend to be superior on more complex mathematics reasoning tasks, such as high school math and word problems involving multiple steps (Hedges & Nowell, 1995; Hyde, Fennema, & Lamon, 1990). Research suggests a genetic link to the pattern of male mathematical superiority (Berk, 1997), while Jacklin (1989) suggests that society's gender-stereotyping beliefs and the greater perceived value of math to boys lies behind the male–female differences. This results in lower mathematics confidence among females, higher parental and teacher expectations for males, and greater male enrollment in higher-level math courses and such math-related classes as chemistry and physics. In other words, it may be societal beliefs that discourage girls and ultimately diminish their mathematical abilities.

As with reading and spelling, children enter school with a good deal of quantitative reasoning ability. Words like *lots* and *little* are attached to quantities at young ages, and between ages two and three children begin to count with the conventional string of number words. Even before learning these number words, however, we find that two and a half year olds can do nonverbal calculations (for example, laying out two disks to match two that had been hidden from view). At this age children also begin to lay out the correct number of disks if they see one disk being added to or subtracted from one or two hidden disks. By four years old, children can do this task with sums up to four or five (Huttenlocher, Jordan, & Levine, 1994).

By age three, most children have established accurate one-to-one correspondence between objects while counting. Within the next year, the principle of cardinality, that the last number in a sequence indicates the quantity of items in the set, is grasped. At the same time, children realize that if two groups of objects match up (e.g., every plate has a cupcake), then each set must contain the same number of items (Fuson, 1988). Children's nonverbal solutions to addition and subtraction problems remain superior to their verbal number-fact knowledge or story problem solving until they are about five and a half to six and a half years old (Levine, Jordan, & Huttenlocher, 1992). Unfortunately, too rapid a transition to working with numerical symbols is believed to

suppress this nonverbal reasoning and slow or disrupt the math acquisition process (Fuscon, 1988). Let us ex-amine how mathematics abilities typically are acquired and how the patterns of students with learning disabilities differ.

Typical Mathematics Acquisition. For formal mathematics instruction to proceed smoothly, it is important for the young child to be able to do the following:

- match objects by size, shape, and color
- sort objects by size, shape, and color names
- compare sets of objects by quantity (more/most, lots/little) and size (bigger/smaller, taller/shorter)
- recognize that additional items result in more than one had before and that removing items results in less than before
- recognize that if nothing has been added or taken away, the same amount remains
- recognize that parts can come together to make a whole
- arrange a series of objects by size
- match each item of one kind with a single item of another kind (for example, one napkin per person)
- recognize the amount of "one"
- match sets of objects by amount
- model the adding or subtracting of one or two objects from a set
- match a spoken number with the correct number of objects
- recognize that the last number in a counting sequence names the quantity in the whole set
- point to the correct numeral when named
- name written numerals
- count to ten

- recall the number of objects seen by naming the number or choosing the correct number of objects

- imitate and recall the spatial arrangement of objects

- copy numerals accurately (Doyle, 1978; Resnick, 1989).

Children progress at a faster pace with mathematics calculations once this list of skills has been mastered and once their cognitive abilities have become mature enough to reason flexibly about several pieces of information at once (Arlin, 1981; Piaget, 1976; Riley, 1989). That is, the child must be able to recognize that

1. Even though things look different, they can still be the same. For example, a child should recognize that 2 + 4 is the same as 3 + 3, or when solving 42 – 18 that the value of 42 is unchanged even when 10 sticks are added to the ones pile and only 3 remain in the tens pile. A dime must be recognized as the same as 2 nickles or 10 pennies, and a half-gallon milk container must be appreciated as the same amount as a half-gallon of cider, although they look different. Or 80 floor tiles must be recognized as necessary, whether laying them in a bedroom that measures 8 × 10 or in a 5 × 16 hallway.

2. Things may look the same but still be different. For example, a 4 may represent four objects, or one quarter of the objects (as in $\frac{1}{4}$), or four 10s as in 40.

This type of reasoning is what is involved in making the transition to Piaget's *concrete operations* stage of cognitive development, which generally happens at ages six to seven. It has been found that many children with learning disabilities are two or more years delayed in making this transition, often not having transitioned even at ten to twelve years of age (Derr, 1985; Speece, McKinney, & Appelbaum, 1986). Even when the transition does occur, the learning disabled still may be

less mature in this cognitive flexibility than their nondisabled peers (Riley, 1989).

The typical pace of the mathematics curriculum, through middle school, is depicted in Figure 5–10. Addition and subtraction instruction begins by counting objects rather than numerals. Using fingers to count is natural and provides a transition between counting objects and mental arithmetic reasoning.

When adding two quantities, the child generally begins by creating and counting two separate sets of objects (or fingers). Then these sets are combined, and the newly combined set is recounted. For subtraction, children count out a starting set. Then they remove the specified number of objects and recount the remainder. Sufficient practice with counting objects eventually leads to using the count words themselves (*one, two, three,* and so on) as objects to count; in this way, mental counting becomes possible. By age six or seven, children can mentally "count on" by starting at the end of one addend and then counting on by ones enough times to add the second addend (5 + 3 = 5 . . . 6, 7, 8). By about nine years of age children can compute subtraction problems mentally by counting up from the smaller number or counting down from the larger quantity. In both mental addition and subtraction, children tend to automatically convert the problem to require fewer counts (for example, 5 + 3 rather than 3 + 5; 9 – 2 = 9 . . . 8, 7 rather than counting fingers between 2 and 9). When multiplication is called for, children generally approach it as repeated addition (5 books + 5 books + 5 books . . .) until their math facts become automatic in the intermediate grades (Resnick, 1989). Even if skilled at more efficient strategies, average achievers still will apply lower level strategies at times (Garnett, 1992).

The word problems children encounter in school rely heavily on language reasoning. Their aim is to help children learn to select relevant information and ignore the irrelevant when solving similar problems in practical situations. Students typically are able to solve word problems easily if the story describes an increase or decrease in quantity that corresponds with what the child is to do (add or subtract). It is not until eight or nine

Middle School

Masters order of operations in complex problems; multiplies/divides two fractions; adds, subtracts, multiplies divides decimals to the thousandth; understands real, rational, irrational numbers and different number bases; calculates square and cube roots; estimates percentages/proportions; calculates discount, sales tax, restaurant tip; understands markup, commission, simple interest, compound interest, percent increase/decrease; understands angles (complementary, supplementary, adjacent, straight, congruent . . .); calculates volume of a cylinder; calculates arc/circumference of circle; understands equilateral, isosceles, scalene, obtuse figures; organizes sets of data; graphs coordinates, transformations, reflections, rotations, equations with two variables; solves equations by substitution; begins to learn about conditional probability, permutations, factorial notation, relative frequency, normal curve, pythagorean theorem; deepens understanding of previously taught skills and concepts

Fifth Grade

Multiplies three digit numbers (962×334); can work harder division problems ($102 \div 32$); adds, subtracts, multiplies mixed numbers; divides a whole number by a fraction; represents fractions as decimals, ratios, percents; adds, subtracts, multiplies, with decimals; understands use of equations, formulas, "working backward"; estimates products/quotients; begins to learn about exponents, greatest common factor, bases, prime factors, composite numbers, integers; understands percent, ratios; understands mean, median, mode; measures area/circumference of a circle, perimeter/areas of triangles and parallelograms, volume of cube; performs metric conversions; uses compass, protractor; reads scale drawings

Fourth Grade

Adds columns of 3 or more numbers; multiplies three digit by two digit numbers (348×34); performs simple division ($44/22$); reduces fractions to lowest terms; adds/subtracts fractions with different denominators ($3/4 + 2/3$); adds/subtracts decimals; converts decimals to percents; counts/makes change for up to $20.00; estimates time; can measure time in hours, minutes, seconds; understands acute, obtuse, right angles; computes area of rectangles; identifies parallel, perpendicular, intersecting lines; calculates weight in tons, length in meters, volume in cubic centimeters

Third Grade

Understands place value to thousands; adds and subtracts four digit numbers (e.g., $1,017 - 978$); learns multiplication facts to 9×9; solves simple multiplication and division problems ($642 \times$ or $\div$ 2); relates division to repeated subtractions; counts by 4s, 1000s; learns harder Roman numerals; introduction to fractions (adds/estimates/orders simple fractions; understands mixed numbers; reads fractions of an inch) and geometry (identifies hexagon, pentagon); understands diameter, radius, volume, area; understands decimals; begins to learn about negative numbers, probability, percentage, ratio; solves harder number story problems

Second Grade

Identifies/writes numbers to 999; Adds/subtracts two and three digit numbers with and without regrouping (e.g., $223 + 88$, $124 - 16$); multiplies by 2, 3, 4, 5; counts by 3s, 100s; reads/writes Roman numerals to XII; counts money and makes change up to $10.00; recognizes days of the week, months, and seasons of the year on a calendar; tells time to five minutes on a clock with hands; learns basic measurements (inch, foot, pint, pound); recognizes equivalents (e.g., two quarters = one half; four quarts = one gallon); divides area into 2/3, 3/4, 10ths; graphs simple data

First Grade

Counts/reads/writes/orders numbers to 99; begins learning addition and subtraction facts to 20; performs simple addition/subtraction problems (e.g., $23 + 11$); understands multiplication as repeated addition; counts by 2s, 5s and 10s; identifies odd/even numbers; estimates answers; understands 1/2, 1/3, 1/4; gains elementary knowledge of calendar (e.g., counts how many days to birthday), time (tells time to half hour; understands schedules; reads digital clock), measurement (cup, pint, quart, liter, inch, cm, kg, lb), and money (knows value of quarter; compares prices); solves simple number story problems; reads bar graphs and charts.

Kindergarten

Matches/sorts/names objects by size, color and shape; recites and recognizes numbers 1–20; one-to-one correspondence; counts/adds up to nine objects; knows addition/subtraction facts to six; evaluates objects by quantity, dimensions, size (e.g., more/less, longer/shorter, tall/tallest, bigger/same); writes numbers 1–10; understands concepts of addition and subtraction; knows symbols +, −, =; recognizes whole vs. half; understands ordinals (first, 5th); learns beginning concepts of weight, time (e.g., before/after; understands lunch is at 12:00; tells time to the hour), money (knows value of pennies, nickels, dimes), and temperature (hotter/colder); aware of locations (e.g., above/below, left/right, nearest/farthest); interprets simple maps, graphs and tallies.

Figure 5–10   Sequence of mathematics development.

years of age, however, that children learn to interpret problems where the language may indicate a decrease, yet the correct operation is the opposite, addition (Resnick, 1989):

Ana went shopping. She spent $3.50 and then counted her money when she got home. She had $2.35 left. How much did Ana have when she started out? (p. 165)

"Combine" situations, where two items (apples and oranges) get renamed into a new category (how much "fruit" is there altogether?) also are difficult for the young elementary school student. Good math students are aided in solving word problems by paraphrasing them in their own words, visualizing the problems using illustrations or mental imaging, setting a problem-solving plan, estimating the answers, and evaluating their answers (Montague, 1992).

Resnick (1989) suggests that school drills and exercises exacerbate math disabilities by forcing children to memorize numerals and calculate with them before their intuitive sense of quantities is firmly established. Children's informal counting methods often are suppressed ("stop counting on your fingers"), and too little oral discussion or demonstration ensues regarding the quantitative reasoning behind the operations. Resnick comments that encouragement of counting up or down actually can speed up the memorization of a number fact because the child generates and practices the correct answer so often, while fully comprehending the logic behind it.

Mathematics Patterns of Students with Learning Disabilities. Rourke (1993) identifies characteristic arithmetic disabilities that relate to a variety of information-processing weaknesses:

1. *Spatial organization:* misaligning numbers in columns; confusing directionality, as in wondering which way a 6 faces, misreading numbers (71 for 17), or subtracting the minuend from the subtrahend:

$$\begin{array}{r} 36 \\ -18 \\ \hline 22 \end{array}$$

2. *Alertness to visual detail:* misreading mathematical signs, omitting a necessary detail (dollar sign, decimal)

3. *Procedural errors:* missing or adding a step; misapplication of a rule that applies to another operation, as in adding the carried number in two-column addition before multiplying:

$$18 \times 8 = \begin{array}{c} 6 \\ 18 \\ \times\ 8 \\ \hline 4 \end{array} = \begin{array}{c} 78 \\ \times\ 8 \\ \hline 564 \end{array}$$

4. *Failure to shift psychological set:* continuing to apply a previous procedure (for example, addition) when one should shift to another procedure (for example, subtraction)

5. *Graphomotor:* printing large, crowded, poorly formed numbers so that the child can't read his or her own writing while calculating; at an earlier age this might manifest itself as disorganized one-to-one correspondence when counting objects (Košč, 1981)

6. *Memory:* displaying poor recall of number facts

7. *Mathematical judgment and reasoning:* giving unreasonable answers and being unaware of the incongruity (10 + 9 = 109); not generalizing a known skill to a new, slightly different problem

Language weaknesses present additional deterrents to mathematics achievement (Badian, 1983; Košč, 1981):

- poor ability to verbally express and reason about mathematical terms and relationships (numerals, operational symbols, operations)

- poor ability to read mathematical symbols

We often don't recognize how essential language is to mathematics operations. Even seemingly simple calculations involve using language to systematize the recall and application of large numbers of steps, rules, and math facts. For example, as many as thirty-three steps are involved in simply solving $62 \times 96 =$ (Strang & Rourke, 1985a). The first step involves interpreting the sign, the second step is remembering to start at the right side of the problem, and so forth.

Figure 5–11 illustrates the mathematical calculations of nine-year-old Gregg; he is so confused by numerical operations that he inappropriately applies strategies from one type of solution to another. Occasionally he adds correctly. At other times he arrives at the right answer but for the wrong reason. For example, in problem 5, Gregg borrows 10 from the 3 in the tens column, adds it to the 2 in the ones column, and then carries the 1 once he adds 12 + 7. The answer is correct, but Gregg set up the problem as though it were subtraction. In problem 9, Gregg began adding with the left column, recording the 2 for 12 (8 + 4), and carrying the 1. In problem 11 he forgets to carry the 1 and demonstrates his confusion about how 3s and 5s are formed. The same thing recurs in problem 14, but this time he carries. Gregg's poor comprehension of numerical concepts is illustrated in how he recorded dictated numbers (problems 3a, 5a, 6a): "one hundred and fifty six plus twenty three," "three thousand, two hundred and thirty-four," and "four thousand one hundred."

The judgments involved in word problems prove particularly troublesome to youngsters with learning disabilities. The greater the reading demands in word problems, the less likely that students will reason appropriately, make use of relevant information, and ignore what is extraneous (Lee & Hudson, 1981, in Stone & Michals, 1986). Irrelevant numerical information in these problems appears to cause even more confusion for students than does irrelevant linguistic information (Englert, Culatta, & Horn, 1987).

In one-third to one-half or more of children with learning disabilities, math and reading disabilities go hand in hand, although their severity levels may differ (Ackerman & Dykman, 1995; Badian, 1983). This coexistence occurs because the child's information-processing weaknesses carry through all academic subjects and, especially at higher levels, both reading comprehension and math share much in common with respect to necessary language, attention, and reasoning skills (Johnson & Myklebust, 1967; Speece, McKinney, & Appelbaum, 1986).

The Intermediate Grades

A dramatic shift in school expectations begins when a child enters the intermediate grades (grades 3, 4, 5). By fourth grade it is expected that students have become more independent in their studies, an expectation that increases with each year of school. These students' reading, comprehension, and learning strategies typically are mature enough to handle learning through independent reading and research. Their handwriting, spelling, and written expression are sophisticated enough so that written tests and short essays can be used to assess knowledge. Learning has become more self-directed, and assignments require long-term planning and organization. The basic skills developed in the primary grades form the foundation on which much more complex comprehension and written expression skills are now built. These skills, in turn, are used to tackle content area subjects, such as social studies and science.

The student with learning disabilities who cannot read or comprehend well, spell, or put thoughts into writing is at a terrible disadvantage. This child does not have the basic skills with which to learn new content or express what is known. It is not uncommon for intellectual potential to begin to decline, due to diminishing motivation and cumulative underexposure to reading content, vocabulary, and concepts essential for new learning (Stanovich, 1986).

Some children do manage to get by in the primary grades but then develop large gaps in the intermediate grades when faced with more complex comprehension, written expression, and math requirements. By this time also, the student's weaknesses and failure experiences frequently result in lowered self-confidence, zeal to achieve, and know-how in getting along with others. The agony of these poor self-perceptions and ineffec-

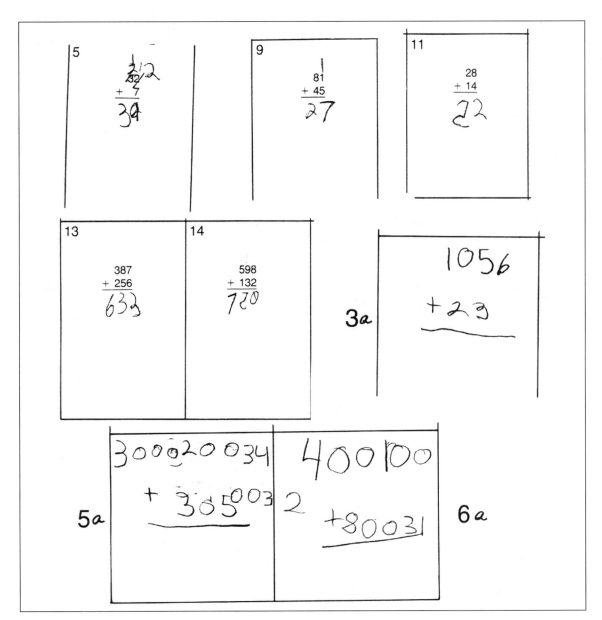

Figure 5–11 Mathematical calculations of a nine-year-old student with learning disabilities.

tual interpersonal relationships may prove to be even more devastating to future adjustment than the academic weaknesses themselves. We will examine the difficulties children with learning dis-

abilities in the intermediate grades face with reading comprehension, content area learning, written language, and mathematics relative to their normally achieving peers.

Reading Comprehension

The ultimate goal of reading is to gain meaning. Without decoding skills there can be no reading comprehension, but without comprehension skills even good decoding ability is useless. Once children become competent decoders, reading can become a tool for learning.

By age six to seven children generally have become sensitive to such characteristics of stories as the main character, sequence of events, inferences, the motives and feelings of characters, and sentence order (Brown, Armbruster, & Baker, 1986; Mandler & Johnson, 1977; Paris & Lindauer, 1976). As they get older, children become more efficient at recognizing and recalling facts, recognizing and inferring main themes and relationships, drawing conclusions, making judgments and generalizations, predicting outcomes, applying what has been learned, and following directions. Because most students by the intermediate grades are good decoders, the instructional focus shifts to helping children develop strategies for detecting meaning from prose as well as strategies for independent study: skimming, using reference materials, outlining, summarizing, altering reading rate and focus as the purpose of reading changes, use of headings, note taking, and so on.

The reading comprehension of some students with learning disabilities is hampered by weak decoding skills. They expend so much time and energy struggling over decoding words that they cannot simultaneously attend to or remember the passage's message. Spear and Sternberg (1987) explain that because these students' decoding requires such conscious effort, they use up the residual capacity that the normal reader has available to allocate to higher-level comprehension. Although the poor reader does use context in a compensatory fashion to speed word recognition, this too depletes cognitive resources that could have been used to organize the information for recall. Moreover, because of their early reading failures, children with learning disabilities have been deprived of the opportunity to learn comprehension and memory strategies that typical learners deduce as they gain skill in reading.

When reading as the tool for gaining meaning is eliminated (for example, via lectures or tapes), students who decode poorly often can comprehend well and no longer miss out on learning opportunities. Nevertheless, listening is not the same as learning through reading. Because the speaking vocabulary used in lectures seldom is as complex as the reading vocabulary, students miss out on vocabulary expansion. In addition, detailed information is harder to recall by listening than by reading, unless a tape is replayed several times; unfortunately, unlike the automatic rereading when something has made no sense, students tend not to take the time to replay parts of tapes. Consequently, over time, these students may not develop a rich enough knowledge base to support comprehension and recall of the increasingly complex content in the upper grades (Snider & Tarver, 1987).

For other students with learning disabilities the comprehension problem goes far beyond decoding. These students have difficulty with comprehension because they don't understand the language of instruction or they apply inefficient learner strategies. These factors deter learning the content in most subject areas, whether by reading or by listening.

Linguistic Deficits. Language weaknesses very often persist well beyond the primary grades. These children may not understand the vocabulary and grammar they are reading. They also may have difficulty comprehending the order of words in sentences and be overloaded by the sheer number of words in sentences. These difficulties create problems because the curriculum expects students to deal with lengthy pieces replete with high-level vocabulary, antonyms, synonyms, homonyms, idioms, metaphors, morals, proverbs, and poetry.

The linguistic difficulties of students with learning disabilities make it difficult for them to automatically gain meaning from what they read. Such language expression weaknesses as poor grammar, word usage, articulation, or word finding also make it hard for these children to communicate what has been comprehended. All these language weaknesses require extensive intervention by both the speech-language pathologist and the teacher.

Inefficient Learner Strategies. Some students with learning disabilities approach learning tasks inefficiently but otherwise have good learning abilities. Other students' inefficient strategies are caused by information-processing weaknesses such as inadequate selective attention, weak visual and holistic processing strategies, or weak language-processing and analytic/sequential strategies. Yet other students apply inefficient strategies because their cognitive styles (for example, preference for dealing with concepts versus details) are mismatched with curricular expectations. Inefficient learner strategies interfere with all aspects of attending to, comprehending, remembering, and communicating knowledge. Therefore, high priority must be placed on matching school tasks to students' preferred learning strategies and on directly teaching students how to attend, think, commit to memory, and retrieve information more effectively. For example, Johnson, Graham, and Harris (1997) found that the comprehension of students with learning disabilities could equal that of typical learners when the LD students were taught how to recognize the structural elements of stories (e.g., time, place, problem, ending). The typical evolution of "knowing how to know" as well as the metacognitive training that helps students become more aware of what they need to do to learn more effectively are explored in Chapter 6.

Content Area Learning

Comprehension, whether through reading or hearing, depends on how well children attend to, conceptualize, organize, store, and retrieve information. When linguistic skills and learner strategies are inefficient, both reading and listening comprehension are likely to be problematic. These comprehension difficulties interfere with achievement in all classes, including learning of content in science and social studies.

A youngster's ability to understand and remember, whether through reading or through listening, also is dependent on the expectations, cultural background, vocabulary, and prior knowledge that he or she brings to the reading or listening task. We often refer to this knowledge as the child's *schema*. The richer the student's background schema, the more readily new information will be linked with the existing knowledge and comprehended; this comprehension, in turn, further enriches and expands the child's schema. Snider and Tarver (1987) explain that we come to understand novel information by reasoning by analogy. We connect the new to the old by comparing the two sets of information: if the two appear linked, the new information is incorporated into the existing schema; if there is no connection, then a new schema is created.

It makes sense that the more vocabulary and background knowledge one knows, the better reading and listening comprehension will be. Knowledge does beget knowledge. "Readers need to bring knowledge and experience to their reading if they are to learn from it" (Chall, 1983a, p. 21). Unfortunately, many students with learning disabilities have deficient vocabulary and knowledge bases, which in turn limit how much sense they can make of new information. This insufficient base limits how memorable new information will be because there is less of a schema to which new information can be linked. Even if a schema does exist, it seems that, instead of letting the new information modify the old, students with learning disabilities may tend to use the old information to distort the new (Weisberg, 1988). This further deters and confuses their learning.

Modifying the language of instruction, encouraging more appropriate learning strategies in content area instruction, and offering prior familiarization with essential vocabulary and background knowledge are important if the student with learning disabilities is to make progress. When this is not done, students who are learning disabled are likely to become less knowledgeable with time in relation to their peers. This in turn makes them less interesting people and less apt to strike a social chord with others.

Written Language

Written language is the highest level of language accomplishment (Johnson & Myklebust, 1967).

It requires that a child translate his or her language comprehension, reasoning, and expression skills into the symbol system we use for reading. People with learning disabilities continue to experience lifelong difficulties in this skill area. We will explore how written expression skills typically are acquired and the ways in which the development of students with learning disabilities can differ.

Typical Written Language Acquisition. Figure 5–12 depicts the typical curriculum's sequence for developing written expression skills. For most children composing begins by using invented spellings even before they enter school. In the intermediate grades, students continue to sharpen their spelling and handwriting skills while developing a greater understanding of the ideational aspects of written expression and its mechanical rules. Spelling instruction is combined with vocabulary study, with a special emphasis on word derivatives, prefixes, suffixes, and roots (Henderson & Beers, 1980). The mechanical rules of writing that receive attention include capitalization, punctuation, and grammar. The ideational aspect of written language can be divided into five categories (MacArthur & Graham, 1987; Poteet, 1980):

1. *Story:* how well the child names and describes the objects, characters, time and setting; presents a plot, action, and ending; and addresses more abstract issues such as theme, morality, precursor events, goals for different characters, and personal reactions of characters.

2. *Fluency:* the number of words that are written. These generally increase with age, as do the number of words per sentence. Hermreck (1979) reports that the average number of words written about a picture increases from 83 words in third grade to 94 words in fourth grade, 141 words in fifth grade, and 200 words in sixth grade (in Poteet, 1980).

3. *Cohesion:* the ease with which the reader can understand what the student has written because there is a logical transition of sentences, ideas, and events throughout the story.

4. *Reality:* how realistic the author's perceptions are.

5. *Style:* the student's unique ways of writing. Style includes the appropriate use of different sentence forms, the tone conveyed, and the vocabulary chosen to express thoughts.

Most students have well-developed story schema by school entry, and by the end of their primary years they are able to produce well-formed narrative compositions. As students mature they increase in ability to include in their writing inferential thinking, critical evaluation, and abstract issues and language (for example, metaphors; plays on words). Students also become able to proofread their work more critically and to make modifications where appropriate. The ability to plan and revise one's writing using notes generally is established by the time one enters middle school. Prior to age ten, however, children generally equate planning with production and therefore use their planning time to generate first drafts (Montague, Graves, & Leavell, 1991).

Written Language Patterns of Students with Learning Disabilities. Students with reading and spelling difficulties have a hard time with written expression. Their level of achievement in written assignments is significantly poorer than their peers in a number of ways: the vocabulary they use, idea generation, the maturity of themes (they use descriptions of objects, characters, or settings and free associations instead of action sequences; stories may not contain a beginning, middle, and end and a conflict or problem to resolve; characters' motives, thoughts, feelings, and relationships are neglected; the location and time of the scene may not be set; causal and temporal relationships may not be described). In addition, they have difficulty with spelling, grammar, organization, cohesion, and the use of description and comparison/contrast. Fewer words, number

Middle School
Develops increasing sophistication in ideas and expression; accurate/effective/appropriate choice of words and phrases; edits to improve style and effect; avoids wordiness and unnecessary repetition; uses complex sentences; avoids vagueness and omissions; develops paragraphs with details/reasons/examples/comparisons; checks for accuracy of statements; connects ideas with transition words; develops paragraphs with topic sentences; adds introduction and conclusion; checks reasoning; uses several sources to prepare a report; makes a bibliography; capitalizes first word of a quote/adjectives of race and nationality; punctuates appropriately; learns to use footnotes; learns notetaking skills

Fifth Grade
Varies type of sentences, including imperative; subjects and verbs agree; uses compound subjects and predicates; ideas are clearly stated in more than one paragraph; keeps to the topic; uses antonyms/prefixes/suffixes/contractions/compound words/ words with sensory images/rhyme and rhythm; greater precision in choice of words; uses dictionary for definitions/syllables/pronunciation; capitalizes names of streets/places/persons/countries/ oceans/trade names/beginning items in outlines/titles with a name (e.g., President Roosevelt); uses quotation marks or underlining for titles; classifies words by parts of speech; uses subheads in outlines; writes from outline; writes dialogue; recognizes topic sentences; enjoys writing/receiving letters; keeps a diary

Fourth Grade
Writes in cursive; develops interesting paragraphs and a sense of the writing process (outline first, write, revise); chooses words that appeal to the senses or that precisely explain a point; capitalizes names of cities/states/organizations; uses apostrophe to show possession, hyphen to divide word at end of line, exclamation point, colon after salutation, quotation marks, comma before quotation in a sentence, period after outline items or Roman numerals; uses command sentences; avoids sentence fragments; selects appropriate title; makes simple outline; writes/tells stories that have character and plot

Third Grade
Writes with both printing and cursive; writes short passages expressing a central idea; sequences ideas well and uses expanded vocabulary; identifies/uses various sentence forms (e.g., declarative, interrogative/exclamatory); combines short, choppy sentences into longer ones; uses interesting beginning and ending sentences; avoids run-on sentences; uses synonyms; distinguishes meaning and spelling of homonyms; uses the prefix "un" and the suffix "less"; capitalizes month/day/common holidays/first word in a line of verse/"Dear"/ "Sincerely;" adds period after abbreviations/initials; uses apostrophe in common contractions (e.g., isn't); adds commas in a list; indents; spells many words in sight vocabulary (including irregular words such as "eight"); proofreads own and others' work

Second Grade
Writes letters legibly and uses appropriate size; understands how writing should be laid out (e.g., margins); combines short sentences into paragraphs; spelling and grammatical expression continue to improve; uses words with similar and opposite meanings in writing; alphabetizes; capitalizes important words in book titles, proper names, Mr./Mrs./Miss/Ms.; adds question mark at the end of a question; adds comma after salutation and closing of a letter; adds comma between the month/year and city/state; avoids running sentences together with "and"; begins to use cursive; begins to develop proofreading skills

First Grade
Uses traditional as well as invented spellings; works on copying letters and words; writes simple sentences; begins to write short poems, invitations, compositions; tries to use words that describe what the child sees, hears, feels as well as how things look, act, feel; capitalizes the first word of a sentence, first and last names, names of streets/towns/the school, and I; adds a period at the end of sentences and after numbers in a list; prints on the line

K
Develops ability to hold and use pencils; traces/copies/writes letters, name, and simple sight words; writes short "stories" using dashes for words or invented spellings

Figure 5–12 Sequence of written expression development.

of ideas, and pertinent details are expressed. Capitalization, punctuation, revising, irrelevancies, and redundancies are typical problems. These students tend to use a "knowledge-telling" strategy rather than theme development, they do not distinguish in importance among major and minor ideas, and they tend to be most concerned with what to say next rather than with how their ideas relate to a major premise. They most often appropriate virtually no time for planning in advance of writing and, when they sit down to write, simply write whatever comes to mind. Interferences from the mechanical aspects of writing (handwriting, spelling, capitalization, punctuation) reduce the length and quality of the finished product (Englert & Thomas, 1987; Graham, 1990; Laughton & Morris, 1989; Montague, Maddux, & Dereshiwsky, 1990; Montague, et al., 1991; Nodine, Barenbaum, & Newcomer, 1985; Poplin et al., 1980; Thomas, Englert, & Gregg, 1987).

Students with visual-processing difficulties but good language abilities may express themselves well in writing, although spelling may be poor. The child with motor-production difficulties also may compose well if only he or she would persist with the arduous writing task, or use a tape recorder. Hermreck (1979) found that students with poor handwriting produced only about half the number of words written by their peers, although productivity did rise some by sixth grade (in Poteet, 1980).

The student with language disturbances is the most severely disabled in written expression because the ideational aspect of writing is impaired. This child may not be able to elaborate ideas orally in a fluent, flexible, and creative way, let alone translate them into writing. When a twelve year old's comprehension of grammatically ambiguous statements is equivalent to that of typical five- to six-year-old children, or the child's comprehension of multiple meanings of words equals that of the seven- to eight-year-old child (Wiig, Semel, & Abele, 1981), this youngster will have only a slim chance of mastering high-level written expression skills unless the child's underlying language disabilities are remediated.

Children whose written expression difficulties are related to attention problems or to unique cognitive styles may succeed when taught systematic methods for writing, beginning with brainstorming and ending with editing. If these students are impulsive, they tend to cover a complex topic in several short paragraphs, dealing only with the major issues and overlooking relevant details. The overly reflective student, on the other hand, may dwell so much on details that the same topic takes pages to cover, and the main issues never become clear. These students need to be made aware of their cognitive styles and taught how to incorporate more appropriate styles into their thinking and writing.

In remediating written language difficulties, teachers have been encouraged to concentrate initially on the ideational aspects rather than on the spelling, handwriting, or mechanical rules (Englert et al., 1988; Graves, 1983). Without appropriate ideas to express, the latter skills are useless. Besides the joy of composing and the opportunity writing provides to systematically develop one's thinking, improving written expression is particularly important in the intermediate grades because this is the major means by which students tend to be evaluated.

Mathematics

Third grade appears to be a period in which children make the transition from "counting up" math facts to recalling number facts automatically. Roughly half of third graders count, and half retrieve facts from memory. By fourth to sixth grades, the automaticity of children's math fact retrieval closely resembles that of adults (Ashcraft & Fierman, 1982; Resnick, 1989). Unfortunately, this automaticity is not achieved by many students with learning disabilities.

The math curriculum in the intermediate grades becomes more difficult conceptually. It relies more on reading of word problems and instructions, which in itself may be difficult for the student with learning disabilities. In addition, mathematics concepts become integrated to a far greater extent into the social studies and science curricula, thereby creating further problems.

Whereas many youngsters discover some aspects of how to read for themselves, discovery is harder when it comes to math calculations. Students must be systematically taught how and why they calculate as they do. The learning of number facts needs to be committed consciously to memory and drilled. There is much debate about whether we should stress number sense or number facts first, since automaticity in either one will enhance the other (Resnick, 1989).

Certainly, the more automatic a child's number facts, the more energy a child can devote to mathematical reasoning when solving problems (Zentall & Ferkis, 1993). Nevertheless, many children have such difficulty learning math facts that experts have advised us to concentrate on helping children understand basic mathematical relationships and problem-solving processes, and leave the computing to portable charts or calculators (Capps & Hatfield, 1977; Gawronski & Coblentz, 1976; Teitelbaum, 1978). Some suggest that charts and calculators may in fact help children improve their knowledge of math facts because the correct fact is given to the student and mislearning from faulty calculations is avoided (Beardslee, 1978; Creswell & Vaughn, 1979; Garnett, 1989). Math educators point out that computers are making it increasingly important for students to first and foremost comprehend mathematical relationships so that they can better judge the accuracy of their computer calculations, whether as a telemarketer, supermarket checkout person, or home cable TV shopper.

The student who cannot understand basic math relationships also often finds it particularly difficult to judge spatial directions and time. This child has trouble finding his or her way around a city, getting to class on time, judging when to go home for dinner, and knowing how much longer before his or her birthday. This youngster also may have a hard time imitating rhythms in music class and on the dance floor (Wolf, 1967). Social difficulties are common because of associated difficulties in interpreting the moods, feelings, and nonverbal cues of others, communicating feelings with appropriate affect, and timing the give and take in social interactions (Ozols & Rourke, 1985; Rourke, 1987, 1993; Strang & Rourke, 1985b). These *nonverbal learning disabilities* are common among students with mathematical reasoning deficits. Their poor social perception and judgment often are accompanied by motor incoordination, poor handwriting, marked slowness of performance, attention difficulties, visual-spatial-organizational deficits, motor and tactile perception problems, poor categorization and nonverbal reasoning, and increasing difficulty as tasks become more novel and complex (Denckla, 1991; Gross-Tsur et al., 1995; Harnadek & Rourke, 1994; Rourke & Conway, 1997).

The Middle and High School Years

Despite years of intensive individualized instruction, many adolescents with learning disabilities still lag behind their peers in reading and written expression. Delays of up to four years on standardized achievement tests are not unusual (Forell & Hood, 1985; Shepard & Smith, 1983). This makes it particularly difficult to access the curriculum, since reading and writing are the expected ways to do so. It is no wonder that failure or below-average performance is common in content area classes (Donahoe & Zigmond, 1990).

Like reading and writing, math skills too remain a focus of remediation. Basic skill instruction is particularly relevant for individuals who have only recently been identified as LD or for whom the quantity or quality of previous remedial effort has been insufficient. Such instruction takes advantage of the sudden and dramatic acceleration in learning that some students experience during adolescence (Epstein, 1980; Stanford Research Institute Report, 1974, in Deshler, 1978). On the other hand, when teenagers continue to be plagued by severe learning problems, a one-sided emphasis on basic skill attainment may deprive them of opportunities to acquire important knowledge in content areas and to prepare sufficiently for the vocational, independent living, social, and leisure time activities of adulthood (Edgar, 1987). A basic skill emphasis may prove more frustrating and less rewarding than programming that provides for tutoring in content area subject matter, learning strategy instruction, and building of compensatory skills that help students learn to work around their weaknesses.

Lieberman (1981) asserts that by ages fourteen to sixteen emphasis should be placed on teaching students how to live with their disabilities instead of focusing solely on remediation of the disabilities. Because disabilities often persist into adulthood, students must use their secondary school years to develop ways of compensating for their weaknesses, building learning strategies, enhancing their strengths, and selecting realistic educational and vocational goals that capitalize on their areas of competence and reduce the impact of their learning disability on future adjustment. These students will need direct tutorial and learning strategy assistance to master and generalize difficult course content. They need instructors to teach more mature social behaviors and to promote students' talents. They also need help learning how to get organized, work independently, plan ahead, adhere to time lines, and use their time wisely. To accomplish all this, basic competencies in reading, writing, and math must be built within a context that emphasizes transition planning.

Academic Competency

In the secondary school years, it is important to plan for the time that remains until students leave school by considering the various school programming options. Involving the adolescent in the actual planning, monitoring, and evaluation process is critical. Most teenagers intensely dislike being different or conspicuous in any way. Asking them to do anything out of the ordinary (such as meeting with the special education teacher, dictating exams, or getting time extensions on tests) can easily be viewed as threatening (Reetz & Hoover, 1992). A radical departure in programming from that of one's peers (such as job apprenticeships) may be unthinkable. By working as a team with students, the school staff can establish rapport, engage cooperation, build personal responsibility and independence, and convey confidence in students' opinions and in their ability to exercise some control over their lives.

Unfortunately, very often the student with learning disabilities is not included in his or her educational or transition planning (Grigal et al., 1997; Houck, Geller, & Engelhard, 1988). Involvement of youth in making decisions about their programs is especially critical given statistics that the average national dropout rate for students with learning disabilities is 39 percent compared to an overall dropout rate of 11 percent (*Condition of Education*, 1994; *Digest of Educational Statistics*, 1996). It appears that the continued academic frustration faced by students with learning disabilities in high school, inappropriate courses, insufficient remedial and counseling services, and their older age (due to retentions), contribute to this dropout rate. Zigmond and Thornton (1985) found that 90 percent of their students with learning disabilities who had repeated a grade left school before graduation; the national dropout rate for students with learning disabilities who have been retained is about 44 percent (*Condition of Education*, 1994). Unfortunately, dropping out of high school does not bode well for these individuals' future vocational success. In the general population, the unemployment rate of people who drop out of high school is one and one-half times that of a high school graduate; dropouts earn 67 percent of the salary of high school graduates (*Condition of Education*, 1996, 1997). Therefore, persisting through high school is important. In Levin and colleagues' study (1985), the higher the reading and math achievement at the end of ninth grade, the more likely the student was to continue in high school.

Most teenagers with learning disabilities attend general education classes and receive support services from special education teachers and consultants to the classroom teacher. Unfortunately, these students' general education class teachers often feel ill-prepared to modify the content area instruction, to supplement the student's basic skill instruction, or to decide on reasonable testing and grading options. It also is difficult for them to find the time to do this planning, as many already teach up to 120 pupils per day. The LD consultant's ability to aid the regular classroom teacher is similarly hampered by the large numbers of students to be served and unfamiliarity with the regular class content.

When LD teachers provide direct services to students with learning disabilities, they generally report doing more basic skill instruction than tutoring or learning strategy work (Houck et al., 1988; Sands, Adams, & Stout, 1995). They often attempt to cover all grounds, and to increase chances that the student will apply the new skills, by using the course material for instruction. Nevertheless, with the pressure to help students pass their courses and state competency tests, LD teachers often are forced to devote more time than they would wish to content area tutoring (Schumaker et al., 1983). Unfortunately, in doing so they forgo important basic skill and strategy instruction on "how to learn," which might have helped these students to become more independent in their learning.

Because of growing national concern over the poor basic skill competencies of high school graduates in general, many states have instituted more rigorous coursework requirements in English, math, social studies, the sciences, and foreign language for high school graduation. Some also are dropping basic courses, because they feel students with disabilities can be accommodated and supported within the higher-level courses (CEC Today, 1996). In addition, minimum competency testing (MCT) programs have been established in most states. In order to ensure accountability for students with special needs the 1997 reauthorization of the Individuals with Disabilities Education Act (IDEA) mandates that by 1998 children with disabilities be included in state- and districtwide assessment programs. Educators applaud including students with disabilities in statewide assessment programs because teachers and schools must be held accountable for solid teaching, and funding sources can't be allowed to forget about the progress of students with disabilities (Ysseldyke, Thurlow, & Silverstein, 1994). Nevertheless, there is serious concern that instituting higher standards and requiring students to pass competency tests as a condition for graduation will increase the number of students with learning disabilities who face retention, tenuous chances for graduation, and the probability of dropping out

(McLeskey & Grizzle, 1992). For example, in a study of over 1,000 Florida tenth graders with disabilities, Algozzine and colleagues (1988) found that 51 percent would not earn a high school diploma because of failure on the MCTs. In contrast, 91 percent of students without disabilities would graduate after taking MCTs.

MCT programs were stimulated by the reports of a number of commissions that faulted our educational system for the United States's declining economic and political status in the world. The view that our nation could prosper and be secure only if business, university faculties, and the military had an expanded supply of well-educated young people was best articulated in *A Nation at Risk* (1983), a report of the National Commission on Excellence in Education:

Our Nation is at risk. Our once unchallenged preeminence in commerce, industry, science, and technological innovation is being overtaken by competitors throughout the world. This report is concerned with only one of the many causes and dimensions of the problem, but it is the one that undergirds American prosperity, security, and civility. We report to the American People that while we can take justifiable pride in what our schools and colleges have historically accomplished and contributed to the United States and the well-being of its people, the educational foundations of our society are presently being eroded by a rising tide of mediocrity that threatens our very future as a Nation and a people. What was unimaginable a generation ago has begun to occur—others are matching and surpassing our educational attainments. (p. 5)

There was no paucity of data to support this alarm. National testing in the 1980s indicated that the average seventeen year old could not understand moderately complicated reading information or math beyond reading simple graphs and solving basic algebraic equations (Dossey et al., 1988; National Assessment of Educational Progress, 1985). Only 65 percent of seventeen-year-old students could write a clear paragraph for a job application, and well-reasoned compositions were beyond the means of most (Applebee, Langer, & Mullis, 1986). The National Assessment of Educational Progress of American history found that the average seventeen-year-old student could answer only about half of the basic items regarding United States democratic principles and history; 40 percent of these students, for example, did not understand the system of checks and balances among the branches of the federal government (Ravitch & Finn, 1987). The 1990 NAEP math reports indicated that fewer than half of high school seniors had a thorough grasp of decimals, percents, and fractions; only 5 percent showed an understanding of geometry and algebra.

The public's outrage over declining SAT scores, and the poor showing of African Americans and Hispanics on these tests, only added fuel to the fire (Hodgkinson, 1986). The laxity in our high schools was further reflected in a homework survey of seniors in over 1,000 high schools (Keith & Page, 1985). These students reported doing less than three hours of homework a week, yet their average grade was close to a B. Only about 20 percent of seniors reported having a C or lower average. Even low-ability seniors who reported doing no homework at all received better than a C average.

It is not surprising that many worried that between the years 2011 and 2030, the nearly 70 million Americans who would retire would depend on a shrinking number of young Americans to support their retirement, and many of that group would be educationally at risk (Hodgkinson, 1986). In response to these concerns, in 1994 Congress allocated major funding to the Goals 2000 program, which encouraged states to adopt educational content and performance standards. Among the eight objectives of Goals 2000 are that all children will start school ready to learn; that students will demonstrate competence over challenging subject matter in grades four, eight, and twelve; and that a 90 percent high school graduation rate would be met by the year 2000. The National Assessment of Educational Progress (1994) indicates that we have a long way to go before we meet these goals; for example, 93 percent of seventeen year olds cannot solve multistep problems or use beginning algebra, and 59 percent cannot understand and summarize complex reading information.

In states that have instituted MCTs, these tests have been used to identify students in need

of remedial instruction, to provide an early warning of problems, and to gauge school performance. In twenty states, MCTs also represent the criteria for awarding high school diplomas (*CEC Today*, 1996). These exit standards tend to be geared toward seventh-to-ninth-grade knowledge and skills.

With growing reliance on passing MCTs for graduation, it has been suggested that schools will need to develop more comprehensive curricula, including alternative paths to a diploma, if the eligibility of students with learning disabilities for postschool employment and educational opportunities is not to be endangered (Bassett & Smith, 1996). The Council for Exceptional Children (CEC) has taken issue with establishing common standards for every student:

> . . . we strongly oppose singular standards to measure achievement. The abilities of our students vary greatly, and curricula and assessment must relate to such variability. . . . Singular criteria for curricula and assessment to determine competence, graduation, or program evaluation is immoral, poor educational practice, a violation of student and societal needs, and contrary to the fundamental tenets of our society. . . . Measures of achievement and competency must reflect individually determined curricula. . . . Graduation, including a diploma, should be granted to all students who satisfactorily complete their individually determined curricula. (Cain et al., 1984, pp. 488–489)

The CEC's statement added that our schools must develop a student's individual aspirations and talents, even if these do not coincide with the standard curriculum. Moreover, development of personal and social skills is critical so that individuals with disabilities can contribute as independently as possible to good citizenry. Sleeter (1986) warned that minimum competency reforms not be allowed to further stratify our population so that the learning disabled end up failing, in the lowest-paying jobs, and in the least advantaged social groups. Likewise, the reforms may aggravate race stratification, because far more African Americans and Hispanics fail the tests than whites (MacMillan, Balow, & Widaman, 1988).

In over 85 percent of states where MCTs have been established, provision has been made for alternate ways of meeting MCT requirements (Ysseldyke et al., 1994). Some states, for example, permit content area tests to be read aloud by a reader and students to respond orally, in order to work around their reading and writing difficulties. Others allow time modifications for students who process information slowly. Modifications in the test format itself may increase the pass rate for students with learning disabilities: for example, ordering items from easiest to hardest, using unjustified margins to help guide the eye, marking answers in the test booklet instead of the confusing "bubble" sheet, setting reading comprehension passages within shaded boxes apart from the test items, including more examples, and using arrows to indicate continuation to the next page or stop signs to indicate the end (Beattie, Grisé, & Algozzine, 1983). Additional testing modifications include administering fewer subsections per testing session, individual or small-group administration in less distracting settings, and modified methods for recording answers (the proctor, a word processor). The 1997 IDEA reauthorization requires that the student's Individualized Education Program (IEP) specify any modifications necessary for the administration of state- or districtwide assessments of student achievement. If the IEP team determines that the student will not participate in a particular assessment, the IEP must state why that achievement assessment is inappropriate and how the student will be assessed.

When special education students do not meet MCT requirements, they still can obtain a modified high school diploma certifying that they attended school and met the requirements of their IEPs. In the following pages we explore the reading, written language, and mathematics instructional needs of adolescents with learning disabilities.

Reading. Although the reading skills of the typical middle school or high school student generally range across several grade levels, most students have mastered sufficient decoding and comprehension skills to engage actively and independently in content area studies. They can compare and evaluate information from a variety of sources. When topics are to be researched in depth, as in term papers (for example, the church's role as depicted in *The Wives of Bath*), students begin to learn to synthesize information from several sources, form hypotheses, and critically evaluate the literature (Chall, 1983a). Not only are the assigned readings more complex but also students are expected to read more and to rely more on reading to gain a good deal of information. Faced with more challenging material, secondary level students learn to monitor and evaluate their understanding automatically as they read. By the time they enter junior high school, students generally have gained insight into the way the text's structure can facilitate their comprehension (for example, differentiating main idea sentences from supporting detail sentences, identifying different levels of importance of ideas, using text organization to aid comprehension) (Taylor & Samuels, 1983). If comprehension falters, then they know to compensate in some manner (for example, reread, scan forward for clarification, use a dictionary, ask the teacher). Those who are successful readers also know how to activate their background knowledge so that what they are reading makes more sense and becomes more memorable (Bransford, Stein, & Vye, 1982).

In contrast, many adolescents with learning disabilities are still acquiring essential reading skills. Problems may continue in basic sight vocabulary, word-attack skills, reading rate, memory for sounds, ability to generalize to words with similar orthography, phoneme segmentation, vocalization during silent reading, and ability to gain meaning from long sentences or paragraphs (Horn, O'Donnell, & Vitulano, 1983). Many students plateau at the fourth and fifth grade reading levels early in high school and show little further progress (Schumaker et al., 1983; Warner et al., 1980).

Achievement levels in third grade seem to have particular predictive value; if reading is still poor at the end of third grade, then the prognosis for rapid subsequent gains is bleak (Badian, 1988). For example, Rutter and his colleagues' (1976) large-scale study of nine- to eleven-year-old Isle of Wight children, who were over two years behind expected reading levels for their age and intelligence, found that at ages fourteen to fifteen these students had achieved the reading equivalency of a nine-year-old child. In contrast, children who were less bright but who read as would be expected for their intelligence had made more rapid progress.

Even if decoding has become automatic, many students with learning disabilities tend not to monitor their reading for comprehension (for example, not taking note of inconsistencies in passages) (Bos & Filip, 1984). Several of Bos and Filip's students did not think it at all unusual that the passage they had read made no sense. Teenagers with learning disabilities also have been found to be less efficient at scanning a text for specific information (Garner & Reis, 1981). Frequently they do not have an awareness of how the text's organization could help them learn, and they do not self-question or activate prior knowledge to make the information more meaningful.

Many characteristics of our schools actually promote reading problems for teenagers who are learning disabled. These include an overemphasis on literal comprehension, poorly organized and written teaching materials, inadequate diagnostic and instructional techniques, and a lack of overall comprehensive planning for teaching reading at the secondary level (Lindsey & Kerlin, 1979). Perhaps most devastating is the assumption of many that if students haven't learned to read by now they never will. All students can learn something, particularly when provided intensive training at the proper instructional level, in an approach drastically different from the one in which failure was most recently experienced. According to Cunningham, Cunningham, and Arthur (1981, p. 13): "Most dyslexia is only terminal if you believe it is!"

Levin, Zigmond, and Birch (1985) found that their teenagers with learning disabilities did make reading progress after four years of special education, despite the fact that they had not begun special education until junior high school. They had improved from the early sixth to mid-eighth grade reading levels. Nearly half of this gain occurred in the first year of special help. Levin and colleagues comment that it is not clear whether students plateau after the first year of remediation or whether the gains actually are equivalent from year to year, with the greater gains when students are first introduced to special education merely reflecting an accumulation of readiness skills that students had not previously been able to apply.

A critical element in the reading remediation process is student cooperation. If the student is not highly motivated to continue working at a task, additional remedial efforts at the secondary level are no more likely to succeed than did earlier ones. Either way, accommodations still need to be made to ensure opportunities to learn in the content areas. This may involve modifications such as listening to tapes, a computer synthesized voice reading the text, or readers, instead of reading independently. Curriculum materials also can be rewritten at lower readability levels. Students must be committed to whatever approach is chosen, and the objectives must coincide with each individual's realistic educational-vocational goals. A useful way of enhancing secondary reading success is to coordinate reading remediation with tutoring in the content area subject matter. Listening comprehension in class, study skills (note-taking, outlining), and test-taking strategies are equally important to develop.

Encouraging reading, any reading at all, is very important. The less one reads, the less the foundation upon which new learning can be built. Consequently, students with learning disabilities may become less and less knowledgeable and capable of absorbing knowledge as time passes. Unfortunately, teachers may play a role in this cumulative information deficit. A survey of nearly 200 middle school and high school social studies and special education teachers found that they very seldom presented contemporary social issues (for example, nuclear weapons, cults, the Ku Klux Klan, prayer in the schools, world hunger, censorship, women's rights) to their students, except when these came up during current events discussions and in response to student questions (Fine, 1987). Special education teachers discussed such issues least, with the exception of substance abuse, child abuse, teenage pregnancy, and social welfare programs.

Although teachers in Fine's survey considered contemporary social issues to be important, they indicated that they felt unprepared, or only somewhat prepared, to deal with this content. If teenagers with learning disabilities are not getting this type of information independently through reading, or in the classroom through discussions or structured lessons, then they are being denied access to the rich historical, cultural, and political background that is every citizen's concern.

Written Language. Facility with written expression is important in both academic and out-of-school situations. Not only is writing the way in which students most commonly demonstrate what they have learned, writing also is a valuable aid in organizing thought. For individuals who lack the capacity and confidence to express themselves in writing, the experience can be highly frustrating.

Writing problems are prevalent and difficult to remediate because proficiency in this area relies on an expanded experiential and knowledge base and the development of adequate language, reading, and self-monitoring skills, all of which may be problematic. For the most part, adolescents with learning disabilities have progressed beyond their elementary school writing performance in that they write stories rather than descriptions, and their stories are longer. Perhaps because of continuing difficulty in abstract reasoning, they tend to omit information related to time context, goals, internal reactions of characters, and endings. They tend not to elaborate on ideas, are not creative, and do not organize ideas or clarify connections by using transition words to signal relationships (for example, *although, however*) (Vallecorsa & Garriss, 1990; Wong et al., 1991).

Compared with nondisabled peers, adolescents with learning disabilities often write at a slower pace and have a more limited vocabulary, and a higher frequency of mechanical errors (spelling, capitalization, and punctuation) (Myklebust, 1973). They also are less competent at monitoring and revising their writing errors (Deshler, 1978; MacArthur, Schwartz, & Graham, 1991). A study of seventh and eighth graders with learning disabilities found that these students tended to make only one significant change when revising their writing: improving handwriting quality. They did make minor word and phrase changes, but these had no effect on meaning. The percentage of spelling, capitalization, and punctuation errors remained the same. Although these students would add information, they tended not to reorganize, improve beginnings and endings, or delete insignificant or irrelevant details (MacArthur, Graham, & Schwartz, 1991).

The writing samples throughout this chapter give you some idea of the written language quality of students with learning disabilities. These writing weaknesses often are exacerbated by the tendency for earlier remedial efforts to have focused primarily on reading and spelling. Despite these interventions, spelling generally continues to lag behind these students' reading skills (Rutter et al., 1976). The spelling of Craig, a bright thirteen year old who has had difficulty mastering the visual and orthographic aspects of spelling, is illustrated in Figure 5–13. He spells a second grade word list with less than 40 percent accuracy. All errors are good phonetic equivalents. Note how Craig spells *come, said, we,* and *went.* This is remarkable in that he no doubt has read these words thousands of times.

Experts recommend that efforts to improve writing skills first should focus on building motivation to write and confidence that one's thoughts are worthy of communication. Intensive remediation begins by showing students just how much they already do know and how information obtained through listening, speaking, and reading can be used in learning to write (Graves, 1983; Hillocks, 1986; Murray, 1984). The mechanics of writing follow.

Because of their written language difficulties, most students with learning disabilities require modifications on tests, such as extended time periods, the option of oral exams, multiple-choice instead of short-answer formats, or permis-

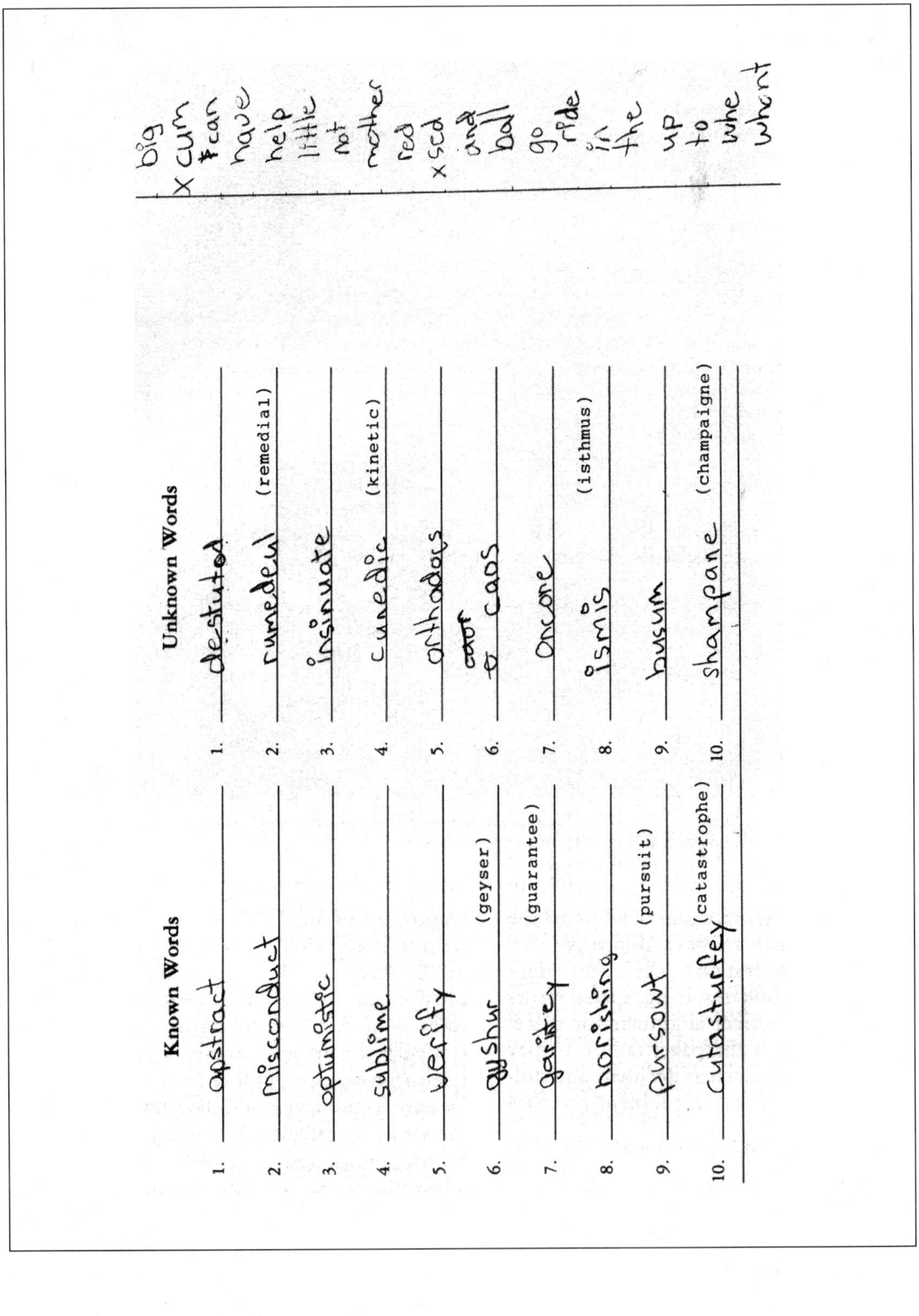

big
X cum
≠can
have
help
little
not
mother
red
X scd
and
ball
go
ride
in the
up
to
whe
when

Known Words

1. abstract
2. misconduct
3. optimistic
4. sublime
5. verify
6. gyshur (geyser)
7. garintey (guarantee)
8. borishing
9. pursowt (pursuit)
10. cutasturfey (catastrophe)

Unknown Words

1. destuted
2. rumedeul (remedial)
3. insinuate
4. cunedic (kinetic)
5. orthodacs
6. coot / c caos
7. oncore
8. ismis (isthmus)
9. busum
10. shampane (champaigne)

Figure 5–13 Good phonetic equivalents of Craig, a bright, thirteen year old with learning disabilities.

sion to respond in outline form. Strategies for dealing with the written language needs of teenagers will be explored further in Chapter 10.

Mathematics. The current proliferation of minicalculators notwithstanding, comprehension of basic arithmetic operations is still essential for successful daily living. Even if one does carry a calculator, it will not be very helpful unless the user understands which operations are to be performed and in what order. In addition, the individual still needs to evaluate the reasonableness of the answers and whether or not to recalculate.

Adolescents with learning disabilities display all levels of mathematical ability and skills. Often math achievement is observed to reach somewhat higher levels than reading achievement (Fletcher, 1985; Rutter et al., 1976). While some students who in their earlier years were hindered by memory (e.g., weak recall of number facts) and attention (e.g., confusing signs) difficulties become more capable of handling more abstract, less memory-related high school math, for many others math achievement peaks at approximately a fifth grade level (Cawley et al., 1996; Garnett, 1992). Ackerman and Dykman (1995) explain that many elementary students who are initially identified for their reading disabilities, years later show math deficiencies as well because the same weak verbal memory skills that prevent rapid access to reading words also preclude automatized number recall. Because these students can't retrieve math facts quickly, they need to "count up"; this counting consumes their short-term memory, taking resources away from their ability to reason about the math concepts. The better developed a student's language and perceptual skills, the greater the math progress is likely to be (Harnadek & Rourke, 1994).

Like the elementary school student, the teenager continues to have difficulty with computational operations, choice of algorithms (rules), ignoring extraneous information in word problems, solving problems with multiple steps and mixed operations, computing at a reasonable speed, incorrect alignment of figures on the page, failure to pay attention to details such as decimals and dollar signs, and subtraction problem reversals as in

$$\begin{array}{r} 25 \\ -16 \\ \hline 11 \end{array}$$

(Algozzine et al., 1987; Cox, 1975; Sharma, 1981; Zentall & Ferkis, 1993). For some teenagers, the problem is not so much with math strategies as with efficiently transforming these strategies when new problems are encountered (for example, failing to recognize that because a numeral multiplied by 1 remains the same, no calculation is necessary; failing to use multiplication instead of addition when the same number reappears several times in long addition columns) (Swanson & Cooney, 1985).

There continues to be much controversy over whether, during the secondary school years, we should stress memorization of math facts, which will make the quantitative reasoning task easier, or whether we should stress the reasoning component, which in itself encourages integration of the math facts. In reality, the average adult uses both strategies; when recall of number facts fails them, they turn to counting strategies as an efficient back-up system (Garnett, 1992). While students with learning disabilities readily can compensate for computational weaknesses with calculators, developing their mathematical understanding and logical reasoning is critical if they are to function adequately in the everyday world.

Given that the math abilities of many students with learning disabilities may ceiling at a fourth or fifth grade level, learning functional life skills must be given some priority. This includes learning to follow the measurements in recipes, understand the library's Dewey decimal system, use calculators, budget, make change, figure tax and interest, compute sale prices and sales tax, calculate payroll deductions and hours worked, read charts and maps, plan on quantities of food or materials to buy, meet health-related needs (such as measuring fat intake, timing medication), and keeping score in games (Miller, 1996; Schwartz & Budd, 1981; Zentall & Ferkis, 1993).

Transition Planning

The 1997 reauthorization of IDEA requires that, beginning at age fourteen, and updated annually thereafter, the IEP address the course of study that will meet the student's transition needs. Beginning at age sixteen, or younger if necessary, transition services must be delineated that will prepare the student to function in his or her home, job, and community. This plan should address postsecondary education plans, job placement and evaluation, community living plans, interagency responsibilities and linkages, as well as everyday concerns such as shopping, leisure time activities, cooperation with coworkers, community travel, and money management. As comprehensive a plan as possible needs to be developed, in light of the fact that many students with learning disabilities, particularly those who choose not to continue their schooling after high school, are likely to become unemployed or underemployed young adults who continue to live with their parents (Blackorby & Wagner, 1996).

With the passage of the Educational Amendments of 1974 (PL 93-380) came the concept of *career education,* a continuous process starting in early childhood that is intended to prepare individuals for a wide variety of social, personal, economic, avocational, and leisure time roles. *Vocational education,* preparing students for entry into one specific job, is just one subcomponent of career education. As currently offered, vocational education typically provides little for the adolescent with learning disabilities. Existing courses, especially those originally developed for intellectually less capable students, are too watered down or menial in scope. On the other hand, career exploration and vocational education courses offered to the entire student body often present the same reading, writing, and coping problems that make survival in other content area courses difficult (Evers & Bursuck, 1993; Okolo & Sitlington, 1986). In general, the vocational preparation that students with learning disabilities are getting is insufficient in quantity and quality to break the cycle of low employment status after they leave high school (Edgar, 1987; Okolo & Sitlington, 1986; Rusch & Phelps, 1987; Shapiro & Lentz, 1991).

When special care is taken to ensure a good match between career education efforts and student needs, school dropout rates have been shown to decline and students develop the skills employers value (West, 1991). Mathews, Whang, and Fawcett's (1982) study details student characteristics that call for intensified efforts in this area. They found that although high school students with learning disabilities were as adept as non-LD adolescents at some tasks (getting a job lead from a friend, telephoning a potential employer to arrange an interview whether or not an opening existed, accepting a suggestion from an employer, and complimenting a coworker on a job well done), they performed significantly worse on seven important job-related skills: participating in a job interview, accepting criticism from an employer, providing constructive criticism to a coworker, explaining a problem to a supervisor, writing a request for interview letter in response to a help wanted ad, and writing a letter to follow up a job interview. Similarly, Roessler and Johnson (1987) found that although adolescents with learning disabilities benefited from videotaped vignettes in learning how to respond more positively to a supervisor (greater response length, more appropriate questions asked), they still communicated with too little energy and interest.

In a nationwide survey of high school seniors, those with learning disabilities expressed significantly lower expectations for reaching high occupational positions than did their nondisabled peers (Rojewski, 1996). Clearly, broader programs are necessary that include occupational awareness and exploration, career and vocational assessment, communications courses (including job interviewing, conversing with coworkers) career guidance, survival reading, writing, and math skills relevant to vocational and daily life (reading want ads, completing job applications, writing a resumé, balancing a checkbook, reading a bus schedule, and building self-confidence, positive work habits, and attitudes (Okolo & Sitlington, 1986; Washburn, 1975; Woodward, 1981).

Such broad training, rather than narrow training to do just one job, makes sense in view of rapidly changing technology and the fact that the students of today will change jobs, if not careers, at least three or four times during their lives. In merely the six- to twenty-four-months postgraduation, Shapiro and Lentz (1991) found that over half of their vocational-technical program graduates were employed in jobs bearing no resemblance to their high school training.

Because postschool employment success will depend on the ability to acquire new skills independently and adapt to changing work situations, a curriculum that encourages students to make job-related decisions, learn new tasks independently, evaluate performance, and decide on needed adjustments is critical (Mithaug, Martin, & Agran, 1987). In addition, an approach that stresses social skill development is essential because the ability to get along is often weighed as heavily as technical competence by those making hiring/firing decisions. Jobs most often are lost because of deficiencies in interpersonal and social skills rather than in work skills (Okolo & Sitlington, 1986; Roessler & Johnson, 1987). One of the best ways to teach these skills is by building into the curriculum job shadowing, community service and paid work opportunities, or supervised internship rotations in a number of community sites. There is considerable evidence that work-study programs lower dropout rates, affect school and work attitudes positively, and improve achievement and postschool employment rates (Berk, 1997; Evers, 1996; Fourqurean et al., 1990). In addition to these options, counselors need to be ready to encourage the possibility of higher education for applicants with learning disabilities who, given specific curriculum modifications and supports, have a reasonable chance for success.

The Adult Years

Studies of both school age students and adults with learning disabilities find that those who have the least severe learning problems, who have the highest intelligence, who come from enriched, supportive homes, and who benefited from intensive intervention have the most favorable outcomes (Bruck, 1985; Finucci, Gottfredson, & Childs, 1985; Levin et al., 1985; Muehl & Forell, 1973). These advantages have helped these individuals to remediate some weaknesses, compensate for others, and develop alternate routes to success.

A number of studies have reported the outlook for the adults with learning disabilities whom they studied to be quite favorable. Despite lingering spelling and reading difficulties, of Rawson's (1968) subjects (average IQ 131), 86 percent had earned college degrees, and all but two held jobs that put them in the top two socioeconomic levels. Similarly, a follow-up study of Gow School graduates, a boarding school attended by middle to high socioeconomic status, average to high intelligence boys with learning disabilities, found that 50 percent had earned at least a bachelor's degree, and approximately 8 percent had graduate degrees; an additional 38 percent had some college or technical training beyond high school. Only 6 percent had not graduated from high school. An unusually high percentage of the college students had majored in business (over 40 percent) rather than more traditional arts and sciences areas, and 65 percent worked in managerial and sales positions. Only 18 percent entered professional or technical fields (predominantly teachers, designers, computer specialists), versus 53 percent of the control subjects (predominantly physicians and lawyers). Forty-eight percent considered their spelling below average, and 36 percent had unfavorable attitudes toward reading; those with the lowest achievement levels in school were the ones who reported the greatest continuing difficulties in these areas (Childs et al., 1982; Finucci, 1986; Finucci et al., 1985).

Bruck (1985) reported similar favorable results with a group of young adults of middle socioeconomic status. Eighty percent had graduated from high school, 58 percent entered college, 31 percent entered graduate school, and only 11 percent were unemployed. Likewise, in a follow-up of average-intelligence young adults who had severe reading disorders as children, Balow and Blomquist (1965) found that 83 percent had graduated from high school, over half had gone on to college or vocational education, and all were vocationally successful. Despite their earlier reading disorders, all had achieved at least average adult reading levels. Nevertheless, these people had not liked school, did not read for pleasure, and had adopted negative, defeatist attitudes toward life. They did not feel as though they were masters of their own destinies. Rogan and Hartman's (1976) follow-up of average-intelligence adults with about three years of private school, remedial education found that 69 percent had graduated from high school, 36 percent had completed college, another 16 percent were attending college, and 8 percent completed or were pursuing graduate study. Sixty percent of the group were employed, primarily in clerical and unskilled jobs. Only 13 percent were in professional jobs. Fifty-five percent were independent of parental supervision, and 15 percent had married. The incidence of adult criminal offenses was very low, 6 percent. Personality tests, however, suggested high vulnerability to stress among this group.

Despite the favorable outcomes just reviewed, these are far outnumbered by reports of unfavorable outcomes in adulthood. Persistent learning and adjustment difficulties characterize individuals who did not have the benefit of the intellectual, socioeconomic, or schooling advantages described. Because the discrepancy between academic demands and the individual's achievement tends to become larger as students with learning disabilities get older, for many, their learning weaknesses become even more pronounced in adulthood (Cone et al., 1985; Shepard & Smith, 1983; Trites & Fiedorowicz, 1976).

The great heterogeneity of the adult LD population is evident in Johnson's (1986) findings. Adults with average to above average intelligence varied from reading no more than a few words to reading at the twelfth grade level. However, even the latter readers were inefficient and still erred on third and fourth grade words. Although letter reversals were infrequent, these adults still tended to identify words by looking at the first and final sounds and then guessing from context. Errors were most frequent on vowels and

medial portions of words. Phoneme segmentation (analyzing words into their separate syllables and phonemes) proved to be difficult for some. Nonphonetic spelling was common, with frequent omissions of syllables and sounds. Bruck's (1990, 1993b) studies of college students with learning disabilities find that some read only as well as sixth graders, read slower than sixth graders, and need to rely to an unusual extent on context, sound, and syllable information to assist word recognition; other college students have reached eleventh grade reading levels, but their spelling remains inferior to that of sixth graders who read at the eleventh grade level. In another study, despite reading levels below the 50th percentile, college students with learning disabilities showed reading comprehension equal to that of their nondisabled peers, but they needed 25 percent extra reading time to achieve this parity (Mosberg & Johns, 1994).

Liberman and her colleagues (1985) report that adults in a community literacy class had persisting problems with the phonological structure of our language. Only 58 percent of the time could these adults identify the initial, medial, or final sound they heard in words. Although some sight recognition had been mastered, decoding unfamiliar words continued to be a struggle. In yet another study, adults with language deficits had not even made an average of one to one and a half year's gain in reading and math ability since identification at about age ten. Although most were high school graduates, at the average age of twenty-seven they still read at about second grade levels. Math skills averaged a mid-fourth grade level. Spelling was the greatest weakness, at times being bizarre (Frauenheim & Heckerl, 1983). Reversals when reading letters and words continued (*on-no, saw-was*) because of confusion over recall of sounds and analysis of sound order in words. Amount of special reading assistance and the age at which assistance began were unrelated to adult reading levels (Frauenheim, 1978). Even when adults' reading difficulties have been remediated to a considerable extent, continued slow reading, slow response time, phonemic awareness, and word finding, comprehension difficulties are not unusual (Felton, Naylor, & Wood, 1990; Pennington et al., 1990; Shaywitz, Fletcher, & Shaywitz, 1995; Silver & Hagin, 1964, 1966; Wolf, 1991). Mancele's story (below) illustrates how difficult spelling continues to be for many adults with learning disabilities and how compromised are their potentials when appropriate intervention is not offered.

Apparently, many youngsters with learning disabilities do not outgrow their problems. As adults, their persistent learning and adjustment difficulties often lead to poor vocational success and less satisfaction with oneself and one's interpersonal relationships. A key to enhancing their vocational and personal adjustment is to encourage participation in postsecondary educational opportunities.

Postsecondary Educational Opportunities

States permit students with learning disabilities to remain in public education to age twenty-one and sometimes even longer, thereby allowing extra time for degree completion. One goal of the high

---

Mancele

My disability in reading, writing, and spelling affected me in two ways. first I had no confidents in myself and the second is the fear I had inside of me.

My fear was and still is so grete [great] that if someone asked me to read, spell, or write down directions, I would break out in a sweat. The fear was divercateing [devastating] to me. About school I don't remember my early years because I don't thing I was taught anything to remember anything about school. However, from the sixth or seven grade, I new I had a problem. I was tested and put into what was called an opportunity class, they call it.

They sed that it would be a special class to help me. Most of the "opportunity" class was made up of young black men. We had the "opportunity" of running movies all day for other classes in our school. This was our opportunity for learning. The classes were taught by one teacher. He was suppose to teach us in all subjects, math sceance [science] and Enlish, Histery, etc. The movies were fun to show, however the only thing I learned was showing movies. So my seventh and eighth grade Education was a lost, too. Most of our tests in class were motobowt [multiple] chosuis [choice]. I got good marks some B, too. I became putty [pretty] good in taking tests. Even on my spelling lists I got 75% or 80% carick [correct]. I could menerize [memorize] anything for a short time, but in two weeks after I forget it all. Because I menorize it. It did not matter what order it was in or giving it to me. I learn the sound of each word, then the letters. But didn't know the words themself. I graduated from High school knowing I could not read or spell afbulb [above] third grade. When I had to write a book reported, the pain in my head would come and I would pannick. I would pick out key words in some books I knew, and picked out key sentence, then put them together for my book report. "So now they say I have a learning disability. I say I wasn't taught."

Source: Reprinted by permission of Mancele W. Simmons Jr.

school's IEP transition plan is to increase the chances of students with learning disabilities taking advantage of postsecondary educational opportunities. This is important because the more schooling one has completed, the greater one's chances for higher-level employment. National statistics indicate that the unemployment rate in the first few years after graduating high school is 37 percent for students who do not continue their education (*Condition of Education*, 1997). Those who find work tend to be in low-paid, unskilled jobs.

Those students who continue with their schooling beyond high school are more often those with higher intellectual, reading, and math capabilities, those who had the social skills and confidence to participate in high school extracurricular activities, and those who used community resources for job assistance and information (Miller, Snider, Rzonca, 1990). High school graduates with learning disabilities have a number of opportunities for postsecondary education: schooling through military enlistment; technical schools (one-year business school; medical or legal secretarial training; cosmetology); government-funded transition program grants; two-year colleges; community, state, and private colleges; night school classes; and modified university programs. PL 95-602 made available evaluation, counseling, and vocational training services of the Office of Vocational and Educational Services for Individuals with Disabilities to students whose severe learning disabilities pose a substantial impediment to employment. Moreover, PL 98-199 authorized postsecondary educational and transition programs for special education graduates in order to promote competitive and supportive employment.

But all this is not enough. National data indicate that only 30 percent of students with learning disabilities enroll in postsecondary education within five years of leaving high school; this contrasts with 68 percent of students without disabilities (Blakorby & Wagner, 1996). This appears related to the lower educational and occupational aspirations among the learning disabled (Rojewski, 1996); the need for vocational rehabilitation counselors to plan alternatives because of the

paucity of remedial, vocational, independent living, and social-skill training programs; and inadequate collaboration between vocational rehabilitation and special education personnel (Dowdy, 1996). Opportunities to learn necessary survival skills also are severely lacking: for example, handling money and banking, reading manuals, writing memos and letters, looking up telephone numbers, reading a menu or street sign, making change, following recipes, using thermometers, and setting alarm clocks (Hoffman et al., 1987; Johnson & Blalock, 1987). What help is available often is open only to those who can afford private fees.

Support groups and counseling needs also require attention. Smith (1988) summarizes studies documenting the unhappiness of adults with learning disabilities regarding family relationships, dependency on others, conversational problems, shyness, lack of self-confidence, frustration, making and keeping friends, and controlling emotions and tempers. Certainly, service options must be expanded in this direction as well. High school dropouts in particular need encouragement to enroll in GED (General Education Development exam) classes in order to earn a high school equivalency diploma and increase their employment opportunities.

At the college level admissions and services have increased markedly for the learning disabled, in part due to nondiscriminatory admissions and teaching procedures, and in part because these students can now take untimed SATs. The more time students with learning disabilities spend on the SAT, the more their scores increase. These increases average thirty- to thirty-eight-points per section above what would be expected simply from taking the test again (Centra, 1986). The scores of nondisabled students taking untimed SATs do not improve to any significant extent.

Colleges that receive federal financial assistance cannot discriminate against the learning disabled in their recruitment, admissions, or teaching procedures (Section 504, Rehabilitation Act of 1973). These colleges have special offices that coordinate support services such as academic advising, tutoring, and counseling. Many colleges offer special learning centers, courses, or even a separate academic track emphasizing reading, writing, spelling, computer, and study skill instruction. Taped texts, tape recording of lectures, and notetakers are offered. Students are encouraged to explore various exam options with their professors such as untimed tests, multiple-choice/outline/essay exams, rephrasing of questions, papers, projects, take-home or oral exams, using scribes or word processors, and quieter, less distracting test locations. Some colleges reduce the number and difficulty level of courses in which a student initially enrolls, permit students to audit classes before taking them, or encourage students to attend more than one section of the class in order to get the same message in different ways. They provide proctors when necessary for reading or writing exams, priority course registration, substitutions for required courses (for example, substituting a multicultural course for the foreign language requirement), proofreaders to assist with grammar, spelling, and punctuation on papers, and advance copies of syllabi so students can get a headstart on the readings. It is not unusual for students to enroll in summer courses in order to reduce their academic year load. It is typical for students to take more than four years to graduate.

Those working with college students who are learning disabled are frequently struck by their disorganization, inability to plan time, and disabling anxiety about failure. These attributes often keep students from attempting to study in more than a cursory way or from doing things to make learning easier (for example, buying a highlighted used text, auditing a course before taking it). College students with learning disabilities often live under the illusion that good students read material only once in order to master it. They are so disheartened at not remembering much after the first reading, or at taking so long to read, that they give up. The compulsivity, rigor, self-discipline, and study strategies of the good student come as shocking surprises to the learning disabled. Their poor self-concepts, the hope that their problems will disappear, fearfulness about disclosing their disability, and lack of appropriate assertiveness all deter these students from asking professors for program modifications that might

facilitate success. The student's social-emotional adjustment certainly is highly related to his or her probability of success.

Bireley and Manley (1980) report that the attributes most likely to lead to success in their college program are independence, motivation, acceptance of the need to expend more time and energy when studying, and the ability to plan study time, evaluate progress realistically, and match personal strengths to course requirements when choosing among courses. Self-advocacy skills, the ability to handle frustration, and the nurturing provided by mentor relationships also are important. Students who thrive at the most competitive of colleges exhibit an "extraordinary drive and determination, . . . together with their exceptional intelligence [that] enables them to accomplish more with their disability than others for whom things have come easier. Such proven resiliency becomes a critical factor in meeting future challenges successfully" (Shaywitz & Shaw, 1988, p. 84).

Summary

Learning disabilities present lifelong learning challenges. While academic development is the primary focus of schooling, by the high school years transition planning for adult life becomes equally important. In order to maximize success as an adult, whether vocationally or in independent living, postsecondary education is critical.

Students with learning disabilities have difficulty with the information processing involved in many academic tasks. Though improvement is the rule, particularly when the student has received extensive remediation at the elementary level, many adolescents with learning disabilities still lag academically, and further progress is slow. Variability between these students in achievement levels and strength/weakness patterns is great.

Programming efforts at the secondary level have focused primarily on the continued development of basic reading, comprehension, written language, and mathematics skills. Tutoring has been provided for content area classes and study and test-taking strategies have been emphasized. Teachers attempt to encourage students' strengths by working around their weaknesses, developing compensatory skills, intensifying career education, and promoting an adequate knowledge and skills base.

While implementation of more rigorous standards for graduation and minimum competency testing help the learning disabled by increasing accountability for program quality, at the same time they may diminish the chances for these youngsters to earn the same academic diploma as their peers. This in turn impacts their future educational and vocational opportunities.

Because learning disabilities follow teenagers into adulthood, adults may curtail their postsecondary education, which unfortunately hampers their vocational options and life adjustment. Studies find that those adults with the most favorable outcomes have less severe learning difficulties, choose vocations that capitalize on their strengths, have high intelligence levels that help them compensate for weaknesses, and have benefited from supportive and stimulating home and school environments.

Chapter Six

Learning Strategy and Information-Processing Development

By definition, students with learning disabilities are bright enough to have learned the basic skills and information expected within their schools' curricula. Yet their achievement in one or more academic areas falls far short of expectation. Despite adequate learning opportunities, these students have failed to remember the information to which they have been exposed. These memory difficulties of the learning disabled appear related to a number of factors: an insufficient knowledge base to which new knowledge can be anchored, poor use of strategies to aid storage and retrieval, and the interference of various information-processing inefficiencies with the processing of information in the first place.

Despite their uneven learning patterns, the learning strategies and information-processing skills of most individuals with learning disabilities still develop in the same order as would typically be expected, although at a much slower rate. When compared with those of younger typical learners who achieve at similar levels, the learning patterns of the learning disabled often appear qualitatively unusual and more immature. For example, ninth grade Tony reads as many words correctly in a minute as a fourth grader, yet the fourth grader quickly sounds out words he has never seen before. Tony cannot. He attacks unknown words haltingly, and most often simply skips over them, hoping that this won't interfere with his understanding. Tony still exhibits dynamic reversals in his spelling (for example, *gril* for *girl*), only 40 percent of the words in his essays are spelled correctly, and the rest often don't phonetically approximate the sound of the word. By contrast, the fourth grader spells 80 percent of the words in his essays correctly, and his misspelled words sound as one would expect (for example, *brue* for *brew*).

This chapter presents our current understanding of how attention and memory, learning strategies, and perceptual, motor, and language abilities develop from the preschool years through adulthood. Delays in these abilities can affect the efficiency of processing and acquisition of knowledge, as well as the ability to communicate what is known. It is important for us to become aware of the typical order of development in these areas so that delays can be detected and the most appropriate interventions planned, in order to promote progress in basic information acquisition, thinking skills, and learning strategies.

Attention, Memory, and Learning Strategies

We have noted that attention disorders are major contributors to learning disabilities. Therefore, it is important for us to be alert to students' inefficient attention processes so that we can try to modify either the attention-getting aspects of our instruction or the students' response patterns. Enhancement of attention is a primary concern for teachers because, without adequate attention, there will be incomplete memory for content, limited systematic, logical reasoning, and disorganized, immature problem-solving and learning approaches.

Each time a student's attention is not engaged and maintained, an opportunity for learning has been lost. Unfortunately, many such lost opportunities may create wide gaps in knowledge and skills among people who otherwise had good potential for learning. These knowledge and skill vacuums, in turn, make new knowledge less meaningful and therefore less memorable.

Try your hand at the mind challengers in Figure 6–1. What did you have to do to solve these problems? Clearly, you had to simultaneously attend to, read, reason about, and hold in memory the figural aspects and word meanings, while you searched your mind for familiar English sayings; you also substituted new approaches when others did not work. Students with learning disabilities have difficulty combining new information with the old, coordinating perceptual and verbal problem solving, and monitoring dif-

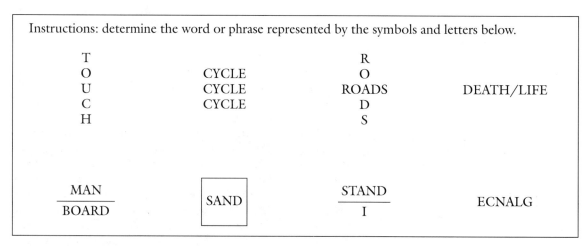

Figure 6–1 Mind challengers. *Source:* unknown.

ferent paths toward a solution. Let us explore how attention, problem-solving, memory, and learning strategies typically develop, and the differences often found among the learning disabled.

Attention and Problem Solving

The attention of the typical preschooler tends to be incomplete, unsystematic, and redundant (Smith, 1991). The preschooler's gaze most often is arrested by eye-catching features of stimuli; other parts are ignored. Certain features are inspected repeatedly, even though they had been fully understood on the first glance. Attention often flits from feature to feature without consistent direction or organization, and distractibility is high. Moreover, the young child's rate of gathering information is limited and variable (Kinsbourne & Caplan, 1979).

Preschoolers attend and learn better when color and shape attributes of tasks are used to grab their attention, when handling objects, when the positions of objects are changed, when tasks are systematically explained, when three-dimensional materials are used, when task-relevant features are accentuated, and when recognition rather than recall is required (Smith, 1991). Examining compound rather than single attributes of objects further helps to sustain attention; novelty serves an attention-arousing role until ages four or five, when preference for familiarity takes over (Zeaman & Hanley, 1983). By age five, children generally can attend to a single activity for about seven minutes when playing (Stodolsky, 1974).

When engaged in problem solving, four- to six-year-old children generally consider only one dimension of a problem. By the mid-elementary years they can switch attention to another aspect of the problem and try incorporating this into a solution. Researchers note that by the middle school years the typical child's ability to reflect about at least two components of a solution at once and to control impulsive judgments has matured a great deal (Siegler, 1983; Smith & Caplan, 1988). These children are self-regulated enough to define goals and persist methodically to meet these goals.

When a preschooler has poor attention, this generally is accompanied by high activity levels. These activity levels tend to increase to age three, after which they show a downward trend. This downward trend continues into adolescence, possibly because the ability to focus and sustain attention continues to mature and because peers, parents, and teachers become less accepting of annoying interruptions (Bryant & McLoughlin, 1972; Epstein, Bursuck, & Cullinan, 1985; Menkes, Rowe, & Menkes, 1967). Nevertheless, the "frantic to-and-fro purposeless motor activity" of the five- or six-year-old hyperactive child may still evidence itself in adolescent finger or object tapping, chair rocking, leg wagging, grimacing, facial tics (Wilcox, 1970, p. 7), poor concentration, poor sustained effort, restlessness, excitability, disruptiveness, and aggression (Brown & Wynne, 1984; Cannon & Compton, 1981; Epstein et al., 1985).

Continuing their earlier behavior patterns, adolescents with learning disabilities tend to be more distractible and impulsive than their peers and less able to focus and sustain attention. They appear to use fewer mental strategies, also called *executive functions* or *control processes,* to monitor their learning: these include among other things decision making, problem solving, time management, trying new strategies when old ones fail, or simply asking questions when information is not understood. When control processes are not used, comprehension and recall suffer. Often these students are aware of the need to use such strategies but are inefficient at it (Bauer, 1987).

Teenagers with learning disabilities frequently do not monitor their comprehension so as to shift strategies when understanding breaks down. They also often fail to take advantage of the organization given to class materials by either the teacher or the text (for example, headings) in order to aid comprehension (Ellis, 1996). Many have trouble asking questions that would clarify their assignments and simplify their lives. Many are unaware that they can manipulate course content to better fit their individual styles of understanding, storing, and reproducing information. Many problem-solving skills that could enhance reading comprehension may be lacking; these include knowing how to narrow a problem to manageable proportions and summarize it succinctly, how to reread when information isn't understood the first time around, how to set reading goals, how to locate relevant books and other sources of information, how to use a table of contents and an index to locate information, how to scan a passage for information, how to discriminate what is relevant from what is irrelevant, how to critically evaluate what is read in order to select or reject information, how to underline or take notes efficiently from a number of sources, how to combine this information into an orderly presentation, and how to keep an open mind for evidence that may modify the solution to a problem (Thomas & Robinson, 1977).

Students with learning disabilites often are unaware of logical inconsistencies in a reading passage. They may even be unaware that a page is missing from a reading passage, may attempt a game with insufficient information about the rules, may predict and evaluate their correct spellings less accurately, may not correct spellings that they know are wrong, and may not allocate study time according to task difficulty (Lloyd & Loper, 1986). They are less adept than their peers at strategies that would help them detect errors in their work. Conceptually, these students tend to be less mature about what academics are all about. For example, when asked by one researcher, "What is good writing?" an answer like "good posture, sit up straight," was not uncommon (Graham, Schwartz, & MacArthur, 1993).

As in reading, it is not uncommon for children with math disorders to use immature strategies such as counting all items in two sets rather than counting on from one set to the other; they also don't use backups when they don't know a math fact (such as tallies on paper, counting subvocally) (Jordan, 1995). Montague and Applegate (1993) found that their middle school children with learning disabilities relied on a trial and error approach to math problems. They did not paraphrase to help understand a problem and did not attempt graphic illustrations to help interpret, set up, or solve problems.

The inefficiencies of students with learning disabilities carry over into their everyday lives. Juggling such everyday tasks as classes, assignments, and social relationships is nearly impossible. Mindy's story (page 195) illustrates how the psychological aspects of a learning disability only complicate further the ability to focus attention on the important tasks at hand.

Psychologists frequently are troubled by these students' declines in performance on intelligence tests in adolescence, when compared with their earlier performance. Some experts have suggested that these lower cognitive scores reflect a developmental lag in logical reasoning and abstract thinking skills (Brutten, Richardson, & Mangel, 1973; Myklebust, 1973); others have blamed school failure for contributing to declines in personal motivation to grow and develop (Deshler, 1978). Most agree, however that the deficient reading skills themselves, in combination with school programs that overemphasize remediating deficits instead of developing areas of strength, result in underexposure of students to a broad array of information, language, and ideas that could stimulate cognitive development (Stanovich, 1986; Woodward, 1981).

Table 6–1 lists many thinking skills that need to be encouraged in adolescents with learning disabilities. While application of these skills requires prior knowledge as a foundation, prior knowledge is not sufficient (French & Rhoder, 1992). Thinking means being able "to 'find' that prior knowledge in memory when it is useful and integrate it with new information" (p. 14). The thinker "prepares to think, thinks, rethinks, checks, rechecks, and concludes" (p. 15). Beyond this, the creative thinker restructures his or her relationship to a situation by breaking with previous understandings and believing that one's intelligence is malleable, that one can learn through sharing with others, and that one's own opinions can transform expert knowledge (Greeno, 1989).

Although Wiig, Lapointe, and Semel (1977) suggest that by the teenage years the critical period for improvement in thinking skills already has passed, research on critical thinking and problem-solving skills suggests that some students continue to be responsive to this type of instruction (Niedelman, 1991). A Stanford Research Institute report, "Compensatory Education in Early Adolescence"

Mindy

On October 24, 1974, I was born with birth complications. These problems resulted in me becoming epileptic and learning disabled.

I didn't know anything was "wrong" with me until I reached school age. In kindergarten, I had further difficulties and needed to have my head shaved. This is when I really began to feel different than the other kids. Even my teacher labeled me as a problem child, ridiculed me and accused me of not paying attention (when I actually was having petite mal seizures). Thankfully, I repeated kindergarten and had a teacher that was more understanding of my behaviors. She encouraged me to focus on my strengths rather than my weaknesses. Unfortunately, repeating this grade and a fall birthday, makes me two years older than my peers.

As I progressed in school, the kids started to tease and make fun of me. In fifth grade, I was becoming depressed over how I was being treated until I wrote a letter to my classmates, explaining the story of my life. This seemed to help them understand why it took me longer to learn and needed special help.

As a teenager I had to struggle with being accepted. I just couldn't seem to find my place among the other students. Nobody wanted me to participate in their study groups, teams or social gatherings. My teachers saw me as a burden to have in their classrooms. Successes were few for me at that time.

My low self-esteem makes me susceptible to the influence of other students. I find myself doing things that I wouldn't do normally just to have some friends that will accept me.

Another difficult issue of my disorder is my exaggerated emotions. I seem be overly sensitive to most people and take on their problems as my own. These feelings keep me from focusing on my own tasks. I become overwhelmed and distracted when it comes to life's daily routines.

Even though I have been labeled as having learning disabilities, I think in some ways I have greater learning abilities than people who are non-disabled. I am able to accept other people and see them as who they are rather than what their obstacles are. Because of problems in my life, I have been able to develop a strong and supportive group of individuals who are helping me to learn to accept myself. The non-acceptance of myself is the greatest disability I need to over come.

Source: Reprinted by permission of Mindy Quinn Buchtel.

(1974, in Deshler, 1978), suggests that with certain older pupils intensive educational efforts may be just as effective as early intervention is with others because some students during this period experience accelerated rates of cognitive growth.

Studies have found that the attention, reasoning, and problem-solving weaknesses of the adolescent often continue to adversely affect learning, performance, and social interactions, even into adulthood (Hechtman, Weiss, & Perlman, 1984a). Slow information processing also continues to be a problem for adults with learning disabilities (Shaywitz, Fletcher, & Shaywitz, 1995; Winters, Patterson, & Shontz, 1989).

Table 6–1   Thinking skills

1. Observing
2. Describing
3. Developing concepts
4. Interpreting concepts
5. Differentiating and defining
6. Questioning
7. Hypothesizing
8. Comparing and contrasting
9. Evaluating
10. Testing and making judgments
11. Forming supportive arguments
12. Persuading
13. Generating new ideas
14. Transforming/recombining old and new ideas
15. Generalizing
16. Predicting and explaining
17. Organizing materials, ideas, and tasks
18. Problem solving
    - identifying the problem
    - analyzing the problem
    - developing options
    - decision making
    - executing the decision
    - evaluating the decision
19. Deciding how to go about remembering
20. Deciding time management

Source: Adapted from Alley, G., and Deshler, D. (1979). *Teaching the learning disabled adolescent: Strategies and methods.* Denver: Love Publishing Company; French, J. N., and Rhoder, C. (1992). *Teaching thinking skills: Theory and practice.* New York: Garland.

Miles (1986), for example, found that even on a simple computer game requiring one to indicate whether a star is above a plus or to move the mouse to a figure's left or right ear, college students with learning disabilities required more time then their peers. Over time, these cumulative information-processing deficits are suspected to contribute to intellectual declines in comparison to nondisabled adults who had been equivalent in intelligence as children (Silver & Hagin, 1964, 1966).

Familiarity with the normal developmental sequence in which attention, memory, and problem-solving processes develop can be of great value to the teacher in guiding instruction. Researchers speak of two types of memory: short term and long term. Memory development begins with maturation of the basic processes of recognition and recall (Flavell, 1977; Flavell & Wellman, 1977). Then knowledge influences learning, and finally memory strategies enhance learning even further. Because many students with learning disabilities are too immature to use strategies to interact intellectually with material in an intensive, planful, and goal-directed manner, very explicit teacher direction regarding what to attend to and precisely how to go about problem solving is important during instruction.

Short- and Long-Term Memory

The preschooler selects certain features of the environment to attend to and ignores others. Interestingly, comparisons of visual and auditory memory between older preschoolers and adults indicate virtually no differences in the qualitative or quantitative encoding of perceptual information at the time it is seen or heard. Capacity and decay rates for the raw visual percept or sound pattern are similar across ages, and auditory information persists slightly longer than does the visual (Bauer, 1987; Kail & Siegel, 1977). This passive process of accumulating and holding onto segments of information as they arrive is called *short-term memory.*

Generally short-term memory lasts only one-quarter of a second to 25 seconds (Siegler, 1983). In order for short-term information, which is limited to 3 to 15 chunks of meaningful information (Baddeley, 1994), to be understood and maintained, it must be restructured in some way, such as by association or repetition. This simultaneous processing and maintenance of information is referred to as *working memory.*

Berk (1997) illustrates the effects of working memory's limited capacity by describing the novice bicycle rider who has no attentional resources left over to look at the scenery because he is so engrossed in controlling the pedals, steering, and balancing. In contrast, the experienced bicyclist can easily chew gum, talk to another rider, and deliver papers all at the same time because cognitive energy does not need to be shared with controlling the activity of riding itself. Even though adults and young children have equal capacities to take in short-term information, adults absorb more because their past knowledge makes the information more meaningful, they are faster at deploying strategies to help remember the information, and the knowledge and strategies permit more abstract, efficient, and effective thought; these in turn free up cognitive resources for other purposes. Baddeley (1986) explains that if a task draws on too much of the attentional pool in our working memory, then only a small amount of additional information will be able to be attended to and held. But when tasks with which we have greater facility are automatically processed, they do not draw much attentional resources; therefore attention can be reallocated to other cognitive operations, and the capacity of our working memory to consider more information is increased (Klatzky, 1984). This reasoning has found support in PET and MRI evidence showing reductions in brain activation with more practice; this activity reduction presumably frees up the brain to allocate energy to other concurrent activities (Matarazzo, 1992).

Clearly, in order to store information in *long-term memory,* a person needs to activate multiple cognitive abilities, such as perception, language, thought, prior memories, and strategies to process the information meaningfully. Because older people are better able to simultaneously engage these multiple abilities, they remember better than do younger people, despite equivalent short-term memory spans. Let us now further examine the influence of recognition, recall, knowledge, and strategies on a student's short- and long-term memory for school content.

Recognition and Recall

The basic memory processes of recognition and recall mature during the first two years of life. Young infants demonstrate their attention and *recognition* abilities when novelty, movement, and changes in the complexity of visual patterns elicit an *orienting reaction:* increased alertness, decreased sucking, and heart rate deceleration (Pick et al., 1975). Before one year of age the ability to *recall* will emerge: the ability to retrieve a thought from memory when the object of thought is physically absent (for example, remembering that one's favorite teddy bear is near the crib and purposefully crawling from the kitchen to the bedroom to fetch it) (Flavell, 1977; Berk, 1997). Recall is always harder than recognition. A one-and-one-half-year-old child, for example, may recognize a ball by pointing to it when asked, "Show me the picture of the ball," but will find it harder to demonstrate recall when asked "What is this?"

As the basic processes of recognition and recall mature during the first two years of life, infants become able to handle more complex and greater numbers of stimuli. At 11 months of age, for example, an infant can imitate a two-step event immediately after seeing it (for example, unfolding a hinged track and releasing a car down the incline). By 20 months children can reproduce a three-step event when they have seen and imitated it only once. This progresses to five steps at 24 months and eight steps at 30 months. Remarkably, 13-month-olds can still reproduce 40 to 50 percent of these events one week later; their ability to maintain these memories is evident even after an eight-month delay. The infant's recall will be better the more the steps need to be produced in a particular order, the more experience a child has with the steps, and when a reminder cue is used (Bauer, 1996). Once infants are able to recall events, ideas, and objects, even in their absence, the development of their basic recognition and recall processes is complete.

Knowledge

What we already know influences the information we will pay attention to, store, and retrieve. We all know too well that the way we remember a situation is not really the way it was to begin with. With time, we alter and reshape our memory of any event or piece of information. When we come across a new situation or piece of information, we evaluate it in terms of what we already know. For example, if we have heard a nasty rumor about someone, this information will continue to invade our thoughts about that person for a time, despite new evidence that invalidates the rumor. The new knowledge we learn always becomes altered through changing meanings, inferences, embellishment, the need to fit it to previous knowledge, integration, rehearsal of some but not other aspects, reorganization, and recomprehending of previous experiences (Paris & Lindauer, 1977). This continual reshaping of our memory for events and information over time influences what new information we will consider meaningful enough to learn. It also results in memory representations that are conceptually simpler, easier to label, and consistent with our attitudes, temperaments, characters, developmental abilities, social backgrounds, and historical information. Brainerd and Reyna's (1993) *fuzzy-trace theory* suggests that we recall vague gists about information over time but lose the verbatim details. It makes sense that the deeper and more complexly information is processed to begin with, the longer it will be remembered.

Categorization, seeing the sameness between objects and events, is essential to promoting acquisition of knowledge. When a child encounters unfamiliar objects, events, or ideas, he or she will understand them far better if they can be linked with categories of knowledge that already are organized in ways that makes sense. When a child can categorize, new vocabulary can be linked more easily to known meanings, grammar can be generalized from a known phrase to a new phrase, and a child can even judge whether what he or she is about to do is likely to have the same consequences as other actions that already have been categorized as "good or bad," "safe or unsafe." There is evidence that as early as one year of age infants begin to categorize (Rescorla, 1981; Ross, 1980). Categorization ability continues to develop through the preschool and elementary

school years (Perlmutter & Myers, 1979; Scott, Serchuk, & Mundy, 1982; Whitney & Kunen, 1983).

Clearly, memory is not an isolated mental faculty or a passive storehouse of experience. It is a complex combination of an individual's information-processing abilities, personality, and experiences. It is easy to see how information that is already stored can be influential in guiding attention, giving meaning to, and ultimately storing, transforming, and retrieving new information. Therefore, the more knowledge a child has, the more the child can learn. Exposure to a broad range of knowledge, and practice with categorization skills, can help to make subsequent information more attention arousing, meaningful, and memorable.

The inefficient memories of students with learning disabilities are due in part to their inflexibility in activating and coordinating the knowledge they have already stored (Ashbaker & Swanson, 1996). Mary Anne's story (page 199) humorously illustrates how important it is to avoid assuming that our students have the necessary background information for a lesson. Teachers of the learning disabled know that, if their lesson is to stick, they must begin by activating any relevant background information the student may have.

Strategies

Even though preschoolers can describe good strategies to us, they seldom will use them to purposefully remember something (Paris & Lindauer, 1977; Sands & Doll, 1996). Because their short-term recall naturally is better for items that come later in a sequence (these items require less rehearsal to hold in memory than do earlier items), teaching sequences need to be kept short in order to aid recall (for example, teach numbers six through ten only after one through five have been mastered, instead of all ten numerals at once).

Efficient long-term storage of information requires memory strategies such as visualization or verbal rehearsal for which preschoolers are still too immature. Even after explicit instruction, they use

Mary Anne

In the twenty-five years I have taught children with learning disabilities, I have learned to always expect the unexpected and never, NEVER assume a student has prior knowledge of a subject, no matter how old, how intelligent, or how "streetwise" s/he is.

I can recall junior high students who didn't know the difference between the white and yellow pages of the phone book because they have never had the opportunity to use one. (If you can't read, you call the operator for a phone number.)

I remember the high school dropout who was learning how to plan and prepare a meal in a life-skills class. After the class selected burgers and fries as their main course, they had to construct a grocery list—rolls, ground hamburger, potatoes. . . . "Potatoes?" one young man inquired. "What do you need potatoes for?"

"The fries!" came the response.

"No kidding! Fries are made out of potatoes?"

But my favorite story came from a seventeen-year-old student, deficient in both auditory and visual processing, who shared his experience at his sisters's wedding with me: "My Ma says to me to stop by the drug store on the way to the reception and pick up a card for my sister. So I did, and I picked out this card with lots of pretty flowers on it cause I thought she'd like it. But when I got to the wedding reception, and my sister opened up the card, she started laughing, and she passes it around, and everybody starts laughing. So I says, 'What's so funny!'. . . . How was I supposed to know it was a "symphony" card! . . . But my ma said it was o.k. cause my sister only stayed married for six months anyway."

Source: Reprinted by permission of Mary Anne Coppola.

these strategies poorly. Not until the early school years are children more apt to use memory strategies on their own initiative. By age eight children have discovered a good deal about strategies, and by age ten they actually are likely to use the strategies they describe (Sands & Doll, 1986). It is not until the middle school to high school years, however, that these memory strategies become highly developed (Berk, 1997; Hagen, Jongeward, & Kail, 1975). Research Box 6–1 summarizes the order in which these memory strategies mature.

Flavell (1971) referred to "knowing how to go about learning and desiring to do so" as *metacognition*. Metacognition involves both knowledge of cognitive strategies that can be helpful (e.g., rehearsal) and monitoring the executive processes (strategy selection and modification) that direct the problem-solving approach. Children's metacognitive maturation is accompanied by a developmental trend toward greater reflectivity with the years (Berk, 1997; Smith & Caplan, 1988).

Typical learners vary greatly with respect to which memory strategies they choose to use and when and how they will use them (Butterfield, Wambold, & Belmont, 1973). Students with learning disabilities generally are far less mature in their repertoire, awareness, and use of these memory strategies. Often they do not use spontaneous verbal rehearsal efficiently, organize information for recall, use memory cues unless prompted, or use all the available cues; they seem unaware of how memory could be facilitated or which strategies are appropriate on different types of tasks (Owings et al., 1980).

RESEARCH BOX 6–1

The Maturation of Metacognitive Abilities

Older children automatically store, retain, and retrieve information better and differently than younger children because their knowledge base, conceptual systems, and strategic processing are more highly developed. For example, when they encode information, older children (ages seven to eight) are more selective and more exhaustive with respect to the relevant features. The fund of basic knowledge and relationships they have internalized help them to interpret situations as analogous, thereby enhancing their reasoning. Younger children (ages four to six), on the other hand, need to literally see the similarities between objects to draw the analogies (Siegler, 1989). The older child's knowledge and conceptual advantages make information more memorable because it is more familiar, meaningful, conceptually interrelated, and subject to the child's inferential ability and ability to fill in the gaps (Flavell & Wellman, 1977). Consequently, more and varied cues are available to aid recall.

Below age five, children seldom use deliberate plans to remember. When told to memorize, they perceive the information in an idle, purposeless fashion. As children mature, they begin to recognize that intensive, persistent, planned, goal-directed, intellectual interaction with the information will aid memory and retrieval (Paris & Lindauer, 1977). The younger elementary school child can be "trapped" into adopting appropriate memory strategies by the nature of the task, by the type of question, quality of pretraining, and by heightening motivation in order to counteract fatigue, boredom, and distractibility. Nevertheless, these children do not automatically seek out the best strategy for learning. The young child may not even use the same strategy on successive problems of the same type. The child may apply a strategy perfectly under one set of conditions but show no evidence of using that same strategy, or any strategy, under another set of conditions (Spiker & Cantor, 1983). For example, even when elementary and middle school students notice that they do not remember information they have read, many do not intentionally reinspect those portions of the text that could provide the information; when asked about this, many claim that it takes too much time or that "it is illegal" (Garner & Alexander, 1989, p. 145).

Research has found that after age five and through the teenage years, the automatic use and efficiency of memory strategies increase (Paris & Lindauer, 1977). Older children are more likely than younger ones to try alternate strategies when their initial strategy does not produce correct performance (Siegler, 1989). These strategies combine with a child's maturing knowledge base, conceptual abilities, and awareness of how memory works to increase memory abilities with age. Berk (1997) and Smith (1994) have summarized how children's awareness and use of memory strategies mature over time.

Naming and Verbal Rehearsal

Rehearsal efforts do little to aid memory until about six years of age. By first grade, children are transitioning toward spontaneous rehearsal; those who do rehearse are better at recalling items such as picture sequences. Although nonrehearsers can be induced to rehearse with minimal instruction and demonstration, and their memory will then equal that of

(Continues on following page)

RESEARCH BOX 6–1   *(Continued from preceding page)*

rehearsers, over half of these children revert to not rehearsing on other tasks. Spontaneous verbal rehearsal during memory tasks increases noticeably between ages five and ten. Younger children will verbalize stimulus names only while the stimuli are present, but older children will verbalize even in their absence. At ages eight to ten children tend to rehearse one item on a list at a time; but by sixth grade children will rehearse words in groups, thereby getting better at remembering lists of information.

Clustering in Order to Organize Material

By age four, children will group objects in order to help them remember (for example, cans in which M&Ms versus pegs have been hidden). They will not spontaneously cluster more abstract, verbal information. However, when instructed to group such information into categories, four year olds can generate the categories and their recall will improve. Nevertheless, they abandon this strategy when no longer directed to do so because it is so effortful. By second grade, being instructed to categorize helps more than repetition when learning lists of information. Until third grade, children's inclination is to use association as a memory aid (for example, linking *monkey* with *banana*), instead of studying same-category information together (for example, recalling all *animals* as a category and *foods* as another category). By eight years old and older, children automatically will think categorically, for example asking category questions in the game Twenty Questions ("Is it fruit?"); six year olds, on the other hand, will ask questions that confirm or eliminate one hypothesis at a time ("Is it a banana?" "Is it an apple?").

Elaborating through Associations

As six- through twelve-year-old children get better at inferring and elaborating on the meaning of stories, their memory for the content improves because they are processing this information more deeply. Recall also improves during these years because the children become able to use implied cues to access prior knowledge; at younger ages the cues need to be present in order to spur recall (for example, an empty cage to cue an animal name), yet the cue might be ignored or even named instead of the word to be recalled. Elaboration ability accelerates after age eleven and gradually continues to develop until adulthood. The richer the associations created with the information, the more children will rehearse this information as a cluster while studying and create multiple ways to cue their memory.

Visual Imagery

Preschoolers cannot generate images when told to do so. While six and seven year olds can generate these images, they are inefficient at using them to memorize information. By age eight, however, children can apply self-generated images to help themselves learn such things as object and picture names. Mental imagery increases in effectiveness until age eleven, when it becomes an effective strategy for recalling verbal, in addition to visual, material.

(Continues on following page)

RESEARCH BOX 6–1   *(Continued from preceding page)*

Monitoring Comprehension

First and second graders are less adept than third graders at judging whether they have understood incomplete directions for a game. Only by watching a partial demonstration or trying the task themselves can the younger children evaluate whether they need more information. Even sixth graders may not automatically recognize inconsistencies in a text they read; detection does increase by age twelve, if children are forewarned of the inconsistencies. An increase can be noted from second to fifth grade in children's ability to attend to the context if it will help memory, and to ignore the context when it is not helpful. Sixth graders also will reduce their reading speed and look back through material that is unclear to a greater extent than third graders; younger children may show puzzled expressions, but they have trouble explaining what is wrong. Interestingly, incidental learning rises until age eleven but declines thereafter because children get better at keeping their attention from being drawn to irrelevant aspects of tasks.

Highlighting and Recording Information

When told to do anything they wish to improve recall of a passage, fifth graders are far less likely to underline or take notes when compared to middle school and high school students. When these strategies are used automatically, they aid recall far more than when directed by an adult. The older students are more likely to paraphrase and reorganize the text as they underline or take notes, and they have more foresight about keeping written records of past problem-solving attempts so as not to repeat these or skip possible solutions.

Awareness of How Memory Works

Three- and four-year-old children understand that noise, lack of interest, and thinking about other things can hinder attentiveness to a task. By age five, they are aware that their memory is limited, and that the number of items to be learned will determine whether the task is easy or hard, as will the familiarity of the items, the amount of study time available, and whether recognition or recall is required. At about this time children recognize that optimal learning involves concentration, motivation, and avoidance of distractions. The ability to sense when they have studied well enough to remember a set of items improves noticeably through the elementary years, as does recognition that categorizable items in a list, opposites, or linking information through a story makes information more memorable than unrelated items. Similar improvements are seen in children's recognition that information too similar to the target information can interfere with memory, and that it is easier to recall something in one's own words than in others' words. As children become older, they can think of more ways to remember something, and these usually rely on self-responsibility ("I'll write it down") than external aids ("I'll ask mom to remind me"). Older students are more aware of and sensitive to the need to memorize; for example, they recognize that items not recalled on tests need more study than ones that were recalled. They also learn much better when they report using cognitive strategies, and they have a more realistic and accurate picture of their memory abilities and limitations than do younger children.

Research indicates that students with learning disabilities tend to spend less time studying information before indicating that they are ready to recall it, and then they recall less well than their peers (Dallago & Moely, 1980; Wong & Wilson, 1984). They often don't recognize that if they slowed down as the list of items to learn gets longer, their recall would increase. Instead they study at a constant rate (Bauer, 1987). Often, these students do not monitor their level of understanding of incoming information (Bos & Filip, 1984) or actively reason about the material; the text may be approached as though it contains random details to be memorized. The most frequent response to a comprehension question is to apply no line of reasoning at all (Kavale, 1980b). Hughes (1996) reports that in his interviews with college students with learning disabilities, they described their memorization strategy for tests as simply rereading the book.

Piaget (1976) believed that the more aware students are of their reasoning processes, the more knowledge they will be able to learn and then generalize to new situations. Subsequent studies have confirmed this belief (Ryan, Short, & Weed, 1986). For example, training Joey to ignore distractions (for example, to turn the TV off while studying) will be more effective if Joey understands why distractions do not help him problem solve. Praising Joey for turning the TV off, without explaining why that was a wise move, will not be as effective.

Because of the poor problem-solving approaches of students with learning disabilities, an important goal for teachers is to help these students employ more efficient metacognitive strategies by teaching what Bryant (1980) calls "LD efficient" lessons. Others call this process *metacognitive training*. Much of metacognitive training is built on Flavell's notion that mental and memory abilities are one and the same:

It has long been clear that what we know and how we think profoundly determines what and how we perceive, or speak, or imagine, or problem-solve, or predict; it is now becoming equally clear that all that knowledge and all that thinking also profoundly shape what and how we learn and remember. . . . Memory itself is mostly applied cognition. . . . The human mind

knows more and thinks better as it grows older, and these changes in *what* it knows and how it thinks have powerful effects on what it learns and remembers, *how* it learns and remembers, and even perhaps *when* it learns and remembers. (1971, p. 273)

Therefore, memory is "the development of intelligent structuring and storage of input, intelligent search and retrieval operations, and intelligent monitoring and knowledge of these storage and retrieval operations—a kind of 'meta-memory.' " (p. 277)

Examples of metacognition include knowing that one is forgetful and therefore writing reminder notes, recognizing one's strengths and weaknesses and choosing college courses or a vocation with these in mind, noting the necessity to prepare differently for essay and true–false tests, knowing to think about all alternatives before choosing an answer, or evaluating when note taking will be useful and when it will not (Flavell, 1976; Palincsar, 1986). Samuels (1986) explains that metacognitive skills are used in school

when a student must decide what the teacher wants; how much specificity and how much general overview the task requires; whether the task is one of importance; how much study is enough in order to do well on the test; when a comprehension breakdown occurs; what strategies are available to overcome a comprehension barrier; if the task is big, how does one approach it; what are the author's major and minor points; how this new information fits in with what is already known; should prior knowledge be altered in light of new information or should this new information be rejected? . . . The student is required to be aware of and to exert some control over the internal workings of the mind. . . . Knowledge of metacognitive skills and strategies allows students who are at first unsuccessful in school tasks to continue until they do achieve success. (p. 11)

These types of metacognitive behaviors are a subset of the broad category we refer to as good study skills. Both tend to automatically become better with age because the older youngster is more active, flexible, organized, and efficient in learning and retrieval strategies (Hagen et al., 1975).

Flavell's notions about metacognition are particularly relevant to the learning disabled because, when these youngsters are taught more efficient use of their cognitive abilities, they often do perform at higher skill levels and learn more intelligently (Lucangeli, Galderisi, & Cornoldi, 1995; Schumaker et al., 1983; Worden, 1986). The more automatic and effortless these strategies become, the better the learning because more attention can be devoted to the content and less to the strategy (Berk, 1997; Flavell, 1977; Flavell & Wellman, 1977). We find that learning strategies are most effective when self-generated, because they comfortably match the individual's learning style (Hagen, 1971; Levin, 1976). However, when students don't self-generate these approaches as they get older, they need to be taught. Early adolescence has been suggested as a prime time for such instruction because students are developmentally mature enough not only to profit from such training but also to apply what they have learned to new circumstances (Rohwer, 1971).

Visual imagery, verbal mediation, self-monitoring, and modeling are among the methods that have helped youngsters with learning disabilities learn to attend to the appropriate elements of their assignments, to organize them for recall, and then to retrieve them. Simple memory strategies incorporated into classroom lessons by teachers will improve learning for all children, but the learning disabled will experience particularly marked gains (Bulgren, Schumaker, & Deshler, 1994). Bulgren and colleagues found that the passing rates of students with learning disabilities on a social studies test increased from 11 to 77 percent when the teacher incorporated memory strategies into the lesson. If the teacher simply repeated the information, recall did not improve.

The more adept students become at using memory strategies, the more independent they can become as learners. Teachers are cautioned, however, that training in the use of these strategies must be extensive, or the strategies must be kept simple, because, until the strategy becomes automatic, processing resources may be diminished and attention diverted from the academic content (Worden, 1986).

Deshler and Schumaker (1986) suggest that students with learning disabilities should be expected to learn and intensively practice only three or four new strategies each year if these are to become automatic approaches to new learning. The more difficult of these strategies, such as those depicted in Figure 6–2, require at least a fourth to fifth grade reading competency to use them profitably for learning (Lenz, 1992). When introduced to these systems over several years, students develop breadth in strategies, each new strategy building in a synergistic fashion on previous ones. These strategies are most helpful when students are told why a strategy will be helpful and given feedback that it indeed is working to improve their skills (Schunk & Rice, 1992). Teaching these strategies is critical because research suggests that students with learning disabilities can remember just as well as their peers, provided the information is stored meaningfully and deeply in the first place (Brainerd, Kingma, & Howe, 1986).

Visual Imagery. Teaching youngsters to mentally imagine the material they are studying has been very helpful in aiding language acquisition, reading comprehension, and learning of prose and word pairs, among other things (Clark et al., 1984; Ferro & Pressley, 1991; Lesgold, McCormick, & Golinkoff, 1975; Levin et al., 1974; Moeser & Bregman, 1973; Rose, Cundick, & Higbee, 1983). Levin's (1973) study, for example, found that the reading comprehension of poor readers increased when they thought of a picture to associate with each sentence in a passage. Because children below the age of eight have difficulty creating images to mirror what they have read, imagery becomes a helpful technique only for slightly older children (Pressley, Johnson, & Symons, 1987).

It frequently has been found that picture cues assist learning for some youngsters more than do verbal instructional approaches (Ferro & Pressley, 1991; Paivio, 1969; Pressley, 1977). Picture cues apparently help students generate inferences, which later serve as useful retrieval cues (Pressley & Miller, 1987). When students describe the images to themselves and store this verbal information, then they have both visual and verbal cues to call on to help their recall. Figure 6–3 illustrates the type of visual images that

Multipass: A Textbook Reading Strategy

Survey the chapter using TISOPT

    T = Title read and paraphrased

    I = Introduction read verbatim and paraphrased

    S = Summary read verbatim and paraphrased

    O = Organization analyzed by reading headings

    P = Pictures examined

    T = Table of contents examined

Size up the information in the chapter using IQ-WHO

    I = Illustrations interpreted

    Q = Questions at the end of the chapter read and paraphrased

    W = Words in italics defined

    H = Headings: for each, do RASPN

        R = Read a heading

        A = Ask self a question based on heading topic

        S = Scan for the answer

        P = Put answer in own words

        N = Note important information

    O = Other clues that textbook employs are identified and used

Sort out what has been learned from what needs to be learned using RAMS

    R = Read the question

    A = Answer the question if known

    M = Mark the question to indicate status

    S = SEARCH for the answer

        S = Select a single heading

        E = Examine the content carefully

        A = Answer question if possible

        R = Repeat under another heading if needed

        C = Check with someone if still not found

        H = Hassle questions clarified with teacher

RIDER: A Visual Imagery Strategy for Reading Comprehension

    R = Read (the sentence)

    I = Image (make an image or picture in your mind)

    D = Describe (describe how the new image is different from the last sentence)

    E = Evaluate (as you make the image, check to make sure it contains everything necessary)

    R = Repeat (as you read the next sentence repeat the steps to RIDE)

DEFENDS: A Writing Strategy for Defending a Position

    D = Decide on exact position

    E = Examine the reasons for the position

    F = Form a list of points that explain each reason

    E = Expose position in the first sentence

    N = Note each reason and supporting points

    D = Drive home the position in the last sentence

    S = SEARCH for errors and correct

        S = See if it makes sense

        E = Eject incomplete sentences

        A = Ask if it's convincing

        R = Reveal COPS errors & correct

            C = Capitalization

            O = Overall appearance

            P = Punctuation

            S = Spelling

        C = Copy over neatly

        H = Have a last look

(Continues on following page)

Figure 6–2   The learning strategies approach. *Source:* Ellis, E. S., & Lenz, B. K. (1987). A component analysis of effective learning strategies for LD students. *Learning Disabilities Focus, 2,* 97–101. Reprinted by permission of the Division of Learning Disabilities.

WRITER: A Monitoring for Written Errors Strategy

  W = Write on every other line

  R = Read the paper for meaning

  I = Interrogate yourself using "COPS" questions

   C = Have I capitalized the first word and all proper nouns?

   O = How is the overall appearance?

   P = Have I used end punctuation, commas, and semicolons correctly?

   S = Do the words look like they are spelled right, can I sound them out, or should I use the dictionary?

  T = Take the paper to someone to proofread again

  E = Execute a final copy

  R = Reread your paper a final time

RAP: A Paraphrasing Strategy for Reading Comprehension

  R = Read a paragraph

  A = Ask yourself what were the main idea and two details

  P = Put main idea and details in your own words

FIST: A Self-Questioning Strategy for Reading Comprehension

  F = First sentence in the paragraph is read

  I = Indicate a question based on information in the first sentence

  S = Search for the answer to the question

  T = Tie the answer to the question with a paraphrase

PREPARE: A Strategy for Preparing for Class

  P = Plan locker visits

  R = Reflect on what you need and get

  E = Erase personal needs

  P = PSYC self up

   P = Pause for attitude check

   S = Say a personal goal related to the class

   Y = Yoke in negative thoughts

   C = Challenge self to good performance

  A = Ask self where class has been and where class is going

  R = Review notes and study guide

  E = Explore meaning of teacher's introduction

Figure 6–2 *Continued*

students can create for themselves to help remember typical social studies content. Teacher-prepared visual aids that simplify text into images also facilitate attention, comprehension, and learning (Bergerud, Lovitt, & Horton, 1988).

Verbal Mediation. The powerful effect of self-verbalization on learning was demonstrated years ago by Bandura, Grusec, and Menlove (1966). As children observed a scene, they either verbalized the model's actions, just watched, or verbalized irrelevant material. The investigators found that imitation of the model's behavior occurred more often with appropriate verbalization, less with just watching, and least with inappropriate verbalization. Verbal self-instruction, self-questioning techniques, and mnemonics have since been identified as powerful mediators for learning.

Verbal Self-Instruction. Donald Meichenbaum (1977) applied Bandura's, Vygotsky's (1962), and Luria's (1961) principles about the self-regulatory function of speech to help students focus attention on task-relevant stimuli and behaviors in a more mature, instrumental, organized, and self-guided fashion. First students observe the instructor modeling task-appropriate behaviors such as sizing up the problem, focusing on relevant aspects, doing the task, self-evaluating performance, and correcting errors. Students next go through three stages of performing the task: (1) under the instructor's verbal directions; (2) on their own while self-

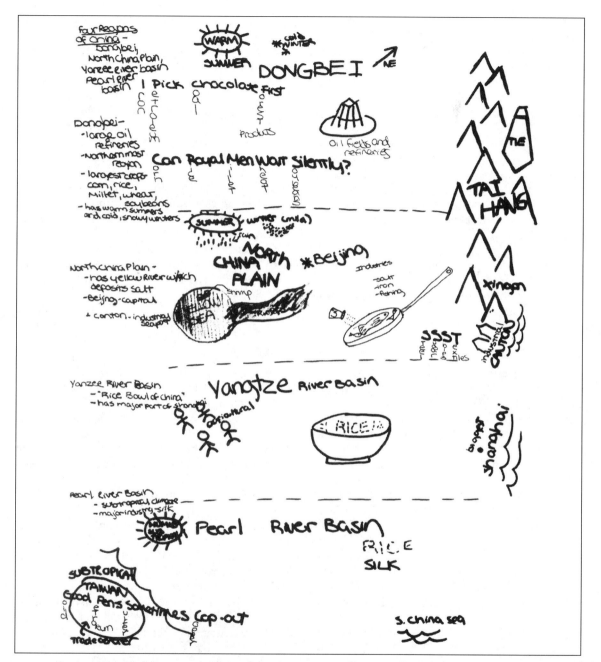

Figure 6–3 Images of China. This ninth grader has arranged the geographic regions of China from north to south along the page. Pictures are used to aid recall (e.g., a bowl of rice to represent "Rice Bowl of China"; stick figures of farmers to depict an agricultural society; fish being salted in a frying pan to depict the salt, fishing, and iron industries). Frequent use has been made of mnemonics (e.g., first letters of words in sentences spur recall of industrial products; a drawing of a necktie helps to recall the name of the "Tai" Hang mountain region).

instructing aloud or in a whisper; and (3) on their own while self-instructing silently.

Use of steps 2 and 3 increases automatically as preschoolers get older (Flavell & Wellman, 1976). By the age of three and a half, most children already give themselves verbal self-instructions. By age five, these overt self-verbalizations as a child tries to understand a problem typically become inaudible to others (Tarnopol & Tarnopol, 1977). The more the five year old verbalizes silently to himself or herself, the better the child's ability to memorize (Adler, 1993). At this age self-generated instructions facilitate problem solving just as much as do instructions that adults ask children to repeat (Miller, Shelton, & Flavell, 1970). By the early elementary years self-verbalization becomes a reliable tool in aiding memory (Adler, 1993).

Meichenbaum's method appears to be most useful to youngsters who don't spontaneously analyze their experience in verbal terms and therefore don't approach problem solving in a planful manner. By literally talking to themselves, impulsive children can increase their problem-solving skills dramatically (Meichenbaum & Goodman, 1971; Orbach, 1977; Weithorn & Kagan, 1978). This method also has improved the attention to task and math productivity of children who are learning disabled, number and quality of revisions while composing, essay length, spelling, capitalization and punctuation, handwriting accuracy, math operations, main idea identification, and reading comprehension as every few sentences are paraphrased; when students talk themselves through a task with encouraging self-statements, success also increases (Graham & MacArthur, 1988; Kamann & Wong, 1993; Leon & Pepe, 1983; Rose et al., 1983; Schunk & Cox, 1986; Schunk & Rice, 1993; Wood, Rosenberg, & Carran, 1993).

With one exception, as overt or inner speech increases, so does task success (Garrity, 1975; Jensen, 1971; Sheingold & Shapiro, 1976). The exception is when a three-and-a-half-year-old or younger child is using self-commands to inhibit a motor activity. Often these self-commands end up generating the very motor activity the child wanted to inhibit (Luria, 1977). For example, the preschooler who approaches the hot stove and says "no touch," often goes ahead and touches. But, by age four to four and a half, the language content of a self-instruction overcomes the motor discharge aspect and the preschooler obeys the "no touch" self-verbalization. This is why mothers of three-year-old children warn Aunt Fritzie to put all her breakables out of reach before they arrive for their Sunday visit. No amount of telling Robin not to touch will help. In fact, telling Robin "don't touch" propels her toward these treasures. A year later, however, Aunt Fritzie no longer has to clear the decks. A simple reminder is enough; Robin eyes all the treasures but resists touching.

Meichenbaum's approach also has been used successfully to teach students cognitive strategies for monitoring their inappropriate behavior tendencies. The student's behavior is broken down into small units, and he or she is made aware of the sequence of situations that typically result in specific, inappropriate behavioral and cognitive reactions. Verbal self-instructions then help the youngster to interrupt a chain of events early and alter responses that he or she typically would have made. Larson and Gerber (1987), for example, found that intensive use of these strategies to analyze interpersonal interactions decreased the numbers of negative behavior reports about incarcerated delinquents with learning disabilities.

Research has found that teaching a child to say inhibiting instructions to oneself ("I'm not going to look at what Joey is doing") may be even more helpful in maintaining attention to a task than task-facilitative self-instructions ("I'm going to look at my work") (Patterson & Mischel, 1976). It may be that inhibition self-instructions prove to be the most beneficial because inhibiting behavior appears to be neurochemically much harder than actually attending to something.

Meichenbaum (1976) suggests using his method to turn around the negative self-statements with which students who are learning disabled often approach tasks ("I'll never be able to do that"). Such thoughts only contribute to inadequate performance and need to be replaced with positive self-statements such as "Now I'm getting it," "I can handle this." The PREPARE strategy in Figure 6–2 incorporates this type of approach (PSYC) to boost a "can do" attitude.

Self-Questioning Techniques. A variety of procedures that use questioning to aid reading comprehension will be discussed in Chapter 10. These strategies, for example those in Figure 6–4, have resulted in improved comprehension in content area subject matter and in solution of math word problems (Hutchinson, 1993; Palincsar, 1986; Simmonds, 1992; Wong & Jones, 1982; Wong et al., 1986). Most often these techniques focus on helping the student learn to survey the task, clarify the purpose, summarize the main idea and details, clarify ambiguities (by rereading, asking for help), recite important facts, and heighten interest and evaluation by predicting what might happen next.

Mnemonics. Mnemonic strategies also have been found to be helpful with the learning disabled. Many of us use mnemonics daily in the form of acronyms to remember our grocery list (for example, PEAR = popcorn, eggs, applesauce, raisins). Ellis and Lenz (1987) illustrate the use of this *first-letter* method in memorizing the major fatal diseases at the turn of the century (syphilis, typhoid, rabies, influenza, polio, diabetes). When combined, the first letter of each item forms the word STRIP + D. This, when used in a sentence that relates to the topic, facilitates recall: "If you got any of these diseases in 1900, you had to go and *STRIP* at the *Doctor's.*"

Figure 6–2 illustrates further uses of acronyms to enhance organized approaches to learning. Another example, the PLEASE strategy, when taught to sixth graders with learning disabilities, improved composition quality in only half a school year (Welch, 1992):

P = Pick a topic,

L = List your ideas about the topic,

E = Evaluate your list,

A = Activate the paragraph with a topic sentence,

S = Supply supporting sentences,

E = End with a concluding sentence, and
    Evaluate your work.

Self-Questions for Representing Algebra Word Problems

1. Have I read and understood each sentence? Are there any words whose meaning I have to ask?
2. Have I got the whole picture, a representation, for this problem?
3. Have I written down my representation on the worksheet? (goal; unknown(s); known(s); type of problem; equation)
4. What should I look for in a new problem to see if it is the same kind of problem?

Self-Questions for Solving Algebra Word Problems

1. Have I written an equation?
2. Have I expanded the terms?
3. Have I written out the steps of my solution on the worksheet? (collected like terms; isolated unknown(s); solved for unknown(s); checked my answer with the goal; highlighted my answer)
4. What should I look for in a new problem to see if it is the same kind of problem?

Figure 6–4 Self-questions on prompt cards. *Source:* Hutchinson, N. L. (1993). Effects of cognitive strategy instruction on algebra problem solving of adolescents with learning disabilities. *Learning Disability Quarterly, 16,* p. 39.

Another mnemonic device, the *keyword method*, is illustrated in Figures 6–5, 6–6, and 6–7. In Figure 6–5, for example, Mastropieri and colleagues (1985) used a picture to focus on the keyword *rain*, which would then remind the student of the vocabulary word *ranid*. *Ranid* means *frog*. Emphasis was on learning the keyword to cue recall of the vocabulary word and its meaning. Junior high school students with learning disabilities practiced several such vocabulary items at a time. Students who studied the same pictures without being told the mnemonic (rain) spent 43 percent longer in training than did those in the mnemonic condition, yet the recall of students who were given the mnemonic was nearly 80 percent compared with 31 percent for the nonmemnonic group. The interesting part of this study is that, in a replication, and in another study (King-Sears, Mercer, & Sindelar, 1992) in which students had to figure out

Wisconsin (whisk broom)   Madison (maid)

Figure 6–6   Mnemonic illustration depicting Madison as capital of Wisconsin. Wisconsin is recalled by associating it with the keyword *whisk broom*, and Madison with the keyword *maid*. *Source:* Mastropieri, M. A., Scruggs, T. E., Bakken, J. P., & Brigham, F. J. (1992). A complex mnemonic strategy for teaching states and their capitals: Comparing forward and backward associations. *Learning Disabilities Research & Practice, 7*, p. 97. Reprinted by permission of the Division of Learning Disabilities.

RANID   {rain}   frog

Figure 6–5   Pictorial mnemonic keyword vocabulary illustration. The word *ranid*, which means "frog," is recalled by associating a similar-looking keyword, *rain*, with a scene of a frog enjoying the rain. *Source:* Mastropieri, M. A., Scruggs, T. E., Levin, J. R., Gaffney, J., & McLoone, B. (1985). Mnemonic vocabulary instruction for learning disabled students, *Learning Disability Quarterly, 8*, 57–63, p. 58. Reprinted by permission of the Division of Learning Disabilities.

how the keywords related or create their own keywords and illustrations, the students did not learn as well as when the experimenter or teacher actually provided the illustration and explanation. While students enjoy generating their own mnemonics, and their products do enhance memory beyond typical teaching strategies, many children find the process difficult and the pace is so slow that a substantial amount of content that could have been learned during this time is sacrificed (Fulk, Mastropieri, & Scruggs, 1992; King-Sears et al., 1992; Scruggs & Mastropieri, 1992).

The keyword method has proved helpful in mastering mathematics, English and foreign language vocabulary (e.g., the Italian word *fonda*, meaning *bag*, is depicted as a phone within a bag), and high school science and history content as

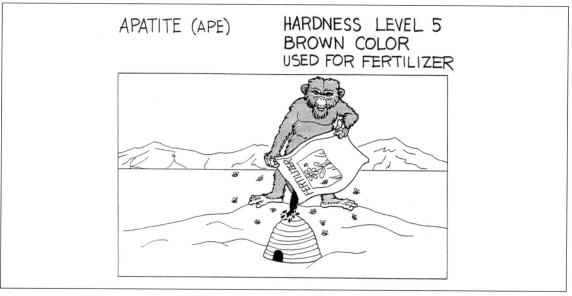

Figure 6–7 Mnemonic instruction. The properties of the mineral *apatite* are learned with this mnemonic: *ape,* both the ape and apatite are brown; the hardness level of apatite is *five,* which rhymes with hive; and it is used for *fertilizer. Source:* Scruggs, T. E., Mastropieri, M. A., Levin, J. R., McLoone, B., Gaffney, J. S., & Prater, M. A. (1985). Increasing content-area learning: A comparison of mnemonic and visual-spatial direct instruction. *Learning Disabilities Research, 1,* p. 20. Reprinted by permission.

well (Bulgren et al., 1995; Scruggs & Mastropieri, 1990). For example, Levin and colleagues' (1983) study found that students' memory for social studies information about the town of Fostoria (keyword, *frost*), which was noted for its abundant natural resources, advances in technology, wealth, and growing population, was aided by depicting crowds of people, scattered money, oil pumps, and computers all covered with frost.

Yet another mnemonic variation uses segments of words that must be memorized (for example, Concord is the capital of New Hampshire) to form a phrase or sentence that will cue recall (for example, "The old man walked his *ham*ster down the street with a *cord* around its neck"). This method is illustrated in Figure 6–6. When Scruggs and colleagues (1992) used this method to present middle school students with a map of mnemonically coded 18th century North American battle sites (see example in right column),

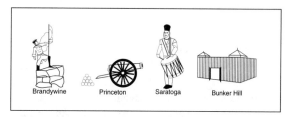

versus not coded battle sites (below),

the mnemonic condition resulted in significantly better ability to locate specific battles on a map and indicate whether the British (colored red in all conditions) or Americans (colored blue) had won.

Finally, the *pegword method* also is quite effective. This involves choosing a word that relates to each item in a numbered list, so as to rhyme with the designated number, such as *hive* with *five* in Figure 6–7, the first ten amendments to the Constitution, or the order of admission of states to the United States. Mnemonic methods have been shown to increase information acquisition beyond that accomplished by typical instructional techniques (Bulgren et al., 1994; Scruggs & Mastropieri, 1990). For example, when students with learning disabilities were taught the names and numbers of 8 presidents for each of two weeks, Mastropieri, Scruggs, and Whedon (1997) found that the traditional method of rehearsing the name and number while looking at the presidents' pictures resulted in recall of 3.8 presidents' names and 5 numbers. On the other hand, when using mnemonics (for example, Franklin Pierce, the 14th president, depicted by a purse being pierced by a fork), students on average recalled 11 presidents' names and 9.6 numbers.

Self-Monitoring. Many metacognitive training studies have taught students how to monitor their classroom behavior and scan material appropriately before deciding on answers. One approach, for example, used the visual prompt and self-monitoring sheet in Figure 6–8 to increase on-task behavior of teenagers with learning disabilities. Using a cassette tape with or without headphones, the students heard a tone at random intervals averaging every one to two and one-half minutes. When hearing this prompt, they checked their self-monitoring sheets. The tones were faded over time. In most studies that have focused on improving attention to task, attention has improved 50 to 100 percent by asking children to periodically record whether they are attending (Reid, 1996). In addition to on-task behavior, math, reading, and spelling have benefited from training students to periodically monitor a number of behaviors, such as inappropriate self-verbalizations, productivity, attention, task accuracy, delay of responding while examining alternatives, breaking tasks down into parts, examining and

recalling details, looking for similarities and differences, and systematically eliminating alternatives (Blick & Test, 1987; Brown & Alford, 1984; Reid, 1996; Rooney, Polloway, & Hallahan, 1985; Salend, Whittaker, & Reeder, 1993). Teaching a student to monitor his or her strategies has more long-lasting effects than merely instructing the student to take more time before answering (Egeland, 1974).

Self-monitoring strategies have been effective in additional ways: by helping students to learn to detect their own errors; to attend to task during independent seatwork so that the number of times the adult initiates assistance and the duration of adult-student interactions are reduced; to decrease inappropriate verbalization in the classroom; to improve reading comprehension, the quality of written compositions, handwriting, assignment and homework completion, and more (Blandford & Lloyd, 1987; Digangi, Maag, & Rutherford, 1991; Graves, 1986; Martin & Manno, 1995; Reid, 1996; Rooney & Hallahan, 1988; Salend et al., 1991). In addition, requiring students to actually graph their on-task behavior after using self-monitoring cards has been found to be very helpful in increasing their on-task behavior, productivity, and accuracy (Digangi et al., 1991).

Modeling. Most metacognitive training strategies incorporate some modeling. Watching others perform correctly can have a strong vicarious effect on learning strategies. Several studies have successfully used modeling to increase reflectivity in impulsive children with learning disabilities, especially when the child actually imitates the model's actions (Cullinan, Kauffman, & LeFleur, 1975; Nagle & Thwaite, 1979; Ridberg, Parke, & Hetherington, 1971). Modeling has been effective in enhancing reading comprehension, computation skills, question asking and answering behavior (after watching, rehearsing, and receiving feedback during videotaped segments of classmates' questioning behavior), problem-solving skills, and more (Jenkins et al., 1987; Kanpczyk, 1991; Mastropieri, Scruggs, & Shiah, 1991; Montague, Applegate, & Marquard, 1993; Rivera & Smith, 1988; Simmonds, 1990). Modeling seems to

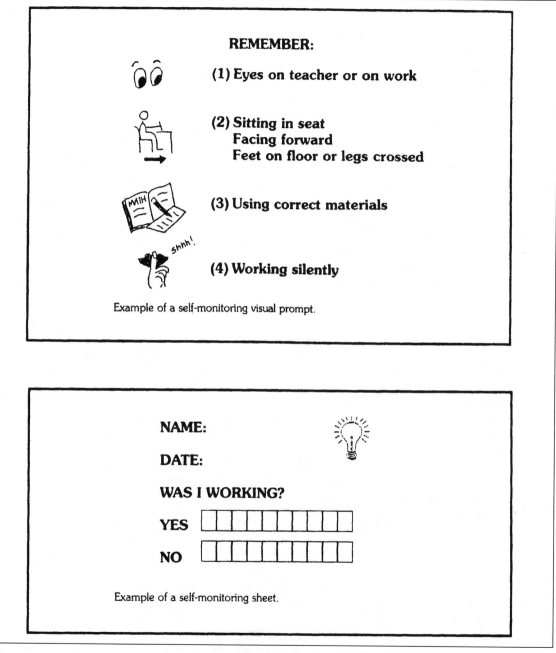

REMEMBER:

(1) Eyes on teacher or on work

(2) Sitting in seat
Facing forward
Feet on floor or legs crossed

(3) Using correct materials

(4) Working silently

Example of a self-monitoring visual prompt.

NAME:

DATE:

WAS I WORKING?

YES

NO

Example of a self-monitoring sheet.

Figure 6–8   Example of an effective self-monitoring aid. *Source:* Prater, M. A., Chilman, R. J. B., Temple, J., & Miller, S. R. (1991). Self-monitoring of on-task behavior by adolescents with learning disabilities. *Learning Disability Quarterly, 14,* p. 169. Reprinted by permission of the Council for Learning Disabilities.

work because attention is drawn to aspects of tasks that students ordinarily would not have noticed. For this same reason, problem solving in a group can be especially beneficial to youngsters with learning disabilities because these students profit from having their attention drawn to the strategies and reasoning used by their peers. A particularly powerful form of modeling with respect to eliciting behavior change is watching carefully edited videotapes of oneself acting appropriately in a given situation. This is accompanied by discussion of the target behavior, role play, and teacher reinforcement (Clark et al., 1992).

Other Metacognitive Approaches. Other metacognitive approaches that can help students to spontaneously analyze their experiences, form rules for active problem solving, and make information more memorable include the following:

- elaborating ideas by adding meaningful enhancements. This is among the most used and effective—but latest to mature—strategies (Berk, 1997; Paris & Haywood, 1973). Students with learning disabilities tend not to self-generate these associations spontaneously (Wiig & Semel, 1975);

- chunking or clustering (as in telephone numbers). Because students with learning disabilities often do not respond to the grouping of material, even if the material is organized into categories, methods have been developed to draw their attention to these categories so as to facilitate recall (Gelzheiser, Shepherd, & Wozniak, 1986; Parker, Freston, & Drew, 1975);

- paraphrasing material;

- developing uniquely personal approaches to material; sometimes these will work better than suggestions imposed by the teacher;

- reviewing material at distributed intervals;

- using associations;

- reviewing relevant known information before beginning to study new information, so that a schema is generated within which to organize the new content;

- highlighting relationships in the material;

- generating principles and inferences that are linked with specific content;

- stopping to draw conclusions;

- creating new ideas;

- making judgments;

- distinguishing between different requirements for multiple choice versus essay exams, and planning one's studies accordingly (Hughes, 1996).

Reports of applications of these metacognitive approaches abound in our journals. They even have been awarded such special names as meta-listening, metacomprehension, and metamemory, depending on the skill being enhanced. Despite the enthusiasm for learning strategy training, generalization of these strategies to novel tasks on which strategy training has not occurred has been disappointing (Berk, 1997; Schumaker et al., 1983; Short & Ryan, 1984; Wong, 1987). Consequently, we continue to seek better ways to encourage students to actively apply these powerful tools to their everyday problem solving.

Chapter 10 will present more specific strategies for developing study skills, test-taking skills, and transfer of school knowledge to survival skills important for employment and independent living.

Visual-Perceptual, Motor, and Language Development

Given the abundant evidence that a learning strategies approach can improve attention and learning, it is believed that many students with learning disabilities may be impaired in learning strategies alone, rather than in their basic ability to learn (Adelman & Taylor, 1983; Deshler & Schumaker, 1986; Torgesen, 1980). These students' underachievement is believed to be due solely to the inefficient way in which they go about learning. To better understand the difference between learning strategy inefficiencies and ability deficits, consider the times you haven't remembered the names of people you were introduced to. You complain about your awful memory, but you know very well that your memory is good. What really happened is that you just never consciously bothered to remember. You never repeated, organized, or rehearsed the names so as to remember them for more than a few seconds. Had the people you were introduced to been particularly notable physically, famous, or of interest in some other way, you might have made more of an effort to remember their names.

Unfortunately, many students with learning disabilities are not lucky enough to be impaired at only the learning strategy end. Many have basic ability delays in attention, visual-perceptual, motor, and language development that make it hard to absorb information, to pull stored information from memory, and to demonstrate one's knowledge and thoughts to others. Academic achievement suffers because these insufficiently developed information-processing skills cannot support higher level achievement; moreover, because these information-processing skills are not automatic, they compete with incoming information for attentional resources in students' working memories.

Research finds that the greater the neurological involvement in childhood, the greater the academic deficits that persist into adulthood (Silver & Hagin, 1964, 1966; Spreen & Haaf, 1986). Youngsters who underachieve in all academic areas tend to have both visual-perceptual and language impairments (Fletcher, 1985; Fletcher & Satz, 1985; Shafrir & Siegel, 1994). Those who experience reading and spelling disabilities, yet no difficulty with arithmetic, tend to have language weaknesses but perceptual strengths. Youngsters with arithmetic disabilities, but adequate reading and spelling, tend to have the opposite pattern (perceptual weaknesses but language strengths); these youngsters often experience greater social and emotional difficulties than do those with perceptual strengths.

Despite the above group trends, there is a great deal of variability within each group (Fletcher & Morris, 1986). The strength/weakness patterns that contribute to a specific student's

learning disabilities frequently are not this clear-cut. In addition, with the passing of time, maturation and compensation tend to refine and integrate many cognitive and information-processing functions, so these weaknesses are manifested in more subtle ways in teenagers or adults. With time, patterns can also change.

Although patterns can change, one cannot sit back and wait for development to take its course. It is important to identify, remediate, and develop compensations for any information-processing inefficiencies that are interfering with success on classroom tasks. For example, when a child's spelling difficulty is caused by poor perception of the order of sounds in words, the child must be helped to develop phoneme segmentation skills through phonological awareness training and continued phonetic instruction in reading and spelling. When a weak pencil grasp contributes to poor writing, this skill must be taught. In the case of poor social communication, the teacher might observe a student's social interactions and point out precisely what, in that situation, the student might have said differently. For example, when someone says "Hi," you say "Hi" back; when your friend asks if you're going to the dance, you answer the question instead of kidding him about his girlfriend. When your friend calls you an "idiot," it means that you are appreciated. It is not an insult, and you should not slug him. Likewise, when a novel is linguistically too difficult, the teacher might assign an easier version to facilitate comprehension, while also directly teaching the harder vocabulary, grammar, and idioms.

Wade and Kass (1987) showed that reading progress of eight- to eleven-year-old children was enhanced far more when information-processing skills also were reinforced during reading instruction than when the children received only standard academic remediation. In this study, children practiced several information-processing skills: haptic discrimination (attending to how their hand movements felt when writing words from memory); visualization of wholes versus parts (pointing to words while reading; recognizing prefixes, suffixes, syllabication, and inflections; finding words in the text after exercises highlighted specific definitions, antonyms, and synonyms); figure-ground discrimination of important from unimportant details (drawing a picture about the story and then writing a title for it); and homework that combined these skills. Because Wade and Kass's students were using relevant classroom material to sharpen their information-processing skills, these activities proved valuable. A good rule of thumb for teachers is to train only those information-processing skills that have immediate, direct transfer value to obvious skills needed for academic progress.

When persistent information-processing problems interfere with learning, the teacher needs to modify the tasks that prove troublesome in order to circumvent the source of difficulty. The teacher might, for example, assign a version of *Romeo and Juliet* that does not use Elizabethan vocabulary. The student with continuing left–right confusions in driver education might be told to wear a *ring* on his *right* hand in order to help differentiate directions. When concentration appears to be a problem, the instructor might consider shorter lectures, less distracting study environments, more varied teaching formats, previewing content, activity-oriented instruction, or learning strategy instruction. In the case of persistent language delays, a high school student might meet the foreign language requirement by substituting American Sign Language classes. For the student who finds writing particularly trying because of time pressures and the basic manipulative difficulty, typing may be an alternative, provided that the perceptual and coordination demands of typing do not preclude it from being a workable solution.

To be sensitive to delays in basic information-processing abilities, it is necessary to appreciate the normal course of development of these skills. Before we describe this development, it is important to recognize that children do not develop smoothly, each month being able to do something in a more complex way than the previous month. Instead, development is characterized by spurts and plateaus. One day two-and-a-half-year-old Elana has only thirty words in her vocabulary; the next day she awakens and miraculously uses fifteen new words. One week four-year-old Jeffrey thinks that a deck of cards is for tossing around the room; the next week he actually can play Old Maid. One evening six-and-one-half-year-old Leah tries to read a book, gives up in frustration, and begs her mother to read to her. The next morning she awakens able to read that book all by herself. While Elana is making these enormous language strides, her motor development may remain rather static. While Jeffrey's attending ability is mushrooming, his toileting skills unfortunately may slip a bit. All these ups and downs are to be expected.

Spurts in young children's development, veritable cognitive explosions, are especially evident at ages two and six. This enormous growth in language, perception, thought, attention, and coordination corresponds with natural spurts in brain growth: myelinization, synapse formation, new neuronal branching, increasing dendrite length, and the development of folds as the cortex grows (Epstein, 1980; Rourke et al., 1983). Sudden increases in attention, judgment, planning, and organization occur at periodic intervals during development, but especially at ages fourteen to sixteen and in early adulthood (Epstein, 1980).

Students with learning disabilities, whether qualitatively different in their information processing or merely immature in comparison to their peers, will benefit from being exposed to the next most difficult task dictated by normal developmental progressions (Brainerd, Kingma, & Howe, 1986; Fygetakis & Ingram, 1973; Wiig et al., 1977; Wiig & Semel, 1976). Therefore, familiarity with the typical development of information-processing skills helps us to plan the next higher objective for remedial attention. It also gives us ideas on how to identify and capitalize on students' strengths during instruction. In the remainder of this chapter we shall contrast the normal development of visual-perceptual, motor, and language skills, from infancy through adulthood, with that of students with learning disabilities.

Visual Perception

Visual perception is the process whereby a person detects and gains meaning from visual material. The sequence in which visual-perceptual skills are acquired is important to appreciate because children with learning disabilities who are maturing slowly in these areas tend to resolve their lags in a way that follows the normal continuum of development. Understanding the order in which visual-perceptual skills develop helps to direct our assessments and guide remedial planning. For example, because a preference for matching by shape occurs earlier than matching by color, the preschooler with perceptual delays should be taught to match shapes first and then colors. Shapes, rather than colors, then become excellent cues to incorporate into more conceptual types of matching activities (for example, match fruits that are *round* before those that are *red*).

Knowledge of the order of visual-perceptual development gives us many remedial hints: help students discriminate verticals, perpendiculars, up–down, and asymmetrical figures before left–right reversal figures, diagonals, or symmetrical figures; draw attention to the borders of objects, designs, and letters first, then to the internal elements, and finally to both combined; focus on three-dimensional before two-dimensional perceptions (Smith, 1991). To illustrate, consider position in space, which is such a salient dimension for young children that it is not uncommon for older preschoolers to outperform college students when playing a game in which position is the cue to be discovered (Zeaman & Hanley, 1983). Next time you're playing with a one year old, pick up any object and place it to the infant's left. Now to the right. Now out of reach in the center. Now to the right again. You'll be surprised by the delighted chuckles that this simple maneuver provokes. Because position is such a salient element for older preschoolers, we find that concentration games are excellent ways to reinforce their basic concepts.

Researchers have discovered that newborns and young infants have a great deal of visual-perceptual ability—much more ability than we thought in the past. For example, by two months of age infants can discriminate colors, by three months familiar and unfamiliar faces, by four months simple shapes, and by six months differences among sets having different numbers of objects (Berk, 1997; Smith, 1991). Likewise,

preschoolers make quite complex visual discriminations relatively early. By ages three to four children can distinguish numbers and letters from scribbles and pictures. Letter discrimination begins by distinguishing letters with straight lines from those with curves. Older preschoolers will shift their focus to the internal elements of the figures, but by six years of age, they orient themselves to both the outer configuration and internal elements, which sharpens their letter recognition and copying (Akshoomoff & Stiles, 1995; Smith, 1994). It is not until age seven that form discriminations that differ in rotation, reversal, and perspective become easy for children (Gibson et al., 1962). At this age, 85 percent of children finally can point to their left and right sides accurately (Nichols & Chen, 1981). These developmental trends help to explain why young children find letters that look similar so confusing. Therefore, when first learning to read and print, children will frequently miscall reversible letters and write letters backward, left–right mirror images being the most difficult. These reversals normally disappear by the mid-elementary school years, although they do persist longer for the child with learning disabilities.

Gibson and colleagues (1962) believe that the frequency of reversals in preschoolers is due to their lack of experience with left–right transformations being distinctive features that must be taken into account. Until school age, when the way a letter faces actually changes its name (*p-q, b-d*), left–right orientation is not an important characteristic. A toy truck is a truck, no matter what the orientation, whether on its side or upside down. Up-down transformations are not as troublesome as left–right transformations, Gibson believes, because children have had more experience with them (it is important if a cup of milk is turned upside down, but there is no consequence if it faces left or right). Miles and Ellis (1981) explain in another way: "up" remains "up" and "down" remains "down" whichever way one is facing; however, if one turns around, one has to shift one's account of what is on the left and what is on the right. Miles and Ellis found that even in typical college students, a decision about whether one item was to the left or right of another took longer than above–below decisions. Other theories for children's reversal tendencies include the finding that discrimination is more difficult when two figures face one another around a symmetrical axis (Huttenlocker, 1967) or when the two figures' missing lines are in line with one another (Bryant, 1974). Casey (1986) points out that the very activity of learning to read will help to sharpen children's sensitivity to mirror images and left versus right.

Because visual perception of form and space develops so early in life, simple types of visual processing do not appear at fault when preschoolers with learning disabilities cannot match colors and shapes or differentiate between letters. If these simple visual perceptions had not already developed by preschool age, a child hardly could realize where a step is, avoid walking into a wall, or discriminate a cup from a plate. Even if a child is delayed in developing these perceptual abilities, sufficient catch-up generally occurs before school begins and during the early elementary school years so that the visual processing of letter forms usually is not a major deterrent to reading progress.

Visual-perceptual theorists in the 1950s and 1960s had urged teachers to incorporate movement into instruction because they believed that movement is essential to early learning. Recent studies, however, show that movement is not essential to the development of simple visual perceptions. The early theorists had suggested that infants who are delayed in their sense of touch, balance, and reflexes will have particular difficulty organizing information perceived through their sensorimotor explorations (crawling, mouthing, touching); this, in turn, would adversely affect their perceptual sense of space and time as well as reasoning ability (Ayres, 1975; Kephart, 1960; Morrison, 1986). To the contrary, however, studies find that simple visual perceptions are learned at such a young age, that movement in space and handling of objects are not yet possible. In fact, these studies find that visual matching of objects is almost always more accurate than matching through touch. Handling will facilitate more complex discriminations at later preschool ages, but only because handling enhances the child's attention and allows for scanning different features than the eye; handling is neither a primary nor necessary mechanism for complex visual discriminations (Cratty, 1970; Gibson, 1969; Pick et al., 1975; Zaporozhets, 1965).

Chapter 4 described the relationship between learning disabilities and visual-perceptual weaknesses that are more complex than the simple processes just described: right hemisphere strategy weaknesses, slow visual information processing. When students have weaknesses in these more complex perceptual abilities, these weaknesses continue to be evident throughout the teenage and adult years (Shafrir & Siegel, 1994; Spreen & Haaf, 1986). But these weaknesses have only a mild-to-moderate impact on learning. Visual-perceptual skills tend to reach "good enough" thresholds during the primary grades so that learning can proceed despite the continued perceptual interference with sight vocabulary, irregular spellings, the grasp of main ideas, and mathematics concepts.

Motor Development

Many children with learning disabilities have fine- and gross-motor coordination difficulties. As preschoolers they did not progress as expected in activities such as working puzzles, stacking blocks, drawing people, or copying designs. In elementary school, this poor coordination continues to be evident in their handwriting, art, gym, and playground activities. Motor incoordination can be a source of great frustration in demonstrating what one knows if the movements involved in drawing or writing are not automatic and efficient. Besides speech, motor movements are the child's second major way of demonstrating his or her knowledge to others.

Although fine-motor coordination generally improves with age, difficulties often persist into adolescence and adulthood (Menkes et al., 1967; Rourke, 1993; Spreen & Haaf, 1986). These problems are evident in the illegibility and poor spacing of written school or work assignments. Fortunately, tape recorders and computers, make these fine-motor weaknesses fairly manageable to work around.

Understanding the normal sequence of motor development is important in order to alert us to children's delays and help us plan appropriate remedial objectives. For example, such knowledge can help a teacher decide whether to encourage spontaneous or imitative drawing, which forms to concentrate on first, in which sport the child is likely to be most successful, and whether delays are so severe that adaptive physical education, keyboarding instruction, or a voice-activated computer are warranted.

Fine-Motor Development. Fine-motor function traditionally refers to the use of the muscles of the hand. Although certain tasks are called "fine-motor," they usually involve skills that go far beyond hand-muscle movements. For example, when a child draws, he or she uses the muscles of the upper arm to position the hand, and the muscles of the trunk and legs to maintain balance in the chair. Just to pick up, use, and release the pencil, the child must engage the motor system as well as his or her tactile and proprioceptive sensations about the position of joints and limbs, and the points at which the pencil touches the skin. Furthermore, the child must use conceptual, visual-perceptual, and language skills to guide the drawing activity. Table 6–2 traces the development of manipulatory and drawing skills from the time that eye tracking becomes continuous (4–8 weeks) through school entrance. In the last chapter you saw illustrations of typical handwriting development in subsequent years.

Long before they can copy designs, children spontaneously scribble and draw dots, zig-zags, loops, circles, and vertical, horizontal, and diagonal lines (Kellogg & O'Dell, 1969). Once they begin to copy figures, children master verticals first, then horizontals, followed by diagonals, circles, squares, and triangles. This parallels the same trend in the visual discrimination development of preschoolers, with verticals and horizontals being much easier for children than diagonals.

As children mature they begin to draw pictures of the people and objects around them. Children's approaches to drawing a human figure have long fascinated parents, teachers, and psychologists; the child's product generally is a good reflection of overall cognitive awareness, visual-motor development, emotional stability, and social maturity. Children's drawings often suggest the thoughts and attitudes they have about themselves, about their friends, about parents and siblings, and about the world.

Kellogg and O'Dell (1969) found that the first step in developing the ability to draw human figures is a scribble, which the child achieves at approximately two years of age. By age three the child can draw an oval and during that year experiments with circles that contain markings. These marks then begin to represent facial features. At the same time children begin to make drawings that Kellogg and O'Dell refer to as *suns*. Children then combine the two forms, resulting in a sun containing some facial features and rays that represent arms and legs. After age three, children generally add about one more feature every three months, particularly eyes, nose, mouth, body, and legs (Harris, 1963).

By the time a child enters kindergarten, the human figures are fairly sophisticated, containing more detail, proportion, and two-dimensional parts. Besides the head, eyes, nose, mouth, body, and legs, it is common for a five year old to add arms, hair, feet, fingers, and one item of clothing. Two-dimensional arms and legs, a neck, hands, ears, eyebrows, pupils, five fingers, arms drawn down, and two to three clothing items are not unusual. More features are added with maturation: feet in two dimensions, arms attached at shoulder, nostrils, elbows, knees, two lips, greater proportionality, more clothing items, and perhaps even a profile drawing (Koppitz, 1968).

By kindergarten age children typically can copy the individual lines that make up letters. They quickly learn to copy letters and short words. With time the print becomes smaller, letters stay on the line, and the spacing becomes uniform. By third grade children are ready to make the transition from manuscript to cursive, and by sixth grade many children have developed their own personal handwriting style.

Gross-Motor Development. Gross-motor function is the earliest developmental ability evaluated at birth. Although abnormalities at this time may

Table 6–2   Development of manipulatory and drawing skills

Age	Manipulatory Skill	Drawing Skill
8–12 weeks	• Moves extremities in response to rattle	
12 weeks	• Looks at own hand and holds it aloft while sweeping at an object Glances back and forth from hand to object	
24 weeks	• Grasps and lifts objects in a palm grasp	

28 weeks	• Is able to reach with both hands
	  Transfers an object from hand to hand
	  Resecures an object after dropping it	

40 weeks	• Holds objects between finger and thumb, replacing the palm grasp	
48 weeks	• Reaching is well coordinated	
12 months		• Uses crayons to make marks on paper

15 months	• Makes a tower of two cubes
	  Takes six cubes in and out of cup
	  Manipulates and drinks from a cup
	  Takes off shoes
	  Throws and retrieves objects
	  Opens doors
	  Imitates sweeping, combing hair
		• Imitates a horizontal scribble (ᴎᎷᎿ)

18 months	• Makes a tower of three to four cubes
	  Turns pages of a book, several at a time
		• Scribbles spontaneously
		  Makes strokes imitatively

18–21 months	Strings beads	• Imitates a vertical stroke (|)

2 years	• Places circle, triangle, and square in formboard puzzle
	  Makes a tower of six to seven cubes
	  Aligns two or more cubes to make a train
	  Puts on and takes off pants
	  Removes coat or dress unassisted
	  Throws ball overhand
		• Imitates V stroke
		  Imitates circular stroke

2 ¼ years		• Imitates horizontal strokes

2 ½ years	• Obtains own drink of water with cup
	  Dries own hands
	  Stacks five rings on peg by size
		• Imitates H strokes
		  Copies vertical line

3 years	• Makes a tower of nine cubes
	  Imitates a cube bridge
	  Dresses self
		• Copies circle
		  Copies horizontal lines
		  Imitates cross

(Continues on following page)

Table 6–2   *Continued*

Age	Manipulatory Skill	Drawing Skill
3½ years		• Imitates X
4 years	• Puts ten or more pellets into a bottle in two to five seconds	• Draws person with two parts Copies cross Copies diagonal line
4½ years	• Buttons Cuts, pastes	• Copies square 20 percent of children print letters
5 years	• Ties shoes	• Copies X Copies triangle
6 years		• Copies diamond Copies rectangle with embedded diagonals

Source: Adapted from Gard, A., Gilman, L., and Gorman, J. (1980). *Speech and language development chart:* Salt Lake City, UT: Word Making Publications; Gesell, A. (1940). *The first five years of life.* New York: Harper & Row; Hynd, G. W., and Willis, W. G. (1988). *Pediatric neuropsychology.* New York: Grune & Stratton; Knobloch, H., and Pasamanick, B. (1974). *Gesell and Amatruda's developmental diagnosis.* New York: Harper & Row; Telzrow, C. F., & Hartlage, L. C. (1983). Evaluation and programming for infants and preschoolers with neurological and neuropsychological impairments. In C. R. Reynolds & J. H. Clark (Eds.), *Assessment and programming for young children with low-incidence handicaps.* New York: Plenum Press.

reflect some brain dysfunction, academic learning would be affected only if high-level reasoning areas of the brain also had been impaired. Because the auditory, sensory, and associative areas essential to academic and cognitive performance are located near the areas of the brain involved in motor function, an insult or developmental delay in any area important to higher-level cognitive processes could affect nearby motor areas as well. Therefore, an important reason for noting motor delays is to alert us to potential difficulties in higher-level cognitive functions as well.

There is no evidence that an abnormality in the ability to perform a smooth motor act causes cognitive disabilities. Rather, when the two coexist, they seem to be caused by a brain insult or general delay that resulted in both disabilities. Especially because poor motor performance may reflect or be associated with other information-processing weaknesses, it is essential to analyze the source of motor delays and intervene as soon as possible.

Despite the fact that poor motor coordination will not itself cause a learning disability, it can make demonstrating knowledge extremely difficult. Because much of preschool education is activity oriented, a child may feel frustrated about her inability to build a house as perfectly as everyone else. When she cuts out her Valentine, the edges are scraggly, and she is all too aware of how sloppy the end product appears. Playground activities (swings, monkey bars, sliding boards) that other children delight in may prove frightful to this child. When she trips over a friend who is playing on the floor, inadvertently knocks over someone's block tower, is so slow that she's always "it" in "cat and mouse," or chooses to paint abstract streaks of color on the easel while everyone else's artwork is becoming more representational, peer interactions and self-concept can begin to erode. Although gross-motor coordination generally improves with age, these weaknesses remain evident throughout the school years. One need only look at the gymnasium or dance floor to see how clumsy behavior can interfere with peer relationships and have a negative impact on self-esteem. Teenagers with learning disabilities often express lower self-perceptions about their physical abilities than do their non-LD classmates (Kistner et al., 1987); when peers perceive these students as particularly unathletic, this also diminishes their social status in the classroom (Conderman, 1995). Incoordination continues to follow the student into adulthood (Menkes et al., 1967; Spreen & Haaf, 1986), where, fortunately, the penchant for spectator sports makes these difficulties easier to live with.

How do we track motor development? The earliest assessment of motor function in infants involves evaluation of the *primitive reflexes*. These are involuntary motor responses elicited by particular peripheral stimuli. An example is the asymmetrical tonic neck reflex. When an infant is laid on his or her back with the head turned to one side, the arm and leg will extend on the side to which the baby is facing. The arm and leg on the opposite side will flex. These reflexes form the substrate for the development of voluntary motor movement. They facilitate the development of grasping, controlling the head and trunk, extending the limbs, and coordinating movements of different body parts. These primitive reflexes, along with attributes such as motor strength, muscle tone, and deep tendon reflexes, are used to predict future neurological development. If the primitive reflexes persist too long and don't become integrated with more complex motor patterns, the maturation of voluntary motor processes becomes disrupted (Hynd & Willis, 1988). Nevertheless, these types of neurological abnormalities at birth generally are not prognostic of learning disabilities (Nichols & Chen, 1981; Werner, 1980; Yang, Ting, & Kennedy, 1968). This is most likely because (1) these neurological indicators do not reflect the brain areas involved in high-level academic reasoning, and (2) the brain's high-level reasoning areas can be modified by enriching environmental influences, whereas

no other brain area can take over for deficits on the motor strip.

Beyond the immediate neonatal period, motor activity becomes more varied and voluntary. Table 6–3 lists the age at which approximately 50 percent of all children attain specific motor milestones.

There has been much discussion about whether the side of the body that one prefers to use has anything to do with learning disabilities. *Laterality* or *dominance*, the preference for one side of the body in hand, foot, eye, and ear use, became a major issue as a result of Orton's (1937) work. Orton proposed that failure to establish a consistent preference for one body side corresponds with the brain's failure to develop the necessary superiority of one hemisphere over another in language and visuospatial functions. This, however, has not been shown to be true. Good learners often display this *mixed laterality* or *mixed dominance*. In fact, in a study of over 30,000 children, left- or right-handedness bore no relationship to learning disabilities; yet, among the 3,000 left-handed seven-year-old children, three-quarters were mixed dominant for eye, hand, or foot movements (Nichols & Chen, 1981). Left- and right-handedness, a sign of hemispheric motor dominance, appears to be related to learning disabilities only when the choice of hand has been forced by brain injury that affected higher cognitive abilities as well (Hicks & Kinsbourne, 1978b, Kinsbourne & Caplan, 1979).

Handedness develops at different rates in different individuals. The earliest indication of handedness is the tonic neck reflex, in which many infants show a more frequent reflex to the right (Gesell & Ames, 1947). If both parents are right-handed, newborns will tend to turn their heads to the right more frequently than to the left as a spontaneous reaction to tactile stimulation (Liederman & Kinsbourne, 1980). Another early indicator of handedness is the length of time that one-and-a-half- to four-month-old infants grasp a rattle in their left or right hand (Caplan & Kinsbourne, 1976).

Before handedness is fully established, the normal child goes back and forth between use of one or both hands (Gesell & Ames, 1947). Infants

Table 6–3   Gross-motor landmarks

Age	*Skill*
Prone and Upright Posture	
16 weeks	• Raises head when lying on stomach; head is almost perpendicular to surface
20 weeks	• Makes compensatory head movements when pulled from lying on back to a sitting posture
24 weeks	• Rolls over
	Supports self on extended arms in the prone position
28 weeks	• In a sitting position, holds trunk erect momentarily
36 weeks	• Holds trunk erect indefinitely
40 weeks	• Holds trunk erect and maintains balance as turns to side to pick up an object
44 weeks	• Goes from sitting to prone to sitting positions
Sitting, Crawling, Standing, Walking, and Running	
12 weeks	• Supports much of weight on legs when held vertically
28 weeks	• Sits alone
	Crawls with abdomen in contact with floor
	Supports full weight when held vertically
36 weeks	• In creeping position, supports weight on toes
	Pulls self into a standing position but has insufficient motor control to lower self
48 weeks	• Pulls to standing and is able to walk holding on to furniture
12–18 months	• Walks alone with elevation of arms; feet are wide-based for support
18 months	• Walks sideways and backward
21 months	• Walks up three steps alone
2 years	• Runs
	Goes up and down stairs placing both feet on each step
2–3 years	• Kicks a ball on the floor
	Balances on one foot for one second
	Imitates crossing of the feet
3 years	• Walks up stairs using alternating feet, but comes down stairs placing both feet on each step
	Rides tricycle
	Balances on each foot for 2 seconds
4 years	• Somersaults
	Balances well on toes
	Walks a straight line 3 meters long
	Hops on one foot
	Touches fingers to thumb in succession
	Balances on one foot for up to 10 seconds
	Walks up and down stairs one step per foot
4–5 years	• Skips
	Catches a bounced ball

Sources: Adapted from Gesell, A. (1940). *The first five years of life*. New York: Harper & Row; Hynd, G. W., & Willis, W. G. (1988). *Pediatric neuropsychology*. New York: Grune & Stratton: Knobloch, H., and Pasamanick, B. (1974). *Gesell and Amatruda's developmental diagnosis*. New York: Harper & Row; Telzrow, C. F., and Hartlage, L. C. (1983). Evaluation and programming for infants and preschoolers with neurological and neuropsychological impairments. In C. R. Reynolds & G. H. Clark (Eds.), *Assessment and programming for young children with low-incidence handicaps*. New York: Plenum Press.

seem to grasp primarily with their right hands, but they reach and swipe at objects with their left hands (Young, 1977). Gesell and Ames observed that this left-handed reaching gives way, after the first six months of life, to periods of right-handedness, left-handedness, and bilaterality. Right-handedness generally becomes predominant at around four years of age but can be established as late as ten years of age. In most cases, children reach eight to nine years of age before they use the right hand for all purposes (Belmont & Birch, 1963). The majority of left-handed children exhibit varying degrees of ambidexterity throughout life, in part because of society's strong encouragement to use the right hand.

Preschoolers who establish consistent hand preference early, especially girls, may also display precocious mental and motor development (Gottfried & Bathurst, 1983). Even if children have not established hand dominance until age nine, however, as long as brain development has been normal they most likely will not have learning difficulties (Kaufman, Zalma, & Kaufman, 1978).

More boys than girls are left-handed (Teng et al., 1979). We already have learned that more boys than girls are identified as learning disabled. It is important to remember that the left-handedness did not cause these boys to become learning disabled. If the two are related, it is because the brain differences that caused the boys' learning problems most likely also caused them to become left-handed.

Remediation of motor delays warrants the attention of parents and preschool teachers, as well as occupational and physical therapists when appropriate. Although gross-motor function develops largely with neurological maturity, some aspects can be influenced through teaching. Familiarity with the sequence of normal motor development helps one choose the most appropriate and least frustrating teaching objectives. Gains from such training will help children more effectively demonstrate the concepts they understand (for example, drawing shapes on the blackboard reflective of their accurate shape perception; stacking blocks as high as they can count), take pride in their motor accomplishments, and interrelate more effectively through the motor activities involved in play. We now know not to be concerned about mixed dominance and to be patient if a child is developing handedness at a slow rate. When handedness remains undefined, fine-motor activities with both hands are encouraged; as the fine-motor skills strengthen, the child's natural hand preference is likely to become more apparent.

Language Development

Because words are merely symbols for concepts, language reception, processing, and expression weaknesses can have a significant impact on a person's thinking, problem solving, listening comprehension, speaking, and social interactions. Visual perception, memory, and regulation of one's activities also will suffer if a person's use of self-verbalization is too weak to help guide attention and memory. For many preschoolers who have language difficulties, these delays persist into the elementary years and beyond so that language cannot be used effectively to facilitate learning.

Language deficits continue to characterize many adolescents with learning disabilities. Word-finding and phonemic awareness difficulties persist beyond adolescence into adulthood, as do problems in comprehending difficult grammatical constructions (Felton, Naylor, & Wood, 1990; Whitehouse, 1983; Wiig & Semel, 1975; Wolf, 1991). These individuals' expressive language often contains inappropriate grammar, incomplete and less sophisticated sentences, and word distortions (for example, *bucker* for *buckle*) especially when faced with new, difficult vocabulary (Johnson & Blalock, 1987; Stirling & Miles, 1988). Although the vocabularies of typical students generally double between third and seventh grades (Jenkins, Stein, & Wysocki, 1984), this often does not occur among youngsters with learning disabilities. The result of these persisting weaknesses is poor facility in communication, reading, listening comprehension, and written language. These reading and writing difficulties further limit opportunities for higher-level language development.

The language weaknesses of as many as half of young children are still evident in adulthood and often accompany overall low adult functioning (Hall & Tomblin, 1978; Johnson, 1980; Menkes et al., 1967; Spreen & Haaf, 1986). These deficits can be subtle, or they may be quite apparent in word-retrieval problems and difficulty understanding/participating in conversations, shifting conversational topics, understanding jokes, detecting teasing, and following directions (Blalock, 1982; Johnson & Blalock, 1987; Lapadat, 1991; Scarborough, 1984; Wiig & Semel, 1980).

Because of the critical impact of language skills on learning and adjustment, it is essential for teachers, parents, and speech-language pathologists to monitor the student's acquisition of language, to assess whether language delays are compounding or creating other developmental delays, and to intervene as soon as possible. Early intervention is essential because by the time children enter school, most of their peers will have mastered the major linguistic forms used by adults; and they will be able to use this sophistication to facilitate their academic progress.

Although theorists still disagree about how language actually is acquired, most learning disabilities experts have adopted the interactionist view. This view is a compromise between the environmentalist perspective that children must hear words and be reinforced for repeating them in order to develop language concepts and speech (Skinner, 1959) and the nativist perspective that the environment merely triggers a natural unfolding so that children generate word combinations that they have never heard before (such as "Mommy all gone," "baby cry," "no go," "no night-night") (Braine, 1963; Brown & Bellugi, 1964; Chomsky, 1968; Lenneberg, 1967). Interactionists postulate that language is acquired as children's reasoning processes direct which language to take in from the environment and then how to transform this language based on their own knowledge and thoughts. They believe that language and thought develop both independently and simultaneously, each influencing the other's continued development (Piaget, 1962).

According to Piaget and Inhelder (1969), language becomes possible once children can represent their thoughts in language, at about one and a half to two years of age. At this age children can easily imagine people or objects in their absence, play "pretend," scribble images from

memory, try to communicate about past events, and imitate a past routine (for example, throwing food over the highchair's tray and delightedly anticipating some adult reaction). Basically, without thought as a prerequisite, children cannot develop meaningful language (Flavell, 1977). But once they begin to acquire language, children use it to further shape their thoughts (Bruner, Olver, & Greenfield, 1966). "Our thinking is enriched or brought into focus by language" (MacNamara, 1972, p. 1).

Myklebust (1960), in applying the interactionist perspective to learning disabilities, proposed that infants cannot develop comprehension of the spoken word (*receptive language*) until their experiences have acquired enough meaningfulness to be reflected in thought (*inner language*). Only after developing receptive skills do children learn to symbolize experiences through words (*expressive language*). "Output follows input, so the child speaks only after he comprehends. . . . A word without meaning is not a word" (pp. 231–232). Eventually, inner language incorporates thinking in words, using mental trial and error to problem solve, grouping and classifying experiences, and talking to oneself. Enhancement of either the inner, receptive, or expressive processes will enhance the others as well (Myklebust, 1954).

Inner language disturbances are the most debilitating of all language disorders. Children with inner language disturbances do not gain meaning from experience. Consequently, even if they do acquire some language, they cannot use it to represent thoughts. Receptive disorders always result in expressive disorders because children cannot respond meaningfully unless they understand what the other person has said. Their poor comprehension also impairs self-monitoring of what they are trying to say. Denckla (1977) points out that even when the disorder is primarily expressive, the limited practice in conversational give and take eventually impairs comprehension as well.

The interactionist view that language and thought are intimately intertwined has provided a valuable framework for evaluating students' language progress and remediating language disorders. The interactionist theory suggests several ways in which the development of youngsters who do not think or express themselves as intelligently as we would wish can be facilitated: teaching better use of language to express meaningful thoughts, teaching specific language through which children can better reason, and making experiences more meaningful so that relevant words can be better understood and in turn used to convey meaning. We shall examine the typical stages of language development and how language weaknesses impact the student with a learning disability.

Language acquisition, whether receptive or expressive, can be broken down into five components: phonology, morphology, syntax, semantics, and pragmatics. *Phonology* refers to individual sounds; *morphology* refers to meaningful units within words; *syntax* refers to grammatical sentence rules; *semantics* refers to the meaning of words and phrases; and *pragmatics* refers to the ability to engage in conversational speech. Although phonetic and morphological weaknesses tend to resolve themselves within the elementary school years, syntax often takes longer to acquire, and semantics and pragmatics may present life-long difficulties. A weakness in any one of these areas may affect proficiency in another. For example, if Steve has difficulty formulating the /s/ phoneme, he will be unable to express the plural morpheme, even if he understands it. If, at an older age, Steve is unable to understand the semantics of idioms ("go jump in the lake," "drop dead"), then his pragmatic ability to converse with peers will be seriously hampered.

Because language delays affect thought, learning, and social interactions, early intervention is critical. The majority of language-delayed children will acquire speech sounds, morphemes, and syntax in the same developmental order as do typical children, although at a slower rate (Bloom, 1978; Ingram, 1976). Therefore, keeping normal language acquisition patterns in mind when planning interventions makes much sense.

Phonology.   *Phonemes* are the smallest units of sound that go into forming words. They carry no meaning. For example, the words *cat* and *that* are each made up of three phonemes, /c/ or /th/ , /a/ , /t/, none of which have meaning by them-

selves. When phonemes are interchanged, however, they affect meaning (e.g., changing b-a-t to c-a-t). By six years of age, children usually have mastered pronunciation of the phonemes of the English language. Frequently parents report that children who are slow to pick up prereading skills were delayed as infants in vocalization, auditory discrimination, and articulation.

Vocalization.   One of the first signs of a potential language disorder may be subtle abnormalities in a child's crying patterns (Wiig & Semel, 1980). Lester (1987) found that infant crying patterns were correlated with the children's developmental progress at one and a half and five years of age. Apparently these crying patterns are influenced by the same neurophysiological immaturities that underlie later developmental delays.

Children typically begin vocalizing using one or two different sounds during the first month after birth. At approximately three months of age they vocalize to an adult's social smile, and by four months they respond with a meaningful smile and vocalize back when talked to. Pleasure, displeasure, eagerness, satisfaction, and anger are evident in these vocalizations. Laughing aloud begins at four to six months, as does babbling repeated syllables and sounds. By approximately eight months the baby's babbling begins to sound like adult inflection patterns. It is at nine to ten months that the child can vocalize all sounds and imitate a number of syllables (Wiig & Semel, 1980).

Auditory Discrimination.   It is remarkable that within the first few days after birth, newborns can discriminate not only speech sounds (for example, /b/ /g/) but also their native language from other languages (Mehler et al., 1988; Molfese & Molfese, 1985). Their left hemisphere electroencephalograms actively respond to speech signals such as syllables and words. Nonspeech sounds (music, noise) create greater activation of the right hemisphere (Molfese, 1973; Molfese, Freeman, & Palermo, 1975). It is amazing that language development at age three can be predicted with considerable accuracy from these early measures (Molfese & Molfese, 1985). By two months infants indicate recognition of words that they've heard embedded within rhythmic clauses, but they do not yet recognize single words to which they have been exposed (Mandel, Jusezyk, & Nelson, 1994). By three to four months the infant clearly attends to spoken voices and soon after can discriminate strangers' voices, localize the source of sounds, play purposefully with noise-making toys, and respond appropriately to friendly or angry voices (Wiig & Semel, 1980). By four and one-half months infants listen longer to their own name than to any other name (Azar, 1996). In the second half of their first year, babies indicate discrimination of familiar words, and they prefer speech with natural pauses (Berk, 1997).

Parents recall that, as preschoolers, their young children with learning disabilities commonly experienced difficulty telling apart similar-sounding phonemes within words. For example, the words *bat* and *pat* might be mistaken as the same. The words *sat* and *pat* were less likely to be mistaken because their phonological features are more distinct. Tallal's (1980) research suggests that because these children tend to be slow information processors, they may have an easier time discriminating sounds that persist longer (/s/ and /m/ versus /b/ and /t/).

By three years of age children's growing phonological awareness is evident as they recite nursery rhymes and play with words beginning with the same sounds (e.g., *deanut, dutter, dandwich*) or other nonsense words (Catts, 1991; Maclean, Bryant, & Bradley, 1987). This sensitivity to rhyme is predictive of the emergence of phonological segmentation skills and the ability to read simple words over the next fifteen months. Rhyming and segmentation skills also correlate strongly with vocabulary and grammatical development during the preschool years, and first grade reading ability (Berk, 1997; Blachman, 1991). The important insight that words are composed of smaller isolated phonemic units is difficult for young children because they are accustomed to thinking of words in terms of their meanings, not in terms of a sequence of merged sounds. Since words' sounds fold into one another, this obscures the segmental nature of the speech stream (Catts, 1991; Griffith & Olson, 1992).

Persistent weaknesses in listening to individual sounds in words can disrupt not only decoding and spelling progress but also social communication, as in understanding "plays on words" (for example, "What did the judge say when the skunk entered the courtroom? Odor in the court"). Yet, these same students may be just as good as their typical peers in interpreting lexical jokes ("Why did the farmer name his hog Ink? Because he kept running out of the pen." "What has eighteen legs and catches flies? A baseball team.") or cognitive incongruity jokes ("What did the newscaster say after he announced that the world had come to an end? Stay tuned, news at eleven.") (Bruno, Johnson, & Simon, 1987, 1988).

Articulation. Children's speech at one year old is often unintelligible, with the exception of a few words. By two years old their speech is 65 percent intelligible, 70 percent at two and one half years, 80 percent at three years, and very intelligible by four and one half years. The hardest sounds to articulate appear to be /f/, which is mastered at five to six years, /v/th/l/zh/sh/, which are mastered at around six and one half years, and /z/s/th/r/hw/, which are mastered at approximately seven and one half years (Gard, Gilman, & Gorman, 1980; Wiig & Semel, 1976).

Persistent articulation difficulties tend to resolve themselves by adolescence and, when unaccompanied by other delays, are not highly related to future learning disabilities. This is because articulation disorders represent a motor-movement or motor-planning difficulty and do not involve higher-level perceptual and cognitive abilities (Eisenson, 1972). Articulation errors, however, can seriously disturb communication with others. One of the first signs of such motor difficulty may be sucking problems at birth (Tarnopol & Tarnopol, 1977). If a child has difficulty discriminating phonemes, this also will be reflected in articulation errors.

For many children discrimination and articulation of individual sounds are easy, but they have difficulty detecting and imitating transitions from one phoneme to another in consonant clusters, syllables, and words (for example, *saw* is easy; *straw* is harder). Some may articulate acceptably in single-word utterances but make distortions in connected speech (sentences and phrases). Poor perception of sound sequences and rhythms can result in such articulation patterns as poor fluency; sound reversals (*aminal* for *animal*); jerky, irregular speech; cluttered incomprehensible speech; difficulty monitoring one's own or interpreting others' pitch and loudness; rhyming difficulty; and difficulty sequencing sounds correctly in words. The preschooler whose articulation disorder is caused by this type of conceptual inability to analyze the order of sounds in words is at high risk for developing a learning disability.

Morphology.   *Morphemes* are the smallest meaningful units in words. For example, the word *cats* is composed of two morphemes: the word /cat/ and the /s/ that gives the word its plural meaning. Other morphemes that lend meaning to words include prefixes (*un*dress), verb tense forms (walk*ed*), person (he walk*s*), and so on. Only when the child understands the meanings of morphemes will he or she be able to string several together to make meaningful sentences (Brown, 1973).

Children's understanding of language is well developed even before they can express themselves in single words. Somewhere between four to six months of age the infant will look in response to his or her own name. By approximately nine months the infant can respond to "give me" requests and directions such as "put the spoon in the cup," "stir," and "no-no" (Gard et al., 1980; Wiig & Semel, 1980).

The baby's first true word is acquired between ten and eighteen months of age. Soon after the infant's first birthday, most children can say ten words; this expands to thirty to fifty words by one and one half years of age. This vocabulary nearly doubles every six months so that, by age four, a child has a speaking vocabulary of 1000 to 1500 words (Gard et al., 1980; Eisenson, 1972; Lennenberg, 1967). Among children's first words are those conveying common actions (*bye-bye*) and objects that they can act on (*bottle, sock*) (Nelson, 1973). Other early words are based on perceptual attributes that are meaningful to a baby (*up* for movement; *mmm* for taste) (Clark, 1973). Table 6–4 details the typical progression of recep-

tive and expressive language from one to seven years of age.

Table 6–5 describes the course of morphological and syntactic acquisition from age one and a half years on. It indicates that by the time youngsters enter kindergarten they have mastered very sophisticated word formation rules. These rules enable children to generate grammatical forms for words they have never before encountered.

Many children with learning disabilities experience significant delays understanding or expressing such morphological rules as third-person verb forms, verb tenses, possessives, singular/plural, irregular plurals and past-tense forms, comparatives/superlatives, and prefixes (Vogel, 1974; Wiig & Semel, 1976; Wiig, Semel, & Crouse, 1973). For some, these difficulties relate to limitations in auditory perception of unstressed (for example, word endings) or low information-carrying parts of phrases and sentences (for example, articles and prepositions) (Wiig & Semel, 1980). When a child has difficulty grasping the meaning of certain word forms, he or she will not use these forms to convey meaning in spoken messages.

Unfortunately, the weak vocabularies of many youngsters with learning disabilities provide a limited foundation on which new vocabulary and knowledge can be built. Although vocabulary instruction can still be undertaken successfully in adolescence, students with learning disabilities tend to have more difficulty acquiring new vocabulary than do their nondisabled peers (Griswold, Gelzheiser, & Shepherd, 1987). They frequently benefit when texts are rewritten in easier vocabulary, and when shorter sentences are used that eliminate unimportant details. These students often require special help in learning the new symbol systems introduced at the secondary level, such as in foreign languages and geometry.

Syntax.   *Syntax* refers to the way words are strung together into meaningful sentences. This grammatical structure is critical to meaning. For example, "You will go with daddy" demands a different response than "Will you go with daddy?"

Although a child begins to speak in single words at around one year of age, it is only at eigh-

Table 6–4   Emergence of language skills from one to seven years of age

Age	*Receptive Skills*	*Expressive Skills*
1–1½ years	• Comprehends approximately 50 words Recognizes own name Recognizes familiar sounds (telephone, door bell) Stops activity in response to "no" Follows simple one-step commands Points to objects when named Understands most simple questions Points to own nose, eyes, and other body parts on request	• Says *mama* or *dada* or other first word (usually an animal, food, or toy) Imitates words such as *baby, more, apple, up* Tries to sing simple tunes such as "Jack and Jill" Says 2 words in a single utterance Uses meaningful gestures such as pointing to make wants known Extensive vocalization and echoing responses Identifies 2 or more objects or pictures when asked "what's this" Uses 3 to 20 words including *all gone, more* Uses 2-word phrases and short sentences Uses jargon Clearly pronounces 4 to 7 words
1½–2 years	• Comprehends approximately 300 words Responds to play requests such as "Put the doll in the chair," "Wipe the doll's nose" Listens to simple, short stories Shakes head yes/no appropriately Points to 5 parts of a doll such as *hand, mouth,* and *eyes* on request Points to 2 to 5 pictures of objects on request (*dog, shoe*) Discriminates between 2 related requests such as "Give me the cup; Give me the plate" Responds to simple requests for actions such as "Pick up the hat," "Give daddy the cup"	• Uses approximately 50 recognizable words Combines 2 words to describe ideas or events such as "Daddy bye-bye" Verbalizes "no" Uses words to make wants known ("cookie," "milk") Speaks 10 words with clear pronunciation Verbalizes immediate experiences Names 1 to 3 pictured objects (*car, doll*) Attempts to describe past experiences Marked decrease in sound and word repetition; has discarded jargon Names 3 related objects such as socks, shoes, pants Responds to basic questions such as "What is your name?" and "What does the doggie say?"
2–2½ years	• Comprehends approximately 500 words Listens to 5- to 10-minute story Identifies pictured objects on request when their function is indicated as in "Show me the one that you wear" or "Show me the one that you eat" Carries out series of 2 related commands Has concept of *one* and *all*	• Uses 200 intelligible words Combines 3 to 4 words in sentences Indicates age by holding up fingers Tells how common objects such as *fork, cup, shoe,* are used Names 6 objects by use Answers "where," "what . . . doing," and "what do you (hear) with" questions Verbalizes toilet needs Counts to 3 Tells own sex

(Continues on following page)

Table 6–4   *(Continued from preceding page)*

Age	Receptive Skills	Expressive Skills
2½–3 years	• Comprehends approximately 900 words Points to pictures of 10 objects described by their use Listens to 20-minute story Knows *in/on/under/big/little*	• Uses 500 intelligible words Answers "what (runs)" questions Answers simple "who," "why," "where," "how many" questions Answers one of three questions: "What do you do when you're hungry, sleepy, cold?" (2 by age 3½; 3 by age 4) Asks simple questions: "What's that?" Asks yes/no questions: ("Is he sleeping?")
3–3½ years	• Comprehends 1200 words Knows *in front of, behind, hard/soft, rough/smooth, circle/square* Responds to commands involving 3 actions or objects	• Combines 4 to 5 words in sentences Uses 800 words Responds to "How . . . " questions Names 8 to 10 pictures States action Supplies last word ("Stoves are . . . ") Counts 3 objects and points to each
3½–4 years	• Comprehends 1500 to 2000 words Recognizes one color	• Uses 1000 to 1500 words Can do simple verbal analogies ("Daddy is a man, mommy is a . . . ") Responds to "how much," "how long," and "what if" questions Relates two events in correct sequence Tells story mixing real and unreal Long, detailed conversations Repeats 12 to 13 syllable sentences Asks "how," "why," "when" questions and expects detailed explanations
4–4½ years	• Understands concept of number 3 Knows *between, above, below, top, bottom* Points to 9 shapes when named	• Combines 4 to 7 words in sentences Responds to "how far" questions Defines simple words Counts 4 objects Rote counts to 10
4½–5 years	• Comprehends 2500 to 2800 words Recognizes 2 to 3 primary colors Knows *heavy/light, loud/soft, like/unlike, long/short*	• Combines 5 to 8 words in sentences Uses 1500 to 2000 words Names one color Answers complex comprehension questions Answers simple "when," "how often" questions Asks meaning of words Tells long story accurately Counts 10 objects Can name objects as *first/middle/last* Repeats days of week in sequence

(Continues on following page)

Table 6–4   *(Continued from preceding page)*

Age	Receptive Skills	Expressive Skills
5–6 years	• Comprehends 13,000 words Understands *opposite of, A.M./P.M., yesterday/tomorrow, more/less, some/many, several/few, most/least, before/after, now/later, across* Comprehends number concepts to 10 Points to penny, nickel, dime, quarter Points to half, whole, right, left Points to numerals 1 to 25 Can classify same objects by shape and color	• Can answer "what happens if" questions Counts 12 objects Rote counts to 30 Names basic colors Names 5 letters of alphabet States similarities and differences of objects Describes location or movement: *through, away, from, toward, over* Names positions of objects: *first, second, third* Names days of week in order
6–7 years	• Comprehends 20,000 to 26,000 words Understands rough time intervals and seasons Aware of others' speech errors	• Uses 10,000 words States preceding and following numbers and days of week Tells address Recites the alphabet Rote counts to 100

Sources: Adapted from Berk, L. E. (1997). *Child Development* (4th ed.). Boston: Allyn & Bacon. Gard, A., Gilman, L., & Gorman, J. (1980). *Speech and language development chart.* Salt Lake City, UT: Word Making Productions. Wiig, E. H., & Semel, E. M. (1980). *Language assessment and intervention for the learning disabled.* Columbus, OH: Charles E. Merrill, pp. 15–17.

teen to twenty-four months of age that the child begins to understand basic grammatical relations so as to combine two words at a time ("Mommy bye-bye"). Children acquire these initial word combinations from imitation and reduction of adult speech into high-information nouns and verbs. "Do you see the milk" is imitated as "see milk" rather than as "you the." They also make deductions from other combinations that they could not have heard (*all gone, night-night*) (Brown & Bellugi, 1964). At two to two and a half years of age, the child's sentences begin to contain subjects and predicates ("Mommy going"; "bottle fall down"). From then on sentences become more and more complex. By age three, the child has mastered subject, predicate, and object relationships and can combine these in phrases (Menyuk, 1969). Agreement between subject and verb typically occurs between three and a half to four years of age (Sabatino & Sed-

lack, 1986). By kindergarten age, the typical child has mastered many of the more complex grammatical rules of adult language.

Some students with learning disabilities have *surface structure* difficulties. They comprehend the meanings of words but get confused by the sheer number of words in a sentence or the word order. These students must take time to translate the words and sentence structure into meaning (Wiig & Semel, 1980).

The syntax comprehension difficulty of children with learning disabilities is reflected in their expressive language. They omit words, add inappropriate words, use incorrect grammar, and distort the order of words and phrases (Johnson & Myklebust, 1967). As preschoolers they often speak in no more than two- or three-word sentences and have great difficulty expressing thoughts or having language aid their conceptual processes.

Table 6–5   Order of morphological and syntactic development

	Approximate Age of Acquisition
• Negation ("no bed"); possessive emerging ("daddy car") Uses pronoun and name for self ("me Tommy") 33% of utterances are nouns	1½–2 years
• Articles *a, the; in/on* Present progressive "ing" on verbs Regular plural form emerging (*cat/cats*); irregular past tense emerging Some contractions in habitual phrases (*don't, can't, it's, that's*) 25% of utterances are nouns, 25% verbs	2–2½ years

• Auxiliary *is/am* + "ing" ("boy *is* runn*ing*")
Is + adjective ("bell is red"); *'s* for possession ("daddy*'s* car")
Regular past tense verbs (*walk/walked*); future tense emerging
    (*do, can, will*)
Pronouns (*I, me, you, mine*); contracted form of is (*he's
    running*)
Imperatives (*go, get it, don't*); *not* emerging
Adverbs of location emerging (*here, there*)
	2½–3 years

• *Is* at beginning of questions *Won't, can't, and* as a conjunction; superlative "est" (*fattest*) Present progressive *are* + "ing" ("boys are running") Regular plurals (*cat/cats*); irregular plurals emerging (*child/children*)	3–3½ years
• Pronouns (*he, she*); *myself* emerging *Got* ("I got it"); conjunction *because* emerging *Was, were* questions emerging (was he there?)	3½–4 years
• *If, so; our, they, their; could, would* Irregular plurals (*child/children*); comparative "er" emerging (*smaller*) Passive voice emerging ("The dog was killed by the boy.")	4–4½ years
• Adjective/noun agreement; noun derivation "-er" (*painter, farmer*)	4½–5 years
• Adverbial endings emerging	5–6 years

• Noun derivation "ist" (*bicyclist*); homonyms emerging
Perfect tense emerging (*have, had*)
Consistently correct morphology (including passive voice,
    irregular past tense, comparatives (*bigger*), adverbial
    endings (*slowly*)
	6–7 years

Sources: Adapted from Gard, A., Gilman, L., & Gorman, J. (1980). *Speech and language development chart.* Salt Lake City, UT: Word Making Productions; Wiig, E. H., & Semel, E. M. (1980). *Language assessment and intervention for the learning disabled.* Columbus, OH: Charles E. Merrill.

Semantics. *Semantics* provides the meaningful connection between words and sentences and other ideas or events. Unless a child has some system of meaning, language is of no use, and he or she will be incapable of understanding it or using it for communication. Toddlers often express semantic content through single words. For example, the context will determine what is meant by "cookie": "I want a cookie," "There is a cookie," or "The cookie fell on the floor" (Bloom, 1970). Toddlers rapidly learn to express ideas about what is going on in the here and now. By the early elementary school years children can express very complex ideas about past and future events as well.

Children with learning disabilities often have semantic difficulties understanding and remembering words that sound alike (*two, too*), words that have dual meanings (*draw a check* versus *write a check*), adjectives that are not easily described (shape and time concepts), complex verbs (*evading* versus *running away*), comparative relations (*smaller than*), pronouns, and strings of adjectives, adverbs, and prepositions (Wiig & Semel, 1976). Idioms, metaphors, morals, and proverbs often present lifelong problems. These *deep structure* problems include difficulty interpreting negatives, "wh" questions, linguistic rules, "this, that, these, those" referants, word sequences, and poor ability to hold onto what one has heard in short-term memory (Abrahamsen & Sprouse, 1995; Wiig & Semel, 1980). It is no wonder that comprehending poetry, colloquial language, and symbolic literature elude the student with a learning disability.

Word-finding problems, a common characteristic of individuals with learning disabilities, can stem from perceptual confusions between similar-sounding words, poor cuing of recall due to syntax weaknesses, and semantic problems that limit the richness of or access to stored knowledge about the word: these semantic weaknesses include concrete and narrow word meanings, limited visualization of language content, weak categorizing ability, narrow word associations, and poor analysis of concepts and words (Jansky & de Hirsch, 1973; Wiig & Semel, 1980). These children's narrow, imprecise attribution of meaning to vocabulary and vocabulary to meaning limits their expressive abilities (McGinnis, 1963). They erroneously associate their words with others in the same semantic category (*tiger* for *lion; paper fork* instead of *plastic fork*), opposites (*aunt* for *uncle*), those with similar phonemes (*cake* for *steak*), or they repeat the same word over and over again (Wiig & Semel, 1980).

Individuals with word-finding difficulties who do have good comprehension and a rich vocabulary encounter expressive problems because they lack the semantic flexibility to retrieve the specific word they are looking for. Therefore, their verbal fluency, flexibility, and creativity in elaborating on concepts is diminished (Wiig & Semel, 1980). Their difficulty in choosing words may cause them to substitute inappropriate words, resort to synonyms, talk around and around a topic, gesture, try to define the words, stall ("you know"; "uhm"; "wait a minute"), use imprecise words ("whatchamacallit"), or change the topic. It is not uncommon for friends to become impatient and implore "hurry up and say what you mean." After finally finding the right words, the friend may retort, "Why didn't you just say that in the first place?" All this only exacerbates the student's frustration and creates more word-finding difficulties.

Naming difficulties and learning disabilities often go hand in hand because both require accurate retrieval (for example, of words, letter sounds, and numeral names). If children are inaccurate or slow namers, this certainly will affect their reading and calculation accuracy and speed. The slower the reading speed, the fewer words students can read before they need to pause to assimilate the information. This breaks up the language into unnatural units and hinders comprehension. Slow naming also interferes with verbal rehearsal, so that memory for what one has heard or read and planful approaches to tasks may be compromised.

Pragmatics. *Pragmatics* is competence in interpersonal communication. Pragmatics combines all the previous skills so that words can be adjusted to the particular person being spoken to, what was just said, the topic of conversation, the goal of the discussion, and the time and setting (Lapadat, 1991). Early signs of pragmatic competence include responding to facial expressions, comprehending parental gestures, and, at seven to nine months of age, looking at family members when named. Interacting reciprocally through peek-a-boo and pat-a-cake emerge around nine months old, and by one to one and one half years old it is clear that the child perceives others' emotions (Gard et al., 1980).

Weak pragmatic speech is believed to be a major contributor to the social problems of students with learning disabilities (Bryan, 1977; Mathinos, 1991). These students tend not to make use of the speaker's *prosody* or style (speed, pitch, stress patterns, duration of individual words, intonation, and pauses between words), and the context in which speech is occurring, in order to help them comprehend. Typical learners begin to be adept at using prosodic cues to enhance comprehension after age ten: for example, he showed *her* baby pictures versus he showed her *baby* pictures; big *green // house* versus big *// greenhouse*. Although children with reading disabilities can perceive these types of prosodic cues, they are poorer at interpreting what they mean (Mann, Cowin, & Schoenheimer, 1989). This lack of appreciation is unfortunate because prosodic cues offer an important, additional means for holding information in memory. For example, recall the number of times you struggled to recall a poem's last line, and you finally resorted to "dum, dum-dum, dum-*dum,* dum." Somehow this prosody brought back the poem's words. Teachers of the learning disabled need to be careful not to limit students' comprehension by using sentences whose meaning depends on subtle prosodic cues.

By the time a student reaches high school, lectures become a primary means for conveying information (Moran, 1980; in Bos & Vaughn, 1994). Even in the adult work environment, listening can dominate anywhere from 30 to 65 percent of an average day (Nichols & Stevens, 1957). Teenagers with learning disabilities frequently exhibit listening deficiencies (Schumaker, Wildgen, & Sherman, 1982), yet because of their reading difficulties, these students need to rely on their auditory skills (lectures, books on tape) even more so than their nondisabled peers. Among Ackerman and colleagues' (1996) teenagers with reading delays, for example, only a handful showed listening comprehension above a sixth grade level. As a group, these teenagers' comprehension was more like that of a fourth grader.

According to Wilkinson, Stratta, and Dudley (1974), effective listening is a complicated procedure that requires processing through many different channels:

1. *The linguistic channel:* comprehending single and multiple meanings of words or phrases (for example, *what a trip*);

2. *The paralinguistic channel:* understanding the tone, quality, loudness, speed, and pauses in an individual's voice and speech;

3. *The visual channel:* gaining information from the speaker's appearance;

4. *The kinesic channel:* comprehending nonverbal cues such as posture, facial expressions, nature of eye contact, and gestures.

The nonverbal patterns described above often are defined by one's culture. Wilkinson and colleagues make the telling point that had the Americans who met the Japanese emissaries before Pearl Harbor understood that to them a smile is merely the accompaniment of any social act, as opposed to a means of conveying friendship or pleasure, they might have been less likely to be "lulled into a false sense of security" (p. 280).

Listening, like all other aspects of communication, is a two-way process. Because teachers rely heavily on the lecture method, they need to assess the kind and clarity of instructions they give, the amount of time they spend introducing new vocabulary, the degree to which they elicit a background schema that makes new information more meaningful and memorable, the way they organize their material, their pacing, the nature of the questions they ask to stimulate thinking and check comprehension, the clarity of their examples, and their use of concrete illustrations for abstract points. Many students with learning disabilities require this type of directed teaching in order to listen effectively (Bos & Vaughn, 1994). To complicate the matter, modern technology has provided a myriad of mechanisms to further strain listening capabilities: radios, TV, telephone answering devices, and tape recorders.

For students with pragmatic difficulties, imperceptions also may occur with nonverbal stimuli; when an adult places a hand on the student's shoulder, this may be interpreted as a warning when it really was meant to convey "Hi there." Similarly, Juli may misunderstand the immediacy implied in her mother's "Can you clear your place?"; Juli cheerfully responds "Yes," and her plate remains where it was. These same imperceptions are evident in nonverbal aspects of communication, such as staring, standing too close when speaking, or difficulty taking another's perspective. In one study, for example, teenagers with learning disabilities were less sensitive than typical learners to the listener's need for more explicit information when they described a film or explained how to solve a problem (Caro & Schneider, 1983; in Ripich & Griffith, 1988).

Clearly, teenagers with different types of language disabilities will be "out of it" at different times. It is frustrating for them to be able to understand much of the time but be absolutely lost at other times. When this occurs on a daily basis, it is understandable that self-doubt regarding one's cognitive abilities builds. It is very easy for the teacher to misinterpret the student's variability as being due to inattentiveness or laziness.

Because poor listening skills and oral communication can have a definite impact on peer acceptance, teacher evaluation, social–emotional development, and future job adjustment, intervention and instructional modifications deserve serious consideration. Signs of pragmatic difficulties can be noted as early as the preschool years, and these children need help learning to respond appropriately in social situations. They can be taught, for example, to whisper in a movie theater, to add inflections when relating a story rather than speaking in a monotone, and to read body language to judge whether jumping into a guest's lap is appropriate. Teenagers can be taught how to take turns in conversations and to be aware of scaring people by standing too close, or annoying people by interrupting at the wrong times. Fortunately, listening skills can be effectively trained, and they should become a greater focus of our instructional programs (Childers, 1970; Cunningham, Cunningham, & Arthur, 1981; Erickson, 1954; Pratt, 1956; Schumaker et al., 1983).

In some cases students already do possess good listening and speaking competencies, but they employ engagement-producing and -maintaining utterances (such as offering necessary information) less consistently and frequently than do their nondisabled peers. This results in conversations that are only slightly more than a monologue, which in turn reduces the responsiveness and informativeness of the conversational partner (Mathinos, 1991). These students can use our help in learning to clarify the norms and goals in various types of interactions, and the strategies they possess that can help to achieve these goals. They also need our help in building the confidence to use their conversational abilities as a vehicle for enriching their personal lives.

Summary

Despite adequate intellectual resources and learning opportunities, students with learning disabilities have difficulty learning basic skills and retaining information. These memory difficulties appear to relate to an insufficient knowledge base to which new information can be anchored, poor use of strategies to aid storage and retrieval, and the interference of various information-processing inefficiencies with the processing of information. For the most part these students' learning strategies and information-processing skills develop in the same order as would typically be expected, although at a slower rate. When compared with younger typical learners who are achieving at similar levels, the patterns of the learning disabled often tend to be qualitatively more immature.

The first signs of learning disabilities frequently become apparent in the preschool years.

Delays in attention, memory, learning strategies, visual-perceptual, motor, or language abilities contrast with pockets of strength. These uneven patterns continue into elementary school and beyond, interfering in subtle or more pervasive ways with achievement and adjustment.

It is important to be aware of the normal sequence of learning strategy and information-processing development, so that we can detect weaknesses that need to be strengthened and design appropriate learning objectives and remedial strategies. In addition to remediating these areas of weakness, attention and memory will improve as we help students to gain more knowledge and store this knowledge in a deeper, more meaningful way; in this way the old information can guide attention to the new information, give it meaning, help it to be stored, and cue its retrieval. The more knowledge a student has, the more the student can learn. Likewise, the more strategically the student approaches learning, and the more automatic the information-processing skills used to reason, the better the learning outcome.

Chapter Seven

Social–Emotional Development

The social adjustment of individuals with learning disabilities is just as important to deal with as their academic achievement because success in life often has far more to do with how people feel about themselves and are accepted by others than with their ultimate level of academic achievement. Unfortunately, behavioral disturbances are more frequent among students with learning disabilities than among their nondisabled peers, especially among males. These students tend to be less accepted by peers and adults, to interact awkwardly with others, to be socially imperceptive, and to respond to failure by no longer trying. Often the origins of their difficulties are apparent in the preschool years, and these difficulties continue year after year, even into adulthood. Consequently, the social–emotional concerns of students with learning disabilities need to be addressed in just as intense a manner as the academic concerns, to ensure that these children grow up with enough personal strengths to pursue areas of talent, to persist in things that are hard, to be motivated to undertake challenges, and to be content interpersonally with their employers, families, and friends.

In this chapter we shall describe typical patterns of social development, so that we can take note of early signs of deviancy or delay and intervene accordingly. We shall explore the development of temperament and social skills in the preschooler and then describe typical patterns among elementary school children, teenagers, and adults. Excerpts of Joseph Lair's story about his life are reprinted in the following pages. Joe was finally identified as learning disabled at age 21. He traces his childhood years and the anguishes he now faces as an adult, beginning school as an eager student, then becoming a class clown, isolate, bully, drug and alcohol addict, and finally a store owner in and out of love relationships. His words attest to the serious responsibility of parents and teachers to help children with the social side of learning disabilities.

Joe

I like to call it an adventure because that's what living with a learning disability feels like to me today. It's an adventure like living one of the *Raiders of the Lost Ark* movies. I never know what's going to happen until it does (p. 7).

The day that changed my life happened in spelling class. Since spelling was one of my most defeating subjects I had taken to getting sick the day of spelling tests and that was that. After missing several spelling test days, my friends started teasing me. I started getting embarrassed and very uncomfortable. . . .

I always tried to study for tests, but it seemed like I never made any headway. I just couldn't get the words, and even the ones I knew how to spell regularly came hard for me in a test (p. 13).

Edith, the girl who sat in front of me, looked around and stuck out her tongue at me. I don't know why she did that, but she did it all the time. Spelling was the first thing we did on that morning. That was fine with me—get it over with.

I pulled my tablet of paper towards me and numbered one through ten on a piece of paper. My hand started to sweat so I wiped it on my pants. Mrs. Pendelton called out the first word and the pencils around me started scratching away. I spelled the word. We went on down the list. After she called out the last word and everyone had finished she told us to pass our papers to the person in front of us. I passed mine to Edith and the guy from the front seat came back and dropped his paper off with me. We started correcting each other's papers. The tenth word was *themselves*. Mrs. Pendelton spelled it out and after she was finished she asked if anyone in class had gotten that word right.

Some hands went up, but not Edith's. Mrs. Pendelton congratulated the two or three who had gotten the word right. Then Edith's hand went up.

"Mrs. Pendelton, guess what? Joe didn't use any vowels in *themselves*."

Edith held up my paper for the teacher to see and looked back and laughed at me. I died. Then I looked around and the whole class was looking at me and they were all laughing. And things changed forever right then and there. . . .

The day of that defeat marked a turning point where I took my first step into a downward spiral (p. 14).

● ● ●

I was sitting in school and I couldn't convince anyone that I was able to do anything. And the harder I tried, the worse it got.

It was in the fifth grade that I first realized that I was being overlooked because I was labeled lazy or lacking incentive. I was able to see that, as I was watching my friends leave

(Continues on following page)

Joe *(Continued from preceding page)*

me behind and it hurt. When the pain and fear became overwhelming, I reached out to my friends the only way I could think of, I became a clown. I could disrupt a classroom at any moment. The teachers hated it, but my classmates loved it and I started getting some status. Even Kevin started leaving me alone most of the time. He even stopped kicking me in the back. It was great (pp. 16–17).

In the classroom a lot of my behavior is very learning disabled. I have a limited attention span and have a hard time keeping quiet. I wiggle and fidget, I chew gum, I daydream, sometimes I'll say things out loud inappropriately, responding to a half-heard phrase the teachers said, and I'm often entirely out of context. It's very embarrassing (p. 70).

Study halls were nothing but social situations for me. I didn't understand what I was supposed to do in a study hall. I could not grasp how to study and study halls were so quiet they drove me crazy. Quiet is a form of deprivation for me. A study hall was like being in a deprivation tank (p. 111).

I always would end up in the bonehead reading section . . . All of my friends were over on the other side and I was over with those "others." I hated being over with the other kids. They were the ones the "cool" kids picked on. It was a pain to be with them. I was really scared about something rubbing off on me. And I am sure now that they all felt the same about me. . . .

It was funny. I always knew I had a problem learning like everyone else but I always knew I wasn't dumb. I was scared all the time of being thought dumb but in my heart I knew I wasn't. I hated being set apart. It made every day so tense for me (p. 17).

So, like a lot of learning disabled kids, I was beginning a career of sticking out, being different. I was noisy, not because I wanted the negative attention it got me, but because I needed and wanted acceptance from my peers and couldn't figure out how to be one of them. With no built in road-map, unable to understand the strange land I was in, things seemed to be getting worse and worse (p. 29).

• • •

I felt different enough from my classmates that stress began piling upon stress. Soon I couldn't trust anything. If a teacher were to ask me what county I lived in I could be thinking "Gallatin County" but out might pop, "America."

This began to happen often. The classroom would be disrupted and the teacher would be mad. I would be embarrassed but the students thought I was great. This could happen to me everyday and countless times in a day. I didn't want to be a smart Alec but the teacher thought I did and my classmates thought I did. If the principal became involved he thought I did, and heck, even my parents began to think I did.

I literally, by then, had little control over my tongue. I still don't today. I hear things and I respond with an inability to screen what I'll say. I don't want to do this and I do my utmost to safeguard myself but I have no protection. Given enough time something inane will always pop out. I've even stopped going to certain business meetings because of a fear

(Continues on following page)

Joe *(Continued from preceding page)*

of making an ass of myself. This is painful, but this is a fact and I have to accept it. . . . I don't know where the wires are crossed, but crossed they are (p. 20).

[There were] times when I would do or say something and my friends would look at me like I was from another planet. It would mostly happen to me when I would come upon a group of my friends somewhere and try to join into the conversation. . . . I would listen in a group and then give the group my ideas. When I did that, the conversation would die and they would all look at me.

I'd die a thousand deaths. . . .

I thought people were starting to laugh at me and maybe even call me dumb, stupid or retarded. I was never sure, but to me it felt that way, and I started to react to these feelings. What I started doing was going totally nuts every time the word dumb or any synonym of it was associated with me. I beat up people for even thinking I was dumb.

A close friend took me aside one day and talked to me about how many people were scared of me and asked me if that was what I wanted. The answer was easy, "No, I don't want anyone scared of me." So I came up with another answer and that was the one I stayed with for a long time. I just went quiet, and just didn't join into things as much . . . I hated the part of me that I couldn't seem to control (pp. 21–22).

• • •

When I was a little kid I loved telling jokes more than anything in the whole world. I loved to make people laugh. It was a pleasure to me to make people laugh. As I was growing up I was pretty good at it, too. I was like everyone else in the world. I loved to make people laugh, but if they were laughing at me it wasn't funny.

As I moved into my eighth grade year I became something to laugh at. I was becoming goofy. I was watching my friends start to relate to the teachers in an adult way and I would try to talk to teachers in the same way. It just didn't work.

I would crack a joke in class and instead of getting my friends to laugh they were starting to tell me to be quiet. My jokes weren't getting the response I was wanting anymore. I was really getting scared about what to do with myself. I had cruised for a long time on my ability to get people to laugh. It was scary to think that it wasn't working anymore.

I started to try to keep my mouth shut in class and it worked sometimes. I was able to be quiet. My problem started coming from the teachers. If I was quiet they would start asking me questions again. For instance, I would be sitting in math class and the teacher would ask me a question. I hadn't spouted off to him in [a] couple of months so he thought it was probably safe to ask me [a] question. So he asked me to answer a question. I had no idea how to answer it. Not one clue.

Now I was in trouble as far as I was concerned and the class was waiting for my answer. I was screwed. I was going to look stupid. I was looking stupid right now!

"Joe, do you know the answer? We've gone over it twice now during class, how about an answer."

(Continues on following page)

Joe   *(Continued from preceding page)*

Great, we've gone over it twice. Now I really feel stupid. I was in the batter's box and I was striking out. The teacher looked at me and I think he saw and smelled the fear coming out of me. He heaved a sigh and called on the dumbest person in the class. The one person we all picked on in the hallway and the lunch room.

"Richard, tell me the answer?" Richard knew the answer. I slid down in my chair and died. I was humiliated Richard had known the answer and he had made me look stupid. . . .

The thing that was scaring me the most was watching my friends talking to adults and seeing the adults relate right back to them on the same level. When I would try and talk with adults or teachers, all I got was weird looks. . . .

I'd start quoting facts no one wanted to hear. I'd make up facts a lot of times. I'd lie to get accepted, and the sad thing was that everyone knew it. I could see it in their faces.

I don't know why I talked like I did. It made me sound even more immature than I was, but even though I knew it sounded wrong I couldn't stop. I just wanted to be accepted and I thought that was the way to sound grown up. I heard my folks talking facts and figures all the time. I thought I sounded just like them. I didn't. (pp. 34–35).

• • •

I wanted to be with my friends who were on the other side of the building. It just didn't seem fair . . . even in the shop classes I was having trouble. It was seeming harder for me than the regular classes. I wasn't able to follow the directions that the teacher was giving.

Verbal directions have always been hard for me. I just can't seem to filter out the information from the spoken word. It usually seems like a different language to me. I hear it and then have to take it to the translation department inside of my brain. In that process something is always lost and I only get part of the information . . .

I was desperately trying to find some way to fit in and all I was doing was getting egg on my face. I would go and find my friends at a party and try to hang out with them. I was not welcomed any more. They were talking about things and classes that I was no longer a part of.

I was totally lost. I was going farther and farther down a road that I didn't like and I was getting into more and more trouble. I was starting to get caught skipping classes and my parents weren't happy with me. I was feeling angrier and I wasn't having much luck expressing it.

I would be in class, trying to listen to the teacher and not be a nuisance and something, anything, would happen and I'd get mad. I would be in the hall walking just after class and rage would start welling up in me. I would reach over and smack a locker and bust up my knuckles.

The people around me would look at me like I was a totally freaked out person. The sad fact was that I was feeling freaked out. . . .

The school part of me was in the toilet and home was going down fast. I was pulling farther away from everybody around me and I wasn't talking to people anymore. Not talking was driving me crazy, but I was scared to open up.

(Continues on following page)

Joe   *(Continued from preceding page)*

There were people who were reaching out to me and trying to help me, but I'd just blow them off as fast as I could (pp. 37–39).

· · ·

Some of my friends were starting to change towards me. It hurt to see them start moving on to other friends. I would talk to them during school and try to make plans with them for the weekend and I always got the same response. "Well. Give me a call and we'll see if we can get together."

I'd call them and they'd be gone already. I'd tell their parents it was me and to have them call me back, but they never did (p. 36).

Simply put, I was so afraid of rejection that just the fear of any of my friends leaving me, kept me always on guard. Somewhere deep inside of me I was so sure there would come a day when, BANG, the person was going to be gone.

Getting through the "friendship minefield" seemed too dangerous to even try. It still does, sometimes, today.

I would go to great lengths to not make mistakes. I would avoid any situation where I felt unsure of myself.

When I was a kid I went to a couple of dances and when I was out on the dance floor I felt so stupid. I couldn't keep track of the music, my feet and the person I was dancing with all at the same time. It drove me crazy. So after a couple of dances I just avoided them. I ended up making a story about bad knees and not being able to dance.

One day in high school I was sitting bored with another lecture from one of the older teachers. I'd gotten totally spaced out and my mind was off in orbit visiting the spaceship Enterprise.

I guess I was really out there because the guy behind had to hit me twice on the shoulder to get my attention. I jerked myself back up in the seat and looked at the teacher. The teacher always reminded me of TOUCHÉ TURTLE one of my favorite cartoon characters. He had a skinny face, no neck, and a jutting upper lip that looked like a snapping turtle.

"Ahh, Mr. Lair has rejoined us, how nice."

"What, turtle face?"

I waited for the class to start laughing and it didn't happen. Part of me was puzzled but I didn't pay any attention to it. I ended up getting two hours of detention for my cruel, albeit LD remark (p. 41).

My inappropriate social behavior has always been the thing that has brought me the most pain and the thing I always get defensive about first. Living life is my biggest problem (p. 43).

I just don't read the cues other people can read, like body language, facial expression, tension in the air. [I learned] to not react, to just be still and not to say or do anything when I first come into a group. I learned to step back from things and try and get the lay of the land before I start to participate . . .

(Continues on following page)

Joe   *(Continued from preceding page)*

I still find myself standing on the shore so many times with everybody on the island pointing to the bridge but I'm not able to find it (pp. 51–52).

• • •

There are times when I have to pull the reins so tight on my brain that I almost stall out. My brain and following directions just don't agree. I can't understand what it is they want from me. I read what the directions say and then start trying to follow them. It just doesn't work and I get so confused so fast . . .

Whenever my brain gets information it slows down . . .

It was probably the reason I lost some of the jobs I lost. In the restaurant when I was a cook the boss would start calling out orders and my brain was slowing down with each order. What my boss needed was me acknowledging each order given. What was going on with me was I felt like I was a prize fighter and each order was a punch coming in. I was punch drunk within ten minutes of being up on the line.

The same thing happens to me when I get in an argument with someone. They start reeling off information as fast as their brain can process it and there I am with my brain starting to hit the emergency brakes. Then the person is starting to want feedback from me and I'm stuck up in my brain trying to sort out the information that has just arrived.

At work even today it's a problem. A large shipment will come in and I'm looking at all the boxes and I know how much I ordered. My brain starts slowing down with what I think is an overwhelming task. My co-workers look at all the fun it's going to be to see the new things that have arrived. They also see the newness of something to do. I see boxes and how overwhelming it all is (p. 58).

• • •

Wherever I went I brought my mess with me.

That mess, I was learning, was my perpetually low self-esteem. I viewed life as a continuing battle and I was always losing. I would wake up in the morning, put on my bulls-eye and people would shoot at it, of course. Then I'd sit back and say to myself, "See I was right, they were out to get me." I was the one who did this to myself—all I had to do was take off the bulls-eye. . . .

A few people tried to tell me I wasn't wearing the right clothes but I didn't believe them mainly because I'd dressed that way for a long time, it was security for me, and I wasn't ready to give it up. For me to give up dressing the way I did would entail change, and that was unacceptable because it terrified me . . .

Change was death, they were one and the same. I would only give up something as a last recourse. I love familiarity, I find comfort in it. I can drive the same way to work forever and not find anything wrong with it. I love having things at home in the same place. I love consistency. . . .

I need things to be the same for a very basic reason. I don't know how to learn things very well (p. 50).

(Continues on following page)

Joe   *(Continued from preceding page)*

• • •

. . . living is what is kicking my butt, and I struggle with it every day (p. 23).

I'm still learning that as a learning disabled person I spend so much energy protecting myself. I still live in such fear of being thought stupid most of the time, and it strongly influences everything I do and all of my decisions (p. 25).

As the pressure mounts my brain slows down. I can feel it happening. It's like words have to fight their way through mud or molasses. And finally my brain shuts down entirely (p. 28).

The first lesson I learned and one I'm still learning is how hard it is for me to get to work on time. Time, like I've already said, is something that I just don't get and I wish I really did. It would make life much easier. . . .

I expect the help to be on time and I think I should set the example, but it hasn't worked out yet. I'm still usually ten or fifteen minutes late and it's a problem. I've tried the same games with my clock that everyone uses. I've made solemn vows not to be late again and they only last three or four days. I've come to work to find a shivering employee who has no key waiting for me to let her in. I've lost jobs because of this.

Another problem is orderliness. I don't pick up things around the store. I pick up things when it's overwhelming, but I just don't see how messy it is until it's reached overwhelming proportions . . .

Anger is another problem. It's been a part of me since I was little kid. I can be doing almost anything and all of a sudden I'm angry. I can't for the life of me tell you why, but one second I'm fine and the next I'm angry. I've tried all my life to control this, I work on it every day. When it's the worst is when I'm doing something and become frustrated. Watch out! I'm a stick of dynamite waiting to blow up.

I couldn't even find one thing in a grocery store. No one believed me when I said I didn't know how to shop, but I really didn't. It's almost impossible to convince people you can't do something that they take for granted. . . .

I have a problem with walking the aisles of the bigger places, I can't seem to get through the process of looking. There's too much for me to take in when I'm in the big places. They have so much to choose from that it almost kills me to make a decision. In the

(Continues on following page)

Before we describe a litany of social–emotional adjustment difficulties among individuals with learning disabilities, it is important to recognize that, as in all areas of LD research, this outcome is not a sure thing. Considering the fact that about 75 percent of individuals with learning disabilities tend to distinguish themselves socially in one way or another from their classmates (fewer social interactions and less befriended, poorer social perception and problem-solving, more hyperactive, distractible, anxious, and rejected), view themselves as deficient academically, or are cognizant of their social skill weaknesses (Kavale & Forness, 1996; Wright-Strawderman & Watson, 1992), nevertheless the majority overall seem to have adjusted reasonably well.

Despite low self-concepts regarding school functioning, we find that these feelings often do

Joe *(Continued from preceding page)*

smaller places I have two or maybe three things to choose from and that's manageable for me . . .

In order to stay relaxed I've had to see that some things that I do in life are not age appropriate. I've made the conscious decision to continue doing them because they're a part of who I am—like blowing bubbles or playing with my yoyo at work. I have a friend who's just like me. . . .

This is one part of being LD. I love being this child-like way. It makes it all worthwhile. I hope this part of me never grows up. And I hope I can continue to stay loose and relaxed about being this way (pp. 55–56).

• • •

My mentor Jerry and I often talk about how getting out of bed in the morning is an incredibly hard thing for us. When we wake up in the morning we both have to laugh at how our day immediately assails us and then paralyzes us. We have had to learn to cope by breaking it into simple things. The process starts with, "Okay, reach over and turn the alarm off. Into the bathroom, take a shower, brush your teeth. Keep going, don't let your mind run away. Start getting positive thoughts going through your brain. You're okay. You're okay." We both have seen that it's necessary to get positive thoughts going through our brain as fast as possible when we first wake up. . . .

Today I was sitting with some friends and we were talking about how hard it is to remember and act upon the belief that "fundamentally all is well." . . .

It's real simple for me to see how unmanageable my life is. I can't keep a checkbook balanced. I always have to wear something on my left hand to know what way is right or left. I'm daily apologizing at least a dozen times for making LD inappropriate comments. I have a total inability to structure my time. I'm at the mercy of whatever wind happens to blow through my life. I've tried keeping my mouth shut in business meetings and social events where I fear I'd embarrass myself. But that is no way to live. I need to be able to speak up and not just keep my opinions to myself because I count (p. 115).

"For what I am today shame on a lot of things. If I stay that way, shame on me" (p. 47).

Source: Lair, J. T. (1992). *Cookie and me.* Bozeman, MT. Reprinted by permission.

not spill over into overall dissatisfaction with one's worth as an individual (Bear, Juvonen, & McInerney, 1993; Bear & Minke, 1996; Kistner et al., 1987; Kloomok & Cosden, 1994). Many of these youngsters are as well liked as their nondisabled peers or other low achievers (Bear et al., 1993; Prillaman, 1981; Sainato, Zigmond, & Strain, 1983; Sater & French, 1989; Vaughn & Haager, 1994). Moreover, some are popular, especially

when compared with other low achievers (Coleman & Minnett, 1993; Perlmutter et al., 1983; Sabornie, Marshall, & Ellis, 1990; Siperstein & Goding, 1983). Even in studies that find a greater frequency of children with learning disabilities being rejected, the majority in fact are not rejected. According to their parents, nearly half of students with learning disabilities are rated as having balanced, well-adjusted personalities

(Fuerst, Fisk, & Rourke, 1989; Porter & Rourke, 1985).

In some studies, students who are learning disabled have been just as attuned to others' feelings, thoughts, intentions, and motives as their non-LD counterparts (Cartledge, Stupay, & Kaczala, 1986; Horowitz, 1981; Maheady, Maitland, & Sainato, 1984). Many are typical in their peer-interactions, numbers of friends, abilities to cope with conflict, and positive regard for themselves and others (Bruck & Hébert, 1982; Bryan, Werner, & Pearl, 1982; Carlson, 1987; Cartledge et al., 1986). Many of these students' conversational interactions are just as mature, positive, cooperative, considerate, and persuasive as those of their non-LD peers (Boucher, 1986; Markoski, 1983). Many are highly motivated and recognize that a combination of ability and hard work can lead to success (Durrant, 1993). Many succeed despite their learning disabilities because they put forth far greater effort than their typical classmates.

Many personal, family, teacher, and peer factors influence whether any one child will experience social and emotional adjustment difficulties. Unfortunately, if due to the differences of those with learning disabilities, others decide to limit their interactions or interact differently with these students, they will be denied important opportunities to develop such important social skills as trust, humor, understanding different perspectives, handling conflict resolution, aggression, competition, and managing their emotional responses (Odom et al., 1992; Wiener, 1987). Immaturity in these social skills in turn invites rejection and isolation. Because the learning disabled are at greater risk socially and emotionally, and because their social and emotional problems may persist into adulthood, it is important to understand the origins of these difficulties so that we can intervene positively.

In Chapters 11 and 12 you will learn about the parental and school attributes that best promote intellectual, academic, and positive social–emotional development in the child. Our task here is to better understand the normal progression of social maturity and the way in which difficult temperaments and learning disabilities can contribute to adjustment problems, so that we can take note of early signs of deviancy or delay and plan for the most appropriate play activities, family interactions, and instructional environments.

The Preschooler

We begin with a look at infant and preschool social–emotional development. It is at this young age that children's temperaments, and the feedback they get from parents, teachers, and peers, begin to shape attitudes and behavior patterns that can exacerbate children's learning difficulties or give them the motivation to persist despite adversity and frustration—to look on the brighter side of things and eventually succeed.

Normal Progression of Social Maturity

The process of learning to feel content with oneself and one's relationships with others begins at birth. Harbingers of a safe, secure, trusting, "can do" outlook on life, or an outlook that is troubled, are quite apparent in observations of parent–infant interactions (Nichols & Chen, 1981). These interaction patterns, in turn, forecast the child's academic and social–emotional adjustment.

What is the typical progression of social–emotional development in the preschooler? From birth to one and a half years of age, children gradually gain a sense of trust in their parents' ability to support their needs (Erikson, 1963). Hartup (1989) characterizes children's relationships with their parents as "vertical" attachments; the parents have greater knowledge and social power, and the children submit to parental control and depend on parental nurturance. Protection and security are provided so that the child's social skills can evolve in a predictable, facilitative environment.

Beginning social skills are already apparent at five to fourteen weeks of age, when infants begin showing orienting responses to other babies (Beckman & Lieber, 1992). By three months the beginnings of conversational turn-taking are evident in the ebbs and flows of mother–child vocalizations and pauses; these eventually transition into turn-taking games such as peekaboo and pat-a-cake (Berk, 1997). Usually around seven months of age, infants begin to develop *object permanence;* they know that something exists, even when it is out of sight. At this time "mother" is such a salient memory that infants demonstrate their attachment by being uncomfortable in their mother's absence and putting up a terrible fuss when she leaves (Ainsworth et al., 1978). At this age children play parallel to others and will flit from one activity to another as their whims and fancies direct. Mothers observe that their children, well before age two, will display caring behaviors such as hugging, kissing, patting, and offering verbal comfort or advice to someone who is crying, ill, or injured (Zahn-Waxler et al., 1992).

By the time preschoolers reach two years of age, they can keep at least two pieces of information in mind at once and imitate activities that they have witnessed (for example, pretending to stir food in a pot and then lick the spoon). They connect two words when speaking, and their reasoning abilities evolve rapidly. With this greater use of language and symbolic play come more frequent and longer play interactions with other children, though for the most part each is doing his or her "own thing" (Hartup, 1989). Two year olds make choices about what they want to do, begin to exercise self-restraint, and show clear pride in accomplishing what they set out to do (for example, grabbing the pen from the desk and scribbling on the wall) (Erikson, 1963). As children get older, they begin to engage in complementary play; they exchange roles, play games, and actively direct and organize their play (Beckman & Lieber, 1992). The quality of these children's pretend play and turn-taking in play is a significant predictor of social competence (Odom, McConnell, & McEvoy, 1992). At this age children successfully negotiate entering a group that is already playing by suggesting a new twist to the game.

Initiative and autonomy continue to develop as the child's cognitive, language, and motor skills mature. Children begin to set challenges for themselves. By two and a half years of age the preschooler is content to follow another child in exploring different toys or even venturing out of the room, away from his or her mother; the child recognizes that mom is still there, available if

needed, and feels comfortable with this greater freedom. Tantrums and resistance to parental limits are typical during what has been called the "terrible two's."

From age three on, children's cooperative play increases and friendships become evident. Eighty percent of children express at least one strong preference for a peer, and reciprocal interactions with partners occupy about 30 percent of play. These friendships constitute "horizontal" attachments through which social skills mature and develop. The relationships are characterized by generally positive interactions, cooperation and competition, as well as reciprocity. Although friends tend to disagree with each other more often than children who aren't friends, they also tend to disengage more often and more rapidly from the conflict, their conflicts are less aggressive, rejecting, and angry, the outcomes more often are equal, and the friends are more likely to stay near each other and interact once again when it is all over. Preschoolers whose reciprocal preferences are maintained for a year tend to have higher social competence (Hartup, 1989; Hartup et al., 1988; Odom et al., 1992). Close friendships, from preschool through adolescence, rarely cross sexes (Farmer & Farmer, 1996; Thorne, 1986).

Children who use the most positive initiations towards their peers are the most likely to receive positive responses in turn. In the preschooler, these positive initiations include sharing, suggesting a play idea, showing affection, offering assistance, and joining in rough and tumble play (Odom et al., 1992).

The quality of the very young child's vertical and horizontal relationships will affect his or her long-term social competence. These are the experiences from which children learn to model behavior, expect good or bad consequences, trust or mistrust, approach or withdraw, and so forth. The more securely attached a child is, the more likely he or she is to be enthusiastic, motivated, attentive to problem solving, and open to teaching attempts (Sroufe & Fleeson, 1986). This type of positive outlook, openness, and persistence can do much to help a child tackle his or her difficulties and learn to work around them. Consequently, it is our responsibility to help facilitate these interpersonal successes with just as much earnestness as we encourage acquisition of preacademic knowledge.

Temperament

The parents' ability to adapt to their child's unique temperament is critical to the social–emotional adjustment of the child with learning disabilities. Often these children have unique temperaments that present challenges for their parents.

It is now a well-documented finding that children come into this world with temperaments that are uniquely their own. The "how" of their behavior is fairly consistent from one setting to another and, in many instances, persists into the elementary school years and beyond (Smith 1997). Because temperament can persist, it has a powerful impact on children's adjustment in learning and interpersonal situations. Much research has been done to determine the origin of these styles and the role of parental temperaments in modifying their children's styles. Thomas and Chess (1977), for example, followed a number of children from infancy through adolescence. On

the basis of the nine categories described in Table 7–1, they classified the infants into three styles: the easy child, the difficult child, and the slow-to-warm-up child. The easy child was characterized by "regularity, positive approach to new stimuli, high adaptability to change and mild or moderately intense mood which is preponderantly positive" (p. 23). Difficult children had traits of "irregularity in biological functions, negative withdrawal to new stimuli, nonadaptability or slow adaptability to change, intense mood and expressions which are frequently negative" (p. 23). Slow-to-warm-up children were characterized "by mild intensity of reactions, whether positive or negative, and by less tendency to show irregularity of biological functions" (p. 23).

Thomas and Chess's difficult children were at greater risk for future behavior problems. However, this was not a certain outcome, and temperament traits did change over time. The stability of traits and the child's outcome appeared to be the result of an interaction between temperament, the child's abilities and motivation, and environmental influences. A good fit between the temperament of the parent and the temperament of the child facilitated the child's development. Many

Table 7–1   Nine categories of temperament and their definitions

1. *Activity.* The amount of physical motion during such activities as eating, playing, and studying.
2. *Rhythmicity.* The regularity of such physiologic functions as hunger, sleep, and elimination.
3. *Approach/Withdrawal.* The tendency to initially approach or withdraw from a new stimulus, be it, for example, a new person, classroom, food, toy, or teaching method.
4. *Adaptability.* The ease with which a child adjusts over time to new or altered situations, such as a new school, schedule, or altered rules in a game.
5. *Intensity.* The level of emotional energy expressed in both positive and negative circumstances.
6. *Mood.* The amount of joyful and friendly versus unhappy and unpleasant behavior in a variety of situations.
7. *Persistence.* The length of time a child pursues an activity despite obstacles such as a difficult task or more desirable options.
8. *Distractability.* The extent to which extraneous stimuli divert the attention and behavior of the child.
9. *Threshold.* The intensity level of stimulation before a child will indicate sensitivity to such changes as lighting, sound, texture of clothing, odors, people's moods, and pain.

Source: Adapted from Thomas, A., & Chess, S. (1977). *Temperament and development.* New York: Brunner/Mazel. Reprinted by permission.

studies have demonstrated this potential to modify difficult temperaments over time (Matheny, Wilson, & Nuss, 1984; Smith, 1997).

When difficult temperament traits do persist, however, these frequently are associated with school learning, emotional, and social difficulties (Chess, Thomas, & Cameron, 1976; Keogh, 1982; Lerner, Lerner, & Zabski, 1985; Martin, Nagle, & Paget, 1983; Martin et al., 1988; Maziade et al., 1990; Mevarech, 1985; Pullis & Cadwell, 1982; Schor, 1985). Temperamentally difficult infants elicit more confrontations with their mothers and, when approached by strangers, respond in a less friendly and more fearful manner than easier infants (Berberian & Snyder, 1982; Lee & Bates, 1985). As preschoolers these children wrestle, hit, jump, push, beat, fuss, cling, and disobey more than do children with easier temperaments. They spend less time simply sitting and are more likely to be the target of parental criticism (Smith, 1997). In the preschool classroom, the more difficult the temperament, the greater the nonacademic behavior contacts initiated by the teacher, and the greater the criticism (Paget, Nagle, & Martin, 1984). Not surprisingly, peers choose to spend less time interrelating with those classmates who have the more difficult temperaments (Keogh & Burstein, 1988). Withdrawn and apathetic preschoolers too have their problems with low frequency and initiation of peer interaction (Kohn & Parnes, 1974). Although preschoolers with more mild developmental delays do establish peer preferences, all too often these are not reciprocated (Odom et al., 1992).

Parents of many students with learning disabilities describe their children as having been "difficult" infants and preschoolers. Raising a child who is hyperactive is particularly trying from day one: parents are exhausted from rocking their colicy baby who seldom sleeps and always cries; parents feel helpless and incompetent when nothing can make their infant happy; they continually worry about what catastrophe has occurred with the babysitter in their absence; they must turn down invitations to join their friends at a restaurant for fear of their child's out of control behavior; parents cannot enjoy a supermarket or mall visit without anticipating a major temper tantrum

or disaster (e.g., child running ahead into an elevator or getting lost in a store); simply going to a movie or reading a book quietly with their child is frustrated by unexpected interruptions; preschool teacher conferences are dreaded, siblings complain, dinnertime is filled with conflict, and grandparents blame the parents. It takes a very special parent to maintain an accepting, peaceful, and positively encouraging attitude and atmosphere, while setting the firm limits and structure that will promote more acceptable behavior. The constant shifting of plans and approaches to meet the hyperactive child's needs is wearing, and makes families feel out of control most of the time. One mother of a ten-year-old child, who still could not do math problems without jumping up and flailing his arms and legs and yelling aloud for "joy" with each problem's completion, recently remarked that not one day has gone by in her son's life that has not witnessed a major trauma. She is worn down and tired of needing to be on guard all the time. While she recognizes that her adaptations are helping her son to develop in positive directions, she also sadly recognizes that progress is slow and that they all have a long way to go.

The child who was premature at birth also presents rearing difficulties and is at risk for learning and adjustment difficulties. These infants tend to be highly sensitive, overreactive to environmental stimulation, and easily stressed (Als, 1985). As with the hyperactive child, in order to reach some equilibrium, these children require adults to sensitively structure their interactions with different environments and people, and to offer support when the children are disorganized and overwhelmed.

Poor parent–child interactions and out of control, unstructured environments that do not facilitate adaptive behaviors can be avoided if parents modulate their behavior in response to their child's disorganization and discomfort. Unfortunately, parents of a neurologically immature or hyperactive baby often will misinterpret the baby's withdrawal, crying, flailing, or flacid responses, thinking that the child does not enjoy the mother's cooing and hugging or the dad's jostling. The parent feels rebuffed. Yet the child is doing the best he can; he cannot muster the animated and well-modulated responses of the more integrated newborn. Because the well-integrated child's behavior is perceived as loving and interested, this child is easier for parents to become attached to. The more we can help parents understand that we are dealing here with different levels of neurological organization or different temperaments, not love, the better parents will be able to cope and patiently guide their children toward more integrated, harmonious interactions.

The Elementary School Student

When six- to eight-year-old children are interviewed about how they view friendships, they generally emphasize playmate relations and sharing. In contrast, nine- to eleven-year-old children point to the reciprocity in their friendships; they value the understanding that friends offer one another, being able to depend on their help, and the companionship that can be counted on from friends when lonely (Youniss, 1980).

Doll (1996) summarizes studies showing that, by first grade, one-third of children have at least one mutual friend. By the time children burst onto the playground for recess, they've already negotiated who will play what with whom. As the elementary school years continue, mutual friendships persist over longer periods and the children spend more time together. The adequacy of these peer friendships is a powerful predictor of future socioemotional adjustment and the child's motivation to succeed academically.

The social status of children relates directly to the quality of their social behaviors: helpfulness, conformity to rules, friendliness. Those who are rejected by peers tend to be more aggressive and engage in inappropriate social interactions. The importance of social skills as a major focus of school programming stems from research showing that early social competencies tend to be stable across settings and ages; childhood peer relationships are strong predictors of adolescent and adult outcomes, including school dropout, emotional problems, and trouble with the law (Odom et al., 1992).

Unfortunately, many factors can deter positive social relationships from developing for children with learning disabilities, including their information-processing inefficiencies, inattentiveness, physical activity and restlessness, unique cognitive styles, maturational lags, unique temperaments, reactions to failure experiences, and the quality of past family support and social learning opportunities. These students' articulation and motor problems often make social conversation with peers and participation in sports difficult; such things as sloppy dress and misbuttoned shirts open them to derision. They also tend to differ from their classmates by engaging in fewer task-oriented behaviors; being more hyperactive, anxious, and obsessive; being more disruptive and less cooperative; showing immature social adaptation; having difficulty accepting others, expressing feelings, maintaining a positive attitude, and helping others; and having particularly weak self-esteem regarding intellectual, physical, school, and social abilities (Bender & Golden, 1988; Bryan, 1974a; Bryan & Wheeler, 1972; Bursuck, 1989; Cooley & Ayers, 1988; Fisher, Allen, & Kose, 1996; Gresham & Reschly, 1986; LaGreca & Stone, 1990; Merrell et al., 1992; Michaels & Lewandowski, 1990; Rogers & Saklofske, 1985; Sobol et al., 1983).

Unfortunately, the negative self-evaluation that may accompany being identified as learning disabled can further decrease overall self-esteem and self-perceptions of academic potential (Heyman, 1990). It is not surprising that one out of every three or four children who are learning disabled describes himself or herself as depressed (Wright-Strawderman & Watson, 1992).

Life in the classroom tends to be different for students with learning disabilities than for their classmates. They often are ignored by teachers and peers when they initiate verbal interactions, are judged more negatively by teachers, and more often are objects of negative, nonsupportive statements, criticisms, warnings, behavioral corrections, or negative nonverbal reactions from their teachers (Bryan, 1974a, 1978; Bryan & Wheeler, 1972; Bursuck, 1989; Chapman, Larsen, & Parker, 1979; Dorval, McKinney, & Feagans,

1982; Garrett & Crump, 1980; Keogh, Tchir, & Windeguth-Behn, 1974; McKinney & Feagans, 1983; Siperstein & Goding, 1983, 1985).

In comparison to typical students, teachers rate the learning disabled as more distractible, hyperactive, acting out, anxious, shy, withdrawn; and less self-confident, persistent, cooperative, assertive, self-controlled, adaptable to new situations, or socially outgoing (Bender & Smith, 1990; Cardell & Parmar, 1988; Epstein, Cullinan, & Nieminen, 1984; Haager & Vaughn, 1995; Hoyle & Serafica, 1988). At times, teachers rate females as worse than males with learning disabilities in their social perception, negativity, and antisocial behaviors; some studies find that disliked females are less accepted and more rejected by classmates than are disliked males (Center & Wascom, 1986; Stiliadis & Wiener, 1989; Swanson & Malone, 1992). When classmates are asked questions such as "Whom would you like/not like to sit beside or invite to a party?" and "whom do you know/like the most/least?" research consistently shows that the student with learning disabilities is less well-known and popular, less accepted, more rejected, more ignored, and more likely to play alone (Bryan, 1974b; Bursuck, 1989; Gottlieb et al., 1986; Haager & Vaughn, 1995; LaGreca & Stone, 1990; Sabornie et al., 1990; Sale & Carey, 1995; Stiliadis & Wiener, 1989; Stone & LaGreca, 1990). The more this student's attributes are valued by his or her classmates (for example, intelligence, good looks, academic or athletic ability) the higher the social status among peers (Bursuck, 1983; Horowitz, 1981; Siperstein & Goding, 1983).

Life outside the classroom also is different for students with learning disabilities than for their peers. They tend to engage in fewer extracurricular activities and only infrequently socialize with classmates outside of school (Hoyle & Serafica, 1988). Often their motor incoordination, poor tactile perception, and spatial disorganization distinguish them from their peers (Harnadek & Rourke, 1994). They are extremely slow at doing most anything (Gross-Tsur et al., 1995). Strangers, whether adults or peers, judge students with learning disabilities more negatively after merely observing their nonverbal behaviors (Bryan & Perlmutter, 1979; Bryan, Sherman, & Fisher, 1980; Perlmutter & Bryan, 1984).

Parents, too, often regard their children with learning disabilities differently. Some parents may express less affection for their offspring with learning disabilities than for their other children (Owen et al., 1971). This may be evident as early as infancy, at which time mothers demonstrate less responsiveness to these babies' needs (Nichols & Chen, 1981). Some parents expect even less of their children with learning disabilities than the children expect of themselves (Chapman & Boersma, 1979). One study found that mothers of children with learning disabilities downplayed their children's successes by attributing them to luck, and compounded their failures by blaming them on poor ability. Mothers of typical children, on the other hand, demonstrated precisely the opposite attribution patterns, crediting success to their children's abilities and failures to bad luck (Pearl & Bryan, 1982). In general, parents of children who are learning disabled rate them as being more anxious, depressed, moody, brooding, uncommunicative, withdrawn, impulsive, distractible, active, and inattentive when compared with their peers; they are rated as having lower self-esteem and frustration tolerance, and greater somatic concerns (fatigue, headaches) and temper outbursts (Eliason & Richman, 1988; Haager & Vaughn, 1995; McConaughy & Ritter, 1986; Porter & Rourke, 1985).

The social–emotional characteristics of some students with learning disabilities do resolve themselves with time (Vaughn & Hogan, 1994), but for others they persist so that, when they enter new social settings, such as a new classroom each September, their social isolation recurs (Bryan, 1976; Odom et al., 1992). Three factors appear to be influential in perpetuating these difficulties: language disabilities, social imperceptions, and *learned helplessness* (feeling that it's not worth trying). Some experts observe that students who are learning disabled often do know appropriate social skills but, because of these factors, fail to use the right skills at the right times (Bryan & Perlmutter, 1979; Spekman, 1981).

Language Disabilities and Social Relationships

The speech of many students with learning disabilities contrasts sharply with the excellent conversational skills of these students' nondisabled peers. Even if on the surface the conversations of students with learning disabilities appear to be no different from those of non-LD students, one nevertheless often detects subtle qualitative differences.

Knight-Arests's (1984) study is an excellent illustration of the language difficulties with which many elementary school children must cope. When required to teach the experimenter how to play checkers, the learning disabled used more sentences than the control children but provided fewer items of information. Their vocabulary was restricted, repetitive, less meaningful, and less mature, and their sentences were shorter, grammatically simpler, and less concise. Although they knew how to play checkers, they had difficulty describing the overall game plan and strategies. Instead, isolated aspects of the game were highlighted. When the experimenter asked for clarification, the children frequently repeated what they had just said rather than reformulating or expanding on it. On the whole, these students preferred to demonstrate moves rather than verbalize strategies. In fact, often the students got sidetracked into playing the game by themselves and neglected the person they were to instruct.

Studies find that youngsters who are learning disabled often cannot adjust their language to the age level of those with whom they are speaking (for example, using a baby voice with an adult, not using simple language with a baby), to what was just said, or to the topic, goal, time, or setting. Their speech may be characterized by non-sequiturs, repetitive statements, rote verbosity, and little or no intonation. They have trouble interpreting and inferring from what others say, taking turns in conversations, and taking other's perspectives. Their sentences often are shorter and less complex than those of their nondisabled peers, and they use inadequate eye contact and facial and body gestures to help get their message across. Children with learning disabilities also tend not to provide age-appropriate descriptive

information about objects and events so as to keep conversations going. Understanding idioms (for example, "Keep your nose clean"), humor, and ambiguous sentences (for example, "They fed her dog biscuits") can be particularly problematic, and immature syntax, semantics, and planning of communication strategies further deter communication. The language skills of students with learning disabilities also are complicated by word finding problems: they sometimes have difficulty responding swiftly or choosing the right words, even if they are sensitive to the line and flow of conversation. It is not surprising that the conversations of children with learning disabilities are characterized by high proportions of silence (Boucher, 1984; Bruno, Johnson, & Simon, 1988; Bryan & Pflaum, 1978; Gross-Tsur et al., 1995; Harnadek & Rourke, 1994; Leong, 1986; Mathinos, 1988; Noel, 1980; Olsen, Wong, & Marx, 1983; Wong & Wong, 1980).

It has been found that the verbal communications of students with learning disabilities often may be more negative and competitive (versus considerate) than that of their peers. This in turn elicits competitiveness from peers (Bryan et al., 1976; Moore & Simpson, 1983).

Donahue (1986) reviews studies suggesting that, as speakers, children with learning disabilities do tend to be sensitive to the listener's need for more information. However, as listeners, they are less likely to recognize that a situation calls for clarification, so they don't ask questions. When they do question, it often is done in such a way that the questions achieve no purpose and do not give the speaker an opportunity to respond: " . . . and the substitute teacher we have—do you like her?—I don't—I mean I really can't stand her because . . . " (Mathinos, 1988, p. 442). These students' communication styles neither sustain nor heighten their control over conversations (Bryan, Donahue, & Pearl, 1981; Byran et al., 1981; Donahue, Pearl, & Bryan, 1980). Interviews indicate that these children are well aware of their difficulties in conversational interaction.

Donahue concludes that the histories of social failure in students with learning disabilities may lead them to doubt their comprehension skills and overestimate the speaker's ability to provide adequate messages. The student, in effect, shifts responsibility for successful exchanges to the speaker. This deferential communication style occurs with peers, adults, and even with these children's own mothers (Bryan et al., 1984). As might be expected, students with learning disabilities are less persuasive than their peers because they tend to give up their own viewpoints in favor of those expressed by others. Because of this deferential role, they are less likely to have their opinions accepted or to assume a leadership role in a group (Bryan, Donahue, & Pearl, 1981).

Commenting on the communication style of the student with a learning disability, Donahue (1986) states that:

. . . The LD conversational partner [is] eager to fulfill conversational responsibilities, while compensating for linguistic inadequacies. Like the tennis player with a limited set of strokes, the LD child seems to hover on the edge of the interaction, watching for an easy opening into the conversation. By seeking out opportunities for participating that provide rich linguistic and contextual support, the LD child gives the appearance of keeping the conversational ball in play. Meanwhile, he or she is equally adept at avoiding those contexts that demand linguistic fluency and conversational initiative. (p. 281)

It is easy to see how language disabilities can interfere with building friendships, peer acceptance, and an adequate self-image.

Social Imperceptions

The social relationships of students with learning disabilities often are hampered by lack of insight into the affect, attitudes, intentions, and expectations communicated by others' verbal and nonverbal behaviors. This ability to take others' perspectives is called *decentering*. Children become able to decenter once they are mature enough to recognize the complex linguistic and nonlinguistic rules that govern communication. This decentering skill typically develops from five to seven years of age, and shows marked increases between ages eight and eleven to thirteen (Flavell et al., 1968; Wiig, 1990). At this same time children naturally transition from being impulsive to

reflective, and they become able to consider more than one side of an issue. In addition, from ages seven to eight and eleven to thirteen children experience a progressive increase in the ability to simultaneously consider several hypotheses regarding the significance of various events and choose the best solutions (Wiig, 1990). Certainly all this cognitive and strategy growth helps with their maturing social relationships.

Unfortunately, some students with learning disabilities are delayed in shifting to these other-oriented strategies and therefore have difficulty understanding the cognitive and affective positions of others (Bruininks, 1978a; Gerber & Zinkgraf, 1982). Their poor comprehension of social rules only exacerbates their isolation, shyness, and withdrawal (Gross-Tsur et al., 1995). Various studies have found that students with learning disabilities may be less accurate than their peers at analyzing a social problem into its important components; foreseeing the possible consequences of various solutions; interpreting nonverbal cues of affection, gratitude, and anger; asking forgiveness; interpreting a character's facial expression (fear, surprise, disgust), gesture, and posture; or describing/explaining a character's feelings. Even interpreting the humor in cartoons presents great difficulty at times (Bryan, 1977; Harnadek & Rourke, 1994; Holder & Kirkpatrick, 1990; Leong, 1986; Nabuzoka & Smith, 1995; Pickering, Pickering, & Buchanan, 1987; Shondrick et al., 1992; Tur-Kaspa & Bryan, 1994). Edmonson and colleagues (1974) found that the social judgments of their elementary school students with learning disabilities were equivalent to those of typical children who were two to four years younger.

When children are poor at perspective taking, they have less insight into what is going on socially and how they are doing within groups. As a result, both the affective and cognitive quality of their interactions suffers (Bryan et al., 1980). This may be why children who are learning disabled at times make more negative statements than their peers, laugh inappropriately, generate fewer alternatives to resolve interpersonal conflicts, tend to use less positive, outgoing, assertive, or rule-oriented means to resolve conflicts (they are more egocentric, demanding, or accommodating), and have difficulty adapting to novel and complex situations, instead overrelying on rote behaviors (Bryan, 1978; Bryan & Pflaum, 1978; Carlson, 1987; Harnadek & Rourke, 1994). These students also fail to use such social ingratiation tactics as acting interested in another speaker through eye contact and smiling (Bryan & Sherman, 1980). It is not surprising that poor social perception has been related to poorer peer acceptance (Stiliadis & Wiener, 1989).

At times students who are learning disabled seem very aware of their lower status and behavioral functioning among peers, and at other times they unrealistically overestimate this status (Bruininks, 1978a,b; Horowitz, 1981; Garrett & Crump, 1980; Smith & Nagle, 1995). They often try very hard to succeed socially and cannot understand the reactions and rebuffs they get from others (Walbrown et al., 1979).

The problem-solving strategies of many students with learning disabilities are too weak to help them clarify their social perceptions. We already have learned that these students are less likely to ask questions to clarify information. In addition, they tend to gather irrelevant information in conversations and contribute contradictory information (Speckman, 1981). By attending to the wrong details in social circumstances, they are unlikely to predict consequences accurately within these situations (Bruno, 1981). When asked what they would do in certain situations (for example, "It's your first day in a new school and the children go out to play at recess"), students with learning disabilities may give the correct solutions but offer reasons similar to those of younger children ("I'd go out to play because it's boring to stay inside" versus "because I'd make friends") (Oliva & LaGreca, 1988). Oliva and LaGreca suggest that if the initial social strategies of students with learning disabilities don't work, they may experience more difficulty than the non-LD child in deciding on alternate actions, because they are less clear about their goals in these situations.

Evidence suggests that the social imperceptions of many youngsters with learning disabilities may reflect immature development rather than a true deficiency. When they interact with younger children, or when they are explicitly told what the social expectations are (for example, "Make this lady like you so that she'll come to our school next year"), the social behavior of students with learning disabilities can be indistinguishable from that of non-LD children (Bryan & Perlmutter, 1979; Perlmutter & Bryan, 1984). It may be that these children have accurate social knowledge and an adequate repertoire of alternative solutions to handle social situations, but they are immature in assessing which solutions are the best in specific circumstances (Stiliadis & Wiener, 1989; Tur-Kaspa & Bryan, 1994). When this is the case, Perlmutter (1986) suggests that instead of training these children's social skills, we should be teaching children to better understand the demands of various social situations so that they can apply the skills they do have more appropriately.

Learned Helplessness

Apparently preschoolers and kindergartners do not think about whether their abilities and effort influence their successes and failures. First and second graders, however, do connect their successes and failures to the personal effort they put into trying; older youngsters add ability to the equation. As a result of this reasoning, children's self-confidence in their ability and expectations for success tend to remain high until around second grade, when they begin comparing their performance to others in their class. For the learning disabled, it does not take long before they blame their failures on poor ability, self-confidence plummets, and with it plummets effort as well (Weiler, 1992).

Given their repeated academic and social failures, it is no wonder that children with learning disabilities often give up. While a first or second grader may try to succeed because effort is seen as related to success, continuing failure experiences often teach the child that his or her efforts are unlikely to lead to success; these children believe that their inabilities make success unreachable.

Table 7–2 explains why, since these youngsters no longer see any use in trying, they have adopted a "learned helpless" attitude toward achievement (Dweck, 1975). Studies find that as

Table 7–2   Student motivation as related to the attributional process

Type of Achievement Related to Expectations of Society and Schools	Type of Adult Feedback ---- Attribution Made by Child	Type of Affect Associated with Internal Evaluation of Performance	Child's Understanding of His or Her Role in Cause-Effect Relationships	Expectations and Probability of Subsequent Behavior
High achiever	Success is positively valued by our society. Success is defined by schools as desirable	Positive feedback from adults. The child receives positive labels such as smart, gifted, etc. Child accepts and internalizes positive labels. ---- The cause of success is attributed by the child to ability and effort.	The positive effects of pride, accomplishment, and competence are associated with successful performance. The child self-reinforces his or her performance with internal positive self-statements. The child's self-concept is enhanced.	The child perceives that his or her effort determines positive outcome. Energy is seen as a means of solving problem.	The child has expectancy of success for future performance. Increased probability of future success serves as an incentive to work harder.
Low achiever	Failure is negatively valued by our society. Failure is defined by schools as undesirable.	Negative feedback from adults. The child receives negative labels such as slow, learning problems, etc. Child accepts and internalizes negative labels. ---- The cause of failure by the child is attributed to lack of ability.	The negative effects of frustration, shame, indifference are associated with failure. Internal statements of the child are primarily negative, reflecting his or her lack of ability. The child's self-concept is decreased.	No causal relationship is perceived between effort and outcome by the child. Therefore, the child considers effort a waste of energy. Energy is spent on avoiding the task.	The child has expectancy of failure in future. Increased probability of failure, therefore, no incentive to expend effort.

Source: Grimes, L. (1981). Learned helplessness and attribution theory: Redefining children's learning problems. *Learning Disability Quarterly, 4*(1), p. 92. Reprinted by permission.

many as 70 percent of children with learning disabilities believe they have little control over success (Kavale & Forness, 1996). They no longer are intrinsically motivated to prove their competence, and are defeated even before they begin to learn because they believe that their "stupidity" or external factors (for example, "the teacher is too picky") preclude success (Adelman, 1978; Halmhuber &

Paris, 1993; Lewis & Lawrence-Patterson, 1989; Licht et al., 1985; Pearl, Bryan, & Donahue, 1980). Any amount of effort or strategizing appears useless because the child expects failure even on tasks with which he or she has no basis to make a judgment.

The lower the child's self-concept, the more he or she uses poor ability to explain failures and the less persistent the child is likely to be (Butkowsky & Willows, 1980; Licht et al., 1985; Marsh, 1986; Pearl, Bryan, & Herzog, 1983). This helpless attitude persists, even in circumstances where the outcomes could be positive. Given these negative attitudes, it is not at all surprising that over a two-year period Kershner (1990) found self-concept to be a far more powerful predictor of academic progress than IQ for elementary and high school students with learning disabilities.

Unlike poor achievers, good achievers are internally motivated. They have learned to attribute success to personal effort; for them, it is always worth trying because success is likely. When they fail, they blame it on bad luck, external factors beyond their control, or personal effort ("I deserve an F because I went to the movies instead of studying"). Although students with learning disabilities do recognize that diminished effort contributes to their failure, they often attribute failure to their personal deficiencies. Even when they are successful, they often give their ability little credit; instead these students tend to attribute their success to luck or to factors beyond their control, such as others' motives ("the teacher was being nice to me") (Kavale & Forness, 1996; Lewis & Lawrence-Patterson, 1989; Jacobsen, Lowery, & Ducette, 1986; Palmer et al., 1982; Pearl, 1982; Rogers & Saklofske, 1985; Sobol et al., 1983). As a result, they see no purpose in struggling with difficult tasks, putting time into studying, trying to be organized, or observing how popular peers get along so that they too can try similar strategies.

Because the initial performance of the student with learning disabilities often is diminished by low motivation, motivational techniques produce greater increments in performance for students with learning disabilities than for typical learners (Adelman & Chaney, 1982). Pearl, Bryan, and Smiley (in Bryan, 1986) illustrate this point in a study of boys with learning disabilities who performed poorly on sit-ups and shuttle runs. These boys could achieve typical performance levels only when motivated by instructions suggesting that they were the type of people who could do very well, or that the apple juice they just drank would give them extra energy to do well. Many children with learning disabilities require these teacher-directed efforts to motivate them. In the following pages we will explore how extrinsic motivators can be built into our interventions, the best types and frequency of rewards, what to do about grading, and how to help students develop greater intrinsic motivation.

Extrinsic Motivation.   Extrinsic incentives help children who avoid challenges put more effort into learning. If the desired goal is within the student's capabilities, then incentives are likely to result in better learning (Bauer, 1987). Examples of extrinsic motivators include giving praise, charting successes, and earning stars, candy, time to play tapes, or more recess time. Point systems that reward children for improved attention and learning have particularly powerful effects on their learning rates and spontaneous use of learning strategies (Brigham, Graubard, & Stans, 1972; Hallahan et al., 1978; Heiman, Fischer, & Ross, 1973). Often these points are accumulated and then traded in for a prize or privilege. In one study, daily reinforcement of a whole class's decreased reading error rate was less time consuming for the teacher, easier to implement, and just as effective as graphing and reinforcing each individual's daily progress (Thorpe, Chiang, & Darch, 1981).

Contracting is another useful motivational strategy because the youngster actually makes his or her own decisions about what to achieve and what the consequence will be. The success of contracting is attributed to the *Premack Principle:* when the student completes x, y, z activities, he or she earns the privilege of doing a, b, or c, which are more highly valued activities. These positive consequences are strong incentives for a student to put effort into less-favored learning activities.

External reinforcement also can come from classroom materials and assignments that are of high interest and that value the student's linguistic and cultural background (for example, taking oral histories of relatives, writing essays or posting signs in the student's native language, studying famous people who share the same background). Material of personal interest is particularly important to students with learning disabilities because they learn less when the material being studied is uninteresting and irrelevant (Heavey et al., 1989).

After years of failure, it cannot be expected that any short period of extrinsic reinforcement will create a new motive system that causes the youngster to appreciate his or her own capabilities or value learning for learning's sake. A student's response to extrinsic motivators is a very individual thing. Not all incentives will induce all children to put more energy into learning, so parents and teachers must search for the incentive that best matches the student's interests. Once a successful extrinsic reinforcer is found, it needs to be maintained for a time and then withdrawn at a slow pace, in order to prevent reversal of the behavior changes (Ayllon, Layman, & Kandel, 1975). The types and frequency of incentives

---

RESEARCH BOX 7–1

Why Rewards at Times May Reduce Motivation

Rewards at times may produce a disincentive toward engaging in a certain behavior (for example, reading) rather than enhancing one's motivation to do so. Eisenberger and Cameron (1996) point out that this happens when people are told to expect a tangible reward for simply engaging in the activity, rather than being rewarded only if the activity is completed or if the performance is of high quality. Verbal rewards, being unexpected, do not seem to have this negative effect on motivation. Malouf (1983) offers several reasons why tangible rewards may be disincentives:

1. **Self-Perception or Attributions**
   - Remember that rewards are extrinsic reinforcers. Therefore, if a person is already intrinsically motivated, offering a reward serves to decrease the individual's incentive to engage in that behavior when the reward is no longer delivered.
   - A person may value a behavior more highly if he or she perceives that it is his or her own choice rather than influenced by external factors. Adelman and Taylor (1990) explain that if students perceive a reward to be coercing compliance, thereby limiting personal control and self-determination, then the result may be psychological reactance against the behavior being reinforced.
   - If the rewards have no relationship to the activity (for example, money for attempting art work versus more paints and brushes), then the target behavior may be reduced because the individual will attribute his or her behavior to the consequences, which are irrelevant to the behavior itself. When a goal becomes construed as only a means to an end, that goal loses some of its value. It can undermine a student's intrinsic motivation; learning is redirected toward getting rewards (stars, grades), and learning for learning's sake declines.

(Continues on following page)

RESEARCH BOX 7–1 *(Continued from preceding page)*

2. **Competing Responses**
   - Rewards may elicit competing responses that are incompatible with task motivation. For example, if the individual is frustrated because he or she can't delay gratification until the reward is received, then the task actually becomes associated with unpleasant stimuli. Alternatively, if the reward becomes a distraction or its anticipation engenders much excitement, then this may impair task performance, which in turn reduces motivation. When learning is dependent on rewards, students may focus primarily on getting the reward in the easiest way; the more salient the extrinsic reward, the more likely the interference with learning.

3. **Reinforcement Contrast**
   - Rewards may be compared with one's previous reward history, so that a particular reward may not be perceived as a reward and behavior may be suppressed.

Certainly this research cautions us to be more aware of the types of contingency systems we establish at home and in the classroom, so that they are in fact motivation enhancers rather than deterrents to performance. If tangible rewards are used, it is best if they are unexpected, not salient enough to distract the child from the task at hand, and awarded contingent on completing a task or doing it well (for example, finishing a whole story or reading a few pages with good quality versus simply staring at and flipping pages) (Eisenberger & Cameron, 1996).

we use, and the types of grading systems we develop, can have a great impact on student achievement.

Types and Frequency of Incentives. What types of rewards are best? Big ones? Little ones? Frequent ones? Infrequent ones? You might be surprised to learn that for the hyperactive student, positive reinforcement at times may increase impulsivity, thereby distracting the student from the task at hand (Douglas & Parry, 1983). In addition, under some circumstances, rewarding a person for engaging in a behavior actually may reduce motivation to continue engaging in that behavior. Research Box 7–1 presents several hypotheses about why a reward may occasionally provoke the unintended consequence of reducing student motivation.

It has been found that praise, especially at the secondary level, is useful only if it is used sparingly, when only 5 to 10 percent of the student's responses are praised (Stallings, 1975). When used more often, praise loses its potency. In addition, the perfunctory comments we tend to make as a student is leaving class, such as "You did a good job today," are useless because they are neither targeted to a specific positive behavior nor timed to coincide with the behavior being reinforced (Brophy, 1981). When we do praise, the praise must be well timed and targeted. In order to prevent rewards or praise from reducing student motivation, Malouf (1983) and Sprick (1996) suggest three guidelines:

1. Refrain from introducing rewards, and even very much praise, when initial levels of

student motivation or interest are high. Only use rewards when they are needed. Showing sincere interest in the activity is sufficient.

2. Use the least powerful reward that is effective. The weakest (least salient or attention-getting) reward or praise necessary for behavior change will minimize the degree to which students will attribute their behavior to external inducements and stop working in the absence of these inducements. For example, breaking assignments into manageable components, creating a quieter study space, or setting up an attention self-monitoring system may be sufficient to help a child persist. If powerful rewards must be employed, these should be faded gradually over time. Lower-level reinforcers (tangible reinforcers, tokens) should be used only when higher-level reinforcers (for example, task completion, pleasure in achievement) are ineffective. Praise and social approval are viewed as medium-level reinforcers.

3. Apply reward procedures that focus on what the child did (rather than what the child gets) in order to foster student self-perceptions of independence, competence, and task enjoyment. If rewards are related to the content of the tasks (for example, a bound journal for completing writing assignments), then students are more likely to perceive the reward as inherent in the task.

Grading Systems. Competition for grades, as a form of external reinforcement, has become a subject of concern in recent years. The philosophy in many classrooms is that competition for grades will enhance performance. Unfortunately, the truth is that competition is only fun for those who do well. Since many students with learning disabilities do not feel themselves capable of succeeding, even if they were to put greater effort into work, they are not motivated by the competitive classroom structure. Lavoie (1986) explains that:

Many well-intentioned teachers emphasize competition in their classroom in the mistaken belief that they are preparing the child for the intense competition that he will face in society. In their zeal to replicate the "big, bad world" these teachers have created classroom environments wherein the level and intensity of competition far exceeds that of the adult world. Our society does require competition in order to achieve success but this competition has two fundamental components: a) adults do not compete unless they elect to and b) we compete only against our peers and equals. Most classroom competitive activities (for example, spelling bees, mathematics games) do not meet those criteria. (p. 63)

It should come as no surprise that, in addition to feeling ill-equipped to compete academically, some students with learning disabilities have greater test anxiety than typical students; their performance diminishes when they know they are being evaluated (Bryan, Sonnefeld, & Grabowski, 1983; Gottlieb, 1982). For both reasons, it would seem that we must find alternatives for our competitive system, in which the success of one student depends on the failure of another. A cooperative learning structure, in which students help one another to succeed (see Chapter 12), may alleviate some of the evaluation stress experienced by students with learning disabilities and promote better performance. Cooperative learning strategies are particularly useful in promoting achievement motivation, intrinsic motivation, task persistence, positive attitudes toward a subject and instructor, and, most important, higher levels of self-esteem (Johnson & Johnson, 1986). Portfolio assessment is another alternative, with grades being awarded on the basis of an individual's progress toward concrete, creative, thoughtful, and meaningful goals, be it performances, demonstrations, projects, or oral reports. A recent national survey found that, instead of grades, 45 percent of elementary schools and 18 percent of high schools permit narrative evaluations; 25 percent of school systems permit pass–fail options (Polloway et al., 1994).

Surveys indicate that grading adaptations for students with disabilities often are permitted by school districts: for example, grading for effort or improvement, or weighting grades according to ability (Bursuck et al., 1996). Lieberman (1986a) proposes an interesting grading option when tests are used for evaluation purposes. Basically, the student, teacher, and parents meet to decide which of three levels of tests is most appropriate given the course content and the competition from typical peers.

Level one:	regular test
Level two:	somewhat less abstract, requiring fill-ins and short written explanations
Level three:	most concrete, requiring the least amount of student output (true–false, multiple-choice)

The highest grade obtainable on a level three test would be a C+, level two a B+, and level one an A. If the student does well on any given level, he or she can choose to take the next higher test. The best of the two grades is what counts. Lieberman comments

"Think about it—if a kid has the option to either make a C+ on a level three test or to fail a level one test, what choice do you think he will make?" (p. 423).

Like Lieberman's system, contracting also can be used to award grades based on whether agreed-on goals have been met: for example, x amount of work earns a certain grade, y amount of work earns another. Another option is to give students opportunities to raise their grades to a level with which they are satisfied: for example, more homework, correcting homework after teacher feedback, completing projects in addition to or in lieu of tests, retaking the test and counting the average grade or the higher of the two grades. Finally, teachers can institute a grading option that involves a grading conference at the end of each quarter. Students present their own estimate of their grades to the teacher on a self-assessment sheet such as that in Figure 7–1. The self-assessment promotes a feeling of control, ownership, and participation. Even when students are disappointed with their grade, they know exactly what they need to do to improve progress the next time around (Ryan, 1991).

Intrinsic Motivation. The best form of motivation comes from within the student. Youngsters who gain satisfaction from engaging in tasks with

responsibility, creativity, and effort can perform equivalently to those who are 20 IQ points brighter (Paris & Haywood, 1973). Several studies have found that persistence and task orientation make significant contributions to the prediction of achievement, sometimes over twice that made by IQ alone (Martin & Holbrook, 1985; Mevarech, 1985). No body of literature attests to this fact better than the significantly higher numbers of Chinese Americans and Japanese Americans than whites in managerial, professional, and technical occupations, despite average IQ scores (Flynn, 1991). For students with learning disabilities, if intellectual or basic learning ability is limited, high motivation can go a long way toward overcoming these weaknesses. This same high motivation may result in a student with learning disabilities achieving at grade level; ironically, the student's high motivation masks the constant struggle, frustration, and inordinate effort needed to keep up.

The very best teacher of internal motivation is the student's family. Children model their families' striving for autonomy and success. After a while they no longer associate their pleasure in achieving with the standing ovations upon speaking their first baby words, the hugs when they first learned the alphabet, or the praise when they first risked riding a two-wheel bike. Achievement becomes a highly valued entity in its own right. Yet when school learning comes hard to these children, they blame their failure on external factors or on being inferior human beings. In extreme cases, they find it safer to expect little, try nothing, and be helpless. The higher the students' feelings of competence and the more they perceive their family and school contexts as involved and supportive of autonomy in learning and behavior, the higher their achievement is likely to be (Deci et al., 1992).

It is a very difficult process to change the attitudes of students who are learning disabled so that they will see their efforts as more likely to lead to success (Bryan, 1986). These students express less optimism about the likelihood of future improvements in performance than do their non-LD peers, and when evaluating their performance they recall doing worse than they actually did; they find it extremely hard to take personal credit for success. Bryan (1986) explains that "Not

English 9   **Self-Assessment**

Name _____ Date _____

WRITING / READING (circle one)

A) Write your quarter goals here.

   1. _____

   2. _____

   3. _____

   4. _____

   5. _____

For each goal, tell what % you believe you've achieved and state why. (e.g., If you were to receive credit for 4 pieces of writing and you did 3, you achieved 75% of that goal.)

   1. _____% _____

   2. _____% _____

   3. _____% _____

   4. _____% _____

   5. _____% _____

B) Write down, in a sentence, your assessment of your effort and attitude this quarter.

C) On a scale of 1–10, assess the QUALITY of your work.

D) Select your best writing/reading and explain why it's your best.

E) GRADE DESIRED FOR WRITING/READING (circle one)

F) Set two goals for yourself next quarter.

   1. _____

   2. _____

Figure 7–1 Grading conference worksheet. *Source:* Ryan, D. (1991, Winter). Management and evaluation revisited. *The School Psychologist, 9* (1), 19. Reprinted by permission.

expecting to be in control of learning, the learning disabled may wait to be rescued. Given the belief that one is not in control of one's destiny, that increased effort will not help one face adversity, there is no reason to seek alternative strategies when faced with difficulty" (p. 227).

The learned helplessness of students with learning disabilities can begin to be turned around by the nature of their parents' and teachers' feedback. When we help the learning disabled to attribute success to very specific abilities and efforts, rather than to luck, and failure to something other than uncontrollable external sources and their own negative self-worth, then the students stand a chance to regain their interest, enthusiasm, and motivation to put energy into learning. This is why Dweck (1975) suggests that teachers attribute students' successes and failures to the amount of effort they put into learning rather than giving general praise or reproofs ("good try at sounding out" versus "you're great"). Because these children do not believe that they are capable, general praise means little. Instead, praising effort shifts attention to what can be done to achieve.

There is evidence that when students who are learning disabled begin to attribute their successes to effort, they begin to persist longer on difficult tasks and are more strategic in going about learning (Adelman and Chaney, 1982; Schunk & Cox, 1986). Moreover, if we help students analyze their assignments into subcomponents that are perceived to be easier, or suggest specific strategies to strengthen, students are more likely to see that effort could lead to success (Aponik & Dembo, 1983; Paris & Oka, 1986). In this way, students learn not to blame their inability, to try specific ways of overcoming their cognitive inefficiencies, and to see themselves as responsible for these successes and capable of meeting further challenges.

Clearly, positive self-attributions are important for encouraging a style of interacting with the world that is oriented toward doing one's best. Fortunately, direct attribution training can have fairly long-term positive effects. In such training students discuss their beliefs about what causes success and failure, they compare results when they use different strategies on tasks, and the teacher uses his or her own errors to model attributing failure to a strategy inefficiency that can be corrected (Borkowski, Weyhing, & Turner, 1986). The attribution statements teachers make about students are specific to *new* tasks, because these attributions are easier to modify than a long history of failure on something old. Borkowski and colleagues comment that attribution retraining "needs to be intensive, prolonged and consis-

tent in order to combat the debilitating, negative beliefs about self-efficacy" (p. 135).

Finally, there is no better way to build intrinsic motivation than to encourage students' talents, build personal satisfaction by incorporating personally meaningful ethnic and native language–related material into the curriculum, and accommodate the child's weaknesses so that the regular curriculum becomes more easily accessible. Adelman and Taylor (1986) comment that

Schools have the responsibility not only to help individuals overcome learning problems but also to facilitate ongoing development and provide opportunities for creative growth through enrichment activity. The fact that a person has a problem learning to read doesn't alter the fact that he or she can learn a variety of other things—and undoubtedly wants to. To find the time for remediation, it may be tempting to set aside enrichment and even some developmental learning opportunities; to do so, however, deprives individuals of other important experiences. It may also negatively affect their attitude toward the school, toward the teacher, and toward overcoming their problems. At the very least, school programs that overstress problem remediation risk becoming tedious and disheartening. (p. 604)

Because students' abilities and talents play a large part in their future vocational and social adjustment, these deserve just as much nurturing as their weaknesses. How else will students learn to see themselves as capable and worthy?

The Secondary School Student

Even if a child had been able to maintain a positive self-concept and get along socially throughout the preschool and elementary years, by adolescence there is a high probability that the indirect effects of a learning disability will impact negatively on self-perceptions and motivation. The world of the adolescent raises issues for the secondary educator that are far broader than those of the elementary school child. These include the adolescent's physical changes, emerging sexuality, social role redefinitions, school transitions, vocational interests and talents, future expectations, leisure time interests, and preparedness for independent living. Important also is developing cognitively challenging, student-centered, and structured learning environments that match both the adolescent's peer orientation, and the adolescent's desire for increased autonomy and control in decision making (Eccles et al., 1993). The development of social skills is an especially important priority at this point because social skills are so highly related to one's degree of satisfaction in all aspects of life. The link between juvenile delinquency and learning disabilities also needs to be understood, and preventive planning instituted.

Although unique and different in many ways, adolescence does not wholly transform a person's personality from what it was as a child. Despite modifications with time, many temperament traits tend to persist (Smith, 1997). "Marked changes do occur but continuity of development is the rule" (Schmid, 1979, p. 383). Youngsters with learning disabilities who were socially "savvy" as children tend to continue to function satisfactorily as adolescents. In fact, some of them use their superior social skills to compensate for deficits in other areas. For those who never developed these social skills, however, and for those who continue to be slow to adapt, overreactive, distractible, moody, and so on, adolescence can be particularly trying. These youngsters are tackling important personal issues without the tools to either facilitate their learning or ease the transition.

Despite the popular notion that adolescence is a time of severe psychological storm and stress for the teenager, and interpersonal conflict and disorganization for his or her family, this turmoil is true in less than 20 percent of cases. Numbers of family conflicts do not increase dramatically in adolescence, although the foci of conflicts do change (Powers, Hauser, & Kilner, 1989). Hartup (1989) summarizes work indicating that the "perceived" decrease in affection and closeness toward parents during adolescence actually represents a transformation in relationships rather than detachment or termination of relationships. The teenager continues to call on his or her parents during times of stress and gains security from the parents' presence. Teenagers trust that their parents will be there when needed. Figure 7–2 poignantly depicts the continued support and direction that teenagers look for from their parents while they are struggling to gain greater personal autonomy, participation in rule making and

decision making, and understanding of the inconsistencies in life.

While temperament traits and family relations in most cases remain stable, adolescence nevertheless is a period of great physical, social, and emotional change. It is a time when young people engage in many important developmental tasks: learning to accept one's changing physique; becoming comfortable with one's sexuality and behaving in a socially responsible manner; becoming less emotionally dependent on parents and other adults, and forming an adult identity; preparing for adulthood through the development of new, more mature, and intimate relations with peers of both sexes; selecting a career and preparing for eventual economic independence; and developing an ideology, ethical code, or set of values by which to live (Havighurst, 1972; Powers et al., 1989).

With adolescent changes comes confusion (Sprinthall & Sprinthall, 1981). The body is changing, but so is the mind. A cognitive leap in reasoning ability accompanies adolescence. The ability of teenagers to perceive the difference between objective reality and subjective perception is sharpened: what really is happening versus what someone thinks is happening. Adolescents become sensitive to the differences in feelings and emotions between themselves and others and, as a result, more often can take another person's perspective. They think about possibilities, alternatives, values, and family issues from a more objective stance. They become more alert to the symbolic as well as literal meaning of situations, noting that people don't always mean what they say. It comes as a shock that adults are not always right and in fact often work hard to cover up their mistakes. With the teenager's maturation in reasoning skills comes a time of sorting out who the individual is relative to all these new perspectives on the world.

It is understandable that the teenager's thinking is likely, for a time, to become highly egocentric. If evaluation of the external world can fluctuate between the real and the subjective, then so can one's view of oneself. With this comes excessive self-consciousness, a deep-rooted belief in one's personal uniqueness and insight, a strong desire for independence (so as to depend on the one reality that can be trusted), and the belief that

Memo From A Child To: Parents

1. Don't spoil me. I know quite well that I ought not to have all I ask for—I'm only testing you.

2. Don't be afraid to be firm with me. I prefer it, it makes me feel secure.

3. Don't let me form bad habits. I have to rely on you to detect them in the early stages.

4. Don't make me feel smaller than I am. It only makes me behave stupidly "big."

5. Don't correct me in front of people if you can help it. I'll take much more notice if you talk quietly with me in private.

6. Don't make me feel that my mistakes are sins. It upsets my sense of values.

7. Don't protect me from consequences. I need to learn the painful way sometimes.

8. Don't be too upset when I say "I hate you." Sometimes it isn't you I hate but your power to thwart me.

9. Don't take too much notice of my small ailments. Sometimes they get me the attention I need.

10. Don't nag. If you do, I shall have to protect myself by appearing deaf.

11. Don't forget that I cannot explain myself as well as I should like. That is why I am not always accurate.

12. Don't put me off when I ask questions. If you do, you will find that I stop asking and seek my information elsewhere.

13. Don't be inconsistent. That completely confuses me and makes me lose faith in you.

14. Don't tell me my fears are silly. They are terribly real and you can do much to reassure me if you try to understand.

15. Don't ever suggest that you are perfect or infallible. It gives me too great a shock when I discover that you are neither.

16. Don't ever think that it is beneath your dignity to apologize to me. An honest apology makes me feel surprisingly warm towards you.

17. Don't forget I love experimenting. I couldn't get along without it, so please put up with it.

18. Don't forget how quickly I am growing up. It must be very difficult for you to keep pace with me, but please do try.

19. Don't forget that I don't thrive without lots of love and understanding, but I don't need to tell you, do I?

20. Please keep yourself fit and healthy. I need you.

Figure 7–2   A teenager's list. This list, which appeared in *New York Magazine* in a health club ad, describes what one teenager wanted from his or her parents. *Source: New York Magazine,* April 11, 1988, p. 114. Reprinted by permission.

everyone, even perfect strangers, are peering at, evaluating, and waiting for the teenager's every action. Such questioning of oneself, yet focusing on what the world is thinking and doing, results in an unusual vulnerability to peer influence.

In talking about their friendships, twelve- to fourteen-year-old adolescents stress cooperation, mutual give and take, and trust that one can reveal feelings to friends, negotiate differences, and feel understood. Sharing of the same interests and activities often is the catalyst for beginning and maintaining relationships in adolescence (Youniss, 1980).

Despite close friendships, at some point in adolescence teenagers should begin to view themselves as unique and separate from their peer groups. The problem here, of course, is that adolescents with learning disabilities often never truly develop significant peer group attachments in the first place. This diminishes their opportunity to experience new roles and explore new relationships. It also removes the one major buffer and support system society provides for easing the transition from childhood identity to a new and more separate sense of self. According to Cook (1979), youngsters who find themselves in this position often tend to make one of two debilitating decisions. Either they remain excessively attached to and dependent on parental support and authority or they separate prematurely from family, without first establishing wider social horizons. The latter decision can result in drifting from one adopted role to another without ever having come to grips, even temporarily, with the basic questions "Who am I?" and "Where am I going?"

The teenager's psychological and physical maturity have a significant impact on his or her adaptive functioning, emotional well-being, and self-image (Powers et al., 1989). At a time when peer-group relations are of prime importance, the adolescent with learning disabilities, who by definition is not developing entirely "on time," often is at a distinct disadvantage. In spite of sincere intentions, some of these adolescents, by both words and mannerisms, fail to attract others. Problems in interpersonal relationships appear to be related to their behavioral difficulties, learned helpless attitudes, and social imperceptiveness.

Behavioral Difficulties

Despite the litany of negative characteristics reported by many studies, these are not true of all teenagers who are learning disabled and certainly not even of the majority. Porter and Rourke (1985) found that nearly half of the students in their study had normal personality characteristics on rating scales completed by their mothers. Other studies find that often these youngsters are no different from their nondisabled peers in popularity, perceptions of social acceptance, number of mutual and best friends, how often they hang around with friends, how often they have friends over or receive phone calls from friends, and incidence of depression or alcohol abuse (Deshler et al., 1980; Maag & Reid, 1994; Sabornie & Kauffman, 1986; Vaughn et al., 1993). In Conderman's (1995) study of middle school students, 50 to 70 percent of students with learning disabilities held positions of at least average social status. Several studies have found that teenagers with learning disabilities frequently express the same degree of general satisfaction with themselves as do their nondisabled classmates (Kistner et al., 1987; Silverman & Zigmond, 1983; Tollefson et al., 1982). Despite their low feelings of academic competence, a large percentage of adolescents with learning disabilities nevertheless have average global self-concepts (Montgomery, 1994).

Despite these positive reports, as a group, teenagers with learning disabilities are at greater risk for personal maladjustment and antisocial behavior than nondisabled adolescents. These difficulties seem to be greatest for those students who have the most severe learning disabilities and neurological involvement (Spreen, 1982). Frequently conduct problems appear as the teenagers' earlier hyperactivity and attention deficits subside (Epstein, Bursuck, & Cullinan, 1985; Epstein, Cullinan, & Lloyd, 1986). At times, girls with learning disabilities appear to have a harder time adjusting and making friends than do males who are learning disabled (Conderman, 1995; Ryckman & Peckham, 1986).

Students with learning disabilities are bright enough to perceive that they are different from their peers, and this hurts. Frequently they will disguise their feelings of inadequacy by claiming that a school assignment was "too dumb"; by purposely completing work sloppily; by becoming the class clown; by avoiding challenges within their grasp, for fear of failing; by using verbal intellectualism and becoming an "expert" in an area of personal strength in order to sidetrack attention from a disability; and by projecting their own weaknesses onto the shortcomings of a school, teacher, or parent (Ferraro, 1992). Given the great effort that goes into trying to cope with oneself, one's schoolwork, family, and friendship relationships, it is not surprising that teenagers with learning disabilities are more often depressed than their typical classmates (Dalley et al., 1992).

Studies report that, as a group, teenagers with learning disabilities involve themselves in more classroom disturbances than do their non-LD classmates. Teachers report defiance, resistance, unethical behavior, poor emotional control, hyperactivity, expansiveness, and inability to delay gratification. Direct observation, however, does not always support these teachers' perceptions (Bender, 1987; Heavey et al., 1989; Hiebert, Wong, & Hunter, 1982; Perlmutter et al., 1983).

Teenagers with learning disabilities also are rated as having less on-task behavior; class observation often finds these students passively off task (not making eye contact with the learning task), although not disturbing others. In the study by Perlmutter and colleagues, special education teachers rated the students with learning disabilities as more anxious, withdrawn, aggressive, or disruptive than did their regular class teachers. The non-LD classmates liked their non-LD peers better and rated the students with learning disabilities as more aggressive and disruptive; they liked the more withdrawn of the students with learning disabilities the best. Twenty-two of the twenty-eight adolescents with learning disabilities were in the bottom half of popularity; six were in the top quartile.

In Porter and Rourke's (1985) study, mothers rated one quarter of their teenagers with learning disabilities as being depressed (moody, brooding) or worried (poor interpersonal relationships, self-blame, low self-esteem); 13 percent as having somatic concerns (headaches, fatigue, gastrointestinal discomfort); and 17 percent as distractible (restless) or showing some antisocial

behavior (lying, stealing, temper tantrums, destruction of property, low frustration tolerance, impulsivity). Other parents have rated their teenagers who are learning disabled as being unusually immature, anxious, hostile, withdrawn, aggressive, cruel, hyperactive, and uncommunicative (McConaughy, 1986; Ritter, 1989). Yet other parents describe these teenagers as being less self-satisfied (ashamed, lacking self-confidence), less flexible (rigid, unimaginative), and lower in sociability (unfriendly, distant, unpopular) (Pihl & McLarnon, 1984; Raviv & Stone, 1991).

About half of studies of substance use find no differences between teenagers with learning disabilities and their peers, while half report greater use among those with learning disabilities (Katims, Zapata, & Yin, 1996). At least one study reports greater self-reports of victimization by classmates (being threatened, physically assaulted, having possessions removed from them) (Sabornie, 1994). Not surprisingly, these youngsters tend to participate less in organized extracurricular school or community activities, to have fewer social contacts with friends, to turn less often to peers for help and support, to report more loneliness, and to be less well-liked and more rejected by classmates (Conderman, 1995; Deshler et al., 1980; Geisthardt & Munsch, 1996; McConaughy, 1986; Sabornie, 1994).

Learned Helplessness

Greater dependence and questioning of one's own intelligence seem to be characteristics that often differentiate the adolescent who is learning disabled from others (Schumaker et al., 1983). During adolescence the typical teenager integrates his or her childhood personality with new biological drives and broader social opportunities (Erikson, 1963). The adolescent slowly and consciously decides who he or she is and in what direction to head. Such understandings generally evolve from a sense of competence and mastery. But with their unsuccessful school histories, most teenagers with learning disabilities have few positive experiences to draw on to construct such a mental image of themselves.

As with the elementary school child, many teens who are learning disabled continue to hold attributions for success and failure that are different from that of their classmates. They attribute their failure to basic inability. At the same time, they fail to credit themselves with successes actually achieved, instead attributing the successes to luck or other external factors beyond their control (such as easy test questions) (Aponik & Dembo, 1983; Bender, 1987; Tollefson et al., 1982). These teenagers tend to be more anxious than their non-LD peers about the possibility of failure. They see themselves as academically less competent and view their future chances for academic success as bleak. If they succeed at a task, they know that a new, more difficult task will follow. Anticipating future failure, they may simply refuse to do the assigned work; "If I didn't try, I didn't really fail" (Ferraro, 1992; Kistner et al., 1987; Margalit & Shulman, 1986). Often these students' parents and teachers hold equally low academic expectations for them (Hiebert et al., 1982).

A survey of nearly 500 seniors with learning disabilities clearly reflected their learned helplessness. They responded more positively than their non-LD peers to the following statements:

1. Good luck is more important than hard work for success.

2. Every time I try to get ahead, something or somebody stops me.

3. Planning only makes a person unhappy, since plans hardly ever work out anyway.

4. People who accept their condition in life are happier than those who try to change things (Gregory, Shanahan, & Walberg, 1986).

These students saw less practical utility in their courses than did their nondisabled peers, were less interested in the courses, and had poorer attitudes toward working hard in school.

Whereas schools should be encouraging these students' talents, and indeed their talents can be extraordinary (for example in business, the arts, music, computer technology, athletics), schooling instead focuses on their weaknesses. The talents are given short shift. Unless an extracurricular activity is specifically designated in the IEP, teenagers with learning disabilities may be excluded from athletics, cheerleading, art contests, set design, and so on because of school "no pass, no play" policies. Even if their talents do continue to develop, in time the adolescents' feelings of cognitive incompetence may generalize to these talents, causing them to pursue achievements in these areas with too little determination and ambition. This helplessness often generalizes to social interactions as well, in that these students do not believe that it is within their control to negotiate successful relationships with others.

The incongruity in schools' neglect to nurture students' talents is that, as adults, these same people will be encouraged to specialize. In a way, these teenagers have already specialized, but at too young an age; their uneven abilities clash with the school curriculum's intent to make everyone well-rounded.

In offering these teenagers help, we must be careful not to offer so much support and help that we inadvertently endanger the development of these students' independence, their ability to cope alone under pressure, or their desire to strive for goals. Margalit and Shulman (1986) found that adolescents with learning disabilities felt lower levels of autonomy (desire to control their behavior without interference from others). They felt less able to function without proximity to their parents, to assert their own needs in the face of group demands, and to face traumatic situations alone. Tollefson and colleagues (1982) speculate that the sheltered environment provided by special education might feed these attitudes of learned helplessness, dependence, and insecurity. Therefore, Carlson (1985) urges high school special educators not to lower curriculum requirements or modify standard materials for the student who is learning disabled unless absolutely necessary. Carlson explains that future employers are not likely to modify work materials and expectations; students must be taught that to remain competitive they must work hard to succeed at what is required, in the required way.

Social Imperceptiveness

Although social perception does increase with age, many teenagers with learning disabilities continue to lag significantly behind their peers (Axelrod, 1982; Holder & Kirkpatrick, 1990; Jackson, Enright, & Murdock, 1987; Pearl et al., 1991; Sisterhen & Gerber, 1989; Tur-Kaspa & Bryan, 1994). Wiig and Harris (1974), for example, found that these adolescents were less able to understand subtle communications in affective situations; expressions that were viewed as negative by both the investigators and nondisabled peers were judged to be positive by students with disabilities. Similarly, Pearl and Cosden (1982) found that adolescents with learning disabilities were consistently less accurate than their non-LD peers in interpreting subtle facial, behavioral, or verbal cues in soap operas depicting interactions between a man and a woman (feelings of insecurity, feelings about each other, about someone else). In the study by Perlmutter and colleagues (1983), when teenagers rated how well they liked others and how well others liked them, the most well-liked of the students with learning disabilities were those who perceived their status within the group most accurately; only six of twenty-eight teenagers with learning disabilities showed such accurate social perception. This social imperceptiveness even extends to difficulty distinguishing between positive and negative attention. Often these students will adopt attention-getting strategies that evoke negative attention, and then wonder what went wrong. In the meantime, their feelings of inadequacy are only reinforced (Ferraro, 1992). Perlmutter and colleagues suggest that perhaps teenagers with learning disabilities prefer to befriend younger junior high school students because of their immaturity in evaluating and responding to age-appropriate situations.

Because social perception is such an integral part of all human interaction, deficits in this area can be the most debilitating of all learning disabilities (Johnson & Blalock, 1987; Minskoff, 1980a). Teachers who are sensitive to these issues can develop mentoring relationships that help adolescents meet some of their emotional needs, particularly for self-esteem and esteem of others. Group counseling can help in this process, and social skills training classes that focus on both verbal and nonverbal social perception and communication skills have produced modest improvements (Berg & Wages, 1982; Forness & Kavale,

1996; Minskoff, 1980ab; Schumaker et al., 1983). Goldstein and his colleagues' (1980) fifty basic social skills that they develop through modeling, role playing, immediate feedback, and real-life application assignments are presented in Table 7–3. Similar techniques can be used to teach anger control, moral reasoning, problem solving, stress management, empathy, and cooperation; these are all lessons from which students with learning disabilities can benefit (Goldstein, 1988). Figure 7–3 illustrates the specificity involved in this type of social skill strategy training.

The goal of these interventions is to ease the transition of adolescents with learning disabilities into broader social circles by helping them to

---

Getting Help

Body Basics
  Face the person
  Make eye contact
  Use a serious voice tone
  Have a serious facial expression
  Keep a straight body posture

Other Skill Steps
  Say the person's name
  Ask if the person has time to help you
  Explain your problem
  Ask for advice
  Listen carefully to the person's advice
  Ask questions if you do not understand
  Do the task while the person watches, if
  needed
  Ask for feedback if needed
  Thank the person

Figure 7–3 Behavioral steps of a social skills strategy. *Source:* Schumaker, J. B. (1992). Social performance of individuals with learning disabilities. Through the looking glass of KU-IRLD research. School *Psychology Review, 21,* 387–399. Copyright 1992 by the National Association of School Psychologists. Reprinted by permission of the publishers.

Table 7–3   Social skills

Group I. Beginning Social Skills
1. Listening
2. Starting a conversation
3. Having a conversation
4. Asking a question
5. Saying thank you
6. Introducing yourself
7. Introducing other people
8. Giving a compliment

Group II. Advanced Social Skills
9. Asking for help
10. Joining in
11. Giving instructions
12. Following instructions
13. Apologizing
14. Convincing others

Group III. Skills for Dealing with Feelings
15. Knowing your feelings
16. Expressing your feelings
17. Understanding the feelings of others
18. Dealing with someone else's anger
19. Expressing affection
20. Dealing with fear
21. Rewarding yourself

Group IV. Skill Alternatives to Aggression
22. Asking permission
23. Sharing something
24. Helping others

25. Negotiation
26. Using self-control
27. Standing up for your rights
28. Responding to teasing
29. Avoiding trouble with others
30. Keeping out of fights

Group V. Skills for Dealing with Stress
31. Making a complaint
32. Answering a complaint
33. Sportsmanship after the game
34. Dealing with embarrassment
35. Dealing with being left out
36. Standing up for a friend
37. Responding to persuasion
38. Responding to failure
39. Dealing with contradictory messages
40. Dealing with an accusation
41. Getting ready for a difficult conversation
42. Dealing with group pressure

Group VI. Planning skills
43. Deciding on something to do
44. Deciding what caused a problem
45. Setting a goal
46. Deciding on your abilities
47. Gathering information
48. Arranging problems by importance
49. Making a decision
50. Concentrating on a task

Source: Goldstein, A., Sprafkin, R., Gershaw, N., & Klein, P. (1980). *Skill-streaming the adolescent: A structured learning approach to teaching prosocial skills.* Champaign, IL: Research Press, pp. 84–85. Reprinted by permission.

read environmental cues accurately and respond more appropriately. Moreover, greater understanding of others, cooperativeness, and verbal/nonverbal behaviors that communicate trustworthiness should help the adolescent be perceived as more supportive and caring, thereby enhancing his or her social acceptance. This point is particularly important in view of Tubbs and Moss's (1977) contention that people who most easily acquire peer acceptance are the ones who enhance the self-esteem of those with whom they associate. Finally, grooming, neatness of clothing, posture, and general attractiveness, all of which contribute to popularity, are objectives not to be overlooked (Conderman, 1995; Schumaker, Wildgen, & Sherman, 1982).

At the very least, social skills programs provide a ready-made group experience for those whose own social circles are limited. Because adequate social skills are vital to personal and vocational adjustment in later life, opportunities to participate in such groups, or to enter mentoring or counseling relationships, should be a priority.

Learning Disabilities and Juvenile Delinquency

Poor academic achievement, lack of motivation, and *short attention span* are terms that occur frequently in the folders of both juvenile delinquents (JD) and adolescents with learning disabilities. Other similarities include low frustration tolerance, negative self-concept, greater prevalence of males than females, and less skillfulness in social problem solving: poor perspective taking; poor impulse control; trouble defining the nature of a problem; and inability to generate multiple and effective solutions, evaluate consequences, select adaptive solutions, understand relevant social cues, or monitor performance (Larson, 1988; Mauser, 1974; Schumaker et al., 1982). Several studies have found that severe hyperactive symptoms and conduct problems (aggressive-defiant behaviors) in one's early years are important predictors of antisocial behavior in adolescence and adulthood (Gittelman et al., 1985; Loney et al., 1983; Weiss & Hechtman, 1993).

The incidence of learning disabilities found in various studies of delinquents is disconcerting: 18 to 55 percent (Bryan, Pearl, & Herzog, 1989; Campbell & Varvariv, 1979; Hollander, 1986; Keilitz & Dunivant, 1986). Studies often find that teens who are learning disabled, and especially those diagnosed with attention deficit hyperactivity disorder, report more trouble with the law—arrests, convictions, and incarcerations—than do their non-LD peers (Bryan et al., 1989; Gregory, Shanahan, & Walberg, 1986; Mannuzza et al., 1989; Spreen, 1982; Zimmerman et al , 1981). While different studies will find that delinquents with learning disabilities have more, less, or the same incidence of serious and violent crimes as delinquents without learning disabilities, once found guilty the learning disabled tend to have greater recidivism and parole failure (Keilitz & Dunivant, 1986; Larson, 1988; Zimmerman et al., 1981).

An LD/JD link is not surprising in that both are more prevalent where there is severe family disorganization, such as in cases of divorce, separation, child abuse, alcoholism, economic hardships, criminal behavior, poor school attendance, or limited diagnostic or remedial attention (Hollander, 1986). Nevertheless, when these influences are held constant, youth who are learning disabled or have attention deficits still are at greater risk for delinquency than their non-LD peers (Keilitz & Dunivant, 1986; Satterfield, Hoppe, & Schell, 1982). Three major hypotheses have been put forward for this higher incidence of delinquency among the learning disabled: the school failure hypothesis, the differential treatment hypothesis, and increased susceptibility to delinquent behavior.

The School Failure Hypothesis. The school failure rationale proposes that the negative social acceptance that follows poor academic achievement erodes self-confidence to the point that, given the proper psychological and environmental incentives, the youngster may engage in delinquent behavior. In support of this hypothesis, several studies have found that white youth from higher socioeconomic status families engaged in more delinquent behavior than did youth from low-income families. This may reflect the frustration and disappointment of youngsters from higher socioeconomic status families at not having been able to live up to expectations set for them by their families and social milieu (Bryan et al., 1989; Keilitz & Dunivant, 1986).

School failure, we have noted, increases the chances of school dropout; school dropout, in turn, is a strong correlate of delinquency (West, 1984). Some experts believe that failing students turn to delinquency because it provides at least one peer group in which a youth can be recognized. Larson (1988), however, noting that delinquency rates peak prior to dropping out, suggests that these students' poor social adjustment and delinquency may be what actually influences the school failure and dropping out, rather than the other way around.

Differential Treatment Hypothesis. The differential treatment hypothesis was proposed after several studies found that for comparable offenses adolescents with learning disabilities and/or hyperactivity were arrested or brought before judges more often than their non-LD peers (Broder et al., 1981; Weiss and Hechtman, 1993; Zimmerman et al., 1981). This increased vulnerability is believed to reflect both these youths' weaknesses (poor expressive capabilities, ineptness at presenting oneself in a positive manner, inability to anticipate the consequences of one's actions or to reason about abstract ideas such as the protection afforded by the right of silence), and factors inherent in the judicial system itself (highly cognitive, strategy-oriented procedure; verbal mode of interaction; paternalistic attitude of judges). With the exception of one study (Spreen, 1981), this "preferential treatment" of the learning disabled does not seem to carry over into more severe dispositions from the courts than for delinquents without learning disabilities (Keilitz & Dunivant, 1986).

Increased Susceptibility to Delinquent Behavior. There is evidence that because of the linguistic differences, social imperceptiveness, poor learning from experience, and impulsivity of the student with learning disabilities, messages often do not get through quite the way they were intended. Factors that might restrain a nondisabled peer from committing an antisocial act simply do not have the same effect on an individual with learning disabilities, thereby increasing susceptibility to delinquent behavior (Murray, 1976; Waldie & Spreen, 1993). It is easy to see how trouble with the law can ensue from immaturities in social judgment, such as in interpreting others' mood or message, interpreting situations and choosing the best solutions, generating alternatives, negotiating, engaging in mutual problem solving, dealing with anger, showing concern about wrongdoing, evaluating and anticipating consequences, taking the perspective of others, controlling impulsive behavior, standing up for what one thinks is right, giving and accepting negative feedback, resisting peer pressure, and yielding to antisocial acts that one doesn't want to commit (cheating, stealing, defacing school property, making prank phone calls, using illicit drugs) (Bryan et al., 1989; Bryan, Pearl, & Fallon, 1989;

Bryan et al., 1982; Heavey et al., 1989; Larson, 1988; Schumaker et al., 1982).

Susceptibility to delinquent behavior also may be greater among teenagers with learning disabilities because their level of moral reasoning tends to be immature for their age. In the elementary school years children judge right and wrong on the basis of whether their personal needs will be satisfied and whether authorities will reward or punish them for their act. With maturity, however, children begin to respond to moral dilemmas with less egocentricity. They become more sensitive to group norms for behavior, to the need to be fair to the rights of others, and to the need to obey rules for the sake of society's welfare (Kohlberg, 1981). This also involves judging right and wrong based on sensitivity to others' circumstances and perspectives, and taking responsibility for maintaining relationships, even if this means compromising some societal rules (Gilligan, 1982; Walker, 1989). Unfortunately, many teenagers with learning disabilities are not yet ready to judge rightness according to responsibilities within relationships and the values of the community (Derr, 1986). Loyalty to others and commitment to contributing to society are unimportant to them. Instead, teenagers with learning disabilities tend to reason from an egocentric perspective, following rules only when these meet their own needs and desires; slipping into delinquency may be the end result.

Classroom discussions about moral dilemmas have been successful in increasing the level of moral reasoning of both typical learners and juvenile delinquents (Hayden & Pickar, 1981; Jennings & Kohlberg, 1983). During these discussions, students at lower moral reasoning stages are exposed to the higher-level reasoning of others. Over time, they tend to incorporate this reasoning into their own frameworks. Brier (1994) found that this type of training, along with vocational education and basic skills tutoring, reduced recidivism significantly among adjudicated sixteen to twenty-one year olds.

Other techniques for trying to prevent or deal with delinquency include encouraging youths' talents, adopting a "bookless" approach to learning when reading is poor, and training cognitive problem solving (Feindler, Marriott, & Iwata,

1984; Larson & Gerber, 1987; Silberberg & Silberberg, 1971). While greater academic achievement alone does not appear to reduce recidivism, the relationships built with LD specialists during intensive special education are associated with less relapse into delinquent patterns (Crawford, 1981; Keilitz & Dunivant, 1986; Larson, 1988). Camping programs that emphasize exposure to vocational opportunities, health care, recreation, fellowship, and leadership also have succeeded in reducing delinquent activity (Unkovic, Brown, & Mierswa, 1978).

The question of a link between learning disabilities and juvenile delinquency takes LD out of the protected realm of academia and introduces a host of other professionals, such as police officers, probation workers, and juvenile court judges. While this link makes preventive measures incumbent upon our schools, in the process we must remember to be particularly cautious about making predictions. In most cases youth who are learning disabled do not get in trouble with the law. These teenagers already have a difficult enough time functioning and being accepted without being earmarked as potential delinquents.

The Adult

We have seen that learning disabilities tend not to disappear with age, and that their influence can continue into adulthood. Exactly how vocational and social adjustment will be affected depends on the adult's strengths and weaknesses, past academic, social, and emotional experiences, and the expectations of the settings in which the adult lives, works, and plays. It is important to develop a greater understanding of the difficulties faced by individuals with learning disabilities in adulthood so that we might intervene preventatively in schools, as well as intensify adult services.

Despite persistent weaknesses, many adults with learning disabilities do go on to postsecondary education, get good jobs, raise their children well, get along with their spouses and friends, and contribute to the betterment of their communities. Others, however, do not. The more successful adults seem to have compensated for their learning difficulties through adequate intelli-

gence, motivation, instruction, and emotional support. These individuals had made conscious decisions to take charge of their lives and engage in whatever adaptations were necessary in order to move ahead. They strove to excell, set goals for themselves, worked very hard, chose educational and work environments where their strengths would be optimized, and continually worked on upgrading their skills. Of greatest importance, these individuals surrounded themselves with supportive, helpful friends, family, and mentors; and they learned to look at their LD experience in a positive, productive manner that facilitated living with and confronting the expected challenges (Gerber, Ginsberg, & Reiff, 1992).

Unfortunately, more often than not adults with learning disabilities have not had the advantage of adequate schooling and emotional supports to continue to grow personally, academically, and intellectually. When learning problems persist into adulthood, it is understandable that many people will choose to curtail their participation in postsecondary education. In turn, their vocational success suffers, and poor interpersonal relations are exacerbated. Fortunately, today's adult with learning disabilities has many more vocational and independent living options than in the past that can help promote maximal adjustment.

Vocational Adjustment

Vocational adjustment is one of the keys to successful life adjustment. The type of job and level of income a person can maintain affect all facets of life: the home one buys, educational opportunities for one's children, vacations, clothing, recreational luxuries, social status, personal satisfaction, stress level regarding meeting everyday needs, and so forth. Job success is more highly related to how much schooling a person pursues than to any other factor. In turn, how much schooling one will pursue is related to one's intelligence and family attitudes toward education. Correlations of adult IQ with occupational status indicate that the two share only 20 to 25 percent of attributes in common, leaving much room for factors such as persistence in school to augment occupational success (Barrett & Depinet, 1991). Interestingly, this level of correlation between IQ and job success is reached as early as the second grade (O'Connor & Spreen, 1988).

Unfortunately, as many as 39 percent of young adults with learning disabilities drop out of high school (*Digest of Educational Statistics*, 1996), and only 30 percent of LD graduates (versus 68 percent of the general population) continue their education after graduation (Blackorby & Wagner, 1996). These decisions compromise their vocational futures. The high school drop out earns 32 percent less than the person who persists through high school; the student who has some college experience earns about 20 percent more than the high school graduate, and 72 percent more once he or she graduates college (*Condition of Education*, 1997). Zigmond and Thornton (1985) report that students with learning disabilities who had graduated from high school one and a half to two years earlier fared nearly as well as non-LD graduates in their rate of employment (74 percent versus 87 percent). However, only half of dropouts, whether LD or non-LD, were successful in finding employment. Because both dropouts and graduates who were learning disabled had the same reading or math skills, achievement differences could not explain the low employment of dropouts. Zigmond and Thornton postulate that those who remained in school learned an important lesson, "stick-to-itiveness"; when hiring, employers are far more concerned about dependability, task persistence, and proper attitudes than achievement levels. National data and the results from other studies support these conclusions, finding that high school dropouts are employed at about 21 percent lower rates than those who graduate (*Condition of Education*, 1996; Sitlington & Frank, 1993).

It is predicted that high school dropouts will soon be 60 percent less likely to be employed than graduates, because the diploma is becoming the required credential for most jobs (West, 1991). Therefore, postsecondary vocational or academic education is more important than ever in the competition for jobs. Unskilled work opportunities are increasingly rare, approximately 5 percent in today's work world. Success on skilled jobs, whether blue collar or white collar, manual or nonmanual, depends in part on quite sophisticated reading, comprehension, and computation

abilities (Lerner, 1981; Okolo & Sitlington, 1986). As one gets promoted to higher-level jobs, the need for analytic reading skills and computer literacy increases.

Unfortunately, the reading skills of many students with learning disabilities do not become proficient enough to ensure their success in postsecondary education. Poor reading skills severely limit academic aspirations, slacken the pace through school, hamper postschool academic achievements, and narrow vocational options. Even among economically advantaged, bright private school graduates, the best predictor of which students ultimately would graduate from college was their reading achievement level at the time of private school entry and subsequent grades (Finucci, 1986). While 53 percent of high school graduates attend college for one or more years, and 27 percent complete college, only about 19 percent of young adults with learning disabilities pursue a postsecondary academic experience; another 18 percent pursue some postsecondary vocational experience (*Condition of Education*, 1996; *Digest of Educational Statistics*, 1996).

It is understandable that many young adults with learning disabilities, especially those who were hyperactive as children, severely language or reading disabled, or more seriously involved neurologically, end up in lower vocational placements than would be expected from their intelligence (Borland & Heckman, 1976; Spreen, 1982; Weiss & Hechtman, 1993; Zangwill, 1978). When compared with non-LD adults who earn the same amount, have held the same number of full-time jobs, and have spent the same amount of time unemployed, adults with learning disabilities tend to have significantly lower job status (White et al., 1980). They often aspire to lower-level occupations, are less satisfied with their employment circumstances, find themselves in entry-level (service worker, laborer) and part-time positions, work for lower earnings than would otherwise be expected (in three-quarters of cases earning only minimal wage), and have frequent job changes and periods of unemployment (Edgar, 1987; Hoffman et al., 1987; Johnson & Blalock, 1987; Rojewski, 1996; Sitlington, Frank, & Carson, 1993; Spreen, 1982; White, 1985; White et al., 1980; Zigmond & Thornton, 1985).

It should come as no surprise that many of the adults in these studies expressed disappointment in themselves. They lacked the zeal to achieve and felt inadequate, guilty, and embarrassed. They feared that their disabilities would be discovered by unknowing employers, and they developed maladaptive interaction patterns. Denckla and Heilman (1979) comment that even if a child with learning disabilities does eventually outgrow his or her delays, the prior emotional pressures may still be a hindrance in reaching adult potential. It is not unusual for these emotional pressures to create personality abnormalities and even to disrupt a marriage and family (Lenkowsky & Saposnek, 1978; Schwartz, Gilroy, & Lynn, 1976).

Clearly, there is a need for a much earlier and more intensive emphasis on vocational preparation at the secondary level and on schooling modifications that support high school graduation and aspirations for postsecondary education. Increased support for the development of these students' positive self-concept, motivation, self-awareness, self-advocacy skills, independence, and responsibility is equally essential.

Those adults who ultimately are seen as successful are the ones who understand and accept their learning disabilities, feel that odds can be overcome, develop realistic goals and compensatory strategies, take an active approach to problem solving and goal setting, persevere through setbacks and learn from these experiences, choose study and work environments that capitalize on their talents and minimize their weaknesses, involve themselves in hobbies and community activities, and are proactive in nurturing supportive, mentor relationships (Spekman, Goldberg, & Herman, 1992; Vogel, Hruby, & Adelman, 1993; Werner, 1993). The more education these adults complete, the more satisfied they tend to be with their employment and with life in general (Rogan & Hartman, 1990).

Social–Emotional Adjustment

The power of emotional factors, relative to intellectual factors, in influencing life adjustment cannot be stressed enough. The correlation between IQ and everyday life performance as an adult is no more than about .20 (McClelland, 1973). IQ tests measure knowledge and problem-solving abilities, but do not adequately reflect the creativity, practical application of knowledge, and personality attributes so important to vocational and social success: ambition, integrity, agreeableness, leadership, responsibility, dependability, organization, extroversion, emotional stability, sensitivity, trustworthiness, optimism, willingness to try hard, eagerness to accept and attack challenges, feelings of being capable and supported even through failure, knowing how to ask for and use help (Azar, 1995; Zigler & Trickett, 1978). It is personality attributes such as these that help individuals through life, despite less academic knowledge or problem-solving ability.

Critchley (1970) writes:

A dyslexic of sufficient ability, who is also fortunate in being endowed with unusual personality traits of application, concentration and ambition may in time overcome many of his problems even without specialized tuition [tutoring]. "Ego-strength" is what the psychiatrists call this quality, more familiar to us as "guts." (p. 100)

Unfortunately, many learning disabled are particularly handicapped in the emotional-social realm. Their learning weaknesses may have caused, aggravated, or in part resulted from social relationship and personal difficulties. As with the adolescent who is learning disabled, the LD adult may be less able to interpret the emotions, attitudes, and intentions that others communicate through language, facial expressions, or body posture. The adult's inappropriate responses to everyday conversation, verbal subtleties, nonverbal cues, and expressions of affection or approval may result in rejection by others, feelings of insecurity, and atypical personality development. The reactions of others to the adult's continuing inattentiveness and impulsivity, coupled with ineffective family support systems, further diminish self-esteem and feelings of control. As a result, the individual is less able to call on positive emotional strengths for support in his or her drive to continue learning, to become vocationally successful, to live independently, and to have meaningful leisure time activities.

Follow-up studies of children with learning disabilities often find social–emotional difficulties and loneliness persisting into adulthood (Bruck, 1985; Vogel & Forness, 1992). In Bruck's follow-up of mild to severely disabled young adults of average intelligence, the more severe the childhood adjustment difficulties, the more likely they were to experience social and emotional problems as adults. Although moderated with time, nearly 50 percent or more of those who had personal adjustment difficulties or poor peer and family relations as children still continued to have difficulties as young adults. Females had more difficulty overcoming their earlier adjustment problems than did males. Interviews with the learning-disabled and control adults revealed no differences in delinquent acts or alcohol and drug abuse. However, differences were apparent in same-sex peer relationships and greater difficulty controlling tempers and dealing with frustration in constructive ways. The amount of education one had completed was a better predictor of adult social–emotional outcome than was the severity of the learning disability itself.

Weintraub and Mesulam (1983) vividly describe the social isolation, loneliness, depression, and extreme shyness of adults with persistent, severe math and visuospatial disabilities. These adults avoided eye contact, used a flat tone to communicate their feelings (at times compensating with exaggerated gestures), and had difficulty identifying the affect conveyed by others' voices. In the follow-up study by White and others (1980), 20-year-old young adults with learning disabilities were found to be less involved in recreational activities and social organizations, less satisfied with their contacts with relatives, using more prescription drugs, more often convicted of crimes, less satisfied with their school experiences, and having fewer plans for future education and training. Their number of friends, contacts with relatives, arrests, and time spent in jail did not differ from that of non-LD adults. Most telling are the responses of 560 adults with learning disabilities to a survey conducted by the Learning Disabilities Association of America. Despite the fact that nearly half were unemployed, and many of those who were employed were not satisfied with their work, the respondents ranked social relationships as the area in need of most assistance. Other concerns were, in descending order of urgency, career counseling, development of self-esteem and confidence, ability to overcome dependence, survival, vocational training, job procurement and retention, reading, spelling, management of personal finances, and organizational skills (Chelser, 1982).

Follow-ups of children who had been hyperactive have received much attention (not all of these children had learning disabilities). As adults, one-third to one-half of these individuals continue with their underachievement, social–emotional immaturity, poor self-esteem, restlessness, impulsivity, and attentional difficulties. The greater the emotional instability and poor frustration tolerance in childhood, the poorer the adult outcome (Wender, 1976). Borland and Heckman (1976) report that hyperactive boys became hyperactive men. They had trouble sitting still to watch television; were nervous, restless, and quick-tempered; and had difficulty concentrating. Despite normal intelligence and equal educational levels, their socioeconomic job status was lower than that of their brothers and fathers. In another study, hyperactive young adults were less successful than the nonhyperactive controls; they had more frequent job changes, more debt, residential moves, and problems with aggression, all of which suggested a more impulsive life-style. They also had more car accidents than control subjects, more suicide attempts, psychiatric symptoms, and immature personality traits. Even when ratings by employers were equivalent to those of nonhyperactive adults, self-ratings on social interaction, self-esteem, and competence measures remained inferior to control subjects (Hechtman, Weiss, & Perlman, 1984a; Weiss & Hechtman, 1986). Antisocial personality disorders and drug abuse have been noted in one in five or six of these adults (Mannuzza et al., 1993).

It has been found that the lower the socioeconomic status of young adults who had been diagnosed as hyperactive as children, and the more troubled the mental health of their family members, the higher the involvement with police and drugs and the more difficult their educational, work, and emotional adjustment. Sometimes, given time for maturation, young adult hyperactive individuals who have had much involvement with alcohol, drugs, the courts, and police (for example, for thefts), will no longer distinguish themselves from control subjects in these and other respects (serious psychiatric disturbances, work adjustment, independent living adjustment) (Hechtman, Weiss, & Perlman, 1984b; Weiss & Hechtman, 1993).

Having taken stimulant medication in childhood appears unrelated to adult drug or alcohol abuse, academic and work achievement, or antisocial and personality disorders (Feldman, Denhoff, & Denhoff, 1979; Hechtman, Weiss, & Perlman, 1984a). However, in Hechtman and colleagues' study, adults who had received stimulant medication in childhood had fewer car accidents, less delinquency, and better social skills and self-esteem than did those who had been untreated as children.

Richard Devine, a college graduate who is severely reading disabled and a talented goldsmith describes the terrible emotional strains that accompany a learning disability in the following way:

I have experienced first-hand the anguish, anger, despair and utter frustration of the inarticulate child who cannot tell the literate person that literacy is not the only level on which he exists; that he is a whole person with many ways of giving and receiving information other than by reading and writing; and that the social environment's demand for functional literacy tends to overshadow all the other potentials an individual may possess. . . . Functional literacy is not the only measure of an individual and never was. My argument is with the world of education which tends sometimes to forget the relative narrowness of its focus and thereby does many of us a grave disservice. . . . It is possible to achieve a successful, fulfilling life even without the ability to read. . . . The educational system could deal with the dyslexic child by working with the strengths and talents of that individual child instead of concentrating on his or her inability to read and thus destroying the child's faith in him/herself. [I] successfully completed high school and obtained a college degree even though [I am] functionally illiterate. [I] learned with [my] heart, my hands, my mind, and my will, and not through literacy. . . . everyone has skills and talents, even if they are not those which our society and its educational machinery traditionally values. . . . There is a person inside the person the school and society is trying to teach. We must learn to respect and re-value that person. It is only because the system's view of literacy is so inflexible that dyslexia is regarded as a "learning disability" at all. What an incredibly narrow view of learning this is, and what an incredibly limiting view of the human potential! (Devine & Rose, 1981)

Sarah's story below portrays the negative impact that social–emotional anguishes accompanying a learning disability can have on life suc-

---

Sarah and Marc

Sarah never read until she was eleven years old. Her one and only dream in life was to become a lawyer. But she almost did not make it to law school because her self-concept was so poor that she could not admit to others that she was learning disabled.

Sarah had taken the academic route of the intellectual, hoping that her bank of facts would prove her worth and intelligence and see her through any social encounters. She seldom dated, had few friends, and felt comfortable only among adults with whom she was assured of no ridicule or rebuffs. Sarah never asked for help in college and made it through with a low B average. Her law boards too were only average. Although she was exceptionally bright in verbal conceptual abilities, she was hampered on all tests and assignments by a very slow reading speed and spelling and handwriting no better than a seventh grader's. Because of her overanalytic, detail-bound conceptual style, she often missed the main themes and could not organize major, relative to minor, points. She always depersonalized

(Continues on following page)

Sarah and Marc   *(Continued from preceding page)*

conversations and turned them into intellectual, political discussions. For example, when asked to write an essay about how the saying "no man is an island" applied to her life, Sarah wrote about Locke's philosophy of a state.

At Sarah's law school interview, she was told in no uncertain terms that she was too dumb to either apply to law school or become a lawyer. Her college grades and law boards were given as examples. When Sarah then explained her learning disability, no one believed her—it had been a secret for too long. To counter the law school's rejection, Sarah's parents begged her to ask for recommendations from all the politicians and lawyers with whom she had interned over the years. They had all evaluated her contributions highly, in spite of her weaknesses. Sarah was afraid to ask them for recommendations, feeling that she would lose the esteem of the only people who made her feel competent. She decided not to pursue law school any further. She would give up her dream because she could risk no more deprecation.

Sarah's parents finally prevailed on her to consider her future before her pride. She confided in those whose esteem she most needed to retain. She found that they had known all along that something was wrong with her; she had required more tutelage in her apprenticeships than had any of her predecessors. Nevertheless, her dedication was outstanding, and her work showed progress. Therefore, they wrote Sarah her recommendations and she was admitted to law school. She also began intense reading, spelling, and written language remediation.

Unlike Sarah, Marc, who had a very similar learning disability, learned early in life that others would always note his weaknesses. There was no escaping it, so he made no attempt to hide his disability. He conferenced with college professors before beginning each course; he worked out compensatory exam writing and grading systems. He did not leave anything to chance. When he wrote an exam, he sprawled in big letters at the top: "Dr. _____ , please remember that I am a dyslexic. You agreed to grade me as follows. . . . If you have any questions please contact me at . . . " Well Marc, like Sarah, got Bs, but he was a personality-plus person. In his junior year of college he was elected president of the Student Senate. He was admitted to law school and negotiated for extended time for briefs, oral exams, and a four- instead of three-year schedule. He even made Law Review. Today Marc is a successful lawyer. He says he would "die" without the spellchecker on his computer. Marc feels like a valued individual in spite of his continuing disabilities, and he never hesitates to ask for help. Sarah is just finishing law school. She does not plan to venture out on her own. She has a place waiting for her in her father's law firm.

cess. Her story contrasts with that of Marc, who learned to cope with his disability far more successfully.

Although Sarah's and Marc's learning disabilities affected their learning similarly, they came to grips with these problems in different ways. Their different feelings of self-worth—not their IQs or academic or problem-solving skills—created Marc's greater chance for successful vocational and social adjustment in adult life.

Unfortunately, there is a dearth of programs preparing personnel to deal with adults who are learning disabled and their very complicated service requirements. Given this state of affairs, the imperative is all the greater for teachers and families to work preventatively during the high school years by implementing appropriate transition plans. Many investigators agree that social–emotional adjustment, often more than the learning disability itself, is the best predictor of whether children will grow up to be happy, fulfilled adults.

Vocational Options

Adults with learning disabilities have more opportunities to enter vocations that capitalize on their stronger abilities today than in the past. This is due to increases in programming at the high school level for transition needs, increased postsecondary educational options and government-funded vocational education programs, and lowering of employment barriers to the disabled. Now that severe learning disabilities are recognized as a handicapping condition, discrimination in employment is prohibited by any program receiving federal financial assistance, if the individual is otherwise qualified for the job (Section 504, The Rehabilitation Act of 1973; PL 93-112).

In 1990, the Americans with Disabilities Act (ADA) extended many of the requirements of Section 504 to private employers of more than fifteen people. These employers are required to provide reasonable accommodations to qualified persons with disabilities in order to enable them to be hired, to function, and to be promoted in the workplace. The ADA very broadly defines a person with disabilities as someone who has a physical or mental impairment which substantially limits one or more major life activity (such as walking, talking, breathing, or working), or who may be discriminated against because of a previous record of such impairment or the appearance of an impairment (such as a burn on the face, when, in fact, the burn is not limiting).

According to ADA, an employer cannot ask applicants if they have a disability or give tests to screen out people with disabilities. An employer can only ask if an applicant needs accommodations to successfully complete the job requirements. These accommodations may include, for example, provision of a spell checker or help with editing when report writing is part of the job; taped or written instructions for persons with auditory processing problems; a checklist of responsibilities for persons with sequencing problems. These modifications cannot impose an undue hardship on the employer.

Despite these opportunities, we have learned that adults with learning disabilities tend to have significantly lower job status, earnings, and job stability than expected, and they tend to be less satisfied with their employment. One continuing barrier is the fact that vocational training programs, employment bureaus, vocational aptitude tests, and job applications have tended to overemphasize reading, other academic competencies, and fast work speed even if these are not skills needed on the job (Evers, 1996; Silberberg & Silberberg, 1978). The paucity of special educators with knowledge about adult needs, or vocational counselors and adult educators with knowledge about the particular needs of the learning disabled, does not help matters. Nor does the paucity of assessment instruments designed to evaluate the strengths, weaknesses, and needs of these adults. All too often evaluators resort to tests designed for school-age children, whose content, reliability, and validity for adults is questionable at best. Inappropriate tests may open the door for misdiagnosis and misdirection. Finally, we have not yet studied in which types of occupations adults with different strength/weakness patterns are likely to succeed. And we have failed to establish sufficient transitional work settings (where supervision and instruction are intensified) or job coaching opportunities in typical employment situations.

An acknowledged social barrier is the unwillingness of employers to hire the learning disabled. In a 1987 survey of 326 employers, only half said they would hire persons with learning disabilities. Five percent even said that they would fire a worker if it was discovered that the individual had a learning disability (Minskoff et al., 1987). This certainly raises the question of whether applicants with learning disabilities should disclose their disability to employers. One recent study found that only 20 percent of college graduates were willing to disclose their learning disabilities to employers, thereby forfeiting accommodations that have the potential to help them be more efficient and effective workers (Greenbaum, Graham, & Scales, 1996). Given the protections of ADA, Goodman and Brown (1992) recommend honesty about the disability, because difficulties encountered at the interview or on the job may otherwise be misinterpreted as laziness or lack of a work ethic. Clearly, in addition to earlier and more appropriate career education, we have much work to do in the public sensitivity arena as well.

Independent Living Options

Many adults with learning disabilities experience great difficulty breaking away from home. In a study of twenty- to twenty-seven-year-old young adults with learning disabilities, for example, 54 percent were still living with their parents (Cobb & Crump, 1984). This percentage is typical of follow-up studies and national data (Blackorby & Wagner, 1996; Sitlington & Frank, 1993; Schalock et al., 1992). Longer-term follow-up into the thirties indicates that, in time, over three-quarters of adults with learning disabilities do live independently (Rogan & Hartman, 1990). Recognizing the need for support in this area, the high school's transition plan, the State/Federal Program of Vocational Rehabilitation, and nonprofit agencies are providing increased opportunities for adults with learning disabilities to make systematic transitions to independent living. Supervision and counseling provided in group homes or special apartment complexes help the adult learn how to take responsibility for daily living needs (cooking, cleaning, clothing, shopping), leisure time activities (sports, clubs), and developing a social network (dates, friendships). These support services help the adult with learning disabilities to self-evaluate behavior, to learn important work habits (punctuality, respect for property, conformity to rules, appropriate grooming), to become more socially competent, to pursue appropriate goals, and to become involved in fulfilling leisure-time interests and community activities. The importance of these social-emotional needs cannot be overstated. Often these attributes, more than the learning disabilities themselves, mean the difference between success or failure in postsecondary education, in gaining or losing jobs, and in managing the important personal, family, and community responsibilities that accompany being an independent, self-supporting adult. It also is important to remember that the personality and behavioral styles of the adult with learning disabilities eventually become powerful influences on the behaviors that his or her children adopt as their own, so systematic intervention is important.

As educators, we must be sensitive to predictable adult issues and work preventively both before and after young adults graduate from high school. To facilitate this transition, some LD teachers are assuming the role of transition specialists, actively developing interagency relationships that will contribute to the future life-style of graduates who are learning disabled.

Summary

It is not uncommon for the uneven academic development of the school-age child to be accompanied by uneven development in social and emotional areas as well. Precursors to social and emotional adjustment difficulties are apparent as early as the preschool years, when some children's difficult temperaments, inattention, and high activity levels require very patient, positive, structured, and understanding parenting to moderate these attributes. By the elementary school years, the uneven development of many children with learning disabilities, together with their disappointment in not living up to their own, their parents', or their schools' expectations, frequently results in poor self-esteem, self-doubt, poor motivation, unhappiness, and limited friendships. When these students constantly fail, are perceived negatively by others, are awkward in social relationships, and give up, their chances for successful life adjustment diminish. Parents and teachers must help these children to become more conversationally appropriate, more socially insightful, and more trusting that with effort success is possible. This involves maximizing opportunities for social learning and positive personal-social adjustment, offering social skills training programs, encouraging talents, modifying grading systems, developing cooperative learning systems, using extrinsic motivators where necessary, and encouraging intrinsic motivation.

While many students with learning disabilities have personal, family, and school resources that help support their self-esteem and motivation, for others the social and emotional problems of the elementary school years only compound themselves in adolescence. The way these adolescents feel about themselves and the way they relate to others color not only their academic performance and interpersonal interactions but also their potential for future personal and vocational satisfaction. Given the link between LD and JD in some students, continued educational and juvenile justice efforts must be made at professional and governmental levels to implement effective prevention and treatment programs. Developing the social repertoires of adolescents with learning disabilities is critical so that they will avoid delinquency and adjust favorably to adult work, family, and social situations and not find themselves treated differentially by employers, peers, and authorities.

Learning disabilities are lifelong. Many of these adults, due to excellent schooling, motivation, intelligence, and family support succeed very well in employee, spouse, parent, and friendship relationships. For others however, despite substantial gains, the residuals of the learning disability are still apparent in less than optimal adult vocational, social, and independent living adjustment. Because of increasing attention to social and emotional concomitants of learning disabilities during the school years, as well as a fuller range of postsecondary educational, independent living, career planning, and vocational opportunities, there is growing optimism that these individuals in the future may more successfully meet life's challenges as adults.

**Part Four
The Task**

Chapter Eight

Assessment

The nature and severity of a person's learning disorders will depend on the interaction between his or her personal characteristics (cognitive abilities, information-processing strengths/weaknesses, personality, motivation, social–emotional maturity, achievement, cognitive style, knowledge), the characteristics of required tasks (how well tasks match the person's abilities and style), and the characteristics of the settings in which the individual lives, studies, and plays (attitudes, interaction patterns, quality of learning through home and school experiences). A multidimensional assessment framework is essential to discover how the strengths of the student can best be matched with task and setting attributes that are most likely to promote academic and social growth. The multiple perspectives that must be taken into account, together with technical and conceptual concerns about many of the assessment devices currently in use, make assessment far from a simple matter.

Assessment is the process of gathering data for the purpose of clarifying strengths and weaknesses and making decisions that will facilitate the individual's growth educationally and psychologically. Contrary to popular opinion, assessment is not the same as testing; testing is just one part of the assessment process. Many other means of data collection are involved in assessment: observing interactions among the student, parents, teachers, and peers; interviewing the student and significant others in his or her life; examining school records and past evaluation results; evaluating developmental and medical histories; using information from checklists completed by parents, teachers, or the student; evaluating curriculum requirements and options; evaluating the student's style and rate of learning during trial teaching periods; using task analysis to identify which criteria still have to be mastered; and collecting data on peer acceptance, classroom climate, and teacher attitudes toward a student with disabilities. Prerequisites for appropriate assessment include being aware of multiple assessment purposes, models, and methods, as well as securing sufficient training to evaluate and plan in a team context and across multiple domains.

Assessment Purposes

Assessment can facilitate different kinds of decisions, each of which may require different sets of information. Salvia and Ysseldyke (1995) identify a number of types of decisions that call for different types of assessment: referral, screening, identification, instructional planning, and pupil progress. Additional reasons for assessment include developing and evaluating new assessment and intervention strategies, and conducting research that might lead to a better understanding of the characteristics and intervention needs of individuals with learning disabilities. The particular purpose for assessment dictates the assessment techniques we ultimately choose to use.

Referral

One type of decision that needs to be made is whether a teacher should seek assistance from other school personnel in dealing with a particular student. Each year 3 to 5 percent of pupils are referred for psychological and educational assessment (Salvia & Ysseldyke, 1995). When pupils referred for reading and learning disabilities are tested, anywhere from half to three-quarters are identified as requiring special education (Fugate, Clarizio, & Phillips, 1993; Shinn, Tindal, & Spira, 1987). Often as many as five different professionals are involved in the testing, which accounts for over 40 percent of the cost of educating a student with learning disabilities (Shepard & Smith, 1983). Unfortunately, the assessment process is so time consuming that it significantly cuts into the time that remains for school personnel to invest in remediating students' difficulties.

In order to address the issue of too much time and money being borrowed from intervention for the sake of testing, some school systems have developed *prereferral* or *teacher assistance teams*. These teams consist of experienced general and special education teachers, and other specialists, who consult with classroom teachers regarding a student's difficulty in the classroom. In group or one-on-one consultation, team members clarify questions, suggest interventions, and assess the need for more in-depth assessment after monitoring the outcome of recommended program modifications. The teacher essentially takes on a researcher role in experimenting with various interventions. Subsequent referral rates and numbers of students identified with a disability do decline when prereferral teams are available to advise the classroom teacher (Graden, Casey, & Bonstrom, 1985; Henning-Stout, Lucas, & McCary, 1993; Lloyd et al., 1988). In addition, the quality of referral appears to become more accurate, in that a greater percentage of the smaller group ultimately referred for LD evaluation are identified for special education services (Dangel & Ensminger, 1988).

The success of prereferral teams suggests that regular class teachers are capable of personalizing the learning environment for students with learning disabilities, so that fewer students enter the referral process. The more constructive regular classroom environments become, the more special education can be reserved for those who really need it (Algozzine & Ysseldyke, 1986). Therefore, the first priority of assessment needs to be consultation regarding how one might modify regular classroom tasks and settings to best meet the needs of the student who demonstrates academic weaknesses.

Screening

Another purpose of assessment is to identify students who lag sufficiently behind their peers to warrant additional instruction or assessment. Typically, screening is accomplished by administering norm-referenced tests to groups of students. These tests compare an individual with others of the same age who have similar sociocultural and experiential backgrounds. Achievement tests, for example, might identify Nadine as having learned less than expected, given her cognitive abilities, age, grade, years of schooling, and quality of home and school background. Further assessment might then be recommended to determine the specific factors contributing to her underachievement. As a preliminary measure, vision and hearing screenings are conducted routinely in schools to identify visual or auditory acuity problems that could interfere with students' learning and adjustment.

Identification

To comply with state and federal laws and regulations, school personnel assess pupils for the purpose of identifying students as having a disability and developing a general framework for intervention. Once identified as disabled, the 1997 reauthorization of IDEA requires that every three years a decision be made by the Individualized Education Plan (IEP) team and parents about whether reassessment is necessary to determine if the child continues to have a disability, and if the student is in the best program.

Instructional Planning

Assessment data are collected to assist educational personnel in planning programs that will enhance the psychological adjustment and educational achievement of students with learning disabilities. Within this assessment goal, emphasis is placed on determining precisely which skills students have and have not mastered and how they approach learning tasks. The results help teachers design both what and how to teach. Chapter 1 addressed the assessment issues involved in identifying students as learning disabled. Our primary concern in this chapter is with psychoeducational planning. Assessment practices that merely lead to identification are not sufficient for designing instructional programs and for planning day-to-day teaching modifications.

Pupil Progress

Once programs are implemented, pupil progress must be evaluated to determine any necessary pro-

gram modifications. IDEA mandates that the IEP be reviewed annually for children with disabilities. Teacher-constructed measures, standardized tests, classroom observation, and behavior checklists often are used to assess students' academic and social progress. Systematic monitoring of progress in the classroom, as often as once or twice weekly, has been associated with significantly higher rates of student learning (Fuchs & Fuchs, 1986; Zigmond & Miller, 1986). Data-based monitoring approaches, especially those that use graphs to analyze performance trends and provide feedback to pupils, are far more effective than informal observation in augmenting achievement.

Data on pupil progress also are gathered to evaluate the effectiveness of intervention programs for different types of students. The school, for example, might evaluate the effectiveness of different classroom organization patterns in helping children maintain attention, or the effectiveness of different reading programs, compared to prestated objectives. Pupil progress evaluations also address whether a student with learning disabilities may make more progress in a more or less restrictive setting. Clearly, analyses of pupil progress provide not only specific, programmatically useful information on student skills, strategies, and behaviors, but also information on important curriculum and setting modifications.

Models of Assessment

There are a number of philosophical models of assessment. Some focus primarily on the learner and how the development of particular skills can augment success. Other models focus on how to modify tasks and settings to best accommodate the needs of the learner.

Each assessment model varies in emphasis, in measures used, and in how the results affect intervention strategies. As each model provides only a partial view of the individual and his or her needs, in assessing pupils with learning disabilities we must employ multiple models so that interventions can focus as necessary on learner, task, or setting characteristics. The various models are used in a complementary fashion to promote many different types of intervention efforts on behalf of students with learning disabilities.

Focus on the Learner

When the focus is on the student, the basic assumption is that the problems originate within the individual. The primary concern is with identifying and remediating these deficits. The medical and information-processing models both emphasize these learner-based problems.

Medical Model.   In this model a problem is defined in terms of biological symptoms of pathology. The model assumes that the student's problems have biological causes, and that one's experiential background is irrelevant to assessment and intervention. Brain injury due to oxygen deprivation at birth, for example, can be diagnosed without reference to one's background. Background characteristics are pertinent to the medical model only when they actually caused the biological symptoms, for example when drinking during pregnancy caused fetal alcohol syndrome and its consequent cognitive and attentional deficits.

Because many biological problems can go unrecognized, screening within the school serves an important function. It can identify students who are at risk for learning problems because of a medical condition (for example, a visual or hearing impairment, cardiac-related lethargy, or hyperactivity due to biochemical irregularities) and then refer them for more thorough medical or neuropsychological assessment. Interventions within the medical model involve treatment of the biological conditions, such as prescribing glasses, hearing devices, a special diet, appropriate exercise regimens, or drugs.

Information-Processing Model.   This model defines a problem in terms of information-processing weaknesses: visual-perceptual, motor, language, or attention and memory deficits. As in the medical model, process deficits too can go unrecognized. A student with learning disabilities might be viewed as lazy, insolent, or of low ability, when in fact information-processing disabilities are interfering with learning and behavior. There-

fore, screening is an important function. Assessment, for example, may uncover the fact that Joanie does well on aurally presented and verbal tasks but has problems with fine-motor coordination. Although Joanie has good language and mathematical reasoning, she does very poorly in school because tests and homework require writing. Within this model, intervention might consist of giving Joanie lessons to strengthen her fine-motor coordination (remediation of deficit) and making tests and classwork primarily oral (compensation for deficit). Joanie's social studies report, for example, might be tape recorded instead of handwritten. Because intervention focuses on both remediation (building up deficits) and compensation (working around deficits by capitalizing on strengths), assessment within the information-processing model identifies both strengths and weaknesses.

The information-processing model has been criticized because in most cases it is impossible to break complex school tasks and student behaviors down into the separate information-processing skills that contribute to achievement, and then independently assess and remediate each. On most tasks all processes play a role to varying degrees. Complicating the matter is the fact that the reliability and validity of information-processing measures are for the most part poor (Salvia & Ysseldyke, 1995; Sattler, 1992). Often the test items assess a student on obtuse tasks that bear a questionable relationship to skills needed on the actual academic tasks. This results in invalid diagnostic conclusions and remedial recommendations that may be irrelevant educationally and perhaps even harmful if attention is diverted from more appropriate teaching objectives. As we gain sophistication in identifying the precise process deficits that impede performance on particular educational tasks, support for incorporating information-processing assumptions into remedial planning certainly will increase. Blachman's (1993) work relating phoneme segmentation ability to reading readiness is a good example of progress in this direction. Nevertheless, as with the medical model, assessments that focus on processing factors alone are far too narrow to lead to comprehensive educational and psychological interventions.

Focus on the Learner's Interactions with Tasks

The basic concern in the task analysis model is with how the student relates to specific aspects of academic, social, and daily living tasks.

Task Analysis Model. Educators apply the task analysis model to classroom academic tasks in order to discover which task attributes best match the abilities of a student with learning disabilities, and which task modifications will best match the student's learning styles. Because the real curriculum is used, the relationship between assessment and intervention is much closer than in the information-processing model.

Teachers use the task analysis model to ascertain whether their students' abilities are sufficient to support progress in the curriculum of the grade. When a task proves too difficult for a student, it is analyzed into its component parts to determine which subskills the student has and hasn't mastered. For example, if division is a prob-lem, one needs to assess whether subskills of the division process (addition, multiplication, subtraction) have been mastered. As illustrated in Table 8–1, if a child cannot write or name letters, we need to find out whether he or she can point to letters when the teacher dictates them and whether the child can discriminate, draw, or repeat letters accurately. A teenager who is having difficulty preparing for tests might be asked the questions in Figure 8–1, in order to ascertain which aspects of test preparation are most troublesome. Once we are certain about which subskills the student already knows, the task analysis offers a logical progression of subsequent teaching objectives.

Tasks also can be analyzed along process dimensions from most to least difficult (Sperry, 1974):

- *Expressive/receptive:* It is harder to express what one knows than to deal with the same material receptively. For example, communicating knowledge through essays

Table 8–1 Task analysis of letter naming

Memory	Modality Input-Output	Task Requirements
Recall	Auditory-motor	Write the letter "C" when "C" is dictated by the teacher
Recall	Visual-oral	Read the letter "C" when presented on a card
Recognition	Auditory-motor	Teacher says "C"; student points to the "C"
Recognition	Visual-oral	Teacher points to a "C" and asks "Is this a 'C'?"; student responds yes or no
No Memory		
Discrimination	Visual-motor	Student matches the "C" with another "C" among several distractor letters
Discrimination	Auditory-vocal	Teacher says the sounds *C—C* or the words *cat—cat* "are they the same or different?" *C—P* or *cat—pat* "are they the same or different?"; student responds
Repetition	Auditory-vocal	Teacher says "C"; student repeats "C"
Repetition	Visual-motor	Student copies a model of "C"

Easier ⟷ Harder

Checklist for Assessing Students' Examinations

Student Name: _____ Date: _____ Examiner: _____

Type of Test:

Multiple Choice _____ Short Answer _____ Essay _____ Standardized _____

Class Test _____ % of Grade _____

Subject: _____

Test Preparation

Interview the student by asking the open-ended question first, followed by the probe question as required.

Tell me how you study: _____

_____

_____

_____

_____

_____

Probes:

1. Do you usually study in a special place? Yes _____ No _____ Where? _____

2. Do you have a special time for studying? Yes _____ No _____ When? _____

3. How long can you study before you take a break? _____ hours _____ minutes

4. When you know you have a test coming up a week away, when do you start studying for it? _____

5. Do you usually find yourself having to cram the night before? Yes _____ No _____ For how long can you cram before you can't concentrate any longer? _____ hours _____ minutes

6. Do you prefer to study in a quiet place, with music playing or in front of the television set? _____
   What do you normally do? _____

7. Do you sit at a desk, in an easy chair or lie on the bed or the floor when you study? _____

8. Do you study from your notebook? _____ textbook? both? _____ Which do you like best? _____
   _____

9. Tell me what goes through your head as you study. _____
   _____

10. When you study, do you try to figure out what information is most important? Yes _____ No _____ or
    to predict what questions will be on the test? Yes _____ No _____ How do you do that? _____
    _____

11. Which subjects do you find the easiest to study? _____
    _____
    Why? _____

12. Which subjects do you find the hardest to study? _____
    _____
    Why? _____

Test-Taking Behavior

Evaluate the student's performance in each area by marking a ✓ in the appropriate column:

	Excellent	Adequate	Inadequate	Notes
• Punctuality				
• Equipped (e.g., pen, pencil)				
• Motivation				
• Planning of time				
• Checking of work				
• Accuracy of prediction of grade				
• Anxiety Level	High	Moderate	Low	

(Continues on following page)

Figure 8–1 Checklist for assessing students' examinations. *Source:* Wiener, J. (1986). Alternatives in the assessment of the learning disabled adolescent: A learning strategies approach. *Learning Disabilities Focus, 12,* 97–107, p. 102. Reprinted by permission of the Division for Learning Disabilities.

Test Product					
Analyze a recent examination or test by examining the areas listed below and questioning the student when clarification is needed. Evaluate the student's performance in each area by marking a ✓ in the appropriate column:					
	Excellent	Adequate	Inadequate	Not Applicable	Notes
• Handwriting: Neatness 　　　　　Legibility 　　　　　Speed • Accuracy of Reading 　of Questions • Comprehension of 　Subtleties of Questions • Spelling • Grammar • Punctuation • Appropriateness of 　Vocabulary to Discipline • Sequencing & 　Organization of 　Thoughts • Relevance of Answers • Conceptualization 　of Answers • Elaboration of Answers					
Comments: _____ _____					

Figure 8–1 *Continued*

is harder than recognizing the information in multiple-choice format. Spelling a word is harder than recognizing whether a word is correctly spelled.

- *Social/nonsocial:* Because of greater distractions and fewer reinforcers, working in a group is more difficult than maintaining attention in a one-on-one situation.

- *Abstract/concrete materials and responses:* Adding numerals is harder than adding with blocks.

- *Verbal/nonverbal materials and responses:* Language tasks often are harder than visual-motor tasks. For example, a child may be able to match the word *cat* with another printed *cat,* locate it among three *bats,* and copy the word *cat.* However, retrieving the language to read this symbol

is more difficult. For most children, recalling both the language and the visual symbols to write them down, as in spelling *cat,* is the most difficult task of all.

- *Symbolic/nonsymbolic materials and responses:* After one brother hits his little brother, it is hard for him to understand how the concept "pick on people your own size" pertains to his punishment; the simple, concrete rule "hitting is wrong" is easier to comprehend. Understanding language that is translated into a new symbol system (printed words) is more difficult than comprehending the same words when listening.

- *Sequential/static items and responses:* Dealing with elements in a series is more difficult than dealing with each in isolation (for example, it is harder to learn all twenty-six letters of the alphabet or twenty capitals of states at once than it is to study four at a time).

- *Long-term memory/short-term memory/no memory:* Remembering something for a long period of time is more difficult than remembering it for the moment; not having to remember is easiest of all, as in open-book exams.

These types of analyses, done as needed in the classroom, help us to determine appropriate remedial objectives, as well as the compensatory approaches that will help students work around their weaknesses by capitalizing on their strengths.

Focus on the Learner's Interactions with Settings

Another way of assessing the student with learning disabilities is to broaden the process to include the various settings to which the student relates. Here the basic assumption is that problems relate to the individual's interactions with settings. Three assessment models place primary emphasis on learner-setting interactions: the social systems model, the ecological assessment model, and the behavioral assessment model.

Social Systems Model. In the social systems model, the primary focus is on whether an individual conforms to the specific role expectations of a given setting (Mercer, 1979). The student with learning disabilities interacts with a variety of social systems (family, classrooms, religious settings, stores) and assumes a variety of social roles, such as both son and brother in a family social system. Because each social role in each social system carries different expectations for behavior, the definition of what is considered normal behavior will vary from setting to setting. The most powerful people in a given setting determine what is acceptable for various roles in that setting. For example, the school principal and teachers define standards for acceptable academic progress within a school. Within a classroom, a teacher's expectations about appropriate behavior for students,

coupled with the teacher's tolerance level, might determine whether a child is considered to be hyperactive. Thus, a person's behavior may be considered typical in one setting but judged atypical in another setting. It is not uncommon for a teenager with learning disabilities to be considered typical in art and mechanical drawing classes but atypical in English or algebra classes.

Assessment within the social systems model looks at the role expectations for the diversity of settings with which the student is likely to interact. Functioning well within any social system involves developing positive interpersonal ties with individuals in the system and attaining the skills necessary for functioning in particular roles in these settings. Intervention within the social systems model is aimed at helping the student develop the relevant interpersonal ties (for example, with teachers and peers) and role skills (for example, academics, paying attention) necessary for success.

Ecological Assessment Model. The ecological model is concerned primarily with how the structural, affective, and organizational components of settings influence individual behavior. A basic premise of this model is that each environment will exert dependable enduring influences on the behavior of all individuals within that setting. To illustrate, the participants in a third grade reading group generally behave in consistent ways when in that group, even though the participants change throughout the morning. These consistent ways of behaving (listening when someone else reads aloud, answering questions) are different from the way these children act in other environments, such as the cafeteria or playground. A lack of adaptive fit between an individual's behavior and a particular setting is cause for concern. Because this model assumes that people try to achieve harmonious relationships with their environments, an environmental intervention that helps one child behave more appropriately (for example, small-group versus large-group instruction) might be effective with other children as well.

The ecological model leads educators to examine how an individual's behavior is linked with the environment immediately surrounding that behavior. Assessment focuses on the objective components of the environment (Gump, 1978): objects in the environment (number of books, educational games, bright colors, busy bulletin boards), the curriculum, people (teacher, peers, support personnel), adult or peer praise and criticism, time schedules, seating arrangements, and more. The subjective components of the environment (that is, the environment from the perspective of participants within that setting) also are investigated (Walberg, 1977). Participants, for example, may describe the environment as "boring," "fun," "threatening," "warm," "hostile," "organized," or "chaotic."

Within the ecological model, educators can assess a whole organization, its interlocking systems (a school district and its building support staff, interrelationships among administration and teachers), and how these influence a student's behavior within a given setting. Conoley (1980), for example, offers an excellent example of the effect on a boy's learning when his first grade classroom moved into a new building due to a school closing.

Intervention within the ecological model focuses on changes in the structural, affective, and organizational components of the environment. Craig, for example, was anxious about getting to his last class on time without dropping his books. Craig was a hemiplegic whose last class necessitated climbing forty-two stairs. Overwrought with concern, he had trouble paying attention throughout the day. A shift to another social studies class on the first floor solved the problem. Another example of an ecological change that can alter individual behavior is organizing cooperative learning activities so that the peer acceptance of a student with learning disabilities might be enhanced.

Behavioral Assessment Model. Behavioral approaches incorporate both the social systems and ecological assessment models while measuring student, peer, and teacher behaviors in natural settings. Systematic observation, for example, might take place in the classroom, school halls, cafeteria, playground, home, and neighborhood and in assessment environments specifically structured to include role playing or trial teaching.

The importance of assessing pupils in their natural settings cannot be stressed enough. When

a child is tested by a strange adult in a strange room with a strange set of questions and tasks that may be irrelevant to the actual curriculum, inappropriate inferences may be made about the child's problems. In addition, the much higher rate of verbal and nonverbal reenforcement in the testing situation, when compared with the classroom, may result in an overestimate of the child's capabilities in day-to-day situations.

Behavioral assessment is not necessarily limited to behavioral actions that can be observed. It also may focus on cognitive (thoughts, images), affective (feelings, subjective interpretations), physiological (heart rate increase prior to a test), and structural (arrangement of desks) components of the interaction between learners and settings. Consequently, a multitude of measurement strategies can be used in the behavioral assessment model, including interviewing, rating scales, observations in natural or testing situations, self-evaluation, and biofeedback monitoring. Interventions are based on a broad social learning approach that aims to shape a youngster's behavior by manipulating environmental antecedents and consequences (Keller, 1981).

Focus on the Learner in a Broader Sociocultural Context

This focus includes a diverse set of approaches designed to be more responsive to the cultural pluralism that exists in this country and others. It attempts to interpret assessment results in a way that is not biased by the dominant culture, which, in America, is the middle class and Anglo American tradition. This pluralistic effort to consider test results within the appropriate sociocultural context arose from concerns about test discrimination and overrepresentation of minorities in special education classes (Mercer, 1979; Oakland & Laosa, 1977).

Pluralistic Model. In the pluralistic model, a student is defined as having a problem only when poor performance persists despite controlling for sociocultural bias. The pluralistic model assumes that potential for learning is distributed in the same way in all racial, ethnic, and cultural groups.

Individual differences in learning potential will exist within each of these groups, but differences in test performance between cultural groups are assumed to be due to biases in the tests and testing procedures we use.

The pluralistic model assumes that tests assess what the individual has learned about the cultural heritage represented in the test's construction. Therefore, the model assumes that all tests are culturally biased. People socialized in the same cultural heritage as the test's norm sample will tend to perform better on a test than those not reared in that cultural tradition. The latter perform poorly because of differences in their socialization, not because of differences in their learning potential. To illustrate, knowing who wrote *Romeo and Juliet,* a question on an intelligence test, depends on a particular cultural heritage. Assessment in the pluralistic model attempts to control for such cultural biases in test instruments and procedures.

In order to deal with the issue of sociocultural bias, *culture-free tests* were developed in the 1950s. However, these measures failed because they did not predict school performance (the goals of which are determined by the dominant culture) and because sociocultural differences could not be eliminated from the measures (Cronbach, 1975; Sattler, 1992). That sociocultural differences exist on so-called culture-free tests should not be surprising, because all test questions and materials must be developed within some cultural context. A test cannot be developed within a cultural vacuum.

Two alternatives to culture-free tests are development of *culture-fair tests* or many *culture-specific tests.* A culture-fair test would balance items across cultural groups. This approach, however, would not predict performance in our predominantly middle-class, white American schools. In fact, contrary to expectations, African American and lower socioeconomic status children actually do better on culturally loaded tests than on culture-fair tests, and on verbal tests than on nonverbal tests (Aiken, 1987; Anastasi, 1982). It seems that they benefit from exposure to the majority culture's vocabulary and information, and that they perform less well when required to

rely on a type of analytic or abstract reasoning that has not been specifically taught (Eysenck, 1984a: Jensen, 1984). Culture-specific tests suffer from the same problem as culture-fair tests—low predictability to school performance. In addition, a separate African American or Hispanic test would continue to ignore the considerable heterogeneity that exists within each of these groups.

A comprehensive assessment that includes all the various domains of assessment can effectively address the broad focus suggested by the pluralistic model. Nonbiased assessment is a process rather than a set of instruments. Jessica's story (page 291) is a good example of how assessment within the pluralistic model can ensure the fairness and effectiveness of assessment and intervention decisions regardless of ethnicity and sociocultural background.

Mercer's (1979) System of Multicultural Pluralistic Assessment (SOMPA) and Feuerstein's Learning Potential Assessment Device (LPAD), though not complete assessment systems, are perhaps the most far-reaching attempts thus far to deal with the issues of pluralistic assessment and nondiscriminatory testing. The SOMPA is a norm-based system that addresses how well a pupil adapts to both the dominant core society and the individual's own sociocultural setting. Besides screening for health problems, and adaptive behavior in school and nonschool roles, performance on the Wechsler Intelligence Scale for Children-Revised (WISC-R) is interpreted as measuring not the child's intelligence, but rather the child's adaptation to the student role in the school's social system (the test predicts well to schools, which reflect the dominant core culture's values, beliefs, and academic role expectations). The SOMPA then tries to estimate the individual's intelligence more fairly by comparing his or her intelligence test performance only with children who share a similar sociocultural background. This intelligence estimate can be useful for identifying socioculturally diverse students as learning disabled because IQs are adjusted upward and discrepancies between intelligence and achievement become more evident.

The LPAD has been used by Feuerstein (1979) in Israel to shed light on the process by

Jessica

Jessica, a seven-year-old girl, was referred to Syracuse University's Psychoeducational Teaching Laboratory by her very concerned mother, who did not believe the school's judgment that Jessica was mentally retarded. Jessica's father had died within the past few months. He had battled cancer for five years, and all family activities revolved around his needs; his bed had been in the middle of the living room. Jessica's mother was on public assistance. Their home was barren; there were no toys or books. When we arrived at their home for a visit, we found Jessica and her two brothers amusing themselves by throwing themselves against a wall and seeing who could rebound farthest. None of the children had ever been enrolled in preschool education.

Jessica had performed within retarded ranges on the school's standardized intelligence test. The psychologist indicated that Jessica's responses were random on many tasks; she seemed not to know what she was to do. Taking a cue from this comment, and considering Jessica's home background, we wondered whether lack of prior exposure to similar tasks may have influenced Jessica's poor performance. Consequently, we spent about fifteen minutes playing the same kinds of games with Jessica that she had to play on the IQ test. Jessica was encouraged to verbalize her problem-solving strategies while sequencing pictured events (Jessica put together the sequence of making a pizza, building a skyscraper, and an imminent storm), to point out similarities between two objects (Jessica grouped pictures of vehicles, flowers, and birds), to copy designs from one place to another, and so on. We then readministered the intelligence test, reminding Jessica to approach the questions in the same ways in which we had just been playing. Jessica achieved a score well within average ranges. Her cultural experiences, not her cognitive abilities, had been tapped the first time around. In fact, the discrepancy between Jessica's higher intelligence and very slow learning rate over the subsequent months eventually led to an LD identification. A pluralistic approach to assessment helped to sort this out.

which culturally disadvantaged children learn best, as well as these students' degree of cognitive modifiability. Its reliability, validity, and the utility of training on its information-processing tasks in order to increase achievement have yet to be demonstrated (Frisby & Braden, 1992). The LPAD examiner tests the student's initial grasp of the tasks' principles, then teaches through a variety of strategies matched to a pupil's learning styles and sociocultural background, notes the amount and nature of effort required to teach the student, and then posttests to measure the amount of gain that the student makes on new tasks as a result of sharpening his or her information-processing skills. These certainly are very different roles from those assumed in the usual testing situation. Research Box 8–1 explores additional issues and methods related to intelligence testing of socioculturally diverse populations.

Assessment Methods

Given the need to intervene with students who are learning disabled at learner, task, and setting levels, the need for a multidimensional assessment approach is clear. Assessment can involve tasks conducted with students or strategies that focus

RESEARCH BOX 8–1

Intelligence Testing of Socioculturally Diverse Populations

Intelligence tests have been said to be biased against ethnic minorities because these groups generally score significantly lower than white middle-income Americans. Studies find, however, that these tests fulfill their purpose of predicting achievement and adult success just as well for African Americans and Hispanics as they do for whites (Barrett & Depinet, 1991; Neisser et al., 1996). Interestingly, on items thought to be culturally unfair, there are no significant differences between African Americans and whites (Koh et al., 1984; Sattler, 1992). If African American, rather than white, examiners test African American students, the scores are no higher (Jensen, 1984; Sattler, 1992).

What we have been referring to as bias within IQ tests is in reality a reflection of several factors:

1. One factor is the pervasive influence of low socioeconomic status on learning school-type content, limiting test-taking skills, and reducing motivation in testing situations (Sattler, 1992). Poverty and ethnic minority status are often inextricably linked (Natriello, Pallas, & McDill, 1990). When African American and white children of equal socioeconomic status are compared, their performance becomes more similar (.5–.7 of a standard deviation apart instead of 1 standard deviation apart), although the scores still represent a significant difference (Eysenck, 1984a). Cultural differences may well influence these persistent discrepancies (Neisser et al., 1996).

2. Another factor is the biased interpretation of these tests by examiners. Historically, more minority children who tested low have been referred for placement in classes for the mentally retarded than white children with the same low scores (Mercer, 1973).

3. The role of genetic influences in IQ test differences continues to be hotly debated (Herrnstein & Murray, 1994; Reynolds & Brown, 1984).

Because of their poor performance on IQ tests, disproportionate numbers of children from low-income and nonwhite families historically have been placed in classes for the mildly mentally retarded (Argulewicz, 1983; Brosnan, 1983; Dunn, 1968; National Center for Education Statistics, 1992; Office of Civil Rights, 1992; Patrick & Reschly, 1982). When Jane Mercer (1970, 1973) tallied the races of Riverside, California, special class students (IQ 79 or below), she found three times more Mexican American and two and one-half times more African American students than would be expected from their percentage in the general population. However, when she used the American Association on Mental Deficiency's definition of retardation, that both intellectual and adaptive (daily living) skills must be deficient to be identified as mentally retarded, the majority of the youngsters had to be declassified because their adaptive skills were normal and their IQs were within normal limits relative to special test norms constructed only from their own cultural group's IQ test performance (Mercer & Lewis, 1978). In another study, 67 percent of mildly retarded

(Continues on following page)

RESEARCH BOX 8–1   *(Continued from preceding page)*

youngsters were declassified after adaptive behavior measurement proved that, in the non-school world, these students functioned normally (Coulter, Morrow, & Tucker, 1978).

Unfortunately, placements in special classes for the mentally retarded are not associated with any higher academic achievement, and in fact sometimes are associated with lower achievement, than had the children remained in regular classes (Carlberg & Kavale, 1980; Gottlieb, Rose, & Lessen, 1983). Therefore, in the *Larry P. v. Riles* case, October 1979, California's Federal District Court Judge Robert Peckham ruled that IQ tests for placing African American children in programs for the retarded are discriminatory, and he banned their use (a statewide injunction had been in effect since 1974). Less than a year after this decision, Illinois' Federal District Court Judge John F. Grady upheld the use of IQ tests with African American children provided that these tests were not the sole criteria for determination of an educational program (*PASE v. Hannon*, 506 F. suppl. 831; N. D. Ill. 1980). Florida and Georgia had similar rulings (Reschly, Kicklighter, & McKee, 1988). On September 26, 1986, Judge Peckham barred all California public schools from administering IQ tests to African American students for any special education reason. Instead he recommended that measures of adaptive behavior, academic achievement, classroom performance, personal history, development, and instruments designed to pinpoint strengths and weaknesses in various areas be used. In response, *Crawford et al. v. Honic et al.* was filed in California in 1988 by African American families who claimed that their civil rights had been violated by being barred from voluntarily taking IQ tests (for example, for determination of giftedness). This resulted in Judge Peckham's reversing his ban for three specific children to take an IQ test for LD identification purposes (August 31, 1992). On the grounds of this reversal, the California Association of School Psychologists continues to contest the state's ban on IQ testing for African American children. Despite reductions due to litigation, racial and ethnic minorities have continued to be overrepresented in classes for the retarded in many parts of the country (Artiles & Trent, 1994; Chinn & Hughes, 1987; MacMillan, Hendrick, & Watkins, 1988).

What happened to those students who, due to the above actions, were declassified as mentally retarded? Did their special educational needs magically disappear? They did not, and many quickly found their way into classes for the learning disabled (Gottlieb et al., 1994; Tucker, 1980; Wright & Santa Cruz, 1983). As a result of increasing cautiousness in identifying socioculturally diverse children as mentally retarded, there is concern about whether the "LD" label is becoming another subtle form of discrimination that reduces teacher, student, and parent aspirations and motivation.

For those declassified children who could not demonstrate significant ability-achievement discrepancies for LD identification, the only option was regular class placement without special educational services (Forness, 1985). Unable to pass these classes' minimum competency tests, a high proportion of these youngsters and those for whom English is a second language have ended up retained, dropping out, or being denied high school diplomas (Gersten & Woodward, 1994; MacMillan et al., 1988). This is a problem across the

(Continues on following page)

RESEARCH BOX 8–1 *(Continued from preceding page)*

entire country. Exacerbating this situation is the seemingly greater reluctance of educators to refer language-minority children and socioculturally diverse children of low socioeconomic status or intelligence to special education or special classes than white children of similar intelligence (Flynn, 1984; Frame, Clarizio, & Porter, 1984; Gersten & Woodward, 1994; Tomlinson et al., 1977). MacMillan and others raise the question of whether our efforts to normalize the school experiences of children from multicultural backgrounds actually has reduced their educational opportunities, a de facto reverse racism.

The use of intelligence tests in LD identification of the socioculturally diverse child is troublesome because, if these tests underestimate their intelligence, we might deny these youngsters educational opportunities from which they could benefit. Adaptive behavior measures provide one alternative for estimating expected achievement of these students, as do dynamic assessment (which evaluates a child's learning ability after modification of instructions and strategies), Mercer's (1979) Estimated Learning Potential score (which adjusts IQ upward based on urban acculturation, socioeconomic status, family structure, and size), and Kaufman and Kaufman's (1983) Kaufman Assessment Battery for Children (which provides intelligence norms for African American and white children of various socioeconomic levels, and adjusts IQ upward by moving highly verbal and school-related items to another scale). The latter two measures, however, do not predict school achievement as well as do standard IQ measures (Sattler, 1992).

After reading about all these machinations, the reader probably would agree that it is a shame that whether or not students fit a label is what, in many cases, will determine whether they get the special help they need. Under IDEA's 1997 reauthorization, children with developmental delays can receive special education until age nine, after which a specific disability identification is to be decided upon.

on the students' interactions with a variety of tasks and settings.

Tests used in assessment have been categorized as either norm-referenced or criterion-referenced measures. Tests that have been standardized on a normative group, in order to compare an individual's performance to that of his or her peers, are called *standardized* or *norm-referenced tests*. In contrast, *criterion-referenced tests* are intended to measure whether a person has mastered very specific skills. A test that shows Brett to have mastered math better than 15 percent of children at his grade level nationally is norm-based. A test that indicates that he can add two-digit numbers, but not when regrouping is required, is criterion-referenced. The norm-referenced test will judge Brett's knowledge of letter sounds by sampling a few letters and comparing his percentage correct with that of the standardization sample. In contrast, the criterion-referenced test is likely to ask Brett to give all twenty-six letter sounds.

Norm-referenced tests are most useful for screening and identification purposes, whereas criterion-referenced measures are most useful for identifying what to teach. How to teach is best ascertained by using *informal evaluation strategies* designed to address the specific questions raised about the student's interactions with tasks and settings. *Curriculum-based assessment*, which uses informal, criterion-referenced strategies to measure progress over time in the classroom curriculum, is among the most instructionally relevant forms of assessment. The most recently developed system to assess student products in daily class work is *authentic assessment*.

Norm-Referenced Measures

Publishers have flooded the market with norm-referenced tests. In order for these tests to be useful in the decision-making process, they must meet several criteria: (1) reliability—consistency of scores from one testing time to another; (2) validity—the test measures what it is supposed to measure; (3) standardized administration procedures (if all examiners use similar procedures, a more accurate estimate of the student's performance relative to the normative group is possible); and (4) norms based on an appropriate comparison group (similar sociocultural and educational background).

Just because a test is published does not mean it is any good. Unfortunately, a large proportion of our tests have been standardized poorly, are not reliable measures, do not validly measure the attributes they purport to test, and are invalid for instructional programming or LD identification purposes. Often these tests are not normed with a group that is similar in ethnic-cultural background to the students being assessed. If ever concerned about a test's technical adequacy for a specific purpose, one can consult Salvia and Ysseldyke (1995), Sattler (1992), or the most recent edition of the Buros Mental Measurements Yearbook. These sources are revised periodically and offer outstanding test critiques by experts in the field.

An important function of well-constructed norm-referenced measures is screening children who might be at risk for psychological and educational problems. However, assessment teams cannot limit themselves to the use of norm-referenced tests alone because these measures sample too few skills to be of much help in planning specifically *what* and *how* to teach students. Additional assessment approaches, such as criterion-referenced and informal evaluation strategies, are necessary. After standard administration, for example, the examiner might apply informal evaluation

methods to the items on which the student erred to discover exactly what subcomponents of the task the student has mastered, which aspects are difficult and why, and how rapidly the student could learn the task and generalize this knowledge to new items given various instructional strategies (Smith, 1980).

Criterion-Referenced Measures

Criterion-referenced tests provide information on *what* to teach. Only a few norm-referenced tests are detailed enough to allow for interpretation in a criterion-referenced way. A criterion-referenced test can be normed, although norms are not critical to its purpose.

Students' scores on criterion-referenced achievement measures can be affected by the amount of overlap that exists between their curriculum and the test items (Bell, Lentz, & Graden, 1992; Good & Salvia, 1988). More often than not, test items do not correspond with what has been taught in the classroom (Shriner & Salvia, 1988). On math tests, for example, more than half the content may be derived from topics never covered by the text (Freeman et al., 1980). On reading tests, only in first and second grades does a large percentage of the content overlap with the vocabulary taught in the students' readers (Shapiro & Derr, 1987). Likewise, the problem-solving strategies called for on the test may differ from those practiced in the classroom. When there is little test/curriculum overlap, tests may underestimate the actual skills children learned in the classroom. If, however, we want to determine how well children can generalize their classroom learning to new material and problems, then the less the test and curriculum overlap the better.

Although criterion-referenced tests do not provide information on how to teach, applying informal evaluation strategies to items on which the student had difficulty can serve this purpose.

Informal Evaluation Strategies

A variety of nonstandardized assessment strategies can provide information about both *what* and *how* to teach. Figures 8–2 and 8–3, for example,

Gaining Information from Text

Student Name: _____ Date: _____ Examiner: _____

Text: Subject _____ Grade Level _____

Select a chapter of a textbook in a content subject such as history, geography, or science. The textbook should be one currently in use in the student's program.

Word Identification

Ask the student to read aloud a passage of about 200 words. Note the number of words identified correctly.

_____ % of words identified correctly

If the student identified 90% or more of the words correctly, proceed with the assessment. If the student identified less than 90% of the words correctly, select an easier textbook. Hesitations and self corrections should not be counted as errors.

Survey of Strategies

Tell the student to show you how he/she would study the chapter in order to learn the material for a test. Ask him/her to verbalize his/her thoughts during the course of reading. Note the strategies employed by placing a ✓ in the blank space.

- Skimmed: introduction   _____
            headings   _____
            figures and illustrations   _____
            italics   _____
            conclusion   _____
  prior to reading the chapter
- Read the chapter from beginning to end   _____
- Began to read chapter, then gave up   _____
- Spontaneously asked himself/herself questions while reading   _____
- Used study questions as a guide for reading   _____
- Picked out the main ideas or important points while reading   _____
- Paraphrased main ideas or important points   _____
- Looked up unknown words in the dictionary   _____
- Underlined or highlighted important information   _____
- Made notes   _____
- Predicted questions that might be on an examination   _____

Other: _____

_____

_____

Probes

Some students have strategies in their repertoire that they do not use unless directed to do so. Select a different chapter in the same textbook and rate the student's skill on the following directed procedures.

	Excellent	Adequate	Inadequate	Notes
Getting appropriate information from				
introduction				
headings				
figures & illustrations				
italics				
conclusions				
Self-questioning				
Paraphrasing of main ideas				
Identifying words not understood				
Looking words up in the dictionary				
Predicting examination questions				

Comments: _____

_____

_____

_____

Figure 8–2   Interview questions on gaining information from text. *Source:* Wiener, J. (1986). Alternatives in the assessment of the learning disabled adolescent: A learning strategies approach. *Learning Disabilities Focus, 12,* 97–107, p. 106. Reprinted by permission of the Division for Learning Disabilities.

Interview Questions on Essay/Project/Report Writing

Student Name: _____ Date: _____ Examiner: _____

The Task Environment

1. How did you select the topic/book? _____
_____

2. Are you interested in it?
   very interested _____ somewhat interested _____ not at all interested _____

3. What did the teacher do when giving out the assignment? _____
_____

		Yes	No	Notes
Probes	• give oral guidelines	_____	_____	
	• give written guidelines	_____	_____	
	• select the topic/book	_____	_____	
	• provide structure	_____	_____	
	• increase your interest	_____	_____	
	• specify length	_____	_____	

4. Who are you expecting to read the essay? _____

Previous Knowledge

5. Have you previously been taught to write essays/projects/reports?
   Yes _____ No _____ What were you taught? _____
_____

6. What did you know about the topic before you started? _____
_____

7. What do you think are the expectations of your reader/teacher? _____
_____

Planning

8. Did you have a plan for writing the essay/project/report? Yes _____ No _____
   What was it? _____

9. When did you begin thinking about the topic? _____

10. Did you do any research? Yes _____ No _____ What resources did you use? _____

11. How much time did you have for writing (i.e. ___ between date assignment was given and assignment due)?
    _____ days. How did you use that time? _____
_____

12. Did you make an outline? Yes _____ No _____ What kind of thinking did you do first? _____
_____

   What was your organizational plan (outline)? _____
_____

Translating/Reviewing

13. How many drafts did you write? one _____ two _____ three _____

14. How long did it take to write each one?
    1. _____ hrs/mins   2. _____ hrs/mins   3. _____ hrs/mins

15. Did you write your first draft with pencil? _____ pen? _____ typewriter? _____ word processor? _____

16. Did you double space your first draft? Yes _____ No _____

17. Did you read your first draft over? Yes _____ No _____
    What kind of changes did you make? _____

18. Did you ask a friend or family member to read the first draft and make suggestions?
    Yes _____ No _____ What kind of suggestions did they have? _____
_____

19. Did you proof read the final draft? Yes _____ No _____

Evaluating

20. How did you feel about the essay/project/report in the end? _____
_____

21. What grade did you think you would get? _____ Why? _____
_____

22. What was the teacher's evaluation? _____
_____

Figure 8–3 Interview questions on essay/project/report writing. *Source:* Wiener,
J. (1986). Alternatives in the assessment of the learning disabled adolescent: A
learning strategies approach. *Learning Disabilities Focus, 12,* 97–107, p. 100.
Reprinted by permission of the Division for Learning Disabilities.

illustrate how we might begin to identify the nature of a secondary school student's learning difficulties, and how to intervene, by merely interviewing the student on a number of areas critical to success.

Task analysis, another informal evaluation procedure, assesses mastery of subskills by breaking down complex instructional goals into their component skills. In this way, a pupil's current knowledge can be pinpointed and the next skill to be taught is identified.

Systematic observation of the student in the classroom also can provide information about what and how to teach both academic and behavioral goals. Classroom observation has the advantage of assessing the problem in the setting where it occurs rather than generalizing from a strange testing situation.

Trial teaching is an assessment strategy that gets directly at the how-to-teach question (Prasse & Reschly, 1986; Salvia & Ysseldyke, 1995; Smith, 1980). A variety of instructional techniques are systematically tried and evaluated, including varying materials, methods of presentation or response, and types of feedback. In trial teaching, the focus of assessment becomes the responsiveness of the student's perceptions, problem solving, and memory to instruction, and how well the student applies this learning to novel tasks. The goal is to shed light on the extent and type of supports that will contribute best to a student's learning, as well as obstacles to avoid (Meltzer & Reid, 1994; Zigmond & Miller, 1986).

Trial teaching evaluation strategies are variously referred to as *direct, formative, process,* or *dynamic assessment.* Instead of measuring only abilities that are already developed, these approaches venture into what Vygotsky (1962) called "the zone of proximal development." They reveal the level of performance a child might reach with appropriate help from an adult.

In dynamic assessment, the educator essentially observes a student's performance on various classroom tasks and formulates hypotheses regarding characteristics that might facilitate success (for example, listening to a tape while reading, giving cues to connect new information with the child's prior knowledge, reducing distractors, corrective feedback, self-monitoring attention) or get in the way of a student's success (for example, too rapid presentation rate, discovery learning approach, anxiety, writing versus dictating). These hypotheses are then validated by manipulating the tasks (Meichenbaum, 1976; Smith 1980). To enhance story comprehension, for example, the child might listen to the examiner read the passage, instead of reading it himself or herself, and then respond to the questions. Instead of conducting a math fact quiz under time pressure, the time element may be eliminated. One might try guiding attention (for example, point to each word while reading), teaching self-verbalization (for example, help the student reason aloud), or enhancing motivation (for example, offer points or stickers for increased effort). Throughout this process, it is important to remember that the instructional modifications determined for one task, for example, success on social studies homework, may not be appropriate for the same child on other tasks (for example, science homework), or for different children on the same task (Levin, 1976).

Those who use nonstandardized assessment procedures generally assume that the student's abilities may be masked by environmental variables, such as inappropriate task content, strategies, or settings. Theoretically, the nonstandard techniques "peel away the veil" that has made a student's abilities inaccessible, so that underlying problem-solving abilities are revealed. Having removed task and setting barriers to the expression of one's intelligence, we gain ideas about how to continue to overcome these barriers, thereby building bridges toward success.

Although time consuming, informal strategies are necessary components in an assessment system designed to develop individual psychoeducational intervention plans. They are well-suited for assessing pupil progress and are of particular value in curriculum-based assessment.

Curriculum-Based Assessment

Curriculum-based assessment, commonly referred to as CBA, uses the actual classroom content to assess how students are progressing relative to their classmates, all of whom have been exposed to similar educational programming. Several investigators have found that decoding and reading comprehension progress can be reliably and validly reflected in the number of words a child reads accurately from a classroom reader in one minute (Shinn et al., 1992). Spelling progress can be reliably assessed by measuring the number of correct letter pairs in a two-minute spelling list drawn from the curriculum, and math progress can be assessed by the number of correct digits in a two-minute sample of curriculum problems. Progress in written language can be ascertained from the number of words written in three minutes in response to a story starter or topic sentence. Another means of evaluating progress is tallying the school day on which a child achieves a specific lesson's objective (1–180 for first grade, 181–360 from second grade, and so forth) (Peterson et al., 1985). When the same measures are administered to a random sample of children in each grade in the fall, winter, and/or spring of each year, then it is easy to keep track of how well any youngster is progressing relative to his or her classmates and the other children in the school (Shinn, 1988).

CBA is an excellent tool for evaluating classroom behavior as well. For example, a student's behavior might be rated at ten-second intervals for one minute, followed by a one-minute rating of the behavior of a same-sex student in the class. This two-minute process is repeated until all same-sex students have been rated once. Ratings might tabulate how often the student distracts others vocally, is out of place, has unacceptable physical contact with a person or a person's property, or is off task (Germann & Tindal, 1985). The target child's data are then compared with those of his or her classmates to determine behavioral progress and areas for intervention.

With some training, teachers are able to conduct these assessments themselves, within minutes. This frees the psychologist and special educators to shift time from assessment to intervention. These simple measures very easily distinguish those students who lag so far behind their peers that a more comprehensive evaluation is desirable to determine eligibility for special education services (Marston, Tindal, & Deno, 1984). CBA also distinguishes those who are learning disabled from slow learners, because their rate of progress is slower than that of slow learners. With CBA, repeated measurements are simple and practical, so that change can be monitored frequently against a predicted "aimline" on a graph (Germann & Tindal, 1985; Shinn, Tindal, & Stein, 1988). In this way program modifications can be instituted as soon as necessary rather than waiting until failure on standardized tests administered at the end of the year. Research indicates that teachers using CBA, particularly in combination with analysis of the students' skills, do engage in more frequent and specific instructional modifications (Fuchs et al., 1990; Fuchs, Fuchs, & Stecker, 1989). CBA also is useful for determining when children receiving special education are ready to benefit from being grouped for instruction with their nondisabled peers (Shinn, Rodden-Nord, & Knutson, 1993).

CBA has the advantage of shifting the problem-solving focus toward program evaluation (e.g., phonics instruction is increasing decoding ability) rather than being quick to blame the pupil for his or her academic delays (e.g., "Sue doesn't know her letter sounds; she's two grade levels behind her classmates") (Bursuck & Lessen, 1987). For example, if CBA shows that the number of words read accurately, or minutes spent on task, increase faster in Ms. Tatlock's room than in Mr. Delman's room, and both classes are composed of similar kinds of students, then this suggests that Mr. Delman's teaching materials and methods, rather than his students, should become the focus of assessment. An added advantage of CBA is that it circumvents the pitfalls of tests, on which items are unlikely to correspond with the actual classroom curriculum, or for which norm groups are poorly matched to the experiences of youngsters in a particular school. Specific areas of achievement and behavior become the focus, rather than testing for global patterns of disability.

CBA's objective measurement of progress is important because teachers tend to overestimate the amount that has been mastered, thereby giving students insufficient practice for these concepts (Deno, 1985). With CBA, teacher referrals for special education evaluation are reduced by as much as half, and the referrals more accurately forecast a potential learning disability (Marston, Mirkin, & Deno, 1984). Without CBA, teachers tend to over-refer male students, males with behavior problems, African Americans, low-income youngsters, and those with less appealing physical appearances (Bennett & Ragosta, 1984; Shinn, et al., 1987). CBA has been implemented extensively by some school districts, especially at the elementary level, and has been associated with higher levels of student achievement (Fuchs et al., 1992).

Authentic Assessment

In recent years there has been a shift away from traditional standardized and paper-pencil classroom tests, toward strategies that are believed to better reflect learning outcomes that are "worthwhile, significant, and meaningful—in short, authentic" (Archbald & Newmann, 1988, p. 1). These include exhibits, demonstrations, performances (art, music, plays), experiments, debates, oral reports, written reaction papers to readings, portfolios of work samples, and more. Portfolios can include seminal works that demonstrate motivation and mastery, multiple examples of concrete progress toward a goal, or evolving perceptions, strategies, and thoughts as one progresses toward completion (Miller, 1992). These techniques refocus attention onto student-selected work that students value as important and reflective of their learning, rather than assessing only final outcomes of the teacher's choosing.

Elliott (1991) explains that the products students generate in authentic assessment involve the application of knowledge, creativity, specific strategies, higher-level thinking, and problem-solving skills to substantive, high-quality instructional activities—with initiative and responsibility. The quality of the product is evaluated against preexisting criteria that are articulated on a profile developed through consensus of expert teachers. Students' ultimate grades are determined by their progress relative to these standards and preset

learning objectives. Another grading alternative is to evaluate the child's progress over time against the standard set by the child in earlier portfolio items. This method helps students feel successful because individual progress is recognized no matter how the child's achievements compare to that of peers. There is some evidence that portfolio data lead to more numerous, specific, and detailed instructional recommendations than do more traditional evaluation methods (Rueda & Garcia, 1997).

Authentic assessment encourages students to self-evaluate and offers a form of feedback that makes much more sense and is more instructionally useful than that garnered from tests. Authentic assessment approaches have been received with much excitement among educators, and there is recognition that reliability and validity considerations are just as important here as with other types of assessment approaches (Gresham, 1991).

Multidimensional Assessment Approaches

The Individuals with Disabilities Education Act (IDEA) mandates that multidimensional, nondiscriminatory assessment procedures be employed in evaluating students. It also requires that multiple perspectives be represented within the assessment and planning processes. The primary goal of assessment with a student who has a learning disability is to plan effective psychoeducational programs that will help the individual to develop educationally and personally. To do this evaluators need to recognize that learning does not occur in isolation. It is influenced by many of the student's characteristics and by how these interact with the particular characteristics of various tasks and settings. Therefore, evaluators need to gain as much information about the student in as many domains as possible: a picture of the total person. This process necessitates a team approach to assessment and decision making. The parents and, to as great an extent as possible, the student are very important members of this assessment and planning process.

Multiple Dimensions

Although IDEA'S identification procedures require that "no single procedure is used as the sole criterion for determining an appropriate educational program for a child" (PL 94-142, Federal Register, December 29, 1977, p. 65082), a thorough assessment of the learning program of a student with learning disabilities will necessitate far more than two measures, and these measures must span many assessment domains. To be identified as learning disabled, the student's information-processing difficulty must be found to significantly deter school learning in one or more areas (reading, reading comprehension, written language, math computation and applications, listening, speaking) compared with expectations given one's intelligence and background experiences.

Assessment should include consideration of the student's interactions with the curriculum and settings to which he or she relates, and the student's as well as significant others' subjective impressions concerning all these influences. In line with this ecological perspective, IDEA requires that students' academic performance be observed in their regular classrooms by a team member other than the regular classroom teacher. If an individual is less than school age, or out of school, then the observation occurs in an environment appropriate for someone that age.

IDEA also requires that the testing materials not be racially or culturally discriminatory and that "tests and other evaluation materials are provided and administered in the child's native language or other mode of communication" (PL 94-142, Federal Register, December 29, 1977, p. 65082). There is disagreement, however, as to what constitutes an unbiased assessment. Reschly (1980) proposed that unbiased assessment be defined as testing that leads to effective intervention, whereas biased assessment is testing that leads ethnic and racial minorities to be exposed differentially to ineffective education. Using a broad range of strategies to examine the multiple dimensions discussed in the following pages, we discover ways to maximize students' development by modifying task expectations and relevant settings to better match what the students already know, what they are ready to learn, and how they learn best.

Multiple Perspectives

IDEA'S regulations require participation of a multidisciplinary team including at least one professional with knowledge in the area of suspected disability, the child's regular classroom teacher (if the child is not in a regular class, then a regular classroom teacher qualified to teach a child of this age), and at least one person qualified to conduct individual diagnostic examinations of children (such as a school psychologist, learning disability specialist, speech-language pathologist, or reading specialist) (PL 94-142, Federal Register, December 29, 1977, pp. 65082–3). Most often, an even wider range of professionals within the school are involved, including administrators, social workers, nurses, and occupational and physical therapists. Participation of teachers in the assessment process is important not only because they can offer valuable information about the student but also because, during this process, their levels of commitment to the recommended interventions can be explored.

During an assessment, information about the student is customarily gathered from the student's parents. Parent involvement is built into IDEA. Parents have the right to request timely evaluations, participate in the development of their children's individualized education programs, request mediation, and if necessary an impartial hearing, if they disagree with the findings, petition the state educational agency if they disagree with the hearing officer's decision, request a free and independent assessment, engage a lawyer, have access to all public records, receive a written notice of evaluation procedures and an invitation to participate in identification and placement decisions, receive written notices of school placement decisions and a copy of the evaluation report, consent to initial evaluation or placement in special eduaction, and sign their children's IEPs. Parental perspectives deserve much respect because they certainly are the ones who know the pupil most directly, for the longest duration, and over the widest range of settings.

Because evaluators are merely making reasoned inferences about the problem, they also should invite the student to become a partner in the assessment. When using task analysis procedures, for example, an evaluator might ask the youngster how he or she attempted to solve the problem. What was the student doing, attending to, and thinking? Which learning strategies are easiest for him or her to use? Which might he or she be most likely to remember to use? The student also might provide a wish list describing how he or she would want the school's curriculum or teacher/peer characteristics to change. Allowing students to choose among alternative interventions often is associated with more rapid gains than when student preferences are not considered (Kosiewicz, Hallahan, & Lloyd, 1981). It has been found that students are interested in and capable of involvement in decisions about their school placement, and for most the experience does not seem to be psychologically negative (Taylor, Adelman, & Kaser-Boyd, 1985). IDEA mandates that teenagers must be invited to participate in their transition planning. Nevertheless, students of all ages too seldom are invited in on the discussions. This results in unfortunate misunderstandings (for example, "I'm stupid"), no role in decision making, and little commitment to put effort into helping the intervention succeed (Schneider, 1984; Taylor et al., 1985). Barry's and Rachael's stories (pages 303–304) present a humorous look at what can happen when we consult with the students we are evaluating. Robin's story (page 304) is one that is familiar to many special educators.

When teachers, parents, and significant others in the environment are positively involved in the problem identification, assessment, and decision-making process, they are more likely to involve themselves constructively in the intervention process as well (Keller, 1980, 1981). If they are merely recipients of the assessment information and a set of recommendations, the likelihood of follow-through is reduced. Therefore, it is wise to rotate the chair of assessment and planning teams, and rotate membership, so that abdication of decision making and follow-through is less likely.

The choice of examiners is important as well. There is evidence that the more familiar the examiner and student are with one another (for example, teacher versus psychologist doing the testing; psychologist making a home visit or phone call to the student prior to testing, or playing/talking for a time before testing), the more likely it is that the student will perform to capacity in the assessment situation (Derr-Minneci & Shapiro, 1992; Fuchs, Zern, & Fuchs, 1983).

A team approach to assessment saves time and cost. The team decides which members need to be involved and which measures should be used. Such coordination avoids the all too frequent redundancy of several professionals assessing the same skill; this is an obvious waste of everyone's time and energy and leads students to think "Something must really be very wrong with me." A team approach is critical to ensuring that multiple perspectives regarding the strengths and weaknesses of the learner, task, and setting are considered.

Assessment Domains

A single chapter on assessment cannot possibly do justice to all the measures available. Therefore, in this section we will restrict ourselves to exploring the various evaluation domains and the types of assessment tools employed in each. In Chapter 9 we will describe how team members divide responsibilities for assessment and intervention across these domains.

Any team member who assesses a student must have the necessary training and expertise to do so. A particular credential does not make a person an expert in assessment. Individuals engaged in assessment must be well versed in special education, skilled in establishing rapport with students, familiar with appropriate strategies and tools for the specific kinds of decisions they need to make, and clear about the behaviors sampled by their measures.

Because the learning disabled may be able to demonstrate their capabilities when asked in one way but not another, it is particularly important that the assessment instruments selected maxi-

Barry

Barry, a bright eleventh grader who read accurately but slowly and spelled no better than a second grader, was being evaluated at Syracuse University's Psychoeducational Teaching Laboratory. His teachers did not understand the nature of his learning disability and were seeking instructional direction. Barry's goal was to enroll in the army on graduation; this was something that disappointed his parents, who were both college graduates. Yet they could see no alternative.

Barry's major difficulty in school was with written expression. His spelling was terrible, and his teachers graded off for this. In his classes, Barry's teachers used overheads when lecturing. Unfortunately, Barry was so slow in copying these that he seldom had an accurate set of notes to study from.

Informal assessment and task analysis indicated that Barry could spell with good phonetic equivalents, but he could recall very few irregular spellings. When a word was flashed for one second, he caught only the first two letters. He was unable to recall the word as a whole.

It was hypothesized that Barry had a severe memory difficulty for visual images. In fact, to his dismay, he could not even imagine in his head what his girlfriend looked like. During trial teaching in spelling, when he was asked to close his eyes and image a word, he was unable to do so.

By coincidence, on the day of Barry's last session at the laboratory, a new test of visual-perceptual skills arrived. Barry was the perfect candidate to try it out, and he agreed. With one exception, Barry performed below the performance expected of an eight year old on all subtests: matching patterns, recalling a specific figure he had just seen, finding a hidden figure, and deciding which figure when completed would look like the model. To our surprise, however, he got every item correct that required recalling a sequence of up to 9 +'s and −'s (for example, + + − + − − + +−), by finding this pattern among three distractors. Given Barry's inability to recall even two letters in a word, we were taken aback and confronted Barry with "How *did* you *do* that?" He smiled sheepishly and replied, "Simple, I just looked at the last two things in the line!" And, in fact, if one looks at just the last two +'s or −'s in the row, one can be correct on all but two items! Had we not asked Barry, who knows what kind of conclusions we would have come to.

Barry began using a word processor in high school to correct his spelling, and his teachers made a separate set of their notes for him so that he wouldn't have to copy from the overhead. In addition, spelling was no longer graded in his written work. Once Barry understood his disability, he felt so much better about himself that he changed his career goals. Today Barry is a sophomore in a community college.

mize students' opportunities to demonstrate their knowledge and problem-solving abilities. The formats of typical reading comprehension and spelling tests depicted in Tables 8–2 (page 305) and 8–3 (page 306) and Figure 8–4 (page 307) illustrate this point. The student may answer comprehension questions after orally or silently reading a passage, may point to the correct picture

Rachael and Robin

Rachael turned five right before entering kindergarten. At the beginning of the year she printed her name in capitals from left to right, often reversing letters. Rachael's teacher noted that her drawing ability was far beyond age expectations; it showed excellent attention to detail and appreciation for spatial relationships. Rachael understood left and right on her body as well as in space. After her first two months of school, Rachael continued to reverse letters and began to sign her name from right to left on the paper (ЈƎHƆAЯ). When the teacher corrected her, Rachael would respond "I know," in a put-out manner. The next day she would again print her name from left to right under one picture and from right to left under another.

In time, Rachael's letter reversals became consistent: when she wrote from left to right they always were correctly oriented; when she wrote from right to left they were mirror images. Rachael's consistency in letter orientation at any one time, together with her drawing talents, would lead one to believe that she had good visual discrimination abilities and a good understanding of directionality. Therefore, the left/right orientation problems in signing her name made no sense. The teacher continued to remind Rachael to begin writing from the left.

Shortly thereafter, the teacher noted Rachael's excellent memory and backward sequencing skills; Rachael wrote her name on the right side of the page and reversed, but, as the teacher had directed, she began from the left with the "Ј" in the center of the page. She then continued in reverse order toward the right, ending with "Я." Exasperated, the teacher asked Rachael to please clarify her confusion about the matter. Rachael responded, "Well isn't this the way I'm supposed to write my name in Hebrew?" Her excellent understanding of directionality, for all this time, actually had presented itself as a deficit in the classroom. Because she had been told so often by the teacher to write from left to right, she had decided to do it that way in "Hebrew" also, still reversing all letters.

Although Rachael's case is unique, it does illustrate the worthiness of consulting with students whose thinking processes we're attempting to second guess. Robin, for example, an eighth grader, did not agree with the assessment team's recommendation for resource room services. She recognized her need for assistance but refused to leave her classroom for this help because she viewed it as stigmatizing. Instead, she suggested after-school tutoring; she was willing to spend extra time at the academics in order to avoid what she felt was a devaluing recommendation by the assessment team. Robin's commitment to this choice was more likely to lead to increased effort and progress than if she had been forced to receive instruction in the resource room.

after reading silently, or may add the missing word in a sentence. In one spelling test the student writes dictated words. On another test he or she merely points to the one spelling among four that is correct. Clearly, each task taps different abilities in the student, and only some of these abilities are the same as those required in the classroom. Therefore, the evaluator needs to know not only the technical aspects of test administration, scoring, interpretation, reliability, and validity but also

Table 8–2   Representative item from a reading comprehension test

The student answers oral questions after reading a passage.

> Mary was going downtown to watch the parade. She skipped and ran along the street because she could hardly wait to get there. She was early and found a good place to stand.
>
> Pretty soon she could hear the music of the bands coming down the main street. The men of the first band were dressed in scarlet, with white feathers in their hats. The men of the second band were clad in dark blue, with red feathers in their caps.

1. Why did Mary go downtown? (*to see the parade*)
2. Had the parade started before she got there? (*no*)
3. What did she hear after she found a place to stand? (*music* or *bands*)
4. What came first in the parade? (*band*)

Source: From *Diagnostic Reading Scales* devised by George D. Spache. Reprinted by permission of the publisher, CTB/McGraw-Hill, Del Monte Research Park, Monterey, CA 93940. Copyright © 1972, 1981 by McGraw-Hill, Inc. All rights reserved. Printed in the U.S.A.

the intelligent use of test information and how to complement this with informal evaluation strategies that reveal more about how a student goes about learning. In addition, the evaluator must be sensitive to what is expected in the regular curriculum and the tremendous variability that is typical among children and teenagers as they develop. The strengths and weaknesses of a particular student must be judged accordingly. We will discuss necessary initial steps in evaluation and each of the domains that should be considered.

Initial Steps

The assessment process is initiated by a referral from the student, parent, teachers, or others in the student's environment. In school districts where prereferral teams or other prereferral formats are used (for example, teachers must document that the problem has persisted despite three systematic attempts to resolve it), regular classroom teachers have become much more capable of solving problems than they often are given credit for. As a result, referrals are maintained at more manageable levels, and much more time is available for support staff to work on serious problems or to

collaborate with the teaching staff on program development. This format provides a very different mind-set from the usual referral procedure. Here the teacher is more likely to perceive himself or herself as a responsible part of the problem-solution process; the problem does not exist solely within the student—its solution is within the modifications a teacher chooses to make in his or her curriculum, teaching strategies, classroom organization, and so forth.

If a referral for formal assessment is initiated, necessary initial steps for team members include examination of available records, interviews with the student and relevant others, and observations in the pupil's natural settings. One important goal of these procedures is to evaluate past learning opportunities to gain a perspective on possible reasons behind a student's skill weaknesses and how modifiable these may be. Marcus, for example, transferred school systems in the middle of second grade and experienced immediate difficulty in reading because he did not know the sounds of letters. When he was given the word *sand* to read he just stared at it and guessed. An analysis of Marcus's previous curriculum showed that he had been taught, through a whole lan-

Table 8–3   Representative items from spelling tests

In the first format the student writes dictated words. In the second format the student points to the correct spelling.

go	Children *go* to school.
cut	Mother will *cut* the cake.
nature	The study of *nature* is interesting.
reasonable	His request was *reasonable* and just.
appropriation	Congress made an *appropriation* for schools.

bok	boc
booke	book

aciletate	facilitate
fasilitate	facilitait

Source (top): Jastak, S., & Wilkinson, G. S. (1984). *Wide Range Achievement Test—Revised*. Wilmington, DE.: Jastak Associates, Inc. Reprinted by permission. NOTE (bottom): Test item similar to Peabody Individual Achievement Test—Revised.

guage approach, to look at words and recognize them from their overall configuration. During such teaching, most children begin to figure out the sounds that individual letters make on their own. However, Marcus was not this type of learner. The referral process was halted at this point, so that the new teacher could intensify the phonics instruction in her own whole language program. Marcus required more practice and a more systematic approach than most of his peers, yet once he learned this material he retained it relatively well. What initially looked like a disability was largely a lack of opportunity to learn, and further assessment was avoided. Clearly, appropriate use of these initial steps can make the total assessment process more efficient.

Referrals.   The structure of a referral form is important because its questions can influence the referral source's view of the problem and com-

municate the source's significant role in contributing to the assessment process. For example, the questions might cue the person to consider the problem as interactional if it asks about how the curriculum, settings, and teacher or parent may have influenced the student. The form might require stating the problem in descriptive terms, so that the antecedents of a problem are considered, rather than speaking only of generalities (for example, "When Terry is left out by her peers she tends to become vocal about telling them what to do; the peer response is even more rejection" versus "Terry isn't liked because she's bossy"). A referral form might also focus on a student's strengths, thereby suggesting that it is important to attend to the brighter side of things as well. By asking about strategies that have and haven't worked, and best guesses as to why, the form suggests that the purpose of the assessment process is collaboration in development of appropriate

See the boy with the hat.

"Please hurry up. We want to be sure to

_____ there on time," said Dad.

Splash! Jimmy stepped into a deep puddle.

His sneaker was all _____ .

Figure 8–4   Representative items from reading comprehension tests. In one format the student identifies the appropriate picture. In the second format, the student fills in the blanks. *Source* (top): Dunn, L. M., & Markwardt, F. C. (1989). *Peabody Individual Achievement Test—Revised.* Circle Pines, MN: American Guidance Service. Reprinted by permission.

programming, as opposed to only LD identification. Clearly, care must be taken to develop a referral form that fosters the positive involvement of others in programming.

Records.   Examination of school records often provides clues as to when a problem began. Was the child absent during presentation of key material that is pertinent to current concepts being taught? Are there clues about family-school personalities and relationships that might be improved or used to maximize subsequent intervention? Is the family different from the dominant school culture, so that sociocultural background needs to be considered during assessment? What medical and developmental history data are available? Such data, in addition to grades and yearly achievement test scores, can provide useful clues as to what important questions need to be asked and what kinds of measures are needed. The accuracy of all this information must be ascertained as well. Are the facts verifiable, or are inferences based on tenuous information?

Interviews.   Interviews with teachers, parents, the referred student, and relevant others are extremely important to the assessment process. The purposes of an interview are to obtain a chronology and history of relevant events, clarify the referral reasons, specify perceptions regarding the problem, obtain descriptions of strengths that could be utilized in programming, learn about the individuals' beliefs and expectations, and determine the initial assessment times, places, and goals. The interview can generate clues to a variety of domains of concern by obtaining thorough descriptive information about the student and the student's interactions with different tasks and settings. Like the referral format, an interviewer's wording of questions, follow-up responses, tone of voice, facial expressions, body posture, motivational style, or personal biases can influence the interviewee's responses, subsequent behaviors, and attitudes (Sattler, 1992). For example, teachers' expectancies regarding their ability to have an impact on children's problems increase when interview questions require behavioral descriptions of children's interactions with settings. In contrast,

more general, open-ended questions tend to result in teacher judgments that view the problems as existing entirely within the child (Tombari & Bergan, 1978).

Given that by the year 2000 38 percent of children under age eighteen will be of non-European heritage, yet 80 percent of educators will be white, interviewers must be particularly sensitive listeners, be open to different belief systems, be willing to compromise their opinions for the best interest of the family, respect families' cultural frameworks (for example, should an Asian or Hispanic family not share the interviewer's value for independence), and be mindful of the style and norms for social interaction, behavior, dress, and pace with which families will feel most comfortable (Dennis & Giangreco, 1996).

Naturalistic Observation.   The use of observation early in the assessment process is important in order to provide information about how a problem manifests itself in the actual settings. Often observation shows that formal assessment is not needed; the problem might be resolved instead through consultation with the teacher and others in the pupil's environment.

When used early and systematically in the assessment process, observation creates a valuable baseline for follow-up after intervention. Teachers appreciate the time taken by the team to observe in class. In addition, parents often perceive direct observation as an indication of genuine interest in their child; they view conclusions drawn from observation as more relevant than those drawn from standardized tests that are difficult to understand. Observation also teaches the assessment team more about the perspectives and frustrations of individuals in the student's environment.

The referred student is not the only focus of observation. Extensive observation of typical students is important because it informs the team of the typical behaviors of students in various settings and grades, about the settings themselves (very important when making placement decisions), and about expectations of personnel for the students in these various settings. This information helps the team to determine whether the behavior of a student with learning disabilities is atypical and to predict how the behavior may change over time in a given classroom.

Classroom norms are easy to collect at the same time that one observes the referred student. For example, for a few minutes daily, the referred student and randomly selected nonreferred students might be rated on the number of minutes spent in and out of seat in various classes, positive and negative comments directed toward them by teachers, nature of student behaviors that elicit these comments, number of math problems completed independently, minutes attending to task in different seating arrangements, and so forth.

Developing local norms on a wide range of referral issues is an effective strategy for understanding the extent of an individual student's problems and how this changes over time relative to one's peers. Stevie, a bright fifth grader, is an interesting case in point. Stevie was referred for evaluation because his parents believed that he was irresponsible. He was lazy about making breakfast for his parents, washing the dishes, taking out the garbage, making the beds, emptying the kitty litter, and so forth. Both parents worked and expected Stevie to assume more than a child's share of responsibilities. When Stevie's parents were disbelieving that the problem was really with their expectations, Stevie's classmates were asked to list all the jobs they were expected to do. These were put on a master list, and each child had to indicate whether he or she did the job never, sometimes, once a week, two to three times a week, or every day, and how often their parents needed to remind them to do the jobs. Stevie's parents finally were convinced when they saw that Stevie had twice as many responsibilities as the average student (an amazing fifty-six) and that he required as many reminders as the girls, but fewer than any other boys.

A variety of methods exist for measuring behavior during observation, including giving a detailed narrative description, recording the number of intervals (for example, class periods) during which a particular behavior occurred, recording the number of times a behavior was observed within a certain time period, and recording whether the behavior occurred at a specified interval (for example, every fifth minute), how long the behavior continued, or the length of time

between an event (for example, teacher direction) and a behavior (for example, student compliance). Professional staff, teachers, parents, the student, aides, and volunteers may be trained in systematic observation procedures that measure their own and/or the target person's behaviors (for example, the number of positive versus negative comments by the adult or student). Their involvement in these observational systems helps pave the way for involvement in subsequent interventions. Malcolm's teachers, for example, rated how many minutes he was on task for two weeks. The average time was found to be five minutes per class period. Because paying attention for an entire class period, the current criterion for earning points, seemed to be an unreasonable expectation for Malcolm at this time, Malcolm's teachers decided to award points for ten minutes of good attention. Expectations were then increased slowly. Likewise, in rating how many temper tantrums Alfonso had at home, and comparing this with Alfonso's own ratings of how often he felt like throwing a tantrum, Alfonso's parents realized that he was indeed showing a good deal of self-control; the suggestion that they should praise this self-control rather than punish the outbursts became easier for his parents to accept.

As in Alfonso's case, self-monitoring by youngsters can be helpful in offering information, developing self-control, and maintaining intervention effects (Shapiro & Kratochwill, 1988). For example, students can chart the number of days they complete their homework or how often the questions they ask their parents or teachers are responded to or ignored. Self-monitoring is particularly effective when behaviors that occur infrequently and that are unlikely to be observed (for example, the times a student feels panicky or the urge to fight) are the objects of assessment.

Observers need thorough training on techniques, ethical issues, and issues of confidentiality. All observers, including professional staff, need frequent "booster" training and reliability checks with another observer because observational reliability and validity often slip with time (Repp et al., 1988).

Analogue Observation.   Instead of using naturalistic settings, analogue observations provide a controlled situation in which the behaviors of concern are easier to observe (for example, ascertaining learning styles or strategies, determining increments in learning when students are offered incentives; role playing responses to various social dilemmas).

In the Psychoeducational Teaching Laboratory at Syracuse University, for example, evaluators occasionally observe parent–child interactions through a sequence of free play between the parent and child, the child playing while the parent completes forms at one side of the room, the parent and child working on a cooperative task (parent turns the knob that makes a horizontal line and the child turns the knob that makes a vertical line on a magnetic board, so as to create a triangle), cleaning up materials, or the parent tutoring the student. Indices of dependence/independence, response to authority and demands for compliance, reward/discipline patterns and responses, and so forth are charted. Particularly telling are the observations of parent reactions as they watch the assessment through a one-way mirror and subsequently interact with their child.

Multicultural and Linguistic Diversity

A student's language and sociocultural background will influence assessment results in all domains. When there is considerable discrepancy between the student and the school in language and sociocultural background, the team must be especially cautious in the interpretation of assessment information.

Primary Language. Assessment of primary language is not only common-sense, but also a requirement under IDEA. Assessment must be conducted in the youngster's primary language. When a student is non-English or limited-English speaking, the team should avoid norm-referenced tests of achievement and ability. Although interpreters have been suggested, there are many problems with such attempts. Items do not have the same meaning in both languages, item difficulties change with translations, and translations may not be in the same dialect, or combination of lan-

guages, that the student is used to speaking. Evaluation of discrepancies between intelligence and achievement for these students is best accomplished by comparing stronger and weaker skill areas, such as adaptive behavior with reading. If decisions must be made about intellectual ability, the team can use nonverbal tests, though these are less predictive of school functioning than are verbal measures (Gerken, 1978; Mercer, 1979; Wilen & Sweeting, 1986).

Although it is generally accepted that it is best to teach reading, writing, math, and content area material to non-English speaking children in their native language, while they also learn English, the research is still equivocal on this point (Gersten & Woodward, 1994). Some evidence suggests that development of language, conceptual, and academic abilities in one's primary language may generalize more readily to the second language than if we try to teach these skills in the second language. The affective benefit to students of having their language respected and used as a tool for learning is equally important (Ambert, 1991; Langdon, 1992). If the assessment team suspects that a language disability exists in the student's native language, then English language remediation would be in order, rather than waiting for English to be acquired merely through exposure.

Collier and Hoover (1987) point out that when a nonnative student finally becomes conversationally proficient in English, this still does not mean that the youngster has the cognitive-academic language proficiency to do well on standard tests or school tasks. Bilingual students who appear facile with English continue to score lower on verbal tests than on nonverbal tests (Jensen, 1984). This is because, although everyday conversational proficiency often is acquired in one and a half to two years of exposure to English, it may take five to seven years before the American cultural and language nuances are integrated sufficiently to learn and problem solve to one's full potential (Collier & Hoover, 1987).

At times children who have grown up in English-speaking environments also have language problems because they have been exposed to learning strategies that prove disadvantageous in our highly language-loaded classrooms. Collier and Hoover offer this example:

Many Native American children are taught primarily to use kinesthetic strategies, that is do as the knowledgeable one does, with a minimum of oral direction. Young girls learn to weave by watching a weaver and weaving on a small scale loom. The oral instruction is not how to weave, but stories and information about sheep, patterns, history, and so on. These are effective strategies within the context, but will not be as effective in the highly oral/aural instruction of the American public school classroom. The teacher will need to provide direct instruction in listening to directions, in following directions, and in monitoring one's own written and oral responses without concrete or kinesthetic cues. (p. 44)

Clearly, extent of English proficiency and the degree to which this matches classroom expectations are extremely important to consider in evaluations.

Sociocultural Background. When we use the term *sociocultural background,* we are referring to socioeconomic status, race, and ethnicity. None of these variables alone is sufficient to explain a child's achievement because the variability within a group is often as large or larger than the differences between groups. Therefore, we always must avoid unwarranted generalizations and instead specify the actual factors that may influence a particular student's achievement, such as family structure and size, urbanization, family interaction patterns, home language, past learning experiences, emotional concerns, culturally rooted reticence to display one's knowledge, different valuing of school work, extent of physical interaction encouraged with learning tasks, socialization experiences, and the extent of prior familiarity with testing and test-type materials. When these factors are not taken into account, assessment observations can be misinterpreted, and inappropriate identification and programming may occur (Collier & Hoover, 1987; Mercer, 1979; Oakland, 1980; Reschly, 1978). Maria's story (page 312) illustrates this point. Deyhle (1987)

offers the additional example of Navajo second graders, who did not seem to understand the concept of evaluation for the purpose of demonstrating competence. Therefore, they did not relate to tests as tasks on which one should attempt to do one's best. Unless sensitive to this cultural attribute, an assessment team may underestimate such a student's abilities and knowledge. Because the information-processing weaknesses associated with learning disabilities are far more prevalent among lower-income individuals and among racial and ethnic minorities, and because greater proportions of these youngsters are identified as learning disabled, it is particularly important to be alert to whether sociocultural factors are biasing our assessment findings. Special sensitivity also is required in designing program modifications and transition plans, so that this planning matches the family's culturally based goals and aspirations.

Language Domain

We have learned that language competence is critical to academic success. Assessment in the language domain evaluates listening vocabulary, expressive vocabulary (both spoken and written), auditory discrimination, rhyming and phonemic awareness, syntactic and semantic knowledge, articulation, auditory sequencing and memory, reasoning through language, and pragmatic speech. Besides using tests to evaluate these skills, speech-language pathologists find that spontaneous language samples are the best way to evaluate a student's conversational abilities. Issues of reliability and validity are just as important in these informal techniques as with more standardized measures (Messick, 1995).

Educational Domain

A wide variety of group-administered general achievement tests are used by schools as screening devices. It is important to examine the test content closely to determine how well it matches the school's curriculum. The less well it matches, the more poor scores may reflect past learning opportunities rather than inability. For example, when

Maria

Maria was five years old and failed her school screening test. On subsequent evaluation with the school psychologist, she scored within retarded ranges on both intelligence and adaptive behavior measures. A class for the mentally retarded was recommended. Very upset, Maria's father referred her for an independent evaluation.

A home visit found that Maria's mother spoke only Italian. Her Dad, an American, spoke only Italian in the home until a year ago, when he realized that Maria needed an English language model to enhance acquisition of English. One year of English was not sufficient, however, to allow Maria to perform well on the highly verbal intelligence test she had been administered. Her mother, noting that Italian mothers are overprotective, explained that there were many items on the adaptive behavior measure that she had never given Maria an opportunity to do: cut with scissors, use a knife, play unsupervised outside, help with simple cooking. Maria's mother took pride in her management of the house and boasted that Maria did not have to do anything for herself, even pick up toys. TV was not allowed because it would warp Maria's mind; Italian fairy tales were substituted for the American. Consequently, Maria could not identify Goldilocks, Little Red Riding Hood, and Ernie on a standardized test. She did, however, recognize more advanced characters to whom she had been introduced in school: George Washington, Abraham Lincoln. But these successes could not count on the test because they were beyond her earlier failure level.

Giving Maria's parents guidelines regarding home stimulation (*Sesame Street,* English books) and out-of-home activities (visiting the zoo and library, attending parades and fairs), as well as independent tasks to encourage, increased her adaptive behavior into the low average range within a short period of time. Maria benefited greatly from exposure to regular kindergarten, though two years later her English is still hesitant at times when playing with her friends. Maria doesn't always comprehend teacher directions, continues to speak English with an Italian accent, and has trouble segmenting words into their component sounds. Daily language therapy has been instituted to try to remediate these weaknesses. Certainly, her language and cultural background put her at a disadvantage in school. Coming from a warm, loving background in which her parents do everything in their power to help Maria succeed, Maria remains a happy, well-adjusted, delightful little girl.

students are instructed with concrete math materials, yet are asked to do traditional paper-pencil calculations on tests, the poor scores do not validly reflect their math competencies. Because group-administered tests do not allow for observation of an individual's performance, they do not offer information about how a student attempts to solve problems, which is just as important as determining what is and is not known.

Individually administered general achievement batteries also are common for screening purposes. Typically, these scores provide inflated estimates of a student's actual ability to perform in the classroom because the tests have an easier response format and capitalize on the heightened attention and motivation in the one-to-one testing situation (Coleman & Harmer, 1982). Because of this overestimation, these tests are useful for guiding further assessment but are inadequate for determining instructional grouping or specific strengths and weaknesses.

A variety of individual diagnostic achievement tests give information about a student's strengths and weaknesses in reading, written language, and mathematics abilities. The test user should not get caught up with grade equivalent scores on these measures because such scores are not very useful or accurate. All that a second grade equivalent score tells us is that the student performed as well as the average second grader taking the test. Because a second grade score is based merely on the total number of items correct, it does not indicate how an individual's performance across the range of items departs from what is typical for a second grader. Therefore, just because a fifth grader earns a third grade equivalent reading score, he or she may not be reading in all respects like a third grader. Another problem is that minor successes and failures can create major fluctuations in grade-level estimates. For example, it is quite possible to earn a score one or two grade levels higher or lower by getting only two or three more items right or wrong. This small increment is virtually meaningless, in that differences in the curriculum easily could account for successes or failures on these items, as could high or low motivation on a particular testing day. Besides, as students get older, a spread of several grade levels in an achievement area is quite common among average students. Therefore, standard scores and percentiles are the measures of choice because they use a uniform metric to reflect the degree to which a student's performance departs from that of one's peers.

Scores on various achievement tests of the same skill can vary greatly because of different items, formats, and norms (Daub & Colarusso, 1996; Slate, 1996). For example, on one test the child may read aloud but on another he or she reads silently. Different oral reading tests will count different errors: mispronunciations, word omissions, insertions, substitutions, repetitions, word-order changes, disregard of punctuation, or hesitations. Some tests assess literal, inferential, and listening comprehension skills, word-attack skills, nonsense word reading, or reading rate,

whereas others do not. Some math tests sample understanding of fractions, algebra, geometry, arithmetic reasoning, and application of this knowledge to measurement, problem solving, graphs, tables, money, budgeting, and time; the majority, however, sample only number knowledge and computation, rather than the breadth of the curriculum (Parmar, Frazita, & Cawley, 1996). Clearly, one type of item or format may be harder than the other for particular students. When different tests are used and the child's performance accurately reflects his or her skills (for example, names all letters but reads no words), standard scores can vary by as much as thirty-five points due to the test differences (Schultz, 1988). Because such variability can greatly affect interpretations and recommendations, knowledge of which tests score high or low at which ages, and for which types of students, is critical. The test of choice is the one that best matches the student's curriculum, response style, and the specific questions being asked about the student's abilities.

Task analysis, trial teaching, and assessment of performance in classroom texts and books of varying interest and difficulty levels are encouraged in order to gain valid information about a student's academic achievement. Informal writing samples, when analyzed relative to one's classmates' performance, are extremely instructive because written language tests are particularly unsophisticated in helping with instructional recommendations.

Finally, because the work, study, and attending weaknesses of students with learning disabilities often contribute to their school failure, these learning styles also need to be a major focus of assessment. Informal assessment strategies, observational data, interview data, and checklists such as those presented earlier in this chapter can provide very useful information in this regard.

Intellectual Domain

First a word of caution. Intelligence is not a thing that exists as a trait within the individual. It is a construct based on performance on a wide variety of tasks that predict school success. Intelligence tests are merely small samples of behavior, and intelligence test scores do change; they are not fixed for life. Intelligence tests do have excellent predictive validity after the preschool years for success on school work and verbal tasks (Sattler, 1992). However, the tests are not very good at predicting an individual's ability to survive interpersonally or occupationally (Mercer, 1979; Oakland, 1980). Given their predictive validity to school learning, Mercer argues that intelligence measures are most appropriately viewed as indices of adaptive fit to the student role in a school setting.

The Stanford-Binet Fourth Edition and the Wechsler Intelligence Scale for Children III (WISC-III) are the most frequently used tests for school-age children. Their subtests measure skills in verbal comprehension, nonverbal reasoning, perceptual organization, acquired knowledge, and memory with high reliability and validity. In contrast to the WISC-III, the Stanford-Binet Fourth Edition has only one timed subtest, which means that students can take as long as they wish to solve problems and administration time frequently is unduly long. When considered together with other evidence, those subtests on the Wechsler scales that rely on good focused attention (doing math calculations mentally, remembering strings of dictated digits) offer useful information about the youngster's attention/distractibility, anxiety, sequencing ability, symbolic ability, and memory skills (Reynolds & Kaufman, 1990; Sattler, 1992).

Although subtest scatter on the Wechsler scales (large discrepancies in subtest scores) frequently has been considered an index of neurological impairment and learning disabilities, Kaufman (1979a, b) cautions that this scatter must be compared to what is normal for typical children. He points out that the fifteen point discrepancy between the verbal scale and performance scale (blocks, puzzles), which we consider to be a "significant difference," occurs in approximately 25 percent of children; nearly half of children have discrepancies of ten or more points (a score of 100 is average). Only a range of twenty-two or more points between the two scales is considered to be abnormal (Kaufman, 1981a). While three scaled score points is considered to be a significant deviation of any one subtest from a person's mean subtest score (ten is average), a range of seven scaled

score points between the highest and lowest subtest score actually is typical of the average child. Clearly, because unevenness in verbal and perceptual abilities is so common, these patterns have diagnostic significance only if a student's degree of fluctuation is highly unusual in the normal population. Kaufman suggests that in most cases a person's profile patterns be evaluated for their educational rather than diagnostic significance; the patterns should be used to provide hypotheses about strengths that can be used in teaching.

Various Wechsler Intelligence Scale profiles have been related to unique cognitive styles and processing patterns in students with reading and learning disabilities (Rourke, 1993; Keogh & Hall, 1974; Kirby & Das, 1977; Smith et al., 1977). Although these patterns do reflect individual strengths and weaknesses, they alone are not valid for diagnosing a specific type of learning disability. This is because even students with learning disabilities who show very similar Wechsler patterns nevertheless can end up being extremely heterogeneous in their achievement, and those with different patterns can end up being no different in achievement (Dundon et al., 1986; Joschko & Rourke, 1985; Kaufman, 1981b).

No one intelligence pattern has been identified as unique to learning disabilities. A synthesis of ninety-four studies of Wechsler patterns showed that, as a group, students with learning disabilities do not have greater verbal-performance discrepancies than do typical students (Kavale & Forness, 1984). As a group, the learning disabled showed no unique patterns and, in fact, showed less variability than the non–learning disabled. Clearly heterogeneity is common within both the LD and non-LD populations.

As our concepts of intelligence broaden to take into account environmental influences, new theories of intelligence are emerging. Sternberg (1986), for example, is developing a measure that taps information-processing abilities, the automaticity of skills gained through prior experience, and the ability to generalize these skills to practical, everyday problems. Gardner (1983) believes that American schools are wasting human potential by focusing primarily on linguistic and logical-mathematical intelligences, and he urges educational programs to develop five additional types of intelligences: spatial (sculptors, surveyors), musical (composers, singers), bodily-kinesthetic (athletes, craftspersons, dancers), interpersonal (sensitivity to others), and intrapersonal (awareness of one's own feelings). These newer concepts of intelligence hold promise for benefiting the learning disabled by highlighting nonschool factors relevant to adjustment and also nonacademic talents that tend to be overlooked.

Perceptual-Motor Domain

Measures in the perceptual-motor domain generally have inadequate norms, reliability, and validity. These measures frequently are used in the process-deficit model to infer information-processing strengths and weaknesses related to achievement. Because motor problems are so frequent among the brain injured, fine-motor measures often are used to screen for students whose learning problems may possibly be of neurological origin. Although these measures are not valid for the purpose of diagnosing a neurological impairment or predicting school achievement, they can guide programming efforts in curriculum areas that require manual dexterity (for example, handwriting, keyboarding, auto mechanics, drafting). Perceptual measures also are helpful in alerting us to the possibility that perceptual weaknesses are interfering with achievement, particularly in the early school years (for example, misalignment of math calculations because of poor spatial judgment, difficulty discriminating reversible letters).

Medical-Developmental Domain

It is important for evaluators to determine whether medical, sensory, or health factors relate to learning problems. This can be done by examining medical records and using medical-developmental history checklists to gather this information from knowledgeable sources (parents, doctors). One limitation of interviews regarding health history is the questionable accuracy of retrospective reports about events in the student's life.

Besides standard medical procedures, a variety of medical-developmental screening measures

also are available. These include screening devices for visual or hearing impairment, physical and neurological problems, and attention deficits and hyperactivity.

The use of neuropsychological assessment with children has increased in recent years, and it is proving helpful in clarifying the strength-weakness patterns of youngsters with learning disabilities. These batteries assess one's balance, coordination, and fine-motor dexterity, but also sample a broad range of intellectual, language, perceptual, problem-solving, and memory abilities. Neuropsychological batteries frequently make use of standardized instruments from other domains but interpret them with respect to the brain regions associated with particular tasks. Often comparisons are made between left and right hemisphere integrity (linguistic and analytic-sequential processing versus spatial and holistic processing), and front-back integrity (motor, sensory, and planning functions versus visual-processing abilities). While these procedures offer clues to the nature of the information-processing disorders underlying a learning disability, their validity for educational program planning is only now beginning to be researched.

As part of the assessment it is also helpful to examine the learning histories of a student's relatives, parents, and siblings. This information offers very useful insights into the possible relationship of the student's learning difficulties to hereditary factors, which interventions succeeded for others, and which of these might be worth trying if the student's learning patterns are similar.

Adaptive Behavior Domain

Adaptive behavior is defined as the degree to which the individual meets the standards of personal independence and social responsiblility expected of his or her age and cultural group. Evaluators are concerned with a pupil's adaptive fit not only to the student role but also to nonacademic roles both inside and outside the school setting. IDEA requires that assessment of adaptive behavior also address nonschool settings, and a special focus on this domain occurs during the transition planning period.

Adaptive behavior measures, such as the Vineland Adaptive Behavior Scales, are helpful in assessing nonschool role functioning. Peer sociometric scales that evaluate a child's popularity (for example, "Name three children that you would most/least like to do a project with") also can be used to assess a student's adaptation to a specific peer group. In addition, checklists are available to compare ratings obtained from teachers, parents, the student, and sometimes peers. Because these ratings are influenced by the rater's attitudes, often ratings of the same student by different adults do not correspond with one another (Elliot, Busse, & Gresham, 1993; Haager & Vaughn, 1995). This lack of correspondence offers insights into those environments in which adult attitudes are most likely to facilitate the student's continued emotional, social, and academic growth.

Adaptive behavior measures often are used when intelligence test estimates are questioned. When used in this way, interpretation must take into account factors that can underestimate adaptive skills: cultural factors (for example, lack of independence due to family overprotectiveness); a new immigrant's limited familiarity with American culture (for example, handling currency, using checks) (Wilen & Sweeting, 1986). Classroom observations that rate this student's adjustment against that of peers who share the same cultural background can be very helpful in sorting out the cultural influences on adaptive functioning.

Socioemotional Domain

Personality assessment has undergone tremendous change over the past two decades. Mischel (1979) strongly challenged the assumptions of personality models that suggested that problems exist solely within the individual. Very briefly, when an individual scores high on a particular personality trait, that individual also should score high on another measure of the same trait. Yet such consistency is rarely found. If you examine your own behavior, you'll find that you behave quite assertively in one set of circumstances, yet you might be meek or dependent in another. This

is because different situations have different influences on personality variables. Consequently, personality assessment now emphasizes assessment of settings and interactions of persons with settings rather than personal traits alone.

In addition to adaptive behavior measures, there are numerous behavior checklists, and teacher and parent rating scales that are helpful in examining socioemotional concerns. Self-concept measures also can be helpful in gaining an understanding of how students feel about themselves relative to school, home life, and peers, although students frequently inflate their self-evaluations, perhaps as a self-protective coping strategy (Alvarez & Adelman, 1986). Despite this, measures with adequate behavioral and situational specificity can aid evaluators in planning appropriate goals and interventions to meet a student's interpersonal and emotional needs.

Projective measures, which assume that students will assign their own thoughts, feelings, needs, and motives to ambiguous, essentially neutral stimuli (ink blots, pictures, their own drawings, play activities), have a long history of use. Unfortunately, these tests often do not have norms, and they have little or no evidence for reliability and validity. A basic problem is that the underlying personality characteristics supposedly measured by these devices are unverifiable. Consequently, rating scales, checklists, and direct observation in natural and analogue settings may provide far more useful and verifiable information about how students feel about themselves, how they relate to others, and how they deal with stressful or unpleasant situations.

Setting Domain

The importance of assessing settings should be obvious. It is surprising that in spite of the need to examine settings themselves, as well as a learner's interactions with settings, few strategies have been developed for this purpose. Because many decisions with students who have learning disabilities involve consideration of programming in multiple settings, evaluators must thoroughly understand those settings and how their structure and social climate may either help or hinder the student's development.

Class placement decisions necessarily involve an assessment of potential classroom environments to determine which will be the least restrictive educationally. Chapter 12 is devoted to the many setting variables that need to be examined in comprehensive assessments: the kinds of curricula and instructional strategies used in various settings, the openness of teachers and peers to a student with learning problems, organization of instruction, seating arrangements, distractions, and so forth. In like manner, Chapter 11 will address the important variables that need to be assessed in the student's most important setting, the home, in order to foster maximal academic and personal growth.

Summary

A variety of decisions that we make on behalf of students involve assessment, whether by means of informal consultation or by formal evaluation. The purpose for evaluation, whether screening, identification, instructional planning, or charting pupil progress, will influence the kinds of assessment strategies chosen. Different models of assessment help evaluators focus on the learner, the learner's interactions with tasks, the learner's interactions with settings, or the learner within broader sociocultural contexts. Each model tends to use a different set of assessment instruments, and each is better suited to address a particular purpose for assessment. Evaluation with norm-referenced measures, criterion-referenced measures, informal evaluation techniques, curriculum-based assessment strategies, or authentic assessment constitutes only a portion of the assessment process. Referral forms, records, interviews, consultation, and observation in natural or analogue settings also are important means of aiding decision making. Regardless of the method chosen to collect information, attention to issues of reliability, validity, relevance of content, and appropriateness of the comparison group is important.

Comprehensive assessment of students with learning problems is best implemented within a team approach that applies multiple perspectives to multiple assessment domains: primary language and sociocultural background, language skills, achievement, intelligence, perceptual-motor skills, medical developmental history, adaptive behavior, socioemotional adjustment, and settings. With such a comprehensive analysis of the student's characteristics, the tasks the student is expected to accomplish, and the settings in which the student lives and learns, it is more likely that the positive attributes of each can be identified and combined to facilitate the student's academic, personal, and social growth.

Chapter Nine

Planning Educational Interventions

This chapter focuses on planning the most appropriate educational interventions for students with learning disabilities, which is not a simple matter. It involves planning individualized instruction, adapting instruction to each student's learning ability and style, coordinating the roles of various professionals, and deciding among service delivery options. To determine which teaching objectives, strategies, and environments are most appropriate for a student, information gained from the assessment process must be considered along with the school's curriculum and possible curriculum modifications, teaching materials and strategies, instructional models, human resources, teaching settings, and the peers in various classes.

Because of the great heterogeneity among the learning disabled, planning educational interventions that will best match their abilities and learning styles is a highly individualized process. Many of these students have severe skill and/or behavioral deficits that make them hard to teach. Others have milder weaknesses that respond rapidly to appropriately structured learning tasks and settings. The uniqueness of each student's learning patterns necessitates teacher flexibility and creativity within an educational environment that encourages teachers to modify their programs as often as necessary.

Planning Individualized Instruction

Individualized instruction tailors an educational program to a student's specific needs. It is a process in which goals are set and the teacher's methods and materials are revised as necessary to facilitate the student's progress. "How can I change *what* I am teaching, and *how* I am teaching" is asked, answered, and asked again repeatedly during the school year.

The "Animal School" story below, humorously illustrates what can happen when pupil and program characteristics are mismatched. Like the animals, when a student must learn something that he or she is not ready to learn, or learn it in a way that is not natural, failure is predictable. This failure experience in turn may deter achievement in other academic and social areas as well. Important components of individualized instruction

include the individualized education program, diagnostic-prescriptive teaching, the instructional model, and one's choice of materials.

The Individualized Education Program

Following the multidisciplinary assessment and determination that a youngster has a learning disability, the Individuals with Disabilities Education Act (IDEA) requires that the student receive an Individualized Education Program (IEP). The specific nature of the program is set down in a written IEP statement that is developed and reviewed annually by the student's parents or

The Animal School

Once upon a time, the animals decided they must do something heroic to meet the problems of "a new world." So they organized a school.

They adopted an activity curriculum consisting of running, climbing, swimming, and flying. To make it easier to administer the curriculum all the animals took all the subjects.

The duck was excellent in swimming, in fact better than his instructor; but he made only passing grades in flying and was very poor in running. Since he was slow in running, he had to stay after school and also drop swimming in order to practice running. This was kept up until his web feet were badly worn and he was only average in swimming. But average was acceptable in school so nobody worried about that except the duck.

The rabbit started at the top of the class in running, but had a nervous breakdown because of so much make-up work in swimming.

The squirrel was excellent in climbing until he developed frustration in the flying class where his teacher made him start from the ground up instead of from the tree top down. He also developed a "charlie horse" from over-exertion and then got C in climbing and D in running.

The eagle was a problem child and was disciplined severely. In the climbing class he beat all the others to the top of the tree, but insisted on using his own way to get there.

At the end of the year, an abnormal eel that could swim exceedingly well, and also run, climb, and fly a little, had the highest average and was valedictorian.

The prairie dogs stayed out of school and fought the tax levy because the administration would not add digging and burrowing to the curriculum. They apprenticed their children to a badger and later joined the groundhogs and gophers to start a successful private school.

Source: Reavis, G. H. (1953). The animal school. *Educational Forum, 17* (2), p. 141. Reprinted by permission of Kappa Delta Pi Honor Society in Education.

guardians, the student's special education teacher at least one of the student's regular education teachers (if the student is participating in the regular education environment), an individual who can interpret the instructional implications of the evaluation results, an administrative representative of the school who is qualified to provide for or supervise special education programming and is knowledgeable about the general curriculum and available resources (principal, pupil personnel director), the student (when appropriate), and appropriate related services personnel. According to the 1997 amendments to IDEA, the IEP should include:

1. the student's present level of educational performance and educational needs

2. a statement of academic and behavioral annual goals (for example, complete the second grade reading curriculum; attend to task for twenty minutes)

3. a statement of short-term objectives (for example, master the short vowel sounds *e, i,* and the blends *th, bl, pr, nd;* increase sight vocabulary from fifty to one hundred words)

4. the specific education and related services to be provided, by whom, where, and how often (for example, resource room for one hour daily, speech therapy for forty-five minutes twice weekly)

5. specification of materials and methods to be used and why

6. objective evaluation criteria and the timeline for determining whether instructional objectives are being achieved

7. the projected date for initiation of services and their expected duration

8. an explanation of how the student's disability affects his or her involvement and progress in the general curriculum, and the extent to which the student will participate in the regular educational program or another least restrictive environment.

9. any modifications the student will need to participate in state- or districtwide assessments. If the student will not participate in the assessment, a statement of why the assessment is inappropriate and how the student will be assessed must be included.

10. how the student's parents will be regularly informed of progress and proposed program changes.

Planning the IEP is facilitated when the student's evaluation has clarified his or her abilities and learning styles, other contributors to the learning problem, and the program characteristics that may best match the student's needs. Beginning at age fourteen, the IEP must specify the academic and/or vocational course of study that the student will follow to prepare for his or her transition needs after high school. For students who are sixteen years of age, or younger if necessary, a comprehensive transition service plan is specified in the IEP to facilitate the student's adaptation to postsecondary education and to adult vocational, independent living, and community participation roles. The transition responsibilities of various professionals and community agencies are specified. Students must be invited to their transition planning meetings. If they do not attend, school personnel must take steps to ensure that the student's preferences and interests are considered.

Class placement decisions during the IEP process consider the setting in which the goals, methods, and materials specified in the IEP can best be implemented, given the physical, organizational, and human characteristics of alternative settings. Chapter 12 will explore the educational and social advantages/disadvantages of particular settings that need to be carefully weighed when making placement recommendations. Foremost among these considerations are the degree of integration with typical peers and the training and personal attributes of the teacher.

As the severity of a student's learning disabilities increases, so does the likelihood of placement in settings that decrease the frequency of interaction with typical peers. Placement options, from least to most segregated and specialized, include:

1. full-time regular class with the general education teacher providing an appropriately personalized environment; consultation is received from a teacher assistance team, LD teacher, or other specialist ("teacher consultant" model)

2. full-time regular class with direct services offered several times weekly in the classroom by an itinerant LD or other specialist ("push in" model)

3. full-time regular class with a full-time special educator as co-teacher

4. part-time regular class with one to three periods daily in a resource room or learning center ("pull out" model)

5. part-time regular class and part-time special class

6. full-time special class

7. removal from the home school to a special class in another building

8. special public or private school

9. residential setting

10. homebound/hospital placement

The teacher is by far the most important element in the teaching process, far more important than any single method or material. Teachers have different teaching styles just as students have different learning styles. When the teacher and student styles and personality characteristics are not well matched, then even the most appropriate material is unlikely to capture the attention, interest, and energy of the student. For example, when the teacher prefers to teach in large groups, a child who works best in a smaller group setting will not benefit maximally from this teacher's approach. An impulsive teacher might bombard some students with more information than they can comfortably handle. An overly detailed, slow-placed, reflective teacher is likely to bore the student with an attention deficit disorder. Moreover, a teacher who feels uncomfortable teaching a student with learning disabilities and assigns the responsibility to the aide is likely to subtly communicate his or her feelings to classmates and limit the student's

academic and social opportunities. Clearly, the quality of the teacher–student relationship is critical to building the student's self-concept, interest in learning, and willingness to collaborate in instructional planning. It is equally important that the peer group be age appropriate, provide an appropriate academic and social model, and be open to including students who learn in different ways.

When the IEP calls for the student to be included in a regular classroom, it is important that the student's skills be compatible with the instructional opportunities in that class. With certain modifications, the student should be able to participate in class as fully as any other student. When classmates are working on fractions, for example, a student with learning disabilities who is present during that time period also should be able to benefit from this instruction when provided appropriate accommodations, such as a calculator. When classmates are tackling word problems, the student with learning disabilities could work around his or her reading weakness by having the same problems set up in numeral form, or by working with a peer. Similarly, a student with written-expression difficulties might take multiple choice or oral American history tests in order to compensate for the writing problem posed by short-answer questions. Or the ninth grader with vocabulary and reading deficits may read an easier version of *Romeo and Juliet,* which still affords him or her the opportunity to participate fully in class discussions.

The schedules of students with learning disabilities must be planned carefully so that they are included in general education classes for those periods from which they can derive most benefit and enjoyment. They should participate in special education services at times when inclusion is inappropriate. As students become older, they tend to be increasingly sensitive to the stigma of leaving their classes for special help. For this reason, many schools attempt to minimize "pull out" programs by having the special educator provide services in the regular classroom itself. Because these "push in" programs can be equally stigmatizing, however, co-teaching arrangements in the regular classroom may be a better option. Although coteaching has yet to be evaluated, it does hold promise, especially if the special educator also teaches some high achievers, so that his or her help is positively valued by all. Regardless of the system adopted, the regular and special education teachers must regularly plan, coordinate, and evaluate a pupil's program so that teaching objectives, methods, and materials complement one another and aid the student's inclusion in the regular curriculum.

Although the IEP is intended to serve as a guide to instruction and as an index of progress toward meeting instructional objectives, it unfortunately usually serves only a broad administrative purpose. Many professionals complain that the IEP is cumbersome to complete. Teachers report that, after writing the IEP, it is seldom consulted again until the next annual IEP review (Pugach, 1982). In addition, few teachers are well trained in translating assessment information into curriculum plans and writing instructional objectives (Smith, 1990). Teachers frequently feel that the time spent preparing the IEP is not worth the effort. In reality, the IEP can establish and monitor quantity and place of teaching but not quality. For example, it can establish that all teachers must give Carlos untimed tests. But it cannot make sure that Mr. Kram, the biology teacher, will not be so angered by what he perceives as an unfair practice that he grades Carlos lower or otherwise treats him differently in class. Likewise, Mrs. Small, a very well-meaning resource teacher, may use the phoneme awareness strategies suggested in the IEP, but her lack of training with this approach may cause her to present the phonemes in the wrong sequence, so that her student's confusion only mounts. Or Allison, who does indeed get her one hour of resource help and half hour each of speech and occupational therapy daily, may be missing out on so much of the regular class that all this special help only makes it more difficult for her to keep up. The quality of instruction all these children receive can only be guaranteed by the willingness of all their teachers to take time to collaborate with one another and engage in ongoing, diagnostic-prescriptive teaching.

Diagnostic-Prescriptive Teaching

Teachers systematically use *diagnostic-prescriptive teaching* to try out various instructional recommendations. Five steps guide the diagnostic-prescriptive teaching process:

1. Observe and analyze the nature of the student's abilities and learning styles and how these relate to performance on different types of tasks.

2. Scrutinize the nature of the current curriculum and setting, and possible modifications.

3. Consult with the student whenever possible, present choices for curriculum and setting modifications, and decide together which ones to try.

4. Set short-term goals, make the modifications, and teach.

5. Evaluate progress after a reasonable time interval; if unsuccessful retrace steps 1 through 4.

Diagnostic-prescriptive teaching is essentially a continuous test-teach-test process. Teddy's story illustrates how important such teaching is to instructional decisions. It points out that when an intervention works one time, we should neither assume that it will always be necessary, nor that it will always work. Teddy's assessment had concluded that he was delayed in language skills. At seven years old, Teddy could name only the letters of the alphabet that appeared in his name. Learning letter names and sounds was one of the annual goals listed on Teddy's IEP. When Teddy's teacher task-analyzed letter naming, she found that Teddy did remember a great deal about letter names. His problem was that he remembered in a different way from the way she had been asking him to remember. Whenever the teacher named letters for him, and he was asked to point to them, Teddy demonstrated 100 percent accuracy. He also could copy letters well. Teddy's problem appeared only when he was asked to retrieve the letter names from memory.

The teacher's task analysis of letter naming suggested that she should experiment with methods that paired Teddy's weaker naming skills with his stronger receptive language, visual discrimination, and copying abilities. The teacher had Teddy draw, trace, paste, construct, and copy letters as she named them, and he repeated their names. A computer program that named letters as he typed also was used. Because Teddy was good at distinguishing the sounds of initial consonants in words, the teacher tried relating the letter form to a key word that began with the same letter and also had its shape. *Snake,* for example, begins with a "sss" sound, and a snake can be shaped into an *s.* Similarly, elephant begins with a short *e* sound, and the elephant's trunk can be curled into the shape of an *e.* This method worked well. Teddy was not introduced to phonetic reading until he became proficient in retrieving letter sounds. Instead, he was taught to compensate for his disability by learning to recognize words by sight.

Could Teddy's teacher assume that he would be a poor namer on all tasks? Would he always need to go through such elaborate teaching modifications? No. We cannot generalize from one task to another unless we test out our assumptions all over again. Surprisingly, Teddy was excellent at naming his numerals. Why the discrepancy? Perhaps numerals are more meaningful to Teddy than letter names; after all, one apple is one real thing, whereas an *s* refers to nothing concrete. Perhaps Teddy finds nine numerals easier to master than twenty-six letters. The teacher could test out this hypothesis by reducing the number of letter names that she expects Teddy to master at any one time. In diagnostic-prescriptive teaching, hunches gained from one set of circumstances are experimented with on other tasks as well, to determine whether these generalizations are warranted.

Consider Teddy four years later. He is now in a sixth grade classroom. He is being instructed in reading at a beginning third grade level and is progressing well in a series that teaches reading through word families (*sight, might; cable, table*). Math, always a strength for him, is suddenly becoming troublesome. Teddy can solve the multiplication problems that the teacher drills on the blackboard, but his homework papers contain many errors. A comparison of the boardwork and homework shows that the latter requires extensive reading of word problems, whereas the boardwork does not. When Teddy's parents were asked to help by reading the problems and directions to him, he once again achieved well in math. Because of this, Teddy's teachers wondered whether reading also should be eliminated in his science and social studies assignments. When they explored this question, it was found that the social studies material was indeed too difficult. The science assignments, however, were all group experiments, and Teddy let others do the reading for him. For his independent science projects, Teddy was quick to enlist the librarian's aid in finding books that were short and that used an easier reading vocabulary.

Clearly, the diagnostic-prescriptive teaching process involves a good deal of clinical intuition and guesswork, a skill that comes with adequate training and many years of teaching experience. Curriculum-based assessment approaches can be particularly helpful in offering teachers frequent checks on whether their approaches are in fact producing the anticipated gains. The way in which teachers go about analyzing student needs, matching the curriculum to these needs, and deciding among programming options reflects the influence of several instructional models.

Instructional Models

Several schools of thought regarding instructional planning have come in and out of fashion in the brief history of the learning disabilities field. The most prominent among these are the developmental, behavioral, underlying process training, and cognitive psychology viewpoints, and more recently the constructivist school of thought. Each differs from the other on questions of what and how children should be taught.

The *developmentalists* follow a maturational lag perspective regarding learning disorders. They advocate teaching only those academic objectives that the student is absolutely ready to master. They maintain that because children's cognitive growth proceeds in invariant stages, these stages must be passed through in an orderly fashion, each stage readying the child for the next. Mastering lower-level components of higher-level skills is the first step toward academic progress. For example, learning to segment words into syllables and syllables into phonemes would precede learning to sound out and blend the individual sounds in words.

In contrast to the developmentalists, *behaviorists* believe that when tasks and environments are carefully structured and designed with the appropriate rewards and consequences, the child can master even skills that he or she is not prepared to understand. So children could be taught to sound out words, even if they did not understand how all of these sounds follow one another in a logical sequence. Direct instruction of key curriculum objectives is the focus. Teachers try to make learning errorless so children won't learn from their errors. Teacher planning and control are implicit in behavioral approaches, for example, the use of a teacher-controlled remote control device on desks of inattentive children that credits points for appropriate attending and deducts points when off task.

The *process training* theorists stress that efficient acquisition of higher-level skills can occur only if the underlying information-processing deficits are remediated. They therefore advocate capitalizing on the student's stronger modalities for academic instruction (for example, using language strengths to dictate compositions), while at the same time spending a good deal of time shoring up important weaknesses (for example, intensifying handwriting instruction to aid writing development, or practicing revisualization of orthographic patterns to aid memory for irregular spellings). It is believed that if learning must depend primarily on the weaker information-processing skill, then progress will be extremely difficult. For example, when a student has a visual-processing deficit, teaching reading through a sight word approach would be counterproductive. It would be wiser to capitalize on the child's language strengths by means of a phonics approach and, as needed, to add compensatory approaches such as listening to textbooks on tape. Hartlage and Telzrow (1986) explain that "giving [these

youngsters] more of something they cannot do not only fails to produce the desired learning effect, but also serves as a regular reminder of their weakest performance areas" (p. 62).

In a manner reminiscent of the process-training theorists' concern for remediating information-processing weaknesses, the *cognitive psychology* focus is on improving students' inefficient learning strategies. Specific techniques are taught that help students activate their background knowledge, abilities, interests, and learning strategies in order to attend to, comprehend, store, and remember new material more efficiently and effectively.

The *constructivist* perspective takes issue with the direct instruction approach because it involves teacher direction, rules, drill, and practice. Constructivists view the child as an active rather than passive "meaning maker" who learns more deeply and more eagerly when encouraged to select, organize, connect, and make sense of information and ideas based on his or her prior knowledge and experience. Children learn from their errors, and discovery approaches are encouraged. Instruction is believed best when it takes place in what Vygotsky (1962) describes as the "zone of proximal development," just a bit beyond what the child already knows. Children's active learning is scaffolded with teacher support and guidance, which is diminished as the child's competence increases.

In actual practice, these different instructional models are combined to various degrees. Most often, a focus on one model, to the exclusion of the others, is unjustified. Easier skills generally are taught before harder ones (developmental model), for example, numbers one through ten before eleven through twenty, or comprehension of story line before inferential reasoning. New skills generally are approached through the student's stronger abilities, modalities, and learning styles (underlying process and cognitive psychology models). Instruction frequently incorporates both active, discovery learning (constructivist model) as well as learning strategy instruction (behavioral and cognitive psychology models), while important weaknesses are concurrently remediated (underlying process model). For example, a student with language deficits may have texts rewritten in easier language, but vocabulary development nevertheless would remain a priority. Vocabulary growth might be encouraged through a high-interest literature-based program that encourages classmates to read, interpret, and compose using cooperative learning strategies. Similarly, a student who cannot recall material for tests because he is a global thinker and does not attend to relevant details may study from the teacher's outline. At the same time, however, he receives instruction in how to take notes and sort out essential from nonessential information. Joanie, who can't distinguish beginning, middle, and ending sounds in words, may be taught reading by emphasizing words' visual features. But her phonemic awareness would receive remediation as well, in the expectation that these gains would promote reading acquisition; she also might be encouraged to discover phonological principles for herself by using invented spellings in her writing. The practice of not ignoring weaker information-processing areas while teaching through the strengths is supported by several studies showing marked gains when development of the weaker areas continues to be stimulated (Bakker, 1984; Bakker & Vinke, 1985; Bakker et al., 1981; Zihl, 1981).

Ideally, the skills taught, whether in stronger or weaker areas, should be those with which the students are ready to succeed, ones that will not present an enormous struggle (developmental and constructivist models). The student practices at one level until he or she is proficient enough to move on to the next more difficult objective. This approach takes less time and results in less faulty learning (and the need to later unlearn error patterns) than when the youngster is forced to learn things that he or she is not ready to understand— for example, confusing soft *a, e,* and *i* sounds because all were taught simultaneously rather than one at a time; or being taught to blend sounds even though the child does not understand that a reading word is bounded by space . . . this child has not mastered prerequisite readiness skills such as pointing successively to each word while "reading" a memorized poem, because he doesn't comprehend the correspondence between oral and written words.

There will always be a small number of students with learning disabilities who do not have the necessary information-processing integrity to make much progress when taught according to the above developmental model. For these students, instruction must be "forced," in the same way that teachers initially force students to the next step on a skill hierarchy (behavioral model). Consider the adult who can't read or calculate beyond the second grade level but who must develop survival reading and math skills: reading road signs and bus directions, using the telephone directory, passing the written portion of a driver's exam, completing a job application, planning a budget, dealing with taxes, counting change. In these cases, departures from normal developmental practices typical at the student's ability level (second grade goals and methods) are encouraged to meet the real-life demands. For example, the essential words could be taught as sight words rather than through phonetic analysis, the person could carry index cards to match against bus signs, or the individual could use a calculator instead of struggling with computations.

Whether developmental, process training, cognitive psychology, or constructivist models are guiding a particular intervention, behavioral principles nevertheless are often apparent in the way in which materials and methods are planned. Behavioral strategies are among the most consistently effective of all intervention approaches (Forness et al., 1997). These principles are summarized in Table 9–1.

Adelman's (1971) teaching model (Figure 9–1) presents a sequence of intervention approaches for students with learning disabilities that incorporates elements of the various instructional philosophies just described. Adelman describes three types of children:

Type I	No ability disorder but learning is slow in a non-personalized instructional program
Type II	Minor disorders can be compensated for in the appropriate learning environment
Type III	Severe ability and/or behavioral deficits as well

Because the difficulties of Type I and II students can be ameliorated by appropriately matching the learning environment to their needs,

Table 9–1   Behavioral principles that guide effective instruction

Principle	*Example*
• Systematically reinforce (repeat, attend to, praise) appropriate responses and do not reinforce errors	• Praise "sitting in seat" behavior and ignore times out of the seat
• Pair neutral events with positive reinforcers so that the neutral behavior takes on positively reinforcing value	• Pair working hard with praise
• Highlight cues that differentiate stimuli and pair them with different responses	• The letter *b* points to the right, say "b"; and *d* points to the left, say "d"; make all *b*s red during instruction while *d*s remain black
• Model appropriate responses	• "Listen to how I would talk through this algebra problem aloud"; "watch how I organize my desk"
• Make positive outcomes contingent on the less valued behaviors, to encourage less valued behaviors	• Make free time contingent on one-half hour of library research
• Shape correct responses by means of successive approximations	• Ignore the fact that Juanita does not intersect the l and o of the letter *b* until she can draw each individual element correctly; first teach Juanita to sit politely beside classmates in the lunchroom and then help her practice conversation entry skills
• Carefully control the rate of presentation of new materials	• Introduce only four new social studies concepts or spelling patterns daily
• Distribute practice over time rather than massing it	• Review class notes daily rather than cramming the night before the exam
• Preplan relearning and generalization of skills	• Periodically insert mastered material into classwork in order to review and encourage application of this information to new contexts
• Continually measure/evaluate interventions and outcomes	• Evaluate retention of spelling words when taught by different methods; evaluate time on task when different types of reinforcers are used
• Present information systematically so that easier subskills precede harder ones	• Teach subtraction before division

Adelman believes that these pupils' difficulties are due primarily to what we have described as task- or setting-based causes. The source of the learning disability is, for the most part, a deficiency in the learning environment. The Type III student is the one who has a learner-based disability. Any one student can vary between being a Type I, II, or III student in different subject areas, depending on the abilities and learning styles tapped by various aspects of the curriculum, whether teacher characteristics match the student's needs, and the nature of different classrooms.

Adelman's hierarchy of personalized learning environments begins at Step 1, where the Type I child's program is altered in the context of the regular classroom. A wide range of individual differences in development, motivation, and performance are accommodated, whether through active, discovery oriented (constructivist model), or direct instruction methods (behaviorist and cognitive

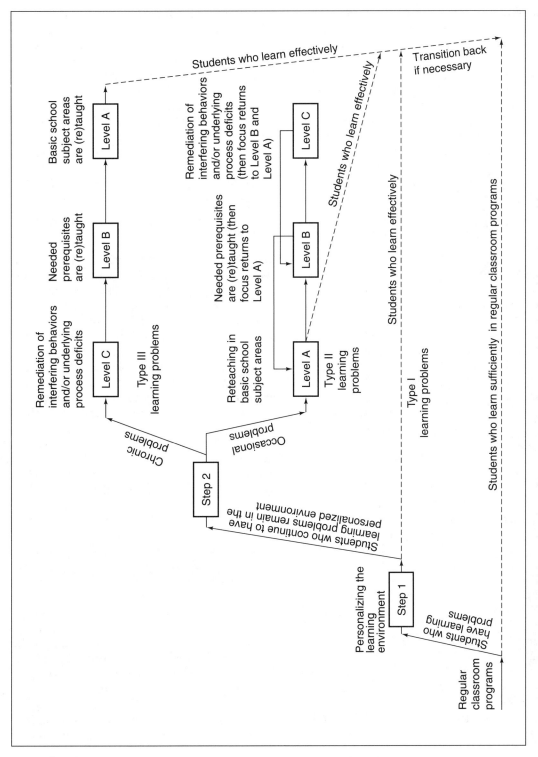

Figure 9–1   Sequential and hierarchical teaching strategies for remedying school learning problems. Adapted from Adelman, H. S. (1971). The not so specific learning disability population. *Exceptional Children, 37*, p. 531. Reprinted by permission.

psychology models). By capitalizing on a child's strengths and fostering each youngster's desire to learn, this classroom environment becomes the prototype for prevention of learning disabilities.

Type II youngsters may function effectively at Step 1 in most areas of learning but encounter occasional problems. At this point, the teacher must decide whether to delay some instruction until the student becomes more ready to deal with it (e.g., paper and pencil addition, but without regrouping) (developmental approach). When a decision is made not to delay instruction, the student will require a different level of programming, Step 2 (behavioral approach).

Step 2 has three levels, each of which requires different types of teaching. At Level A the basic skills, content, and concepts of the school subject are retaught, such as number facts to ten. The reteaching involves qualitatively different explanations, techniques, materials, and remedial approaches from those that had been used previously (e.g., sorting concrete objects, playing number games, and working with a calculator versus doing calculations by hand). If reteaching is unsuccessful, Level B is initiated. Level B involves the reteaching of prerequisites needed for success at Level A, such as mastering comprehension of quantities to five before attempting six through ten. When Level B is successful, the teacher returns to Level A. If Level B is unsuccessful, the teacher goes to Level C, where any interfering behavior or information-processing deficits are remediated. The teacher, for example, assesses the child's counting and one-to-one correspondence ability, comprehension of more and less, and ability to copy numerals, and works with the child on identified problems. Once the child is successful at Level C, the teacher returns to Levels B and A.

The Type III student has severe, pervasive learning difficulties that necessitate resolution of interfering behaviors or information-processing deficits first (process training approach). The child begins at Level C (remediating weaknesses), then moves to Level B, and finally to Level A. Despite their Type II needs, most of these children will still have some achievement areas that are developing normally or that require only a Level A or B intervention.

Whereas the Type I child may require the indirect services of an LD consultant to the regular classroom teacher, the Type II student usually requires some daily direct special education services. The Type III child requires far more specialized and intense special education services.

To maximize students' motivation to put effort into their studies, students must understand how the program relates to their strengths, weaknesses, and interests, and how they are progressing. It is important that they be given an opportunity to indicate their preferences for various methods and materials.

Materials

Research on most special education programs is conducted in an unsystematic fashion, and many years after their publication. Therefore, very few data are available to substantiate any one program's approach as better than another's. Would children with learning disabilities automatically learn this information or develop these strategies as they grew older, even if they had never been exposed to a particular program? Does one program's method work best for one or another type of student or teacher? Research addressing these issues is sparse.

Given this limited program efficacy research, teachers for the most part choose materials based on what worked best for them in the past with students who had similar learning challenges. Teachers choose materials that best suit their teaching styles and organizational preferences, that they are trained to use, and that are readily available. In most cases teachers need to adapt any materials even before teaching begins because the majority of materials have been developed for students who do not find learning difficult. No one material or method will be right for all students taught by the teacher. Nor is it likely that any one program will contain exactly the right material to address the strengths and weaknesses of even one student with learning disabilities. The teacher, in the end, mixes parts of different programs, modifies, and improvises.

Traditional commercial programs prepared for the general education curriculum do simplify the teacher's job by organizing a complex set of skills and materials. However, these materials tend to be insufficient in many ways for students with special education needs: they provide only limited examples and insufficient background information; they tend not to deepen understanding by connecting new concepts to a variety of ideas and topics; they broadly survey a field by tackling too many objectives and information, rather than intensively teaching only essential skills; they do not describe strategies sufficiently, and provide for too little guided practice and active learning applications; they contain infrequent systematic reviews (Simmons, Fuchs, & Fuchs, 1991; Zentall & Ferkis, 1993). Since students with learning disabilities often bring limited background knowledge to text learning, the fact that many texts lack organization and coherence, and leave it to the student to fill in the gaps, doesn't help matters any (Kintsch, 1994).

Because no published material is likely to be perfect, the experienced teacher takes a good deal of time to scrounge, cut, and paste from all sorts of materials to create supplemental explanatory, practice, and review activities. In Emmy's story (below), her resource teacher shares the exhausting process of adapting instruction and materials to meet Emmy's needs. Doing this daily for a year took its toll, and the next academic year Emmy's LD teacher transferred to a regular first grade to get a breather.

Budgetary matters are a realistic concern in choosing instructional materials. Without proof about which programs teach best, how can the teacher choose wisely? Teachers need to look beyond attractive packaging and marketing in order to evaluate how the program fits the needs of their particular students. We will explore general guidelines for selecting materials and the options offered by computer-assisted instruction.

Emmy

I first met Emmy two years before I started working with her. She used to hang around outside my classroom door hoping to catch a glimpse of one of the boys that I worked with. She appeared to be a typical teenage girl. She was fashionably dressed, giggley, and persistent.

 I came in contact with Emmy again during a summer meeting. She was to be one of my students come September. All I really knew about her was that she was coming from our self-contained classroom. I learned that she had been in a similar setting for all of her school career. Now she was a 13-year-old girl who read and wrote at a second grade level and whose math skills were at the fourth grade level. It was decided that it was time for an educational change. That September she was to be mainstreamed for English, science, and all of her specials. She would receive reading instruction and support for her courses in the resource room for three periods each day. She would receive individual math instruction by the math teacher.

 My first reaction when I heard all this was no way. How could I meet all the needs of this child plus the needs of my other resource students? I was also very nervous about the situation because of all the attention her case was receiving. I thought for sure I would have six different people peering over my shoulder keeping an eye on my every move. Then I

(Continues on following page)

Emmy   *(Continued from preceding page)*

thought of Emmy. No one had ever given her the chance in a regular program. With modifications and the support of the people who were going to be working with her we might be able to help her be successful.

I met with all of Emmy's teachers the first week of school in order to ask for their input and review modifications. While all seemed more than willing to be flexible, I felt as if there was really no true understanding of Emmy's needs or what would be required of them in order for the program to work. We started out okay. Content area objectives were cut to the essential concepts and facts. I received notes ahead of time from the science teacher—once, and the books the English teacher would be using. I found out as weeks went by that her teachers were more than willing to allow modifications in her program, but no one was willing to do any of the modifying.

At first I thought I could do it all. As the year went on it became clear that one person could not be responsible for all of the changes. In science alone individual notecards had to be made for each chapter, vocabulary cards were made from class notes, separate readings from low level books had to be found, and tests had to be modified. In English short stories had to be taped, vocabulary units had to be retaught and modified along with all of the teacher's exams. Individual summaries were written for each chapter of the novels that were assigned and study guides were made to help prepare Emmy for the exams. Along with supplementing the content areas, I was also responsible for working on Emmy's reading and writing. If Emmy was one of five students, I know I could have done much more with her. But the truth was she was one of twenty-five.

At first the modifications helped Emmy be successful and feel good about herself. She worked hard and was into it. As the year went on, though, it became increasingly difficult to meet all of her needs by myself. Everyone was feeling overwhelmed, Emmy, myself, her teachers, and her mom. Every success was wonderful, but every disappointment was equally devastating and frustrating. Emmy was not always the easiest person to bring out of a bad or down mood. Many times she was unhappy with her grades, which was very frustrating for me. At times I could not blame her though; it had to be so frustrating. The most frustrating for me was the fact that the testing that I did at the end of the year showed little or no growth on the cognitive portion of the tests. I know that Emmy made a lot of gains that school year, but the one thing everyone usually focuses on showed that she didn't.

I don't want people to think it was a terrible year, because it wasn't. It was exhausting and exhilarating all at the same time. A regular rollercoaster. The tests might not have shown any growth, but I knew better. I always look at my students as very unique individuals. They do not just grow as students, they grow as people. That's how I judge growth and success. Emmy, in my eyes, grew by leaps and bounds. When I see her once a week, now a freshman in high school, I am very proud of her. She helps me after school in my classroom. She has joined groups, works on committees, works with a tutor, and I think has come to realize that she's an okay person and can succeed at many things. I am very proud to have been a part of that.

Source: Reprinted by permission of Mary Ellen Koloski.

Chapter 10 will present more specific program options and strategies for pupils with different types of learning disabilities.

Guidelines for Selecting Materials. Because of their slow progress, students with learning disabilities usually are instructed on the same objectives over and over again. Therefore, materials need to be innovative in how they present routine objectives. They also must help to expand a student's breadth of knowledge, curiosity, and thinking skills. It is important that published materials contain a stated rationale that matches that of the teacher, that students have the necessary readiness skills to benefit from the program, that the materials be of high interest, and that they contain no subtle bias toward or against a particular racial, ethnic, socioeconomic, gender, or disability group. The ideal curriculum integrates basic skills instruction with content area instruction. In this way reading, writing, and math skills are reinforced through content area materials and vice versa.

In choosing materials for a student with learning disabilities, the teacher must make certain that the content is conceptually challenging, despite the student's weaknesses in taking in or communicating information. To maintain interest and success, subject matter, concepts, and language levels need to be equivalent to the conceptual, vocabulary, and maturity levels of the student, while the reading, spelling, or composition requirements are geared toward the student's lower competencies in these areas. Thypin (1979) demonstrates how reading material can be at a high content and abstraction level yet low reading level and vice versa:

	Reading Level	Content Level
(1) The question is to be or not to be	First grade	High school
(2) Homo sapiens are omnivorous bipeds among the cohabiting stalagmites	High school	Fourth grade

Clearly, just because a student can't read or write well does not mean that he or she must be exposed to less intellectually stimulating content. It is our responsibility to ensure that, in our quest to build basic skills, students are not denied the opportunity to become just as knowledgeable as their nondisabled peers. This knowledge is the necessary foundation for acquiring further knowledge and reasoning abilities, as well as a common ground for interchanges with classmates. This means that, as needed, teachers need to find easier reading levels of texts for students, and even rewrite texts into simpler language, while maintaining critical information. Table 9–2 presents additional criteria for exemplary curriculum materials.

Teachers also need to enlist the help of assistive technology whenever necessary to help their students succeed. For example, talking calculators (increases accuracy in writing down answers), a pocket speller or thesaurus, wireless transmitter and receiver (headset) to make the teacher's voice more salient, or a variable-speech-control tape recorder to slow down and speed up playback of books on tape have been very helpful to students with learning disabilities. One of the more exciting developments in recent years is the expansion of published computer-assisted instructional tools for the learning disabled, and the ease with which teachers can create these tools themselves.

Computer-Assisted Instruction. A visit to Mr. Delman's resource room reveals an air of involvement and excitement. Mr. Delman is working with a group of four sixth graders, while eight other students are engrossed at computer screens. At the first computer, two students take turns blowing up rockets by quickly typing answers to flashed multiplication facts. At the second terminal, a heavy game of "Rob the Boss' Office" requires students to compose sentences that direct the robber's actions. The computer recognizes most of their words and creates a matching graphic. Right now, however, the screen is flashing "Beg your pardon?" and the boys are busy searching for the correct spelling of a word in the dictionary. Mike and Lynn have a spelling quiz tomorrow. At their terminal the spelling words they've entered flash one at a time; Mike and Lynn have to type the word right after it has

Table 9–2 Selected criteria for exemplary curriculum materials

1. Have a logical, hierarchical sequence of instructional objectives against which a student's current level of functioning can be compared
2. Incorporate styles of information presentation and reinforcement activities that are adaptable to different students' learning styles (projects, lectures, slides or transparencies, independent study modules, educational games, role-playing, workbooks, term papers, community service projects)
3. Rehearse the same objectives in multiple ways
4. Allow students to proceed at their own pace, backtracking over easier objectives when the student has difficulty learning the material, speeding up coverage of objectives that are mastered more easily, or skipping objectives already mastered
5. Present content and directions in a consistent and simple fashion
6. Offer teachers ideas for task analysis and individualization of teaching and reinforcement strategies
7. Pretest for where teaching should begin
8. Have built-in evaluation mechanisms for determining mastery of instructional objectives
9. Have built-in periodic rechecks on retention of previous learning, and provide opportunities for relearning in a novel format
10. Include several evaluation formats (projects; multiple-choice, essay, or open-book exams; oral reports; homework assignments; self-corrected assignments)
11. Include charts to facilitate student and teacher progress monitoring
12. Have built-in components that enhance student motivation
13. Be flexible so that different teaching methods may be used with the same materials
14. Be adaptable to individual, small-group, or large-group work
15. Help students transfer skills to related contexts and practice practical applications

disappeared from the screen. Finally, Jessica and Lindsey are partners on a research project about quasars. They composed their paper on the word processor and are now making the changes suggested in an editing session with Mr. Delman.

As the cost of computers has come within reach of school district budgets, scenes such as this have become commonplace. There is no question that computer-assisted instruction is an effective aid to learning and practicing basic academic skills, such as word recognition and elementary mathematics (Jones, Torgesen, & Sexton, 1987; Koscinski & Gast, 1993). Professional journals abound with success stories.

The question of which skills are most benefited by computer-assisted instruction has not yet received sufficient scrutiny. Some studies find that computer-assisted instruction is superior to traditional instruction, some that traditional instruction is superior, and some show no difference (Koscinski & Gast, 1993). In one study, forty minutes of daily computerized math work was twice as effective for eleven- and twelve-year-old students with learning disabilities than equal instructional time in the resource room (Trifiletti, Frith, & Armstrong, 1984). Similarly, Horton, Lovitt, and Slocum (1988) found that high school students learned the locations of twenty-eight Asian cities better when using a one-half hour computerized map tutorial than when they used the traditional approach of referencing an atlas and transcribing their findings onto a map.

There is some evidence that computer reading programs develop decoding and vocabulary skills better than they develop comprehension skills (Swanson & Trahan, 1992). In one study, the science learning of high school students was enhanced when several features were added to the computerized version of the text: speech synthesis, glossary, questions linked back to the answer in the text, highlighting of main ideas, supplementary explanations that summarized important ideas (MacArthur & Haynes, 1995).

Another study found that typing on the computer the word that matched a picture aided spelling acquisition more than pressing a key to select the correct word (Cohen, Torgesen, & Torgesen, 1988). Data also point to more optimal learning outcomes in some areas when computer-assisted instruction supplements rather than supplants classroom instruction and is preceded by explicit strategy instruction on the part of the teacher (Lieber & Semmel, 1985; Woodward et al., 1986). For example, Kerchner and Kistinger (1984) found that the quantity and quality of students' written work improved faster when the teacher combined prewriting and editing conferences with the work on the word processor, rather than using the word processor alone.

Computers with synthesized speech output are enormously helpful to students with reading disabilities, who can now scan text into the computer, with the computer highlighting words as it reads the text back aloud in a voice of the student's choosing. For students with written language difficulties, speech recognition software can now learn to interpret the student's voice-input so that the student simply talks into the computer, pausing for about one-tenth of a second between words, and the computer types out what was said. This technology is associated with reading recognition, comprehension, vocabulary, and spelling gains in school children and with enhanced quality and proofreading of compositions among college students with learning disabilities (Herbert & Murdock, 1994; Higgins & Boone, 1991; Higgins & Raskind, 1995; Olsen, Foltz, & Wise, 1986; Raskind & Higgins, 1995; Rosegrant, 1986; van Daal and van der Leij, 1992).

Computers have the advantage of systematically applying procedures known to enhance achievement: instruction and practice on preplanned goals; individualized program development; ability to measure student responses and provide immediate feedback; mastery learning (presenting an objective until a certain criterion of mastery and automaticity is achieved); controlled rate/quantity/sequence of presentation; controlled response to student answers; encouragement of independent work; ability to readjust difficulty levels based on student responses; ability to review concepts in a format that simulates real-life decisions, thereby encouraging generalization and active learning. Motivation enhancement is one of the most important attributes of computerized instruction. It has been found that engaged time on the computer tends to be very high, 80 to 90 percent, in comparison with engaged time of 15 to 50 percent in standard academic activities (Cosden et al., 1987).

Computer programs range from simple drill work, problem-solving practice, and word processing to complex data-base and design/drafting systems. The drill and practice programs reinforce previously learned rote material so that the student can become more automatic in responding. As the computer speeds up, the student is encouraged to increase his or her speed of information retrieval and problem solving. The more automatic these functions can become, the more open and flexible a student will be in higher-order thinking; in other words, as cognitive energy expended on such basics as decoding diminishes, intrusions on a student's ability to optimize his or her higher-level reasoning abilities also diminish (Patterson & Smith, 1986). These computer programs provide as much repetition as a student requires until mastery is attained. Such extensive reinforcement is something that students who are learning disabled require; yet, without the computer, and within the school's curriculum and time constraints, it is virtually impossible for teachers to accomplish this on their own. Let us examine our current technology more closely.

Drills. Drills do not have to be dry and boring. They can generate excitement by means of arcade type game formats that combine spectacular graphics, colors, moving objects, sounds, a fast pace, and harder and harder challenges that keep the student involved. Besides the keyboard and mouse, joysticks and even light pens (that light up the screen wherever the screen is touched) add to the excitement of these exercises. Tape recorders can be attached to computers to synchronize sound with the computer image, and speech synthesizers will read the screen's text aloud phonetically. Drill and practice embedded within computer games seem to be far more motivating than a nongame computer format (Malouf, 1987–88).

Problem-Solving Practice. Problem-solving practice and exposure to new content also can occur in a gamelike format, with the branching of material being determined by the student's previous response. Exciting simulations are available that teach problem solving by pretending that the student is driving a car, conducting a science experiment, deciding moves in an important historical battle, and more. Even a game that requires the student to find the hidden treasure and escape from an evil monster can be the medium for some wonderful problem-solving practice: the student must evaluate risk probabilities (what are the risks of being captured if I enter the forbidden chamber?), plan ahead (what is my strategy?), draw maps, analyze clues, interpret complex directions, organize a strategy, take notes to recall previous moves, use logic, sustain attention, and so forth. Such simulations also offer much practice in basic skills, such as reading instructions on the screen, composing spellings and grammatically correct instructions to be recognized by the computer, typing, calculating how many miles to run or feet to climb, and encouraging eye-hand coordination and rapid reaction time.

Word Processing. Word processing has meant the difference between success and failure for many students with learning disabilities. Whether the student's weakness is spelling, revising, or the actual act of writing, word processing can help. Word processors help compensate for spelling weaknesses because the spell checker detects all but homonym errors, and students are fairly successful in choosing the correct suggested spelling of a word (MacArthur et al., 1996). Students find revisions easier with word processing because they can get all their ideas down on paper and then easily add, delete, and move them around. Even a thesaurus is available to suggest alternatives for overused words, and proofreading programs suggest punctuation, capitalization, grammar, and style changes. Given the slow typing of many students with learning disabilities, abbreviations can be most helpful: students can create their own abbreviations for frequently used words or phrases, and the computer automatically expands the text.

Many students with learning disabilities produce far more text on a computer than had they written the papers by hand (MacArthur, 1988). Quantity, however, does not imply quality. Unless these programs use revision prompts (a set of questions and suggestions about the text—for example, "Does this paragraph make a clear point?") or are coordinated with teacher instruction in the writing process, students will tend to limit themselves to mechanical revisions or minor changes in wording (Daiute, 1986; Kerchner & Kistinger, 1984; MacArthur, 1988; MacArthur & Graham, 1987). Only instruction in how to make revisions that affect meaning, syntax, and organization will alter the quality of students' writing, no matter how much they enjoy the word processor.

MacArthur (1988) lauds the ease with which computers lend themselves to publishing of student works. In the course of preparing materials for "publication," students benefit from learning to gather, select, and organize information, write clearly and for an audience, as well as revise and edit. The monitor, being upright and visible to everyone, makes it easy for students to engage in collaborative writing, revising, and editing activities and for the teacher to observe how a student goes about composing.

It should be noted that not all students with learning disabilities will automatically "take to" the computer. Many will require structured word processing and keyboarding instruction because they have difficulty teaching themselves harder word processing commands and are frustrated by their slow typing (MacArthur & Shneiderman, 1986).

Data Base Management Systems. Some students will be exposed to data base systems that electronically sort and file statistics (bank statements, sports scores, library checkouts). Because such programs are very common tracking devices in business and industry, an introduction to their use for maintaining lists, analyzing trends, and organizing information may be helpful to particular students.

Graphic Design. The person who is interested in graphic or architectural design will be delighted with the time savings of computer-generated designs. Even the future landscaper can design a landscape on the computer and check on how it will look five, ten, and fifteen years from now; the plants grow in seconds before one's eyes.

Authoring Systems. Some students with learning disabilities are just as capable of creating their own computer programs as are students with no learning difficulties (Hearne et al., 1988). Mather and Bos (1994) review the value of teaching students to author programs: gains in personal-social confidence, logical-analytical reasoning, task persistence when faced with frustration, creativity, organization, cooperation and sharing of ideas, attention to detail, positive attitude toward learning, ability to follow directions, independent work habits, and the willingness to ask for help. In particular, when permitted to author their own quizzes, students learn a great deal of content in the process.

Concerns. One of the problems with computer-assisted instruction is that it is all too easy for the busy teacher to occupy students with motivating programs and then offer little teacher assistance (Cosden et al., 1987). Magical as they are, computers are product oriented and cannot substitute for the teacher's ability to observe the quality of a student's strategies. Computers respond to right and wrong answers and have no way of recognizing whether the student has given the right answer but for the wrong reason. Only teacher observation can detect this. Conversely, when a response

is wrong, the student may need teacher assistance to generate a new strategy. It is essential for teachers to work with the student at the computer, observing the student's methods, reinforcing appropriate strategies, and modifying those that are inadequate (Howell, Sidorenko, & Jurica, 1987). When teachers do this, student learning from the software program is increased.

Special educators raise the additional concern that computer software relies too heavily on drill and practice rather than on more intellectually challenging material. Often the drill software is poorly constructed and is insufficiently individualized (Cosden et al., 1987; Woodward & Carnine, 1988). Mather and Bos (1994) warn that ten to fifteen minutes a day is sufficient drill and practice time for most students. Too much can get boring and reduce students' enthusiasm for using computers as a learning tool.

The success of any computer program will depend on the ability of the teacher to choose programs that address relevant curricular objectives with a presentation style and content appropriate to the student's background knowledge, interests, and needs. This includes making sure that the graphics are not too confusing, distracting, or overstimulating for the student; that the reading and comprehension requirements are appropriate to the student's instructional level; that the memory demands are within a student's capabilities; and that the presentation rate is suited to the student's information-processing speed and reaction time (Taymans & Malouf, 1984). Teachers also need to check on students' typing proficiency because some youngsters are frustrated when the typing slows them down. As with any classroom instruction, computer-assisted instruction will be most beneficial when teachers set performance criteria and then systematically chart student progress toward these goals.

Finally, Hearne and colleagues (1988) make an important point. They urge educators to use the computer to enhance talents, not just to remediate deficits. "If students concentrate exclusively on their disabilities, they remain ignorant of their own abilities, and thus their talents lay dormant" (p. 489).

Adapting Instruction to Learner Ability and Style

Translating information from the assessment process to wise decisions about teaching goals, materials, and strategies is much easier said than done. Although matching tasks to students' abilities and unique learning styles began with the pioneers in learning disabilities, it is still more an art than a science. Research Box 9–1 discusses why research on these matches, officially called *aptitude by treatment interactions (ATI)*, is so hard to conduct. We have learned from ATI research that there are a few methods that are likely to benefit most children, such as teaching phonics, using teacher directed instruction, heightening motivation, and developing learning strategies. In general, however, discovering optimal child-task matches is an individualized process that continues over time. This is because not all methods work for all children, the same method does not work on all curriculum objectives for any one child, and the same materials or methods may, after some time, no longer work for a given child.

The nature of the requirements students face in the classroom is important to scrutinize because these play an important role in optimizing or detering student progress. Although adhering to rigid curriculum demands may be good for some children, Liza's story (pages 338–340) is an example of how lack of flexibility may foster perceived

RESEARCH BOX 9–1
Aptitude by Treatment Interaction Research

Aptitude by treatment interaction (ATI) research on how to match child and task characteristics is extremely difficult to conduct. To begin with, the tests used to categorize students as one or another type of learner often are not reliable or valid for the purpose. Besides, it is nearly impossible to categorize groups of children as similar learners (for example, auditory or visual learning preferences) because children can differ in so many ways that affect learning: for example, their motivation, their funds of information, styles of learning, and instructional backgrounds. Therefore, one type of instruction will have nearly as many effects on the children in a study as there are children. For these reasons, studies that make rather gross discriminations among children on the basis of a few test scores, and then compare the effects of different teaching methods, often show modest or no differences in outcome between groups (Kavale & Forness, 1987; Larrivee, 1981). Most children will learn from the instruction given, and their preferred modalities may direct learning, even when the teaching method is intended to capitalize on their weaker modalities (Tarver & Dawson, 1978). Although some children probably did benefit more from one type of instruction than they would have from another, since they did not receive both types of instruction there is no way of finding this out. The group data also mask the great gains of some children because of the less remarkable gains of others. To complicate the matter even further, most studies can't be compared because of differences in design and children studied. The majority of these studies have been conducted on a short-term basis in the laboratory. In most cases researchers don't know whether this laboratory instruction transfers to classroom skills and behaviors and how long its positive effects persist.

(Continues on following page)

or actual failure. Because of Liza's uniqueness, neither her parents nor her teachers could ever rest easy, thinking that all her problems were behind her. In a similar way, teachers must continually stay on top of task content and process modifications for students with learning disabilities so that the possibility of steady progress is maximized.

Matching Task Content to Student Readiness

The comment "My child can't remember anything" is commonly heard. Yet there is no such thing as a child who can't remember anything. Some children may not learn what they are expected to learn for their age and intelligence levels, but they certainly can learn more fundamental skills that are easier for them. When task content is matched to what the student is absolutely ready to learn, then learning is facilitated. The achievement of higher-level goals will occur more rapidly and completely when we build the background foundation first (Kinsbourne & Caplan, 1979).

Developmental theorists warn against teaching too much, too soon, thereby bypassing mastery of important basic skills. When such teaching does take place, then faulty habits are learned; these only need to be unlearned later on. The child who has put inordinate effort into learning,

---

RESEARCH BOX 9–1 *(Continued from preceding page)*

Because of these factors, aptitude by treatment interaction studies should be conducted in the classroom where they measure individual children's progress, rather than the group's progress (Guralnick, 1978; Kratochwill, Brody & Piersel, 1979; Lovitt, 1975a, b; Wilson & Baddeley, 1986). These studies should teach with one method and then switch methods, so that the efficacy of different approaches with the same child can be compared. In this way researchers can discover what really works, and to what degree, for particular children. The heterogeneity of a group of children would no longer mask individual gains.

A more recent approach to ATI research is to administer extensive neuropsychological, information-processing, psychological, and educational batteries to students with learning disabilities and then apply statistical procedures to classify these children into subgroups. Lyon (1985), for example, provided a one hour weekly phonics program to eleven- and twelve-year-old students reading at the third grade level. Students with normal perceptual and language profiles, despite reading delays, made the greatest gains in word recognition (nearly one year). Nearly eight months' gain was evidenced by students with weaknesses in some but not all language areas. Finally, students with significant deficits in auditory comprehension, auditory memory, and sound blending made no gains. In other words, the more severe one's language impairment, the less the benefit from phonics instruction. More of this type of well-designed research is beginning to shed light on the value of matching particular teaching techniques to students' specific modality preferences (see Research Box 10–1 for a review of ATI reading research). In the meantime, we know too little about how learner, teacher, classroom environment, and educational approaches interact to be certain of more than a handful of instructional recommendations for any one child. Trial teaching with continuous progress monitoring is the pragmatic way to make such educational decisions until ATI variables are better understood.

Liza

Liza was born full term and healthy, although her mother was hospitalized with toxemia one week before delivery. At age five, Liza was enrolled in a small private school because her listening and expressive language skills were weak. She had not uttered single words until age two and had not combined words until age two and one-half. When she entered speech therapy at age three and one-half, she could produce almost no consonant sounds. She referred to her sister Julie as "oo-ee," *bye-bye* was "i-i," and *bottle* was "o-u." She was able to say "ma-ma" and "da-ee."

Fearing that Liza might encounter academic difficulties, her parents thought that a private school's small-group setting would be to her benefit. By May of her kindergarten year, Liza's teacher's support of *any* verbalizations she made ended happily. Liza had progressed from not even being brave enough to call out "Bingo" when she won a game at the beginning of the year, to constantly yelling "Hey Mrs. Thomas!" from anywhere in the room by the end of the year. All were delighted with this change.

But first grade required work and not talk. In early October the school's team told Liza's mother that she had an insolent, disobedient child who knew what to do but wouldn't do it and who destroyed the class with her disturbing chatter. Simply put, she was hyperactive and emotionally disturbed and was potentially excludable from school. The message was clear: the mother was to go home and have a talk with Liza. Liza should *pay attention* to the teacher, follow directions, and stop annoying others.

This type of behavior was a problem specific to the school. Although Liza chattered a lot at home, she was not a disturbance in that context. Her mother's message to the team was equally clear: "for my $4800 a year it had better be your (teachers') attitudes and task modifications that alter my daughter's school behavior." Two hours later, the team and mother agreed on what types of modifications they would make to help Liza attend better and talk less: turn her desk to the wall with her back to the others, instruct her in small groups rather than all by herself so that she would have an opportunity to learn how to listen in a group, tell her the *rules* of when talking is allowed and not allowed, compliment her on good listening, get her attention before talking to her, and ask her to repeat directions. By the next conference the mother was amused to hear from the team, "I don't know what you did but Liza has been a changed child since the very day following our conference!"

Liza's idiosyncrasies followed her wherever she went. Her chatter and inattention were predictable. Her parents decided to explore second grade in their local public school. They found that although Liza had completed all her first grade work at the private school, most of her suburban peers in the public school had already completed second grade work. If enrolled with these children, Liza would be looked on as an underachiever among her peers. Liza's parents decided to enroll her in the public school's first grade instead. They reasoned that she had an August birthday and was somewhat immature anyhow. Liza became the brilliant class leader! She still talked a lot, didn't modulate her voice well, and couldn't judge when not to talk, but the teacher didn't notice in that large group. She still

(Continues on following page)

Liza   *(Continued from preceding page)*

needed to hear directions twice, but the teacher repeated them automatically anyhow because of the noise in the classroom.

What is Liza?—emotionally disturbed, an underachiever relative to her peers and intelligence level (learning disabled), gifted? She is none of these; she is just a delightfully unique little girl who needed to find the right match between her strengths and weaknesses and school environment to facilitate her development.

The story doesn't end all that simply. Just as the resolved weaknesses of children with learning disabilities reappear periodically and interfere with progress, so Liza's uniqueness creates continual challenges. When in third grade, there was some concern that Liza was not being challenged enough in reading and math because she was being taught the curriculum of children one year younger. Her social maturity was excellent and in some ways distanced her from her peers. Yet she didn't seem to understand their joking. Her handwriting also did not progress, so she began seeing a resource teacher twice a week. Liza was not as adept at poetry, composition, and playing with words as her classmates. She also was too loud in the lunchroom.

Yet, even in third grade Liza's parents knew that she would be okay. Aware of her stumbling blocks, she nevertheless thought of herself as a lovable, beautiful, capable child. She tried very hard and seldom was defeated by disappointment. Liza's biggest trauma at the end of third grade was her strong desire to go to overnight camp at an age when most other children wouldn't consider it, but she didn't know whether camp was worth giving up thumbsucking or whether the energy of hiding the thumbsucking under her blankets for four weeks was worth it!

Liza is now 20 years old and a junior architecture student at an Ivy League college. Her language lags are evident even today in that her math SAT scores were 780, but the best she could do on the verbal SAT, even after one thousand dollars of tutoring, was 590. All SAT achievement tests were in the 600 to 700 range, but Spanish barely broke 450. Liza just finished a series of voice lessons with a radio/TV coach, because her sorority sisters commented once too often on how young her enunciation and voice quality sound.

Liza's interest in architecture began in seventh grade when the math her friends were doing fascinated her. But the guidance counselor would not allow Liza into their honors class because of Liza's merely average academic record. Liza fought back tears with her counselor and, when in January a student moved away and left a vacant seat, the counselor gave in. Having missed half the content, and with private tutoring from the head of the high school math department, Liza mustered only an 80 average at the end of the year. Again her counselor wanted to drop her from the class, and again Liza protested. "I'd rather be the dumbest person in the honors class than the smartest person in the dumb class." It was in that next year that Liza became a 99th percentile math student eligible to try out for the Johns Hopkins Gifted and Talented Search.

Ninth grade brought with it 90s in all honors classes, although Spanish grades were in the 80s. Liza preplanned for Spanish vocabulary tests by systematically studying five

(Continues on following page)

Liza   *(Continued from preceding page)*

flashcards per day. If she tried to cram the day before a test, it never worked. To improve her Spanish, she lived with a family in Spain that summer, and to improve her writing, the following summer she enrolled in a private school summer program. Well, her Spanish did not improve—the family had learned English at Liza's expense. But Liza's motivation to write and publish soared following the positive feedback she received in her writing program. By the time Liza applied to college, she had published 23 stories in national magazines and had won two national essay contests. How can that be, given her language lags? It seems that Liza's short sentences and simple vocabulary, coupled with her astute observations and quick wit, make for light, easy, enjoyable reading.

Liza panicked when she got to college because she was unaware that there was a two-year language requirement for graduation. She would not only have to pass four Spanish courses, and a written and oral exam, but she also would have to earn a 550 on the SAT Spanish achievement test. For the first time in her life she gave in and submitted her credentials regarding a language disability to the disability services office. In the meantime, Liza was required to enroll in the beginning Spanish class. So she enrolled in the third level class in an attempt to get through this requirement faster. The disability committee members said that they would not make a determination until the end of the semester. Panicked throughout and motivated to move on, Liza studied hard, earned an A, and passed out of the language requirement at the end of the semester, the same day she received a letter from the disability office that waived her language requirement!

Liza's motivation pulls her through over and over again. She can't draw well, but practices and practices, and has improved to an A-level in her studio classes. She can't memorize art history facts well, so out come the flashcards again—this time ten per day. Having succeeded despite much frustration, Liza's attitude toward life is happy and optimistic. With effort she knows she can do anything. Her bubbly, cheery personality attracts many friends. She has suffered too much to speak ill of anyone—they know that—and they love the quirks that make her fun and unique.

yet continually fails, may finally lose the motivation to try. Consequently, teaching the right material at the right time is critical.

By comparing a student's skills with the scope and sequence charts contained in commercial curricula, teachers can discover if the curriculum is appropriately matched to what the student is ready to learn. These charts, when used along with task analysis, evaluation of past learning opportunities, and consultation with the student, help to determine the most logical goals for teaching.

Matching Task Processes to Student Learning Styles

Besides modifying the curricular content to teach the right objective at the right time, the teacher's methods must fit well with the student's learning styles. In the following pages we shall explore how we might modify instruction to match the most common learning styles among students with learning disabilities: poor attention, slow information processing, performance deterioration as practice continues, modality preferences, impulsive and low conceptual level styles, and poor generalization of what has been learned. Chapters 6 and 7 have already dealt with two other common characteristics: metacognitive weaknesses and low motivation; additional approaches to these problems will be addressed in subsequent chapters as well.

Matching Tasks to Students' Attending Strategies. Results of numerous studies show that students with learning disabilities tend to have so much more off-task and distractible behavior than their peers that learning opportunities are severely compromised (Bender & Smith, 1990). Because these students' attention tends to vary from one time to another, teachers often perceive a student's capabilities as being greater than they really are. Ross and Ross (1976) vividly describe these misperceptions.

A teacher who sees a child act like a disorganized tornado for the first two weeks of school and then suddenly switch to being obedient and industrious has a hard time believing that the child's behavior is out of his control. Furthermore, his grades often fluctuate from high to low, so that the teacher usually concludes that having done it once he could do it again if he wanted to. (p. 43)

But many children cannot do it again even if they wanted to. Often their good days and bad days reflect the ups and downs of their attention. Unevenness in performance is common. They may be able to sustain attention to activities that are highly stimulating and interesting (for example, a computer game), but not to activities that are less interesting and more effortful (for example, seatwork). These students need teachers to make special efforts to modify settings, task characteristics, instructions, and explanations so that the school content engages their interest and participation more than do the distractors.

With respect to maximizing attention-sustaining setting variables, it is important to recognize that these students' attention and related activity levels typically vary greatly across settings. A hyperactive child, for example, is not hyperactive all the time. To illustrate, Kalverboer's (1976)

observations of 117 children in six different situations found only one child who was consistently among the 20 percent most active in each setting. Similarly, Porrino and colleagues (1983), after monitoring motor activity twenty-four hours daily for one week, found their hyperactive boys to be far more active than typical boys during reading and math lessons, but their activity levels did not differ during lunch, recess, or physical education. Interestingly, research suggests that fewer than 25 percent of children with Attention Deficit Hyperactivity Disorder meet these criteria both at home and at school (Szatmari, Offord, & Boyle, 1989). Keeping this variability in mind, teachers must take time to observe children carefully in various settings and then develop the kind of environment in which each student shows the greatest tendency to focus and sustain his or her attention. This includes scrutinizing the content matter, methods (for example, seatwork versus cooperative learning groups), structure provided by the teacher, peer characteristics, teacher attitudes, seating arrangements, and ambient noise, to name just a few variables.

Maximizing attention-sustaining task variables is equally important. The behavior and achievement of students with learning disabilities tend to vary more as a function of instructional variables than do those of their peers. Therefore, to increase learning teachers must capture and sustain the attention of students with learning disabilities by carefully adjusting task difficulty, their instructions, activity versus book learning, learning load, the highlighting of distinctive features, use of concrete objects and multimodal learning, presence of distractors, task organization, and the presentation of similar information.

Reducing Task Difficulty. When students with learning disabilities are involved in low cognitive demand tasks (drawing pictures, free-play activities), their attention can be every bit as engaged as that of non-LD students. But as task demands get harder (copying letters from the blackboard) and harder (reading, mathematics), time on task progressively decreases (Krupski, 1985). This pattern has been attributed to these children's natural avoidance when demands are too taxing or to children having learned to avoid even manageable tasks because of their history of failure. Therefore, in order to maximize their attention, the learning disabled can benefit from sensitive adjustments of task difficulty.

Directed Instruction on How to Perform Tasks. It is important for teachers' instructions to specifically direct students' attention to how to perform the required tasks. O'Shea, Sindelar, and O'Shea (1987), for example, influenced recall of story content by instructing eleven- to thirteen-year-old students with learning disabilities to read a story and "try to remember as much about the story as you can." In contrast, students told to read "as quickly and correctly as you can" had lower comprehension. Another way teachers can cue appropriate attention, at times even augmenting the memory performance of students with learning disabilities to equal that of typical learners, is by building verbal labeling into tasks (Torgesen & Goldman, 1977). In one study Torgesen (1977b) found that poor readers could memorize picture cards better when instructed to label the cards as the experimenter sorted them into categories. They learned even more when instructed to sort the cards into the categories themselves.

Experienced teachers have discovered many additional ways of enhancing students' attention and recall by means of their instructions. Teachers, for example, can instruct students to apply new ideas to a practical problem in a different setting, to use mnemonic tricks (for example, the first letters of the Great Lakes spell "HOMES"), to memorize related vocabulary pairs rather than single words, to actively question the meaning while reading, to immediately rehearse what has been seen or heard, to review small amounts of material at frequent intervals, and to attend to the organization of the information presented to gain main and subordinate ideas. Lloyd and Loper's (1986) study is typical of self-monitoring research indicating that, when teachers instruct students to self-record their attention or academic output, students increase both their attention to task and their academic productivity.

Activity-Based Instruction. Activity-based instruction has been shown to benefit the content learning of students with learning disabilities more than textbook approaches involving teacher presentation and worksheets (Scruggs et al., 1993). While we know that instructing students via demonstrations does draw attention and teach, active imitation of these demonstrations increases student learning and retention considerably (Bauer, 1996).

Avoidance of Overloading. Students with learning disabilities often attend exclusively to the perceptual characteristics of materials and neglect to use their past knowledge to think through solutions (Reid, 1980). It is common for these children's attention to become overloaded when they have to attend to more than three or four elements or ideas at a time. Johnson and Myklebust (1967), for example, pointed out that some children cannot monitor for meaning while reading aloud because they are overloaded with too much stimulation. To work around this, they might tape their voices reading aloud and later close the book and listen to the tape in order to gain the meaning.

The helpfulness of not overloading students with too much to look at, listen to, or think about at once is illustrated in Bryant and Gettinger's (1981) study. These investigators found that both typical children and those who were learning disabled were better at learning to associate geometric figures with nouns (a task simulating sight word reading) when only one figure (versus all) appeared on a card and when they mastered one pair at a time (instead of running through all items on the list until mastery was reached). Looking at one figure at a time reduced the complexity of what they had to look at, and mastering one pair at a time reduced the potential for the incomplete recall of one item to interfere with the recall of another item on the list. The students with learning disabilities exhibited more marked improvement than did typical learners under these conditions, which reflects their greater sensitivity to such task variables.

Bryant and Gettinger suggest that this overloading may be due to distractibility, which causes the child to process irrelevant information; slow processing speed; failure to process input and output automatically; or a tendency to fatigue early. When a student is distracted or overloaded by the perceptual features of tasks, the teacher easily can divide the task into more manageable chunks (for example, cutting a calculation worksheet into quarters, limiting review to only four math fact cards at one time, giving two rather than four choices on a multiple-choice test, presenting three choices per item rather than the whole list on a matching test).

Since overloading can occur when students must engage in too much new learning or too many memory searches at once, teachers need to determine the optimum unit size for each pupil and limit material accordingly. Bryant (1980), for example, found that temporarily dropping learned items from lists of new items facilitated mastery. In another study, Bryant, Drabin, and Gettinger (1981) taught students with learning disabilities three spelling words on each of three consecutive days. They found that 62 percent of the students achieved the criterion for mastery. However, the percentage reaching criterion on the original nine words decreased to 30 percent when given one additional word to learn each day and to 17 percent when given two additional words to learn each day. Bryant's research suggests that the optimal unit size for instruction may be five new words at a time for reading but only three for spelling (Bryant, 1980).

The benefit of reducing the memory load required at one time comes up repeatedly in the LD literature. For example, breaking lectures into several natural segments, and stopping to ask students questions about each segment before going on, increases acquisition of social studies content (Hudson, 1997). Even computer-assisted vocabulary instruction has been shown to produce faster learning when ten rather than twenty-five words are practiced at a time (Johnson, Gersten, & Carnine, 1987). In another computer study, children with learning disabilities learned the seven South American countries much faster (eight minutes versus twenty-two minutes) in a presentation format where many questions about all preceding countries had to be answered correctly before a new country was introduced. This was in contrast to a presentation format in which all seven countries were presented in sequence with one question between each; the remaining questions were asked at once, and when an error was made the computer returned to that country's initial item and began again (Gleason, Carnine, & Vala, 1991). Likewise, with learning science facts, Scruggs and colleagues (1985) found that students could recall only about one fourth of the information when they were taught three attributes about each of eight minerals. However, when the same period of time was devoted to just four minerals, students remembered much more. The implication for the classroom is that in order to avoid overloading, information should be broken into smaller segments to be learned at separate intervals. Recent brain studies suggest that, with such spacing, memory for the task actually consolidates and becomes stronger (Karni et al., 1995).

For the student who becomes overloaded with a barrage of materials and verbal directions, brevity, simplicity, clarity, and directness are important; excess, irrelevant, vague, and distracting information, such as interesting tangents, needs to be eliminated.

Drawing Attention to Distinctive Features. It is helpful when academic tasks can be structured so as to draw attention to the tasks' most important features. Vertical discriminations, for example, are much easier for young children than are horizontal discriminations (Davidson, 1935; Hendrickson & Muehl, 1962). Therefore, children will find the left–right discrimination between b-d much easier when the two are lined up, one on top of the other b
d (Pick & Pick, 1970). On the other hand, the up–down difference between p-b is much more noticeable if the letters remain horizontally placed. Similarly, Gheorghita (1981) reports that her students with reading disabilities found it easier to read words vertically,

t
a
b
l
e

than horizontally. She claims that vertical positioning broke up the tendency to scan too quickly from left to right. An alternate explanation might be that attention to one phoneme at a time was facilitated by such a display. Clearly, at times the way teachers arrange tasks can help draw students' attention to the critical features.

Another way to build attention-getters into tasks is to note the student's preferences for color, shape, or size. As noted in Chapter 6, these preferences change with age, as one or another attribute draws more attention. These preferences can then be used to aid concept attainment (Odom & Corbin, 1973; Suchman & Trabasso, 1966a, b). When teaching the difference between the numerals 1 and 2, for example, teachers can make materials more distinctive by varying the sizes (big 1, small 2), shapes (the 1 is pasted on a square background, the 2 on a circular background), or colors (red 1, yellow 2). Researchers, for example, have successfully used color to improve children's attention to details in letter formation and to similarities in spellings (Zentall, 1989; Zentall & Kruczek, 1988). Simply highlighting the last part of a text helps ten to eleven year olds maintain attention and remember the information (Belfiore et al., 1996). This same principle applies equally well to secondary students. The democratic leaders' names, for example, might be written on circular backgrounds, and the nondemocratic rulers might be written on square backgrounds. All foreign language words with accents or irregular conjugations could be printed on pink index cards. The nonaccent or regular words would be on white cards.

Use of Concrete Objects. The well-known fact that the attention of immature children is best grabbed by three-dimensional rather than two-dimensional objects also can be capitalized on in teaching. For example, a block with a 3 painted on it is likely to draw more attention than a piece of paper with a 3 on it. Concrete objects are likely to draw greater attention than abstract symbols. For this reason, children both with and without learning disabilities will improve in calculation accuracy when number fact problems are transformed into stories referring to objects; moreover, encourag-

ing young children with language delays to use their fingers to count can raise their accuracy to that of their typical learning peers (Jordan, 1995). Likewise, concrete manipulatives added to math instruction enhances children's recognition of the operations necessary to solve story problems (Marsh & Cooke, 1996).

Illustrating this principle on the computer, Ceci and Baker (1989) found that children with learning disabilities could not anticipate in what direction to move a stimulus in order to catch moving circular and square cues of different colors and sizes. But when the identical task was repeated, and the cues became large/small, blue/white bees or butterflies, and the stimulus to be moved became a net, then the children easily could guide the net to the point where they thought the bee or butterfly would fly. With these concrete stimuli, the performance of the children with learning disabilities became just as good as that of typical learners.

Multimodal Learning. Special education has placed long-standing value on multimodal learning, teaching through several modalities at once in the hope that each will draw attention to different elements of the task. While multimodal instruction is helpful to most students, there are those children for whom multimodal input is overstimulating; they will attend much better when attention requirements are reduced to one stimulus in one modality at one time. For example, Montali and Lewandowski (1996) found that bimodal presentation of science and social studies material on a computer (the computer highlighted each word as it was read by its synthesized voice) increased the comprehension of most secondary students with learning disabilities to equal that of their nondisabled classmates. Some students, however, did best simply listening to the text, while others did better reading it on the computer. The typical learners were not benefited any more by the bimodal presentation than by simply reading the material. Therefore, we must be careful to teach through multiple modalities only when this is unlikely to overwhelm the student's attention. The Basic Behavioral Science Task Force of the National Advisory Mental Health Council (1996), in fact, advises that teachers who give two directions at once do so via two modalities (one modality per direction) rather than through the same modality, in order to reduce competition for the one modality's attention and increase the child's chances of remembering each discrete direction.

Reducing Distractors. Students with learning disabilities at times may learn just as much information as non-LD students, but what they learn may be incidental information that is not central to the intended objectives (Pelham, 1979). Because these students' attention can be drawn away to irrelevant aspects of an assignment, the correct response often is competing for attention with irrelevant responses. Therefore, distractors must be minimized. For example, many children with learning disabilities become distracted by the pictures in their reading books and then read slower and less accurately (Harber, 1983; Rose, 1986; Rose & Furr, 1984). They gather comprehension clues from the pictures and then guess at the words rather than trying to analyze the words phonetically. Therefore, in some cases word recognition gains will be more rapid if pictures are eliminated. Similarly, Radosh and Gittleman (1981) found that typical learners had more math calculation errors when their problems were bordered by drawings of appealing toys, animals, and objects than when bordered by abstract paintings or no border. Hyperactive children, however, experienced far greater distraction with all but the blank border. Interestingly, story composition too may be inhibited for some children by simply asking them to draw a picture about a topic before beginning to write (Barenbaum, Newcomer, & Nodine, 1987). Clearly, attention on the teacher's part to reducing distractors can be most helpful to a student's learning.

Increasing Task Organization. One important way of reducing distractions is to organize information for students so that associations make the information more meaningful. Suiter and Potter (1978), for example, gave children with learning disabilities forty pictures of objects to remember. Some children were shown the pictures in groups of four objects belonging to the same cat-

egory (food, animals, toys). The remaining children also were shown four pictures at a time, but no two belonged to the same category. Those who received the organized presentation recalled the information significantly better. Likewise, elementary students could comprehend a passage better when information pertinent to the question (for example, which house to buy based on the electrical savings from fewer windows) was centralized in one place in the text rather than distributed randomly throughout the text (Simmons, Kameenuî, & Darch, 1988). Frequently, we find that when a teacher creates handouts that organize the information clearly into categories (crops, religions, rivers), this is very helpful to the student with learning disabilities. Giving the student a known vocabulary word to associate with a new one (for example, *fail-fallacy*), or a high-interest association for new information (for example, *humiliated*—"I feel humiliated if people stare when I *hum* loudly while wearing my walkman") are other ways of sparking attention and helping a student memorize because new information is linked with prior understandings.

Studies find that the achievement of students with learning disabilities is greater when the teacher organizes information so that key concepts are continually repeated (for example, state a concept, give an example, restate the concept), or the student is familiarized with the order in which a lesson's concepts will be developed (for example, a diagram of the headings). The same lesson produces far more learning when the teacher explains the lesson's organization at the outset, announces when transitions occur, points out how different segments relate to one another, and once again reviews the organization at the end (Zigmond et al., 1986).

Reducing Similar Information. At times the presence of similar information distracts the youngster with learning disabilities from learning more than it distracts the typical student (Cermak et al., 1981; Mauer & Kamhi, 1996). Consequently, the reduction of similar items that may confuse learning or retrieval often is necessary. For example, a kindergarten teacher might elect not to teach *b* at the same time as *d*. Only when the student has learned to efficiently retrieve the sound of *b* would *d* be introduced. The same principle would hold true for introducing 6 versus 9, and sounding out short /e/ versus /i/. Likewise, the junior high teacher might purposely separate the teaching of the word *latitude* from *longitude*, or *homogeneous* from *heterogeneous*.

Matching Time Limits to Information-Processing Speed.   Professionals are becoming increasingly sensitive to the differences between students in their information-processing time. Even when they can read words perfectly, students with learning disabilities may take far longer than typical readers to read a word or indicate whether they had seen a specific word (Cermac & Miliotis, 1987; Elbert, 1984). Even a simple sorting task is executed more slowly by youngsters with learning disabilities (Copeland & Reiner, 1984). Yet, when given unlimited time to show what they know, these students' performances can increase dramatically, often equalling those of their nondisabled peers; in contrast, typical students benefit only marginally from extended time (Alster, 1997; Runyan, 1991).

When students need longer periods of time to solve certain types of problems, they will be penalized by timed assignments and tests. Therefore, we must decide on time limits that will give each youngster a reasonable opportunity to show his or her knowledge. During lectures, time limits must be sufficient to allow opportunities for verbal rehearsal of the material that has been heard; this may involve the teacher talking more slowly and pausing more often (for example, ten-minute lecture followed by three-minute group work to discuss the main ideas). A similar approach with college students, in which the instructor paused for two minutes at about seven-minute intervals was helpful in facilitating immediate recall of the content and completeness of lecture notes (Ruhl & Suritsky, 1995). Just as more time is helpful in facilitating access to lecture material, we have noted previously that some students need phonemes to be sustained longer, or longer time spans to survey visual material.

Finally, a very important variable to keep in mind while teaching is to adjust our wait time after questions and comments to many students' need to take longer to retrieve information (because they take longer to process our message, have naming difficulties, or store information in an incomplete or disorganized fashion). In the typical classroom, teachers often wait less than one second for students to respond to their questions or comments before they repeat or rephrase what they had said (Honea, 1982; Lehr, 1984). For lower-achieving students, they tend to wait even less time, as though they don't expect an appropriate response (Good, 1980). If we increase wait time by even a few seconds, we are likely to increase students' opportunities for participation and discover that they know a great deal more than we had thought (Lehr, 1984).

Matching Task Repetitions to Students' Practice Needs.   It would seem axiomatic that "practice makes perfect." But surprisingly, this may not always be so for the learning disabled. Why is it that Leah can read the word *friend* with no problem at all in the first paragraph but can't even guess what it might be when she sees *friend* again two pages later? Why is it that Nicholas's invented spellings and reversals deteriorate by the fifth line he writes (see Figure 9–2)? When Nicholas was asked this question, he answered, "My brain went on pause." As Nicholas implied, it appears that some students become overwhelmed and worn down by too much practice, to the point that they can no longer call to mind what they do know. Continuous scanning of their memories for auditory information seems to be particularly troublesome (Farnham-Diggory & Gregg, 1975; Lehman & Brady, 1982). It seems that switching from one to another modality does not aid recovery. Likewise, children with learning disabilities may not improve motor performance with practice (for example, accuracy on a sorting task), as do those with normal learning abilities (Copeland & Reiner, 1984; Wozniak, 1972). On a simple reaction time task on which students were to release a key when a target light appeared, the time students with learning disabilities took to notice and react became longer as trials continued (Pihl & Niaura, 1982). Therefore, we must be careful that the number of repetitions of tasks assigned to students

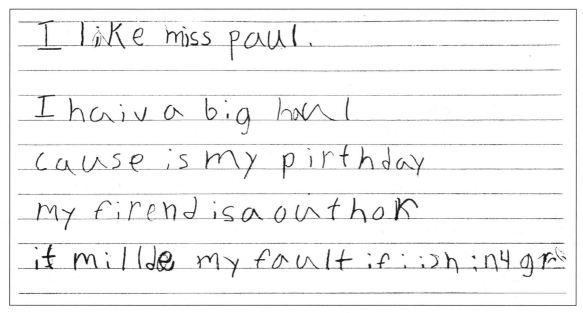

I like miss paul.

I haiv a big hanl
cause is my pirthday
my firend isa outhok
it millde my fault if i sh in4 gr

Figure 9–2 Invented spellings and reversals get worse as writing continues. This exercise required Nicholas, who is nine years old, to compose sentences from a list of *au* words. His last sentence reads, "it will be my fault if I stay in 4th grade."

does not overwhelm and exhaust them. Writing twenty spelling words ten times each, all in one sitting, may in fact do more harm than good. While students with learning disabilities need far more repetitions than typical students before the information "sticks," these repetitions need to be in small doses at distributed intervals.

Matching Tasks to Students' Stronger Modalities. The idea of matching task attributes to youngsters' stronger information-processing modalities makes intuitive sense, yet only recently has the research become more consistent in supporting this practice (see Research Boxes 9–1 and 10–1). Studies using more sophisticated statistical procedures suggest that when teaching techniques are carefully selected to match students' modality strengths, these are highly beneficial; the mismatches (for example, teaching an auditory learner reading through a visual approach) generally produce minimal gains.

Some studies have suggested that, due to their written language difficulties, oral recall of themes after children with learning disabilities read stories is better than written recall (Fuchs & Maxwell, 1988); or that when auditory memory is a strength, listening to taped words or passages enhances sight vocabulary, reading comprehension, and reading rate (Freeman & McLaughlin, 1984; Rose & Sherry, 1984; Torgesen, Dahlem, & Greenstein, 1987). Phonics instruction, too, appears to promote reading progress best with students who are stronger in the language areas (Lyon, 1985).

Many studies have demonstrated marked increases in performance when tasks are modified to work around the student's weaker information-processing skills. For example, Graham (1990) found that children with learning disabilities dictated longer and higher-quality essays in comparison with their handwritten essays; dictation was up to seven times faster. Nevertheless, Johnson

(1993) warns us not to automatically assume that such compensations will produce better performance. In some cases students with reading difficulties will comprehend better when reading than listening because of the heavy language and memory load entailed in listening. They also may do better at writing answers than dictating because writing permits more time for monitoring and revising one's language. Therefore, we can't jump to conclusions without systematically testing out our assumptions.

Rourke, Fisk, and Strang (1985) urge that even if instruction is proceeding well through the student's strengths, educators must not ignore the weaknesses. A child who is a good phonetic analyzer, for example, will continue to be a slow, laborious reader unless he or she develops sight recognition skills. If the analytic skills are encouraged through instruction and rapid visual recognition is ignored, then the gap between the child's processing strengths and weaknesses is only widened, and reading will remain inefficient. A balanced focus between strengths and weaknesses must be achieved.

In keeping with this reasoning, Bakker and Vinke (1985) specifically adapted remedial techniques to challenge poor readers' weaker information-processing capabilities. Children with right hemisphere weaknesses were tutored with perceptually complex texts: letters within words were printed in a mixture of capitals and lowercases, some children saw three print sizes, texts were illustrated, and exercises were perceptually challenging (for example, finding five letters embedded in drawings; looking at richly illustrated packs of letter cards). In contrast, tutoring for children with left hemisphere weaknesses used one common typeface and no illustrations, and instead highlighted the verbal features of the reading task: blanks had to be completed with words that rhymed with a preceding word, exercises required finding the one in four words that did not fit phonetically, and vocabulary comprehension was stressed. Bakker and Vinke found that perceptual stimulation arrested the continued strengthening of left hemisphere electroencephalograms in children with right hemisphere weaknesses, and verbal stimulation was associated with reading gains in children with left hemisphere weaknesses. In addition, strong reading and spelling gains were apparent in children whose weaker right hemispheres were directly stimulated through visual half-field techniques. Certainly this research is provocative. It highlights the notion that although we may introduce new concepts through stronger modalities, it is important to try to strengthen the weaker information-processing skills as well.

Matching Tasks to Students' Cognitive Styles. Many students have difficulty breaking away from their preferred way of perceiving their environments. McKenney and Keen's (1976) study, for example, found that three-fourths of subjects used one problem-solving style on all types of problems. Only one-fourth switched styles to more appropriately match task requirements (in Ewing, 1977).

Because individuals have difficulty altering their conceptual styles, learning can be facilitated when teachers alter their materials and methods to be more congruent with student cognitive styles. For example, it has been found that students with learning disabilities who attributed success to their own efforts benefited more when encouraged to study spelling words any way they wished or to self-correct context clue exercises. Conversely, students who attributed success to external factors benefited more when the teacher told them precisely how to study the spelling words ("Trace each word; write it three times") or specifically pointed out and corrected their reading errors (Bendell, Tollefson, & Fine, 1980; Pascarella & Pflaum, 1981).

In another study, Maier (1980) matched a story comprehension task to the inefficient, inactive learning styles of fourth graders with language and learning disabilities. One-third of the way through the story she told the children, "Now you will hear the problem." Two-thirds of the way through she told them, "Now you will hear how he solved the problem." Given this organization and focus, the experimental group was able to recall and infer better than students not given this structure. Similarly, Dyck and Sundbye (1988) found that story comprehension improved when inference questions guided children to elaborate at the end of each episode of a story, or when elaborations were added to the text. For students with simultaneous processing preferences, Carnine (1989) found that learning was facilitated when they were made aware of how parts related to the whole, as in learning Central American countries better when presented on a map rather than as individual countries, or when they learned math facts as a sequence (6 + 1 = 7, 6 + 2 = 8, 6 + 3 = 9) rather than individually.

A number of researchers have explored ways of matching task attributes to the cognitive styles of impulsive or reflective and low or high conceptual level learners. The teacher's modeling of appropriate behaviors is particularly important for these students. Yando and Kagan (1968), for example, found that students who were taught by reflective teachers showed greater increases in reflective style than did those who were taught by impulsive teachers. Similarly, Scott and Sigel (1965, in Coop & Sigel, 1971) taught fifteen science concepts to children in grades four, five, and six. Half the children were taught by an inquiry method and half by a conventional direct approach. On a cognitive style test at the end of the school term, children tended to respond in the same style as they had been instructed. Coop and Sigel suggest that because a student may not be able to break away from his or her preferred mode of perceiving a situation, teachers should explain content from a perceptual framework that accommodates the student's style, while at the same time being alert that their own styles provide appropriate models.

Impulsive and Reflective Learners. Youngsters with impulsive conceptual styles do not stop to reflect about alternative answers. This tendency in part is due to their global, rather than detail-oriented, approach to tasks. Glancing at a word or getting the gist of a story takes them less time than attending to each of the parts.

Impulsive students commonly do not double-check their work. They ignore details, write before thinking and planning, leave off word endings, do not organize compositions, copy sloppily from the board, and do not self-correct. On the

other hand, they might be able to summarize the main idea of a passage quickly, remember general concepts very well, and overview situations with a great deal of insight. Because our curricula usually call for detail analysis, the true capabilities of the impulsive student may not be tapped much of the time.

Whenever possible, tasks must be modified to use these students' preferred style of problem solving and minimize the style's interfering effects. For example, when teaching word-attack skills, the teacher might tell the impulsive second grader the whole word and afterwards ask the student to describe why the parts combine to sound as they do, rather than the other way around; working from the parts to the whole would be difficult for the impulsive child. The teacher might approach the rules for regrouping in multiplication by pasting a number fact chart and a list of calculation steps on the fourth grader's desk. The child would then use this as a reference for organizing problem solving. Attention to details during reading might be facilitated by having the child skim pictures and the text's main ideas to guess the details; the child then reads the passage to see whether he or she was on target. Pictures might be covered over on a page so that the student is forced to attend to the individual words to derive meaning. The child also might correct his or her own papers, underline word endings, and outline stories to help adapt attention to the more detail-oriented strategy that schools emphasize.

Teaching impulsive students specific strategies for executing school tasks, and why and when these are important, has been very helpful in promoting their success (Kurtz & Borkowski, 1987). Moreover, Yap and Peters (1985) suggest that we should not hesitate to give impulsive students honest feedback when they are doing poorly; because impulsive students are naturally less attuned to errors, this feedback will increase both their effort and success.

The schools' bias in favor of the reflective student does not mean that the reflective student always has an easy time of it. The reflective style means taking longer to discover main points. The student's overly analytic approach may induce him or her to try to learn every detail in a textbook, which is overwhelming and counterproductive when only understanding of major points is expected. These students get bogged down with text vocabulary, up to 80 percent of which is unimportant and used only on the page where it is introduced (Bloom, 1976). Reflectivity also is a clear disadvantage on timed tests when students spend too much time pondering the ramifications of every multiple-choice question. The reflective student might be at a further disadvantage on drills and games that call for more rapid information processing (Coop & Sigel, 1971). For this type of student, explicit directions regarding which concepts and vocabulary to study, group study sessions that help highlight the most important information, outlines during lectures that guide attention to relationships between themes and topics, instruction in a note-taking method that organizes details into broader categories, written composition formats that emphasize main ideas and clincher sentences, and extended time on tests can be beneficial.

Low and High Conceptual Level Learners.   Many students with learning disabilities are low conceptual level learners. During instruction, they prefer highly structured tasks and explicit teacher directions. They have difficulty generating new concepts on their own and thinking of alternative solutions to problems. For these youngsters, directly teaching pertinent facts and key concepts, giving rules before instead of after examples, and using lecture rather than discovery methods match their styles and promote more rapid learning. They profit best when their attention is specifically directed to what's important, when they are instructed to repeat facts or ideas in their own words, when they are given immediate feedback, and when practice is made very systematic. Hunt's (1974) work suggests that these methods may be just what the problem learner needs to promote greater integration of information and generalization. When, instead of asking children "What do you think?," teachers expand their students' thinking by actually giving them more alternatives to think about and guiding them through structured question-

ing, acquisition of information is no longer left to chance. In effect, teachers are increasing their students' conceptual flexibility by prompting more thoughts with which to reason more intelligently.

All too often, instead of instructing students in the precise criteria to be learned, teachers expect them to assimilate information on their own. Marc is a good example. Marc is a bright twelve year old who attends a private school with other bright youngsters. His reading, math, and comprehension skills are excellent. His spelling, however, is terrible. Marc's teachers asked his parents to have him evaluated for a learning disability. Trial teaching approaches were used during the evaluation, and no difficulty with learning to spell either phonetic or nonphonetic words could be found. Marc learned well with typical teaching methods and was even able to generalize spelling forms learned on one word to new words (such as commercial to superficial). When these findings were shared with his teachers, they commented, "But we never teach spelling as a subject; these children just pick it up." Well, this student did "soak up" most information but not spelling. Marc needed directed teaching in spelling all along.

Many studies have supported the effectiveness of teacher-directed instruction with well-sequenced, structured materials and high levels of student involvement (White, 1988). This involves beginning a lesson with a statement of goals and a short review of relevant information from previous lessons, presenting material in short steps with practice after each step, giving clear and detailed instructions and explanations, asking questions to check for understanding and obtain feedback, and guiding practice with explicit instruction (Rosenshine, 1986). Guiding the student's attention to essential parts of the task, teaching appropriate strategies, allaying the student's frustration, questioning to deepen comprehension, and modeling strategic processing such as shifting to a new approach when another hasn't worked are important. The analogy of the teacher as offering the necessary "scaffolding" to help the student progress to the next higher level of competence has become an important concept in learning disabilities. As the student becomes more independent, the teacher's "scaffolding" is gradually pulled away.

Applying the careful sequencing and structure of direct instruction, teacher modeling, and "think alouds" to math problem solving has helped students with learning disabilities identify the correct operations for solving math word problems (Case, Harris, & Graham, 1992; Wilson & Sindelar, 1991). Likewise, Gold and Fleisher (1986) found comprehension to be facilitated when passages were organized deductively (main idea is stated in the first sentence) rather than inductively (main idea is stated at the end or implied). In one study, when a computerized study guide provided the sequence of main ideas in a chapter, more learning occurred than from independent note taking (Horton et al., 1989). In another investigation, study guides that referred middle and high school students to the specific page and paragraph in the text where the answer could be found improved students' responses to factual questions (Horton, Lovitt, & Christensen, 1991). Some students with learning disabilities have been found to profit best when, after a reading error, the teacher simply supplies the correct word rather than having the child sound out the word (Rose, McEntire, & Dowdy, 1982). Critical reasoning training too (for example, just because two things happen together doesn't mean that one causes the other; just because someone who is important says something is good or bad doesn't mean it's right) has been found to transfer better to novel tasks when teachers specifically state the rules and follow these with examples than when they simply lead a discussion and rely on workbook exercises (Darch & Kameenui, 1987).

Explicit direction from the teacher regarding the purpose for reading, which content to focus on, and how one will be tested helps all students' recall, but especially those with learning disabilities (Wong, Wong, & LeMare, 1982). Hansen and Pearson (1983) found that poor readers significantly improved their ability to answer inference questions when specifically made aware of the importance of comparing the new information with what they already knew, and

when a prereading discussion was used to highlight similar events in the students' lives. Of more interest, however, is the finding that this technique actually hampered good readers' acquisition of literal knowledge.

Kintsch (1994) summarizes research indicating that, when students have little background knowledge about the information they will be reading, the text needs to be as explicit and coherent as possible and offer full explanations. The good learner, on the other hand, benefits when the text leaves out explanations and connecting inferences; this forces the student to read more actively, fill in the reasoning gaps, engage in elaborating on the text's knowledge, and ultimately to learn more. Therefore, it is important for teachers to be sensitive to when more information is needed, and when leaving the student to figure something out on his or her own would be more helpful.

Direct instruction will be critical for the majority of students with learning disabilities. We must be very careful not to expect students to learn information incidentally or to generate their own strategies, unless they are quite ready to do so. When Suzie struggles to create a mnemonic for the thirteen colonies, make one up for her. When Rufus can't get the point of a chemistry experiment and is disorganized throughout, give him a list of what he should expect to see at every step and why. Instruction that gives these students direction on what to attend to and guides them in thinking about information certainly will give them more options with which to think more intelligently. Active teacher questioning and offering of clues can improve students' recall beyond that when simply given the information, because the students are guided to generate more meaningful conclusions and to deepen their understandings through uncovering relationships between new and prior information (Scruggs & Mastropieri, 1993).

Fortunately, as students get older they do become able to operate at higher levels of conceptual complexity, reflectivity, and independence. Therefore, teachers need to be ready to reduce their support to students when appropriate, for example, encouraging them to create their own mnemonics, study strategies, and study schedules and then inviting the teacher's feedback.

Building Generalization into Tasks. When Marc was asked if he would remember to apply the new spelling words he had learned to his English compositions, he responded "No." Students with learning disabilities have predictable problems automatically transferring learned knowledge, strategies, social skills, and behaviors to new situations (Ayllon & Roberts, 1974; Darch & Carnine, 1986; DuPaul & Eckert, 1994; Mastropieri et al., 1992; Montague, 1992; Scruggs & Mastropieri, 1990). With respect to strategy use, for example, although Griffey, Zigmond, and Leinhardt (1988) found that the reading comprehension of poor readers improved with self-questioning techniques, this only happened when students were specifically reminded to use these strategies. Clearly, any instruction is useful to students only if it will be applied when needed in new situations, and teachers are responsible for making sure that this happens.

To better understand the kind of reminders that everyone uses to cue generalization of knowledge, recall an experience taking a French, or any other, final exam in a strange (chemistry) lecture hall. Did you do poorly and then blame it on the room? If so, your blaming may have been justified. After all, the room was not filled with "French cues" that would facilitate recall. You might have looked around the room during the exam, hoping to reconstruct the teacher's voice as she conjugated the verb *être* on the blackboard. But it is hard to imagine this when all you see are chemistry molecules and formulas. With insufficient environmental cuing, you may not have been able to recover from memory what you knew you had put there. This same kind of stimulus interference occurs with the learning disabled. Therefore, it is important for the teacher to think of ways to help students generalize academic objectives, whether it be transferring headings taught in English class to math assignments, or applying an operation learned in math class when at the grocery store.

Generalization is hard for students with learning disabilities because it involves recognizing the sameness between a new situation and the familiar task with which a particular strategy, piece of information, or behavior had been useful. It also involves reformulating the original strategy, information, or behavior so that it is appropriate in the new situation. The more automatic this transfer becomes, the more capacity remains for higher-order analysis, planning, and monitoring of the work at hand (Gelzheiser, Shepherd, & Wozniak, 1986).

Table 9–3 presents several ways in which research suggests that generalization might be enhanced. Metacognitive strategies also can be very helpful in promoting generalization. In contrast to direct instruction, in which the teacher's goal is to explicitly draw the student's attention to important content, to direct the student to repeat the information, and to provide feedback and structured practice, metacognitive instruction helps the student learn how to learn on his or her own: to actively transform new information into something concrete and familiar; to relate the new information to something already known; to retrieve the new information by systematically searching this richer meaning base; to choose strategies because one knows why and when each can be helpful. When teachers give explicit metacognitive strategy instruction, explain when, where, and how to use these strategies, why each step is important, and how to modify strategies as needed, generalization of strategic approaches to new situations has increased (Chan, 1991; Kurtz & Borkowski, 1987).

Checklists on which students self-monitor their behavior (for example, "Did I write a neat paper, volunteer to answer a question during science, hand in math homework when it is due"?) also can be particularly helpful in facilitating transfer (Anderson-Inman, 1986). Students record the use of a strategy on their checklist and hand the checklist in with the assignment. The teacher's role is to remind students to use the strategy, to identify specific contexts in which the strategy could be applied, to determine the helpfulness of the strategy in attaining goals, and to point out cues that will help trigger use of the strategy (Deshler & Schumaker, 1986). Students brainstorm ways to adapt

Table 9–3   Approaches that increase generalization of learning

- Teachers should focus on conceptual models such as advance organizers that forecast what is to be learned and encourage students to meaningfully relate the forthcoming information to information that is already known.
- Teachers should teach fewer principles, but broadly develop these principles' general applications, rather than teaching more principles with fewer applications.
- Teachers should use many examples to deepen the potential application of the skills being learned. Examples should progress from easiest to most difficult.
- Problem-solving strategies should be taught and integrated within the regular curriculum. Teacher-guided exercises should help students reflect on why the strategies were helpful and where else they could be applied.
- Students should be taught to cue teachers when the students use appropriate task strategies, so that they can benefit from reinforcement.
- Teachers should use consistency and structure in initial teaching but then vary formats, procedures, and examples to promote generalization.
- The same information should be instructed by many people, in as many settings and conditions as possible.
- Teachers initially should use a consistent schedule to reinforce generalization but then change to delayed and intermittent reinforcement, so that the tendency to generalize independently is strengthened.
- Students should be taught to use verbal mediation to help them generalize.
- Students should be instructed to self-report generalization and to apply self-recording and self-reinforcement techniques.
- Information should be taught in connection with naturally occurring stimuli (peers, physical stimuli) and natural settings so that less generalization needs to occur. The teacher should build the connection between the standard curriculum and how this content is important to everyday life.

Sources: Adapted from Cronin, M. E. (1996). Life Skills curricula for students with learning disabilities: A review of the literature. *Journal of Learning Disabilities, 29,* 53–68; Niedelman, M. (1991). Problem solving and transfer. *Journal of Learning Disabilities, 24,* 322–329; Stokes, T. F., and Baer, D. M. (1977). An implicit technology of generalization. *Journal of Applied Behavior Analysis, 10,* 349–367. Wong, B. Y. L. (1994). Instructional parameters promoting transfer of learning strategies in students with learning disabilities. *Learning Disabilities Quarterly, 17,* 110–120.

the strategies and then report back regarding their successes.

Researchers have emphasized that solid, well-understood knowledge is a necessary support for higher-level problem solving and transfer. Deepening one's understanding of basic information and how it can be applied is of special importance to students with learning disabilities. This is because the recall difficulties of some students who are learning disabled may relate to a lack of "richness of meaning" when information is being stored in the first place (Brainerd, Kingma, & Howe, 1986; Kail & Leonard, 1986). Consider Alex, who met Dede at a school dance. If Alex had known more about Dede (for example, her sports interests, where she goes to high school, her favorite music, her family, her tough school subjects), then perhaps he would have remembered her name when he bumped into her two weeks later at the movies. In other words, the more associations we can offer students that will elaborate an idea or piece of information, the more likely the student will be to remember it in a new situation. Likewise, the more we help students think of ways to retrieve the information (visualize the setting where you learned it, focus on the first sound of the word, recall some piece of information linked to it), the more accessible this information will be when needed in new situations.

Combinations of these techniques have succeeded in helping students generalize computational skills, correct spellings, main idea detection strategies in science and social studies, reading comprehension techniques, social skills, and more, from special education to the regular classroom and from the classroom to beyond the school (Anderson-Inman, 1986; Blankenship & Baumgartner, 1982; Clement-Heist, Siegel, & Gaylord-Ross, 1992; Jenkins et al., 1987; Palincsar & Brown, 1984; Wong et al., 1986). Some students merely require frequent reminders to generalize the skills taught in one setting to a similar task in a different setting. Other students with learning disabilities, however, require months of systematic teaching and transfer procedures.

Defining and Coordinating Intervention Roles

The heterogeneous needs of students with learning disabilities require expertise from many different professionals. However, the involvement of so many individuals has resulted in some difficulty with role definition. In addition to school personnel, medical specialists play an important role in preventing or alleviating disease processes that can interfere with learning. The family, of course, carries major responsibility for their child's growth and development. The family is the primary monitor and advocate for school interventions and the primary teacher and model for children's achievements, attitudes, and behaviors.

School-Based Personnel

The general education teacher, LD specialist, reading and math specialist, speech-language pathologist, transition specialist, and school psychologist, among others, have expertise that can serve the learning disabled. Their efforts benefit these students during the assessment, planning, and intervention process. Unfortunately, the overlapping roles of all these professionals can confuse decisions about who is responsible for teaching what, often leading to duplication of services and role conflicts.

Some experts have suggested that schools should permit those with the greatest competencies in a specific area to deal with those problems, regardless of their professional titles (Abrams, 1976; Larsen, 1976; Lieberman, 1980b). At the elementary school level, for example, a school counselor may be the most appropriate individual to counsel some children, while the physical education teacher's rapport may be more appropriate with other children. It makes sense that the high school general education teacher, who knows the most about his or her subject matter, should take responsibility for teaching this content to the student with learning disabilities. In contrast, the special education teacher, who knows more about basic reading, math, spelling, writing, and study skill instruction, should take responsibility for these aspects of the student's education. Because aides and volunteers are not trained in these domains, they should be used to free the professional staff to work with students who require the greatest instructional expertise. With over 80,000 paraprofessionals involved with disabled students in the public schools, intensified preservice and inservice training programs are necessary in order to help these individuals acquire the essential skills for working with students who have learning disabilities (McKenzie & Houk, 1986).

As in the teaching process, during the assessment phase as well team members should be able to shift roles flexibly, depending on the questions being asked about a student and the specialists' area of expertise. By flexibly matching staff competencies to student needs, we can use the variety of expertise in our schools to our students' best advantage.

The General Education Teacher. The general education teacher has primary responsibility for most students with learning disabilities; this is where, in 1995–96, 81 percent of these youngsters spent 40 percent or more of their school day (U.S. Department of Education, 1997). The regular class teacher is responsible for conferring with prereferral teams when a problem is noticed, and attempting program modifications in the classroom. If these modifications are not successful, the teacher refers these children for evaluation, and the teacher joins in the assessment process.

The regular class teacher's instructional responsibilities to a student with learning disabilities are detailed by the IEP. The regular class teacher, however, often merely provides information to the IEP process on current student performance rather than becoming actively involved in formulating the instructional goals (Pugach, 1982). This is unfortunate in that general education teachers have considerable knowledge about the student with learning disabilities, given that they are the ones who spend the most instructional time with these students. Also, they are the ones who must be committed to carrying out the goals of the IEP.

Although great responsibility for the learning disabled is placed on general education teachers, their day to day responsibilities preclude sufficient time for planning of special programs; even if sufficient time were available, the university curriculum often has not prepared these teachers for such planning. In fact, a 1987 survey of state departments of education found that only twenty-nine states required elementary education teachers to take any coursework in reading, usually only two courses; no state required a course in teaching writing (Nolen, McCutchen, & Berninger, 1990). Likewise, in a survey of 440 teachers, Lyon, Vaasen, and Toomey (1989) found that about 80 to 90 percent of respondents had no university experiences geared toward dealing with cultural diversity among students.

To help general education teachers deal with a wider array of abilities and learning styles in their classrooms, university teacher-preparation programs are increasingly requiring special education and multicultural coursework of their students. To increase the fund of content area knowledge on which these teachers can draw in their teaching, universities also are requiring increased intensity in subject matter studies. Reports calling for educational reform agree that universities must institute higher standards in teacher education and demand greater teaching aptitude from their graduates. School districts in recent years have intensified inservice education efforts as well, to help teachers understand the unique needs of students with learning disabilities, how to adapt teaching methods and materials appropriately and creatively, and how to adapt programming to the increasing cultural diversity in today's classrooms. Generally, giving a single lecture on how to teach learning strategies or recommending a book will be insufficient to help a teacher effectively implement a new program. Extensive staff training, on the other hand, especially when hands on and practical, results in excellent gains (Deshler & Schumaker, 1986). More often than not, however, general education teachers continue to feel that they lack sufficient knowledge or skills to plan for and instruct the learning disabled; they rely heavily on the learning disabilities teacher instead of adapting instruction on their own (Vaughn & Schumm, 1995).

The Learning Disabilities Specialist. The LD specialist is expected to be skilled in classroom observation, interviewing, assessment, specialized teaching, consulting and teaming with other professionals, and nurturing positive attitudes among school personnel toward students with learning disabilities. Students with learning disabilities who are placed in general education classes benefit from the LD specialist's consultation with the regular class teacher, "push-in" services provided in the regular classroom, or services provided in a resource room for one or more periods each day. Only 19 percent of students who are learning disabled are taught by LD teachers full-time in special classes, schools, hospitals, or at home (U.S. Department of Education, 1997).

LD teachers generally remediate basic skill weaknesses, teach learning strategies, and provide tutorial help in classroom subjects. In many states LD teachers teach their own special sections of secondary content area classes (McKenzie, 1991). The techniques these teachers use are intended to be special, not just a repetition of regular class instruction. After all, students are identified as learning disabled because they require a quality and intensity of instruction that differs from the instruction that benefits the typical student. Unfortunately, classroom observations often have been disappointing in that special educators' instructional adaptations frequently are not special; they merely mimic what already is being done in the regular classroom (Haynes & Jenkins, 1986). Zigmond (1990), for example, reports an observational study of high school resource rooms in which 85 percent of the time students were engaged in independent seatwork and receiving little instruction.

LD specialists also assess students and provide inservice training to the school staff. Given the large numbers of youngsters with learning disabilities being educated in regular classes, the LD teacher's consultation role is of prime importance. However, the need to help students pass minimum competency tests, the daily academic pressures, the lack of scheduled planning periods, and the reluctance of general educators to take responsibility for the student with special needs often prevent spending sufficient time in consultation (Idol-Maestas & Ritter, 1985; Voltz, Elliott, & Cobb, 1994). In those districts where consulting teachers have conferred for several years with classroom teachers, significant increases in the progress of students with disabilities have been apparent (Knight et al., 1981). These students' gains appear to reflect both the knowledge acquired by the general education teacher from the consultant and the teacher's increased involvement in the youngster's referral, assessment, curriculum development, implementation of recommendations, and evaluation of progress.

Despite consultation from LD teachers, general educators are not becoming more willing or able to accommodate the exceptional learner at a fast enough pace (Zigmond, 1996), and LD teachers are picking up the slack by tutoring students in their regular classwork. One national survey reported that 27 percent of LD teachers at the junior high school level and 47 percent at the senior high level spent most of their time engaged in subject matter tutoring (Wells et al., 1983). Although tutoring is certainly called for, other personnel, or even peer tutors, are capable of serving this function as well or better than the LD teacher. After all, the LD teacher is not an expert in content areas and does not have sufficient time to offer more than cursory help to students who

must meet daily, pressing classroom demands. Zentall and Ferkis (1993), for example, report that special education teachers often lack confidence in their math knowledge and therefore give less attention to this subject area.

The more LD teachers tutor, the less time they can invest in doing what they are most qualified to do—remediate the weaknesses (for example, reading, math, written expression, learning strategies) that make the tutoring necessary in the first place. Many LD teachers try to do both by addressing the basics within the context of the classroom content. This is entirely appropriate as long as the goal is clear—assisting basic learning abilities more so than teaching of content. Gains in basic learning skills have more potential benefits than learning one piece of content. Because some states are requiring special education teachers to complete an undergraduate content area major or to become certified in regular education as well, new teachers are in a better position to integrate specialized basic instruction with support in content area subject matter.

LD teachers express frustration about the unrealistic expectations placed on them, inadequate support systems, inadequate accommodations for students with learning disabilities in the regular classroom, and insufficient time to instruct students intensively (Houck, Geller, & Engelhard, 1988). They also are frustrated that the more they tutor, the more dependent students become on them and the less initiative general education teachers take to deal with individual differences in their classrooms.

Clearly, because LD teachers address a broad spectrum of academic and social needs, they require broad training. Nevertheless, very few states specifically require course work pertaining to remedial reading, learning theory, program planning, speech/language development and disorders, math remediation, or consultation (Carpenter, 1985; Idol & West, 1987; Leigh & Patton, 1986). Lack of preparation is apparent in the area of curriculum development as well (Sands, Adams, & Stout, 1995). Assessment skills also tend to be underdeveloped. Shepard and Smith (1983) found that the majority of clinicians sampled in Colorado used technically inadequate instruments, were unaware of this inadequacy, did not understand the statistics for test interpretation, did not apply their clinical judgment to validate test results, and, more often than not, inappropriately identified students as learning disabled. These findings have been replicated a number of times (Bennett & Shepherd, 1982; Davis & Shepard, 1983).

Some experts believe that special educators should be given the opportunity to teach up and down the regular grades in order to develop a sense of how normal development proceeds, which academic objectives are paramount at different ages, how the patterns of students with learning disabilities differ, and which curriculum goals would be the most important. To develop more uniform LD teacher training, certification standards, criteria for employment, and standards for monitoring professional practices, in 1992 the Council for Exceptional Children's Division for Learning Disabilities (DLD) published *The DLD Competencies for Teachers of Students with Learning Disabilities.*

The Reading and Math Specialists. The reading and math teachers engage in remediation and also help to organize and evaluate general education's reading and math programs. Because their remedial role overlaps the LD teacher's role, these specialists have had difficulty demarcating their respective teaching domains.

The LD specialist often has an advantage over the reading or math teacher in acquiring jobs servicing youngsters with learning disabilities because IDEA requires that a student who is learning disabled receive services from a certified special education teacher. The LD teacher has a special education degree, but the reading or math teacher usually does not. Because the reading and math teachers are not legally required to teach the learning disabled, they frequently end up working primarily with unidentified students who are less severe underachievers. They naturally are puzzled by the inconsistency in a law that was designed to provide greater educational opportunities for the disabled but that stipulates that services be provided by special education teachers who may have less expertise in a specific area of remediation.

The Speech-Language Pathologist. The speech-language pathologist (communicative disorders specialist) is trained to evaluate and work with students who have articulation, voice, fluency (stuttering), or language development disorders. As we have noted, many students' learning disabilities relate to difficulties in these areas. Therefore, the speech-language pathologist plays an important role in targeting emergent literacy skills in young children, such as comprehension and rhyming, before these children even experience learning difficulties in school. Upon school entry, the speech-language pathologist's role is critical in supporting the linguistic growth that can accelerate learning and social adjustment.

The speech pathologist also is faced with a role definition conflict with the LD specialist. For example, experts in both speech pathology and learning disabilities urge their respective colleagues to engage in phonemic awareness training in order to increase reading readiness (Blachman, 1991, 1993; Catts, 1991). In addition, because of state caseload requirements that can number as many as fifty to ninety pupils weekly, the speech pathologist often is precluded from offering daily therapy to students with learning disabilities who could benefit from such help. As a result, language development instruction often falls to the LD teacher who has a more reasonable caseload, usually of twenty to twenty-five students. Universities and state certification regulations are addressing the need to increase LD coursework on the part of speech-language pathology students and reading and math specialists so that they will be prepared to better meet the needs of the learning disabled.

The School Psychologist. The school psychologist traditionally provides assessment and counseling to students and consultation to the classroom teacher. IDEA states that the school psychologist must be involved in the decision making of the multidisciplinary group that determines the presence of a handicapping condition but need not actually conduct the LD assessment. Because the school psychologist is well versed in normal child development, handicapping conditions, and the physical, organizational, and human aspects of a school environment that affect learning and behavior, the student with learning disabilities can benefit directly and indirectly from the psychologist's assessments, psychological services, teacher consultation, inservice training, and program efficacy research.

The Vocational Educator.   As youngsters with learning disabilities reach secondary school age, they need to look toward the future. Because of their learning difficulties, many students do not choose to continue with formal education after high school. For these individuals, high school vocational education offers invaluable opportunities for skill development, career exploration, and training in how to get along on a job. Often employment prior to graduation is an excellent predictor of later vocational success (Rusch & Phelps, 1987). Vocational educators, to be successful, require consultation from special educators because they have little preparation for working with students with special needs, and often they have neither college nor education backgrounds. Not surprisingly, observations in their classes find little individualization. The teaching methods are very much like those in the academic classrooms in which the students have failed (seatwork, lecture, large-group instruction, minimal supervision, textbooks, and workbooks) (Evers, 1996).

It is critical to attend not only to the vocational adjustment of students with learning disabilities but also to their independent living, leisure, and social adjustment needs. This necessitates that school personnel become active change agents in broader contexts (family, industry, legislation) so that, on leaving high school, sufficient personal and community supports exist to promote the self-sufficiency and satisfaction of the young adult with learning disabilities. The IEP's transition plan is designed to assist in this process.

Other Specialists.   The school's audiologist evaluates whether hearing or auditory-processing difficulties may be contributing to the problems of a youngster with learning disabilities and intervenes accordingly. The audiologist's findings can guide a teacher in modifying instructional approaches and seating arrangements. The occupational therapist, physical therapist, and adaptive physical education teacher also are invaluable resources for students with persistent coordination and self-help difficulties.

The social worker helps deal with family issues that can have an impact on learning, and the services of the rehabilitation counselor are available to help students make the transition to the adult world of work and independent living. Finally, the school's guidance and administrative personnel not only help establish the organizational framework for service delivery but also provide important personal support to students and teachers.

Medical Specialists

IDEA mandates that any medical factors relevant to a handicapping condition must be explored and treated by appropriate medical personnel. These include the ophthalmologist and optometrist, who help students use their eyes more comfortably; the allergist, who may alleviate physical conditions that distract a student from learning; the endocrinologist, who treats glandular disorders; the geneticist, who evaluates inherited learning patterns; the otologist, who diagnoses and treats hearing disorders; and others. The pediatrician and the neurologist are the most frequently consulted when learning disabilities are suspected.

The Pediatrician.   The pediatrician is one of the first professionals to see a child after birth and the individual who will track a child's development into adolescence. The pediatrician attends to conditions that can affect learning such as vision or hearing disorders, malnutrition, and endocrine or metabolic disorders. It is natural for parents to turn to the pediatrician for advice regarding their children's physical needs, academic and behavioral concerns, and advice regarding the question of medication for attention deficits and hyperactivity. Therefore, pediatricians should not shy away from dealing with the child's functional development. Pediatricians have a responsibility to communicate their findings to educators, to encourage families to pursue assessment and special teaching programs, and to be knowledgeable about the services available in the community.

Recognizing that parents will consult physicians on educational issues, medical schools commonly offer courses and clinical rotations relevant to assessment and treatment of learning and behavior problems. Continuing education programs for practicing physicians also frequently offer seminars on the learning disabled and attention deficit hyperactivity disorder.

The Neurologist. The neurologist is frequently called on when a student has a learning problem. Although not enough is known yet about brain-behavior relationships to have the neurological information suggest more than very general educational directions, the neurologist can detect and treat ongoing neurological disease and seizure disorders, explore the family history of learning disorders, prescribe medication for attention deficits and hyperactivity, and look for signs of brain injury. The neurologist's job is complicated because the child's nervous system is still developing, and it is sometimes difficult to discriminate slow development from actual damage to the nervous system. In addition, neurological abnormalities are so common among both good and poor learners that it is difficult to ascertain whether any abnormalities that are found are in fact related to the learning problems. Advances in techniques for studying brain structure, function, and neurochemistry forecast a more diagnostically and instructionally relevant role for the neurologist in the future.

The Family

Academic and social learning is a lifelong process that can be facilitated or impeded by familial circumstances. The family system bears the major responsibility for positive interventions and influences on a child's life. For this reason, IDEA encourages parental involvement in identification, placement, and programming decisions. Over the years, government funds have been provided to large numbers of parents to receive training pertinent to their children's disabilities.

As professionals begin to approach learning disabilities from a more ecological perspective, they are more often viewing these students' problems as residing within a malfunctioning system rather than within the individual alone. Because the family network strongly shapes a youngster's attitudes and habits, problem resolution becomes the responsibility of the whole family and not just the child. The child will change as the family changes. Chapter 11 is devoted to the critical role that the family plays as model, advocate, and teacher in a student's life.

Developing Partnerships between Special and General Education

For students with learning disabilities to benefit maximally from the talents of the various school professionals, increasing partnerships between special and general education need to be a school-wide priority. In 1986, Madeleine Will, assistant secretary for the Office of Special Education and Rehabilitative Services, U.S. Department of Education, called for stronger partnerships to be built between special and general education, and for services to be determined on the basis of a student's educational needs rather than disability category. Will reasoned that if we could build greater sensitivity to special needs within the regular classroom, the stigmatization of the disabled would decline and achievement expectations would increase as students with disabilities become more included in the regular classroom. Prevention of failure would be the focus rather than attention to students only after failure has set in. Will emphasized that this proposal "does not mean the consolidation of special education into regular education" (p. 415). Her proposal has become known as the *Regular Education Initiative*.

With the regular education initiative serving as the catalyst, many experts proceeded to propose that, instead of just lowering barriers between special and general education, special education should merge with regular education into a unified service delivery system. With flexible curricula and grouping of pupils, it was believed that most instruction could be delivered to heterogeneous groups of students within the context of the regular classroom.

These experts argued that a merger of special and general education would avoid several issues that currently plague special education:

overidentification and misidentification of students (with greater sensitivity and appropriate services available in the regular classroom context, labels would no longer be necessary); exclusion of some students from general education; the increasing need for alternative special education placements; poor coordination and sharing of programing among regular and special educators; regular educators being excused from trying to work more effectively with a wider range of students; overly bureaucratic approaches to special education; escalating costs due to the operation of two separate systems; and the enormous time spent testing for identification purposes which, in a merger, could be reallocated to teaching (Hagerty & Abramson, 1987; McKinney & Hocutt, 1988; Pugach, 1987; Reschly, 1987a; Reynolds, Wang, & Walberg, 1987; Shepard, 1987; Stainback & Stainback, 1984). Stainback and Stainback (1984) offer an eloquent argument for the merger of the regular and special education systems:

While labels have created a wellspring of pity and sympathy that has resulted in strong federal and state support for special education (Deno, 1970), no student should have to be categorized, labeled, and pitied in order to receive a free and appropriate education. All students should be entitled to a free and appropriate education without any student being subjected to the de-individualizing and stereotyping impact of a pity-evoking label. . . . The issue is not whether there are differences among students. There obviously are differences, even extreme differences. It is also clear that because of these differences some students may need adaptations or modifications in their educational experiences. However, this should not be used as a justification to label, segregate, or maintain a dual system of education. With careful planning, it should be possible to meet the unique needs of all students within one unified system of education—a system that does not deny differences, but rather a system that recognizes and accommodates for differences. (pp. 108–109)

Many educators believe that the Stainbacks' proposal is premature. "Regular education has a history of being reluctant to meet the needs of all students. Agreeing with them [the Stainbacks] about the nature of the beast, I do not believe it is time to place our handicapped children in the cage with it" (Mesinger, 1985, p. 511). Lieberman (1985) sums up many educators' concerns about the Stainbacks' proposal. "Of course they are right; but being right and being real are very different (p. 513). . . . Spouses who maintain separate strong identities, while choosing to be married, are probably less at risk for divorce. . . . A separate identity for special education must be maintained in order for the marriage to occur and succeed" (p. 516). The Stainbacks (1985) respond that general educators are more disposed to individualization than in the past. The proposed merger represents a "long needed reunion of a common family unit that has been broken apart by misunderstandings (p. 518). . . . a major goal for educators should be to make 'what is right, real' " (p. 520).

The Council for Exceptional Children's Division for Learning Disabilities (DLD) published a response to the Regular Education Initiative in May of 1986. While commending the recommendation for more cooperative planning between regular and special education, DLD expressed concern that the Regular Education Initiative was not based on research comparing various models for serving the broad range of students with learning difficulties.

We emphasize . . . [that learning disabled] pupils frequently require specialized services and techniques which go beyond the instructional practices available within regular class settings. The assumption that all pupils can be served well within regular programs is inconsistent with achievement evidence nationally. (p. ii)

The Learning Disabilities Association of America (1993) issued a statement sharing similar concerns, as did the National Joint Committee on Learning Disabilities (1992): "The desire to include all students within regular education should not overshadow the fact that some students with learning disabilities need to learn different content in different ways" (p. 3).

The Council for Learning Disabilities Position Statement (1993) is similar in tone: "The Council supports the education of students with learning disabilities in general education classrooms *when deemed appropriate* by the Individual Education Program (IEP) team. . . . One policy that the Council cannot support is the indiscriminate full-time placement of ALL students with learning disabilities in the regular classroom. . . ." The statement goes on to share the Council's grave concern about any policy that dictates class placement without evaluating each student's programming on an individual basis. Many professionals agree that the general education classroom placement is not always the preferred option for all students because many regular class teachers tend not to individualize instruction for the student with learning disabilities (Baker & Zigmond, 1990; Jenkins & Pious, 1991; Vaughn & Schumm, 1995). In fact, in 1993 the American Federation of Teachers called for a moratorium on inclusion until the effects on all students can be assessed and the responsibilities of general education teachers delineated.

The move toward increased excellence and accountability in general education presents another obstacle to implementation of the Regular Education Initiative. Shepard (1987) noted, "Brave talk about teachers learning to adapt to a wider range of differences is unrealistic when the sanctions for failing to teach or failing to learn are serious" (p. 329). Educators express concern that the national push toward higher student achievement will decrease the variety of curricular options in regular education; increase the number of students failing to meet the higher academic requirements; increase the consultation requirements of special educators and decrease time spent in direct service; increase the need for special education for students who fail; promote separate classes; increase tracking; increase school dropouts; reduce eligibility for postsecondary programs due to rising standards; lower expectations for low-income students; lead to less individualization; foster a feeling that special education students are not worthy; increase the number of special education programs that are watered-down versions of the core curriculum, irrespective of student needs; and preclude sufficient help for those with severe, intense learning disabilities (Boyer, 1983; Council for Exceptional Children, DLD position paper, May 1986; Goodlad, 1984; National Coalition of Advocates for Students, 1985; National Joint Committee on Learning Disabilities, 1992; Pugach & Sapon-Shevin, 1987; Shepard, 1987; Snow, 1984; Sapon-Shevin, 1987; Sizer, 1984).

Ironically, general educators, who are the ones most affected by these proposals and whose cooperation is most needed, have not had significant input into these debates (McKinney & Hocutt, 1988). The few surveys of general education teachers that have been conducted find that they are not particularly supportive of educating all students with disabilities within the mainstream (Coates, 1989; Semmel et al., 1991).

Several educators comment that appropriate partnerships between general and special education would develop faster if university training were not segregated into two separate systems and if separate state certification requirements were eliminated (Hagerty & Abramson, 1987; Pugach, 1987). Then perhaps teachers no longer would view special and general education as two separate entities.

Because of the overlapping instructional needs of students with learning disabilities, those with mild disabilities, and students who underachieve for other reasons, alternative classification systems have been explored that have the potential for breaking down barriers between special and general education. In Massachusetts, for example, students are identified by the percent of time they require for individualized instruction outside of the regular classroom. The percentage time system provides school systems with a financial incentive to offer the student as much special service as needed. It also works to the advantage of the pupil who previously was ineligible for identification as disabled but would benefit from a few hours of services (counseling, occupational therapy) weekly. Other states (for example, New York) combine both categorical and noncategorical options by retaining the traditional categories for federal financial reimbursement purposes yet grouping students for instruction based on common needs rather than labels.

These noncategorical options seem attractive because they address labeling concerns while defining teaching needs with the individual, rather than the diagnostic category, in mind. It is up to future research to ascertain whether these noncategorical systems facilitate individualization of instruction or help teachers, peers, and others to treat exceptional students with any greater sensitivity than in a system based on labels.

Despite the disparity in opinions regarding merging special and general education systems, the move to include students with special needs in the general classroom for all instruction—*inclusion*—is in full swing. The research to date on student progress in inclusive versus pull out or special class placements will be explored in Chapter 12. In spite of all the disagreements regarding how special services should be provided, this debate has helped all school professionals recognize that each can play some important role in the education of students with learning disabilities.

Summary

To develop appropriate individualized instructional programs for students, the assessment team's information is translated into an Individualized Education Program (IEP). Through the planning process involved in writing the IEP, goals are set, evaluation criteria are established, and which types of services, by whom, and with how much participation in general education or another least restrictive environment are specified. A transition service component is designed for secondary students.

Daily lesson planning is the teacher's responsibility. This is not an easy task, especially considering that no one packaged program is likely to suit the uneven development of the student with learning disabilities. To ascertain precisely what and how to teach, teachers engage in ongoing, diagnostic-prescriptive teaching. They generally follow an eclectic instructional model that addresses both the student's weaker and stronger skill areas. Published materials must be creatively adapted to the unique needs of each student. In recent years, computer technology has added an exciting new dimension to teaching options.

When the classroom tasks are well matched to what the student is ready to learn and how he or she prefers to go about learning, academic progress can be maximized. Scope and sequence charts, task analysis, evaluation of previous learning opportunities, and consultation with the student help us select the objectives that the student is most ready and willing to learn. Such common factors as the student's poor attention, slow information-processing speed, performance deterioration as practice continues, modality preferences for processing information, weak ability to generalize, and unique cognitive styles need to be considered when deciding how to approach instruction. The more we know about the unique learning styles of our students with learning disabilities, the better we can plan our teaching modifications.

The regular classroom teacher tends to spend more school hours with the student with learning disabilities than do other professionals. The LD teacher, reading and math teachers, speech pathologist, vocational educator, and school psychologist offer important assessment services, remedial and tutorial instruction, and teacher consultation. Medical personnel also play an important role in the service delivery network, as do individuals in the student's social system: family, close friends, relatives, and others. To make the talents of all school professionals available to the learning disabled, many educators are calling for greater partnerships between general and special education, and more flexible service delivery within the context of the regular classroom.

Instructional Strategies

Effective matches between student, material, and strategy are extremely important in the teaching of students with learning disabilities. In this chapter we will discuss general instructional approaches available to teachers at the preschool, elementary, and secondary levels. No one chapter or even book could do justice to all there is to know about instructional strategies. Therefore, this chapter's purpose is to offer a sampling in order to help the reader appreciate the variety of materials and methods that are available. The excerpt from Lederer's *The World According To Student Bloopers,* pages 364–366, is a humorous look at the kinds of spelling, sequencing, and reasoning confusion that characterize many of our students who are learning disabled. As you read this and smile, try to keep in mind that it is with this same type of sensitivity, appreciation, and light-heartedness that we need to approach even the most challenging of our students.

Preschool Programming

Parents and professionals need to intervene as soon as possible when they detect developmental delays or irregularities in the behavior or cognitive styles of preschoolers. Parents cannot afford to wait and see whether preschoolers will automatically outgrow their weaknesses; they may not. Intervention not only offers these children a head start in overcoming their weaknesses but also encourages continued growth in areas of strength that can help compensate for weaknesses. With appropriate programming, the risk of a serious learning disorder may

The World According to Student Bloopers

One of the fringe benefits of being an English or history teacher is receiving the occasional jewel of a student blooper in an essay. I have pasted together the following "history" of the world from certifiably genuine student bloopers collected by teachers throughout the United States, from eighth grade through college level. Read carefully, and you will learn a lot.

The inhabitants of ancient Egypt were called mummies. They lived in the Sarah Dessert and traveled by Camelot. . . . The Egyptians built the Pyramids in the shape of a huge triangular cube. The Pramids are a range of mountains between France and Spain.

The Bible is full of interesting caricatures. In the first book of the Bible, Guinesses, Adam and Eve were created from an apple tree. . . . Jacob, son of Isaac, stole his brother's birth mark. . . . One of Jacob's sons, Joseph, gave refuse to the Israelites.

Pharaoh forced the Hebrew slaves to make bread without straw. Moses led them to the Red Sea, where they made unleavened bread, which is bread made without any ingredients. . . . David was a Hebrew king skilled at playing the liar. He fought with the Philatelists, a race of people who lived in Biblical times. Solomon, one of David's sons, had 500 wives and 500 porcupines.

Without the Greeks we wouldn't have history. The Greeks invented three kinds of columns—Corinthian, Doric, and Ironic. They also had myths. . . . One myth says that the mother of Achilles dipped him in the River Stynx until he became intollerable. Achilles appears in *The Iliad,* by Homer. Homer also wrote *The Oddity,* in which Penelope was the last hardship that Ulysses endured on his journey. Actually, Homer was not written by Homer but by another man of that name.

Socrates was a famous Greek teacher who went along giving people advice. They killed him. Socrates died from an overdose of wedlock.

In the Olympic Games, Greeks ran races, jumped, hurled the biscuits, and threw the java. . . . The government of Athens was democratic because people took the law into their own hands. . . .

Eventually, the Ramons conquered the Greeks. History calls people Romans because they never stayed in one place for very long. . . . Julius Caesar extinguished himself on the battlefields of Gaul. The Ides of March murdered him because they thought he was going to be made king. Nero was a cruel tyranny who would torture his poor subjects by playing the fiddle to them.

Then came the Middle Ages. King Alfred conquered the Dames, King Arthur lived in the Age of Shivery, King Harold mustarded his troops before the Battle of Hastings, Joan of Arc was cannonized by Bernard Shaw. . . . Finally, Magna Carta provided that no free man should be hanged twice for the same offense.

In midevil times most of the people were alliterate. The greatest writer of the time was Chaucer, who wrote many poems and verses and also wrote literature. . . .

(Continues on following page)

The World According to Student Bloopers   *(Continued from preceding page)*

The Renaissance was an age in which more individuals felt the value of their human being. Martin Luther was nailed to the church door at Wittenberg for selling papal indulgences. . . . It was an age of great inventions and discoveries. Gutenberg invented the Bible. Sir Walter Raleigh is a historical figure because he invented cigarettes. Another important invention was the circulation of blood. Sir Francis Drake circumcised the world with a 100-foot clipper.

The government of England was a limited mockery. . . . When Elizabeth exposed herself before her troops, they all shouted, "hurrah." Then her navy went out and defeated the Spanish Armadillo.

The greatest writer of the Renaissance was William Shakespeare. . . . He lived at Windsor with his merry wives, writing tragedies, comedies, and errors. In one of Shakespear's famous plays, Hamlet rations out his situation by relieving himself in a long soliloquy. . . . Romeo and Juliet are an example of a heroic couplet. Writing at the same time as Shakespear was Miguel Cervantes. He wrote *Donkey Hote*. The next great author was John Milton. Milton wrote *Paradise Lost*. Then his wife died and he wrote *Paradise Regained*.

During the Renaissance America began. Christopher Columbus was a great navigator who discovered America while cursing about the Atlantic. His ships were called the Nina, the Pinta, and the Santa Fe. Later, the Pilgrims crossed the Ocean, and this was known as Pilgrims Progress. . . . Many of the Indian heroes were killed, along with their cabooses, which proved very fatal to them. The winter of 1620 was a hard one for the settlers. Many people died and many babies were born. Captain John Smith was responsible for all this.

One of the causes of the Revolutionary Wars was the English put tacks in their tea. . . . Finally, the colonists won the War and no longer had to pay for taxis.

Thomas Jefferson . . . and Benjamin Franklin were two singers of the Declaration of Independence. . . . Franklin died in 1790 and is still dead.

George Washington married Martha Curtis and in due time became the Father of Our Country. Then the Constitution of the United States was adopted to secure domestic hostility. . . .

Abraham Lincoln became America's greatest Precedent. . . . Abraham Lincoln wrote the Gettysburg Address while traveling from Washington to Gettysburg on the back of an envelope. He also freed the slaves . . . and the Fourteenth Amendment gave the ex-Negroes citizenship. But the Clue Clux Clan would torcher and lynch the ex-Negroes and other innocent victims. It claimed it represented law and odor. On the night of April 14, 1865, Lincoln went to the theater and got shot in his seat by one of the actors in a moving picture show. The believed assinator was John Wilkes Booth, a supposingly insane actor. This ruined Booth's career.

(Continues on following page)

The World According to Student Bloopers   *(Continued from preceding page)*

Meanwhile in Europe, . . .

Bach was the most famous composer in the world, and so was Handel. Handel was half German, half Italian, and half English. He was very large. . . . Beethoven wrote music even though he was deaf. He was so deaf he wrote loud music. . . .

France was in a very serious state. . . . During the Napoleonic Wars, the crowned heads of Europe were trembling in their shoes. Then the Spanish gorillas came down from the hills and nipped at Napolean's flanks. . . .

The sun never set on the British Empire. . . . Queen Victoria was the longest queen. She sat on a thorn for sixty-three years. Her death was the final event which ended her reign.

The nineteenth century was a time of many great inventions and thoughts. . . . Samuel Morse invented a code of telepathy. Louis Pasteur discovered a cure for rabbis. . . . Madman Curie discovered radium. . . .

The First World War, caused by the assignation of the Arch-Duck by a surf, ushered in a new error in the anals of human history.

Source: Lederer, R. (1987). *VERBATIM, The Language Quarterly.* Copyright 1987 by *VERBATIM®, The Language Quarterly.* Used by permission.

be reduced, offering the youngster a greater chance of reaching his or her potential. Because inappropriate social skills tend to be fairly stable once established, the preschool years are not too early to begin work on how to form and maintain relationships with peers. Heavy emphasis on social skill development in the preschool years has a greater chance of success than in later years, when negative behavior patterns already have become well-established (Odom, McConnell, & McEvoy, 1992).

Preschool programming also needs to focus on the child's attending abilities, use of visual- and auditory-processing skills to gain information, and the ability to communicate through language and motor production. Although language and attending abilities have the most to do with severe learning disorders, inefficiencies in visual and motor processes do nevertheless interfere with acquisition and communication of knowledge. The preschool years are also an important time for shaping appropriate learning strategies, motiva-

tion to learn, and positive attitudes toward one's self, peers, and those in authority. All this learning occurs primarily through play. This is a time when children develop at their own pace as we present them with learning opportunities that they are ready to grasp. Preschool is not the time to rush a child into the academic work of school (Zigler, 1987). When we do rush these children too fast, we may in fact harm their overall development (Winn, 1983).

Some preschoolers with delayed development can learn quite well when we personalize their learning environments by introducing learning objectives very systematically, in a way that matches their learning abilities and styles. For other preschoolers, learning is harder. They need to be taught and retaught very basic skills that are fundamental to later academic knowledge (for example, names of colors and shapes, classification skills). Both types of children require directed instruction because they tend not to discover relationships for themselves or to generalize what they have learned to new situations. For example, Sasha might be able to count to ten, yet not recognize that this skill can be applied to count out four napkins for the four children at his snack table. Because of their immature attention and information-processing skills, these children tend to need very special encouragement and exciting activities in order to stay with a task.

The preschool teacher needs to be aware of the fact that preschoolers seldom use deliberate plans to remember and will not simply "remember" because they are told to do so; they will learn best from playing with toys while the teacher mediates the experience (Berk, 1997; Newman, 1990; Paris & Lindauer, 1977). Therefore, it is up to the teacher to make tasks memorable by making learning active and fun, and purposely drawing the preschooler's attention to the most important task attributes. Child development literature suggests that teachers of three-year-old children should highlight color attributes over form (e.g., in teaching names of fruits, exaggerate discussion of color, not shape, differences). By age four, however, children prefer form to color (e.g., highlight shape distinctions of different animals). We know that preschoolers attend better when allowed to handle an object (versus merely watching the teacher's demonstration), when the task is explained to them (versus learning through discovery), when objects are three- versus two-dimensional (alphabet blocks versus printed letters), and when relevant features are accentuated (for example, learning colors by searching for animals under colored boxes, rather than by simply naming colors displayed by the teacher) (Pick, Frankel, & Hess, 1975). Teaching sequences for preschoolers need to be kept short (for example, master numbers one to five before introducing six to ten), because preschoolers recall best what comes last in a series; this information has had the least opportunity to decay, while earlier information requires rehearsal to avoid decay, a strategy for which preschoolers are still too young.

The preschool is an ideal setting for building learning readiness through modeling adult and peer behavior, playing group games, playing

with attention-getting materials, and taking part in teacher-directed lessons. Specific goals need to be set to help preschoolers acquire skills that they have not yet mastered; nonsensical remediation approaches, such as crawling or eye-tracking exercises, that do not relate directly to preacademic objectives should be avoided. Early assessment and intensive remedial programming by specialists such as speech-language pathologists, occupational therapists, and physical therapists are very much in order for children with significant delays.

The preschool program generally varies between independent, teacher–child, small-group, and large-group activities. Group activities use a variety of means to encourage such social behaviors as listening, sharing, turn taking, and attending: games, songs, circle time discussions, physical education, dancing, snacktime, and listening to records or stories. Group activities also are used to expand a child's preliteracy skills, breadth of knowledge, inquisitiveness, and problem-solving abilities. Children, for example, might learn the principles of gravity by dropping objects of various sizes and weights, or discover the effect of temperature changes on solids and liquids by making jello, or learn about nesting and child rearing behaviors by raising gerbils. They can listen to predictable books and finish the sentences, discuss the theme, or reenact the story.

Individual classroom time usually is spent in visual-motor activities (clay work, coloring, cutting, tracing), language activities (labeling shapes, colors, sizes; categorizing; sequencing; telling about events), and school readiness activities (counting blocks, conservation exercises, matching alphabet letters, jingles, songs, poems, and stories containing rhyming, alliterative, or nonsense sound sequences) intended to enhance knowledge and sharpen the child's information reception, expression, and thinking skills. Introduction of learning strategies, such as self-instructing aloud during problem solving or stopping, looking, and listening before responding, are important. Most activities have multiple purposes. Coloring, for example, is an eye-hand coordination activity, a language activity (naming colors), a visual-perceptual activity (noting differences among shades of colors), a following directions activity, a sustained attention training activity, and a conceptual and planning activity (considering whether to depart from the color of real objects when choosing crayons; deciding on the sequence in which segments will be colored).

Because preschool teachers realize that multiple strategies often are needed to engage student attention and learning, they frequently set themes that pervade the child's day. For example, when Kasy does not learn to label and sequence several animals through the Gingerbread Man story, she may learn these skills by singing the Gingerbread Man song, portraying a character in a Gingerbread Man skit, baking gingerbread and animal cookies, or drawing, cutting, pasting, tracing, and coloring Gingerbread Man and animal figures. It takes a great deal of ingenuity for the preschool teacher to think of multiple ways to reinforce a concept so that when one way doesn't draw a child's attention, interest, and participation, another will.

Children who make insufficient gains through typical preschool activities may benefit from many packaged visual-motor and language development programs that can be adapted to their learning needs and styles. In the area of language development, for example, children make greater gains when they receive structured, individualized interventions (Kavale, 1981b). These language programs stimulate children's receptive, reasoning, and expressive language in several ways: they build vocabulary; model the construction of syntactically accurate sentences; encourage problem solving and communication of information through dialogues; analyze sentence structure; and develop such skills as description, classification, logical reasoning, facility with opposites, synonyms, analogies, absurdities, rhymes, and ability to describe functional relationships. For children with severe language delays, the simultaneous use of sign and oral language has encouraged both receptive and expressive language development. In these cases, signing is used all the time in class, and typical students too seem to enjoy this addition to their communicative ability.

A wealth of ideas for encouraging language, visual-motor (buttoning, cutting, drawing), and gross-motor (hopping, climbing steps) develop-

ment were suggested in the teaching guides written by the pioneers in learning disabilities and their students: Barsch (1967), Frostig & Maslow (1973), Furth & Wachs (1974), Johnson & Myklebust (1967), Kephart (1971). These books are seminal even today, and they form the foundation for the hundreds of preschool development books and programs that are currently marketed.

Intervention within a preschool program is only the beginning of a long educational process. It has been found that gains are better the earlier individualized intervention begins, especially before age three, and the longer the intervention continues, especially when into the elementary grades (Caldwell, 1974; Cicirelli, Evans, & Schiller, 1970; Guralnick, 1991). Although at times the intellectual gains are lost once special intervention is terminated, most often there is some persistence (Aiken, 1987; Bronfenbrenner, 1975; Campbell & Ramey, 1994; Lazar & Darlington, 1982; McCarthy, J., 1980). When compared with children who did not have the advantage of preschool education, benefits may become apparent years later in many ways: fewer of these children being retained or assigned to special classes, higher academic achievement and motivation, greater homework completion and high school graduation rates, greater enrollment in postsecondary education, higher competence in skills of everyday life, higher earnings and employment rates, lower use of welfare assistance, fewer encounters with the law, and fewer early pregnancies (Berrueta-Clement et al., 1984; Campbell & Ramey, 1994; Lazar & Darlington, 1982; Neisser et al., 1996; Schweinhart & Weikart, 1980; Zigler, Taussig, & Black, 1992).

Preschool programs with highly structured goals (including task analysis and detailed measurement of outcomes), reinforcements, and teacher direction tend to benefit children more in the important areas of intelligence, language, visual perception, and school readiness than do more open, less academically structured programs (Karnes, Hodgins, & Teska, 1969; White, 1984). These differential patterns of gain are most apparent in children from low-income families (Casto & Mastropieri, 1986). Several studies have found that lower functioning preschoolers will benefit most when teachers also actively mediate their social and cognitive development by talking through, suggesting, and actively guiding the children's awareness of memory strategies, making choices and comparisons, changing perspectives, planning ahead, using senses, identifying and understanding feelings, and the like. The higher functioning of preschoolers with developmental delays, however, are familiar with these strategies, and benefit most from simply the direct instruction approach without the additional teacher mediation (Cole et al., 1993). Programs that are less structured and more flexible seem to encourage children to take greater responsibility for success and to be more independent and cooperative (Stallings, 1974). These attributes too are important to later school success.

The family plays a very important part in the maintenance of gains from the preschool program. Therefore, a family-centered rather than child-centered focus, beginning before age three, is the most effective means of enhancing long-term effects, especially given the need for support with difficult issues faced by many of these families: unemployment, poverty, illegal drugs, homelessness, violence in the street and at home, poor health care and nutrition (Bronfenbrenner, 1975; Caldwell, 1974; Rossetti, 1986; Zigler & Styfco, 1994). By working with both parents and children, parent–child relationships are strengthened, and parents feel supported and enabled to become more competent and independent in their efforts to encourage their children's motivation and learning. Family involvement that focuses on supporting relationships, rather than on asking the parent to become the actual therapist or teacher, helps build parents' self-confidence, coping abilities, and satisfaction with the parenting role, which in turn impacts positively on their children's development and social competence (Guralnick, 1991).

Elementary School Programming

The achievement of the elementary school student with learning disabilities is uneven across aca-

demic areas because of the different information-processing skills, cognitive styles, and background experiences that the child brings to school tasks. Consequently, the teacher must adapt the curriculum to what the child already knows, what he or she still needs to learn, and how he or she learns best. At times, minor program modifications are sufficient. At other times, very special approaches are needed. Despite publication of special materials and approaches, teachers still find themselves mixing and matching from several programs so that the children's precise needs are addressed. The elementary school program emphasizes reading decoding and comprehension, written language (composition, handwriting, spelling), mathematics, content area instruction, and social–emotional adjustment. Often physical education, art, and music instruction also must be adapted to the individual needs of the student with learning disabilities.

The teaching objectives to which we apply the materials and strategies discussed in this chapter are enumerated in the Scope and Sequence charts contained in published programs. Our intervention strategies generally capitalize on children's strengths to promote progress by working around their information-processing weaknesses. Our strategies also try to shore up these weaknesses. The best way to determine which materials and approaches will be most effective is to try each out for a number of weeks, chart progress, and then evaluate the learning outcome.

Reading

Reading intervention is a priority because difficulties in this area inevitably create problems in other academic areas as well. Some general approaches to reading instruction emphasize the meaning of the language that is being read (whole-word, whole-language, and language experience approaches), while others stress the ability to break the phonetic code (phonics and linguistic approaches). An approach that integrates both meaning- and phonics-based methods is advocated by many experts because fluent reading necessitates the recognition of words at a glance, the automatic analysis, sequencing, and retrieval of sounds, and the ability to gain meaning from words. Therefore, no one process can be concentrated on to the exclusion of another. A study that taught children to read pseudowords by a whole-word or analytic-phonic method illustrates this point. Vellutino and Scanlon (1986) found that the method by which children were taught created a generalized strategy with which children subsequently approached new words. Although the children who received whole-word training at first learned more rapidly than children who received the phonemic segmentation training, the latter group eventually became as good as or better than the whole-word group. However, the combination of both training methods produced the most learning. Each seemed to contribute something important at different stages of reading, thereby complementing one another. Vellutino and Scanlon, as do many other experts, believe that an overemphasis on one process, to the exclusion of the other, might create an information-processing bias that could impair fluency in word identification.

The whole-language approach to reading and writing (Goodman, 1986), which focuses on whole-word recognition and meaning, has become very popular in recent years. In whole-language reading, the interpretive potential of authentic literature is emphasized. Literature is meant to be savored and transformed by the reader, not read and memorized for tests. The whole-language movement has brought fresh life to many classrooms: student immersion in good literature and a language-rich environment, greater appreciation of literature and emphasis on comprehension, more active classroom participation in creative activities, early emphasis on daily writing, alleviation of good readers' boredom when subjected to intensive phonic drills, enhancement of comprehension skills, expanded linguistic and conceptual knowledge (Mather, 1992). With these positives, however, has come intense debate about a one-sided emphasis on whole-language in beginning reading instruction. The whole-language approach focuses on the meaning in text by having students read good literature instead of the isolated words, sounds, or uninspiring vocabulary—controlled stories characterizing traditional code-emphasis reading approaches. The latter approaches fragment language arts into hierarchies of discrete skills. The assumption in the whole-language approach is that children will learn phonetic rules naturally, without systematic instruction, by being immersed in a print-rich environment that invites guessing words from context and from one's own experiential and conceptual knowledge. Teachers may at times teach phonics, but not in a preplanned fashion, and only within an authentic language context, for example, giving a student a phonic spelling hint while writing.

The majority of students do intuitively discover the relationship between spoken and written words and learn to read regardless of the specific teaching method. This is especially true of students who enter school with good phonemic awareness (Griffith & Olson, 1992). Good readers use syntactic and semantic (meaning-based) as well as graphophonic (code-based) cues to aid word recognition, and consequently to access meaning. Whereas good readers have both avenues available to them when they fail to recognize a word, the poor reader does not.

What happens to students with learning disabilities who cannot master the alphabetic code without explicit instruction? These students are likely to continue guessing at words from context, and have no alternative strategy to decipher a new word when contextual cues are insufficient. Consequently, the whole purpose of reading, which is to reconstruct meaning from print, suffers.

The student who does not naturally crack the code with exposure to print requires systematic, explicit skill-by-skill phonics instruction to become a fluent, proficient reader. This does not preclude whole-language instruction, as long as supplemental phonics instruction is offered and the literature being read is appropriate to the student's language comprehension. Research Box 10–1 further explores the importance of phonic training in the reading development of students with learning disabilities.

Whether a classroom is whole-language literature based, or whether it uses traditional basal readers that tend to control for vocabulary difficulty, in many cases the phonetic aspects of the reading vocabulary will not be sufficiently controlled for students with learning disabilities. In learning to read, children are faced with a multitude of different word types, and they must infer a good many phonic rules on their own. Given the abundant evidence that many students with learning disabilities are deficient in ability to segment words into individual sounds and in ability to access the phonetic code even once it has been memorized, they are unlikely to intuit these phonics skills unless very systematically taught.

For most children with learning disabilities, phonetic approaches that teach listening to, identifying, blending, and sequencing of individual sounds in words work better in the long run than methods that do not incorporate phonics instruction. Liberman (1985) points out that the strings of letters that form our printed words are poorly suited to apprehension by whole-word approaches alone. How confusing it would be to try to learn the different "names" for *hit, hut, bit, but, bat, hat* when they all look so much alike. Our alphabetical system was meant to help us figure out words that

look this similar and also words that we've never seen before. A whole-word approach would be of little value in either case. Because it is essential to go beyond the visual shape of a word to decipher its internal aspects, phonic skill instruction is critical.

Research Box 10–1 explains that the optimal timing for the introduction of phonics instruction will depend on the student's specific strengths and weaknesses. If the student has language and auditory analysis strengths, phonetic instruction is likely to lead to immediate success, while the weaker sight recognition skills receive remedial attention. If the student is weak in phonetic analysis, blending, sound retrieval, or linguistic skills, however, then building a whole-word foundation first may be best, while remedial attention is given to sharpening the child's awareness of sounds in words and retrieval of sounds from memory (using, for example, Rosner's Perceptual Skills Curriculum, Rhyme and Reason in Reading and Spelling, or Lindamood's Auditory Discrimination in Depth). The downside of this temporary "look-say" approach is that children are encouraged to

---

RESEARCH BOX 10–1
Research Matching Reading Methods with Students' Information-Processing Strengths

Studies conducted in the classroom that tested phonic against whole-word approaches to reading generally have found that the phonic emphasis has an advantage, especially for children who are at risk for learning difficulties (Bateman, 1968b; Bliesmer & Yarborough, 1965; Felton, 1993; Guyer & Sabatino, 1989; Potts, 1968; Silberberg, Iversen, & Goins, 1973; Stahl & Miller, 1989). Developing the ability to segment words into syllables and syllables into their component sounds, and then to blend these sounds together, is essential to reading achievement. Approaches that emphasize meaning (using a whole-word strategy) rather than phonics have been found to be less successful than those that, early on, systematically teach word recognition and decoding (Adams, 1990; Anderson et al., 1985; Chall, 1983a; Finn, 1986). Spelling also benefits more from a code emphasis approach, whereas comprehension appears to be developed equally well through either method (Adams, 1990). Bateman's study is of particular interest because it used several instructional

(Continues on following page)

RESEARCH BOX 10–1   *(Continued from preceding page)*

approaches throughout first grade and analyzed the data separately for auditory and visual learners. Even the visual learners, who theoretically were mismatched with the phonetic teaching technique, profited more in reading and spelling from a phonic approach than from a whole-word approach; "breaking the code" was facilitated by concentrating instruction on sound-symbol relationships. Even when this skill doesn't come easily to visual learners, it is essential to reading progress and will benefit them in the long run.

There is abundant evidence regarding the positive effects on reading achievement of readying children for phonics through phonemic awareness instruction, for as little as two 15 to 20 minute sessions weekly: teaching such basic phonics readiness skills as, from easiest to hardest, recognizing which word sounds longer (*spaghetti* or *train*), segmenting sentences into words and words into syllables, rhyming, blending phonemes, syllable splitting (*b/ack*), segmenting phonemes within words, and substituting one phoneme for another within a word (Berninger, 1990; Bradley & Bryant, 1978, 1983; Griffith & Olson, 1992; Hurford et al., 1994; Litcher & Roberge, 1979; Lundberg, Frost, & Petersen, 1988; Tornéus, 1984; Vandervelden & Siegel, 1997; Vellutino & Scanlon, 1987; Wallach & Wallach, 1979; Williams, 1984). For example, Bradley and Bryant (1985) report that when beginning readers who experienced difficulty detecting sounds in words were taught to categorize words by matching initial, medial, and final sounds, or rhymes, these children made greater gains on reading and spelling tests than did control children (who received no training or were taught to categorize the same words conceptually, for example, *animals*). When the sound categorization instruction was combined with plastic letters to represent the sounds, progress was even better. Four years after completion of the study, the differential effects of this instruction were still evident (Bradley, 1988). Similarly, Ball and Blachman (1991) and Tangel and Blachman (1992) found that instructing kindergartners on phoneme segmentation and letter names and sounds produced greater increases in word identification and spelling over a seven- and eleven-week period than did traditional kindergarten letter/sound instruction and language activities. Gains from continuing this type of intervention into first grade were evident (Blachman, 1994; Tangel & Blachman, 1995). In spite of the generally facilitative effect of phonemic awareness training, Torgesen, Wagner, and Rashotte (1994) report that 30 percent of their young subjects were resistant to this type of training and required far more intensive intervention.

Phonetic decoding efficiency is important because the more fluently one reads, the more effectively the text is comprehended (Vellutino, 1991). When word identification is slow and cumbersome, comprehension suffers because cognitive resources need to be expended on decoding rather than on comprehension. Skilled readers automatically apply their phonic skills to process nearly all the letters and words they see in a text; when they do need to apply guessing strategies, these are successful only about 25 percent of the time. Skilled readers do not need to use context to guide decoding because word identification is so automatic.

The battles rage on between whole-language and code-emphasis advocates, with many experts recommending an eclectic approach. Unfortunately, experimental studies of the effi-

(Continues on following page)

RESEARCH BOX 10-1   *(Continued from preceding page)*

cacy of the two approaches for different types of learners are important, but very hard to run: children improve just because the teachers know they're being studied (Hawthorne Effect), diagnostic instruments for defining a child as one or another type of learner are of questionable reliability and validity, it is difficult to homogeneously group very heterogeneous children for instruction, and it is difficult to get adequate control groups. Generalizations are hard to make because children's characteristics differ vastly from study to study, as do the nature and intensity of the instructional programs. Even when one program is found to be superior, it is difficult to determine which aspects accounted for the good learning. Furthermore, all programs teach, and it is hard to sort out how much of any difference that is found could be due to the teacher characteristics rather than to the program.

Despite these research issues, it is generally accepted among LD experts that phonemic awareness and phonic instruction are essential for reading progress. Which specific approach to phonetic instruction is best for different types of learners (for example, picture cues for the child with visual strengths, only auditory stimuli for children who get overloaded by too much to attend to at once, manipulatives for the child with attention deficits) remains for future research to sort out. Whether phonics instruction for the child with weaknesses in this area should be offered first, or after success with an alternate reading approach, is a question that currently is being investigated. Lyon (1985) reports that after twenty-six one-hour sessions with a phonics approach (letter and sound clusters are systematically blended), word-recognition gains were apparent only in children who had no information-processing weaknesses or in children who had strengths in blending, naming, auditory discrimination, language comprehension, and auditory memory. In contrast, children who were weak in these language skills benefited (after thirty hours of instruction) only if phonemic analysis and blending practice came *after* learning the whole-word units to which the phonics skills would be applied: pairing words with pictures, pointing to words when named, reading the words in isolation and in short sentences, analyzing root words, endings, and syllables.

In summary, even if phonemic awareness is not a strength, it still seems to be essential to beginning reading instruction for youngsters who do not intuitively crack the code. Exactly where in the teaching sequence to introduce phonic instruction, however, depends on analysis of the child's strength and weakness patterns; with some children a foundation must first be set in a way that organizes the child's thinking, for example, learning the whole-word units first and then analyzing them phonetically. While developing these phonic competencies, code-oriented theorists emphasize that students also should benefit from immersion in excellent literature that encourages vocabulary enrichment, reading for comprehension, use of context to monitor story lines and make predictions, and an understanding of how reading and writing are related (Chall, 1983a; Hatcher, Hulme, & Ellis, 1994; Mather, 1992; Pressley & Rankin, 1994; Spear-Swerling & Sternberg, 1994; Vellutino, 1991). Adams (1990) concludes that reading achievement will be superior when systematic decoding instruction accompanies a meaning emphasis approach, as well as language enrichment, and practice with text reading.

guess from context, a habit that may interfere with applying the phonetic skills they are learning concurrently. In addition, the great variety of words that need to be learned by sight can be quite confusing. The same concerns apply to the language experience approach, in which the child uses his or her linguistic, cognitive, and cultural knowledge to orally relate stories and personal experiences (Stauffer, 1980). These are recorded verbatim by the teacher. The child listens to the teacher read the selection, and then the child reads it. The child's attention is drawn by the teacher to individual words. Motivation to read is built by activities such as illustrating, editing, and marking permanent wall charts or books of one's "writing." The more a child dictates and reads the transcriptions, the more automatic knowledge the child presumably absorbs about our alphabetic system.

Because linguistic approaches cluster sounds into word families (*pat, rat, cat*), this approach can be very helpful to the child who is unable to analyze and sequence the individual phonemes in a word (Goswami, 1989). Word stems like *ick* are taught as sight words, and then individual sounds are substituted at the beginning of the stems: *pick, kick, sick*. Stems are taught that can be placed at the beginning (e.g., *un, dis*), end, or middle of words. There is a definite sequence to the presentation of words: regular spelling patterns first, followed by irregular patterns. Once the child has mastered consonant and vowel sounds, Adams (1990) urges educators to focus on common letter pairs rather than the individual letters; the more familiar the child is with common orthographic sequences, the more sight word recognition will increase. Once the phonic code is mastered, the major focus of reading instruction can shift to the very purpose for reading—comprehension.

It makes sense to teach reading, whenever possible, in the context of good literature and content materials, rather than just using word lists, since poor readers' word recognition is aided by the semantic and syntactic cues in a passage (Krieger, 1981). Moreover, reading in context reinforces the purpose for reading, gaining meaning. It also provides excellent models for language development.

Unfortunately, poor readers all too often have an impoverished understanding of what reading is all about. Palincsar & Klenk (1992) quote one child as saying that reading is "a piece of paper—on a piece of paper." Another described good readers as being children who read "fast and loud" (p. 218). It is the teacher's responsibility to not let the severity of a child's learning disability alienate him or her from literacy experiences and from the ultimate objective of reading—gaining meaning and knowledge.

For many children with learning disabilities, a wise match between a reading program's approach and their learning strengths will lead to reading progress. For children with severe deficits, however, the curriculum generally needs to be modified dramatically to include special reading strategies.

We will next describe several special reading strategies available to educators. The building of comprehension skills will be discussed when special approaches to content area instruction are explored. Research Box 10–2 discusses the best way of offering students feedback when they make reading errors.

Special Reading Strategies.   The structure of English written language does not make it easy to crack the code that maps our oral words to print. Major obstacles need to be overcome in learning to read English: English spelling does not always correspond with the expected letter sound (an *a* can sound like a long *a* as in *bake*, a short *a* as in *back*, *e* as in *language*, *i* as in *stomach*, or *u* as in *infamy*); several letters may represent one sound (the *o* sound in *although* is spelled *ough*); the same letter combinations may sound different depending on the word (b*ea*t, h*ea*lth); one-half of all words contain silent letters; and only one half of all words follow phonetic rules. These obstacles prove especially difficult for the child with learning disabilities who may have trouble remembering letter sounds and revisualizing how words should look.

Several specialized reading approaches have been used with severely disabled readers. These methods can replace the standard program or be used to reinforce its objectives. Many of these methods follow a multisensory approach similar

RESEARCH BOX 10–2
Providing Feedback to Students on Their Reading Errors

How should we respond when a child makes a decoding error? Pany and McCoy (1988) summarize common arguments against interrupting students to correct their oral reading errors: the reader will rely increasingly on the teacher and diminish his or her self-monitoring during reading; correction detracts from the real purpose of reading–meaning; feedback is disruptive, and impairs comprehension. Countering these arguments, however, Pany and McCoy found that third graders with learning disabilities who were corrected for every error decreased their oral reading errors, increased comprehension, and could recall the words two to three days later significantly better than students who received no feedback or were corrected only when their errors altered meaning (about half of all errors). Pany and McCoy's error correction procedure first cued the child to "try another way," then asked "What sounds does _____ make?"; if the child was still unsuccessful, the adult supplied the word.

Many of our special reading strategies are successful for the same reason as Pany and McCoy's technique: they offer very precise feedback that immediately corrects errors and prevents a student from practicing/learning his or her mistakes. Subsequent drills on these words help promote retention (Rosenberg, 1986).

Another technique, constant time delay, avoids practicing and learning one's errors altogether. A nearly errorless method, in constant time delay, a reading word is presented to a student and the teacher simultaneously reads the word aloud. On subsequent trials, the teacher waits a designated number of seconds (usually three to five) for the student to read the word; if the student is unsuccessful, the teacher reads the word aloud. This method has resulted in more rapid learning of sight words, word definitions, math facts, spelling words, and science, social studies, and health facts than when students are prompted toward the correct response (Keel & Gast, 1992; Koscinski & Hoy, 1993; Mattingly & Bott, 1990; Wolery et al., 1991). Retention over time seems to be good, and the material is generalized to other tasks and settings. When constant time delay procedures have been implemented within a group setting, elementary and high school students who were not being asked to respond to the target information also learned a good deal through observation, provided that their attention was cued by being required to write the word or orally repeat the question while waiting for their peer's response.

---

to that advocated by the pioneers in learning disabilities. Their premise is that when children actively involve all senses in the learning process, then attention to appropriate elements of the learning task is likely to be facilitated. Unlike typical reading programs that require children to read words, some multisensory methods approach reading by first having the child learn to spell the word orally or write it from memory. Although using all senses may be beneficial for many children, the choice of multisensory methods needs to be evaluated carefully because indiscriminate bombardment may overload some children to the point that they literally tune out (Johnson & Myklebust, 1967; Kirk & Kirk, 1971; Montali & Lewandowski, 1996).

The Elkonin Method. Blachman's (1991) "say-it-and-move-it" activity is an adaptation of Elkonin's (1963, 1973) method of helping children differentiate among sounds in words. Children are given sheets of paper with counters and a picture placed on the top half, and squares that represent phonemes on the bottom half. Teachers model slowly saying sounds (e.g., *eee*) and words (e.g., *sssuuunnn*) as they move a counter corresponding with each phoneme into a different square. Children learn to represent one, then two, and finally three phoneme combinations and words with these counters, using a slow blending strategy. Eventually, letters are substituted for the counters. Sustainable sounds precede stop consonants in this process, and words can be built by substituting different letters. Beck and Juel (1995) point out that until children learn to blend, their knowledge of individual letter sounds will have little practical value. Over time picture cues, squares, and counters can be eliminated and replaced with simply saying the word slowly and writing it. Many studies have validated the efficacy of this procedure for increasing phonemic awareness and generalizing learned skills to new words and spellings. When training continues into the first and second grades, children using these techniques outperform those who received traditional instruction on word recognition, spelling, and invented spelling tasks (Ball & Blachman, 1991; Blachman, 1993; Tangel & Blachman, 1992).

The Fernald Approach. The VAKT (Visual-Auditory-Kinesthetic-Tactile) method was developed by Grace Fernald (1943) for students with very severe reading delays. Words are taught through a multisensory approach that focuses more on the whole word than on individual sounds. Some research has supported the efficacy of this approach and its incorporation of tracing to aid memory (Hulme, 1981; Thorpe & Borden, 1985). In Fernald's method, a short story is dictated by the child. The teacher then writes each word that the child wants to learn on a strip of paper in large cursive writing. The child traces each word with two-finger contact while slowly saying the word in syllables. Tracing is repeated until the child demonstrates that he or she can

write the word from memory without the model. When all the words have been learned, the teacher types the story so that the child can read it in print. As the child's word bank builds, writing of stories is encouraged and VAKT is used to learn any new words. When the child becomes more skilled, the child abandons the tracing and learns words by looking at, saying, and copying them, and then writing them without a model.

The Gillingham-Stillman Method. Gillingham and Stillman's (1970) multisensory approach to reading, spelling, and writing, and Slingerland's (1974) adaptation, are based on Orton's (1937, 1966) theories. Like the Elkonin method, this is an alphabetic system, stressing letters and their corresponding sounds. Spelling and writing are used to promote reading acquisition. This highly structured approach requires that the child be given instruction five times a week for at least two years, working through a fixed sequence of phonetic rules.

Each sound is learned one at a time using auditory, visual, and kinesthetic stimuli and some tracing. When shown the letter *a*, for example, the student recites as many ways to pronounce the *a* as he or she has been taught (for example, *a* says ă as in *sat; a* followed by a consonant and *e* says ā as in *bake*). These single sounds are then blended into sound clusters and finally into short words.

For word analysis, the teacher initially dictates words as the child points to them. The child then reads words that contain the learned phonemes. The teacher creates reading passages using the phonics skills the student has mastered. Finally, the Simultaneous Oral Spelling process is introduced. The teacher says the word, followed by the child saying the word, naming the letters, and then writing the letters as he or she names them subvocally. In both reading and spelling, nonsense words are interspersed with real words in order to check on generalization of phonetic rules.

Research has supported the effectiveness of spelling instruction as a means of facilitating word recognition (Ehri & Wilce, 1987). In their study, for example, van Daal and van der Leij (1992) required children to read or type the word that was present on a computer screen, or they could type the word once it had disappeared. Children could press a button to hear a voice pronounce the word on the screen. Both the spelling and reading methods proved effective in promoting sight word recognition.

The Neurological Impress Method, Choral Reading, Repeated Readings, and Previewing. The neurological impress method makes use of auditory modeling by having the student and teacher read a passage aloud several times in unison (Heckelman, 1969). The child points to the words as they are read. At first the teacher's voice is louder and faster than the child's. As the child's confidence and sight recognition increase, the teacher's volume decreases and his or her reading begins to lag behind the student's.

A variation of the neurological impress method is *choral reading,* in which several students read aloud as a group (Bos, 1982). *Repeated readings* on one's own also have improved reading performance, even on new passages containing the same vocabulary; for most children three readings are sufficient to reach an adequate reading rate and maximum comprehension of the material (O'Shea, Sindelar, & O'Shea, 1987; Rashotte & Torgesen, 1985). Another variation, *silent previewing* of a reading selection, has been shown to increase the number of words students subsequently read correctly. *Previewing by listening* may be an even more effective strategy than previewing through silent reading (Rose, 1984; Rose & Sherry, 1984; Salend & Nowak, 1988). Previewing by listening is cost and time effective and can be incorporated with ease into the classroom routine. Peers or aides can serve as readers, and taped passages can be listened to independently. Previewing by listening, followed by repeat readings, is an excellent strategy for improving reading rate; a criterion of three successive improvements in reading rate before moving on to another passage appears to maintain student motivation and result in rate gains (Weinstein & Cooke, 1992). In one study, teenagers who read along with a tape once a day for three to seven days significantly improved the rate and accuracy of their sight recognition (Freeman & McLaughlin, 1984). This method

fostered independence in self-correction, and it had the added advantage of being self-paced.

Other Methods. Several programs teach a prescribed sequence of phonics or linguistic skills, while narrowing the memory load for students who can deal with only a limited amount of new information at a time. Programs like *Reading Mastery* (formerly Distar), *Corrective Reading,* or *Recipe for Reading* initially restrict the load to nine or eleven sounds. Once the student has mastered these sounds, then more phonemes gradually are added. Reading gains in these tightly controlled programs often are well beyond what would be expected from typical classroom programs (Gersten, Woodward, & Darch, 1986). *Patterned books* also have been useful to students with learning disabilities in that the same sentences and phrases reappear throughout the book. As the teacher reads these books aloud, students join in at those times when they can predict what comes next. Basically, the flow of the language facilitates identification of unknown words (Bos & Vaughn, 1994). *Reading Recovery* slowly introduces the alphabet to beginning readers while working one-on-one with the teacher over a twelve to fifteen week period. Hundreds of simple books, particularly patterned books, are read and reread, brief stories are written, words are built with magnetic letters, and a variety of strategies are taught with much teacher scaffolding. *Reading Recovery* has been effective in preventing reading disabilities among at risk children (Clay, 1991).

Many of these special programs introduce letter-sound correspondences by associating a letter with an object that is shaped like the letter and begins with that sound, thereby aiding recall of the letter's shape and sound, as in

 and (Isgur, 1975).

Frequently puppets that are named after letters and contain the printed letter on their clothing (for example, *Mr. M*) are used to relate prepared tales that reinforce the letter-sound association. In addition, specific letters can be color-coded to draw attention and distinguish them from others.

When no system has succeeded in teaching the child letter-sound associations, the teacher might resort to the *Peabody Rebus Reading Program,* in which traditional printed words are replaced with "rebus" symbols (Woodcock & Clark, 1969). For example the word *bottlecap* may be represented by 🍾🧢, *brain* by b 🐀, and *bread* by 🍞. The rebus symbol provides an easier link to the spoken word than does the printed word. As the program progresses, many rebuses transition into sight words, so that the child eventually can read over one hundred printed words. By helping the child access printed, meaningful sentences, the rebus program provides beginning readers with a valuable idea of what reading for meaning is like.

Today's teacher has a myriad of special reinforcement methods available to add variety, excitement, challenge, and individualization to the learning process. These include the computer, tape recorder, educational games, filmstrips, overhead transparencies, records or tapes with accompanying books, and tachistoscopes that flash words at fixed rates. Educational TV is popularly used, as are teaching machines. These machines vary from simple "language masters" (a child writes and tape records a word on a computer card and then simultaneously sees and hears it as it runs through the machine), to more complex talking typewriters or computers that speak the name of the letter a child has typed as it flashes on the screen.

Written Language

Written language skills most often present the greatest stumbling block for the student who is learning disabled because the language processes involved in reading, spelling, listening, speaking, and thinking must complement and support one another all at once. The whole-language approach offers an outstandingly rich language environment for learning about authoring and writing. The quality literature to which students are exposed provokes ideas for writing and offers superb models for the craft of writing: text organization, cohesion, appropriateness of voice, and understanding of different writing purposes and styles. Even in non–whole-language programs, it is estimated that the learning transfer between reading and writing is about 30 percent (Shanahan & Tierney, 1990). Palincsar and Perry (1995), for example, remark on their seven year olds' "aha" when the children's invented spellings were transcribed into conventional spellings; the children finally recognized that their writing actually represented reading words that could be sounded out. The fruitfulness of creating language-rich programs in which reading and writing naturally reinforce one another is evident.

Vygotsky's (1978) theories of learning have had an important impact on the whole-language movement. Vygotsky viewed learning as a social event in which the teacher's modeling of strategies, through demonstration, discussion, and explanation, plays a critical role. The teacher's questioning and guidance provide the necessary support for the student to progress to the next higher level of development. Students also benefit from discussions and feedback from their peers. When applying Vygotsky's principles, teachers and students discuss what they are learning and how they are going about learning; the intent is for such dialogue to not only guide the learner but also to be internalized as "inner talk" that will guide the student even in the teacher's absence.

Using a whole-language approach, Bos (1991) describes the reading-writing connection that a teacher can foster by means of *Literature Circles.* Basically, children choose from among books recommended by the teacher and form Literature Circles in which five or six students meet to discuss a work as they are reading it. The teacher models and guides the students in relating this literature to their own personal experiences, knowledge, other readings, and to their own writing. If the author is local, the author could be invited to offer his or her own perspective on the piece. Students might wish to write or enact a dramatization of the story, create a new ending, write a new story borrowing the same theme or characters, tell the story from a different character's perspective, research and write a report on the setting or one of the characters (particularly if historical fiction), or even have one of their own works be the subject of the Literature Circle. Establishing "reader's" and "author's" chairs have been popular ways for students to read to others in their group, especially their own works (Palincsar & Klenk, 1992). The ensuing discussion addresses issues beyond the literal meaning of the text and offers an excellent opportunity for peer feedback for revisions.

Bos also describes the value of using Literature Circles to read sets of texts that are related by common themes (e.g., survival, divorce), authors, characters, cultures, or text structure (e.g., cumu-lative patterns where one event causes another to happen). Each student in the Circle could read the same or different text, or the teacher could read one book aloud while students read other members of the set independently. The teacher again helps students make comparisons between texts and authors and relate this to their own writing.

Clearly, the best environment for developing writing skills is one that encourages the student to use language for a variety of purposes and audiences through reading, writing, listening, and speaking. Figure 10–1 reprints an excellent

---

Storytelling and Writing Time

One story the children worked with was entitled, "Franklin in the Dark" (Bourgeois & Clark, 1986). (Franklin is a turtle whose fear of dark places has led him to imagine that his own shell is inhabited by monsters, ghosts, and other unsavory characters.) Each child had been given a three-ring binder that served as a personal journal in which they would maintain their writings and revisions. As a prelistening activity, the children wrote journal entries about the things they were afraid of—or, in the case of 10-year-old boys who claimed to be fearless, about the fears of family members. After encouraging the children to share their journal entries (an opportunity for reading self-generated text), the teacher introduced the book. The children were asked to identify the genre, with supporting evidence, and to make predictions about the story. An illustration on the book cover, depicting a desolate turtle dragging his shell behind him, prompted the children to suggest that this would be a make-believe story.

After generating a series of predictions, the children listened as the teacher began to read . . . the children actively participated, spontaneously demonstrating their knowledge of story structure and their personal constructions of meaning: "Franklin is the name of the character." "His problem is he's afraid of the dark; that's my problem too!" "He oughta get hisself a night light." The student who made this suggestion later reminded everyone, with considerable pride, that he had predicted the author's solution.

As the teacher read the story, she called the children's attention to the story elements that they had been listening for in previous stories. She revisited their predictions, but she also called the children's attention to how Franklin might be feeling as he journeyed the world over, discovering that everyone he met had learned to deal with fear of some kind. "How would you feel if you were Franklin at this point?" "How," she asked, "does the

(Continues on following page)

Figure 10–1   The whole-language environment. *Source:* Palincsar, A. S., & Klenk, L. (1992). Fostering literacy learning in supportive contexts. *Journal of Learning Disabilities, 25,* 220–221. Copyright 1992 by PRO-ED, Inc. Reprinted by permission.

author tell you that Franklin is surprised with what he is learning?" The teacher invited the children to join her in a second reading. The illustrations and predictable text supported the children in their choral reading.

Following the reading, the teacher introduced a writing activity by sharing her own fear of swimming, and by inviting the children to help her think of solutions to the problem. Then the children were asked to write a response to the story of Franklin in their journals. The response could be to write about solutions to the fear they had raised earlier, or to write a new story in which they were the character seeking help with a fear.

In a future session, the children shared their journal entries with their classmates. The writing process continued as, with the assistance of the teacher, the children edited their entries to substitute conventional spellings for inventions. Revisions were completed at this mechanical level over several months. . . . As we explored a variety of themes with the students, none seemed as appealing as those that dealt with people. Influenced by the topics the students chose to discuss and write about, we settled on themes related to friendship. This meant that we would explore friendship through both the writing and the reading that we did. Also, with this theme we chose to focus more systematically on planning, organizing, and revising one's writing. To facilitate this, the teachers began by composing a story with the children, first discussing some events they would possibly like to write about, then listing all the ideas they had for this story, and finally enlisting the children's help as they transformed the ideas into text. The children easily assumed ownership of the story, choosing ideas from their list and organizing these ideas into a story.

To foster a similar process of planning and organization among the students, we encouraged them to work in triads before they began their writing, to list—as the teacher had—ideas they would like to weave into their stories, and to help one another think of interesting ways to assemble those ideas. Following this pattern, with the teacher initially modeling, and the students planning collaboratively and then writing independently, the students were asked to select one from several writings that they would like to revise to make more interesting, exciting, or complete. The teacher once again used his writing and thought aloud, using a form of self-questioning, about how he might revise his writing. As the students began to get the gist of the teacher's activity, they added additional questions about the teacher's writing and suggested additional revisions.

To reinforce the concept of their classrooms as communities of inquiry, the students engaged in a variety of joint projects. For example, they assembled a class book entitled "Our School" for the purpose of informing new students about life at their school. They wrote a chapter about school rules, took photos of their favorite people and places in the school, planned and conducted interviews with significant people in the school, and wrote about those people and places. During a unit on whales, the students created a mural depicting the things they both wondered and learned about as they read and listened to information about whales from multiple sources, including books, newspapers, journals, videotapes, and tape recordings.

Throughout our instruction, we placed considerable emphasis on communicating to the children that they were capable of learning from print—even though they were not yet conventional readers—by listening to text, and studying the pictures from children's nature magazines, trade books, and newspaper articles.

Figure 10–1   *(Continued)*

illustration of this type of environment. Spiegel (1992) and Palincsar and Klenk (1992) comment positively on the excitement generated by such an integrated approach, the flexibility in materials and activities, the increase in students' recreational reading, the high level of student and teacher choice, the encouragement to take risks by trying out new readings and ways of writing, the focus on each child as a unique individual, the increase of humor in the classroom, the greater interest in learning to read (especially from self-generated text), the increase in unsolicited writing, the heightened interest in sharing and displaying one's knowledge, the improvement in conventional spellings and more complete expression of thoughts in writing, the greater opportunity to reveal strategies students have generated independently, and the fostering of pride in one's products even if less than perfect.

In the whole-language approach, writing is viewed as a process of communication among a community of readers and writers. Even before children can read or spell they are encouraged to use invented spellings ("spell it the way you hear it") to begin communicating through writing. This approach, however, does not negate the need for clearly defined objectives for writing instruction and very specific teacher-directed instruction.

Many children with learning disabilities appropriate very little time to planning in advance of writing, and when they sit down to write they frequently simply write whatever comes to mind (Montague, Graves, & Leavell, 1991). These types of students have an extremely impoverished understanding of written language. Palincsar and Klenk (1992) quote several of these children as describing writing in the following ways: "good writers have strong muscles so that they can do cursive," the way to become a good writer is "to practice and hope and hold your pencil right," and writing is "copying the morning news" and "doing your five times each" (spelling list) (p. 218). This lack of understanding contributes to depressed writing competence. While a whole-language environment can build enthusiasm for writing, promote eagerness to try out different forms of writing, provide models for good writing,

and spark ideas, the majority of students with learning disabilities will require very specialized instruction in written expression, spelling, and penmanship.

Written Expression. Beyond expository writing (e.g., compositions, poetry, short stories), written expression skills are important throughout the school years for notetaking, completing written homework assignments, essay exams, term papers, and letter writing. Graves and Montague (1991) point out the added benefits of knowing written story structure, including enhanced ability to evaluate and appreciate literature, plays, movies, television shows, and stories told by friends, as well as the therapeutic value of writing about plots, characters, thoughts, and feelings that relate directly to the student's experiences.

Many of our written expression instructional goals are identical to the oral language goals of speech-language specialists: enriched vocabulary, logical organization of thoughts, inferential reasoning, syntax, ability to use synonyms, and comprehension of metaphors and idioms. Teachers need to make the appropriate referral if students' written expression skills require reinforcement through oral expression as well.

It is important that teachers ascertain whether students' written expression difficulties are due to lack of experiences, weaknesses in language skills, or production difficulties (handwriting, punctuation, capitalization, and spelling). For those who lack motivating experiences to write about, the teacher can introduce particularly exciting literature, provide enriching experiences such as field trips, discussions, and movies, or encourage creative fantasies. The teacher also can help students to be creative about recounting their everyday activities, provide books, newspapers, magazines, posters, or student-generated stories to stimulate ideas, or suggest story enders (e.g., " . . . and waved goodbye to the new friends," " . . . and no longer was afraid of the sea monster," " . . . and after the journey became a much wiser person"). It has been suggested that story enders induce more goal-directed strategies for generating content than do story starters (Montague et al., 1991).

Other students have the experiences to relate but are reluctant to write them down. They may need instruction in such prerequisite skills as idea and theme development, vocabulary, cohesion (logical, clear sequence of events), grammar, and the mechanical rules of writing (handwriting, punctuation, capitalization, paragraph construction, and spelling).

Whatever approach is taken to enhancing written expression, it is important for teachers to remember that their red marks are likely to discourage the writing efforts of students with learning disabilities. Therefore, it is best for written feedback to be given on positive aspects of the student's work, and constructive feedback to be given through conferences with the student. It is equally important that teachers focus on very specific goals in each assignment while overlooking others. Before starting written assignments, students should be told whether their teacher is concerned with content and organization or mechanics. Then students can direct their energies selectively to clarity in thinking, expression of ideas, and creativity, or to grammar, spelling, and mechanical rules.

Maintaining a writing notebook or personal journal has become a popular way of encouraging the development of written expression. Students enjoy writing down personal experiences and reactions that are important to them. The teacher reads the notebook or journal once every four to six weeks and invites students to leave a note telling the teacher what to look for. After reading the work, the teacher may add a personal reaction to the content of entries, but not corrections. The personal nature of the work is respected.

Another unique idea that heightens motivation for writing is periodically giving children ten minutes to write notes to one another; couriers are selected to pass the notes. Implicit in this activity is a heightened motivation to sharpen one's writing skills because what is passed is intended to be read.

Since students with learning disabilities tend to cut their writing short, we find that simply encouraging them to "write some more" can result in longer and higher-quality productions. While students tend to add few new ideas, they do add elaborations to what was already said (Graham, 1990). Strategy instruction also is extremely helpful to increasing reflection, planning, and the ultimate quality of works: for example, STOP (**S**uspend judgement so as to consider each side before taking a posistion, **T**ake a side, **O**rganize ideas, **P**lan more as you write) and DARE (**De**velop your topic sentence, **A**dd supporting ideas, **R**eject arguments for the other side, **E**nd with a conclusion) (De La Paz & Graham, 1997).

Another way to encourage writing is to have the student dictate into a tape recorder. The tape is then transcribed by the student or someone else. The teacher uses this piece for further instruction on written expression competencies. Although for some children dictation has improved the length and quality of compositions, for other students it has led to no change or to less cohesion in writing (Graham, 1990; MacArthur & Graham, 1987; Montague et al., 1991; Newcomer, Barenbaum, & Nodine, 1988). Therefore, before dictation is used on an ongoing basis, teachers need to compare a student's dictated and written products to see which method is likely to promote the most mature writing.

Mather and Lachowicz (1992) suggest a "shared writing" approach in which the teacher and student alternate writing sentences to form a composition. While students can pair with peers as well, the involvement of the teacher is particularly beneficial because the teacher can use his or her sentences to model organization, punctuation, vocabulary, and spelling. A variation of this approach, the *dialogue journal,* involves the teacher and student in a written conversation that is sustained over a period of time (Gaustad & Messenheimer-Young, 1991). Topics are usually initiated by the student. The teacher reads the student's entry and responds in writing, extending the dialogue with additional ideas or questions. The teacher tries to expand on those constructions with which the student has difficulty. Instead of correcting the student's writing, the teacher counts on his or her modeling and the motivation implicit in such an approach to accelerate writing progress.

One very helpful way of facilitating written language development is by means of what we call the *writing process,* especially when this is accompanied by direct instruction (Graham et al., 1992; Zaragoza & Vaughn, 1992). In the writing process, students are given at least thirty minutes daily to write on topics of their choice. They are to focus on the most important element in writing, the message, and worry about the mechanics only after the message is down on paper. The teacher sets the right tone by also writing at the same time as the students.

During the writing process, a relaxed, informal atmosphere is established in the classroom, and students are encouraged to work in small groups if they wish, read their works to each other, solicit feedback from their peers, and so forth. An individual file is maintained that contains works in progress, a list of ideas for future writing topics, the dates students conference with the teacher about their work, and perhaps a list of writing and spelling skills that they have mastered (Bos & Vaughn, 1994). The writing conference is critical to the writing process. This is where the student reads the piece to the teacher, describes difficulties, asks for input, and learns to self-evaluate; the teacher helps the student to explore a few (not all) well-chosen problem areas. The student takes the lead in indicating which aspects of the work to attend to. Ideally, theme development is the initial focus. If teachers hone in on mechanical errors too soon, this may disrupt students' thought and sentence flow in subsequent writing; they may give up if they feel overburdened by too much to concentrate on at once. Skill lessons in the classroom can be developed around the needs that become evident through these conferences.

Bos and Vaughn describe the stages entailed in the writing process: prewriting, composing, revising, editing, and publishing. The *prewriting stage* begins with topic selection, a task that can be hard for students who appreciate neither how much they already know nor what they would want to share with others. To help students brainstorm topics, the teacher might have them list on a piece of paper things of interest about themselves, their family, and friends: hobbies, activities, stories about past happenings. After sharing this list with a partner or the class, the student selects three topics he or she is most interested in writing

about. This process of topic selection contrasts with the picture cues or story starters that teachers typically give students. The process of self-selection communicates not only that we have confidence in students' choices but also that we trust they do have something worthwhile to share. Topic selection is facilitated by offering a range of writing styles, including stories, mysteries, observation of situations, and factual descriptions. Moreover, students are alerted to alternative topics as they read or listen to one another's writing.

The *brainstorming phase* is extremely important before writing begins, in order to get down the major ideas one wishes to communicate and to sequence them logically. Brainstorming might involve simply recording a title; notes on "where," "when," "who," "what happened"; and an ending. A more visual way to brainstorm, depicted in Figure 10–2, has been helpful in increasing children's planning time before writing and the quality of their pieces. Notecards are another means of organizing the content. The use of story grammar cue cards, such as that depicted in Figure 10–3, also have facilitated higher-quality stories in students with learning disabilities. Students check the appropriate story parts as they plan, and once again as they write.

Composing comes next. After composing, reading one's work to others elicits comments and questions that cue the author about revisions that he or she might make. *Revising* is the most difficult of all writing tasks. Many students are relieved to have gotten anything down on paper, let alone have to revise it. At this point the student may need to go back to the prewriting stage to confer with others or seek more information. The focus during revisions is still on content, organization, and theme development.

The revision process offers a unique opportunity to reflect on both one's writing and ideas. Unfortunately, most students do little revision beyond correction of mechanical errors, so that the quality of their composition does not improve (MacArthur, Schwartz, & Graham, 1991). To help students identify problems and try alternatives to improve their works, MacArthur and colleagues demonstrated the usefulness of a peer editor strategy in which student pairs read their

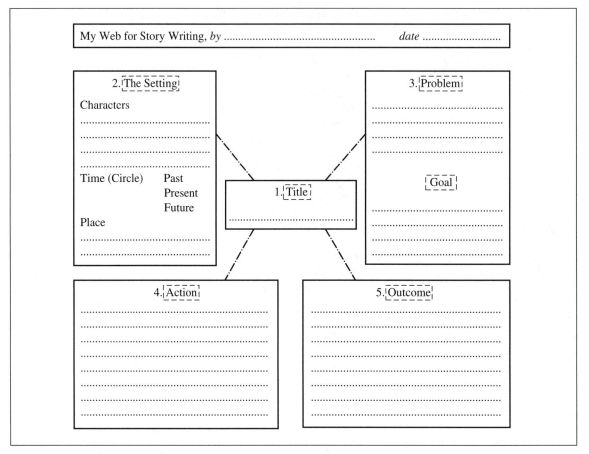

My Web for Story Writing, *by* .... *date* ....

2. The Setting

Characters

....

....

....

Time (Circle)   Past
                Present
                Future

Place

....

....

1. Title

....

3. Problem

....

....

Goal

....

....

4. Action

....

....

....

....

....

....

....

5. Outcome

....

....

....

....

....

....

....

Figure 10–2   Prestructured story web form. *Source:* Zipprich, M. A. (1995). Teaching web making as a guided planning tool to improve student narrative writing. *Remedial and Special Education, 16,* p. 6. Copyright 1995 by PRO-ED, Inc. Reprinted by permission.

works to each other, comment on what they like best in the partner's work, and record revision questions and suggestions that deal with the need for greater clarity or detail in particular sections. Following this discussion, students revise their work and meet once again to edit for mechanical errors: complete sentences, capitalization, punctuation, spelling.

During the following stage, *editing,* attention is turned to spelling, capitalization, punctuation, and language (noun-verb agreement, synonyms). Students are taught to circle misspelled words,

draw boxes around punctuation that may be wrong, and underline sentences that don't sound quite right. Enlisting the help of peer editors makes this process more interesting.

Bos and Vaughn (1994) stress that it is important to *publish* pieces a student writes every few weeks. This involves preparing the piece with a cover and circulating it to others in and beyond the class. Publishing confirms a student's hard work and provides an audience for one's thoughts. Through publishing the broader school community and family become involved in a positive way

	Check as I plan	Check as I write
Characters		
Setting		
Problem		
Plan		
Ending		

Figure 10–3 Story grammar cue card. *Source:* Graves, A., & Montague, M. (1991). Using story grammar cueing to improve the writing of students with learning disabilities. *Learning Disabilities Research & Practice, 6,* p. 247. Reprinted by permission.

with a student's writing. Students' revisions have been shown to improve when they are given such a sense of purpose in writing for an authentic reason and real audience (MacArthur et al., 1991).

Clearly, the writing process takes much time and organization to set up. But once it is working well, the payoffs are evident. Students with a few years' experience with the process would never dream of just sitting down and writing. They begin their research weeks before, carefully organize their notes, brainstorm, and revise their brainstorming before they write. Once these students start to compose, they are relaxed about knowing what they want to say, and in what order. The writing flows much more easily. Phone calls become commonplace, especially between teenagers, asking friends to listen and give feedback before they revise. When an atmosphere of mutual trust and respect is built within the classroom, this type of sharing becomes possible and fun. Students' self-esteem is heightened as they begin to see themselves as writers who have valuable thoughts to share, and control over how they say it.

Spelling. The majority of children with learning disabilities require very directed spelling instruc-

tion because they do not automatically discover spelling relationships through their reading. Whereas the typical elementary school student can spell 70 to 80 percent of his or her sight words (Smith, 1997), we generally find that students with learning disabilities can spell only 30 to 40 percent of the words that they recognize by sight. Spelling problems may be experienced for a number of reasons: trouble recalling which letters go with which sounds, difficulty determining the sequence of sounds heard in a word, trouble recalling typical orthographic patterns, trouble recalling irregular spelling patterns that must be memorized visually (for example, the spelling of *rough* must be memorized; it can't be sounded out), or poor mastery/misapplication of rules. Obviously, the instructional method chosen depends on the teacher's analysis of why the child is experiencing spelling difficulties. For example, if a student can't analyze where sounds are positioned in words, then helping the child learn to segment words into their individual sounds would be an important component of spelling instruction.

Children develop spelling skills in a predictable order, first by translating phonemes to letters and next by internalizing standard orthography. It is important that children be able to read and understand the words being instructed in spelling. Therefore, exercises that encourage composition and attention to orthography are likely to be more useful than weekly spelling lists that are unrelated to one's reading and writing. In addition, incorporating previously mastered spelling words into the everyday curriculum is essential to retention. This review does not have to be a drudgery. Computers can be used. Games can be used (for example, concentration, crossword puzzles, hangman, word lotto). Many students enjoy exercises that capitalize on their visual capacities, for example, filling in various missing letters in the word (first the vowels, then the consonants). Many also enjoy closing their eyes, imagining how the word looks, spelling it aloud, and then writing it down. Those who have difficulty maintaining the word's image are aided by imagining large black glossy letters on the blackboard, each letter being pounded onto a theater marquis, or even a floodlight illuminating the letters one by one

(Pressley et al., 1990). Children also enjoy choosing the one word among four that looks like it is spelled correctly.

Research has found that children benefit from correcting their own spelling tests, from the teacher's help comparing their incorrect spellings with the correct spellings, and from using a dictionary after underlining words in essays about which they are uncertain (Pressley et al., 1990). The common method of writing each word ten times often does not work because students tend to copy rather than to commit the word to memory. Sara, for example, would copy the first letter of a word ten times down the column, then the second letter, and so forth. Certainly this was accomplishing nothing. She began to make much greater progress when she was shown how to fold her paper into a five-column accordion; she copied the word in column 1, then folded over the paper and wrote the word from memory in column 2. She then checked her word against the model in column 1. Sara was told to continue this process until the word was spelled correctly three times. Sara's spelling progress also was facilitated when the target words were selected from words she could read or from her own essays.

The school's reading and language arts curricula include weekly spelling objectives that can be reinforced with special teaching strategies. In applying these strategies, it is important that spelling goals be limited to only a few words, orthographic patterns, or phonetic rules at a time in order to avoid overloading the student. It is helpful if the phonic rules and irregular spellings to be taught are drawn from the spelling vocabulary that the child has used in his or her writing, since children will tend to reuse these same words again and again.

The Elkonin Method. Elkonin's method of teaching phonemic awareness is a powerful tool for enhancing spelling acquisition. Several studies have found improvement in both accurate and invented spellings (words that sound as they should but look different) following a "say-it-and-move-it" procedure that uses disks to represent the phonemes heard in words (Ball & Blachman,

1991; Blachman, 1993; Tangel & Blachman, 1992).

The Fernald and Gillingham-Stillman Approaches. The Fernald remedial reading strategy also has been used successfully with students who have spelling disabilities. In this method students use all their senses (looking, saying, tracing, writing) in acquiring the spellings of words they choose to learn. Writing the word from memory is emphasized. The Fernald method might be appropriate for the student with stronger visual-processing skills because of its whole-word emphasis. The Gillingham-Stillman approach, on the other hand, might best benefit the student whose strength is analyzing and sequencing the sounds of letters in words. The Gillingham-Stillman method actually uses oral and written spelling as a means of teaching reading. Emphasis is placed on listening to the word being pronounced very slowly and then determining which letter sound is heard first, second, third, and so forth. If the child misspells orally, then the teacher might write down the misspelling so that the student can read the misspelling and learn why it was incorrect. After the oral spelling becomes accurate, the student locates a letter card for the first letter, names the letter, and writes it; then the second letter card is found, and so forth. Techniques that simply have children say the letters as they write the word a number of times also accelerate spelling progress (Kearney & Drabman, 1993).

Linguistic Approach. Linguistic approaches to spelling use word families *(bought, sought, thought; picture, torture, future)* and also group morphemes into a systematic instructional approach (for example, adding common prefixes or word endings to stems: *un-, dis-, -s, -ed, -ing*). Arranging words by their common spelling patterns has been found to be a beneficial instructional method, especially when the teacher helps the child recognize that the rhyming elements are spelled alike (Englert, Hiebert, & Stewart, 1985; Hanna, Hodges, & Hanna, 1971; Lovitt, 1975b). It enables the child with learning disabilities to more readily generalize these word forms to others that follow the same orthographic patterns or rules (for example, double the consonant before adding "ing" if preceded by a short vowel). The linguistic approach, when combined with specially constructed activities, can help a child learn to monitor his or her spelling according to the syntactic *(they're, their, there; its, it's)* and semantic *(new, knew; one, won; plain, plane)* aspects of a sentence.

Contingent Imitation Modeling. Several studies have found that when a teacher points out and imitates a misspelling, then models the correct spelling and draws a child's attention to the discrepancies, spelling improves (Fulk & Stormont-Spurgin, 1995).

Other Methods. The constant time delay strategy (see Research Box 10–2), computer-assisted instruction, variations of a five-step procedure (say, write and say, check, trace and say, write and check), and naming letters instead of words while writing also have been found to benefit the spelling of students with learning disabilities. There appears to be no particular advantage among writing, tracing, or keyboarding words on the computer. However, there are some children for whom writing the words may be more effective than simply moving around letter tiles (Fulk & Stormont-Spurgin, 1995). Finally, Wong's (1986) seven-step cognitive strategy is particularly interesting; while concentrating on structural word analysis, the child is taught to ask: (a) Do I know this word?; (b) How many syllables do I hear in this word? (write down the number); (c) I'll spell out the word; (d) Do I have the right number of syllables down?; (e) If yes, is there any part of the word for which I'm not sure of the spelling? (underline and try again); (f) Now, does it look right to me?; (g) When I finish spelling, I'll tell myself I'm a good worker. I've tried hard at spelling.

Handwriting. Despite the availability of word processors, handwriting difficulties still will interfere with productivity in note taking and essay exams and will negatively influence the judgment of teachers when grading exams or an employer when reading a job application. Therefore, every

effort must be made to help the student's handwriting become as fluent and legible as possible.

A classic study of penmanship from the early grades to adulthood found that the letters *a, e, r,* and *t* accounted for about 50 percent of all malformed letters (Newland, 1932). Other common deterrents to legibility include poor spacing between letters and words, failure to connect lines within letters, failure to close letters (for example, *o*), not crossing letters (for example, *t, x*), failure to stay on a line, and variability in size of letters.

The goals of handwriting instruction include holding and directing a writing utensil with appropriate pencil grip, posture, and paper position, as well as correctly, easily, quickly, and legibly forming manuscript (printing) and cursive writing. There is some controversy about whether children with writing disabilities should be taught manuscript or cursive writing first. Students typically begin with manuscript and then make the transition to cursive writing by the third grade. Manuscript generally is easier to learn and more closely resembles the print found in books. When the child has struggled to finally master the manuscript form, school personnel might suggest not making the transition to cursive writing, which would create another struggle. They point out that the signature is the only time that cursive is required in adult life. Advocates of cursive writing, on the other hand, point out that cursive helps limit reversals because all letters are formed from left to right; its connected letters and continuous writing rhythm also help to eliminate irregular spacing and to make writing faster. If the child with learning disabilities learns cursive writing from the beginning, then he or she will not have to transfer from one system to another (Johnson & Myklebust, 1967).

Whether manuscript or cursive is chosen, the instructional approach of teachers will vary, depending on whether the child's handwriting difficulties are caused by weaknesses in revisualization of letter forms, motor coordination, or spatial judgment (Gerard & Junkala, 1980). When, for example, the difficulty is at the perceptual end, the student may require instruction in recognizing and recalling the size, shape, and direction of letters. Instruction eventually addresses such pro-duction skills as the spacing, formation, and orga-nization of letters on the page. Proper positioning of the writing instrument (pencil held lightly be-tween the thumb and first two fingers), paper (right-handers' paper slanted clockwise; left-han-ders' paper slanted counterclockwise), arms (fore-arms on the table, elbows extended slightly), and body (hips touching the back of the chair, feet on the floor, torso leaning slightly forward in a straight line) also affects the child's ability to write.

Often workbook exercises in which students copy a model or follow dotted lines do not offer sufficient instruction to result in fluent, legible handwriting. The teacher often needs to supple-ment or replace the published programs with some of the following instructional steps:

1. The teacher models the correct formation of one letter at a time; letters should be organized by type of stroke (circular, crossed lines).

2. The distinguishing features of the letter are discussed (for example, "hills" for *m* and *h,* "valleys" for *u* and *w*), highlighted (for example, color-coding), and contrasted with other letters; the teacher may model self-correction of his or her own errors.

3. The child might draw the letter very large on a chalkboard or easel to have gravity help with the direction of the strokes; fingerpaints, tracing in sand or shaving cream, tracing bumpy letters created by writing with a grease pencil on paper placed over a mesh screen, and tracing letters formed by dropping glitter on wet glue also are helpful. Eventually the transition to paper and pencil is made. The child is always to say the letter name while tracing or writing.

4. As needed, the teacher physically guides the child's hand, verbally prompts the hand movements, and uses dots, arrows, or associations of the letter strokes with an object to direct letter formation; the child is instructed to say the letter name at the same time.

5. The child is shown how to talk to himself or herself, thereby self-directing the letter formation. Figure 10–4 is an example of the improvement in numeral formation and reversals when nine-year-old Diane was taught to say "over and down" and "around and down" as she drew 7s and 9s, respectively. Two weeks later Diane still remembered this self-verbalization strategy and the reversals did not reappear.

6. After accurately copying the letter a number of times (while saying the letter name), the child writes the letter from memory several times.

7. The child compares the letter with the model, describing areas for improvement and praising correct features.

8. The above process is repeated for letter combinations and then words.

9. Once accuracy is achieved, fluency may be increased by having the child periodically graph the time it takes to copy a paragraph neatly.

The *trace and fade method* is an interest-ing approach to handwriting that maximizes the modeling principle by decreasing visual sup-ports in a more gradual way than suddenly shift-ing from copying words to writing from memory. The child traces a letter or word, then inserts a piece of tracing paper between the model and the product, shifts the paper, and traces again. More and more tracing paper is inserted, until the model's image finally fades away. The child is left forming letters or words from memory. Layers of scotch tape also can be used to gradually fade the model's image.

Particularly useful methods in handwriting instruction are those that build both appropriate learning strategies and motivation: these methods include teaching students to recognize their errors, reinforcing self-instruction and self-correc-tion procedures, using programmed materials with rewards for correct responses, or making positive outcomes (free time) contingent on good handwriting quality (Brigham et al., 1972; Hop-kins, Schutte, & Garton, 1971; Kosiewicz et al.,

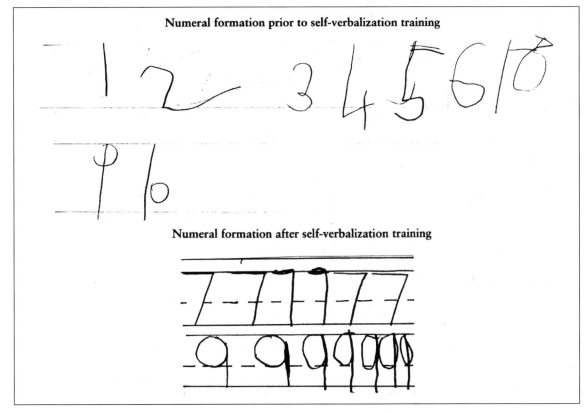

Figure 10–4   Numeral formation before and after self-verbalization training

1982; Tagatz et al., 1969). To ensure success, these methods typically begin with letter forms and gradually progress to words, then to short phrases, and finally to sentences.

Teaching handwriting is an area in which the teacher can be especially creative: developing templates in the form of letters, creating dot-to-dot letters, using acetate for tracing, varying the color paper for different letters, and using paper with different-sized lines to help children stay within boundaries. Also available are sticks for tracing letters in dirt, paint brushes for painting with water on the playground, dough to form letter cookies, pencil grippers that help shape children's pencil grips (and scotch tape to hold the paper in the correct position). Many special commercially prepared materials and programs provide systematic writing exercises and can even turn the paper yellow with a gray dot when the writing instrument goes where it is supposed to. Moreover, our computer technology permits students to draw letters on the screen with a mouse or computer pen. When this is printed out, students take great pride in a computer product that looks like their own handwriting.

Content Area Instruction and Reading Comprehension

In the elementary school, content area instruction occurs primarily in social studies and science courses. By fourth and fifth grade, textbooks might be introduced in these classes and the student may be required to engage in short independent research projects and written assignments. It is critical that the reading, written expression, and study skill weaknesses of the student with learning disabilities not be allowed to interfere with acquiring content or demonstrating knowledge in these areas. Unfortunately, when these basic skills prevent students from fully accessing the broader curriculum, they become less knowledgeable with the years, less prepared for subsequent classes, and less able to interface with their peers around topics of mutual interest or concern.

To evaluate whether the content area textbook is appropriate for a student, the teacher must check vocabulary, sentence complexity, extent of expected prior knowledge, and whether the readability level is appropriate for the student. To evaluate the reading level of the material, the teacher can employ one of several readability formulas described later in this chapter. Texts that teach well highlight important relationships, avoid overloading the student with insignificant concepts and details, give concrete examples for complex concepts, and also provide visual aids, self-checks, interesting content and style, and examples of practical applications of information. When any of these criteria are unmet, the teacher must make the necessary accommodations to meet particular students' needs.

Unfortunately, the student with learning disabilities frequently is disadvantaged by textbooks that are poorly organized, have a stilted writing style, and cover too many facts in too little conceptual depth (Ciborowski, 1995; Harniss et al., 1994). Studies of major elementary science and reading textbooks find that teachers are offered little information about how to adapt lessons to include children with disabilities; science texts, for example, often contain only ideas for supplemental activities, many of which are inappropriate, impractical, and even dangerous (Parmar & Cawley, 1993; Schumm et al., 1994).

Another common problem for students who are learning disabled is that their texts are too difficult for them to read independently. In these cases, a teacher or peer can read the content to the student before class, rewrite the material in vocabulary that the student can manage, or help the student create an outline so that only key words need to be read. If writing is problematic, the student might tape record answers to homework assignments or tests. A teacher, peer, or parent could then transcribe these answers; because the answers represent the youngster's natural language and thoughts, they become ideal material for further instruction in reading, spelling, and written language.

Despite these accommodations, a student still may be unable to comprehend the text's material because its vocabulary and sentence structure are too difficult. This is especially true of social studies and science texts, where experts suggest a "less is more" policy for students with learning disabilities (Carnine et al., 1994; Shepard & Adjogah, 1994). Rather than overwhelm students by covering all topics in a text, these experts suggest that teachers spend more time on carefully chosen topics and study them in greater depth, so that students develop some higher-order meanings rather than learn only superficially. At Syracuse University's Psychoeducational Teaching Laboratory, teachers are helped to rewrite texts, assignments, and tests into vocabulary and sentence complexity/length that matches the student's abilities; illustrations are retained and the simplified version is simply pasted over the old print so the student's text looks like everyone else's. Only essential points about essential topics are retained in order to focus the student's learning and avoid bombardment by too much information.

Comprehension difficulties can involve far more than poor vocabulary, syntax, and semantics, and getting overloaded by too much information, however. Also common are weaknesses identifying details and main ideas, sequencing events, organizing ideas, drawing inferences (using comparison-contrast, cause-effect, conditional relationships, figurative language, style), reaching conclusions, and applying information, especially when higher levels of problem solving and information evaluation are called for.

Since the ultimate purpose of reading is comprehension, opening children's minds to new information, thoughts, ideas, and reasoning abilities, one would think that a major portion of the school day would be spent discussing readings, ideas, and their implications; introducing new vocabulary; building a background to which to link new ideas; and generating prereading questions to stimulate a purpose for reading. Yet, with the exception of whole-language programs, classroom observation indicates that this seldom occurs (Durkin, 1984). More often than not, comprehension exercises are left to worksheets and tests. Therefore, the student who has difficulty not only reading and writing but also comprehending is at a triple disadvantage.

Several approaches can aid comprehension under these circumstances. Most often these methods apply schema theory to create a purpose for reading and a framework within which students can organize and interpret the new information. They also teach self-questioning strategies and encourage the thinking skill goals and metacognitive strategies described in Chapter 6, which are invaluable in aiding comprehension and memory.

Schema Theory. Research on schema theory has established that comprehension will improve as one's fund of relevant background information and awareness of text organization is heightened (Rumelhart, 1980). Applications of schema theory have proved valuable in improving the comprehension of students who find it difficult to locate, interpret, or remember important information and ideas in what they read.

One way to increase comprehension is to activate students' background knowledge. In this way new information can be linked to something that is already familiar and understood, and the new information becomes more memorable. Activating background knowledge is particularly helpful to inferential comprehension because the information is not literally stated in the text; the child's prior knowledge will help the child to infer what is meant. Bos and Vaughn (1994) illustrate the application of background schema in the example of a student reading "Pat watched her father talk on the CB radio and watched the sun come up over the mountains." When asked at what time of day the story took place, a student can respond correctly only if he or she already knows that the sun rises in the morning and then bothers to activate this knowledge.

Bos and Vaughn discuss three ways to help activate background knowledge before a student reads the text: brainstorming, prereading plan, and schema activation. In *brainstorming,* the teacher selects a word, phrase, picture, or excerpt from the reading passage and asks students to list as many words or phrases as they can associate with this stimulus. These lists are compiled into categories on the blackboard. Titles for the categories are discussed, and the underlying ideas are clarified. Then students proceed to read the passage. The *prereading plan* expands on brainstorming by asking students to reflect on what triggered their associations. This discussion generates further insights and associations. For the student who has little knowledge to offer, some basic concept instruction will be necessary before the student actually reads. The *schema activation* strategy encourages students to discuss something that they have done that is similar to the event they will read about in the story and to hypothesize what will happen in the story. The main ideas are explicitly stated before students read, and discussion revolves around what they would do/feel/think in similar circumstances.

In addition to techniques that activate background knowledge, we have found that comprehension can be increased by alerting students to the text's organizational structure. Basically these strategies teach *story grammar,* the essential components of typical narratives and how these components interrelate (Griffey, Zigmond, & Leinhardt, 1988). Carnine and Kinder (1985), for example, found that when students were taught to ask themselves a series of text organization questions as they read, they approached new material with a greater ability to gain information. Questions included:

1. *Who* is the story about?
2. *What* is he or she trying to do?
3. *What happens* when he or she tries to do it?
4. What happens *in the end?*

Teachers also can highlight organizational structure by manipulating magnetic or cardboard figures depicting a story's events as the student listens to the story; comprehension increases (Chan, Cole, & Morris, 1990).

Another way to encourage more active involvement in the comprehension process is to teach children to differentiate between questions whose answers easily can be found in one place in the text, those that are hidden in the text, and those that require the reader to rely entirely on what he or she already knows. Children do this by self-verbalizing answers to three self questions: How will I answer this question? Where is the answer to the question found? Is my answer correct? Teaching these types of discriminations enhances children's comprehension, presumably because they discover where one can go to find answers, including one's own mind (Graham & Wong, 1993).

Finally, Bos and Vaughn (1994) describe a variation of the *RAP* procedure presented in Figure 6–2. Here, elementary school children paraphrase the main ideas and details of a paragraph by dictating into a tape recorder. In a study following a similar procedure, children had to write a brief statement summarizing each paragraph immediately after reading it. Comprehension improved significantly (Jenkins et al., 1986). Teachers also can use story retelling strategies to alert students to the fact that narratives can be organized into such components as the setting, problem, goals, sequence of events (initiating events, reactions, outcomes), and an ending. With *story maps* (see Figure 10–5) students can map these relationships, thereby clarifying story components (Bos & Vaughn, 1994).

Questioning Strategies.   The more we predict what is to come and question ourselves as we read, the more likely we are to comprehend. Teaching questioning strategies to students with learning disabilities is particularly important because these students tend not to spontaneously monitor their comprehension as they read. One such technique, *Multipass,* was described in Figure 6–2. Another technique, *SQ3R,* teaches the child to survey the reading materials first (chapter title, introductory statement, main headings, illustrations, summary) (Robinson, 1961). Then the student reads the end of the chapter questions to discover the pur-

pose for reading or formulates his or her own questions from the headings (for example, who, what, where, when, why, how). The 3 Rs follow: *R*ead the material to find the answers to these questions, *R*ecite the answers to the questions, and *R*eview the material to check for accuracy or gain new information and ideas. Adaptations of the SQ3R technique have been widely used. In one adaptation, *directed reading-thinking activities,* students make predictions about what they will be reading and generate questions (Stauffer, 1969). They then read to determine if they were accurate and to answer their questions. The teacher follows up with questions that require interpretation.

The teacher also can enhance the student's comprehension and retention of information by assigning short segments of passages and then immediately following each with a *reciprocal questioning* technique between teacher and pupil. The questions progress to higher-level question types only when the child is ready to handle such thinking: knowledge (facts, sequence of information, categories, methods), comprehension (interpret ideas, inference), application, analysis (of content, relationships, structure), synthesis (apply own ideas regarding the material or a solution, generalize), and evaluation (analyze and make judgments about conclusions) (Bloom et al., 1956). Manzo's (1969) *request* technique, for example, has the child and teacher ask each other questions after each has read the material silently. First the child asks the teacher questions, which gives the teacher an opportunity to model appropriate answers. If the teacher is uncertain of an answer, he or she checks in the text. Next, the teacher gets to model appropriate question types by asking the child. This questioning process aids evaluation and retention of information. Similarly, *elaborative interrogation,* in which the teacher's questions guide students to reason out why a fact is true, leads to greater long-term recall than merely being told the reason (Scruggs, Mastropieri, & Sullivan, 1994).

In a group questioning technique called *reciprocal teaching,* the teacher and students take turns leading class discussions regarding the content of texts they are reading or listening to. The

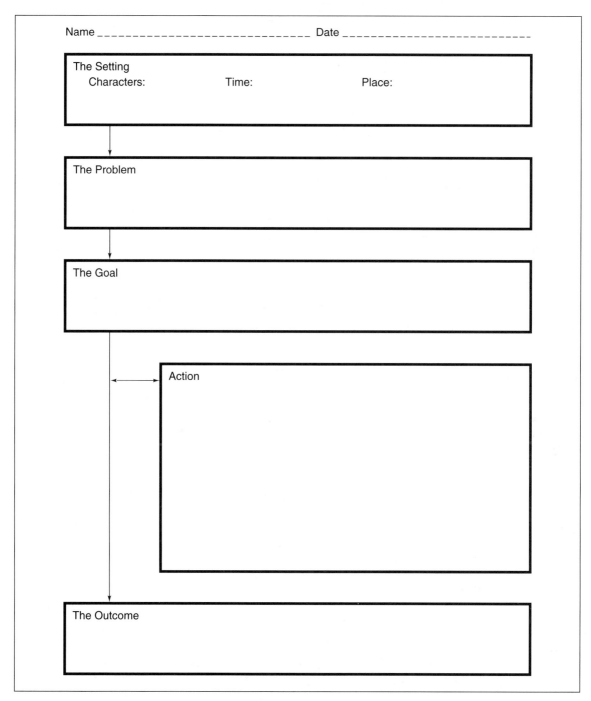

Figure 10–5 Story map. *Source:* Idol, L., & Croll, V. J. (1987). Story-mapping as a means of improving reading comprehension. *Learning Disability Quarterly, 10,* p. 216. Reprinted by permission.

teacher initially models and labels different comprehension strategies to help guide the leader's discussion: questioning, summarizing, clarifying, predicting. The ensuing discussion focuses on the content of the text, inferences, disagreements in interpretation, arriving at a group summary of the gist of the segment read, and predicting what will come next. Palincsar and Klenk (1992) found that recall of text, summarizing the gist of the material, and application of this knowledge to a novel situation increased when using reciprocal teaching, and these comprehension gains were maintained for six months to a year. The value of this strategy is that it sharpens a child's ability to engage in intentional learning from text, to use higher levels of discourse, and to self-monitor one's comprehension processes. Several of these comprehension strategies can be combined for the benefit of students with learning disabilities, for example, using strategy cue cards and story mapping in the context of reciprocal teaching activities (Englert et al., 1994).

Mathematics

Many children with learning disabilities have difficulty understanding basic number concepts, time, measurement, money, fractional units, or computational processes. These children also have little success with solving word problems because these require reading in addition to abstract reasoning, mathematical reasoning, and computation skills. To choose the best remediation approach, the teacher must determine exactly what the student has and has not mastered in the program's scope and sequence chart and then identify what may be interfering with the child's mathematical progress, such as difficulty with size and spatial relations, logical reasoning, motor movements in writing numerals, reading, recall of number facts, inattentiveness to details, or poor past teaching. A planning technique that is particularly helpful is to listen to students as they problem solve aloud. We find from this that students' errors usually are not random. They are trying to apply a rule, but they do so in a faulty manner. As the child talks through his or her reasoning, step by step, the teacher can gain an understanding of why the

errors are occurring and design the most fitting instructional approach.

Computations are only one aspect of a mathematics curriculum. Students must learn how to apply this knowledge in everyday situations, estimate the reasonableness of their answers, read tables and graphs, reason about geometric principles, deal with time and measurement, and handle money. Therefore, it is important that the math instruction for students with learning disabilities be put into a meaningful framework to help these skills transfer to real-life problem solving.

As with traditional reading curricula, the classroom's math curriculum frequently does not meet the needs of the student with learning disabilities. Often the reading vocabulary is too difficult, too many concepts are introduced at once with insufficient practice being offered on any one concept, little practical application of these skills is built in, and students may be unprepared for the concepts taught (Blankenship, 1984). Therefore, the teacher may need to use alternate approaches designed specifically for students with disabilities. The teacher will find him or herself using ingenuity in helping students who have difficulty with various aspects of math, as in:

- aligning calculations (use graph paper, turn lined paper sideways)
- remembering number facts (use a tachistoscope, computer drills, number line, fact sheet, or a matrix pasted to the desk; teach how to count on from the highest number and to count by 2s, 3s, 4s, 5s, and 10s; teach rounding to the nearest 5 or 10 and then adding or subtracting from the answer the amount that was rounded; teach "count-bys" to calculate multiplication facts (counting by 2s, 3s, 4s, etc.); reduce the number of addition facts to be learned by teaching doubles for numbers one through nine (5 + 5), then double plus 1 (5 + 6 is calculated as 5 + 5 + 1), doubles plus 2 (5 + 7 is calculated as 5 + 5 + 2), add 1/subtract 1 before doubling [6 + 8 is calculated as $(6 + 1) + (8 - 1) = 7 + 7$], and going through 10 [9 + 5 is calculated as $(10 + 5 = 15) - 1$] (Pressley et al., 1990)

- reading word problems (transcribe them into numerals; teach cue words such as "altogether" and "left"; reduce sentence length and vocabulary complexity; eliminate extraneous information)

- comprehending word problems (paraphrase them; draw a representation of the problem; estimate an answer before calculating; personalize word problems to the child's interests and real life surroundings) (Pressley et al., 1990)

- attending to all elements of a problem (set up lists of steps or self-checking devices)

- becoming overloaded by too many problems on a page (cut each worksheet into four segments)

- understanding tens and ones places in borrowing (enact the calculation using groups of ten tongue depressors banded together and single tongue depressors)

- understanding what a numerical problem really means (draw a picture of it, make up a story problem about it)

- conceptualizing fractions (enact by sharing food or toys, using a measuring cup)

- showing disinterest and lack of perceived relevance (build math story problems into other subject matter lessons) (Cawley, 1984)

- calculating, despite good conceptual and practical understanding of the problem (use calculators).

There has been great reluctance on the part of teachers to use calculators, even when the computation process is so arduous for the child that it draws the child's attention away from math concepts and applications (Suydam, 1982). Nevertheless, research consistently shows that in the early elementary years calculators in fact increase skill acquisition, attitudes toward math, and self-confidence (Hembree, 1986). It seems that calculators help students avoid being sidetracked by complicated computation processes, so that they are freed up to reason more intelligently about the

mathematical concepts. This mathematical reasoning, rather than calculation ability, should be at the forefront of classroom math objectives. After all, even calculators are useless if one cannot reason whether to add or subtract, or whether the calculator's answer appears reasonable.

Unfortunately, even the instruction of good math students suffers from a paucity of practice in quantitative reasoning. Stipp (1992) reports that when second graders were asked the following question, 90 percent of the children gave the answer "36," despite having scored above average on a standardized achievement test: There are 26 sheep and 10 goats on a ship. How old is the captain?

Clearly, traditional "drill and kill" math teaching, in which children memorize rules and do routine exercises in preparation for achievement tests, has not resulted in facility with higher-order quantitative reasoning. In order to develop such reasoning Stipp describes teaching within the *constructivist* model, which encourages teachers to let their students learn math by wrestling with personally engaging problems, thereby constructing their own knowledge and basic quantitative understandings. Students grapple as a group with interesting problems, problem solve aloud, and try different approaches. For example, they might build a scale model of a pencil from Gulliver's land of the giants, given only the clue of the size of a paperclip. They might also calculate in what year women swimmers might surpass men's records, given that the two have been getting closer. Such active learning engenders excitement and basic conceptual development, but must be accompanied by teacher feedback and systematic calculation and application practice for students who do not discover relationships for themselves. Besides this active learning, several special approaches incorporating concrete materials and behavioral techniques have benefited the mathematics attainment of students with learning disabilities.

Concrete Materials. Many children have difficulty understanding that the numerals on paper actually represent real things. Until they can comprehend this relationship, paper-pencil adding of numerals serves no purpose and, in fact, will only confuse the child further. These students benefit from seeing and manipulating the quantities and algorithms about which they are reasoning, thereby learning to associate these quantities and processes with the numerals and operations (Marsh & Cooke, 1996; Peterson, Mercer, & O'Shea, 1988). Concrete materials help children reason about the logical relationships represented by numerals: largest–smallest, first-last-next, more than–less than, and so forth. For impulsive students, touching the real objects, in contrast to counting pictures, will slow their counting speeds so that their accuracy increases.

Concrete objects should be the focus of beginning instruction in all areas, not just operations. Understanding the time we wake up, go to school, go to bed, day of the week, months of the year, and moving the hands of a real clock, for example, are important for instruction of time concepts, as are real money for money concepts (for example, set up a class store) or real tools for measuring (for example, weigh or measure ingredients in recipes and the amount of cloth needed for a doll's blanket). The more this practice can occur with real-life activities, the more likely it is that the utility of the number concepts will be understood and that they will be applied when needed in practical circumstances. It generally is recommended that children learn mathematics principles first using manipulative devices, next pictures of objects and tallies, and finally numbers only (Miller & Mercer, 1993). *Cuisenaire rods* and *Stern's Structural Arithmetic* are commonly used concrete approaches in which children actively manipulate concrete materials while engaging in activities to discover number concepts, facts, and problem-solving approaches.

Behavioral Techniques. Behavioral methods systematically sequence the order of presentation of math skills and give students immediate feedback on accuracy. In the *Sullivan Basal Math Program,* for example, students progress through a series of programmed workbooks that teach addition, subtraction, multiplication, division, fractions, and decimals. The student progresses at his or her own rate. Because the workbooks are self-correcting, they provide immediate feedback con-

cerning right or wrong responses. When each workbook is completed, the teacher administers a test to check for mastery. Because the program does not require any reading, it is useful for students whose mathematical difficulties are complicated by their inability to read directions and word problems. However, because it doesn't teach the basic concepts underlying computations, the program needs to be supplemented with materials that highlight these relationships.

Another approach based on behavioral principles is the *Distar Arithmetic Program I, II, III* in which, like its counterpart reading program, the teacher must adhere to a prescribed set of verbal instructions. The child is actively involved by responding orally and in writing to a rapid presentation of problems. The fast-paced activity and motivation implicit in this approach helps to engage students' attention. Whether it is appropriate for students with learning disabilities who process information very slowly and have trouble responding to aural directions needs to be evaluated on an individual basis.

Cawley's Project Math is a program designed to overcome the problems associated with traditional curricula. It teaches to mastery, reduces the level of reading demands, and ties ongoing assessment to a number of excellent instructional modifications.

Constant time delay also is a very effective strategy. The teacher shows the child a math fact. If the child doesn't respond correctly within about three seconds, the teacher simply supplies the answer. The student then repeats the teacher's model and the teacher proceeds to a new math fact. Three to six facts are taught as a set, in a near errorless fashion (Koscinski & Hoy, 1993). In a variation, Williams and Collins (1994) encouraged students to use their fingers, poker chips, or a number line if they could not provide the number fact within the designated time.

Finally, cognitive behavior modification techniques are particularly helpful when applied to mathematics instruction. After the teacher models a problem-solving procedure by talking it through aloud, the student and teacher repeat the process together; then the child self-instructs aloud as problem solving continues, and finally self-instruction becomes inaudible (Leon & Pepe, 1983). A variant of this approach was used by Case and others (1992) to help children learn to identify the correct operation to use in word problems. The instructor modeled self-instructions for problem definition ("What is it I have to do?") and planning ("How can I solve this problem?". . . . by looking for important words). This was followed by a five-step strategy: read the problem, circle the key words, draw a picture representing the problem, write an equation, solve the problem. Next came self-evaluation ("How am I doing? Does this make sense?") and self-reinforcement ("I did a nice job; I got it right").

Social–Emotional Adjustment

Oliver Wendell Holmes once attended a meeting in which he was the shortest man present. "Doctor Holmes," quipped a friend, "I should think you'd feel rather small among us big fellows." "I do," retorted Holmes, "I feel like a dime among a lot of pennies" (Canfield & Wells, 1976, p. 55).

We are all perceived differently by our friends, our family, and people we meet. Certain attributes are noticed by some individuals and not by others. These men focused on how Holmes was different from them, equating the difference with inferiority. Holmes was able to change their observation to reflect self-worth. Similarly, the teacher who focuses attention on the strengths of individuals with learning disabilities and on their many similarities to others, rather than on their differences, can help to counter the many negative stereotypes applied to children with disabilities. The teacher plays a significant role in developing students' positive self-images. The better children feel about themselves, the more likely they will be to use their strengths to their benefit and to face up to, and try to overcome, weaknesses. We have learned that the student with learning disabilities is in jeopardy of social failure as a result of academic failure, social imperceptiveness, language difficulties, and more. Because one's feelings of self-worth and social skills play a significant role in present and future adjustment, teachers have an important responsibility to develop programming in this area. Let us explore a few approaches.

Multicultural Education. Students cannot feel good about themselves unless the school environment is one that is equitable and just, one that appreciates the unique contributions offered by individuals from different racial, ethnic, income, exceptionality, and sexual orientation groups. A wide diversity of students are part of our classrooms, and all students must feel welcomed and valued in order to feel open to expressing their views, and motivated and able to learn. Unfortunately, much of the school curriculum is written from the white perspective: white generals, white explorers, white inventors. This one-sided emphasis needs to be balanced by the teacher so that students learn to appreciate and take pride in the strengths of every individual's history and culture. This means that teachers must deal with the struggles and hopes of all Americans within the classroom by:

1. incorporating ethnic information into topics being taught (e.g., the roles of African American brigades and Native Americans during the Civil War)

2. examining history and knowledge from different vantage points (e.g., examining the "discovery" of America from a Sioux's perspective; recognizing varying student perspectives on an issue)

3. using teaching strategies that match children's learning styles and promote progress (e.g., cooperative learning)

4. helping create school cultures that promote equity (e.g., rethink instructional grouping practices or academic eligibility criteria for sports participation) (Banks, 1993).

Multicultural education recognizes not only cultural differences but also the value of a child's language. If everyone in Mr. Shulman's class is told to speak only English, and Juan just arrived from Mexico, it will not be long before he feels that his language and culture are being denied, so he must be inferior. The more we incorporate Juan's language and culture in instruction, the more his self-esteem and motivation rise, and the more familiar, meaningful, and memorable the lessons become. This extends to exams as well, in which Juan, even once he becomes conversationally fluent in English, is asked questions and given the opportunity to respond in both English and Spanish; this is necessary because Juan may be unfamiliar with the vocabulary on the test. This type of respect for diversity should pervade the entire school climate, so that Native American handicrafts are introduced in art class; African drumming, the blues, cajun music, or jazz in music class; dramatic presentations focusing on historical and contemporary cultures in drama club; traditional foods in health class; oral histories of grandparents or fables and folktales in English class to explore the similarities and differences among people of different cultures; and so forth.

In discussing issues of diversity, teachers worry that if they permit students to speak their minds, some contributions may be understood as bigoted. They worry that talking about differences will only exacerbate them and lead to discord in the classroom. This is not true, however, provided that teachers convey that different students' opinions matter to them, that there is no "right" or "wrong," that we don't need to agree on everything, that put-downs or preaching are not permitted, and that listening to others with respect and without interruption promotes understanding whether or not consensus is reached. Open, honest conversations can be the beginning of greater understanding and promote the social integration and achievement of students from underrepresented groups.

Peer-Mediated Approaches. In addition to building a multiculturally sensitive environment, teachers can help students with learning disabilities be accepted and develop friendships by judiciously pairing children for instruction, projects, seatwork, and special privileges. Fox (1989) found peer pairings in which children discovered areas of mutual interest to be of particular benefit to the social acceptance of students with learning disabilities. *Peer tutoring* also has been shown to benefit friendships, social skills, classwork, and positive attitudes and interactions between children with

disabilities and their typical peers (Warger, 1991). The child with learning disabilities can be tutored by a classmate, tutor that classmate when appropriate, or tutor younger children. Classmates also can be used successfully as peer trainers to help manage the nonacademic behavior of a student with learning disabilities, to model how to achieve academic and behavioral goals, and to increase play interactions and sharing (Lloyd et al., 1988; McEvoy, Odom & McConnell, 1992). Dohrn and Bryan (1994) describe their success with teaching peer tutors to use attribution statements to help the learning disabled feel more capable and try harder (e.g., "You're really trying hard," "Try this strategy"). The mutual give and take that develops in such situations goes a long way toward making youngsters with learning disabilities feel worthwhile, and helping them find at least one friend to whom they are important.

A variation of peer tutoring, *classwide peer tutoring,* is another interesting means of stimulating social and academic gains. In classwide peer tutoring, the class is randomly divided into two or more teams that compete for points. Two to four times a week, tutor pairs within teams ask one another prescribed questions from study guides, listen to one another read, dictate spelling words, and so on, for twenty to thirty minutes. Halfway through the session, tutors and tutees switch roles. Tutors award two points for correct answers on the first try, and one point on the second attempt (after the tutor has modeled the correct response). The teacher circulates throughout the room, awarding points for tutor-tutee cooperation and appropriate behavior. Such systems have been successful in raising students' classroom grades and self-concept, increasing time on task, decreasing behavior problems, increasing opportunities for direct feedback, and increasing reading, math, and spelling accuracy (Delquadri et al., 1986; Ginsburg-Block & Fantuzzo, 1997; Maheady, Harper, & Sacca, 1988; Warger, 1991). Even at the junior high and high school level, truancy and tardiness decreased and failing grades on quizzes were virtually eliminated by using classwide peer tutoring. And with the elimination of school failure comes the enhancement of one's self-esteem. In Chapter

12 we will explore another peer-mediated instructional model—cooperative learning.

Social Skills Building Programs. Social skills programs help children learn to appreciate the worthiness of their own and others' ideas, feelings, and attributes. They use discussion and systematic teaching to help children define their personal and interpersonal problems, identify long- and short-range goals, generate alternative solutions to problems, choose the best option based on predicted consequences, act on this option, and evaluate the outcome. In the course of the program, students are helped to become more sensitive to their own and others' needs, to cope more effectively with emotional upsets, to adapt to new situations, to interpret environmental and interpersonal cues so as to judge which behaviors are appropriate, to communicate more effectively and honestly with others, to give positive feedback, to give and accept negative feedback appropriately, to initiate and maintain conversations, to resolve conflicts with others (negotiate, resist peer pressure), and to maintain friendships (Vaughn, Levine, & Ridley, 1986). One technique, for example, that helps students avoid behavioral outbursts when feeling anxious, angry, or frustrated is to teach them to identify the body reactions that reflect these feelings, and then say three statements:

(present) (1) *I feel* . . . (angry).
(past) (2) *because* . . . (Ronnie called me "stupid").
(future) (3) *I want* . . . (him to stop).

Through these statements students become aware of their typical behavior patterns when these feelings are aroused, and they are guided toward more appropriate behavioral decisions that accomplish the desired end. Table 7–3 and Figure 7–3 offered samples of additional objectives emphasized within these social skills programs.

Many of these programs combine behavior modification and social-learning theory principles to achieve the targeted goals. They reinforce behaviors as they approximate the goal, reinforce behaviors incompatible with inappropriate behaviors, and use contracts, modeling, self-evaluation,

and self-management, all while keeping track of the frequency or duration of the targeted behaviors. LaGreca and Mesibov (1981), for example, describe how students learned greeting, joining, and conversational skills by observing leaders model appropriate and inappropriate skills, discussing how and when to use these, role playing, critiquing videotapes, and practicing in and out of sessions, followed again by discussion. Goldstein and Gallagher (1992) describe their use of *script training,* in which teachers teach children scripted roles for everyday situations: going to dinner, shopping, waiting as a customer at a hamburger stand. The teacher provides initial modeling and direct instruction on what to do and say. The teacher then prompts students to stay in their roles and maintain communication as they enact their roles.

Bessell and Palomares's (1972) *Human Development Program* is more informal than those just described. Children sit in a "magic circle" and share their feelings and attitudes while becoming attuned to what other members of the group are feeling. The teacher acts as facilitator to get the group started and encourages participation, without being overly directive. Anyone may suggest topics for discussion. If they wish, children can "pass" when it is their turn to contribute to the group. Children are not permitted to comment on each others' statements, so that no value judgments occur. With such safety measures built in, children who choose to listen eventually become participants.

A very different approach is taken by Dinkmeyer's (1970) *Developing Understanding of Self and Others* (DUSO). DUSO contains pre-planned lessons using puppets, songs, and role playing. Topics are designed to enhance the emotional and social development of elementary school students by discussing similarities and differences among children, helping, sharing, independence, decision making, feelings, and so forth. In the upper elementary grades this program transitions into *Toward Affective Development* (TAD), which covers more sophisticated topics.

Although social skills programs do improve target skills during the training sessions, most often the programs are only moderately successful because the learned behaviors do not generalize to interactions within everyday situations (Berler, Gross, & Drabman, 1982; DuPaul & Eckert, 1994; Forness & Kavale, 1996). This happens in part because of short-lived programs that do not incorporate practice of precise enough skills in real-life situations, and in part because students with learning disabilities may have the appropriate social repertoires in their behavior but misjudge in which situations these should be applied. Therefore, Perlmutter (1986) urges that social skills training emphasize how to better understand which social situations call for which behaviors. Moreover, Forman (1987) argues that because social problems occur in real relationships between people, they are best taught in the naturalistic context, by involving all members in that relationship. In this way, everyone shares responsibility, not just the child with learning disabilities.

Classroom Environment. Teachers should systematically plan to devote time daily to the type of learning just described. Helping children to better appreciate themselves and others, however, is not something that can be limited to a twenty-minute curriculum slot. The teacher must model respect, trust, honesty, and positive expectations throughout the school day. These are reflected in the teacher's behaviors (grading only items that children get right, eliminating red pencils, using progress charts) and the types of activities that the teacher encourages, such as participating in daily group problem solving, discussing items anonymously dropped into a problem box, sharing family trees, picking a student of the week, including the child in curriculum decisions, sharing the successes of individual children, putting on plays, role playing, using puppets, having each child write something good about the student on his or her right and then having the class guess which statement describes whom, and so forth. Specifically creating a situation in which the student is perceived as valuable because of a learned skill he or she then teaches to the class also is helpful in building social acceptance (Vaughn, McIntosh, & Spencer-Rowe, 1991). One of the best ways to

promote positive self-esteem and social relationships is to substitute cooperative for competitive learning systems (see Chapter 12) and to build on students' talents rather than always focusing on their weaknesses.

One interesting activity specifically geared toward cooperative behavior is to have each child award one point at the end of the day to a classmate who was helpful to him or her. The helpful act is reported to the class, and if the child requests it, the class can vote to award up to two points. The teacher also can award one point to anyone who is observed being helpful to another. Over time, points accumulate and the teacher auctions items collected from the children's and teacher's homes. Children bid with their points, go home with trinkets they won, and come to school the next day ready to be helpful.

Helpfulness breeds gratitude, friendship, and good feelings about oneself. When the child's self-confidence and trust in others is built, he or she is more likely to try harder to succeed in all ways. The teacher can be instrumental in raising this motivation by giving the student feedback that suggests that effort and specific behaviors can lead to success.

Besides the classroom and special education teachers, the school psychologist and guidance counselor can provide counseling. The art, gym, and music teachers can enhance students' self-esteem by helping them achieve in areas in which they show promise. Often the school custodian is one of the most valued pals that students have, and the librarian can guide students to books in which characters have learned to cope with situations with which the students themselves are grappling. A popular author of this type in recent years is Judy Blume. Her *Tales of a Fourth Grade Nothing, Blubber,* and other titles present situations that are all too familiar to many. Students can be helped through trying times when they read these books, dramatize them, incorporate them into art projects, and discuss the characters' solutions or feelings and how these pertain to real situations in the children's lives. The cartoon in Figure 10–6 depicts the attitude with which we hope our students will leave school.

Figure 10–6 Self-concept: An important goal of schooling. *Source:* © 1971 by United Feature Syndicate. Reprinted by permission.

Secondary School Programming

Students who are learning disabled are likely to develop additional difficulties on entering secondary school. The adolescent not only experiences learning-related problems but also must concurrently deal with the changes in his or her body, emotional needs, and social environment. Like the nondisabled student, the adolescent with learning disabilities does not always pass smoothly through these changes. Disruptions in his or her life patterns and adjustment are to be expected.

If individualizing instruction was difficult at the elementary school level, it is even more so at the secondary level. Gaps between one's achievement and that of classmates often widen with the years, and greater variability in program requirements must be dealt with. Strengths must be enhanced, and compensations must be developed. Provided that the adolescent is motivated to try to overcome his or her weaknesses, remedial programming is also important. Remedial sessions in reading, mathematics, written language, and survival skills are the customary interventions offered to students who are learning disabled, together with academic tutoring, transition planning, and learning-strategy instruction. Only recently have educators turned their attention to other critical needs: instruction in speaking, thinking, and social skills.

Reading

The primary goals of secondary level reading instruction are to help students cope with the secondary school's academic requirements and to prepare the student for everyday reading demands as an adult. Reading can be taught in isolation, through the content areas, or both. Some strategies developed for younger learners continue to be useful with secondary students, although most are too immature and require retailoring for adolescents.

Those students who are severely reading disabled still need to be taught basic decoding and comprehension strategies. When a student struggles to decode material that is too hard, comprehension and acquisition of fundamental knowledge and concepts will suffer because the student can't devote energy to understanding the content at the same time as decoding. To cope with this problem, high interest–low reading level texts have been developed for these students. Instead of being limited to reading content that is far below their intellectual maturity, teenagers can read content area books and classics written at easier levels, or material about the major disasters of the world, rock stars, unexplained phenomena, biographies, foods, and other age-appropriate topics. Even *Time Magazine* and *Sports Illustrated* have photo-packed versions *"For Kids"* that are abbreviated into a few pages of short excerpts on newsbreaking stories. These materials use easier reading vocabulary and shorter sentences to convey sophisticated content with mature print size, appearance, and format.

Special attention at the secondary level must be given to rebuilding positive attitudes toward reading, since the attitude with which students leave high school tends to characterize their orientation toward reading throughout adulthood (Ribovich & Erikson, 1980). To help prepare them for secondary school and adult reading needs, a large majority of teenagers with learning disabilities require instruction in vocabulary development, reading rate, and the comprehension skills needed to read for meaning.

Vocabulary.   You are familiar with studies showing that our words guide our thinking, and that the ability to name and verbally rehearse what we see and hear enhances our memory capacities. The implication is that building the vocabularies of students with learning disabilities, and facility in translating new information into one's own words, is important. Providing teenagers with opportunities to use new words in everyday language or to read new words through a broad range of

reading materials will strengthen their ability to communicate orally, to read, to comprehend, to recall information, and to write meaningfully.

A technique called *SSR* (sustained silent reading) can help with vocabulary development by encouraging the student to read anything he or she wishes for a set period of time each day, without interruptions. The student is neither questioned nor tested on the material. Reading is for enjoyment alone, and vocabulary, comprehension, and positive attitudes toward reading tend to increase (Cline & Kretke, 1980; Minton, 1980).

The *language experience approach* is also helpful in expanding oral and reading vocabularies. In this approach the student discusses an event or idea that he or she would like to write about and then dictates it to the teacher. The teacher encourages incorporation of new vocabulary words and develops a classroom environment in which students feel secure enough to try these words, and even new thinking, without fearing negative reactions (Deighton, 1970). The student then transcribes the piece, which can be used for further instruction in any number of areas: vocabulary development, comprehension, written organization, sentence structure, and so forth.

Whenever new vocabulary is introduced, it needs to be used in as rich a variety of meaningful contexts as possible, to help the student to understand its connotations and extended meanings (Adams, 1990). That is why interactive techniques such as those depicted in Figures 10–7, 10–8, and 10–9 are more helpful in building vocabulary knowledge than is typical definition instruction (see explanation of these strategies on page 410) (Bos & Anders, 1990). By activating students' background knowledge and developing conceptual understandings about a vocabulary word, these strategies help increase comprehension.

Reading Rate.   Reading rate is a significant problem for students with learning disabilities. Horton, Lovitt, and Christensen (1991) report that the reading rate of their secondary students with learning disabilities ranged from 32 to 152 words per minute, in comparison with 93 to 187 words per minute for teenagers without disabili-

Relationship Chart for the Chapter on Fossils

Key
+ = positive relationship
− = negative relationship
0 = no relationship
? = uncertain

Important Ideas

Important Words	Type of life		Location			Extinct?	
	Plant	Animal	Sea	Land	Lakes	Extinct	Not extinct
Trilobites							
Crinoids							
Giant cats							
Coral							
Bryozoans							
Guide fossils							
Dinosaurs							
Fresh water fish							
Brachiopods							
Small horses							
Ferns							
Enormous winged bugs							
Trees							

Figure 10–7 Semantic-feature analysis. *Source:* Bos, C. S., & Anders, P. L. (1987). Semantic feature analysis: An interactive teaching strategy for facilitating learning from text. *Learning Disabilities Focus, 3*, p. 57. Reprinted by permission of the Division for Learning Disabilities.

ties. Because the faster one reads, the more attention can be freed up for comprehension, increasing reading rate is an important goal (Snider & Tarver, 1987).

For the most part, students with learning disabilities tend not to adjust their reading rates to the difficulty of the material and the purpose for reading. Consequently, reading for pleasure is

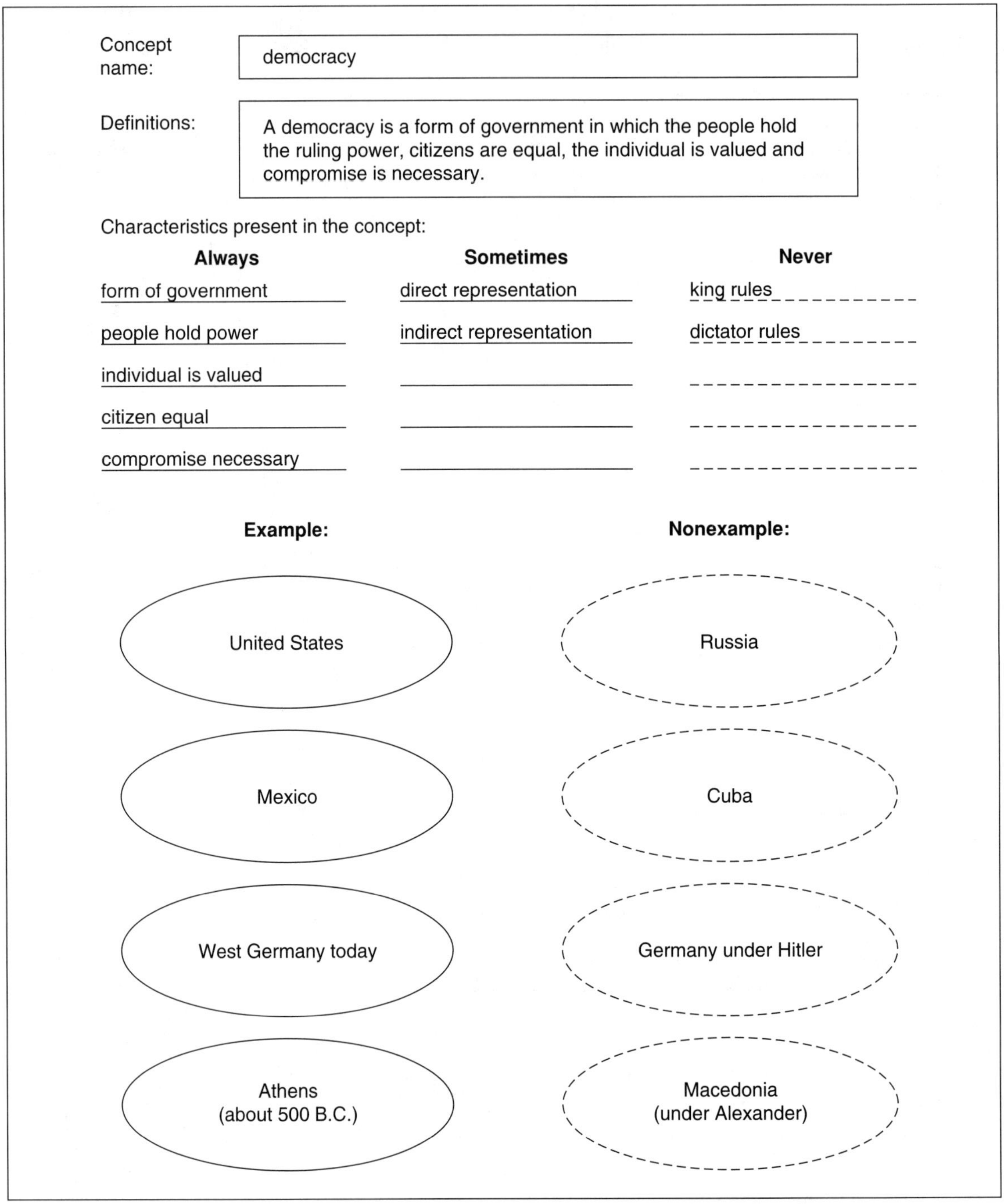

Concept name: democracy

Definitions: A democracy is a form of government in which the people hold the ruling power, citizens are equal, the individual is valued and compromise is necessary.

Characteristics present in the concept:

Always	Sometimes	Never
form of government	direct representation	king rules
people hold power	indirect representation	dictator rules
individual is valued		
citizen equal		
compromise necessary		

Example:

- United States
- Mexico
- West Germany today
- Athens (about 500 B.C.)

Nonexample:

- Russia
- Cuba
- Germany under Hitler
- Macedonia (under Alexander)

Figure 10–8 Concept diagram. *Source:* Bulgren, J., Schumaker, J. B., & Deschler, D. D. (1988). Effectiveness of a concept teaching routine in enhancing the performance of LD students in secondary-level mainstream classes. *Learning Disability Quarterly, 11,* p. 6. Reprinted by permission.

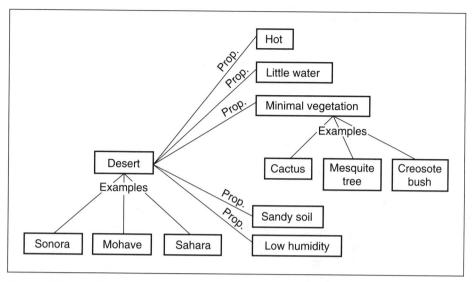

Figure 10–9   Semantic map of student's concept of deserts. *Source:* Anders, P. L., & Bos, C. S. (1984). In the beginning: Vocabulary instruction in content classes. *Topics in Learning Disabilities, 3(4),* p. 59. Copyright 1984 by PRO-ED, Inc. Reprinted by permission.

curtailed. Even simple assignments become major projects because these students don't realize that they can gain a great deal of information in a brief time from well-organized skimming. Teachers need to clarify the difference between skimming and reading for details, and help students choose which to use for particular types of reading. This assistance is essential because students with learning disabilities often are not very mature in recognizing how their learning strategies need to be altered to meet task demands.

Thomas and Robinson (1972) have divided skimming into three useful levels:

Level I   Scanning for points that are easily recognizable
Level II   Scanning for a specific answer to a question
Level III Scanning for information that goes beyond simple answers to questions (the author's style or main idea; reviewing class notes)

When you opened this textbook and flipped through it for the first time, what enticed you to stop and look at a page? Illustrations, case studies, and headings may have caught your eye. If so, you were scanning on Level I. You scanned on Level II

if you wondered whether the text would address the adult with learning disabilities. It is at this level that students who are learning disabled begin to have difficulties. They often seem to be unaware of the common organization of text material, not knowing where to look first. Therefore, they have trouble previewing the questions they will be asked, selecting from the questions keywords to search for in the passage, locating the paragraphs containing this information, and then deciding whether to read more intensively. Unless explicitly taught, they often do not realize that chapter introductions and conclusions summarize the content, as should each paragraph's topic and concluding sentence. Scanning at Level III is most difficult of all because it requires intensive reading and good comprehension. Students with learning disabilities often require assistance in judging which reading passages are most important to spend time on and reread, and which can be passed over quickly.

Reading Comprehension.   Comprehension problems are the most frequent and debilitating reading difficulties at the secondary level because language weaknesses, inefficient learner strategies, and decoding struggles usually persist beyond the elementary school years. Unfortunately, extraction of facts from texts often is complicated by poorly written, disorganized texts that vary widely in reading levels. Our science and social studies texts often consist of incomprehensible lists of unnecessary details that have little coherence and ramble from one topic to another (Calfee & Chambliss, 1988). Anthologies can have a reading range of nine grade levels, and business and vocational texts often are written far above the students' reading levels (Aukerman, 1972). In addition, because textbooks are not simply "talk written down," their sentence patterns and vocabulary differ from students' customary language use. Interpretation cannot be aided by the social context or the intonation cues (pauses, rate, emphasis) that help when the material is imparted orally (McCormick & Moe, 1982).

Partly because of an overemphasis on the easiest type of comprehension, literal comprehension, by content area teachers, students with learning disabilities often receive instruction on only a limited range of comprehension skills. It is essential to broaden these skills to enable students to profit maximally from the information to which they are exposed and to increase chances for these concepts to generalize to practical applications.

Traditionally, the approach to reading comprehension has been "bottom-up" in nature. That is, students read the words in the text and use these to derive meaning. This approach has not worked for adolescents with learning disabilities, in part because of language and reasoning difficulties, and in part because, even if students have cracked the decoding code, most remain such slow readers that integration of the information is hampered. Consequently, "top-down" approaches to comprehension have been developed. Top-down approaches are conceptually driven, in that the teacher helps a student's prior knowledge and reasoning ability guide the reading and comprehension process. Students, for example, are helped to analyze the selection's conclusions with reference to their own experiences, ideas, and feelings. Comprehension exercises are then geared

toward a number of objectives, including the ability to:

1. Paraphrase information

2. Associate, generalize, and infer based on information given

3. Deal with main ideas and details

4. Make comparisons (for example, relationship between elements, overall structure)

5. Interpret figurative language (metaphors), ambiguous statements

6. Interpret causal relations

7. Be sensitive to sequence (for example, events, methods, processes)

8. Interpret anaphoras or pronominalization (a word or pronoun that substitutes for a preceding word or group of words; for example, I did *it*).

9. Separate fact from fiction, reality from fantasy

10. Evaluate author bias and style

11. Be cognizant of the setting, theme, plot, character development, resolution (Pearson and Johnson, 1978)

According to schema theory, when questions anticipating the text's content are discussed before reading, and background associations are stimulated, students will approach their reading preset to organize information in a way that addresses the comprehension skills listed above and enhances memory. Decoding too will prove to be less of an obstacle because the students can guess at the words as they anticipate the context.

The top-down questioning strategies described for the elementary school student are equally appropriate with more mature secondary level materials. Mutual questioning, for example, can take place between the teacher and the student, as the teacher carefully controls the level of cognitive ability required in asking or responding to questions. The student needs to become facile in answering questions at easier comprehension levels before he or she can succeed at higher levels. Scruggs and Mastropieri (1993), for example, describe the teacher's active prompting in their *elaborative integration* strategy. The teacher asks questions and offers prompts that help students elaborate on information by discovering relationships with their prior knowledge. For example, "Why would changing climate have caused the dinosaur to die out?" . . . (prompt) "Remember, we said dinosaurs may have been cold-blooded." Such coaching is very effective in improving comprehension and reasoning.

Students also benefit from being taught to use self-questioning techniques, such as questioning themselves about the main idea, and who, what, when, where, why, or how. This is followed by reading the passage and underlining or recording the answers (Clark et al., 1984; Wong & Jones, 1982). Story grammar training and techniques that require generating main idea summary sentences are particularly helpful (Bridge et al., 1984; Gurney et al., 1990; Pressley et al., 1990). Summarization techniques help students learn to discriminate and organize information so that key points are condensed into units that are likely to be remembered. Sheinker and Sheinker (1989), for example, recommend that students practice skimming a passage, listing the key points, combining related points into single statements, crossing out least important points, numbering the remaining points in logical order, and finally transforming these points in the numbered order into a cohesive paragraph.

Questioning and summarizing strategies aid comprehension by actively involving students in applying their reasoning skills to reading material. As comprehension increases, so does memory for the information presented. It is common for students with learning disabilities to require reminders to apply these strategies to content area material and to experiences outside of school. The next section presents several examples of schema theory applications that facilitate comprehension and memorization of content area material.

Reinforcing Reading and Comprehension through Content Area Instruction. Content area teachers often are confused about how to meet the needs of the adolescent with learning disabilities in their classroom. Several strategies are available for increasing reading and comprehension abilities while simultaneously enhancing learning of course content.

Reading. Suppose that you need to select one of five available American history textbooks to use with your students who are learning disabled. How do you determine if the readability level will be suitable? Just because a text is written for use at a certain grade level does not mean that it is written at a level appropriate for students at that grade. Even at the elementary levels, Gickling and Thompson (1985) report that random passages selected from first and second grade readers typically range in grade level difficulty from 1.5 to 3.5. Those from the intermediate grades range in difficulty level from 4.0 to 9.0, and high school texts often extend into college difficulty levels. Given this variability, the best way to assure that the reading material is appropriate for a student is to use a readability formula, conduct an informal reading inventory within the curriculum materials themselves, or use the Cloze procedure. It is equally important to consider whether the text is interesting to the student, relevant, and up to date.

Readability formulas offer rough estimates of the reading grade level of written materials by considering factors such as average numbers of syllables or letters per word, sentence length, and extent of unfamiliar vocabulary. Readability formulas appropriate at the secondary level include Dale and Chall's (1948) formula, Flesch's (1951) Reading Ease Formula, the SMOG Grading Formula (McLaughlin, 1969), and Fry's (1968) formula, which appears in Figure 10–10. Each formula yields somewhat different grade level estimates. Because readability formulas do not take into account the complexity of a passage's syntax and organization (Cullinan & Fitzgerald, 1984; Klare, 1984), they should be used as only one piece of evidence in judging text appropriateness.

The *Informal Reading Inventory* asks the student vocabulary, fact, sequence, and inference questions after he or she has read a portion of the text silently. If over 90 percent of the responses are

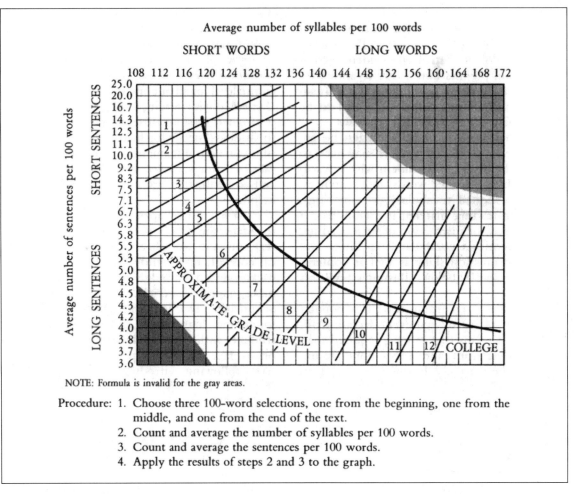

Average number of syllables per 100 words

SHORT WORDS   LONG WORDS

NOTE: Formula is invalid for the gray areas.

Procedure: 1. Choose three 100–word selections, one from the beginning, one from the middle, and one from the end of the text.
2. Count and average the number of syllables per 100 words.
3. Count and average the sentences per 100 words.
4. Apply the results of steps 2 and 3 to the graph.

Figure 10–10 Fry graph for estimating readability. *Source:* Fry, E. *Reading instruction for classroom and clinic.* Copyright © 1972 by McGraw-Hill, Inc. Used with the permission of McGraw-Hill Book Company.

correct, the student is capable of independently comprehending the material. Roughly 75 to 90 percent correct represents an appropriate instructional level. Anything below 75 percent is far too difficult. Moreover, if the student can read less than about 95 percent of the words correctly, then the text is too difficult (Galeese, 1973). The teacher should also check to see whether the student is capable of using the table of contents, glossary, index, charts, and so forth independently.

For homework, class assignments, and drill work (for example, spelling, phonics, and sight-word practice), Gickling and Thompson (1985) suggest that the student's responses should be correct 70 to 85 percent of the time. Gickling and Thompson found that if the material was either too difficult or too easy, the percentages of task completion, comprehension, and on-task behavior were relatively low. The authors hypothesize that if material is too easy, students are left with large percentages of unused time, which increases their off-task behavior. When material is too difficult, frustration causes task avoidance, again leading to off-task behavior. When material was at an instructional level, however, task completion, comprehension, and on-task behavior were maintained at consistently high levels. Therefore, it is very important for us to control the difficulty level of both texts and assignments so that a student is sufficiently challenged and reinforced by success to remain task-oriented. A tenth grader, for example, may be assigned an easier version of *Hamlet* that avoids Shakespeare's vocabulary, but enables the student to understand the themes and participate in class discussions.

In the *Cloze procedure,* every fifth word of a 250-word passage is occluded. The student fills in the blanks orally or in writing. The teacher then can judge whether the student's comprehension permits him or her to anticipate a significant enough portion of the text (usually around 50 percent) for the text to be appropriate for instructional purposes.

When these techniques suggest no appropriate textbook, the teacher may need to rewrite the text for the student who is learning disabled (shorter words and sentences, less sophisticated vocabulary and sentence structure). Once the reading material is established, it can be used for instruction of basic reading, comprehension, vocabulary, spelling, and written expression skills as well as content.

Although tape recording texts is a popular practice to circumvent decoding difficulties, tapes alone are unlikely to be panaceas because more is required than simply a verbatim tape. In one experiment in which students listened to a verbatim text, used a text in which the most important information was marked in color, and completed a fifteen-item worksheet (marks appeared in the text indicating when to answer each question), recall improved over a reading-only condition. Nevertheless, recall was still at a failure level for all but one student (Torgesen, Dahlem, & Greenstein, 1987). Because tapes of original versions of texts are not adapted to students' needs for help in organizing or summarizing information, simplifying vocabulary and sentence structure, reread-

ing, and so forth, they are not likely to be very helpful.

When using tapes, teachers may need to adapt the tape's content (reorganize it, present only the most important information, paraphrase using easier vocabulary and syntax), highlight the text, develop study guides focusing on critical content, teach study skills, and provide background knowledge and vocabulary to make taped material more meaningful. Schumaker, Deshler, and Denton (1984), for example, found that students with learning disabilities improved on average 51 to 84 percent on chapter tests following introduction of recorded materials that summarized and highlighted the most important information in the text. The most crucial information also was highlighted in the actual text, and worksheets helped students identify the critical points. Further, students were taught to overview chapter content, study intensively while taking notes, self-test, and rehearse the salient facts. Simply providing verbatim recordings of the chapters did not increase these students' performance on tests.

Bos and Vaughn (1994) offer the following suggestions for recording tapes:

1. Do not record a chapter verbatim; instead read the key sections and paraphrase those of lesser importance.

2. Provide a short advanced organizer on the tape (outline of what's to come).

3. Insert questions or reminders that will encourage the listener to stop and think.

4. Read at a comfortable rate and in a natural tone of voice.

The decision about whether to use tapes is best made by evaluating comprehension after a student reads and listens to a variety of actual and adapted classroom materials.

Recorded books will be useful when a student can benefit from listening to the original version of a novel or textbook, or simply when used for leisure time enjoyment. Recorded books are available from Recording for the Blind (Princeton, NJ), the American Printing House for the Blind (Louisville, KY), the Library of Congress

(National Library Service for the Blind, Washington, DC), and most public libraries. These organizations maintain novels, daily newspapers, and weekly magazines (*Time, Newsweek*) on tape. To keep up to date with world events and the richness of our literature, the poor or reluctant reader should be encouraged to borrow these tapes. Teachers might encourage parents to try one on the next long family drive. Mary Shelley's *Frankenstein,* on a lonely highway at night, is a particularly exciting one to start with. Read by real actors, these books provide an important access to our rich cultural heritages. Cassette players that play at half speed and allow for easier relistening also are available from the above organizations.

Comprehension.   Craig, a high school senior with inconsistent comprehension in lectures, was concerned about his ability to handle large lecture situations in college. Therefore, Craig's resource teacher decided to take him to a psychology lecture at a local university. During the lecture the teacher constructed comprehension questions to ask Craig later. To her surprise, Craig's comprehension was 100 percent; the lecture happened to be on teenage sexuality! Although most lectures are likely to be far less captivating in content, Craig's experience illustrates how activating background knowledge and interest can greatly enhance comprehension of new material. This is the objective behind schema theory approaches to comprehension.

In recent years schema theory has been used to develop a number of comprehension-enhancing techniques that in turn result in greater memory for content. *Semantic feature analysis* is a strategy that has helped students more effectively learn vocabulary and concepts needed for comprehending content area texts (Bos et al., 1989; Bos & Anders, 1987). The teacher gives each student a chart, such as that in Figure 10–7, listing main ideas and related vocabulary or concepts. The main ideas are introduced, and students then share their current knowledge about these concepts, the aim being to generate the meanings of the concepts. Once these meanings have been established, the teacher guides the students in discovering the meaning of each vocabulary word or concept, whether from background knowledge or from looking in the text. Then students predict how each word might relate to the main ideas by marking each box with a +, −, ?, or O (no relationship). Finally, students read to confirm or disconfirm their predictions. Once everyone has finished reading, the reasons for changes on the chart are discussed by the group. This technique has been found to be more effective in building vocabulary and comprehension than is direct instruction of word meanings on the part of the teacher or looking words up in a dictionary and writing a sentence using each word. A logical follow-up activity involves presenting sentences with blanks that are to be completed by referring to the chart (for example, "Some extinct animals that lived in lakes are _____ , _____ , and _____ ").

Bulgren, Schumaker, and Deshler (1988) describe another concept learning strategy, also based on schema theory. Using the diagram in Figure 10–8 to teach the concept of democracy, for example, they define the concept and then list attributes that always, sometimes, or never characterize the concept. Next students generate examples and nonexamples of the concept. Teaching also can begin with the examples, which are then used to build the characteristics, or with a listing of the characteristics in order to build the definition. Used with high school students, this technique significantly improved scores on unit tests.

Semantic mapping, as depicted in Figure 10–9, is another means to help students organize concepts and related vocabulary. Prior to reading, the teacher writes the key concept on the board and helps students generate ideas related to the main theme. After brainstorming, students might consult the text's illustrations, headings, and bold print terms for additional clues. These are drawn branching from the key concept and, whenever possible, are organized by category. The map serves as an organizing guide when reading. After reading, the map can be revised (Scanlon et al., 1992).

The ability of students to make inferences from unfamiliar content is enhanced simply by probing background knowledge with a few questions prior to reading: "Tell me what you know about . . . " (Carr & Thompson, 1996). When students have little background information to bring to a lesson, it is helpful for teachers to offer relevant prior knowledge (Snider, 1989) and to hand out *advance organizers*. An advance organizer is an outline of the lesson's content. Students refer to the outline as the teacher relates the topic to previous lessons, forecasts the new information, clarifies concepts that will be learned, defines new terms, and builds interest and a purpose in reading. The advance organizer also is helpful to students in organizing their notetaking. Both the quality and the quantity of learning by the teenager with learning disabilities have been shown to improve with the use of such organizers (Billingsley & Wildman, 1988; Darch & Gersten, 1986; Lenz, Alley, & Schumaker, 1987).

Finally, Bos and Vaughn (1994) describe how teachers can create *structured overviews* by merely listing lecture or text concepts on the blackboard and having students generate related vocabulary from their background knowledge. What if the concepts are too technical for students to know? The teacher then would list the words on the board and discuss the meanings of each. The interesting part involves rearranging this vocabulary until a map is created that links related ideas to one another. The map is revised while reading and serves as a blueprint for studying. The reasons for these linkages are explored. Billingsley and Wildman (1988) explain why such techniques are helpful in guiding subsequent comprehension, notetaking, discussion of new ideas and reactions, and studying for tests:

1. Familiarity with the major ideas prior to reading helps students evaluate how each new sentence can be integrated with the text's overall organization.

2. Because readers do not have to identify the text's organization, the processing load is decreased and more attention can be directed toward monitoring comprehension.

3. Readers who lack the necessary background knowledge for comprehension have been given a schema to use as they read.

Bos and Vaughn suggest several additional tools that students can use independently to enhance comprehension as they read: fill in an outline provided by the teacher, underline key points in the text, use margin notes to highlight important information, and complete a study guide that asks several questions about each section of the text. Malone and Mastropieri (1992) found that teaching students to ask two questions after reading each paragraph, and self-monitor this strategy, significantly increased comprehension:

(a) "Who or what is the paragraph about?"

(b) "What is happening to them?"

Also useful are summarization procedures that teach students to select or create topic sentences, to compare and contrast key words or phrases while reading, to differentiate important details from those that did not contribute to passage meaning, to delete redundancies, to write a sentence summarizing the meaning of each paragraph, to orally summarize a passage, to record the answers to "wh" questions (who, what, where, when, why) as one reads, or to simply reread (Gajria & Salvia, 1992; Weisberg 1988). A variation of the RAP procedure (Figure 6–2), in which students followed RAP by circling the main idea in the passage and linking it with the details, has been shown to enhance both literal and inferential comprehension (Boyle, 1996).

Charts, diagrams, or graphs also are helpful comprehension enhancers. These devices help the teacher be more systematic and thorough in presentations, reduce the information to a manageable load, stimulate student interest, highlight the important information, compensate for disorganized texts, provide a model for organizing notes, and aid memory by highlighting the spatial arrangement (Crank & Bulgren, 1993). In at least one study such diagrams were even more helpful on tests than were study guides on which students answered a series of questions (Bergerud, Lovitt, & Horton, 1988). Bimodal presentation of science and social studies passages via computer, with a digitized voice reading the words as they are highlighted, is another powerful strategy for increasing the comprehension of students (Montali & Lewandowski, 1996). Finally, the thinking skills goals and metacognitive strategies enumerated in Chapter 6 have been very helpful to the progress of students with learning disabilities. Students with learning disabilities, when directly taught, can learn to reason logically by analogy and to critically evaluate information based on the evidence (Leshowitz et al., 1993).

Besides focusing comprehension exercises around reading materials, teachers need to make a concerted effort to use oral class time to increase comprehension through listening exercises. Purposes for listening are set, the student listens, and questions pertaining to the comprehension objectives listed on page 406 are asked (Cunningham & Cunningham, 1976). Manzo (1975) provides a guided listening procedure for developing these skills, in order to increase the amount of information students internalize, remember, and can think about in the absence of teacher guidance. Note-taking too is predicated on good listening skills. The more intelligently a youngster can pick up information from the environment, the greater the likelihood of success in school and in everyday life.

Written Language

Written language remains one of the most unsuccessful areas for adolescents with learning disabilities. Spelling remediation (for example, teaching word derivatives and prefixes, suffixes, and roots) and handwriting instruction need to continue when appropriate. Students also need to build compensations by learning to use a dictionary, using the spell check on a computer, learning to check for homonyms or real-word substitutions that spell checkers won't catch, proofing by reading compositions backward (errors are more difficult to overlook because the student is not distracted by the context), using a misspeller's dictionary if the regular dictionary is too difficult (see Figure 10–11), and learning to type. Typing is a welcome relief for some students who are learning disabled. For others, however, it presents the same fine-motor difficulties as does handwriting (MacArthur & Shneiderman, 1986).

Incorrect	Correct	Incorrect	Correct
kitastrofy	**catastrophe**	koming	**coming**
kitin	**kitten**	kommunist	**communist**
kiyoty	**coyote**	koris	**chorus**
klak	**claque**	korz	**corps**
kleeg	**klieg**	kraft	**craft**
kleek	**clique**	Kremlen	**Kremlin**
klorine	**chlorine**	kriptic	**cryptic**
knifes	**knives**	kronic	**chronic**
knoted	**knotted**	Krushchev	**Khrushchev**
knowlege	**knowledge**	Kugele	**cudgel**
kolic	**colic**	kwik	**quick**
kolyumnist	**columnist**	kwire	**choir**
komfortable	**comfortable**	kwire	**quire**

Look-Alikes or Sound-Alikes

kernel (seed) • **colonel** (officer)

key (with lock) • **quay** (dock)

kill (murder) • **kiln** (oven)

knave (fool) • **nave** (part of church)

knead (to press) • **need** (must have)

kneel (to rest on the knees) • **Neal** (man's name)

knew (did know) • **gnu** (animal) • **new** (not old)

knight (feudal rank) • **night** (opposite of day)

knit (form fabric) • **nit** (insect)

knock (to strike) • **nock** (notch of an arrow)

knot (what you tie) • **not** (no)

know (to understand) • **no** (opposite of yes)

knows (understands) • **noes** (negatives) • **nose** (on face)

kohl (eye shadow) • **coal** (fire) • **koel** (a cuckoo)

kola (a nut or tree) • **cola** (a drink)

kris (cheese; dagger) • **crease** (fold)

Figure 10–11   Sample page from a Misspeller's Dictionary. *Source:* Krevisky, J., & Linfield, J. L. *The Bad Speller's Dictionary.* (1963). New York: Random House, p. 81. Copyright © 1963, 1967 by Innovation Press. Reprinted by permission of Random House, Inc.

Conceptual writing is the main priority to attend to. Students with learning disabilities often approach writing as though it were simply talk written down. They have a poor sense of the audience's perspective and therefore omit temporal, sequential, and organizational words that would help the reader.

These students often require special help learning to repeat words and synonyms when needed for clarity (when the referents for words like *he, these, that, the same* are unclear) and to use transitional ties that add cohesion to their text (e.g., *therefore, similarly, however, on the other hand, furthermore, for example, first/second/finally, in other words, to summarize, later, so far, until now*) (Gregg, 1986).

Hillocks (1986) concludes that the most effective written language teaching activity for high school students is one that emphasizes the need to problem solve by gathering, analyzing, and reorganizing information. The traditional emphasis on handwriting, grammar, spelling, and punctuation will not excite students about writing nor stimulate them to develop conceptually or stylistically. With this in mind, a useful technique for simply encouraging writing is Allington's *uninterrupted silent sustained writing* (USSW). Several times a week, for five or ten minutes, students write anything that comes to mind. They write quickly, without making corrections. Best of all, the product need not be shared with anyone! USSW's objective is simply to get students over the hurdle of unwillingness even to try to write. Keeping personal journals can have the same beneficial outcomes. *Interactive journal writing,* in which students and teachers converse via a journal, has helped students apply their oral language proficiency to their writing. In interactive journals, teachers are more natural in their discourse and avoid asking questions, expecting replies, and evaluating responses. The conversational give and take encourages students to use higher-level discourse in their writing (Rueda, 1992).

Another approach in which content is the focus and spelling, punctuation, and handwriting are disregarded until after the student's ideas are developed is presented in Table 10–1. Try constructing your own essay following this approach. This method provides a systematic technique that guides the student to express his or her own thoughts in a cohesive manner.

Writing instruction necessarily incorporates prewriting (idea generation, organization, goal

identification), drafting, and revising stages (content first, then mechanics and grammar). These, in combination with the word processor, can be particularly effective (Kerchner & Kistinger, 1984; MacArthur, 1988). Reynolds and her colleagues (1988) found that brief instruction in COPS (see Figure 6–2) and the self-check statements presented in Table 10–2 were helpful to students with learning disabilities when revising their writing. Simply offering students story starters or story enders also improves the quality of students' writing (Graves, Semmel, & Gerber, 1994).

Story grammar cue cards such as that in Figure 10–3 can be helpful in producing longer and higher-quality stories among teenagers, especially when more detailed cueing is used (for example, "Tell the characters' thoughts, feelings, emotions, and reasons for doing what they do. Make them think and feel just as real people do") (Montague & Leavell, 1994). Students' compare/contrast essays have improved in clarity, appropriateness of content, and logically ordered ideas when students are taught to follow a planning diagram that clarifies the topic, thesis, different categories of compare/contrast ideas, and the conclusion (Wong et al., 1997). Peer-editing strategies that use interactive dialogues or respond to specific questions about each others' work (e.g., "Is there anything that is not CLEAR?" "Where could more DETAILS and information be added?") also produce higher-quality products that are maintained in the absence of peer editor support (MacArthur et al., 1991; Wong et al., 1996). Similarly, instructional dialogues with the teacher that identify ambiguities in one's writing help to promote clarity in teenagers' revisions (Wong et al., 1991). Further, Espin and Sindelar (1988) suggest that listening to a taped version of one's writing may help students detect their syntactic errors.

The need to teach the teenager with learning disabilities how to write cannot be overemphasized. On high school graduation, the student will apply for jobs or take advantage of postsecondary educational opportunities. In either case, the written product will play a large part in determining the individual's future options. Besides, the better developed and organized one's writing,

Table 10–1   Method for teaching written composition skills

Steps	*Description*
I	Write a short, simple, declarative sentence that makes one statement. This should be a sentence about an idea you have and not merely a description of how something looks or directions on how to make something.
II	Write three sentences about your subject in Step I that are clearly and directly about the entirety of that subject and not just some small aspect of it. A key to this step would be to think of the questions someone would typically ask about your subject.

    A) _____

    B) _____

    C) _____

III	Write four or five sentences about each of the three sentences in Step II.

    A) _____

        1) _____

        2) _____

        3) _____

        4) _____

    B) _____

        1) _____

        2) _____

        3) _____

        4) _____

    C) _____

        1) _____

        2) _____

        3) _____

        4) _____

IV	Make the material in the four or five sentences in Step III as concrete and specific as possible. Go into detail. Give examples. Don't ask, "What will I say next?" Say some more about what you have just said. Your goal is to say a lot about a little, not a little about a lot. Kerrigan stresses the importance of details. Avoid abstract terms.
V	In the first sentence of the second paragraph and every paragraph following, insert a clear reference to the idea in the preceding paragraph. In this step, relate each paragraph to the preceding paragraph and provide smooth transitions in the composition.
VI	Make sure every sentence in your theme is connected with, and makes clear reference to, the preceding sentence. Once again, the importance of clear references is emphasized.

Source: Adapted from Kerrigan, W. J., & Metcalf, A. A. (1987). *Writing to the point: Six basic steps (4th ed.)* New York: Harcourt Brace Jovanovich.

Table 10–2   Evaluative and directive phrases (adapted from Bereiter & Scardamalia, 1982)

Evaluative Phrases	*Directive Phrases*
A. Readers won't see why this is important.	1. I'd better leave this part out.
B. People may not believe this.	2. I'd better say more.
C. People won't be very interested in this part.	3. I'd better cross this sentence out and say it in a different way.
D. People may not understand what I mean here.	4. I'd better change the wording.
E. This is good.	5. I think I'll leave it this way.
F. This could be said more clearly.	6. I'd better support what I'm saying with facts.
G. Even I am confused about what I am trying to say.	7. I'd better move this sentence.
H. This doesn't sound quite right.	
I. This sentence states the topic.	
J. This sentence sums up what I have said.	
K. This sentence doesn't follow a logical order.	
L. This shows what I really think.	
M. This does not sound like a conclusion.	

Source: Reynolds, C. J., Hill, D. S., Swassing, R. H., & Ward, M. E. (1988). The effects of revision strategy instruction on the writing performance of students with learning disabilities. *Journal of Learning Disabilities, 21,* p. 541. Copyright 1988 by PRO-ED, Inc. Reprinted by permission.

the more aware one becomes of the organization of text and oral language, so that understanding and recall of what one has read or heard improves.

Mathematics

In high school, mathematics may become particularly difficult even for those students with learning disabilities who were able to manage math at the elementary level. This is because the subject matter (algebra, geometry, trigonometry) demands a new vocabulary (for example, *sin, pi*), very sophisticated logical and perceptual reasoning, the learning of new symbols (for example, $\sqrt{\ }$, γ), and the solution of complex word problems. Mathematics remediation methods specifically designed to meet the needs of the secondary level student have focused primarily on the teaching of problem-solving strategies. These include self-checking techniques, listing problem-solving steps, or verbal self-instruction methods. Cawley's *Project Math,* for example, combines visual aids with an active verbal problem-solving approach.

By far the greatest problem that students with learning disabilities face in mathematics is word problems. First, the problems must be read. Second, not all the information is usually given. Students must apply some additional knowledge to solve the problem. The necessary math vocabulary, which is embedded in the problem, must be translated into a math operation, and then the problem's solution must be translated back into language. Word problems also contain extraneous information that sidetracks the student from correct solutions. Some experts advocate transcribing word problems into a simple listing of the data that need to be calculated (Shaw, 1981), and others stress the importance of instructing students in word problems as a means of increasing both their math vocabulary and their preparation for similar real-life problem solving (Sharma, 1981). After all, a good number of the mathematical applications in real life are in word form. Real-life mathematical problems are even more difficult because they are presented orally and solved mentally (for example, estimating whether you have sufficient money when the salesperson tells you the cost of two items; determining how much time you have to make the next train after you call the dispatcher to find out the departure time).

For adolescents who continue to have great difficulty with very basic mathematical reasoning and computations, Schwartz and Budd (1981) recommend focusing on math skills that will be functional in adult life. The goals they suggest are found in Figure 10–12. Schwartz and Budd emphasize the importance of teaching students to estimate answers before solving problems, so that they learn to evaluate the reasonableness of their solutions. In teaching these "survival" skills, it is best to practice the operations within real-life con-

texts. Even science and social studies content can be adapted to reinforce essential math skills: for example, working with population statistics, stock pages in the newspaper, and science measurements.

Study and Test-Taking Skills

Students with learning disabilities, especially those with attention deficits, routinely forget to write down assignments, complete homework, or hand it in on time. They have great difficulty using their time wisely, breaking down long-term assignments into manageable pieces, developing reasonable time lines, and following through. Unless tasks are novel, highly interesting, or subject to

---

Consumer Skills
  Making change
  Determining cost of sale items utilizing
    percentages (e.g., "25% off")
  Determining tax amounts
  Doing cost comparisons
  Buying on "time"
  Balancing a checkbook
  Determining total cost of purchases

Homemaking Skills
  Measuring ingredients
  Budgeting for household expenses
  Calculating length of cooking and baking
    time when there are options (e.g., for a
    cake using two 9" round pans vs. two 8"
    round pans)
  Measuring material for clothing
    construction
  Doing cost comparisons

Health Care
  Weighing oneself and others
  Calculating caloric intake
  Determining when to take medication

Auto Care
  Calculating cost of auto parts
  Measuring spark plug gaps
  Determining if tire pressure is correct
  Figuring gas mileage

Home Care
  Determining amount of supplies (paint, rug
    shampoo) to buy
  Determining time needed to do projects
  Measuring rods and drapes
  Finding cost of supplies
  Finding cost of repairs

Vocational Needs
  Calculating payroll deductions
  Determining money owed
  Knowing when to be at work
  Doing actual math for various jobs

Figure 10–12 Content for teaching functional math. *Source:* Schwartz, S. E., & Budd, D. (1981). Mathematics for handicapped learners: A functional approach for adolescents. *Focus on Exceptional Children 13 (7)*, pp. 7–8. Reprinted by permission of Love Publishing, Denver, Colorado.

rewards or penalties, students have difficulty persisting—or even getting started. Certainly, if these students are to retain what they are taught, they must develop good study skills. This includes note taking, outlining, library, and test-taking skills. The key word to success in each of these areas is *organization*.

It is critical for students to develop a well-planned time schedule and a disciplined study approach. It is helpful for students to write down the essential activities for that particular day and a quick reminder of what needs to be done one day, two days, or weeks from now on 3″ × 5″ index cards. Post-its are also great for this purpose, especially when placed judiciously in spots where they are likely to be seen. When students with learning disabilities share their time-reminder cards with parents or teachers, realistic daily and long-term goals can be set, as well as rewards for meeting these goals (for example, time to work out or go to a movie). A well-organized notebook, complete with weekly and monthly calendars, also is essential. A helpful approach is to assign students with learning disabilities to observe their peers' study habits and then generate academic aids that they think would work for themselves.

An approach that has a particularly good chance of success is *coaching*, because it details what must be done on a daily basis to reach long-term goals, and students are actively involved in the decision-making process. Students who volunteer to meet with a "coach" determine long-term goals (e.g., attend a moderately competitive college, make the soccer team, get a specific job) (see Figure 10–13) and then meet with the coach ten to fifteen minutes daily to monitor the previous day's progress and to plan exactly what to do for the following day (see Figure 10–14). The coach can be a caring teacher, sports coach, teacher aide—anyone with whom the student gets along well and whom the student trusts. Barriers to reaching goals (e.g., skipping classes, failure to complete homework) are discussed and worked on, and environmental supports decided upon. The daily goals involve not only task completion and good grades, but also behavioral commitments such as participating in class discussions. Students' self-evaluation and verbal commitment

are important keys to success, as are the daily enthusiasm and encouragement on the part of the coach (Guare & Dawson, 1995). This type of strategy presents a strong model for learning habits that, hopefully, will persist long after the coaching relationship has ended.

Note-Taking Skills. When you open one of your textbooks you are apt to find the trails of a yellow marking pen. But for students with language weaknesses, underlining texts may not be beneficial, even when the books are within their readability ranges. They may still have to go back and reread all the material when exam time nears, in order to understand the context of the underlined phrases. Note taking can be an effective alternative strategy for facilitating recall (Saski, Swicegood, & Carter, 1983). Note taking forces a student to paraphrase, organize, and elaborate on new information. It involves detecting key concepts, differentiating important from unimportant details, and summarizing pertinent information. When processed in such an active manner, the information is more likely to become meaningful and memorable. Although no one note-taking method has proved to be the most effective, any note-taking strategy is generally better than none at all (Devine, 1981).

As in note taking from text, note taking during lectures alleviates the need to concentrate on memorizing content at the moment. Research has found a positive relationship between the amount of information students record in notes and their subsequent test performance. Students who take notes during lectures recall more information than students who merely listen (Hughes & Suritsky, 1994). Note taking during lectures, however, can be particularly problematic for students who are learning disabled because it requires attending, listening, paraphrasing, comprehending, identifying the information instructors deem important, and writing, all at the same time. In their study of college students with learning disabilities, Hughes and Suritsky found that they record significantly fewer information units from lectures in their notes and fewer units that the instructor had cued as important. They used fewer abbreviated words and wrote slower.

Long-Term Goals Planning Sheet

Student's Name: **Leah Brody**   Date: **November 18, 1997**

What is your long-term goal?

Goal 1: **Pass English in order To be eligible to try out for the volleyball team**

What do you need to do to meet your goal?

1. **Take notes in class**
2. **write down all assignments**
3. **do homework**
4. **hand in homework**
5. **revew before Tests**

Are there barriers you need to overcome in order to meet your goal?	How can you overcome these barriers?
1. **trouble taking notes and listening at the same time**	**ask the teacher for her nAtes.**
2. **watching TV instead of doing homework**	**watch TV only after finishing homework**
3. **not studying for tests**	**study with a friend**

What environmental supports or modifications are necessary in order to help you meet these goals?

The teacher needs to share her notes
My parents need to drive me to my friend's home

What is your long-term goal?

Goal 2:

What do you need to do to meet your goal?

1.
2.
3.
4.
5.

Are there barriers you need to overcome in order to meet your goal?	How can you overcome these barriers?
1.	
2.	
3.	

What environmental supports or modifications are necessary in order to help you meet these goals?

Do you think these are realistic goals?

✓ Yes

_____ No—How can they be modified?

Figure 10–13   Long-term goals planning sheet used in coaching. *Source:* Adapted from Dawson, P., & Guare, R. (1997). Reproduced with permission of Multi-Health Systems, Inc. 908 Niagara Falls Blvd., North Tonawanda, NY 19120-2060. (800) 456–3003.

Coach Monitoring Sheet

Name: Leah Brody   Date: November 28, 1997

THE BIG PICTURE:

Upcoming tests/quizzes:		Long-term assignments:		Other responsibilities:	
Subject:	Date:	Assignment:	Date Due:	Task:	Date:
English	Dec. 1	Shakespeare Paper	Dec. 15	Apply for Xmas break job	Dec. 5
Math	Dec. 3	Science project	Dec. 17	Invite friends to birthday party	Dec. 10
Earth Science	Dec. 3				

TODAY'S PLANS:

What are you going to do?	When will you do it?	Did you do it?	How did you do?*
Academic Tasks:			
1. English homework	1. today 7:00 – 7:45 pm	Yes No	1 2 3 ④ 5
2. Shakespeare note cards	2. Saturday afternoon	Yes No	1 2 3 4 5
3. go to library for science	3. Thursday night	Yes No	1 2 3 4 5
4. project	4.	Yes No	1 2 3 4 5
5. review for math quiz	5. today 7:45 – 8:15 pm	Yes No	1 2 ③ 4 5
6.	6.	Yes No	1 2 3 4 5
Behavioral:			
1. talk on phone only when	1. every day	Yes No	① 2 3 4 5
2. homework is done	2.	Yes No	1 2 3 4 5

*Use this scale to evaluate: 1—Not well at all; 2—So-so; 3—Average; 4—Very well; 5—Excellent

GENERAL OBSERVATIONS REGARDING GOALS/PERFORMANCE:

I have trouble getting started with homework and then rush it so I can watch my favorite TV shows

Figure 10–14 Coach monitoring sheet for daily tasks. *Source:* Adapted from Dawson, P., & Guare, R. (1997) Reproduced with permission of Multi-Health Systems Inc. 908 Niagara Falls Blvd., North Tonawanda, NY 19120-2060. (800) 456–3003.

Although it is the student's responsibility to take notes, it is the teacher's responsibility to give lectures that are so well organized that relationships are clear to students. Bos and Vaughn (1994) suggest that we incorporate several helpful techniques when we lecture: use advance organizers, link information from the previous lecture with the current lecture, use words that cue an important concept ("in summary," "this is impor-

tant to remember"), repeat key ideas and phrases and give students time to write them down, stress important ideas by varying voice quality, number the points being made (first, second) or use temporal cues (next, finally), write important ideas and technical words on the board, present examples and nonexamples of a concept, use pictures and diagrams to illustrate relationships among ideas, ask questions during the lecture that will relate the new information to students' background knowledge, ask questions to test student comprehension, encourage question asking, provide many examples, and allow time at the end of the lecture for students to review their notes and ask questions. If we follow these suggestions, students certainly will have an easier time taking notes.

Teachers also can help by providing structured lessons on note taking as well as reinforcement for taking organized and thorough notes. Videotaped or audiotaped lectures are particularly helpful in teaching note taking because students can replay the tape for different purposes: for example, to listen to details or to listen for cue words that alert the listener to a major point that is about to be made.

Sheinker and Sheinker (1989) stress the importance of teaching students to recognize and note the signals authors give readers regarding what they think is important: headings, bold print, italics, listed and numbered items, asterisks. They also suggest mapping to help students connect the major ideas to a topic and then subdivide these ideas into subordinate ideas and details. Along the same lines, Seidenberg (1991) encourages structured lessons, such as that in Figure 10–15, to help students recognize and organize main ideas and details. This same structure can be used to enumerate description, sequence, causality, and comparison/contrast statements. These Detail Boxes are accompanied by exercises in which students detect a sentence that is not relevant to a main idea in a paragraph, select which sentences could be added to a paragraph, reorder sentences to form a paragraph, compose paragraphs, and write summary statements. As students become aware of how main ideas and

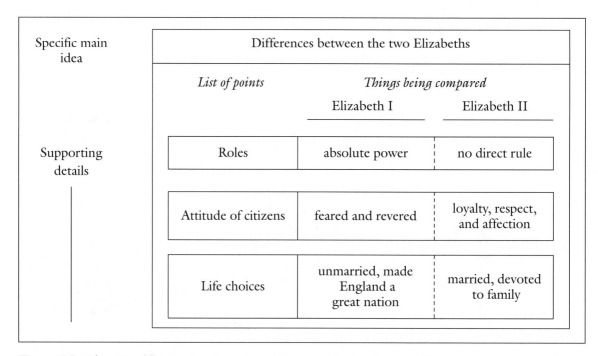

Figure 10–15 Detail box comparison chart. *Source:* Seidenberg, P. L. (1991). *Reading, writing, and studying strategies: An integrated curriculum:* Gaithersburg, MD: Aspen Pub., p. 268. © 1991, Aspen Publishers, Inc. Reprinted with permission

subordinate information interrelate, their comprehension increases, as does their recall.

Teaching students to use two-column note-taking systems also is helpful. The student takes notes in a broad right-hand column and uses the narrower left-hand column to list key concepts that summarize the information in the right-hand column. When studying, the right-hand information is occluded, and the left-hand column is used to trigger these details (Devine, 1981). In three-column systems, the far-left column is used for related notes from the text. Some students find it helpful to open their notebooks and use the right-hand page for the two-column system and the left-hand page for text notes. The left-hand column also could be used to identify known information that is relevant to the topic at hand, comments, questions to ask the teacher, gaps, future assignments, and so forth. Rereading of notes immediately after taking them is important in order to fill in gaps and label the key concepts.

Students benefit best when they use their own words in note taking, rather than those of the author, and experiment with a format that suits their own style. Reducing notes to the essential points, organizing the information, classifying ideas, reciting the material, and reviewing it are essential in order to have note taking benefit the learner (Askov & Kamm, 1982).

There is evidence that students who take lecture notes in class usually learn more than those who just listen (Carrier, 1983; Suritsky & Hughes, 1991). Students seem to learn more from recording and reviewing their own notes than from working with someone else's. Nevertheless, there are some students who will benefit best from listening only: those with poor short-term memories, low general ability, and little prior knowledge about the instructional content. For these students note taking creates an additional processing burden.

If, after systematic instruction, the student is still an inefficient note taker, the teacher may wish to give the student a copy of his or her lecture notes or permit the student to use a carbon or photocopy of a peer's notes. Teacher-prepared guides on which students merely fill in key words also can be helpful.

Outlining Skills. Outlining is a useful tool for identifying the main ideas of a passage or taking notes in class. By design, outlines assist the adolescent in organizing ideas about what he or she is about to write, what an author has written, or what a lecturer is saying. Fisher (1967) suggests that the student ask several questions while outlining:

I. Does this reflect an important component of the topic?
   A. Does this help develop the main heading?
      1. Does this detail,
      2. as well as this detail, relate to the subdivision in sequential order?

Teachers can structure assignments and lessons to allow the student opportunities to learn outlining as a skill for organizing information. The inverse of Fisher's technique, working from details to subheadings to main ideas, is an alternate method for organizing notes.

Many students find outlining from a text tedious. They may have difficulty sorting the material into superordinate categories or may get bogged down in the mere mechanics of writing and spelling. An excellent substitute for outlining is a method taught in a study skills course at Brown University. Students simply pencil notes in the margins of their text. These can easily be erased later on. The method teaches that there are only seven types of questions a student will ever be asked:

1. *Definition-identification*—explicit definition of ideas and the person/group that originated or supported the idea

2. *Cause-effect*—identify causal relations

3. *Location-spatial relations*—geographical and nongeographical (for example, molecular structure, location of different cell types in the brain)

4. *Time-temporal relations*—specific dates or time periods and relationships (for example, how the past influences the present and future)

5. *Method*—how something is accomplished or resolved (for example, what political policies achieve a goal)

6. *Type*—into what subtypes has the writer subdivided the main idea?

7. *Motive*—why? what was the context, climate behind a relationship?

First the student prereads ten pages of topic sentences, introductions, summaries, and illustrations to help forecast which of these categories will be most relevant. If a topic sentence is weak, then the student instead reads the last sentence of that paragraph. This prereading process takes about five minutes. Next, the student reads the text, continually asking oneself if the information is important enough to memorize for a test. If so, the student jots down the category of the information in the margin and what it should trigger. For example, for Madame Curie a student would record "ID (identification): discoverer of radium." For the date and cause of the Civil War, the student would record "Time: Civil War" and "Cause: Civil War." As the student records these, he or she simultaneously verbalizes the answer. When the bottom of the page is reached, the student reads all notations and checks to see if he or she can generate the information asked for. If not, then the corresponding sentences are reread, and the student verbalizes the information and places a checkmark next to the notation, indicating that this had been difficult to memorize.

Students proceed like this for ten pages. At the end of ten pages, they review their recall of the triggers on each page. It is recommended that students then reward themselves with a fifteen-minute break. If there is specific information that continues to be difficult to trigger, this should be written in a notebook in sentence form, preceded by its chapter heading.

When students follow this system judiciously, it is virtually foolproof in generating improved performance on exams. Just think about what is happening. Students are organizing information into more memorable categories as they read. They are self-questioning as they read. And they are rehearsing the information three times for memory: as they make notations, at the end of every page, and after every ten pages. Try this for your next exam in this course. You'll be surprised how easily you'll recall and organize the informa-

tion. It should be noted that this method is exciting to teenagers, not tedious, because they recognize how well they are memorizing as they go along. And every ten pages they have permission to take a break!

Library Skills.   Libraries can be a source of information or a source of confusion for anyone, and especially for the student with learning disabilities. Students need to become comfortable with the library's organization (Dewey Decimal System, card or computer catalogue) and reference aids (indexes to periodicals, dictionaries, encyclopedias, almanacs, atlases, computer search systems) to use libraries profitably. The teacher can undertake a variety of activities to promote library use and to facilitate the student's view of the library as an ally rather than enemy. Opportunities to use the library's multimedia materials also can motivate adolescents to become involved in learning. For many students with learning disabilities these materials, rather than reading, may become the primary tool for acquiring knowledge throughout life. When students don't become comfortable with a library during their school years, an important avenue for lifelong learning may be shut off.

Test-Taking Skills.   Having taken many quizzes and exams, you undoubtedly have discovered test-taking strategies that work for you. In contrast, most adolescents with learning disabilities need to be taught test-taking strategies to enable them to, at the least, accurately show what they do know (Scruggs & Mastropieri, 1988). When students with learning disabilities are taught these strategies, their test scores benefit more than do the scores of nondisabled students, who already apply many of these approaches automatically.

Alley and Deshler proposed a five-step procedure for preparing for tests, which appears in Table 10–3. Table 10–3 also illustrates Carman and Adams's SCORER technique, which is helpful to the student during tests. Sheinker and Sheinker (1989) urge students to star the twenty-five most important items in their notes and study primarily these. This makes the job of studying realistic, focuses the student on essential details,

Table 10–3   Procedure for preparing for tests and the SCORER technique

Preparing for tests

1. The student should ask the teacher exactly what material will be on the test and what aspects of it will come from the notes, lectures, or textbooks. The student should also ask what the format of the test will be: true-false, essay, short answer, or multiple choice.
2. The student should obtain copies of previous exams (and their answer sheets) from other students who have taken the course or from teachers themselves. Students should be "test wise" and know what type of questions are usually on the exams and which topics are emphasized.
3. The student should be instructed in setting up and following a study schedule. This alleviates some of the necessity of cramming for tests, an ineffective method for all students—especially for LD students who have reading problems. A brief review of the material following each class helps the student remember the content.
4. The student should understand testing terms such as *compare, contrast, illustrate, briefly describe, define,* and *elaborate.* The student should also note the relative point value the teacher places on different test items. This is an indication of how much information is needed to adequately answer the questions and how much time the student should spend answering it.
5. Students should be encouraged to approach the testing situation with a positive mental attitude. Discussing feelings ahead of time can be helpful and provides the teacher with an opportunity to reinforce the student's abilities and positive outlook toward the test.

SCORER technique

S = *schedule* your time. How many questions are there, and how much time is there to complete the exam?

C = *cue* words. *All, never,* and *always* rarely indicate a true answer on a true-false test but *usually* or *sometimes* often do.

O = *omitting* or setting aside the difficult questions. Answer the easiest questions first and then go back.

R = *read* the directions and examples carefully.

E = *estimate* the approximate range of possible answers for a question; e.g., the area of a shoe box will be in square inches, so answers in square feet may be disregarded. You should also "guesstimate" the answer if credit is not taken off for doing so.

R = *review* your work. Make sure all questions are answered with the correct letter or number and be very cautious about changing answers without substantiation for the new choice.

Sources: Alley, G., & Deshler, D. (1979). *Teaching the LD adolescent: Strategies and methods.* Denver: Love Publishing Company; Carman, R. A., & Adams, W. R., Jr. (1972). *Study skills: A student's guide for survival.* New York: Wiley.

gives time for more repetition of this information, and avoids overload from trying to remember everything. The mnemonic memorization strategies presented in Chapter 6 can be particularly helpful because secondary teachers tend to prepare exams asking primarily for the recall or recognition of facts (Putnam, Deshler, & Schumaker, 1992). Finally, permitting students to bring one 8 1/2" × 11" cheat sheet into the examination has much merit; by the time the student has selected the most important points to add to his or her cheat sheet, the information often is memorized.

This method teaches students that comprehension of the main ideas is more important than memory for details, as long as they know where to go to find specific information when they need it.

To test students fairly and maximize their success on classroom tests and tests used for grade promotion or graduation, we must help students communicate their knowledge as competently as possible. Because students with learning disabilities typically perform poorly on multiple-choice or short-answer tests, Dalton and colleagues (1995) suggest that teachers use hands-on performance assessments whenever possible. Students are far more successful on such assessments. Though not as successful as hands-on assessment, filling in answers on diagrams or writing simple yes/no responses to questions about diagrams also results in better demonstration of knowledge than standard testing techniques.

Transition Planning

Planning ahead for postsecondary educational and career opportunities is an important part of the high school program. Adolescents also need to learn practical life skills with which to survive in their own as well as adult worlds. Presumably, this has been the intention of their reading (reading a menu, directions on prescriptions, credit card rules), comprehension (figuring out how to work a voting booth and whom to vote for), math (budgeting, completing a tax return), written language (completing a job application, writing a cover letter when returning a mail order item), and study skills (studying for a driver's test) curricula throughout school. Yet many secondary students with learning disabilities are weak in these basic skills or do not transfer them from the classroom to practical life. These weaknesses, compounded by social and emotional difficulties, frequently forecast a less than adequate life adjustment, making transition planning a necessity.

A priority of transition planning is career and vocational education, and preparation for postsecondary education options. Students with learning disabilities who have some experience in vocational education or paid outside work during

high school are more successful in the job market than those who haven't had these opportunities (Evers, 1996). Unfortunately, many of the currently existing vocational education programs are geared toward students who are less bright or who are delinquents. Because these programs may be inappropriate for students who are learning disabled, and many adolescents with learning disabilities don't want to be part of these groups, they often forgo prevocational experiences. Yet other programs may be inappropriate because they are geared toward the mid-range high school student, are academically oriented, and are directed toward higher-level occupations and continued postsecondary education (e.g., Tech-Prep programs). Consequently, many students with disabilities continue to be underrepresented in vocational programs (Evers, 1996).

In the absence of appropriate vocational programs, flexible schedules can be arranged so that students actually apprentice on community jobs during the school day, or students can participate in school-operated small businesses. Job clubs, where long- and short-term goals are established and the meeting of goals rewarded, represent another way to explore talents and careers, and to gain self-confidence by sharing information among peers, taking field trips to job sites, and participating in informational interviews (Lindstrom, Benz, & Johnson, 1996). Interview skills (timeliness, appearance, posture, politeness, conversational skills) and resume writing should be important goals of these programs, as should role playing various employment situations: teaching students how to accept a compliment, how to compliment or constructively criticize a coworker, how to accept instruction and criticism from a supervisor, or how to explain a problem to a supervisor (Whang, Fawcett, & Mathews, 1984). These experiences all have potential for increasing students' job retention.

Money management and budgeting are other important areas for transition planning. Opening, maintaining, and balancing a bank account can be learned by using actual bank checks and bankbooks or by using a variety of commercially published materials.

Given that students with learning disabilities have so much to prepare for, teaching goals and materials must have very practical, everyday value and be taught whenever possible in natural rather than simulated settings (Cronin, 1996). This includes preparing students for skills essential to independent living, such as cooking, cleaning, shopping, spending leisure time, developing hobbies, and accessing community activities. A good example of how reading, writing, and problem solving can be taught within a practical context is making use of the driver's manual for instruction. Because a major move toward independence for many high school students is obtaining a driver's license, the driver's manual can be turned into a motivating instructional tool. Reading and math lessons can be structured using concepts to be learned such as parking requirements, distances to remain behind a moving vehicle, meaning of signs, and also informal problem solving such as how to get the car for a Saturday night date. This instruction can be quite helpful, since passing the written test, let alone the performance test, is difficult for many teenagers.

The student and family's involvement in transition planning is essential, as is the involvement of relevant adult service organizations, employers, and postsecondary educational institutions. Family involvement is critical because, despite the school's transition plan, after graduation, significant numbers of students with learning disabilities remain at home, and the responsibility for guidance is largely up to their families.

Social–Emotional Adjustment

Although school generally is viewed as a place for learning facts, it must be remembered that "education is essentially a social process" (Stanford & Roark, 1974, p. viii). It is the quality of human interactions, more than academic knowledge or even intelligence, that makes for life success. Adolescents spend a great deal of time and energy pondering the answers to such questions as, "Will I be invited to the party?" "Do you think he (or she) really likes me?" "Will I make the team?" The social development aspect of secondary school is a critical stepping stone toward adult emotional and social adjustment. The more positive the student's social relationships and the higher his or her self-esteem, the more likely the student is to be successful in life. Unfortunately, positive social relationships and self-esteem don't come easily to many students with learning disabilities. Poor social skills handicap them probably more than any other skill deficit.

The school's role in building social relationships, thinking skills, speaking skills, and self-esteem is important to the enhancement of these students' social–emotional adjustment. Wiener (1987) cautions that because it is peers who choose to ignore or treat students with learning disabilities differently (thereby affording these youngsters fewer opportunities for social learning), interventions must be directed at more than the student who is learning disabled. The interactions of the student with his or her peers, family, and teachers must be studied to determine whether peers also should be involved in social skills programming, families in counseling, or teachers in consultation because they interact differently with the student who is learning disabled.

Social Relationship Programming. Teachers need to help students with learning disabilities practice acceptable social behaviors. This is particularly important for students who have insufficient opportunities to interact with nondisabled students because of the time spent in special education. Environments that are conducive to sharing feelings help youngsters learn much about themselves and the willingness of others to listen. Group discussions, for example, have helped promote positive social–emotional growth and self-understanding among adolescents (Wanat, 1983). Students learn to engage in behavior that satisfies their personal needs without impinging on the needs of others. This requires them to use decision-making skills that carefully consider the implications of alternative actions, a process that is difficult for many adolescents who are learning disabled.

Debono (1977) emphasizes the importance of helping students acquire lateral methods for problem solving—in other words, shifting from vertical thinking ("digging the same hole deeper") to lateral thinking ("digging a hole somewhere else"). Students need to be shown how to think in a variety of ways about a single issue, to monitor their thoughts, to evaluate their choices and probable consequences, and to regulate their thoughts positively and appropriately (for example, "My stomach isn't in a knot because I'm *nervous* about tennis tryouts. It's because I'm *excited*!"). Students need to be taught how to recognize the sameness between new and old situations, so that tried and proven approaches will be attempted. Students also need to learn the value of challenging assumptions in their daily lives so they can look at information in a new light and gain new insights. Brainstorming sessions can help develop these skills, as can development of the thinking skills listed in Table 6–1. Brainstorming sessions can be quite effective, provided that the basic rules for brainstorming are followed:

1. Criticism is not allowed. No one should criticize the ideas of another.

2. "The wilder the idea the better." Freedom of expression stimulates more creative ideas.

3. Generate a vast number of ideas. Come up with as many as you can and make sure someone or something (tape recorder, videotape) is recording them.

4. Expand on each other's ideas. Try combining and improving on others' suggestions (Osborn, 1963).

Formal thinking skills programs also can be helpful, but only if they are strongly connected to the actual knowledge, behaviors, and situations to which these skills are intended to be applied (Niedelman, 1991).

Besides discussions and brainstorming, other methods that have been successful in teaching social skills include chaining of behavior segments, modeling, shaping, cuing, verbal rehearsal, role playing, and videotapes to help students observe and practice new behaviors (Schumaker

& Hazel, 1984). Goldstein's (1988) *Prepare Curriculum,* for example, uses a structured format to teach cooperation and interpersonal skills, in addition to such skills as anger control, stress management, moral reasoning, and empathy.

Curricula that develop nonverbal skills in socially imperceptive adolescents are equally important. Minskoff (1980a), for example, offers a detailed approach to learning about body language cues, use of space, cosmetics, clothing, and sensitivity to vocal pitch, loudness, pause, and rate. Her teaching sequence involves discrimination of these social cues, followed by understanding their meaning, their appropriate usage, and their application to actual social problems.

Unfortunately, social skill gains from such programs are for the most part modest, and generalization to everyday circumstances is limited (DuPaul & Eckert, 1994; Forness & Kavale, 1996). Besides issues regarding the validity of social skill measurement instruments, Forness and Kavale raise questions about whether intervention programs are too short-lived, poorly applied, or not sufficiently targeted to the specific needs of students to be able to turn around years of social skill deficits. Research suggests that, if we are going to teach social skills, these behaviors must be socially meaningful and we must plan specifically for generalization by doing the teaching as much as possible in natural environments and in conjunction with alterations of consequences in these environments (DuPaul & Eckert, 1994). One way of doing this is by establishing networks of students without disabilities who provide social support during school activities to students with disabilities for the purpose of increasing their participation and acceptance. The nondisabled students make a serious commitment to this activity, meeting weekly to problem solve and develop strategies for mediating the social relationships of their peers with disabilities (Haring, 1992). Alternatively, Perlmutter (1986) points out that weak results may be due to students' inability to judge when a particular behavior is appropriate even though they may have appropriate behaviors in their social repertoires. Therefore, Perlmutter urges us to consider decreasing time spent teaching social behaviors and instead spending more time helping students to analyze which social environments call for which interaction patterns.

Speaking Skills Training.   Edmund Muskie said, "Never say anything that doesn't improve upon silence." Unfortunately, students with learning disabilities often violate this adage. Alley and Deshler (1979) suggest several important strategies for teaching students to respond to questions or converse more appropriately:

1. *Waiting time.* Students should be encouraged to organize their thoughts before speaking. Teachers can reinforce students when they are successful in controlling irrelevant or inappropriate comments.

2. *Rehearsal.* Students rehearse what they want to say to a teacher, friend, potential employer, or even in a speech and receive feedback from the class. Strategies can be discussed to assist the students in real situations.

3. *Interpersonal sensitivity.* Teachers can help students discover how their speech affects listeners and then model what makes a person interesting to listen to (for example, maintaining good eye contact and showing enthusiasm and genuine interest in the conversations of others).

4. *Surface counseling.* Teachers are responsible for giving accurate feedback to their students by sharing what behavior they observed, which behaviors affect the peer group in particular ways, and the teachers' own reactions to the behaviors.

When speaking skills improve, students' social relationships also benefit.

Building Self-Esteem.   Students' self-esteem will differ, based on whether they are reflecting on their academic abilities, athletic skills, attractiveness, sociability, or overall worth as individuals.

When we intervene to raise a student's academic self-esteem, this may have some positive spillover to global self-esteem; however, increases in global self-esteem will not generalize in the opposite direction (Strein, 1993). Therefore, we must identify our self-esteem goals carefully and be very targeted in our programming.

The teacher has many options for enhancing various aspects of a student's self-esteem. This is especially important given our inclusive education practices: there is evidence that scholastic environments, in which average skill levels are higher than the student's, are associated with lower academic self-concepts, somewhat lower grades, and lower educational and occupational aspirations (Strein, 1993). In addition to the activities suggested below, teachers can help prevent such self-esteem losses by creating a cooperative rather than competitive class environment, decreasing emphasis on letter grades in favor of mastery-oriented learning and evaluation, recognizing and valuing individual differences, and decreasing undue social comparison. Involving students in community service activities on a regular basis also is effective in bolstering social skills, self-esteem, positive connections, confidence, and a sense of pride and belonging (Yoder, Retish, & Wade, 1996).

Directed Writing Activity.   If you ever have dug through attic treasures and unearthed an old diary, you probably discovered that underneath all the dust and cobwebs was an insightful incantation of feelings, thoughts, and experiences. Teachers too can encourage students to jot down reactions to their daily lives in a journal format. Alley and Deshler (1979) suggest that students write daily reactions to both a positive and a negative experience and focus on their own abilities and shortcomings. If the journals are not totally private, then they should be read by the teacher at least once a week and the issues discussed with the student.

Self-Determination Training.   One goal of education is to facilitate greater autonomy and ability to govern one's life. But many students with learning disabilities view their lives as controlled by others and place the responsibility for their actions on someone else: "Sue didn't sit with me at lunch because she's ashamed to be seen with me." The student who accepts more responsibility for his or her own actions might say, "If I want Sue to sit with me at lunch, I think I should ask her, or get there early enough to be sure there's room for me at the table."

Felton and Davidson (1973) suggest teaching students how to identify and apply the fundamental concept of locus of control to their daily lives. Role playing and simulations can help students discover whether their locus of control is coming from outside or from inside themselves. The value of internal control is highlighted and support is offered as problems and action plans are identified.

A number of self-determination curricula have been developed. In addition, modeling, giving students opportunities for choice, helping students attribute success to their own efforts and abilities, and positive reinforcement of motivation, self-esteem, and internal locus of control are effective strategies (Field, 1996). In one intervention, for example, Kamann and Wong's (1993) students increased their math performance by learning to use empowering self-statements: "I'm saying [negative] things that don't help me. . . ." "I can stop and think more helpful thoughts." "Take it step by step." "I did really well in not letting this get the best of me." "Good for me! I did a good job." Self-determination skills are essential to effective participation in transition planning, to overcoming learned helplessness, and to making important decisions about one's life. Students who act according to their personal preferences and interests, make independent decisions about how to act in various situations, believe they can influence outcomes with their actions, and apply an accurate understanding of their strengths and limitations in making decisions are more likely to be employed one year out of high school, earn higher wages, have a savings or checking account, and express a preference to live outside their parents' home (Wehmeyer & Schwartz, 1997).

Q-sort. Kroth (1973) suggests using a Q-sort, the sorting of descriptive adjectives into piles, to enable students to analyze their perceptions of their "existing" behavior and their "ideal" behavior. Students then select a behavior that they wish to change and are reinforced for progress toward this goal.

Assertiveness Training. Assertive behavior is characterized as honest and straightforward expression to others and ourselves about how we feel. It is simply a tool for social contact that is open, direct, spontaneous, and appropriate (Rimm & Masters, 1974). Assertive does not mean aggressive. With assertiveness training, students learn to feel better about themselves and less anxious about sharing their feelings and ideas (Fensterheim & Baer, 1975; Smith, 1975). In contrast, the nonassertive student often gets hurt. Assertiveness training ties into the locus of control concept because nonassertive students allow others to shape their goals. Assertive students more often make their own decisions and, from this, gain self-satisfaction. Essential components of assertive behavior include:

1. good eye contact, appropriate body language, and facial expression consistent with verbal expression (for example, not smiling when you are dissatisfied);

2. spontaneous reactions to others' actions, and judgment about the most appropriate timing of comments;

3. honest content that communicates what the student is feeling ("I am angry with you for breaking my watch" rather than "You are so clumsy!");

4. gauging the intensity of one's response to a situation (not "blowing up" when someone bumps you in line) (Alberti & Emmons, 1978).

Through assertiveness training, students learn to substitute positive, honest, open behaviors for nonassertive, self-destructive actions.

Values Clarification. "School is boring. Should I quit?" "Why do I bite my nails?" "Do I really care what my friends think of me?" These and hundreds more personal and theoretical questions are asked by adolescents who are trying to clarify the values they've incorporated from their parents, friends, and teachers and from their own experiences (Simon, Have, & Kirschenbaum, 1972). When students become clear about what they prize, what they believe, and how they want to behave—and when they act accordingly—important choices and social interactions are facilitated. Teachers and counselors can help by being good listeners and reflectors of a student's feelings.

Summary

Special interventions for students who are learning disabled begin in the preschool years and often continue beyond the secondary school years. Materials and approaches are chosen on the basis of what students need to learn, how they learn best, and what learning strategies need to be taught. Exactly which materials and approaches will teach which students best is the focus of much current research. Some students with learning disabilities require moderate task modifications to be successful, whereas others require intense remedial and compensatory efforts.

The teacher is the key to good teaching, and the student's family is the key to supporting a youngster's efforts. Both the teacher and the family have the responsibility to attend as much to the affective development as to the academic development of the youngster.

This chapter reviewed approaches for academic and affective development at the preschool, elementary, and secondary school levels. These approaches help to facilitate academic, daily living, and vocational preparation by remediating weaknesses, capitalizing on students' strengths, and teaching students ways to work around their weaknesses.

**Part Five
The Setting**

Chapter Eleven

The Family

Just as characteristics of the curriculum can help to prevent, exacerbate, or overcome learning disabilities, so can the student's home environment. By far a student's most important setting is his or her family. The members of the youngster's family, especially his or her parents, provide the surroundings that will nurture the student's intellectual and learning abilities, as well as social attitudes, behaviors, and feelings of self-worth. Fostering children's intellectual competencies is very important, but so is supporting their personal-social adjustment. No matter what children's abilities, they will have a much easier time if they learn to trust others, listen and learn from others, and get along by telling the truth, following the rules, and acting in considerate, helpful, and altruistic ways. The parents' example and child-rearing patterns are paramount in teaching children positive values, assertiveness, self-confidence, and achievement orientation, all qualities important for school performance and life adjustment.

Because the family greatly influences the development of students with learning disabilities, it is important for teachers to get to know parents and encourage their participation in the assessment, planning, and intervention process. Parents can be valuable resources to teachers; conversely, teachers need to be prepared to meet parental needs for information and emotional support. Because families greatly affect their children's learning progress and social adjustment, teachers need to learn how to assess family systems and how to help parents make better use of their strengths, minimize their weaknesses, and become better teachers, advocates, and sources of support for their children. We begin by exploring the family's role in promoting their children's academic and social learning.

Families and Learning

Parents are truly children's first teachers, and home is the child's first school. Children come into the world with certain potentials, but it is how they learn in their "first school" that will most affect their ultimate cognitive development. Throughout their children's lives, parents serve as models for behavior and stimulate their children to interact with and learn from the world. The more teachers understand how the cognitive, academic, and social difficulties of the child with learning disabilities may relate to the family environment, the more they can help plan family interventions aimed at increasing youngsters' academic and social-learning opportunities.

Cognitive and School Achievement

Early childhood is an important time. It is often during the preschool years that parents of a child with learning disabilities first note delays in development. Parents can do much during this period to maximize their child's opportunities for cognitive and social–emotional development.

Many family factors play a role in the developmental progress of children: the home press for achievement, language models, encouragement of independence and exploration beyond the home, intellectual interests/activities in the home, work habits modeled at home, father presence, parental employment, quantity of activities with adults, positive affect in the home, avoidance of punishment, organization of time and objects in the home, appropriate play materials, books, the behaviors of siblings and secondary caregivers, traumatic events (for example, death of a parent, divorce, birth of a sibling, moving), and the parents' initiative, energy level, learning and teaching styles, task orientation, emotional and verbal responsiveness, interpersonal skills, and involve-

ment with the school (Bradley & Caldwell, 1978; Christenson et al., 1997; Lorsbach & Frymier, 1992; Walberg & Marjoribanks, 1976). The intellectual, academic, and social–emotional declines experienced by many children who live with neglect, alcoholic or abusive parents, or divorce speak to the powerful influence of family factors (Gelardo & Sanford, 1987; Guidubaldi et al., 1983; Tharinger & Koranek, 1988).

The way in which environmental stimulation affects child development has received much research attention over the years. Provence and Lipton's (1962) vivid descriptions of children raised in an orphanage shocked the world into recognizing exactly how powerful maternal deprivation can be in causing developmental delays. But the home need not be as barren as the orphanage in order to produce children who fall behind. The intellectual competence and attending ability of infants has been associated with the amount and nature of auditory and kinesthetic stimulation, the variety of social and play activities, maternal responsiveness to the infant's stress vocalizations, maternal consistency, the amount of time parents and infants spend gazing at one another, the extent to which caretakers talk to infants, and the variety and responsiveness of toys (for example, newspaper crackles when touched by the child) (Fletcher, Levin, & Landry, 1984; White, 1980; Yarrow, Rubenstein, & Pederson, 1975). When these factors reduce an infant's competence, the delays tend to persist throughout subsequent years (White, 1980).

Early intervention projects have attempted to influence the family history of children who, because of family and socioeconomic circumstances, are at high risk for retardation or school failure. The interventions have either enrolled the child in a preschool program or intervened directly with parents by nurturing their parenting abilities.

Research has shown that preschool programs produce gains in such skills as memory and abstract reasoning when compared to no intervention. Although at times the intellectual gains are lost once the program is stopped, in most cases there is some persistence (Aiken, 1987; Bronfenbrenner, 1975; Campbell & Ramey, 1994; Lazar

& Darlington, 1982; McCarthy, J., 1980). Lasting benefits frequently become apparent years later in the form of higher school achievement, high school graduation rates, earnings, and employment rates; and fewer retentions, special class placements, encounters with the law, and early pregnancies (Berrueta-Clement et al., 1984; Campbell & Ramey, 1994; Neisser et al., 1996).

Gains in home-based intervention programs also are long-lasting, often persisting six to seven years or more after the intervention has ended (Garber, 1987; Haskins, 1989; Levenstein, O'Hara, & Madden, 1983; Rossetti, 1986). Studies suggest that home-based programs can be successful with children even if initiated as late as the sixth grade. The support, modeling, and information parents receive in home-based interventions seem to foster parental awareness of their children's potential, commitment to becoming primary educators in their children's lives, and confidence in their parenting skills. When mothers receive home visits from preschool educators, the mothers have increased their involvement with their youngsters, emotional and verbal responsiveness, provision of appropriate play material, and organization of their children's physical environments. Whitehurst and colleagues (1988), for example, taught parents how to enrich reading experiences with their children by asking open-ended questions, expanding on their children's answers, suggesting alternative possibilities, and posing progressively more challenging questions. Within one month, these parents' two- and three-year-old children had progressed six to eight months in verbal skills beyond that of the control group. To the extent to which parental gains persist beyond termination of the preschool intervention, children's gains are likely to persist as well (Zigler, 1987). The earlier that either home-based or school-based intervention occurs, the greater the benefits (Bronfenbrenner, 1975). It is unfortunate that preschool participation for low-income children remains low (45%); this contrasts with 73 percent attendance among families with incomes over $50,000 (Dwyer, 1996).

Clearly, parents can be very successful change agents in their children's lives. They can do much to promote developmental and behav-

ioral gains beyond what can be accomplished by preschool education alone (Moreland et al., 1982; Wells & Forehand, 1981). Consequently, most center-based preschool programs try to incorporate a strong parent-involvement component, and PL 99–457 provides for support services such as social skills training, parent consultation, and prevention activities with families of infants and preschoolers. For school-age children with disabilities, IDEA mandates involving parents in their children's program planning.

In the following pages we will explore the relationship of socioeconomic factors, parent–child interactions, and physical surroundings to children's cognitive, academic, and social development. We have found that socioeconomic factors are far more predictive of learning and adjustment difficulties than the birth trauma a child had experienced, but an even stronger predictor is the nature of the parent–child relationship.

Socioeconomic Status and Achievement. Over and over again, studies show that parental socioeconomic status and educational levels are extremely predictive of children's developmental and academic outcomes, and even their educational and occupational attainments as adults (Broman, Bien, & Shaughnessy, 1985; Gottlieb et al., 1994; Haywood & Switzky, 1986; Kopp & Kaler, 1989; Lorsbach & Frymier, 1992; O'Connor and Spreen, 1988). Just as the example in Research Box 11–1 illustrates how variables associated with higher socioeconomic status can make up for poor schooling, we have striking evidence that these factors also can overcome the effects of birth trauma on later school failure. One of the earliest of these studies, the Kauai study, followed every child born in 1955 on the island of Kauai, Hawaii, until 32 years of age. One of the most startling conclusions reached was that the effects of socioeconomic status are more powerful than those of perinatal complications (Werner, 1989; Werner, Bierman, & French, 1971; Werner & Smith, 1977). By twenty months of age, children who had experienced the most severe perinatal complications, but who grew up in upper-middle-income homes, nearly equaled the intelligence levels of children who had experienced no perinatal stress but were living in lower-socioeconomic-level homes. By age ten, the former children had achieved above-average IQs. But the children from low-income homes who had experienced severe perinatal complications remained significantly delayed in intelligence, language, perceptual, reading, and social skills (Werner, 1980).

The Collaborative Perinatal Project, which followed the children of nearly 50,000 women receiving prenatal care in twelve university medical centers through age eight, supported the Kauai findings (Broman et al., 1985; Nichols & Chen, 1981). Again, learning disorders were more strongly related to socioeconomic status than to amount of perinatal stress, with a greater proportion of children with learning disabilities coming from lower-income families. Similarly, high-socioeconomic status homes help children overcome the effect on IQ of cytomegalovirus at birth, but low-income homes may not (Hanshaw et al., 1976). Likewise, many studies show that

high-risk or malnourished adopted infants develop normally if raised in higher-socioeconomic-status families (Siegel, 1981; Stigler et al., 1982; Winick, Meyer, & Harris, 1975). An unusual percentage of students with learning disabilities come from families where educational stimulation is lacking and economic and family difficulties are pervasive (Toro et al., 1990).

Berk (1997) reviews literature suggesting that the harsh life conditions of the lower-income parent, the powerlessness and lack of influence in one's job, the authoritarian model presented by employers, and the lack of higher education that would refocus values onto abstract ideas may result in lower-income parents using authoritarian methods to enforce external characteristics in their children such as obedience, neatness, and cleanliness. In contrast, higher-income parents tend to value internal characteristics such as curiosity, happiness, and self-control, which they encourage in their children through verbal praise,

RESEARCH BOX 11–1
Home Teaching Helps Make Up for Poor Teaching

An interesting natural experiment regarding the value of encouraging whole-word versus phonic approaches to reading occurred in Israel in the 1940s and 1950s (Feitelson, 1973). Because of the influence of a prominent educator, the whole-word, language experience approach was instituted in schools. Children were expected to infer the phonetic rules on their own. This method worked just fine for the largely middle-income European Jews living in Israel at the time. However, with mass immigration of lower-socioeconomic-status Jews from the Arab countries in the early 1950s, reading failure rates soared to 50 percent.

Investigation of the matter revealed that the whole-word method actually did not work well for most children. Children from European backgrounds nevertheless read well because their parents had taught them phonics at home. Because the families from Arab countries did not value education to the same extent and had lower parental educational levels, they did not supplement their children's schooling at home. Consequently, their children failed reading, and the failure of the whole-word teaching strategy finally became evident. The home press for education among the better-educated European Jews not only overcame their children's inadequate schooling but also masked the ineffectiveness of the teaching methods to which the children were being exposed.

explanations, and mutual problem solving. These variations in child rearing certainly can set different educational paths, as can living in "urban war zones" where fear for one's safety, withdrawal, depression, and aggression sap motivation and concentration (Osofsky, 1995). The more a child's environment promotes intellectual stimulation, feelings of personal value, and control, the more likely the child is to overcome the effects of a poor start in life.

Parent–Child Interaction and Achievement. It is known that homes in which a parent is an alcoholic, is abusive to the children, or is absent for long periods of time (for example, because of divorce) are particularly detrimental to children's intellectual, academic, and social–emotional development (Bergman, 1981; Svanum, Bringle, & McLaughlin, 1982; Tharinger & Koranek, 1988). But even if the home situation is not this severe, certain parental interaction patterns can greatly

deter child development. In contrast, a positive, stable, stimulating, and supportive adult relationship can render children resilient to the effects of negative environments.

Examine the difference between the drawings in Figures 11–1 and 11–2. Both Eden and Rebecca are eight years old, of above average intelligence, and they have been raised in middle-income homes. Every child in Eden's family has inherited a phonological processing disorder, which results in serious reading delays. Eden's parents understand this and are supportive and hopeful. In her family picture Eden depicts her father presenting flowers to her nine-month pregnant mother, and a happy Eden playing ball with her sister. In her replies to incomplete sentence stems, Eden reflected her satisfaction with herself and her family, and her continuing high academic and personal self-esteem: *Boys think I* am pretty; *My father never* shouts; *People are always* nice; *I know I can* read; *My family* is important to me; *At*

Figure 11–1   Eden.

Figure 11–2   Rebecca.

home I like to play with my sisters; *Other children* play with me; *I wish I could stop* I don't know anything I wish I could stop.

Rebecca's pictures depict a different situation, although she has the same kind and severity of learning disability as Eden. Rebecca's mother is a history professor, her father a physics professor, and her brother's academic career is as stellar as would be expected in that family. Rebecca's parents cannot accept her differences. They are disappointed and angry, they let her know it, and her pictures show it. While Eden's parents work cooperatively with the school to develop appropriate programming, Rebecca's parents demand this help. Their dissatisfaction with the school's slowness in responding to their requests has resulted in Rebecca's ambivalence toward investing energy in work required by teachers whom her parents do not respect. In Rebecca's family drawing, her cats are more animated than the people. Although it is dinnertime, there is virtually no food on the table. Rebecca's parents and brother are together, while she draws herself segregated, looking on from the doorway. Rebecca angrily scribbled over her self-portrait. In response to questions about her drawings she stated: "I'm pretty stupid"; "I wish I could get out of the family"; "I'm sad because my mom and dad yell and scream"; "My brother's mean to me"; "I get spanked because I didn't change the cats' compost"; "My mom and dad wish for me to get away for real and in the picture"; "There's a blizzard outside but the sun's on the cat"; "My parents hate all of us."

Eden and Rebecca's examples illustrate why parent–child interactions and stimulation within the home are far more powerful influences on child development than factors associated with poverty or perinatal stress (Barrett & Depinet, 1991; Bee et al., 1982; Haywood & Switzky, 1986). Christenson and colleagues (1997) review research indicating that 60 percent of a child's achievement is related to family process variables, whereas only 25 percent is predicted from health or socioeconomic status. For example, in the Kauai study, both perinatal stress and socioeconomic status were less related to low achievement than was the degree of educational stimulation and emotional support in the home, including parental emphasis on intellectual pursuits; the amount parents read to themselves and their child; numbers of books, magazines, and learning supplies in the home; and parental interest in the child's schooling and homework. Homes that were positive in these features produced the children with the highest academic achievement. There were many examples of children who had experienced oxygen deprivation at birth and yet, at ten years of age, performed academically at their grade level with an IQ only a few points lower than children of the same social status who had experienced no perinatal stress. Siegel (1981) too found that infants who were born at risk for developmental problems were developing normally at age two if raised in stimulating home environments. Infants who were not identified at risk, but who showed delays at two years of age, tended to come from homes that provided less stimulation. Similarly, a follow-up of hyperactive children found that biological factors were less important than home environment in predicting educational outcomes, drug use, high school graduation, college attendance, and independent living (Landers, 1987). School achievement and social adjustment are higher when children bring with them from home a sense of competence, positive self-concept, stability, awareness, interest, and a mental set that values learning (Bell, Abrahamson, & McRae, 1977). Southeast Asian boat children exemplify this point: despite harrowing

escapes and relocation, their strong family support system, including family commitment to spend time on homework, has helped these children overcome insurmountable odds and achieve well above their American-born peers (Caplan, Choy, & Whitmore, 1992). The positive effects of intimate, nurturing, and stimulating relationships between mothers and their children are evident well into adolescence and beyond (Garber, 1987). Nick's story (page 437) illustrates how important loving parents are in helping children get through the anger and frustration that often accompany a learning disability.

Poor parent–child relationships impact all areas of a child's development. Matheny, Wilson, and Thoben (1987), for example, found that toddlers growing up in homes characterized by noise and confusion, other things being equal, developed more difficult temperaments. An adult style that consists of many commands, requests, directions, and instructions has been associated with slower vocabulary acquisition (Nelson, 1973). Parents whose communications to their preschoolers tend to be prohibitions ("stop that," "don't . . . ") rather than responses to child initiations, asking questions, or repeating, paraphrasing, and extending their children's statements, have children with lower IQs (Hart & Risley, 1992). Likewise, parents who are less involved with their children, who communicate lower expectations, who neither monitor how constructively children's time is spent nor set clear and consistent limits, and who are least accepting, nurturent, encouraging, involved with the school, and emotionally responsive to the child's needs have children with the most academic difficulties (Christenson et al., 1997). An unusual percentage of children who are identified as learning disabled come from homes that are unstable and that experience unexpected numbers of tragedies such as job loss, serious illness, or death (Lorsbach & Frymier, 1992).

Most studies of parent–child interactions have focused on maternal behavior, particularly in infancy. In the Collaborative Perinatal Project, eight-month-old children whose mothers had the following attributes were most likely to be identified as learning disabled or hyperactive at age seven: spoke harshly or negatively to their babies;

Nick

Nick's mother shares the following introduction to Nick's journal entry:
Nick was in the fifth grade at the time of this journal entry, in complete despair over his inability to make any sense out of the class he was in. The teacher Nick had for the mainstreamed portion of his school day seemed certain she could handle Nick's slow work pace and misunderstanding of class assignments by making him sit on a bench during recesses. He didn't tell me about the benchings at first, apparently quite sad that the year was beginning so badly. That year remains in his memory as one of his worst, and he still shakes his head when he thinks of that teacher. Nick has shown us an incredible spirit in the face of many not so happy experiences and I tip my hat to him for his incredible determination.

Nick's Journal Entry
The hardest thing I ever had to do is get a good grade on my vocabulary test. Because I have a hard time remembering things. I study and study and I can't get it. I try hard but I need *more time*. My mom has been a big help. Now I have to do a poem. I can't do it see I told you now I have to sit on the bench. I wish I could slap myself and get rid of my learning problems, but Mrs. Saunders doesn't understand. My mom and my dad will talk to her and my dad has been a big help too. I've been on the bench for two weeks. This is getting me really mad. My friend understands why doesn't Mrs. Saunders understand. I hope I pass fifth grade. I'm really scared. Somebody help me. Alls Mrs. Saunders does is putting people on the bench. She yells at everybody. Now Matt is dead. I know Matt tried. He didn't mean to. I'm not having very much fun this year. I hate myself. Life isn't fair. I'm not happy. But when I'm around my dad he makes me feel really good. I love him very very much. He is the best dad in the world. I feel like I'm in jail and I will never get out. I want to tell her what I feel like but she will yell at me. I'm to get up my guts and tell her. I'm really sad with a capital S. I'm going to be dead again in about 3 seconds. I'm at the library now. Maybe I will talk to Mrs. Saunders.

Mom I hope you read this I love you mom and Dad. Now I'm going to study hall.

Source: Reprinted by permission of Rita and Nick Ter Sarkissoff.

made more critical statements about their babies; handled the babies in a remote, impersonal, rough, and clumsy manner; were unhelpful in orienting the children toward the testing materials; were slow in recognizing and responding to the children's needs (comforting, hunger, wet diapers); were indifferent to what or how their children were doing with the test materials; neglected the children's physical needs (inadequately dressed, body odor, sores, rashes, didn't bring clean diapers) (Nichols & Chen, 1981). Keogh and Becker (1973) point out that there are also parents of children with learning disabilities who are overly anxious and understanding about their children's problems; consequently, they fail to communicate high enough expectations and do not push their children to work to the best of their ability.

The importance of the mother as a language model has received special attention because of the relationship between language development and academic readiness. Language modeling occurs when parents repeat a word the child has uttered (for example, *ball*), expand it ("Yes, that's a ball"), or use the word in a question ("Did you find a ball?"). Conversations at home should be children's best source of linguistic and cognitive enrichment because the frame of reference shared with their parents allows children to explore ideas and events with more personal meaning than conversations held with strange teachers (Tizard & Hughes, 1985). Yet some mothers of language-impaired and hyperactive children may not be optimal language models because they tend to degrade the language they use with their children (Barkley, Cunningham, & Karlsson, 1983; Leonard, 1982).

Parents' distinctive interaction patterns become evident shortly after birth in the synchrony between the newborn's movements and the parents' reaction (Austin & Peery, 1983; Kato et al., 1983; Peery, 1980). In the following example, Tronick (1989) describes how the affective communications of mothers and their infants influence one another's emotional experiences and behavior.

Imagine two infant-mother pairs playing the game peek-a-boo. In the first, the infant abruptly turns away from his mother as the game reaches its "peak" of intensity and begins to suck his thumb and stare into space with a dull facial expression. The mother stops playing and sits back watching her infant. After a few seconds the infant turns back to her with an interested and inviting expression. The mother moves closer, smiles, and says in a high-pitched, exaggerated voice, "Oh, now you're back!" He smiles in response and vocalizes. As they finish crowing together, the infant reinserts his thumb and looks away. The mother again waits. After a few seconds the infant turns back to her, and they greet each other with big smiles.

Imagine a second similar situation except that after this infant turns away, she does not look back at her mother. The mother waits but then leans over into the infant's line of vision while clicking her tongue to attract her attention. The infant, however, ignores the mother and continues to look away. Undaunted, the mother persists and moves her head closer to the infant. The infant grimaces and fusses while she pushes at the mother's face. Within seconds she turns even further away from her mother and continues to suck on her thumb. (p. 112)

We can see from this example that babies are active, not passive, in signaling what they need from the environment. Clearly, the first child's mother, in tune with the infant's signals, is providing a more positive, less stressful environment than the second mother. Because the second mother disregards her infant's message ("Please stay away; I'm overaroused; I need time to quiet down and regulate my emotional state"), their interactions are likely to be more negative, and sadness and disengagement from the caretaker may follow. Tronick illustrates the parent's responsibility to turn the baby's negative states into positive states and promote positive communication:

The six-month-old infant stretches his hands out toward the object [which is just out of reach]. Because he cannot get hold of it, he becomes angry and distressed. He looks away for a moment and sucks on his thumb. Calmer, he looks back at the object and reaches for it once more. But this attempt fails too, and he gets angry again. The caretaker watches for a moment, then soothingly talks to him. The infant calms down and with a facial expression of interest gazes at the object and makes another attempt to reach for it. The caretaker brings the object just within the infant's reach. The infant successfully grasps the object, explores it, and smiles. . . . the caretaker is responsible for the reparation of the infant's failure into success and the simultaneous transformation of his negative emotion into a positive emotion. (p. 113)

Just as parents' actions must be guided by the baby's emotional state, infants use the emotional state of their caretakers to guide their actions ("I'll crawl over there if mom looks encouraging, but not if mom looks fearful") (Campos et al., 1983). If what the baby senses in the caretaker is continual depression, intrusiveness, and mistimed interactions, the baby is likely to reciprocate with negative affect. This infant gets little guidance about how to face stress and repair his or her negative affective states. The baby also does not develop trust for the input of caretakers or a representation of himself or herself as effective, capable of positive interactions, and capable of turning negative into positive states (Emde, 1983; Gianino & Tronick, 1988). Instead, the baby works to regulate negative states by turning away, escaping, or becoming perceptually unavailable. As the baby reduces interactions with objects and people, the potential for compromising cognitive development increases. In addition, the more comfortable the child finds disengagement, the more it becomes a regular way of functioning.

What the child learns in interactions with his or her caretakers is a style of approach or withdrawal, anticipation of pleasure or stress from new situations, which is likely to continue throughout childhood and even into adulthood. When parents are attentive, warm, stimulating, flexible, supportive, accepting, and actively engage and support their children in solving problems, this is reflected in higher intellectual and academic competencies throughout childhood (Bayley & Schaeffer, 1964; Belsky, 1981; Estrada et al., 1987). These children seem to feel safe exploring the wider world because the parent represents a stable emotional base to support their experiences; they become friendlier, more enthusiastic, and more attractive playmates (Beckman & Lieber, 1992; Hartup, 1989).

Beckman and Lieber review research supporting the important role of the father as well in children's development. Fathers tend to engage in more rough and tumble play and play involving objects than do mothers (who are more instructive, directive, and engage in more fantasy play). The father's kind of play is invaluable because it is closer to what children need for interactions with peers.

It is important to remember that parent–child interaction is a two-way process and that relationships can be hampered by characteristics of the child, not just the parents. If a child with a learning disability has a difficult or "slow-to-warm-up" temperament, this makes the caretaker's responsibility all the more difficult. In addition, central nervous system damage can disrupt the body movements that constitute early nonverbal communication between children and their mothers; this in turn could reduce optimal parental stimulation for cognitive and social development (Thoman, 1978). Finally, factors such as low birth weight, prematurity, serious neonatal illness and the resulting parent–infant separation after birth, developmental delays, and difficulty controlling behavior may predispose a child to be the one targeted for neglect or maltreatment in abusive families (Gelardo & Sanford, 1987).

Werner's (1993) Kauai study showed that, despite the odds, there is always hope that youngsters will prove resilient to the adversities in their lives. In their early 30s, three of four Kauai individuals with learning disabilities had grown into responsible adults who held down jobs, had stable marriages, and were caring parents. Werner identified several protective factors that served as buffers: temperaments that elicited positive responses; skills, values, and motivation that put personal abilities to good use; parental caregiving styles that fostered competence and self-esteem; maternal postsecondary education; rules and structure in the home; maternal employment (for girls); supportive adults who fostered trust and faith; availability of opportunities at major life transitions.

Because appropriate parenting can do much to make up for both a poor start in life and the correlates of poverty, teachers must be sensitive to parents' circumstances, and, when appropriate, provide parents with information on how to interact with their children more productively. This may be as simple as suggesting that parents talk more with their children, use different words, and take turns in play because these relate to higher intelligence in preschoolers (Hart & Risley, 1992); or that they regularly read and discuss stories with their children because these increase language development (Taverne & Sheridan, 1995); or that parents periodically discuss future educational plans with their children because this is associated with lower dropout rates (National Center for Education Statistics, 1992).

If parents are not ready or able to provide the necessary supports, then it is important that teachers help students connect with other resources who can give positive attention, especially in times of crisis, provide nurturance, be positive role models, and establish close bonds: a friend, relative, neighbor or favorite teacher, or contacts within church groups, the YMCA, 4-H, and extracurricular activities. Werner's (1989) follow-up of the children of Kauai found that these supports, when available to children who had very positive personal characteristics, helped those in the most high-risk circumstances to be resilient enough to succeed academically and grow "into competent young adults who loved well, worked well, and played well" (p. 108D). The lifeguard story (below) illustrates how sometimes these supports come from the most unexpected sources.

The "Lifeguard" Who Cared

A child with a learning disability who also comes from a broken home, has attended three schools in his first four years of formal education, and somehow missed attending kindergarten may likely walk into his newest school with feelings of anger and lack of trust of both his fourth grade peers and school staff.

John is the student. In a small group setting, when he read orally, he would mimic the voice of a sassy four year old; when asked to complete a written task, his work was not legible; when contributing to an oral discussion, his answers were not appropriate. Finally, approximately six weeks after the school year began, John expressed his feelings of anger, sadness and fear through tears. The wall had finally been broken and there was a break through—a tiny twinkle at the end of the tunnel.

John described the playground rules as stupid, his peers as aggressive, and his new neighborhood without any friends. John said the classroom assignments were too difficult, and in general, life was rotten. When asked what he would like to do, he stated he wanted to build a go-cart assisted by the "lifeguard" who works in front of the school. The "lifeguard" happened to be the school crossing guard. Not only did he assist the students with pedestrian safety and serve as the "welcome wagon" to all entering the school, but Howard, the crossing guard, also displayed his handmade wooden toys on the school sidewalk.

Through several brief conversations and a letter to John's mother, arrangements were made for John to spend thirty to forty-five minutes every Friday afternoon in the resource classroom with the school crossing guard, Howard. Howard was aware of John's needs and interests and gave John the opportunity to design something to be constructed out of wood. John chose a helicopter, drew a picture, and after the first session, Howard returned with the wooden pieces cut for a helicopter. The next five to six Fridays were spent sanding, hammering, and painting.

Of course, the final product, an army-green helicopter, went home with one happy boy. More importantly and throughout the weeks when John and Howard were a team, John's attitude changed in everything he did from reading to writing to oral responses to less aggression on the playground. The relationship John developed with Howard was not only a nurturing one for John, but served as a grandfather-grandson relationship for Howard. Their weekly session was not contingent upon anything, which eliminated any pressure for John, and also gave him a feeling of control. Howard was more than willing to give a little of his time each week and walked out of the resource room with a grin of satisfaction just as big as John's smile of success and security.

Source: Reprinted by permission of Ellen Peterson.

Physical Surroundings and Achievement. Books, magazines, learning supplies, and many more aspects of children's physical learning environments are related to school success. In a survey of nearly 500 seniors with learning disabilities, students reported fewer and less adequate facilities for study and intellectual stimulation, and lower parental interest in their schooling and personal lives, than did their peers (Gregory, Shanahan, & Walberg, 1986). The National Center for Education Statistics (1992) reports that those parents who discuss future educational plans, restrict television viewing, and set rules about minimum grade-point averages are least likely to have children who drop out of high school.

One factor in the home's physical environment that has received much recent attention is television. Estimates of children's average viewing time range from eleven to twenty-eight hours a week (Huston, Watkins, & Kunkel, 1989). Over 40 percent of fourth graders and eighth graders watch three or more hours of television a day (*Condition of Education*, 1996). Children spend more time watching television than any other activity except sleeping. Children from African American, less well-educated, or lower-income families rely more heavily on television for education, entertainment, aesthetics, and knowledge about the world than do their more educated, affluent, or white counterparts. Yet commercial TV networks average less than one hour per week of informative programming geared toward children; this contrasts with public television's twenty-seven hours. Despite the excellent programming on some cable channels, these may be financially inaccessible to low-income and minority children. By the age of eighteen, the average child is estimated to have witnessed over 13,000 killings and over 101,000 violent episodes on television (Huston et al., 1989).

What is the effect of television on children? Early research indicated that watching TV for more than ten hours a week is associated with lower school achievement (Williams et al., 1982). However, it is now apparent that even one hour of TV watching per day is associated with lower academic achievement (*Condition of Education*, 1996). As viewing time increases, verbal fluency

and imaginativeness have been found to decrease (*The School Psychologist*, 1983). A small causal effect of television violence on aggressive behavior, acceptance of violence, reduced sensitivity to the suffering of others, and more fearfulness of the world has been demonstrated repeatedly (Drabman & Thomas, 1976; Feinbloom, 1976; Huston et al., 1989; Liebert, Neal, & Davidson, 1973; Pallak & Kaplinski, 1985). In one study, the more violent the programs watched at age eight, the more aggressive the youngsters were at age nineteen, the more serious the crimes for which they were convicted at age thirty, and the more harshly they punished their own children (Huesmann et al., in Eron & Huesmann, 1987). It seems that the more true-to-life children believe television aggression to be, and the more they identify with the TV characters, the more aggressive they are likely to become. Young children tend to accept much of what they see on television as realistic and do not distinguish fantasy from reality. Because they are too young to fully grasp the relationship between aggressive acts and the motives that prompted them, they may learn that disobedient attitudes and verbal/physical attacks are acceptable in our society (*The School Psychologist*, 1983).

TV also generates value lessons. Despite efforts to more accurately represent family types (for example, single-parent families) and individual roles (for example, women and people from diverse cultural groups as professionals), many TV programs nevertheless "convey a highly stereotyped and distorted social world in which being male, youthful, beautiful, and white are valued, and being female, old, handicapped, dark-skinned, or foreign are not valued" (Huston et al., 1989, p. 425). This prevents young people from gaining insights into new role possibilities, inhibits women and racial and ethnic minorities from striving to achieve positive self-images, and deters the public from accepting and understanding the goals of culturally diverse persons and women (Eron & Huesmann, 1987).

Williams's (1986) study of a small Canadian town just before TV reception became available and two years later sums up our concerns about TV viewing. After TV, grade school children showed a decline in reading fluency and creative thinking, a rise in sex-stereotyped attitudes, and increased verbal and physical aggression during spontaneous play. Community participation by adolescents and adults also showed a marked drop.

Although the above studies have not related specifically to the learning disabled, they are troublesome and suggest that the viewing choices of a child who is learning disabled must be monitored carefully. In the event that the student's viewing patterns lead to secondary attitudinal and behavioral problems, this would further aggravate the learning problems. Parents need to be encouraged to limit the number of hours their children watch TV, ban some programs, discuss violent episodes, and encourage shows that are designed to teach and that depict cooperative and nonstereotypic behavior. Research has shown that children will model the latter attitudes and behaviors (Huston et al., 1989). Although educational programming, such as *Sesame Street,* increases vocabulary and readiness skills, some professionals have cautioned that fast-paced TV programs may reinforce hyperactivity, echoic speech, or impulsive cognitive styles in some preschoolers (Halpern, 1975). There is some evidence that rhythmic, fast-tempo musical backgrounds detrimentally impact visual attention span and learning (Wakshlag, Reitz, & Zillman, 1982). On the other hand, slow-paced television shows, such as *Mister Rogers' Neighborhood,* are believed by some to lengthen children's attention spans, increase reflectivity, and result in greater retention of information (Singer & Singer, 1979).

To mitigate the negative effects of TV viewing, school curricula have been developed to demystify what students are seeing. These curricula describe how TV shows are produced, distinguish between reality and fantasy on TV, examine special effects (disappearing acts, violence) and how these distort reality, explore the consequences of TV behavior if it were real, and help children understand the purpose for airing commercials and the advertisers' motives and techniques (Sprafkin, Gadow, & Kant, 1987–1988).

Social Development

Although social problems with parents, teachers, and peers certainly do not trouble every student with a learning disability, they nevertheless are more prevalent than in students having no academic difficulties. When present, social difficulties must be taken seriously. Intervention involves attending to the environmental as well as student aspects of the problem because social difficulties do not develop in a vacuum; the environment plays an important role in shaping children's self-concepts and behaviors.

We will review how children learn to interact successfully within society, to adopt socially acceptable attitudes and behaviors. We also will examine the part parents play in fostering or impeding this social learning process in the child with learning disabilities.

Normal Patterns of Prosocial Development. The behavior of children who act in a prosocial (socially acceptable) manner is influenced by their ability to judge what is right and wrong according to societal standards. As with other areas of development, moral judgments change with age.

In his classic investigations on moral reasoning, Jean Piaget (1948) asked children questions about what they would do in certain situations and why. Piaget noted that children under the age of seven or eight often do not understand why something is right or wrong; rather, they accept some external source, such as a parent or an older child, as the authority. This frequently results in very rigid interpretations of rules, with a particular act being judged as wrong under all circumstances. For example, when Ronnie takes Anna's toy, this is judged to be wrong because adults say it is wrong. The fact that Ronnie took the toy in retaliation for Anna having taken his toy is not considered. Likewise, children consider lying wrong because they expect a parent to punish them. Mitigating factors such as the intentions of the speaker (sparing someone hurtful information) or the speaker's ignorance of the truth are not considered by this younger age group. That is why, at young ages, a white lie is judged to be just as serious as a lie told in order to hurt someone. Another characteristic of young children is their concreteness in judging the magnitude of a lie or misdeed. When a tray accidentally is dropped and a dozen glasses break, this is judged as deserving a more severe punishment than accidentally dropping one glass. Likewise, these children base their judgments of a lie on how far the lie departs from the truth. More than one six-year-old child thought that saying that he or she saw a cow in the street, when in truth it was a dog, was a greater lie than pretending to have good marks in school. The "cow for a dog" lie created a more obvious discrepancy from the truth.

In children over age eight, Piaget noted a gradual shift toward conforming to the behavioral rules established by groups and greater self-reliance on following these rules. The parent is no longer seen as the final authority in making moral judgments about behavior, and the child tends to vacillate between considering and not considering specific circumstances or motives.

By age eleven or twelve, a child begins to understand that rules arise out of mutual consent, a give and take with others. Still behaving in accord with the group's expectancies, the child begins to realize the social value of these rules and how rules make life easier for people. Lying begins to be regarded as wrong because the world couldn't operate if everyone told lies. Who could be trusted? The twelve-year-old child is equitable in judging punishments, taking into account the intentions of the perpetrator and whether the misdeed was warranted. Not until late adolescence do youngsters fully understand that rules preserve society and that one is obliged to follow laws for that reason (Sprinthall & Sprinthall, 1981).

This developmental progression in moral reasoning is extremely important for teachers to share with parents. With greater understanding of their youngster's current moral reasoning level, parents can better decide how to encourage their child's growth in social maturity and how to deal with wrongdoing.

Prosocial Development and the Student with Learning Disabilities. Just as the academic achievement of a student who is learning disabled is delayed, the child's ability to make social judgments also may be more like that of a younger child. A nine-year-old child, for example, still may rely almost entirely on authority figures to cue appropriate ways to act. Unfortunately, this is an almost impossible way to function in school, where numerous situations arise that demand immediate decisions and actions, perhaps about issues on which the child's authority figures have never made a ruling.

Consider a ten-year-old impulsive child who must make a social judgment, for example, determining whether lying to avoid hurting someone's feelings is more correct than telling the truth. The child has difficulty focusing on several aspects of the problem at once and delaying a response until he or she has considered the alternatives and anticipated the consequences. Among other things, the child must look at the situation from another's perspective, evaluate verbal and nonverbal situational cues, and choose which words to use, all skills with which many children who are learning disabled have difficulty. Clearly this child is at a disadvantage in contemplating which actions are most appropriate; poor decisions and negative feedback from adults and peers come as no surprise.

When the teacher knows the students' stage of moral reasoning, the teacher's interactions can be geared in a way that will help the children progress to higher moral reasoning levels. That is, when Sasha reacts negatively to Alec's too-aggressive albeit affectionate bear hug, or when Danny needs to learn how much teasing and roughhousing his friends will tolerate, the teacher must select a response that fits the youngsters' moral reasoning levels. For young children, behavior modification techniques and simply stating what is right or wrong work well because these children choose their behaviors on the basis of adults' rules and anticipated consequences. Elementary school children, very aware of social obligations to the groups with which they interact, benefit from explicit reminders about these expectations and instructions to model their peers' behaviors. In contrast, the older youngster, who recognizes the benefits of laws in our society, may benefit from mutual agreements (for example, about not talking out in class, or goals for grades) and contracting for specific positive consequences if the agreements are fulfilled. Reasoning with a youngster at a level that is over one level above his or her current moral reasoning maturity is generally to no avail because the message will not be understood.

It is important that the teacher's understanding of a student's moral reasoning be communicated to the student's parents, so that their approaches will be facilitative of development in this area. At the same time, teachers need to assess whether family factors also play a role in disrupting a child's social development.

Children learn from their parents by identification (wanting to be like them), by modeling (imitating them), and through direct training. Some data suggest that children with learning disabilities and their parents may not be as effective as other families in these three processes. In addition, mismatches between parent–child temperaments can have an adverse impact on prosocial development.

Identification and Modeling. Parents are high-status people in their children's lives; children literally watch their parents as a way of learning. When the father always lends a helping hand in neighborhood projects, his son sees this model, wants to be like his dad, and most likely will help other children in the neighborhood or, as an adult, be active in neighborhood causes. A daughter may be tempted to lie but then resists because she recalls her parents' example and fears the loss of her parents' respect if she does not do the right thing. These processes of identification and modeling are fostered by warmth and support on the part of parents, which in turn foster in their children such prosocial traits as kindness, honesty, generosity, resistance to cheating and lying, obedience to rules, and consideration of the rights and welfare of others (Baumrind, 1975; Becker, 1964). The more attachment and emotional security there is in the home, and the lower the level of family dysfunction, the more competent the child's behavior toward peers (Odom, McConnell, & McEvoy, 1992).

In order for parents to promote modeling of appropriate behaviors, they not only must have favorable attitudes toward their child but they also must arouse the child's attention toward processing of the modeled behavior, facilitate the child remembering the behavior through overt or covert verbal rehearsal, encourage actual practice of the behavior, and give incentives for adopting this behavior (Bandura, 1969). Parents use these processes in influencing their children, although most often they do so unconsciously.

It should come as no surprise that some children with learning disabilities have difficulty attending to, interpreting, and retaining modeled behavior and verbal explanations (Schwartz & Bryan, 1971). Bryan (1977), for example, found that children with learning disabilities were not as adept as controls at interpreting what a model was doing and what emotions the model was expressing. Consequently, parents of children with learning disabilities may need to explain more, highlight important aspects, help the child verbally rehearse and role play what has been said, and provide support when information-processing or motivational problems present obstacles.

Although parental warmth and support promote identification and modeling, several studies find these qualities to be less than satisfactory in some parents of children with learning disabilities. At times parents describe their family systems as more chaotic, disturbed, less structured, less emotionally stable, less enmeshed, more rigid, and more disengaged than typical families (Amerikaner & Omizo, 1984; Michaels & Lewandowski, 1990; Owen et al., 1971). Parents often have more negative reactions toward their children with learning disabilities, are more negative/harsh/remote, communicate lower expectations, and provide less affection and caregiving (Chapman & Boersma, 1979; Nichols & Chen, 1981; Owen et al., 1971; Tollison, Palmer, & Stowe, 1987). At times this affection is transferred to a sibling who has higher verbal ability, perseveres in school tasks, and worries the parent less (Owen et al., 1971). Pearl and Bryan (1982) found that mothers of children with learning disabilities viewed their children's successes less positively and their failures more negatively than did mothers of nondisabled children. The children's successes were attributed more to luck and less to ability than were the successes of typical children, and their failures were attributed more to inability and less to bad luck. Frequently, parents of the learning disabled even expect less of these youngsters than the youngsters expect of themselves (Chapman & Boersma, 1979; McLoughlin et al., 1987).

There is evidence that for infants who were born prematurely or were very ill at birth, the origins of these parent–child interaction patterns may appear as early as the first few weeks of life. Mothers of ill and premature infants have been found to touch, smile at, look at, speak to, and hold their babies close less often than do mothers of healthy newborns (Rossetti, 1986). The separation of high-risk infants in newborn intensive care nurseries, as well as the anxiety, shock, guilt, and powerlessness that accompany the birth of a baby who differs from the baby that was envisioned, clearly limits the development of normal caregiving and attachment patterns.

An additional difficulty for children with learning disabilities is that some parents may themselves be poor models. In fact, the mothers in Pearl and Bryan's study actually evaluated their own abilities as poorly as those of their children who were learning disabled. Because learning disorders often show a hereditary pattern, children and parents often share similar cognitive problems and inappropriate behavioral styles (Cantwell, 1975; Decker & DeFries, 1980; Morrison & Stewart, 1971; Owen et al., 1971; Pearl & Bryan, 1982). Consequently, at times parents will have to evaluate and modify their own behavior before being able to optimize their help for their children.

Direct Training. Direct training, through teaching and discipline, is another way in which parents influence the attitudes and behaviors they wish to instill in their children. It seems that clear expectations offer a consistent family structure that has a stabilizing influence on children's development (Rappaport, 1981). In addition, research has found that threats of punishment or power exhortations are less effective than explanations and reasoning about why the child should behave in a certain way. Positive reinforcement and flexibility that balances adult with child needs are important to maximize children's social and emotional development.

Baumrind (1972, 1975), in investigating child-rearing practices among middle-socioeconomic-status parents, identified three general patterns: authoritative, authoritarian, and permissive. *Authoritative* parents were controlling and de-

manding. They had high demands for obedience, academic achievement, and sharing in household tasks. Yet at the same time these parents were warm, were open to discussing a child's reasons for not wanting to comply, and responded positively to their children's independent behavior. *Authoritarian* parents, on the other hand, were more punitive and rejecting. They too had high standards for behavior, but these were absolute. Power measures, unaccompanied by reasoning and communication, were used to establish compliance. These parents valued compliance for its own sake, and there was little verbal give and take with their children. *Permissive* parents, in contrast, were very accepting of all their children's impulses and did not enforce rules or standards for conduct and achievement.

Baumrind found a correlation between parental authoritative patterns and children's behaviors that were socially responsible, independent, friendly to peers, cooperative, achievement oriented, dominant, and purposeful. Authoritative parents who also valued nonconformity produced the most dominant and purposeful children in the study. In contrast, children of authoritarian parents tended to be discontent, withdrawn, and distrustful. Children of permissive parents were the least self-reliant, self-controlled, and explorative.

Baumrind identified several adult practices and attitudes that facilitated the development of socially responsible, assertive, cooperative, purposeful, confident, altruistic, creative, cognitively challenging, and independent behavior in children:

1. adult modeling of socially responsible and self-assertive behavior, especially if the adult is seen as powerful and a strong support/advocate for the child;

2. firm enforcement policies that reward socially responsible behavior and punish deviant behavior and are accompanied by explanations consistent with the parents' principles;

3. accepting but not overprotective or passive-acceptant parental attitudes; approval is conditional on the child's behavior;

4. high demands for achievement and conformity with parental policies, accompanied by openness to the child's rationale and encouragement of independent judgment; and

5. provision of a complex, stimulating environment that offers challenge and excitement as well as security.

Berk (1997) adds that parents who tell children *why*, and not just *what*, to do provide a rationale for future actions when children are faced not only with a particular task, but also with new problems. Powers, Hauser, and Kilner's findings (1989) also support the relationship between the development of autonomy in youngsters and having parents with greater self-awareness; parents who appreciate individual differences yet preserve connectedness in family relationships; parents who explain more, are curious, and use family discussions to problem solve; and parents who are accepting, empathic, supportive, and authoritative.

Baumrind's findings hinted at the nonfacilitative effects of overprotectiveness on children's social development. In Nichols and Chen's (1981) Collaborative Perinatal Project, mothers who were overdemonstrative to their eight-month-old infants—frequently fondling and caressing them, using terms of endearment, talking only about their children's good qualities and glossing over, ignoring, or explaining away less desirable behaviors—more often had children who displayed learning difficulties and hyperactivity at age seven. This highlights the importance of keeping a balanced view of one's child, offering encouragement where needed but also noting areas that require correction. Robynn's mother (below) describes how her daughter let her know that she had to begin letting go.

The attitudes and styles of many parents are indeed very well suited to facilitating the development of their children with learning disabilities (Elardo and Freund, 1981; Humphries & Bauman, 1980; Lyytinen et al., 1994). Nevertheless, considering that some parents of children with

Robynn

Although students with learning disabilities don't always say or do things the way others do, they certainly get their points across.

My teenage daughter was diagnosed as learning disabled when she was three years old. Our suspicions were first aroused by her lack of verbal expression. Of course, this turned out to be just a symptom of a far greater problem.

Verbal aptitude has always eluded Robynn. She speaks slowly and often the right words just don't come to her. But when she wants to get a point across, she figures out which words to put together.

Being an overprotective mother, I have always monitored Robynn's comings and goings. In trying to protect her from the world, I have often hovered too long over her.

One day she had had enough. She wanted to tell me that she wanted some more independence, that I was smothering her with my protective arms. For lack of those words, she said, "You make me feel like I'm still inside of you." I understood exactly what she was feeling. She couldn't have said it better.

Source: Reprinted by permission of Irene Hershkowitz.

learning disabilities are not as warm, supportive, structured, and goal directed as one would wish, that some parents are poor models, and that some youngsters with learning disabilities do not learn well from modeling, many factors that contribute to positive encouragement and good discipline may be lacking in many of these children's home environments. For example, Frick and Lahey (1991) found that parents and other relatives of children with attention-deficit hyperactivity disorder (ADHD) themselves were characterized by a high rate of ADHD; dysfunctional patterns in parent–child relations were common, with these parents being more directive, controlling, and negative, and less rewarding and responsive than parents of control subjects.

At times the disorganization of children with learning disabilities and their families may become a vicious cycle: the child's behavior causes disruption in the family, which in turn is increasingly unable to provide the structure and discipline the child needs. Studies on temperament show how this vicious cycle may develop and how academic and social success depends a great deal on the interaction of the child's unique characteristics with those of the family.

Parent–Child Temperament Match. We have noted that the child brings to the family environment cognitive or behavioral styles that are uniquely his or her own. This *temperament* is the "how rather than the what (abilities and content) or the why (motivations) of behavior" (Thomas & Chess, 1977, p. 9). Thomas and Chess's work (1977, 1984) vividly illustrates the benefits of a good fit between parent and child temperaments, how parental practices can modify a child with a hard-to-live-with temperament, and conversely how parental practices may create even more problems. The distractible child, for example, is put under undue stress when parents expect concentration for excessive periods of time. The same is true of the highly active child whose parents restrict mobility (as in requiring sitting through dinner instead of allowing for needed activity by letting the child help serve and clear). Likewise, the very goal-directed, persistent child whose parents abruptly terminate a project to do something

else as a family is not likely to be in a cooperative or pleasant mood. The emotional adjustment of the very capable child is similarly disrupted when parents do not value or encourage the hard work he is putting forth, as is the adjustment of the child with learning disabilities when parental achievement expectations are unreasonable. When at age three a child's temperament and adjustment are considered along with level of parental conflict and later elementary school adjustment, Thomas and Chess (1984) found that 34 percent of the eventual variance in this child's adult temperament and adjustment is predictable. Therefore, very early attention to stresses and strains caused by parent–child temperament mismatches is critical.

The way in which each family member's traits interact with another's has been described by Cameron (1977, 1978) as analogous to the origins of an earthquake. The child's temperament is akin to the fault lines. Environmental events, particularly parenting styles, are akin to the strain. Just as earthquakes result from the match between faults and strains, so behavior difficulties arise from a mismatch between certain child temperaments and certain styles of parenting. The story of Norman (page 448) is a good example of how temperament and environment interact, sometimes to the detriment of the child. Norman's temperament and life experiences are like those frequently associated with children with learning disabilities. When these children grow up in warm, supportive homes that arrange the environment to help them, rather than imposing unreasonable pressures and standards, they have a better chance of avoiding secondary problems such as poor self-image and depression. But if their homes are hostile and critical and parental expectations are beyond the children's capabilities, then the outcome is likely to be bleaker.

Interestingly, the same home environment can affect different children in different ways, from the shaping of personality to the facilitation of cognitive gains (Plomin, 1988). Although we used to assume that a family offered the same environment to all its children, there appear instead to be different environments for each child in the family. It seems that each child experiences

Norman

Norman was seen at age seventeen by one of us (S.C.), who had followed him since age four and a half because of persistent behavior disturbance. At age seventeen he had already dropped out of two colleges in one year, and was planning to go abroad for a work-study program. He was in good contact but dejected and depressed. He was extraordinarily self-derogatory, said he could not finish anything he started, was lazy, and didn't know what he wanted to do. "My father doesn't respect me, and let's face it, why should he." He talked of "hoping to find myself" in a vague, unplanned way.

Norman had always been a highly distractible child with a short attention span. Intelligent and pleasant, the youngest in his class throughout his school years due to a birth date, he started his academic career with good mastery. However, at home his parents were impatient and critical of him even in his preschool years because of his quick shifts of attention, dawdling at bedtime, and apparent "forgetfulness." By his fifth year he showed various reactive symptoms such as sleeping difficulties, nocturnal enuresis, poor eating habits, and nail tearing. Year by year his academic standing slipped. His father, a hard-driving, very persistent professional man, became increasingly hypercritical and derogatory of Norman. The father equated the boy's short attention span and distractibility with irresponsibility and lack of character and willpower. He used these terms openly to the boy and stated that he "disliked" his son. The mother grew to understand the issue, but no discussion with the father as to the normalcy of his son's temperament and the impossibility of the boy's living up to his standards of concentrated hard work succeeded in altering the father's attitude. He remained convinced that Norman had an irresponsible character and was headed for future failure—indeed a self-fulfilling prophecy. There were several times when the boy tried to comply with his father's standards and made himself sit still with his homework for long periods of time. This only resulted in generalized tension and multiple tics and Norman could not sustain this effort so dissonant with his temperament—another proof to himself and his father of his failure. Direct psychotherapy was arranged in early adolescence, but Norman entered this with a passive, defeated attitude and the effort was unsuccessful. His subsequent development was all too predictable.

Source: Thomas & Chess, 1977, pp. 167–169. Reprinted by permission.

the family environment in a different way, perhaps because of differential parent behavior and affection toward the child, the child's perception of differences in treatment, birth order and gender differences, experiences outside the family, peer interactions, and so forth (Plomin, 1989). Given the challenges posed by a child with learning disabilities, it may happen that a parent–child match that was perfect for all the other siblings needs to be rethought and reworked when it comes to the child with a learning disability.

Family Adjustment

Researchers have described a number of parental reactions to having a child who is disabled, some of which may contribute to poor family relationships and diminution in achievement. Other reactions may interfere with the evaluation and delivery of services to the student with learning disabilities. When sensitive to the reactions of family members, teachers are in an excellent position to offer the necessary support.

Parental Adjustment

Many parents are superb observers of their child's behavior. Even before the evaluation results are in, they can estimate their child's developmental levels fairly accurately and pinpoint weaknesses. Confirmation of their suspicions comes as a relief (Faerstein, 1986). Other parents, however, may experience shock, anger, guilt, denial, or sorrow on first learning that their child has a learning disability. As bearers of bad tidings, the school personnel, family physician, or other professionals at times become objects of the parents' anger. A parent may also blame himself or herself, or the spouse, or may review past actions and events repeatedly in an attempt to pinpoint a cause for the child's problems. When parents deny that a problem exists at all, this response is usually followed by a search for a more favorable opinion from other professionals.

It is not uncommon for a professional in the learning disabilities field to have been the fourth or fifth person to evaluate a child in the parents' search to find someone who will tell them that there is or is not a problem, what the cause is, or what the cure is. In a field that has so many unanswered questions, obtaining a second opinion may be prudent, but this "shopping" becomes problematic when it interferes with making definitive intervention plans and with fully accepting the child no matter what his or her abilities.

In finally coming to grips with the reality of having a child with a disability, many parents have had to "mourn" the loss of the ideal concept they had envisioned for their child. Some parents react to their own anger and disappointment by becoming overprotective or overindulgent. Unfortunately, overprotection and overinvolvement deprive students with learning disabilities of important learning experiences; can make the students feel fragile, weak, and incapable; and withdraw them from learning to deal with conflicts and problem solving (such as arguing with siblings) independent of parental interference. The overindulgent parent, on the other hand, does not provide the guidance and limits that all children need.

In some cases parents react by placing educational responsibility on the child and not involving themselves at all. Some parents are unconcerned about intellectual striving, whereas others will push until the child rebels. Klein and her colleagues (1981a, b) point out that some parents' adverse attitudes toward authority lead them to communicate dissatisfaction with the school system to their children. Their children in turn get the message to resist the school curriculum or teachers because these are to blame for the children's problems. In other cases parents deny the gravity of the problem, and schooling suffers because the children are not held responsible for learning in an active and motivated way. Other families may work to preserve the child's learning problem in order to deflect attention from problems in the family, to have a mission, or to feel needed (Falik, 1995). It is easy to see how these parental attitudes can exacerbate the child's learning and attitudinal problems.

It is important for us to be wary that our professional attitudes do not add to a parent's feelings of frustration, anger, inadequacy, or guilt about the child's poor progress. Faerstein (1986), for example, documents mothers' anger at knowing something was wrong yet being told by professionals that the problem did not exist or would go away. With reduced support from others, increased isolation, and frustration that their perceptions were being discounted, the mothers' anger at times got displaced onto the children. Having a child with a learning disability can stress a family system, and teachers need to be appropriately sensitive and supportive (Dyson, 1996). When teachers are alert to parental feelings, patiently weather a family's emotional crisis, and remain available for support, they can become invaluable resources to the family.

Sibling Adjustment

Siblings are affected by their learning-disabled brothers or sisters, and they in turn influence the behavior of the child with learning disabilities. Most siblings are not told much about the problem and may regard it as mysterious. When given no explanation by their parents, children are left to form conclusions based on their own experiences, fantasies, and maturity levels. Unfortunately, these conclusions may be very anxiety provoking. Children may conclude that their sibling's problem is their fault or is an infectious or fatal disease. Honest parental explanations about the strengths and weaknesses of a sibling with learning disabilities can do much to avoid such guilt and confusion.

Some anger is not uncommon among siblings. They often resent the increased attention and time the child who is learning disabled gets from his or her parents, especially if the rules and discipline are different. They also may be embarrassed by their brother's or sister's behavior or poor achievement and respond with hostility.

Siblings of students with disabilities often experience greater than typical stress (Hannah & Midlarsky, 1985). They are asked to assume some responsibility for their disabled sibling while at the same time facing decreased parental support for themselves. Often the needs of the child with the disability dictate family life, whether it be daily schedules, vacation decisions, monetary and time allocations, or the like. Compensating for the lowered expectations of the child who is disabled, parents often put undue pressure for achievement on the nondisabled sibling, whether it be in academic, athletic, or social areas. Increased anxiety, withdrawal, depression, aggression, poor peer relations, and reduced academic and cognitive efficiency have been reported in up to 25 percent of siblings of children with a wide variety of disabilities. On the other hand, siblings can show psychological benefits, such as greater tolerance and understanding for people's differences, greater patience and compassion, dedication to altruistic goals, and even enhanced self-concepts because, in comparison with the sibling with a learning disability, they feel normal and competent.

Certainly parents need to be alert to potential adjustment problems on the part of their nondisabled children, accept their negative feelings, and take time to listen to their concerns and respond to their needs. Including siblings as much as possible in discussions and planning makes them feel less neglected and invites their help in promoting their sister's or brother's development. It is critical that parents guard against siblings' diminished self-concept due to not feeling special, identification with the disabled brother or sister, or adopting the stressful roles of mediator or super achiever (Atkins, 1991). Moreover, parents need to be alert that teachers do not lower their expectations for typical children because of their familiarity with the performance of a sibling who is learning disabled (Richey & Ysseldyke, 1983).

Special care must be taken so that every child in the family gets all the nurturing he or she needs. This does not mean, however, that everyone gets the same thing. When Miriam charges that it is unfair for Gabe to get one hour alone nightly with their mother doing homework, the mother must explain that "fairness" means that everyone gets what he or she needs (Lavoie, 1986). Because each individual's needs are different, Miriam is fortunate not to need this tutoring, but she does get what she needs in other ways: the special lunch out with Mom when Miriam's best friend turned on her, the special advice from her Dad when she decided to join boys' Little League and, ever since, her cheering family in attendance at every Thursday night game. These are things that her brother did not need.

Parents must be cautioned that the child with learning disabilities will suffer if compared to a higher-achieving sibling, especially if that brother or sister is younger. Instead, the sibling relationship needs to be nurtured. The child who is learning disabled has much to gain from siblings. They may be good models for social and study behavior, and they provide excellent peer experiences. Their love and acceptance can do much to make home a happy place for the child who is learning disabled, somewhere where the youngster can feel safe and important.

Family Assessment

One of the most important yet most difficult tasks of a teacher is to assess family factors that may be exacerbating students' difficulties. Despite time and training constraints, such assessments are important because the family plays a primary role in fostering the intellectual stimulation and social skills needed for success in and out of school. PL 99-457 in fact mandates the assessment of family strengths and needs pertinent to enhancing the development of the preschool child with disabilities; its Individualized Family Service Plan is designed to address identified issues.

At least one study has shown that, for older elementary and younger middle school children, the child's satisfaction with family life is far more related to overall self-concept, intrinsic motivation, and extraversion than is the child's satisfaction with friends (Huebner, 1991). The influence of teachers and schools on child development also is far less powerful than the influence of family factors such as amount of time encouraged for homework and TV viewing, parental concern about education, parents treating children as individuals, discipline patterns, parental social awareness, and structure and orderliness of the home (Barrett & Depinet, 1991). Among individuals of equal ability, Barrett and Depinet found that the most significant predictor of adult occupational status was the parents' attitude toward education. Therefore, family assessment and intervention are critical.

An ecological approach to family assessment is important because the student's behavior is affected not only by individual family members, but also by relatives, friends, and neighbors; the student in turn influences this system and its members. A broad view of this interaction can help a teacher and family decide how to intervene. For example, a visit to six-year-old Becky's home helped shed light on why Becky always appeared fearful and withdrew from academic and social participation at school. Becky's parents revealed that an ex-convict, who had been in prison for child molestation, had just moved his trailer next to their property. At night he would parade outside nude, build bonfires on his property, and peer into neighbors' windows. Becky's fear was so great that she would enter only those portions of her mobile home with windows facing away from this man's trailer. Knowing of this situation helped the teacher decide to relax academic pressures and create opportunities for Becky to draw and talk about her fears. The teacher also helped the parents obtain representation through legal aid services.

Ideally, family assessment should center around the family's emotional atmosphere, methods of discipline, prosocial modeling, and attitudes toward learning, as well as the student's broader social context. Emotional factors include the warmth and affection between family members, stressors (for example, financial, emotional, illness, isolation, divorce, job dissatisfaction), the support and encouragement given to children, the fostering of independence, hostility between certain individuals, and attitudes toward the student's disability. Methods of discipline involve evaluating such factors as how rules are established and maintained, negotiation, coercion, compliance, and use of corporal punishment. Prosocial modeling involves assessment of the behaviors and attitudes that the child may model or be reinforced for from parents, siblings, babysitters, relatives, neighbors, peers, and so on. Assessment of attitudes toward learning includes attitudes toward different school subjects, teachers, the school administration, parent expectations of the school, and whether academic achievement is valued. Assessment also should include information about health history, nutrition, accidents, possible toxins in parental workplaces, and the family history of learning problems.

Special emphasis in the assessment process needs to be placed on identifying the support systems available to help families cope during difficult times. Researchers find that the ability to cope with the stress of a child with a disability is more difficult in lower-income and single-parent households. Twenty-one percent of children now live in poverty (*Condition of Education,* 1996), and it is estimated that 40 to 50 percent spend at least part of their childhoods living in a single-parent family (Hollander, 1986). Eighty-seven percent of single-parent families are headed by mothers

(*Information Please Almanac,* 1997), and single mothers are at greater risk than married mothers for anxiety, depression, and health problems that in turn affect their relations with their children (Guidubaldi et al., 1983; McLoyd, 1989). With the increasing number of single-parent households, and with well over half of women in the workforce, finding adequate day care becomes an additional stressor.

Hoffman's (1989) literature review indicates that a mother's working is detrimental to the child's emotional or academic adjustment under the following circumstances: the mother works more than 40 hours a week, child-care arrangements are inadequate, there is no father or other adult support, the child is disabled or chronically ill, the mother's preference is not to work, and work hours are inflexible. These situations create stress and dissatisfaction in the mother and in turn affect her children.

Studies find that working outside the home is beneficial to most women's self-esteem and sense of satisfaction, provided that they wish to be employed, are satisfied with the quality of their job, and have stable child-care arrangements. If a father shares child-care responsibilities, this further relieves the strain and enhances the mother's mental health. Research finds that psychosomatic symptoms, depression, and general stress are lower among employed mothers, and that employment offers support during stressful periods in these women's lives. It seems that employment provides a particularly important buffer for mothers of "difficult" infants, enabling the employed mothers to function more effectively. This maternal satisfaction in turn has a positive impact on parent–child interactions (for example, higher levels of interaction and verbal stimulation), as well as on the youngster's achievement, adjustment, and adult accomplishments. Children of working mothers tend to be more independent and to have less stereotyped views of sex roles. Their mothers tend to adopt warm but firm (authoritative) parenting styles and are more likely to perceive positive qualities in their children and to emphasize independence. Several studies have found maternal employment to be especially beneficial to daughters, perhaps because it facilitates

rejection of traditional sex-role ideology and reinforces the concept of women being as competent as men.

In both single- and dual-wage families, the greater the father's involvement in child care, the higher the child's intelligence, academic achievement, and social maturity. This has been related to the increased sense of self-esteem that the father gains from the parenting role.

Marital satisfaction appears to be no different in dual- or single-career families, except where, in a dual-career marriage, a spouse's employment is resented or the father resents the child-care responsibilities, worries that his own career may suffer, or interprets maternal employment as failure in his breadwinner role. This threat to the father's morale has been observed to strain father–son relationships in particular. When marital stress does occur, its impact appears less pervasive in dual-career families than in single-career families.

The role satisfaction of mothers who are full-time homemakers is equally important to assess. The mother's satisfaction can be affected by the fact that she lives in a world in which nearly 70 percent of mothers work outside the home (*Information Please Almanac,* 1997). Daughters exacerbate the homemaker's role conflict when they view her role as inconsistent with the adult roles to which they aspire. Moreover, the family's reinforcement of traditional father roles contrasts sharply with the more helpful role expectations of fathers in dual-employed families. Hoffman's research review finds greater stress and depression among women who desired employment yet remained homemakers. These mothers tend to be less responsive toward their infants, and mother–child relationships are disrupted. Often these children are less independent than children of employed mothers because of the mother's encouragement of dependency. Several studies have found that part-time employment mediates the stresses of both full-time homemaking or full-time work, resulting in more positive outcomes for family life and child development than either full-time pattern.

Family assessment may be done not only by the teacher but also by a school social worker or psychologist using home observation, interviews, and questionnaires that parents, significant others, or the children complete. Variations among different respondents' answers shed light on the implicit or explicit messages children receive when interacting with each of these individuals and on the interaction patterns and attitudes that may be promoting or deterring youngsters' academic and social–emotional adjustment.

As parents get to know and trust the teacher through informal contacts, they may be more willing to share their family experiences and collaborate in intervention efforts. With the benefit of the parents' information, teachers can provide for types of intellectual stimulation and emotional support not present in the home. They can help parents become better models, teachers, and advocates. They also can provide the family with needed emotional support and information.

Family Intervention

How can school personnel intervene to help parents become more able models, teachers, and advocates? One of the major ways of doing this is by listening and learning about the parents' perspectives and then offering feedback and information. Because different cultures interpret disabilities in different ways, school personnel must be particularly sensitive to parents' belief systems. For example, Hispanic parents whose children already exceed parental levels of English speaking and reading ability do not view their children as disabled. In fact, the very term stigmatizes the whole family because of their strongly enmeshed family identity; their parameters of "normalcy" are much wider than those used by the educational system (Harry, 1992a). Clearly, we must learn to value the positions of those who hold different perspectives, while also helping them to understand the perspectives of the school personnel.

Even if parents understand the cultural meanings conveyed by the term learning disabilities, many have never heard of such terms as phonics, receptive language, or criterion-referenced tests. The conference at which the parents initially learn the results of the schools' evaluation and recommendations can provide for their informational needs while also building a relationship of trust and understanding between home and school. Most important for continued dialogue regarding assessment and intervention is for the parent's input to be heard, considered, and valued in the problem-solving process. Harry (1992b), for example, suggests that at the IEP meeting parents be invited to present their own report on the child's progress and needs.

Rockowitz and Davidson (1979) emphasize that information at the IEP meeting must be imparted in clear, understandable terms; strengths must be emphasized, not only weaknesses; recommendations must be offered; and, most important, the conference must elicit information and participation from the family and, whenever possible, the student. When the group is kept small (two or three professionals at most) and privacy/freedom from interruption are ensured, parental feedback is facilitated. Based on their experiences when first told that their child had a learning disability, parents have recommended the following: professionals should use less jargon; both parents should be included in the meetings; relevant reading material should be available; parents should receive written reports; advice should be offered for home management; and information about the child's social progress should be emphasized as well (Dembrinski & Mauser, 1977).

At Syracuse University's Psychoeducational Teaching Laboratory, feedback usually is accomplished by explaining, interpreting, and eliciting opinions and information from parents during extended home visits and as they observe the evaluation through a one-way mirror. Most often a "draft" report is mailed to parents prior to the conference. The parents then come to the conference ready to engage in dialogue, questions, or rebuttals. Rather than being primarily information giving, the conferences tend to be working sessions that clarify basic understandings and intervention plans. The report is then revised, based on new information or plans arrived at during the meeting.

At parent conferences, teachers and other school professionals must be prepared to clarify for parents the possible reasons for their child's learning difficulty. Parents also want to know what services are available in the school and community, and the long-range forecasts for their child's school, work, and life adjustment. While long-range prediction for the individual child is always uncertain due to the range of learner, task, and setting factors that can buffer or exacerbate the impact of a learning disability, parents should be told about group research results in a way that is hopeful and instructive about what they can do to help. Parents want the best for their children, and we must help them be both good planners and patient because there are no quick solutions. As educators, we also have a responsibility to inform parents about the controversial therapies that tout quick solutions but have no research support (e.g., visual training, scotopic sensitivity correction, patterning, medication for vestibular dysfunctions, applied kinesiology, auditory sensitivity treatment, trace element deficiency and allergy treatments; Silver, 1995).

Once a course of action has been decided upon teachers and parents need feedback from one another as to how things are going. This is best done through notes, phone calls, or conferences at predetermined intervals.

Parents also may request help with problems at home such as increasing the child's academic motivation, providing structure for a child with an attention deficit, organizing their child's approach to homework, or improving methods of discipline. A teacher, for example, can help parents learn to model academic interest by pointing out that if parents themselves read more, talk favorably about academic achievement, show an interest in their child's school work by reviewing school papers, praise academic effort and independence, help establish a set homework time and area, develop positive contingencies for homework completion, and provide learning games and activities at home, this will encourage their child's efforts in school. Parents can be helped to model flexibility in problem solving, so their children will try new methods. For the inattentive, hyperactive child the teacher can recommend a consistent daily routine that is explained clearly and repeat-

edly. Because impulsivity and hyperactivity can be augmented by anxiety, parents also must be helped to eliminate avoidable stressors at home. Moreover, parents need to be sensitized to matching their behaviors to their child's abilities. For example, when parents speak with a child who has difficulty with auditory processing or organization, they may need to speak slowly, use shorter sentences, and repeat often. For teenagers who have difficulty remembering all they need to do in a day, the parents can learn to help by suggesting metamemory strategies. If the child is insistent that rock and roll music helps him stick with his homework, parents should be helped to investigate with a mini-experiment before simply saying "no." Teachers can also help parents adopt the role of "coach," thereby helping their children learn to work more independently; stepping back and letting go can be the most difficult task of all.

Most important, the teacher must communicate to parents how critical they are in promoting their child's feelings of self-worth. By providing a warm, supportive home atmosphere, they can help their child feel loved and wanted rather than a disappointment to them because of the academic failures. There is usually some activity that the child with learning disabilities is good at, and parents are the perfect people to provide opportunities for their child to shine. It is important that parents not spend so much time remediating the academic weaknesses that they overlook nurturing their child's talents, strengths, and social relationships.

Parents also need emotional support from the school in dealing with their own adjustment to having a child who is disabled. School personnel can recommend books to parents that explain LD terminology in everyday language, the roles of various professionals, causation, and ideas about home and school management. Individual sessions with parents are useful, as are small informational groups and workshops held after school hours or as part of PTA programs.

Parents themselves have organized to hold informational meetings, to provide emotional support to one another, and to increase advocacy for quality services. The value of parents meeting other parents of students with learning disabilities cannot be underestimated. Parents learn that others have gone through similar experiences, that others too have been frustrated by their child's behavior and are sad or angry at their situation. By listening to how others have coped, they become aware of a broader range of goals and methods and can decide on those that best fit their child's needs. Parents also share behavior management techniques with one another, provide information about community services, and band together to advocate for new services and legislative action. A teacher or member of the school system, when part of such a parent group, is a valuable source of information and support.

Not to be overlooked is the parent as a valuable asset to teachers. Often the behaviors teachers report observing in school do not occur in the home. Parents can offer tips to teachers on how they would handle such behavior. Parents also can serve as powerful reinforcers of their children's in-school behavior. Schumaker, Hovell, and Sherman (1977), for example, found that parental awarding of privileges when their junior high student brought home daily records of improved behavior (for example, points awarded for speaking courteously to the teacher, raising hand before speaking) had a positive impact on social behaviors in the classroom and grades. Teachers also may encourage parents to observe in class to learn about their children's behavior across settings. Home–school linkages appear to be most satisfactory when contacts are face to face, informal, and personal (brief exchanges at school drop-off/pick-up times, volunteering in the classroom, home visits) rather than structured conferences or impersonal notes and phone calls (Fuqua, Hegland, & Karas, 1985). Additional means for encouraging parent–teacher interaction include newsletters, school open houses (scheduled to accommodate parental work schedules), family nights that include meals and child care, and bulletin boards that post information pertinent to parents. With sufficient education and support and positive home–school linkages, parents can become excellent teachers and advocates for their children.

Parents as Teachers

The role of the parent as teacher and provider of services is appropriate for some parents. Considering the gap between the number of children requiring learning disabilities services and the limited time of professionals, parents can be important additional resources if given appropriate training. Barkley (1987), for example, has developed an effective parent-training sequence to deal with very difficult hyperactive children. Using systematic behavior modification principles, Barkley teaches parents to attend to their child's positive behaviors, to ignore the negative, to set up token systems and time-out procedures, and to apply these principles to manage the child's behavior in public places.

Preschool programs that incorporate a home-based parent-training component promote long-lasting gains, presumably because parents have become better teachers. Parent tutoring has also improved skills in their children such as reading rate, comprehension, and visual-motor performance, when parents receive counseling or special training (for example, on how to correct errors and make praise contingent on academic performance) (Maryam & White, 1988; Shapiro & Forbes, 1981; Thurston & Dasta, 1990).

With respect to academic tutoring, research suggests that parental involvement in academic activities, especially homework completion, can noticeably affect achievement (Keith et al., 1993). Nevertheless, there are compelling reasons why some parents should not provide these services to their children. The home should be the primary source of love and support for every child. It may be asking too much of a child to fail in school and then come home and once again fail before the most important people in the student's life, his or her family. A youngster needs time to refuel, and, depending on the individual situation, this may be a more appropriate function for the family.

Teachers must understand that some parents, for various reasons, may not be suited to the role of academic teacher. Their desire for academic success may make teaching sessions torture for both parent and child, with the parent getting more upset with each unsuccessful attempt on the child's part. Because heredity is one cause of learning disabilities, the parent also might have the same learning or behavioral problems as the child, thereby making teaching impractical or troublesome. In comparison with parents of typical achievers, when teaching their children with learning disabilities, some parents have been observed to teach for less time, to provide more negative feedback, to be more directive and less encouraging of higher-level thinking, to communicate lower expectations, and to have a more negative tone and less mutual involvement, thereby fostering the child's dependence, lack of effort, and avoidance of challenge (Lyytinen et al., 1994). Moreover, parents often feel ill-equipped to help their children with homework and would prefer to assist with experiential practice, homework that promotes life skills (Kay et al., 1994). Other parents may simply be too overwhelmed with reality (food, clothing, shelter) to have energy for a teaching role. Clearly, educators must balance the fact that parents are powerful teachers and models in their own right against the dangers of placing added burdens on already burdened families.

Some parents have a view of their role that does not include acting as teacher, but they are nevertheless interested in their child's education. Even if they do not directly help the child with homework, parents can help their child establish a routine time and place for homework, complete a homework calendar, gather necessary materials to assist in homework completion, monitor distractions (for example, television and noise from siblings), provide snacks, sign completed homework, and praise homework completion. Teachers must be careful not to undermine parents' important nurturing function with a direct tutoring job for which some may have little inclination and few skills.

Parents as Advocates

Parents are the most important advocates a youngster has. They are committed to the child for the long haul, from birth to maturity, and their advocacy should be encouraged.

The parental advocacy role begins when a problem is recognized with the development of one's child. This leads to a search for an evaluation and finally a search for services. IDEA supports intensive parent involvement in the educational process by mandating that schools obtain parental consent for assessment, provide parents access to records, and encourage parental participation in planning for their child's needs. When parents are involved in their children's schooling, their children show improvement in grades, attendance, achievement, behavior, self-esteem, attitude toward schoolwork, homework completion, and classroom participation, and even greater enrollment in postsecondary education (Christenson et al., 1997).

Unfortunately, school participation levels of parents whose children have learning disabilities have tended to be low, with parents believing that they have little to contribute (Abramson et al., 1983). Mothers are more involved than fathers, and parents tend to become less involved as their children get older (Cone, Delawyer, & Wolfe, 1985). The incomplete understanding of educational issues and due process rights, and the low levels of involvement of parents from minority backgrounds, lower-income parents, and parents with lower educational levels are particularly troublesome (Brantlinger, 1987; Cone et al., 1985; Lynch & Stein, 1987). Even when they do participate, parents tend to be too passive during planning conferences, asking too few questions and contributing little (Vaughn et al., 1988).

Parental advocacy should not stop at attending meetings. Compliance by the school district to the letter of the law does not guarantee that the student with learning disabilities is receiving adequate services. It is the parents' role to watch over the initial evaluation to ensure that it is adequately done by competent personnel and that the subsequent instructional program is appropriate. School personnel are not perfect, and well-meaning people can make mistakes. Parents ideally should be partners in the problem-solving process from the outset of evaluation, including the process of monitoring progress and future planning.

An important area for parental advocacy involves creation of services where none existed before. Frustrations in trying to obtain professional help have led parents to form parent-professional organizations, the most prominent of these being the Learning Disabilities Association of America (LDA). The marked strains of daily life involved in raising children with attention-deficit hyperactivity disorders propelled parents to form another national organization Children with Hyperactivity and Attention Disorders (CHAD). Local affiliates of these and other groups have offered needed personal support to parents; they also have been powerful advocates for legislation of services to the learning disabled, including vocational training and transitional living services.

Professionals can encourage parental involvement. But they also can place roadblocks in parents' way: intimidating parents; having too many people at a conference; using poor eye contact; rustling papers during a conference, which suggests that they would rather be somewhere else; getting angry or defensive; or quoting regulations to show that parents must do as they say (McLoughlin, McLoughlin, & Steward, 1979). Providing communication in the language of the home, respecting cultural differences, actively inviting parental input, making transportation available to meetings, and providing bilingual facilitators when necessary can go a long way toward establishing positive home–school linkages. To help ensure the school's responsibility to invite parental involvement, IDEA requires that written notice about evaluations and services be provided to parents in their native language if feasible.

No one can put in as many hours, be as committed to a child with a disability, or be as potent an influence as a parent. Therefore, it is important that professionals do all they can to encourage a parent's involvement and to provide parents with information to enhance their advocacy and teaching efforts.

Summary

Learning disabilities may be exacerbated, greatly ameliorated, or perhaps even prevented by the family. The impact of the family, especially the parents, on a youngster's intellectual, academic, and social development is great. Parents have the responsibility to observe, stimulate, and oversee the development of their offspring with kindness, respect, and warmth. Parents influence their children's attitudes, work habits, values, and learned skills through their own attitudes toward learning, through the amount of intellectual stimulation provided in the home, through the kind of modeling they provide, and through their warmth, acceptance, and support. Higher-socioeconomic-status homes are more successful when it comes to producing academically achieving children, even when these children had experienced severe trauma at birth. Far more powerful than the influence of socioeconomic status, however, is the nature of the parent–child relationship. The probability for overcoming the risk factors posed by biological and socioeconomic conditions is excellent in homes that offer high-quality family environments.

Through the processes of identification, modeling, and discipline, parents can instill in their children honesty, consideration of others, respect for rules, and independence. These are all attitudes that aid the student in his or her social relationships with adults and peers and ultimate life adjustment. Some families of children with learning disabilities may lack the skills and resources to be effective models or to provide the discipline and support that would help their child. Unfortunately, unless lessons taught in school are complemented by similar teaching at home, they are likely to go unlearned.

Teachers can help parents become better informed and more effective parents in a number of ways. One is by supporting parents through emotional crises and helping parents work through the many ramifications of having a child with learning disabilities. Teachers also can provide information about learning disabilities and methods for modeling, discipline, and making the home more conducive to learning. Parents as advocates and teachers are a natural answer to the shortage of services and personnel to teach students with disabilities. But the teacher role does not suit every parent, so professionals need to carefully assess which intervention plans will best match different families' life-styles, personalities, and needs.

Chapter Twelve

The School

One of the major premises of this text is that students live and learn in a variety of settings, each of which has its own interactional and organizational patterns that affect different students in different ways. In this chapter we shift our focus from family settings to ways in which school settings affect the academic achievement and social–emotional adjustment of students with learning disabilities.

From kindergarten through twelfth grade, the average youngster spends about 14,000 hours in classroom settings. Certainly, the school is a powerful influence in the student's life; it is because of the school's academic expectations that the child with learning disabilities is singled out.

From a social systems perspective, students with learning disabilities are victims of the demands our society places on its citizens to achieve academically. This demand is clearly reflected in states' compulsory education laws and minimum competency standards for graduation. When children cannot gain these skills, they may be viewed as failures by others. Unfortunately, the school setting emphasizes some skills while awarding less value to others that may be strengths for these students, such as street smarts, musical or artistic talent, mechanical prowess, or athletic ability.

Although over the years human behavior has been viewed as originating primarily within the person, as we saw in Chapter 11, behavior is highly influenced by one's environment. Person-centered views of human behavior cannot account for all possible ways in which an individual might behave in all possible situations. The context or setting in which the behavior occurs is important in its own right. This point was illustrated many years ago in a famous study by Hartshorne and May (1928). Although we commonly think of honesty or dishonesty as a trait that exists within a person, these researchers found that honest and dishonest behavior in elementary school children varied greatly, depending on the circumstances.

The learning and behavior of students with learning disabilities are influenced by the hundreds of variables operating in a given classroom at any given time. Joshua and Dale, for example, are of similar ages and family background. Because of their short attention spans, their academic achievement has suffered, and both are considered to be learning disabled. Joshua's classroom is very traditional, with seats placed in rows and few out-of-seat activities. Joshua's school includes very few children with special education needs in general education classes, so Joshua spends most of his day in his special education classroom. Dale, on the other hand, attends an open classroom in a school that believes strongly in including children with disabilities full-time in the general education classroom.

Joshua and Dale, despite the similarities in their backgrounds and behaviors, are likely to have very different school experiences. In Joshua's case, the school setting has helped him to focus attention and to make academic progress. However, he has not learned to socialize in the same way as his typical peers. On the other hand, Dale seems to be slipping further and further behind academically. She continually is distracted and cannot draw conclusions or learn on her own. She needs constant teacher direction. Yet, Dale is a very popular girl. She has above-average numbers of social contacts with different children each day. Her classmates like her company, and she has learned to dress and behave just as they do and to share their interests. Gradually, the similarities between Joshua and Dale fade. This is due to differences in their classrooms' physical, organizational, and human environments.

This chapter will help us understand exactly how school interventions can best meet the needs of students who are learning disabled by considering the effects of the school's physical, organizational, teacher, and peer characteristics. These dimensions interact with student characteristics in a way that can optimize or impede their learning.

Physical Characteristics

Many aspects of the classroom physical environment must be attended to beyond establishing minimum standards for class size, acoustics, lighting, and heating. Educators had assumed that, as long as these basic requirements were fulfilled, they could turn their attention to other psychological, instructional, and social variables (Weinstein, 1979). However, we have learned that it does matter where a student sits, what shape the classroom is, whether there is noise in the background, and more. A number of studies have investigated the impact on students' learning of ambient (nonarchitectural) aspects of classrooms such as background noise, and designed (architectural) aspects such as school size. An even more paramount concern, of course, is safety. When studies suggest that as few as 30 to 35 percent of parents feel that their children are very safe when in school or walking to school (Osofsky, 1995), it is no wonder that learning is compromised.

The Ambient Classroom Environment

Since Strauss and Lehtinen's (1947) pioneering times, professionals have recommended reducing excessive distractions in the classroom for youngsters with learning disabilities. This typically involves the reduction of extraneous noise and visual stimulation by means of three-sided cubicles, and trying to keep class decorum in check so that disturbances are minimized. At times, limiting high-appeal distractors (such as jewelry, vivid colors, or clutter) is recommended to help the hyperactive child stay on task (Barkley, 1981).

Studies find that visual and noise distractions, especially intense or meaningful noise, are disruptive to students' performance. Generally, the level of disruption tends to be similar for both children with and without learning disabilities.

Background Noise. Quieter classroom environments appear to benefit most students, whether learning disabled or not (Aylward & Whitehouse, 1987). Research has found that background noise, especially meaningful noise, will lower performance for most children (Ackerman & Dykman, 1993; Bremer & Stern, 1976; Sykes et al., 1971; Whalen et al., 1979; Zentall & Zentall, 1976), although there are some exceptions (Abikoff et al., 1996).

Weinstein (1970) offered three possibilities for depressed performance in noisy environments:

1. The noise interferes with communication in the classroom, so that children are unable to attend to or even hear the teacher and consequently miss essential instruction.

2. Less communication is possible in noisy than in quiet environments, as illustrated in Bronzaft and McCarthy's (1975) study where teachers had to stop instructing for thirty seconds about every four and a half minutes while an elevated train passed by.

3. Children in perpetually noisy environments develop an auditory screening process that filters out relevant as well as irrelevant sounds.

Staples (1996) adds that poorer learning in high noise conditions also may relate to the negative effect on the child's emotional state of these psychological stressors, which are outside the child's control, annoying, distressing, and perhaps even appraised as threatening. At Syracuse University's Psychoeducational Teaching Laboratory, for example, we once worked with a child who asked with every passing airplane whether a bomb was going to be dropped on us. It was not difficult to understand why, with these concerns, he would have difficulty attending to the task at hand.

The detrimental effects of external classroom noise have been examined in a series of fascinating studies of disruptions caused by airplane, train, and other noises (Crook & Langdon, 1974; Hygge, 1993; Kyzar, 1977). Bronzaft and McCarthy's (1975) study, for example, was with students attending an elementary school located very close to an elevated train line. The noise level in the classrooms nearest the train tracks was so high when a train was going by that teachers had to scream to be heard by nearby children. When the reading achievement of children in classrooms on the near and far sides of the building was compared, the scores of students on the noisy side were significantly lower.

When noise in the classroom exceeds that common in even the loudest of classrooms, there is some evidence that distractible children will take longer to complete educational tasks than will nondistractible children (Somervill et al., 1974). Surprisingly, however, listening to one's favorite rock music actually may facilitate accuracy in particular circumstances for children with ADHD, although this music seems to make no difference in the task performance of typical students (Abikoff et al., 1996) Abikoff and colleagues explain that this positive effect may be due to the music's appeal, or to the added stimulation it provides to children whose central nervous systems are underaroused; it could be that such pleasant, highly salient stimuli keep children from drifting off task, thereby increasing focused and effortful behavior.

Noise in the classroom also has been studied from the standpoint of whether the noise is meaningful (talking, voices) or nonmeaningful (random and unintelligible). Meaningful noise in the classroom appears to lower the performance of children more than does unintelligible noise of similar intensity, whether the children are learning disabled or not (Cherry & Kruger, 1983; Joiner & Kottmeyer, 1971; Nober & Nober, 1975). In Cherry and Kruger's study, subjects with learning problems were disrupted even more than their peers under all noise conditions.

Visual Distractions. As with noise, most studies find that both students with learning disabilities and typical students are hampered to similar extents on educational tasks by excessive visual distractions (Aylward & Whitehouse, 1987; Carter & Diaz, 1971; Patton, Routh, & Offenbach, 1981; Somervill et al., 1974). McNellis (1987), for example, found that children with learning disabilities were just as distracted as non-LD children on several visual tasks: reading "color" words painted in the wrong color (for example, the word *blue* was drawn in green); copying figures on a background of wavy, intersecting lines; naming pictures while ignoring embedded objects or words; and finding and outlining simple geometric forms obscured within a background of lines and shading. Interestingly, use of three-sided cubicles and other methods to minimize visual distractions may not always lead to better performance (Somervill, Warnberg, & Bost, 1973).

Some research on another visual aspect of the environment, lighting, suggests that classroom lighting may not always be optimal for learning purposes. Kasik, Sabatino, and Spoentgen (1987), for example, review evidence that the light at the sides of a classroom with standard ceiling fixtures is 50 percent that in the center. Fluorescent lighting too is only one tenth as bright as being in the shade on a sunny day. In addition, a small and controversial body of research has argued that there is a relationship between standard cool white fluorescent lighting in the classroom and the incidence of hyperactivity in children (Mayron et al., 1976; Ott, 1976; Painter, 1976). Because of difficulties in experimental design in the latter studies, however, the decrease in hyperactive behaviors when fluorescent lights were removed or when full-spectrum fluorescent lights were substituted (with lead foil shielding the cathode ends and grounded aluminum screening preventing low-frequency electromagnetic radiation) cannot be linked for sure to the experimental treatment. The decrease in hyperactivity could be due to other variables, such as observer bias or the positive effect on the children of being in an experiment. In a better-controlled study in which, unbeknown to the observers, the lighting in the classrooms was switched every other week, no differences in hyperactivity were revealed in relation to standard fluorescent lighting or lighting that controlled for emission of soft X rays and radio frequencies (O'Leary, Rosenbaum, & Hughes, 1978).

Color, another aspect of our visual environment, has yet to attract serious research attention. Designers have long used color to create certain moods in homes and offices. Only recently has this practice expanded to other institutions, where light pink purportedly helps calm violent behavior in prisons and light green helps relax muscles when exercising. Exactly how color may affect classroom performance has yet to be studied.

The Designed Environment

Designed aspects of the school setting that have been investigated include school and classroom size and design. These studies suggest that the student with learning disabilities will benefit from smaller schools and class size, the more positive teacher and student attitudes in open-space designs, small-group seating arrangements that require teachers to move around to supervise, pleasant surroundings, and sitting front and center.

School and Class Size. School buildings come in a tremendous variety of sizes, from the once widespread one-room schoolhouse to mammoth high schools that house thousands of students under one roof. The ecological investigations of Roger Barker and his colleagues noted that small schools give the student a better chance of participating in most aspects of school life, thereby fostering a spirit of challenge, action, close cooperation among peers, and high self-esteem (Barker & Gump, 1964). They also afford the teacher the opportunity to employ more of the effective teaching strategies discussed later in this chapter and to develop more powerful, intense interactions with students. These results have stood up well in subsequent studies (Glass et al., 1982).

There also is a strong and clear relationship between class size and academic achievement, with students in classrooms of fifteen to twenty or fewer pupils achieving significantly higher than pupils in classes of twenty-five or more (Glass & Smith, 1979). It seems that, in smaller classes, teachers are more likely to individualize instruction and to have higher morale and more favorable attitudes toward students, which in turn relate to higher student self-concept, interest, and participation (Smith & Glass, 1980).

School and Classroom Design. The design of school buildings and classrooms has changed greatly through the years. Getzels (1974) argues that changes in classroom design are not merely the product of architectural and engineering advances but these changes actually mirror changing views of the learner. The rectangular classroom design of the turn of the century reflected the then-current notion of the child as an "empty" learner, one who must sit still and be "fed" information that others decide is important. These early classrooms featured long rows of chairs fastened tightly to the floor, with a raised platform in the front of the room for the teacher. In contrast, the square classrooms of the 1930s, with movable seats and the teacher's desk at the side of the room, reflected the progressive education movement and its image of the child as an active learner. The open-plan classroom design of the late 1960s reflects still a different concept of the child, as a "vital entity, perpetually in motion, that must be given an effective opportunity to remain in motion if it is to function and continue to live" (Getzels, 1974, p. 535). Getzels highlights the transaction between the learner and the educational setting: "The classrooms we build for our children are not only places where the lessons intended by the teacher are taught. These classrooms teach lessons of their own; they tell the child who he is supposed to be . . . and how he is supposed to learn" (p. 538). An assortment of school and classroom design variables have been shown to influence students' attitudes, behaviors, and achievement.

Open-Space Schools. George (1975) reported that over 50 percent of all schools built in this country between 1967 and 1970 were open in design. The particular design of these open-space schools varies widely, but they are generally characterized by a lack of interior walls and by instructional areas ranging in size from two ordinary classrooms to over thirty (Weinstein, 1979). There is an important distinction between open *space* and open *education.* The former is what we are discussing here, an architectural variable. The latter is an instructional variable in which students self-pace and self-initiate educational activities, with the teacher acting as a facilitator for their learning.

Studies of student movement and behavior patterns in open-space schools show that more classroom areas, particularly library areas, are used in these schools, and less time is spent at desks (Beeken & Jansen, 1978; Rothenburg & Rivlin, 1975). Interaction between peers is more frequent, but seemingly at some expense to individual contact with the teacher. Less time is spent reading and writing in open-space schools than in traditional classrooms, although no consistent differences in academic achievement or student creativity between the two designs have been shown (George, 1975).

Both teachers' and students' attitudes toward school appear to be influenced favorably by open-space schools, particularly with regard to satisfaction, ambition, feelings of autonomy, willingness on the part of students to take risks, and feelings of cooperation and caring among teachers and students (Cohen, 1973; George, 1975; Meyer, 1971; Trickett, 1978). Weinstein (1979) notes that the enthusiasm and ambition of the class may reflect teacher self-selection rather than the open plan itself. That is, teachers in open-space schools may differ in attitude from other teachers, and it is these attitudes that influence their selection to teach in these innovative settings.

Studies show that students with learning disabilities who are hyperactive and distractible are not necessarily at a disadvantage with the increased freedom in open-space classrooms (Flynn & Rapoport, 1976; Jacob, O'Leary, & Rosenblad, 1978). Nevertheless, recognizing that some students need greater structure, consistency, and teacher direction than is typical in the open-setting's relaxed structure, researchers have suggested design alternatives in the form of graduated degrees of open-to-structured learning areas.

Furniture Arrangement. The arrangement of furniture and the use of space in the classroom also affect student behavior (Kritchevsky & Prescott, 1969; Weinstein, 1977). Zifferblatt (1972), for example, looked at the relationship between classroom furniture arrangement and student behavior in two third grade classrooms in which the teachers had similar instructional styles, curricula, and classroom activities. In one class-room the attention spans of students appeared much shorter, and they had more inappropriate movement around the classroom and loud conversation. In this classroom, as many as twelve student desks were clustered together and there were no clear boundaries or barriers for specific classroom activities. The teacher's desk was in the center of the room, enabling her to manage most classroom activities from her seat, thus decreasing individual contact with students.

In the classroom where behavior was not a problem, the desks were situated in less accessible areas of the room, providing some degree of privacy for the students. The desks were arranged so that only two or three children could work together. The teacher's desk was located in a corner so that she was unable to direct activities from the desk and had to move around the classroom. Several bookcases, serving as barriers, helped limit classroom-wide movement and activity.

Zifferblatt concluded that the differences in behavior observed in these two classrooms were due to differences in the way classroom space was arranged and used. Zifferblatt's findings were replicated in a study that found clusters or circles of desks associated with significantly more on-task behavior than when desks were arranged in rows (Rosenfield, Lambert, & Black, 1985). Studies like these have clear implications for students with learning disabilities, who often need nondistracting seating arrangements and close, personal contact with the teacher to help them stay on task.

Pleasantness of Surroundings. It seems that children persist more at educational tasks when they are in pleasant surroundings. Early work by Mintz (1956) and Maslow and Mintz (1956) found a relationship between an ugly environment and feelings of discontent, the desire to escape, and fatigue. Building on this, Santrock (1976) had first and second graders perform a motor task in a school room that was decorated with happy, sad, or neutral pictures. The results indicated that these environments had a significant impact on persistence on the motor task, with students working longest in the "happy" room setting.

More recent evidence from a number of studies suggests that, when teachers induce positive moods among students of any age (for example, "close your eyes and think about something that makes you happy"), the amount, accuracy, and rate of learning and retention on that task may improve (Bryan, Mathur, & Sullivan, 1996).

Seating Location. Where students sit has an important effect on their classroom experiences. Early studies by Walberg (1969) and Adams and Biddle (1970) noted a "front and center" phenomenon: students who sit in the front-center portion of the classroom seem to place significantly higher value on learning, are more attentive, engage in more on-task behavior, and interact more with the classroom teacher. This "front and center" phenomenon has generally been confirmed (Koneya, 1976; Schwebel & Cherlin, 1972), with a few exceptions (Delefes & Jackson, 1972). Weinstein (1979) concluded that "the weight of the evidence seems to indicate that a front-center phenomenon facilitates achievement, positive attitudes, and participation, at least for those somewhat predisposed to speak in class . . . [and] it seems reasonable to hypothesize that teachers attend more to students in the front and center" (p. 580).

In light of these findings, teachers need to reexamine the common practice of isolating children with learning disabilities in the far reaches of the classroom because of their high distractibility. This placement may result in far less supervision and encouragement from the teacher, especially in traditional classrooms where the teacher spends most class time in the front of the room. The diminished interaction with the teacher may outweigh any advantages of reduced distractions.

Organizational Characteristics

Organizational aspects of school settings include the procedures for allocating resources, developing curriculum, identifying students in need of special services, assigning pupils and teachers to classrooms, and devising general rules. When school personnel assume that identification as disabled and receiving special education services outside the regular classroom can help the student with learning disabilities receive more appropriate educational services, this must be weighed against the stigma and isolation that also can accompany these services. In response to this concern, alternatives for service provision that do not necessitate removal from the educational mainstream have been encouraged. These include the model of coteaching by general and special educators, "push in" models whereby special educators deliver services in the student's classroom rather than having to "pull out" the child, and consultation services provided by the special educator to the general education teacher. These approaches seem to work well in meeting the needs of many students with learning disabilities while complying with the "least restrictive environment" mandate of the Individuals with Disabilities Education Act (IDEA). Because the mainstream environment is not the least restrictive for every student with learning disabilities, the needs of each learner must be assessed carefully before deciding which placement is likely to provide the most appropriate program. This includes ascertaining in which setting the student is likely to be encouraged to spend the most time on the most appropriate tasks, feel better about himself or herself, and reach the highest possible levels of academic, social, and prevocational adjustment. In the following pages we will explore the impact of various identification, placement, and instructional organization options on the academic and social–emotional growth of the student with learning disabilities.

Identification

In most states special services are provided primarily to students who have been formally identified as disabled. Identification qualifies school systems for funds distributed by federal and state education agencies, though these reimbursements represent only a fraction of the 100 percent increase in costs over the cost of services to the typical student. Identification also helps to project numbers of personnel needed, and serves as a rallying point for advocacy to increase research,

funding, and service provision. Against this justification for identification, the educator must weigh a variety of potential disadvantages: reduced parent and teacher expectations, reduced achievement if students are homogeneously grouped for instruction, and the tendency to overlook task and setting contributors to the student's difficulties, thereby moving students out of the regular classroom too hastily.

There is concern that teacher, parental, and peer attitude changes, when a child is identified as learning disabled, may negatively affect the student. Once children have been identified as learning disabled, this has been shown to reduce mothers' evaluations of their children's well-being in comparison to the attitudes of mothers toward equally low-achieving, but unidentified children (Coleman, 1983). Likewise, when children are told that another has ADHD, they have been observed to become less friendly in their interactions with that child, talk less, become less involved in a mutual task, and make the child with ADHD work harder (Milich, McAninch, & Harris, 1992). The children with ADHD in turn see themselves as less capable and perceive the other child as mean. The label "learning disabled" can also negatively influence the attitudes of peers and exert a biasing effect on teacher judgments of a student's behavior and potential failure (Clark, 1997; Foley, 1979; Foster, Schmidt, & Sabatino, 1976; Sutherland & Algozzine, 1979).

The negative judgments of children with disability labels is disconcerting because a sizable and controversial body of research has found that in some, but not all, cases a teacher's expectations about a student's ability can influence the teacher's behavior toward the student, the student's classroom behavior, and the student's ultimate performance (Alexander & Strain, 1978; Dusek, 1975; Meyers, Sundstrom, & Yoshida, 1974; Rosenthal & Jacobson, 1968; Rosenthal & Rosnow, 1969). This so-called "self-fulfilling prophecy" is operative when the teacher knows that the student is disabled but is not yet familiar with the child, or when the youngster's behavior actually matches the teacher's prior expectations; once teachers get to know children, they form their expectations on the basis of the actual behaviors they observe

(Brophy, 1983; Reschly & Lamprecht, 1979). The more closely acquainted teachers are with their pupils, the smaller the expectancy effect (Raudenbush, 1984). Nevertheless, any expectancy gained from the label may take some time to counteract (Ysseldyke & Foster, 1978). Remember the last time you heard a nasty rumor about a friend and subsequently learned it was unfounded? Despite this knowledge, it probably took you a long time to stop doubting the person and begin believing what you saw rather than what you heard.

There are other disadvantages to handicapping classifications besides the potential biasing effect on family, teacher, and peer attitudes. Major among these is the mistake of assuming that group homogeneity will be increased by grouping students together for all instruction because they have the same disability classification or because they achieve equally poorly in one subject area ("ability grouping") (Balow, 1964; Chandler, 1966; Hallahan & Kauffman, 1977; Richey & McKinney, 1978; Wilhelms & Westby-Gibson, 1961). When students are grouped on the basis of one criterion, such as disability or level of reading achievement, this does not make them any more alike on any other characteristic (for example, math achievement). Such tracking results in lower achievement than had the children been educated with their nontracked peers, and perhaps received a few minutes of daily extra assistance (Dawson, 1987; Jenkins et al., 1994; Persell, 1979). It seems that teachers pace instruction differently for different ability groups, with the instructional pace for higher-ability groups at times being as much as thirteen times faster than for lower-ability groups (Shavelson, 1983). Obviously, students being taught at a slower pace will be exposed to less of the curriculum, thereby falling further and further behind. Instruction in lower-ability groups has been differentiated from that in higher-ability groups in a number of other ways: more teacher interruptions, more teacher time spent managing the class, less clarity of directions, lower task orientation, lower teacher enthusiasm, and poorer student attention to task, confidence, work habits, and independence (Dawson, 1987). In addition to reduced richness of curriculum

content, course selection also is more limited (Hallinan & Sorensen, 1983; Lee & Bryk, 1988). Certainly, all this fosters an inferior quality of education.

Despite their label, pupils who are learning disabled remain just as diverse in learning styles, behavior, and instructional needs as many of their nondisabled peers. In fact, a review of forty-seven studies comparing typical learners and those with learning disabilities found that 23 percent of the children with learning disabilities in some areas scored above the average performance of the nondisabled group (Weener, 1981). Often the achievement test scores of students with learning disabilities are indistinguishable from those of low achievers who are not identified as disabled. Unfortunately, in actual practice, teachers' choices of teaching objectives, methods, and materials are largely irrelevant to an LD identification, or to designation for remedial services. Observation in forty self-contained classes for the mildly mentally retarded, learning disabled, or emotionally disturbed, for example, found that the teachers for the most part taught similarly no matter which type of student was in their class (Algozzine, Morsink, & Algozzine, 1988). Instruction in many resource programs also may be no different than that in the regular class (Haynes & Jenkins, 1986; Zigmond, 1990).

One must wonder then whether grouping the learning disabled together for instruction, because of the label's implicit assumption of homogeneity, might not offer very much that is special, and might in fact limit learning opportunities in areas in which these students otherwise might have progressed well. Among the worst aspects of segregating these students for instruction is that they lose access to the regular education curriculum. Consequently, the learning disabled become less knowledgeable about science, social studies, and today's social concerns (drugs, women's issues, pollution) and fads (rock groups, fashion). This puts students at a disadvantage because their paucity of background knowledge makes them less and less prepared over time to integrate a wide array of information. They also become less able to communicate effectively with typical peers because they have less in common.

Another disadvantage of identification is that it implies that inborn characteristics are sufficient to explain why the student who is learning disabled is having so much difficulty. In some instances, the real reasons for the student's lack of success might be found in the instructional strategies and human interactions in the pupil's classroom. A further fallacy is that a disability label implies consistent behaviors from situation to situation. Supposedly, an individual with learning disabilities is learning disabled not only in school but also at home, on the playground, and in the community. Yet students with mild learning disabilities are often indistinguishable from other children in nonschool settings and excel in nonacademic areas such as athletics and the arts. Disability classifications do not describe the student, and the classification itself tells us nothing about how to intervene. It is in response to these concerns that noncategorical options for assigning pupils to programs according to their instructional needs, rather than disability category, have arisen in recent years.

Placement

A second broad aspect of the organizational environment of schools concerns how schools arrange classroom placements for students who have special learning needs. A range of placement possibilities exists, from regular classroom placement with no support services to special schools that are devoted exclusively to pupils with learning disabilities. The "place" in which services are offered is not the critical factor here; it is what goes on in these placements that is important. The choice of an effective placement for a particular student depends on a good understanding of the least restrictive environment concept and a comparison of the supports available through special class placements, inclusive service models (educating students fulltime in the regular classroom), and resource rooms. Although research to date finds that students with learning disabilities tend to benefit more academically, socially, and emotionally when receiving services in a special education setting, newer service models attempt to incorporate the benefits of the special education setting

into the mainstream environment, which has its own potential benefits.

The Least Restrictive Environment. IDEA mandates that students with disabilities be educated in as near normal a setting as possible—the "least restrictive environment" (LRE). IDEA's LRE provision states that

to the maximum extent appropriate, children with disabilities . . . [be] educated with children who are not disabled, and [that] . . . removal. . . . from the regular educational environment [occur] only when the nature or severity of the disability of a child is such that education in regular classes with the use of supplementary aids and services cannot be achieved satisfactorily. (IDEA reauthorization, 1997)

Courts have ruled that if schools move students to restrictive settings, they must be able to justify those placements with concrete data (Yell, 1994). If gaps in the continuum of services exist, and the appropriate placement for a particular child is not available in the district, the school must make other arrangements for an appropriate placement (for example, pay for a private school, contract with another school district). Legislative comments on IDEA stress that

where a child with disabilities is so disruptive in a regular classroom that the education of other students is significantly impaired, the needs of the child with disabilities cannot be met in that environment. Therefore regular placement would not be appropriate to his or her needs. (34 C. F. R. § 33.552, comments)

IDEA reflects the view that although many students with special needs can be appropriately educated in the regular classroom setting, some have needs best met in some form of special education setting. Based on insights from educational research, Heron and Skinner (1981) define the least restrictive environment "as that educational setting which maximizes the learning disabled student's opportunity to respond and achieve, permits the regular education teacher to interact proportionally with all the students in the classroom, and fosters acceptable social relations between nonhandicapped and learning disabled students" (p. 116.)

It is important to remember that "inclusion" and "least restrictive" are not synonymous. At times, education in the mainstream might be restrictive for a student with learning disabilities for a variety of reasons: for example, lack of preparation of regular classroom teachers to deal with the student's needs, teacher unwillingness to individualize for a student with a disability, inappropriate class structure and curriculum, and poor quality of peer modeling in the regular classroom. Therefore, placement considerations must be based on both student needs and school resources.

Special Class Placement. The appropriateness of placing students with special educational needs in special classes has long been debated among educators. As in many areas of education, policy decisions often come before empirical evidence is complete. Influential articles, particularly Dunn's (1968) on the detrimental aspects of special class placements for children with mild disabilities, paved the way for a gradual retreat from the special class concept. Has this been a wise course of action? Are the needs of particular students with special educational needs better met in the regular or special education classroom?

Contrary to research with children of below-average intelligence, who develop no better socially and often worse academically in a special class than in a regular class, studies with the learning disabled show academic and social gains favoring special classes (Carlberg & Kavale, 1980; Dawson, 1987; Gottlieb, Rose, & Lessen, 1983; Madden & Slavin, 1983; Wang & Baker, 1985–1986). Special classrooms might benefit students with learning disabilities more than they benefit the mildly retarded because the learning disabled have the cognitive potential to make more rapid academic progress when exposed to more intense instruction. In special classes teacher–pupil ratios are two to three times lower than in regular classes, which maximizes the possibility of intensive, individualized instruction. Bryan's (1974a) study illustrates how this might happen. She found that students with learning disabilities in the regular class spent 14 percent of their time waiting for the teacher to get organized. In the LD classroom only 3 percent of their time was spent waiting. In the LD class-

room there was greater on-task behavior, more positive reinforcement from the teacher, and more interaction with the teacher than in the regular classroom. Bryan and Wheeler (1976), too, reported several more positive types of teacher–child interaction in LD classrooms than in regular classrooms: greater frequency of completed interactions (student spoke, teacher responded), fewer teacher instructions geared to the whole group, more frequent and longer duration of communications (often up to one minute), and greater number of adult initiations to which children responded. Wagner (1990; in Rieth & Polsgrove, 1994) reports that students with learning disabilities educated in special classes fail less often than do those educated in mainstream classes; this in turn may reduce the chance of school dropout.

What about the social or affective development of youngsters with learning disabilities in special and regular classes? Several studies have found beneficial effects of special class placement on the general and academic self-concepts of students with learning disabilities (Battle & Blowers, 1982; Boersma, Chapman, & Battle, 1979; Coleman, 1983; Coleman & Minnett, 1993; Ribner, 1978). Yauman's (1980) study found that students with learning disabilities in special classes maintained as good a self-concept as typical children in regular classes, despite significantly lower reading achievement, which usually correlates with lower self-concept. The students with learning disabilities who remained in regular classes but received daily tutoring had significantly lower self-concept scores than the typical children, even though their reading achievement scores were higher than those of the students in LD classes. Likewise, Kistner and colleagues (1987) found that those elementary and middle school students with learning disabilities who had higher IQs, who were more skilled academically, and who spent the least number of hours a day in special classes were the ones who consistently viewed their self-concepts in all areas as more negative than did students who were less skilled but spent more time in special classes.

It has been suggested that the lower self-concepts in regular classes may be due to students comparing themselves unfavorably against their higher-functioning classmates, and to the regular class competition that sets criteria for achievement that students with learning disabilities have difficulty meeting. Access to more homogeneous or multiple reference groups (as in resource programs) increases the possibility for positive judgments of self-worth because youngsters can compare their performance to peers who also experience learning difficulties (Coleman, 1983; Coleman & Minnett, 1993). Since the ability to make social comparisons and normative judgments is fully developed around age ten, it is in the intermediate grades that exposure to more competent peers is most likely to begin to undermine a child's perceived competence (Butler & Marinov-Glassman, 1994). The challenge for educators is to determine what it is that makes the special class effective and how to incorporate more of these benefits into the mainstream environment.

Inclusive Service Models. Studies showing that special classes for the mildly retarded did not result in special outcomes, together with philosophical awakenings related to civil rights activism, brought about profound changes in long-established practices in special education. One change was *mainstreaming*, at least part-time placement of students with disabilities in the regular classroom, as promoted through PL 94-142, now IDEA. Since passage of PL 94-142, many advocates of mainstreaming have become strong proponents of *inclusion*, including students with disabilities full-time in regular classes with appropriate special education supports provided in that setting.

While the long-term effects of part-time mainstreaming or full inclusion have not been fully evaluated, what we know so far is that:

1. regular classroom teachers, especially at the secondary level, tend to be hesitant and fearful about providing for the needs of special students in their classrooms; even if they feel positively about including students with special needs, in reality they make few instructional adaptations, resist making adaptations, feel inadequately prepared, fear lawsuits, have safety concerns (e.g., getting everyone out during a fire drill), complain about workload and added paperwork, are not keen on team teaching, and feel that the needed adaptations aren't feasible in the regular classroom (Hannah & Pliner, 1983; Mesinger, 1985; Minke et al., 1986; Salend, 1984; Schumm & Vaughn, 1995; Vaughn, Schumm et al., 1996). Bender, Vail, and Scott (1995) found that one-third or fewer of mainstream elementary and middle school teachers used adaptations such as specialized grading systems, student self-monitoring, token economies, behavioral contracts, advanced organizers, or direct and daily progress measurement. Scanlon, Deshler, and Schumaker's (1996) secondary inclusive teachers were willing to spend only about five minutes daily on strategy instruction to help with content learning, and implementation rate was variable, perhaps because the teachers felt compelled to "move on" in the curriculum even when not all students were ready to do so; classroom observations indicated that teaching practices typically were aimed at the class as a whole, and students with learning disabilities received little individual attention or feedback with regard to their performance. Schumm and Vaughn's research review indicates that some general education teachers objected to adaptations because they call attention to students with disabilities; most often pressure to cover content precluded adaptations, and any adaptations tended to be incidental and not carefully planned; 98 percent of teachers felt competent to plan for general education students, but only 39 percent felt competent to plan for special education students. In Gajria, Salend, and Hemrick's (1994) study, teachers in grades seven to twelve were willing to alter design elements of tests (e.g., typewritten, spacing of items) that are useful for the whole class, but they were reluctant to provide modifications geared toward particular individuals' needs (e.g., modify reading level of a test, develop alternative scoring criteria, provide a sample

test or a model of a correct response, provide an answer check sheet listing the components expected on essay questions);

2. students with learning disabilities who are mainstreamed into regular classrooms generally need some special education support services to maintain the academic gains they had made in the special classroom (Lieberman, 1985; Ritter, 1978). Reading gains are greater if *both* the regular and special education teachers take responsibility for teaching than if only one does (Marston, 1996);

3. as discussed earlier, the academic achievement of mainstreamed students with learning disabilities may suffer relative to their progress in segregated environments;

4. the popularity of students with learning disabilities in the regular classroom tends to be low and they are more frequently rejected (Haager & Vaughn, 1995; Sale & Carey, 1995; Vaughn, Elbaum, & Schumm, 1996);

5. mainstreaming may not result in greater social interaction with nondisabled students, greater social acceptance, or modeling of typical peers' behaviors (Gresham, 1982; Guralnick & Groom, 1988). Jenkins, Speltz, and Odom (1985) conclude that mere proximity between the disabled and nondisabled is insufficient to accelerate the development of the disabled beyond that expected in segregated settings. For students with disabilities to benefit from integration, the classroom organization must specifically preplan for modeling to occur (for example, by using cooperative learning principles or assigning modeling roles to the nondisabled). In contrast to school-age students, integrated preschool settings tend to be particularly facilitative of social and behavioral progress (Buysse & Bailey, 1993);

6. the self-perceptions and teacher perceptions of mainstreamed students who are learning disabled tend to be lower than in more

segregated environments (Battle & Blowers, 1982; Morrison, 1985). Even if the overall, physical ability, appearance, or friendship self-concepts of mainstreamed students are equivalent to their typical classmates, academic, intellectual, and social self-concepts tend to be lower (Smith & Nagle, 1995; Vaughn, Elbaum, & Schumm, 1996). Remedial help has a positive effect on self-concept (Chapman, 1988);

7. given the mainstream emphasis on learning the regular curriculum, yet the less than satisfactory postschool employment histories and earnings of many young adults with learning disabilities, some individuals wonder whether exposure to the regular curriculum is in the best interest of all students with learning disabilities (Edgar, 1987). Intensified vocational preparation and transition services may benefit some students more, which again raises the specter of separate programs and segregation;

8. mainstreaming may affect the parent as well as the child. On bulletin board displays of student work, at open house curriculum presentations, and in other ways parents are reminded of the discrepancy between their child and the typical classmates. Sharing their child's stigma, parents may feel less respected or accepted by other parents. In addition, because their interests and concerns are different from those of the typical student's parents, their isolation may grow over time (Turnbull & Blacher-Dixon, 1980);

9. some parents and teachers have expressed concern that typical children's achievement will be negatively affected by the inclusion of students with learning disabilities in their classrooms (Vaughn, Schumm et al., 1996). These concerns, however, are not justified. Studies at the preschool and elementary levels have found that typical students make no fewer developmental and academic gains in integrated settings than when students with disabilities are not included in the class

(Affleck et al., 1988; Odom, DeKlyen, & Jenkins, 1984; Pomplun, 1996).

In general, research suggests that if inclusion is to work for students with learning disabilities, special education intervention or general educator training to help plan teaching modifications is essential. Children with disabilities cannot merely be added on to the existing mainstream program as an appendage (Stainback & Stainback, 1985). The general education teacher must be willing to forgo the rigid lockstep system dictated by each grade's curriculum and be flexible regarding what students are ready to learn, how they will learn, the rate at which they will learn, and grading. The system must make adjustments to accommodate the individual with special needs.

Advocates of inclusion have argued that its rationale does not need to be verified by research studies—it is simply ethically wrong to isolate individuals from the regular classroom and peers. It also has been argued that classroom management for the student with learning disabilities actually may be easier in the mainstream. Kirk (1986) explains that self-contained classes are difficult to manage because the teacher must divide his or her time among ten to twelve different students. Because each student with a learning disability has unique needs that make it difficult to group for instruction, a special class teacher could have as many as twelve reading and twelve math groups a day, each consisting of only one pupil. With barely enough time to get through these groups, little time is left for expanding students' knowledge (for example, science, social studies, enrichment activities, social skills training).

When deciding on class placements, the practical thing is to determine what is right for each individual child given the student's age, needed curriculum modifications, social skills, numbers of pupils in the regular class, attitude and competency of the regular class teacher, and the family support system. Even if a full-time special education class is the placement of choice, it still is common for students to be mainstreamed for art, physical education, music, library, field trips, and perhaps even homeroom. If students are ready to

be included in an academic subject area, they are mainstreamed for this as well. Sansone and Zigmond (1986) point out that if students with disabilities are to gain socially from their mainstream interactions, then they should be mainstreamed into grade-appropriate classes, be assigned to the same class of students for all mainstream activities, and attend the full sequence of scheduled instruction in each subject (for example, all three music classes per week, not just one).

Extensive inservice training is essential to modify mainstream teachers' attitudes, build a repertoire of accommodations that require little preplanning, and teach useful interventions that can be implemented for the class as a whole (Schumm et al., 1995). The success of students with learning disabilities in mainstream classes has been facilitated by teaching regular educators how to implement study skills instruction such as note taking, memory strategies, test-taking skills, organization, time management, listening comprehension, reading in content areas, and vocabulary development (Smith, 1987). Preparing students for mainstreaming by specifically teaching them the requisite social skills for effective social interaction and peer acceptance also is important (Gresham, 1982, 1984). These include how to interact positively with others, obey class rules, and display appropriate work habits. It also may involve weaning the student from supports that may no longer be present in the mainstream, such as small-group instruction, token systems, and frequent teacher attention (Salend, 1984). Encouragement of skills in athletics, game playing, and conversation also is important because being perceived as competent in these areas will facilitate social integration and popularity with classmates (Cartledge, Frew, & Zaharias, 1985; Conderman, 1995). Maher (1982) adds that regular class placement can be far more successful academically if teachers and pupils jointly set instructional goals, measure goal attainment, and meet weekly to discuss progress and instructional plans.

Inclusive service models are more likely to succeed if the nondisabled students also are prepared to serve as friends, role models, peer tutors, or teammates on projects. Group discussions, disability simulations, and films and books about the disabled have been helpful in fostering more positive attitudes among nondisabled classmates. Techniques that pair the student who is learning disabled with a popular peer, and that create opportunities to showcase children's individual talents, are particularly effective in improving peer popularity (Vaughn, Lancelotta, & Minnis, 1988).

The most common method for providing service to mainstreamed students has been through "pull out" services offered in the resource room. Models in which the special educator coteaches with the general educator, comes into the class to deliver services, or consults on program modifications are increasing in popularity, however.

Pull out Services. Currently, approximately 80 percent of students with learning disabilities are educated in the mainstream for 40 percent or more of the school day. Of these, about one-half are "pulled out" for special instruction in the resource room for less than 21 percent of the school day; the other half receive resource room instruction for 21 to 60 percent of the school day. (*U.S. Office of Education*, 1997). The *resource room* concept emerged as an alternative to the segregated special classroom. The resource room is a *pull out* service that allows the student to leave the regular classroom for one or more periods a day to receive individual or small group instruction from a special education teacher. Often students with different types of disabilities but similar instructional needs are grouped together for resource room instruction.

Research has supported the effectiveness of resource room services as a means of increasing students' achievement and on-task behavior (O'Connor, Stuck, & Wyne, 1979; Sindelar & Deno, 1978). Marston (1987–1988), for example, found that elementary school children at risk for special education identification progressed at twice the rate when receiving daily resource room help than when receiving only regular education instruction. Gains in the resource setting, however, do not always transfer to the regular classroom (Anderson-Inman, 1987). Resource services do not appear to diminish the peer acceptance or overall self-concept of mainstreamed stu-

dents with learning disabilities; however, academic, social, and behavioral self-concepts tend to be low regardless of the setting in which these children are educated (Prillaman, 1981; Sheare, 1978; Smith & Nagle, 1995). Some studies suggest that resource services may enhance teacher and student perceptions of progress and personal social adjustment (Kistner et al., 1987; Quinn & Wilson, 1977; Strang, Smith, & Rogers, 1978).

Despite the success of resource programs, pulling students out of their regular classes for special education services does have disadvantages. When a child is pulled out of class he or she can feel disconnected and confused, may get a watered-down curriculum, and may miss out on important classwork (necessitating extra time playing catchup). The student also misses out on enjoyable subject areas like art, physical education, and music in which success could provide just the motivation needed to persist with the harder academic challenges. Time is also wasted going from class to class. In addition, many children are sensitive to the stigma of leaving class and are confused by frequent disruptions in their instruction. Moreover, pull out programs make it difficult for special and general educators to coordinate instruction, and they absolve classroom teachers from the need to take their instructional responsibilities toward low-achieving students seriously (Jenkins & Heinen, 1989). Albinger (1995) reports the poignant stories of children pulled out of regular classes for resource services who fabricated tales to hide where they had been. While the stories they constructed protected them from their perceptions of others' reactions, the fabrications became even bigger concerns than the learning problems themselves (for example, Kim told her friends for 2½ years that she takes piano lessons when out of the classroom; now she worries that someday someone will ask to hear her play).

There certainly should be something very special, intense, individualized, and qualitatively different about pull out programs to justify removing a student from his or her regular class. Yet observers have found that in many cases materials and practices that did not work in the regular classroom are continued in the resource room

(Licopoli, 1984; Thurlow et al., 1983b). Zigmond (1990), for example, observed that resource teachers instructed for less than 40 percent of the time, mainly on worksheets; 23 percent of the time teachers didn't interact with students at all, and 28 percent of the time was spent giving directions without any modeling. Often, instead of stressing basic remediation or study-strategy training, resource teachers complain that they must spend a good deal of time tutoring in order to ensure that students will pass the regular curriculum. Though these students may pass, they still have not gained the skills necessary to function more independently in the mainstream classroom.

Push in Models.   In order to deal with criticisms leveled at the pull out model, *push in models* have been developed to try to provide high-quality, individualized educational experiences for children within their regular classes. Special education teachers may come into the regular class to instruct one or more children. Alternatively, special education teachers may teach their own regular class or team teach in an integrated general education class. When coteaching, the two teachers divide responsibilities according to those children and subject areas with which they feel most competent. In these circumstances special educators often make sure to teach the "high" group in at least one subject area, coach an athletic team, advise the yearbook staff, or work with some other school activity. This helps the teacher avoid being stigmatized as the teacher of the "dummies," and alleviates the embarrassment and reduced motivation that could result from being taught by the special educator. Vaughn and colleagues (1996) report that general education teachers who cotaught felt that inclusion had benefited their students with learning disabilities socially and academically; they viewed the inclusion of these children in the class as an asset.

One organizational framework that has been reported to improve achievement is the nongraded (multiage) class, where students are regrouped for instruction in each subject based on skill level (Gutierrez & Slavin, 1992). Alternatively, Algozzine and Ysseldyke (1986) suggest that every student in the school, disabled or not, be assigned to one period a day devoted to special education or enrichment activities.

A three-year comparison of resource programs and programs where special educators or trained regular educators taught elementary students with learning disabilities full-time in regular classes showed equivalent academic gains (Affleck et al., 1988). Another study in which special education teachers taught their own regular classes found peer popularity of their students with learning disabilities to be greater than in regular classes taught by general educators (students here needed to go to resource settings for special instruction) (Madge, Affleck, & Lowerbraun, 1990).

At least one study has indicated that elementary school students prefer their classroom teacher for special help more so than specialists (Jenkins & Heinen, 1989). Some children view specialists coming into the classroom to offer services as embarrassing, whereas others see leaving the class as more embarrassing. While students of all ages like their general education teachers to make instructional accommodations for them, they are more sensitive about adaptations in tests, textbooks, and homework assignments (Vaughn, Schumm, & Kouzekanani, 1993). Jenkins and Heinen recommend that we consult the student when there is a choice of services and ask which option he or she prefers.

In the *teacher consultant model,* the stigma for the student is reduced because the special educator does not serve students with disabilities directly. Instead, the special educator works to improve the skills of the general education teachers who are instructing these students in the regular classroom. The teacher consultant requires very special training in collaborative problem-solving skills (questioning, listening, strategizing), the regular curriculum, the demands of large-group instruction, and curricular adaptation and behavior change in the regular classroom (Huefner, 1988)

In comparing the teacher consultant model with the resource room model, several studies have found equivalent gains in the academic performance of children with disabilities (Schulte, Osborne, & McKinney, 1990). General education teachers voice the need for more consultation help from special education teachers (Schumm & Vaughn, 1995). In fact, even when general education teachers who have agreed to coteach feel positively about inclusion and their teaching competencies, Minke and colleagues (1996) report that these teachers nevertheless think that the regular class is inappropriate for students with mild disabilities and that more resources are needed.

In conclusion, the pull out, push in, coteaching, and teacher consultant models are organizational characteristics of the school setting that have the potential to benefit students with learning disabilities. Their strength lies in the fact that students can receive support from special educators for their learning problems yet maximize the time spent with typical peers. Which particular model ultimately will prove to be the most effective, what about these programs is responsible for the gains, and whether these gains are any greater than those in special classes is up to future research to assess.

On page 478 Emmy describes the hard work and pleasure that accompanied her transition from the special class to a regular class placement—in Emmy's words, her "baptismal" day. In Chapter 9 Emmy's resource teacher described how grueling it was to serve Emmy within regular classes. Yet it was worth it. Emmy had been placed in a special class in first grade because she could not read. Her self-confidence diminished from year to year because of an overprotective teacher who hesitated to challenge the children. Basic skills stood still. With much effort on everyone's part, Emmy was included full time in regular classes in sixth grade. Now a high school junior who continues to receive resource room support and spends three hours a day on homework, Emmy is active in afterschool activities, walks with a bounce, smiles, speaks spontaneously to others, no longer stares at the floor when spoken to, has a date for the senior prom, and recently celebrated another "Baptismal Day"—she was elected to the National Honor Society!

Organization of Instruction

Classroom teachers use a myriad of approaches to deliver instruction to students, depending on their instructional aims, organizational preferences, and personal styles. Teachers differ from one another regarding the use of class time, the pace of instruction, the way in which the curriculum is structured and delivered, the way students progress through the curriculum, and the way they are grouped for instruction. Each of these factors influences whether a teacher will be effective in maximizing student learning.

Exactly how should teachers organize their instruction? What variations in instructional procedures will affect student outcome most positively? Much research has attempted to delineate the specific practices that make schools effective. Those factors found to maximize students' learning in the classroom are listed in Table 12–1.

This effective schools research refutes the notion that schools are relatively powerless in the face of other variables that affect achievement, for example, a youngster's family background. Schools can do much to enhance student achievement when they promote appropriate changes in the system itself, organization of instruction, and teaching strategies.

Much of the effective schools research has been conducted schoolwide, with only occasional reference to pupils with special educational needs (Morsink et al., 1986). The limited information we do have, however, suggests disappointing implementation of effective teaching strategies by special educators. There is too little time spent in direct instruction, too little time on task, too little active student responding, too little teacher feedback, and too little teacher attention or praise contingent on appropriate student behaviors. Nevertheless, our growing knowledge about how to effectively organize schools and instruction increases the potential for more effective special and regular education programming in the future. In applying these blueprints for enhancing academic performance, Bickel and Bickel (1986) warn educators not to implement these processes in unbridled fashion, lest we narrow the curriculum

Table 12–1 Characteristics of effective schools, classrooms, and instruction

Educational Leadership and Support

- Principal demonstrates commitment to goals and flexibility in pursuing them
- Clear, reasonable, orderly, disciplined, and consistent school policies
- The staff agrees to emphasize basic skills
- Support for small class size
- Staff development through inservice programs
- Principal protects the school day for teaching, minimizing teachers' administrative chores and classroom interruptions
- Principal makes sure teachers have necessary materials and assistance
- Principal builds morale of teachers
- Encouragement of teacher involvement in formulating school teaching policies and selecting textbooks

Orderly and Positive School Climate

- High levels of informal interaction with desirable activities
- School policies emphasize shared responsibility for the overall school climate
- A safe and comfortable environment is created in which students perceive the school's expectations for academic success
- Establish a positive, expectant, and orderly classroom environment
- Convey enthusiasm, "ham" it up, use humor and vocal expressiveness
- Reward using content-related praise ("That's right, a triangle has three sides"), activity reinforcers (free time, time with coach), exchangeable reinforcers (points, holes punched in a ticket), tangible reinforcers (pencils, magazines); when possible offer choice of reinforcers
- Reward group task completion at times instead of each individual; encourage self-praise
- Correct papers marking accurate answers rather than errors; errors are then corrected by students to yield perfect papers
- Small-group and individualized instruction establishes closer teacher-student social ties and involvement than recitations, which place the teacher at the center of control
- Incorporate students' ideas as a way of letting them know their ideas are valued
- Encourage creative experiences

High Achievement Expectations

- Set high but attainable goals; assign appropriate and frequent homework
- Outcomes are emphasized more than are procedures
- Administrators and teachers communicate expectations for success
- The mission of schooling is consistently communicated to students and the community
- The staff is serious, businesslike, and purposeful about the task of teaching
- The staff expects students to learn, holds them accountable for learning, and rewards it
- Communicate high expectations by seating lower-ability students close to the teacher
- Attend as much to low- as high-ability students
- Call on low- as much as high-ability students and give them equal quality of feedback
- Wait up to five seconds for low-ability students to respond to questions; provide clues and follow-up questions when students have difficulty answering questions

(Continues on following page)

Table 12–1 *(Continued)*

- Praise contingent on specific, appropriate responses (not general praise); avoid overcriticizing, especially via sarcasm or personal attacks
- Demand equal levels of effort from low- and high-ability students
- Provide feedback to parents about the quality of student work

Systematic Monitoring of Student Performance

- Performance is monitored through classroom questions, homework, frequent essays, quizzes
- Continual monitoring of individual and class progress; rapid feedback on homework
- Weekly and monthly reviews of student progress
- Use mastery learning to assess student progress after blocks of instruction
- Graph student progress
- Monitor independent work to increase time that student is engaged (move about to check accuracy, ask questions, give feedback)
- Grading motivates students if tied to objective performance and used judiciously

Emphasis on Basic Skills

- Communicate basic skills as the primary mission of schooling consistently to the student
- Increase silent reading time, which increases vocabulary and reading fluency (elementary school students average only seven to eight minutes a day of silent reading)

Organization of Instruction

- Systematic, preplanned structure to the learning process and time management
- Allocate time for instruction in proportion to the priority of the subject area
- Increase time allocated to instruction (teachers deliver instruction about 80 percent of the time they allocate; large variability exists across teachers)
- Increase time that student is engaged during time allocated for instruction; engaged time influences achievement of low-ability more than high-ability students
- Increase time on task during which a student experiences a high rate of success
- Increase practice related to materials on which evaluation will occur
- Maintain 90 to 100 percent success on practice activities before moving on to new objectives
- Make assignments neither too easy nor too hard, or on-task behavior will decrease
- The more content covered, the more is learned; as much as 80 percent of reading achievement can be related to pacing, with higher-ability groups being paced up to fifteen times faster than lower-ability groups
- Pace instruction rapidly but in small steps; vary the pace to allow students time to absorb the material
- Use both whole-class and small-group instruction
- Determine number and size of instructional groups based on student skill and characteristics as well as content; cross-age grouping is encouraged
- Use different groupings for different subjects
- Shift group membership frequently based on reassessment
- Select group membership on the basis of feedback during instruction (vs. tests)
- Teaching in small (two or less) and medium (three to nine) groups maintains attention better than large groups (ten or more)

(Continues on following page)

Table 12–1 *(Continued)*

- Classes should be heterogeneous with 1/3 or fewer being low-ability students
- Large or small heterogeneous groups are well suited to teaching material requiring no prior knowledge
- Small heterogeneous learning groups are effective for helping one another practice skills
- Homogeneous grouping for reading instruction is effective when coordinated with related heterogeneous activities; grouping also may be done by interest in different topics
- Hold two reading sessions a day for low-ability groups rather than one long session
- Avoid extreme heterogeneity in classes (for example, ten grade levels)
- Limit ability grouping to only a few groups, to allow adequate direct instruction time
- Decrease the use of worksheets to 50 percent (these often constitute 70 percent of daily reading time yet contribute little to yearly reading gains)
- Teach important subjects in both the morning and the afternoon
- Reduce transition time between activities (for example, reinforce students for getting materials quickly, rearrange seating to make access to materials easier)
- Shorten recess or free time
- Streamline organizational activities (for example, passing out papers; correcting papers) by increasing student self-management (for example, correcting own spelling papers, charting own progress)
- Develop cooperative learning environments, peer tutoring

Teacher Strategies
- Take an active, teacher-directed role in instruction, including extended time blocks to develop concepts and actively elicit student responses
- There should be greater teacher-directed instruction than independent work
- Check for understanding of new content and assignments by reviewing the previous day's lessons through questioning and quizzes
- Give oral or written frequent, detailed, and meaningful feedback, correction, and reteaching
- Use distributed, varied, and cumulative review
- Correct student errors immediately; keep corrections to thirty seconds or less to avoid the rest of the class becoming off task
- Assign independent practice to students
- Explicitly teach strategies and scaffold instruction
- Relate new academic content to a student's own life and previous learning
- Provide guided practice and drill; use a variety of activities and learning strategies
- Model the new process or product a student is expected to learn; clarify quality work criteria and how the work will be judged
- Provide choices so students have options for how to complete assignments; solicit student suggestions
- Begin work on assignments in class so assistance can be provided
- Use many detailed and redundant explanations when introducing a new concept, especially concrete and everyday examples and nonexamples
- Circulate among students as they do independent work, check student work, and give frequent, brief contacts to on-task students
- Provide daily opportunities to read easy material (96 percent accuracy level)

(Continues on following page)

Table 12–1 *(Continued)*

- Keep initial stages of learning at close to 80 percent accuracy; homework and seatwork at over 90 percent accuracy; high error rates correlate negatively with achievement
- Unknown material should range from 15 to 30 percent of the total material presented
- 50 or more repetitions, spread over several teaching sessions, may be necessary to reach automaticity
- Give clear instructions and demonstrate often; signal transition between key ideas
- Actively elicit student responses in small-group discussion (avoid passive listening)
- Use games and exercises that have a high response format rather than activities that require students to wait for a turn and listen to others
- Use a variety of learning modalities
- Use frequent comprehension checks, at least one question every two minutes; call on a student after rather than before the question has been asked, in order to maintain class attention
- Redirect questions back to the group
- Encourage students to paraphrase and summarize
- Use higher-order questions that stimulate application, analysis, and synthesis of knowledge
- Follow a set teaching sequence: overview, relationship to prior learning, key questions, demonstration, concrete and meaningful examples, practice, test, review, feedback
- Attention and success are increased by spending time discussing the goals of a lesson, how they fit with the scheme of things, and what to focus on for success
- Waiting three or more seconds after asking a question leads to more appropriate and higher-level responses, greater variety of responses, and more confidence in responding (teachers typically wait only one second)

Sources: Berliner (1984); Bickel & Bickel (1986); Brigham, Scruggs, & Mastropieri (1992); Carnine (1994); Dawson (1987); Englert (1984); Fisher, Berliner, Filby, Marliave, Cahan, & Dishaw (1980); Gersten, Woodward, & Darch (1986); Gickling & Thompson (1985); Glass, Cahan, Smith, and Filby (1982); Gottlieb (1984); Hudson (1996); Lipham (1981); Lloyd & Loper (1986); Purkey & Smith (1983); Rademacher, Schumaker, & Deshler (1996); Samuels & Miller (1985); Shapiro (1992); Shavelson (1983); Sikorski, Niemiec, & Walberg (1996); Stevens & Rosenshine (1981); White (1986); Wilson & Wesson (1986).

too much and ignore other important functions of schooling, such as developing students' higher-order cognitive reasoning and social skills. Two of the effective schools variables most highly related to academic outcome are the amount of structure provided through direct instruction and the amount of engaged time productively spent on task.

Direct Instruction. The achievement and social adjustment of students is enhanced when student needs and program characteristics are well-matched. For students with learning disabilities, this generally means structuring instruction and concentrating on teaching a few major criteria well (so that they will be applied as appropriate beyond the classroom), rather than teaching many concepts superficially.

Depending on their goals and teaching styles, teachers may organize instruction into teacher-directed group activities, teacher-directed individual activities, free-play situations (where children can choose among all activities available), and free-choice situations (where students are free to choose their activity but only from those that have been prepared by the teacher). Either a closed (teacher-directed) or open (free-choice) approach may be appropriate in different subject

Emmy

A baptismal battle for me was when I got out of being in one class all day. Now I am in regular classes this year. Last year I had no homework, and this year I have a lot. Last year if I did not want to do something I did not have to do it. If I do not do something this year I lose grades and only get half credit. I like this year alot better But it is a lot harder for me. I did not think I would ever get out of being in the same room all day. my grades have been very good. I have been really happy with them.

Now all I have to do is get my Reading and my other skills up there, and I will feel better about myself and school. maybe it will help me do better. I guess I have come a long way so far, I wish I could come even farther. I wish I was smart.

Source: Reprinted by permission of "Emmy."

areas, depending on the needs and characteristics of the student.

In the late 1960s and early 1970s, it was in vogue to replace the traditional, teacher-directed approach with self-paced, self-initiated student learning. This *open-education* instructional system was expected to foster more creativity and psychological well-being (happiness, self-esteem, lower anxiety) and yet be as effective as the traditional approach in fostering academic achievement (Lerner, 1981). Hyperactive and distractible children had the potential to be less disruptive in open-education classrooms because there was an expectation for active involvement and less need for children to focus on only one source of instruction; attention and learning could be self-paced (McNew, 1984). Nevertheless, study after study has found that psychological well-being has not been superior in the open-education classroom and that achievement in reading, mathematics, and other subjects has been inferior to that in the traditional classroom (Bell, Sipursky, & Switzer, 1976; Bennett, 1976; Ward & Barcher, 1975; Wright, 1975).

Lerner (1981) and others believe that students in traditional classes fare better academically than those in open-education systems because they spend more time working directly on academic tasks instead of being less goal oriented, waiting for teacher attention, and interacting socially with peers. Time on classroom and homework tasks is one of the most powerful predictors of achievement in all areas. Therefore, more traditional organization of instruction, or more teacher guidance in classrooms with constructivist philosophies, may benefit students with learning disabilities who require consistent teacher direction to focus attention appropriately, to remain on task, and to comprehend and remember what they are being taught.

Given the huge amount of material covered in textbooks (for example, 300 new science words per text in sixth grade and 3,000 terms and symbols in tenth grade), it is advisable for teachers to pick among topics, simplify the material, and teach a few "big" things well rather than covering many topics poorly (Woodward & Noell, 1991). Because texts "mention" so much, teachers can devote on average less than thirty minutes in instructional time per year to 70 percent of the topics covered (Porter, 1989). Such teaching for exposure rather than depth accomplishes little with respect to maximizing chances that the new information or skill will be remembered and applied in practical situations. Our students will be far better educated if we help them understand a few "big" ideas well rather than lots of things poorly (Carnine, 1994).

Engaged Time on Tasks. Research shows that when greater amounts of time are allocated to instruction, when students spend more of this time engaged on task, and when more of the engaged time results in successful learning experiences, the greater the academic gains (Anderson, 1984; Borg, 1980; Fisher et al., 1980; Guthrie, 1980). For example, Mevarech (1985) found that 20 percent of the variability in math achievement of second and fourth graders could be explained from observations of time on task. Unfortunately, students' daily amounts of academic learning time is shockingly low. Studies report that students are allocated approximately 50 to 60 percent of the school day for instruction yet are actually on task for only about 40 percent of the day (Rich & Ross, 1989). Almost three hours of every school day are spent in nonlearning time, which decreases in the following order: procedures (distributing worksheets, collecting students' materials, managing behavior, making announcements, clarifying classroom rules); waiting for instruction or one's turn; transitions between subjects or settings; free time; interruptions by teachers, students, or the public address system; eating/snack time. Rosenshine's (1980) findings are particularly bleak: of the 330 minutes a student was in school per day, instruction was allocated for only 170 minutes (52 percent), taught for only 135 minutes (41 percent), and attended to for only 93 minutes (28 percent). In their six-month observation of regular classes, Baker and Zigmond (1990) found that one-third of the instructional time was spent waiting for teacher directions, getting and putting away materials, and lining up and moving to new activities. There was no intensity or urgency in the learning that was taking place.

Observing a thirty-minute reading group of fourth to sixth grade students with learning disabilities, Miramontes, Cheng, and Trueba (1984) found that the individual reading time of each student ranged from a minimum of twelve seconds to a maximum of eighty-eight seconds. Of the thirty minutes available for reading instruction, only 23 percent was spent directly on reading; the rest of the time was spent waiting, attending to interruptions, giving directions, and asking or responding to questions. Time spent in writing activities is no more encouraging. Englert and her colleagues' (1988) review reports that students in the elementary grades composed only once every eight days, that only 3 percent of their time was spent in writing activities of a paragraph or more in length, and that students seldom wrote, edited, or revised for a sustained period of time. Instead, short sentences and paragraphs were the norm for answering teacher questions. Thoughtful development of ideas based on one's background knowledge generally was not encouraged.

When comparing the percentage time on task in the regular classroom to that in the resource room, some studies favor the regular class, others favor the resource setting, and yet others find no differences (Rich & Ross, 1989; Thurlow et al., 1983a). Thurlow and her colleagues (1983b) found that the time third and fourth graders had allocated to reading instruction and the time they actually spent in individual instruction was ten times greater in the resource room than in the regular classroom. Nevertheless, even in the resource room students spent more than half of their allocated instructional time looking for materials, raising hands, and engaging in other noninstructional activities. The students averaged less than fifteen minutes a day practicing reading. Haynes and Jenkins (1986) report equally low levels of engaged academic time in the resource room.

In a similar observational study in special classes for the learning disabled, it was found that students averaged only twenty-seven minutes of reading per day (Zigmond, Vallecorsa, & Leinhardt, 1982). In contrast, fifty-five minutes per day were spent simply waiting (for the teacher, for the rest of the class, for equipment) or in management tasks (getting ready, finding materials, putting things away). Clearly, regardless of the setting in which pupils are educated, too many opportunities for learning are being wasted.

If students could spend only a few of the wasted minutes just described in additional reading each day, their reading achievement probably would be affected positively. Allington's (1984) simple mathematics dramatizes this point. Beginning with an assumption that the student who is learning disabled may lose fifteen minutes of learning time daily when going from the regular class to a resource room, Allington states that:

Fifteen minutes a day is not much time but it translates into forty-five hours a year—a full two weeks of instructional days. Over a K–12 school experience, a total of 130 days are lost at 15 minutes a day—more than two-thirds of a school year! Nearly a year of instruction lost just in the time it takes to leave the regular education class, walk to the resource room, be greeted and have the day's instructional activity commence, and then to return to the regular classroom and begin to work there. (p. 95)

Homework is another avenue for increasing time on task. Time spent on homework is known to correlate positively with academic achievement (Polloway, Foley, & Epstein, 1992). A national survey of seniors in over 1,000 high schools found that grades and achievement test scores increased as the number of hours put into homework increased (Keith & Page, 1985). Homework was able to compensate partially for low ability, in that the average low-ability student who completed three to five hours of homework a week achieved higher grades than the average-ability student who did no homework at all. The more able students reported doing more homework than those who were lower in ability. Over half of the seniors reported doing less than three hours of homework a week. A 1990 survey of thirteen and seventeen year olds found that only about one-third of students spent as much as one hour or more per night on homework. Yet 40 to 50 percent watched television three to five hours per day (U.S. Department of Education, 1991). Most students perceive extracurricular activities and being with friends as more important than doing homework (Gajria & Salend, 1995).

Survey results from nearly 500 seniors who were learning disabled are equally discouraging (Gregory, Shanahan, & Walberg, 1986). Gregory and colleagues found that these students did significantly less homework than their nondisabled counterparts. Although the learning disabled engaged in homework only one to three hours per week, they watched TV for two to three hours daily and participated in extracurricular activities for an additional two to three hours a day.

Reluctance to do homework (complaining, avoiding beginning homework, taking unusually long to complete homework) and distractibility (daydreaming, being drawn off task by noises, completing homework only if someone is in the room or working with the student), poor study skills, forgetting to bring home assignments and materials, problems estimating time for homework, not checking to see whether homework is complete and failing to hand it in, frustration due to task difficulty and quitting, failing to break projects and reports into more manageable segments to work on a little at a time, and receiving less help and encouragement from parents but more criticism are common among students with learning disabilities (Bryan & Sullivan-Burstein, 1997; Epstein et al., 1993; Gajria & Salend, 1995). These unfortunately limit their opportunities for learning. Polloway and colleagues (1992) make several recommendations that could help these students with homework completion: make parents sign a diary of homework assignments; focus assignments on proficiency and maintenance-type tasks rather than new learning, so that 80 percent success is likely; help parents to set schedules and contingencies that encourage homework completion; teach students independent study skills. Bryan and Sullivan-Burstein (1997) also report that assigning meaningful tasks and graphing homework completion are very effective strategies.

As would be expected, assigning more homework does affect achievement of students with learning disabilities (Rosenberg, 1989). Another way to impact achievement is to make a concerted effort to decrease classroom time spent on class management, waiting, making transitions, and so forth. Aides, foster grandparents, and student teachers also can be used to help increase the time students spend actively engaged in instructional programs (Wilson & Wesson, 1986). A fourth promising approach is classwide peer tutoring, in which student pairs take turns listening to one another read and asking questions daily (Simmons et al., 1994). Presumably because of the daily increased opportunity to respond (in one study reading aloud increased from 2 percent of the time in group reading lessons with the teacher to 27 percent of the time during classwide peer tutoring; silent reading increased from 4 percent to 34 percent of the allocated time), remarkable increases in reading, spelling, math, and comprehension accuracy have been reported (Delquadri et al., 1986).

Research indicates that peer tutoring is effective for increasing the academic skills of both tutors and tutees; students with disabilities benefit from the tutoring role, and they do quite well at it with appropriate training and supervision (Cook et al., 1985–1986; Mathes & Fuches, 1984). In Mathes and colleagues' (1994) structured peer tutoring system, for example, the stronger reader reads for five minutes, followed by the weaker reader reading the same text. Errors are pointed out and tutors encourage tutees to figure out a hard word and reread the sentence before they tell them the word. The lower achiever then retells what had been read. After each paragraph the student stops to summarize the main idea in ten words or less. The student then predicts what will be read in the next paragraph, and the process begins anew. Points are awarded for good performance. Short training periods appear sufficient to teach appropriate helping behaviors to tutors (Bentz & Fuchs, 1996). Such training is important because often the stronger student will dominate, cut short explanations, convey faulty logic, and create confusion that only hampers the learning process (Pressley et al., 1996).

Various reports recommending educational reform have urged that the school day and year be lengthened and that more demanding requirements for homework be instituted (Cain et al., 1984). While increasing time on task by means of homework is likely to increase academic gains, simply manipulating the school day or year may not (MacKenzie, 1983). Such lengthening can succeed only if we make better use of this extended time. We have seen that there is plenty of opportunity for doing just that within the current school day without necessitating extensions (Bickel & Bickel, 1986; Wilson & Wesson, 1986).

Finally, the extent to which a teacher emphasizes different subject areas also impacts achievement (Cooley & Leinhardt, 1980). It is within the teacher's power to determine what is taught and for how much time it is taught. A teacher's choice of content is influenced by the perceived effort required to teach a subject, the perceived difficulty of the subject matter, and the teacher's personal enjoyment when teaching a subject (Schwille et al., 1981, in Berliner, 1984). Whether students maximize their engagement with the material that is presented and experience success will depend on the degree to which teachers incorporate the effective schools strategies in their instruction.

Human Characteristics

The character of an environment will reflect the attitudes and behaviors of its members. The most important members of the school environment are, of course, the classroom teacher and students. In this section we will look at attributes of classroom teachers and peers that can affect the academic and social success of students. We will find that many students with learning disabilities have difficulty drawing positive responses from their classmates and establishing friendships. In addition, teacher–student interactions tend not to be optimal in many general education classes. Given these findings, priority in our schools needs to be placed on finding ways to help children with learning disabilities be more valued, accepted, and befriended so that the resulting boost to self-esteem can motivate persistence and positively impact their life adjustment. Carol Blatt's story (pages 482 and 483) is a wonderful example of how one special teacher at the right time, and much personal strength, can help the student with a severe learning disability find satisfaction.

Teacher Characteristics

The teacher's attitudes and personality characteristics are key to setting a positive tone in the classroom. Goodlad (1984) found that teachers whose styles were predominantly positive spent about 10 percent of their time dealing with behavior problems. In contrast, those whose styles were predominantly negative spent about 42 percent of their time managing students' inappropriate behaviors. Clearly the classroom climate is influenced at least in part by the teacher's attitudes, and both can be key contributors to the success or failure of the student with learning disabilities. We shall explore a number of variables that have been

The Force IN Me That Said—You Are a Fighter and Survivor So Don't Give Up Regardless How Difficult Success Is

My name is Carol. I was born on March 27, 1955. I could not complete anything that I had to write down in elementary school and I was a very slow writer and reader however as the school system I was in was concerned I did not exist. When I entered the Sixth Grade and mathematically I had the skills of a sixth grader but I could not write anything down on paper and yet I had no trouble verbalizing what should have been written down on paper. My family was told by a school system who had not woken up until I had completed the

(Continues on following page)

The Force IN Me   *(Continued from preceding page)*

sixth grade for the first time that they sensed that a problem existed and I could not enter Junior High School. My mother said you have just woken up now and told us that there is problem well you will not hold her over and she will go onto Junior High School. In Junior High School Grade Seven I was placed in a class whereby all that the other children did not want to learn. After be exposed to one more year of the School systems inability to educate me my parents placed me in a private school.

Now to chapter two of my life—Grade Eight and the initial installment of you are a fighter, you will never give up and you will succeed regardless how difficult success is for you I walked into my Eighth Grade Homeroom and gradually came to know someone one who was also my Eighth Grade English teacher who continually instilled in me that you can learn regardless how difficult the work gets, you can be taught anything regardless how difficult and that even if it takes you twice as long or even three times as long you will succeed. She became the person who helped me with anything in Grades 8 to 12 that was difficult and frustrating for me to achieve and throughout all this and what she wrote in my school year book in Grade 12—DESPITE HOW DIFFICULT THE TASK, YOU ARE A FIGHTER AND YOU WILL NOT JUST SURVIVE BUT SUCCEED.

Now onto part three my parents had no expectations of my becoming anything but I told my sister that I wanted to go onto college and she told my parents that I had to be given that chance. I also new that when I completed college I wanted to educate those children like myself that no other teachers can educate. Despite the endless obstacles I was faced with in college and Section 504 not coming into play until after I completed college I was still determined to succeed. All those subjects that I could relate to real life experiences including most of the Education courses I received A+ in college. After I had to leave Student Teaching as a result of my disability and not abilities I took a course the following semester titled Introduction to Special Education. IT was the second time that the University gave this course which I got an A+ in and I read a book BY Mr. Gardner titled "Your Neurologically and Learning Disabled Child" a book for Parents to share with there Learning Disabled Child. From this book that I learned who I was and again what flashed back to me you are a fighter, survivor and you will succeed.

Shortly after reading this book that allowed me to understand who I was and why I continued to come upon obstacles in all parts of my life. With the voice within in me that comes through everytime I come upon an obstacles that says you will succeed and don't give up. I have continued to make many strives until today. It is my goal to do whatever I can to educate young LD Children . . . So Ends my vignette of where I am today a teaching for 15 years with a Master's Degree, 4 City Education Licenses, Permanent State Certification in both Elementary and Special Education and probably as many people have told me that I am the first person who is an LD Adult who is working toward a Degree in Educational Administration and Supervision. This Degree has taken me a long time to achieve I am currently still working toward this degree very part time and at my own pace and I will not stop until I have completed this degree. The End.

Source: Reprinted by permission of Carol Blatt.

found to influence teachers' attitudes and behaviors with regard to students with disabilities.

Attitudes toward Special Students. Much of the success of inclusion efforts hinges on the attitudes of general education teachers toward youngsters with disabilities. The greater the number of special education courses and workshops completed by a teacher, coteaching experiences with special educators, and the teacher's confidence regarding his or her teaching ability, the more willing the teacher is to include students with disabilities and adapt instruction (Alexander & Strain, 1978; Hannah & Pliner, 1993; Minke et al., 1996; Stephens & Braun, 1980).

While the teacher attitude research of the 1970s and 1980s suggested that regular classroom teachers were very negative or hesitant about accepting special students in their classes, the attitude in the 1990s has softened considerably. Teachers tend to accept those students with milder disabilities more easily, especially when the students will fit nicely into established instructional groupings (Alexander & Strain, 1978; Bryan & Pearl, 1979; Cartledge et al., 1985; McIntosh et al., 1993; Panda & Bartel, 1972; Rodden-Nord, Shinn, & Good, 1992; Vaughn, Schumm et al., 1996; Wiener, 1987). Special education teachers, however, tend to have a more favorable attitude toward the intelligence, task orientation, and motivation of exceptional students, as well as the potential for including these students in the regular classroom (Moore & Fine, 1978; Parish et al., 1977; Pullis, 1985).

Perlmutter and colleagues (1983), for example, report that regular class teachers rate teenagers who are learning disabled lower in intelligence, performance, and comprehension than do these same teens' special education teachers; the LD teachers appear to be more sensitive to the youths' personal difficulties, thereby rating them lower on these attributes than do regular class teachers. In Martin, Nagel, and Paget's (1983) study, first grade teachers indicated that they prefer those students who are more approachable, persistent, and adaptable. They would prefer to eliminate from their classes children with more active and distractible temperaments. If students

with learning disabilities sense the general education teacher's ambivalence, negativism, lack of understanding, and support, this could impact their performance.

Certainly building sensitivity among the school staff toward special-needs students is of prime importance. The impact of positive teacher attitudes on students is evident in Bear and Minke's (1996) study. Bear and Minke found that LD students who acknowledged academic problems, yet perceived their teachers' feedback and grading as positive, rated themselves just as smart and good at schoolwork as did their non-LD classmates. Likewise, when placed with general education teachers who were accepting of learning disabilities, LD students were not less well-liked or known than their peers; 90 percent had a mutual best friend (Vaughn, McIntosh, et al., 1993). Barbara Eddinger's poignant letter to her son's teacher, pages 485 and 486, is an especially moving appeal to the teacher to set aside typical biases and give her son a chance to grow and develop in this teacher's classroom.

Teacher–Student Interaction. Generally, teacher–student interactions appear to be more numerous, more positive, and of higher quality when the student with learning disabilities is being taught by a special education teacher (Dembo et al., 1978), although the child certainly is not purposely singled out or made to feel different in the regular classroom (Vaughn & Schumm, 1996). Some studies find that students with learning disabilities tend to have a lower rate of interaction with the teacher than their typical peers because the LD students tend not to ask for assistance or volunteer to answer questions, and teachers tend not to check on these students' learning (McIntosh et al., 1993). When more frequent interactions are found, these seem to be precipitated by differential teacher behavior related to the student's LD identification, or to student characteristics (difficult temperaments, distractibility, low frustration tolerance) that elicit teacher attention, criticisms, corrections, and warnings (Bryan, 1978; Chapman, Larsen, & Parker, 1979; Fellers & Saudargas, 1987; Keogh & Burstein, 1988; Pullis, 1985; Siperstein & Goding, 1983, 1985;

Dear Regular Education Teacher:

My son will be in your class next year. He has just finished a wonderful year in the Resource Room, and with the Regular Education Initiative at the doorstep of our school, he will be mainstreamed into your class. You will be the one who touches his life most in school, even though the special education teacher will be there to help you.

My son is a fine boy. You will like him. He wants to do well but he does not read well. His language skills are also quite low. He doesn't spell well and he doesn't know all his math facts yet. He sometimes has a hard time understanding when instructions are given too fast and too many are given at once. He may get mixed up at times, but he always tries hard. He won't cause any trouble. Please don't let him give up; the special education teacher is still there to help him. He won't often ask for your help. He'll be quiet.

For his sake, please don't accept sloppy work. His markovers and misaligned work are part of his learning disability but he can copy the work. Maintain high standards for him. Give pencil grades and expect him to improve. Use the improved grade as the permanent grade. He can do well if we set high standards for him.

It might be a helpful realization for you, as a regular education teacher, to consider the area of fairness. When a special education student is only required to do ten questions or half the homework, the other students often resent this. The realization that this may be the fair way must come from the heart of the teacher and be explained to the class from the beginning. Fairness is not having everything the same for every student, fairness is providing what each student needs to be successful. All students need to know that this is the standard.

Another idea which may be helpful is to talk to all students about individual strengths and weaknesses. Some strengths are very visible, like academics and sports. Some strengths are less obvious, like kindness and the desire to work hard.

Learning disabilities are handicaps that others may not be able to see but are very real. These hidden handicaps are affecting every part of my son's life. No student wants to fail and failing is what he and others like him have done. They need to achieve success at their own level and to be able to be proud of their effort. Praise the effort!

School is often a tough time for these kids and it is important that some part of each school day is enjoyable, or at least that students like my son understand the reason they are there: to teach them how to learn, to teach them the job skills they will need, to teach them how to get along with others, and to teach them how to follow instructions. Often these students will not learn or retain the information offered in the regular education classroom as readily as other students. They need to know there are reasons to keep trying. Always praise their efforts!

My last suggestion for you comes from the heart of a mother. I am working very hard to give you a whole human being. He is sensitive, loving, hard working, and desires very much to please you, his teacher. He'll try hard for you. Please help me give this child a sense of self-worth, of value to his life. He has faith in his family to love and support him and faith in his school to teach him the best way they can. He will learn at his own rate and in time he will get there. Please don't be frustrated or discouraged. He feels that enough for both of you. Try as hard as you can to help me build that self-esteem he so desperately needs to

(Continues on following page)

Dear Regular Education Teacher *(Continued from preceding page)*

survive. Offer information; you may find a spark of interest there. Try to share your love of learning with him, and if you find that spark, encourage him to branch out even if his specific interest does not fit into the curriculum.

Next to his parents, I believe you, his teacher, have the hardest job. Thank you for helping me to shape a positive, productive, whole person through your understanding, love, and encouragement.

Thank you for being willing to listen to the mother who is sharing her son with you this school year, so we can be prepared and confident through the sometimes tough but successful days together.

Source: Eddinger, B. A. (July/August, 1990), *LDA Newsbriefs,* p. 15. Reprinted with permission of *LDA Newsbriefs.*

Slate & Saudargas, 1986). Campbell, Endman, and Bernfeld (1977), for example, report that a hyperactive child's presence in a classroom was associated with increased disruptiveness in classmates and negative feedback from the teacher toward both the hyperactive child and the class. Vaughn and Schumm (1996) review studies indicating little praise for students with learning disabilities by regular class teachers, little feedback, and low expectations. In Alves & Gottlieb's (1986) study, the general education teacher asked fewer academic questions of the students with learning disabilities and gave them less extended feedback (for example, shorter explanations, fewer clues, fewer repetition of questions). Alves and Gottlieb explain that teachers may avoid such interaction in whole-class situations because they think that the slower students will take longer to arrive at answers or bore their classmates, in either case increasing the risk of class disruption.

Many studies have found that regular class teachers tend not to individualize instruction for students with learning disabilities or to systematically monitor learning, despite recognizing the desirability of doing so (Vaughn & Schumm, 1996). Adaptations remain infrequent even when teachers are given intensive training on how to

adapt a child's curriculum (Zigmond, 1996). Despite specific direction on making adaptations, teachers' adaptations tend not to be "special"; instead, teachers simply extend timelines to reach instructional objectives, delete an objective, lower the goals, or move the child out of the regular class for instruction (Fuchs et al., 1995). A recent national survey found that 66 percent of general education teachers thought it unfair to adapt tests for the learning disabled alone (Jayanthi et al., 1996).

Since teaching to the whole group is the norm, teachers are more apt to adopt practices that improve instruction for all learners, rather than implement a practice that meets the needs of only the learning disabled (Vaughn & Schumm, 1996). For example, teachers seem more than willing to implement the cooperative learning strategies described in Research Box 12–1. Among typical students, these techniques have been related to higher achievement and more positive social interaction than have traditional competitive learning systems. The achievement of students with disabilities in cooperative learning groups tends to be the same as in competitive systems, but achievement increases when cooperative learning includes individual accountability and group rewards (Jenkins et al., 1991; Johnson & Johnson, 1983, 1986; Johnson et al., 1986; Stevens & Slavin, 1991; Tateyama-Sniezek, 1990).

The willingness of a teacher to implement special strategies will make a big difference to a child with disabilities in that classroom, as will the teacher's sensitivity to how the teacher's behavior can be influenced by factors such as student gender, attractiveness, social class, and achievement level.

Teacher Nonverbal Behavior. Nonverbal behavior refers to those aspects of communication between people that do not involve written or spoken words. Teachers communicate positive and negative judgments to children through their facial expressions, body movements, and postures (Brophy & Good, 1974; Richey & Richey, 1978). These in turn affect students' self-esteem, how well they like their teachers, and their judgments of teacher performance (Brophy & Good, 1974;

RESEARCH BOX 12–1
Cooperative Learning Techniques

In cooperative learning every member of a group participates in activities that can be successfully completed only through interdependent and cooperative behavior. These strategies have been very successful in promoting social interaction, while avoiding the competitive atmosphere of the typical classroom. Positive effects due to the cooperative reward structure have been apparent on student achievement, race relations, mutual concern, self-esteem, time on task, perspective taking, and cooperativeness (Slavin, 1980).

Cooperative learning techniques can differ in subject matter, the way in which students help one another, the way in which groups interact, whether students or teachers choose the groups, whether grades or rewards are based on individual or group performance, and the amount of environmental modification, teacher preparation, or financial support required. It is common for students to be graded individually, although group scores are computed to determine which team has excelled. Grades may be assigned on the basis of test performance, accuracy of homework, individual effort, individual contribution to the group, individual improvement, or cooperativeness in the group. If individual scores are used to compute the group's score, it is wise to compare each student's performance against that of a student of equal ability in each of the other groups (for example, the top scorer in each team on the previous quiz, the second best scorers, and so forth). The highest scorer is assigned the maximum number of points (for example, 10), the second highest scorer 1 or 2 points lower, and so on. In this way each student, whether of high or low ability, is equally valued within the group because he or she has the opportunity to contribute the same number of points to the group's overall performance as anyone else. Because the group outcome depends on every individual's success, group members are motivated to encourage and help one another to excel (for example, explain information in a way that makes more sense than the teacher's explanations, quiz one another, demonstrate how to go about researching a topic). A modification of this approach is to assign students to heterogeneous groups to coach one another for a test. When the test is taken, "improvement

(Continues on following page)

RESEARCH BOX 12–1 *(Continued from preceding page)*

points" are awarded to each student based on comparison with past test grades. The improvement points are then tallied for each group. Because the student with learning disabilities has a good chance of contributing more improvement points to group scores than do typical learners, teammates are motivated to help the student prepare.

Groups of four students have been found to be optimum, composed of one high achiever, two average achievers, and one low achiever. A group may remain together for four to six weeks or even a whole marking period. The social skills necessary for successful cooperation must be taught, such as refraining from interruption, how to disagree agreeably, responding to others' suggestions, how to reach consensus, abiding by time limits, sharing feelings, generating memory strategies, how to ask for ideas or help, how to expand on someone else's ideas.

Inclusion of students with learning disabilities in cooperative groups is easier when these students are pretrained in the academic or cooperative skills required. In addition, the nondisabled need reassurance that their grades will not be negatively affected by such inclusion. This can be accomplished by keeping the requirements for the student who is learning disabled reasonable, offering bonus points to groups that include members with disabilities, and training students in peer-tutoring strategies (Johnson & Johnson, 1986). Bohlmeyer and Burke (1987) and Slavin (1983) offer comprehensive reviews of cooperative learning techniques. We will explore several of these.

Jigsaw
In Jigsaw, students are assigned heterogeneously (gender, race, ability levels) to groups of three to six students to teach each other some classroom content. Each person in the group is given a specific set of information to teach the others. In a social studies unit, for example, one student may be assigned social customs, another the nation's agriculture, another religious beliefs, and so forth. A biography might be divided into the person's youth, family, schooling, accomplishments, and so on. Students responsible for the same lessons across different groups get together to clarify their understanding of the materials and discuss how to make their teaching most interesting. Then they return to their groups to teach their sections. Finally, all students are quizzed on the entire content. Team scores may or may not be used. A variation of this technique is for all students to study all the content, but individuals are responsible for focusing on different aspects on the test.

Group Investigation
In Group Investigation, the class is assigned a general area of study, with each group being responsible for researching a specific topic. Students can choose the group that most interests them, although the teacher does encourage heterogeneity of ability, gender, and ethnicity within groups. The teacher sets up learning stations in order to facilitate the students' research activities. Once each group has gathered sufficient information, the group plans a report and presents it to the class. The class members are responsible for learning the materials presented by all groups.

(Continues on following page)

RESEARCH BOX 12–1 *(Continued from preceding page)*

Co-op Co-op

Co-op Co-op is a combination of Group Investigation and Jigsaw. Each group is assigned a subtopic to research, but then the group divides once again to research relevant mini-topics. The subgroups present their information to the group, which integrates it into a presentation to be made to the entire class. All students are ultimately responsible for all the material.

Student Team Learning

In Student Team Learning, group members are responsible for teaching one another the content, and the groups compete for mastery. If the groups are heterogeneously formed, the average quiz grade of team members can be the basis for group points. At other times students of equal ability engage in an academic tournament. The score each student earns is added to an overall team score. The winning team is recognized in some fashion, such as an announcement in the school newspaper. Grades, however, are based on students' individual quiz performance.

Circles of Learning

As in Student Team Learning, group members teach one another from a packet of information provided to each group. Group members sit in a circle facing each other and are responsible for sharing materials and helping one another. While individual tests are administered, group rewards also can be earned. For example, bonus points can be awarded to each member of a group if all members reach a certain criterion. Classwide cooperation can be encouraged by giving the entire class a reward if each group reaches a set criterion.

Small-Group Mathematics

Here the teacher decides on homogeneous or heterogeneous groupings and assigns students to groups after students submit names indicating whom they would and would not prefer to work with. Groups are composed of four members who work as a group to solve each math problem. Students are encouraged to share leadership, build on others' ideas, and confirm that everyone understands the problem's solution before moving on.

Team-Assisted Individualization

Also designed for mathematics instruction, Team-Assisted Individualization teams consist of four or five heterogeneously placed students. Students within teams are divided into dyads or triads. Students work their own problems. Then their partners check their accuracy, and team members monitor one another's progress. When students have questions, they consult their team members first. If still unclear, they consult the teacher. The program is individually paced so that when they feel they are ready, students take the test that matches their instructional objectives. At the end of each week, team scores are compiled based on the average number of units covered by each team's members. The team reaching the criterion number of units established by the teacher wins some form of recognition (for example, a certificate).

Chaikin et al., 1978). In Woolfolk and Brooks's (1985) study, direct and frequent teacher eye contact improved student attention, intensified participation, increased the amount of information retained, and boosted students' self-esteem.

There is evidence that the lower social status of students with learning disabilities in their classrooms is highly correlated with teacher attitudes toward these children (Garrett & Crump, 1980). Bryan (1974b) demonstrated one nonverbal way in which teachers may communicate these preferences to a child's classmates: teachers ignored the verbal initiations of students with learning disabilities significantly more often than the initiations of good learners. Likewise, Lyon (1977) found that pupils whose personal attributes were rated low by the teacher received significantly greater amounts of negative nonverbal behaviors from the teacher, such as avoiding eye contact, frowning, and lack of physical contact or encouragement. Unfortunately, other students take note of these teacher behaviors and adjust their attitudes about the social desirability of the student with learning disabilities accordingly (Foley, 1979). These teacher and peer attitudes in turn can greatly influence the way students with learning disabilities feel about themselves.

We know that children who give more positive nonverbal behaviors to teachers are more often liked by teachers and judged to be brighter (Good & Brophy, 1972). Unfortunately, many students with learning disabilities are not likely to initiate positive nonverbal interactions that would favorably alter teachers' attitudes toward them.

Gender Differences. The gender of the student seems to influence both the quality and quantity of interaction between students and teachers (Washington, 1979). In both elementary and secondary schools, males are disciplined more often than females and receive both more teacher approval and criticism (Brophy & Good, 1974; Carrier, 1983). Teachers also are more likely to use harsh or angry tones when talking with males than females, even when each has exhibited equivalent misbehavior (Brophy & Good, 1974). Moreover,

teachers tend to grade boys, but not girls, lower than their achievement warrants (Carrier, 1983). Shinn, Tindal, and Spira (1987) report that although equal numbers of their male and female subjects showed poor reading achievement, far more males were referred to special education.

Good and Brophy (1978) maintain that it is the disruptive behavior of boys that brings them more negative feedback, not an overt gender bias on the part of teachers. Brophy and Good (1974) explain that teachers generally interact more (both positively and negatively) with boys because boys stand out more; they provide more intense stimuli for teachers to react to. Regardless of the reason, sex is likely to play a role in the interactions of teachers with students who are learning disabled, the majority of whom are boys.

The gender of the teacher is an equally important factor to consider when looking at the ecology of the classroom. McIntyre (1988) found that female teachers were far more likely than male teachers to refer children displaying high levels of problem behaviors for alternative educational services; these more often will be males, due to their higher activity levels. Interestingly, McIntyre wondered whether students with learning disabilities who have male teachers might be denied access to special education services because their teachers believe that they have the situation under control.

Attractiveness. Several studies have reported that students whose appearance is odd or unattractive are more likely to receive poor grades, to be involved in negative interactions with teachers, to elicit lower teacher expectancies, and to be referred to special education (Ross & Salvia, 1975; Salvia, Algozzine, & Sheare, 1977). The physical appearance of students with learning disabilities appears to be an important influence on social status among their peers (Odom, McConnell, & McEvoy, 1992). It seems that some students who are learning disabled may be at risk for negative evaluation in this area because their social imperceptiveness is such that they can appear quite unkempt, and at times their cognitive disabilities are accompanied by subtle physical differences.

Social Class, Race, and Cultural Differences. A relationship between social class, race, cultural background, and teacher–student interactions also has been observed. Several studies have found that teachers hold more negative attitudes toward and have lower expectations of African American, Hispanic, and lower-income students (Jackson & Cosca, 1974; Rist, 1970; Smith, 1988). All other factors being equal, these students are referred for special education services at higher than expected rates (Bennett & Ragosta, 1984; Chinn & Hughes, 1987; Shinn et al., 1987). Teachers seem to give more praise, rewards, approval, support, and nonverbal reinforcement to middle-income children; they more often neglect, punish, and misunderstand lower-socioeconomic-status and African American children, especially boys (Brophy & Good, 1974; Smith 1988). In one study, Crowl and MacGinitie (1974) found that experienced white teachers listening to taped responses to school questions assigned significantly higher grades to responses given by white than African American boys, even though the boys gave identical answers. Similarly, Carter (1977, in Sattler, 1992) found that teachers' attitudes toward Hispanic American third and fourth graders became less favorable as these children's accents increased. This held true, to a lesser extent, even for Hispanic American teachers.

Ambert's (1991) research review reports that teachers display their bias against Hispanic American and African American students in a number of ways: isolating these students, communicating lower expectations, avoiding interaction and eye contact, leaving them out of class activities, calling on and praising them less often, not helping to develop their ideas as fully, not responding as positively to their comments, and asking them fewer questions. This type of bias against children from low-socioeconomic-status, racial, and culturally different backgrounds is particularly relevant to learning disabilities because the characteristics associated with learning disabilities are prevalent among students in these groups (Toro et al., 1990), and many students with learning disabilities come from culturally and linguistically diverse backgrounds.

Teachers need to learn to value the contribution that students from diverse backgrounds bring to the class and find ways for these students to feel comfortable sharing their rich heritages. The more multiculturalism is built into the curriculum and the more individual variability is respected, the more the personal self-worth and academic motivation of those who are in the minority are fostered.

Teachers must try to modify their programs to fit with the learning and behavioral styles brought to the classroom by students from various backgrounds. This includes learning which cultures tend to respect competitiveness and which cooperativeness, for which cultures time tends to "run" and for which it "walks" (for example, hurrying or taking forever to get through a test), in which cultures passive activity is favored and in which people are always talking and on the move, which prefer to stand close to and touch others and which prefer distance (e.g., for example, Latin Americans versus Anglo Americans), which seek eye contact and which feel that eye contact is disrespectful (e.g., Latin Americans versus Asian Americans), which prefer nonverbal to verbal communication, and so forth (Chamberlain & Medinos-Landurand, 1991). Teachers must be wary not to expect a child to behave in a certain way merely because of generalizations about a particular cultural group. There is tremendous heterogeneity within cultures, and each child must be approached as an individual within an ecosystem that may be uniquely his or her own.

As teachers learn to appreciate the origins of children's individual styles, they will be less likely to misjudge and respond to these students as indifferent, insolent, or arrogant. They also will be more apt to modify classroom patterns to match these students' natural preferences. For example, Mitchell (1992) describes how a Chicago school encouraged peer tutoring and close mentoring relationships by building on the "brotherhood" and "sisterhood" that united these African American students. These kinship bonds were associated with more positive decision making, achievement motivation, and numbers of students enrolling in postsecondary schooling. Likewise, Jordan,

Tharp, and Baird-Vogt (1992) describe the benefits to Hawaiian students when the teachers learned to behave more like these students' mothers: expecting children to handle major responsibilities and letting them decide how to get the job done. The children's pride, investment, and participation increased as the teacher withdrew from detailed supervision, minimized verbal directions, and presumed that the children would follow through responsibly by organizing and assigning tasks among themselves (e.g., setting up the room and learning centers, sweeping, straightening lockers).

Such class restructuring draws children's home and school lives closer together, thereby affirming their culture. This valuing can be conveyed in may ways: encouraging students to use their native language among themselves in school or to write in this language; posting signs or providing books in these languages; displaying pictures of their native countries; recruiting tutors or guest speakers who share similar backgrounds; and so forth (Langdon, 1992). When classrooms become responsive to the unique, culturally bound skills and behaviors that children bring with them, the schooling experience is less likely to be devalued as irrelevant and meaningless; conversely, children no longer feel the pressure to reject their culture in favor of the attitudes of the dominant culture. Feeling less alienated and more respected, positive energy can be devoted to managing the social and academic challenges of the school.

Achievement Differences.   Most research suggests that teacher behavior toward high- and low-achieving students differs more in the quality than the quantity of interaction. When frequency of interaction does differ, it usually favors the high achievers (Alves & Gottlieb, 1986). Higher-achieving students are more active participants in the classroom and receive more positive teacher contact and feedback. Teachers smile, nod, maintain eye contact, call on, give feedback to, and lean forward toward the pupil more often when they are told that he or she is a high than low achiever (Brophy, 1982; Good & Brophy, 1978; Parker et al., 1989).

Good (1981) summarizes additional ways in which studies have found teachers to treat low achievers differently from high achievers; paying less attention to them; waiting less time for them to answer questions; interrupting them more frequently; failing to provide clues or ask follow-up questions when the student is uncertain; criticizing more often for incorrect responses and praising less often for correct or marginal responses; requiring less work and effort from them; seating low-ability students farther away from the teacher, making it more difficult to monitor their learning; and providing these students with less accurate and detailed feedback. Because students with learning disabilities are low achievers in some areas, they are ready candidates for triggering these types of teacher biases.

Peer Characteristics

Peer relationships are an important part of the human aspect of the classroom setting. Research in this area indicates that students with learning disabilities do form friendship clusters with students who are like themselves (Farmer & Farmer, 1996). However, these students experience difficulty establishing friendships and drawing positive responses from typical peers. In fact, these children are rejected by their peers more often than one would expect (Bryan, 1976; Cartledge et al., 1985; Haager & Vaughn, 1995; LaGreca & Stone, 1990; Morrison, 1985; Parish, Ohlsen, & Parish, 1978; Sabornie et al., 1990; Sale & Carey, 1995; Wiener, 1987). At times, students with learning disabilities seem to be aware of their lower status, and at other times they are not (Bruininks, 1978a; Horowitz, 1981).

Why do peers react less favorably to their classmates who are learning disabled? For one thing, it is well known that popularity often is related to academic and athletic ability (Conderman, 1995; Hartup, 1983). In these respects, students with learning disabilities are disadvantaged before they even begin to get to know their peers. Low achievement, physical incoordination, reluctance to go out for sports, or school "pass and play" policies limit their social status. Further, some students who are learning disabled have attributes that make social communication and friendships difficult: comprehension and oral language difficulties, social imperceptiveness, poor perspective taking, learned helplessness, immaturity, impulsiveness, and poor social ingratiation tactics. When Perlmutter and colleagues (1983) found that nineteen of twenty-eight teenagers with learning disabilities were rated as average to well-liked in a lower-track classroom, they suggested that the greater homogeneity in that setting helped these students understand social cues more accurately; therefore, their social skills were more appropriate. With respect to the finding that girls with learning disabilities tend to be weaker in social status than boys, Perlmutter (1986) suggests that only the more severely involved girls are identified LD because girls are less disruptive in their behavioral styles than boys. Therefore, those who are identified are even more discrepant from their peers than boys with learning disabilities. We know that the more unusual a child is relative to his or her peer group, the more likely that person is to be rejected (Hartup, 1983).

Rejection of students with learning disabilities also may be a function of the identification process. When classmates are aware that these students have been identified by the school as academically less adequate than others, the social status of the student with learning disabilities can be affected negatively.

The reports that the self-concepts of students with learning disabilities tend to be lower in mainstream environments than in more segregated environments may relate to these students' social isolation or rejection, as well as to anticipation of critical evaluation by more academically superior peers. That students with learning disabilities are sensitive to peer evaluation was evident in Gottlieb's (1984) study where students made significantly more oral reading errors when reading in a group of more skilled peers than in a group of peers similar in ability. Gottlieb conjectures that depressed academic performance amid a higher-functioning peer group may only feed teachers' unnecessarily negative perceptions of students with learning disabilities, which further aggravates peer perceptions.

Exciting possibilities for modifying peer attitudes toward classmates with special needs are provided by *cooperative learning,* where the cooperative work of the group, including the student with learning disabilities, is necessary to ensure success at a task. Cooperative learning strategies seem to help students with disabilities to be viewed by their classmates either neutrally or as worthwhile, competent people, rather than being rejected (Johnson & Johnson, 1983, 1986). Teacher ratings of student self-concept and behavior show improvement favoring cooperative over competitive learning environments (Lloyd et al., 1988; Tateyama-Sniezek, 1990). Cooperative strategies have increased the nondisabled students' openness to sitting by and playing, talking, or working with students who are learning disabled. The student with a learning disability, in turn, seems to exhibit more positive social behaviors (listening, questioning, working together) (Bryan, Cosden, & Pearl, 1982). In an interesting study of cooperative swim instruction, where the goal was to have student pairs learn to swim by helping one another, more friendly interactions between boys with and without learning disabilities ensued during a later free-swim period than when the instructional focus had been on individual swimming achievement (Martino & Johnson, 1979).

Peer tutoring also has been successful in enhancing social acceptance and interaction among students with disabilities and their classmates, especially when specific social interaction strategies are taught, such as "Stay with your friend, play with your friend, and talk with your friend" (English et al., 1997; Greenwood, Carta, & Hall, 1988). Moreover, teachers can help facilitate friendship by pairing children for activities, designing activities that invite interaction among classmates, placing particular students' desks near each other, allowing quiet talk in the classroom so children can negotiate whom to play with on the playground and what to play, not withdrawing children for special assistance at times of high peer interaction, encouraging students to "first ask three others, and then ask me," and not instituting academic remediation or punishments during recess and play times (Doll, 1996). All these strategies help children become known to one another, which is critical in view of the tendency for students with learning disabilities to have lower rates of peer interaction than their typical classmates (McIntosh et al., 1993). Vaughn and colleagues (1993) found that the more highly students of all ages rated "knowing" students with learning disabilities, the better the LD students were liked. Because "likes attract" when it comes to friendship groups (Farmer & Farmer, 1996), and even preschoolers tend to select nondisabled or older, more mature children as play partners (Odom et al., 1992), teachers need to make very concerted efforts to help the learning disabled become befriended by their peers. The affective education strategies described in Chapter 10 can do much to facilitate this social integration.

Summary

The culture of the school, its organizational and interactional patterns, plays a significant role in students' academic and social adjustment. It is in this context that students are identified as learning disabled; schools can and do make a difference.

The physical, organizational, and human environments of school and classroom settings can affect students either positively or negatively. While background noise and visual distractions tend to diminish performance of all pupils equally, students with learning disabilities are the ones who can least afford any more lost opportunities for learning. Small schools seem to promote greater participation and feelings of responsibility among students. Open-space schools, although providing opportunities to develop students' self-direction in learning, have a decreased amount of structure and consistency, just the opposite of what students with learning disabilities generally require. Studies in classroom design and seating arrangement show that students seated near the front and center of the room interact more with the teacher. In addition, direct instructional approaches benefit students with learning disabilities more than do free-choice instructional approaches.

The most visible organizational attribute of schools relates to identification and placement. Students with learning disabilities generally benefit academically and socially from separate special classes. However, concerns with segregation have resulted in students with learning disabilities being included in regular classes whenever possible, with the necessary support services. Inclusion enables special students to benefit from interaction with their nondisabled peers and to access the regular curriculum.

Human attributes of the school setting include the attitudes and behaviors of teachers and peers. Many students with learning disabilities are not viewed in a particularly positive manner by general education teachers and classmates. Curricula that are sensitive to the various cultural backgrounds in the classroom, cooperative learning techniques, and peer tutoring have been helpful in enhancing the acceptance and social integration of students with learning disabilities.

The climate of the school setting is an important factor in "making it or breaking it" for students with learning disabilities. Evaluation of the physical, organizational, and human attributes of school settings is important in order to suggest modifications that can provide more academically and socially productive environments for these students.

References

Abikoff, H. (1979). Cognitive training interventions in children: Review of a new approach. *Journal of Learning Disabilities, 12,* 123–135.

Abikoff, H., Courtney, M. E., Szeibal, P. J., & Koplewicz, H. S. (1996). The effects of auditory stimulation on the arithmetic performance of children with ADHD and nondisabled children. *Journal of Learning Disabilities, 29,* 238–246.

Abrahamsen, E. P., & Sprouse, P. T. (1995). Fable comprehension by children with learning disabilities. *Journal of Learning Disabilities, 28,* 302–308.

Abrams, J. C. (1976). More on interdisciplinary cooperation. *Journal of Learning Disabilities, 9,* 603–604.

Abramson, M., Willson, V., Yoshida, R. K., & Hagerty, G. (1983). Parents' perceptions of their learning disabled child's educational performance. *Learning Disability Quarterly, 6,* 184–194.

Ackerman, P. T. (1995). Reading-disabled students with and without comorbid arithmetic disability. *Developmental Neuropsychology, 11,* 351–371.

Ackerman, P. T., & Dykman, R. A. (1993). Phonological processes, confrontational naming, and immediate memory in dyslexia. *Journal of Learning Disabilities, 26,* 597–609.

Ackerman, P. T., Dykman, R. A., & Gardner, M. Y. (1990a). Counting rate, naming rate, phonological sensitivity, and memory span: Major factors in dyslexia. *Journal of Learning Disabilities, 23,* 325–327, 319.

Ackerman, P. T., Dykman, R. A., & Gardner, M. Y. (1990b). ADD students with and without dyslexia differ in sensitivity to rhyme and alliteration. *Journal of Learning Disabilities, 23,* 279–283.

Ackerman, P. T., Dykman, R. A., Oglesby, D. M., & Newton, J. E. O. (1994). EEG power spectra of children with dyslexia, slow learners, and normally reading children with ADD during verbal processing. *Journal of Learning Disabilities, 27,* 619–630.

Ackerman, P. T., Weir, N. L., Metzler, D. P., & Dykman, R. (1996). A study of adolescent poor readers. *Learning Disabilities Research & Practice, 11,* 68–77

ACLD Newsbriefs. (1982, January/February). *142.* Learning Disabilities Association of America.

Adams, M. J. (1990). *Beginning to read: Thinking and learning about print.* Cambridge, MA: MIT Press.

Adams, R. S., & Biddle, B. J. (1970). *Realities of teaching: Explorations with video tape.* New York: Holt, Rinehart, & Winston.

Adelman, H. S. (1971). The not so specific learning disability population. *Exceptional Children, 37,* 528–533.

Adelman, H. S. (1978). The concept of intrinsic motivation: Implications for practice and research with the learning disabled. *Learning Disability Quarterly, 1,* 43–54.

Adelman, H. S., & Chaney, L. A. (1982). Impact of motivation on task performance of children with and without psychoeducational problems. *Journal of Learning Disabilities, 15,* 242–244.

Adelman, H. S., & Taylor, L. (1983). *Learning disabilities in perspective.* Glenview, IL: Scott, Foresman.

Adelman, H. S., & Taylor, L. (1986). Moving the LD field ahead: New paths, new paradigms. *Journal of Learning Disabilities, 19,* 602–608.

Adelman, H. S., & Taylor, L. (1990). Intrinsic motivation and school misbehavior: Some intervention implications. *Journal of Learning Disabilities, 23,* 541–550.

Adler, N. E., Boyce, T., Chesney, M. A., Cohen, S., Folkman, S., Kahn, R. L., & Syme, S. L. (1994). Socioeconomic status and health: The challenge of the gradient. *American Psychologist, 49,* 15–24.

Adler, S. (1979). Megavitamin treatment for behaviorally disturbed and learning disabled children. *Journal of Learning Disabilities, 12,* 678–681.

Adler, T. (1992, November). Prenatal cocaine exposure has subtle, serious effects. *Monitor.* American Psychological Association, 17.

Adler, T. (1993, June). Kids' memory improves if they talk to themselves. *Monitor, 8,* American Psychological Association.

Affleck, J. Q., Madge, S., Adams, A., & Lowenbraun, S. (1988). Integrated classroom versus resource model: Academic viability and effectiveness. *Exceptional Children, 54,* 339–348.

Aiken, L. R. (1987). *Assessment of intellectual functioning.* Boston: Allyn & Bacon.

Ainsworth, M. D. S., Blehar, M., Waters, E., & Wall, S. (1978). *Patterns of attachment: A psychological study of the strange situation.* Hillsdale, NJ: Lawrence Erlbaum.

Akshoomoff, N. A., & Stiles, J. (1995). Developmental trends in visuospatial analysis and planning: I. Copying a complex figure. *Neuropsychology, 9,* 364–377.

Alajouanine, Th., & Lhermitte, F. (1965). Acquired aphasia in children. *Brain, 88,* 653–662.

Alberti, R. D., & Emmons, M. L. (1978). *Your perfect right: A guide to assertive behavior* (3rd ed.). San Luis Obispo, CA: Impact Publishers.

Albinger, P. (1995). Stories from the resource room: Piano lessons, imaginary illness, and broken-down cars. *Journal of Learning Disabilities, 28,* 615–621.

Alexander, C., & Strain, P. S. (1978). A review of educator's attitudes toward handicapped children and the concept of mainstreaming. *Psychology in the Schools, 15,* 390–396.

Alexander, D., Gray, D. B., & Lyon, G. R. (1993). Conclusions and future directions. In G. R. Lyon, D. B. Gray, J. F. Kavanagh, & N. A. Krasnegor (Eds.), *Better understanding learning disabilities: New views from research and their implications for education and public policies.* Baltimore: Paul H. Brookes.

Algozzine, B., Morsink, C., & Algozzine, K. M. (1988). What's happening in self-contained special education classrooms? *Exceptional Children, 55,* 259–265.

Algozzine, B., O'Shea, D. J., Crews, W. B., & Stoddard, K. (1987). Analysis of mathematics competence of learning disabled adolescents. *Journal of Special Education, 21,* 97–107.

Algozzine, B., O'Shea, D. J., Stoddard, K., & Crews, W. B. (1988). Reading and writing competencies of adolescents with learning disabilities. *Journal of Learning Disabilities, 21,* 154–160.

Algozzine, B., & Ysseldyke, J. E. (1986). The future of the LD field: Screening and diagnosis. *Journal of Learning Disabilities, 19,* 394–398.

Allen, J. E. (1969). *The right to read—Target for the 70's.* Washington, DC: U.S. Department of Health, Education, and Welfare, Office of Education.

Alley, G., & Deshler, D. (1979). *Teaching the learning disabled adolescent: Strategies and methods.* Denver: London Publishing Co.

Allington, R. L. (1984). So what is the problem? Whose problem is it? *Topics in Learning & Learning Disabilities, 3*(4), 91–99.

Als, H. (1985). Patterns of infant behavior: Analogues of later organizational difficulties? In F. H. Duffy & N. Geschwind (Eds.), *Dyslexia: A neuroscientific approach to clinical evaluation.* Boston: Little, Brown.

Alster, E. H. (1997). The effects of extended time on algebra test scores for college students with and without learning disabilities. *Journal of Learning Disabilities, 30,* 222–227.

Alvarez, V., & Adelman, H. S. (1986). Overstatements of self-evaluations by students with psychoeducational problems. *Journal of Learning Disabilities, 19,* 567–571.

Alves, A. J., & Gottlieb, J. (1986). Teacher interactions with mainstreamed handicapped students and their nonhandicapped peers. *Learning Disability Quarterly, 9,* 77–83.

Aman, M. G., & Werry, J. S. (1982). Methylphenidate and diazepam in severe reading retardation. *Journal of the American Academy of Child Psychiatry, 21,* 31–37.

Ambert, A. N. (1991). *Bilingual education and English as a second language: A research handbook, 1988–1990.* New York: Garland.

American Academy of Ophthalmology. (1981). *Policy statement: Learning disabilities, dyslexia, and vision.* San Francisco, American Academy of Ophthalmology. In N. Flax, R. Mozlin, & H. Solan (1984). Learning disabilities, dyslexia, and vision. *Journal of the American Optometric Association, 55,* 399–403.

American Academy of Pediatrics. (1976). Committee on Nutrition. Megavitamin therapy for childhood psychoses and learning disabilities. *Pediatrics, 58,* 910–912.

American Council on Education, and Education Commission of the States. (1988). *One-third of a nation: A report of the Commission on Minority Participation in Education and American Life.* Washington, DC.: author.

American Psychiatric Association. (1994). *Diagnostic and statistical manual of mental disorders* (IV ed.). Washington, DC.

Amerikaner, M. J., & Omizo, M. M. (1984). Family interaction and learning disabilities. *Journal of Learning Disabilities, 7,* 540–543.

Ames, L. B. (1968). Learning disabilities: The developmental point of view. In H. R. Myklebust (Ed.), *Progress in learning disabilities* (Vol. 1). New York: Grune & Stratton.

Ames, L. B. (1977). Learning disabilities: Time to check our roadmaps? *Journal of Learning Disabilities, 10,* 328–330.

Ames, L. B. (1983). Learning disability: Truth or Trap? *Journal of Learning Disabilities, 16,* 19–20.

Ames, L. B. (1986). Ready or not: How birthdays leave some children behind. *American Educator, 10*(3), 30–33.

Amos, K. (1980). Competency testing: Will the LD student be included? *Exceptional Children, 47,* 194–197.

Anastasi, A. (1982). *Psychological testing* (5th ed.) New York: Macmillan.

Anderson, J. M., Milner, R. D. G., & Strich, S. J. (1967). Effects of neonatal hypoglycemia on the nervous system: A pathological study. *Journal of Neurology, Neurosurgery, and Psychiatry, 30,* 295–310.

Anderson, L. W. (Ed.). (1984). *Time and school learning: Theory, research, and practice.* New York: St. Martin's Press.

Anderson, R. C., Hiebert, E. H., Scott, J. A., & Wilkinson, I. A. G. (1985). *Becoming a nation of readers: The report of the Commission on reading.* Pittsburgh, PA: National Academy of Education.

Anderson-Inman, L. (1986). Bridging the gap: Student-centered strategies for promoting the transfer of learning. *Exceptional Children, 52,* 562–572.

Anderson-Inman, L. (1987). Consistency of performance across classrooms: Instructional materials versus setting as influencing variables. *Journal of Special Education, 21,* 9–29.

Annett, M. (1985). *Left, right, hand and brain: The right shift theory.* Hillsdale, NJ: Lawrence Erlbaum.

Aponik, D. A., & Dembo, M. H. (1983). LD and normal adolescents' causal attributions of success and failure at different levels of task difficulty. *Learning Disability Quarterly, 6,* 31–39.

Applebee, A., Langer, J., & Mullis, I. V. S. (1986). *The writing report card: Writing achievement in American schools.* Princeton, NJ: Educational Testing Service.

Archbald, D. A., & Newmann, F. M. (1988). *Beyond standardized testing: Assessing authentic academic achievement in the secondary school.* Reston, VA: National Association of Secondary School Principals.

Argulewicz, E. N. (1983). Effects of ethnic membership, socioeconomic status, and home language on LD, EMR, and EH placements. *Learning Disability Quarterly, 6,* 195–200.

Arlin, P. K. (1981). Piagetian tasks as predictors of reading and math readiness in grades K–1. *Journal of Educational Psychology, 73,* 712–721.

Artiles, A. J., & Trent, S. C. (1994). Overrepresentation of minority students in special education: A continuing debate. *The Journal of Special Education, 27,* 410–437.

Ashbaker, M. H., & Swanson, H. L. (1996). Short-term memory and working memory operations and their contribution to reading in adolescents with and without learning disabilities. *Learning Disabilities Research & Practice, 11,* 206–213.

Ashcraft, M. H., & Fierman, B. A. (1982). Mental addition in third, fourth, and sixth graders. *Journal of Experimental Child Psychology, 33,* 216–234.

Askov, E. N., & Kamm, K. (1982). *Study skills in the content areas.* Boston: Allyn & Bacon.

Atkins, S. P. (1991). Siblings of learning disabled children: Are they special, too? *Child and Adolescent Social Work, 8,* 525–533.

Aukerman, R. C. (1972). *Reading in the secondary school classroom.* New York: McGraw-Hill.

Austin, A. M. B., & Peery, J. C. (1983). Analysis of adult-neonate synchrony during speech and nonspeech. *Perceptual and Motor Skills, 57,* 455–459.

Axelrod, L. (1982). Social perception in learning disabled adolescents. *Journal of Learning Disabilities, 15,* 610–613.

Ayllon, T., Layman, D., & Kandel, H. J. (1975). A behavioral-educational alternative to drug control of hyperactive children. *Journal of Applied Behavior Analysis, 8,* 137–146.

Ayllon, T., & Roberts, M. D. (1974). Eliminating discipline problems by strengthening academic performance. *Journal of Applied Behavior Analysis, 7,* 71–76.

Aylward, E. H., & Whitehouse, D. (1987). Learning disability with and without attention deficit disorder. In S. J. Ceci (Ed.), *Handbook of cognitive, social, and neuropsychological aspects of learning disabilities* (Vol. 2). Hillsdale, NJ: Lawrence Erlbaum.

Ayres, A. J. (1975). Sensorimotor foundations of academic ability. In W. M. Cruickshank & D. P. Hallahan (Eds.), *Perception and learning disabilities in children* (vol. 2). Syracuse, NY: Syracuse University Press.

Azar, B. (1995, March). Psychological damage by toxicants being researched. *Monitor,* American Psychological Association, 25.

Azar, B. (1995, July). Which traits predict job performance. *Monitor.* American Psychological Association, 30–31.

Azar, B. (1996, January). Sound patterns: Learning language keys. *Monitor.* American Psychological Association, 20.

Baddeley, A. (1994). The magical number seven: Still magic after all these years? *Psychological Review, 101,* 353–356.

Baddeley, A. D. (1981). Cognitive psychology and psychometric theory. In M. P. Friedman, J. P. Das, & N. O'Connor (Eds.), *Intelligence and learning.* New York: Plenum.

Baddeley, A. D. (1986). *Working memory.* London: Oxford University Press.

Badian, N. A. (1983). Dyscalculia and nonverbal disorders of learning. In H. Myklebust (Ed.), *Progress in learning disabilities* (Vol. 5). New York: Grune & Stratton.

Badian, N. A. (1988). The prediction of good and poor reading before kindergarten entry: A nine-year follow-up. *Journal of Learning Disabilities, 21,* 98–103, 123.

Badian, N. A. (1993). Predicting reading progress in children receiving special help. *Annals of Dyslexia, 43,* 90–109.

Badian, N. A. (1996). Dyslexia: A validation of the concept at two age levels. *Journal of Learning Disabilities, 29,* 102–112.

Baker, J. G., Ceci, S. J., & Herrmann, D. (1987). Semantic structure and processing: Implications for the learning disabled child. In H. L. Swanson (Ed.), *Advances in learning and behavioral disabilities: Memory and learning disabilities.* Greenwich, CT: JAI Press.

Baker, J. M., & Zigmond, N. (1990). Are regular education classes equipped to accommodate students with learning disabilities? *Exceptional Children, 56,* 515–526.

Baker, L. A., Decker, S. N., & DeFries, J. C. (1984). Cognitive abilities in reading-disabled children: A longitudinal study. *Journal of Child Psychology and Psychiatry, 25,* 111–117.

Bakker, D. J. (1970). Temporal order perception and reading retardation. In D. J. Bakker & P. Satz (Eds.), *Specific reading disability: Advances in theory and method.* Rotterdam: Rotterdam University Press.

Bakker, D. J. (1972). *Temporal order in disturbed reading: Developmental and neuropsychological aspects in normal and reading retarded children.* Rotterdam: Rotterdam University Press.

Bakker, D. J. (1983). Hemispheric specialization and specific reading retardation. In M. Rutter (Ed.), *Developmental neuropsychiatry.* New York: Guilford Press.

Bakker, D. J. (1984). The brain as dependent variable. *Journal of Clinical Neuropsychology, 6,* 1–16.

Bakker, D. J., Bouma, A., & Gardien, C. J. (1990). Hemisphere-specific treatment of dyslexia subtypes. A field experiment. *Journal of Learning Disabilities, 23,* 433–438.

Bakker, D. J., & de Wit, J. (1977). Perceptual and cortical immaturity in developmental dyslexia. In L. Tarnopol & M. Tarnopol (Eds.), *Brain function and reading disabilities.* Baltimore: University Park Press.

Bakker, D. J., & Licht, P, (1986). Learning to read: Changing horses in mid-stream. In G. Th. Pavlidis & D. F. Fisher (Eds.), *Dyslexia: Its neuropsychology and treatment.* New York: John Wiley & Sons.

Bakker, D. J., Moerland, R., & Goekoop-Hoefkens, M. (1981). Effects of hemisphere-specific stimulation on the reading performance of dyslexic boys: A pilot study. *Journal of Clinical Neuropsychology, 3,* 155–159.

Bakker, D. J., Smink, T., & Reitsma, P. (1973). Ear dominance and reading ability. *Cortex, 9,* 301–312.

Bakker, D. J., Teunissen, J., & Bosch, J. (1976). Development of laterality-reading patterns. In R. M. Knights & D. J. Bakker (Eds.), *The neuropsychology of learning disorders: Theoretical approaches.* Baltimore: University Park Press.

Bakker, D. J., & Vinke, J. (1985). Effects of hemisphere-specific stimulation on brain activity and reading in dyslexics. *Journal of Clinical and Experimental Neuropsychology, 7,* 505–525.

Ball, E. W., & Blachman, B. A. (1988). Phoneme segmentation training: Effect on reading readiness. *Annals of Dyslexia, 38,* 208–225.

Ball, E. W., & Blachman, B. A. (1991). Does phoneme awareness training in kindergarten make a difference in early word recognition and developmental spelling? *Reading Research Quarterly, 26,* 49–66.

Balow, B., & Blomquist, M. (1965). Young adults ten to fifteen years after severe reading disability. *Elementary School Journal, 66,* 44–48.

Balow, I. H. (1964). The effects of homogeneous grouping in seventh grade arithmetic. *Arithmetic Teacher, 11,* 186–191.

Bandura, A. (1969). *Principles of behavior modification.* New York: Holt, Rinehart and Winston.

Bandura, A., Grusec, J. E., & Menlove, F. L. (1966). Observational learning as a function of symbolization and incentive set. *Child Development, 37,* 499–506.

Banks, J. A. (1993). Multicultural education: Characteristics and goals. In J. A. Banks & C. A. McGee Banks (Eds.), *Multicultural education: Issues and perspectives* (2nd ed.). Boston: Allyn & Bacon.

Baratz, J. C., & Shuy, R. D. (Eds.). (1969). *Teaching black children to read.* Washington, DC: Center for Applied Linguistics.

Barenbaum, E., Newcomer, P., & Nodine, B. (1987). Children's ability to write stories as a function of variation in task, age, and developmental level. *Learning Disability Quarterly, 10,* 175–188.

Barker, R. G., & Gump, P. (1964). *Big school, small school.* Stanford, CA: Stanford University Press.

Barkley, R. A. (1977). A review of stimulant drug research with hyperkinetic children. *Journal of Child Psychology and Psychiatry, 18,* 137–165.

Barkley, R. A. (1981). *Hyperactive children: A handbook for diagnosis and treatment.* New York: Guilford Press.

Barkley, R. A. (1987). *Defiant children: A clinician's manual for parent training.* New York: Guilford Press.

Barkley, R. A. (1991). Attention deficit hyperactivity disorder. *Psychiatric Annals, 91,* 725–733.

Barkley, R. A., Cunningham, C. E., & Karlsson, J. (1983). The speech of hyperactive children and their mothers: Comparison with normal children and stimulant drug effects. *Journal of Learning Disabilities, 16,* 105–110.

Barkley, R. A., DuPaul, G. J., & McMurray, M. B. (1990). Comprehensive evaluation of attention deficit disorder with and without hyperactivity as defined by research criteria. *Journal of Consulting and Clinical Psychology, 58,* 775–789.

Barkley, R. A., Karlsson, F., Strzelecki, E., & Murphy, J. V. (1984). Effects of age and Ritalin dosage on the mother-child interactions of hyperactive children. *Journal of Consulting and Clinical Psychology, 52,* 750–758.

Barnes, A. B., Colton, T., Gundersen, J., Noller, K. L., Tilley, B. C., Strama, T., Townsend, D. E., Hatab, P., & O'Brien, P. C. (1980). Fertility and outcome of pregnancy in women exposed in utero to diethylstilbestrol. *New England Journal of Medicine, 302,* 609–613.

Barrett, G. V., & Depinet, R. L. (1991). A reconsideration of testing for competence rather than for intelligence. *American Psychologist, 46,* 1012–1024.

Barsch, R. H. (1967). *Achieving perceptual motor efficiency.* Seattle: Special Child Publications.

Bartel, N. R., & Bryen, D. N. (1982). Problems in language development. In D. D. Hammill & N. R. Bartel (Eds.), *Teaching children with learning and behavior problems* (3rd ed.). Boston: Allyn & Bacon.

Basic Behavioral Science Task Force of the National Advisory Mental Health Council (1996). Basic behavioral science research for mental health: Perception, attention, learning, and memory. *American Psychologist, 51,* 133–142.

Bassett, D. S., & Smith, T. E. C. (1996). Transition in an era of reform. *Journal of Learning Disabilities, 29,* 161–166.

Bateman, B. (1965). An educator's view of a diagnostic approach to learning disorders. In J. Hellmuth (Ed.), *Learning Disorders* (Vol. 1). Seattle: Special Child Publications.

Bateman, B. (1968). The efficacy of an auditory and a visual method of first grade reading instruction with auditory and visual learners. In H. Smith (Ed.), *Perception and reading.* Newark, DE: International Reading Association.

Bateman, B. (1974). Educational implications of minimal brain dysfunction. *Reading Teacher, 27,* 662–668.

Battle, J., & Blowers, T. (1982). A longitudinal comparative study of the self-esteem of students in regular and special education classes. *Journal of Learning Disabilities, 15,* 100–102.

Bauer, P. J. (1996). What do infants recall of their lives? Memory for specific events by one to two year olds. *American Psychologist, 51,* 29–41.

Bauer, R. H. (1979a). Recall after a short delay and acquisition in learning disabled and nondisabled children. *Journal of Learning Disabilities, 12,* 596–607.

Bauer, R. H. (1979b). Memory, acquisition, and category clustering in learning disabled children. *Journal of Experimental Child Psychology, 27,* 365–383.

Bauer, R. H. (1987). Control processes as a way of understanding, diagnosing, and remediating learning disabilities. In H. L. Swanson (Ed.), *Advances in learning and behavioral disabilities: Memory and learning disabilities.* Greenwich, CT: JAI Press.

Baumrind, D. (1972). Socialization and instrumental competence in young children. In W. W. Hartup (Ed.), *The young child: Reviews of research* (Vol. 2.) Washington, DC: National Association for the Education of Young Children.

Baumrind, D. (1975). The contributions of the family to development of competence in children. *Schizophrenia Bulletin, 14,* 12–37.

Bayley, N. (1943). Size and body build of adolescents in relation to rate of skeletal maturing. *Child Development, 14,* 47–89.

Bayley, N. (1949). Consistency and variability in the growth of intelligence from birth to eighteen years. *Journal of Genetic Psychology, 75*, 165–196.

Bayley, N., & Jones, M. C. (1955). Physical maturing among boys as related to behavior. In W. E. Martin & C. B. Stendler (Eds.), *Reading in child development,* New York: Harcourt, Brace & Co.

Bayley, N., & Schaeffer, E. S. (1964). Correlations of maternal and child behaviors with the development of mental abilities. *Monographs of the Society for Research in Child Development, 29*(6).

Bear, G. G., Juvonen, J., & McInerney, F. (1993). Self-perceptions and peer relations of boys with and boys without learning disabilities in an integrated setting: A longitudinal study. *Learning Disability Quarterly, 16*, 127–136.

Bear, G. G., & Minke, K. M. (1996). Positive bias in maintenance of self-worth among children with LD. *Learning Disability Quarterly, 19*, 23–32.

Beardslee, E. C. (1978). Teaching computational skills with a calculator. In M. Suydam & R. Reys (Eds.), *Developing computational skills: 1978 yearbook.* Reston, VA: National Council of Teachers of Mathematics.

Beattie, S., Grisé, P., & Algozzine, B. (1983). Effects of test modifications on the minimum competency performance of learning disabled students. *Exceptional Children, 6,* 75–77.

Beck, I. L., & Juel, C. (1995). The role of decoding in learning to read. *American Educator, 19*(2), 8, 21–25, 39–42.

Becker, W. C. (1964). Consequences of different kinds of parental discipline. In M. L. Hoffman & L. W. Hoffman (Eds.), *Review of child development research* (Vol. 1). New York: Russell Sage Foundation.

Beckman, P. J., & Lieber, J. (1992). Parent-child social relationships and peer social competence of preschool children with disabilities. In S. L. Odom, S. R. McConnell, & M. A. McEvoy (Eds.). *Social competence of young children with disabilities: Issues and strategies for intervention.* Baltimore: Paul H. Brookes.

Bee, H. L., Barnard, K. E., Eyres, S. J., Gray, C. A., Hammond, M. A., Spietz, A. L., Snyder, C., & Clark, B. (1982). Prediction of IQ and language skill from perinatal status, child performance, family characteristics, and mother-infant interaction. *Child Development, 53,* 1134–1156.

Beeken, D., & Janzen, H. L. (1978). Behavioral mapping of student activity in open-area and traditional schools. *American Educational Research Journal, 15,* 507–517.

Belfiore, P. J., Grskovic, J. A., Murphy, A. M., & Zentall, S. S. (1996). The effects of antecedent color on reading for students with learning disabilities and co-occuring attention-deficit/hyperactivity disorder. *Journal of Learning Disabilities, 29,* 432–438.

Bell, A. E., Abrahamson, D. S., & McRae, K. N. (1977). Reading retardation: A 12 year prospective study. *Journal of Pediatrics, 91,* 363–370.

Bell, A. E., Sipursky, M. A., & Switzer, F. (1976). Informal or open-area education in relation to achievement and personality. *British Journal of Educational Psychology, 46,* 235–243.

Bell, P. F., Lentz, F. E., & Graden, J. L. (1992). Effects of curriculum-test overlap on standardized achievement test scores: Identifying systematic confounds in educational decision making. *School Psychology Review, 21,* 644–655.

Bell, R. Q., & Waldrop, M. F. (1989). Achievement and cognition correlates of minor physical anomalies in early development. In M. H. Bornstein & N. A. Krasnegor (Eds.), *Stability and continuity in mental development: Behavioral and biological perspectives.* Hillsdale, NJ: Lawrence Erlbaum.

Bell, R. W., Miller, C. E., Ordy, J. M., & Rolstein, C. (1971). Effects of population density and living space upon neuroanatomy, neurochemistry, and behavior in the C57B1/10 mouse. *Journal of Comparative and Physiological Psychology, 75,* 258–263.

Bellinger, D., Leviton, A., Waternaux, C., Needleman, H., & Rabinowitz, M. (1987). Longitudinal analyses of prenatal and postnatal lead exposure and early cognitive development. *The New England Journal of Medicine, 316,* 1037–1043.

Belmont, L., & Birch, H. G. (1963). Lateral dominance and right-left awareness in normal children. *Child Development, 34,* 257–270.

Belsky, J. (1981). Early human experience: A family perspective. *Developmental Psychology, 17,* 3–23.

Bendell, D., Tollefson, N., & Fine, M. (1980). Interaction of locus-of-control orientation and the performance of learning disabled adolescents. *Journal of Learning Disabilities, 13,* 83–86.

Bender, W. N. (1987). Secondary personality and behavioral problems in adolescents with learning disabilities. *Journal of Learning Disabilities, 20,* 280–285.

Bender, W. N., & Golden, L. B. (1988). Adaptive behavior of learning disabled and non-learning disabled children. *Learning Disability Quarterly, 11,* 55–61.

Bender, W. N., & Smith, J. F. (1990). Classroom behavior of children and adolescents with learning disabilities: A meta-analysis. *Journal of Learning Disabilities, 23,* 298–305.

Bender, W. N., Vail, C. O, & Scott, K. (1995). Teachers' attitudes toward increased mainstreaming: Implementing effective instruction for students with learning disabilities. *Journal of Learning Disabilities, 28,* 87–94, 120.

Bennett, N. (1976). *Teaching styles and pupil progress.* Cambridge, MA: Harvard University Press.

Bennett, R. E., & Ragosta, M. (1984). *A research context for studying admissions tests and handicapped populations.* Princeton: Educational Testing Service.

Bennett, R. E., & Shepherd, M. J. (1982). Basic measurement proficiency of learning disability specialists. *Learning Disability Quarterly, 5,* 177–184.

Benton, A. (1962). Dyslexia in relation to form perception and directional sense. In J. Money (Ed.), *Reading disability progress and research needs in dyslexia.* Baltimore: Johns Hopkins Press.

Benton, A. (1973). Minimal brain dysfunction from a neuropsychological point of view. *Annals of the New York Academy of Sciences, 205,* 29–37.

Benton, A. L., & Pearl, D. (1978). *Dyslexia: An appraisal of current knowledge.* New York: Oxford University Press.

Benton, C. D. (1969). Dyslexia and dominance: Some second thoughts. *Journal of Pediatric Ophthalmology, 6,* 220–222.

Bentz, J. L., & Fuchs, L. S. (1996). Improving peers' helping behavior to students with learning disabilities during mathematics peer tutoring. *Learning Disability Quarterly, 19,* 202–215.

Bentzen, F. (1963). Sex ratios in learning and behavior disorders. *American Journal of Orthopsychiatry, 33,* 92–98.

Berberian, K. E., & Snyder, S. S. (1982). The relationship of temperament and stranger reaction for younger and older infants. *Merrill-Palmer Quarterly, 28,* 79–94.

Bereiter, C., & Scardamalia, M. (1982). From conversation to composition: The role of instruction in a developmental process. In R. Glaser (Ed.), *Advances in instructional psychology* (Vol. 2). Hillsdale, NJ: Erlbaum.

Berg, R. C., & Wages, L. (1982). Group counseling with the adolescent learning disabled. *Journal of Learning Disabilities, 15,* 276–277.

Bergerud, D., Lovitt, T. C., & Horton, S. (1988). The effectiveness of textbook adaptations in life science for high school students with learning disabilities. *Journal of Learning Disabilities, 21,* 70–76.

Bergman, L. R. (1981). Is intellectual development more vulnerable in boys than in girls? *Journal of Genetic Psychology, 138,* 175–181.

Berk, L. E. (1997). *Child Development* (4th ed). Boston: Allyn & Bacon.

Berler, E. S., Gross, A. M., & Drabman, R. S. (1982). Social skills training with children: Proceed with caution. *Journal of Applied Behavior Analysis, 15,* 41–53.

Berlin, C. I., Hughes, L. F., Lowe-Bell, S. S., & Berlin, H. L. (1973). Dichotic right ear advantage in children 5 to 13. *Cortex, 9,* 394–402.

Berliner, D. C. (1984). The half-full glass: A review of research on teaching. In P. L. Hosford (Ed.), *Using what we know about teaching.* Alexandria, VA: Association for Supervision and Curriculum Development.

Berninger, V. W. (1990). Multiple orthographic codes: Key to alternative instructional methodologies for developing the orthographic-phonological connections underlying word identification. *School Psychology Review, 19,* 518–533.

Bernstein, B. (1960). Language and social class. *British Journal of Sociology, 11,* 271–276.

Berrueta-Clement, J. R., Schweinhart, L. J., Barnett, W. S., Epstein, A. S., & Weikart, D. P. (1984). *Changed lives: The effects of the Perry preschool program on youths through age 19.* Ypsilanti, MI: High/Scope Press.

Bessell, H., & Palomares, U. (1972). *Human development program.* San Diego: Human Development Training Program.

Betts, E. A. (1936). *The prevention and correction of reading difficulties.* San Francisco: Row.

Bever, T. G., & Chiarello, R. J. (1974). Cerebral dominance in musicians and nonmusicians, *Science, 185,* 537–539.

Bickel, W. E., & Bickel, D. D. (1986). Effective schools, classrooms, and instruction: Implications for special education. *Exceptional Children, 52,* 489–500.

Bigler, E. D. (1992). The neurobiology and neuropsychology of adult learning disorders. *Journal of Learning Disabilities, 25,* 488–506.

Bijou, S. W. (1970). What psychology has to offer education—now. *Journal of Applied Behavior Analysis, 3,* 65–71.

Billingsley, B. S., & Wildman, T. M. (1988). The effects of prereading activities on the comprehension monitoring of learning disabled adolescents. *Learning Disabilities Research, 4,* 36–44.

Bireley, M., & Manley, E. (1980). The learning disabled student in a college environment: A report of Wright State University's program. *Journal of Learning Disabilities, 13,* 7–10.

Blachman, B. A. (1984). Relationship of rapid naming ability and language analysis skills to kindergarten and first grade reading achievement. *Journal of Educational Psychology, 76,* 610–622.

Blachman, B. A. (1991). Early intervention for children's reading problems: Clinical applications of the research in phonological awareness. *Topics in Language Disorders, 12,* 51–65.

Blachman, B. A. (1993). Early literacy acquisition: The role of phonological awareness. In G. Wallach & K. Butler (Eds.), *Language learning disabilities in school-age children and adolescents: Some underlying principles and applications.* Columbus, OH: Charles Merrill.

Blachman, B. A. (1994). What we have learned from longitudinal studies of phonological processing and reading, *and* some unanswered questions: A response to Torgesen, Wagner, and Rashotte. *Journal of Learning Disabilities, 27,* 287–291.

Black, F. W. (1973). Neurological dysfunction and reading disorders. *Journal of Learning Disabilities, 6,* 313–316.

Blackorby, J., & Wagner, M. (1996). Longitudinal postschool outcomes of youth with disabilities: Findings from the National Longitudinal Transition Study. *Exceptional Children, 62,* 399–413.

Blackwell, S. L., McIntyre, C. W., & Murray, M. E. (1983). Information processed from brief visual displays by learning-disabled boys. *Child Development, 54,* 927–940.

Blalock, J. W (1982). Persistent auditory language deficits in adults with learning disabilities. *Journal of Learning Disabilities, 15,* 604–609.

Blandford, B. J., & Lloyd, J. W. (1987). Effects of a self-instructional procedure on handwriting. *Journal of Learning Disabilities, 20,* 342–346.

Blankenship, C. S. (1984). Curriculum and instruction: An examination of models in special and regular education. In J. F. Cawley (Ed.), *Developmental teaching of mathematics for the learning disabled.* Rockville, MD: Aspen.

Blankenship, C. S., & Baumgartner, M. D. (1982). Programming generalization of computational skills. *Learning Disability Quarterly, 5,* 152–162.

Blatt, B. (1970). *Exodus from pandemonium: Human abuse and a reformation of public policy.* Boston: Allyn & Bacon.

Blatt, B. (1979). Bandwagons also go to funerals: Unmailed letters 1 and 2. *Journal of Learning Disabilities, 12,* 222–224.

Blick, D. W., & Test, D. W. (1987). Effects of self-recording on high-school students' on-task behavior. *Learning Disabilities Quarterly, 10,* 203–213.

Bliesmer, E. P., & Yarborough, B. H. (1965). A comparison of ten different beginning reading programs in first grade. *Phi Delta Kappan, 46,* 500–504.

Bloom, B. S. (1976). *Human characteristics and school learning.* New York: McGraw-Hill.

Bloom, B. S., Englehart, M. D., Furst, E. J., Hill, W. H., & Krathwohl, D. R. (1956). *Taxonomy of educational objectives, Handbook I: Cognitive domain.* New York: David McKay.

Bloom, L. (1970). *Language development: Form and function in emerging grammars.* Cambridge, MA: MIT Press.

Bloom, L. (1978 December). *LD cubed.* Paper presented at the meetings of the New York Association for the Learning Disabled. New York City.

Boder, E. (1971). Developmental dyslexia: Prevailing diagnostic concepts and a new diagnostic approach. In H. R. Myklebust (Ed.), *Progress in learning disabilities* (Vol. II). New York: Grune & Stratton.

Boder, E. (1973). Developmental dyslexia: A diagnostic approach based on three atypical reading-spelling patterns. *Developmental Medicine and Child Neurology, 15,* 663–687.

Boersma, F. J., Chapman, J. W., & Battle, J. (1979). Academic self-concept change in special education students: Some suggestions for interpreting self-concept scores. *Journal of Special Education, 13,* 433–442.

Bohlmeyer, E. M., & Burke, J. P. (1987). Selecting cooperative learning techniques: A consultative strategy guide. *School Psychology Review, 16,* 36–49.

Bond, G. L., & Tinker, M. A. (1973). *Reading difficulties: Their diagnosis and correction* (3rd ed.). New York: Appleton-Century-Crofts.

Book, R. M. (1980). Identification of educationally at-risk children during the kindergarten year: A four-year follow-up study of group test performance. *Psychology in the Schools, 17,* 153–158.

Borg, W. R. (1980). Time and school learning. In C. Denham & A. Lieberman (Eds.), *Time to learn.* Washington, DC: National Institute of Education.

Borkowski, J. G., Weyhing, R. S., & Turner, L. A. (1986). Attributional retraining and the teaching of strategies. *Exceptional Children, 53,* 130–137.

Borland, B. L., & Heckman, H. K. (1976). Hyperactive boys and their brothers. *Archives of General Psychiatry, 33,* 669–675.

Bortner, M., Hertzig, M. D., & Birch, H. G. (1972). Neurological signs and intelligence in brain-damaged children. *Journal of Special Education, 6,* 325–333.

Bos, C. S. (1982). Getting past decoding: Assisted and repeated readings as remedial methods for learning disabled students. *Topics in Learning & Learning Disabilities, 1*(4), 51–57.

Bos, C. S. (1991). Reading-writing connections: Using literature as a zone of proximal development for writing. *Learning Disabilities Research & Practice, 6,* 251–256.

Bos, C. S., & Anders, P. L. (1987). Semantic feature analysis: An interactive teaching strategy for facilitating learning from text. *Learning Disabilities Focus, 3,* 55–59.

Bos, C. S., & Anders, P. L. (1990). Effects of interactive vocabulary instruction on the vocabulary learning and reading comprehension of junior-high learning disabled students. *Learning Disability Quarterly, 13,* 31–42.

Bos, C. S., Anders, P. L., Filip, D., & Jaffe, L. E. (1989). The effects of an interactive instructional strategy for enhancing reading comprehension and content area learning for students with learning disabilities. *Journal of Learning Disabilities, 22,* 384–390.

Bos, C. S., & Filip, D. (1984). Comprehension monitoring in learning disabled and average students. *Journal of Learning Disabilities, 17,* 229–233.

Bos, C. S., & Fletcher, T. V. (1997). Sociocultural considerations in learning disabilities inclusion research: Knowledge gaps and future directions. *Learning Disabilities Research & Practice, 12,* 92–99.

Bos, C. S., & Vaughn, S. (1994). *Strategies for teaching students with learning and behavior problems* (3rd ed). Boston: Allyn & Bacon.

Boucher, C. R. (1984). Pragmatics: The verbal language of learning disabled and nondisabled boys. *Learning Disability Quarterly, 7,* 271–286.

Boucher, C. R. (1986). Pragmatics: The meaning of verbal language in learning disabled and nondisabled boys. *Learning Disability Quarterly, 9,* 285–294.

Bowers, P. G., & Swanson, L. B. (1991). Naming speed deficits in reading disability: Multiple measures of a singular process. *Journal of Experimental Child Psychology, 51,* 195–219.

Boyer, E. L. (1983). *High school: A report of the Carnegie Foundation for the Advancement of Teaching.* New York: Harper & Row.

Boykin, A. W. (1994). Harvesting talent and culture: African-American children and education reform. In R. Rossi (Ed.), *Schools and students at risk: Context and framework for positive change.* New York: Teachers College Press.

Boyle, J. R. (1996). The effects of a cognitive mapping strategy on the literal and inferential comprehension of students with mild disabilities. *Learning Disability Quarterly, 19,* 86–98.

Bradley, L. (1988). Making connections in learning to read and spell. *Applied Cognitive Psychology, 2,* 3–18.

Bradley, L., & Bryant, P. E. (1978). Difficulties in auditory organization as a possible cause of reading backwardness. *Nature, 271,* 746–747.

Bradley, L., & Bryant, P. E. (1983). Categorizing sounds and learning to read—A causal connection. *Nature, 301,* 419–421.

Bradley, L., & Bryant, P. (1985). *Rhyme and reason in reading and spelling.* Ann Arbor, MI: University of Michigan Press.

Bradley, R. H., & Caldwell, B. M. (1978). Screening the environment. *American Journal of Orthopsychiatry, 48,* 114–130.

Braine, M. (1963). The ontogeny of English phrase structure: The first phase. *Language, 39,* 1–13.

Brainerd, C. J. (1985). Model-based approaches to storage and retrieval development. In C. J. Brainerd & M. Pressley (Eds.), *Basic processes in memory development: Progress in cognitive developmental research.* New York: Springer-Verlag.

Brainerd, C. J., Kingma, J., & Howe, M. L. (1986). Long-term memory development and learning disability: Storage and retrieval loci of disabled/nondisabled differences. In S. J. Ceci (Ed.), *Handbook of cognitive, social, and neuropsychological aspects of learning disabilities* (Vol. 1). Hillsdale, NJ: Lawrence Erlbaum.

Brainerd, C. J., & Reyna, V. F. (1993). Memory independence and memory interference in cognitive development. *Psychological Review, 100,* 42–67.

Brandt, I. (1981). Brain growth, fetal malnutrition, and clinical consequences. *Journal of Perinatal Medicine, 9,* 3–26.

Bransford, J. D., Stein, B. S., & Vye, N. J. (1982). Helping students learn how to learn from written texts. In M. H. Singer (Ed.), *Competent reader, disabled reader.* Hillsdale, NJ: Lawrence Erlbaum.

Brantlinger, E. A. (1987). Making decisions about special education placement: Do low-income parents have the information they need? *Journal of Learning Disabilities, 20,* 94–101.

Bremer, D. A., & Stern, J. A. (1976), Attention and distractibility during reading in hyperactive boys. *Journal of Abnormal Child Psychology, 4,* 381–387.

Brenner, A. (1982). The effects of megadoses of selected B complex vitamins on children with hyperkinesis: Controlled studies with long-term follow-up. *Journal of Learning Disabilities, 15,* 258–264.

Bridge, C. A., Belmore, S. M., Moskow, S. P., Cohen, S. S., & Matthews, P. D. (1984). Topicalization and memory for main ideas in prose. *Journal of Reading Behavior, 16,* 61–80.

Brier, N. (1994). Targeted treatment for adjudicated youth with learning disabilities: Effects on recidivism. *Journal of Learning Disabilities, 27,* 215–222.

Brigham, F. R., Scruggs, T. E., & Mastropieri, M. A. (1992). Teacher enthusiasm in learning disabilities classrooms: Effects on learning and behavior. *Learning Disabilities Research & Practice, 7,* 68–73.

Brigham, T. A., Graubard, P. S., & Stans, A. (1972). Analysis of the effects of sequential reinforcement contingencies on aspects of composition. *Journal of Applied Behavior Analysis, 5,* 421–429.

Broder, P. K., Dunivant, N., Smith, E. C., & Sutton, P. L. (1981). Further observations on the link between learning disabilities and juvenile delinquency. *Journal of Educational Psychology, 73,* 838–850.

Broman, S., Bien, E., & Shaughnessy, P. (1985). *Low achieving children: The first seven years.* Hillsdale, NJ: Lawrence Erlbaum.

Bronfenbrenner, U. (1975). Is early intervention effective? *Exceptional infant: Assessment and intervention* (Vol. 3). New York: Brunner/Mazel.

Bronzaft, A. L., & McCarthy, D. P. (1975). The effect of elevated train-noise on reading ability. *Environment and Behavior, 7,* 517–527.

Brophy, J. (1981). Teacher praise: A functional analysis. *Review of Educational Research, 51,* 5–32.

Brophy, J. (1982). Successful teaching strategies for the inner-city child. *Phi Delta Kappan, 63,* 527–530.

Brophy, J. E. (1983). Research on self-fulfilling prophecy and teacher expectations. *Journal of Educational Psychology, 75,* 631–661.

Brophy, J., & Good T. (1974). *Teacher-student relationships.* New York: Holt, Rinehart, & Winston.

Brosnan, F. L. (1983). Overrepresentation of low-socioeconomic minority students in special education programs in California. *Learning Disability Quarterly, 6,* 517–525.

Brown, A. L. (1975). The development of memory: Knowing, knowing about knowing, and knowing how to know. In H. W. Reese (Ed.), *Advances in child development and behavior* (Vol. 10). New York: Academic Press.

Brown, A. L., Armbruster, B. B., & Baker, L. (1986). The role of metacognition in reading and studying. In J. Orasanu (Ed.), *Reading comprehension: From research to practice.* Hillsdale, NJ: Lawrence Erlbaum.

Brown, B., Haegerstrom-Portnoy, G., Adams, A. J., Yingling, D. D., Galin, D., Herron, J., & Marcus, M. (1983). Predictive eye movements do not discriminate between dyslexic and control children. *Neuropsychologia, 21,* 121–128.

Brown, R. (1973). *A first language: The early stages.* Cambridge, MA: Harvard University Press.

Brown, R., & Bellugi, U. (1964). Three processes in the child's acquisition of syntax. *Harvard Education Review, 34,* 133–151.

Brown, R. T., & Alford, N. (1984). Ameliorating attentional deficits and concomitant academic deficiencies in learning disabled children through cognitive training. *Journal of Learning Disabilities, 17,* 20–26.

Brown, R. T., & Sleator, E. K. (1979). Methylphenidate in hyperkinetic children: Differences in dose effects on impulsive behavior. *Pediatrics, 64,* 408–411.

Brown, R, T., & Wynne, M. E. (1984). An analysis of attentional components in hyperactive and normal boys. *Journal of Learning Disabilities, 17,* 162–166.

Bruck, M. (1985). The adult functioning of children with specific learning disabilities: A follow-up study. In I. E. Siegel (Ed.), *Advances in applied developmental psychology* (Vol. 1). Norwood, NJ: Ablex.

Bruck, M. (1990). Word-recognition skills of adults with childhood diagnoses of dyslexia. *Developmental Psychology, 26,* 439–454.

Bruck, M. (1993a). Component spelling skills of college students with childhood diagnoses of dyslexia. *Learning Disability Quarterly, 16,* 171–184.

Bruck, M. (1993b). Word recognition and component phonological processing skills of adults with childhood diagnoses of dyslexia. *Developmental Review, 13,* 258–268.

Bruck, M., & Hébert, M. (1982). Correlates of learning disabled students' peer-interaction patterns. *Learning Disability Quarterly, 5,* 353–362.

Bruininks, R. H., Glaman, G. M., & Clark, C. R. (1973). Issues in determining prevalence of reading retardation. *The Reading Teacher, 27,* 177–185.

Bruininks, V. L. (1978a). Actual and perceived peer status of learning disabled students in mainstream programs. *Journal of Special Education, 12,* 51–58.

Bruininks, V. L. (1978b). Peer status and personality characteristics of learning disabled and nondisabled students. *Journal of Learning Disabilities, 11,* 484–489.

Bruner, J. S., Olver, R. R., & Greenfield, P. M. (1966). *Studies in cognitive growth.* New York: Wiley.

Bruno, R. M. (1981). Interpretation of pictorially presented social situations by learning disabled and normal children. *Journal of Learning Disabilities, 14,* 350–352.

Bruno, R. M., Johnson, J. M., & Simon, J. (1987). Perception of humor by regular class students and students with learning disabilities or mild mental retardation. *Journal of Learning Disabilities, 20,* 568–570.

Bruno, R. M., Johnson, J. M., & Simon, J. (1988). Perception of humor by learning disabled, mildly retarded, and nondisabled students. *Learning Disability Focus, 3,* 114–123.

Brutten, M., Richardson, S. O., & Mangel, C. (1973). *Something is wrong with my child.* New York: Harcourt, Brace, Jovanovich.

Bryan, J. H., & Perlmutter, B. (1979). Immediate impressions of LD children by female adults. *Learning Disability Quarterly, 2,* 80–88.

Bryan, J. H., & Sherman, R. (1980). Immediate impressions of nonverbal integration attempts by learning disabled boys. *Learning Disability Quarterly, 3,* 19–28.

Bryan, J. H., Sherman, R., & Fisher, A. (1980). Learning disabled boys' nonverbal behaviors within a dyadic interview. *Learning Disability Quarterly, 3,* 65–72.

Bryan, J. H., Sonnefeld, L. J., & Grabowski, B. (1983). The relationship between fear of failure and learning disabilities. *Learning Disability Quarterly, 6,* 217–222.

Bryan, T. (1974a). An observational analysis of classroom behaviors of children with learning disabilities. *Journal of Learning Disabilities, 7,* 26–34.

Bryan, T. (1974b). Peer popularity of learning disabled children. *Journal of Learning Disabilities, 7,* 621–625.

Bryan, T. (1976). Peer popularity of learning disabled children: A replication. *Journal of Learning Disabilities, 9,* 307–311.

Bryan, T. (1977). Learning disabled children's comprehension of nonverbal communication. *Journal of Learning Disabilities, 10,* 501–506.

Bryan, T. (1978). Social relationships and verbal interactions of learning disabled children. *Journal of Learning Disabilities, 11,* 107–115.

Bryan, T. (1986). Personality and situational factors in learning disabilities. In G. Th. Pavlidis & D. F. Fisher (Eds.), *Dyslexia: Its neurology and treatment.* New York: John Wiley.

Bryan, T., Cosden, M., & Pearl, R. (1982). The effects of cooperative models on LD and NLD students. *Learning Disability Quarterly, 5,* 415–421.

Bryan, T., Donahue, M., & Pearl, R. (1981). Learning disabled children's peer interactions during a small-group problem-solving task. *Learning Disability Quarterly, 4*(1), 13–22.

Bryan, T., Donahue, M., Pearl, R., & Herzog, A. (1984). Conversational interactions between mothers and learning-disabled or nondisabled children during a problem-solving task. *Journal of Speech and Hearing Disorders, 49,* 64–71.

Bryan, T., Donahue, M., Pearl, R., & Sturm, C. (1976). Learning: An observational study of children's communications. *Journal of Learning Disabilities, 9,* 661–669.

Bryan, T., Donahue, M., Pearl, R., & Sturm, C. (1981). Learning disabled children's conversational skills—The "TV talk show." *Learning Disability Quarterly, 4,* 250–259.

Bryan, T., Mathur, S., & Sullivan, K. (1996). The impact of positive mood on learning. *Learning Disability Quarterly, 19,* 153–162.

Bryan, T., & Pearl, R. (1979). Self-concepts and locus of control of learning disabled children. *Journal of Clinical Child Psychology, 8,* 223–226.

Bryan, T., Pearl, R., & Fallon, P. (1989). Conformity to peer pressure by students with learning disabilities: A replication. *Journal of Learning Disabilities, 22,* 458–459.

Bryan, T., Pearl, R., & Herzog, A. (1989). Learning disabled adolescents' vulnerability to crime: Attitudes, anxieties, experiences. *Learning Disability Quarterly, 5,* 51–60.

Bryan, T., & Pflaum S. (1978). Social interactions of learning disabled children: A linguistic, social, and cognitive analysis. *Learning Disability Quarterly, 1*(1), 70–79.

Bryan, T., & Sullivan-Burstein, K. (1997). Homework how-to's. *Teaching Exceptional Children, 29,* 32–37.

Bryan, T., Werner, M., & Pearl, R. (1982). Learning disabled students' conformity responses to prosocial and antisocial situations. *Learning Disability Quarterly, 5,* 344–352.

Bryan, T., & Wheeler, R. (1972). Perception of children with learning disabilities: The eye of the observer. *Journal of Learning Disabilities, 5,* 199–206.

Bryan, T., & Wheeler, R. A. (1976). Teachers' behaviors in classes for severely retarded, multiply trainable mentally retarded, learning disabled, and normal children. *Mental Retardation, 14*(4), 41–45.

Bryant, N. D. (1980). Modifying instruction to minimize the effects of learning disabilities. *Forum,* 19–20.

Bryant, N. D., Drabin, I. R., & Gettinger, M. (1981). Effects of varying unit size on spelling achievement in learning disabled children. *Journal of Learning Disabilities, 14,* 200–203.

Bryant, N. D., & Gettinger, M. (1981). Eliminating differences between learning disabled and non-disabled children on a paired-associate learning task. *Journal of Educational Research, 74,* 342–346.

Bryant, N. D., & McLoughlin, J. A. (1972). Subject variables: Definition, incidence, characteristics, and correlates. In N. D. Bryant & C. E. Kass (Eds.), *Final report: Leadership training institute in learning disabilities* (Vol. 1). Tucson: University of Arizona, Department of Special Education, 27.

Bryant, P. (1974). *Perception and understanding in young children.* New York: Basic Books.

Bryant, P. E., & Bradley, L. (1983). Auditory organization and backwardness in reading. In M. Rutter (Ed.), *Developmental neuropsychiatry.* New York: Guilford Press.

Bryant, S. K., McIntyre, C. W., Murray, M. E., & Blackwell, S. L. (1983). Rate of visual information pick-up in learning disabled and normal boys. *Learning Disability Quarterly, 6,* 166–171.

Bryden, M. P. (1970). Laterality effects in dichotic listening: Relations with handedness and reading ability in children. *Neuropsychologia, 8,* 443–450.

Bryden, M. P., & Allard, F. (1976). Visual hemifield differences depend on typeface. *Brain and Language, 3,* 191–200.

Buchsbaum, M., & Wender, P. (1973). Average evoked responses in normal and minimally brain dysfunctioned children treated with amphetamine: A preliminary report. *Archives of General Psychiatry, 29,* 764–770.

Bulgren, J. A., Hock, M. F., Schumaker, J. B., & Deshler, D. D. (1995). The effects of instruction in a paired associates strategy on the information mastery performance of students with learning disabilities. *Learning Disabilities Research & Practice, 10,* 22–37.

Bulgren, J., Schumaker, J. B., & Deshler, D. D. (1988). Effectiveness of a concept teaching routine in enhancing the performance of LD students in secondary-level mainstream classes. *Learning Disability Quarterly, 11,* 3–17.

Bulgren, J. A., Schumaker, J. B., & Deshler, D. D. (1994). The effects of a recall enhancement routine on the test performance of secondary students with and without learning disabilities. *Learning Disabilities Research & Practice, 9,* 2–11.

Bursuck, W., Polloway, E. A., Plante, L., Epstein, M. H., Jayanthi, M., & McConeghy, J. (1996). Report and grading and adaptations: A national survey of classroom practices. *Exceptional Children, 62,* 301–318.

Bursuck, W. D. (1989). A comparison of students with learning disabilities to low achieving and higher achieving students on three dimensions of social competence. *Journal of Learning Disabilities, 22,* 188–194.

Bursuck, W. D., & Lessen, E. (1987). A classroom-based model for assessing students with learning disabilities. *Learning Disabilities Focus, 3,* 17–29.

Butkowsky, I. S., & Willows, D. M. (1980). Cognitive-motivational characteristics of children varying in reading ability: Evidence for learned helplessness in poor readers. *Journal of Educational Psychology, 72,* 408–422.

Butler, R., & Marinov-Glassman, D. (1994). The effects of educational placement and grade level on the self-perceptions of low achievers and students with learning disabilities. *Journal of Learning Disabilities, 27,* 325–334.

Butterfield, E. C., Wambold, C., & Belmont, J. M. (1973). On the theory and practice of improving short-term memory. *American Journal of Mental Deficiency, 77,* 654–669.

Buysse, V., & Bailey, D. B. (1993). Behavioral and developmental outcomes in young children with disabilities in integrated and segregated settings: A review of comparative studies. *The Journal of Special Education, 26,* 434–461.

Byrne, B., Freebody, P., & Gates, A. (1992). Longitudinal data on the relations of word-reading strategies to comprehension, reading time, and phonemic awareness. *Reading Research Quarterly, 27,* 141–151.

Cain, L., Melcher, J., Johns, B., Ashmore, J., Callahan, C., Draper, I., Beveridge, P., & Weintraub, T. (1984). Reply to "A Nation at Risk." *Exceptional Children, 50,* 484–494.

Calanchini, P. R., & Trout, S. S. (1971). The neurology of learning disabilities. In L. Tarnapol (Ed.), *Learning disorders in children: Diagnosis, medication, education.* Boston: Little, Brown.

Caldwell, B. M. (1974). A decade of early intervention programs: What have we learned? *American Journal of Orthopsychiatry, 44,* 491–496.

Calfee, R., & Chambliss, M. (1988). Beyond decoding: Pictures of expository prose. *Annals of Dyslexia, 38,* 243–257.

Calfee, R. C., Chapman, R., & Venezky, R. L. (1972). How a child needs to think to read. In L. W. Gregg (Ed.), *Cognition and learning in memory.* New York: Wiley.

Calfee, R. C., Lindamood, P., & Lindamood, C. (1973). Acoustic-phonetic skills and reading—Kindergarten through twelfth grade. *Journal of Educational Psychology, 64,* 293–298.

Cameron, J. R. (1977). Parental treatment, children's temperament, and the risk of childhood behavioral problems: 1. Relationships between parental characteristics and changes in children's temperament over time. *American Journal of Orthopsychiatry, 47,* 568–576.

Cameron, J. R. (1978). Parental treatment, children's temperament, and the risk of childhood behavioral problems: 2. Initial temperament, parental attitudes, and the incidence and form of behavioral problems. *American Journal of Orthopsychiatry, 48,* 140–147.

Campbell, F. A., & Ramey, C. T. (1994). Effects of early intervention on intellectual and academic achievement: A follow-up study of children from low-income families. *Child Development, 65,* 684–698.

Campbell, P. B., & Varvariv, D. S. (1979). *Psychoeducational diagnostic services for learning disabled youths: Validation analysis.* Princeton, NJ: Educational Testing Service.

Campbell, S. B., Endman, M. W., & Bernfield, G. (1977). A three-year follow-up of hyperactive preschoolers into elementary school. *Journal of Child Psychology and Psychiatry, 18,* 239–249.

Campos, J. J., Barrett, K. C., Lamb, M. E., Goldsmith, H. H., & Stenberg, C. (1983). Socioemotional development. In P. H. Mussen (Ed.), *Handbook of child psychobiology (Vol. 2): Infancy and developmental psychobiology.* New York: Wiley.

Canfield, J., & Wells, H. C. (1976). *100 ways to enhance self-concept in the classroom: A handbook for teachers and parents.* Englewood Cliffs, NJ: Prentice-Hall.

Cannon, I., & Compton, C. (1981). School dysfunction in the adolescent. In C. Larson & P. Larson (Eds.), *Neurological impairments—*

A proposal for service. New York: NYALD Developmental Disabilities Act Grant Contract No. 171365.

Cantwell, D. P. (1975). Familial genetic research with hyperactive children. In D. P. Cantwell (Ed.), *The hyperactive child: Diagnosis, management, current research.* New York: Spectrum Publications.

Caplan, N., Choy, M. H., & Whitmore, J. K. (1992). Indochinese refugee families and academic achievement. *Scientific American, 266*(2), 36–42.

Caplan, P. J. (1977). Sex, age, behavior, and school subjects as determinants of report of learning problems. *Journal of Learning Disabilities, 10,* 314–316.

Caplan, P. J., & Kinsbourne, M. (1974). Sex differences in response to school failure. *Journal of Learning Disabilities, 7,* 232–235.

Caplan, P. J., & Kinsbourne, M. (1976). Baby drops the rattle: Asymmetry of duration of grasp by infants. *Child Development, 47,* 532–534.

Capps, L. R., & Hatfield, M. M. (1977). Mathematical concepts and skills: Diagnosis, prescription, and correction of deficiencies. *Focus on Exceptional Children, 8,* 1–8.

Cardell, C. D., & Parmar, R. S. (1988). Teacher perceptions of temperament characteristics of children classified as learning disabled. *Journal of Learning Disabilities, 21,* 497–502.

Carlberg, C., & Kavale, K. (1980). The efficacy of special versus regular class placement for exceptional children: A meta-analysis. *Journal of Special Education, 14,* 295–309.

Carlson, C. L. (1987). Social interaction goals and strategies of children with learning disabilities. *Journal of Learning Disabilities, 20,* 306–311.

Carlson, C. L., & Bunner, M. R. (1993). Effects of methylphenidate on the academic performance of children with attention-deficit hyperactivity disorder and learning disabilities. *School Psychology Review, 22,* 184–198.

Carlson, S. A. (1985). The ethical appropriateness of subject-matter tutoring for learning disabled adolescents. *Learning Disability Quarterly, 8,* 310–314.

Carman, R. A., & Adams, W. R., Jr. (1972). *Study skills: A student's guide for survival.* New York: Wiley.

Carmon, A., Nachshon, I., & Starinsky, R. (1976). Developmental aspects of visual hemifield differences in perception of verbal material. *Brain and Language, 3,* 463–469.

Carnine, D. (1989). Designing practice activities. *Journal of Learning Disabilities, 22,* 603–607.

Carnine, D. (1994). Introduction to the mini-series: Diverse learners and prevailing, emerging, and research-based educational approaches and their tools. *School Psychology Review, 23,* 341–350.

Carnine, D., & Kinder, D. (1985). Teaching low-performing students to apply generative and schema strategies to narrative and expository material. *Remedial and Special Education, 6*(1), 20–30.

Carnine, D., Miller, S., Bean, R., & Zigmond, N. (1994). Social studies: Educational tools for diverse learners. *School Psychology Review, 23,* 428–441.

Carpenter, R. L. (1985). Mathematics instruction in resource rooms: Instruction time and teacher competence. *Learning Disability Quarterly, 8,* 95–100.

Carr, S. C., & Thompson, B. (1996). The effects of prior knowledge and schema activation strategies on the inferential reading comprehension of children with and without learning disabilities. *Learning Disability Quarterly, 19,* 48–61.

Carrier, C. A. (1983). Notetaking research: Implications for the classroom. *Journal of Instructional Development, 6*(3), 19–25.

Carter, J. L., & Diaz, A. (1971). Effects of visual and auditory background on reading test performance. *Exceptional Children, 38,* 43–50.

Carter, R. B. (1977). A study of attitudes: Mexican American and Anglo American elementary teachers' judgments of Mexican American bilingual children's speech. *Dissertation Abstracts International, 37,* 4941A–4942A.

Cartledge, G., Frew, T., & Zaharias, J. (1985). Social skill needs of mainstreamed students: Peer and teacher interactions. *Learning Disability Quarterly, 8,* 132–140.

Cartledge, G., Stupay, D., & Kaczala, C. (1986). Social skills and social perception of LD and nonhandicapped elementary-school students. *Learning Disability Quarterly, 9,* 226–234.

Case, L. P., Harris, K. R., & Graham, S. (1992). Improving the mathematical problem-solving skills of students with learning disabilities: Self-regulated strategy development. *The Journal of Special Education, 26,* 1–19.

Casey, M. B. (1986). Individual differences in selective attention among prereaders: A key to mirror-image confusions. *Developmental Psychology, 22,* 58–66.

Casto, G., & Mastropieri, M. A. (1986). The efficacy of early intervention programs: A meta-analysis. *Exceptional Children, 52,* 417–424.

Catts, H. W. (1991). Facilitating phonological awareness: Role of speech-language pathologists. *Language, Speech, and Hearing Services in Schools, 22,* 196–203.

Cawley, J. F. (1984). An integrative approach to needs of learning disabled children: Expanded use of mathematics. In J. F. Cawley (Ed.), *Developmental teaching of mathematics for the learning disabled.* Rockville, MD: Aspen.

Cawley, J. F., Parmar, R. S., Fan Yan, W., & Miller, J. H. (1996). Arithmetic computation abilities of students with learning disabilities: Implications for instruction. *Learning Disabilities Research & Practice, 11,* 230–237.

CEC Today. (1996, September). States act to include students with disabilities in standards. 1, 9. Council for Exceptional Children.

Ceci, S. J. (1983). Automatic and purposive semantic processing characteristics of normal and language/learning-disabled children. *Developmental Psychology, 19,* 427–439.

Ceci, S. J. (1984). A developmental study of learning disabilities and memory. *Journal of Experimental Child Psychology, 38,* 352–371.

Ceci, S. J. (1991). How much does schooling influence general intelligence and its cognitive components? A reassessment of the evidence. *Developmental Psychology, 27,* 703–722.

Ceci, S. J., & Baker, J. G. (1989). On learning . . . more or less: A knowledge × process × context view of learning disabilities. *Journal of Learning Disabilities, 22,* 90–99.

Cegelka, P. (1981). Career education. In A. Blackhurst & W. Berdine (Eds.), *An introduction to special education.* Boston: Little, Brown.

Center, D. B., & Wascom, A. M. (1986). Teacher perceptions of social behavior in learning disabled and socially normal children and youth. *Journal of Learning Disabilities, 19,* 420–425.

Centra, J. A. (1986). Handicapped student performance on the Scholastic Aptitude Test. *Journal of Learning Disabilities, 19,* 324–327.

Cermac, L. D., & Miliotis, P. (1987). Information processing deficits in children with learning disabilities. In H. L. Swanson (Ed.), *Advances in learning and behavioral difficulties: Memory and learning disabilities.* Greenwich, CT.: JAI Press.

Cermak, L. S. (1983). Information processing deficits in children with learning disabilities. *Journal of Learning Disabilities, 16,* 599–605.

Cermak, L. S., Goldberg-Warter, J., Deluca, D., Cermak, S., & Drake, C. (1981). The role of interference in the verbal retention ability of learning disabled children. *Journal of Learning Disabilities, 14,* 291–295.

Chaikin, A. L., Gillen, B., Derlega, V. S., Heinen, J. R. K., & Wilson, M. (1978). Students' reactions to teachers' physical attractiveness and non-verbal behavior: Two exploratory studies. *Psychology in the Schools, 15,* 588–595.

Chalfant, J. C. (1985). Identifying learning disabled students: A summary of the National Task Force Report. *Learning Disabilities Focus, 1,* 9–20.

Chall, J. (1983a). *Stages of reading development.* New York: McGraw-Hill.

Chall, J. S. (1983b). Literacy: Trends and explanations. *Educational Researcher, 12*(9), 3–8.

Chamberlain, P., & Medinos-Landurand, P. (1991). Practical considerations for the assessment of LEP students with special needs. In E. V. Hamayan & J. S. Damico (Eds.), *Limiting bias in the assessment of bilingual students.* Austin, TX: Pro-Ed.

Chan, D. M. (1986). Curriculum development for limited English proficient exceptional Chinese children. *Rural Special Education Quarterly, 8,* 26–31.

Chan, L. K. S. (1991). Promoting strategy generalization through self-instructional training in students with reading disabilities. *Journal of Learning Disabilities, 24,* 427–433.

Chan, L. K. S., Cole, P. G., & Morris, J. N. (1990). Effects of instruction in the use of a visual-imagery strategy on the reading-comprehension competence of disabled and average readers. *Learning Disability Quarterly, 13,* 2–11.

Chandler, T. A. (1966). The fallacy of homogeneity. *Journal of School Psychology, 5,* 64–67.

Chapman, J. W. (1988). Learning disabled children's self-concept. *Review of Educational Research, 58,* 347–371.

Chapman, J. W., & Boersma, F. J. (1979). Learning disabilities, locus of control, and mother attitudes. *Journal of Educational Psychology, 71,* 250–258.

Chapman, R. B., Larsen, S. C., & Parker, R. M. (1979). Interactions of first-grade teachers with learning disordered children. *Journal of Learning Disabilities, 12,* 225–230.

Characteristics of At-Risk Students in NELS:88. (1992). Washington, DC: U.S. Department of Education, Office of Educational Research and Improvement.

Chase, C. H., & Tallal, P. (1991). Cognitive models of developmental reading disorders. In J. E. Obrzut & G. W. Hynd (Eds.), *Neuropsychological foundations of learning disabilities: A handbook of issues, methods, and practice.* New York: Academic Press.

Chase, H. P. (1973). The effects of intrauterine and postnatal undernutrition on normal brain development. *Annals of the New York Academy of Sciences, 205,* 231–244.

Chelser, B. (1982). ACLD vocational committee completes survey on LD adult. *ACLD Newsbriefs,* No. 146, 5, 20–23.

Cherkes-Julkowski, M., Gertner, N., & Norlander, K. (1986). Differences in cognitive processes among handicapped and average children: A group learning approach. *Journal of Learning Disabilities, 19,* 438–445.

Cherry, R. S., & Kruger, B. (1983). Selective auditory attention abilities of learning disabled and normal achieving children. *Journal of Learning Disabilities, 16,* 202–205.

Chess, S., Thomas, A., & Cameron, M. (1976). Temperament: Its significance for early schooling, *New York University Education Quarterly, 7*(3), 24–29.

Chiarenza, G. A. (1990). Motor-perceptual function in children with developmental reading disorders: Neuropsychophysiological analysis. *Journal of Learning Disabilities, 23,* 375–385.

Childers, P. R. (1970). Listening is a modifiable skill. *The Journal of Experimental Education, 38*(4), 1–3.

Children's Defense Fund. (1996). *The state of America's Children Yearbook, 1996.* Washington, DC.

Childs, B., & Finucci, J. M. (1983). Genetics, epidemiology, and specific reading disability. In M. Rutter (Ed.), *Developmental neuropsychiatry.* New York: Guilford Press.

Childs, B., Finucci, J. M., Pulver, A. E., & Tielsch, J. (1982). *The natural history of specific reading disability: Education outcomes.* Unpublished manuscript, John Hopkins University, Department of Pediatrics, Baltimore.

Chinn, P. C., & Hughes, S. (1987). Representation of minority students in special education classes. *Remedial and Special Education, 8,* 41–46.

Chomsky, N. A. (1968). *Language and mind.* New York: Harcourt Brace Jovanovich.

Christenson, S. L., Hurley, C. M., Sheridan, S. M., & Fenstermacher, K. (1997). Parents' and school psychologists' perspectives on parent involvement activities. *School Psychology Review, 26,* 111–130.

Ciborowski, J. (1995). Using textbooks with students who cannot read them. *Remedial and Special Education, 16,* 90–101.

Cicirelli, V. G., Evans, J. W., & Schiller, J. S. (1970). The impact of Head Start: A reply. *Harvard Educational Review, 40*(1), 105–129.

Clark, E. (1973). What's in a word? On the child's acquisition of semantics in his first language. In T. E. Moore (Ed.), *Cognitive development and the acquisition of language*. New York: Academic Press.

Clark, E., Kehle, T. J., Jenson, W. R., & Beck, D. E. (1992). Evaluation of the parameters of self-modeling interventions. *School Psychology Review, 21,* 246–254.

Clark, F. L., Deshler, D. D., Schumaker, J. B., Alley, G. R., & Warner, M. M. (1984). Visual imagery and self-questioning: Strategies to improve comprehension of written material. *Journal of Learning Disabilities, 17,* 145–149.

Clark, M. D. (1997). Teacher response to learning disability: A test of attributional principles. *Journal of Learning Disabilities, 30,* 69–79.

Clay, M. M. (1991). *Becoming literate: The construction of inner control*. Portsmouth, NH: Heinemann.

Clayman, C. B. (Ed.). (1988). *The American Medical Association guide to prescription and over-the-counter drugs*. New York: Random House.

Clement-Heist, K., Siegel, S., & Gaylord-Ross, R. (1992). Simulated and in situ vocational social skills training for youths with learning disabilities. *Exceptional Children, 58,* 336–345.

Clements, S. D. (1966). *Minimal brain dysfunction in children: Terminology and identification. Phase one of a three-phase project* (NINDS Monograph No. 3, U.S. Public Health Service Publication No. 1415). Washington, DC: U.S. Government Printing Office.

Clements, S. D., Davis, J. S., Edgington, R., Goolsby, C. M., & Peters, J. E. (1971). Two cases of learning disabilities. In L. Tarnopol (Ed.), *Learning disorders in children: Diagnosis, medication, education*. Boston: Little, Brown.

Cline, R. K. J., & Kretke, G. L. (1980). An evaluation of long term SSR in the junior high school. *Journal of Reading, 23,* 503–506.

Coates, R. D. (1989). The Regular Education Initiative and opinions of regular classroom teachers. *Journal of Learning Disabilities, 22,* 532–536.

Cobb, R. M., & Crump, W. D. (1984). *Post-school status of young adults identified as learning disabled while enrolled in public schools: A comparison of those enrolled and not enrolled in learning disabilities programs* (Final report). Washington, DC: Office of Special Education and Rehabilitation Services, Division of Educational Services (ERIC Document Reproduction Service No. ED 253 029).

Cohen, A. H. (1988). The efficacy of optometric vision therapy. *Journal of the American Optometric Association, 59,* 95–105.

Cohen, A. L., Torgesen, J. K., & Torgesen, J. L. (1988). Improving speed and accuracy of word recognition in reading disabled children: An evaluation of two computer program variations. *Learning Disability Quarterly, 11,* 333–341.

Cohen, E. G. (1973). Open-space schools: The opportunity to become ambitious. *Sociology of Education, 46,* 1–8.

Cohen, S. A. (1971). Dyspedagogia as a cause of reading retardation: Definition and treatment. In B. Bateman (Ed.), *Learning disorders* (Vol. 4). Seattle: Special Child Publications.

Cohn, R. (1964). The neurological study of children with learning disabilities. *Exceptional Children, 31,* 179–185.

Colarusso, R. P., Martin, H., & Hartung, J, (1975). Specific visual perceptual skills as long-term predictors of academic success. *Journal of Learning Disabilities, 8,* 651–655.

Cole, K. N., Dale, P. S., Mills, P. E., & Jenkins, J. R. (1993). Interaction between early intervention curricula and student characteristics. *Exceptional Children, 60,* 17–28.

Coleman, J. C., & Sandhu, M. (1967). A descriptive relational study of 364 children referred to a university clinic for learning disorders. *Psychological Reports, 20,* 1091–1105.

Coleman, J. M. (1983). Handicapped labels and instructional segregation: Influences on children's self-concepts versus the perceptions of others. *Learning Disability Quarterly, 6,* 3–11.

Coleman, J. M., & Dover, G. M. (1993). The RISK screening test: Using kindergarten teachers' ratings to predict future placement in resource classrooms. *Exceptional Children, 59,* 468–477.

Coleman, J. M., & Minnett, A. M. (1993). Learning disabilities and social competence: A social ecological perspective. *Exceptional Children, 59,* 234–246.

Coleman, M., & Harmer, W. R. (1982). A comparison of standardized tests and informal placement procedures. *Journal of Learning Disabilities, 15,* 396–398.

Coleman, P. D., & Riesen, A. H. (1968). Environmental effects on cortical dendritic fields: 1. Rearing in the dark. *Journal of Anatomy, 102,* 363–374.

Coll, C. T. G. (1990). Developmental outcome of minority infants: A process-oriented look into our beginnings. *Child Development, 61,* 270–289.

Colletti, L. F. (1979). Relationship between pregnancy and birth complications and later development of learning disabilities. *Journal of Learning Disabilities, 12,* 659–663.

Collier, C., & Hoover, J. J. (1987). Sociocultural considerations when referring minority children for learning disabilities. *Learning Disabilities Focus, 3,* 39–45.

Colligan, R. (1977a). Concurrent validity of the Myklebust Pupil Rating Scale in a kindergarten population. *Journal of Learning Disabilities, 10,* 317–320.

Colligan, R. C. (1977b). The Minnesota Child Development Inventory as an aid in the assessment of developmental disability. *Journal of Clinical Psychology, 33,* 162–163.

Colligan, R. C. (1981). Prediction of reading difficulty from parental preschool report: A 3-year follow-up. *Learning Disability Quarterly, 4,* 31–37.

Coltheart, M., Masterson, J., Byng, S., Prior, M., & Riddoch, J. (1983). Surface dyslexia. *Quarterly Journal of Experimental Psychology, 35A,* 469–495.

Compensatory education in early adolescence. (1974). Menlo Park, CA: Stanford Research Institute.

Conderman, G. (1995). Social-status of sixth- and seventh-grade students with learning disabilities. *Learning Disability Quarterly, 18,* 13–24.

Condition of Education. (1980, 1994, 1996, 1997). Washington, DC: U.S. Department of Education, National Center for Education Statistics.

Cone, J. D., Delawyer, D. D., & Wolfe, V. V. (1985). Assessing parent participation: The Parent/Family Involvement Index. *Exceptional Children, 51,* 417–424.

Cone, T. E., & Wilson, L. R. (1981). Quantifying a severe discrepancy: A critical analysis. *Learning Disability Quarterly, 4,* 359–371.

Cone, T. E., Wilson, L. R., Bradley, C. M., & Reese, J. H. (1985). Characteristics of LD students in Iowa: An empirical investigation. *Learning Disability Quarterly, 8,* 211–220.

Conners, C. K. (1970). Symptom patterns in hyperkinetic, neurotic, and normal children. *Child Development, 41,* 667–682.

Conners, C. K. (1975). Controlled trial of methylphenidate in preschool children with minimal brain dysfunction. *International Journal of Mental Health, 4,* 61–74.

Conners, C. K. (1980). *Food additives and hyperactive children*. New York: Plenum Press.

Conners, C. K., Goyette, C. H., Southwick, D. A., Lee, J. M., & Andrulonis, P. A. (1976). Food additives and hyperkinesis: A controlled double-blind experiment. *Pediatrics, 58,* 154–166.

Conoley, J. C. (1980). Organizational assessment. *School Psychology Review, 9,* 83–89.

Cook, L. D. (1979). The adolescent with a learning disability: A developmental perspective. *Adolescence, 14,* 697–706.

Cook, S. B., Scruggs, T. E., Mastropieri, M. A., & Casto, G. C. (1985–1986). Handicapped students as tutors. *Journal of Special Education, 19,* 486–492.

Cooley, E. J., & Ayres, R. R. (1988). Self-concept and success-failure attributions of nonhandicapped students and students with learning disabilities. *Journal of Learning Disabilities, 21,* 174–178.

Cooley, W. W., & Leinhardt, G. (1980). The instructional dimensions study. *Educational Evaluation and Policy Analysis, 2*(1), 7–25.

Coop, R. H., & Sigel, I. E. (1971). Cognitive style: Implications for learning and instruction. *Psychology in the Schools, 8,* 152–161.

Copeland, A. P., & Reiner, E. M. (1984). The selective attention of learning-disabled children: Three studies. *Journal of Abnormal Child Psychology, 12,* 455–470.

Cosden, M. A., Gerber, M. M., Semmel, D. S., Goldman, S. R., & Semmel, M. I. (1987). Microcomputer use within microeducational environments. *Exceptional Children, 53,* 399–409.

Coss, R. G., & Globus, A. (1978). Spine stems on tectal interneurons in Jewel fish are shortened by social stimulation. *Science, 200,* 787–790.

Cott, A. (1985). *Dr. Cott's help for your learning disabled child.* New York: Times Books.

The Council of Learning Disabilities Position Statement. (1993). *Learning Disability Quarterly, 16,* 126.

Coulter, W. A., Morrow, H. W., & Tucker, J. A. (1978). *What you always wanted to know about adaptive behavior but were too hostile and angry to ask.* Paper presented at the meeting of the National Association of school Psychologists, New York, NY.

Cox, L. S. (1975). Diagnosing and remediating systematic errors in addition and subtraction computations. *The Arithmetic Teacher, 22,* 151–157.

Crank, J. N., & Bulgren, J. A. (1993). Visual depictions as information organizers for enhancing achievement of students with learning disabilities. *Learning Disabilities Research & Practice, 8,* 140–147.

Cratty, B. (1970). *Perceptual and motor development in infants and children.* New York: Macmillan.

Cravioto, J. (1972). Nutrition and learning in children. In N. S. Springer (Ed.), *Nutrition and mental retardation.* Ann Arbor, MI: Institute for the Study of Mental Retardation and Related Disabilities.

Cravioto, J., & Arrieta, R. (1983). Malnutrition in childhood. In M. Rutter (Ed.), *Developmental neuropsychiatry.* New York: Guilford Press.

Cravioto, J., & DeLicardie, E. R. (1975). Environmental and nutritional deprivation in children with learning disabilities. In W. M. Cruickshank & D. P. Hallahan (Eds.), *Perceptual and learning disabilities in children: Vol. 2. Research and Theory.* Syracuse: Syracuse University Press.

Crawford, D. (1981). A summary of the results and recommendations from the Learning Disabilities Research and Development Project (National Institute for Juvenile Justice and Delinquency Prevention, Law Enforcement Assistance Administration, U.S. Department of Justice Grant Nos. 76-JN-99-0021 and 78-JN-AX-0022). Presented to the Federal Coordinating Council, Washington, DC, December 16.

Creswell, J. L., & Vaughn, L. R. (1979). Hand-held calculator curriculum and mathematical achievement and retention. *Journal for Research in Mathematics Education, 10,* 364–367.

Critchley, M. (1970). *The dyslexic child.* Springfield, IL: Charles C Thomas.

Cronbach, L. J. (1975). Five decades of public controversy over mental testing. *American Psychologist, 30,* 1–14.

Cronin, M. E. (1996). Life skills curricula for students with learning disabilities: A review of the literature. *Journal of Learning Disabilities, 29,* 53–68.

Crook, M. A., & Langdon, F. J. (1974). The effects of aircraft noise in schools around London Airport. *Journal of Sound and Vibration, 34,* 221–232.

Crowl, T. K., & MacGinitie, W. H. (1974). The influence of students' speech characteristics on teachers' evaluation of oral answers. *Journal of Educational Psychology, 66,* 304–308.

Cruickshank, W. M. (1967). The development of education for exceptional children. In W. M. Cruickshank & G. O. Johnson (Eds.), *Education of exceptional children and youth* (2nd ed.). Englewood Cliffs, NJ: Prentice-Hall.

Cruickshank, W. M. (1972). Some issues facing the field of learning disability. *Journal of Learning Disabilities, 5,* 380–388.

Cruickshank, W. M. (1976). William M. Cruickshank. In J. M. Kauffman & D. P. Hallahan (Eds.), *Teaching children with learning disabilities: Personal perspectives.* Columbus, OH: Charles E. Merrill.

Cruickshank, W. M., Bentzen, F. A., Ratzeburg, F. H., & Tannhauser, M. T. (1961). *A teaching method for brain-injured and hyperactive children.* Syracuse: Syracuse University Press.

Cruickshank, W. M., Bice, H. V., & Wallen, N. E. (1957). *Perception and cerebral palsy.* Syracuse: Syracuse University Press.

Cullinan, B., & Fitzgerald, S. (1984). *Background information bulletin on the use of readability formulae.* Urbana, IL: National Council of Teachers of English.

Cullinan, D., Kauffman, J. M., & LaFleur, N. K. (1975). Modeling: Research with implications for special education. *Journal of Special Education, 9,* 209–221.

Cunningham, J. W., Cunningham, P. M., & Arthur, S. V. (1981). *Middle and secondary school reading.* New York: Longman.

Cunningham, P. M., & Cunningham, J. W. (1976, December). Improving listening in content area subjects. *NASSP Bulletin,* pp. 26–31.

D'Angelo, K., & Mahlios, M. (1983). Insertion and omission miscues of good and poor readers. *The Reading Teacher, 36,* 778–782.

Daiute, C. (1986). Physical and cognitive factors in revising: Insights from studies with computers. *Research in the Teaching of English, 20,* 141–159.

Dalby, J. T., & Gibson, D. (1981). Functional cerebral lateralization in subtypes of disabled readers. *Brain and Language, 14,* 34–48.

Dale, E., & Chall, J. S. (1948, January 27). A formula for predicting readability. *Educational Research Bulletin,* pp. 11–20, 28, 37–54.

Dallago, M. L. L., & Moely, B. E. (1980). Free recall in boys of normal and poor reading levels as a function of task manipulations. *Journal of Experimental Child Psychology, 30,* 62–78.

Dalley, M. B., Bolocofsky, D. N., Alcorn, M. B., & Baker, C. (1992). Depressive symptomatology, attributional style, dysfunctional attitude, and social competency in adolescents with and without learning disabilities. *School Psychology Review, 21,* 444–458.

Dalton, B., Tivnan, T., Riley, M. K., Rawson, P., & Dias, D. (1995). Revealing competence: Fourth-grade students with and without learning disabilities show what they know on paper-and-pencil and hands-on performance assessments. *Learning Disabilities Research & Practice, 10,* 198–214.

Dangel, H. L., & Ensminger, E. E. (1988). The use of a discrepancy formula with LD students. *Learning Disabilities Focus, 4,* 24–31.

Darch, C., & Carnine, D. (1986). Teaching content area material to learning disabled students. *Exceptional Children, 53,* 240–246.

Darch, C., & Gersten, R. (1986). Direction-setting activities in reading comprehension: A comparison of two approaches. *Learning Disability Quarterly, 9,* 235–243.

Darch, C., & Kameenui, E. J. (1987). Teaching LD students critical reading skills: A systematic replication. *Learning Disability Quarterly, 10,* 82–91.

Das, J. P., Kirby, J., & Jarman, R. F. (1975). Simultaneous and successive syntheses: An alternative model for cognitive abilities. *Psychological Bulletin, 82,* 87–103.

Das, J. P., Kirby, J. R., & Jarman, R. F. (1979). *Simultaneous and successive cognitive processes.* Orlando, FL: Academic Press.

Das, J. P., & Varnhagen, C. K. (1986). Neuropsychological functioning and cognitive processing. In J. E. Obrzut & G. W. Hynd (Eds.), *Child neuropsychology: Vol. 1. Theory and research.* New York: Academic Press.

Daub, D., & Colarusso, R. P. (1996). The validity of the WJ-R, PIAT-R, and DAB-2 reading subtests with students with learning disabilities. *Learning Disabilities Research & Practice, 11,* 90–95.

Davenport. J. W. (1976). Environmental therapy in hypothyroid and other disadvantaged animal populations. In R. N. Walsh & W. T. Greenough (Eds.), *Environments as therapy for brain dysfunction.* New York: Plenum.

Davidoff, J. B., Cone, B. P., & Scully, J. P. (1978). Developmental changes in hemispheric processing for cognitive skills and the relationship to reading ability. In A. M. Lesgold, J. W. Pellegrino, S. Fokkema, & R. Glaser (Eds.), *Cognitive psychology and instruction*. New York: Plenum.

Davidson, H. P. (1935). A study of the confusing letters b, d, p, and q. *Journal of Genetic Psychology, 47,* 458–468.

Davis, H., & Davis, P. A. (1936). Action potentials of the brain in normal persons and in normal states of cerebral activity. *Archives of Neurology and Psychiatry, 36,* 1214–1224.

Davis, W. A., & Shepard, L. A. (1983). Specialists' use of tests and clinical judgment in the diagnosis of learning disabilities. *Learning Disability Quarterly, 6,* 128–138.

Dawson, M. M. (1987). Beyond ability grouping: A review of the effectiveness of ability grouping and its alternatives. *School Psychology Review, 16,* 348–369.

Deci, E. L., Hodges, R., Pierson, L., & Tomassone, J. (1992). Autonomy and competence as motivational factors in students with learning disabilities and emotional handicaps. *Journal of Learning Disabilities, 25,* 457–471.

Dearborn, W. F. (1933). Structural factors which condition special disability in reading. *Proceedings of the American Association for Mental Deficiency, 38,* 266–283.

Debono, E. (1977). Information processing and new ideas—Lateral and vertical thinking. In S. J. Pames, R. B. Noller, & A. M. Biondi (Eds.), *Guide to creative action*. New York: Charles Scribner & Sons.

Decker, S. N., & DeFries, J. C. (1980). Cognitive abilities in families with reading disabled children. *Journal of Learning Disabilities, 13,* 517–522.

Decker, S. N., & DeFries, J. C. (1981). Cognitive ability profiles in families of reading-disabled children. *Developmental Medicine and Child Neurology, 23,* 217–227.

DeFries, J. C., & Gillis, J. J. (1991). Etiology of reading deficits in learning disabilities: Quantitative genetic analysis. In J. E. Obrzut & G. W. Hynd (Eds.), *Neuropsychological foundations of learning disabilities: A handbook of issues, methods, and practice*. San Diego, CA: Academic Press.

de Hirsch, K. (1963). Psychological correlates of the reading process. *Bulletin of the Orton Society, 13,* 59–71.

Deighton, L. C. (1970). Developing vocabulary: Another look at a problem. In A. V. Olson & W. S. Ames (Eds.), *Teaching reading skills in secondary schools: Readings*. Scranton, PA: Intext Educational Pub.

Déjèrine, J. (1891). Sur un cas de cécité verbale avec agraphie suivi d'autopsie. (An autopsy study of a case of cessation of speech and agraphia.) *Comptes Rendus Hebdomadaires des Séances et Mémoires de la Société de Biologie, 3,* 197–201.

Del Dotto, J. E., & Rourke, B. P. (1985). Subtypes of left-handed learning-disabled children. In B. P. Rourke (Ed.), *Neuropsychology of learning disabilities*. New York: Guilford Press.

Delacato, C. H. (1966). *Neurological organization and reading*. Springfield, IL: Charles C Thomas.

De La Paz, S., & Graham, S. (1997). Strategy instruction in planning: Effects on the writing performance and behavior of students with learning difficulties. *Exceptional Children, 63,* 167–181.

Delefes, P., & Jackson, B. (1972). Teacher-pupil interaction as a function of location in the classroom. *Psychology in the Schools, 9,* 119–123.

Delgado-Gaitan, C., & Trueba, H. T. (1985). Ethnographic study of participant structures in task completion: Reinterpretation of "handicaps" in Mexican children. *Learning Disability Quarterly, 8,* 67–75.

Delquadri, J., Greenwood, C. R., Whorton, D., Carta, J. J., & Hall, R. V. (1986). Classwide peer tutoring. *Exceptional Children, 52, 6,* 535–542.

Dembo, M. M., Yoshida, R. K., Reilly, T., & Reilly, V. (1978). Teacher-student interaction in special education classrooms. *Exceptional Children, 45,* 212–213.

Dembrinski, R., & Mauser, A. (1977). What parents of the learning disabled really want from professionals. *Journal of Learning Disabilities, 10,* 578–584.

Denckla, M. B. (1977). Minimal brain dysfunction and dyslexia: Beyond diagnosis by exclusion. In M. E. Blaw, I. Rapin, & M. Kinsbourne (Eds.), *Child neurology*. New York: Spectrum Publications.

Denckla, M. B. (1979). Childhood learning disabilities. In K. M. Heilman & E. Valenstein (Eds.), *Clinical neuropsychology*. New York: Oxford University Press.

Denkla, M. B. (1991). Academic and extracurricular aspects of nonverbal learning disabilities. *Psychiatric Annals, 21,* 717–724.

Denckla, M. B., & Heilman, K. M. (1979). The syndrome of hyperactivity. In K. M. Heilman & E. Valenstein (Eds.), *Clinical neuropsychology*. Oxford: Oxford University Press.

Denckla, M. B., LeMay, M., & Chapman, C. A. (1985). Few CT scan abnormalities found even in neurologically impaired learning disabled children. *Journal of Learning Disabilities, 18,* 132–135.

Denckla, M. B., & Rudel, R. (1974). Rapid (automatized) naming of pictured objects, colors, letters, and numbers by normal children. *Cortex, 10,* 186–202.

Denckla, M. B., Rudel, R. G., & Broman, M. (1981). Tests that discriminate between dyslexic and other learning-disabled boys. *Brain and Language, 13,* 118–129.

Dennis, M. & Whitaker, H. A. (1976). Language acquisition following hemidecortication: Linguistic superiority of the left over the right hemisphere. *Brain and Language, 3,* 404–433.

Dennis, R. E., & Giangreco, M. F. (1996). Creating conversation: Reflections on cultural sensitivity in family interviewing. *Exceptional Children, 63,* 103–116.

Dennis, W. (1960). Causes of retardation among institutional children: Iran. *Journal of Genetic Psychology, 96,* 47–59.

Deno, S. L. (1985). Curriculum-based measurement: The emerging alternative. *Exceptional Children, 52,* 219–232.

Deno, S., Mirkin, P. K., & Chiang, B. (1982). Identifying valid measures of reading. *Exceptional Children, 49,* 36–45.

Denson, R., Nanson, J. L., & McWatters, M. A. (1975). Hyperkinesis and maternal smoking. *Canadian Psychiatric Association Journal, 20,* 183–187.

Derienzo, P. J. (1981). *A predictive validity study of the Gesell School Readiness Test*. Unpublished master's thesis, Syracuse University.

Derr, A. M. (1985). Conservation and mathematics achievement in the learning disabled child. *Journal of Learning Disabilities, 18,* 333–336.

Derr, A. M. (1986). How learning disabled adolescent boys make moral judgments. *Journal of Learning Disabilities, 19,* 160–164.

Derr-Minneci, T. F., & Shapiro, E. S. (1992). Validating curriculum-based measurement in reading from a behavioral perspective. *School Psychology Quarterly, 7,* 2–16.

Deshler, D. D. (1974). *Learning disability in the high school student as demonstrated in monitoring of self-generated and externally generated errors*. Unpublished doctoral dissertation, University of Arizona.

Deshler, D. D. (1978). Psychoeducational aspects of learning disabled adolescents. In L. Mann, L. Goodman, & J. L. Wiederholt (Eds.), *Teaching the learning disabled adolescent*. Boston: Houghton Mifflin.

Deshler, D. D., & Schumaker, J. B. (1986). Learning strategies: An instructional alternative for low-achieving adolescents. *Exceptional Children, 52,* 583–590.

Deshler, D. D., Schumaker, J. B., Warner, M. M., Alley, G. R., & Clark, F. L. (1980). *An epidemiological study of learning disabled adolescents in secondary schools: Social status, peer relationships, activities in and out of school, and time uses* (Research Report No. 19). Lawrence, KS: The University of Kansas Institute for Research in Learning Disabilities.

Deshler, D. D., Warner, M. M., Schumaker, J. B., & Alley, G. R. (1983). Learning strategies intervention model: Key components and current status. In J. D. McKinney & L. Feagans (Eds.), *Current topics in learning disabilities*. Norwood, NJ: Ablex.

Deuel, R. K. (1995). Developmental dysgraphia and motor skills disorders. *Journal of Child Neurology, 10,* S6–S8.

Devine, R., & Rose, D. (1981). *To learn to learn, or to learn to read*. Proposal to produce a one-hour, broadcast-quality videotape on dyslexia, Rochester, NY.

Devine, T. G. (1981). *Teaching study skills: A guide for teachers.* Boston: Allyn & Bacon.

Deyhle, D. (1987). Learning failure: Tests as gatekeepers and the culturally different child. In H. E. Trueba (Ed.), *Success or failure?* Rawley, MA: Heinle & Heinle.

Digangi, S. A., Maag, J. W., & Rutherford, R. B. Jr. (1991). Self-graphing of on-task behavior: Enhancing the reactive effects of self-monitoring on on-task behavior and academic performance. *Learning Disability Quarterly, 14,* 221–230.

Digest of Educational Statistics. (1996). National Center for Educational Statistics. Washington DC: U.S. Department of Education.

DiLollo, V., Hanson, D., & McIntyre, J. S. (1983). Initial stages of visual information processing in dyslexia. *Journal of Experimental Psychology, 9,* 923–935.

Dimond, S. J., & Beaumont, J. G. (Eds.). (1974). *Hemisphere function in the human brain.* London: Elek.

Dinkmeyer, D. (1970). *Developing understanding of self and others (DUSO).* Circle Pines, MN: American Guidance Service.

DiPasquale, G. W., Moule, A. D., & Flewelling, R. W. (1980). The birthdate effect. *Journal of Learning Disabilities, 13,* 234–238.

Divoky, D. (1974). Education's latest victim: The "LD" kid. *Learning, 3*(2), 20–25.

Dohrn, E., & Bryan, T. (1994). Attribution instruction. *Teaching Exceptional Children, 26*(4), 61–63.

Dolan, A. B., & Matheny, A. P. (1978). A distinctive growth curve for a group of children with academic learning problems. *Journal of Learning Disabilities, 11,* 490–494.

Doll, B. (1996). Children without friends: Implications for practice and policy. *School Psychology Review, 25,* 165–183.

Donahoe, K., & Zigmond, N. (1990). Academic grades of ninth-grade urban learning-disabled students and low-achieving peers. *Exceptionality, 1,* 17–27.

Donahue, M. (1986). Linguistic and communicative development in learning-disabled children. In S. J. Ceci (Ed.), *Handbook of cognitive, social, and neuropsychological aspects of learning disabilities* (Vol. 1). Hillsdale, NJ: Lawrence Erlbaum.

Donahue, M., Pearl, R., & Bryan, T. (1980). Learning disabled children's conversational competence: Responses to inadequate messages. *Applied Psycholinguistics, 1,* 387–403.

Donofrio, A. F. (1977). Grade repetition: Therapy of choice. *Journal of Learning Disabilities, 10,* 349–351.

Dool, C. B., Stelmack, R. M., & Rourke, B. P. (1993). Event-related potentials in children with learning disabilities. *Journal of Clinical Child Psychology, 22,* 387–398.

Dorval, B., McKinney, J. D., & Feagans, L. (1982). Teacher interaction with learning disabled children and average achievers. *Journal of Pediatric Psychology, 7,* 317–330.

Dossey, J. A., Mullis, I. V. S., Linquist, M. M., & Chambers, D. L. (1988). *The mathematics report card: Are we measuring up?* Princeton, NJ: Educational Testing Service.

Douglas, V. I. (1972). Stop, look and listen: The problem of sustained attention and impulsive control in hyperactive and normal children. *Canadian Journal of Behavioral Science, 4,* 259–282.

Douglas, V. I. (1975). Are drugs enough? To treat or to train the hyperactive child. *International Journal of Mental Health, 4,* 199–212.

Douglas, V. I. (1976). Perceptual and cognitive factors as determinants of learning disabilities: A review chapter with special emphasis on attentional factors. In R. M. Knights & D. J. Bakker (Eds.), *The neuropsychology of learning disorders: Theoretical approaches.* Baltimore: University Park Press.

Douglas, V. I., Barr, R. G., O'Neill, M. E., & Britton, B. G. (1986). Short term effects of methylphenidate on the cognitive, learning and academic performance of children with attention deficit disorder in the laboratory and the classroom. *Journal of Child Psychology and Psychiatry, 27,* 191–211.

Douglas, V. I., & Parry, P. A. (1983). Effects of reward on delayed reaction time task performance of hyperactive children. *Journal of Abnormal Child Psychology, 11,* 313–326.

Dowdy, C. A. (1996). Vocational rehabilitation and special education: Partners in transition for individuals with learning disabilities. *Journal of Learning Disabilities, 29,* 137–147.

Doyle, B. A. (1978). *Math readiness skills.* Paper presented at the national meetings of the National Association of School Psychologists, New York City.

Drabman, R., & Thomas, M. H. (1976). Does watching violence on television cause apathy. *Pediatrics, 57,* 329–331.

Duffy, F. H., & McAnulty, G. B. (1985). Brain electrical activity mapping (BEAM): The search for a physiological signature of dyslexia. In F. H. Duffy & N. Geschwind (Eds.), *Dyslexia: A neuroscientific approach to clinical evaluation.* Boston: Little, Brown.

Dundon, W. D., Sewell, T. E., Manni, J. L., & Goldstein, D. (1986). The Bannatyne recategorization assessment procedure: Is it valid for individual diagnosis of LD children? *Learning Disability Quarterly, 9,* 208–213.

Dunn, H. G., McBurney, A. K., Ingram, S., & Hunter, C. M. (1977). Maternal cigarette smoking during pregnancy and the child's subsequent development; II. Neurological and intellectual maturation to the age of 6 1/2 years. *Canadian Journal of Public Health, 68,* 43–50.

Dunn, L. M. (1968). Special education for the mildly retarded—Is much of it justifiable? *Exceptional Children, 35,* 5–22.

DuPaul, G. J., Barkley, R. A., & McMurray, M. B. (1991). Therapeutic effects of medication on ADHD: Implications for school psychologists. *School Psychology Review, 20,* 203–219.

DuPaul, G. J., & Eckert, T. L. (1994). The effects of social skills curricula: Now you see them, now you don't. *School Psychology Quarterly, 9,* 113–132.

DuPaul, G. J., & Eckert, T. L. (1997). The effects of school-based interventions for attention deficit hyperactivity disorder: A meta-analysis. *School Psychology Review, 26,* 5–27.

Durkin, D. (1984), Is there a match between what elementary teachers do and what basal reader manuals recommend? *The Reading Teacher, 37,* 734–744.

Durrant, J. E. (1993). Attributions for achievement outcomes among behavioral subgroups of children with learning disabilities. *The Journal of Special Education, 27,* 306–320.

Dusek, J. B. (1975). Do teachers bias children's learning? *Review of Educational Research, 45,* 661–684.

Dweck, C. S. (1975). The role of expectations and attributions in the alleviation of learned helplessness. *Journal of Personality and Social Psychology, 31,* 674–685.

Dwyer, K. (1996, February). Goals 2000: Midterm progress report. *Communiqué,* 1, 4. National Association of School Psychologists.

Dyck, N., & Sundbye, N. (1988). The effects of text explicitness on story understanding and recall by learning disabled children. *Learning Disabilities Research, 3,* 68–77.

Dykman, R. A., & Ackerman, P. T. (1991). Attention deficit disorder and specific reading disability: Separate but often overlapping disorders. *Journal of Learning Disabilities, 24,* 96–103.

Dykman, R. A., Ackerman, P. T., Clements, S. D., & Peters, J. E. (1971). Specific learning disabilities: An attentional deficit syndrome. In H. R. Myklebust (Ed.), *Progress in learning disabilities* (Vol. 2). New York: Grune & Stratton.

Dykman, R, A., Ackerman, P. T., Holcomb, P. J., & Boudreau, A. Y. (1983). Physiological manifestations of learning disability. *Journal of Learning Disabilities, 16,* 46–53.

Dykman, R. A., Ackerman, P. T., & McCray, D. S. (1980). Effects of methylphenidate on selective and sustained attention in hyperactive, reading disabled, and presumably attention-disordered boys. *Journal of Nervous and Mental Disease, 168,* 745–752.

Dyson, L. L. (1996). The experiences of families of children with learning disabilities: Parental stress, family functioning, and sibling self-concept. *Journal of Learning Disabilities, 29,* 280–286.

Eames, T. H. (1934). Low fusion convergence as a factor in reading disability. *American Journal of Ophthalmology, 17,* 709–710.

Eames, T. H. (1955). The relationship of birth weight, the speeds of object and word perception, and visual acuity. *Journal of Pediatrics, 47,* 603–606.

Eccles, J. S., Midgley, C., Wigfield, A., Buchanan, C. M., Reuman, D., Flanagan, C., & MacIver, D. (1993). Development during adolescence: The impact of stage-environment fit on young adolescents' experiences in schools and in families. *American Psychologist, 48,* 90–101.

Edfeldt, A. W. (1959). *Silent speech and silent reading.* Stockholm: Almquist & Wiksell.

Edgar, E. (1987). Secondary programs in special education: Are many of them justifiable? *Exceptional Children, 53,* 555–561.

Edmonson, B., dcJung, J., Leland, H., & Leach, E. (1974). *The test of social inference.* New York: Educational Activities, Education Daily, July 13, 1981.

Egeland, B. (1974). Training impulsive children in the use of more efficient scanning techniques. *Child Development, 45,* 165–171.

Eggert, G. H. (1977). *Wernicke's works on aphasia: A sourcebook and review.* The Hague: Mouton Publishers.

Ehri, L. C. (1989). The development of spelling knowledge and its role in reading acquisition and reading disability. *Journal of Learning Disabilities, 22,* 356–365.

Ehri, L. C., & Wilce, L. S. (1987). Movement into reading: Is the first stage of printed word learning visual or phonetic? *Reading Research Quarterly, 20,* 163–179.

Eimas, P. D. (1969). Multiple-cue discrimination learning in children. *Psychological Record, 19,* 417–424.

Eisenberger, R., & Cameron, J. (1996). Detrimental effects of reward: Reality or myth? *American Psychologist, 51,* 1153–1166.

Eisenson, J. (1954). *Examining for aphasia.* New York: The Psychological Corporation.

Eisenson, J. (1968). Developmental aphasia: A speculative view with therapeutic implications. *Journal of Speech and Hearing Disorders, 33,* 3–13.

Eisenson, J. (1972). *Aphasia in children.* New York: Harper.

Ekel, G. J. (1974). Use of conditioned reflex methods in Soviet behavioral toxicology research. In C. Xintras, B. L. Johnson, & I. de Groot (Eds.), *Behavioral toxicology.* Washington, DC: U.S. Department of Health, Education, and Welfare.

Elardo, R., & Freund, J. H. (1981). Maternal child-rearing styles and the social skills of learning disabled boys: A preliminary investigation. *Contemporary Educational Psychology, 6,* 86–94.

Elbert, J. C. (1984). Short-term memory encoding and memory search in the word recognition of learning-disabled children. *Journal of Learning Disabilities, 17,* 342–345.

Elbert, T., Pantev, C., Wienbruch, C., Rockstroh, B., & Taub, E. (1995). Increased cortical representation of the fingers of the left hand in string players. *Science, 270,* 305–307.

Eliason, M. J., & Richman, L. C. (1988). Behavior and attention in LD children. *Learning Disability Quarterly, 11,* 360–369.

Elkind, D., & Weiss, J. (1967). Studies in perceptual development, III: Perceptual explorations. *Child Development, 38,* 553–563.

Elkonin, D. B. (1963). The psychology of mastering the elements of reading. In B. Simon & J. Simon (Eds.), *Educational psychology in the U.S.S.R.* London: Routledge & Kegan Paul.

Elkonin, D. B. (1973). U.S.S.R. in J. Downing (Ed.), *Comparative reading.* New York: Macmillan.

Elliott, S. N. (1991). Authentic assessment: An introduction to a neobehavioral approach to classroom assessment. *School Psychology Quarterly, 6,* 273–278.

Elliott, S. N., Busse, R. T., & Gresham, F. M. (1993). Behavior rating scales: Issues of use and development. *School Psychology Review, 22,* 313–321.

Ellis, E. S. (1996). Reading strategy instruction. In D. D. Deshler, E. S. Ellis, & B. K. Lenz (Eds.), *Teaching adolescents with learning disabilities: Strategies and methods* (2nd ed.). Denver: Love Publishing.

Ellis, E. S., & Lenz, B. K. (1987). A component analysis of effective learning strategies for LD students. *Learning Disabilities Focus, 2,* 94–107.

Elterman, R. D., Abel, L. A., Daroff, R. B., Dell'Osso, L. F., & Bornstein, J. L. (1980). Eye movement patterns in dyslexic children. *Journal of Learning Disabilities, 13,* 11–16.

Emde, R. N. (1983). The prerepresentational self and its affective core. *The Psychoanalytic Study of the Child, 38,* 165–192.

Englemann, S., Carnine, D., & Steely, D. G. (1991). Making connections in mathematics. *Journal of Learning Disabilities, 24,* 292–303.

Englert, C. S. (1984). Effective direct instruction practices in special education settings. *Remedial and Special Education, 5*(2), 38–47.

Englert, C. S., Culatta, B. E., & Horn, D. G. (1987). Influence of irrelevant information in addition word problems on problem solving. *Learning Disability Quarterly, 10,* 29–36.

Englert, C. S., Hiebert, E. H., & Stewart, S. R. (1985). Spelling unfamiliar words by an analogy strategy. *The Journal of Special Education, 19,* 291–306.

Englert, C. S., Raphael, T. E., Anderson, L. M., Anthony, H. M., Fear, K. L., & Gregg, S. L. (1988). A case for writing intervention: Strategies for writing informational text. *Learning Disabilities Focus, 3,* 98–113.

Englert, C. S., Tarrant, K. L., Mariage, T. V., & Oxer, T. (1994). Lesson talks as the work of reading groups: The effectiveness of two interventions. *Journal of Learning Disabilities, 27,* 165–185.

Englert, C. S., & Thomas, C. C. (1987). Sensitivity to text structure in reading and writing: A comparison between learning disabled and non-learning disabled students. *Learning Disability Quarterly, 10,* 93–105.

English, K., Goldstein, H., Shafer, K., & Kaczmarek, L. (1997). Promoting interactions among preschoolers with and without disabilities: Effects of a buddy skills-training program. *Exceptional Children, 63,* 229–243.

Epstein, H. T. (1980). Some biological bases of cognitive development. *Bulletin of the Orton Society, 30,* 46–62.

Epstein, H. (1985). Multimodality, crossmodality, and dyslexia. *Annals of Dyslexia, 35,* 35–49.

Epstein, M. H., Bursuck, W., & Cullinan, D. (1985). Patterns of behavior problems among the learning disabled: Boys aged 12–18, girls aged 6–11, and girls aged 12–18. *Journal of Learning Disabilities, 8,* 123–129.

Epstein, M. H., Cullinan, D., & Lloyd, J. W. (1986). Behavior-problem patterns among the learning disabled: III. Replication across age and sex. *Learning Disability Quarterly, 9,* 43–54.

Epstein, M. H., Cullinan, D., & Nieminen, G. (1984). Social behavior problems of learning disabled and normal girls. *Journal of Learning Disabilities, 17,* 609–611.

Epstein, M. H., Polloway, E. A., Foley, R. M., & Patton, J. R. (1993). Homework: A comparison of teachers' and parents' perceptions of the problems experienced by students identified as having behavioral disorders, learning disabilities, or no disabilities. *Remedial and Special Education, 14,* 40–50.

Erickson, A. G. (1954). Can listening efficiency be improved? *Journal of Communication, 4,* 128–132.

Erikson, E. H. (1963). *Childhood and society.* New York: W. W. Norton.

Eron, L. D., & Huesmann, L. R. (1987). Television as a source of maltreatment of children. *School Psychology Review, 16,* 195–202.

Espin, C. A., & Sindelar, P. T. (1988). Auditory feedback and writing: Learning disabled and nondisabled students. *Exceptional Children, 55,* 45–51.

Estrada, P., Arsenio, W. F., Hess, R. D., & Holloway, S. D. (1987). Affective quality of the mother-child relationship: Longitudinal consequences for children's school-relevant cognitive functioning. *Developmental Psychology, 23,* 210–215.

Eustis, R. S. (1947). Specific reading disability. A familial syndrome associated with ambidexterity and speech defects and a frequent cause of problem behavior. *New England Journal of Medicine, 237,* 243–249.

Evers, R. B. (1996). The positive force of vocational education: Transition outcomes for youth with learning disabilities. *Journal of Learning Disabilities, 29,* 69–78.

Evers, R. B., & Bursuck, W. (1993). Teacher ratings of instructional and setting demands in vocational education classes. *Learning Disability Quarterly, 16,* 82–92.

Ewing, D. W. (1977). Discovering your problem-solving style. *Psychology Today, 11*(7), 69–73, 138.

Eysenck, H. (1984a). The effect of race on human abilities and mental test scores. In C. R. Reynolds & R. T. Brown (Eds.), *Perspectives on bias in mental testing*. New York: Plenum Press.

Eysenck, H. (1984b). Recent advances in the theory and measurement of intelligence. *Early Child Development and Care, 15,* 97–116.

Faerstein, L. M. (1986). Coping and defense mechanisms of mothers of learning disabled children. *Journal of Learning Disabilities, 9,* 8–11.

Falik, L. H. (1995). Family patterns of reaction to a child with a learning disability: A mediational perspective. *Journal of Learning Disabilities, 28,* 335–341.

Farmer, T. W., & Farmer, E. M. Z. (1996). Social relationships of students with exceptionalities in mainstream classrooms: Social networks and homophily. *Exceptional Children, 62,* 431–450.

Farnham-Diggory, S. (1978). *Learning disabilities: A psychological perspective*. Cambridge: Harvard University Press.

Farnham-Diggory, S., & Gregg, L. W. (1975). Short term memory functioning in young readers. *Journal of Experimental Child Psychology, 19,* 279–298.

Fawcett, A. J. & Nicolson, R. I. (1994). Naming speed in children with dyslexia. *Journal of Learning Disabilities, 27,* 641–646.

Federal Register (1977, Thursday, December 29) (65082-65085) Washington, DC.

Feinbloom, R. I. (1976). Children and television. *Pediatrics, 57,* 301–303.

Feindler, E. L., Marriott, S. A., & Iwata, M. (1984). Group anger control training for junior high school delinquents. *Cognitive Therapy and Research, 8,* 299–311.

Feingold, B. F. (1975). *Why your child is hyperactive*. New York: Random House.

Feingold, B. F. (1976). Hyperkinesis and learning disabilities linked to the ingestion of artificial food colors and flavors. *Journal of Learning Disabilities, 9,* 551–559.

Feitelson, D. (1973). Israel. In J. Downing (Ed.), *Comparative reading: Cross-national studies of behavior and processes in reading and writing*. New York: Macmillan.

Feldman, S., Denhoff, E., & Denhoff, J. (1979). The attention disorders and related syndromes: Outcome in adolescence and young adult life. In E. Denhoff & L. Stern (Eds.), *Minimal brain dysfunction: A developmental approach*. New York: Mason.

Fellers, G., & Saudargas, R. A. (1987). Classroom behaviors of LD and nonhandicapped girls. *Learning Disability Quarterly, 10,* 231–236.

Felton, G. S., & Davidson, H. R. (1973). Group counseling can work in the classroom. *Academic Therapy, 8,* 461–468.

Felton, R. H. (1993). Effects of instruction on the decoding skills of children with phonological-processing problems. *Journal of Learning Disabilities, 26,* 583–589.

Felton, R. H., Naylor, C. E., & Wood, F. B. (1990). Neuropsychological profile of adult dyslexics. *Brain and Language, 39,* 485–497.

Felton, R. H., & Wood, F. B. (1989). Cognitive deficits in reading disability and attention deficit disorder. *Journal of Learning Disabilities, 22,* 3–13, 22.

Fennell, E. B., Satz, P., & Morris, R. (1983). The development of handedness and dichotic ear listening asymmetries in relation to school achievement: A longitudinal study. *Journal of Experimental Child Psychology, 35,* 248–262.

Fensterheim, H., & Baer, J. (1975). *Don't say yes when you want to say no*. New York: Dell.

Fernald, G. M. (1943). *Remedial techniques in basic school subjects*. New York: McGraw-Hill.

Ferraro, M. G. (1992, May/June). Learning disabled/gifted and talented: Nature's incongruity. *LDA Newsbriefs*, pp. 8–9.

Ferro, S. C., & Pressley, M. G. (1991). Imagery generation by learning disabled and average-achieving 11- to 13-year-olds. *Learning Disability Quarterly, 14,* 231–239.

Feuerstein, R. (1979). *The dynamic assessment of retarded performers: The learning potential assessment device, theory, instruments, and techniques*. Baltimore: University Park Press.

Field, S. (1996). Self-determination instructional strategies for youth with learning disabilities. *Journal of Learning Disabilities, 29,* 40–52.

Filipek, P. A. (1995). Neurobiologic correlates of developmental dyslexia: How do dyslexics' brains differ from those of normal readers? *Journal of Child Neurology, 10* (Supplement 1), S62–S69.

Filskov, S. B., Grimm, B. H., & Lewis, J. A. (1981). Brain-behavior relationships. In S. B. Filskov & T. J. Boll (Eds.), *Handbook of clinical neuropsychology*. New York: Wiley.

Fine, E. (1987). Are we preparing adolescents with learning disabilities to cope with social issues? *Journal of Learning Disabilities, 20,* 633–634.

Finger, S. (1978). *Recovery from brain damage: Research and theory*. New York: Plenum.

Finger, S., & Almli, C. R. (1984). *Early brain damage: Vol. 2. Neurobiology and behavior*. New York: Academic Press.

Finn, C. E. (1986). *What works: Research about teaching and learning*. Washington, DC: U.S. Department of Education.

Finucci, J. M. (1978). Genetic considerations in dyslexia. In H. R. Myklebust (Ed.), *Progress in learning disabilities* (Vol. IV). New York: Grune & Stratton.

Finucci, J. M. (1986). Follow-up studies of developmental dyslexia and other learning disabilities. In S. D. Smith (Ed.), *Genetics and learning disabilities*. San Diego: College-Hill Press.

Finucci, J. M., Gottfredson, L. S., & Childs, B. (1985). A follow-up study of dyslexic boys. *Annals of Dyslexia, 35,* 117–136.

Fischer, F. W., Liberman, I. Y., & Shankweiler, D. (1978). Reading reversals and developmental dyslexia: A further study. *Cortex, 14,* 496–510.

Fishbein, D., & Meduski, J. (1987). Nutritional biochemistry and behavioral disabilities. *Journal of Learning Disabilities, 20,* 505–512.

Fisher, B. L., Allen, R., & Kose, G. (1996). The relationship between anxiety and problem-solving skills in children with and without learning disabilities. *Journal of Learning Disabilities, 29,* 439–446.

Fisher, C. W., Berliner, D. C., Filby, N. N., Marliave, R., Cahen, L. S., & Dishaw, M. M. (1980). Teacher behaviors, academic learning time, and student achievement: An overview. In C. Denham & A. Lieberman (Eds.), *Time to learn*. Washington, DC: National Institute of Education.

Fisher, D. F., & Athey, I. (1986). Methodological issues in research with the learning disabled: Establishing true controls. In G. T. Pavlidis & D. F. Fisher (Eds.), *Dyslexia: Its neuropsychology and treatment*. New York: John Wiley.

Fisher, J. A. (1967). *Learning and study skills: A guide to independent learning*. Des Moines, IA: Drake University Reading and Study Skills Clinic.

Fisher, J. H. (1905). Case of congenital word-blindness (inability to learn to read). *Ophthalmic Review, 24,* 315–318.

Fisher, K. (1985, December). Measuring effects of toxic chemicals: A growing role for psychology. *Monitor*, pp. 13–14.

Fitzgibbons, D., Goldberger, L., & Eagle, M. (1965). Field dependence and memory for incidental material. *Perceptual and Motor Skills, 21,* 743–749.

Flavell, J. H. (1971). What is memory development the development of? *Human Development, 14,* 272–278.

Flavell, J. H. (1976). Metacognitive aspects of problem solving. In L. B. Resnick (Ed.), *The nature of intelligence*. Hillsdale, NJ: Lawrence Erlbaum.

Flavell, J. H. (1977). *Cognitive development*. Englewood Cliffs, NJ: Prentice-Hall.

Flavell, J. H., Botkin, P. T., Fry, C. L., Wright, J. W., & Jarvis, P. E. (1968). *The development of role-taking and communication skills in childhood*. New York: John Wiley & Sons.

Flavell, J. H., & Wellman, H. M. (1976). Metamemory. In R. V. Kail & J. W. Hagen (Eds.), *Memory in cognitive development*. Hillsdale, NJ: Lawrence Erlbaum.

Flavell, J. H., & Wellman, H. (1977). Metamemory. In R. V. Kail & J. W. Hagen (Eds.), *Perspectives on the development of memory and cognition*. Hillsdale, NJ: Lawrence Erlbaum.

Flax, N. (1973). The eye and learning disabilities. *Journal of Learning Disabilities, 6,* 328–333.

Flax, N., Mozlin, R., & Solan, H. (1984). Learning disabilities, dyslexia, and vision. *Journal of the American Optometric Association, 55,* 399–403.

Flesch, R. (1951). *How to test readability.* New York: Harper & Row.

Fletcher, J. (1991). Qualitative descriptions of error recovery patterns across reading level and sentence type: An eye movement analysis. *Journal of Learning Disabilities, 24,* 568–575.

Fletcher, J. M. (1985). External validation of learning disability typologies. In B. P. Rourke (Ed.), *Neuropsychology of learning disabilities.* New York: Guilford Press.

Fletcher, J. M., Espy, K. A., Francis, D. J., Davidson, K. C., Rourke, B. P., & Shaywitz, S. E. (1989). Comparisons of cutoff and regression-based definitions of reading disabilities. *Journal of Learning Disabilities, 22,* 334–338, 355.

Fletcher, J. M., Francis, D. J., Rourke, B. P., Shaywitz, S. E., & Shaywitz, B. A. (1993). Classification of learning disabilities: Relationships with other childhood disorders. In G. R. Lyon, D. B. Gray, J. F. Kavanagh, & N. A. Krasnegor (Eds.), *Better understanding of learning disabilities: New views from research and their implications for education and public policies.* Baltimore: Paul H. Brookes.

Fletcher, J. M., Levin, H. S., & Landry, S. H. (1984). Behavioral consequences of cerebral insult in infancy. In C. R. Almli & S. Finger (Eds.), *Early brain damage; Vol. 1. Research orientations and clinical observations.* New York: Academic Press.

Fletcher, J. M., & Morris, R. (1986). Classification of disabled learners: Beyond exclusionary definitions. In S. J. Ceci (Ed.), *Handbook of cognitive, social, and neuropsychological aspects of learning disabilities.* Hillsdale, NJ: Lawrence Erlbaum.

Fletcher, J. M., & Satz, P. (1979a). Unitary deficit hypotheses of reading disabilities: Has Vellutino led us astray? *Journal of Learning Disabilities, 12,* 155–159.

Fletcher, J. M., & Satz, P. (1979b). Has Vellutino led us astray? A rejoinder to a reply. *Journal of Learning Disabilities, 12,* 168–171.

Fletcher, J. M., & Satz, P. (1980). Developmental changes in the neuropsychological correlates of reading achievement: A six-year longitudinal follow-up. *Journal of Clinical Neuropsychology, 2,* 23–37.

Fletcher, J. M., & Satz, P. (1985). Cluster analysis and the search for learning disability subtypes. In B. P. Rourke (Ed.), *Neuropsychology of learning disabilities.* New York: Guilford Press.

Flowers, D. L. (1993). Brain basis for dyslexia: A summary of work in progress. *Journal of Learning Disabilities, 26,* 575–582.

Flynn, J. M., Deering, W., Goldstein, M., & Rahbar, M. H. (1992). Electrophysiological correlates of dyslexia subtypes. *Journal of Learning Disabilities, 25,* 133–141.

Flynn, J. R. (1991). *Asian Americans: Achievement beyond IQ.* Hillsdale, NJ: Erlbaum.

Flynn, N. M., & Rapoport, J. L. (1976). Hyperactivity in open and traditional classroom environments. *Journal of Special Education, 10,* 285–290.

Flynn, T. M. (1984). IQ tests and placement. *Integrated Education, 21,* 124–126.

Foley, J. M. (1979). Effect of labeling and teacher behavior in children's attitudes. *American Journal of Mental Deficiency, 83,* 380–384.

Forell, E. R., & Hood, J. (1985). A longitudinal study of two groups of children with early reading problems. *Annals of Dyslexia, 35,* 97–116.

Forman, E. A. (1987). Peer relationships of learning disabled children: A contextualist perspective. *Learning Disabilities Research, 2,* 80–90.

Forness, S. R. (1985). Effects of public policy at the state level; California's impact on MR, LD, and ED categories. *Remedial and Special Education, 60*(3), 36–43.

Forness, S. R., & Kavale, K. A. (1996). Treating social skill deficits in children with learning disabilities: A meta-analysis of the research. *Learning Disability Quarterly, 19,* 2–13.

Forness, S. R., Kavale, R. A., Blum, I. M., & Lloyd, J. W. (1997). Mega-analysis of meta-analysis: What works in special education and related services. *Teaching Exceptional Children, 29,* 4–9.

Foster, G. G., Schmidt, C. R., & Sabatino, D. (1976). Teacher expectancies and the label "Learning Disabilities." *Journal of Learning Disabilities, 9,* 111–114.

Fourqurean, J. M., Meisgeier, C., Swank, P. R., & Williams, R. E. (1990). Correlates of postsecondary employment outcomes for young adults with learning disabilities. *Journal of Learning Disabilities, 24,* 400–405.

Fox, B., & Routh, D. K. (1983). Reading disability, phonemic analysis, and dysphonetic spelling: A follow-up study. *Journal of Clinical Child Psychology, 12,* 28–32.

Fox, C. L. (1989). Peer acceptance of learning disabled children in the regular classroom. *Exceptional Children, 56,* 50–59.

Frame, R. E., Clarizio, H. F., & Porter, A. (1984). Diagnostic and prescriptive bias in school psychologists' reports of a learning disabled child. *Journal of Learning Disabilities, 17,* 12–15.

Francis, D. J., Shaywitz, S. E., Steubing, K., Shaywitz, B. A., & Fletcher, J. M. (1994). Measurement of change: Assessing behavior over time and within a developmental framework. In G. R. Lyon (Ed.), *Frames of reference for the assessment of learning disabilities: New views on measurement issues.* Baltimore, MD: Brookes.

Fraser, D., Kidd, B. S. L., Kooh, S. W., & Paunier, L. A. (1966). New look at infantile hypercalcemia. *Pediatric Clinics of North America, 13*(2), 503–525.

Frauenheim, J. G. (1978). Academic achievement characteristics of adult males who were diagnosed as dyslexic in childhood. *Journal of Learning Disabilities, 11,* 476–483.

Frauenheim, J. G., & Heckerl, J. R. (1983). A longitudinal study of psychological and achievement test performance in severe dyslexic adults. *Journal of Learning Disabilities, 16,* 339–347,

Freeman, D., Kuhs, T., Porter, A., Knappen, L., Floden, R., Schmidt, W., & Schwille, J. (1980). *The fourth grade mathematics curriculum as inferred from textbooks and tests.* Report No. 82. East Lansing: Michigan State University, Institute for Research on Teaching.

Freeman, F. W. (1965). *Reference manual for teachers. Grades one through four.* Columbus, OH: Zaner-Bloser.

Freeman, R. D. (1971). Special education and the electroencephalogram: Marriage of convenience. In D. Hammill & N. Bartel (Eds.), *Educational perspectives in learning disabilities.* New York: Wiley.

Freeman, T. J., & McLaughlin, T. F. (1984). Effects of a taped-words treatment procedure on learning disabled students' sight-word oral reading. *Learning Disability Quarterly, 7,* 49–54.

French, J. N., & Rhoder, C. (1992). *Teaching thinking skills: Theory and practice.* NY: Garland.

Frick, P. J., & Lahey, B. B. (1991). The nature and characteristics of attention-deficit hyperactivity disorder. *School Psychology Review, 20,* 163–173.

Frisby, C., & Braden, J. P. (1992). Feuerstein's dynamic assessment approach: A semantic, logical, and empirical critique. *The Journal of Special Education, 26,* 281–301.

Frith, U. (1983). The similarities and differences between reading and spelling problems. In M. Rutter (Ed.), *Developmental neuropsychiatry.* New York: Guilford Press.

Frith, U. (1985). Beneath the surface of developmental dyslexia. In K. E. Patterson, J. C. Marshall, & M. Coltheart (Eds.), *Surface dyslexia: Neuropsychological and cognitive studies of phonological reading.* Hillsdale, NJ: Lawrence Erlbaum.

Frostig, M. (1967). Testing as a basis for educational therapy. *Journal of Special Education, 2,* 15–34.

Frostig, M. (1976). Marianne Frostig. In J. M. Kauffman & D. P. Hallahan (Eds.), *Teaching children with learning disabilities: Personal perspectives.* Columbus, OH: Charles E. Merrill.

Frostig, M., & Horne, D. (1964). *The Frostig program for the development of visual perception: Teacher's guide.* Chicago: Follett.

Frostig, M., Lefever, D. W., & Whittlesey, J. R. B. (1961). A developmental test of visual perception for evaluating normal and neurologically handicapped children. *Perceptual and Motor Skills, 12,* 383–394.

Frostig, M., Lefever, D. W., & Whittlesey, J. R. B. (1964). *The Marianne Frostig developmental test of visual perception.* Palo Alto, CA: Consulting Psychologists Press.

Frostig, M., & Maslow, P. (1973). *Learning problems in the classroom.* New York: Grune & Stratton.

Frostig M., & Maslow, P. (1979). Neuropsychological contributions to education. *Journal of Learning Disabilities, 12,* 538–552.

Fuchs, D., & Fuchs, L. S. (1986). Test procedure bias: A meta-analysis of examiner effects. *Review of Educational Research, 56,* 243–262.

Fuchs, D., Fuchs, L. S., Hodge, J. P., & Mathes, P. G. (1994). Importance of instructional complexity and role reciprocity to classwide peer tutoring. *Learning Disabilities Research & Practice, 9,* 203–212.

Fuchs, D., Zern, D. S., & Fuchs, L. S. (1983). A microanalysis of participant behavior in familiar and unfamiliar test conditions. *Exceptional Children, 50,* 75–77.

Fuchs, L. S., & Fuchs, D. (1986). Effects of systematic formative evaluation: A meta-analysis. *Exceptional Children, 53,* 199–208.

Fuchs, L. S., Fuchs, D., Hamlett, C. L., & Ferguson, C. (1992). Effects of expert system consultation within curriculum-based measurement, using a reading maze task. *Exceptional Children, 58,* 436–450.

Fuchs, L. S., Fuchs, D., Hamlett, C. L., Phillips, N. B., & Karns, K. (1995). General educators' specialized adaption for students with learning disabilities. *Exceptional Children, 61,* 440–459.

Fuchs, L. S., Fuchs, D., Hamlett, C. L., & Stecker, P. M. (1990). The role of skills analysis in curriculum-based measurement in math. *School Psychology Review, 19,* 6–22.

Fuchs, L. S., Fuchs, D., & Stecker, P. M. (1989). Effects of curriculum-based measurement on teachers' instructional planning. *Journal of Learning Disabilities, 22,* 51–59.

Fuchs, L. S., & Maxwell, L. (1988). Interactive effects of reading mode, production format, and structural importance of text among LD pupils. *Learning Disability Quarterly, 11,* 97–105.

Fuerst, D. R., Fisk, J. L., & Rourke, B. P. (1989). Psychosocial functioning of learning-disabled children: Replicability of statistically derived subtypes. *Journal of Consulting and Clinical Psychology, 57,* 275–280.

Fugate, D. J., Clarizio, H. F., & Phillips, S. E. (1993). Referral-to-placement ratio: A finding in need of reassessment? *Journal of Learning Disabilities, 26,* 413–416.

Fulk, B. J. M., Mastropieri, M., & Scruggs, T. E. (1992). Mnemonic generalization training with learning disabled adolescents. *Learning Disabilities Research & Practice, 7,* 2–10.

Fulk, B. M., & Stormont-Spurgin, M. (1995). Spelling interventions for students with disabilities: A review. *The Journal of Special Education, 28,* 488–513.

Fuqua, R. W., Hegland, S. M., & Karas, S. C. (1985). Processes influencing linkages between preschool handicap classrooms and homes. *Exceptional Children, 51,* 307–314.

Furlong, M. J., & Yanagida, E. H. (1985). Psychometric factors affecting multidisciplinary team identification of learning disabled children. *Learning Disability Quarterly, 8,* 37–44.

Furth, H. G., & Wachs, H. (1974). *Thinking goes to school.* New York: Oxford University Press.

Fuson, K. C. (1988). *Children's counting and concepts of number.* New York: Springer-Verlag.

Fygetakis, L. J., & Ingram, D. (1973). Language rehabilitation and programmed conditioning: A case study. *Journal of Learning Disabilities, 6,* 60–64.

Gadow, K. D. (1983a). Effects of stimulant drugs on academic performance in hyperactive and learning disabled children. *Journal of Learning Disabilities, 16,* 290–299.

Gadow, K. D. (1983b). Pharmacotherapy for learning disabilities. *Learning Disabilities, 2,* 127–140.

Gadow, K. D, (1986). *Children on medication: Vol. 1. Hyperactivity, learning disabilities, and mental retardation.* San Diego: College-Hill.

Gajria, M., & Salend, S. J. (1995). Homework practices of students with and without learning disabilities: A comparison. *Journal of LEarning Disabilities, 28,* 291–296.

Gajria, M., Salend, S. J., & Hemrick, M. A. (1994). Teacher acceptability of testing modifications for mainstreamed students. *Learning Disabilities Research & Practice, 9,* 236–243.

Gajria, M., & Salvia, J. (1992). The effects of summarization instruction on text comprehension of students with learning disabilities. *Exceptional Children, 58,* 508–516.

Galaburda, A. M. (1986). Animal studies and the neurology of developmental dyslexia. In G. Th. Pavlidis & D. F. Fisher (Eds.), *Dyslexia: Its neuropsychology and treatment.* New York: John Wiley & Sons.

Galaburda, A., & Livingstone, M. (1993). Evidence for a magnocellular defect in developmental dyslexia. *Annals of the New York Academy of Sciences, 682,* 70–82.

Galaburda, A. M., Sherman, G. F., Rosen, G. D., Aboitiz, F., & Geschwind, N. (1985). Developmental dyslexia: Four consecutive patients with cortical anomalies. *Annals of Neurology, 18,* 222–233.

Galeese, B. (1973). *Informal reading inventory program.* The University of Michigan, Office of Instructional Services, School of Education.

Gallagher, J. J. (1966). Children with developmental imbalances: A psychoeducational definition. In W. M. Cruickshank (Ed.), *The teacher of brain-injured children: A discussion of the bases for competency.* Syracuse: Syracuse University Press.

Galler, J. R., Ramsey, F., & Solimano, G. (1985). A follow-up study of the effects of early malnutrition on subsequent development. II. Fine motor skills in adolescence. *Pediatric Research, 19,* 524–527.

Garber, H. L. (1987). *The Milwaukee Project: Preventing mental retardation in children at risk.* Washington, DC: American Association on Mental Deficiency.

Gard, A., Gilman, L., & Gorman, S. (1980). *Speech and language development chart.* Salt Lake City, UT: Word Making Productions.

Gardner, H. (1983). *Frames of mind: The theory of multiple intelligence.* New York: Basic Books.

Garner, R., & Alexander, P. A., (1989). Metacognition: Answered and unanswered questions, *Educational Psychologist, 24,* 143–158.

Garner, R., & Reis, R. (1981). Monitoring and resolving comprehension obstacles: An investigation of spontaneous text look-backs among upper-grade good and poor comprehenders. *Reading Research Quarterly, 16,* 569–582.

Garnett, K. (1989, winter). Math learning disabilities. *The Forum,* 11–15.

Garnett, K. (1992). Developing fluency with basic number facts: Intervention for students with learning disabilities. *Learning Disabilities Research & Practice, 7,* 210–216.

Garnett, K., & Fleischner, J. E. (1983). Automatization and basic fact performance of normal and learning disabled children. *Learning Disability Quarterly, 6,* 223–230.

Garrett, M. K., & Crump, W. D. (1980). Peer acceptance, teacher preference, and self-appraisal of social status among learning disabled students, *Learning Disability Quarterly, 3*(3), 42–48.

Garrity, L. (1975). An electromyographical study of subvocal speech and recall in preschool children. *Developmental Psychology, 11,* 274–281.

Gaustad, M. G., & Messenheimer-Young, T. (1991). Dialogue journals for students with learning disabilities. *Teaching Exceptional Children, 23,* 28–32.

Gawronski, J. D., & Coblentz, D. (1976). Calculators and the mathematics curriculum. *Arithmetic Teacher, 23,* 510–512.

Geffner, D. S., & Hochberg, I. (1971). Ear laterality performance of children from low and middle socioeconomic levels on a verbal dichotic listening task. *Cortex, 7,* 193–203.

Geisthardt, C., & Munsch, J. (1996). Coping with school stress: A comparison of adolescents with and without learning disabilities. *Journal of Learning Disabilities, 29,* 287–296.

Gelardo, M. S., & Sanford, E. E. (1987). Child abuse and neglect: A review of the literature. *School Psychology Review, 16,* 137–155.

Gelzheiser, L. M., Shepherd, M. J., & Wozniak, R. H. (1986). The development of instruction to induce skill transfer. *Exceptional Children, 53,* 125–129.

George, P. S. (1975). *Ten years of open space schools: A review of the research.* Gainesville, FL: Florida Educational Research and Development Council, University of Florida.

Gerard, J. A., & Junkala, J. (1980). Task analysis, handwriting, and process based instruction. *Journal of Learning Disabilities, 13,* 49–58.

Gerber, M. M. (1984). Orthographic problem-solving ability of learning disabled and normally achieving students. *Learning Disability Quarterly, 7,* 157–164.

Gerber, P. J., Ginsberg, R., & Reiff, H. B. (1992). Identifying alterable patterns in employment success for highly successful adults with learning disabilities. *Journal of Learning Disabilities, 25,* 475–487.

Gerber, P. J., & Zinkgraf, S. A. (1982). A comparative study of social-perceptual ability in learning disabled and nonhandicapped students. *Learning Disability Quarterly, 5,* 374–378.

Gerken, K. (1978). Performance of Mexican-American children on intelligence tests. *Exceptional Children, 44,* 438–443.

Germann, G., & Tindal, G. (1985). An application of curriculum-based assessment: The use of direct and repeated measurement. *Exceptional Children, 52,* 244–265.

Gersten, R., & Woodward, J. (1994). The language-minority student and special education: Issues, trends, and paradoxes. *Exceptional Children, 60,* 310–322.

Gersten, R., Woodward, J., & Darch, C. (1986). Direct instruction: A research-based approach to curriculum design and teaching. *Exceptional Children, 53,* 17–31.

Geschwind, N. (1968). Neurological foundations of language. In H. R. Myklebust (Ed.), *Progress in learning disabilities* (Vol. 1). New York: Grune & Stratton.

Geschwind, N. (1985). Biological foundations of reading. In F. H. Duffy & N. Geschwind (Eds.), *Dyslexia: A neuroscientific approach to clinical evaluation.* Boston: Little, Brown.

Geschwind, N. (1986). Dyslexia, cerebral dominance, auto-immunity, and sex hormones. In G. Th. Pavlidis & D. F. Fisher (Eds.), *Dyslexia: Its neuropsychology and treatment.* New York: John Wiley & Sons.

Geschwind, N., & Behan, P. (1982). Left-handedness: Association with immune disease, migraine, and developmental learning disorder. *Proceedings of the National Academy of sciences* (USA), *79,* 5097–5100.

Gesell, A. L. (1939). *Biographies of child development.* New York: Harper.

Gesell, A. L., & Ames, L. B. (1947). The development of handedness. *Journal of Genetic Psychology, 70,* 155–175.

Getman, G. N. (1977). Searching for solutions or perpetuating problems? *Academic Therapy, 13,* 185–196.

Getzels, J. W. (1974). Images of the classroom and visions of the learner. *School Review, 82,* 527–540.

Gheorghita, N. (1981). Vertical reading: A new method of therapy for reading disturbances in aphasics. *Journal of Clinical Neuropsychology, 3,* 161–164.

Gianino, A., & Tronick, E. (1988). The mutual recognition model: The infant's self and interactive regulation coping and defense. In T. H. Field, P. M. McCabe, & N. Schneiderman (Eds.), *Stress and coping across development.* Hillsdale, NJ: Lawrence Erlbaum.

Gibson, E. J. (1969). *Principles of perceptual learning and development.* New York: Appleton-Century-Crofts.

Gibson, E. J., Gibson, J. J., Pick, A. D., & Osser, H. A. (1962). Developmental study of the discrimination of letter-like forms. *Journal of Comparative and Physiological Psychology, 55,* 897–906.

Gibson, E. J., & Levin, H. (1975). *The psychology of reading.* Cambridge, MA: MIT Press.

Gickling, E. E., & Thompson, V. P. (1985). A personal view of curriculum-based assessment. *Exceptional Children, 52,* 205–218.

Gillespie, P. H., Miller, T. L., & Fielder, V. D. (1975). Legislative definitions of learning disabilities: Roadblocks to effective service. *Journal of Learning Disabilities, 8,* 660–666.

Gilligan, C. (1982). *In a different voice: Psychological theory and women's development.* Cambridge, MA: Harvard University Press.

Gillingham, A., & Stillman, B. (1970). *Remedial training for children with specific disability in reading, spelling, and penmanship.* Cambridge, MA: Educator's Publishing Service.

Ginsburg-Block, M., & Fantuzzo, J. (1997). Reciprocal peer tutoring: An analysis of "teacher" and "student" interactions as a function of training and experience. *School Psychology Quarterly, 12,* 134–149.

Gittelman, R., Klein, D. F., & Feingold, I. (1983). Children with reading disorders—II. Effects of methylphenidate in combination with reading remediation. *Journal of Child Psychology and Psychiatry, 24,* 193–212.

Gittelman, R., Mannuzza, S., Shenker, R., & Bonagura, N. (1985). Hyperactive boys almost grown up: 1. Psychiatric status. *Archives of General Psychiatry, 42,* 937–947.

Glass, G. V., Cahan, L. S., Smith, M. L., & Filby, N. N. (1982). *School class size: Research and policy.* Beverly Hills, CA: Sage Publications.

Glass, G. V., & Smith, M. L. (1979). Meta-analysis of research on class size and achievement. *Educational Evaluation and Policy Analysis, 1,* 2–16.

Glazzard, M. (1977). The effectiveness of three kindergarten predictors for first-grade achievement. *Journal of Learning Disabilities, 10,* 95–99.

Glazzard, P. H. (1981). Teacher rating and reading readiness as predictors of vocabulary and comprehension achievement in first, second, third and fourth grade. *Learning Disability Quarterly, 3,* 35–45.

Glazzard, P. H. (1982). Long-range kindergarten prediction of reading achievement in first through sixth grade. *Learning Disability Quarterly, 5*(1), 85–88.

Gleason, M., Carnine, D., & Vala, N. (1991). Cumulative versus rapid introduction of new information. *Exceptional Children, 57,* 353–358.

Godfrey, J. F., Syrdal-Lasky, A. K., Millay, K. K., & Knox, C. M. (1981). Performance of dyslexic children on speech perception tests. *Journal of Experimental Child Psychology, 32,* 401–424.

Goethe, K. E., & Levin, H. S. (1984). Behavioral manifestations during the early and long-term stages of recovery after closed head injury. *Psychiatric Annals, 14,* 540–546.

Gold, J., & Fleisher, L. S. (1986). Comprehension breakdown with inductively organized text: Differences between average and disabled readers. *Remedial and Special Education, 7*(4), 26–32.

Gold, R. F. (1978). Constitutional growth delay and learning problems. *Journal of Learning Disabilities, 11,* 427–429.

Goldberg, E., & Costa, L. D. (1981). Hemisphere differences in the acquisition and use of descriptive systems. *Brain and Language, 14,* 144–173.

Goldman, P. S., Crawford, H. T., Stokes, L. P., Galkin, T. W., & Rosvold, H. E. (1974). Sex-dependent behavioral effects of cerebral cortical lesions in the developing rhesus monkey. *Science, 186,* 540–542.

Goldsmith, H. H., & Gottesman, I. I. (1981). Origins of variation in behavioral style: A longitudinal study of temperament in young twins. *Child Development, 52,* 91–103.

Goldstein, A. P. (1988). *The prepare curriculum: Teaching prosocial competencies.* Champaign, IL: Research Press.

Goldstein, A. P., Sprafkin, R. P., Gershaw, N. J., & Klein, P. (1980). *Skill-streaming the adolescent: A structured approach to teaching prosocial skills.* Champaign, IL: Research Press.

Goldstein, D., & Dundon, W. D. (1987). Affect and cognition in learning disabilities. In S. J. Ceci (Ed.), *Handbook of cognitive, social, and neuropsychological aspects of learning disabilities* (Vol. II). Hillsdale, NJ: Lawrence Erlbaum.

Goldstein, H., & Gallagher, T. M. (1992). Strategies for promoting the social-communicative competence of young children with specific language impairment. In S. L. Odom, S. R. McConnell, & M. A.

McEvoy (Eds.), *Social competence of young children with disabilities: Issues and strategies for intervention*. Baltimore: Paul H. Brookes.

Goldstein, K. (1936). The modifications of behavior consequent to cerebral lesions. *Psychiatric Quarterly, 10,* 586–610.

Goldstein, K. (1942). *Aftereffects of brain injuries in war*. New York: Grune & Stratton.

Good, R. H., III, & Salvia, J. (1988). Curriculum bias in published, norm-referenced reading tests: Demonstrable effects. *School Psychology Review, 17,* 51–60.

Good, T., & Brophy, J. (1972). Behavioral expression of teacher attitudes. *Journal of Educational Psychology, 63,* 617–624.

Good, T., & Brophy, J. (1978). *Looking in classrooms*. New York: Harper & Row.

Good, T. L. (1980). Classroom expectations: Teacher-pupil interactions. In J. H. McMillan (Ed.), *The social psychology of school learning*. New York: Academic Press.

Good, T. L. (1981), Teacher expectations and student perceptions: A decade of research. *Educational Leadership, 38,* 415–422.

Goodlad, J. I. (1984). *A place called school*. New York: McGraw-Hill.

Goodman, C. H., & Brown, D. S. (1992, July/August). Learning disabilities and the workplace. *LDA Newsbriefs,* 9.

Goodman, K. S. (1976). Reading: A psycholinguistic guessing game. In H. Singer & R. Ruddell (Eds.), *Theoretical models and processes of reading* (2nd ed.). Newark, DE: International Reading Association.

Goodman, K. S. (1986). *What's whole in whole language?* Portsmouth, NH: Heinemann.

Goodman, K. S., & Goodman, Y. M. (1977). Learning about psycholinguistic processes by analyzing oral reading. *Harvard Educational Review, 47,* 317–333.

Goodman, K. S., & Goodman, Y. (1979). Learning to read is natural. In L. B. Resnick & P. A. Weaver (Eds.), *Theory and practice of early reading* (Vol. 1). Hillsdale, NJ: Lawrence Erlbaum.

Goodman, Y. M., & Burke, C. L. (1972). *Reading miscue inventory manual: Procedure for diagnosis and evaluation*. New York: Macmillan.

Goswami, U. (1989, March). *Orthographic units and transfer in reading*. San Francisco: American Educational Research Association.

Gottesman, R. L., Croen, L., & Rotkin, L. (1982). Urban second grade children: A profile of good and poor readers. *Journal of Learning Disabilities, 15,* 268–272.

Gottfried, A. W., & Bathurst, K. (1983). Hand preference across time is related to intelligence in young girls, not boys. *Science, 221,* 1074–1076.

Gottlieb, B. W. (1982). Social facilitation influences on the oral reading performance of academically handicapped children. *American Journal of Mental Deficiency, 87,* 153–158.

Gottlieb, B. W. (1984). Effects of relative competence on learning disabled children's oral reading performance. *Learning Disability Quarterly, 7,* 108–112,

Gottlieb, B. W., Gottlieb, J., Berkell, D., & Levy, L. (1986). Sociometric status and solitary play of LD boys and girls. *Journal of Learning Disabilities, 19,* 619–622.

Gottlieb, J., Alter, M., Gottlieb, B. W., & Wishner, J. (1994). Special education in urban America: It's not justifiable for many. *The Journal of Special Education, 27,* 453–465.

Gottlieb, J., Rose, T. L., & Lessen, E. (1983). Mainstreaming. In K. T. Kernan, M. J. Begab, & R. B. Edgerton (Eds.), *Environments and behavior: The adaptation of mentally retarded persons*. Baltimore: University Park Press.

Goyette, C. H., Conners, C. K., Petti, T. A., & Curtis, L. E. (1978). Effects of artificial colors on hyperkinetic children: A double-blind challenge study. *Psychopharmacology Bulletin, 14*(2), 39–40.

Graden, J. L., Casey, A., & Bonstrom, O. (1985). Implementing a pre-referral intervention system: Part II. The data. *Exceptional Children, 51*(6), 487–496.

Graham, L., & Wong, B. Y. L. (1993). Comparing two modes of teaching a question-answering strategy for enhancing comprehension: Didactic and self-instructional training. *Journal of Learning Disabilities, 26,* 270–279.

Graham, S. (1990). The role of production factors in learning disabled students' composition. *Journal of Educational Psychology, 82,* 781–791.

Graham, S., & MacArthur, C. (1988). Improving learning disabled students' skills at revising essays produced on a word processor: Self-instructional strategy training. *The Journal of Special Education, 22,* 133–152.

Graham, S., MacArthur, C., Schwartz, S., & Page-Voth, V. (1992). Improving the compositions of students with learning disabilities using a strategy involving product and process goal setting. *Exceptional children, 58,* 322–334.

Graham, S., Schwartz, S. S., & MacArthur, C. A. (1993). Knowledge of writing and the composing process, attitude toward writing, and self-efficacy for students with and without learning disabilities. *Journal of Learning Disabilities, 26,* 237–249.

Graves, A., & Montague, M. (1991). Using story grammar cueing to improve the writing of students with learning disabilities. *Learning Disabilities Research & Practice, 6,* 246–250.

Graves, A., Semmel, M., & Gerber, M. (1994). The effects of story prompts on the narrative production of students with and without learning disabilities. *Learning Disability Quarterly, 17,* 154–164.

Graves, A. W. (1986). Effect of direct instruction and metacomprehension training on finding main ideas. *Learning Disabilities Research, 1,* 90–100.

Graves, D. H. (1983). *Writing: Teachers and children at work*. Portsmouth, NH: Heinemann Educational Books.

Green, M. (1974). Sublingual provocative testing for foods and FD & C dyes. *Annals of Allergy, 33,* 274–281.

Green, O. C., & Perlman, S. M. (1971). Endocrinology and disorders of learning. In H. R. Myklebust (Ed.), *Progress in learning disabilities* (Vol. II). New York: Grune & Stratton.

Greenbaum, B., Graham, S., & Scales, W. (1996). Adults with learning disabilities: Occupational and social status after college. *Journal of Learning Disabilities, 29,* 167–173.

Greeno, J. G. (1989). A perspective on thinking. *American Psychologist, 44,* 134–141.

Greenough, W. T. (1976). Enduring brain effects of differential experience and training. In M. R. Rosenzweig & E. L. Bennett (Eds.), *Neural mechanisms of learning and memory*. Cambridge, MA: MIT Press.

Greenough, W. T., & Juraska, J. M. (1979). Experience-induced changes in brain fine structure: Their behavioral implications. In M. E. Hahn, C. Jensen, & B. C. Dudek (Eds.), *Development and evolution of brain size: Behavioral implications*. New York: Academic Press.

Greenwood, C. R., Carta, J. J., & Hall, R. V. (1988). The use of peer tutoring strategies in classroom management and educational instruction. *School Psychology Review, 17,* 258–275.

Gregg, N. (1986). Cohesion: Inter and intra sentence errors. *Journal of Learning Disabilities, 19,* 338–341.

Gregory, J. F., Shanahan, T., & Walberg, H. (1986). A profile of learning disabled twelfth-graders in regular classes. *Learning Disability Quarterly, 9,* 33–42.

Gregory, S. C., & Bunch, M. E. (1959). The relative retentive abilities of fast and slow learners. *Journal of General Psychology, 60,* 173–181.

Gresham, F. M. (1982). Misguided mainstreaming: The case for social skills training with handicapped children. *Exceptional Children, 48,* 422–433.

Gresham, F. M., (1984). Social skills and self-efficacy for exceptional children. *Exceptional Children, 51,* 253–261.

Gresham, F. M. (1991). Alternative psychometrics for authentic assessment? *School Psychology Quarterly, 6,* 305–309.

Gresham, F. M., MacMillan, D. L., & Bocian, K. M. (1997). Teachers as "tests": Differential validity of teacher judgments in identifying students at-risk for learning disabilities. *School Psychology Review, 26,* 47–60.

Gresham, F. M., & Reschly, D. J. (1986). Social skill deficits and low peer acceptance of mainstreamed learning disabled children. *Learning Disability Quarterly, 9,* 23–32.

Griffey, Q. L., Zigmond, N., & Leinhardt, G. (1988). The effects of self-questioning and story structure training on the reading comprehension of poor readers. *Learning Disabilities Research, 4,* 45–51.

Griffith, P. L. (1991). Phonemic awareness helps first graders invent spellings and third graders remember correct spellings. *Journal of Reading Behavior, 23,* 215–233.

Griffith, P. L., & Olson, M. W. (1992). Phonemic awareness helps beginning readers break the code. *The Reading Teacher, 45,* 516–523.

Griffiths, A. D., & Laurence, K. M. (1974). The effect of hypoxia and hypoglycaemia on the brain of the newborn human infant. *Developmental Medicine and Child Neurology, 16,* 308–319.

Grigal, M., Test, D. W., Beattie, J., & Wood, W. M. (1997). An evaluation of transition components of individualized education programs. *Exceptional Children, 63,* 357–372.

Grissom, J. B., & Shepard, L. A. (1989). Repeating and dropping out of school. In L. A. Shepard & M. L. Smith (Eds.), *Flunking grades: Research and policies on retention.* London: Falmer Press.

Griswold, P. C., Gelzheiser, L. M., & Shepherd, M. J. (1987). Does a production deficiency hypothesis account for vocabulary learning among adolescents with learning disabilities? *Journal of Learning Disabilities, 20,* 620–626.

Groenendaal, H. A., & Bakker, D. J. (1971). The part played by mediation processes in the retention of temporal sequences by two reading groups. *Human Development, 14,* 62–70.

Gross-Tsur, V., Shalev, R. S., Manor, O., & Amir, N. (1995). Developmental right-hemisphere syndrome: Clinical spectrum of the nonverbal learning disability. *Journal of Learning Disabilities, 28,* 80–86.

Gruber, E. (1962). Reading ability, binocular coordination and the ophthalmograph. *Archives of Ophthalmology, 67,* 280–288.

Guare, R., & Dawson, P. (1995, November). "Coaching" teenagers with attention disorders. *Communiqué, 9.* National Association of School Psychologists.

Guidubaldi, J., Perry, J. D., Cleminshaw, H. K., & McLoughlin, C. S. (1983). The impact of parental divorce on children: Report of the nationwide NASP study. *School Psychology Review, 12,* 300–323.

Guralnick, M. J. (1978). The application of single-subject research designs to the field of learning disabilities. *Journal of Learning Disabilities, 11,* 415–421.

Guralnick, M. J. (1991). The next decade of research on the effectiveness of early intervention. *Exceptional Children, 58,* 174–183.

Guralnick, M. J., & Groom, J. M. (1988). Peer interactions in mainstreamed and specialized classrooms: A comparative analysis. *Exceptional Children, 54,* 415–425.

Gurney, D., Gersten, R., Dimino, J., Carnine, D. (1990). Story grammar: Effective literature instruction for high school students with learning disabilities. *Journal of Learning Disabilities, 23,* 335–342, 348.

Guthrie, J. (1980). Time in reading programs. *The Reading Teacher, 33,* 500–502.

Gutierrez, R., & Slavin, R. E. (1992). Achievement effects of the nongraded elementary school: A best evidence synthesis. *Review of Educational Research, 62,* 333–376.

Guyer, B. P., & Sabatino, D. (1989). The effectiveness of a multisensory alphabetic phonetic approach with college students who are learning disabled. *Journal of Learning Disabilities, 22,* 430–434.

Haager, D., & Vaughn, S. (1995). Parent, teacher, peer, and self-reports of the social competence of students with learning disabilities. *Journal of Learning Disabilities, 28,* 205–215, 231.

Haber, R. N., & Haber, L. R. (1981). The shape of a word can specify its meaning. *Reading Research Quarterly, 16,* 334–345.

Hagen, J. W. (1971). Some thoughts on how children learn to remember. *Human Development, 14,* 262–271.

Hagen, J. W., Jongeward, R. H., & Kail, R. V. (1975). Cognitive perspectives on the development of memory. In H. W. Reese (Ed.), *Advances in child development and behavior* (Vol. 10). New York: Academic Press.

Hagerty, G. J., & Abramson, M. (1987). Impediments to implementing national policy change for mildly handicapped students. *Exceptional Children, 53,* 315–323.

Hall, P. K., & Tomblin, J. B. (1978). A follow-up study of children with articulation and language disorders. *Journal of Speech and Hearing Disorders, 43,* 227–241.

Hallahan, D. P., & Cruickshank, W. M. (1973). *Psycho-educational foundations of learning disabilities.* Englewood-Cliffs, NJ: Prentice-Hall.

Hallahan, D. P., & Kauffman, J. M. (1977). Labels, categories, behaviors: ED, LD, and EMR reconsidered. *Journal of Special Education, 11,* 139–149.

Hallahan, D. P., Kneedler, R. D., & Lloyd, J. W. (1983). Cognitive behavior modification techniques for learning disabled children: Self instruction and self-monitoring. In J. D. McKinney & L. Feagans (Eds.), *Current topics in learning disabilities.* Norwood, NJ: Ablex.

Hallahan, D. P., Tarver, S. G., Kauffman, J. M., & Graybeal, N. L. (1978). A comparison of the effect of reinforcement and response cost on the selective attention of learning disabled children. *Journal of Learning Disabilities, 11,* 430–438.

Hallinan, M. T., & Sorensen, A. B. (1983). The formation and stability of ability groups. *American Sociological Review, 48,* 838–851.

Halmhuber, N. L., & Paris, S. G. (1993). Perceptions of competence and control and the use of coping strategies by children with disabilities. *Learning Disability Quarterly, 16,* 93–111.

Halpern, W. (1975). Turned on toddlers. *Journal of Communication, 25,* 66–70.

Hammack, F. M. (1986). Large school systems' dropout reports: An analysis of definitions, procedures, and findings. In G. Natriello (Ed.), *School dropouts: Patterns and policies.* New York: Teachers College Press.

Hammill, D. D. (1972). Defining "LD" for programmatic purposes. *Academic Therapy, 12,* 29–37.

Hammill, D. D. (1976). Defining "LD" for programmatic purposes. *Academic Therapy, 12,* 29–37.

Hammill, D. D. (1990). On defining learning disabilities: An emerging consensus. *Journal of Learning Disabilities, 23,* 74–84.

Hammill, D. D., & Larsen, S. C. (1974a). The relationship of selected auditory perceptual skills and reading ability. *Journal of Learning Disabilities, 7,* 429–436.

Hammill, D. D., & Larsen, S. C. (1974b). The effectiveness of psycholinguistic training. *Exceptional Children, 41,* 5–14.

Hammill, D. D., & Larsen, S. C. (1978). The effectiveness of psycholinguistic training: A reaffirmation of position. *Exceptional Children, 44,* 402–414.

Haney, W. (1981). Validity, vaudeville and values: A short history of social concerns over standardized testing. *American Psychologist, 36,* 1021–1034.

Hanna, P. R., Hodges, R. E., & Hanna, J. S. (1971). *Spelling: Structure and strategies.* Boston: Houghton-Mifflin.

Hannah, M. E., & Midlarsky, E. (1985). Siblings of the handicapped: A literature review for school psychologists. *School Psychology Review, 14,* 510–520.

Hannah, M. E., & Pliner, S. (1983). Teacher attitudes toward handicapped children: A review and synthesis. *School Psychology Review, 12,* 12–25.

Hansen, J., & Pearson, P. D. (1983). An instructional study: Improving the inferential comprehension of good and poor fourth-grade readers. *Journal of Educational Psychology, 75,* 821–829.

Hansen, R. C. (1985). Acutane (isotretinoin) revisited: Severe birth defects from acne therapy. *Southern Arizona Medicine, 42,* 363–365.

Hanshaw, J. B., Scheiner, A. P., Moxley, A. W., Gaev, L., Abel, V., & Scheiner, B. (1976). School failure and deafness after "silent" congenital cytomegalovirus infection. *The New England Journal of Medicine, 295,* 468–470.

Hanson, C. L. (1990). Understanding insulin-dependent diabetes mellitus (IDDM) and treating children with IDDM and their families.

In S. W. Henggeler & C. M. Borduin (Eds.), *Family therapy and beyond: A multisystemic approach to treating the behavior problems of children and adolescents*. Pacific Grove, CA: Brooks/Cole.

Harber, J. R. (1983). The effects of illustrations on the reading performance of learning disabled and normal children. *Learning Disability Quarterly, 6,* 55–60.

Hardyck, C., & Petrinovich, L. F. (1977). Left-handedness. *Psychological Bulletin, 84,* 385–404.

Haring, N. G., & Lovitt, T. C. (1967). Operant methodology and educational technology in special education. In H. G. Haring & R. L. Schiefelbusch (Eds.), *Methods in special education*. New York: McGraw-Hill.

Haring, T. G. (1992). The context of social competence: Relations, relationships, and generalization. In S. L. Odom, S. R. McConnell, & M. R. McEvoy (Eds.), *Social competence of young children with disabilities: Issues and strategies for interaction*. Baltimore: Paul H. Brookes.

Harley, J. P., Matthews, C. G., & Eichman, P. (1978). Synthetic food colors and hyperactivity in children: A double-blind challenge experiment. *Pediatrics, 62,* 975–983.

Harley, J. P., Ray, R. S., Tomasi, L., Eichman, P. L., Matthews, C. G., Chun, R., Cleeland, C. S., & Traisman, E. (1978). Hyperkinesis and food additives: Testing the Feingold hypothesis. *Pediatrics, 61,* 818–822.

Harnadek, M. C. S., & Rourke, B. P. (1994). Principle identifying features of the syndrome of nonverbal learning disabilities in children. *Journal of Learning Disabilities, 27,* 144–154.

Harniss, M. K., Hollenbeck, K. L., Crawford, D. B., & Carnine, D. (1994). Content organization and instructional design issues in the development of history texts. *Learning Disability Quarterly, 17,* 235–248.

Harris, A. J. (1957). Lateral dominance, directional confusion and reading disability. *Journal of Psychology, 44,* 283–294.

Harris, A. J. (1962). *Effective teaching of reading*. New York: David McKay.

Harris, A. J., & Sipay, E. R. (1979). *How to teach reading: A competency-based program*. New York: Longman.

Harris, D. (1963). *Children's drawings as measures of intellectual maturity*. New York: Harcourt, Brace & World.

Harris, E. L. (1986). The contribution of twin research to the study of the etiology of reading disability. In S. D. Smith (Ed.), *Genetics and learning disabilities*. San Diego: College Hill Press.

Harris, R. (1983). Clinical neurophysiology in paediatric neurology. In E. M. Brett (Ed.), *Paediatric neurology*. Edinburgh: Churchill Livingstone.

Harry, B. (1992a). Making sense of disability: Low-income, Puerto Rican parents' theories of the problem. *Exceptional Children, 59,* 27–40.

Harry, B. (1992b). Restructuring the participation of African-American parents in special education. *Exceptional Children, 59,* 123–131.

Hart, B., & Risley, T. R. (1992). American parenting of language-learning children: Persisting differences in family-child interactions observed in natural home environments. *Developmental Psychology, 28,* 1096–1105.

Hartlage, L. C., & Green, J. B. (1971). EEG differences in children's reading, spelling, and arithmetic abilities. *Perceptual and Motor Skills, 32,* 133–134.

Hartlage, L. C., & Green, J. B. (1972). The EEG abnormalities and WISC subtest differences. *Journal of Clinical Psychology, 28,* 170–171.

Hartlage, L. C., & Telzrow, C. F. (1982). Specific medical findings which predict specific learning outcomes. In W. M. Cruickshank & J. W. Lerner (Eds.), *Coming of age: Vol. 3. The best of ACLD*. Syracuse: Syracuse University Press.

Hartlage, L. C., & Telzrow, C. F. (1986). *Neuropsychological assessment and intervention with children and adolescents*. Sarasota, FL: Professional Resource Exchange.

Hartshorne, H., & May, M. A. (1928). *Studies in deceit*. New York: Macmillan.

Hartup, W. W. (1983). Peer relations. In E. M. Hetherington (Ed.), *Handbook of child psychology: Socialization, personality, and social development* (Vol. 4). New York: Wiley.

Hartup, W. W. (1989). Social relationships and their developmental significance. *American Psychologist, 44,* 120–126.

Hartup, W. W., Laursen, B., Stewart, M. I., & Eastenson, A. (1988). Conflict and the friendship relations of young children. *Child Development, 59,* 1590–1600.

Haskins, R. (1989). Beyond metaphor: The efficacy of early childhood education. *American Psychologist, 44,* 274–282.

Haslam, R. H. A., Dalby, J. T., & Rademaker, A. W. (1984). Effects of megavitamin therapy on children with attention deficit disorders. *Pediatrics, 74,* 103–111.

Hatcher, P. J., Hulme, C., & Ellis, A. W. (1994). Ameliorating early reading failure by integrating the teaching of reading and phonological skills: The phonological linkage hypothesis. *Child Development, 65,* 41–57.

Havighurst, R. J. (1972). *Developmental tasks and education*. New York: David McKay.

Hayden, B., & Pickar, D. (1981). The impact of moral discussions on children's level of moral reasoning. *Journal of Moral Education, 10*(2), 131–134.

Haynes, M. C., & Jenkins, J. R. (1986). Reading instruction in special education resource rooms. *American Educational Research Journal, 23,* 161–190.

Haywood, H. C., & Switzky, H. N. (1986). The malleability of intelligence: Cognitive processes as a function of polygenic-experiential interaction. *School Psychology Review, 15,* 245–255.

Head, H. (1915). Hughlings Jackson on aphasic and kindred affections of speech. *Brain, 38,* 1–190.

Head, H. (1920a). Aphasia: An historical review. *Brain, 43,* 390–411.

Head, H. (1920b). Aphasia and kindred disorders. *Brain, 43,* 87–165.

Head, H. (1923). Speech and cerebral localization. *Brain, 46,* 355–528.

Head, H. (1926). *Aphasia and kindred disorders of speech*. London: Cambridge University Press.

Hearne, J. D., Poplin, M. S., Schoneman, C., & O'Shaughnessy, E. (1988). Computer aptitude: An investigation of differences among junior high students with learning disabilities and their non-learning-disabled peers. *Journal of Learning Disabilities, 21,* 489–492.

Heavey, C. L., Adelman, H. S., Nelson, P., & Smith, D. C. (1989). Learning problems, anger, perceived control, and misbehavior. *Journal of Learning Disabilities, 22,* 46–50, 59.

Hebert, B. M., & Murdock, J. Y. (1994). Comparing three computer-aided instruction output modes to teach vocabulary words to students with learning disabilities. *Learning Disabilities Research & Practice, 9,* 136–141.

Hécaen, H., & Albert, M. L. (1978). *Human neuropsychology*. New York: Wiley.

Hechtman, L. (1985). Adolescent outcome of hyperactive children treated with stimulants in childhood: A review. *Psychopharmacology Bulletin, 21,* 178–191.

Hechtman, L., Weiss, G., & Perlman, T. (1984a). Young adult outcome of hyperactive children who received long-term stimulant treatment. *Journal of the American Academy of Child Psychiatry, 23,* 261–269.

Hechtman, L., Weiss, G., & Perlman, T. (1984b). Hyperactives as young adults: Past and current substance abuse and antisocial behavior. *American Journal of Orthopsychiatry, 54,* 415–425.

Heckelman, R. C. (1969). A neurological impress method of remedial reading. *Academic Therapy, 4,* 277–282.

Hedges, L. V., & Nowell, A. (1995). Sex differences in mental test scores, variability, and numbers of high-scoring individuals. *Science, 269,* 41–45.

Heider, E. R. (1971). Information processing and the modification of an "impulsive conceptual tempo." *Child Development, 42,* 1276–1281.

Heilman, K. M., & Valenstein, E. (1979). *Clinical neuropsychology*. Oxford: Oxford University Press.

Heiman, J. R., Fischer, M. J., & Ross, A. O. (1973). A supplementary behavioral program to improve deficient reading performance. *Journal of Abnormal Child Psychology, 1,* 390–399.

Helveston, E. M., Weber, J. C., Miller, K., Robertson, K., Hohberger, G., Estes, R., Ellis, F. D., Pick, N., & Helveston, B. H. (1985). Visual function and academic performance. *American Journal of Ophthalmology, 99,* 346–355.

Hembree, R. (1986). Research gives calculators a green light. *Arithmetic Teacher, 34*(1), 18–21.

Henderson, E. H. (1980). Developmental concepts of word. In E. H. Henderson & J. W. Beers (Eds.), *Developmental and cognitive aspects of learning to spell: A reflection of word knowledge.* Newark, DE: International Reading Assoc.

Henderson, E. H., & Beers, J. W. (Eds.). (1980). *Developmental and cognitive aspects of learning to spell: A reflection of word knowledge.* Newark, DE: International Reading Association.

Henderson, L., & Chard, J. (1980). The reader's implicit knowledge of orthographic structure. In U. Frith (Ed.), *Cognitive processes in spelling.* London: Academic Press.

Hendrickson, L. N., & Muehl, S. (1962). The effects of attention and motor response pretraining on learning to discriminate b and d in kindergarten children. *Journal of Educational Psychology, 53,* 236–241.

Henker, B., & Whalen, C. K. (1989). Hyperactivity and attention deficits. *American Psychologist, 44,* 216–223.

Henning-Stout, M., Lucas D. A., & McCary, V. L. (1993). Alternative instruction in the regular classroom: A case illustration and evaluation. *School Psychology Review, 22,* 81–97.

Hermreck, L. A. (1979). *A comparison of the written language of LD and non-LD elementary children using the Inventory of Written Expression and Spelling.* Unpublished master's thesis, University of Kansas, Lawrence.

Heron, T. E., & Skinner, M. E. (1981). Criteria for defining the regular classroom as the least restrictive environment for LD students. *Exceptional Children, 4*(2), 115–121.

Herrnstein, R. J., & Murray, C. (1994). *The bell curve: Intelligence and class structure in American life.* New York: Free Press.

Hickman, J. (1989). Teenage pregnancy and births. *The School Psychologist, 43*(5), 14.

Hicks, R. E., & Kinsbourne, M. (1978a). Differences: Left-handedness. In M. Kinsbourne (Ed.), *The asymmetrical function of the brain.* New York: Cambridge University Press.

Hicks, R. E., & Kinsbourne, M. (1978b). Human handedness. In M. Kinsbourne (Ed.), *The asymmetrical function of the brain.* New York: Cambridge University Press.

Hiebert, B., Wong, B., & Hunter, M. (1982). Affective influences on learning disabled adolescents. *Learning Disability Quarterly, 5,* 334–343.

Hier, D. B. (1979). Sex differences in hemisphere specialization: Hypothesis for the excess of dyslexia in boys. *Bulletin of the Orton Society, 29,* 74–83.

Hier, D. B., LeMay, M., Rosenberger, P. B., & Perlo, V. P. (1978). Developmental dyslexia: Evidence for a sub-group with a reversal of cerebral asymmetry. *Archives of Neurology, 35,* 90–92.

Higgins, E. L., & Raskind, M. H. (1995). Compensatory effectiveness of speech recognition on the written composition performance of postsecondary students with learning disabilities. *Learning Disability Quarterly, 18,* 159–174.

Higgins, K., & Boone, R. (1991). Hypermedia CAI: A supplement to an elementary school basal reader program. *Journal of Special Education Technology, 11 (1),* 1–15.

Hillocks, G. C. (1986). *Research on written composition.* Urbana, IL: National Council of Teachers of English.

Hines, M. (1990). Gonadal hormones and human cognitive development. In J. Balthazart (Ed.), *Hormones, brains, and behaviors in vertebrates: 1. Sexual differentiation, neuroanatomical aspects, neurotransmitters, and neuropeptides.* Basel, Switzerland: Karger.

Hinshelwood, J. (1896). A case of dyslexia: A peculiar form of word-blindness. *Lancet, 2,* 1451–1454.

Hinshelwood, J. (1898). A case of "word" without "letter" blindness. *Lancet, 1,* 422–425.

Hinshelwood, J. (1899). "Letter" without "word" blindness. *Lancet, 1,* 83–86.

Hinshelwood, J. (1907). Four cases of congenital word-blindness occurring in the same family. *British Medical Journal, 2,* 1229–1232.

Hinshelwood, J. (1911). Two cases of hereditary congenital word-blindness. *British Medical Journal, 1,* 608–609.

Hinshelwood, J. (1917). *Congenital word blindness.* London: H. K. Lewis.

Hiscock, M. (1982). Verbal-manual time sharing in children as a function of task priority. *Brain and Cognition, 1,* 119–131.

Hodgkinson, H. L. (1986, May 14). Here they come, ready or not. *Education Week,* pp. 13–87.

Hoffman, F. J., Sheldon, K. L., Minskoff, E. H., Sautter, S. W., Steidle, E. F., Baker, D. P., Bailey, M. B., & Echols, L. D. (1987). Needs of learning disabled adults. *Journal of Learning Disabilities, 20,* 43–52.

Hoffman, L. W. (1989). Effects of maternal employment in the two-parent family. *American Psychologist, 44,* 283–292.

Holder, H. B., & Kirkpatrick, S. W. (1990). Interpretation of emotion from facial expressions in children with and without learning disabilities. *Journal of Learning Disabilities, 24,* 170–177.

Hollander, H. E. (1986). Learning disability among seriously delinquent youths: A perspective. In G. Th. Pavlidis & D. F. Fisher (Eds.), *Dyslexia: Its neuropsychology and treatment.* New York: John Wiley & Sons.

Holmes, J. M. (1987). Natural histories in learning disabilities: Neuropsychological difference/environmental demand. In S. J. Ceci (Ed.), *Handbook of cognitive, social and neuropsychological aspects of learning disabilities* (Vol. 2). Hillsdale, NJ: Lawrence Erlbaum.

Honea, J. M., Jr. (1982). Wait-time as an instructional variable: An influence on teacher and student. *Clearing House, 56,* 167–170.

Honzik, M. P. (1957). Developmental studies of parent-child resemblance in intelligence. *Child Development, 28,* 215–228.

Honzik, M. P., Macfarlane, J. W., & Allen, L. (1948). The stability of mental test performance between two and eighteen years. *Journal of Experimental Education, 17,* 309–324.

Hopkins, B. L., Schutte, R. C., & Garton, K. L. (1971). The effects of access to a playroom on the rate and quality of printing and writing of first and second grade students. *Journal of Applied Behavior Analysis, 4,* 77–87.

Horn, A. (1941). *The uneven distribution of the effects of specific factors* (Southern California Educational Monographs No. 12). Los Angeles: University of Southern California Press.

Horn, W. F., O'Donnell, J. P., & Vitulano, L. A. (1983). Long-term follow-up studies of learning disabled persons. *Journal of Learning Disabilities, 16,* 542–555.

Horn, W. F., & Packard, T. (1985). Early identification of learning disabilities: A meta-analysis. *Journal of Educational Psychology, 77,* 597–607.

Horowitz, E. C. (1981). Popularity, decentering ability, and role-taking skills in learning disabled and normal children. *Learning Disability Quarterly, 4*(1), 23–30.

Horton, S. V., Lovitt, T. C., & Christensen, C. C. (1991). Matching three classifications of secondary students to differential levels of study guides. *Journal of Learning Disabilities, 24,* 518–529.

Horton, S. V., Lovitt, T. C., Givens, A., & Nelson, R. (1989). Teaching social studies to high school students with academic handicaps in a mainstreamed setting: Effects of a computerized study guide. *Journal of Learning Disabilities, 22,* 102–107.

Horton, S. V., Lovitt, T. C., & Slocum, T. (1988). Teaching geography to high school students with academic deficits: Effects of a computerized map tutorial. *Learning Disability Quarterly, 11,* 371–379.

Houck, C. K., Geller, C. H., & Engelhard, J. (1988). Learning disabilities teachers' perceptions of the educational programs for adolescents with learning disabilities. *Journal of Learning Disabilities, 21,* 90–97.

Howell, R., Sidorenko, E., & Jurica, J. (1987). The effects of computer use on the acquisition of multiplication facts by a student with learning disabilities. *Journal of Learning Disabilities, 20,* 336–341.

Hoyle, S. G., & Serafica, F. C. (1988). Peer status of children with and without learning disabilities—A multimethod study. *Learning Disability Quarterly, 11,* 322–332.

Hudson, P. (1996). Using a learning set to increase the test performance of students with learning disabilities in social studies class. *Learning Disabilities Research & Practice, 11,* 78–85.

Hudson, P. (1997). Using teacher-guided practice to help students with learning disabilities acquire and retain social studies content. *Learning Disability Quarterly, 20,* 23–32.

Huebner, E. S. (1991). Correlates of life satisfaction in children. *School Psychology Quarterly, 6,* 103–111.

Huefner, D. S. (1988). The consulting teacher model: Risks and opportunities. *Exceptional Children, 54,* 403–414.

Hughes, A. (1996). Memory and test-taking strategies. In D. D. Deshler, E. S. Ellis, & B. K. Lenz (Eds.), *Teaching adolescents with learning disabilities: Strategies and methods* (2nd ed.). Denver: Love Publishing.

Hughes, C. A., & Suritsky, S. K. (1994). Note-taking skills of university students with and without learning disabilities. *Journal of Learning Disabilities, 27,* 20–24.

Hughes, M., & Sussman, H. M. (1983). An assessment of cerebral dominance in language-disordered children via a time-sharing paradigm. *Brain and Language, 19,* 48–64.

Hulme, C. (1981). *Reading retardation and multi-sensory teaching.* London: Routledge & Kegan Paul.

Humphreys, P., Kaufmann, W. E., & Galaburda, A. M. (1990). Developmental dyslexia in women: Neuropathological findings in three patients. *Annals of Neurology, 28,* 727–738.

Humphries, T. W., & Bauman, E. (1980). Maternal child rearing attitudes associated with learning disabilities. *Journal of Learning Disabilities, 13,* 54–57.

Hunt, D. E. (1974). Learning styles and teaching strategies. *High School Behavioral Science, 2,* 22–34.

Hunt, D. E., Joyce, B. R., Greenwood, J., Noy, J. E., Reid, R., & Weil, M. (1974). Student conceptual level and models of teaching: Theoretical and empirical coordination of two models. *Interchange, 5,* 19–30.

Hurford, D. P., Johnston, M., Nepote, P., Hampton, S., Moore, S., Neal, J., Mueller, A., McGeorge, K., Huff, L., Awad, A., Tatro, C., Juliano, C., & Huffman, D. (1994). Early identification and remediation of phonological-processing deficits in first-grade children at risk for reading disabilities. *Journal of Learning Disabilities, 10,* 647–659.

Hurford, D. P., Schauf, J. D., Bunce, L., Blaich, T., & Moore, K. (1994). Early identification of children at risk for reading disabilities. *Journal of Learning Disabilities, 27,* 371–382.

Huston, A. C., Watkins, B. A., & Kunkel, D. (1989). Public policy and children's television. *American Psychologist, 44,* 424–433.

Hutchinson, N. L. (1993). Effects of cognitive strategy instruction on algebra problem solving of adolescents with learning disabilities. *Learning Disability Quarterly, 16,* 34–63.

Huttenlocher, J. (1967). Discrimination of figure orientation: Effects of relative position. *Journal of Comparative and Physiological Psychology, 63,* 359–361.

Huttenlocher, J., Jordan, N. C., & Levine, S. C. (1994). A mental model for early arithmetic. *Journal of Experimental Psychology: General, 123,* 284–296.

Hyde, J. S. Fennema, E., & Lamon, S. J. (1990). Gender differences in mathematics performance: A meta-analysis. *Psychological Bulletin, 107,* 139–155.

Hygge, S. (1993). A comparison between the impact of noise from aircraft, road traffic and trains on long-term recall and recognition of a text in children aged 12–14 years. In H. Ising & B. Krupp (Eds.), *Larm und Krankheit: Noise and disease.* Stuttgart, Germany: Gustav Fischer Verlag.

Hynd, G. W., Marshall, R., & Gonzalez, J. (1991). Learning disabilities and presumed central nervous system dysfunction. *Learning Disability Quarterly, 14,* 283–296.

Hynd, G. W., & Willis, W. G. (1988). *Pediatric neuropsychology.* New York: Grune & Stratton.

Hynd, G. W., Voeller, K. K., Hern, K. L., & Marshall, R. M. (1991). Neurobiological basis of attention-deficit hyperactivity disorder (ADHD). *School Psychology Review, 20,* 174–186.

Idol, L., & West, J. F. (1987). Consultation in special education (Part II): Training and practice. *Journal of Learning Disabilities, 20,* 474–494.

Idol-Maestas, L., & Ritter, S. (1985). A follow-up study of resource consulting teachers. *Teacher Education and Special Education, 8*(3), 121–131.

Ilg, F., & Ames, L. (1964). *School readiness.* New York: Harper & Row.

Ilg, F. L., Ames, L. B., & Apell, R. (1965). School readiness as evaluated by Gesell developmental, visual, and projective tests. *Genetic Psychology Monographs, 71,* 61–91.

Ingram, T. T. S. (1976). Speech disorders in childhood. In E. H. Lenneberg & E. Lenneberg (Eds.), *Foundations of language development* (Vol. 2). New York: Academic Press.

Ingram, T. T. S., Mason, A. W., & Blackburn, I. (1970). A retrospective study of 82 children with reading disability. *Developmental Medicine and Child Neurology, 12,* 271–279.

Interagency Committee on Learning Disabilities Report. (1987). *A Report to the U.S. Congress.* Washington, D.C.: U.S. Department of Health and Human Services.

Isaacson, R. L., & Spear, L. P. (1984). A new perspective for the interpretation of early brain damage. In S. Finger & C. R. Almli (Eds.), *Early brain damage: Vol 2. Neurobiology and behavior.* New York: Academic Press.

Isgur, J. (1975), Establishing letter-sound associations by an Object-Imaging-Projection method. *Journal of Learning Disabilities, 8,* 351.

Jacklin, C. N. (1989). Female and male: Issues of gender. *American Psychologist, 44,* 127–133.

Jacklin, C. N., & Maccoby, E. M. (1982). Length of labor and sex of offspring. *Journal of Pediatric Psychology, 7,* 355–360.

Jacks, K. B., & Keller, M. E. (1978). A humanistic approach to the adolescent with learning disabilities: An educational, psychological, and vocational model. *Adolescence, 13,* 59–68.

Jackson, G., & Cosca, C. (1974). The inequality of educational opportunity in the Southwest: An observational study of ethnically mixed classrooms. *American Educational Research Journal, 11,* 219–229.

Jackson, H. (1931). *Selected writings of John Hughlings Jackson* (2 vols.). London: Hodder & Stoughton.

Jackson, S. C., Enright, R. D., & Murdock, J. Y. (1987). Social perception problems in learning disabled youth: Developmental lag versus perceptual deficit. *Journal of Learning Disabilities, 20,* 361–364.

Jacob, R. G., O'Leary, K. D., & Rosenblad, C. (1978). Formal and informal classroom settings: Effects on hyperactivity. *Journal of Abnormal Child Psychology, 6,* 47–59.

Jacobsen, B., Lowery, B., & DuCette, J. (1986). Attributions of learning disabled children. *Journal of Educational Psychology, 78,* 59–64.

Jansky, J., & de Hirsch, K. (1973). *Preventing reading failure: Prediction, diagnosis, intervention.* New York: Harper & Row.

Jayanthi, M., Epstein, M. H., Polloway, E. A., & Bursuck, W. D. (1996). A national survey of general education teachers' perceptions of testing adaptations. *The Journal of Special Education, 30,* 99–115.

Jenkins, J. R. & Heinen, A. (1989). Students' preferences for service delivery: Pull-out, in-class, or integrated models. *Exceptional Children, 55,* 516–523.

Jenkins, J. R., Heliotis, J., Haynes, M., & Beck, K. (1986). Does passive learning account for disabled readers' comprehension deficits in ordinary reading situations? *Learning Disability Quarterly, 9,* 69–76.

Jenkins, J. R., Heliotis, J. D., Stein, M. L., & Haynes, M. C. (1987). Improving reading comprehension by using paragraph restatements. *Exceptional Children, 54,* 54–59.

Jenkins, J. R., Jewell, M., Leicester, N., Jenkins, L., & Troutner, N. M. (1991). Development of a school building model for educating students with handicaps and at-risk students in general education classrooms. *Journal of Learning Disabilities, 24,* 311–320.

Jenkins, J. R., Jewell, M., Leicester, N., O'Connor, R. E., Jenkins, L. M., & Troutner, N. M. (1994). Accommodations for individual differences without classroom ability groups: An experiment in school restructuring. *Exceptional Children, 60,* 344–358.

Jenkins, J. R., & Pious, C. G. (1991). Full inclusion and the REI: A reply to Thousand and Villa. *Exceptional Children, 57,* 562–564.

Jenkins, J. R., Pious, C. G., & Peterson, D. L. (1988). Categorical programs for remedial and handicapped students: Issues of validity. *Exceptional Children, 55,* 147–158.

Jenkins, J. R., Stein, M. L., & Wysocki, K. (1984). Learning vocabulary through reading. *American Educational Research Journal, 21,* 767–787.

Jenkins, J. R., Speltz, M. L., & Odom, S. L. (1985). Integrating normal and handicapped preschoolers: Effects on child development and social interaction. *Exceptional Children, 52,* 7–17.

Jennings, W. S., & Kohlberg, L. (1983). Effects of a just community programme on the moral development of youthful offenders. *Journal of Moral Education, 12,* 33–50.

Jensen, A. (1963). Learning ability in retarded, average, and gifted children. *Merrill-Palmer Quarterly, 9,* 123–140.

Jensen, A. (1971). The role of verbal mediation in mental development. *Journal of Genetic Psychology, 118,* 39–70.

Jensen, A. R. (1984). Test bias: Concepts and criticisms. In C. R. Reynolds & R. T. Brown (Eds.), *Perspectives on bias in mental testing.* New York: Plenum Press.

John, E. R., Karmel, B. Z., Corning, W. C., Easton, P., Brown, D., Ahn, H., John, M., Harmony, T., Prichep, L., Toro, A., Gerson, I., Bartlett, F., Thatcher, R., Kaye, H., Valdes, P., & Schwartz, E. (1977). Neurometrics. *Science, 196,* 1393–1410.

John, E. R., Prichep, L. S., Friedmen, J., Ahn, H., Kaye, H., & Baird, H. (1985). Neurometric evaluation of brain electrical activity in children with learning disabilities. In F. H. Duffy & N. Geschwind (Eds.), *Dyslexia: A neuroscientific approach to clinical evaluation.* Boston: Little, Brown.

Johnson, D., & Myklebust, H. (1967). *Learning disabilities: Educational principles and practices.* New York: Grune & Stratton.

Johnson, D. J. (1980). Persistent auditory disorders in young dyslexic adults. *Bulletin of the Orton Society, 30,* 268–276.

Johnson, D. J. (1986). Remediation for dyslexic adults. In G. Th. Pavlidis & D. F. Fisher (Eds.), *Dyslexia: Its neuropsychology and treatment.* New York: John Wiley & Sons.

Johnson, D. J. (1993). Relationships between oral and written language. *Social Psychology Review, 22,* 595–609.

Johnson, D. J., & Blalock, J. W. (Eds.). (1987). *Adults with learning disabilities: Clinical studies.* Orlando, FL: Grune & Stratton.

Johnson, D. W., & Johnson, R. T. (1986). Mainstreaming and cooperative learning strategies. *Exceptional Children, 52,* 553–561.

Johnson, D. W., Johnson, R. T., Warring, D., & Maruyama, G. (1986). Different cooperative learning procedures and cross-handicap relationships. *Exceptional Children, 53,* 247–252.

Johnson, G., Gersten, R., & Carnine, D. (1987). Effects of instructional design variables on vocabulary acquisition of LD students: A study of computer-assisted instruction. *Journal of Learning Disabilities, 20,* 206–213.

Johnson, G. O. (1962). Special education for the mentally handicapped—a paradox. *Exceptional Children, 29,* 62–69.

Johnson, L., Graham, S., & Harris, K. R. (1997). The effect of goal setting and self-instruction on learning a reading comprehension strategy: A study of students with learning disabilities. *Journal of Learning Disabilities, 30,* 80–91.

Johnson, R. T., & Johnson, D. W. (1983). Effects of cooperative, competitive, and individualistic learning experiences on social development. *Exceptional Children, 49,* 323–329.

Joiner, L. M., & Kottmeyer, W. A. (1971). Effect of classroom noise on number identification by retarded children. *California Journal of Educational Research, 22,* 164–169.

Jones, D. R. (1980). The dictionary: A look at "Look it up." *Journal of Reading, 23,* 309–312.

Jones, K. M., Torgeson, J. K., & Sexton, M. A. (1987). Using computer guided practice to increase decoding fluency in learning disabled children: A study using the Hint and Hunt I program. *Journal of Learning Disabilities, 20,* 122–128.

Jordan, C., Tharp, R. G., & Baird-Vogt (1992). "Just open the door": Cultural compatibility and classroom rapport. In M. Saravia-Shore & S. F. Arvizu (Eds.), *Cross-cultural literacy: Ethnographies of communication in multiethnic classrooms.* New York: Garland.

Jordan, N. C. (1995). Clinical assessment of early mathematics disabilities: Adding up the research findings. *Learning Disabilities Research & Practice, 10,* 59–69.

Jorgenson, C. B., Jorgenson, D. E., Gillis, M. K., & McCall, C. M. (1993). Validation of a screening instrument for young children with teacher assessment of school performance. *School Psychology Quarterly, 8,* 125–139.

Jorm, A. F., & Share, D. L. (1983). Phonological recoding and reading acquisition. *Applied Psycholinguistics, 4,* 103–147.

Jorm, A. F., Share, D. L., Maclean, R., & Matthews, R. (1986). Cognitive factors at school entry predictive of specific reading retardation and general reading backwardness: A research note. *Journal of Child Psychology and Psychiatry, 27,* 45–54.

Joschko, M., & Rourke, B. P. (1985). Neuropsychological subtypes of learning-disabled children who exhibit the ACID pattern on the WISC. In B. P. Rourke (Ed.), *Neuropsychology of learning disabilities.* New York: Guilford Press.

Jost, H., & Sontag, L. W. (1944). The genetic factor in autonomic nervous system function. *Psychosomatic Medicine, 6,* 308–310.

Juel, C. (1988). Learning to read and write: A longitudinal study of 54 children from first through fourth grades. *Journal of Educational Psychology, 80,* 437–447.

Kagan, J. (1965). Reflection-impulsivity and reading ability in primary grade children. *Child Development, 36,* 609–628.

Kagan, J., & Kogan, N. (1970). Individual variation in cognitive processes. In P. H. Mussen (Ed.), *Carmichael's manual of child psychology* (Vol. 1). New York: John Wiley & Sons.

Kagan, J., Rosman, B. L., Day, D., Albert, J., & Phillips, W. (1964). Information processing in the child: Significance of analytic and reflective attitudes. *Psychological Monographs, 78* (1, No. 578).

Kail, R., & Leonard, L. B. (1986). Sources of word-finding problems in language-impaired children. In S. J. Ceci (Ed.), *Handbook of cognitive, social, and neuropsychological aspects of learning disabilities* (Vol. 1). Hillsdale, NJ: Lawrence Erlbaum.

Kail, R. V., & Siegel, A. W. (1977). The development of anemonic encoding in children: From perception to abstraction. In R. V. Kail & J. W. Hagen (Eds.), *Perspectives on the development of memory and cognition.* New York: John Wiley & Sons.

Kaliski, L. (1962). Arithmetic and the brain-injured child. *Arithmetic Teacher, 9,* 245–251.

Kalverboer, A. F. (1976). Neurobehavioral relationships in young children: Some remarks on concepts and methods. In R. M. Knights & D. J. Bakker (Eds.), *The neuropsychology of learning disorders: Theoretical approaches.* Baltimore: University Park Press.

Kamann, M. P., & Wong, B. Y. L. (1993). Inducing adaptive coping self-statements in children with learning disabilities through self-instruction training. *Journal of Learning Disabilities, 26,* 630–638.

Kamhi, A. G., Catts, H. W., & Mauer, D. (1990). Explaining speech production deficits in poor readers. *Journal of Learning Disabilities, 23,* 632–636.

Kamphaus, R. W., Frick, P. J., & Lahey, B. B. (1991). Methodological issues and learning disabilities diagnosis in clinical populations. *Journal of Learning Disabilities, 24,* 613–618.

Karnes, M., Hodgins, A., & Teska, J. (1969). The effects of preschool interventions: Evaluations over two years. In M. B. Karnes et al., *Investigations of classroom and at-home interventions: Research and development program on preschool disadvantaged* (Final report, Vol. 1). Washington, DC: Office of Education, Bureau of Research.

Karni, A., Meyer, G., Jezzard, P., Adams, M. M., Turner, R., & Ungerleider, L. G. (1995). Functional MRI evidence for adult motor cortex plasticity during motor skill learning. *Nature, 377,* 155–158.

Karpati, G., & Frame, B. (1964) Neuropsychiatric disorders in primary hyperparathyroidism. *Archives of Neurology, 10,* 387–397.

Kasik, M. M., Sabatino, D. A., & Spoentgen, P. (1987). Psychosocial aspects of learning disabilities. In S. J. Ceci (Ed.), *Handbook of cognitive, social, and neuropsychological aspects of learning disabilities* (Vol. 2). Hillsdale, NJ: Lawrence Erlbaum.

Kaswan, J., Haralson, S., & Cline, R. (1965). Variables in perceptual and cognitive organization and differentiation. *Journal of Personality, 33,* 164–177.

Katims, D. S., Zapata, J. T., & Yin, Z. (1996). Risk factors for substance use by Mexican American youth with and without learning disabilities. *Journal of Learning Disabilities, 29,* 213–219, 212.

Kato, T., Takahaski, E., Sawada, K., Kobayashi, N., Watanabe, T., & Ishi, T. (1983). A computer analysis of infant movements synchronized with adult speech. *Pediatric Research, 17,* 625–628.

Katz, P. A., & Deutsch, M. (1963). Relation of auditory-visual shifting to reading achievement. *Perceptual Motor Skills, 17,* 327–332.

Katz, R. B., Shankweiler, D., & Liberman, I. Y. (1981). Memory for item order and phonetic recoding in the beginning reader. *Journal of Experimental Child Psychology, 32,* 474–484.

Kaufman, A., Zalma, R., & Kaufman, N. (1978). The relationship of hand dominance to the motor coordination, mental ability and R-L awareness of young normal children. *Child Development, 49,* 885–888.

Kaufman, A. S. (1976). Verbal-performance IQ discrepancies on the WISC-R. *Journal of Consulting and Clinical Psychology, 44,* 739–744.

Kaufman, A. S. (1979a). *Intelligent testing with the WISC-R.* New York: Wiley.

Kaufman, A. S. (1979b). WISC-R research: Implications for interpretation. *School Psychology Digest, 8,* 5–27.

Kaufman, A. S. (1981a). The impact of WISC-R research for school psychologists. In C. R. Reynolds & T. B. Gutkin (Eds.), *A handbook of school psychology.* New York: John Wiley & Sons.

Kaufman, A. S. (1981b). The WISC-R and learning disabilities assessment: State of the art. *Journal of Learning Disabilities, 14,* 520–526.

Kaufman, A. S., & Kaufman, N. L. (1983). *Kaufman Assessment Battery for Children.* Circle Pines, MN: American Guidance Service.

Kavale, K. (1981a). The relationship between auditory perceptual skills and reading ability: A meta-analysis. *Journal of Learning Disabilities, 14,* 539–546.

Kavale, K. (1981b). Functions of the Illinois Test of Psycholinguistic Abilities (ITPA): Are they trainable? *Exceptional Children, 47,* 496–510.

Kavale, K. (1982a). The efficacy of stimulant drug treatment for hyperactivity: A meta-analysis. *Journal of Learning Disabilities, 15,* 280–289.

Kavale, K. (1982b). Meta-analysis of the relationship between visual perceptual skills and reading achievement. *Journal of Learning Disabilities, 15,* 42–51.

Kavale, K. A. (1980a). Learning disability and cultural-economic disadvantage: The case for a relationship. *Learning Disability Quarterly, 3,* 97–112.

Kavale, K. A. (1980b). The reasoning abilities of normal and learning disabled readers on measures of reading comprehension. *Learning Disability Quarterly, 3*(4), 34–45.

Kavale, K. A. (1987a). On regaining integrity in the LD field. *Learning Disabilities Research, 2,* 60–61.

Kavale, K. A. (1987b). Theoretical issues surrounding severe discrepancy. *Learning Disabilities Research, 3,* 12–20.

Kavale, K. A., & Forness, S. R. (1983). Hyperactivity and diet treatment: A meta-analysis of the Feingold hypothesis. *Journal of Learning Disabilities, 16,* 324–330.

Kavale, K. A., & Forness, S. R. (1984). A meta-analysis of the validity of Wechsler Scale profiles and recategorizations: Patterns or parodies? *Learning Disability Quarterly, 7,* 136–156.

Kavale, K. A., & Forness, S. R. (1987). Substance over style: Assessing the efficacy of modality testing and teaching. *Exceptional Children, 54,* 228–239.

Kavale, K. A., & Forness, S. R. (1996). Social skill deficits and learning disabilities: A meta-analysis. *Journal of Learning Disabilities, 29,* 226–237.

Kavale, K. A., & Reese, J. H. (1992). The character of learning disabilities: An Iowa profile. *Learning Disability Quarterly, 15,* 74–94.

Kay, P. J., Fitzgerald, M., Paradee, C., & Mellencamp, A. (1994). Making homework at home: The parent's perspective. *Journal of Learning Disabilities, 27,* 550–561.

Kearney, C. A., & Drabman, R. S. (1993). The write-say method for improving spelling accuracy in children with learning disabilities. *Journal of Learning Disabilities, 26,* 52–56.

Keel, M. C., & Gast, D. L. (1992). Small-group instruction for students with learning disabilities: Observational and incidental learning. *Exceptional Children, 58,* 357–368.

Keilitz, I., & Dunivant, N. (1986). The relationship between learning disability and juvenile delinquency. Current state of knowledge. *Remedial and Special Education, 7*(3), 18–26.

Keir, E. H. (1977). Auditory information processing and learning disabilities. In L. Tarnopol & M. Tarnopol (Eds.), *Brain function and reading disabilities.* Baltimore: University Park Press.

Keith, R. W., & Engineer, P. (1991). Effects of methylphenidate on the auditory processing abilities of children with attention deficit-hyperactivity disorder. *Journal of Learning Disabilities, 24,* 630–636.

Keith, T. Z., Keith, P. B., Troutman, G. C., Bickley, P. G., Trivette, P. S., & Singh, K. (1993). Does parental involvement affect eighth-grade student achievement? Structural analysis of national data. *School Psychology Review, 22,* 474–496.

Keith, T. Z., & Page, E. B. (1985). Homework works at school: National evidence for policy changes. *School Psychology Review, 14,* 351–359.

Keller, H. R. (Ed.). (1980). Behavioral assessment. *School Psychology Review, 9,* 3–89, 93–98.

Keller, H. R. (1981). Behavioral consultation. In J. C. Conoley (Ed.), *Consultation in schools: Theory, research, technology.* New York: Academic Press.

Kellogg, R., & O'Dell, S. (1969). *Analyzing children's art.* Palo Alto, CA: National Press Books.

Kemler Nelson, D. G., & Smith, J. D. (1989). Analytic and holistic processing in reflection-impulsivity and cognitive development. In T. Globerson & T. Zelniker (Eds.), *Cognitive style and cognitive development.* Norwood, NJ: Ablex.

Keogh, B. K. (1973). Perceptual and cognitive styles: Implications for special education. In L. Mann & D. A. Sabatino (Eds.), *The first review of special education.* Philadelphia: JSE Press.

Keogh, B. K. (1982). Children's temperament and teachers' decisions. In R. Porter & G. M. Collins (Eds.), *Temperamental differences in infants and young children* (CIBA Foundation Symposium 89). London: Pitman.

Keogh, B. K. (1987a). Learning disabilities: In defense of a construct. *Learning Disabilities Research, 3,* 4–9.

Keogh, B. K. (1987b). Response (to Senf). In S. Vaughn & C. S. Bos (Eds.), *Research in learning disabilities: Issues and future directions.* Boston: College-Hill.

Keogh, B. K., & Babbitt, B. C. (1986). Sampling issues in learning disabilities research: Markers for the study of problems in mathematics. In G. Th. Pavlidis & D. F. Fisher (Eds.), *Dyslexia: Its neuropsychology and treatment.* New York: John Wiley.

Keogh, B. K., & Becker, L. D. (1973). Early detection of learning problems: Questions, cautions, and guidelines. *Exceptional Children, 40,* 5–11.

Keogh, B. K., & Burstein, N. D. (1988). Relationship of temperament to preschoolers' interactions with peers and teachers. *Exceptional Children, 54,* 456–461.

Keogh, B. K., & Hall, R. J. (1974). WISC subtest patterns of educationally handicapped and educable mentally retarded pupils. *Psychology in the Schools, 11,* 296–300.

Keogh, B. K., Major-Kingsley, S., Omori-Gordon, H., & Reid, H. P. (1982). *A system of marker variables for the field of learning disabilities.* New York: Syracuse University Press.

Keogh, B. K., & Margolis, J. (1976). Learn to labor and to wait: Attentional problems of children with learning disorders. *Journal of Learning Disabilities, 9,* 276–286.

Keogh, B. K., & Smith, C. E. (1967). Visuo-motor ability for school prediction: A seven-year study. *Perceptual and Motor Skills, 25,* 101–110.

Keogh, B. K., Tchir, C., & Windeguth-Behn, A. (1974). Teachers' perceptions of educationally high risk children. *Journal of Learning Disabilities, 7,* 367–374.

Kephart, N. C. (1960). *The slow learner in the classroom.* Columbus, OH: Charles E. Merrill.

Kephart, N. C. (1971). Forward. In T. S. Ball, *Itard, Seguin, and Kephart: Sensory education. A learning interpretation.* Columbus, OH: Charles E. Merrill.

Kerchner, L. B., & Kistinger, B. J. (1984). Language processing/word processing: Written expression, computers and learning disabled students. *Learning Disability Quarterly, 7,* 329–335.

Kershner, J. R. (1977). Cerebral dominance in disabled readers, good readers, and gifted children: Search for a valid model. *Child Development, 48,* 61–67.

Kershner, J. R. (1990). Self-concept and IQ as predictors of remedial success in children with learning disabilities. *Journal of Learning Disabilities, 23,* 368–374.

Kershner, J. R., & Stringer, R. W. (1991). Effects of reading and writing on cerebral laterality in good readers and children with dyslexia. *Journal of Learning Disabilities, 24,* 560–567.

Ketchum, E. G. (1967). Neurological and/or emotional factors in reading disabilities. In J. Figural (Ed.), *Vistas in reading.* Newark, DE: International Reading Association.

Kimura, D. (1967). Functional asymmetry of the brain in dichotic listening. *Cortex, 3,* 163–178.

King, M. L. (1963). *Why we can't wait.* New York: Harper & Row.

King-Sears, M. E., Mercer, C. D., & Sindelar, P. T. (1992). Toward independence with keyword mnemonics: A strategy for science vocabulary instruction. *Remedial and Special Education, 13 (5),* 22–33.

Kinney, D. K., Woods, B. T., & Yurgelun-Todd, D. (1986). Neurologic abnormalities in schizophrenic patients and their families. *Archives of General Psychiatry, 43,* 665–668.

Kinsbourne, M. (1973a). Minimal brain dysfunction as a neurodevelopmental lag. *Annals of the New York Academy of Sciences, 205,* 268–273.

Kinsbourne, M. (1973b). School problems. *Pediatrics, 52,* 697–710.

Kinsbourne, M. (1987). Commentary: Using laterality tests to monitor disabled learners' thinking. In S. J. Ceci (Ed.), *Handbook of cognitive, social, and neuropsychological aspects of learning disabilities.* (Vol.1). Hillsdale, NJ: Lawrence Erlbaum.

Kinsbourne, M., & Caplan, P. (1979). *Children's learning and attention problems.* Boston, MA: Little, Brown.

Kinsbourne, M., & Warrington, E. K. (1963). Developmental factor in reading and writing backwardness. *British Journal of Psychology, 54,* 145–156.

Kintsch, W. (1994). Text comprehension, memory, and learning. *American Psychologist, 49,* 294–303.

Kintsch, W., & Buschke, H. (1969). Homophones and synonyms in short-term memory. *Journal of Experimental Psychology, 80,* 403–407.

Kirby, J. R., & Das, J. P. (1977). Reading achievement, IQ, and simultaneous successive processing. *Journal of Educational Psychology, 69,* 564–570.

Kirby, J. R., & Robinson, G. L. W. (1987). Simultaneous and successive processing in reading disabled children. *Journal of Learning Disabilities, 20,* 243–252.

Kirchner, C., & Peterson, R. (1988). Estimates of race: Ethnic groups in the U.S. visually impaired and blind population. In C. Kirchner (Ed.), *Data on blindness and visual impairment in the U.S.: A resource manual on social demographic characteristics, education, employment and income, and service delivery* (2nd ed.). New York: American Foundation for the Blind.

Kirk, S. A. (1958). *Early education of the mentally retarded: An experimental study.* Urbana, IL: University of Illinois Press.

Kirk, S. A. (1976). Samuel A. Kirk. In J. M. Kauffman & D. P. Hallahan (Eds.), *Teaching children with learning disabilities: Personal perspectives.* Columbus, OH: Charles E. Merrill.

Kirk, S. A. (1986). Redesigning delivery systems for learning disabled students. *LD Focus, 2,* 4–6.

Kirk, S. A., & Elkins, J. (1975a). Characteristics of children enrolled in the child service demonstration centers. *Journal of Learning Disabilities, 8,* 630–637.

Kirk, S. A., & Elkins, J. (1975b). Identifying developmental discrepancies at the preschool level. *Journal of Learning Disabilities, 8,* 417–419.

Kirk, S. A., & Kirk, W. D. (1971). *Psycholinguistic learning disabilities: Diagnosis and remediation.* Urbana: University of Illinois Press.

Kirk, S. A., McCarthy, J. J., & Kirk, W. D. (1968). *Illinois Test of Psycholinguistic Abilities* (rev. ed.). Urbana: University of Illinois Press.

Kistner, J., Haskett, M., White, K., & Robbins, F. (1987). Perceived competence and self-worth of LD and normally achieving students. *Learning Disability Quarterly, 10,* 37–44.

Klare, G. R. (1984). Readability. In P. D. Pearson (Ed.), *Handbook of reading research.* New York: Longman.

Klatzky, R. L. (1984). *Memory and awareness: An information processing perspective.* New York: Freeman.

Klaus, R., & Gray, S. (1968). The early training project for disadvantaged children: A report after five years. *Monographs of the Society for Research in Child Development, 33* (4, Serial No. 120).

Klausmeier, H. J., Feldhusen, J., & Check, J. (1959). *An analysis of learning efficiency in arithmetic of mentally retarded children in comparison with children of average and high intelligence.* Madison: University of Wisconsin Press.

Klein, R. S., Altman, S. D., Dreizen, K., Friedman, R., & Powers, L. (1981a). Restructuring dysfunctional parental attitudes toward children's learning and behavior in school: Family-oriented psychotherapy, Part I. *Journal of Learning Disabilities, 14,* 15–19.

Klein, R. S., Altman, S. D., Dreizen, K., Friedman, R., & Powers, L. (1981b). Restructuring dysfunctional parental attitudes toward children's learning and behavior in school: Family-oriented psychotherapy, Part II. *Journal of Learning Disabilities, 14,* 99–101.

Kloomok, S., & Cosden, M. (1994). Self-concept in children with learning disabilities: The relationship between global self-concept, academic "discounting," nonacademic self-concept, and perceived social support. *Learning Disability Quarterly, 17,* 140–153.

Klorman, R. (1991). Cognitive event-related potentials in attention deficit disorder. *Journal of Learning Disabilities, 24,* 130–140.

Klorman, R., Brumaghim, J. T., Fitzpatrick, P. A., & Borgstedt, A. D. (1990). Clinical effects of a controlled trial of methylphenidate on adolescents with attention deficit disorder. *Journal of the American Academy of Child and Adolescent Psychiatry, 29,* 702–709.

Knapczyk, D. (1991). Effects of modeling in promoting generalization of student question asking and question answering. *Learning Disabilities Research & Practice, 6,* 75–82.

Knight, M. F., Meyers, H. W., Paolucci-Whitcomb, P., Hasazi, S. E., & Nevin, A. (1981). A four year evaluation of consulting teacher service. *Behavior Disorders, 6,* 92–100.

Knight-Arest, I. (1984). Communicative effectiveness of learning disabled and normally achieving 10- to 13-year-old boys. *Learning Disability Quarterly, 7,* 237–245.

Knowlton, M. (1997). Efficiency in visual scanning of children with and without visual disabilities. *Exceptional Children, 63,* 557–565.

Kochanek, T. T., Kabacoff, R. I., & Lipsitt, L. P. (1990). Early identification of developmentally disabled and at-risk preschool children. *Exceptional Children, 56,* 528–538.

Koh, T., Abbatiello, A., & McLoughlin, C. S. (1984). Cultural bias in WISC subtest items: A response to Judge Grady's suggestion in relation to the PASE case. *School Psychology Review, 13,* 89–94.

Kohlberg, L. (1968). Montessori with the culturally disadvantaged: A cognitive-developmental interpretation and some research findings. In R. D. Hess & R. M. Bear (Eds.), *Early education.* Chicago: Aldine.

Kohlberg, L. (1981). *The philosophy of moral development.* San Francisco: Harper & Row.

Kohn, B., & Dennis, M. (1974). Patterns of hemispheric specialization after hemidecortication for infantile hemiplegia. In M. Kinsbourne & W. L. Smith (Eds.), *Hemispheric disconnection and cerebral function.* Springfield, IL: Charles C Thomas.

Kohn, M., & Parnes, B. (1974). Social interaction in the classroom—A comparison of apathetic-withdrawn and angry-defiant children. *The Journal of Genetic Psychology, 125,* 165–175.

Koivisto, M., Blanco-Sequeiros, M., & Krause, U. (1972). Neonatal symptomatic and asymptomatic hypoglycemia: A follow-up study of 15 children. *Developmental Medicine and Child Neurology, 14,* 603–614.

Kok, A., & Rooijakkers, J. A. J. (1985). Comparisons of event-related potentials of young children and adults in a visual recognition and word reading task. *Psychophysiology, 22,* 11–23.

Kolb, B. (1989). Brain development, plasticity and behavior. *American Psychologist, 44,* 1203–1212.

Koneya, M. (1976). Location and interaction in row-and-column seating arrangements. *Environment and Behavior, 8,* 265–282.

Kopp, C., & Kaler, S. R. (1989). Risk in infancy. *American Psychologist, 44,* 224–230.

Kopp, C. B., & Kaler, S. R. (1989). Risk in infancy: Origins and implications. *American Psychologist, 44,* 224–230.

Koppitz, E. M. (1968). *Psychological evaluation of children's human figure drawings.* New York: Grune & Stratton.

Korhonen, T. T. (1995). The persistence of rapid naming problems in children with reading disabilities: A nine year follow-up. *Journal of Learning Disabilities, 28,* 232–239.

Košč L. (1981). Neuropsychological implications of diagnosis and treatment of mathematical learning disabilities. *Topics in Learning & Learning Disabilities, 1*(3), 19–30.

Koscinski, S. T., & Gast, D. L. (1993). Computer-assisted instruction with constant time delay to teach multiplication facts to students with learning disabilities. *Learning Disabilities Research & Practice, 8,* 157–168.

Koscinski, S. T., & Hoy, C. (1993). Teaching multiplication facts to students with learning disabilities: The promise of constant time delay procedures. *Learning Disabilities Research & Practice, 8,* 260–263.

Kosiewicz, M. M., Hallahan, D. P., & Lloyd, J. (1981). The effects of an LD student's treatment choice on handwriting performance. *Learning Disability Quarterly, 4,* 281–286.

Kosiewicz, M. M., Hallahan, D. P., Lloyd, J., & Graves, A. W. (1982). Effects of self-instruction and self-correction procedures on handwriting performance. *Learning Disability Quarterly, 5,* 71–78.

Kratochwill, T. R., Brody, G. H., & Piersal, W. C. (1979). Time-series research: Some comments on design methodology for research in learning disabilities. *Journal of Learning Disabilities, 12,* 257–263.

Kratz, K. E., Sherman, S. M., & Kalil, R. (1979). Lateral geniculate nucleus in dark-reared cats: Loss of Y cells without changes in cell size. *Science, 203,* 1353–1355.

Krech, D., Rosenzweig, M. R., & Bennett, E. L. (1966). Environmental impoverishment, social isolation, and changes in brain chemistry and anatomy. *Physiology and Behavior, 1,* 99–104.

Kreiger, V. K. (1981). A hierarchy of "confusable" high-frequency words in isolation and context. *Learning Disability Quarterly, 4,* 131–138.

Kritchevsky, S., & Prescott, E. (1969). *Planning environments for young children: Physical space.* Washington, DC: National Association for the Education of Young Children.

Kroth, R. (1973). The behavioral Q-sort as a diagnostic tool. *Academic Therapy, 8,* 317–330.

Krupski, A. (1985). Variations in attention as a function of classroom task demands in learning handicapped and CA-matched nonhandicapped children. *Exceptional Children, 52,* 52–56.

Kuder, S. J. (1991). Language abilities and progress in a direct instruction reading program for students with learning disabilities. *Journal of Learning Disabilities, 24,* 124–127.

Kurtz, B. E., & Borkowski, J. G. (1987). Development of strategic skills in impulsive and reflective children. A longitudinal study of metacognition. *Journal of Experimental Child Psychology, 43,* 129–148.

Kyzar, B. L. (1977). Noise pollution and schools: How much is too much? *CEFP Journal, 4,* 10–11.

LaBuda, M. C., & DeFries, J. C. (1988a). Genetic and environmental etiologies of reading disability: A twin study. *Annals of Dyslexia, 38,* 131–138.

LaBuda, M. C., & DeFries, J. C. (1988b). Cognitive abilities in children with reading disabilities and controls: A follow-up study. *Journal of Learning Disabilities, 21,* 562–566.

LaGreca, A. M., & Mesibov, G. B. (1981). Facilitating interpersonal functioning with peers in learning disabled children. *Journal of Learning Disabilities, 14,* 197–199.

LaGreca, A. M., & Stone, W. L. (1990). LD status and achievement: Confounding variables in the study of children's social status, self-esteem, and behavioral functioning. *Journal of Learning Disabilities, 23,* 483–490.

Lahey, B. B., & Carlson, C. L. (1991). Validity of the diagnostic category of attention deficit disorder without hyperactivity: A review of the literature. *Journal of Disabilities, 24,* 110–120.

Lambert, N. M., & Sandoval, J. (1980). The prevalence of learning disabilities in a sample of children considered hyperactive. *Journal of Abnormal Child Psychology, 8,* 33–50.

Landers, S. (1987, November). Differing risk paths seen for hyperactive children. *Monitor,* 19. American Psychological Association.

Langdon, H. W., (1992). *Hispanic children and adults with communication disorders: Assessment and intervention.* Gaithersburg, MD: Aspen.

Lapadat, J. C. (1991). Pragmatic language skills of students with language and/or learning disabilities: A quantitative synthesis. *Journal of Learning Disabilities, 24,* 147–158.

Lapp, E. R. (1957). A study of the social adjustment of slow-learning children who were assigned part-time to regular classes. *American Journal of Mental Deficiency, 62,* 254–262.

Larrivee, B. (1981). Modality preference as a model for differentiating beginning reading instruction: A review of the issues, *Learning Disability Quarterly, 4,* 180–188.

Larsen, S. C. (1976). The learning disabilities specialist: Role and responsibilities. *Journal of Learning Disabilities, 9,* 498–508.

Larsen, S. C. (1978). Learning disabilities and the professional educator. *Learning Disability Quarterly, 1,* 5–12.

Larsen, S. C., & Hammill, D. D. (1975). The relationship of selected visual-perceptual abilities to school learning. *Journal of Special Education, 9,* 281–291.

Larsen, S. C., Rogers, D., & Sowell, V. (1976). The use of selected perceptual tests in differentiating between normal and learning disabled children. *Journal of Learning Disabilities, 9,* 85–90.

Larson, K. A. (1988). A research review and alternative hypothesis explaining the link between learning disability and delinquency. *Journal of Learning Disabilities, 21,* 357–369.

Larson, K. A., & Gerber, M. M. (1987). Effects of social metacognitive training for enhancing overt behavior in learning disabled and low achieving delinquents. *Exceptional Children, 54,* 201–211,

Lassen, N. A., Ingvar, D. H., & Skinhøj, E. (1978). Brain function and blood flow. *Scientific American, 239,* 62–71.

Laughton, J., & Morris, N. C. (1989). Story grammar knowledge of learning disabled students. *Learning Disabilities Research, 4,* 87–95.

Lavoie, R. D. (1986). Toward developing a philosophy of education: A re-examination of competition, fairness and the work ethic. *Journal of Learning Disabilities, 19,* 62–63.

Lazar, I., & Darlington, R. (1982). Lasting effects of early education: A report from the Consortium for Longitudinal Studies. *Monographs of the Society for Research in Child Development, 47* (Serial No. 195).

Learning Disabilities Association of America. (1993). Position paper on full inclusion of all students with learning disabilities in the regular education classroom. *Journal of Learning Disabilities, 26,* 594.

Lee, C. L., & Bates, J. E. (1985). Mother-child interaction at age 2 years and perceived difficult temperament. *Child Development, 56,* 1314–1325.

Lee. V. E., & Bryk, A. S. (1988). Curriculum tracking as mediating the social distribution of high school. *Sociology of Education, 62,* 78–94.

Lee, W. M., & Hudson, F. G. (1981). *A comparison of verbal problem-solving in arithmetic of learning disabled and non-learning disabled seventh grade males* (Research Report No. 43). Lawrence: University of Kansas, Institute for Research in Learning Disabilities.

Lehman, E. B., & Brady, K. McC. (1982). Presentation modality and taxonomic category as encoding dimensions for good and poor readers. *Journal of Learning Disabilities, 15,* 103–105.

Lehmkuhle, S., Garzia, R. P., Turner, L., Hash, T., & Baro, J. A. (1993). A defective visual pathway in children with reading disability. *New England Journal of Medicine, 328,* 989–996.

Lehr, F. (1984). Student-teacher communication. *Language Arts, 61,* 200–203.

Lehrer, G. M. (1974). Measurement of minimal brain dysfunction. In C. Xintras, B. L, Johnson, & I. de Groot (Eds.), *Behavioral toxicology.* Washington, DC: U.S. Department of Health, Education, and Welfare.

Leiderman, J., & Kinsbourne, M. (1980). Rightward motor bias in newborns depends on potential right-handedness. *Neuropsychologia, 18,* 579–584.

Leigh, J., & Patton, J. (1986). State certification standards for teachers of learning disabled students. *Learning Disability Quarterly, 9,* 259–267.

LeMay, M. (1977). Asymmetries of the skull and handedness: Phrenology revisited. *Journal of the Neurological Sciences, 32,* 243–253.

Lenchner, O., Gerber, M. M., & Routh, D. K. (1990). Phonological awareness tasks as predictors of decoding ability: Beyond segmentation. *Journal of Learning Disabilities, 23,* 240–247.

Lenkowsky, L. K., & Saposnek, D. T. (1978). Family consequences of parental dyslexia. *Journal of Learning Disabilities, 11,* 47–53.

Lenneberg, E. H. (1967). *Biological foundations of language.* New York: John Wiley & Sons.

Lennox, W. G., Gibbs, E. L., & Gibbs, F. A. (1945). The brain-wave pattern, an hereditary trait: Evidence from 74 "normal" pairs of twins. *Journal of Heredity, 36,* 233–243.

Lenz, B. K. (1992). Self-managed learning strategy systems for children and youth. *School Psychology Review, 21,* 211–228.

Lenz, B. K., Alley, G. R., & Schumaker, J. B. (1987). Activating the inactive learner: Advance organizers in the secondary content classroom. *Learning Disability Quarterly, 10,* 53–67.

Leon, J. A., & Pepe, H. J. (1983). Self-instructional training: Cognitive behavior modification for remediating arithmetic deficits. *Exceptional Children, 50,* 54–60.

Leonard, L. B. (1982). The nature of specific language impairment in children. In S. Rosenberg (Ed.), *Handbook of applied psycholinguistics: Major thrusts of research and theory.* Hillsdale, NJ: Lawrence Erlbaum.

Leong, C. K. (1976). Lateralization in severely disabled readers in relation to functional cerebral development and synthesis of information, In R. M. Knights & D. J. Bakker (Eds.), *The neuropsychology of learning disorders: Theoretical approaches.* Baltimore: University Park Press.

Leong, C. K. (1986). The role of language awareness in reading proficiency. In G. Th. Pavlidis & D. F. Fisher (Eds.), *Dyslexia: Its neuropsychology and treatment.* New York: John Wiley and Sons.

Lerner, B. (1981). The minimum competence testing movement: Social, scientific, and legal implications. *American Psychologist, 36,* 1057–1066.

Lerner, J. V., Lerner, R. M., & Zabski, S. (1985). Temperament and elementary school children's actual and rated academic performance: A test of a "goodness of fit" model. *The Journal of Child Psychology and Psychiatry, 26,* 125–136.

Lesgold, A. M., McCormick, C., & Golinkoff, R. M. (1975). Imagery training and children's prose learning. *Journal of Educational Psychology, 67,* 663–667.

Lesgold, A. M., & Perfetti, C. A. (1978). Interactive processes in reading comprehension. *Discourse Processes, 1,* 323–336.

Leshowitz, B., Jenkens, K., Heaton, S., & Bough, T. L. (1993). Fostering critical thinking skills in students with learning disabilities: An instructional program. *Journal of Learning Disabilities, 26,* 483–490.

Lester, B. M. (1987). Developmental outcome prediction from acoustic cry analysis in term and preterm infants. *Pediatrics, 80,* 529–534.

Letourneau, J., Lapierre, N., & Lamont, A. (1979). The relationship between convergence insufficiency and school achievement. *American Journal of Optometry and Physiological Optics, 56,* 18–22.

Levenstein, P., O'Hara, J., & Madden, J. (1983). The mother-child home program of the Verbal Interaction Project. In Consortium for Longitudinal Studies (Ed.), *As the twig is bent: Lasting effects of preschool programs.* Hillsdale, NJ: Lawrence Erlbaum.

Levin, E. K., Zigmond, N., & Birch, J. W. (1985). A follow-up study of 52 learning disabled adolescents. *Journal of Learning Disabilities, 18,* 2–7.

Levin, H. S., Handel, S. F., Goldman, A. M., Eisenberg, H. M., & Guinto, F. C., Jr. (1985). Magnetic resonance imaging after "diffuse" nonmissile head injury: A neurobehavioral study. *Archives of Neurology, 42,* 963–968.

Levin, J. R. (1973). Inducing comprehension in poor readers: A test of a recent model. *Journal of Educational Psychology, 65,* 19–24.

Levin, J. R. (1976). What have we learned about maximizing what children learn? In J. R. Levin & V. L. Allan (Eds.), *Cognitive learning in children: Theories and strategies.* New York: Academic Press.

Levin, J. R., Divine-Hawkins, P., Kerst, S. M., & Guttmann, J. (1974). Individual differences in learning from pictures and words: The development and application of an instrument. *Journal of Educational Psychology, 66,* 296–303.

Levin, J. R., Shriberg, L. K., & Berry, J. K. (1983). A concrete strategy for remembering abstract prose. *American Educational Research Journal, 20,* 277–290.

Levine, S. C., Jordan, N. C., and Huttenlocher, J. (1992). Development of calculation abilities in young children. *Journal of Experimental Child Psychology, 53,* 72–103.

Lewis, M., Worobey, J., Ramsay, D. S., & McCormak, M. K. (1992). Prenatal exposure to heavy metals: Effect on childhood cognitive skills and health status. *Pediatrics, 89,* 1010–1015.

Lewis, S. K., & Lawrence-Patterson, E. (1989). Locus of control of children with learning disabilities and perceived locus of control by significant others. *Journal of Learning Disabilities, 22,* 255–257.

Liberman, I. Y. (1985). Should so-called modality preferences determine the nature of instruction for children with reading disabilities? In F. H. Duffy & N. Geschwind (Eds.), *Dyslexia: A neuroscientific approach to clinical evaluation.* Boston: Little, Brown.

Liberman, I. Y., Rubin, H., Duques, S., & Carlisle, J. (1985). Linguistic abilities and spelling proficiency in kindergarteners and adult poor spellers. In D. B. Gray & J. F. Kavanaugh (Eds.), *Biobehavioral measures of dyslexia.* Parkton, MD: York Press.

Liberman, I. Y., & Shankweiler, D. (1985). Phonology and the problems of learning to read and write. *Remedial and Special Education, 6*(6), 8–17.

Liberman, I. Y., Shankweiler, D., Fischer, F. W., & Carter, B. (1974). Reading and the awareness of linguistic segments. *Journal of Experimental Child Psychology, 18,* 201–212.

Liberman, I. Y., Shankweiler, D., Orlando, C., Harris, K. S., & Berti, F. B. (1971). Letter confusions and reversals of sequence in the beginning reader: Implications for Orton's theory of developmental dyslexia. *Cortex, 7,* 127–142.

Licht, B. G., Kistner, J. A., Ozkaragoz, T., Shapiro, S., & Clausen, L. (1985). Causal attributions of learning disabled children: Individual differences and their implications for persistence. *Journal of Educational Psychology, 77,* 208–216.

Licht, R., Bakker, D. J., Kok, A., & Bouma, A. (1988). The development of lateral event-related potentials (ERPS) related to word naming: A four year longitudinal study. *Neuropsychologia, 26,* 327–340.

Licopoli, L. (1984). The resource room and mainstreaming secondary handicapped students: A case study. *Topics in Learning & Learning Disabilities, 3*(4), 1–15.

Lieber, J., & Semmel, M. I. (1985). Effectiveness of computer application to instruction with mildly handicapped learners: A review. *Remedial and Special Education, 6*(5), 5–12.

Lieberman, L. M. (1980a). The implications of noncategorical special education. *Journal of Learning Disabilities, 13,* 65–68.

Lieberman, L. M. (1980b). Territoriality—Who does what to whom? *Journal of Learning Disabilities, 13,* 124–128.

Lieberman, L. M. (1981). The LD adolescent . . . When do you stop? *Journal of Learning Disabilities, 14,* 425–426.

Lieberman, L. M. (1985). Special education and regular education: A merger made in heaven. *Exceptional Children, 51,* 513–516.

Lieberman, L. M. (1986a). Reconciling standards and individual differences. *Journal of Learning Disabilities, 19,* 127.

Lieberman, L. M. (1986b). Profiles: An interview with Laurence M. Lieberman. *Academic Therapy, 21,* 421–425.

Liebert, R. M., Neal, J. M., & Davidson, E. S. (1973). *The early window: Effects of television on children and youth.* New York: Pergamon.

Liederman, J., & Kinsbourne, M. (1980). Rightward motor bias in newborns depends on parental right-handedness. *Neuropsychologia, 18,* 579–584.

Lindsey, J. D., & Kerlin, M. A. (1979). Learning disabilities and reading disorders: A brief review of the secondary level literature. *Journal of Learning Disabilities, 12,* 408–415.

Lindstrom, L. E., Benz, M. R., & Johnson, M. D. (1996). Developing job clubs for students in transition. *Teaching Exceptional Children, 29 (2),* 18–21.

Lipham, J. M. (1981). *Effective principal, effective school.* Reston, VA: National Association of Secondary School Principals.

Litcher, J. H., & Roberge, L. P. (1979). First grade intervention for reading achievement of high-risk children. *Bulletin of the Orton Society, 29,* 238–244.

Lloyd, J. W., Crowley, E. P., Kohler, F. W., & Strain, P. S. (1988). Redefining the applied research agenda: Cooperative learning, pre-referral, teacher consultation, and peer-modulated interventions. *Journal of Learning Disabilities, 21,* 43–52.

Lloyd, J. W., & Loper, A. B, (1986). Measurement and evaluation of task-related learning behaviors: Attention to task and metacognition. *School Psychology Review, 15,* 336–345.

Lockey, S. D., Sr. (1972). Sensitizing properties of food additives and other commercial products. *Annals of Allergy, 30,* 638–641.

Lockey, S. D., Sr. (1977). Hypersensitivity to Tartrazine (FD & C Yellow No. 5) and other dyes and additives present in foods and pharmaceutical products. *Annals of Allergy, 38,* 206–210.

Loney, J., Whaley-Klahn, M. A., Kosier, T., & Conboy, J. (1983). Hyperactive boys and their brothers at 21: Predictors of aggressive and antisocial outcomes. In K. T. Van Dusen & S. A. Mednick (Eds.), *Prospective studies of crime and delinquency.* Boston: Kluwer-Nijhoff.

Lord-Maes, J., & Obrzut, J. E. (1996). Neuropsychological consequences of traumatic brain injury in children and adults. *Journal of Learning Disabilities, 29,* 609–617.

Lorsbach, T. C., & Frymier, J. (1992). A comparison of learning disabled and nondisabled students on five at-risk factors. *Learning Disabilities Research & Practice, 7,* 137–141.

Lou, H. C., Henriksen, L., & Bruhn, D. (1984). Focal cerebral hypoperfusion in children with dysphasia and/or attention deficit disorder. *Archives of Neurology, 41,* 825–829.

Lovegrove, W., Billing, G., & Slaghuis, W. (1978). Processing of visual contour orientation information in normal and reading disabled children. *Cortex, 14,* 268–278.

Lovegrove, W., Slaghuis, W., Bowling, A., Nelson, P., & Geeves, E. (1986). Spatial frequency processing and the prediction of reading ability: A preliminary investigation. *Perception & Psychophysics, 40,* 440–444.

Lovitt, T. C. (1975a). Applied behavior analysis and learning disabilities—Part I: Characteristics of ABA, general recommendations, and methodological limitations. *Journal of Learning Disabilities, 8,* 432–443.

Lovitt, T. C. (1975b). Applied behavior analysis and learning disabilities—Part II: Specific research recommendations and suggestions for practitioners. *Journal of Learning Disabilities, 8,* 504–518.

Lowell, R. (1971). Reading readiness factors as predictors of success in first grade reading. *Journal of Learning Disabilities, 4,* 563–567.

Lubchenco, L. O., & Bard, H. (1971). Incidence of hypoglycemia in newborn infants classified by birth weight and gestational age. *Pediatrics, 47,* 831–838.

Lucangeli, D., Galderisi, D., & Cornoldi, D. (1995). Specific and general transfer effects following metamemory training. *Learning Disabilities Research & Practice, 10,* 11–21.

Luick, A. H., & Senf, G. M. (1979). Where have all the children gone? *Journal of Learning Disabilities, 12,* 285–287.

Lundberg, I., Frost, J., & Petersen, O. (1988). Effects of an extensive program for stimulating phonological awareness in preschool children. *Reading Research Quarterly, 23,* 263–284.

Lundberg, I., Olofsson, A., & Wall, S. (1980). Reading and spelling skills in the first school years predicted from phonemic awareness skills in kindergarten. *Scandinavian Journal of Psychology, 21,* 159–173.

Luria, A. (1961). *The role of speech in the regulation of normal and abnormal behavior.* New York: Liveright Publishing Corp.

Luria, A. R. (1970). The functional organization of the brain. *Scientific American, 222,* 66–78.

Luria, A. R. (1976). *The neuropsychology of memory.* New York: John Wiley & Sons.

Luria, A. R. (1977). Cerebral organization of conscious acts; A frontal lobe function. In L. Tarnopol & M. Tarnopol (Eds.), *Brain function and reading disabilities.* Baltimore: University Park Press.

Luria, A. R. (1980). *Higher cortical functions in man.* New York: Basic Books.

Lykken, D. T., McGue, M., Tellegen, A., & Bouchard, T. J. (1992). Emergenesis: Genetic traits that may not run in families. *American Psychologist, 47,* 1565–1577.

Lynch, E. W., & Stein, R. C. (1987). Parent participation by ethnicity: A comparison of Hispanic, Black, and Anglo families. *Exceptional Children, 54,* 105–111.

Lyon, G. R. (1985). Educational validation studies of learning disability subtypes. In B. P. Rourke (Ed.), *Neuropsychology of learning disabilities.* New York: Guilford Press.

Lyon, G. R. (1995). Research initiatives in learning disabilities: Contributions from scientists supported by the National Institute of Child Health and Human Development. *Journal of Child Neurology, 10,* S120–S126.

Lyon, G. R., Vaasen, M., & Toomey, F. (1989). Teachers' perceptions of their undergraduate and graduate preparation. *Teacher Education and Special Education, 12,* 164–169.

Lyon, S. (1977). Teacher nonverbal behavior related to perceived pupil social-personal attributes. *Journal of Learning Disabilities, 10,* 173–177.

Lyytinen, P., Rasku-Puttonen, H., Poikkeus, A.-M., Laskso, M.-L., & Ahonen, T. (1994). Mother-child teaching strategies and learning disabilities. *Journal of Learning Disabilities, 27,* 186–192.

Maag, J. W., & Reid, R. (1994). The phenomenology of depression among students with and without learning disabilities: More similar that different. *Learning Disabilities Research & Practice, 9,* 91–103.

MacArthur, C. A. (1988). The impact of computers on the writing process. *Exceptional Children, 54,* 536–542.

MacArthur, C. A., & Graham, S. (1987). Learning disabled students' composing under three methods of text production: Handwriting, word processing, and dictation. *Journal of Special Education, 21*(3), 22–42.

MacArthur, C. A., Graham, S., Haynes, J. B., & De La Paz, S. (1996). Spell checkers and students with learning disabilities: Performance comparisons and impact on spelling. *The Journal of Special Education, 30,* 35–57.

MacArthur, C. S., Graham, S., & Schwartz, S. (1991). Knowledge of revision and revising behavior among students with learning disabilities. *Learning Disabilities Quarterly, 14,* 61–73.

MacArthur, C. A., & Haynes, J. B. (1995). Student assistant for learning from text (SALT): A hypermedia reading aid. *Journal of Learning Disabilities, 28,* 150–159.

MacArthur, C. A., Schwartz, S. S., & Graham, S. (1991). Effects of a reciprocal peer revision strategy in special education classrooms. *Learning Disabilities Research & Practice, 6,* 201–210.

MacArthur, C. A., & Shneiderman, B. (1986). Learning disabled students' difficulties in learning to use a word processor: Implications for instruction and software evaluation. *Journal of Learning Disabilities, 19,* 248–253.

MacDonald, G. W., & Cornwall, A. (1995). The relationship between phonological awareness and reading and spelling achievement eleven years later. *Journal of Learning Disabilities, 28,* 523–527.

MacKavey, W., Curcio, F., & Rosen, J. (1975). Tachistoscopic word recognition performance under conditions of simultaneous bilateral presentation. *Neuropsychologia, 13,* 27–33.

MacKenzie, D. E. (1983). Research for school improvement: An appraisal of some recent trends. *Educational Researcher, 12*(4), 5–17.

Mackie, R. P. (1969). *Special education in the United States: Statistics 1948–1966.* New York: Teachers College Press.

Maclean, M., Bryant, P., & Bradley, L. (1987). Rhymes, nursery rhymes, and reading in early childhood. *Merrill-Palmer Quarterly, 33,* 255–281.

MacMillan, D. L., Balow, I. H., & Widaman, K. F. (1988). Local option competency testing: Conceptual issues with mildly handicapped and educationally at-risk students. *Learning Disabilities Research, 3,* 94–100.

MacMillan, D. L., Hendrick, I. G., & Watkins, A. V. (1988). Impact of Diana, Larry P., and P. L. 94–142 on minority students. *Exceptional Children, 54,* 426–432.

MacNamara, J. (1972). Cognitive basis of language learning in infants. *Psychological Review, 79,* 1–13.

Macy, D. J., Baker, J. A., & Kosinski, S. C. (1979). An empirical study of the Myklebust Learning Quotient. *Journal of Learning Disabilities, 12,* 93–96.

Madden, N. A., & Slavin, R. E. (1983). Mainstreaming students with mild handicaps: Academic and social outcomes. *Review of Educational Research, 53,* 519–569.

Maddux, C. D., Green, C., & Horner, C. M. (1986). School entry age among children labeled learning disabled, mentally retarded, and emotionally disturbed. *Learning Disabilities Focus, 2,* 7–12.

Madge, S., Affleck, J., & Lowenbraum, S. (1990). Social effects of integrated classrooms and resource room/regular class placements on elementary students with learning disabilities. *Journal of Learning Disabilities, 23,* 439–445.

Maheady, L., Harper, G. F., & Sacca, M. K. (1988). Peer-mediated instruction: A promising approach to meeting the diverse needs of LD adolescents. *Learning Disability Quarterly, 11,* 108–113.

Maheady, L., Maitland, G. E., & Sainato, D. M. (1984). The interpretation of social interactions by mildly handicapped and nondisabled children. *Journal of Special Education, 18,* 151–159.

Maheady, L., Sacca, M. K., & Harper, G. F. (1988). Classwide peer tutoring with mildly handicapped high school students. *Exceptional Children, 55,* 52–59.

Maher, C. A. (1982). Learning disabled adolescents in the regular classroom: Evaluation of a mainstreaming procedure. *Learning Disability Quarterly, 5*(1), 82–84.

Maier, A. S. (1980). The effect of focusing on the cognitive processes of learning disabled children. *Journal of Learning Disabilities, 13,* 143–147.

Majsterek, D. J., & Ellenwood, A. E. (1995). Phonological awareness and beginning reading: Evaluation of a school-based screening procedure. *Journal of Learning Disabilities, 28,* 449–456.

Malone, L. D., & Mastropieri, M. A. (1992). Reading comprehension instruction: Summarization and self-monitoring training for students with learning disabilities. *Exceptional Children, 58,* 270–279.

Malouf, D. (1983). Do rewards reduce student motivation? *School Psychology Review, 12,* 1–11.

Malouf, D. B. (1987–88). The effect of instructional computer games on continuing student motivation. *Journal of Special Education, 21*(4), 27–38.

Mandel, D. R., Jusczyk, P. W., & Nelson, D. G. (1994). Does sentential prosody help infants organize and remember speech information? *Cognition, 53,* 155–180.

Mandler, J. M., & Johnson, N. S. (1977). Remembrance of things passed: Story structure and recall. *Cognitive Psychology, 9,* 111–151.

Manis, F. R. (1985). Acquisition of word identification skills in normal and disabled readers. *Journal of Educational Psychology, 77,* 78–90.

Manis, F. R., Szeszulski, P. A., Holt, L. K., & Graves, K. (1988). A developmental perspective on dyslexic subtypes. *Annals of Dyslexia, 38,* 139–153.

Mann, C. A., Lubar, J. F., Zimmerman, A. W., Miller, C. A., & Muenchen, R. A., (1992). Quantitative analysis of EEG in boys with attention-deficit–hyperactivity disorder: Controlled study with clinical implications. *Pediatric Neurology, 8,* 30–36.

Mann, L. (1971). Perceptual training revisited: The training of nothing at all. *Rehabilitation Literature, 32,* 322–335.

Mann, L., Davis, C. H., Boyer, C. W., Metz, C. M., & Wolford, B. (1983). LD or not LD, that was the question: A retrospective analysis of child service demonstration centers' compliance with the Federal definition of learning disabilities. *Journal of Learning Disabilities, 16,* 14–17.

Mann, V. A. (1993). Phoneme awareness and future reading ability. *Journal of Learning Disabilities, 26,* 259–269.

Mann, V. A., Cowin, E., & Schoenheimer, J. (1989). Phonological processing, language comprehension, and reading ability. *Journal of Learning Disabilities, 22,* 76–89.

Mannuzza, S., Klein, R. G., Bessler, A., Malloy, P., & LaPadula, M. (1993). Adult outcome of hyperactive boys: Education achievement, occupational rank, and psychiatric status. *Archives of General Psychiatry, 50,* 565–576.

Mannuzza, S., Klein, R. G., Konig, P. H., & Giampino, T. L. (1989). Hyperactive boys almost grown up: IV. Criminality and its relationship to psychiatric status. *Archives of General Psychiatry, 46,* 1073–1079.

Manzo, A. V. (1969). The request procedure. *Journal of Reading, 13,* 123–126.

Manzo, A. V. (1975). Guided reading procedure. *Journal of Reading, 7,* 287–291.

Marcel, T., Katz, L., & Smith, M. (1974). Laterality and reading proficiency. *Neuropsychologia, 12,* 131–139.

Marcel, T., & Rajan, P. (1975). Lateral specialization for recognition of words and faces in good and poor readers. *Neuropsychologia, 13,* 489–497.

Margalit, M., & Shulman, S. (1986). Autonomy perceptions and anxiety expressions of learning disabled adolescents. *Journal of Learning Disabilities, 19,* 291–293.

Markoski, B. D. (1983). Conversational interactions of the learning disabled and nondisabled child. *Journal of Learning Disabilities, 16,* 606–609.

Marsh, H. W. (1986). Self-serving effect (bias?) and academic attributions: Its relation to academic achievement and self-concept. *Journal of Educational Psychology, 78,* 190–200.

Marsh, L. G., & Cooke, N. L. (1996). The effects of using manipulatives in teaching math problem solving to students with learning disabilities. *Learning Disabilities Research & Practice, 11,* 58–65.

Marshall, W., & Ferguson, J. H. (1939). Hereditary word-blindness as a defect of selective association. *Journal of Nervous and Mental Diseases, 89,* 164–173.

Marston, D. (1987–1988). The effectiveness of special education: A time series analysis of reading performance in regular and special education settings. *Journal of Special Education, 21,* 13–26.

Marston, D. (1996). A comparison of inclusion only, pull-out only, and combined-service models for students with mild disabilities. *The Journal of Special Education, 30,* 121–132.

Marston, D., Mirkin, P., & Deno, S. (1984). Curriculum-based measurement: An alternative to traditional screening, referral, and identification. *Journal of Special Education, 18,* 109–117.

Marston, D., Tindal, G., & Deno, S. L. (1984). Eligibility for learning disability services: A direct and repeated measurement approach. *Exceptional Children, 50,* 554–556.

Martin, K. F., & Manno, C. (1995). Use of a check-off system to improve middle school students' story compositions. *Journal of Learning Disabilities, 28,* 139–149.

Martin, R. P., Drew, K. D., Gaddis, L. R., & Moseley, M. (1988). Prediction of elementary school achievement from preschool temperament: Three studies. *School Psychology Review, 17,* 125–137.

Martin, R. P., & Holbrook, J. (1985). Relationship of temperament characteristics to the academic achievement of first-grade children. *Journal of Psychoeducational Assessment, 3,* 131–140.

Martin, R. P., Nagle, R., & Paget, K. (1983). Relationships between temperament and classroom behavior, teacher attitudes, and academic achievement. *Journal of Psychoeducational Assessment, 1,* 377–386.

Martino, L., & Johnson, D. W. (1979). Cooperative and individualistic experiences among disabled and normal children. *Journal of Social Psychology, 107,* 177–183.

Marx, J. L. (1983). The two sides of the brain. *Science, 220,* 488–490.

Maryam, M., & White, K. R. (1988). Parent tutoring as a supplement to compensatory education for first-grade children. *Remedial and Special Education, 9,* (3), 35–41.

Maslow, A. H., & Mintz, N. L. (1956). The effects of esthetic surroundings: 1. *Journal of Psychology, 41,* 247–254.

Mastropieri, M. A., Scruggs, T. E., Bakken, J. P., & Brigham, F. J. (1992). A complex mnemonic strategy for teaching states and their capitals: Comparing forward and backward associations. *Learning Disabilities Research & Practice, 7,* 96–103.

Mastropieri, M. A., Scruggs, T. E., & Shiah, S. (1991). Mathematics instruction for learning disabled students: A review of research. *Learning Disabilities Research and Practice, 6,* 89–98.

Mastropieri, M. A., Scruggs, T. E., & Whedon, C. (1997). Using mnemonic strategies to teach information about U.S. presidents: A classroom-based investigation. *Learning Disability Quarterly, 20,* 13–21.

Matarazzo, J. D. (1992). Psychological testing and assessment in the 21st century. *American Psychologist, 47,* 1007–1018.

Matějček, Z., & Sturma, J. (1986). Language structure, dyslexia, and remediation: The Czech perspective. In G. Th. Pavlidis & D. F. Fisher (Eds.), *Dyslexia: Its neuropsychology and treatment.* New York: John Wiley & Sons.

Matheny, A. P., Jr., Wilson, R. S., & Nuss, S. M. (1984). Toddler temperament: Stability across settings and over ages. *Child Development, 55,* 1200–1211.

Matheny, A. P., Jr., Wilson, R. S., & Thoben, A. S. (1987). Home and mother: Relations with infant temperament. *Developmental Psychology, 23,* 323–331.

Mather, N. (1992). Whole language reading instruction for students with learning disabilities. Caught in the cross fire. *Learning Disabilities Research & Practice, 7,* 87–95.

Mather, N., & Bos, C. S. (1994). Educational computing and multimedia. In C. S. Bos & S. Vaughn (Eds.), *Strategies for teaching students with learning and behavioral problems* (3rd ed.). Boston: Allyn & Bacon.

Mather, N., & Lachowicz, B. L. (1992). Shared writing: An instructional approach for reluctant writers. *Teaching Exceptional Children, 25,* 26–30.

Mathes, P. G., & Fuchs, L. S. (1994). The efficacy of peer tutoring in reading for students with mild disabilities: A best-evidence synthesis. *School Psychology Review, 23,* 59–80.

Mathes, P. G., Fuchs, D., Fuchs, L. S., Henley, A. M., & Sanders, A. (1994). Increasing strategic reading practice with Peabody classwide peer tutoring. *Learning Disabilities Research & Practice, 9,* 44–48.

Mathews, R. M., Whang, P. L., & Fawcett, S. B. (1982). Behavioral assessment of occupational skills of learning disabled adolescents. *Journal of Learning Disabilities, 15,* 38–41.

Mathinos, D. A. (1988). Communicative competence of children with learning disabilities. *Journal of Learning Disabilities, 21,* 437–443.

Mathinos, D. A. (1991). Conversational engagement of children with learning disabilities. *Journal of Learning Disabilities, 24,* 439–445.

Matoušek, M., & Petersén, I. (1973). Frequency analysis of the EEG in normal children (1–15 years) and in normal adolescents (16–21 years). In P. Kellaway & I. Petersen (Eds.), *Automation of clinical electroencephalography.* New York: Raven Press.

Matthews, B. A. J., & Seymour, C. M. (1981). The performance of learning disabled children on tests of auditory discrimination. *Journal of Learning Disabilities, 14,* 9–12.

Mattingly, J. C., & Bott, D. A. (1990). Teaching multiplication facts to students with learning problems. *Exceptional Children, 56,* 438–449.

Mattis, S., French, J. H., & Rapin, I. (1975). Dyslexia in children and young adults: Three independent neuropsychological syndromes. *Developmental Medicine and Child Neurology, 17,* 150–163.

Mauer, D. M., & Kamhi, A. G. (1996). Factors that influence phoneme-grapheme correspondence learning. *Journal of Learning Disabilities, 29,* 259–270.

Mauser, A. J. (1974). Learning disabilities and delinquent youth. *Academic Therapy, 4,* 389–402.

Maxwell, S. E., & Wallach, G. P. (1984). The language-learning disabilities connection: Symptoms of early language disability change over time. In G. P. Wallach & K. G. Butler (Eds.), *Language learning disabilities in school-age children.* Baltimore: Williams & Wilkins.

Mayron, L. W. (1979). Allergy, learning, and behavior problems. *Journal of Learning Disabilities, 12,* 32–42.

Mayron, L. W., Mayron, E. L., Ott, J. W., & Nations, R. (1976). Light, radiation, and academic achievement: Second year data. *Academic Therapy, 11,* 397–407.

Maziade, M., Caron, C. Côté, R., Boutin, P., & Thivierge, J. (1990). Extreme temperament and diagnosis: A study in a psychiatric sample of consecutive children. *Archives of General Psychiatry, 47,* 477–484.

McCall, R. B., Hogarty, P. S., & Hurlburt, N. (1972). Transitions in infant sensorimotor development and the prediction of childhood IQ. *American Psychologist, 27,* 728–748.

McCarthy, M. (1980). Minimum competency testing and handicapped students. *Exceptional Children, 47,* 166–173.

McCauley, C., & Ciesielski, J. (1982). Electroencephalogram tests for brain dysfunction: A question of validity. *Science, 217,* 81–82.

McClelland, D. C. (1973). Testing for competence rather than for "intelligence." *American Psychologist, 28,* 1–14.

McConaughy, S. H. (1986). Social competence and behavioral problems of learning disabled boys aged 12–16. *Journal of Learning Disabilities, 19,* 101–106.

McConaughy, S. H., & Ritter, D. R. (1986). Social competence and behavioral problems of learning disabled boys aged 6–11. *Journal of Learning Disabilities, 19,* 39–45.

McCormick, S., & Moe, A. J. (1982). The language of instructional materials: A source of reading problems. *Exceptional Children, 49,* 48–53.

McCroskey, R. L., & Kidder, H. C. (1980). Auditory fusion among learning disabled, reading disabled, and normal children. *Journal of Learning Disabilities, 13,* 69–76.

McEvoy, M. A., Odom, S., & McConnell, S. R. (1992). Peer social competence intervention for young children with disabilities. In S. L. Odom, S. R. McConnell, & M. A. McEvoy (Eds.), *Social competence of young children with disabilities: Issues and strategies for intervention.* Baltimore: Paul H. Brookes.

McGinnis, M. (1963). *Aphasic children: Identification and education by the association method*. Washington, DC: Volta.

McGue, M. Bouchard, T. J., Jr., Iacono, W. G., & Lykken, D. T. (1993). Behavioral genetics of cognitive ability: A life-span perspective. In R. Plomin & G. E. McClearn (eds.), *Nature, nurture, and psychology*. Washington, DC: American Psychological Association.

McHale, K., & Cermak, S. A. (1992). Fine motor activities in elementary school: Preliminary findings and provisional implications for children with fine motor problems. *American Journal of Occupational Therapy, 46*, 898–903.

McIntosh, D. K., & Dunn, L. M. (1973). Children with major specific learning disabilities. In L. M. Dunn (Ed.), *Exceptional children in the schools: Special education in transition* (2nd ed.). New York: Holt, Rinehart & Winston.

McIntosh, R., Vaughn, S., Schumm, J. S., Haager, D., & Lee, O. (1993). Observations of students with learning disabilities in general education classrooms. *Exceptional Children, 60*, 249–261.

McIntyre, L. L. (1988). Teacher gender: A predictor of special education referral? *Journal of Learning Disabilities, 21*, 382–383.

McKeever, W. F., & Van Deventer, A. D. (1975). Dyslexic adolescents: Evidence of impaired visual and auditory language processing associated with normal lateralization and visual responsivity. *Cortex, 11*, 361–378.

McKenney, J. L., & Keen, P. G. W. (1976). How managers' minds work. *Harvard Business Review, 52*, 14–21.

McKenzie, R. G. (1991). Content area instruction delivered by secondary learning disabilities teachers: A national survey. *Learning Disability Quarterly, 14*, 115–122.

McKenzie, R. G., & Houk, C. S. (1986). Use of paraprofessionals in the resource room. *Exceptional Children, 53*, 41–45.

McKinney, J. D., & Feagans, L. (1983). Adaptive classroom behavior of learning disabled students. *Journal of Learning Disabilities, 16*, 360–367.

McKinney, J. D., & Hocutt, A. M. (1988). Policy issues in the evaluation of the regular education initiative. *Learning Disabilities Focus, 4*, 15–23.

McKinney, J. D., Osborne, S. S., and Schulte, A. C. (1993). Academic consequences of learning disability: Longitudinal prediction of outcomes at 11 years of age. *Learning Disabilities Research & Practice, 8*, 19–27.

McLachlan, J. F. C., & Hunt, D. E. (1973). Differential effects of discovery learning as a function of conceptual level. *Canadian Journal of Behavioral Science, 5*, 152–160.

McLaughlin, H. G. (1969). SMOG grading—A new readability formula. *Journal of Reading, 12*, 639–646.

McLeod, T. M., & Crump, W. D. (1978). The relationship of visuospatial skills and verbal ability to learning disabilities in mathematics. *Journal of Learning Disabilities, 11*, 237–241.

McLeskey, J. (1989). The influence of level of discrepancy on the identification of students with learning disabilities. *Journal of Learning Disabilities, 22*, 435–438, 443.

McLeskey, J. (1992). Students with learning disabilities at primary, intermediate, and secondary grade levels: Identification and characteristics. *Learning Disability Quarterly, 15*, 13–19.

McLeskey, J., & Grizzle, K. L. (1992). Grade retention rates among students with learning disabilities. *Exceptional Children, 58*, 548–554.

McLeskey, J., & Waldron, N. L. (1991). Identifying students with learning disabilities: The effect of implementing statewide guidelines. *Journal of Learning Disabilities, 24*, 501–506.

McLeskey, J., Waldron, N. L., & Wornhoff, S. A. (1990). Factors influencing the identification of black and white students with learning disabilities. *Journal of Learning Disabilities, 23*, 362–366.

McLoughlin, J. A., Clark, F. L., Mauck, A. R., & Petrosko, J. (1987). A comparison of parent-child perceptions of student learning disabilities. *Journal of Learning Disabilities, 20*, 357–360.

McLoughlin, J. A., McLoughlin, R., & Steward, W. (1979). Advocacy for parents of the handicapped: A professional responsibility. *Learning Disability Quarterly, 2*, 51–57.

McLoughlin, J. A., Nall, M., Isaacs, B., Petrosko, J., Karibo, J., & Lindsey, B. (1983). The relationship of allergies and allergy treatment to school performance and student behavior. *Annals of Allergy, 51*, 506–510.

McLoughlin, J. A., Nall, M., & Petrosko, J. (1985). Allergies and learning disabilities. *Learning Disability Quarterly, 8*, 255–260.

McLoyd, V. C. (1989). Socialization and development in a changing economy: The effects of paternal job and income loss on children. *American Psychologist, 44*, 293–302.

McMichael, A. J., Vimpani, G. V., Robertson, E. F., Baghurst, P. A., & Clark, P. D. (1986). The Port Pirie Cohort Study: Maternal blood lead and pregnancy outcome. *Journal of Epidemiology and Community Health, 40*, 18–25.

McMillen, M. M. (1979). Differential mortality by sex in fetal and neonatal deaths. *Science, 204*, 89–91.

McNellis, K. L. (1987). In search of the attentional deficit. In S. J. Ceci (Ed.), *Handbook of cognitive, social, and neuropsychological aspects of learning disabilities* (Vol. 2). Hillsdale, NJ: Lawrence Erlbaum.

McNew, S. (1984). Hyperactivity: The implications of heterogeneity. In E. S. Gollin (Ed.), *Malformations of development: Biological and psychological sources and consequences*. New York: Academic Press.

Medway, F. J. (1985, January). To promote or not to promote? *Principal*, pp. 22–25.

Medway, F. J., & Rose, J. S. (1986). Grade retention. In T. R. Kratochwill (Ed.), *Advances in school psychology* (Vol. 5), pp. 141–175. Hillsdale, NJ: Lawrence Erlbaum.

Mehler, J., Jusczyk, P. W., Lambertz, G., Halsted, N., Bertoncini, J., & Amiel-Tison, C. (1988). A precursor of language acquisition in young infants. *Cognition, 29*, 143–178.

Meichenbaum, D. (1976). Cognitive factors as determinants of learning disabilities: A cognitive-functional approach. In R. M. Knights & D. J. Bakker (Eds.), *The neuropsychology of learning disorders: Theoretical approaches*. Baltimore: University Park Press.

Meichenbaum, D. (1977). *Cognitive-behavior modification: An integrative approach*. New York: Plenum Press.

Meichenbaum, D., & Goodman, J. (1971). Training impulsive children to talk to themselves: A means of developing self control. *Journal of Abnormal Psychology, 77*, 115–126.

Meier, J. H. (1971). Prevalence and characteristics of learning disabilities found in second grade children. *Journal of Learning Disabilities, 4*, 1–16.

Meiners, M. L., & Dabbs, J. M., Jr. (1977). Ear temperature and brain blood flow: Laterality effects. *Bulletin of the Psychonomic Society, 10*, 194–196.

Meltzer, L., & Reid, D. K. (1994). New directions in the assessment of students with special needs: The shift toward a constructivist perspective. *The Journal of Special Education, 28*, 338–355.

Menkes, M. M., Rowe, J. S., & Menkes, J. H. (1967). A 25-year-old follow-up study on the hyperkinetic child with minimal brain dysfunction. *Pediatrics, 39*, 393–399.

Menyuk, P. (1969). *Sentences children use*. Cambridge, MA: MIT Press.

Mercer, C. D., Jordan, L., Allsop, D. H., & Mercer, A. R. (1996). Learning disabilities definitions and criteria used by state education departments. *Learning Disability Quarterly, 19*, 217–232.

Mercer, J. R. (1970). The ecology of mental retardation. In *The proceedings of the first annual spring conference of the institute for the study of mental retardation*. Ann Arbor, MI, pp. 55–74.

Mercer, J. R. (1973). *Labeling the mentally retarded: Clinical and social system perspectives on mental retardation*. Berkeley: University of California Press.

Mercer, J. R. (1979). *Technical manual: System of multicultural pluralistic assessment*. New York: Psychological Corp.

Mercer, J. R., & Lewis, J. F. (1978). *The system of multicultural pluralistic assessment*. New York: Psychological Corp.

Merrell, K. W., Johnson, E. R., Merz, J. M., & Ring, E. N. (1992). Social competence of students with mild handicaps and low achievement: A comparative study. *School Psychology Review, 21*, 125–137.

Mesinger, J. F. (1985). Commentary on "A rationale for the merger of special and regular education" or, Is it time for the lamb to lie down with the lion? *Exceptional Children, 51,* 510–512.

Messer, S. B. (1976). Reflection-impulsivity: A review. *Psychological Bulletin, 83,* 1026–1052.

Messick, S. (1995). Validity of psychological assessment: Validation of inferences from persons' responses and performances as scientific inquiry into score meaning. *American Psychologist, 50,* 741–749.

Messick, S., & Damarin, F. (1964). Cognitive styles and memory for faces. *Journal of Abnormal and Social Psychology, 69,* 313–318.

Messick, S., Heller, K. A., & Finn, J. D. (1982). Introduction: Disproportion in special education. In K. A. Heller, W. H. Holtzman, & S. Messick (Eds.), *Placing children in special education: A strategy for equity.* Washington, DC: National Academy Press.

Mevarech, Z. R. (1985). The relationships between temperament characteristics, intelligence, task-engagement, and mathematics achievement. *British Journal of Educational Psychology, 55,* 156–163.

Meyer, J. (1971). *The impact of the open space school upon teacher influence and autonomy: The effects of an organizational innovation* (ERIC Document Reproduction Service No. ED 062 291).

Meyers, C. E., Sundstrom, P. E., & Yoshida, R. K. (1974). The school psychologist and assessment in special education. *School Psychology Monographs, 2,* 3–57.

Michaels, C. R., & Lewandowski, L. J. (1990). Psychological adjustment and family functioning of boys with learning disabilities. *Journal of Learning Disabilities, 23,* 446–450.

Michaelsson, G., & Juhlin, L. (1973). Urticaria induced by preservatives and dye additives in food and drugs. *British Journal of Dermatology, 88,* 525–532.

Miles, T. R. (1986). On the persistence of dyslexic difficulties into adulthood. In G. Th. Pavlidis & D. F. Fisher (Eds.), *Dyslexia: Its neuropsychology and treatment.* New York: John Wiley & Sons.

Miles, T. R., & Ellis, N. C. (1981). A lexical encoding deficiency II. In G. Th. Pavlidis & T. R. Miles (Eds.), *Dyslexia research and its applications to education.* Chichester: John Wiley & Sons.

Milianti, F. J., & Cullinan, W. L. (1974). Effects of age and word frequency on object recognition and naming in children. *Journal of Speech and Hearing Research, 17,* 373–385.

Milich, R. (1994). The response of children with ADHD to failure: If at first you don't succeed, do you try, try again? *School Psychology Review, 23,* 11–18.

Milich, R., Lindgren, S., & Wolraich, M. (1986). The behavioral effects of sugar: A comment on Buchanan. *American Psychologist, 41,* 218–220.

Milich, R., McAninch, C. B., & Harris, M. J. (1992). Effects of stigmatizing information on children's peer relations: Believing is seeing. *School Psychology Review, 21,* 400–409.

Miller, G. A. (1956). The magical number seven, plus or minus two: Some limits on our capacity for processing information. *The Psychological Review, 63,* 81–97.

Miller, L. K., & Turner, S. (1973). Development of hemifield differences in word recognition. *Journal of Educational Psychology, 65,* 172–176.

Miller, M. A. (1992). In ins and outs of portfolios. *Communiqué,* June, 3–4.

Miller, R. J., Snider, B., & Rzonca, C. (1990). Variables related to the decision of young adults with learning disabilities to participate in postsecondary education. *Journal of Learning Disabilities, 23,* 349–354.

Miller, S. A., Shelton, J., & Flavell, J. H. (1970). A test of Luria's hypotheses concerning the development of verbal self-regulation. *Child Development, 41,* 651–665.

Miller, S. P. (1996). Perspectives on mathematics instruction. In D. D. Deshler, E. S. Ellis, & B. K. Lenz (Eds.), *Teaching adolescents with learning disabilities: Strategies and methods* (2nd ed.). Denver: Love Pub.

Miller, S. P., & Mercer, C. D. (1993). Using data to learn about concrete-semiconcrete-abstract instruction for students with math disabilities. *Learning Disabilities Research & Practice, 8,* 89–96.

Minke, K. M., Bear, G. G., Deemer, S. A., & Griffin, S. M. (1996). Teachers' experiences with inclusive classrooms: Implications for special education reform. *The Journal of Special Education, 30,* 152–186.

Minskoff, E. (1980a). Teaching approach for developing nonverbal communication skills in students with social perception deficits. Part I: The basic approach and body language clues. *Journal of Learning Disabilities, 13,* 118–124.

Minskoff, E. (1980b). Teaching approach for developing nonverbal communication skills in students with social perception deficits. Part II: Proxemic, vocalic, and artifactual cues. *Journal of Learning Disabilities, 13,* 203–208.

Minskoff, E. H., Sautter, S. W., Hoffman, F. J., & Hawks, R. (1987). Employer attitudes toward hiring the learning disabled. *Journal of Learning Disabilities, 20,* 53–57.

Minton, M. J. (1980). The effect of sustained silent reading upon comprehension and attitudes among 9th graders. *Journal of Reading, 23,* 498–502.

Mintz, N. L. (1956). Effects of esthetic surroundings: II. Prolonged and repeated experience in a "beautiful" and "ugly" room. *Journal of Psychology, 41,* 459–466.

Miramontes, O., Cheng, L., & Trueba, H. T. (1984). Teacher perceptions and observed outcomes: An ethnographic study of classroom interactions. *Learning Disability Quarterly, 7,* 349–357.

Mischel, W. (1979). On the interface of cognition and personality: Beyond the person-situation debate. *American Psychologist, 34,* 740–754.

Mitchell, V. (1992). African-American students in exemplary urban high schools: The interaction of school practices and student actions. In M. Saravia-Shore & S. F. Arvizu (Eds.), *Cross-cultural literacy: Ethnographies of communication in multiethnic classrooms.* New York: Garland.

Mithaug, D. E., Martin, J. E., & Agran, M. (1987). Adaptability instruction: The goal of transitional programming. *Exceptional Children, 53,* 500–505.

Moeser, S. D., & Bregman, A. S. (1973). Imagery and language acquisition. *Journal of Verbal Learning and Verbal Behavior, 12,* 91–98.

Molfese, D. (1973). Cerebral asymmetry in infants, children and adults: Auditory evoked responses to speech and musical stimuli. *Journal of the Acoustical Society of America, 53,* 363(A).

Molfese, D. L., Freeman, R. B., Jr., & Palermo, D. S. (1975). The ontogeny of brain lateralization for speech and nonspeech stimuli. *Brain and Language, 2,* 356–368.

Molfese, D. L., & Molfese, V. J. (1985). Electrophysiological indices of auditory discrimination in newborn infants: The bases for predicting later language development? *Infant Behavior and Development, 8,* 197–211.

Monroe, M. (1932). *Children who cannot read.* Chicago: University of Chicago Press.

Montague, M. (1992). The effects of cognitive and metacognitive strategy instruction on the mathematical problem solving of middle school students with learning disabilities. *Journal of Learning Disabilities, 25,* 230–248.

Montague, M. & Applegate, B. (1993). Mathematical problem-solving characteristics of middle school students with learning disabilities. *The Journal of Special Education, 27,* 175–201.

Montague, M., Applegate, B., & Marquard, K. (1993). Cognitive strategy instruction and mathematical problem-solving performance of students with learning disabilities. *Learning Disabilities Research & Practice, 8,* 223–232.

Montague, M., Graves, A., & Leavell, A. (1991). Planning, procedural facilitation, and narrative composition of junior high students with learning disabilities. *Learning Disabilities Research & Practice, 6,* 219–224.

Montague, M., & Leavell, A. G. (1994). Improving the narrative writing of students with learning disabilities. *Remedial and Special Education, 15,* 21–33.

Montague, M., Maddox, C. D., & Dereshiwsky, M. I. (1990). Story grammar and comprehension and production of narrative prose by students with learning disabilities. *Journal of Learning Disabilities, 23,* 190–197.

Montali, J., & Lewandowski, L. (1996). Bimodal reading: Benefits of a talking computer for average and less skilled readers. *Journal of Learning Disabilities, 29,* 271–279.

Montgomery, M. S. (1994). Self-concept and children with learning disabilities: Observer-child concordance across six context-dependant domains. *Journal of Learning Disabilities, 27,* 254–262.

Moore, J., & Fine, M. J. (1978). Regular and special class teachers' perceptions of normal and exceptional children and their attitudes toward mainstreaming. *Psychology in the Schools, 15,* 253–259.

Moore, S. R., & Simpson, R. L. (1983). Teacher-pupil and peer verbal interactions of learning disabled, behavior-disordered, and nonhandicapped students. *Learning Disability Quarterly, 6,* 273–282.

Moreland, J. R., Schwebel, A. I., Beck, S., & Wells, R. (1982). Parents as therapists: A review of the behavior therapy parent training literature: 1975–1981. *Behavior Modification, 6,* 250–276.

Morgan, W. P. (1896). A case of congenital word blindness. *British Medical Journal, 2,* 1378.

Morris, R., Lyon, G. R., Alexander, D., Gray, D. B., Kavanagh, J., Rourke, B. P., & Swanson, H. L. (1994). Editorial: Proposed guidelines and criteria for describing samples of persons with learning disabilities. *Learning Disability Quarterly, 17,* 106–109.

Morrison, D. C. (1986). Neurobehavioral dysfunction and learning disabilities in children. In S. J. Ceci (Ed.), *Handbook of cognitive, social, and neuropsychological aspects of learning disabilities* (Vol. 1). Hillsdale, NJ: Lawrence Erlbaum.

Morrison, F. J. (1987). The nature of reading disability: Toward an integrative framework. In S. J. Ceci (Ed.), *Handbook of cognitive, social, and neuropsychological aspects of learning disabilities* (Vol. 2). Hillsdale, NJ: Lawrence Erlbaum.

Morrison, G. M. (1985). Differences in teacher perceptions and student self-perceptions for learning disabled and nonhandicapped learners in regular and special education settings. *Learning Disabilities Research, 1,* 32–41.

Morrison, J. P., & Stewart, M. A. (1971). A family study of the hyperactive child syndrome. *Biological Psychiatry, 3,* 189–195.

Morrison, J. P., & Stewart, M. A. (1973). The psychiatric status of the legal families of adopted hyperactive children. *Archives of General Psychiatry, 28,* 888–891.

Morrison, J. R., & Stewart, M. D. (1974). Bilateral inheritance as evidence for polygenicity in the hyperactive child syndrome. *Journal of Nervous and Mental Disease, 158,* 226–228.

Morse, W. C., Cutler, R. L., & Fink, A. H. (1964). *Public school classes for the emotionally handicapped: A research analysis.* Washington, DC: Council for Exceptional Children, National Education Association.

Morsink, C. V., Soar, R. S., Soar, R. M., & Thomas, A. (1986). Research on teaching: Opening the door to special education classrooms. *Exceptional Children, 53,* 32–40.

Mosberg, L., & Johns, D. (1994). Reading and listening comprehension in college students with developmental dyslexia. *Learning Disabilities Research & Practice, 9,* 130–135.

Moya, F., & Smith, B. E. (1965). Uptake, distribution and placental transport of drugs and anesthetics. *Anesthesiology, 26,* 465–476.

Muehl, S., & Forell, E. R. (1973). A follow-up study of disabled readers: Variables related to high school reading performance. *Reading Research Quarterly, 9,* 110–123.

Mumbauer, C. C., & Miller, J. O. (1970). Socioeconomic background and cognitive functioning in preschool children. *Child Development, 41,* 471–480.

Murray, C. A. (1976). *The link between learning disabilities and juvenile delinquency: Current theory and knowledge.* Washington, DC: U.S. Government Printing Office.

Murray, D. M. (1984). *A writer teaches writing* (2nd ed.). Boston: Houghton-Mifflin.

Mwamwenda, T., Dash, U. N., & Das, J. P. (1984). A relationship between simultaneous-successive synthesis and concrete operational thought. *International Journal of Psychology, 19,* 547–563.

Myklebust, H. R. (1952). Aphasia in children. *Exceptional Children, 19,* 9–14.

Myklebust, H. R. (1954). *Auditory disorders in children.* New York: Grune & Stratton.

Myklebust, H. R. (1960). *The psychology of deafness: Sensory deprivation, learning, and adjustment.* New York: Grune & Stratton.

Myklebust, H. R. (1965). *Development and disorders of written language: Vol. 1. Picture story language test.* New York: Grune & Stratton.

Myklebust, H. R. (1968). Learning disabilities: Definition and overview. In H. R. Myklebust (Ed.), *Progress in learning disabilities* (Vol. 1). New York: Grune & Stratton.

Myklebust, H. R. (1973). *Development and disorders of written language: Vol. 2. Studies of normal and exceptional children.* New York: Grune & Stratton.

Myklebust, H. R., & Boshes, B. (1969). *Minimal brain damage in children.* Washington, DC: Neurological and Sensory Disease Control Program, Department of Health, Education and Welfare.

Nabuzoka, D., & Smith, P. K. (1995). Identification of expressions of emotions by children with and without learning disabilities. *Learning Disabilities Research & Practice, 10,* 91–101.

Nagle, R. J., & Thwaite, B. C. (1979). Modelling effects on impulsivity with learning disabled children. *Journal of Learning Disabilities, 12,* 331–336.

A nation at risk: The imperative for educational reform. A report to the Nation and the Secretary of Education. (1983). Washington, DC: U.S. Department of Education, The National Commission on Excellence in Education.

National Advisory Committee on Handicapped Children. (1970). *Better education for handicapped children: Second annual report.* Washington, D.C.: U.S. Department of Health, Education, and Welfare.

National Assessment of Educational Progress. (1985). *The reading report card: Progress toward excellence in our schools.* Princeton, NJ: Educational Testing Service.

National Assessment of Educational Progress. (1994). Trends in Academic Progress. Washington DC: National Center for Educational Statistics.

National Center for Educational Statistics. (1992). *NELS: 88: A profile of parents of eighth graders.* Washington, DC: U.S. Government Printing Office.

National Coalition of Advocates for Students. (1985). *Barriers to excellence: Our children at risk.* Washington, DC: U.S. Department of Education.

Natriello, G., Pallas, A. M., & McDill, E. L. (1990). *Schooling disadvantaged children: Racing against catastrophe.* New York: Teachers College Press.

Nazarro, J. N. (Ed.). (1981). *Culturally diverse exceptional children.* Reston, VA: Council for Exceptional Children.

Neisser, U., Boodoo, G., Bouchard, T. J., Boykin, A. W., Brody, N., Ceci, S. J., Halpern, D. F., Loehlin, J. C., Perloff, R., Sternberg, R. J., & Urbina, S. (1996). Intelligence: Knowns and unknowns. *American Psychologist, 51,* 77–101.

Nelson, H. E., & Warrington, E. K. (1976). Developmental spelling retardation. In R. M. Knights & D. J. Bakker (Eds.), *The neuropsychology of learning disorders: Theoretical approaches.* Baltimore: University Park Press.

Nelson, K. (1973). Structure and strategy in learning to talk. *Monographs of the Society for Research in Child Development, 38* (1–2, Serial No. 149).

Newcombe, F., & Ratcliff, G. (1973). Handedness, speech lateralization and ability. *Neuropsychologia, 11,* 399–407.

Newcomer, P. L., Barenbaum, E. M., & Nodine, B. F. (1988). Comparison of the story production of LD, normal-achieving, and low-achieving children under two modes of production. *Learning Disability Quarterly, 11,* 82–96.

Newland, T. E. (1932). An analytical study of the development of illegibilities in handwriting from the lower grades to adulthood. *Journal of Educational Research, 26,* 249–258.

Newman, L. S. (1990). Intentional and unintentional memory in young children: Remembering vs. playing. *Journal of Experimental Child Psychology, 50,* 243–258.

Nichols, P., & Chen, T. (1981). *Minimal brain dysfunction: A prospective study.* Hillsdale, NJ: Lawrence Erlbaum.

Nichols, R. G., & Stevens, L. A. (1957). *Are you listening?* New York: McGraw-Hill.

Nicolson, R. (1981). The relationship between memory span and processing speed. In M. P. Friedman, J. P. Das, & N. O'Connor (Eds.), *Intelligence and learning.* New York: Plenum Press.

Niedelman, M. (1991). Problem solving and transfer. *Journal of Learning Disabilities, 24,* 322–329.

Nober, L. W., & Nober, E. H. (1975). Auditory discrimination of learning disabled children in quiet and classroom noise. *Journal of Learning Disabilities, 8,* 656–659.

Nodine, B. F., Barenbaum, E., & Newcomer, P. (1985). Story composition by learning disabled, reading disabled, and normal children. *Learning Disability Quarterly, 8,* 167–179.

Noel, M. M. (1980). Referential communication abilities of learning disabled children. *Learning Disability Quarterly, 3*(3), 70–75.

Nolen, P., McCutchen, D., & Berninger, V. (1990). Ensuring tomorrow's literacy: A shared responsibility. *Journal of Teacher Education, 41,* 63–72.

Norman, C. A., Jr., & Zigmond, N. (1980). Characteristics of children labeled and served as learning disabled in school systems affiliated with child service demonstration centers. *Journal of Learning Disabilities, 13,* 542–547.

Norman, D. A. (1969). *Memory and attention.* New York: Wiley.

Novitski, E. (1977). *Human genetics.* New York: Macmillan.

O'Connor, P. D., Stuck, G. B., & Wyne, M. D. (1979). Effects of a short-term interaction resource room program on task orientation and achievement. *Journal of Special Education, 13,* 375–385.

O'Connor, S. C., & Spreen, O. (1988). The relationship between parents' socioeconomic status and education level, and adult occupational and educational achievement of children with learning disabilities. *Journal of Learning Disabilities, 21,* 148–153.

O'Leary, D. S., & Boll, T. J. (1984). Neuropsychological correlates of early generalized brain dysfunction in children. In C. R. Almli & S. Finger (Eds.), *Early brain damage: Vol. 1. Research orientations and clinical observations.* New York: Academic Press.

O'Leary, K. D., Rosenbaum, A., & Hughes, P. C. (1978). Fluorescent lighting: A purported source of hyperactive behavior. *Journal of Abnormal Child Psychology, 6,* 285–289.

O'Malley, J. E., & Eisenberg, L. (1973). The hyperkinetic syndrome. *Seminars in Psychiatry, 5,* 95–103.

O'Neill, G., & Stanley, G. (1976). Visual processing of straight lines in dyslexic and normal children. *British Journal of Educational Psychology, 46,* 323–327.

O'Shea, L. J., Sindelar, P. T., & O'Shea, D. J. (1987). The effects of repeated readings and attentional cues on the reading fluency and comprehension of learning disabled readers. *Learning Disabilities Research, 2,* 103–109.

O'Shea, L. J., & Valcante, G. (1986). A comparison over time of relative discrepancy scores of low achievers. *Exceptional Children, 53,* 253–259.

Oakland, T. (1980). An evaluation of the ABIC, pluralistic norms, and estimated learning potential. *Journal of School Psychology, 18,* 3–11.

Oakland, T., & Laosa, L. M. (1977). Professional, legislative, and judicial influences on psychoeducational assessment practices in schools. In T. Oakland (Ed.), *Psychological and educational assessment of minority children.* New York: Brunner/ Mazel.

Obrzut, J. E. (1991). Hemispheric activation and arousal asymmetry in learning-disabled children. In J. E. Obrzut & G. W. Hynd (Eds.), *Neuropsychological foundations of learning disabilities: A handbook of issues, methods, and practice.* San Diego: Academic Press.

Obrzut, J. E., Hynd, G. W., & Boliek, C. A. (1986). Lateral asymmetries in learning disabled children: A review. In S. J. Ceci (Ed.), *Handbook of cognitive, social, and neuropsychological aspects of learning disabilities* (Vol. 1). Hillsdale, NJ: Lawrence Erlbaum.

Odom, R. D., & Corbin, D. W. (1973). Perceptual salience and children's multidimensional problem solving. *Child Development, 44,* 425–532.

Odom, S. L., DeKlyen, M., & Jenkins, J. R. (1984). Integrating handicapped and nonhandicapped preschoolers: Developmental impact on nonhandicapped children. *Exceptional Children, 51,* 41–48.

Odom, S. L., McConnell, S. R., & McEvoy, M. A. (1992). *Social competence of young children with disabilities: Issues and strategies for intervention.* Baltimore: Paul H. Brookes.

Oettinger, L., Majovski, L. V., Limbeck, G. A., & Gauch, R. (1974). Bone age in children with minimal brain dysfunction. *Perceptual and Motor Skills, 39,* 1127–1131.

Office of Civil Rights. (1992). *1992 Office of Civil Rights elementary and secondary school survey.* Washington, DC: U.S. Office of Education.

Okolo, C. M., & Sitlington, P. (1986). The role of special education in LD adolescents' transition from school to work. *Learning Disability Quarterly, 9,* 141–155.

Oliva, A. H., & LaGreca, A. M. (1988). Children with learning disabilities: Social goals and strategies. *Journal of Learning Disabilities, 21,* 301–306.

Oliver, J. M., Cole, N. H., & Hollingsworth, H. (1991). Learning disabilities as functions of familial learning problems and developmental problems. *Exceptional Children, 57,* 427–440.

Olsen, J. L., Wong, B. Y. L., & Marx, R. W. (1983). Linguistic and metacognitive aspects of normally achieving and learning disabled children's communication process. *Learning Disability Quarterly, 6,* 289–304.

Olson, R., Foltz, G., & Wise, B. (1986). Reading instruction and remediation with the aid of computer speech. *Behavior Research Methods, Instruments, and Computers, 18,* 93–99.

Olson, R., Wise, B., Conners, F., Rack, J., & Fulker, D. (1989). Specific deficits in component reading and language skills: Genetic and environmental influences. *Journal of Learning Disabilities, 22,* 339–348.

Olson, R. K., Davidson, B. J., Kliegl, R., & Davis, S. E. (1984). Development of phonetic memory in disabled and normal readers. *Journal of Experimental Child Psychology, 37,* 187–206.

Olson, R. K., Kliegl, R., & Davidson, B. J. (1983). Dyslexic and normal readers' eye movements. *Journal of Experimental Psychology: Human Perception and Performance, 9,* 816–825.

Omenn, G. S., & Weber, B. A. (1978). Dyslexia: Search for phenotypic and genetic heterogeneity. *American Journal of Medical Genetics, 1,* 333–342.

Orbach, I. (1977). Impulsive cognitive style: Three modification techniques. *Psychology in the Schools, 14,* 353–359.

Orton, S. T. (1925). "Word-blindness" in school children. *Archives of Neurology and Psychiatry, 14,* 582–615.

Orton, S. T. (1928). Specific reading disability—strephosymbolia. *The Journal of the American Medical Association, 90,* 1095–1099.

Orton, S. T. (1937). *Reading, writing and speech problems in children.* New York: W. W. Norton.

Orton, S. T. (1966). The Orton Gillingham Approach. In J. Money & G. Shiffman (Eds.), *Disabled reader.* Baltimore: Johns Hopkins Press.

Osborn, A. (1963). *Applied imagination.* New York: Charles Scribner & Sons.

Osgood, C. E. (1957). A behavioristic analysis of perception and language as cognitive phenomena. In J. S. Bruner (Ed.), *Contemporary approaches to cognition.* Cambridge: Harvard University Press.

Osgood, C. E., & Miron, M. S. (1963). *Approaches to the study of aphasia.* Urbana, IL: University of Illinois Press.

Osofsky, J. D. (1995). The effects of exposure to violence on young children. *American Psychologist, 50,* 782–788.

Ott, J. N. (1976). Influence of fluorescent lights on hyperactivity and learning disabilities. *Journal of Learning Disabilities, 9,* 417–422.

Otto, W., McMenemy, R. A., & Smith, R. (1973). *Corrective and remedial teaching: Principles and practices.* Boston: Houghton-Mifflin.

Owen, F. W., Adams, P. A., Forrest, T., Stolz, L. M., & Fisher, S. (1971). Learning disorders in children: Sibling studies. *Monographs of the Society for Research in Child Development, 36*(4, Serial No. 144).

Owings, R. A., Petersen, G. A., Bransford, J. D., Morris, C. D., & Stein, B. S. (1980). Spontaneous monitoring and regulation of learning: A comparison of successful and less successful fifth graders. *Journal of Educational Psychology, 72,* 250–256.

Ozols, E. J., & Rourke, B. P. (1985). Dimensions of social sensitivity in two types of learning-disabled children. In B. P. Rourke (Ed.), *Neuropsychology of learning disabilities.* New York: Guilford Press.

Paget, K. D., Nagle, R. J., & Martin, R. P. (1984). Interrelationships between temperament characteristics and first-grade teacher-student interactions. *Journal of Abnormal Child Psychology, 12,* 547–560.

Painter, M. (1976). Fluorescent lights and hyperactivity in children: An experiment. *Academic Therapy, 12,* 181–184.

Paivio, A. (1969). Mental imagery in associative learning and memory. *Psychological Review, 76,* 241–263.

Palincsar, A. S. (1986). Metacognitive strategy instruction. *Exceptional Children, 53,* 118–124.

Palincsar, A. S., & Brown, A. L. (1984). Reciprocal teaching of comprehension-fostering and comprehension-monitoring activities. *Cognition and Instruction, 1,* 117–175.

Palincsar, A. S., & Klenk, L. (1992). Fostering literacy learning in supportive contexts. *Journal of Learning Disabilities, 25,* 211–225, 229.

Palincsar, A. S., & Perry, N. E. (1995). Developmental, cognitive, and sociocultural perspectives on assessing and instructing reading. *School Psychology Review, 24,* 331–344.

Pallak, M., & Kaplinski, E. (1985, September). TV violence. *Monitor,* p. 38.

Palmer, C. F., & Barba, C. V. (1981). Mental development after dietary intervention: A study of Philippine children. Journal of Cross-Cultural Psychology, *12,* 480–488.

Palmer, D. J., Drummond, F., Tollison, P., & Zinkgraff, S. (1982). An attributional investigation of performance outcomes for learning-disabled and normal-achieving pupils. *Journal of Special Education, 16,* 207–219.

Panda, K. C., & Bartel, N. R. (1972). Teacher perception of exceptional children. *Journal of Special Education, 6,* 261–266.

Pany, D., & McCoy, K. M. (1988). Effects of corrective feedback on word accuracy and reading comprehension of readers with learning disabilities. *Journal of Learning Disabilities, 21,* 546–550.

Paris, S. G., & Haywood, H. C. (1973). Mental retardation as a learning disorder. *Pediatric Clinics of North America, 20*(3), 641–651.

Paris, S. G., & Landauer, B. K. (1976). The role of inference in children's comprehension and memory for sentences. *Cognitive Psychology, 8,* 217–227.

Paris, S. G., & Lindauer, B. K. (1977). Constructive aspects of children's comprehension and memory. In R. V. Kail & J. W. Hagen (Eds.), *Perspectives on the development of memory and cognition.* Hillsdale, NJ: Lawrence Erlbaum.

Paris, S. G., & Oka, E. R. (1986). Self-regulated learning among exceptional children. *Exceptional Children, 53,* 103–108.

Parish, R. S., Ohlsen, R. L., & Parish, J. G. (1978). A look at mainstreaming in light of children's attitudes toward the handicapped. *Perceptual and Motor Skills, 46,* 1019–1021.

Parish, T. S., Eads, G. M., Reece, N. H., & Piscitello, M. A. (1977). Assessment and attempted modification of future teachers' attitudes toward handicapped children. *Perceptual and Motor Skills, 46,* 1019–1021.

Parker, I., Gottlieb, B. W., Davis, S., & Kunzweiller, C. (1989). Teacher behavior toward low achievers, average achievers, and mainstreamed minority group learning disabled students. *Learning Disabilities Research, 4,* 101–106.

Parker, T. B., Freston, C. W., & Drew, C. J. (1975). Comparison of verbal performance of normal and learning disabled children as a function of input organization. *Journal of Learning Disabilities, 8,* 386–393.

Parmar, R. S., & Cawley, J. F. (1993). Analysis of science textbook recommendations provided for students with disabilities. *Exceptional Children, 59,* 518–531.

Parmar, R. S., Frazita, R., & Cawley, J. F. (1996). Mathematics assessment for students with mild disabilities: An exploration of content validity. *Learning Disability Quarterly, 19,* 127–136.

Pasamanick, B., & Knobloch, H. (1960). Brain damage and reproductive causality. *American Journal of Orthopsychiatry, 30,* 298–305.

Pasamanick, B., & Knobloch, H. (1961). Epidemiological studies on the complications of pregnancy and the birth process. In J. Caplan (Ed.), *Prevention of mental disorder in children.* New York: Basic Books.

Pasamanick, B., & Knobloch, H. (1973). The epidemiology of reproductive causality. In S. G. Sapir & A. C. Nitzburg (Eds.), *Children with learning problems: Reading in a developmental-interaction approach.* New York: Brunner/Mazel.

Pascarella, E. T., & Pflaum, S. W. (1981). The interaction of children's attribution and level of control over error correction in reading instruction. *Journal of Educational Psychology, 73,* 533–540.

Patrick, J. L., & Reschly, D. J. (1982). Relationship of state educational criteria and demographic variables to school system prevalence of mental retardation. *American Journal of Mental Deficiency, 86,* 351–360.

Patterson, C., & Mischel, W. (1976). Effects of temptation-inhibiting and task facilitating plans on self-control. *Journal of Personality and Social Psychology, 33,* 209–217.

Patterson, C. J., Kupersmidt, J. B., & Vaden, N. A. (1990). Income level, gender, ethnicity and household composition as predictors of children's school-based competence. *Child Development, 61,* 485–494.

Patterson, J. H., & Smith, M. S. (1986). The role of computers in higher-order thinking. In J. A. Culbertson & L. L. Cunningham (Eds.), *Microcomputers and education: Eighty-fifth yearbook of the National Society for the Study of Education.* Chicago: University of Chicago Press.

Patton, J. E., Routh, D. K., & Offenbach, S. I. (1981). Televised classroom events as distractors for reading-disabled children. *Journal of Abnormal Child Psychology, 9,* 355–370.

Pavlidis, G. Th. (1981). Sequencing, eye movements and the early objective diagnosis of dyslexia. In G. Th. Pavlidis & T. R. Miles (Eds.), *Dyslexia research and its applications to education.* Chichester: John Wiley.

Pavlidis, G. Th. (1986). The role of eye movements in the diagnosis of dyslexia. In G. Th. Pavlidis & D. F. Fisher (Eds.), *Dyslexia: Its neuropsychology and treatment.* New York: John Wiley & Sons.

Pearl, R. (1982). LD children's attributions for success and failure: A replication with a labeled LD sample. *Learning Disability Quarterly, 5,* 173–176.

Pearl, R., & Bryan, T. (1982). Mothers' attributions for their learning disabled child's successes and failures. *Learning Disability Quarterly, 5*(1), 53–57.

Pearl, R., Bryan, T., & Donahue, M. (1980). Learning disabled children's attributions for success and failure. *Learning Disability Quarterly, 3,* 3–9.

Pearl, R., Bryan, T., Fallon, P., & Herzog, A. (1991). Learning disabled students' detection of deception. *Learning Disabilities Research & Practice, 6,* 12–16.

Pearl, R., Bryan, T., & Herzog, A. (1983). Learning disabled and nondisabled children's strategy analysis under high and low success conditions. *Learning Disability Quarterly, 6,* 67–74.

Pearl, R., & Cosden, M. (1982). Sizing up a situation: LD children's understanding of social interactions. *Learning Disability Quarterly, 5,* 371–373.

Pearson, P. D., & Johnson, D. D. (1978). *Teaching reading comprehension.* New York: Holt, Rinehart & Winston.

Peery, J. C. (1980). Neonate-adult head movement: No & yes revisited. *Developmental Psychology, 16,* 245–250.

Pelham, W. E. (1979). Selective attention deficits in poor readers? Dichotic listening, speeded classification, and auditory and visual central and incidental learning tasks. *Child Development, 50,* 1050–1061.

Pelham, W. E. (1993). Pharmacotherapy for children with attention-deficit hyperactivity disorder. *School Psychology Review, 22,* 199–227.

Pelham, W. E., & Bender, M. E. (1982). Peer relationships in hyperactive children: Description and treatment. In K. D. Gadow & I. Bialer (Eds.), *Advances in learning and behavioral disabilities* (Vol. 1). Greenwich, CT: JAI Press.

Pelham, W. E., Bender, M. E., Caddell, J., Booth, S., & Moorer, S. H. (1985). Methylphenidate and children with attention deficit disorder: Dose effects on classroom academic and social behavior. *Archives of General Psychiatry, 42,* 948–952.

Pelham, W. E., Carlson, C., Sams, S. E., Vallano, G., Dixon, J., & Hoza, B. (1993). Separate and combined effects of methylphenidate and behavior modification on boys with attention deficit-hyperactivity disorder in the classroom. *Journal of Consulting and Clinical Psychology, 61,* 506–515.

Penfield, W., & Roberts, L. (1959). *Speech and brain mechanisms.* Princeton: Princeton University Press.

Pennington, B. F. (1986). Issues in the diagnosis and phenotype analysis of dyslexia: Implications for family studies. In S. D. Smith (Ed.), *Genetics and learning disabilities.* San Diego: College Hill Press.

Pennington, B. F. (1995). Genetics of learning disabilities. *Journal of Child Neurology, 10, Supplement #1,* s69–s77.

Pennington, B. F., & Gilger, J. W. (1996). How is dyslexia transmitted? In C. H. Chase, G. D. Rosen, and G. F. Sherman (Eds.), *Developmental dyslexia: Neural, cognitive, and genetic mechanisms.* Baltimore, MD: York Press.

Pennington, B. F., Gilger, J. W., Pauls, D., Smith, S. A., Smith, S. D., & DeFries, J. C. (1991). Evidence for major gene transmission of developmental dyslexia. *Journal of the American Medical Association, 266,* 1527–1534.

Pennington, B. F., Van Orden, G. C., Smith, S. D., Green, P. A., & Haith, M. M. (1990). Phonological processing skills and deficits in adult dyslexics. *Child Development, 61,* 1753–1778.

Pennsylvania Association for Retarded Children v. Pennsylvania. 334 F. Supp. 1257 (E.D. Pa. 1971).

Perfetti, C. A. (1982). Discourse context, word identification, and reading ability. In J. F. LeNy & W. Kintsch (Eds.), *Language and comprehension.* Amsterdam: North-Holland.

Perfetti, C. A. (1984). Some reflections on learning and not learning to read. *Remedial and Special Education, 5*(3), 34–38.

Perfetti, C. A. (1985). *Reading ability.* New York: Oxford University Press.

Perfetti, C. A., Beck, I., Bell, L. C., & Hughes C. (1987). Phonemic knowledge and learning to read are reciprocal: A longitudinal study of first grade children. *Merrill-Palmer Quarterly, 33,* 283–319.

Perfetti, C. A., & Lesgold, A. M. (1977). Coding and comprehension in skilled reading and implications for reading instruction. In L. B. Resnick & P. Weaver (Eds.), *Theory and practice in early reading.* Hillsdale, NJ: Lawrence Erlbaum.

Perlmutter, B. F. (1986). Personality variables and peer relations of children and adolescents with learning disabilities. In S. J. Ceci (Ed.), *Handbook of cognitive, social, and neuropsychological aspects of learning disabilities.* (Vol. 1). Hillsdale, N.J.: Lawrence Erlbaum.

Perlmutter, B. F., & Bryan, J. H. (1984). First impressions, ingratiation, and the learning disabled child. *Journal of Learning Disabilities, 17,* 157–161.

Perlmutter, B. F., Crocker, J., Cordray, D., & Garstecki, D. (1983). Sociometric status and related personality characteristics of mainstreamed learning disabled adolescents. *Learning Disability Quarterly, 6,* 20–30.

Perlmutter, M., & Myers, N. A. (1979). Development of recall in 2- to 4-year-old children. *Developmental Psychology, 15,* 73–83.

Persell, C. H. (1979). *Education and inequality.* New York: Free Press.

Peterson, J., Heistad, D., Peterson, D., & Reynolds, M. (1985). Montevideo individualized prescriptive instructional management system. *Exceptional Children, 52,* 239–243.

Peterson, S. E., DeGracie, J. S., & Ayabe, C. R. (1987). A longitudinal study of the effects of retention/promotion on academic achievement. *American Educational Research Journal, 24,* 107–118.

Peterson, S. K., Mercer, C. D., & O'Shea, L. (1988). Teaching learning disabled students place value using the concrete to abstract sequence. *Learning Disabilities Research, 4,* 52–56.

Pettit, J. M., & Helms, S. B. (1979). Hemispheric language dominance of language-disordered, articulation-disordered, and normal children. *Journal of Learning Disabilities, 12,* 71–76.

Phelps, L. (1995). Psychoeducational outcomes of fetal alcohol syndrome. *School Psychology Review, 24,* 200–212.

Phelps, L., & Cox, D. (1993). Children with perinatal cocaine exposure: Resilient or handicapped? *School Psychology Review, 22,* 710–724.

Piaget, J. (1948). *The moral judgment of the child.* Glencoe, IL: Free Press.

Piaget, J. (1962). *The language and thought of the child.* New York: World Publishing.

Piaget, J. (1976). Piaget's theory. In B. Inhelder, H. H. Chipman, & C. Zwingmann (Eds.), *Piaget and his school: A reader in developmental psychology.* New York: Springer-Verlag.

Piaget, J., & Inhelder, B. (1969). *The psychology of the child.* New York: Basic Books.

Pick, A. D., Frankel, D. G., & Hess, V. L. (1975). Childrens' attention: The development of selectivity. *Review of Child Development Research, 5,* 325–383.

Pick, H. L., Jr., & Pick, A. D. (1970). Sensory and perceptual development. In P. H. Mussen (Ed.), *Carmichael's manual of child psychology* (3rd ed.). New York: John Wiley & Sons.

Pickering, E., Pickering, A., & Buchanan, M. L. (1987). LD and nonhandicapped boys' comprehension of cartoon humor. *Learning Disability Quarterly, 10,* 45–51.

Pihl, R. O., & McLarnon, L. D. (1984). Learning disabled children as adolescents. *Journal of Learning Disabilities, 17,* 96–100.

Pihl, R. O., & Niaura, R. (1982). Learning disability: An inability to sustain attention. *Journal of Clinical Psychology, 38,* 632–634.

Plomin, R. (1988). The nature and nurture of cognitive abilities. In R. J. Sternberg (Ed.), *Advances in the psychology of human intelligence* (Vol. 4). Hillsdale, NJ: Lawrence Erlbaum.

Plomin, R., DeFries, J. C., McClearn, G. E., & Rutter, M. (1997). *Behavioral genetics* (3rd ed.). New York: W. H. Freeman & Co.

Pollitt, E., Gorman, K. S., Engle, P. L., Martorell, R., & Rivera, J. (1993). Early supplementary feeding and cognition: Effects over two decades. *Monographs of the Society for Research in Child Development, 58* (serial No. 235).

Polloway, E. A., Epstein, M. H., Bursuck, W. D., Roderique, T. W., McConeghy, J. L., & Jayanthi, M. (1994). Classroom grading: A national survey of policies. *Remedial and Special Education, 15,* 162–170.

Polloway, E. A., Foley, R. M., & Epstein, M. H. (1992). A comparison of the homework problems of students with learning disabilities and nonhandicapped students. *Learning Disabilities Research & Practice, 7,* 203–209.

Pomplun, M. (1996). Cooperative groups: Alternative assessment for students with disabilities? *The Journal of Special Education, 30,* 1–17.

Poplin, M. S. (1981). The severely learning disabled: Neglected or forgotten? *Learning Disability Quarterly, 4*(4), 330–335.

Poplin, M. S., Gray, R., Larsen, S., Banikowksi, A., & Mehring, T. (1980). A comparison of components of written expression abilities in learning disabled and non-learning disabled students at three-grade levels. *Learning Disability Quarterly, 3*(4), 46–53.

Porges, S. W., Walter, G. F., Korb, R. J., & Sprague, R. L. (1975). The influences of methylphenidate on heart rate and behavioral measures of attention in hyperactive children. *Child Development, 46,* 727–733.

Porrino, L. J., Rapoport, J. L., Behar, D., Sceery, W., Ismond, D. R., & Bunney, W. E. (1983). A naturalistic assessment of the motor activity of hyperactive boys. I. Comparison with normal controls. *Archives of General Psychiatry, 40,* 681 687.

Porter, A. (1989). A curriculum out of balance: The case of elementary school mathematics. *Educational Researcher, 18* (5), 9–15.

Porter, J. E., & Rourke, B. P. (1985). Socioemotional functioning of learning-disabled children: A subtypal analysis of personality patterns. In B. P. Rourke (Ed.), *Neuropsychology of learning disabilities.* New York: Guilford Press.

Poteet, J. A. (1980). Informal assessment of written expression. *Learning Disability Quarterly, 3*(4), 88–98.

Potts, M. (1968). The relative achievement of first graders under three different reading programs. *The Journal of Educational Research, 61,* 447–450.

Powers, S. I., Hauser, S. T., & Kilner, L. A. (1989). Adolescent mental health. *American Psychologist, 44,* 200–208.

Prasse, D. P., & Reschly, D. J. (1986). Larry P.: A case of segregation, esting, or program efficacy? *Exceptional Children, 52,* 333–346.

Pratt, E. (1956). Experimental evaluation of a program for the improvement of listening. *Elementary School Journal, 56,* 315–320.

Pressley, M. (1977). Imagery and children's learning: Putting the picture in developmental perspective. *Review of Educational Research, 47,* 585–622.

Pressley, M., & associates. (1990). *Cognitive strategy instruction that really improves children's academic performance.* Cambridge, MA: Brookline Books.

Pressley, M., Hogen, K., Wharton-McDonald, R., Mistretta, J., & Ettenberger, S. (1996). The challenges of instructional scaffolding: The challenges of instruction that supports student thinking. *Learning Disabilities Research & Practice, 11,* 138–146.

Pressley, M., Johnson, C. J., & Symons, S. (1987). Elaborating to learn and learning to elaborate. *Journal of Learning Disabilities, 20,* 76–91.

Pressley, M., & Miller, G. E. (1987). Effects of illustrations on children's listening comprehension and oral prose memory. In D. M. Willows & A. H. Houghton (Eds.). *The psychology of illustration:* Vol. 1. *Basic research.* New York: Springer-Verlag.

Pressley, M., & Rankin, J. (1994). More about whole language methods of reading instruction for students at risk for early reading failure. *Learning Disabilities Research & Practice, 9,* 157–168.

Pribram, K., & McGuinness, D. (1987). Commentary: Brain function and learning disabilities. In S. J. Ceci (Ed.), *Handbook of cognitive, social, and neuropsychological aspects of learning disabilities* (Vol. 2). Hillsdale, NJ: Lawrence Erlbaum.

Prichep, L., John, E. R., Ahn, H., & Kaye, H. (1983). Neurometrics: Quantitative evaluation of brain dysfunction in children. In M. Rutter (Ed.), *Developmental neuropsychiatry.* New York: Guilford Press.

Prillaman, D. (1981). Acceptance of learning disabled students in the mainstream environment: A failure to replicate. *Journal of Learning Disabilities, 14,* 344–346.

Progress toward a free appropriate public education. A report to Congress on the implementation of public law 94–142: The Education for All Handicapped Children Act. (1979, January). Washington, DC: United States Department of Health, Education, and Welfare, Office of Education.

Provence, S., & Lipton, R. C. (1962). *Infants in institutions.* New York: International Universities Press.

Pugach, M. (1987). The national education reports and special education: Implications for teacher preparation. *Exceptional Children, 53,* 308–314.

Pugach, M., & Sapon-Shevin, M. (1987). New agendas for special education policy: What the national reports haven't said. *Exceptional Children, 53,* 295–299.

Pugach, M. C. (1982). Regular classroom teacher involvement in the development and utilization of IEP's. *Exceptional Children, 48,* 371–374.

Pullis, M. (1985). LD students' temperament characteristics and their impact on decisions by resource and mainstream teachers. *Learning Disability Quarterly, 8,* 109–122.

Pullis, M., & Cadwell, J. (1982). The influence of children's temperament characteristics on teachers' decision strategies. *American Educational Research Journal, 19,* 165–181.

Punnett, A. F., & Steinhauer, G. D. (1984). Relationship between reinforcement and eye movements during ocular motor training with learning disabled children. *Journal of Learning Disabilities, 17,* 16–19.

Purkey, S. C., & Smith, M. S. (1983). Effective schools: A review. *The Elementary School Journal, 83,* 427–452.

Putnam, L. M., Deshler, D. D., & Schumaker, J. B. (1992). The investigation of setting demands: A missing link in learning strategies instruction. In L. J. Meltzer (Ed.), *Strategy assessment and instruction for students with learning disabilities: From theory to practice.* Austin, TX: Pro-Ed.

Pysh, J. J., & Weiss, G. M. (1979). Exercise during development induces an increase in Purkinje cell dendritic tree size. *Science, 206,* 230–232.

Quay, H. C. (1973). Special education: Assumptions, techniques, and evaluative criteria. *Exceptional Children, 40,* 165–170.

Quinn, J. A., & Wilson, B. J. (1977). Programming effects on learning disabled children: Performance and affect. *Psychology in the Schools, 14,* 196–199.

Rack, J. P., & Olson, R. K. (1993). Phonological deficits, IQ, and individual differences in reading disability: Genetic and environmental influences. *Developmental Review, 13,* 269–278.

Rademacher, J. A., Schumaker, J. B., & Deshler, D. D. (1996). Development and validation of a classroom assignment routine for inclusive settings. *Learning Disability Quarterly, 19,* 163–177.

Radosh, A., & Gittleman, R. (1981). The effect of appealing distractors on the performance of hyperactive children. *Journal of Abnormal Child Psychology, 9,* 179–189.

Rafoth, M. A., Dawson, P., & Carey, K. (1988, December). Supporting paper on retention. *Communiqué,* pp. 17–19.

Ramirez, M., & Castaneda, A. (1974). *Cultural democracy, cognitive development, and education.* New York: Academic Press.

Rapoport, J. L., Berg, C. J., Ismond, D. R., Zahn, T. P., & Neims, A. (1984). Behavioral effects of caffeine in children. *Archives of General Psychiatry, 41,* 1073–1079.

Rapoport, J. L., Buchsbaum, M. S., Weingartner, H., Zahn, T. P., Ludlow, C., & Mikkelson, E. J. (1980). Dextroamphetamine. Its cognitive and behavioral effects in normal and hyperactive boys and normal men. *Archives of General Psychiatry, 37,* 933–943.

Rappaport, M. (1981). Prevention of problems in children: The executive function of the family. *The Forum, 7*(2), 11, 22.

Rapport, M. D., Denney, C., DuPaul, G. J., & Gardner, M. J. (1994). Attention deficit disorder and methylphenidate: Normalization rates, clinical effectiveness, and response prediction in 76 children. *Journal of the American Academy of Child and Adolescent Psychiatry, 33,* 882–893.

Rapport, M. D., DuPaul, G. J., Stoner, G., & Jones, J. T. (1986). Comparing classroom and clinic measures of attention deficit disorder: Differential, idiosyncratic, and dose-response effects of methylphenidate. *Journal of Consulting and Clinical Psychology, 54,* 334–341.

Rapport, M. D., Stoner, G., DuPaul, G. J., Birmingham, B. K., & Tucker, S. (1985). Methylphenidate in hyperactive children: Differential effects of dose on academic, learning, and social behavior. *Journal of Abnormal Child Psychology, 13,* 227–244.

Rashotte, C. A., & Torgesen, J. K. (1985). Repeated reading and reading fluency in learning disabled children. *Reading Research Quarterly, 20,* 180–188.

Raskind, M. H., & Higgins, E. (1995). Effects of speech synthesis on the proofreading efficiency of postsecondary students with learning disabilities. *Learning Disability Quarterly, 18,* 141–158.

Ratcliff, G., Dila, C., Taylor, L., & Milner, B. (1980). The morphological asymmetry of the hemispheres and cerebral dominance for speech: A possible relationship. *Brain and Language, 11,* 87–98.

Raudenbush, S. W. (1984). Magnitude of teacher expectancy effects on pupil IQ as a function of the credibility of expectancy induction: A synthesis of findings from 18 experiments. *Journal of Educational Psychology, 76,* 85–97.

Ravitch, D, & Finn, C. E. (1987). *What do our 17-year olds know?* New York: Harper & Row.

Raviv, D., & Stone, C. A. (1991). Individual differences in the self-image of adolescents with learning disabilities: The roles of severity, time of diagnosis, and parental perceptions. *Journal of Learning Disabilities, 24,* 602–611, 629.

Rawson, M. B. (1968). *Developmental language disability: Adult accomplishments of dyslexic boys.* Baltimore: Johns Hopkins Press.

Rayner, K. (1986). Eye movements and the perceptual span: Evidence for dyslexic typology. In G. Th. Pavlidis & D. F. Fisher (Eds.), *Dyslexia: Its neuropsychology and treatment.* New York: John Wiley.

Rayner, K. (1996). What we can learn about reading processes from eye movements. In C. H. Chase, G. D. Rosen, & G. F. Sherman, (Eds.), *Developmental dyslexia: Neural, cognitive, and genetic mechanisms.* Baltimore: York Press.

Rayner, K., & Pollatsek, A. (1987). Eye movements in reading: A tutorial review. In M. Coltheart (Ed.), *Attention and performance. XII: The psychology of reading.* London: Erlbaum Associates.

Raz, S., Lauterbach, M. D., Hopkins, T. L., Porter, C. L., Riggs, W. W., & Sander, C. J. (1995). Severity of perinatal cerebral injury and developmental outcome: A dose-response relationship. *Neuropsychology, 9,* 91–101.

Read, C. (1975). Lessons to be learned from the preschool orthographer. In E. H. Lenneberg & E. Lenneberg (Eds.), *Foundations of language development: A multidisciplinary approach.* New York: Academic Press.

Reetz, L. J., & Hoover, J. H. (1992). The acceptability and utility of five reading approaches as judged by middle school LD students. *Learning Disabilities Research & Practice, 7,* 11–15.

Reid, D. K. (1980). Learning from a Piagetian perspective: The exceptional child. In I. E. Sigel, R. M. Golinkoff, & D. Brodzinsky (Eds.), *Piagetian theory and research: New directives and applications.* Hillsdale, NJ: Lawrence Erlbaum.

Reid, D. K., & Hresko, W. P. (1980). A developmental study of the language and early reading in learning disabled and normally achieving children. *Learning Disability Quarterly, 3*(4), 54–61.

Reid, M. K., & Borkowski, J. G. (1984). Effects of methylphenidate (Ritalin) on information processing in hyperactive children. *Journal of Abnormal Child Psychology, 12,* 169–185.

Reid, M. K., & Borkowski, J. G. (1987). Causal attributions of hyperactive children: Implications for teaching strategies and self-control. *Journal of Educational Psychology, 79,* 296–307.

Reid, R. (1996). Research in self-monitoring with students with learning disabilities: The present, the prospects, the pitfalls. *Journal of Learning Disabilities, 29,* 317–331.

Reitan, R. M. (1974). Methodological problems in clinical neuropsychology. In R. M. Reitan & L. A. Davison (Eds.), *Clinical neuropsychology: Current status and applications.* Washington, DC: Winston.

Repp, A. C., Nieminen, G. S., Olinger, E., & Brusca, R. (1988). Direct observation: Factors affecting the accuracy of observers. *Exceptional Children, 55,* 29–36.

Reschly, D. (1978). *Comparisons of bias in assessment with conventional and pluralistic measures.* Paper presented at meetings of the Council for Exceptional Children.

Reschly, D., & Lamprecht, M. J. (1979). Expectancy effects of labels: Fact or artifact? *Exceptional Children, 46*(1), 55–58.

Reschly, D. J. (1980). School psychologists and assessment in the future. *Professional Psychology, 11,* 841–848.

Reschly, D. J. (1987). Learning characteristics of mildly handicapped students: Implications for classification, placement, and programming. In M. C. Wang, M. C. Reynolds, & H. J. Walberg (Eds.), *The handbook of special education: Research and practice* (Vol. 1). Oxford, England: Pergamon.

Reschly, D. J., Kicklighter, R., & McKee, P. (1988). Recent placement litigation Part II, minority EMR overrepresentation: Comparison of Larry P. (1979, 1984, 1986) with Marshall (1984, 1985) and S-1 (1986). *School Psychology Review, 17,* 22–38.

Rescorla, L. A. (1981). Category development in early language. *Journal of Child Language, 8,* 225–238.

Resnick, L. B. (1989). Developing mathematical knowledge. *American Psychologist, 44,* 162–169.

Reynolds, C. J., Hill, D. S., Swassing, R. H., & Ward, M. E. (1988). The effects of revision strategy instruction on the writing performance of students with learning disabilities. *Journal of Learning Disabilities, 21,* 540–545.

Reynolds, C. R., & Brown, R. T. (Eds.). (1984). *Perspectives on bias in mental testing.* New York: Plenum.

Reynolds, C. R., & Kaufman, A. S. (1990). Assessment of children's intelligence with the Weschler Intelligence Scale for Children—Revised. In C. R. Reynolds & R. W. Kamphaus (Eds.), *Handbook of psychological and educational assessment of children: Intelligence and achievement.* New York: Guilford Press.

Reynolds, M. C., & Balow, B. (1972). Categories and variables in special education. *Exceptional Children, 38,* 357–366.

Reynolds, M. C., & Heistad, D. (1997). 20/20 analysis: Estimating school effectiveness in serving students at the margins. *Exceptional Children, 63,* 439–449.

Reynolds, M. C., Wang, M. C., & Walberg, H. J. (1987). The necessary restructuring of special and regular education. *Exceptional Children, 53,* 391–398.

Reynolds, M. C., Zetlin, A. G., & Wang, M. C. (1993). 20/20 analysis. Taking a close look at the margins. *Exceptional Children, 59,* 294–300.

Ribner, S. (1978). The effects of special class placement on the self-concept of exceptional children. *Journal of Learning Disabilities, 11,* 319–323.

Ribovich, J. K., & Erikson, L. (1980). A study of lifelong reading with implications for instructional programs. *Journal of Reading, 24,* 20–26.

Riccio, C. A., & Hynd, G. W. (1995). Contributions of neuropsychology to our understanding of developmental reading problems. *School Psychology Review, 24,* 415–425.

Rich, H. L., & Ross, S. M. (1989). Students' time on learning tasks in special education. *Exceptional Children, 55,* 508–515.

Richards, G. P., Samuels, S. J., Turnure, J. E., & Ysseldyke, J. E. (1990). Sustained and selective attention in children with learning disabilities. *Journal of Learning Disabilities, 23,* 129–136.

Richardson, J. T. E., & Firlej, M. D. E. (1979). Laterality and reading attainment. *Cortex, 15,* 581–595.

Richardson, S. (1979, October). Address to Grand Rounds, Upstate Medical Center. Syracuse, NY.

Richey, D. D., & McKinney, J. D. (1978). Classroom behavioral styles of learning disabled boys. *Journal of Learning Disabilities, 11,* 297–302.

Richey, H. W., & Richey, M. N. (1978). Nonverbal behavior in the classroom. *Psychology in the Schools, 15,* 571–576.

Richey, L. S., & Ysseldyke, J. E. (1983). Teachers' expectations for the younger siblings of learning disabled students. *Journal of Learning Disabilities, 16,* 610–615.

Ridberg, E. H., Parke, R. D., & Hetherington, E. M. (1971). Modification of impulsive and reflective cognitive styles through observation of film-mediated models. *Developmental Psychology, 5,* 369–377.

Rieth, H. J., & Polsgrove, L. (1994). Curriculum and instructional issues in teaching secondary students with learning disabilities. *Learning Disabilities Research & Practice, 9,* 118–126.

Riley, N. J. (1989). Piagetian cognitive functioning in students with learning disabilities. *Journal of Learning Disabilities, 22,* 444–451.

Rimm, D. C., & Masters, J. C. (1974). *Behavior therapy: Techniques and empirical findings.* New York: Academic Press.

Ripich, D. N., & Griffith, P. L. (1988). Narrative abilities of children with learning disabilities and nondisabled children. Story structure, cohesion, and propositions. *Journal of Learning Disabilities, 21,* 165–173.

Rist, R. C. (1970). Student social class and teacher expectations: The self-fulfilling prophecy in ghetto education. *Harvard Educational Review, 40,* 411–451.

Ritter, D. R. (1978). Surviving in the regular classroom: A follow-up of mainstreamed children with learning disabilities. *Journal of School Psychology, 16,* 253–256.

Ritter, D. R. (1989). Social competence and problem behavior of adolescent girls with learning disabilities. *Journal of Learning Disabilities, 22,* 460–461.

Rivera, D., & Smith, D. (1988). Using a demonstration strategy to teach midschool students with learning disabilities how to compute long division. *Journal of Learning Disabilities, 21,* 77–81.

Robinson, D. L., Haier, R. J., Braden, W., & Krengel, M. (1984). Psychometric intelligence and visual evoked potentials: A replication. *Personality and Individual Differences, 5,* 487–489.

Robinson, F. P. (1961). Study skills for superior students in the secondary schools. *The Reading Teacher,* pp. 29–33.

Rockowitz, R. J., & Davidson, P. W. (1979). Discussing diagnostic findings with parents. *Journal of Learning Disabilities, 12,* 11–16.

Rodden-Nord, K., Shinn, M. R., & Good, R. H., III. (1992). Effects of classroom performance data on general education teachers' attitudes toward reintegrating students with learning disabilities. *School Psychology Review, 21,* 138–154.

Rodier, P. M. (1984). Exogenous sources of malformations in development: CNS malformations and developmental repair processes. In E. S. Gollin (Ed.), *Malformations of development.* New York: Academic Press.

Roessler, R. T., & Johnson, V. A. (1987). Developing job maintenance skills in learning disabled youth. *Journal of Learning Disabilities, 20,* 428–432.

Rogan, L. L., & Hartman, L. D. (1976). *A follow-up study of learning disabled children as adults* (Final report). Washington, DC: Bureau of Education for the Handicapped.

Rogan, L. L., & Hartman, L. D. (1990). Adult outcome of learning disabled students ten years after initial follow-up. *Learning Disabilities Focus, 5,* 91–102.

Rogers, H., & Saklofske, D. H. (1985). Self-concepts, locus of control and performance expectations of learning disabled children. *Journal of Learning Disabilities, 18,* 273–278.

Rohwer, W. D., Jr. (1971). Prime time for education: Early childhood or adolescence? *Harvard Educational Review, 41,* 316–341.

Rojewski, J. W. (1996). Educational and occupational aspirations of high school seniors with learning disabilities. *Exceptional Children, 62,* 463–476.

Rooney, K., Polloway, E. A., & Hallahan, D. P. (1985). The use of self-monitoring procedures with low IQ learning disabled students. *Journal of Learning Disabilities, 18,* 384–389.

Rooney, K. J., & Hallahan, D. P. (1988). The effects of self-monitoring on adult behavior and student independence. *Learning Disabilities Research, 3,* 88–93.

Rose, M. C., Cundick, B. P., & Higbee, K. L. (1983). Verbal rehearsal and visual imagery: Mnemonic aids for learning-disabled children. *Journal of Learning Disabilities, 16,* 352–354.

Rose, T. L. (1984). The effects of two prepractice procedures on oral reading. *Journal of Learning Disabilities, 17,* 544–548.

Rose, T. L. (1986). Effects of illustrations on reading comprehension of learning disabled students. *Journal of Learning Disabilities, 19,* 542–544.

Rose, T. L., & Furr, P. M. (1984). Negative effects of illustrations as word cues. *Journal of Learning Disabilities, 17,* 334–337.

Rose, T. L., McEntire, E., & Dowdy, C. (1982). Effects of two error-correction procedures on oral reading. *Learning Disability Quarterly, 5,* 100–105.

Rose, T. L., & Sherry, L. (1984). Relative effects of two previewing procedures on LD adolescents' oral reading performance. *Learning Disability Quarterly, 7,* 39–44.

Rosegrant, T. J. (1986). Using the microcomputer as a scaffold for assisting beginning readers and writers. In J. L. Hoot (Ed.), *Computers in early childhood education: Issues and practices.* Englewood Cliffs, NJ: Prentice-Hall.

Rosen, L. A., Booth, S. R., Bender, M. E., McGrath, M. L., Sorrell, S., & Drabman, R. S. (1988). Effects of sugar (sucrose) on children's behavior. *Journal of Consulting and Clinical Psychology, 56,* 583–589.

Rosenberg, J. B., & Weller, G. M. (1973). Minor physical anomalies and academic performance in young school children. *Developmental Medicine and Child Neurology, 15,* 131–135.

Rosenberg, M. S. (1986). Error-correction during oral reading: A comparison of three techniques. *Learning Disability Quarterly, 9,* 182–192.

Rosenberg, M. S. (1989). The effects of daily homework assignments on the acquisition of basic skills by students with learning disabilities. *Journal of Learning Disabilities, 22,* 314–323.

Rosenberg, M. S., Bott, D., Majsterek, D., Chiang, B., Gartland, D., Wesson, C., Graham, S., Smith-Myles, B., Miller, M., Swanson, H. L., Bender, W., Rivera, D., & Wilson, R. (1993). Minimum standards for the description of participants in learning disabilities research. *Journal of Learning Disabilities, 26,* 210–213.

Rosenfield, P., Lambert, N. M., & Black, A. (1985). Desk arrangement effects on pupil classroom behavior. *Journal of Educational Psychology, 77,* 101–108.

Rosenshine, B. V. (1980). How time is spent in elementary classrooms. In C. Denham & A. Lieberman (Eds.), *Time to learn.* Washington, DC: National Institute of Education.

Rosenshine, B. V. (1986). Synthesis of research on explicit teaching. *Educational Leadership, 43*(7), 60–69.

Rosenstock, L., Keifer, M., Daniell, W. E., McConnell, R., Claypoole, K., & The Pesticide Health Effects Study Group. (1991). Chronic central nervous system effects of acute organophosphate pesticide intoxication. *Lancet, 338,* 223–227.

Rosenthal, J. H. (1982). EEG-event related potentials in dyslexia and its subtypes. In D. A. B. Lindenberg, M. F. Colien, & E. E. Van Brunt (Eds.), *AMIA Congress, 82.* New York: Masson.

Rosenthal, R., & Jacobson, L. (1968). *Pygmalion in the classroom: Teacher expectations and pupils' intelligence development.* New York: Holt, Rinehart & Winston.

Rosenthal, R., & Rosnow, R. (1969). *Artifact in behavioral research.* New York: Academic Press.

Rosenzweig, M. R. (1966). Environmental complexity, cerebral change, and behavior. *American Psychologist, 21,* 321–332.

Rosenzweig, M. R. (1979). Responsiveness of brain size to individual experience: Behavioral and evolutionary implications. In M. E. Hahn, C. Jensen, & B. C. Dudek (Eds.), *Development and evolution of brain size: Behavioral implications.* New York: Academic Press.

Rosenzweig, M. R., Bennett, E. L., & Alberti, M. (1984). Multiple effects of lesions on brain structure in young rats. In S. Finger & C. R. Almli (Eds.), *Early brain damage: Vol. 2. Neurobiology and behavior.* New York: Academic Press.

Rosenzweig, M. R., Bennett, E. L., & Diamond, M. C. (1972). Brain changes in responses to experience. *Scientific American, 226,* 22–30.

Rosner, J. (1973). Language arts and arithmetic achievement, and specifically related perceptual skills. *American Educational Research Journal, 10,* 59–68.

Ross, A. O. (1976). *Psychological aspects of learning disabilities and reading disorders.* New York: McGraw-Hill.

Ross, D. M., & Ross, S. A. (1976). *Hyperactivity: Research, theory, and action*. New York: John Wiley & Sons.

Ross, G. S. (1980). Categorization in 1- to 2-year olds. *Developmental Psychology, 16*, 391–396.

Ross, M. B., & Salvia, J. (1975). Attractiveness as a biasing factor in teacher judgments. *American Journal of Mental Deficiency, 80*, 96–98.

Rossetti, L. (1986). *High risk infants: Identification, assessment, and intervention*. Boston: College-Hill.

Roth, M., McCaul, E., & Barnes, K. (1993). Who becomes an "at-risk" student? The predictive value of a kindergarten screening battery. *Exceptional Children, 59*, 348–358.

Rothenburg, M., & Rivlin, L. (1975). *An ecological approach to the study of open classrooms*. Paper presented at a conference on ecological factors in human development, University of Surrey, England.

Rourke, B. P. (1976). Reading retardation in children: developmental lag or deficit. In R. M. Knights & D. J. Bakker (Eds.), *The neuropsychology of learning disorders: Theoretical approaches*. Baltimore: University Park Press.

Rourke, B. P. (1987). Syndrome of nonverbal learning disabilities: The final common pathway of white-matter disease/dysfunction? *Clinical Neuropsychologist, 1*, 209–234.

Rourke, B. P. (1993). Arithmetic disabilities specific and otherwise: A neuropsychological perspective. *Journal of Learning Disabilities, 26*, 214–226.

Rourke, B. P., Bakker, D. J., Fisk, J. L., & Strang, J. D. (1983). *Child neuropsychology: An introduction to theory, research, and clinical practice*. New York: Guilford Press.

Rourke, B. P., & Conway, J. A. (1997). Disabilities of arithmetical reasoning: Perspectives from neurology and neuropsychology. *Journal of Learning Disabilities, 30*, 34–46.

Rourke, B. P., Fisk, J. L., & Strang, J. D. (1985). *Neuropsychological assessment of children: A treatment-oriented approach*. New York: Guilford Press.

Rourke, B. P., & Orr, R. R. (1977). Prediction of the reading and spelling performances of normal and retarded readers: A four-year follow-up. *Journal of Abnormal Child Psychology, 5*, 9–20.

Routh, D. K., & Roberts, R. D. (1972). Minimal brain dysfunction in children: Failure to find evidence for a behavioral syndrome. *Psychological Reports, 31*, 307–314.

Rovet, J. F., Ehrlich, R. M., Czuchta, D., & Akler, M. (1993). Psychoeducational characteristics of children and adolescents with insulin-dependent diabetes mellitus. *Journal of Learning Disabilities, 26*, 7–22.

Rubin, R., & Balow, B. (1971). Learning and behavior disorders: A longitudinal study. *Exceptional Children, 38*, 293–299.

Rudel, R. G. (1985). The definition of dyslexia: Language and motor deficits. In F. H. Duffy & N. Geschwind (Eds.), *Dyslexia: A neuroscientific approach to clinical evaluation*. Boston: Little, Brown.

Rudel, R. G., Denckla, M. B., & Spalten, E. (1976). Paired associate learning of Morse Code and Braille letter names by dyslexic and normal children. *Cortex, 12*, 61–70.

Rueda, R., & Garcia, E. (1997). Do portfolios make a difference for diverse students? The influence of type of data on making instructional decisions. *Learning Disabilities Research & Practice, 12*, 114–122.

Rueda, R. S. (1992). Characteristics of teacher-student discourse in computer-based dialogue journals: A descriptive study. *Learning Disability Quarterly, 15*, 187–206.

Ruhl, K. L., & Suritsky, S. (1995). The pause procedures and/or an outline: Effect on immediate free recall and lecture notes taken by college students with learning disabilities. *Learning Disability Quarterly, 18*, 2–11

Rumelhart, D. E. (1980). Schemata: The building blocks of cognition. In R. J. Spiro, B. C. Bruce, & W. F. Brewer (Eds.), *Theoretical issues in reading comprehension*. Hillsdale, NJ: Lawrence Erlbaum.

Rumsey, J. M. Andreason, P., Zametkin, A. J., Aquino, T., King, C., Hamburger, S. D., Pikus, A., Rapoport, J. L., & Cohen, R. M. (1992). Failure to activate left temporoparietal cortex in dyslexia:

An oxygen 15 positron emission tomographic study. *Archives of Neurology, 49*, 527–534.

Runyan, M. K. (1991). The effect of extra time on reading comprehension scores for university students with and without learning disabilities. *Journal of Learning Disabilities, 24*, 104–108.

Rusch, F. R., & Phelps, L. A. (1987). Secondary special education and transition from school to work: A national policy. *Exceptional Children, 53*, 487–492.

Rutter, M. (1978). Prevalence and types of dyslexia. In A. L. Benton & D. Pearl (Eds.), *Dyslexia: An appraisal of current knowledge*. New York: Oxford University Press.

Rutter, M. (1982). Syndromes attributed to "Minimal Brain Dysfunction" in childhood. *American Journal of Psychiatry, 139*, 21–33.

Rutter, M., Tizard, J., Yule, W., Graham, P., & Whitmore, K. (1976). Research report: Isle of Wight studies 1964–1974. *Psychological Medicine, 6*, 313–332.

Ryan, D. (1991). Management and evaluation revisited. *The School Psychologist, 9*(1), 19–20.

Ryan, E. B., Short, E. J., & Weed, K. A. (1986). The role of cognitive strategy training in improving the academic performance of learning disabled children. *Journal of Learning Disabilities, 19*, 521–529,

Ryckman, D. B., & Peckham, P. D. (1986). Gender differences on attribution patterns in academic areas for learning disabled students. *Learning Disabilities Research, 1*, 83–89.

Sabatino, D. A., & Sedlack, R. A. (1986). Specific developmental disorders. In J. M. Reisman (Ed.), *Behavior disorders in infants, children, and adolescents*. New York: Random House.

Sabo, R. (1976, October). *The Feingold diet*. Address to the annual meeting of the School Psychologists of Upstate New York, Syracuse.

Sabornie, E. J. (1994). Social-affective characteristics in early adolescents identified as learning disabled and nondisabled. *Learning Disability Quarterly, 17*, 268–279.

Sabornie, E. J., & Kauffman, J. M. (1986). Social acceptance of learning disabled adolescents. *Learning Disability Quarterly, 9*, 55–60.

Sabornie, E. J., Marshall, K. J., & Ellis, E. S. (1990). Restructuring of mainstream sociometry with learning disabled and nonhandicapped students. *Exceptional Children, 56*, 314–323.

Sacks, O. (1985). *The man who mistook his wife for a hat*. New York: Summit Books.

Safer, D. (1986). Nonpromotion correlates and outcomes at different grade levels. *Journal of Learning Disabilities, 19*, 500–503.

Sainato, D. M., Zigmond, N., & Strain, P. S. (1983). Social status and initiations of interaction by learning disabled students in a regular education setting. *Analysis and Intervention in Developmental Disabilities, 3*, 71–87.

Sale, P., & Carey, D. M. (1995). The sociometric status of students with disabilities in a full-inclusion school. *Exceptional Children, 62*, 6–19.

Salend, S. J. (1984). Factors contributing to the development of successful mainstreaming programs. *Exceptional Children, 50*(5), 409–416.

Salend, S. J., & Nowak, M. R. (1988). Effects of peer-previewing on LD students' oral reading skills. *Learning Disability Quarterly, 11*, 47–53.

Salend, S. J., Whittaker, C. R., Raab, S., & Giek, K. (1991). Using a self-evaluation system as a group contingency. *Journal of School Psychology, 29*, 319–329.

Salend, S. J., Whittaker, C. R., & Reeder, E. (1993). Group evaluation: A collaborative peer-mediated behavior management system. *Exceptional Children, 59*, 203–209.

Salvia, J., Algozzine, R., & Sheare, J. B. (1977). Attractiveness and school achievement. *Journal of School Psychology, 15*, 60–67.

Salvia, J., & Ysseldyke, J. E. (1995). *Assessment in special and remedial education* (6th ed.). Boston: Houghton Mifflin.

Samuels, S. J. (1967). Attentional process in reading: The effect of pictures on the acquisition of reading responses. *Journal of Educational Psychology, 58*, 337–342.

Samuels, S. J. (1973). Effect of distinctive feature training on paired-associate learning. *Journal of Educational Psychology, 64,* 164–170.

Samuels, S. J. (1986). Why children fail to learn and what to do about it. *Exceptional Children, 53,* 7–16.

Samuels, S. J., & Anderson, R. H. (1973). Visual recognition memory, paired-associate learning and reading achievement. *Journal of Educational Psychology, 65,* 160–167.

Samuels, S. J., & Miller, N. L. (1985). Failure to find attention differences between learning disabled and normal children on classroom and laboratory tasks. *Exceptional Children, 51,* 358–375.

Sandberg, D. E., & Barrick, C. (1995). Endocrine disorders in childhood: A selective survey of intellectual and educational sequelae. *School Psychology Review, 24,* 146–170.

Sands, D. J., Adams, L., & Stout, D. M. (1995). A statewide exploration of the nature and use of curriculum in special education. *Exceptional Children, 62,* 68–83.

Sands, D. J., & Doll, B. (1996). Fostering self-determination is a developmental task, *The Journal of Special Education, 30,* 58–76.

Sansone, J., & Zigmond, N. (1986). Evaluating mainstreaming through an analysis of students' schedules. *Exceptional Children, 52,* 452–458.

Santrock, J. W. (1976). Affect and facilitative self-control: Influence of ecological setting, cognition, and social agent. *Journal of Educational Psychology, 68,* 529–535.

Sapon-Shevin, M. (1987). The national education reports and special education: Implications for students. *Exceptional Children, 53,* 300–306.

Saski, J., Swicegood, P., & Carter, J. (1983). Notetaking formats for learning disabled adolescents. *Learning Disability Quarterly, 6,* 265–272.

Sater, G. M., & French, D. C. (1989). A comparison of the social competencies of learning disabled and low achieving elementary aged children. *Journal of Special Education, 23,* 29–42.

Satterfield, J. H., Hoppe, C. M., & Schell, A. M. (1982). A prospective study of delinquency in 110 adolescent boys with attention deficit disorder and 88 normal boys. *American Journal of Psychiatry, 6,* 795–798.

Satterfield, J. H., Schell, A. M., & Barb, S. D. (1980). Potential risk of prolonged administration of stimulant medication for hyperactive children. *Developmental and Behavioral Pediatrics, 1,* 102–107.

Sattler, J. M. (1992). *Assessment of children* (Revised and updated 3rd ed.). San Diego: Sattler, Inc.

Satz, P., Bakker, D. J., Teunissen, J., Goebel, R., & Vander Vlugt, H. (1975). Developmental parameters of the ear asymmetry: A multivariate approach. *Brain and Language, 2,* 171–185.

Satz, P., Taylor, H. G., Friel, J., & Fletcher, J. (1978). Some predictive and developmental precursors of reading disability: A six-year follow-up. In D. Pearl & A. Benton (Eds.), *Dyslexia: A critical appraisal of current theory.* Oxford: Oxford University Press.

Satz, P., Yanowitz, J., & Willmore, J. (1983). Early brain damage and lateral development. In R. Bell, J. Elias, R. Green, & J. Harvey (Eds.), *Interfaces in psychology.* Texas: Texas University Press.

Sawyer, D. J., Dougherty, C., Shelly, M., & Spaanenburg, I. (1990). Auditory segmenting performance and reading acquisition. In C. S. Simon (Ed.), *Communication skills and classroom success: Assessment of language-learning disabled students.* Austin, TX: PRO-ED.

Scanlon, D., Deshler, D. D., & Schumaker, J. B. (1996). Can a strategy be taught and learned in secondary inclusive classrooms? *Learning Disability Research and Practice, 11,* 41–57.

Scanlon, D. J., Duran, G. Z., Reyes, E. I., & Gallego, M. A. (1992). Interactive semantic mapping: An interactive approach to enhancing LD students' content area comprehension. *Learning Disabilities Research & Practice, 7,* 142–146.

Scarborough, H. S. (1984). Continuity between childhood dyslexia and adult reading. *British Journal of Psychology, 75,* 329–348.

Scarr, S., Weinberg, R. A., & Waldman, I. D. (1993). IQ correlations in transracial adoptive families. *Intelligence, 17,* 541–555.

Schalock, R. L., Holl, C., Elliott, B., & Ross, I. (1992). A longitudinal follow-up of graduates from a rural special education program. *Learning Disability Quarterly, 15,* 29–38.

Schiff, M., Duyme, M., Dumaret, A., & Tomkiewicz, S. (1982). How much *could* we boost scholastic achievement and IQ scores? A direct answer from a French adoption study. *Cognition, 12,* 165–196.

Schmid, R. E. (1979). The learning disabled adolescent. In C. Mercer (Ed.), *Children and adolescents with learning disabilities.* Columbus, OH: Charles E. Merrill.

Schneider, B. H. (1984). LD as they see it: Perceptions of adolescents in a special residential school. *Journal of Learning Disabilities, 17,* 533–536.

Schoer, L. (1962). Effect of list length and interpolated learning on the learning and recall of fast and slow learners. *Journal of Educational Psychology, 53,* 193–197.

Schonhaut, S., & Satz, P. (1983). Prognosis for children with learning disabilities: A review of follow-up studies. In M. Rutter (Ed.), *Developmental neuropsychiatry.* New York: Guilford Press.

The School Psychologist. (1983). *37*(4), 2.

Schor, D. P. (1985). Temperament and the initial school experience. *Children's Health Care, 13,* 129–134.

Schulte, A. C., Osborne, S. S., & McKinney, J. D. (1990). Academic outcomes for students with learning disabilities in consultation and resource programs. *Exceptional Children, 57,* 162–172.

Schultz, M. K. (1988, December). A comparison of standard scores for commonly used tests of early reading. *Communiqué,* p. 13.

Schumaker, J. B., Deshler, D. D., Alley, G. R., & Warner, M. M. (1983). Toward the development of an intervention model for learning disabled adolescents: The University of Kansas Institute. *Exceptional Education Quarterly, 4*(1), 45–74.

Schumaker, J. B., Deshler, D. D., & Denton, P. H. (1984). An integrated system for providing content to learning disabled adolescents using an audio-taped format. In W. M. Cruickshank & J. M. Kleibhan (Eds.), *Early adolescence to early adulthood.* Syracuse: Syracuse University Press.

Schumaker, J. B., & Hazel, J. S. (1984). Social skills assessment and training for the learning disabled: Who's on first and what's on second? Part II. *Journal of Learning Disabilities, 17,* 492–499.

Schumaker, J. B., Hazel, J. S., Sherman, J. A., & Sheldon, J. (1982). Social skill performances of learning disabled, non-learning disabled, and delinquent adolescents. *Learning Disability Quarterly, 5,* 388–397.

Schumaker, J. B., Hovell, M. F., & Sherman, J. A. (1977). An analysis of daily report cards and parent-managed privileges in improvement of adolescents' classroom performance. *Journal of Applied Behavior Analysis, 10,* 449–464.

Schumaker, J. B., Wildgen, J. S., & Sherman, J. A. (1982). Social interaction of learning disabled junior high students in their regular classrooms: An observational analysis. *Journal of Learning Disabilities, 15,* 355–358.

Schumm, J. S., & Vaughn, S. (1995). Getting ready for inclusion: Is the stage set? *Learning Disabilities Research & Practice, 10,* 169–179.

Schumm, J. S., Vaughn, S., Haager, D., & Klinger, J. K. (1994). Literacy instruction for mainstreamed students: What suggestions are provided in basal reading series? *Remedial and Special Education, 15,* 14–20.

Schumm, J. S., Vaughn, S., Haager, D., McDowell, J., Rothlein, L., & Saumell, L. (1995). General education teacher planning: What can students with learning disabilities expect? *Exceptional Children, 61,* 335–352.

Schunk, D. H., & Cox, P. D. (1986). Strategy training and attributional feedback with learning disabled students. *Journal of Educational Psychology, 78,* 201–209.

Schunk, D. H., & Rice, J. M. (1992). Influence of reading-comprehension strategy information on children's achievement outcomes. *Learning Disability Quarterly, 15,* 51–64.

Schunk, D. H., & Rice, J. M. (1993). Strategy fading and progress feedback: Effects on self-efficacy and comprehension among students receiving remedial reading services. *The Journal of Special Education, 27,* 257–276.

Schwartz, M. L., Gilroy, J., & Lynn, G. (1976). Neuropsychological and psychosocial implications of spelling deficit in adulthood: A case report. *Journal of Learning Disabilities, 9,* 144–148.

Schwartz, S. E., & Budd, D. (1981). Mathematics for handicapped learners: A functional approach for adolescents. *Focus on Exceptional Children, 13*(7), 1–12.

Schwartz, T. H., & Byran, J. H. (1971). Imitation and judgements of children with language deficits. *Exceptional Children, 38,* 157–158.

Schwebel, A. I., & Cherlin, D. L. (1972). Physical and social distancing in teacher-pupil relationships. *Journal of Educational Psychology, 63,* 543–550.

Schwebel, A. S. (1966). Effects of impulsivity on performance of verbal tasks in middle and lower class children. *American Journal of Orthopsychiatry, 36,* 13–21.

Schweinhart, L. J., & Weikart, D. P. (1980). Young children grow up: The effects of the Perry Preschool Program on youths through age 15. *Monographs of the High/Scope Educational Research Foundation.* Ypsilanti, MI: High/Scope Press.

Schwille, J., Porter, A., Belli, A., Floden, R., Freeman, D., Knappen, L., Kuhs, T., & Schmidt, W. J. (1981). *Teachers as policy brokers in the content of elementary school mathematics* (National Institute of Education Contract No. P-80-0127). East Lansing: Institute for Research on Teaching, Michigan State University.

Science Agenda (1990, August/September), p. 11.

Scott, M. S., Serchuk, R., & Mundy, P. (1982). Taxonomic and complementary picture pairs: Ability in two- to five-year-olds. *International Journal of Behavioral Development, 5,* 243–256.

Scott, N., & Sigel, I. E. (1965). *Effects of inquiry training in physical science on creativity and cognitive styles of elementary school children.* Research report for United States Office of Education.

Scruggs, T. E., & Mastropieri, M. A. (1988). Are learning disabled students "Test-Wise"?: A review of recent research. *Learning Disabilities Focus, 3,* 87–97.

Scruggs, T. E., & Mastropieri, M. A. (1990). Mnemonic instruction for students with learning disabilities: What it is and what it does. *Learning Disability Quarterly, 13,* 271–280.

Scruggs, T. E., & Mastropieri, M. A. (1992). Classroom applications of mnemonic instruction: Acquisition, maintenance and generalization. *Exceptional Children, 58,* 219–229.

Scruggs, T. E., & Mastropieri, M. A. (1993). Special education for the twenty-first century: Integrating learning strategies and thinking skills. *Journal of Learning Disabilities, 26,* 393–398.

Scruggs, T. E., Mastropieri, M. A., Bakken, J. P., & Brigham, F. J. (1993). Reading versus doing: The relative effects of textbook-based and inquiry-oriented approaches to science learning in special education classrooms. *The Journal of Special Education, 27,* 1–15.

Scruggs, T. E., Mastropieri, M. A., Brigham, F. J., & Sullivan, G. S. (1992). Effects of mnemonic reconstructions on the spatial learning of adolescents with learning disabilities. *Learning Disability Quarterly, 15,* 154–162.

Scruggs, T. E., Mastropieri, M. A., Levin, J. R., & Gaffney, J. S. (1985). Facilitating the acquisition of science facts in learning disabled students. *American Educational Research Journal, 22,* 575–586.

Scruggs, T. E., Mastropieri, M. A., & Sullivan, G. S. (1994). Promoting relational thinking: Elaborative interrogation for students with mild disabilities. *Exceptional Children, 60,* 450–457.

Searleman, A. (1977). A review of right hemisphere linguistic capabilities. *Psychological Bulletin, 84,* 503–528.

Segalowitz, S. J., & Bryden, M. P. (1983). Individual differences in hemispheric representation of language. In S. J. Segalowitz (Ed.), *Language functions and brain organization.* New York: Academic Press.

Segalowitz, S. J., & Lawson, S. (1995). Subtle symptoms associated with self-reported mild head injury. *Journal of Learning Disabilities, 28,* 309–319.

Seidenberg, P. L. (1991). *Reading, writing, and studying strategies: An integrated curriculum.* Gaithersburg, MD: Aspen Publishers.

Semmel, M. I., Abernathy, T. V., Butera, G., & Lesar, S. (1991). Teacher perceptions of the Regular Education Initiative. *Exceptional Children, 58,* 9–24.

Semrud-Clikeman, M., Hynd, G., Novey, E., & Eliopulos, D. (1991). Dyslexia and brain morphology: Relationships between neuroanatomical variation and linguistic tasks. *Learning and Individual Differences, 3,* 225–242.

Senf, G. M. (1978). Implications of the final procedures for evaluating specific learning disabilities. *Journal of Learning Disabilities, 11,* 124–126.

Senf, G. M. (1987). Learning disabilities as sociologic sponge: Wiping up life's spills. In S. Vaughn & C. S. Bos (Eds.), *Research in learning disabilities: Issues and future directions.* Boston: College-Hill.

Settipane, G. A., & Pudupakkam, R. K. (1975). Aspirin intolerance: III. Subtypes, familial occurrence, and cross-reactivity with tartrazine. *Journal of Allergy and Clinical Immunology, 56,* 215–221.

Shaffer, D., O'Connor, P. A., Shafer, S. Q., & Prupis, P. (1983). Neurological "soft signs": Their origins and significance for behavior. In M. Rutter (Ed.), *Developmental neuropsychiatry.* New York: Guilford Press.

Shafrir, U., & Siegel, L. S. (1994). Subtypes of learning disabilities in adolescents and adults. *Journal of Learning Disabilities, 27,* 123–134.

Shanahan, T., & Tierney, R. J. (1990). Reading-writing connections: The relations among three perspectives. In J. Zutell & S. McCormick (Eds.), *Literacy theory and research: Analyses from multiple paradigms* (39th Yearbook). Chicago: National Reading Conference.

Shankweiler, D., & Liberman, I. Y. (1976). Exploring the relations between reading and speech. In R. M. Knights & D. J. Bakker (Eds.), *The neuropsychology of learning disorders: Theoretical approaches.* Baltimore: University Park Press.

Shapiro, E. S. (1992). Use of Gickling's model of curriculum-based assessment to improve reading in elementary age students. *School Psychology Review, 21,* 168–176.

Shapiro, E. S., & Derr, T. F. (1987). An examination of overlap between reading curricula and standardized achievement tests. *Journal of Special Education, 21*(2), 59–67.

Shapiro, E. S., & Kratochwill, T. R. (1988). *Behavioral assessment in schools: Conceptual foundations and practical applications.* NY: Guilford.

Shapiro, E. S., & Lentz, F. E. (1991). Vocational-technical programs: Follow-up of students with learning disabilities. *Exceptional Children, 58,* 47–59.

Shapiro, S., & Forbes, R. A. (1981). Review of involvement programs for parents of learning disabled children. *Journal of Learning Disabilities, 14,* 499–504.

Sharma, M. C. (1981). Using word problems to aid language and reading comprehension. *Topics in Learning & Learning Disabilities, 1*(3), 61–71.

Shavelson, R. J. (1983). Review of research on teachers' pedagogical judgments, plans, and decisions. *Elementary School Journal, 83,* 392–413.

Shaw, R. A. (1981). Designing and using non-word problems as aids to thinking and comprehension. *Topics in Learning & Learning Disabilities, 1*(3), 73–80.

Shaw, S. F., Cullen, J. P., McGuire, J. M., & Brinkerhoff, L. C. (1995). Operationalizing a definition of learning disabilities. *Journal of Learning Disabilities, 28,* 586–597.

Shaywitz, B. A., Fletcher, J. M., Holahan, J. M., & Shaywitz, S. E. (1992). Discrepancy compared to low achievement definitions of reading disability: Results from the Connecticut longitudinal study. *Journal of Learning Disabilities, 25,* 639–648.

Shaywitz, B. A., Fletcher, J. M., & Shaywitz, S. E. (1995). Defining and classifying learning disabilities and attention-deficit/hyperactivity disorder. *Journal of Child Neurology, 10* (Supplement 1), S50-S57.

Shaywitz, S. E., & Shaw, R. (1988). The admissions process: An approach to selecting learning disabled students at the most selective colleges. *Learning Disabilities Focus, 3,* 81–86.

Shaywitz, S. E., Shaywitz, B. A., Fletcher, J. M., & Escobar, M. D. (1990). Prevalence of reading disability in boys and girls: Results of the Connecticut Longitudinal Study. *Journal of the American Medical Association, 264,* 998–1002.

Sheare, J. B. (1978). The impact of resource programs upon the self-concept and peer acceptance of learning disabled children. *Psychology in the Schools, 15,* 406–412.

Sheingold, K., & Shapiro, J. (1976). Children's verbal rehearsal in a free-recall task. *Developmental Psychology, 12,* 169–170.

Sheinker, J., & Sheinker, A. (1989). *Metacognitive approach to study strategies.* Gaithersburg, MD: Aspen Publishers.

Shepard, L. A. (1987). The new push for excellence: Widening the schism between regular and special education. *Exceptional Children, 53,* 327–329.

Shepard, L. A., & Smith, M. L. (1983). An evaluation of the identification of learning disabled students in Colorado. *Learning Disability Quarterly, 6,* 115–127.

Shepard, L. A., & Smith, M. L. (1986). Synthesis of research on school readiness and kindergarten retention. *Educational Leadership, 44*(3), 78–86.

Shepard, T., & Adjogah, S. (1994). Science performance of students with learning disabilities on language-based measures. *Learning Disabilities Research & Practice, 9,* 219–225.

Shepherd, M. J., & Gelzheiser, L. M. (1987). Strategies and mnemonics go to school. In H. L. Swanson (Ed.), *Advances in learning and behavioral disabilities: Memory and learning disabilities.* Greenwich, CT: JAI Press.

Shetty, T. (1971). Alpha rhythms in the hyperkinetic child. *Nature, 234,* 476.

Shields, D. T. (1973). Brain responses to stimuli in disorders of information processing. *Journal of Learning Disabilities, 6,* 501–505.

Shinn, M. R. (1986). Does anyone care what happens after the refer-test-place sequence: The systematic evaluation of special education program effectiveness. *School Psychology Review, 15,* 49–58.

Shinn, M. R. (1988). Development of curriculum-based local norms for use in special education decision-making. *School Psychology Review, 17,* 61–80.

Shinn, M. R., Good, R. H., Knutson, N., Tilly, W. D., & Collins, V. L. (1992). Curriculum-based measurement of oral reading fluency: A confirmatory analysis of its relation to reading. *School Psychology Review, 21,* 459–479.

Shinn, M. R., Rodden-Nord, K., & Knutson, N. (1993). Using curriculum-based measurement to identify potential candidates for reintegration into general education. *The Journal of Special Education, 27,* 202–221.

Shinn, M. R., Tindal, G. A., & Spira, D. A. (1987). Special education referrals as an index of teacher tolerance: Are teachers imperfect tests? *Exceptional Children, 54,* 32–40.

Shinn, M. R., Tindal, G. A., & Stein, S. (1988). Curriculum-based measurement and the identification of mildly handicapped students: A research review. *Professional School Psychology, 3,* 69–85.

Shinn, M. R., Ysseldyke, J. E., Deno, S. L., & Tindal, G. A. (1986). A comparison of differences between students labeled learning disabled and low achieving on measures of classroom performance. *Journal of Learning Disabilities, 19,* 545–552.

Shondrick, D. D., Serafica, F. C., Clark, P., & Miller, K. G. (1992). Interpersonal problem solving and creativity in boys with and boys without learning disabilities. *Learning Disability Quarterly, 15,* 95–102.

Short, E. J., & Ryan, E. B. (1984). Metacognitive differences between skilled and less skilled readers: Remediating deficits through story grammar and attribution training. *Journal of Educational Psychology, 76,* 225–235.

Shriner, J., & Salvia, J. (1988). Chronic noncorrespondence between elementary math curricula and arithmetic tests. *Exceptional Children, 55,* 240–248.

Shuell, T. J., & Keppel, G. (1970). Learning ability and retention. *Journal of Educational Psychology, 61,* 59–65.

Sieben, R. L. (1977). Controversial medical treatments of learning disabilities. *Academic Therapy, 13,* 133–147.

Siegel, L. (1981). Infants tests as predictors of cognitive and language development at two years. *Child Development, 52,* 545–557.

Siegel, L. S. (1989). IQ is irrelevant to the definition of learning disabilities. *Journal of Learning Disabilities, 22,* 469–478,486.

Siegler, R. S. (1983). Information processing approaches to development. In W. Kessen (Ed.), *Handbook of child psychology: Vol. 1. History, theory, and methods.* New York: Wiley.

Siegler, R. S. (1989). Mechanisms of cognitive development. *Annual Review of Psychology, 40,* 353–379.

Sikorski, M. F., Niemiec, R. P., & Walberg, H. J. (1996). A classroom checkup: Best teaching practices in special education. *Teaching Exceptional Children, 29*(1), 27–29.

Silberberg, N. E., Iversen, I. A., & Goins, J. T. (1973). Which remedial reading method works best? *Journal of Learning Disabilities, 6,* 547–556.

Silberberg, N. E., & Silberberg, M. C. (1971). School achievement and delinquency. *Review of Educational Research, 41,* 17–33.

Silberberg, N. E., & Silberberg, M. C. (1978). And the adult who reads poorly? *Journal of Learning Disabilities, 11,* 3–4.

Silberman, A. (1976, January). If they say your child can't learn. *McCalls, 103,* 76–81.

Silver, A. A., & Hagin, R. A. (1964). Specific reading disability: Follow-up studies. *American Journal of Orthopsychiatry, 34,* 95–102.

Silver, A. A., & Hagin, R. A. (1966). Maturation of perceptual functions in children with specific reading disability. *The Reading Teacher, 19,* 253–259.

Silver, L. B. (1971). Familial patterns in children with neurologically-based learning disabilities. *Journal of Learning Disabilities, 4,* 349–358.

Silver, L. B. (1977, November). *The faces of MBD—Psychiatric aspects.* Address to SUNY Upstate Medical Center and CIBA conference, Understanding Minimal Brain Dysfunction, Syracuse, NY.

Silver, L. B. (1987). The "magic cure": A review of the current controversial approaches for treating learning disabilities. *Journal of Learning Disabilities, 20,* 498–504.

Silver, L. B. (1988). A review of the Federal government's Interagency Committee on Learning Disabilities Report to the U.S. Congress. *Learning Disabilities Focus, 3,* 73–80.

Silver, L. B. (1995). Controversial therapies. *Journal of Child Neurology, 10,* S96–S100.

Silverberg, R., Bentin, S., Gaziel, T., Obler, L. K., & Albert, M. L. (1979). Shift of visual field preference for English words in native Hebrew speakers. *Brain and Language, 8,* 184–190.

Silverberg, R., Gordon, H. W., Pollack, S., & Bentin, S. (1980). Shift of visual field preference for Hebrew words in native speakers learning to read. *Brain and Language, 11,* 99–105.

Silverman, R., & Zigmond, N. (1983). Self-concept in learning disabled adolescents. *Journal of Learning Disabilities, 16,* 478–482.

Simmonds, E. P. M. (1990). The effectiveness of two methods for teaching a constraint-seeking questioning strategy to students with learning disabilities. *Journal of Learning Disabilities, 23,* 229–232.

Simmonds, E. P. M. (1992). The effects of teacher training and implementation of two methods for improving the comprehension skills of students with learning disabilities. *Learning Disabilities Research & Practice, 7,* 194–198.

Simmons, D. C., Fuchs, D., & Fuchs, L. S. (1991). Instructional and curricular requisites of mainstreamed students with learning disabilities. *Journal of Learning Disabilities, 24,* 354–360, 353.

Simmons, D. C., Kameenuî, E. J., & Darch, C. B. (1988). The effect of textual proximity on fourth- and fifth-grade LD students' metacognitive awareness and strategic comprehension behavior. *Learning Disability Quarterly, 11,* 380–395.

Simner, M. L. (1982). Printing errors in kindergarten and the prediction of academic performance. *Journal of Learning Disabilities, 15,* 155–159.

Simon, S. B., Have, L. W., & Kirschenbaum, H. (1972). *Values clarification: A handbook of practical strategies for teachers and students.* New York: Hart.

Sinclair, E., & Alexson, J. (1986). Learning disability discrepancy formulas: Similarities and differences among them. *Learning Disabilities Research, 1,* 112–118.

Sindelar, P. T., & Deno, S. L. (1978). The effectiveness of prediction of academic performance. *Journal of Learning Disabilities, 15,* 155–159.

Singer, J. L., & Singer, D. (1979). Come back, Mister Rogers, come back. *Psychology Today, 12,* 59–60.

Siperstein, G. N., & Goding, M. J. (1983). Social integration of learning disabled children in regular classrooms. *Advances in Learning and Behavioral Disabilities, 2,* 227–263.

Siperstein, G. N., & Goding, M. J. (1985). Teachers' behavior toward LD and non-LD children: A strategy for change. *Journal of Learning Disabilities, 18,* 139–144.

Sisterhen, D. H., & Gerber, P. J. (1989). Auditory, visual, and multisensory nonverbal social perception in adolescents with and without learning disabilities. *Journal of Learning Disabilities, 22,* 245–249, 257.

Sitlington, P. L., & Frank, A. R. (1993). Dropouts with learning disabilities: What happens to them as young adults? *Learning Disabilities Research & Practice, 8,* 244–252.

Sitlington, P. L., Frank, A. R., & Carson, R. (1993). Adult adjustment among high school graduates with mild disabilities. *Exceptional Children, 59,* 221–233.

Sizer, T. R. (1984). *Horace's compromise: The dilemma of the American high school.* Boston: Houghton-Mifflin.

Skeels, H. M., & Skodak, M. (1966, May). *Adult status of individuals who experienced early intervention.* Paper presented at the 90th annual meeting of the American Association on Mental Deficiency, Chicago, IL. In D. P. Hallahan & W. M. Cruickshank (Eds.), *Psycho-educational foundations of learning disabilities.* (1973). Englewood-Cliffs, NJ: Prentice-Hall.

Skinner, B. F. (1959). *Verbal behavior.* New York: Appleton-Century-Crofts.

Slate, J. R. (1996). Interrelations of frequently administered achievement measures in the determination of specific learning disabilities. *Learning Disabilities Research & Practice, 11,* 86–89.

Slate, J. R., & Saudargas, R. A. (1986). Differences in learning disabled and average students' classroom behaviors. *Learning Disability Quarterly, 9,* 61–67.

Slavin, R. E. (1980). Cooperative learning. *Review of Educational Research, 50,* 315–342.

Slavin, R. E. (1983). *Cooperative learning.* New York: Longman.

Sleeter, C. E. (1986). Learning disabilities: The social construction of a special education category. *Exceptional Children, 53,* 46–54.

Slingerland, B. H. (1974). *A multi-sensory approach to language arts for specific language disability children.* Cambridge, MA: Educator's Publishing Service.

Smead, V. S. (1977). Ability training and task analysis in diagnostic/prescriptive teaching. *Journal of Special Education, 11,* 113–125.

Smith, A. (1984). Early and long-term recovery from brain damage in children and adults. Evolution of concepts of localization, plasticity, and recovery. In C. R. Almli & S. Finger (Eds.), *Early brain damage: Vol. 1. Research orientations and clinical observations.* New York: Academic Press.

Smith, C. R. (1980). Assessment alternatives: Non-standardized procedures. *School Psychology Review, 9,* 46–57.

Smith, C. R. (1985). Learning disabilities: Past and present. *Journal of Learning Disabilities, 18,* 513–517.

Smith, C. R. (1986). The future of the LD field: Intervention approaches. *Journal of Learning Disabilities, 19,* 461–472.

Smith, C. R. (1991, 1994). *Learning disabilities: The interaction of learner, task, and setting* (2nd & 3rd eds.). Boston: Allyn & Bacon.

Smith, C. R. (1997). *Five and fifteen year follow-up of children differing in temperament at birth.* Paper submitted for publication.

Smith, C. R. (1997). Typical development of phonetic approximations in spelling. Manuscript submitted for publication.

Smith, D. D., & Luckasson, R. (1992). *Introduction to special education: Teaching in an age of challenge.* Boston: Allyn & Bacon.

Smith, D. K., Lyon, M. A., Hunter, E., & Boyd, R. (1988). Relationship between the K-ABC and WISC-R for students referred for severe learning disabilities. *Journal of Learning Disabilities, 21,* 509–513.

Smith, D. S., & Nagle, R. J. (1995). Self-perceptions and social comparisons among children with learning disabilities. *Journal of Learning Disabilities, 28,* 364–371.

Smith, G. (1987). Facilitating mainstreaming through a schoolwide study skills program. *Learning Disabilities Focus, 3,* 53–54.

Smith, J. D., & Caplan, J. (1988). Cultural differences in cognitive style development. *Developmental Psychology, 24,* 46–52.

Smith, J. O. (1988). Social and vocational problems of adults with learning disabilities: A review of the literature. *Learning Disabilities Focus, 4,* 46–58.

Smith, M. D., Coleman, J. M., Dokecki, P. R., & Davis, E. E. (1977). Recategorized WISC-R scores of learning disabled children. *Journal of Learning Disabilities, 10,* 444–449.

Smith, M. J. (1975). *When I say no I feel guilty.* New York: Bantam Books.

Smith, M. K. (1988). Effects of children's social class, race, and gender on teacher expectations for children's academic performance: A study in an urban setting. In C. Heid (Ed.), *Multicultural education: Knowledge and perceptions.* Bloomington/Indianapolis: Indiana University Center for Urban and Multicultural Education.

Smith, M. L., & Glass, G. V. (1980). Meta-analysis of research on class size and its relationship to attitudes and instruction. *American Educational Research Journal, 17,* 419–433.

Smith, M. L., & Shepard, L. A. (1987). What doesn't work: Explaining policies of retention in the early grades. *Phi Delta Kappan, 69,* 129–134.

Smith, S. W. (1990). Individualized Education Programs (IEP's) in special education—From intent to acquiescence. *Exceptional Children, 57,* 6–14.

Snider, V. E. (1989). Reading comprehension performance of adolescents with learning disabilities. *Learning Disability Quarterly, 12,* 87–96.

Snider, V. E., & Tarver, S. G. (1987). The effect of early reading failure on acquisition of knowledge among students with learning disabilities. *Journal of Learning Disabilities, 20,* 351–56, 373.

Snow, R. E. (1984). Placing children in special education: Some comments. *Educational Researcher, 13*(2), 12–14.

Snowling, M. J. (1981). Phonemic deficits in developmental dyslexia. *Psychological Research, 43,* 219–234.

Sobol, M. P., Earn, B. M. Bennett, D., & Humphries, T. (1983). A categorical analysis of the social attributions of learning disabled children. *Journal of Abnormal Child Psychology, 11,* 217–228.

Solan, H. A. (1987). A comparison of the influences of verbal-successive and spatial-simultaneous factors on achieving readers in fourth and fifth grade: A multivariate correlational study. *Journal of Learning Disabilities, 20,* 237–242.

Solan, H. A., & Mozlin, R. (1986). The correlations of perceptual-motor maturation to readiness and reading in kindergarten and the primary grades. *Journal of the American Optometric Association, 57,* 28–35.

Somervill, J. W., Jacobsen, L., Warnberg, L., & Young, W. (1974). Varied environmental condition and task performance by mentally retarded subjects perceived as distractible and nondistractible. *American Journal of Mental Deficiency, 79,* 204–209.

Somervill, J. W., Warnberg, L., & Bost, D. E. (1973). Effects of cubicles vs. increased stimulation of task performance by 1st-grade males perceived as distractible and nondistractible. *Journal of Special Education, 7,* 169–185.

Sömmering, S. T. (1791). *Von Baue des Menschlichen Koerpers* (On the structure of the human body). Vol. 5, Part 1. Frankfurt am Main: Barrentropp and Wenner.

Sommers, R. K., & Taylor, L. M. (1972). Cerebral speech dominance in language-disordered and normal children, *Cortex, 8,* 224–232.

Sparrow, S., & Satz, P. (1970). Dyslexia, laterality, and neuropsychological development. In D. J. Bakker & P. Satz (Eds.), *Specific reading disability: Advances in theory and method.* Rotterdam: Rotterdam University Press.

Spear, L. C., & Sternberg, R. J. (1987). An information-processing framework for understanding reading disability. In S. J. Ceci (Ed.), *Handbook of cognitive, social, and neuropsychological aspects of learning disabilities* (Vol. 2). Hillsdale, NJ: Lawrence Erlbaum.

Spear-Swerling, L., & Sternberg, R. J. (1994). The road not taken: An integrative theoretical model of reading disability. *Journal of Learning Disabilities, 27,* 91–103, 122.

Speece, D. L., McKinney, J. D., & Appelbaum, M. I. (1986). Longitudinal development of conservation skills in learning disabled children. *Journal of Learning Disabilities, 19,* 302–307.

Spekman, N. J. (1981). Dyadic verbal communication abilities of learning disabled and normally achieving fourth- and fifth-grade boys. *Learning Disability Quarterly, 4*(2), 139–151.

Spekman, N. J., Goldberg, R. J., & Herman, K. L. (1992). Learning disabled children grow-up: A search for factors related to success in the young adult years. *Learning Disabilities Research & Practice, 7,* 161–170.

Sperry, R. W. (1968). Hemisphere deconnection and unity in conscious awareness. *American Psychologist, 23,* 723–733.

Sperry, V. B. (1974). *A language approach to learning disabilities.* Palo Alto, CA: Consulting Psychologists Press.

Spicker, H. H., & Bartel, N. R. (1968). The mentally retarded. In G. O. Johnson & H. D. Blank (Eds.), *Exceptional children review.* Washington, DC: Council for Exceptional Children.

Spiegel, D. L. (1992). Blending whole language and systematic direct instruction. *The Reading Teacher, 46,* 38–44.

Spiker, C. C., & Cantor, J. H. (1983). Component in the hypothesis testing strategies of young children. In T. J. Tighe & B. E. Shepp (Eds.), *Perception, cognition, and development: Interactional analyses.* Hillsdale, NJ: Lawrence Erlbaum.

Spitz, R. A. (1945). Hospitalism: An inquiry into the genesis of psychiatric conditions in early childhood. *Psychoanalytic Study of the Child, 1,* 53–74.

Sporns, O. (1994). Selectionist and instructionist ideas in neuroscience. In O. Sporns and G. Tononi (Eds.), *Selectionism and the brain.* New York: Academic Press.

Sprafkin, J., Gadow, K. D., & Kant, G. (1987–1988). Teaching emotionally disturbed children to discriminate reality from fantasy on television. *Journal of Special Education, 21*(4), 99–107.

Sprague, R. L., & Sleator, E. K. (1973). Effects of psychopharmacologic agents on learning disorders. *Pediatric Clinics of North America, 20,* 719–735.

Spreen, O. (1981). The relationship between learning disability, neurological impairment, and delinquency: Results of a follow-up study. *The Journal of Nervous and Mental Disease, 169,* 791–799.

Spreen, O. (1982). Adult outcome of reading disorders. In R. N. Malatesha & P. G. Aaron (Eds.), *Reading disorders: Varieties and treatments.* New York: Academic Press.

Spreen, O., & Haaf, R. G. (1986). Empirically derived learning disability subtypes: A replication attempt and longitudinal patterns over 15 years. *Journal of Learning Disabilities, 19,* 170–180.

Sprick, R. S. (1996, September). Is positive reinforcement the same as bribery? *CEC Today,* 14. Council for Exceptional Children.

Spring, C., & Capps, C. (1974). Encoding speed, rehearsal, and probed recall of dyslexic boys. *Journal of Educational Psychology, 66,* 780–786.

Sprinthall, R. C., & Sprinthall, N. A. (1981). *Educational psychology: A developmental approach* (3rd ed.). Reading, MA: Addison-Wesley.

Spurzheim, J. G. (1815). *The physiognomical system of Drs. Gall and Spurzheim.* London: Baldwin, Cradock, & Joy.

Spyker, J. M. (1974). Occupational hazards and the pregnant worker. In C. Xintras, B. L. Johnson, & I. de Groot (Eds.), *Behavioral toxicology.* Washington, DC: U.S. Department of Health, Education, and Welfare.

Sroufe, L. A., & Fleeson, J. (1986). Attachment and the construction of relationships. In W. W. Hartup & Z. Rubin (Eds.), *Relationships and development.* Hillsdale, NJ: Lawrence Erlbaum.

Stage, S. A., & Wagner, R. K. (1992). Development of young children's phonological and orthographic knowledge as revealed by their spellings. *Developmental Psychology, 28,* 287–296.

Stahl, S. A., & Miller, P. D. (1989). Whole language and language experience approaches for beginning reading: A quantitative research synthesis. *Review of Educational Research, 59,* 87–116.

Stainback, S., & Stainback, W. (1985). The merger of special and regular education: Can it be done? A response to Lieberman and Mesinger. *Exceptional Children, 51,* 517–521.

Stainback, W., & Stainback, S. (1984). A rationale for the merger of special and regular education. *Exceptional Children, 51,* 102–111.

Stallings, J. (1974). *Follow through classroom observation evaluation, 1972–1973.* Menlo Park, CA: Stanford Research Institute.

Stallings, J. (1975). Implementation and child effects of teaching practices in follow through classrooms. *Monographs of the Society for Research in Child Development, 40* (Serial No. 163), Nos. 7–8.

Stanford, G., & Roark, A. E. (1974). *Human interaction in education.* Boston: Allyn & Bacon.

Stanley, G., & Hall, R. (1973). Short-term visual information processing in dyslexics. *Child Development, 44,* 841–844.

Stanley, G., Smith, G. A., & Howell, E. A. (1983). Eye-movements and sequential tracking in dyslexic and control children. *British Journal of Psychology, 74,* 181–187.

Stanovich, K. E. (1986). Explaining the variance in reading ability in terms of psychological processes: What have we learned? *Annals of Dyslexia, 35,* 67–96.

Stanovich, K. E. (1982). Individual differences in the cognitive processes of reading: I. Word decoding. *Journal of Learning Disabilities, 15,* 485–493.

Stanovich, K. E. (1988). Explaining the differences between the dyslexic and the garden-variety poor reader: The phonological-core variable-difference model. *Journal of Learning Disabilities, 21,* 590–604.

Stanovich, K. E. (1991a). Conceptual and empirical problems with discrepancy definitions of reading disability. *Learning Disability Quarterly, 14,* 269–280.

Stanovich, K. E. (1991b). Changing models of reading and reading acquisition. In L. Rieben & C. A. Perfetti (Eds.), *Learning to read: Basic research and its implications.* Hillsdale, NJ: Lawrence Erlbaum.

Stanovich, K. E. (1993). A model for studies of reading disability. *Developmental Review, 13,* 225–245.

Stanovich, K. E., Cunningham, A. E., & Cramer, B. B. (1984). Assessing phonological awareness in kindergarten children: Issues of task comparability. *Journal of Experimental Child Psychology, 38,* 175–190.

Staples, S. L. (1996). Human response to environmental noise: Psychological research and public policy. *American Psychologist, 51,* 143–150.

Starck, R., Genesee, F., Lambert, W. E., & Seitz, M. (1977). Multiple language experience and the development of cerebral dominance. In S. J. Segalowitz & F. A. Gruber (Eds.), *Language development and neurological theory.* New York: Academic Press.

Stare, F. J., Whelan, E. M., & Sheridan, M. (1980). Diet and hyperactivity: Is there a relationship? *Pediatrics, 66,* 521–525.

Stauffer, R. (1969). *Directing reading maturity as a cognitive process.* New York: Harper & Row.

Stauffer, R. G. (1980). *The language experience approach to the teaching of reading* (2nd ed.). New York: Harper & Row.

Steg, J. P., & Rapoport, J. L. (1975). Minor physical anomalies in normal, neurotic, learning disabled, and severely disordered children. *Journal of Autism and Childhood Schizophrenia, 5,* 299–307.

Stein, J. F., Riddell, P. M., & Fowler, M. S. (1986). The Dunlop test and reading in primary school children. *British Journal of Ophthamology, 70,* 317–320.

Stephens, R. S., Pelham, W. E., & Skinner, R. (1984). State-dependant and main effects of methylphenidate and pemoline on paired-associate learning and spelling in hyperactive children. *Journal of Consulting and Clinical Psychology, 52,* 104–113.

Stephens, T. M., & Braun, B. L. (1980). Measures of regular classroom teachers' attitudes toward handicapped children. *Exceptional Children, 46,* 292–294.

Stephenson, S. (1907). Six cases of congenital word-blindness affecting three generations of one family. *Ophthalmoscope, 5,* 482–484.

Sternberg, R. J. (1986). *Intelligence applied: Understanding and increasing your intellectual skills.* San Diego: Harcourt Brace Jovanovich.

Sternberg, R. S., & Wagner, R. K. (1982). Automatization failure in learning disabilities. *Topics in Learning & Learning Disabilities, 2,* 1–11.

Stevens, G. D., & Birch, J. W. (1957). A proposal for clarification of the terminology used to describe brain-injured children. *Exceptional Children, 23,* 346–349.

Stevens, R., & Rosenshine, B. (1981). Advances in research on teaching. *Exceptional Education Quarterly, 2*(1), 1–9.

Stevens, R. J., & Slavin, R. E. (1991). When cooperative learning improves the achievement of students with mild disabilities: A response to Tateyama-Sniezek. *Exceptional Children, 57,* 276–280.

Stevenson, H. W., Friedricks, A. C., & Simpson, W. E. (1970). Interrelations and correlates over time in children's learning. *Child Development, 41,* 625–637.

Stevenson, H. W., Parker, T., & Wilkenson, A. (1976). Predictive value of teachers' ratings of young children. *Journal of Educational Psychology, 68,* 507–517.

Sticht, T. G., & James, J. H. (1984). Listening and reading. In P. D. Pearson, R. Barr, M. Kamil, & P. Mosenthal (Eds.), *Handbook of reading research.* New York: Longman.

Stigler, J. W., Lee, S., Lucker, G. W., & Stevenson, H. W. (1982). Curriculum and achievement in mathematics: A study of elementary school children in Japan, Taiwan, and the United States. *Journal of Educational Psychology, 74,* 315–322.

Stiliadis, K., & Wiener, J. (1989). Relationship between social perception and peer status in children with learning disabilities. *Journal of Learning Disabilities, 22,* 624–629.

Stipp, D. (1992, September 11). Reinventing math. *The Wall Street Journal,* p. B4.

Stirling, E. G., & Miles, T. R. (1988). Naming ability and oral fluency in dyslexic adolescents. *Annals of Dyslexia, 38,* 50–72.

Stoch, M. B., Smythe, P. M. Moodie, A. D., & Bradshaw, D. (1982). Psychosocial outcome and CT findings after gross undernourishment during infancy: A 20-year developmental study. *Developmental Medicine and Child Neurology, 24,* 419–436.

Stodolsky, S. S. (1974). How children find something to do in preschools. *Genetic Psychology Monographs, 90,* 245–303.

Stone, A., & Michals, D. (1986). Problem-solving skills in learning disabled children. In S. J. Ceci (Ed), *Handbook of cognitive, social, and neuropsychological aspects of learning disabilities* (Vol. 1). Hillsdale, NJ: Lawrence Erlbaum.

Stone, W. L., & LaGreca, A. M. (1990). The social status of children with learning disabilities: A reexamination. *Journal of Learning Disabilities, 23,* 32–37.

Stott, D. H. (1973). Follow-up study from birth of the effects of prenatal stresses. *Developmental Medicine and Child Neurology, 15,* 770–787.

Strang, J. D., & Rourke, B. P. (1985a). Arithmetic disability subtypes: The neuropsychological significance of specific arithmetical impairment in childhood. In B. P. Rourke (Ed.), *Neuropsychology of learning disabilities.* New York: Guilford Press.

Strang, J. D., & Rourke, B. P. (1985b). Adaptive behavior of children who exhibit specific arithmetic disabilities and associated neuropsychological abilities and deficits. In B. P. Rourke (Ed.), *Neuropsychology of learning disabilities.* New York: Guilford Press.

Strang, L., Smith, M. D., & Rogers, C. M. (1978). Social comparison, multiple reference groups, and the self-concepts of academically handicapped children before and after mainstreaming. *Journal of Educational Psychology, 70,* 487–497.

Strauss, A. A. (1943). Diagnosis and education of the cripple-brained, deficient child. *Exceptional Children, 9,* 163–168, 183.

Strauss, A. A., & Kephart, N. C. (1955). *Psychopathology and education of the brain-injured child: Vol. 2. Progress in theory and clinic.* New York: Grune & Stratton.

Strauss, A. A., & Lehtinen, L. E. (1947). *Psychopathology and education of the brain-injured child.* New York: Grune & Stratton.

Strauss, A. A., & Werner, H. (1942). Disorders of conceptual thinking in the brain-injured child. *Journal of Nervous and Mental Disease, 96,* 153–172.

Strein, W. (1993). Advances in research on academic self-concept: Implication for school psychology. *School Psychology Review, 22,* 273–284.

Streissguth, A. P., Sampson, P. D., & Barr, H. M. (1989). Neurobehavioral dose-response effects of prenatal alcohol exposure in humans from infancy to adulthood. *Annals of the New York Academy of Sciences, 562,* 145–158.

Suchman, R. G., & Trabasso, T. (1966a). Color and form preference in young children. *Journal of Experimental Child Psychology, 3,* 177–187.

Suchman, R. G., & Trabasso, T. (1966b). Stimulus preference and cue function in young children's concept attainment. *Journal of Experimental Child Psychology, 3,* 188–198.

Suiter, M. L., & Potter, R. E. (1978). The effects of paradigmatic organization on verbal recall. *Journal of Learning Disabilities, 11,* 247–250.

Suritsky, S. K., & Hughes, C. A. (1991). Benefits of notetaking: Implications for secondary and postsecondary students with learning disabilities. *Learning Disability Quarterly, 14,* 7–18.

Sutherland, J., & Algozzine, B. (1979). The learning disabled label as a biasing factor in the visual motor performance of normal children. *Journal of Learning Disabilities, 12,* 8–14.

Suydam, M. N. (1982). *The use of calculators in precollege education: Fifth annual state-of-the-art review* (ERIC Document Reproduction Service No. ED 206 454). Columbus, OH: Calculator Information Center.

Svanum, S., Bringle, R. G., & McLaughlin, J. E. (1982). Father absence and cognitive performance in a large sample of six- to eleven-year-old children. *Child Development, 53,* 136–143.

Swanson, H. L. (1983). Relations among metamemory, rehearsal activity and word recall of learning disabled and non-disabled readers. *British Journal of Educational Psychology, 53,* 186–194.

Swanson, H. L. (1986). Multiple coding processes in learning disabled and skilled readers. In S. J. Ceci (Ed.), *Handbook of cognitive, social, and neuropsychological aspects of learning disabilities* (Vol. 1). Hillsdale, NJ: Lawrence Erlbaum.

Swanson, H. L. (1988). Memory subtypes in learning disabled readers. *Learning Disability Quarterly, 11,* 342–357.

Swanson, H. L., & Cooney, J. B. (1985). Strategy transformation in learning disabled and nondisabled students. *Learning Disability Quarterly, 8,* 221–230.

Swanson, H. L., & Malone, S. (1992). Social skills and learning disabilities: A meta-analysis of the literature. *School Psychology Review, 21,* 427–443.

Swanson, H. L., & Trahan, M. F. (1992). Learning disabled readers' comprehension of computer mediated text: The influence of working memory, metacognition and attribution. *Learning Disabilities Research & Practice, 7,* 74–86.

Swanson, J. M., Cantwell, D., Lerner, M., McBurnett, K., & Hanna, G. (1991). Effects of stimulant medication on learning in children with ADHD. *Journal of Learning Disabilities, 24,* 219–230, 255.

Swanson, J. M., & Kinsbourne, M. (1976). Stimulant-related state-dependent learning in hyperactive children. *Science, 192,* 1354–1357.

Swanson, J. M., & Kinsbourne, M. (1980). Food dyes impair performance of hyperactive children on a laboratory learning test. *Science, 207,* 1485–1487.

Swanson, J. M., Kinsbourne, M., Roberts, W., & Zucker, K. (1978). Time-response analysis of the effect of stimulant medication on the learning ability of children referred for hyperactivity. *Pediatrics, 61,* 21–29.

Swanson, L. (1982). Verbal short-term memory encoding of learning disabled, deaf, and normal readers. *Learning Disability Quarterly, 5,* 21–28.

Sweeney, J. E., & Rourke, B. P. (1985). Spelling disability subtypes. In B. P. Rourke (Ed.), *Neuropsychology of learning disabilities.* New York: Guilford Press.

Sykes, D. H., Douglas, V. I., Weiss, G., & Minde, K. K. (1971). Attention in hyperactive children and the effect of methylphenidate (Ritalin). *Journal of Child Psychology and Psychiatry, 12,* 129–139.

Szasz, T. S. (1967). The myth of mental illness. In T. Millon (Ed.), *Theories of psychopathology.* Philadelphia: W. B. Saunders.

Szatmari, P., Offord, D. R., & Boyle, M. H. (1989). Ontario Child Health Study: Prevalence of attention deficit disorder with hyperactivity. *Journal of Child Psychology and Psychiatry, 30,* 219–230.

Tagatz, G. E., Otto, W., Klausmeir, H. J., Goodwin, W. L., & Cook, D. M. (1969). Effect of three methods of instruction upon the handwriting performance of third and fourth graders. In W. Otto & K. Koenke (Eds.), *Remedial teaching: Research and comment.* Boston: Houghton-Mifflin.

Tallal, P. (1980). Auditory temporal perception, phonics, and reading disabilities in children. *Brain and Language, 9,* 182–198.

Tallal, P., & Piercy, M. (1978). Defects of auditory perception in children with developmental dysphasia. In M. A. Wyke (Ed.), *Developmental dysphasia.* New York: Academic Press.

Tallal, P., Stark, R. E., Kallman, C., & Mellits, D. (1980). Developmental dysphasia: Relation between acoustic processing deficits and verbal processing. *Neuropsychologia, 18,* 273–284.

Tangel, D. M., & Blachman, B. A. (1992). Effect of phoneme awareness instruction on kindergarten children's invented spelling. *Journal of Reading Behavior, 24,* 233–261.

Tangel, D. M., & Blachman, B. A. (1995). Effect of phoneme awareness instruction on the invented spelling of first-grade children: A one-year follow-up. *Journal of Reading Behavior, 27,* 153–185.

Tarnopol, L., & Tarnopol, M. (1977). Introduction to neuropsychology. In L. Tarnopol & M. Tarnopol (Eds.), *Brain function and reading disabilities.* Baltimore: University Park Press.

Tarver, S. G., & Dawson, M. M. (1978). Modality preference and the teaching of reading: A review. *Journal of Learning Disabilities, 11,* 5–17.

Tarver, S. G., & Hallahan, D. P. (1974). Attention deficits in children with learning disabilities: A review. *Journal of Learning Disabilities, 7,* 560–569.

Task Force on Pediatric AIDS. (1989). Pediatric AIDS and human immunodeficiency virus infection. *American Psychologist, 44,* 258–264.

Tateyama-Sniezek, K. M. (1990). Cooperative learning: Does it improve the academic achievement of students with handicaps? *Exceptional Children, 56,* 426–437.

Taussig, H. B. (1962). A study of the German outbreak of phocomelia: The thalidomide syndrome. *Journal of the American Medical Association, 180,* 1106–1114.

Taverne, A., & Sheridan, S. M. (1995). Parent training in interactive book reading: An investigation of its effects with families at risk. *School Psychology Quarterly, 10,* 41–64.

Taylor, B. M., & Samuels, S. J. (1983). Children's use of text structure in the recall of expository material. *American Educational Research Journal, 20,* 517–528.

Taylor, E. (1966). *The fundamental reading skill as related to eye movement photography and visual anomalies.* Springfield, IL: Charles C Thomas.

Taylor, H. G. (1984). Early and long-term recovery from brain damage in children and adults: Evolution of concepts of localization, plasticity, and recovery. In C. R. Almli & S. Finger (Eds.), *Early brain damage: Vol. 1. Research orientations and clinical observations.* New York: Academic Press.

Taylor, L., Adelman, H. S., & Kaser-Boyd, N. (1985). Minors' attitudes and competence toward participation in psychoeducational decisions. *Professional Psychology: Research and Practice, 16,* 226–235.

Taymans, J., & Malouf, D. (1984). A hard look at software in computer-assisted instruction in special education. *The Pointer, 28*(2), 12–15.

Teberg, A. J., Walther, F. J., & Pena, I. C. (1988). Mortality, morbidity, and outcome of the small-for-gestational-age infant. *Seminars in Perinatology, 12,* 84–94.

Teitelbaum, E. (1978). Calculators for classroom use? *Arithmetic Teacher, 26,* 18–20.

Telzrow, C. F., Century, E., Redmond, C., Whitaker, B., & Zimmerman, B. (1983). The Boder Test: Neuropsychological and demographic features of dyslexic subtypes. *Psychology in the Schools, 20,* 427–432.

Teng, E. L., Lee, P-H., Yang., K-S., & Chang, P. C. (1979). Lateral preferences for hand, foot and eye, and their lack of association with scholastic achievement, in 4143 Chinese. *Neuropsychologia, 17,* 41–48.

Tharinger, D. J., & Koranek, M. E. (1988). Children of alcoholics—At risk and unserved: A review of research and service roles for school psychologists. *School Psychology Review, 17,* 166–191.

Thatcher, R. W., & John, E. R. (1977). *Functional neuroscience: Foundations of cognitive processes* (Vol. 1). New York: Halsted Press.

Thoman, E. B. (1978). CNS dysfunction and nonverbal communication between mother and infant. In C. L. Ludlow & M. E. Doran-Quine (Eds.), *NINCDS Monograph No. 22: The Neurological Bases of Language Disorders in Children: Methods and Directions for Research.* Bethesda, MD: U.S. Department of Health, Education and Welfare.

Thomas, A., & Chess, S. (1977). *Temperament and development.* New York: Brunner/Mazel.

Thomas, A., & Chess, S. (1984). Genesis and evolution of behavioral disorders: From infancy to early adult life. *American Journal of Psychiatry, 141,* 1–9.

Thomas, C. C., Englert, C. S., Gregg, S. (1987). An analysis of errors and strategies in the expository writing of learning disabled students. *Remedial and Special Education, 8,* 21–30, 46.

Thomas, C. J. (1905). Congenital "word-blindness" and its treatment. *Ophthalmoscope, 3,* 380–385.

Thomas, E. L., & Robinson, H. A. (1972). *Improving reading in every class.* Boston: Allyn & Bacon.

Thomas, E. L., & Robinson, H. A. (1977). *Improving reading in every class: A sourcebook for teachers.* Boston: Allyn & Bacon.

Thorne, B. (1986). Girls and boys together . . . but mostly apart: Gender arrangements in elementary schools. In W. W. Hartup & Z. Rubin (Eds.), *Relationships and development.* Hillsdale, NJ: Erlbaum.

Thorpe, H. W., & Borden, K. S. (1985). The effect of multisensory instruction upon the on-task behavior and word reading accuracy of learning disabled children. *Journal of Learning Disabilities, 18,* 279–286.

Thorpe, H. W., Chiang, B., & Darch, C. B. (1981). Individual and group feedback systems for improving oral reading accuracy in learning disabled and regular class children. *Journal of Learning Disabilities, 14,* 332–334.

Thurlow, M., Graden, J., Greener, J., & Ysseldyke, J. (1983a). LD and non-LD students' opportunities to learn. *Learning Disability Quarterly, 6,* 172–183.

Thurlow, M. L., Ysseldyke, J. E., Graden, J. L., & Algozzine, B. (1983b). What's "special" about the special education resource room for learning disabled students? *Learning Disability Quarterly, 6,* 283–288.

Thurlow, M. L., Ysseldyke, J., Graden, J., & Algozzine, B. (1983c). Instructional ecology for students in resource and other classrooms. *Teacher Education and Special Education, 6,* 248–254.

Thurston, L. P., & Dasta, K. (1990). An analysis of in-home parent tutoring procedures: Effects on children's academic behavior at home and in school and on parents' tutoring behaviors. *Remedial and Special Education, 11,*(4), 41–52.

Thypin, M. (1979). Selection of books of high interest and low reading level. *Journal of Learning Disabilities, 12,* 428–430.

Tizard, B., & Hughes, M. (1985). *Young children learning.* Cambridge, MA: Harvard University Press.

Tollefson, N., Tracy, D. B., Johnson, E. P., Buenning, M., Farmer, A., & Barke, C. R. (1982). Attribution patterns of learning disabled adolescents. *Learning Disability Quarterly, 5*(1), 14–20.

Tollison, P., Palmer, D. J., & Stowe, M. L. (1987). Mothers' expectations, interactions, and achievement attributions for their learning disabled or normally achieving sons. *Journal of Special Education, 21,* 83–93.

Tombari, M. L., & Bergan, J. K. (1978). Consultant cues and teacher verbalizations, judgments, and expectancies concerning children's adjustment problems. *Journal of School Psychology, 16,* 212–219.

Tomlinson, J. R., Acker, A., Canter, A., & Lindborg, S. (1977). Minority status, sex, and school psychological services. *Psychology in the Schools, 14,* 456–460.

Tomlinson, P. C., & Hunt, D. E. (1971). Differential effects of rule-example order as a function of conceptual level. *Canadian Journal of Behavioral Science, 3,* 237–245.

Torgesen, J., & Goldman, T. (1977). Verbal rehearsal and short-term memory in reading disabled children. *Child Development, 48,* 56–60.

Torgesen, J. K. (1977a). The role of nonspecific factors in the task performance of learning-disabled children: A theoretical assessment. *Journal of Learning Disabilities, 10,* 27–34.

Torgesen, J. K. (1977b). Memorization processes in reading-disabled children. *Journal of Educational Psychology, 69,* 571–578.

Torgesen, J. K. (1980). Conceptual and educational implications of the use of efficient task strategies by learning disabled children. *Journal of Learning Disabilities, 13,* 364–371.

Torgesen, J. K. (1987). Thinking about the future by distinguishing between issues that have resolutions and those that do not. In S. Vaughn & C. S. Bos (Eds.), *Research in learning disabilities: Issues and future directions.* Boston: College-Hill.

Torgesen, J. K. (1988). Studies of children with learning disabilities who perform poorly on memory span tasks. *Journal of Learning Disabilities, 21,* 605–612.

Torgesen, J. K., Dahlem, W. E., & Greenstein, J. (1987). Using verbatim text recordings to enhance reading comprehension in learning disabled adolescents. *Learning Disabilities Focus, 3,* 30–38.

Torgesen, J. K., & Houck, D. G. (1980). Processing deficiencies of learning disabled children who perform poorly on the digit span test. *Journal of Educational Psychology, 72,* 141–160.

Torgesen, J. K., Murphy, H. A., & Ivey, C. (1979). The influence of an orienting task on the memory performance of children with reading problems. *Journal of Learning Disabilities, 12,* 396–401.

Torgesen, J. K., Rashotte, C. A., Greenstein, J., & Portes, P. (1991). Further studies of learning disabled children with severe performance problems on the digit span test. *Learning Disabilities Research & Practice, 6,* 134–144.

Torgesen, J. K., Wagner, R. K., & Rashotte, C. A. (1994). Longitudinal studies of phonological processing and reading. *Journal of Learning Disabilities, 27,* 276–286.

Torgesen, J. K., Wagner, R. K., Simmons, K., & Laughon, P. (1990). Identifying phonological coding problems in disabled readers: Naming, counting, or span measures? *Learning Disability Quarterly, 13,* 236–243.

Tornéus, M. (1984). Phonological awareness and reading: A chicken and egg problem? *Journal of Educational Psychology, 76,* 1346–1358.

Toro, P. A., Weissberg, R. P., Guare, J., & Liebenstein, N. L. (1990). A comparison of children with and without learning disabilities on social problem-solving skill, school behavior, and family background. *Journal of Learning Disabilities, 23,* 115–120.

Touwen, B. C. L., & Huisjes, H. J. (1984). Obstetrics, neonatal neurology, and later outcome. In C. R. Almli & S. Finger (Eds), *Early brain damage: Vol. 1. Research orientations and clinical observations.* New York: Academic Press.

Townes, B. D., Trupin, E. W., Martin, D. C., & Goldstein, D. (1980). Neuropsychological correlates of academic success among elementary school children. *Journal of Consulting and Clinical Psychology, 48,* 675–684.

Trammel, D.L., Schloss, P. J., & Alper, S. (1994). Using self-recording, evaluation, and graphing to increase completion of homework assignments. *Journal of Learning Disabilities, 27,* 75–81.

Trickett, E. J. (1978). Toward a social ecological conception of adolescent socialization: Normative data on contrasting types of public school classrooms. *Child Development, 49,* 408–414.

Trifiletti, J. J., Frith, G. H., & Armstrong, S. (1984). Microcomputers versus resource rooms for LD students: A preliminary investigation of the effects on math skills. *Learning Disability Quarterly, 7,* 69–76.

Trites, R. L., & Fiedorowicz, C. (1976). Follow-up study of children with specific (or primary) reading disability. In R. M. Knights & D. J. Bakker (Eds.), *The neuropsychology of learning disorders: Theoretical approaches.* Baltimore: University Park Press.

Tronick, E. Z. (1989). Emotions and emotional communication in infants. *American Psychologist, 44,* 112–119.

Tubbs, S. L., & Moss, S. (1977). *Human communication: An interpersonal perspective.* New York: Random House.

Tucker, J. A. (1980). Ethnic proportions in classes for the learning disabled: Issues in nonbiased assessment. *Journal of Special Education, 14,* 93–105.

Tugend, A. (1985, November 13). Steady rise in learning-disabled spurs review. *Education Week,* pp. 1, 18–20.

Tummer, W. E., & Nesdale, A. R. (1985). Phonemic segmentation skill and beginning reading. *Journal of Educational Psychology, 77,* 417–427.

Tur-Kaspa, H., & Bryan, T. (1994). Social information-processing skills of students with learning disabilities. *Learning Disabilities Research & Practice, 9,* 12–23.

Turkington, C. (1992, January). Diabetes in pregnancy negatively affects child. *Monitor.* American Psychological Association, 16.

Turnbull, A. P., & Blacher-Dixon, J. (1980). Preschool mainstreaming: Impact on parents. In J. J. Gallagher (Ed.), *New directions for exceptional children* (Vol. 1). San Francisco: Jossey-Bass.

Tzavaras, A., Kaprinis, G., & Gatzoyas, A. (1981). Literacy and hemispheric specialization for language: Digit dichotic listening in illiterates. *Neuropsychologia, 19,* 565–570.

Underwood, B. J. (1964). Degree of learning and the measurement of forgetting. *Journal of Verbal Learning and Verbal Behavior, 3,* 112–129.

United States Department of Health, Education, and Welfare. (1977). *Learning disabilities due to minimal brain dysfunction, hope through research.* Washington, DC: National Institution of Health U.S. Government Printing Office.

United States Department of Health, Education, and Welfare. (1979). *Departments of Labor and Health Education, and Welfare Appropriations for 1980, part 5: Hearings before a Subcommittee of the Committee on Appropriations House of Representatives.* Washington, DC: U.S. Government Printing Office.

United States Office of Education. (1970a). *Third Annual Report of the National Advisory Committee on Handicapped Children.* Washington, DC: U.S. Department of Health, Education, and Welfare, June 30.

United States Office of Education. (1970b). *Better education for handicapped children: Annual report fiscal year 1969.* Washington, DC: U.S. Department of Health, Education, and Welfare.

United States Office of Education. (1971–1972). *Estimated number of handicapped children in the United States.* Washington, DC: U.S. Office of Education.

United States Office of Education. (1997). *Nineteenth annual report to Congress on the implementation of the Individuals with Disabilities Education Act.* Washington, DC: U.S. Department of Education.

Unkovic, C. M., Brown, W. R., & Mierswa, C. G. (1978). Counterattack on juvenile delinquency: A configurational approach. *Adolescence, 13,* 401–410.

U.S. Conference of Mayors. (1994). *Status report on hunger and homelessness in America's cities: 1994.* Washington, DC.

Uzgiris, I. C. (1970). Sociocultural factors in cognitive development. In H. C. Haywood (Ed.), *Social-cultural aspects of mental retardation.* New York: Appleton-Century-Crofts.

Valenstein, E., & Heilman, K. M. (1979). Emotional disorders resulting from lesions of the central nervous system. In K. M. Heilman & E. Valenstein (Eds.), *Clinical neuropsychology.* Oxford: Oxford University Press.

Vallecorsa, A. L., & Garriss, E. (1990). Story composition skills of middle-grade students with learning disabilities. *Exceptional Children, 57,* 48–54.

Valus, A. (1986). Achievement-potential discrepancy status of students in LD programs. *Learning Disability Quarterly, 9,* 200–205.

Valverde, F. (1967). Apical dendrite spines of the visual cortex and light deprivation in the mouse. *Experimental Brain Research, 3,* 337–352.

van Daal, V. H. P., & Van der Leij, A. (1992). Computer-based reading and spelling practice for children with learning disabilities. *Journal of Learning Disabilities, 25,* 186–195.

Vandervelden, M. C., & Siegel, L. S. (1997). Teaching phonological processing skills in early literacy: A developmental approach. *Learning Disability Quarterly, 20,* 63–81.

Van der Vlugt, H., & Satz, P. (1985). Subgroups and subtypes of learning-disabled and normal children: A cross-cultural replication. In B. P. Rourke (Ed.), *Neuropsychology of learning disabilities.* New York: Guilford Press.

Vaughn, S., Bos, C. S., Harrell, J. E., & Lasky, B. A. (1988). Parent participation in the initial placement/IEP conference ten years after mandated involvement. *Journal of Learning Disabilities, 21,* 82–89.

Vaughn, S., Elbaum, B. E., & Schumm, J. S. (1996). The effects of inclusion on the social functioning of students with learning disabilities. *Journal of Learning Disabilities, 29,* 598–608.

Vaughn, S., & Haager, D. (1994). Social competence as a multifaceted construct: How do students with learning disabilities fare? *Learning Disability Quarterly, 17,* 253–266.

Vaughn, S., & Hogan, A. (1994). The social competence of students with learning disabilities over time: A within-individual examination. *Journal of Learning Disabilities, 27,* 292–303.

Vaughn, S., Lancelotta, G. X., & Minnis, S. (1988). Social strategy training and peer involvement: Increasing peer acceptance of a female, LD student. *Learning Disabilities Focus, 4,* 32–37.

Vaughn, S., McIntosh, R., Schumm, J. S., Haager, D., & Callwood, D. (1993). Social status, peer acceptance, and reciprocal friendships revisited. *Learning Disabilities Research & Practice, 8,* 82–88.

Vaughn, S., McIntosh, R., & Spencer-Rowe, J. (1991). Peer rejection is a stubborn thing: Increasing peer acceptance of rejected students with learning disabilities. *Learning Disabilities Research & Practice, 6,* 83–88.

Vaughn, S. R., Levine, L., & Ridley, C. A., (1986), *PALS: Problem solving and affective learning strategies.* Chicago: Science Research Associates.

Vaughn, S., & Schumm, J. S. (1995). Responsible inclusion for students with learning disabilities. *Journal of Learning Disabilities, 28,* 264–270, 290.

Vaughn, S., & Schumm, J. S. (1996). Classroom interactions and implications for inclusion of students with learning disabilities. In Speece, D. L., & Keogh, B. (Eds.), *Research on classroom ecologies: Implications for inclusion of children with learning disabilities.* Mahwah, NJ: Lawrence Erlbaum.

Vaughn, S., & Schumm, J. S., Jallad, B., Slusher, J., & Saumell, L. (1996). Teachers' views of inclusion. *Learning Disabilities Research & Practice, 11,* 96–106.

Vaughn, S., & Schumm, J. S., & Kouzekanani, K. (1993). What do students with learning disabilities think when their general education teachers make adaptations? *Journal of Learning Disabilities, 26,* 545–555.

Vellutino, F. R. (1991). Introduction to three studies on reading acquisition: Convergent findings on theoretical foundations of code-oriented versus whole-language approaches to reading instruction. *Journal of Educational Psychology, 83,* 437–443.

Vellutino, F. R., Pruzek, R. M., Steger, J. A., & Meshoulam, U. (1973). Immediate visual recall in poor and normal readers as a function of orthographic-linguistic familiarity. *Cortex, 9,* 370–386.

Vellutino, F. R., & Scanlon, D. M. (1986). Experimental evidence for the effects of instructional bias on word identification. *Exceptional Children, 53,* 145–155.

Vellutino, F. R., & Scanlon, D. M. (1987). Phonological coding, phonological awareness, and reading ability: Evidence from a longitudinal and experimental study. *Merrill-Palmer Quarterly, 33,* 321–363.

Vellutino, F. R., Scanlon, D. M., Small, S. G., & Tanzman, M. S. (1991). The linguistic basis of reading ability: Converting written to oral language. *Text, 11,* 99–133.

Vellutino, F. R., Steger, J. A., DeSetto, L., & Phillips, F. (1975a). Immediate and delayed recognition of visual stimuli in poor and normal readers. *Journal of Experimental Child Psychology, 19,* 223–232.

Vellutino, F. R., Steger, J. A., Kaman, M., & DeSetto, L. (1975b). Visual form perception in deficient and normal readers as a function of age and orthographic-linguistic familiarity. *Cortex, 11,* 22–30.

Vellutino, F. R., Steger, J. A., & Kandel, G. (1972). Reading disability: An investigation of the perceptual deficit hypothesis. *Cortex, 8,* 106–118.

Voeller, K. K. S. (1986). Right-hemisphere deficit syndrome in children. *American Journal of Psychiatry, 143,* 1004–1009.

Vogel, S. A. (1974). Syntactic abilities in normal and dyslexic children. *Journal of Learning Disabilities, 7,* 103–109.

Vogel, S. A., & Forness, S. R. (1992). Social functioning in adults with learning disabilities. *School Psychology Review, 21,* 375–386.

Vogel, S. A., Hruby, P. J., & Adelman, P. B. (1993). Educational and psychological factors in successful and unsuccessful college students with learning disabilities. *Learning Disabilities Research & Practice, 8,* 35–43.

Vogler, G. P., DeFries, J. C., & Decker, S. N. (1985). Family history as an indicator of risk for reading disability. *Journal of Learning Disabilities, 18,* 419–421.

Voltz, D. L., Elliott, R. N., & Cobb, H. B. (1994). Collaborating teacher roles: Special and general educators. *Journal of Learning Disabilities, 27,* 527–535.

von Hilsheimer, G., & Kurko, V. (1979). Minor physical anomalies in exceptional children. *Journal of Learning Disabilities, 12,* 462–469.

Vygotsky, L. S. (1962). *Thought and language.* Cambridge, MA: MIT Press.

Vygotsky, L. S. (1978). *Mind in society: The development of higher psychological processes.* Cambridge, MA: Harvard University Press.

Wade, J., & Kass, C. E. (1987). Component deficit and academic remediation of learning disabilities. *Journal of Learning Disabilities, 20,* 441–447.

Wagner, M. (1990, April). The school programs and school performance of secondary students classified as learning disabled: Findings from the National Longitudinal Transition Study of Special Education Students. Paper presented at the meetings of Division G., American Educational Research Association, Boston.

Wakshlag, J. J., Reitz, R. J., & Zillman, D. (1982). Selective exposure to and acquisition of information from educational television programs as a function of appeal and tempo of background music. *Journal of Educational Psychology, 74,* 666–677.

Walberg, H. J. (1969). Physical and psychological distance in the classroom. *School Review, 77,* 64–70.

Walberg, H. J. (1977). Psychology of learning environments: Behavioral, structural, or perceptual? In L. S. Shulman (Ed.), *Review of research in education* (Vol. 4). Itasca, IL: F. E. Peacock.

Walberg, H. J., & Marjoribanks, K. (1976). Family environment and cognitive development: Twelve analytic models. *Review of Educational Research, 46,* 527–551.

Walbrown, F. H., Fremont, T. S., Nelson, E., Wilson, J., & Fischer, J. (1979). Emotional disturbance or social misperception? An important classroom management question. *Journal of Learning Disabilities, 12,* 645–648.

Waldie, K., & Spreen, O. (1993). The relationship between learning disabilities and persisting delinquency. *Journal of Learning Disabilities, 26,* 417–423.

Walker, L. J. (1989). A longitudinal study of moral reasoning. *Child Development, 60,* 157–166.

Walker, N. M. (1985). Impulsivity in learning disabled children: Past research findings and methodological inconsistencies. *Learning Disability Quarterly, 8,* 85–94.

Wall, W. D. (1945). Reading backwardness among men in the army (1). *British Journal of Educational Psychology, 15,* 28–40.

Wall, W. D. (1946). Reading backwardness among men in the army (2). *British Journal of Educational Psychology, 16,* 133–148.

Wallach, L., Wallach, M. A., Dozier, M. G., & Kaplan, N. E. (1977). Poor children learning to read do not have trouble with auditory discrimination but do have trouble with phoneme recognition. *Journal of Educational Psychology, 69,* 36–39.

Wallach, M. A., & Wallach, L. (1979). *Teaching all children to read.* Chicago: University of Chicago Press.

Walsh, K. W. (1978). *Neuropsychology: A clinical approach.* Edinburgh: Churchill-Livingstone.

Wanat, P. E. (1983). Social skills: An awareness program with learning disabled adolescents. *Journal of Learning Disabilities, 16,* 35–38.

Wang, M. C., & Baker, E. T. (1985–1986). Mainstreaming programs: Design features and effects. *Journal of Special Education, 19,* 503–521.

Ward, W. D., & Barcher, P. R. (1975). Reading achievement and creativity as related to open classroom experience. *Journal of Educational Psychology, 67,* 683–691.

Warger, C. L. (1991). Peer tutoring: When working together is better than working alone. *Research & Resources on Special Education* (Number 30). Reston, VA: ERIC Clearinghouse on Handicapped and Gifted Children.

Warner, M. M., Schumaker, J. B., Alley, G. R., & Deshler, D. D. (1980). Learning disabled adolescents in the public schools: Are they different from other low achievers? *Exceptional Education Quarterly, 1,* 27–36.

Warner, M. M., Schumaker, J. B., Alley, G. R., & Deshler, D. D. (1989). The role of executive control: An epidemiological study of school-identified learning disabled and low-achieving adolescents on a serial recall task. *Learning Disabilities Research, 4,* 107–118.

Washburn, W. Y. (1975). Where to go in voc-ed for secondary LD students. *Academic Therapy, 11,* 31–35.

Washington, V. (1979). Noncognitive effects of instruction: A look at teacher behavior and effectiveness. *Educational Horizons, 57,* 209–213.

Weener, P. (1981). On comparing learning disabled and regular classroom children. *Journal of Learning Disabilities, 14,* 227–232.

Wehmeyer, M., & Schwartz, M. (1997). Self-determination and positive adult outcomes: A follow-up study of youth with mental retardation or learning disabilities. *Exceptional Children, 63,* 245–255.

Weiler, M. D. (1992, September). Strategies for enhancing student motivation. *Communiqué,* pp. 20–21.

Weingartner, H., Rapoport, J. L., Buchsbaum, M. S., Bunney, W. E., Ebert, M. H., Mikkelsen, E. J., & Caine, E. D. (1980). Cognitive processes in normal and hyperactive children and their response to amphetamine treatment. *Journal of Abnormal Psychology, 89,* 25–37.

Weinstein, C. S. (1977). Modifying student behavior in an open classroom through changes in the physical design. *American Educational Research Journal, 14,* 249–262.

Weinstein, C. S. (1979). The physical environment of the school: A review of the research. *Review of Educational Research, 49,* 577–610.

Weinstein, G., & Cooke, N. L. (1992). The effects of two repeated reading interventions on generalization of fluency. *Learning Disability Quarterly, 15,* 21–28.

Weintraub, F. J., & Abeson A. (1974). New education policies for the handicapped: The quiet revolution. *Phi Delta Kappan, 55,* 526–529, 569.

Weintraub, S., & Mesulam, M. M. (1983). Developmental learning disabilities of the right hemisphere: Emotional, interpersonal, and cognitive components. *Archives of Neurology, 40,* 463–468.

Weisberg, R. (1988). 1980s: A change in focus of reading comprehension research—A review of reading/learning disabilities research based on an interactive model of reading. *Learning Disability Quarterly, 11,* 149–159.

Weiss, B., Williams, J. H., Margen, S., et al. (1980). Behavioral responses to artificial food colors. *Science, 207,* 1487.

Weiss, G., & Hechtman, L. (1993). *Hyperactive children grown up (2nd ed.): ADHD in children, adolescents, and adults.* NY: Guilford.

Weithorn, C. J., & Kagen, E. (1978). Interaction of language development and activity level on performance of first-graders. *American Journal of Orthopsychiatry, 48,* 148–159.

Welch, M. (1992). The PLEASE strategy: A metacognitive learning strategy for improving the paragraph writing of students with mild learning disabilities. *Learning Disability Quarterly, 15,* 119–128.

Wells, D., Schmid, R., Algozzine, B., & Maher, M. (1983). Teaching LD adolescents: A study of selected teacher and teaching characteristics. *Teacher Education and Special Education, 6,* 227–234.

Wells, K. C., & Forehand, R. (1981). Child behavior problems in the home. In S. M. Turner, K. S. Calhoun, & H. E. Adams (Eds.), *Handbook of clinical behavior therapy.* New York: John Wiley.

Welton, D. A. (1990). Language as a mirror of culture. *Houghton Mifflin/Educators' Forum,* p. 7.

Wender, P. H. (1976). Hypothesis for possible biochemical basis of minimal brain dysfunction. In R. M. Knights & D. J. Bakker (Eds.), *The neuropsychology of learning disorders: Theoretical approaches.* Baltimore: University Park Press.

Wender, P. H., Reimherr, F. W., Wood, D., & Ward, M. (1985). A controlled study of methylphenidate in the treatment of attention deficit disorder, residual type, in adults. *American Journal of Psychiatry, 142,* 547–552.

Wepman, J. M., & Jones, L. V. (1961). *The language modalities test for aphasia.* Chicago: University of Chicago Education Industry Service.

Wepman, J. M., Jones, L. V., Bock, R. D., & Van Pelt, D. (1960). Studies in aphasia: Background and theoretical formulations. *Journal of Speech and Hearing Disorders, 25,* 323–332.

Werner, E. E. (1980). Environmental interaction in minimal brain dysfunction. In H. E. Rie & E. D. Rie (Eds.), *Handbook of minimal brain dysfunction.* New York: John Wiley & Sons.

Werner, E. E. (1989, April). Children of the Garden Island. *Scientific American, 260,* 106–111.

Werner, E. E. (1993). Risk and resilience in individuals with learning disabilities: Lessons learned from the Kauai longitudinal study. *Learning Disabilities Research & Practice, 8,* 28–34.

Werner, E. E., Bierman, J. M., & French, F. E. (1971). *The children of Kauai.* Honolulu: University of Hawaii Press.

Werner, E. E., & Smith, R. (1977). *Kauai's children come of age.* Honolulu: University of Hawaii Press.

Werner, H. (1937). Process and achievement: A basic problem of education and developmental psychology. *Harvard Educational Review, 7,* 353–368.

Werner, H. (1944). Development of visuo-motor performance on the Marble-Board Test in mentally retarded children. *Journal of Genetic Psychology, 64,* 269–279.

Werner, H., & Bowers, M. (1941). Auditory-motor organization in two clinical types of mentally deficient children. *Journal of Genetic Psychology, 59,* 85–99.

Werner, H., & Strauss, A. A. (1939). Problems and methods of functional analysis in mentally deficient children. *Journal of Abnormal and Social Psychology, 34,* 37–62.

Werner, H., & Strauss, A. A. (1940). Causal factors in low performance. *American Journal of Mental Deficiency, 45,* 213–218.

Werner, H., & Strauss, A. A, (1941). Pathology of figure-background relation in the child. *Journal of Abnormal and Social Psychology, 36,* 236–248.

West, L. L. (1991). *Effective strategies for dropout prevention of at-risk youth.* Gaithersburg, MD: Aspen Publishers.

West, W. G. (1984). *Young offenders and the state: A Canadian perspective on delinquency.* Toronto: Butterworths Press.

Whalen, C. K., & Henker, B. (1976). Psychostimulants and children: A review and analysis. *Psychological Bulletin, 83,* 1113–1130.

Whalen, C. K., Henker, B., Collins, B. E., Finck, D., & Dotemoto, S. (1979). A social ecology of hyperactive boys: Medication effects in structured classroom environments. *Journal of Applied Behavior Analysis, 12,* 65–81.

Whalen, C. K., Henker, B., & Dotemoto, S. (1980). Methylphenidate and hyperactivity: Effects on teacher behaviors. *Science, 208,* 1280–1282.

Whalen, R. J. (1966). The relevance of behavior modification procedures for teachers of emotionally disturbed children. In P. Knoblock (Ed.), *Intervention approaches in educating emotionally disturbed children.* Syracuse: Syracuse University Press.

Whang, P. L. Fawcett, S. B., & Mathews, R. M. (1984). Teaching job-related social skills to learning disabled adolescents. *Analysis and Intervention in Developmental Disabilities, 4,* 29–38.

White, B. L. (1980). Developing a sense of competence in young children by H. Yahrais in *Families today: A research sampler on families and children* (Vol. 1). U.S. Department of Health, Education, and Welfare, National Institute of Mental Health Science Monograph.

White, K. R. (1984). *An integrative review of early intervention.* Logan: Utah State University, Early Intervention Research Institute.

White, O. R. (1986). Precision teaching–precision learning. *Exceptional Children, 52,* 522–534.

White, W. A. T. (1988). A meta-analysis of effects of direct instruction in special education. *Education and Treatment of Children, 11,* 364–374.

White, W. J. (1985). Perspectives on the education and training of learning disabled adults. *Learning Disability Quarterly, 8,* 231–236.

White, W. J., Clark, F. L., Schumaker, J. B., Warner, M. M., Alley, G. R., & Deshler, D. D. (1980). The impact of learning disabilities on post-school adjustment. *Forum, 6*(4), 14–15, 21.

Whitehouse, C. C. (1983). Token test performance by dyslexic adolescents. *Brain and Language, 18,* 224–235.

Whitehurst, G. J., Falco, F., Lonigan, C. J., Fischal, J. E., DeBaryshe, B. D., Valdez-Manchaca, M. C., & Caulfield, M. (1988). Accelerating language development through picturebook reading. *Developmental Psychology, 24,* 552–559.

Whitney, P., & Kunen, S. (1983). Development of hierarchical conceptual relationships in children's semantic memories. *Journal of Experimental Child Psychology, 35,* 278–293.

Whorf, B. L. (1956). *Language, thought, and reality.* New York: John Wiley & Sons.

Wiederholt, J. L. (1974). Historical perspectives on the education of the learning disabled. In L. Mann & D. Sabatino (Eds.), *The second review of special education.* Philadelphia: Journal of Special Education Press.

Wiener, J. (1987). Peer status of learning disabled children and adolescents: A review of the literature. *Learning Disabilitie: Research, 2,* 62–79.

Wiig, E. H. (1990). Linguistic transition and learning disabilities: Strategic learning perspective. *Learning Disability Quarterly, 13,* 128–140.

Wiig, E. H., & Harris, S. P. (1974). Perception and interpretation of nonverbally expressed emotions by adolescents with learning disabilities. *Perceptual and Motor Skills, 38,* 239–245.

Wiig, E. H., Lapointe, C., & Semel, E. M. (1977). Relationships among language processing and production abilities of learning disabled adolescents. *Journal of Learning Disabilities, 10*(5), 292–299.

Wiig, E. H., & Semel, E. M. (1975). Productive language abilities in learning disabled adolescents. *Journal of Learning Disabilities, 8,* 578–586.

Wiig, E. H., & Semel, E. M. (1976). *Language disabilities in children and adolescents.* Columbus, OH: Charles E. Merrill.

Wiig, E. H., & Semel, E. M. (1980). *Language assessment and intervention for the learning disabled.* Columbus: Charles E. Merrill.

Wiig, E. H., Semel, E. M., & Abele, E. (1981). Perception and interpretation of ambiguous sentences by learning disabled twelve year olds. *Learning Disability Quarterly, 4,* 3–12.

Wiig, E. H., Semel, E. M., & Crouse, M. A. B. (1973). The use of English morphology by high-risk and learning disabled children. *Journal of Learning Disabilities, 6,* 457–465.

Wilcox, E. (1970). Identifying characteristics of the NH adolescent. In L. E. Anderson (Ed.), *Helping the adolescent with the hidden handicap.* Los Angeles, CA: Academic Therapy Publications.

Wilen, D. K., & Sweeting, C. V. (1986). Assessment of limited English proficient Hispanic students. *School Psychology Review, 15,* 59–75.

Wilhelms, F. T., & Westby-Gibson, D. (1961). Grouping: Research offers leads. *Educational Leadership, 18,* 410–413, 476.

Wilkinson, A., Stratta, L., & Dudley, P. (1974). *The quality of listening.* London: Macmillan Education.

Will, M. C. (1986). Educating children with learning problems: A shared responsibility. *Exceptional Children, 52,* 411–415.

Williams, D. M., & Collins, B. C. (1994). Teaching multiplication facts to students with learning disabilities: Teacher-selected versus student-selected material prompts within the delay procedure. *Journal of Learning Disabilities, 27,* 589–597.

Williams, J. (1987). Educational treatments for dyslexia at the elementary and secondary levels. In R. Bowler (Ed.), *Intimacy with language: A forgotten basic in teacher education.* Baltimore: Orton Dyslexia Society.

Williams, J. P. (1984). Phonemic analysis and how it relates to reading. *Journal of Learning Disabilities, 17,* 240–245.

Williams, P. A., Haertel, E. H., Haertel, G. D., & Walberg, H. J. (1982). The impact of leisure-time television on school learning: A research synthesis. *American Educational Research Journal, 19,* 19–50.

Williams, T. M. (1986). *The impact of television: A natural experiment in three communities.* Orlando, FL: Academic Press.

Willson, V. L. (1987). Statistical and psychometric issues surrounding severe discrepancy. *Learning Disabilities Research, 3,* 24–28.

Wilson, B., & Baddeley, A. (1986). Single case methodology and the remediation of dyslexia. In G. Th. Pavlidis & D. F. Fisher (Eds.), *Dyslexia: Its neuropsychology and treatment.* New York: John Wiley & Sons.

Wilson, C. L., & Sindelar, P. T. (1991). Direct instruction in math word problems: Students with learning disabilities. *Exceptional Children, 57,* 512–519.

Wilson, R., & Wesson, C. (1986). Making every minute count: Academic learning time in LD classrooms. *Learning Disabilities Focus, 2,* 13–19.

Wilson, R. S., & Matheny, A. P., Jr. (1986). Behavioral genetics research in infant temperament: The Louisville Twin Study. In R. Plomin & J. Dunn (Eds.), *The study of temperament: Changes, continuities, and challenges.* Hillsdale, NJ: Erlbaum.

Winick, M., Meyer, K. K., & Harris, R. C. (1975). Malnutrition and environmental enrichment by early adoption. *Science, 190,* 1173–1175.

Winn, M. (1983). *Children without childhood.* New York: Pantheon Books.

Winters, R. L., Patterson, R., & Shontz, W. (1989). Visual persistence and adult dyslexia. *Journal of Learning Disabilities, 22,* 641–645.

Witelson, S. (1977). Developmental dyslexia: Two right hemispheres and none left. *Science, 195,* 309–311.

Witelson, S. F. (1974). Hemispheric specialization for linguistic and nonlinguistic tactual perception using a dichotomous stimulation technique. *Cortex, 10,* 3–17.

Witelson, S. F. (1976a). Sex and the single hemisphere: Specialization of the right hemisphere for spatial processing. *Science, 193,* 425–427.

Witelson, S. F. (1976b). Abnormal right hemisphere specialization in developmental dyslexia. In R. M. Knights & D. J. Bakker (Eds.), *The neuropsychology of learning disorders: Theoretical approaches.* Baltimore: University Park Press.

Witelson, S. F., & Rabinovitch, M. S. (1972). Hemispheric speech lateralization in children with auditory-linguistic deficits. *Cortex, 8,* 412–426.

Witkin, H. A., Goodenough, D. R., & Karp, S. A. (1967). Stability of cognitive style from childhood to young adulthood. *Journal of Personality and Social Psychology, 7,* 291–300.

Witty, P. A., & Kopel, D. (1936). Studies of eye muscle imbalance and poor fusion in reading disability: An evaluation. *Journal of Educational Psychology, 27,* 663–671.

Wolery, M., Cybriwsky, C. A., Gast, D. L., & Boyle-Bast, K. (1991). Use of constant time delay and attentional responses with adolescents. *Exceptional Children, 57,* 462–474.

Wolf, C. W. (1967). An experimental investigation of specific language disability (dyslexia). *Bulletin of the Orton Society, 17,* 32.

Wolf, M. (1980, 1981). The word retrieval process and reading in children and aphasics. In K. Nelson (Ed.), *Children's language* (Vols. 1 & 2). Hillsdale, NJ: Lawrence Erlbaum.

Wolf, M. (1991). Naming speed and reading: The contribution of the cognitive neurosciences. *Reading Research Quarterly, 26,* 126–141.

Wolf, M., & Obregón, M. (1992). Early naming deficits, developmental dyslexia, and a specific deficit hypothesis. *Brain and Language, 42,* 219–247.

Wolraich, M. L., Wilson, D. B., & White, J. W. (1995). The effect of sugar on behavior or cognition in children: A meta-analysis. *Journal of the American Medical Association 274,* 1617–1621.

Wong, B. Y. L. (1986). A cognitive approach to teaching spelling. *Exceptional Children, 53,* 169–173.

Wong, B. Y. L. (1987). How do the results of metacognitive research impact on the learning disabled individual? *Learning Disability Quarterly, 10,* 189–195.

Wong, B. Y. L., Butler, D. L., Ficzere, S. A., & Kuperis, S. (1996). Teaching low achievers and students with learning disabilities to plan, write, and revise opinion essays. *Journal of Learning Disabilities, 29,* 197–212.

Wong, B. Y. L., Butler, D. L., Ficzere, S. A., & Kuperis, S. (1997). Teaching adolescents with learning disabilities and low achievers to plan, write, and revise compare-and-contrast essays. *Learning Disabilities Research & Practice, 12,* 2–15.

Wong, B. Y. L., & Jones, W. (1982). Increasing metacomprehension in learning disabled and normally achieving students through self-questioning training. *Learning Disability Quarterly, 5,* 228–240.

Wong, B. Y. L., & Sawatsky, D. (1984). Sentence elaboration and retention of good, average, and poor readers. *Learning Disability Quarterly, 6,* 229–236.

Wong, B. Y. L., & Wilson M. (1984). Investigating awareness of and teaching passage organization in learning disabled children. *Journal of Learning Disabilities, 17,* 477–482.

Wong, B. Y. L., & Wong, R. (1980). Role-taking skills in normal achieving and learning disabled children. *Learning Disability Quarterly, 3*(2), 11–18.

Wong, B. Y. L., Wong, R., Darlington, D., & Jones, W. (1991). Interactive teaching: An effective way to teach revision skills to adolescents with learning disabilities. *Learning Disabilities Research & Practice, 6,* 117–127.

Wong, B. Y. L., Wong, R., & LeMare, L. (1982). The effects of knowledge of criterion task on comprehension and recall in normal achieving and learning disabled children. *Journal of Educational Research, 76,* 119–126.

Wong, B. Y. L., Wong, R., Perry, N., & Sawatsky, D. (1986). The efficacy of a self-questioning summarization strategy for use by underachievers and learning disabled adolescents in social studies. *Learning Disabilities Focus, 2,* 20–35.

Wood, D. A., Rosenberg, M. S., & Carran, D. T. (1993). The effects of tape-recorded self-instruction cues on the mathematics performance of students with learning disabilities. *Journal of Learning Disabilities, 26,* 250–258, 269.

Wood, R. W., Weiss, A. B., & Weiss, B. (1973). Hand tremor induced by industrial exposure to inorganic mercury. *Archives of Environmental Health, 26,* 249–252.

Woodcock, R. W., & Clark, C. R. (1969). *Peabody Rebus Reading Program.* Circle Pines, MN: American Guidance Service.

Woodward, D. M. (1981). *Mainstreaming the learning disabled adolescent: A manual of strategies and materials.* Rockville, MD: Aspen Systems Corporation.

Woodward, J., Carnine, D., Gersten, R., Gleason, M., Johnson, G., & Collins, M. (1986). Applying instructional design principles to CAI for mildly handicapped students: Four recently conducted studies. *Journal of Special Education Technology, 8,* 13–26.

Woodward, J., & Noell, J. (1991). Science instruction at the secondary level: Implications for students with learning disabilities. *Journal of Learning Disabilities, 24,* 277–284.

Woodward, J. P., & Carnine, D. W. (1988). Antecedent knowledge and intelligent computer assisted instruction. *Journal of Learning Disabilities, 21,* 131–139.

Woolfolk, A. E., & Brooks, D. M. (1985). The influence of teachers' nonverbal behaviors on students' perceptions and performance. *The Elementary School Journal, 85,* 513–528.

Worden, P. E. (1986). Prose comprehension and recall in disabled learners. In S. J. Ceci (Ed.), *Handbook of cognitive, social, and neuropsychological aspects of learning disabilities* (Vol. 1). Hillsdale, NJ: Lawrence Erlbaum.

Wortis, J. (1956). A note on the concept of the "brain-injured" child. *American Journal of Mental Deficiency, 61,* 204–206.

Wozniak, R. H. (1972). Verbal regulation of motor behavior: Soviet research and non-Soviet replications. *Human Development, 15,* 13–57.

Wright, P., & Santa Cruz, R. (1983). Ethnic composition of special education programs in California. *Learning Disability Quarterly, 6,* 387–394.

Wright, R. J. (1975). The affective and cognitive consequences of an open-education elementary school. *American Educational Research Journal, 12,* 449–465.

Wright-Strawderman, C., & Watson, B. L. (1992). The prevalence of depressive symptoms in children with learning disabilities. *Journal of Learning Disabilities, 25,* 258–264.

Yando, R. M., & Kagan, J. (1968). The effect of teacher tempo on the child. *Child Development, 39,* 27–34.

Yang, D. C., Ting, R. Y., & Kennedy, C. (1968). The predictive value of the neurological examination in infancy and for mental status at four years of age. In R. MacKeith & M. Bax (Eds.), Studies in infancy. *Clinics in Developmental Medicine, 27,* 94–99.

Yap, J. N. K., & Peters, R. DeV. (1985). An evaluation of two hypotheses concerning the dynamics of cognitive impulsivity: Anxiety-over-errors or anxiety-over-competence? *Developmental Psychology, 21,* 1055–1064.

Yarrow, L. J., Rubenstein, J. L., & Pederson, F. A. (1975). *Infant and environment: Early cognitive and motivational development.* Washington, DC: Hemisphere Publishing.

Yasutake, D., & Bryan, T. (1995). The influence of induced positive affect on middle school children with and without learning disabilities. *Learning Disabilities Research & Practice, 10,* 38–45.

Yauman, B. E. (1980). Special education placement and the self-concepts of elementary-school-age children. *Learning Disability Quarterly, 3*(3), 30–35.

Yell, M. L. (1994). Least restrictive environment, inclusion, and students with disabilities: A legal analysis. *The Journal of Special Education, 28,* 389–404.

Yoder, D. I., Retish, E., & Wade, R. (1996). Service learning: Meeting student and community needs. *Teaching Exceptional Children, 28* (4), 14–18.

Yopp, H. K. (1988). The validity and reliability of phonemic awareness tests. *Reading Research Quarterly, 23,* 159–177.

Young, G. (1977). Manual specialization in infancy: Implications for lateralization of brain function. In S. J. Segalowitz & F. A. Gruber

(Eds.), *Language development and neurological theory*. New York: Academic Press.

Youniss, J. (1980). *Parents and peers in social development: A Sullivan-Piaget perspective*. Chicago: University of Chicago Press.

Ysseldyke, J., Algozzine, B., & Epps, S. (1983). A logical and empirical analysis of current practice in classifying students as handicapped. *Exceptional Children, 50,* 160–166.

Ysseldyke, J. E., & Foster, G. G. (1978). Bias in teachers' observations of emotionally disturbed children and learning disabled children. *Exceptional Children, 44,* 613–615.

Ysseldyke, J. E., & Salvia, J. (1974). Diagnostic-prescriptive teaching: Two models. *Exceptional Children, 41,* 181–185.

Ysseldyke, J., Thurlow, M., & Silverstein, B. (1994, March). Making accomodations in assessments of students with disabilities. *Communiqué, 22*(6). National Association of School Psychologists.

Zahn-Waxler, C., Radke-Yarrow, M., Wagner, E., & Chapman, M. (1992). Development of concern for others. *Developmental Psychology, 28,* 126–136.

Zametkin, A. J., Nordahl, T. E., Gross, M., King, A. C., Semple, W. E., Rumsey, J., Hamburger, S., & Cohen, R. M. (1990). Cerebral glucose metabolism in adults with hyperactivity of childhood onset. *New England Journal of Medicine, 323,* 1362–1366.

Zametkin, A. J., & Rapoport, J. L. (1986). The pathophysiology of attention deficit disorder with hyperactivity. A review. In B. B. Lahey & A. E. Kazdin (Eds.), *Advances in Clinical Child Psychology* (Vol. 9). New York: Plenum Press.

Zangwill, O. L. (1978). The concept of developmental dysphasia. In M. A. Wyke (Ed.), *Developmental dysphasia*. New York: Academic Press.

Zangwill, O. L., & Blakemore, C. (1972). Dyslexia: Reversal of eye movements during reading. *Neuropsychologia, 10,* 371–373.

Zaporozhets, A. V. (1965). The development of perception in the preschool child. In P. Mussen (Ed.), European research in cognitive development. *Monographs of the Society for Research in Child Development, 30*(2, Serial No. 100).

Zaragoza, N., & Vaughn, S. (1992). The effects of process writing instruction on three 2nd-grade students with different achievement profiles. *Learning Disabilities Research & Practice, 7,* 184–193.

Zeaman, D., & Hanley, P. (1983). Stimulus preferences as structural features. In T. J. Tighe & B. E. Shepp (Eds.), *Perception, cognition, and development: Interactional analyses*. Hillsdale, NJ: Lawrence Erlbaum.

Zelniker, T., & Jeffrey, W. E. (1976). Reflective and impulsive children: Strategies of information processing underlying differences in problem solving. *Monographs of the Society for Research in Child Development, 41* (5, Serial No. 168).

Zentall, S. S. (1985). A context for hyperactivity. In K. D. Gadow (Ed.), *Advances in learning and behavioral disabilities* (Vol. 4). Greenwich, CT: JAI Press.

Zentall, S. S. (1989). Attentional cuing in spelling tasks for hyperactive and comparison regular classroom children. *Journal of Special Education, 23,* 83–93.

Zentall, S. S., & Ferkis, M. A. (1993). Mathematical problem solving for youth with ADHD, with and without learning disabilities. *Learning Disability Quarterly, 16,* 6–18.

Zentall, S. S., & Gohs, D. E. (1984). Hyperactive and comparison children's response to detailed vs. global cues in communication tasks. *Learning Disability Quarterly, 7,* 77–87.

Zentall, S. S., & Kruczek, T. (1988). The attraction of color for active attention-problem children. *Exceptional Children, 54,* 357–362.

Zentall, S. S., & Zentall, T. R. (1976). Activity and task performance of hyperactive children as a function of environmental stimulation. *Journal of Consulting and Clinical Psychology, 44,* 693–697.

Zeskind, P. S., & Ramey, C. T. (1981). Preventing intellectual and interactional sequelae of fetal malnutrition: A longitudinal, transactional, and synergistic approach to development. *Child Development, 52,* 213–218.

Zifferblatt, S. M. (1972). Architecture and human behavior: Toward increased understanding of a functional relationship. *Educational Technology, 12,* 54–57.

Zigler, E., & Styfco, S. J. (1994). Head Start: Criticisms in a constructive context. *American Psychologist, 49,* 127–132.

Zigler, E., Taussig, C., & Black, K. (1992). Early childhood intervention: A promising preventative for juvenile delinquency. *American Psychologist, 47,* 997–1006.

Zigler, E., & Trickett, P. K. (1978). IQ, social competence, and evaluation of early childhood intervention programs. *American Psychologist, 33,* 789–798.

Zigler, E. F. (1987). Formal schooling for four-year-olds? No. *American Psychologist, 42,* 254–260.

Zigmond, N. (1990). Rethinking secondary school programs for students with learning disabilities. *Focus on Exceptional Children, 23*(1), 1–22.

Zigmond, N. (1996). Organization and management of general education classrooms. In Speece, D. L., & Keogh, B. (Eds.), *Research on classroom ecologies: Implication for inclusion of children with learning disabilities*. Mahwah, NJ: Lawrence Erlbaum.

Zigmond, N., & Miller, S. E. (1986). Assessment for instructional planning. *Exceptional Children, 52,* 501–509.

Zigmond, N., Sansone, J., Miller, S. E., Donahoe, K. A., & Kohnke, R. (1986). Teaching learning disabled students at the secondary school level; What research says to teachers. *Learning Disabilities Focus, 1,* 108–115.

Zigmond, N., & Thornton, H. (1985). Follow-up of postsecondary-age learning disabled graduates and drop-outs. *Learning Disabilities Research, 1,* 50–55.

Zigmond, N., Vallecorsa, A., & Leinhardt, G. (1982). Reading instruction for students with learning disabilities. In K. G. Butler & G. P. Wallach (Eds.), *Language disorders and learning disabilities*. Rockville, MD: Aspen Publishers.

Zihl, J. (1981). Recovery of visual functions in patients with cerebral blindness: Effect of specific practice with saccadic localization. *Experimental Brain Research, 44,* 159–169.

Zimmerman, J., Rich, W. D., Keilitz, I., & Broder, P. K. (1981). Some observations on the link between learning disabilities and juvenile delinquency. *Journal of Criminal Justice, 9,* 1–17.

Zurif, E. B., & Carson, G. (1970). Dyslexia in relation to cerebral dominance and temporal analysis. *Neuropsychologia, 8,* 351–361.

Name Index

Subject Index